Problem-Solving Strategies

D0219312

ActivPhysics OnLine™ Activities for Volume 1

Activ
ONLINE
Physics   www.aw-bc.com/young_geller

SEARS &
ZEMANSKY'S

COLLEGE
PHYSICS

VOLUME ONE

8TH EDITION

Hugh D. Young
Carnegie Mellon University

Robert M. Geller
University of California, Santa Barbara

San Francisco   Boston   New York   Cape Town   Hong Kong   London   Madrid   Mexico City
Montreal   Munich   Paris   Singapore   Sydney   Tokyo   Toronto

Editor-in-Chief:	Adam Black, Ph.D.
Senior Development Editor:	Margot Otway
Project Manager:	Laura Kenney
Project Editors:	Liana Allday, Chandrika Madhavan
Managing Producer:	Claire Masson
Development Associate, Media:	Brad Patterson
Executive Marketing Manager:	Christy Lawrence
Market Development Manager:	Josh Frost
Managing Editor:	Corinne Benson
Production Service:	WestWords, Inc.
Text and Cover Design:	Gary Hespenheide Design
Illustrations:	Rolin Graphics
Photo Research:	Cypress Integrated Systems
Cover Printer:	Phoenix Color Corporation
Printer and Binder:	R.R. Donnelley, Willard
Cover Image:	Ken Findlay/Dorling Kindersley

Photo Credits:	See page C-1.

Library of Congress Cataloging-in-Publication Data

Young, Hugh D.
  Sears & Zemansky's college physics.-- 8th ed. / Hugh D. Young, Robert M. Geller.
    p. cm.
  8th ed. of: College physics.
  Includes bibliographical references and index.
  ISBN 0-8053-7821-9 (alk. paper)
  1. Physics. I. Title: Sears and Zemansky's college physics. II. Geller, Robert M. III. Sears, Francis
Weston, 1898- College physics. IV. Title.

  QC23.2.Y68 2006
  530--dc22

                    2005028757

ISBN 0-8053-9214-9 Volume 1 with MasteringPhysics
ISBN 0-8053-7822-7 Volume 1 without MasteringPhysics
ISBN 0-8053-9384-6 Volume 1 with MasteringPhysics (Instructor's Edition)

www.aw-bc.com

1 2 3 4 5 6 7 8 9 10—DOW—08 07 06 05

Brief Contents

v

Hugh D. Young is Emeritus Professor of Physics at Carnegie Mellon University in Pittsburgh, Pennsylvania. He attended Carnegie Mellon for both undergraduate and graduate study and earned his Ph.D. in fundamental particle theory under the direction of the late Richard Cutkosky. He joined the faculty of Carnegie Mellon in 1956 and has also spent two years as a visiting professor at the University of California, Berkeley.

Hugh's career has centered entirely around undergraduate education. He has written several undergraduate-level textbooks, and in 1973 he became a coauthor of Francis Sears and Mark Zemansky's well-known introductory texts. In addition to fulfilling his role on Sears and Zemansky's *College Physics,* he is currently a coauthor with Roger Freedman on Sears and Zemansky's *University Physics.*

Hugh is an enthusiastic skier, climber, and hiker. He also served for several years as associate organist at St. Paul's Cathedral in Pittsburgh and has played numerous organ recitals in the Pittsburgh area. Hugh and his wife Alice usually travel extensively in the summer, especially in Europe and in the desert canyon country of southern Utah.

Robert M. Geller teaches physics at the University of California, Santa Barbara (UCSB), where he also obtained his Ph.D. under Robert Antonucci in observational cosmology. Currently, he is involved in two major research projects: a search for cosmological halos predicted by the Big Bang, and a search for the flares that are predicted to occur when a supermassive black hole consumes a star.

Rob also has a strong focus on undergraduate education. In 2003, he received the Distinguished Teaching Award at UCSB. He trains graduate teaching assistants on methods of physics education. He is also a frequent faculty leader for the UCSB Physics Circus, in which student volunteers perform exciting and thought-provoking physics demonstrations at elementary schools.

Rob loves the outdoors. He and his wife Susanne enjoy backpacking along rivers and fly fishing, usually with rods she has built and flies she has tied. Their daughter Zoe loves fishing, too, but her fish tend to be plastic and float in the bathtub.

THE MOST RELIABLE FOUNDATION IN PHYSICS, REFINED FOR THE STUDENTS OF TODAY

For more than five decades, Sears and Zemansky's *College Physics* has provided the most reliable foundation of physics education for students around the world. For the **Eighth Edition**, Robert Geller joins Hugh Young to produce a comprehensive update of this benchmark text.

A broad and thorough introduction to physics, this new edition carefully integrates many solutions from educational research to help develop deeper conceptual understanding, stronger quantitative-reasoning skills, and greater confidence in solving problems, while helping students connect what they learn with their other courses and the changing world around them.

The following pages provide an overview of how the book is designed and has been tested to provide students with **more effective instruction** and **more helpful guided practice**.

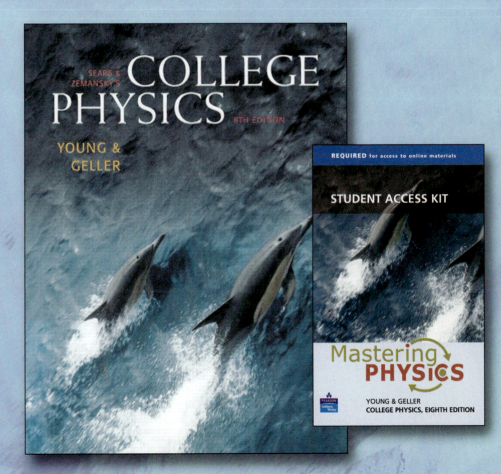

Effective Instruction

An explicit 3-step approach to problem solving is used throughout the book. This provides students with a consistent framework for attacking problems which research shows builds confidence and skill.

EXAMPLE 1.1 **Driving the autobahn**

Although there is no maximum speed limit on the German autobahn, signs in many areas recommend a speed of 130 km/h. Express this speed in meters per second and miles per hour.

SOLUTION

SET UP We know that 1 km = 1000 m. From Appendix B or the inside front cover, 1 mi = 1.609 km. We also know that 1 h = 60 min = 60 × (60 s) = 3600 s.

SOLVE We use these conversion factors with the problem-solving strategy we've outlined above:

$$130 \text{ km/h} = \left(\frac{130 \text{ km}}{1 \text{ h}}\right)\left(\frac{1000 \text{ m}}{1 \text{ km}}\right)\left(\frac{1 \text{ h}}{3600 \text{ s}}\right) = 36.1 \text{ m/s},$$

$$130 \text{ km/h} = \left(\frac{130 \text{ km}}{1 \text{ h}}\right)\left(\frac{1 \text{ mi}}{1.609 \text{ km}}\right) = 80.8 \text{ mi/h}.$$

REFLECT In physics, speeds are often expressed in meters per second, but if you're American, you're probably used to thinking in miles per hour. These calculations show that the number of miles per hour is roughly twice the number of meters per second; that is, a speed of twice 36.1 m/s isn't very different from 80.8 mi/h.

Practice Problem: Suppose you leave the autobahn and reduce your speed to 55 km/h. What is this speed in m/s and mi/h. *Answer:* 55 km/h = 15 m/s = 34 mi/h.

---

① Set Up focuses on the steps students usually skip — sketching a figure, identifying knowns and unknowns, and making simplifying assumptions.

② Solve begins with a plan for solving the problem, addresses common dead ends, and even discusses alternative solutions.

③ Reflect reinforces the importance of considering whether the answer makes sense, and what was learned.

PROBLEM-SOLVING STRATEGY 8.1 **Conservation of momentum**

Momentum is a vector quantity; you *must* use vector addition to compute the total momentum of a system. Using components is usually the simplest method.

SET UP
1. Define the s...
   fying the pos...
   x axis as hav...
   you are using...
2. Treat each o...
   including yo...
   sent all know...
   ponents, or...
   magnitude, a...
   use multiple...
   plete identifi...
   velocity of o...

SOLVE
3. Compute the...
   before and...
   $p_y = mv_y$. S...
   representing...
   line (such as...
   this line can...
4. Determine w...
   conserved, a...
   equates the...
   x component...
   These two e...
   form. In som...

PROBLEM-SOLVING STRATEGY 10.1 **Rotational dynamics**

Our strategy for solving problems in rotational dynamics is similar to Problem-Solving Strategy 5.2 on the use of Newton's second law.

SET UP
1. Sketch the situ...
   $\sum \vec{F} = m\vec{a}$ or...
2. Draw a free-bo...
   extended bodie...
   diagram must...
   and angles tha...
   translational m...
   forces that act...
   (taken to act at...
3. Choose coordi...
   positive sense...
   angular positio...
4. If more than o...
   object. There...
   more objects...
   same object. E...
   two linear acc...
   acceleration.

SOLVE
5. Write a separa...
   each body, inc...
   forces if neces...
   ties. This may...

REFLECT
6. Check particul...
   compare the re...
   expectations. A...

PROBLEM-SOLVING STRATEGY 5.2 **Using Newton's second law**

SET UP
1. Draw a sketch of the physical situation, and identify the moving object or objects to which you will apply Newton's second law.
2. Draw a free-body diagram for each chosen object, showing all the forces acting *on* that object, as described in the strategy for Newton's first law (Problem-Solving Strategy 5.1). Label the magnitudes of unknown forces with algebraic symbols. Usually, one of the forces will be the object's weight; it is generally best to label this as *mg*. If a numerical value of mass is given, you can compute the corresponding weight.
3. Show your coordinate axes explicitly in each free-body diagram, and then determine components of forces with reference to these axes. If you know the direction of the acceleration, it is usually best to take that direction as one of the axes. When you represent a force in terms of its components, cross out the original force so as not to include it twice. When there are two or more objects, you can use a separate axis system for each object; you don't have to use the same axis system for all the objects. But in the equations for each object, the signs of the components *must* be consistent with the axes you have chosen for that object.

SOLVE
4. Write the equations for Newton's second law in component form: $\sum F_x = ma_x$ and $\sum F_y = ma_y$ (Equations 4.8). Be careful not to add x and y components in the same equation.
5. If more than one object is involved, repeat step 4 for each object. In addition, the motions of the bodies may be related. For example, the objects may be connected by a rope. Express these relations in algebraic form as relations between the accelerations of the various bodies. Then solve the equations to find the required unknowns.

REFLECT
6. Check particular cases or extreme values of quantities, when possible, and compare the results for these particular cases with your intuitive expectations. Ask yourself, "Does this result make sense?" Think about what the problem has taught you that you can apply to other problems in the future.

A Problem-Solving Strategy for each major type of problem provides detailed guidance and reinforces the same 3-step approach.

Guided Practice

Worked Examples show the student how the Problem-Solving Strategy and the 3-step approach will build their skill and confidence tackling real problems. These examples go beyond providing a model solution to highlight what students must do (and reject). They even include Pencil Sketches in the Set Up step.

EXAMPLE 6.2 At the end of the tether

A tetherball is attached to a swivel in the ceiling by a light cord of length L. When the ball is hit by a paddle, it swings in a horizontal circle with constant speed v, and the cord makes a constant angle β with the vertical direction. The ball goes through one revolution in time T. Assuming that T, the mass m, and the length L of rope are known, derive algebraic expressions for the tension F_T in the cord and the angle β.

SOLUTION

SET UP Figure 6.5 shows our diagrams. Two forces act on the ball: its weight $\vec{w}$ and the tension force $\vec{F}_T$ exerted by the cord. In our free-body diagram, we point the x axis toward the center of the circle (in the direction of the centripetal acceleration a_{rad}), and we replace the tension force by its x and y components: $F_x = F_T \sin\beta$ and $F_y = F_T \cos\beta$, respectively. The y components of force sum to zero, so the net force on the ball is the x component of tension, which acts toward the center of the ball's circular path.

SOLVE Because the period T is known, we express a_{rad} in terms of T and the radius R of the circle, using Equation 6.2: $a_{rad} = 4\pi^2 R/T^2$. (Note that the radius of the circular path is $L\sin\beta$, not L.)

To find F_T, we use Newton's second law for the x component

$$\sum F_x = ma_x = ma_{rad} \qquad F_T \sin\beta = m\frac{4\pi^2 R}{T^2}.$$

for the radius R of the circle

$$\frac{(L\sin\beta)}{T^2}$$

get

$$\frac{^2 L}{^2}.$$

We're halfway home; the foregoing equation gives the rope tension F_T in terms of known quantities. To obtain an expression for the angle β, we use Newton's second law for the y component of net force. (Remember that this component must be zero $(\sum F_y = 0)$, because there is no y component of acceleration.) Newton's second law yields

$$\sum F_y = F_T \cos\beta + (-mg) = 0.$$

We substitute our expression for F_T into this equation to get

$$m\frac{4\pi^2 L}{T^2}\cos\beta + (-mg) = 0, \qquad \cos\beta = \frac{gT^2}{4\pi^2 L}.$$

So we've succeeded in expressing the tension F_T and the cosine of the angle β in terms of known quantities.

REFLECT For a given length L, $\cos\beta$ decreases and β increases as T becomes smaller and the ball makes more revolutions per second. The angle can never be 90°, however; that would require that $T = 0$, $F_T = \infty$, and $v = \infty$. The relationship between T and β doesn't contain the *mass* of the ball, but the force magnitude F_T is directly proportional to m. When β is very small, F_T is approximately equal to the ball's weight, $\cos\beta$ is approximately unity, and the expression we found above becomes approximately $T = 2\pi\sqrt{(L/g)}$.

Practice Problem: What is the speed v of the ball if $T = 2.0$ s and $L = 2.0$ m? *Answer:* 0.87 m/s.

EXAMPLE 5.11 Toboggan ride with friction

Let's go back to the toboggan we studied in Example 5.6. The wax has worn off, and there is now a coefficient of kinetic friction μ_k. The slope has just the right angle to make the toboggan slide with constant velocity. Derive an expression for the slope angle in terms of w and μ_k.

SOLUTION

SET UP Figure 5.16 shows our sketch and free-body diagram. The slope angle is α. The forces on the toboggan are identified by their magnitudes: its weight (w) and the normal (n) and frictional (f_k) components of the contact force exerted on it by the sloping surface. We take axes perpendicular and parallel to the surface and represent the weight in terms of its components in these two directions as shown.

SOLVE The toboggan is moving with constant velocity and is therefore in equilibrium. The equilibrium conditions are

$$\sum F_x = w\sin\alpha + (-f_k) = w\sin\alpha - \mu_k n = 0,$$
$$\sum F_y = n + (-w\cos\alpha) = 0.$$

Rearranging terms, we get

$$\mu_k n = w\sin\alpha, \qquad n = w\cos\alpha.$$

Note that the normal force n is less than the weight w. When we divide the first of these equations by the second, we find that

$$\mu_k = \frac{\sin\alpha}{\cos\alpha} = \tan\alpha.$$

▲ **FIGURE 5.16** Our diagrams for this problem.

REFLECT The normal force is *not* equal in magnitude to the weight; it is always smaller. The weight w doesn't appear in the expression for μ_k; *any* toboggan, regardless of its weight, slides down an incline with constant speed if the tangent of the slope angle of the hill equals the coefficient of kinetic friction. The greater the coefficient of friction, the steeper the slope has to be for the toboggan to slide with constant velocity. This behavior is just what we should expect.

(b) The forces on the ball (c) Free-body diagram

Conceptual Analysis problems throughout the text help students quickly assess their understanding of each key concept they have just read in the text.

A multiple-choice format (also used in the latest MCAT) is used to probe actively for key misconceptions

Conceptual Analysis 6.2 Skateboarder takes the hills

The following pictures show a skateboarder (seen from the side) moving along a straight or curved track.

▲ **FIGURE 6.3**

Which picture is consistent with the free-body diagram shown in Figure 6.3?

SOLUTION Force $\vec{w}$ has a larger magnitude than force $\vec{F}$. The net force is directed downward, so the acceleration must also be downward. In A, there is no vertical component of acceleration, so this choice cannot be correct. In B, the acceleration is upward, toward the center of the circular path. This would require a net upward force, not downward. The center of the circular path in C is downward from the ball. The acceleration is downward (toward the center), requiring a net downward force, as in Figure 6.3. The correct picture is C.

The answer is embedded in the solution, not listed separately, encouraging the student to read for understanding.

Quantitative Analysis 4.6 Relating graphs and free-body diagrams

An object moves along the x axis. Assuming that the positive coordinate is to the right and that the forces are constant, which of the following graphs of v_x as a function of time is consistent with the forces shown in the free-body diagram in Figure 4.25?

$\vec{F}_1 \qquad \vec{F}_2$

▶ **FIGURE 4.25**

SOLUTION The force diagram shows the larger force to the right, so the acceleration must be to the right also; a_x is positive. This means that the object is either (a) moving toward the left (the negative direction) and slowing down or (b) moving toward the right and speeding up. None of the graphs show leftward, slowing motion. D shows rightward, slowing motion, while A shows a constant velocity. Both B and C show rightward and speeding-up motion, but only C has a constant slope (corresponding to constant acceleration). Since the forces are constant, the acceleration is constant also, as indicated by the straight line in answer C.

Quantitative Analysis problems follow a similar multiple-choice probing format and develop students' math skills and confidence. They focus on helping students see equations as meaningful relationships (rather than black boxes to plug numbers into), and on developing skills of proportional reasoning.

DEVELOPING VISUALIZATION AND MODELING SKILLS

Effective Instruction

Unique, highly effective figures incorporate the latest ideas from educational research.

Extraneous detail has been removed and color is used only for strict pedagogical purposes. In mechanics, color is used to identify the object of interest while all other objects are grayscale. This technique helps students bridge the gap from the real world (photographs throughout the text) to the model they should build (Pencil Sketches).

$v_f = 30$ m/s

AFTER

$m = 0.40$ kg

$45°$

$v_i = 20$ m/s   BEFORE

(a) Before-and-after diagram

$F_{av,y}$ F_{av} θ $F_{av,x}$

(b) Average force on the ba

During each equal time interval Δt, the velocity increases by a fixed amount $\Delta v_x = a_x t$.

$v_x = v_{0x} + \Delta v_x$

Slope $= v_x$

Slope $= v_{0x}$

(a) A race car moves in the x direction with constant acceleration.

(b) The graph of x versus t.

(c) The graph of v_x versus t.

(d) The graph of a_x versus t.

Throughout, figures, models, and graphs are combined to help student "translate" between different representations

The plot with constant acceleration:
$x = x_0 + v_{0x}t = \frac{1}{2}a_x t^2$

The effect of acceleration:
$\frac{1}{2}a_x t^2$

The plot we would get without acceleration:
$x = x_0 + v_{0x}t$

The plot with constant acceleration:
$v = v_{0x} + a_x t$

The added velocity due to acceleration:
$\Delta v_x = a_x t$

The plot without acceleration:
$v_x = v_{0x}$

Blue annotation on the figures guides students in "reading" graphs and interpreting physics figures. This emulates what instructors do at the chalkboard. Research shows students assimilate information more readily in this form than from traditional figures for which explanation is relegated to the text or a long descriptive caption.

(a) Plot of x versus t for an object moving with positive constant acceleration

(b) Plot of v_x versus t for the same object

Unique visual chapter summaries show each concept in words, math, and figures to reinforce how to "translate" between different representations and to address different student learning styles. This approach discourages students from "equation hunting," which traditional chapter summaries — with lists of equations — have been found to promote.

Summary **153**

SUMMARY

Equilibrium of a Particle
(**Section 5.1**) When an object is in equilibrium, the vector sum of the forces acting on it must be zero: $\Sigma \vec{F} = 0$. (Equation 4.3). In component form,

$$\Sigma F_x = 0, \qquad \Sigma F_y = 0. \qquad (4.4)$$

Free-body diagrams are useful in identifying the forces acting on the object being considered. Newton's third law is also frequently needed in equilibrium problems. The two forces in an action–reaction pair never act on the same object.

Applications of Newton's Second Law
(**Section 5.2**) When the vector sum of the forces on an object is not zero, the object has an acceleration determined by Newton's second law, $\Sigma \vec{F} = m\vec{a}$ (Equation 4.7). In component form,

$$\Sigma F_x = ma_x, \qquad \Sigma F_y = ma_y. \qquad (4.8)$$

Pencil Sketches are used consistently in worked examples.

EXAMPLE 10.11 **Playing on a seesaw**

You and a friend play on a seesaw. Your mass is 90 kg, and your friend's mass is 60 kg. The seesaw board is 3.0 m long and has negligible mass. Where should the pivot be placed so that the seesaw will balance when you sit on the left end and your friend sits on the right end?

SOLUTION

SET UP Figure 10.25 shows our sketches. First we sketch the physical situation, and then we make a free-body diagram, placing the pivot at a distance x from the left end. Note that each weight is the corresponding mass multiplied by g, so g will divide out of the final result. Remember that counterclockwise torques are positive and clockwise torques are negative. For the seesaw to be in equilibrium, the sum of the torques about any axis must be zero. We choose to take torques about the pivot axis; then the normal force acting at the pivot doesn't enter into the analysis. The moment arms are x for you and $(3.0\,\text{m} - x)$ for your friend.

SOLVE Your torque is $\tau_{\text{you}} = +(90\,\text{kg})gx$. Your friend is $3.0\,\text{m} - x$ from the pivot, and the corresponding torque is $\tau_{\text{friend}} = -(60\,\text{kg})g(3.0\,\text{m} - x)$. For equilibrium, the sum of these torques must be zero:

$$\tau_{\text{you}} + \tau_{\text{friend}} = 0$$
$$+(90\,\text{kg})gx - (60\,\text{kg})g(3.0\,\text{m} - x) = 0.$$

We divide through by g and solve for x, obtaining $x = 1.2\,\text{m}$.

REFLECT If we put the pivot at the center of the board $(x = 1.5\,m)$, we would have equal moment arms but unequal weights, so it's clear that the pivot must be to the *left* of center.

(a) Sketch of physical situation

(b) Free-body diagram

▲ **FIGURE 10.25**

Practice Problem: If the board has a mass of 20 kg, where should the pivot be placed for balance? *Answer:* 1.24 m from left end.

Pencil Sketches emphasize exactly what to draw and encourage students to always include a sketch when solving real problems — a step that research shows students otherwise skip.

Inspiring examples help students connect physics with their world. In-margin photos with explanatory captions provide diverse, interesting, and self-contained examples of physics at work in the life sciences and in the technological world.

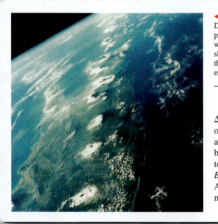

◄ **The day the day got shorter.** The earthquake that caused the devastating tsunami of December 26, 2004, represented a rupture along a 1200 km stretch of the fault where the In plate of the earth's crust dives under the Burma plate, allowing the India plate to move dow ward by about 15 m. This downward shift of mass reduced our planet's moment of inertia slightly. Its angular momentum about its axis of rotation is very nearly constant; to conserv this angular momentum, the speed of rotation increased, shortening the length of the day. S entists estimated that the quake shortened the length of the day by 2.7 microseconds.

The pro ... 0.10 (Σ $\Delta L / \Delta t$). Wh ... he parts e on each oth ... but the angular mom ... le: When bodies A a ... lse, A an together for ... $_{A\text{ on }B}$ on b B; the corre ... ose) is τ_A According t ... ge of ang momentum ...

▲ **A jet-propelled ... jellyfish?** This jellyfish moves by using the same physical principles of propulsion that we see in interplanetary rockets. By forcing water out of its bell in one direction, it is able to move in the opposite direction.

▲ **Falling with style.** This is a gravity map of the earth. Protrusions represent areas of stronger gravity (because of nonuniform mass distribution) and dips show areas of weaker gravity. For example, the Andes represent an area of strong gravity because of the extra mass of the mountain range. The map was made by the Gravity Recovery and Climate Experiment (GRACE) project. To measure gravity, GRACE employs a pair of satellites that orbit the earth in formation while precisely monitoring the distance between them. For instance, as the pair approaches a mountain range, the lead satellite will speed up in response to the mountains' gravitational pull, increasing the distance between the two satellites. As the satellites straddle the mountains, the pull of the extra mass then shrinks the distance between them, and as they pass the mountains, the distance increases again.

PROVIDING THE FIRST PRE-TESTED PROBLEMS AND INDIVIDUALIZED TUTORING

Effective Instruction

The renowned Sears/Zemansky problems, refined over five decades of use, have been enhanced and expanded with many new problem types from educational research. The wealth of 3,000 problems in the **Eighth Edition are the first and only textbook problems to be pre-tested** (before publication) for reliability, difficulty, and duration on thousands of students. *(See pull-out grid inside front cover for more details.)*

Conceptual Questions

Multiple-Choice Problems

Multiple-choice problems test the skills developed by the Qualitative Analysis and Quantitative Analysis problems in the chapter. The multiple-choice format and carefully chosen distractors test conceptual understanding and elicit common misconceptions. They follow the format used in the latest MCAT exams.

Problems

5.1 Equilibrium of a Particle

8. **Muscles and tendons.** The gastrocnemius muscle, in the back of the leg, has two portions, known as the medial and lateral heads. Assume that they attach to the Achilles tendon as shown in Figure 5.40. The cross-sectional area of each of these two muscles is typically 30 cm² for many adults. What is the maximum tension they can produce in the Achilles tendon? (See the previous problem for some useful information.)

▲ **FIGURE 5.40** Problem 8.

Lateral head
Medial head
Achilles tendon

A wealth of additional problems on life-science applications provide motivational examples for students specializing in those fields, and interesting real-world examples for other majors.

General Problems

89. **Automobile air-bag safety.** An automobile air bag cushions the force on the driver in a head-on collision by absorbing her energy before she hits the steering wheel. Such a bag can be modeled as an elastic force, similar to that produced by a spring. (a) Use energy conservation to show that the effective force constant k of the air bag is $k = mv_0^2/x_{max}^2$, where m is the mass of the driver, v_0 is the speed of the car (and driver) at the instant of the accident, and x_{max} is the maximum distance

▲ **FIGURE 7.46** Problem 89.

More advanced General Problems include many **context-rich problems** which require the student to simplify and model more complex **real-world situations**.

Guided Practice

Simpler subproblems are provided upon request when a student gets stuck.

Students select only the specific help they need. Thousands of solution paths are allowed.

See the MasteringPhysics™ brochure for more details on how it enables instructors to quickly build assignments of just the right coverage, difficulty, and duration, and the time-saving and probing diagnostic it provides (including most-common class wrong answers at each step, the detailed work of each student, and even national average comparison data).

MasteringPhysics™ is the most widely used and educationally proven physics homework and tutorial system in the world. NSF-sponsored research and independent studies at a wide range of schools show that students who use **MasteringPhysics™** significantly improve their scores on final exams and conceptual tests such as the Force Concept Inventory. Drawing from the world's largest metadatabase of the step-by-step work of how real students solve problems, accumulated over eight years of research, **MasteringPhysics™** offers unparalleled individualized and adaptive guidance.

Instantaneous feedback is provided with responses specific to the most-common wrong answers.

MasteringPhysics™ provides instructors with more than 4,000 problems from which to build wide-ranging weekly assignments that include:

- end-of-chapter textbook problems
- tutorials for practicing the Problem-Solving Strategies and the Conceptual Analysis and Quantitative Analysis problems in every chapter
- Skill-Building Tutorials for mastering key concepts, and Self-Tutoring Problems for guided practice
- math-specific Skill-Building Tutorials, ranking task problems, and even essay questions

Numerical problems provide randomized numbers and sig-fig feedback, and tutorial problems provide specific feedback for wrong answers and simpler subproblems upon request.

A vector-drawing tool provides grading and feedback on student-drawn free-body diagrams embedded in the tutorials.

Partial credit is provided for the method, not just the final numerical answer.

A graph-drawing tool provides grading and feedback on student-drawn graphs in tutorials that develop graph-reading skills.

Mastering PHYSICS

www.masteringphysics.com

BIO indicates bioscience applications in the list above and highlights bioscience-related problems at the end of each chapter.

Preface

We hear from other instructors that there is a need for a book that places equal emphasis on quantitative, qualitative, and conceptual understanding. With this goal, our new edition builds on the strengths that have made *College Physics* a success for over half a century. Guided by tested and proven innovations in education research, we have revised and enhanced previous material and added new features focusing on more explicit problem-solving steps and techniques, conceptual understanding, and visualization and modeling skills. Our main objectives are to teach a solid understanding of the fundamentals, help students develop critical thinking and quantitative reasoning, teach sound problem-solving skills, and spark the students' interest in physics with interesting and relevant applications.

This text provides a comprehensive introduction to physics at the beginning college level. It is intended for students whose mathematics preparation includes high school algebra and trigonometry, but no calculus. The complete text may be taught in a two-semester or three-quarter course, and the book is also adaptable to a wide variety of shorter courses.

Key Features of the Eighth Edition

- **A systematic approach to problem solving.** To solve problems with confidence, students must learn to approach them effectively at a global level, must understand the physics in question, and must acquire the specific skills needed for particular types of problems. This new edition provides research-proven tools and techniques for meeting each goal.

  - The **worked examples** all follow a consistent and explicit **global problem-solving framework** drawn from educational research. This three-step approach puts special emphasis on how to **set up** the problem before trying to solve it and on the importance of how to **reflect** on whether the answer is sensible.
  - Worked example solutions emphasize the steps and decisions students often omit. In particular, many worked examples include **pencil diagrams:** hand-drawn diagrams that show exactly what a student should draw in the **Set Up** step of solving the problem.
  - **Problem-solving strategies** teach students the tactics to use on particular types of problems—such as problems requiring Newton's second law, energy conservation, etc.—and reinforce the same three-step global approach (Set Up, Solve, Reflect). Adaptive tutorial versions are also available online at www.masteringphysics.com.
  - **Conceptual Analysis** and **Quantitative Analysis** problems help students practice their qualitative and quantitative understanding of the associated physics. The Quantitative Analysis problems focus on the skills of quantitative and proportional reasoning, skills that are key to success on the MCATs. No other introductory physics text addresses this need. The Quantitative Analysis problems use a multiple-choice format to elicit specific common misconceptions. Adaptive tutorial versions are also available online at www.masteringphysics.com.

- **Figures incorporate the latest ideas from educational research.** Extraneous detail has been removed and color is used only for strict pedagogical purposes. For instance, in mechanics, **color is used to identify the object of interest,** while all other objects are in gray scale. Helpful **annotation in blue** is included in figures to help guide students in "reading" graphs and physics figures. This technique emulates what instructors do at the chalkboard when explaining figures. Throughout, **figures, models, and graphs are placed side**

by side to help students understand multiple representations. **Pencil sketches** are used consistently in worked examples to emphasize what students should draw.

- **Unique visual chapter summaries** show each concept in words, math, and figures to reinforce how to "translate" different representations and to address different student learning styles.

- **Rich and diverse end-of-chapter problem sets.** The renowned Sears–Zemansky problems, refined over five decades of use, have been expanded and enhanced for today's courses to provide the largest number and widest variety of problems. These are also the first *pretested* textbook problems available.

  - The more than 3000 problems are the first textbook problems to be pretested on students nationally for reliability, difficulty, and duration, prior to publication. These chapter problems are available online at www .masteringphysics.com, along with 1000 additional adaptive tutorials.

  - New in each chapter is a set of **multiple-choice problems** that test the skills developed by the Qualitative Analysis and Quantitative Analysis problems in the text. The multiple-choice format probes for specific common misconceptions, enabling students to pinpoint their misunderstandings.

  - The general problems contain many **context-rich problems** (also known as **real-world problems**), which require the student to simplify and model more complex real-world situations.

  - The problem sets include more **biomedically oriented problems** than does any other college physics text.

- **Connects physics with the student's world.** In-margin photos with explanatory captions provide diverse, interesting, and self-contained examples of physics at work in the world.

- **Writing that is easy to follow and rigorous.** The writing is friendly, yet focused; it conveys an exact, careful, straightforward understanding of the physics, with an emphasis on the connections among concepts.

Instructor Supplements

The **Instructor Solutions Manuals, Chapters 1–16** (ISBN 0-8053-9218-1) and **Chapters 17–30** (ISBN 0-8053-9379-X), written by Lewis Ford, University of Texas, contain complete and detailed solutions to all end-of-chapter problems. All solutions follow consistently the same Set Up/Solve/Reflect problem-solving framework used in the textbook. As part of the national pretesting of the chapter problems, statistically reliable student-calibrated estimates of difficulty and duration are also provided to help instructors select problems of just the right level and build assignments of appropriate length.

The cross-platform **Instructor Resource CD-ROM** (ISBN 0-8053-9381-1) offers a comprehensive library of more than 200 applets from ActivPhysics OnLine™, as well as all line figures from the textbook in JPEG format. In addition, all the key equations, problem-solving strategies, tables, and chapter summaries are provided in editable Microsoft Word format. In-class weekly multiple-choice questions for use with various Classroom Response Systems (CRSs) are also provided, based on the Conceptual Analysis and Quantitative Analysis questions in the text. The Instructor Solutions Manual is also included in convenient editable Word format and as PDFs.

MasteringPhysics™ (www.masteringphysics.com) is the most advanced, educationally effective, and widely used physics homework and tutorial system in the world. It provides instructors with a library of extensively pretested end-of-chapter problems and rich Socratic tutorials that incorporate a wide variety of answers, wrong-answer feedback, and adaptive help (comprising hints or simpler subproblems upon request). MasteringPhysics™ allows instructors to quickly build wide-ranging homework assignments of just the right difficulty and duration and provides them with efficient tools to analyze class trends—or, indeed, the work of any individual student—in unprecedented detail and to compare results with the national average or with the performance of previous classes.

The **Transparency Acetates** (ISBN 0-8053-9220-3) contain more than 200 key figures from *College Physics,* 8th edition, in full color.

The **Printed Test Bank** (ISBN 0-8053-9219-X) provides more than 2000 multiple-choice questions.

The **Computerized Test Bank** (ISBN 0-8053-9380-3) includes all of the questions from the Printed Test Bank on a cross-platform CD-ROM. More than half of the questions have numerical values that can be randomly assigned for each student.

Student Supplements

The **Student Study Guide, Chapters 1–16** (ISBN 0-8053-9222-X) and **Chapters 17–30** (ISBN 0-8053-9352-8), coaches students through basic principles and problem-solving strategies presented in the text through a series of chapter-by-chapter self-quizzes and helps students resolve difficulties and build confidence in preparation for tackling the end-of-chapter problems.

The **Student Solutions Manuals, Chapters 1–16** (ISBN 0-8053-9370-6) and **Chapters 17–30** (ISBN 0-8053-9221-1), written by Lewis Ford, University of Texas, contain detailed, step-by-step solutions to more than half of the odd-numbered end-of-chapter problems from the textbook. All solutions consistently follow the same Set Up/Solve/Reflect problem-solving framework used in the text, reinforcing good problem-solving behavior.

ActivPhysics OnLine™ (http://www.aw-bc.com/young_geller) is a free, open-access self-study website that provides the most comprehensive library of applets and applet-based tutorials available today. ActivPhysics OnLine was created by the educational pioneers Alan van Heuvelen of Rutgers University and Paul d'Alessandris, Monroe Community College. Throughout *College Physics,* 8th edition, in-margin icons direct the student to specific applets on the ActivPhysics OnLine website for additional interactive help.

ActivPhysics OnLine™ **Workbooks, Volume 1** (ISBN 0-8053-9060-X) and **Volume 2** (ISBN 0-8053-9061-8), by Alan van Heuvelen and Paul d'Alessandris, offer a range of tutorials that use the critically acclaimed ActivPhysics OnLine™ applets to help students develop understanding and confidence. In particular, the tutorials focus on developing intuition, making predictions, testing assumptions experimentally, drawing effective diagrams, understanding key equations both qualitatively and quantitatively, and interpreting graphical information. These workbooks can be used for labs, homework, or self-study.

MasteringPhysics™ (www.masteringphysics.com) is the most advanced, widely used, and educationally proven physics tutorial system in the world. It is the result of eight years of detailed studies of how real students work physics problems and of precisely where they need help. Studies show that students who use MasteringPhysics™ significantly improve their scores on final exams and conceptual tests such as the Force Concept Inventory. MasteringPhysics™ achieves this improvement by providing students with instantaneous feedback specific to their wrong answers, simpler subproblems upon request when they get stuck, and partial credit for their method(s) used. This individualized, 24/7 tutor system is recommended by 9 out of 10 students to their peers as the most effective and time-efficient way to study.

The **Addison-Wesley Tutor Center** (www.aw.com/tutorcenter) provides one-on-one tutoring via telephone, fax, e-mail, or interactive website. Qualified instructors answer questions and give instruction with examples and problems from *College Physics,* 8th edition, as well as help with MasteringPhysics™.

Acknowledgments

I want to extend my heartfelt thanks to my colleagues at Carnegie Mellon for many stimulating discussions about physics pedagogy and for their support and encouragement during the writing of several successive editions of this book. I am equally indebted to the many generations of Carnegie Mellon students who have helped me learn what good teaching and good writing are by showing me what works and what doesn't.

This new edition has developed under the outstanding overall editorial guidance of Adam Black. I'm pleased to acknowledge also the contributors of problems and other essential elements for this edition, including Tom Sandin, Lewis Ford, Wayne Anderson, and Greg Bertoni. Equally important are the efforts of Claire Masson (producer of MasteringPhysics™ for this book and coordinator of pre-publication testing of problems), Josh Frost (analysis of feedback from class-testing of sample material), Christy Lawrence (liaison with the sales representatives about the Sears-Zemansky legacy and the role of this new edition), Chandrika Madhaven (manager of the extensive set of supplements), and Corinne Benson (production supervisor).

Very special thanks are due to the members of the Addison-Wesley editorial team, especially Margot Otway and Laura Kenney, who brought this all together. Their heroic efforts in coordinating the entire project, and their patience and support for the authors when the going was tough, are greatly appreciated. I would also like to thank Jared Sterzer and the folks at WestWords, Inc., for their production expertise. Finally, and most importantly, it is always a joy and a privilege to express my gratitude to my wife Alice and our children Gretchen and Rebecca for their love, support, and emotional sustenance during the writing of several successive editions of this book. May all men and women be blessed with love such as theirs.

—*H.D.Y.*

I would like to thank some of the people who had a great impact on my education and ability to teach others. Henry Abarbanel and Duncan Haldane were the first to show me what physics is all about. My former thesis advisor, colleague, and next-door neighbor Robert Antonucci continues to make physics fun and doesn't mind if I shout questions over the fence. Roger Freedman was first my instructor in graduate school and then a mentor when I began teaching; his lecture notes are as popular among the faculty as his textbooks are throughout the nation. My brother Michael and I went through undergraduate and graduate school together. Only free-dive spearfishing, an activity during which talking is rather difficult, has lessened our nonstop 20-year discussion of physics.

I'd like to thank my brother David (another science teacher) and my parents for their unwavering love and support for all of my pursuits; my father, who used an earlier edition of this text in college, will get this revision free of charge. Finally, I want to thank my wife Susanne for her tremendous support during this project. She's been the first reviewer of many of my ideas, discussing material on hikes or at the beach. I dedicate my contributions in this book to Susanne and my daughter Zoe.

—*R.M.G.*

Reviewers and Classroom Testers

Susmita Acharya, *Cardinal Stritch University*

Hamid Aidinejad, *Florida Community College, Jacksonville*

Alice Hawthorne Allen, *Virginia Tech*

Jim Andrews, *Youngstown State University*

Charles Bacon, *Ferris State University*

Jennifer Blue, *Miami University*

Richard Bone, *Florida International University*

Phillip Broussard, *Covenant College*

Young Choi, *University of Pittsburgh*

Orion Ciftja, *Prairie View A&M University*

Dennis Collins, *Grossmont College*

Lloyd Davis, *Montreat College*

Diana Driscoll, *Case Western Reserve University*

Laurencin Dunbar, *St. Louis Community College, Florissant Valley*

Alexander Dzyubenko, *California State University, Bakersfield*

Robert Ehrlich, *George Mason University*

Mark Fair, *Grove City College*

Shamanthi Fernando, *Northern Kentucky University*

Len Feuerhelm, *Oklahoma Christian University*

Carl Frederickson, *University of Central Arkansas*

Mikhail Goloubev, *Bowie State University*

Alan Grafe, *University of Michigan, Flint*

William Gregg, *Louisiana State University*

John Gruber, *San Jose State University*

Robert Hagood, *Washtenaw Community College*

Scott Hildreth, *Chabot College*

Andy Hollerman, *University of Louisiana, Lafayette*

John Hubisz, *North Carolina State University*

Manuel Huerta, *University of Miami*

Todd Hurt, *Chatham College*

Adam Johnston, *Weber State University*

Roman Kezerashvili, *New York City College of Technology*

Ju Kim, *University of North Dakota*

Jeremy King, *Clemson University*

David Klassen, *Rowan University*

Ichishiro Konno, *University of Texas, San Antonio*

Ikka Koskelo, *San Francisco State University*

Jon Levin, *University of Kentucky*

David Lind, *Florida State University*

Dean Livelybrooks, *University of Oregon, Eugene*

Estella Llinas, *University of Pittsburgh, Greensburg*

Craig Loony, *Merrimack College*

Rafael Lopez-Mobilia, *University of Texas, San Antonio*

Barbra Maher, *Red Rocks Community College*

Dan Mazilu, *Virginia Tech*

Randy McKee, *Tallahassee Community College*

Larry McRae, *Berry College*

William Mendoza, *Jacksonville University*

Anatoli Mirochnitchenko, *University of Toledo*

Charles Myles, *Texas Tech University*

Austin Napier, *Tufts University*

Erin O' Connor, *Allan Hancock College*

Christine O'Leary, *Wallace State College*

Jason Overby, *College of Charleston*

James Pazun, *Pfeiffer University*

Unil Perera, *Georgia State University*

David Potter, *Austin Community College*

Michael Pravica, *University of Nevada, Las Vegas*

Sal Rodano, *Harford Community College*

Rob Salgado, *Dillard University*

Surajit Sen, *SUNY Buffalo*

Bart Sheinberg, *Houston Community College*

Natalia Sidorovskaia, *University of Louisiana*

Chandralekha Singh, *University of Pittsburgh*

Marlina Slamet, *Sacred Heart University*

Daniel Smith, *South Carolina State University*

Gordon Smith, *Western Kentucky University*

Kenneth Smith, *Pennsylvania State University*

Zhiyan Song, *Savannah State University*

Sharon Stephenson, *Gettysburg College*

Chuck Stone, *North Carolina A&T State University*

George Strobel, *University of Georgia*

Cheng Fu Su, *Mississippi State University*

Brenda Subramaniam, *Cypress College*

Mike Summers, *George Mason University*

Eric Swanson, *University of Pittsburgh*

Colin Terry, *Ventura College*

Vladimir Tsifrinovich, *Polytechnic University*

Gajendra Tulsian, *Daytona Beach Community College*

Paige Uozts, *Lander University*

James Vesenka, *University of New England*

Walter Wales, *University of Pennsylvania*

John Wernegreen, *Eastern Kentucky University*

Dan Whitmire, *University of Louisiana, Lafayette*

Sue Willis, *Northern Illinois University*

Jaehoon Yu, *University of Texas, Arlington*

Nouredine Zettili, *Jacksonville State University*

Bin Zhang, *Arkansas State University*

Detailed Contents

* Optional section.

1 MODELS, MEASUREMENTS, AND VECTORS

The study of physics is an adventure. You'll find it challenging, sometimes frustrating, and often richly rewarding and satisfying. It will appeal to your sense of beauty as well as to your rational intelligence. Our present understanding of the physical world has been built on foundations laid by scientific giants such as Galileo, Newton, and Einstein. You can share some of the excitement of their discoveries when you learn to use physics to solve practical problems and to gain insight into everyday phenomena. Above all, you'll come to see physics as a towering achievement of the human intellect in its quest to understand the world we all live in.

In this opening chapter we go over some important preliminaries that we'll need throughout our study. We need to think about the philosophical framework in which we operate—the nature of physical theory and the role of idealized *models* in representing physical systems. We discuss systems of *units* that are used to describe physical quantities, such as length and time, and we examine the *precision* of a number, often described by means of *significant figures*. We look at examples of problems in which we can't or don't want to make precise calculations, but in which rough estimates can be interesting and useful. Finally, we study several aspects of *vector algebra*. We use vectors to describe and analyze many physical quantities, such as velocity and force, that have direction as well as magnitude.

Like these players, you already know a lot of physics. Your brain easily computes forces and motions in complex situations. In this course, your goal is simply to build a conscious model of the physical world you live in.

1.1 Introduction

Physics is an *experimental* science. Physicists observe the phenomena of nature and try to discover patterns and principles that relate these phenomena. These patterns are called *physical theories* or, when they are very broad and well

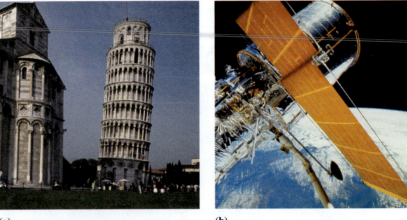

▶ **FIGURE 1.1** Two research laboratories. (a) The Leaning Tower of Pisa (Italy). According to legend, Galileo studied the motion of freely falling objects by dropping them from the tower. He is also said to have gained insights into pendulum motion by observing the swinging of the chandelier in the cathedral to the left of the tower. (b) The Hubble Space Telescope, the first major telescope to operate in space, free from the effects of earth's atmosphere.

(a) (b)

established, *physical laws.* The development of physical theory requires creativity at every stage. The physicist has to learn to ask appropriate questions, design experiments to try to answer the questions, and draw appropriate conclusions from the results. Figure 1.1 shows two famous experimental facilities.

According to legend, Galileo Galilei (1564–1642) dropped light and heavy objects from the top of the Leaning Tower of Pisa to find out whether they would fall at the same rate or at different rates. Galileo recognized that only an *experimental* investigation could answer this question. From the results of his experiments, he had to make the inductive leap to the principle, or theory, that the rate at which an object falls is independent of its weight.

The development of physical theory is always a two-way process that starts and ends with observations or experiments. Physics is not a collection of facts and principles; it is the *process* by which we arrive at general principles that describe the behavior of the physical universe. And there is always the possibility that new observations will require revision of a theory. We can *disprove* a theory by finding a phenomenon that is inconsistent with it, but we can never *prove* that a theory is *always* correct.

Getting back to Galileo, suppose we drop a feather and a cannonball. They certainly *do not* fall at the same rate. This doesn't mean that our statement of Galileo's theory is wrong, but that it is incomplete. One complicating feature is air resistance. If we drop the feather and the cannonball in vacuum, they *do* fall at the same rate. Our statement of Galileo's theory is valid for bodies that are heavy enough that air resistance has almost no effect on them. A feather or a parachute clearly does not have this property.

Every physical theory has a range of validity and a boundary outside of which it is not applicable. The range of Galileo's work with falling bodies was greatly extended half a century later by Newton's laws of motion and his law of gravitation. Nearly all the principles in this book are so solidly established by experimental evidence that they have earned the title **physical law.** Yet there are some areas of physics in which present-day research is continuing to broaden our understanding of the physical world. We'll discuss some examples of these areas in the final four chapters of the book.

An essential part of the interplay of theory and experiment is learning how to apply physical principles to a variety of practical problems. At various points in our study, we'll discuss systematic problem-solving procedures that will help you set up problems and solve them efficiently and accurately. Learning to solve problems is absolutely essential; you don't *know* physics unless you can *do* physics. This means not only learning the general principles, but also learning how to apply them in a variety of specific situations.

▲ **Where are the tunes coming from?**
These dancers may not realize it, but they are enjoying the application of fundamental principles of physics that makes their music possible. In later chapters, we will learn about electric charge and current and about how batteries are used to store electrical potential energy. We will see how this energy can be harnessed to perform the mechanical work of rotating the CD within the CD player. We will learn about lasers and optics, which provide the means to "read" a CD. And we will learn about harmonic motion, sound waves, and how these waves travel through space to bring us these "good vibes."

1.2 Idealized Models

In everyday conversation, we often use the word **model** to mean either a small-scale replica, such as a model train or airplane, or a human figure that displays articles of clothing. **In physics, a *model* is a simplified version of a physical system that would be too complicated to analyze in full without the simplifications.**

Here's an example: We want to analyze the motion of a baseball thrown through the air. How complicated is this problem? The ball is neither perfectly spherical nor perfectly rigid; it flexes a little and spins as it moves through the air. Wind and air resistance influence its motion, the earth rotates beneath it, the ball's weight varies a little as its distance from the center of the earth changes, and so on. If we try to include all these things, the analysis gets pretty hopeless. Instead, we invent a simplified version of the problem. We neglect the size and shape of the ball and represent it as a *particle*—that is, as an object that has no size but is completely localized at a single point in space. We neglect air resistance, treating the ball as though it moves in vacuum; we forget about the earth's rotation, and we make the weight of the ball exactly constant. *Now* we have a problem that is simple enough to deal with: The ball is a particle moving along a simple parabolic path. We'll analyze this model in detail in Chapter 3.

The point is that we have to overlook quite a few minor effects in order to concentrate on the most important features of the motion. That's what we mean by making an idealized model of the system. Of course, we have to be careful not to neglect *too much.* If we ignore the effect of gravity completely, then when we throw the ball, it will travel in a straight line and disappear into space, never to be seen again! We need to use some judgment and creativity to construct a model that simplifies a system without throwing out its essential features.

When we analyze a system or predict its behavior on the basis of a model, we always need to remember that the validity of our predictions is limited by the validity of the model. If the model represents the real system quite precisely, then we expect predictions made from it to agree quite closely with the actual behavior of the system. Going back to Pisa with Galileo once more, we see that our statement of his theory of falling objects corresponds to an idealized model that does not include the effects of air resistance, the rotation of the earth, or the variation of weight with height. This model works well for a bullet and a cannonball, not so well for a feather.

The concept of an idealized model is of the utmost importance in all of physical science and technology. In applying physical principles to complex systems, we always make extensive use of idealized models, and it is important to be aware of the assumptions we are making. Indeed, the *principles* of physics themselves are stated in terms of idealized models; we speak about point masses, rigid bodies, ideal insulators, and so on. Idealized models will play a crucial role in our discussion of physical theories and their applications to specific problems throughout this book.

▲ How can I find lunch in the dark?
Insect-eating bats utilize the laws of physics in their quest for prey in a process known as echolocation. To locate and capture an insect, these flying mammals first emit an extremely rapid series of 20 to 200 bursts of high-frequency sound. Without using a stopwatch or calculator, they are able to determine the insect's position by sensing the direction of the reflected sound waves and the time it takes for these waves to reach their ears. Luckily for us, the sounds they emit are above the range of human hearing, as they can be over 100 decibels, or about as loud as a typical smoke alarm.

1.3 Standards and Units

Any number that is used to describe an observation of a physical phenomenon quantitatively is called a **physical quantity.** Some physical quantities are so fundamental that we can define them only by describing a procedure for measuring them. Such a definition is called an **operational definition.** In other cases, we define a physical quantity by describing a way to *calculate* the quantity from other quantities that we can measure. As an example of an operational definition, we might use a ruler to measure a length or a stopwatch to measure a time interval. As

The meter was originally defined as 1/10,000,000 of this distance.

(a)

(b)

▲ **FIGURE 1.2** The original definition of the meter, from 1791.

▲ **FIGURE 1.3** (a) NIST-F1, the atomic clock that serves as the primary time standard for the United States. This clock is accurate to one part in 10^{15}, meaning that it will neither gain nor lose more than 1 second in 30 million years. (b) This platinum–iridium cylinder, kept in a vault in Sèvres, France, is the standard for the unit of the kilogram. Duplicates are kept at various locations around the world.

an example of a quantity we calculate, we might define the average speed of a moving object as the distance traveled (measured with a ruler) divided by the time of travel (measured with a stopwatch).

When we measure a quantity, we always compare it with some reference standard. When we say that a rope is 30 meters long, we mean that it is 30 times as long as a meterstick, which we *define* to be 1 meter long. We call such a standard a **unit** of the quantity. The meter is a unit of length, and the second is a unit of time.

> **NOTE** ▶ When we use a number to describe a physical quantity, we *must* specify the unit we are using; to describe a distance simply as "30" wouldn't mean anything. ◀

To make precise measurements, we need definitions of units of measurement that do not change and that can be duplicated by observers in various locations. When the metric system was established in 1791 by the Paris Academy of Sciences, the **meter** was originally defined as one ten-millionth of the distance from the equator to the North Pole (Figure 1.2), and the **second** was defined as the time taken for a pendulum 1 meter long to swing from one side to the other.

These definitions were cumbersome and hard to duplicate precisely, and in more recent years they have been replaced by more refined definitions. Since 1889, the definitions of the basic units have been established by an international organization, the General Conference on Weights and Measures. The system of units defined by this organization is based on the metric system, and since 1960 it has been known officially as the **International System,** or **SI** (the abbreviation for the French equivalent, Système International).

Time

From 1889 until 1967, the unit of time was defined in terms of the length of the day, directly related to the time of the earth's rotation. The present standard, adopted in 1967, is much more precise. It is based on an atomic clock (Figure 1.3a) that uses the energy difference between the two lowest energy states of the cesium atom. Electromagnetic radiation (microwaves) of precisely the proper frequency causes transitions from one of these states to the other. One second is defined as the time required for 9,192,631,770 cycles of this radiation.

Length

In 1960 an atomic standard for the meter was established, using the orange-red light emitted by atoms of krypton in a glow discharge tube. In November 1983 the standard of length was changed again, in a more radical way. The new definition of the meter is the distance light travels (in vacuum) in $1/299,792,458$ second. The adoption of this definition has the effect, in turn, of *defining* the speed of light to be precisely 299,792,458 m/s; we then define the meter to be consistent with this number and with the atomic-clock definition of the second. This approach provides a much more precise standard of length than the one based on a wavelength of light.

Mass

The standard of *mass* is the mass of a particular cylinder of platinum-iridium alloy. Its mass is defined to be 1 **kilogram,** and it is kept at the International Bureau of Weights and Measures at Sèvres, near Paris (Figure 1.3b). An atomic standard of mass has not yet been adopted, because, at present, we cannot measure masses on an atomic scale with as great precision as on a macroscopic scale.

TABLE 1.1   **Prefixes for powers of ten**

Power of ten	Prefix	Abbreviation
10^{-18}	atto-	a
10^{-15}	femto-	f
10^{-12}	pico-	p
10^{-9}	nano-	n
10^{-6}	micro-	μ
10^{-3}	milli-	m
10^{-2}	centi-	c
10^{3}	kilo-	k
10^{6}	mega-	M
10^{9}	giga-	G
10^{12}	tera-	T
10^{15}	peta-	P
10^{18}	exa-	E

Prefixes

Once the fundamental units have been defined, it is easy to introduce larger and smaller units for the same physical quantities. One of the great strengths of the metric system is that these other units are always related to the fundamental units by multiples of 10 or 1/10. (By comparison, the English system bristles with inconvenient factors such as 12, 16, and 36.) Thus, 1 kilometer (1 km) is 1000 meters, 1 centimeter (1 cm) is 1/100 meter, and so on.

We usually express these multiplicative factors in exponential notation, sometimes called *powers-of-ten* notation or *scientific* notation. For example; $1000 = 10^3$ and $1/100 = 10^{-2}$. With this notation,

$$1 \text{ km} = 10^3 \text{ m}, \qquad 1 \text{ cm} = 10^{-2} \text{ m}.$$

The names of the additional units are always derived by adding a **prefix** to the name of the fundamental unit. For example, the prefix "kilo-," abbreviated k, always means a unit larger by a factor of 1000; thus,

$$1 \text{ kilometer} = 1 \text{ km} = 10^3 \text{ meters} = 10^3 \text{ m},$$
$$1 \text{ kilogram} = 1 \text{ kg} = 10^3 \text{ grams} = 10^3 \text{ g},$$
$$1 \text{ kilowatt} = 1 \text{ kW} = 10^3 \text{ watts} = 10^3 \text{ W}.$$

Table 1.1 lists the standard SI prefixes with their meanings and abbreviations. Note that most of these are multiples of 10^3.

When pronouncing unit names with prefixes, always accent the *first* syllable: KIL-o-gram, KIL-o-meter, CEN-ti-meter, and MIC-ro-meter. (Kilometer is sometimes pronounced kil-OM-eter.)

Here are a few examples of the use of multiples of 10 and their prefixes with the units of length, mass, and time. Some additional time units are also included. Figure 1.4 gives a partial idea of the range of length scales studied in physics.

Length

$$1 \text{ nanometer } = 1 \text{ nm } = 10^{-9} \text{ m} \quad \text{(a few times the size of an atom)}$$
$$1 \text{ micrometer } = 1 \text{ } \mu\text{m } = 10^{-6} \text{ m} \quad \text{(size of some bacteria and cells)}$$
$$1 \text{ millimeter } = 1 \text{ mm } = 10^{-3} \text{ m} \quad \text{(point of a ballpoint pen)}$$
$$1 \text{ centimeter } = 1 \text{ cm } = 10^{-2} \text{ m} \quad \text{(diameter of your little finger)}$$
$$1 \text{ kilometer } = 1 \text{ km } = 10^{3} \text{ m} \quad \text{(distance traveled in a 10 minute walk)}$$

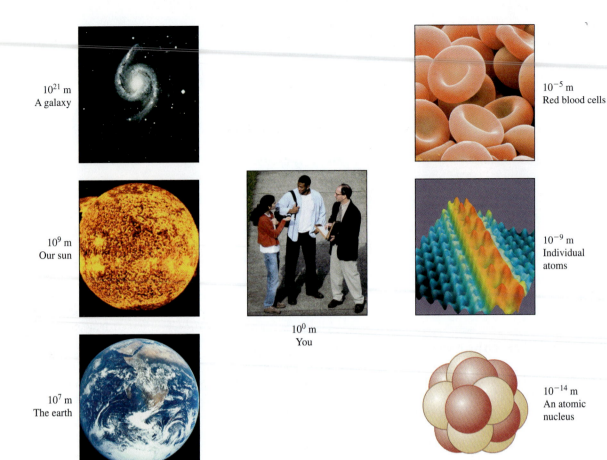

10^{21} m
A galaxy

10^{-5} m
Red blood cells

10^9 m
Our sun

10^{-9} m
Individual
atoms

10^0 m
You

10^7 m
The earth

10^{-14} m
An atomic
nucleus

▲ **FIGURE 1.4** These images show part of the range of sizes with which physics deals.

Mass

1 microgram = 1 μg = 10^{-9} kg   (mass of a 1 mm length of hair)

1 milligram = 1 mg = 10^{-6} kg   (mass of a grain of salt)

1 gram   = 1 g = 10^{-3} kg   (mass of a paper clip)

1 kilogram   = 1 kg = 10^3 g   (mass of a 1 liter bottle of water)

Time

1 nanosecond = 1 ns = 10^{-9} s   (time required for a personal computer to add two numbers)

1 microsecond = 1 μs = 10^{-6} s   (time required for a 10-year-old personal computer to add two numbers)

1 millisecond = 1 ms = 10^{-3} s   (time required for sound to travel 0.35 m)

1 minute   = 1 min = 60 s

1 hour   = 1 h   = 3600 s

1 day   = 1 day = 86,400 s

Finally, we mention the British system of units. These units are used only in the United States and a few other countries, and in most of those countries they are being replaced by SI units. British units are now officially *defined* in terms of SI units, as follows:

> Length: 1 inch = 2.54 cm (exactly).
>
> Force: 1 pound = 4.448221615260 newtons (exactly).

The fundamental British unit of time is the second, defined the same way as in SI. British units are used only in mechanics and thermodynamics; there is no British system of electrical units.

In this book we use SI units for almost all examples and problems, but in the early chapters we occasionally give approximate equivalents in British units. As you solve problems using SI units, try to think of the approximate equivalents in British units, but also try to think in SI as much as you can. Even in the United States, we now use metric units in many contexts; we speak about 4 liter engines, 50 mm lenses, 10 km races, 2 L soda bottles, and so on. The use of SI in everyday life is not far off.

Quantitative Analysis 1.1

SI measurement of hand

With your hand flat and your fingers and thumb close together, the width of your hand is about

A. 50 cm
B. 10 cm
C. 10 mm

SOLUTION If you're not familiar with metric units of length, you can use your body to develop intuition for them. One meter (100 cm) is slightly more than a yard, so the distance from elbow to fingertips is about 50 cm; this eliminates answer A. Ten millimeters (1 cm) is about the width of your little finger. Ten centimeters is about 4 inches and is about the width of your hand.

1.4 Unit Consistency and Conversions

We use equations to express relations among physical quantities that are represented by algebraic symbols. Most algebraic symbols for physical quantities denote both a number and a unit. For example, d might represent a distance of 10 m, t a time of 5 s, and v (for velocity) a speed of 2 m/s.

An equation must always be **dimensionally consistent.** You can't add apples and pomegranates; two terms may be added or equated only if they have the same units. For example, if a body moving with constant speed v travels a distance d in a time t, these quantities are related by the equation

$$d = vt. \quad (\text{distance} = \text{speed} \times \text{time})$$

If d is measured in meters, then the product vt must also be expressed in meters. Using the above numbers as an example, we may write

$$10 \text{ m} = (2 \text{ m/s})(5 \text{ s}).$$

Because the unit $1/\text{s}$ cancels the unit s in the last factor, the product vt does have units of meters, as it must. In calculations, with respect to multiplication and division, units are treated just like algebraic symbols.

NOTE ▶ When a problem requires calculations using numbers with units, *always* write the numbers with the correct units and carry the units through the calculation, as in the preceding example. This provides a very useful check for calculations. If at some stage in a calculation you find that an equation or an expression has inconsistent units, you know you have made an error somewhere. In this book we will always carry units through all calculations; we strongly urge you to follow this practice when you solve problems. ◀

PROBLEM-SOLVING STRATEGY 1.1 **Unit conversions**

Units are multiplied and divided just like ordinary algebraic symbols. This fact gives us an easy way to convert a quantity from one set of units to another. The key idea is that we can express the same physical quantity in two different units and form an equality. For example, when we say that 1 min = 60 s, we don't mean that the number 1 is equal to the number 60, but rather that 1 min represents the same physical time interval as 60 s. In a physical sense, multiplying by the quantity 1 min/60 s is really multiplying by unity, which doesn't change the physical meaning of the quantity. To find the number of seconds in 3 min, we write

$$3 \text{ min} = (3 \text{ min})\left(\frac{60 \text{ s}}{1 \text{ min}}\right) = 180 \text{ s}.$$

This expression makes sense. The second is a smaller unit than the minute, so there are more seconds than minutes in the same time interval.

A ratio of units, such as 1 min/60 s (or 1 min = 60 s), is called a **conversion factor**. A table of conversion factors is given in Appendix E and on the inside front cover. If you are used to English units, it may be useful to realize that 1 m is about 3 ft and that 1 gallon is about 4 liters ($1 \text{ gal} \approx 4 \text{ L}$).

 Inches vs. centimeters

If you express your height both in inches and in centimeters, which unit will give the larger number for your height?

A. The result in centimeters is larger, since you are comparing your height to a unit of length smaller than the inch.
B. Your height in inches is larger, since an inch is larger than a centimeter.
C. Either approach will give the same number, since your height does not depend on the unit used to express it.

SOLUTION Suppose you had a ruler just 1 cm long. To measure the height of a 5 ft person, you would have to move the ruler end-to-end up the person's body about 150 times. However, if your ruler were 1 inch long, you would have to move it just 60 times (5 ft = 60 in). Thus, the smaller your unit of measure, the larger the number you will get when you measure something with it. The correct answer is A.

EXAMPLE 1.1 **Driving the autobahn**

Although there is no maximum speed limit on the German autobahn, signs in many areas recommend a top speed of 130 km/h. Express this speed in meters per second and miles per hour.

SOLUTION

SET UP We know that 1 km = 1000 m. From Appendix E or the inside front cover, 1 mi = 1.609 km. We also know that 1 h = 60 min = 60 × (60 s) = 3600 s.

SOLVE We use these conversion factors with the problem-solving strategy we've outlined above:

$$130 \text{ km/h} = \left(\frac{130 \text{ km}}{1 \text{ h}}\right)\left(\frac{1000 \text{ m}}{1 \text{ km}}\right)\left(\frac{1 \text{ h}}{3600 \text{ s}}\right) = 36.1 \text{ m/s},$$

$$130 \text{ km/h} = \left(\frac{130 \text{ km}}{1 \text{ h}}\right)\left(\frac{1 \text{ mi}}{1.609 \text{ km}}\right) = 80.8 \text{ mi/h}.$$

REFLECT In physics, speeds are often expressed in meters per second, but if you're American, you're probably used to thinking in miles per hour. These calculations show that the number of miles per hour is roughly twice the number of meters per second; that is, a speed of 36.1 m/s isn't very different from 80.8 mi/h.

Practice Problem: Suppose you leave the autobahn and reduce your speed to 55 km/h. What is this speed in m/s and mi/h? *Answer:* 55 km/h = 15 m/s = 34 mi/h.

EXAMPLE 1.2 The age of the universe

The universe is thought to be about 13.7 billion years old. **(a)** What is the age of the universe in seconds? **(b)** Our species evolved about 4.7×10^{12} seconds ago. How many years is that?

SOLUTION

SET UP AND SOLVE We calculate the answer by using the appropriate conversion factors, starting with $1 \, y = 3.156 \times 10^7 \, s$.

Part (a): $13.7 \times 10^9 \, y = (13.7 \times 10^9 \, y)\left(\dfrac{3.156 \times 10^7 \, s}{1 \, y}\right)$

$$= 4.32 \times 10^{17} \, s.$$

Part (b): $4.7 \times 10^{12} \, s = (4.7 \times 10^{12} \, s)\left(\dfrac{1 \, y}{3.156 \times 10^7 \, s}\right)$

$$= 1.5 \times 10^5 \, y.$$

REFLECT These numbers tell us that the universe is about 10^5 times older than the human species. That is, the universe has existed about 100,000 times as long as we have. A handy approximate conversion factor is $1 \, y \approx \pi \times 10^7 \, s$; this is within 0.5% of the correct value.

Practice Problem: The average human life span in the United States is about 76.1 years. Calculate this time in seconds. *Answer:* $2.40 \times 10^9 \, s$.

Consistency of units

When an object moves through air, the air exerts a force on it. (You notice this force when you put your hand out of the window of a moving car.) The strength of the force, which we denote by F, is related to the speed v of the object by the equation $F = bv^2$, where b is a constant. In SI units (kg, m, s), the units of force are $kg \cdot m/s^2$ and the units of speed are m/s. For the preceding equation to have consistent units (the same units on both sides of the equation), the units of b must be

A. kg/m
B. $kg \cdot m/s$
C. kg/m^2

SOLUTION To solve this problem, we start with the equation $F = bv^2$. For each symbol whose units we know (in this case, F and v), we replace the symbol with those units. For example, we replace v with (m/s). We obtain

$$\left(\frac{kg \cdot m}{s \cdot s}\right) = b\left(\frac{m}{s}\right)\left(\frac{m}{s}\right).$$ (Algebraically, units are treated like numbers.)

We now solve this equation for b. When we multiply the equation on both sides by s^2, the seconds (s) cancel, and one of the meter units (m) cancels. We obtain $b = kg/m$, so the correct answer is A.

1.5 Precision and Significant Figures

Measurements always have uncertainties. When we measure a distance with an ordinary ruler, it is usually reliable only to the nearest millimeter, but with a precision micrometer caliper, we can measure distances with an uncertainty of less than 0.01 mm. We often indicate the precision of a number by writing the number, the symbol $\pm$, and a second number indicating the likely uncertainty. If the diameter of a steel rod is given as 56.47 ± 0.02 mm, this expression means that the true value is unlikely to be less than 56.45 mm or greater than 56.49 mm.

When we use numbers having uncertainties or errors to compute other numbers, the computed numbers are also uncertain. It is especially important to understand this when comparing a number obtained from measurements with a value obtained from a theoretical prediction. Suppose you want to determine the value of π (pi), as in Figure 1.5, using the relation of the circumference C of a circle to its diameter D: $C = \pi D$. Then

$$\pi = \frac{C}{D} = \frac{\text{circumference}}{\text{diameter}}.$$

The true value of this ratio, to 10 digits, is 3.141592654. To make your own calculation, you cut a circular piece out of a sheet of plywood and measure its diameter and circumference to the nearest millimeter, using a flexible measuring tape. Suppose you obtain the values 135 mm and 424 mm, respectively. You

135 mm

424 mm

▲ **FIGURE 1.5** Finding π with a plywood disk and a tape measure.

▲ **What went wrong?** While a 0.01% error may sound insignificant, in this case it resulted in a spectacular mishap. In a journey of 500 kilometers, a 0.01% error represents only 50 meters. Yet going 0.01% too far had tragic results in this instance. In physics, measurements can be considerably more precise than ±0.01%. For example, according to the National Institute of Standards and Technology, the mass of the electron has been determined to be $9.1093826 \pm 0.0000016 \times 10^{-31}$ kg. This represents a relative uncertainty of 1.7×10^{-7}, or only ±0.000017%, in measuring the mass of the electron.

punch these numbers into your calculator and obtain the quotient 3.140740741. Does this quantity agree with the true value or not?

First, the last seven digits in this answer are meaningless, because they imply greater precision than is possible with your measurements. The number of meaningful digits in a number is called the number of **significant figures** or **significant digits.** ("Figure" in this context means "digit.") **When numbers are multiplied or divided, the number of significant figures in the result is no greater than in the factor with the fewest significant figures.** For example, $3.1416 \times 2.34 \times 0.58 = 4.3$. Thus your measured value of π using the plywood circle has only three significant figures and should be stated simply as 3.14. Your value *does* agree with the true value, although only to three significant figures.

NOTE ▶ Zero can be a significant figure. The number 0.580 has three significant figures. The initial zero doesn't matter, but the final zero implies that the number is probably between 0.579 and 0.581. Writing 0.58 implies only that the number is probably between 0.57 and 0.59. Leading zeroes aren't significant, but trailing zeroes are. ◀

When you add or subtract, the rule for handling significant figures is slightly different than when you multiply or divide: **When you add or subtract, the answer can have no more decimal places than the term with the fewest decimal places.** For example, $5.232 + 0.31 = 5.54$, not 5.542.

Here's one additional point: In symbolic relationships, when unitless numerical constants appear, usually they should be taken to have infinitely great accuracy, with no uncertainty at all. For example, in the relation $C = 2\pi R$ between the radius R and circumference C of a circle, the factor 2 is taken to be exact, with no uncertainty. It could appropriately be written as 2.000000000000000.

Most examples and problems in this book give data to two or three significant figures (occasionally more). In each problem, your answer should have no more significant figures than the preceding rules allow. You may do the arithmetic with a calculator having a display with 5 to 10 digits. But you should *not* give a 10 digit answer for a calculation using numbers with three significant figures. To do so is not only unnecessary; it is genuinely wrong, because it misrepresents the precision of the results. Always round your answer to keep only the correct number of significant figures.

When we calculate with very large or very small numbers, we can show significant figures much more easily by using powers-of-ten notation, sometimes called *scientific notation,* as we discussed in Section 1.3. For example, the distance from the earth to the sun is about 149,000,000,000 m, but writing the number in this form gives no indication of the number of significant figures. Certainly, not all 12 are significant! Instead, we move the decimal point 11 places to the left (corresponding to dividing by 10^{11}) and multiply by 10^{11}. That is,

$$149{,}000{,}000{,}000 \text{ m} = 1.49 \times 10^{11} \text{ m}. \quad \text{(three significant figures)}$$

In this form, it is clear that we have three significant figures. In scientific notation, a common practice is to express a quantity as a number between 1 and 10, multiplied by the appropriate power of 10.

EXAMPLE 1.3 Mass is energy

The energy E corresponding to the mass m of an electron is given by Einstein's famous equation

$$E = mc^2, \quad \text{(equivalence of mass and energy)}$$

where c is the speed of light. Calculate the value of E for an electron, using powers of ten and three significant figures.

Continued

SOLUTION

SET UP We find the needed numbers inside the front cover or in Appendix E: $m = 9.11 \times 10^{-31}$ kg and $c = 3.00 \times 10^8$ m/s.

SOLVE We use these numbers to calculate the value of E:

$$E = (9.11 \times 10^{-31} \text{ kg})(3.00 \times 10^8 \text{ m/s})^2$$
$$= (9.11)(3.00)^2(10^{-31})(10^8)^2(\text{kg} \cdot \text{m}^2)/\text{s}^2$$
$$= (82.0)(10^{[-31+(2\times8)]})(\text{kg} \cdot \text{m}^2)/\text{s}^2$$
$$= 8.20 \times 10^{-14} \text{ kg} \cdot \text{m}^2/\text{s}^2.$$

REFLECT Most pocket calculators can use scientific notation and do this addition of exponents automatically for you; but you should be able to do such calculations by hand when necessary. Incidentally, the value used for c in Example 1.3 has three significant figures, even though two of them are zeros. To greater precision, $c = 2.997925 \times 10^8$ m/s.

Conceptual Analysis 1.4

Significant figures

To seven significant figures, the speed of light is $c = 2.997925 \times 10^8$ m/s. Which of the following choices is or are correct?

A. $c = 3.0 \times 10^8$ m/s
B. $c = 3.00 \times 10^8$ m/s
C. $c = 3.000 \times 10^8$ m/s

SOLUTION Answer C is incorrect, because when we round to four significant figures, we get 2.998, not 3.000. But A and B are both correct; they represent different levels of precision, even though the numerical value is the same.

1.6 Estimates and Orders of Magnitude

We've talked about the importance of knowing the precision of numbers that represent physical quantities. But there are also situations in which even a very crude estimate of a quantity may give us useful information. Often we know how to calculate a certain quantity but have to guess at the data we need for the calculation. Or the calculation may be too complicated to carry out exactly, so we make some crude approximations. In either case our result is also a guess, but many times such a guess is useful, even if it is uncertain by a factor of 2, or 10, or more. Such calculations are often called **order-of-magnitude estimates.** The great nuclear physicist Enrico Fermi (1901–1954) called them "back-of-the-envelope calculations."

EXAMPLE 1.4   **Espionage**

You are writing an international espionage novel in which the hero escapes across the border with a billion dollars worth of gold in his suitcase. Is this possible? Would that amount of gold fit in a suitcase? Would it be too heavy to carry?

SOLUTION

SET UP AND SOLVE We can guess at both the mass of gold needed and its density. From these numbers we can then find the volume of gold needed.

Gold sells for around $400 an ounce. On a particular day, the price might be $200 or $600, but never mind. An ounce is about 30 grams. Actually, an ordinary (avoirdupois) ounce is 28.35 g; an ounce of gold is a troy ounce, which is 9.45% more. Again, never mind. Ten dollars worth of gold has a mass somewhere around 1 gram, so a billion (10^9) dollars worth of gold is a hundred million (10^8) grams, or a hundred thousand (10^5) kilograms. This corresponds to a weight in British units of around 200,000 lb, or a hundred tons.

We can also estimate the *volume* of this gold. If its density were the same as that of water (1 g/cm^3), the volume would be 10^8 cm^3, or 100 m^3. But gold is a heavy metal; we might guess its density to be 10 times that of water. In fact, it is over 20 times as dense as water. But guessing 10, we find a volume of 10 m^3. Visualize 10 cubical stacks of gold bricks, each 1 meter on a side, and ask whether they would fit in a suitcase!

REFLECT Whether the precise weight is 50 tons or 200 doesn't matter. Either way, the hero is not about to carry it across the border in a suitcase. And 10 cubic meters certainly won't fit in the suitcase!

Practice Problem: Suppose our hero needs only a million dollars, not a billion. Are the answers the same or different? Would he do better if he used cut diamonds instead of gold? *Answer:* Weight is a few hundred pounds; volume is comparable to a small carry-on suitcase. Diamonds would be better.

1.7 Vectors and Vector Addition

Handwritten notation: $\vec{A}$

Ending position

Displacement $\vec{A}$

Starting position

(a)

The displacement depends only on the starting and ending positions—not on the path taken.

$\vec{A}$

Path taken

(b)

If the object makes a round-trip, the total displacement is 0, regardless of the distance traveled.

(c)

▲ **FIGURE 1.6** Displacement is a vector quantity. A displacement vector represents a change in position (distance and direction) of an object from one point in space to another.

Some physical quantities, such as time, temperature, mass, density, and electric charge, can be described completely by a single number with a unit. Many other quantities, however, have a *directional* quality and cannot be described by a single number. A familiar example is velocity. To describe the motion of an airplane, we have to say not only *how fast* it is moving, but also *in what direction*. To fly from Chicago to New York, the plane has to head east, not south. Force is another example. When we push or pull on a body, we exert a force on it. To describe a force, we need to describe the direction in which it acts, as well as its magnitude, or "how hard" the force pushes or pulls. A tow truck usually pulls a stalled car forward, not sideways.

When a physical quantity is described by a single number, we call it a **scalar quantity.** In contrast, a **vector quantity** has both a **magnitude** (the "how much" or "how big" part) and a **direction** in space. Calculations with scalar quantities use the operations of ordinary arithmetic. For example, 6 kg + 3 kg = 9 kg, or $(12\,\text{m})/(3\,\text{s}) = 4\,\text{m/s}$. However, combining vector quantities requires a different set of operations. Vector quantities play an essential role in all areas of physics, so let's talk next about what vectors are and how they combine.

We start with the simplest of all vector quantities: **displacement.** Displacement is simply a change in position of an object, which we will assume can be treated as a pointlike particle. In Figure 1.6a, we represent the object's change in position by an arrow that points from the starting position to the ending position. Displacement is a *vector quantity* because we must state not only *how far* the particle moves, but also *in what direction*. Walking 3 km north from your front door doesn't get you to the same place as walking 3 km southeast.

We usually represent a vector quantity, such as a displacement, by a single letter, such as $\vec{A}$ in Figure 1.6. In this book, we always print vector symbols **in boldface type with an arrow above them,** to remind you that vector quantities have properties different from those of scalar quantities. In handwriting, vector symbols are usually written with an arrow above, as shown in Figure 1.6a, to indicate that they represent vector quantities.

NOTE ▶ When you write a symbol for a vector quantity, *always* put an arrow over it. If you don't distinguish between scalar and vector quantities in your notation, you probably won't make the distinction in your thinking either, and hopeless confusion will result. ◀

A displacement is always a straight-line segment, directed from the starting point to the endpoint, even though the actual path of the object may be curved. In Figure 1.6b, the displacement is still $\vec{A}$, even though the object takes a round-about path. Also, note that displacement is not related directly to the total *distance* traveled. If the particle makes a round trip, returning to its starting point as shown in Figure 1.6c, the displacement for the entire trip is *zero*.

The vector $\vec{A}'$ from point 3 to point 4 in Figure 1.7 has the same length and direction as the vector $\vec{A}$ from point 1 to point 2. These two displacements are equal, even though they start at different points. Thus we may write $\vec{A}' = \vec{A}$. By definition, two vector quantities are equal if they have the same magnitude (length) and direction, no matter where they are located in space. The vector $\vec{B}$, however, is *not* equal to $\vec{A}$, because its direction is *opposite* to that of $\vec{A}$. We define the *negative* of a vector as a vector having the same magnitude as the original vector, but opposite direction. The negative of the vector quantity $\vec{A}$ is denoted $-\vec{A}$. If $\vec{A}$ is 87 m south, then $-\vec{A}$ is 87 m north.

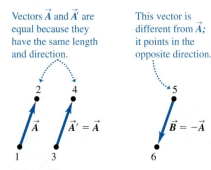

Vectors $\vec{A}$ and $\vec{A}'$ are equal because they have the same length and direction.

This vector is different from $\vec{A}$; it points in the opposite direction.

$\vec{A}$ $\vec{A}' = \vec{A}$ $\vec{B} = -\vec{A}$

▲ **FIGURE 1.7** Two displacement vectors are equal if they have the same length (magnitude) and the same (not opposite) direction.

Thus, the relation between $\vec{A}$ and $\vec{B}$ may be written as $\vec{A} = -\vec{B}$ or $\vec{B} = -\vec{A}$. When two vectors $\vec{A}$ and $\vec{B}$ have opposite directions, we say that they are *antiparallel*.

NOTE ▶ Remember that two vector quantities are equal only when they have the same magnitude *and* the same (not opposite) direction. ◀

We usually represent the magnitude of a vector quantity (its length, in the case of a displacement vector) by the same letter used for the vector, but in light italic type rather than boldface italic. An alternative notation is the vector symbol with vertical bars on both sides. Thus,

Magnitude of $\vec{A} = A = |\vec{A}|$.   (notation for magnitude of a vector quantity)

By definition, the magnitude of a vector quantity is a scalar quantity (a single number) and is always positive. We also note that a vector can never be equal to a scalar, because they are different kinds of quantities. The expression $\vec{A} = 6$ m is just as wrong as "2 oranges = 3 apples" or "6 lb = 7 km"!

Now suppose a particle undergoes a displacement $\vec{A}$, followed by a second displacement $\vec{B}$ (Figure 1.8a). The final result is the same as though the particle had started at the same initial point and undergone a single displacement $\vec{C}$, as shown. We call displacement $\vec{C}$ the **vector sum,** or **resultant,** of displacements $\vec{A}$ and $\vec{B}$; we express this relationship symbolically as

$$\vec{C} = \vec{A} + \vec{B}.\quad\text{(vector sum of two vectors)}$$

The plus sign in this equation denotes the geometrical operation of **vector addition** that we've described; it is *not* the same operation as adding two scalar quantities such as $2 + 3 = 5$.

If we make the displacements $\vec{A}$ and $\vec{B}$ in the reverse order, as in Figure 1.8b, with $\vec{B}$ first and $\vec{A}$ second, the result is the same, as the figure shows. Thus,

$$\vec{C} = \vec{B} + \vec{A}\quad\text{and}\quad \vec{A} + \vec{B} = \vec{B} + \vec{A}.\quad\text{(Vector sum is commutative.)}$$

The last equation shows that the order of the terms in a vector sum doesn't matter; addition of vectors is **commutative.** We draw the tail of the second vector at the point of the first, and the results are the same with either order.

Figure 1.8b also suggests an alternative graphical representation of the vector sum. When vectors $\vec{A}$ and $\vec{B}$ are both drawn with their tails at the same point, vector $\vec{C}$ is the diagonal of a parallelogram constructed with $\vec{A}$ and $\vec{B}$ as two adjacent sides.

Figure 1.9 shows the special cases in which two vectors $\vec{A}$ and $\vec{B}$ are parallel (Figure 1.9a) or antiparallel (Figure 1.9b). When the vectors are parallel, the magnitude of the vector sum equals the *sum* of the magnitudes of $\vec{A}$ and $\vec{B}$; when they are antiparallel, it equals the *difference* of their magnitudes.

(a)

(b)

(c)

▲ **FIGURE 1.8** Vector $\vec{C}$ is the vector sum of vectors $\vec{A}$ and $\vec{B}$. The order in vector addition doesn't matter. (Vector addition is commutative.)

(a) The sum of two parallel vectors

(b) The sum of two antiparallel vectors

▲ **FIGURE 1.9** The vector sum of (a) two parallel vectors and (b) two antiparallel vectors. Note that the vectors $\vec{A}$, $\vec{B}$, and $\vec{C}$ in (a) are not the same as the vectors $\vec{A}$, $\vec{B}$, and $\vec{C}$ in (b).

Conceptual Analysis 1.5

Resultant vector

Two vectors, one with magnitude 3 m and the other with magnitude 4 m, are added together. The resultant vector could have a magnitude as small as

A. 1 m;

B. 3 m;

C. 4 m.

SOLUTION The resultant has the largest magnitude when the two vectors are parallel and the smallest when they are antiparallel— that is, pointing in opposite directions. In the latter case, the resultant will be the difference between their lengths, which is 1 m. Thus, answer A is correct.

To find the sum of these three vectors . . .

we could add $\vec{A}$ and $\vec{B}$ to get $\vec{D}$ and then add $\vec{C}$ to $\vec{D}$ to get the final sum (resultant) $\vec{R}$, . . .

or we could add $\vec{B}$ and $\vec{C}$ to get $\vec{E}$ and then add $\vec{A}$ to $\vec{E}$ to get $\vec{R}$, . . .

or we could add $\vec{A}$, $\vec{B}$, and $\vec{C}$ to get $\vec{R}$ directly, . . .

or we could add $\vec{A}$, $\vec{B}$, and $\vec{C}$ in any other order and still get $\vec{R}$.

(a)   (b)   (c)   (d)   (e)

▲ **FIGURE 1.10** Several constructions for finding the vector sum $\vec{A} + \vec{B} + \vec{C}$.

▲ **Where will it end up?** Although this caribou is trying to swim straight across the river, it will not end up directly across from its starting point. Its final position on the opposite bank can be determined by the addition of two vectors. One represents its movement directly across the river, and a second represents the downstream movement of the water. If it paddles across at the same speed as the river flows, summing these two vectors shows us that it will actually cross the river at a 45° angle. At the other side, it will end up a distance downstream equal to the width of the river, having traveled a distance of $\sqrt{2}$ times the river's width.

When we need to add more than two vectors, we may first find the vector sum of any two, add it vectorially to the third, and so on. Figure 1.10a shows three vectors $\vec{A}$, $\vec{B}$, and $\vec{C}$. In Figure 1.10b, vectors $\vec{A}$ and $\vec{B}$ are first added, giving a vector sum $\vec{D}$; vectors $\vec{D}$ and $\vec{C}$ are then added by the same process to obtain the vector sum $\vec{R}$:

$$\vec{R} = (\vec{A} + \vec{B}) + \vec{C} = \vec{D} + \vec{C}.$$

Alternatively, we can first add $\vec{B}$ and $\vec{C}$ (Figure 1.10c) to obtain vector $\vec{E}$ and then add $\vec{A}$ and $\vec{E}$ to obtain $\vec{R}$:

$$\vec{R} = \vec{A} + (\vec{B} + \vec{C}) = \vec{A} + \vec{E}.$$

We don't even need to draw vectors $\vec{D}$ and $\vec{E}$; all we need to do is draw the given vectors in succession, with the tail of each at the head of the one preceding it, and complete the polygon by a vector $\vec{R}$ from the *tail* of the first to the *head* of the last, as shown in Figure 1.10d. The order makes no difference; Figure 1.10e shows a different order, and we invite you to try others.

NOTE ▶ When adding vectors graphically, always arrange them tip to tail, so that the tip of one points to the tail of the next. The vectors can be in any order. The resultant always points from the tail of the first vector to the tip of the final one. ◀

Quantitative Analysis 1.6

Pythagorean vectors

If you walk 40 m east, then 30 m north, how far from the starting point are you?

A. 10 m
B. 50 m
C. 70 m

SOLUTION The two legs of your trip form the sides of a right triangle; your final displacement is the hypotenuse. Draw a diagram showing the two successive displacements and the vector

sum. You can use the Pythagorean theorem to calculate the length of the vector sum, 50 m.

You can confirm the length of this resultant vector by using what you know about parallel and antiparallel vectors. If the two legs of your trip were antiparallel (rather than at right angles), the resultant would have a magnitude of 10 m. So A can't be right; the correct answer must be larger. If the two legs were parallel (i.e., if you walked 40 m and then continued 30 m in the same direction), the resultant would have a magnitude of 70 m, so C can't be right either; the correct answer must be smaller. That leaves B as the correct answer.

Diagrams for the addition of displacement vectors don't have to be drawn actual size. Often, we'll use a scale similar to those used for maps, in which the distance on the diagram is *proportional* to the actual distance, such as 1 cm for 5 km. When we work with other vector quantities with different units, such as force or velocity, we *must* use a scale. In a diagram for velocity vectors, we might use a scale in which a vector 1 cm long represents a velocity with magnitude 5 m/s. A velocity with magnitude 20 m/s would then be represented by a vector 4 cm long in the appropriate direction.

A vector quantity such as a displacement can be multiplied by a scalar quantity (an ordinary number). As shown in Figure 1.11, the displacement $2\vec{A}$ is a displacement (vector quantity) in the same direction as the vector $\vec{A}$, but twice as long. The scalar quantity used to multiply a vector may also be a physical quantity having units. For example, when an object moves in a straight line with constant velocity $\vec{v}$ for a time t, its total displacement $\vec{d}$ is equal to $\vec{v}t$. The magnitude d of the displacement is equal to the magnitude v of the velocity multiplied by the time t. The directions of $\vec{d}$ and $\vec{v}$ are the same (assuming that t is positive). The units of d are the product of the units of v and t.

We've already mentioned that $-\vec{A}$ is, by definition, a vector having the same magnitude as $\vec{A}$ but opposite direction. This definition provides the basis for defining vector *subtraction*. (See Figure 1.12.) We define the *difference* $\vec{A} - \vec{B}$ of two vectors $\vec{A}$ and $\vec{B}$ to be the vector sum of $\vec{A}$ and $-\vec{B}$:

$$\vec{A} - \vec{B} = \vec{A} + (-\vec{B}). \quad \text{(vector difference)}$$

Multiplying a vector by a positive scalar changes the magnitude (length) of the vector, but not its direction.

$2\vec{A}$ is twice as long as $\vec{A}$.

Multiplying a vector by a negative scalar changes its magnitude and reverses its direction.

$-3\vec{A}$ is three times as long as $\vec{A}$ and points in the opposite direction.

▲ **FIGURE 1.11** The effect of multiplying a vector by a scalar.

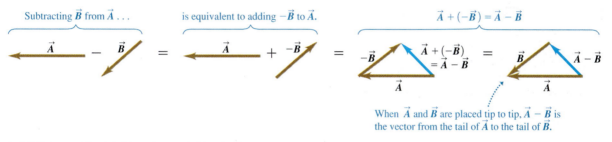

▲ **FIGURE 1.12** The definition of vector subtraction.

EXAMPLE 1.5 Displacement of a cross-country skier

On a cross-country ski trip, you travel 1.00 km north and then 2.00 km east. **(a)** How far and in what direction are you from your starting point? **(b)** What are the magnitude and direction of your resultant displacement?

SOLUTION

SET UP Figure 1.13 is a scale diagram. By careful measurement on the diagram, we find that the distance d from the starting point is about 2.2 km and the angle ϕ is about 63°. But it's much more accurate to *calculate* the result. The vectors in the diagram form a right triangle, and we can find the length of the hypotenuse by using the Pythagorean theorem. The angle can be found by simple trigonometry, from the definition of the tangent function.

SOLVE **Part (a):** Use the Pythagorean theorem to find the length d of the resultant displacement vector (the distance from the starting point):

$$d = \sqrt{(1.00 \text{ km})^2 + (2.00 \text{ km})^2}$$
$$= 2.24 \text{ km}. \quad \text{(Magnitude of displacement vector)}$$

From the definition of the tangent function,

$$\tan\phi = \frac{\text{opposite side}}{\text{adjacent side}} = \frac{2.00 \text{ km}}{1.00 \text{ km}},$$
$$\phi = 63.4°. \quad \text{(direction of displacement vector)}$$

▲ **FIGURE 1.13** A vector diagram, drawn to scale, for a cross-country ski trip.

Part (b): The magnitude of the resultant displacement is just the distance d we found in part (a), 2.24 km. We can describe the direction as 63.4° east of north, or 26.6° north of east. Take your choice!

Continued

REFLECT The method we've used here works only for vectors that form a right triangle. In the next section, we'll present a more general method.

Practice Problem: Your friend skis 3.00 km east and then 1.50 km north. **(a)** How far and in what direction is he from the starting point? **(b)** What are the magnitude and direction of his resultant displacement? *Answers:* (a) 3.35 km, 26.6°; (b) 3.35 km, 26.6° north of east.

1.8 Components of Vectors

We need to develop efficient and general methods for adding vectors. In Example 1.5 in the preceding section, we added two vectors by drawing and measuring a scale diagram or by making use of the properties of right triangles. Measuring a diagram offers only very limited precision, and our example was a special case in which the two vectors were perpendicular. With an angle other than 90° or with more than two vectors, we would get into repeated trigonometric solutions of oblique triangles, which can get horribly complicated.

So we need a simple, but more general, method for adding vectors. The usual method makes use of *components* of vectors. As a prelude to explaining this method, let's review the definitions of the basic trigonometric functions.

For a right triangle, the functions $\sin\theta$, $\cos\theta$ and $\tan\theta$ are defined as follows:

Definitions of trigonometric functions
For the right triangle shown,

$$\sin\theta = \frac{\text{opposite side}}{\text{hypotenuse}}, \qquad \cos\theta = \frac{\text{adjacent side}}{\text{hypotenuse}},$$

$$\tan\theta = \frac{\text{opposite side}}{\text{adjacent side}}. \tag{1.1}$$

From these definitions, we can prove that, for any angle θ,

$$\tan\theta = \frac{\sin\theta}{\cos\theta} \qquad \text{and} \qquad \sin^2\theta + \cos^2\theta = 1.$$

Now, what are components, and how are they used to add and subtract vectors? To define what we mean by components, let's start with a rectangular (Cartesian) coordinate axis system as in Figure 1.14. We can represent any vector lying in the x-y plane as the vector sum of a vector parallel to the x axis and a vector parallel to the y axis. These two vectors are labeled $\vec{A}_x$ and $\vec{A}_y$ in Figure 1.14a; they are called the **component vectors** of vector $\vec{A}$, and their vector sum is equal to $\vec{A}$. In symbols,

$$\vec{A} = \vec{A}_x + \vec{A}_y. \quad \text{(vector } \vec{A} \text{ as a sum of component vectors)}$$

By definition, each component vector lies along one of the two coordinate-axis directions. Thus, we need only a single number to describe each component. When the vector points in the positive axis direction, we define the number A_x to

(a)

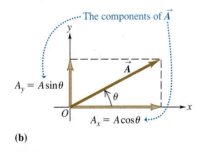

(b)

▲ **FIGURE 1.14** (a) The component vectors of $\vec{A}$ in the direction of the x and y axes. (b) The x and y components of $\vec{A}$.

be the magnitude of $\vec{A}_x$. When $\vec{A}_x$ points in the $-x$ direction, we define the number A_x to be the *negative* of that magnitude, keeping in mind that the magnitude of a vector quantity is always positive. We define the number A_y the same way. The two numbers A_x and A_y are called the **components** of the vector $\vec{A}$. We haven't yet described what they're good for; we'll get to that soon!

NOTE ▶ Be sure that you understand the relationship between $\vec{A}$ (a vector), A or $|\vec{A}|$ (the vector's magnitude), $\vec{A}_x$ (a component vector) and A_x (a component). The following tips are useful:

- A subscript x or y indicates that the quantity is a component vector or component along the x or y axis. Watch for these subscripts!
- A *magnitude* is always positive.
- A *component* is positive if the corresponding component vector points in the positive direction of the axis, negative if the component vector points in the negative direction of the axis. ◀

If, for the vector $\vec{A}$ in Figure 1.14, we know both the magnitude A and the direction, given by the angle θ, we can calculate the components, as shown in Figure 1.14b. From the definitions of the trigonometric cosine and sine functions,

$$\frac{A_x}{A} = \cos\theta \quad \text{and} \quad \frac{A_y}{A} = \sin\theta;$$

$$A_x = A\cos\theta \quad \text{and} \quad A_y = A\sin\theta. \tag{1.2}$$

NOTE ▶ These equations are correct for *any* angle θ, from 0 to 360°, provided that the angle is measured counterclockwise from the positive x axis. This is the usual convention, but sometimes you'll find it more convenient to measure θ from a different axis; then you'll have to identify the appropriate right triangle and use the definitions of the trigonometric functions for that triangle. Be careful! ◀

In Figure 1.15, the component B_x is negative because its direction is opposite that of the positive x axis. This is consistent with Equations 1.2; the cosine of an angle in the second quadrant is negative. B_y is positive, but both C_x and C_y are negative.

We can describe a vector completely by giving either its magnitude and direction or its x and y components. Equations 1.2 show how to find the components if we know the magnitude and direction. Applying the Pythagorean theorem to Figure 1.14, we find

$$A = \sqrt{A_x^2 + A_y^2}. \quad \text{(magnitude of vector } \vec{A}) \tag{1.3}$$

Also, from the definition of the tangent of an angle,

$$\tan\theta = \frac{A_y}{A_x} \quad \text{and} \quad \theta = \tan^{-1}\frac{A_y}{A_x}. \quad \text{(direction of vector } \vec{A}) \tag{1.4}$$

NOTE ▶ There's a slight complication in using Equations 1.4 to find θ. Suppose $A_x = 2$ m and $A_y = -2$ m; then $\tan\theta = -1$. But, as shown in Figure 1.16, there are two angles having tangents of -1, namely, 135° and 315° (or $-45°$). To decide which is correct, we have to look at the individual components. Because A_x is positive and A_y is negative, the angle must be in the fourth quadrant; thus, $\theta = 315°$ (or $-45°$) is the correct value. Most pocket calculators give $\tan^{-1}(-1) = -45°$. In this case, that is

(a)

(b)

▲ **FIGURE 1.15** The components of a vector are numbers; they may be positive or negative.

In this case, $\tan\theta = \dfrac{A_y}{A_x} = -1$.

Two angles have tangents of -1: 135° and 315°. Inspection of the diagram shows that θ must be 315°.

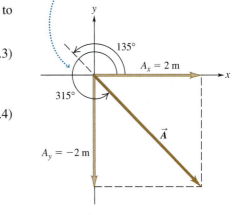

▲ **FIGURE 1.16** Two angles may have the same tangent; sketching the vector shows which angle is correct.

correct; but if, instead, we have $A_x = -2$ m and $A_y = 2$ m, then the correct angle is 135°. You should always draw a sketch to check which of the two possibilities is the correct one. Similarly, when A_x and A_y are both negative, the tangent is positive, but the angle is in the third quadrant. ◄

The next example will give us some practice in finding components of individual vectors; then we'll talk about how the components are used to find vector sums and differences.

EXAMPLE 1.6   **Finding components of vectors**

Raoul and Maria set out walking from their aunt's house. Raoul walks a certain distance straight east and then a certain distance straight north. A crow passing overhead starts from the same point as Raoul, but flies in a straight line. Raoul observes that the crow flies a total distance of 500 m in a direction 35° north of east to reach the same final point as Raoul. Maria starts from the same point as Raoul, but she walks first straight west and then straight south. Her final point is 700 m from the starting point in a direction that is 55° south of west. How far did Raoul walk on the east leg of his trip? How far on the north leg? Similarly, how far did Maria walk on the west leg and how far on the south leg? Express these quantities in terms of displacement vectors and their components, using a coordinate system with the $+x$ axis pointing east and the $+y$ axis pointing north.

SOLUTION

SET UP First we sketch a diagram showing each displacement, as in Figure 1.17. We draw a rectangular coordinate system and label the axes, with the $+x$ axis east and the $+y$ axis north. Be sure to make your sketch large enough so that you will be able to draw and label the components of each vector. Note that the vector representing Maria's displacement lies in the third quadrant, so both the x and y components of this vector will be negative.

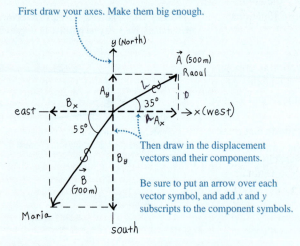
First draw your axes. Make them big enough.

Then draw in the displacement vectors and their components.

Be sure to put an arrow over each vector symbol, and add x and y subscripts to the component symbols.

▲ **FIGURE 1.17** The diagram we draw for this problem.

SOLVE We'll label Raoul's displacement vector $\vec{A}$ and Maria's $\vec{B}$. Then to find the components we use Equations 1.2:

$$A_x = A\cos\theta \quad \text{and} \quad B_x = B\cos\theta$$
$$A_y = A\sin\theta \quad \qquad B_y = B\sin\theta$$

We measure the angles counterclockwise from the $+x$ axis. So the direction of Maria's displacement is $180° + 55° = 235°$. The components of the two displacement vectors are as follows:

Raoul	Maria
$A_x = 500\text{ m }(\cos 35°)$	$B_x = 700\text{ m }(\cos 235°)$
$\quad = 410\text{ m (east)}$	$\quad = -402\text{ m (west)}$
$A_y = 500\text{ m }(\sin 35°)$	$B_y = 700\text{ m }(\sin 235°)$
$\quad = 287\text{ m (north)}$	$\quad = -573\text{ m (south)}$

REFLECT Because Maria walked west and south, the x and y components of her displacement are both negative. To get the correct signs, we must measure the angles counterclockwise from the $+x$ axis.

Practice Problem: Raoul's friend Johnny sets out from his house in the city. His displacement is 600 m 40° north of west. What are the x and y components of his displacement vector? *Answers:* $A_x = -460$ m; $A_y = 386$ m.

Using components to add vectors

Now, at last, we're ready to talk about using components to calculate the vector sum of several vectors. The component method requires only right triangles and simple computations, and it can be carried out with great precision. Here's the basic idea: Figure 1.18a shows two vectors $\vec{A}$ and $\vec{B}$ and their vector sum (resultant) $\vec{R}$, along with the x and y components of all three vectors. You can see from the diagram that the x component R_x of the vector sum is simply the sum

$\vec{R}$ is the sum (resultant) of $\vec{A}$ and $\vec{B}$.

The y component of $\vec{R}$ equals the sum of the y components of $\vec{A}$ and $\vec{B}$.

The same goes for the x components.

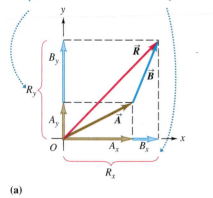

(a)

When we replace a vector with its components, we cross out the original vector with a squiggle for clarity.

(b)

◄ **FIGURE 1.18** (a) When two vectors $\vec{A}$ and $\vec{B}$ are added to give a vector sum (resultant) $\vec{R}$, the sum of their x components is the x component of $\vec{R}$, and the sum of their y components is the y component of $\vec{R}$. (b) When we replace a vector with its components, we cross out the original vector to avoid confusion.

$(A_x + B_x)$ of the x components of the vectors being added. The same is true for the y components. In symbols,

$$R_x = A_x + B_x,$$
$$R_y = A_y + B_y.$$ (components of vector sum)   (1.5)

Once we know the components of $\vec{A}$ and $\vec{B}$, perhaps by using Equations 1.2, we can compute the components of the vector sum $\vec{R}$. Then if the magnitude and direction of $\vec{R}$ are needed, we can obtain them from Equations 1.3 and 1.4, with the A's replaced by R's.

NOTE ▶ As Figure 1.18b shows, when you represent a vector in terms of its components, it's always a good idea to use a squiggly line to cross out the original vector in your diagram. Otherwise there's danger that you'll count the same vector twice when you have to perform a vector addition or some other vector operation. ◄

This procedure can easily be extended to find the vector sum of any number of vectors. Let $\vec{R}$ be the vector sum of $\vec{A}, \vec{B}, \vec{C}, \vec{D}$, and $\vec{E}$. Then

$$R_x = A_x + B_x + C_x + D_x + E_x,$$
$$R_y = A_y + B_y + C_y + D_y + E_y.$$

NOTE ▶ In sums such as this, usually some of the components are positive and some are negative, so be very careful about signs when you evaluate such sums. And remember that x and y components are *never* added together in the same equation! ◄

EXAMPLE 1.7   **Adding two vectors**

Vector $\vec{A}$ has a magnitude of 50 cm and a direction of 30°, and vector $\vec{B}$ has a magnitude of 35 cm and a direction of 110°. Both angles are measured counterclockwise from the positive x axis. Use components to calculate the magnitude and direction of the vector sum (i.e., the resultant) $\vec{R} = \vec{A} + \vec{B}$.

SOLUTION

SET UP We set up a rectangular (Cartesian) coordinate system and place the tail of each vector at the origin, as shown in Figure 1.19a. We label the known magnitudes and angles on our diagram.

SOLVE We find the x and y components of each vector, using Equations 1.2, and record the results in the table shown next. We add the x components to obtain the x component of the vector sum $\vec{R}$, and we add the y components to obtain the y component

Continued

of $\vec{R}$. (But be very careful *not* to add the x and y components together!) The resulting table is as follows:

Magnitude	Angle	x component	y component
$A = 50$ cm	30°	43.3 cm	25.0 cm
$B = 35$ cm	110°	−12.0 cm	32.9 cm
		$R_x = 31.3$ cm	$R_y = 57.9$ cm

Now we use Equations 1.3 and 1.4 to find the magnitude and direction of the vector sum $\vec{R}$. From the Pythagorean theorem,

$$R = \sqrt{R_x^2 + R_y^2} = \sqrt{(31.3 \text{ cm})^2 + (57.9 \text{ cm})^2} = 66 \text{ cm}.$$

From the definition of the inverse tangent,

$$\theta = \tan^{-1}\frac{R_y}{R_x} = \tan^{-1}\frac{57.9 \text{ cm}}{31.3 \text{ cm}} = 62°.$$

Figure 1.19b shows this resultant vector and its components.

REFLECT We used the components of the vector sum $\vec{R}$ to find its magnitude and direction. Note how important it was to recognize that the x component of $\vec{B}$ is negative.

Practice Problem: Find the vector sum of the following two vectors by using components: 45 m, 55°, and 70 m, 135°. *Answers:* magnitude = 90 m; direction = 105°.

(a) Our diagram for this problem

(b) The resultant $\vec{R}$ and its components

▲ **FIGURE 1.19**

EXAMPLE 1.8   **Vector addition helps win a Porsche**

The four finalists in a hog-calling contest are brought to the center of a large, flat field. Each is given a meterstick, a compass, a calculator, a shovel, and (in a different order for each contestant) the following three displacements:

> 72.4 m, 32.0° east of north;
> 57.3 m, 36.0° south of west;
> 17.8 m straight south.

The three displacements lead to the point where the keys to a new Porsche are buried. The finder gets the Porsche. Three of the four contestants start measuring immediately, but the winner first *calculates* where to go. What does he calculate?

SOLUTION

SET UP The situation is shown in Figure 1.20. We have chosen the x axis as east and the y axis as north. This is the usual choice for maps. Let $\vec{A}$ be the first displacement, $\vec{B}$ the second, and $\vec{C}$ the third. We can estimate from the diagram that the vector sum $\vec{R}$ is about 10 m, 40° west of north. The angles of the vectors, measured counterclockwise from the $+x$ axis, are 58°, 216°, and 270°. We have to find the components of each.

SOLVE The components of $\vec{A}$ are

$$A_x = A\cos\theta = (72.4 \text{ m})(\cos 58°) = 38.37 \text{ m},$$
$$A_y = A\sin\theta = (72.4 \text{ m})(\sin 58°) = 61.40 \text{ m}.$$

The table below shows the components of all the displacements, the addition of components, and the other calculations. To find the magnitude R and direction θ, use the Pythagorean theorem $R = \sqrt{R_x^2 + R_y^2}$ and the definition of the inverse tangent,

Continued

$\theta = \tan^{-1}\dfrac{R_y}{R_x}$. Always arrange your component calculations sys-
tematically as in the table. Note that we have kept one too many
significant figures in the components; we'll wait until the end to
round to the correct number of significant figures. Here's the table:

Distance	Angle	x component	y component
A = 72.4 m	58°	38.37 m	61.40 m
B = 57.3 m	216°	−46.36 m	−33.68 m
C = 17.8 m	270°	0.00 m	−17.80 m
		$R_x = -7.99$ m	$R_y = 9.92$ m

$$R = \sqrt{(-7.99 \text{ m})^2 + (9.92 \text{ m})^2} = 12.7 \text{ m}$$

$$\theta = \tan^{-1}\frac{9.92 \text{ m}}{-7.99 \text{ m}} = 129° = 39° \text{ west of north.}$$

REFLECT The losers try to measure three angles and three distances totaling 147.5 m, 1 meter at a time. The winner measures
only one angle and one much shorter distance.

Practice Problem: In a second contest, the three displacements
given are 63.5 m, 52° west of north; 12.6 m straight north; and

▲ **FIGURE 1.20** Three successive displacements $\vec{A}$, $\vec{B}$, and $\vec{C}$ and
the resultant (vector sum) displacement $\vec{R} = \vec{A} + \vec{B} + \vec{C}$.

81.9 m, 41° south of east. What magnitude and direction does the
winner calculate for the displacement to find the Porsche?
Answers: R = 11.9 m and θ = 9.8° south of east.

Our discussion of vector addition has centered mostly on combining
displacement vectors, but the method is applicable to all other vector quantities as
well, including force, velocity, acceleration, and many other vector quantities. In
Chapter 4, when we study the concept of *force* and its effects, we'll make extensive use of the fact that forces can be combined according to the same methods of
vector addition that we've used with displacement.

SUMMARY

Standards, Units, and Unit Conversions

(Sections 1.3 and 1.4) The fundamental physical quantities of mechanics are mass, length, and time; the corresponding SI units are the kilogram (kg), the meter (m), and the second (s), respectively. Other units, related by powers of 10, are identified by adding prefixes: for example, 1 kilometer (km) = 10^3 meters (m). Derived units for other physical quantities are products or quotients of the basic units. For example, the units of speed are meters/second (m/s). Equations must be dimensionally consistent; two terms can be added, subtracted, or equated only when they have the same units.

Significant Figures

(Section 1.5) The uncertainty of a measurement can be indicated by the number of significant figures or by a stated uncertainty. For example, 1.40×10^6 has three significant figures. A typical metric ruler has an uncertainty of 1 mm. When numbers are multiplied or divided in a calculation, the number of significant figures in the result is no greater than in the factor with the least number of significant figures. Thus, the product $3.1416 \times 2.34 \times 0.58 = 4.3$ has only two significant figures, because 0.58 has only two significant figures.

Calculating pi from measured values of radius r and circumference C:

Three significant figures (the leading zero doesn't count)⋯⋯

We are dividing, so the result can have only three significant figures.

$$\pi = \frac{C}{2r} = \frac{0.424 \text{ m}}{2(0.06750 \text{ m})} = 3.14$$

This exact number has no uncertainty and thus doesn't affect the signficant figures in the result.

Four significant figures (the trailing zero counts)

Vector Addition

(Section 1.7) Vector quantities have direction as well as magnitude and are combined according to the rules of vector addition. To add vectors graphically, we place the tail of the second vector at the tip, or point, of the first vector. To subtract vectors, as in $\vec{A} - \vec{B}$, we first obtain the vector $(-\vec{B})$ by reversing the direction of $\vec{B}$. Then we write $\vec{A} - \vec{B} = \vec{A} + (-\vec{B})$ and apply the usual rule for vector addition.

$$\vec{A} + \vec{B} = \vec{A} + \vec{B}$$

To add vectors graphically, arrange them tip to tail in any order.

$$\left(\vec{A} - \vec{B}\right) = \left(\vec{A} + -\vec{B}\right) = \left(\begin{array}{c}\vec{A} - \vec{B} \\ = \vec{A} + (-\vec{B})\end{array}\right)$$

Subtracting $\vec{B}$ from $\vec{A}$ is equivalent to adding $-\vec{B}$ to $\vec{A}$.

Components of Vectors

(Section 1.8) We can represent any vector $\vec{A}$ lying in the x-y plane as the sum of a vector $\vec{A}_x$ parallel to the x axis and a vector $\vec{A}_y$ parallel to the y axis; these are called x and y **component vectors** of $\vec{A}$. If $\vec{A}_x$ points in the positive x direction, we define the number A_x to be its magnitude. If $\vec{A}_x$ points in the $-x$ direction, we define A_x to be the negative of its magnitude. (Remember that a magnitude is always positive.) We define the number A_y the same way. The two numbers A_x and A_y are called the **components** of the vector $\vec{A}$.

Vector addition can be carried out using components of vectors. If A_x and A_y are the components of vector $\vec{A}$, and B_x and B_y are the components of vector $\vec{B}$, the components R_x and R_y of the vector sum $\vec{R} = \vec{A} + \vec{B}$ are given by

$$R_x = A_x + B_x \quad \text{and} \quad R_y = A_y + B_y. \quad (1.5)$$

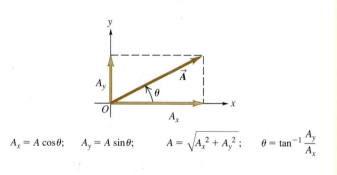

$$A_x = A\cos\theta; \quad A_y = A\sin\theta; \quad A = \sqrt{A_x^2 + A_y^2}; \quad \theta = \tan^{-1}\frac{A_y}{A_x}$$

Conceptual Questions

1. What are the units of the number π?
2. Suppose you are asked to compute the cosine of 3 meters. Is this possible?
3. In the construction business, quantities such as sand, soil, and concrete are normally sold by the "yard." What do you think is meant by this "yard"? What would be its units in scientific terms?
4. (a) Would 200 cm be a reasonable height for an adult male? (b) Is it unusual for a human to have an age of 6×10^8 s? (c) Would 10^6 g be a reasonable mass for an adult person?
5. What physical phenomena (other than those discussed in the text) could be used to define a time standard?
6. Atomic quantities are now used to define the second and the meter. Could some atomic quantity be used for a definition of the kilogram? What advantages (or disadvantages) might this definition have compared with that based on the 1 kg platinum cylinder kept at Sèvres?
7. Suppose your lab partner tells you to calculate the volume of a cone of radius r and height h using the formula $V = \pi r^3 h$. Could this formula be correct?
8. Why is an angle a dimensionless number when measured in radians?
9. How could you determine the average thickness of a page of this textbook with an ordinary ruler?
10. (a) The mass m of an object is proportional to its volume V: $m = kV$. What are the SI units of k? (b) If the distance d an object moves in time t is given by the equation $d = At^2$, find the SI units of A. (c) If the speed v of an object depends on time t according to the equation $v = A + Bt + Ct^4$, what are the SI units of A, B, and C?
11. Based *only* on consistency of units, which of the following formulas could *not* be correct? In each case, A is area, V is volume, C is circumference, and R is radius. (a) $A = 2\pi R$, (b) $V = \frac{4}{3}\pi R^2$, (c) $A = 2\pi R^2$, (d) $V = 6\pi R^3$, (e) $C = \pi R^2$, (f) $V = CA$.
12. Based *only* on consistency of units, which of the following formulas could *not* be correct? In each case, x is distance, v is speed, and t is time. (a) $v = x/t$, (b) $x = vt$, (c) $t = v/x$, (d) $vx = t$, (e) $xt = v$, (f) $v_2^2 = v_1^2 + 2x^2$.
13. (a) In adding scalars, is 1 m + 1 m necessarily equal to 2 m? (b) In adding two vectors, each of magnitude 1 m, does the resultant *necessarily* have a magnitude of 2 m? Explain your reasoning in each case.
14. Is it possible for the magnitude of a vector (a) to be smaller than the magnitude of any of its components or (b) to be equal to the magnitude of one of its components? How?
15. Can you find a single vector that has components different from zero, but a magnitude of zero?

Multiple-Choice Problems

1. Andy Roddick can sometimes serve a tennis ball at 150 mi/h (about 75 m/s). The length of a tennis court is 78 ft. Approximately how long does his opponent have to react, from the instant he sees Roddick hit the ball until the ball reaches the opponent?
   A. 1/10 s   B. 1/3 s   C. 3/4 s   D. 1 s

2. Suppose that bacon is sold for $2 per pound. If you were to buy 1 kilogram of bacon, what would you expect to pay for it?
   A. More than $2
   B. Less than $2
   C. $2

3. The distance from an adult's elbow to her fingertips is closest to
   A. 5 cm   B. 10 cm   C. 50 cm   D. 1 m

4. A vector is directed at an angle θ above the $+x$ axis, pointing into the first quadrant. If the x component of this vector is 10 m, the magnitude of the vector is
   A. greater than 10 m
   B. equal to 10 m
   C. less than 10 m
   D. the same as the y component of the vector

5. A mass of 1.0×10^{-3} μkg is the same as
   A. 10^{-12} g   B. 10^{-6} g   C. 1 kg   D. 1 mg

6. If the vector $\vec{B}$ has a magnitude of 25 m and makes an angle of $30°$ with the $+x$ axis, the vector $-\vec{B}$
   A. has a magnitude of 25 m.
   B. has the same direction as $\vec{B}$, but a magnitude of -25 m.
   C. makes an angle of $-30°$ with the $+x$ axis.
   D. has the opposite direction of $\vec{B}$ and a magnitude of -25 m.

7. If you place an ordinary sugar cube on a laboratory balance, the mass reading will be closest to
   A. 1 mg   B. 1 g   C. 100 g   D. 1 kg

8. The length of a typical sedan car is closest to
   A. 100 cm   B. 100 m   C. 10 m   D. 5 m

9. If vector $\vec{A}$ has components A_x and A_y and makes an angle θ with the $+x$ axis, then
   A. $A = A_x + A_y$ (where A is the magnitude of $\vec{A}$).
   B. $\theta = A_y/A_x$.
   C. $\cos\theta = \dfrac{A_x}{\sqrt{A_x^2 + A_y^2}}$.
   D. $\tan\theta = A_x/A_y$.

10. If the distance d (in meters) traveled by an object in time t (in seconds) is given by the formula $d = A + Bt^2$, the SI units of A and B must be
    A. meters for both A and B.
    B. m/s for A and m/s^2 for B.
    C. meters for A and m/s^2 for B.
    D. m/s^2 for both A and B.

11. The height of a typical adult female is closest to
    A. 1 m.   B. 2 m.   C. 3 m.   D. 4 m.

12. If vector $\vec{A}$ has unity magnitude and makes an angle of $45°$ with the $+x$ axis, then the x and y components of $\vec{A}$ are
    A. $A_x = A_y = 1$.
    B. $A_x = A_y = \dfrac{1}{\sqrt{2}}$.
    C. $A_x = A_y = \frac{1}{2}$.
    D. $A_x = A_y = \sqrt{2}$.

13. If vector $\vec{A}$ has components $A_x = -3$ and $A_y = -4$, then the magnitude of $\vec{A}$ is
    A. 7
    B. -7
    C. $\sqrt{7}$
    D. 5
    E. -5

Problems

1.3 Standards and Units

1.4 Unit Consistency and Conversions

1. • (a) The maximum sodium intake for a person on a 2000 calorie diet should be 2400 mg/day. How many grams of sodium is this per day? (b) The recommended daily allowance (RDA) of the trace element chromium is 120 μg/day. Express this dose in grams per day. (c) An intake of vitamin C up to 500 mg/day is considered safe (although the safety of higher doses has not yet been established). Express this intake in grams per day. (d) The electrical resistance of the human body is approximately 1500 ohms when it is dry. Express this resistance in kilohms. (e) An electrical current of about 0.020 amp can cause muscular spasms so that a person cannot, for example, let go of a wire with that amount of current. Express this current in milliamps.

2. • (a) How many ohms are there in a 7.85-megohm resistor? (b) Typical laboratory capacitors are around 5 picofarads. How many farads are they? (c) The speed of light in vacuum is 3.00×10^8 m/s. Express this speed in gigameters per second. (d) The wavelength of visible light is between 400 nm and 700 nm. Express this wavelength in meters. (e) The diameter of a typical atomic nucleus is about 2 femtometers. Express this diameter in meters.

3. • (a) The recommended daily allowance (RDA) of the trace metal magnesium is 410 mg/day for males. Express this quantity in μg/day. (b) For adults, the RDA of the amino acid lysine is 12 mg per kg of body weight. How many grams per day should a 75 kg adult receive? (c) A typical multivitamin tablet can contain 2.0 mg of vitamin B_2 (riboflavin), and the RDA is 0.0030 g/day. How many such tablets should a person take each day to get the proper amount of this vitamin, assuming that he gets none from any other sources? (d) The RDA for the trace element selenium is 0.000070 g/day. Express this dose in mg/day.

4. • (a) Starting with the definition 1.00 in. = 2.54 cm, find the number of kilometers in 1.00 mile. (b) In medicine, volumes are often expressed in milliliters (ml or mL). Show that a milliliter is the same as a cubic centimeter. (c) How many cubic centimeters of water are there in a 1.00 L bottle of drinking water?

5. •• (a) The density (mass divided by volume) of water is 1.00 g/cm^3. What is this value in kilograms per cubic meter? (b) The density of blood is 1050 kg/m^3. What is this density in g/cm^3? (c) How many kilograms are there in a 1.00 L bottle of drinking water? How many pounds?

6. • (a) To save car rental costs, you take your American car to Europe, where highway speed limits are posted in km/h. Of course, your car's speedometer shows mph. If the speed limit on the autostrada near Rome is posted at 150 km/h, what should be the reading on your American car's speedometer so that you are driving at the posted speed limit? (b) While on vacation in France, you buy a new car and have it shipped home after your revels are over. Of course, the French car's speedometer shows km/h. If the speed limit on the freeway near your home is posted at 65 mph, what should be the maximum reading on your French car's speedometer so that you will not get a speeding ticket?

7. • The Concorde was the fastest airliner used for commercial service. It cruised at 1450 mi/h (about two times the speed of sound, or Mach 2). (a) What was the cruise speed of the Concorde in km/h? (b) What was it in m/s?

8. • **Metric wrenches.** (a) You have a new set of metric wrenches, but need to loosen a $\frac{3}{8}$ inch bolt. To find out which size metric wrench to use, convert the $\frac{3}{8}$ in. to millimeters, accurate to the nearest tenth of a millimeter. (b) If you want to tighten a 12 mm bolt, what size wrench should you use in inches, accurate to the nearest hundredth of an inch? (c) English-unit wrenches often come in $\frac{1}{8}$ inch intervals, not in decimal units. What size wrench should you use in part (b)?

9. • **Gasoline mileage.** You are considering buying a European car and want to see if its advertised fuel efficiency (expressed in km/L) is better than that of your present car. If your car gets 37.5 miles per gallon, how many km/L is this? Consult Appendix E.

10. •• While driving in an exotic foreign land, you see a speed-limit sign on a highway that reads 180,000 furlongs per fortnight. How many miles per hour is this? (One furlong is $\frac{1}{8}$ mile, and a fortnight is 14 days. A furlong originally referred to the length of a plowed furrow.)

11. •• **Fill 'er up!** You fill up your gas tank in Europe when the euro is worth $1.25 and gasoline costs 1.35 euros per liter. What is the cost of gasoline in dollars per gallon? How does your answer compare with the cost of gasoline in the United States? (Use conversion factors in Appendix E.)

12. •• **Bacteria.** Bacteria vary somewhat in size, but a diameter of 2.0 μm is not unusual. What would be the volume (in cubic centimeters) and surface area (in square millimeters) of such a bacterium, assuming that it is spherical? (Consult Appendix A for relevant formulas.)

13. • Compute the number of seconds in (a) an hour, (b) a 24 hour day, and (c) a 365 day year.

14. • **Some commonly occurring quantities.** All of the quantities that follow will occur frequently in your study of physics. (a) Express the speed of light $(3.00 \times 10^8 \text{ m/s})$ in mi/s and mph. (b) Find the speed of sound in air at 0°C (1100 ft/s) in m/s and mph. (c) Show that 60 mph is the same as 88 ft/s. (d) Convert the acceleration of a freely falling body (9.8 m/s^2) to ft/s^2.

1.5 Precision and Significant Figures

15. • Express each of the following numbers to three, five, and eight significant figures: (a) $\pi = 3.141592654 \ldots$, (b) $e = 2.718281828 \ldots$, (c) $\sqrt{13} = 3.605551275. \ldots$

16. • Express each of the following approximations of π to six significant figures: (a) 22/7, (b) 355/113. (c) Are these approximations accurate to that precision?

17. • An angle is given, to one significant figure, as 4°, meaning that its value is between 3.5° and 4.5°. Find the corresponding range of possible values of (a) the cosine of the angle, (b) the sine of the angle, and (c) the tangent of the angle.

18. • **Blood is thicker than water.** The density (mass divided by volume) of pure water is 1.00 g/cm^3, that of whole blood is 1.05 g/cm^3, and the density of seawater is 1.03 g/cm^3. What is the mass (in grams) of 1.00 L of each of these substances?

19. •• **White dwarfs and neutron stars.** Recall that density is mass divided by volume, and consult Appendices A and F as needed. (a) Calculate the average density of the earth in g/cm^3, assuming our planet to be a perfect sphere. (b) In about 5 billion years, at the end of its lifetime, our sun will end up as a white

dwarf, having about the same mass as it does now, but reduced to about 15,000 km in diameter. What will be its density at that stage? (c) A neutron star is the remnant left after certain supernovae (explosions of giant stars). Typically, neutron stars are about 20 km in diameter and have around the same mass as our sun. What is a typical neutron star density in g/cm^3?

20. •• **Atoms and nuclei.** The atom helium (He) consists of two protons, two neutrons, and two electrons. (Recall that density is mass divided by volume, and consult Appendices B and F and Table 1.1 as needed.) (a) The diameter of the He atom is approximately 0.10 nm. Calculate the density of the He atom in g/cm^3 (assuming that it is a sphere), and compare it with that of pure water, which is 1.0 g/cm^3. (b) The diameter of the He nucleus is about 2.0 fm. Assuming the nucleus to be a sphere, calculate its density in g/cm^3 and compare it with that of a neutron star in the previous exercise.

21. •• **Critical mass of neptunium.** In the fall of 2002, a group of scientists at Los Alamos National Laboratory determined that the critical mass of neptunium-237 is about 60.0 kg. (The critical mass of a fissionable material is the minimum amount that must be brought together to start a nuclear chain reaction.) Neptunium has a density of 19.5 g/cm^3. What would be the radius of a sphere made of this material that has a critical mass? (Recall that density is mass divided by volume.)

22. •• **Cell walls.** Although these quantities vary from one type of cell to another, a cell can be 2.0 μm in diameter with a cell wall
BIO 50.0 nm thick. If the density (mass divided by volume) of the wall material is the same as that of pure water, what is the mass (in mg) of the cell wall, assuming the cell to be spherical and the wall to be a very thin spherical shell?

23. •• A brass washer has an outside diameter of 4.50 cm with a hole of diameter 1.25 cm and is 1.50 mm thick. (See Figure 1.21.) The density of brass is 8600 kg/m^3. If you put this washer on a laboratory balance, what will it "weigh" in grams? (Recall that density is mass divided by volume and consult Appendix A as needed.)

1.50 mm

1.25 cm

4.50 cm

▲ **FIGURE 1.21** Problem 23.

1.6 Estimates and Orders of Magnitude

24. • Estimate the total mass of all the humans presently living on earth.

25. •• How many cars can pass though a two-lane tunnel through a mountain in 1 hour at ordinary highway speeds?

26. •• **How many cells in the body?** Although their sizes vary,
BIO cells can be modeled as spheres 2.0 μm in diameter, on the average. About how many cells does a typical human contain, and approximately what is the mass of an average cell?

27. •• How many kernels of corn does it take to fill a 2 L soft-drink bottle?

28. •• How many drops of water are in all the oceans on earth? (The oceans cover about two-thirds of the earth's surface and are about 4,000 m deep, on the average.)

29. • How many dollar bills would you have to stack to reach the moon? Would that be a cheaper way to get there than building and launching a spacecraft (which costs a few billion dollars)?

30. •• **Space station.** You are designing a space station and want
BIO to get some idea how large it should be to provide adequate air for the astronauts. Normally, the air is replenished, but for security, you decide that there should be enough to last for two weeks in case of a malfunction. (a) Estimate how many cubic meters of air an average person breathes in two weeks. A typical human breathes about 1/2 L per breath. (b) If the space station is to be spherical, what should be its diameter to contain all the air you calculated in part (a)?

31. •• **A beating heart.** How many times does a human heart
BIO beat during a lifetime? How many gallons of blood does it pump in that time if, on the average, it pumps 50 cm^3 of blood with each beat?

32. •• How long would it take you to walk to the moon, and how many steps would you have to take, assuming that you could somehow walk normally in space?

33. •• How much would it cost to paper the entire United States (including Alaska and Hawaii) with dollar bills? What would be the cost to each person in the nation?

1.7 Vectors and Vector Addition

34. • On a single diagram, carefully sketch each force vector to scale and identify its magnitude and direction on your drawing: (a) 60 lb at 25° east of north. (b) 40 lb at $\pi/3$ south of west. (c) 100 lb at 40° north of west. (d) 50 lb at $\pi/6$ east of south.

35. •• A runner jogs around a circular track 150 ft in diameter. (a) Clearly sketch this runner's displacement vector when he has completed one-fourth of a lap; one-half of a lap; one lap. (b) Find the magnitude and direction of the runner's displacement vector for each case in part (a).

36. • A ladybug starts at the center of a 12-in.-diameter turntable and crawls in a straight radial line to the edge. While this is happening, the turntable turns through a 45° angle. (a) Draw a sketch showing the bug's path and the displacement vector for the bug's progress. (b) Find the magnitude and direction of the ladybug's displacement vector.

37. • For the vectors $\vec{A}$ and $\vec{B}$ shown in Figure 1.22, carefully sketch (a) the vector sum $\vec{A} + \vec{B}$; (b) the vector difference $\vec{A} - \vec{B}$; (c) the vector $-\vec{A} - \vec{B}$; (d) the vector difference $\vec{B} - \vec{A}$.

$\vec{B}$ (18.0 m)

$\vec{A}$ (12.0 m)   37.0°

▲ **FIGURE 1.22** Problem 37.

38. • **Chin brace.** A person with
BIO an injured jaw has a brace below his chin. The brace is held in place by two cables directed at 65° above the horizontal. (See Figure 1.23.) The cables produce

65°   65°

▲ **FIGURE 1.23** Problem 38.

forces of equal magnitude having a vertical resultant of 2.25 N upward. (a) Make a scale drawing showing both the forces produced by the cables and the resultant force. Estimate the angle carefully or measure it with a protractor. (b) Use your scale drawing to estimate the magnitude of the force due to each cable.

1.8 Components of Vectors

39. • Use a *scale drawing* to find the x and y components of the vectors listed next. For each vector, the numbers given are its magnitude followed by the counterclockwise angle that it makes with the +x axis. (a) Magnitude 9.30 m, angle 60.0°, (b) magnitude 22.0 km, angle 135°, (c) magnitude 6.35 cm, angle 307°.

40. • In each of the cases that follow, the magnitude of a vector is given along with the counterclockwise angle it makes with the +x axis. Use trigonometry to find the x and y components of the vector. Also, sketch each vector approximately to scale to see if your calculated answers seem reasonable. (a) 50.0 N at 60.0°, (b) 75 m/s at $5\pi/6$ rad, (c) 254 lb at 325°, (d) 69 km at 1.1π rad.

41. • In each of the cases that follow, the components of a vector $\vec{A}$ are given. Use trigonometry to find the magnitude of that vector and the counterclockwise angle it makes with the +x axis. Also, sketch each vector approximately to scale to see if your calculated answers seem reasonable. (a) $A_x = 4.0$ m, $A_y = 5.0$ m, (b) $A_x = -3.0$ km, $A_y = -6.0$ km, (c) $A_x = 9.0$ m/s, $A_y = -17$ m/s, (d) $A_x = -8.0$ N, $A_y = 12$ N.

42. • A woman takes her dog Rover for a walk on a leash. To get the little pooch moving forward, she pulls on the leash with a force of 20.0 N at an angle of 37° above the horizontal. (a) How much force is tending to pull Rover forward? (b) How much force is tending to lift Rover off the ground?

43. • If a vector $\vec{A}$ has the following components, use trigonometry to find its magnitude and the counterclockwise angle it makes with the +x axis: (a) $A_x = 8.0$ lb, $A_y = 6.0$ lb, (b) $A_x = -24$ m/s, $A_y = -31$ m/s, (c) $A_x = -1500$ km, $A_y = 2000$ km, (d) $A_x = 71.3$ N, $A_y = -54.7$ N.

44. • Compute the x and y components of the vectors $\vec{A}$, $\vec{B}$, and $\vec{C}$ shown in Figure 1.24.

45. • Vector $\vec{A}$ has components $A_x = 1.30$ cm, $A_y = 2.25$ cm; vector $\vec{B}$ has components $B_x = 4.10$ cm, $B_y = -3.75$ cm. Find (a) the components of the vector sum $\vec{A} + \vec{B}$; (b) the magnitude and direction of $\vec{A} + \vec{B}$; (c) the components of the vector difference $\vec{B} - \vec{A}$; (d) the magnitude and direction of $\vec{B} - \vec{A}$.

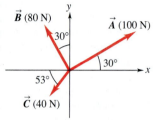

▲ FIGURE 1.24 Problem 44.

46. •• A plane leaves Seattle, flies 85 mi at 22° north of east, and then changes direction to 48° south of east. After flying at 115 mi in this new direction, the pilot must make an emergency landing on a field. The Seattle airport facility dispatches a rescue crew. (a) In what direction and how far should the crew fly to go directly to the field? Use components to solve this problem. (b) Check the reasonableness of your answer with a careful graphical sum.

47. •• Two vectors of equal magnitude act in a vertical plane perpendicular to each other. If their resultant is 75 N directly downward, (a) sketch these two vectors and the resultant, and (b) use components to find the magnitude of each of the two vectors and the angle each makes with the vertical.

48. • Three horizontal ropes are attached to a boulder and produce the pulls shown in Figure 1.25. (a) Find the x and y components of each pull. (b) Find the components of the resultant of the three pulls. (c) Find the magnitude and direction (the counterclockwise angle with the +x axis) of the resultant pull. (d) Sketch a clear *graphical* sum to check your answer in part (c).

▲ FIGURE 1.25 Problem 48.

49. • A disoriented physics professor drives 3.25 km north, then 4.75 km west, and then 1.50 km south. (a) Use components to find the magnitude and direction of the resultant displacement of this professor. (b) Check the reasonableness of your answer with a graphical sum.

50. • A postal employee drives a delivery truck along the route shown in Figure 1.26. Use components to determine the magnitude and direction of the truck's resultant displacement. Then check the reasonableness of your answer by sketching a graphical sum.

▲ FIGURE 1.26 Problem 50.

General Problems

51. • **Baseball mass.** Baseball rules specify that a regulation ball shall weigh no less than 5.00 ounces nor more than $5\frac{1}{4}$ ounces. What are the acceptable limits, in grams, for a regulation ball? (See Appendix E and use the fact that 16 oz = 1 lb.)

52. • A useful and easy-to-remember approximate value for the number of seconds in a year is $\pi \times 10^7$. To how many significant figures is this approximation accurate? (There are 365.24 days in 1 year.)

53. •• **Breathing oxygen.** The density of air under standard laboratory conditions is 1.29 kg/m³, and about 20% of that air consists of oxygen. Typically, people breathe about $\frac{1}{2}$ L of air per breath. (a) How many grams of oxygen does a person breathe

in a day? (b) If this air is stored uncompressed in a cubical tank, how long is each side of the tank?

54. •• **Airline air.** Airliners do not replenish the air in an airplane; they just recycle it. What must be the minimum volume of air in a jumbo jet carrying 300 passengers and crew on a 17-hour international flight if, on the average, people take $\frac{1}{2}$ L of air per breath and use up all of the oxygen in that breath (which is not quite true)? How does this volume compare with that of such an airliner? Neglect any effects due to the reduced pressure in the cabin. (*Hint:* Start by estimating the number of breaths a person takes per minute, and then figure out the number of breaths taken during the flight.)

55. •• **How much blood in a heartbeat?** A typical human contains 5.0 L of blood, and it takes 1.0 min for all of it to pass through the heart when the person is resting with a pulse rate of 75 heartbeats per minute. On the average, what volume of blood, in liters and cubic centimeters, does the heart pump during each beat?

56. •• **Muscle attachment.** When muscles attach to bones, they usually do so by a series of tendons, as shown in Figure 1.27. In the figure, five tendons attach to the bone. The uppermost tendon pulls at 20.0° from the axis of the bone, and each tendon is directed 10.0° from the one next to it. (a) If each tendon exerts a 2.75 N pull on the bone, use vector components to find the magnitude and direction of the resultant force on this bone due to all five tendons. Let the axis of the bone be the $+x$ axis. (b) Draw a graphical sum to check your results from part (a).

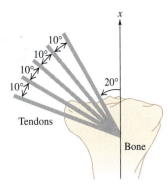

▲ **FIGURE 1.27** Problem 56.

57. •• **Hiking the Appalachian Trail.** The Appalachian Trail runs from Mt. Katahdin in Maine to Springer Mountain in Georgia, a total distance of 2160 mi. If you hiked for 8 h per day, estimate (a) how many steps it would take to hike this trail and b) how many days it would take to hike it.

58. •• For exercise and to conserve gasoline, you walk to and from work, 30 min each way at a regular rate. If you work a five-day week with three weeks of vacation per year, estimate (a) how many miles you walk in a 15 year period and (b) how many coast-to-coast trips across the United States you have walked during that time. (The United States is about 3,000 mi from coast to coast.)

59. •• **Contamination of drinking water.** The Environmental Protection Agency specifies that drinking water should contain no more than 10 $\mu g/L$ of arsenic. If your well contained the maximum allowable amount of arsenic, how much (in g and

μg) of this contaminant would you receive each day if you drank eight 8 oz glasses daily? (Four 8 oz glasses make up a quart, and there are 4 quarts in a gallon. Also, consult Appendix A.)

60. •• **Density of the human body.** (a) Make simple measurements on your own body, and use them to calculate your body's average density (mass divided by volume) in kg/m^3. (b) How does this result compare with the density of water, which is 1000 kg/m^3? Is your result surprising?

61. •• While surveying a cave, a spelunker follows a passage 180 m straight west, then 210 m in a direction 45° east of south, and then 280 m at 30.0° east of north. After a fourth unmeasured displacement, she finds herself back where she started. Use vector components to find the magnitude and direction of the fourth displacement. Then check the reasonableness of your answer with a graphical sum.

62. •• A sailor in a small sailboat encounters shifting winds. She sails 2.00 km east, then 3.50 km southeast, and then an additional distance in an unknown direction. Her final position is 5.80 km directly east of her starting point. (See Figure 1.28.) Find the magnitude and direction of the third leg of the journey. Draw the vector addition diagram, and show that it is in qualitative agreement with your numerical solution.

▲ **FIGURE 1.28** Problem 62.

63. •• **Dislocated shoulder.** A patient with a dislocated shoulder is put into a traction apparatus as shown in Figure 1.29. The pulls $\vec{A}$ and $\vec{B}$ have equal magnitudes and must combine to produce an outward traction force of 5.60 N on the patient's arm. How large should these pulls be?

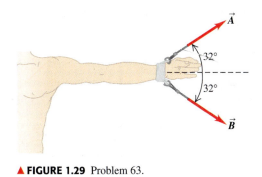

▲ **FIGURE 1.29** Problem 63.

64. •• A boulder of weight w rests on a hillside that rises at a constant angle α above the horizontal, as shown in Figure 1.30. The boulder's weight w is a force on the boulder that has a direction vertically downward. (a) In terms of α and w, what is the component of the weight of the boulder in the direction parallel to the surface of the hill? (b) What is the component of the weight in the direction perpendicular to the surface of the hill? (c) An air-conditioner unit is fastened to a roof that slopes upward at an angle of 35.0° In order that the unit not slide down the roof, the component of the unit's weight parallel to the roof cannot exceed 550 N. What is the maximum allowed weight of the unit?

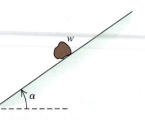

▶ **FIGURE 1.30** Problem 64.

65. •• **Bones and muscles.** A patient in therapy has a forearm
    BIO that weighs 20.5 N and lifts a 112.0 N weight. The only other significant forces on his forearm come from the biceps muscle (which acts perpendicularly to the forearm) and the force at the elbow. If the biceps produce a pull of 232 N when the forearm is raised 43° above the horizontal, find the magnitude and direction of the force that the elbow exerts on the forearm. (*Hint:* The elbow force and the biceps force together must balance the weight of the arm and the weight it is carrying, so their vector sum must be 132.5 N upward.)

66. •• **Googols and googolplexes!** When the mathematician Edward Kasner asked his young nephew to coin a name for the huge number 10^{100}, the boy said *googol*. (a) Express the googol in standard notation as a 1 followed by the appropriate number of zeroes. (b) Approximately how many googols of atoms does our sun contain? For simplicity, assume that the sun consists of only protons and electrons, in equal numbers, which is approximately true. (Consult Appendix F.) (c) The *googolplex* is an even larger number, 10 to the googol power: 10^{googol}. Express the googolplex in scientific notation. If you wrote it in standard notation with a 1 followed by the appropriate number of zeroes, how many zeroes would you need?

2

MOTION ALONG A STRAIGHT LINE

H ow do you describe the motion of a racehorse coming down the homestretch, galloping toward the finish line? When you throw a baseball straight up in the air, how high does it go? How fast do you have to throw it to reach that height? When a glass slips from your hand, how much time do you have to catch it before it hits the floor? These are the kinds of questions you'll learn to answer in this chapter.

We're beginning our study of physics with **mechanics,** the study of the relationships among force, matter, and motion. Our first goal is to develop mathematical methods for *describing* motion; this discipline is called **kinematics.** Later we'll study the more general subject of **dynamics,** the relation of motion to its causes.

Motion is a continuous change of position with time. In this chapter we'll limit our discussion to the simplest possible situation, a single object moving along a straight line. We'll assume that the object can be treated as a particle, as described in Section 1.2. We'll always take the line to be one of the axes of a coordinate system. Then we can describe the position of the particle by its displacement from the origin of coordinates along this line. Displacement is a *vector* quantity, as we discussed in Chapter 1. But when a particle moves along a line that is a coordinate axis, only one component of displacement is different from zero, and the particle's position is described by a single **coordinate.** In Chapter 3 we'll consider more general motions in a plane, in which the particle has two coordinates.

A fall is a classic example of straight-line motion. If air resistance could be neglected, this sky-diver would be accelerating toward the earth at a constant 9.8 m/s². Luckily for him, air resistance exists—and later, when he deploys his parachute, it will give him an *upward* acceleration.

▲ **FIGURE 2.1** Positions of a AA-fuel dragster at two times during its run.

2.1 Displacement and Average Velocity

Suppose a drag racer drives his AA-fuel dragster in a straight line down the track. We'll use this line as the x axis of our coordinate system, as shown in Figure 2.1. We'll place the origin O at the starting line. The distance of the front of the dragster from the origin is given by the coordinate x, which varies with time. Note that x is positive when the car is to the right of O, negative when it is to the left. Suppose that, at a time 1 second $(1.0\ \text{s})$ after the start of the race, the car is at x_1, 19 m to the right of the origin, and that, at 4.0 s after the start, it is at x_2, 277 m from the origin. Then it has traveled a distance of $(277\ \text{m} - 19\ \text{m}) = 258\ \text{m}$ in the direction of increasing x in a time interval of $(4.0\ \text{s} - 1.0\ \text{s}) = 3.0\ \text{s}$. We define the car's **average velocity** during this interval to be a vector quantity whose x component is the change in x $(258\ \text{m})$, divided by the time interval $(3.0\ \text{s})$; that is, $(258\ \text{m})/(3.0\ \text{s}) = 86\ \text{m/s}$.

Now let's generalize this discussion. At time t_1 a point at the front of the car is at position x_1, and at time t_2 it is at position x_2. The displacement during the time interval from t_1 to t_2 is the vector from x_1 to x_2. The x component of this vector is $(x_2 - x_1)$; all other components are zero, because there is no motion in any direction other than along the x axis. For motion in the x direction, we define the average velocity as a vector in the direction from x_1 to x_2, with an x component of average velocity $v_{\text{av},x}$ given by

$$v_{\text{av},x} = \frac{x_2 - x_1}{t_2 - t_1}. \tag{2.1}$$

All other components of the average velocity vector are zero.

Changes in quantities, such as $(x_2 - x_1)$ and $(t_2 - t_1)$, occur so often throughout physics that it's worthwhile to use a special notation. From now on, we'll use the Greek letter Δ (capital delta) to represent a *change* in any quantity. Thus, we write

$$\Delta x = x_2 - x_1. \tag{2.2}$$

Be sure you understand that Δx is *not the product* of Δ and x. It is a *single symbol,* and it means "the change in the quantity x." Here, Δx is the x-component of the displacement of the particle. With this same notation, we denote the time interval from t_1 to t_2 as $\Delta t = t_2 - t_1$.

NOTE ▶ Values such as Δx or Δt always denote the final value minus the initial value, never the reverse. ◀

We can now define the x component of the average velocity.

Definition of average velocity

The x component of an object's average velocity is defined as the x component of displacement Δx, divided by the time interval Δt in which the displacement occurs. We represent this quantity by the letter v, with a subscript "av" to signify "average value" and a subscript "x" to signify "x component." Thus,

$$v_{av,x} = \frac{x_2 - x_1}{t_2 - t_1} = \frac{\Delta x}{\Delta t}. \qquad (2.3)$$

Unit: m/s

When we express distance in meters and time in seconds, a component of velocity is expressed in meters per second (m/s). Other common units of velocity are kilometers per hour (km/h), miles per hour (mi/h), and knots $(6080\ \text{ft/h})$.

In the preceding example, we have $x_1 = 19$ m, $x_2 = 277$ m, $t_1 = 1.0$ s, and $t_2 = 4.0$ s, and Equation 2.3 gives

$$v_{av,x} = \frac{277\ \text{m} - 19\ \text{m}}{4.0\ \text{s} - 1.0\ \text{s}} = 86\ \text{m/s}.$$

In some cases, $v_{av,x}$ is negative, as shown in Figure 2.2. Suppose an official's truck is moving *toward* the origin, with $x_1 = 277$ m and $x_2 = 19$ m. If $t_1 = 6.0$ s and $t_2 = 16.0$ s, then $\Delta x = -258$ m, $\Delta t = 10.0$ s, and the x component of average velocity is -26 m/s. Whenever x is positive and decreasing, or negative and becoming more negative, the object is moving in the negative x direction and $v_{av,x}$ is negative.

We stress again that average velocity is a *vector* quantity, and Equation 2.3 defines the x component of this vector. In this chapter, all vectors have *only one* nonzero component, frequently only an x component. We'll often call x the displacement and $v_{av,x}$ the average velocity, remembering that these are really the x components of vector quantities that, in straight-line motion, have *only x* components. In Chapter 3, displacement, velocity, and acceleration vectors will have two nonzero components.

When we deal with motion along a vertical line, we'll usually use a vertical y axis instead of an x axis, so our components will be called y components. Then Equation 2.3, with the x's replaced by y's, gives the y component of average velocity, $v_{av,y}$.

In Figures 2.1 and 2.2, it doesn't matter whether the car's velocity is or isn't constant during the time interval Δt. Another dragster may have started from rest,

▲ **FIGURE 2.2** Positions of an official's truck at two times during its drive up the racetrack.

reached a maximum velocity, blown its engine, and then slowed down. To calculate the average velocity, we need only the total displacement $\Delta x = x_2 - x_1$ and the total time interval $\Delta t = t_2 - t_1$.

EXAMPLE 2.1   **Swim competition**

During a freestyle competition, a swimmer performs the crawl stroke in a pool 50.0 m long, as shown in Figure 2.3. She swims a length at racing speed, taking 24.0 s to cover the length of the pool. She then takes twice that time to swim casually back to her starting point. Find **(a)** her average velocity for each length and **(b)** her average velocity for the entire swim.

|← 50.0 m →|

▲ **FIGURE 2.3**

SOLUTION

SET UP As shown in Figure 2.4, we choose a coordinate system with the origin at the starting point (often a convenient choice) and x increasing to the right. We add the information given to the diagram we sketch for the problem.

SOLVE Part (a):   For the first length, we have $x_1 = 0$, $x_2 = 50.0$ m, $t_1 = 0$, and $t_2 = 24.0$ s. Using the definition of average velocity given by Equation 2.3, we find that

$$v_{av,x} = \frac{x_2 - x_1}{t_2 - t_1} = \frac{50.0 \text{ m} - 0 \text{ m}}{24.0 \text{ s} - 0 \text{ s}} = 2.08 \text{ m/s.}$$

For the return trip, we have $x_1 = 50.0$ m, $x_2 = 0$, $t_1 = 24.0$ s, and $t_2 = 24.0$ s $+ 48.0$ s $= 72.0$ s. Using the definition of average velocity again, we obtain

$$v_{av,x} = \frac{x_2 - x_1}{t_2 - t_1} = \frac{0 \text{ m} - 50.0 \text{ m}}{72.0 \text{ s} - 24.0 \text{ s}} = -1.04 \text{ m/s.}$$

Part (b):   The starting and finishing points are the same: $x_1 = x_2 = 0$. The average velocity for a round-trip is zero!

▲ **FIGURE 2.4** Our sketch for this problem.

REFLECT The average x component of velocity in part (b) is negative because x_2 lies to the left of x_1 on the axis and x is decreasing during this part of the trip. Thus, the average velocity *vector* points to the right for part (a) and to the left for part (b). The average velocity for the total out-and-back trip is zero because the total displacement is zero.

Practice Problem: If the swimmer could cross the English Channel (32 km), how many hours would she need if she could maintain the same average velocity as for the first 50 m in the pool? (Actual times are around 15 hours.) *Answer:* 4.3 hr.

You may have noticed that we haven't used the term *speed* in our discussion of particle motion. The terms *speed* and *velocity* are often used interchangeably (and erroneously), but there is a very important distinction between them. The average **speed** of a point during any motion is a *scalar* quantity equal to the total *distance* traveled (disregarding the direction of motion) during a specified time interval, divided by the time interval. Average *velocity* is a *vector* quantity, equal to the vector *displacement* of the particle, divided by the time interval. In Example 2.1, the average velocity during the two laps is zero because the total

◄ **Will I ever get there?** Lombard Street in San Francisco is sometimes called "the crookedest street in the world." In descending the hill, a car travels a much greater distance than does a pedestrian walking down the adjacent stairs directly from top to bottom. However, both have moved the same overall distance through space; thus, the driver of the car and the pedestrian have experienced the same displacement. Therefore, if a car and a pedestrian left the top at the same time and arrived simultaneously at the bottom, they would have had the same average velocity (displacement divided by time), even though the car had a greater speed (overall distance traveled, divided by time).

displacement is zero. But the average speed is the total *distance* traveled (100.0 m), divided by the total time (72.0 s): 100.0 m$/72.0$ s $= 1.39$ m/s. The speedometer of a car is correctly named; it measures speed, irrespective of the direction of motion. To make a velocity meter, you would need a speedometer and a compass.

In Example 2.1, we could just as well have chosen the origin to be the other end of the pool and the positive direction for x to be to the left instead of to the right. Then the first x component of velocity would be negative and the second positive.

Conceptual Analysis 2.1

Signs and coordinate choices

You and a friend stand 10 m apart. Your dog, initially midway between you, runs in a straight line toward your friend. Each of you independently defines a coordinate system (position of origin and positive direction for the coordinate x) and calculates the dog's average x component of velocity. (Remember in this context, when we say "velocity," we really mean "x component of velocity.") What can you say with *certainty* about the average velocity?

A. The average velocity you calculate is positive.
B. The average velocity your friend calculates is negative.
C. Neither of you can obtain a negative velocity.
D. Both of you can obtain a negative velocity.

SOLUTION The question makes sense only if the coordinate axis is along the line joining you and your friend. But as Figure 2.5 shows, the axis can point to the left or to the right. If it points to the right, the dog moves in the positive x direction, so Δx is positive; if it points to the left, the dog moves in the negative x direction, so Δx is negative. Either person can choose either axis, so either person can obtain either sign for velocity. Thus, the correct

▲ **FIGURE 2.5** Your choice of coordinate system determines the sign of velocity.

answer is D. Notice that the sign of the average velocity does *not* depend on where you place the origin, but only on the direction you define as positive.

We've described motion of a particle along a straight line by stating the values of the coordinate x at various times t. In mathematical language, we say that x is a *function* of t. It's often useful to represent the relationship of x and t by means of a graph. We choose an axis system in which the coordinate x of the particle is plotted along the vertical axis and time t along the horizontal axis.

Figure 2.6 is a graph of the position of the dragster as a function of time. The curve in the figure *does not* represent the car's path in space; as Figure 2.1 shows,

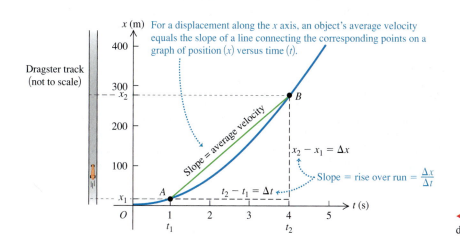

▲ **FIGURE 2.6** Graph of the position of the dragster as a function of time.

the path is a straight line. Rather, the graph is a pictorial way to represent the car's position at various times. Points A and B on the graph correspond to positions x_1 and x_2, respectively. The graph shows that, at time $t = 1.0$ s, the dragster's x coordinate (its displacement from the origin) is $x = 19$ m and that, at time $t = 4.0$ s, it is $x = 277$ m. During the 3.0-s interval from $t = 1.0$ s to $t = 4.0$ s, the x coordinate changes from 19 m to 277 m. The horizontal interval is $\Delta t = 3.0$ s, the vertical interval is $\Delta x = 258$ m. The average velocity $v_{\text{av},x} = \Delta x/\Delta t$ is the vertical side of the triangle (Δx) divided by the horizontal side (Δt). This quotient is the **slope** of the line joining A and B (often described as the "rise" divided by the "run"). Thus, we obtain the following general principle:

> The average velocity between two positions is the slope of a line connecting the two corresponding points on a graph of position as a function of time.

We'll use this fact in the next section when we define instantaneous velocity.

2.2 Instantaneous Velocity

When a particle speeds up or slows down, we can still define its velocity at any one specific instant of time or at one specific point in the path. Such a velocity is called the particle's **instantaneous velocity,** and it needs to be defined carefully.

Suppose we want to find the instantaneous velocity (i.e., the x component) of the dragster in Figure 2.1 at the point x_1. We can take the second point x_2 to be closer and closer to the first point x_1, and we can compute the average velocity over these shorter and shorter displacements and time intervals. Although both Δx and Δt become very small, their quotient does not necessarily become small. We then define the instantaneous velocity at x_1 as the value that this series of average velocities *approaches* as the time interval becomes very small and x_2 comes closer and closer to x_1.

In mathematical language, the instantaneous velocity is called the **limit** of $\Delta x/\Delta t$ as Δt approaches zero or (in the language of calculus) the **derivative** of x with respect to t. Using the symbol v_x with no subscript for instantaneous velocity, we obtain the following definition:

Definition of instantaneous velocity

The x component of instantaneous velocity is the limit of $\Delta x/\Delta t$ as Δt approaches zero:

$$v_x = \lim_{\Delta t \to 0} \frac{\Delta x}{\Delta t}. \qquad (2.4)$$

Like average velocity, instantaneous velocity is a vector quantity. Equation 2.4 defines its x component, which can be positive or negative. In straight-line motion, all other components are zero, and in this case we'll often call v the instantaneous velocity. From now on, when we use the term *velocity,* we'll always mean instantaneous rather than average velocity, unless we state otherwise.

The *sign* of a velocity component always depends on the choice of coordinate system, including the location of the origin and the choice of positive axis directions. We always assume that t_2 is a *later* time than t_1. (We always grow older, not younger.) Thus, Δt is always positive, and v_x has the same algebraic sign as Δx. If the positive x axis points to the right, as in Figure 2.1, a positive value of v_x

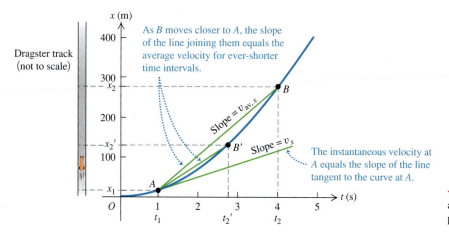

FIGURE 2.7 The relationship of average and instantaneous velocity for a graph of position as a function of time.

means motion toward the right, and a negative value means motion toward the left. But an object can have a positive x and a negative v_x, or the reverse; x tells us where the particle *is,* and v_x tells us how it is *moving.* In Figure 2.2 the object is to the right of O but is moving toward the left, so it has a positive x and a negative v_x. An object to the left of O moving toward the right has a negative x and a positive v_x. Can you see what the situation is when *both* x and v_x are negative?

Figure 2.7 shows the relation of the graph of x vs t to the average and instantaneous velocities. As we saw in Figure 2.6, the average velocity between any two points A and B on a graph of x versus t is the slope of the line connecting the points. To approach the instantaneous velocity, as we just learned, we move x_2 closer and closer to x_1 (and t_2 closer and closer to t_1). Graphically, that means finding the slope for ever smaller intervals as point B approaches point A. As this interval becomes very small, the slope equals that of a line tangent to the curve at point A. Thus,

> **On a graph of a coordinate x as a function of time t, the instantaneous velocity at any point is equal to the slope of the tangent line to the curve at that point.**

As shown in Figure 2.8, if the tangent line slopes upward to the right, its slope is positive, v_x is positive, and the motion of the particle is in the positive x direction. If the tangent slopes downward to the right, the velocity is negative, and the motion of the particle is in the negative x direction. Where the tangent is horizontal, the slope is zero and the velocity is zero.

(a)   (b)

FIGURE 2.8 On a graph of position as a function of time, the slope of the tangent line at any point is the velocity at that point.

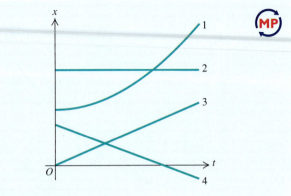

Conceptual Analysis 2.2

Velocity from graphs of position versus time

Figure 2.9 shows graphs of an object's position along the x axis versus time for four separate trials. Which of the following statements is or are correct?

A. The velocity is greater in trial 2 than in trial 3.
B. The velocity is not constant during trial 1.
C. During trial 4, the object changes direction as it passes through the point $x = 0$.
D. The velocity is constant during trials 2, 3, and 4.

(Remember that "velocity" means "x component of velocity.")

SOLUTION The graph of the motion during trial 1 has a changing slope and therefore v_x isn't constant. Trials 2, 3, and 4 all have graphs with constant slope and thus correspond to motion with constant velocity. (The velocity is zero during trial 2, as indicated by the slope of zero, but this value is still constant.) Trial 3 has a positive velocity, while the velocity in trial 4 is negative. Thus, choices B and D are correct.

▲ FIGURE 2.9

EXAMPLE 2.2 Average and instantaneous velocities

A cheetah is crouched in ambush 20.0 m to the east of an observer's vehicle, as shown in Figure 2.10a. At time $t = 0$, the cheetah charges an antelope in a clearing 50.0 m east of the observer. The cheetah runs along a straight line; the observer estimates that, during the first 2.00 s of the attack, the cheetah's coordinate x varies with time t according to the equation

$$x = 20.0 \text{ m} + (5.00 \text{ m/s}^2)t^2.$$

(a) Find the displacement of the cheetah during the interval between $t_1 = 1.00$ s and $t_2 = 2.00$ s. **(b)** Find the average velocity during this time interval. **(c)** Estimate the instantaneous velocity at time $t_1 = 1.00$ s by taking $\Delta t = 0.10$ s.

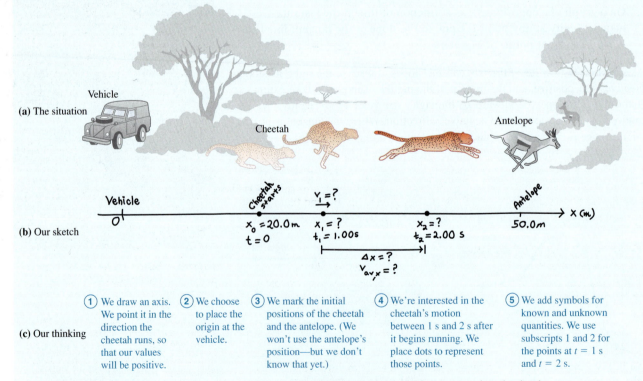

(a) The situation

(b) Our sketch

(c) Our thinking

① We draw an axis. We point it in the direction the cheetah runs, so that our values will be positive.

② We choose to place the origin at the vehicle.

③ We mark the initial positions of the cheetah and the antelope. (We won't use the antelope's position—but we don't know that yet.)

④ We're interested in the cheetah's motion between 1 s and 2 s after it begins running. We place dots to represent those points.

⑤ We add symbols for known and unknown quantities. We use subscripts 1 and 2 for the points at $t = 1$ s and $t = 2$ s.

▲ **FIGURE 2.10** (a) The situation for this problem, (b) the sketch we draw, and (c) the thinking that goes into the sketch.

Continued

SOLUTION

SET UP Figure 2.10b shows the diagram we sketch. First we define a coordinate system, orienting it so that the cheetah runs in the $+x$ direction. We add the points we are interested in, the values we know, and the values we will need to find for parts (a) and (b).

SOLVE Part (a): To find the displacement Δx, we first find the cheetah's positions (the values of x) at time $t_1 = 1.00$ s and at time $t_2 = 2.00$ s by substituting the values of t into the given equation. At time $t_1 = 1.00$ s, the cheetah's position x_1 is

$$x_1 = 20.0 \text{ m} + (5.00 \text{ m/s}^2)(1.00 \text{ s})^2 = 25.0 \text{ m}.$$

At time $t_2 = 2.00$ s, the cheetah's position x_2 is

$$x_2 = 20.0 \text{ m} + (5.00 \text{ m/s}^2)(2.00 \text{ s})^2 = 40.0 \text{ m}.$$

The displacement during this interval is

$$\Delta x = x_2 - x_1 = 40.0 \text{ m} - 25.0 \text{ m} = 15.0 \text{ m}.$$

Part (b): Having the displacement from 1.00 s to 2.00 s, we can now find the average velocity for that interval:

$$v_{av,x} = \frac{\Delta x}{\Delta t} = \frac{40.0 \text{ m} - 25.0 \text{ m}}{2.00 \text{ s} - 1.00 \text{ s}} = \frac{15.0 \text{ m}}{1.00 \text{ s}} = 15.0 \text{ m/s}.$$

Part (c): The instantaneous velocity at 1.00 s is approximately (but not exactly) equal to the average velocity in the interval from $t_1 = 1.00$ s to $t_2 = 1.10$ s (i.e., $\Delta t = 0.10$ s). At $t_2 = 1.10$ s,

$$x_2 = 20.0 \text{ m} + (5.00 \text{ m/s})(1.10 \text{ s})^2 = 26.05 \text{ m},$$

so that

$$v_{av,x} = \frac{\Delta x}{\Delta t} = \frac{26.05 \text{ m} - 25.0 \text{ m}}{1.10 \text{ s} - 1.00 \text{ s}} = 10.5 \text{ m/s}.$$

If you use the same procedure to find the average velocities for time intervals of 0.01 s and 0.001 s, you will get 10.05 m/s and 10.005 m/s, respectively. As Δt gets smaller and smaller, the average velocity gets closer and closer to 10.0 m/s. We conclude that the instantaneous velocity at time $t = 1.0$ s is 10.0 m/s.

REFLECT As the time interval Δt approaches zero, the average velocity in the interval is closer and closer to the limiting value 10.0 m/s, which we call the instantaneous velocity at time $t = 1.00$ s. Note that when we calculate an average velocity, we need to specify two times—the beginning and end times of the interval—but for instantaneous velocity at a particular time, we specify only that one time.

NOTE ▶ Here's a reminder about the term *speed*. It is distance traveled, divided by time taken, on either an average or an instantaneous basis. Speed is a scalar quantity, not a vector; it has no direction. If a race car makes one lap around the Indianapolis race track (2.5 mi in circumference) in 1.00 min ($=1/60$ h), its average speed is $(2.5 \text{ mi})/(1/60 \text{ h}) = 150 \text{ mi/h}$. Its instantaneous speed may or may not be constant, but its velocity is certainly not constant because the car changes direction at the turns. At the end of one lap, the race car is back where it started, so its average *velocity* for one lap is zero. ◀

2.3 Average and Instantaneous Acceleration

When the velocity of a moving object changes with time, we say that the object has *acceleration*. Just as velocity is a quantitative description of the rate of change of *position* with time, acceleration is a quantitative description of the rate of change of *velocity* with time. Like velocity, acceleration is a vector quantity. In straight-line motion its only nonzero component is along the coordinate axis.

To introduce the concept of acceleration, let's consider again the motion of an object (such as the dragster of Section 2.1) along the x axis. As usual, we assume that the object can be treated as a particle. Suppose that at time t_1 the particle is at point x_1 and has an x component of instantaneous velocity v_{1x} and that at a later time t_2 it is at point x_2 and has an x component of velocity v_{2x}.

Definition of average acceleration

The **average acceleration** a_{av} of an object as it moves from x_1 (at time t_1) to x_2 (at time t_2) is a vector quantity whose x component is the ratio of the change in the x component of velocity, $\Delta v_x = v_{2x} - v_{1x}$, to the time interval $\Delta t = t_2 - t_1$:

$$a_{av,x} = \frac{v_{2x} - v_{1x}}{t_2 - t_1} = \frac{\Delta v_x}{\Delta t}. \qquad (2.5)$$

Unit: If we express velocity in meters per second and time in seconds, then acceleration is in meters per second per second $(\text{m/s})/\text{s}$. This unit is usually written as m/s^2 and is read "meters per second squared."

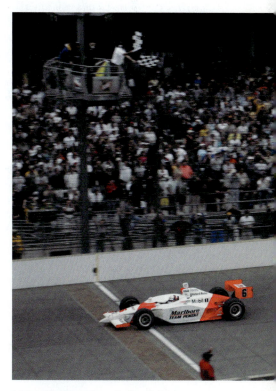

▲ **Haven't I been here before?** Gil de Ferran has just won the 2003 Indianapolis 500 auto race by completing 200 laps of the 2.5-mile oval course more rapidly than anyone else. He did this in under three hours, for an average speed of close to 200 miles per hour for the 500-mile race. However, since he finished the race right where he started, his total displacement during the race was zero. So don't tell him now, but despite his high average speed, his average velocity for the trip was 0 miles per hour!

In straight-line motion, we'll usually call $a_{av,x}$ the average acceleration, although we recognize that it is actually the x component of the average acceleration.

EXAMPLE 2.3 **Acceleration in a space walk**

An astronaut has left the space shuttle on a tether to test a new personal maneuvering device. She moves along a straight line directly away from the shuttle. Her onboard partner measures her velocity before and after certain maneuvers, and obtains the following results:

A. $v_{1x} = 0.8$ m/s, $v_{2x} = 1.2$ m/s; (speeding up)
B. $v_{1x} = 1.6$ m/s, $v_{2x} = 1.2$ m/s; (slowing down)
C. $v_{1x} = -0.4$ m/s, $v_{2x} = -1.0$ m/s; (speeding up)
D. $v_{1x} = -1.6$ m/s, $v_{2x} = -0.8$ m/s. (slowing down)

If $t_1 = 2$ s and $t_2 = 4$ s in each case, find the average acceleration for each set of data.

SOLUTION

SET UP We use the diagram in Figure 2.11 to organize our data.

SOLVE To find the astronaut's average acceleration in each case, we will use the definition of average acceleration (Equation 2.5): $a_{av,x} = \Delta v_x / \Delta t$. The time interval is $\Delta t = 2.0$ s in all cases; the change in velocity in each case is $\Delta v_x = v_{2x} - v_{1x}$.

Part (a): $a_{av,x} = \dfrac{1.2 \text{ m/s} - 0.8 \text{ m/s}}{4 \text{ s} - 2 \text{ s}} = +0.2 \text{ m/s}^2;$

Part (b): $a_{av,x} = \dfrac{1.2 \text{ m/s} - 1.6 \text{ m/s}}{4 \text{ s} - 2 \text{ s}} = -0.2 \text{ m/s}^2;$

Part (c): $a_{av,x} = \dfrac{-1.0 \text{ m/s} - (-0.4 \text{ m/s})}{4 \text{ s} - 2 \text{ s}} = -0.3 \text{ m/s}^2;$

Part (d): $a_{av,x} = \dfrac{-0.8 \text{ m/s} - (-1.6 \text{ m/s})}{4 \text{ s} - 2 \text{ s}} = +0.4 \text{ m/s}^2.$

REFLECT The astronaut speeds up in cases (a) and (c) and slows down in (b) and (d), but the average acceleration is positive in (a) and (d) and negative in (b) and (c). In other words, negative acceleration *does not* necessarily indicate a slowing down.

▲ **FIGURE 2.11** We can use a sketch and table to organize the information given in the problem.

The preceding example raises the question of what the sign of acceleration means and how it relates to the signs of displacement and velocity. Because average acceleration (i.e., the x component) is defined as $a_{av,x} = \Delta v_x / \Delta t$, and Δt is always positive, the sign of acceleration is the same as the sign of Δv_x. Figure 2.12 shows the four possible cases; make sure you understand why the acceleration is positive or negative in each case.

NOTE ▶ As Figure 2.12 shows, the velocity and acceleration of an object do not necessarily have the same sign. For instance, an object that is moving in the positive direction, but slowing down, has positive velocity and negative acceleration. Velocity describes the motion of an object at a given instant of time; acceleration describes how the object's motion is *changing* with time. ◀

The term *deceleration* is sometimes used for a decrease in speed; such a decrease can correspond to either positive or negative acceleration. Because of

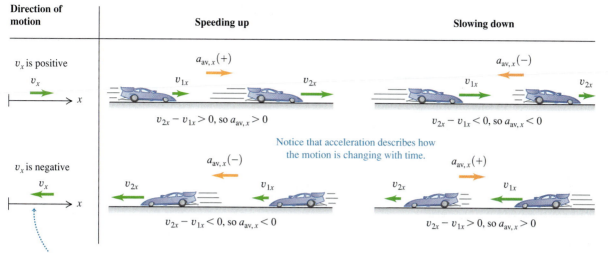

Direction of motion	Speeding up	Slowing down

v_x is positive

$a_{av,x}(+)$

v_{1x} $\qquad$ v_{2x}

$v_{2x} - v_{1x} > 0$, so $a_{av,x} > 0$

$a_{av,x}(-)$

v_{1x} $\qquad$ v_{2x}

$v_{2x} - v_{1x} < 0$, so $a_{av,x} < 0$

Notice that acceleration describes how the motion is changing with time.

v_x is negative

$a_{av,x}(-)$

v_{2x} $\qquad$ v_{1x}

$v_{2x} - v_{1x} < 0$, so $a_{av,x} < 0$

$a_{av,x}(+)$

v_{2x} $\qquad$ v_{1x}

$v_{2x} - v_{1x} > 0$, so $a_{av,x} > 0$

The *direction of the axis* determines the signs of velocity and acceleration.

▲ **FIGURE 2.12** The relationship between the sign of acceleration, the sign of Δv, and the direction chosen as positive.

this ambiguity, we won't use the term in what follows. Instead, we recommend careful attention to the interpretation of the algebraic sign of a_x in relation to that of v_x.

We can now define **instantaneous acceleration,** following the same procedure that we used for instantaneous velocity. Consider the situation shown in Figure 2.13: A sports car has just entered the final straightaway at the Grand Prix. It reaches point x_1 at time t_1, moving with velocity v_{1x}. It passes point x_2, closer to the finish line, at time t_2 with velocity v_{2x}.

To define instantaneous acceleration at point x_1, we take the second point x_2 in Figure 2.13 to be closer and closer to the first point x_1, so the average acceleration is computed over shorter and shorter time intervals. The instantaneous acceleration at point x_1 is defined as the limit approached by the average acceleration when point x_2 is taken closer and closer to point x_1 and t_2 is taken closer and closer to t_1.

▲ **Is this car accelerating?** Shortly after this jet-propelled car reached its top speed, the parachute was deployed to help bring it to a stop. As you know from your study of physics, the car is indeed accelerating while it is slowing down. Because acceleration is defined as a change in velocity per unit time, in this case the car has a negative acceleration component in the forward direction.

Definition of instantaneous acceleration

The x component of instantaneous acceleration is defined as the limit of $\Delta v_x / \Delta t$ as Δt approaches zero:

$$a_x = \lim_{\Delta t \to 0} \frac{\Delta v_x}{\Delta t}. \tag{2.6}$$

Instantaneous acceleration plays an essential role in the laws of mechanics. From now on, when we use the term *acceleration,* we will always mean instantaneous acceleration, not average acceleration.

v_{1x} $\qquad$ v_{2x}

O $\quad$ x_1 $\qquad\qquad$ x_2 $\qquad$ x

◀ **FIGURE 2.13** A race car at two points on the straightaway.

EXAMPLE 2.4 **Average and instantaneous accelerations**

Suppose that, at any time t, the velocity v of the car in Figure 2.13 is given by the equation $v_x = 60.0$ m/s $+ (0.500$ m/s$^3)t^2$. In this equation, v_x has units of m/s and t has units of s. Note that the numbers 60 and 0.50 *must* have the units shown for this equation to be dimensionally consistent.
(a) Find the change in velocity of the car in the time interval between $t_1 = 1.00$ s and $t_2 = 3.00$ s. **(b)** Find the average acceleration in this time interval. **(c)** Estimate the instantaneous acceleration at time $t_1 = 1.00$ s by taking $\Delta t = 0.10$ s.

SOLUTION

SET UP Figure 2.14 shows the diagram we use to establish a coordinate system and organize our known and unknown information.

SOLVE Part (a): We first find the velocity at each time by substituting each value of t into the equation. From these values, we can find the change in velocity in the interval. Thus, at time $t_1 = 1.00$ s,

$$v_{1x} = 60.0 \text{ m/s} + (0.500 \text{ m/s}^3)(1.00 \text{ s})^2 = 60.5 \text{ m/s}.$$

At time $t_2 = 3.00$ s,

$$v_{2x} = 60.0 \text{ m/s} + (0.500 \text{ m/s}^3)(3.00 \text{ s})^2 = 64.5 \text{ m/s}.$$

The change in velocity Δv_x is then

$$\Delta v_x = v_{2x} - v_{1x} = 64.5 \text{ m/s} - 60.5 \text{ m/s} = 4.00 \text{ m/s}.$$

Part (b): The change in velocity, divided by the time interval, gives the average acceleration in each interval.
The time interval is $\Delta t = 3.00$ s $- 1.00$ s $= 2.00$ s, so

$$a_{\text{av},x} = \frac{v_{2x} - v_{1x}}{t_2 - t_1} = \frac{4.0 \text{ m/s}}{2.00 \text{ s}} = 2.00 \text{ m/s}^2.$$

▲ **FIGURE 2.14** Our sketch for this problem.

Part (c): We use the same procedure to approximate the instantaneous acceleration at x_1 by calculating the average acceleration over 0.100 s. When $\Delta t = 0.100$ s, $t_2 = 1.10$ s, and it follows that

$$v_{2x} = 60.0 \text{ m/s} + (0.500 \text{ m/s}^3)(1.10 \text{ s})^2 = 60.605 \text{ m/s},$$
$$\Delta v_x = 0.105 \text{ m/s},$$
$$a_{\text{av},x} = \frac{\Delta v_x}{\Delta t} = \frac{0.105 \text{ m/s}}{0.100 \text{ s}} = 1.05 \text{ m/s}^2.$$

REFLECT If we repeat the calculation in part (c) for $\Delta t = 0.01$ s and $\Delta t = 0.001$ s, we get $a_{\text{av},x} = 1.005$ m/s^2 and $a_{\text{av},x} = 1.0005$ m/s^2, respectively (although we aren't entitled to this many significant figures). As Δt gets smaller and smaller, the average acceleration gets closer and closer to 1.00 m/s^2. We conclude that the instantaneous acceleration at $t = 1.00$ s is 1.00 m/s^2.

As with average and instantaneous velocity, we can gain added insight into the concepts of average and instantaneous acceleration by plotting a graph with velocity v_x on the vertical axis and time t on the horizontal axis. Figure 2.15 shows such a graph for the race car from Figure 2.13. Notice that now we are plotting *velocity* against time, not position against time as before. If we draw a line between any two points on the graph, such as A and B (corresponding to a displacement from x_1 to x_2 and to the time interval $\Delta t = t_2 - t_1$), the slope of that line equals the average acceleration over that interval. If we then take point B and move it closer and closer to point A, the slope of the line AB approaches the slope

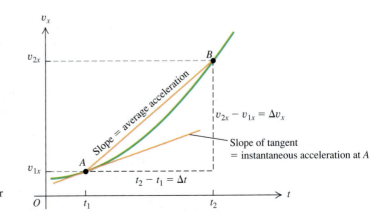

▶ **FIGURE 2.15** A graph of velocity versus time for the motion of the race car in Figure 2.13.

of the line that is tangent to the curve at point *A*. Accordingly, we can interpret a graph of velocity versus time as follows:

> **The average acceleration between any two points on a graph of velocity versus time equals the slope of a line connecting those points.**

> **The instantaneous acceleration at any point on the graph equals the slope of the line tangent to the curve at that point.**

Let's emphasize once again the significance of the *sign* of acceleration. First, the velocity v_x and acceleration a_x of an object don't necessarily have the same sign; they are independent quantities. When v_x and a_x *do* have the same sign, the object is speeding up. If both are positive, the object is moving in the positive direction with increasing speed. If both are negative, the object is moving in the negative direction with a velocity that becomes more and more negative with time, and again the object's speed increases. If v_x is positive and a_x is negative, the object is moving in the positive direction with decreasing speed. If v_x is negative and a_x is positive, the object is moving in the negative direction with a velocity that is becoming less negative, and again the object slows down.

Conceptual Analysis 2.3

Translating a graphical description to a verbal description

Figure 2.16 shows a graph of velocity versus time for a moving object. (Notice that the vertical axis is velocity in this case, not position.) The object moves on an east-west axis, with west chosen as the positive direction. Which of the following verbal descriptions matches the graph?

A. The object speeds up continuously while moving westward.
B. The object moves toward the origin while slowing, then moves away from the origin while speeding up.
C. The object moves in the positive direction while slowing to a stop, then moves east while speeding up.
D. The object moves east while slowing to a stop, then moves west while speeding up.

▲ **FIGURE 2.16**

SOLUTION The direction of motion and the sign of the velocity tell us the same thing; in this case, a positive velocity means that the object is going west and a negative velocity means that it is going east. A large negative velocity means that the object is going east at high speed, while a small negative velocity means that it is going east slowly. Since the vertical axis of this graph represents velocity, the velocity coordinate of any point on the plot tells you the object's direction and speed. The plot starts with a large, negative value of velocity, indicating that the object is moving east fast. When the plot reaches $v_x = 0$ (the point at which it crosses the horizontal axis), the object has slowed to a halt. From there, the object has progressively higher positive values of v_x; it is moving to the west with increasing speed. Thus, A cannot be true, because the object starts with negative v_x. Nor can B be true, since knowing your speed and direction of motion says nothing about where you are. The answer D matches the reasoning given here.

Acceleration and the Human Body

Accelerations require forces; we'll study the relationship between them in Chapter 4. An object subjected to sufficiently large accelerations and the associated forces may suffer damage. The earth's gravitational attraction causes objects to fall with a downward acceleration with a magnitude of about 9.8 m/s^2 (assuming that effects such as air resistance can be neglected). This acceleration is often denoted by g; we'll study its effects in greater detail in Section 2.5. For now, we simply note that $g = 9.8 \text{ m/s}^2$.

Because earth's land life evolved in an environment characterized by this magnitude of acceleration, it isn't surprising that the human body can withstand accelerations on the order of g without damage. Sport cars can accelerate at about $0.5g$, or 4.9 m/s^2. Accelerations on the order of $3g$ in a jet fighter cause serious impairment of the pilot's blood circulation, and above about $5g$ the pilot loses consciousness. The primary function of air bags in cars is to reduce the maximum acceleration during a collision to a value that can be sustained by the body without catastrophic damage. The human body can withstand accelerations on the order of 50*g* for very short time intervals (about 0.05 s).

2.4 Motion with Constant Acceleration

The simplest accelerated motion is straight-line motion with *constant* acceleration. In this case, the velocity changes at the same rate throughout the motion. Figure 2.17 shows four ways to represent the motion of a race car undergoing constant acceleration. Notice that the plot of velocity versus time (Figure 2.17c) is a straight line; that is, its slope is constant. That tells you that the car's velocity changes by equal amounts Δv_x in equal time intervals Δt. This characteristic of motion with constant acceleration makes it easy for us to derive equations for the position x and velocity v_x as functions of time. Let's start with velocity. In the definition of average acceleration (Equation 2.5), we can replace the average acceleration $a_{av,x}$ by the constant (instantaneous) acceleration a_x. We then have

$$a_x = \frac{v_{2x} - v_{1x}}{t_2 - t_1} \quad \text{(for an object moving with constant acceleration).} \quad (2.7)$$

Now we let $t_1 = 0$ and t_2 be any arbitrary later time t. We use the symbol v_{0x} for the velocity (again, the x component) at the initial time $t = 0$; the velocity at the later time t is v_x. Then Equation 2.7 becomes the following:

1.1, 1.3, 1.4–1.6   Act[iv ONLINE Physics

Velocity as a function of time for an object moving with constant acceleration

For an object that has x component of velocity v_{0x} at time $t = 0$ and moves with constant acceleration a_x, we find the velocity v_x at any later time t:

$$a_x = \frac{v_x - v_{0x}}{t - 0}, \quad \text{or}$$

$$v_x = v_{0x} + a_x t. \quad (2.8)$$

Unit: m/s

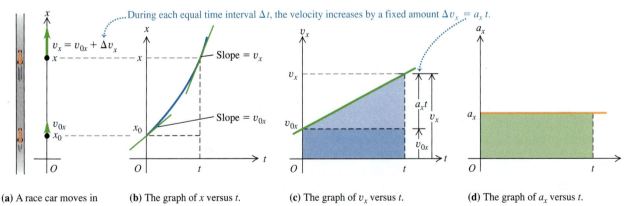

..During each equal time interval Δt, the velocity increases by a fixed amount $\Delta v_x = a_x t$.

(a) A race car moves in the x direction with constant acceleration.

(b) The graph of x versus t.

(c) The graph of v_x versus t.

(d) The graph of a_x versus t.

▲ **FIGURE 2.17** Four ways to represent the motion of a race car moving with constant acceleration.

We can interpret this equation as follows: The acceleration a_x is the constant rate of change of velocity, that is, the change in velocity per unit time. The term $a_x t$ is the product of the change in velocity per unit time, a_x, and the time interval t. Therefore, it equals the *total* change in velocity from the initial time $t = 0$ to the later time t. The velocity v_x at any time t is the sum of the initial velocity v_{0x} (at $t = 0$) and the *change* in velocity $a_x t$. Figure 2.17c shows this analysis in graphical terms. The height v_x of the graph at any time t is the sum of two segments: one with length v_{0x} equal to the initial velocity, the other with length $a_x t$ equal to the change in velocity during time t.

Activ
Physics   1.8, 1.9, 1.11–1.14

EXAMPLE 2.5   Passing speed

A car initially traveling along a straight stretch of highway at 15 m/s accelerates with a constant acceleration of 2.0 m/s^2 in order to pass a truck. What is the velocity of the car after 5.0 s?

SOLUTION

SET UP Figure 2.18 shows what we draw. We take the origin of coordinates to be at the initial position of the car, where $v_x = v_{0x}$ and $t = 0$, and we let the $+x$ direction be the direction of the car's initial velocity. With this coordinate system, $v_{0x} = +15 \text{ m/s}$ and $a_x = +2.0 \text{ m/s}^2$.

▲ **FIGURE 2.18** The diagram we draw for this problem.

SOLVE The acceleration is constant during the 5.0 s time interval, so we can use Equation 2.8 to find v_x:

$$v_x = v_{0x} + a_x t = 15 \text{ m/s} + (2.0 \text{ m/s}^2)(5.0 \text{ s})$$
$$= 15 \text{ m/s} + 10 \text{ m/s} = 25 \text{ m/s}.$$

REFLECT The velocity and acceleration are in the same direction, so the speed increases. An acceleration of 2.0 m/s^2 means that the velocity increases by 2.0 m/s every second, so in 5.0 s the velocity increases by 10 m/s.

Practice Problem: If the car maintains its constant acceleration, how much additional time does it take the car to reach a velocity of 35 m/s? *Answer:* 5.0 s.

Next we want to derive an equation for the *position* x of a particle moving with constant acceleration. To do this, we make use of two different expressions for the average velocity $v_{\text{av},x}$ during the interval from $t = 0$ to any later time t. First, when the acceleration is constant and the graph of velocity vs. time is a straight line, as in Figure 2.17, the velocity changes at a uniform rate. In this particular case, the average velocity throughout any time interval is simply the average of the velocities at the beginning and the end of the interval. Thus, for the time interval from 0 to t,

$$v_{\text{av},x} = \frac{v_{0x} + v_x}{2} \quad \text{(for constant acceleration).} \tag{2.9}$$

(This equation does *not* hold if the acceleration varies with time; in that case, the graph of velocity vs. time is a curve, as in Figure 2.15.)

We also know that v_x, the velocity at any time t, is given by Equation 2.8. Substituting that expression for v_x into Equation 2.9, we find that

$$v_{\text{av},x} = \tfrac{1}{2}(v_{0x} + v_{0x} + a_x t)$$
$$= v_{0x} + \tfrac{1}{2}a_x t. \tag{2.10}$$

We can also get an expression for $v_{\text{av},x}$ from the general definition, Equation 2.1:

$$v_{\text{av},x} = \frac{x_2 - x_1}{t_2 - t_1}.$$

We call the position at time $t = 0$ the *initial position,* denoted by x_0. The position at the later time t is simply x. Thus, for the time interval $\Delta t = t - 0$ and the corresponding displacement $x - x_0$, Equation 2.1 gives

$$v_{av,x} = \frac{x - x_0}{t}. \tag{2.11}$$

Finally, we equate Equations 2.10 and 2.11 and simplify the result to obtain the following equation:

> **Position as a function of time for an object moving with constant acceleration**
> For constant acceleration a_x, we solve
>
> $$v_{0x} + \tfrac{1}{2}a_x t = \frac{x - x_0}{t} \quad \text{to find}$$
>
> $$x = x_0 + v_{0x}t + \tfrac{1}{2}a_x t^2. \tag{2.12}$$

This equation states that if, at the initial time $t = 0$, a particle is at position x_0 and has velocity v_{0x}, its new position x at any later time t is the sum of three terms: its initial position x_0, plus the distance $v_{0x}t$ that it would have moved if its velocity had been constant, plus an additional distance $\tfrac{1}{2}a_x t^2$ caused by the changing velocity.

EXAMPLE 2.6   **Passing distance**

What distance does the car in Example 2.5 travel during its 5.0 seconds of acceleration?

SOLUTION

SET UP We use the same coordinates as in Example 2.5. As before, $v_{0x} = +15$ m/s and $a_x = +2.0$ m/s^2.

SOLVE We want to solve for $x - x_0$, the distance traveled by the car during the 5.0 s time interval. The acceleration is constant, so we can use Equation 2.12 to find

$$\begin{aligned} x - x_0 &= v_{0x}t + \tfrac{1}{2}a_x t^2 \\ &= (15 \text{ m/s})(5.0 \text{ s}) + \tfrac{1}{2}(2.0 \text{ m/s}^2)(5.0 \text{ s})^2 \\ &= 75 \text{ m} + 25 \text{ m} = 100 \text{ m}. \end{aligned}$$

REFLECT If the speed were constant and equal to the initial value $v_0 = 15$ m/s, the car would travel 75 m in 5.0 s. It actually travels *farther,* because the speed is increasing. From Example 2.5,

we know that the final velocity is $v_x = 25$ m/s, so the *average* velocity for the 5.0 s segment of motion is

$$v_{av,x} = \frac{v_{0x} + v_x}{2} = \frac{15 \text{ m/s} + 25 \text{ m/s}}{2} = 20 \text{ m/s}.$$

An alternative way to obtain the distance traveled is to multiply the average velocity by the time interval. When we do this, we get $x - x_0 = v_{av,x}t = (20 \text{ m/s})(5.0 \text{ s}) = 100$ m, the same result we obtained using Equation 2.12.

Practice Problem: If the car in Example 2.5 maintains its constant acceleration for a total time of 10 s, what total distance does it travel? *Answer:* 250 m.

For some problems, we aren't given the time interval for the motion, and we need to obtain a relation for x, v_x, and a_x that doesn't contain t. To obtain such a relation, we can combine Equations 2.8 and 2.12 to eliminate t. This involves a little algebra, but the result is worth the effort!

We first solve Equation 2.8 for t and then substitute the resulting expression into Equation 2.12 and simplify:

$$t = \frac{v_x - v_{0x}}{a_x},$$

$$x = x_0 + v_{0x}\left(\frac{v_x - v_{0x}}{a_x}\right) + \frac{1}{2}a_x\left(\frac{v_x - v_{0x}}{a_x}\right)^2.$$

We transfer the term x_0 to the left side and multiply through by $2a_x$:

$$2a_x(x - x_0) = 2v_{0x}v_x - 2v_{0x}^2 + v_x^2 - 2v_{0x}v_x + v_{0x}^2.$$

Finally, we combine terms and simplify to obtain the following equation:

Velocity as a function of position for an object moving with constant acceleration

For an object moving in a straight line with constant acceleration a_x,

$$v_x^2 = v_{0x}^2 + 2a_x(x - x_0). \qquad (2.13)$$

This equation gives us the particle's velocity v_x at any position x without needing to know the *time* when it is at that position.

EXAMPLE 2.7   Entering the freeway

A sports car is sitting at rest in a freeway entrance ramp. The driver sees a break in the traffic and floors the car's accelerator, so that the car accelerates at a constant 4.9 m/s^2 as it moves in a straight line onto the freeway. What distance does the car travel in reaching a freeway speed of 30 m/s?

SOLUTION

SET UP As shown in Figure 2.19, we place the origin at the initial position of the car and assume that the car travels in a straight line in the $+x$ direction. Then $v_{0x} = 0$, $v_x = 30 \text{ m/s}$, and $a_x = 4.9 \text{ m/s}^2$.

SOLVE The acceleration is constant; the problem makes no mention of time, so we can't use Equation 2.8 or Equation 2.12 by themselves. We need a relation between x and v_x, and this is provided by Equation 2.13:

$$v_x^2 = v_{0x}^2 + 2a_x(x - x_0).$$

Rearranging and substituting numerical values, we obtain

$$x - x_0 = \frac{v_x^2 - v_{0x}^2}{2a_x} = \frac{(30 \text{ m/s})^2 - 0}{2(4.9 \text{ m/s}^2)} = 92 \text{ m}.$$

Alternative Solution: We could have used Equation 2.8 to solve for the time t first:

$$t = \frac{v_x - v_{0x}}{a_x} = \frac{30 \text{ m/s} - 0}{4.9 \text{ m/s}^2} = 6.12 \text{ s}.$$

Then Equation 2.12 gives the distance traveled:

$$x - x_0 = v_{0x}t + \tfrac{1}{2}a_xt^2 = 0 + \tfrac{1}{2}(4.9 \text{ m/s}^2)(6.12 \text{ s})^2 = 92 \text{ m}.$$

▲ **FIGURE 2.19** A car accelerating on a ramp merging onto a freeway.

REFLECT We obtained the same result in one step when we used Equation 2.13 and in two steps when we used Equations 2.8 and 2.12. When we use them correctly, Equations 2.8, 2.12, and 2.13 *always* give consistent results.

The final speed of 30 m/s is about 67 mph, and 92 m is about 100 yd. Does this distance correspond to your own driving experience?

Practice Problem: What distance has the car traveled when it has reached a speed of 20 m/s? *Answer:* 41 m.

Equations 2.8, 2.12, and 2.13, are the *equations of motion with constant acceleration*. Any kinematic problem involving motion of an object in a straight line with constant acceleration can be solved by applying these equations.

Here's a summary of the equations:

Equations of motion for constant acceleration

$$\begin{array}{lll} v_x = v_{0x} + a_x t & \text{(Gives } v_x \text{ if } t \text{ is known.)} & (2.8) \\ x = x_0 + v_{0x}t + \tfrac{1}{2}a_x t^2 & \text{(Gives } x \text{ if } t \text{ is known.)} & (2.12) \\ v_x^2 = v_{0x}^2 + 2a_x(x - x_0) & \text{(Gives } v_x \text{ if } x \text{ is known.)} & (2.13) \end{array}$$

We can get one more useful relationship by equating the two expressions for $v_{av,x}$ given by Equations 2.9 and 2.11, and multiplying through by t. Doing this, we obtain the following equation:

Position, velocity, and time for an object moving with constant acceleration

$$x - x_0 = \frac{v_{0x} + v_x}{2}t. \tag{2.14}$$

This equation says that the total displacement $x - x_0$ from time $t = 0$ to a later time t is equal to the average velocity $(v_{0x} + v_x)/2$ during the interval, multiplied by the time t. Equation 2.14 doesn't contain the acceleration a_x, so it is sometimes useful when a_x is not given in the problem.

Figure 2.20 is a graphical representation of Equations 2.12 and 2.8, respectively, for the case of positive velocity and positive acceleration. In Figure 2.20a, the blue curve represents Equation 2.12. The straight dashed line shows the plot we would get if the acceleration is zero: If $a_x = 0$, then $x = x_0 + v_{0x}t$. For this line, the slope (velocity) is constant. The vertical separation between the two curves represents the term $\frac{1}{2}a_xt^2$, which is the effect of acceleration. In Figure 2.20b, the green curve represents Equation 2.8. Make sure you understand how this graph represents the individual terms of the equation.

The plot with constant acceleration:
$x = x_0 + v_{0x}t + \frac{1}{2}a_xt^2$

The effect of acceleration: $\frac{1}{2}a_xt^2$

The plot we would get with zero acceleration: $x = x_0 + v_{0x}t$

(a) Plot of x versus t for an object moving with positive constant acceleration

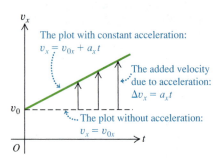

The plot with constant acceleration: $v_x = v_{0x} + a_xt$

The added velocity due to acceleration: $\Delta v_x = a_xt$

The plot without acceleration: $v_x = v_{0x}$

(b) Plot of v_x versus t for the same object

▲ **FIGURE 2.20** The graphical meaning of Equations 2.8 and 2.12 for an object moving with positive velocity and positive constant acceleration.

PROBLEM-SOLVING STRATEGY 2.1 **Motion with constant acceleration**

SET UP

1. You *must* decide at the beginning of a problem where the origin of coordinates is and which axis direction is positive. The choices are usually a matter of convenience; it is often easiest to place the origin at the object's location at time $t = 0$; then $x_0 = 0$. Draw a diagram showing your choices. Then sketch any relevant later positions of the object in the same diagram.
2. Once you have chosen the positive axis direction, the positive directions for velocity and acceleration are also determined. It would be wrong to define x as positive to the right of the origin and velocities as positive toward the left.
3. It often helps to restate the problem in prose first and then translate the prose description into symbols and equations. *When* (i.e, at what value of t) does the particle arrive at a certain point? *Where* is the particle when its velocity has a certain value? (That is, what is the value of x when v_x has the specified value?) The next example asks, "Where is the motorcyclist when his velocity is 25 m/s?" Translated into symbols, this becomes "What is the value of x when $v_x = 25$ m/s?"
4. Either on your diagram or in a list, write known and unknown quantities such as x, x_0, v_x, v_{0x}, and a_x. Write in the values for those that are known. Be on the lookout for implicit information; for example, "A car sits at a stoplight" usually means that $v_{0x} = 0$, and so on.

SOLVE

5. Once you've identified the unknowns, you may be able to choose an equation from among Equations 2.8, 2.12, 2.13, and 2.14 that contains only one of the unknowns. Solve for that unknown; then substitute the known values and compute the value of the unknown. Carry the units of the quantities along with your calculations as an added consistency check.

REFLECT

6. Take a hard look at your results to see whether they make sense. Are they within the general range of magnitudes you expected? If you change one of the given quantities, do the results change in a way you can predict?

EXAMPLE 2.8 **Constant acceleration on a motorcycle**

A motorcyclist heading east through a small Iowa town accelerates after he passes a signpost at $x = 0$ marking the city limits. His acceleration is constant: $a_x = 4.0 \text{ m/s}^2$. At time $t = 0$ he is 5.0 m east of the signpost and has a velocity of $v_x = 15 \text{ m/s}$. **(a)** Find his position and velocity at time $t = 2.0$ s. **(b)** Where is the motorcyclist when his velocity is 25 m/s?

SOLUTION

SET UP Figure 2.21 shows our diagram. The problem tells us that $x = 0$ at the signpost, so that is the origin of coordinates. We point the x axis east, in the direction of motion. The (constant) acceleration is $a_x = 4.0 \text{ m/s}^2$. At the initial time $t = 0$ the position is $x_0 = 5.0$ m, and the initial velocity is $v_{0x} = 15 \text{ m/s}$.

SOLVE **Part (a):** We want to know the position and velocity (the values of x and v_x, respectively) at the later time $t = 2.0$ s. Equation 2.12 gives the position x as a function of time t:

$x = x_0 + v_{0x}t + \frac{1}{2}a_xt^2$
$= 5.0 \text{ m} + (15 \text{ m/s})(2.0 \text{ s}) + \frac{1}{2}(4.0 \text{ m/s}^2)(2.0 \text{ s})^2 = 43 \text{ m}.$

Equation 2.8 gives the velocity v_x as a function of time t:

$v_x = v_{0x} + a_xt$
$= 15 \text{ m/s} + (4.0 \text{ m/s}^2)(2.0 \text{ s}) = 23 \text{ m/s}.$

Part (b): We want to know the value of x when $v_x = 25 \text{ m/s}$. Note that this occurs at a time later than 2.0 s and at a point farther than 43 m from the signpost. From Equation 2.13, we have

$v_x^2 = v_{0x}^2 + 2a_x(x - x_0),$
$(25 \text{ m/s})^2 = (15 \text{ m/s})^2 + 2(4.0 \text{ m/s}^2)(x - 5.0 \text{ m}),$
$x = 55 \text{ m}.$

Alternatively, we may use Equation 2.8 to find first the time when $v_x = 25 \text{ m/s}$:

$v_x = v_{0x} + a_xt,$
$25 \text{ m/s} = 15 \text{ m/s} + (4.0 \text{ m/s}^2)(t),$
$t = 2.5 \text{ s}.$

▲ FIGURE 2.21

Then, from Equation 2.12,

$x = x_0 + v_{0x}t + \frac{1}{2}a_xt^2$
$= 5.0 \text{ m} + (15 \text{ m/s})(2.5 \text{ s}) + \frac{1}{2}(4.0 \text{ m/s}^2)(2.5 \text{ s})^2$
$= 55 \text{ m}.$

REFLECT Do the results make sense? The cyclist accelerates from 15 m/s (about 34 mi/h) to 23 m/s (about 51 mi/h) in 2.0 s while traveling a distance of 38 m (about 125 ft). This is fairly brisk acceleration, but well within the realm of possibility for a high-performance bike.

Practice Problem: If the acceleration is 2.0 m/s² instead of 4.0 m/s², where is the cyclist, and how fast is he moving, 5.0 s after he passes the signpost if $x_0 = 5.0$ m and $v_{0x} = 15 \text{ m/s}$? *Answers:* 105 m, 25 m/s.

EXAMPLE 2.9 **Pursuit!**

A motorist traveling at a constant velocity of 15 m/s passes a school-crossing corner where the speed limit is 10 m/s (about 22 mi/h). A police officer on a motorcycle stopped at the corner starts off in pursuit with constant acceleration of 3.0 m/s² (Figure 2.22a). **(a)** How much time elapses before the officer catches up with the car? **(b)** What is the officer's speed at that point? **(c)** What is the total distance the officer has traveled at that point?

▲ FIGURE 2.22 (a) A diagram of the problem. (b) Graphs of position as a function of time for the police officer and the car.

Continued

SOLUTION

SET UP Both objects move in a straight line, which we'll designate as the x axis. Then all positions, velocities, and accelerations have only x components. We'll omit the subscripts x in our solution; but always keep in mind that when we say "velocity," we really mean "x component of velocity," and so on.

The motorcycle and the car both move with constant acceleration, so we can use the formulas we have developed. We have two different objects in motion; Figure 2.22a shows our choice of coordinate system. The origin of coordinates is at the corner where the policeman is stationed; both objects are at this point at time $t = 0$, so $x_0 = 0$ for both. Let x_P be the police officer's position and x_C the car's position, at any time t. At the instant when the officer catches the car, the two objects are at the same position. We need to apply the constant-acceleration equations to each, and find the time when x_P and x_C are equal. We denote the initial x components of velocities (i.e., x components) as v_{P0} and v_{C0} and the accelerations (x components) as a_P and a_C. From the data given, we have $v_{P0} = 0$, $v_{C0} = 15$ m/s, $a_P = 3.0$ m/s^2, and $a_C = 0$.

SOLVE Applying Equation 2.12 to each object, we find that

$$x_P = x_0 + v_{P0}t + \tfrac{1}{2}a_Pt^2 = 0 + 0 + \tfrac{1}{2}(3.0 \text{ m/s}^2)t^2$$
$$= \tfrac{1}{2}(3.0 \text{ m/s}^2)t^2,$$
$$x_C = x_0 + v_{C0}t + \tfrac{1}{2}a_Ct^2 = 0 + (15 \text{ m/s})t + 0 = (15 \text{ m/s})t.$$

Part (a): At the time the officer catches the car, they must be at the same position, so at this time, $x_C = x_P$. Equating the preceding two expressions, we have

$$\tfrac{1}{2}(3.0 \text{ m/s}^2)t^2 = (15 \text{ m/s})t,$$

or

$$t = 0, 10 \text{ s}.$$

There are *two* times when the two vehicles have the same x coordinate; the first is the time ($t = 0$) when the car passes the parked motorcycle at the corner, and the second is the time when the officer catches up.

Part (b): From Equation 2.8, we know that the officer's velocity v_P at any time t is given by

$$v_P = v_{P0} + a_Pt = 0 + (3.0 \text{ m/s}^2)t,$$

so when $t = 10$ s, $v_P = 30$ m/s. When the officer overtakes the car, she is traveling twice as fast as the motorist is.

Part (c): When $t = 10$ s, the car's position is

$$x_C = (15 \text{ m/s})(10 \text{ s}) = 150 \text{ m},$$

and the officer's position is

$$x_P = \tfrac{1}{2}(3.0 \text{ m/s}^2)(10 \text{ s})^2 = 150 \text{ m}.$$

This result verifies that, at the time the officer catches the car, they have gone equal distances and are at the same position.

REFLECT A graphical description of the motion is helpful. Figure 2.22b shows graphs of x_P and x_C as functions of time. At first x_C is greater, because the car is ahead of the officer. But the car travels with constant velocity, while the officer accelerates, closing the gap between the two. At the point where the curves cross, the officer has caught up to the car. We see again that there are two times when the two positions are the same. Note that the two vehicles don't have the same speed at either of these times.

Practice Problem: If the officer's acceleration is 5.0 m/s^2, what distance does she travel before catching up with the car? What is her velocity when she has caught up? During what time interval is she moving more slowly than the car? *Answer:* 90 m, 30 m/s, 0 to 3 s.

2.5 Proportional Reasoning

The relationships for straight-line motion that we've developed in this chapter offer an ideal background for introducing an analytical technique that is useful in many areas of physics. We'll call this technique **proportional reasoning.** It's particularly useful when we want to describe general relationships between variables, without reference to specific details of numerical values.

Following are some examples of the sort of problems for which proportional reasoning is useful. Some are trivial, but they illustrate the methods we'll describe.

1. Two cars start from rest and have the same acceleration, but car *A* accelerates over a time interval twice as great as car *B*. How are the distances traveled related? Does *A* go twice as far as *B*? Four times as far? Half as far?
2. You have two circles. One has a radius three times the other. Is the area of the larger circle three times as great as the area of the smaller one? Or nine times as great? Or one-third as great?
3. Water flows through a pipe with a certain radius. The pipe is joined to another pipe having a radius twice as large. The volume flow rate (i.e., the number of liters per second) in each pipe is equal to its cross-sectional area times the

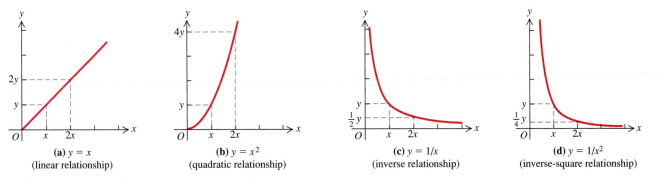

(a) $y = x$
(linear relationship)

(b) $y = x^2$
(quadratic relationship)

(c) $y = 1/x$
(inverse relationship)

(d) $y = 1/x^2$
(inverse-square relationship)

▲ **FIGURE 2.23** Graphs of some simple relationships between two variables.

speed of the water's motion. If the volume flow rate is the same in both pipes, does the water move twice as fast in the larger pipe? Half as fast?

In all of these situations, we have two variables, such as distance and time or the radius and area of a circle, that are related in a simple way. If we call the two variables x and y, the relationship between them often takes one of the following simple forms:

$$y = kx \text{ (linear relation)};$$

$$y = kx^2 \text{ (quadratic relation)};$$

$$y = k/x \text{ (inverse relation)};$$

$$y = k/x^2 \text{ (inverse-square relation)}.$$

In all these forms, k is a constant or a product of constants, and the numerical value of k may or may not be known. Figure 2.23 shows graphs of these four forms of relationship; for simplicity, we have taken the constant k equal to unity in all of them.

Let's see how the preceding relational forms can be applied to Problem 1. From our analysis in this chapter, we know that when an object starts from rest at the point $x = 0$ on the x axis and moves along the axis with constant acceleration a_x, its position x at any time t is given by the simple relation

$$x = \tfrac{1}{2} a_x t^2.$$

We call the two cars A and B; they have the same acceleration a_x. If car A accelerates for a time t_A, it travels a distance x_A given by

$$x_A = \tfrac{1}{2} a_x t_A^2,$$

and if car B accelerates for a time t_B, it travels a distance x_B given by

$$x_B = \tfrac{1}{2} a_x t_B^2.$$

We'd like to get a general relationship between the two distances and the two times that doesn't contain the common acceleration, which may or may not be known. There are two ways to do this: We can divide one of the preceding equations by the other. When we do, the factor $a_x/2$ divides out, and we obtain

$$\frac{x_A}{x_B} = \frac{\tfrac{1}{2} a_x t_A^2}{\tfrac{1}{2} a_x t_B^2} = \frac{t_A^2}{t_B^2} = \left(\frac{t_A}{t_B}\right)^2.$$

Or we can put all the variables in each equation on one side and all the constants on the other side, equate the two resulting equations, and obtain the same result:

$$\frac{x_A}{t_A^2} = \frac{1}{2}a_x \quad \text{and} \quad \frac{x_B}{t_B^2} = \frac{1}{2}a_x, \quad \text{so}$$

$$\frac{x_A}{t_A^2} = \frac{x_B}{t_B^2}, \quad \text{or} \quad \frac{x_A}{x_B} = \left(\frac{t_A}{t_B}\right)^2 \quad (\text{as before}).$$

Either of these procedures can be used to yield a relation that contains only the values of x and t.

Now let's get back to the original problem: If car A travels for twice as much time as car B, then $t_A = 2t_B$, or $t_A/t_B = 2$. This equation becomes

$$\frac{x_A}{x_B} = (2)^2 = 4,$$

and we see that $x_A = 4x_B$; Car A, with twice as much time to accelerate as car B, travels four times as far.

Now let's summarize what we've done:

1. First, we choose the quantities we want to consider as our variables (in this case, x and t) and find an equation relating them (in this case, $x = a_x t^2/2$).
2. Next, we write this equation for two different values of each of the chosen variables (t_A, x_A and t_B, x_B in our example) and then use one of the procedures described above to eliminate the constants and obtain an equation containing only the two values of each variable.
3. Finally, we specify a relation between two values of one variable (in this case, t_A and t_B) and solve for the relation between the corresponding values of the other variable (in this case, x_A and x_B). We don't need the numerical value of a_x (or k in the generic examples in Figure 2.23); everything is done with ratios and proportions. Note, incidentally, that this relation is *quadratic* in form, the second example in the figure.

Here's another example: The same two cars, A and B, have just finished a speed run; they cross the finish line at the same time, with different speeds v_A and v_B. They both apply their brakes as they cross the line, giving them the same (negative) acceleration, and they come to a stop at distances x_A and x_B, respectively, beyond the finish line. If car A has $1\frac{1}{2}$ times the speed of car B at the finish line, by what factor does its stopping distance exceed that of car B?

For Step 1, we choose v and x as our variables; we need to find a relation between them. No times are mentioned in the statement of the problem; this suggests that we use Equation 2.13. Dropping the subscript x to simplify our notation, we write this equation as

$$v^2 = v_0^2 + 2a(x - x_0).$$

We place the origin of coordinates at the finish line (the starting point for our analysis), so that $x_0 = 0$ for both cars. The final velocity is zero (i.e., $v = 0$) for both cars. Thus, the relationship we need is simply

$$v_0^2 = -2ax.$$

That is, a car that crosses the finish line with speed v_0 and brakes with constant (negative) acceleration a travels a distance x before stopping.

For Step 2, we rewrite the preceding equation, placing the variables on the left side and the constants on the right:

$$\frac{v_0^2}{x} = -2a, \quad \text{so} \quad \frac{v_{0A}^2}{x_A} = -2a \quad \text{and} \quad \frac{v_{0B}^2}{x_B} = -2a.$$

Hence $\dfrac{x_A}{x_B} = \left(\dfrac{v_{0A}}{v_{0B}}\right)^2$.

The relationship is again quadratic, but now our variables are x and v instead of x and t.

Finally, for Step 3, if car A is initially moving $1\frac{1}{2}$ times as fast as car B, it travels a distance $\left(\frac{3}{2}\right)^2 = \frac{9}{4}$ as great as car B before stopping.

Here's an alternative language for the relationships we've discovered: In our first example, in which the variables were x and t, we say that x is proportional to t^2; in the second, x is proportional to v^2. The special symbol $\propto$ is often used to represent proportionality; thus, in the above examples, we would write $x \propto t^2$ and $x \propto v^2$, read as "x is proportional to t^2" and "x is proportional to v^2."

Brakes on a wet road

When you are driving your car on wet pavement and need to stop suddenly, the maximum (negative) acceleration you can apply to the car without skidding is about one-third as much as on dry pavement. For a given initial velocity, how does your stopping distance x_w on wet pavement differ from your stopping distance x_d on dry pavement?

A. $x_w = x_d$
B. $x_w = 3x_d$
C. $x_w = 9x_d$

SOLUTION As in the previous example, the variables are related by $v_0^2 = -2ax$. This time we consider the variables to be x and a, and the initial velocity v_0 is constant. Separating constants and variables, we find that

$$xa = -\tfrac{1}{2}v_0^2, \quad \text{so} \quad x_d a_d = -\tfrac{1}{2}v_0^2, \quad x_w a_w = -\tfrac{1}{2}v_0^2,$$

$$x_d a_d = x_w a_w, \quad \frac{x_w}{x_d} = \frac{a_d}{a_w}, \quad \text{and} \quad x \propto \frac{1}{a}.$$

This result confirms our intuition that x varies *inversely* with a: If $a_w = \tfrac{1}{3}a_d$, then $x_w = 3x_d$, and choice B is the correct one. The relation of x to a is shown by the graph in Figure 2.23c.

2.6 Freely Falling Objects

The most familiar example of motion with (nearly) constant acceleration is that of an object falling under the influence of the earth's gravitational attraction. Such motion has held the attention of philosophers and scientists since ancient times. Aristotle thought (erroneously) that heavy objects fall faster than light objects, in proportion to their weight. Galileo argued that an object should fall with an acceleration that is constant and *independent* of its weight. We mentioned in Section 1.1 that, according to legend, Galileo experimented by dropping musket balls and cannon balls from the Leaning Tower of Pisa.

The motion of falling bodies has since been studied with great precision. When air resistance is absent, as in a vacuum chamber or on the moon, Galileo is right: All objects at a particular location fall with the same acceleration, regardless of their size or weight. Figure 2.24 shows an apple and a feather falling in a vacuum chamber; they are released at the same time and fall at the same rate. If the distance of the fall is small compared with the radius of the earth (or of the moon, planet, or other astronomical body on which the fall occurs), the acceleration is constant. In the discussion that follows, we'll use an idealized model in which we neglect air resistance, the earth's rotation, and the decrease in an object's acceleration with increasing altitude. We call this idealized motion **free fall,** although it includes rising as well as falling motion.

The constant acceleration of a freely falling object is called the **acceleration due to gravity,** or the *acceleration of free fall;* we denote its magnitude with the letter g. At or near the earth's surface, the value of g is approximately 9.80 m/s^2, 980 cm/s^2, or 32.2 ft/s^2. Because g is the magnitude of a vector quantity, it is always a *positive* number. On the surface of the moon, the acceleration due to gravity is caused by the attractive force of the moon rather than the earth, and $g = 1.62 \text{ m/s}^2$. Near the surface of the sun, $g = 274 \text{ m/s}^2$.

Activ ONLINE Physics   1.7, 1.10

▲ **FIGURE 2.24** In vacuum, objects with different weights fall with the same acceleration and thus fall side by side.

In the examples that follow, we use the constant-acceleration equations developed in Section 2.4. We suggest that you review the problem-solving strategy discussed in that section before you study these examples.

EXAMPLE 2.10 Falling euro in Pisa

A 2-euro coin is dropped from the Leaning Tower of Pisa. It starts from rest and falls freely. Compute its position and velocity after 1.0, 2.0, and 3.0 s.

SOLUTION

SET UP Figure 2.25 shows the diagram we sketch. Because the motion is downward, we choose a vertical axis; by convention, we call it the y axis rather than the x axis. Choosing this axis means that we will replace all the x's in the constant-acceleration equations by y's. We choose the upward direction to be positive, and we place the origin at the starting point. The position, velocity, and acceleration have only y components. The initial value y_0 of the coordinate y and the initial y component of velocity v_{0y} are both zero. The acceleration is downward (in the negative y direction), so the constant y component of acceleration is $a_y = -g = -9.8 \text{ m/s}^2$. (Remember that, by definition, g itself is *always* positive.)

SOLVE From Equations 2.12 and 2.8, with x replaced by y, we get

$$y = v_0 t + \tfrac{1}{2} a_y t^2 = 0 + \tfrac{1}{2}(-g)t^2 = (-4.9 \text{ m/s}^2)t^2,$$

$$v_y = v_{0y} + a_y t = 0 + (-g)t = (-9.8 \text{ m/s}^2)t.$$

Using subscripts 1, 2, and 3 for the three times, we find that when $t = t_1 = 1.0 \text{ s}$, $y_1 = (-4.9 \text{ m/s}^2)(1.0 \text{ s})^2 = -4.9 \text{ m}$ and $v_{1y} = (-9.8 \text{ m/s}^2)(1.0 \text{ s}) = -9.8 \text{ m/s}$. The coin is therefore 4.9 m below the origin (because y is negative) and has a downward velocity (v_y is negative) with magnitude 9.8 m/s.

The position and velocity at 2.0 and 3.0 s are found in the same way. The results are -19.6 m and -19.6 m/s at $t = 2.0 \text{ s}$ and -44.1 m and -29.4 m/s at $t = 3.0 \text{ s}$.

REFLECT All of our values of y and v_y are negative because we have chosen the positive y axis to be upward. We could just as well have chosen the downward direction to be positive. In that case, the y component of acceleration would have been

The Leaning Tower   Our sketch for the problem

▲ **FIGURE 2.25**

$a_y = g = +9.8 \text{ m/s}^2$. The crucial point is that you *must* decide at the start which direction is positive, and then stick with your decision.

Practice Problem: The coin is released 47 m above the ground. How much time is required for the coin to fall to the ground? What is its velocity just before it strikes the ground? *Answers:* 3.1 s, -30 m/s.

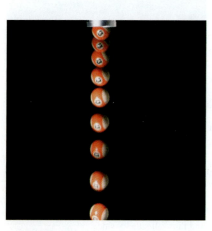

Figure 2.26 is a strobe photograph of a falling ball taken with a light source that produces a series of intense, brief flashes. The flashes occur at equal time intervals, so this photograph records the position of the ball at equal time intervals. Therefore, the average velocity of the ball between successive flashes is proportional to the distance between the corresponding images of the ball in the photograph. The increasing distances between images show that the ball's velocity increases continuously; in other words, the ball accelerates. Careful measurement shows that the change in velocity is the same in each time interval; thus the acceleration is constant.

▲ **FIGURE 2.26** Strobe photo of a freely falling ball.

EXAMPLE 2.11   A ball on the roof

Suppose you throw a ball vertically upward from the flat roof of a tall building. The ball leaves your hand at a point even with the roof railing, with an upward velocity of 15.0 m/s. On its way back down, it just misses the railing. Find **(a)** the position and velocity of the ball 1.00 s and 4.00 s after it leaves your hand; **(b)** the velocity of the ball when it is 5.00 m above the railing; and **(c)** the maximum height reached and the time at which it is reached. Ignore the effects of the air.

SOLUTION

SET UP As shown in Figure 2.27, we place the origin at the level of the roof railing, where the ball leaves your hand, and we take the positive direction to be upward. Here's what we know: The initial position y_0 is zero, the initial velocity v_{0y} (y component) is $+15.0$ m/s, and the acceleration (y component) is $a_y = -9.80$ m/s^2.

SOLVE What equations do we have to work with? The velocity v_y at any time t is

$$v_y = v_{0y} + a_y t = 15.0 \text{ m/s} + (-9.80 \text{ m/s}^2)t.$$

The position y at any time t is

$$y = v_{0y}t + \tfrac{1}{2}a_y t^2 = (15.0 \text{ m/s})t + \tfrac{1}{2}(-9.80 \text{ m/s}^2)t^2.$$

The velocity v_y at any position y is given by

$$v_y^2 = v_{0y}^2 + 2a_y(y - y_0)$$
$$= (15.0 \text{ m/s})^2 + 2(-9.80 \text{ m/s}^2)(y - 0).$$

Part (a):   When $t = 1.00$ s, the first two equations give $y = +10.1$ m, $v_y = +5.20$ m/s.
The ball is 10.1 m above the origin (y is positive), and it has an upward velocity (v is positive) of 5.20 m/s (less than the initial velocity of 15.0 m/s, as expected).

When $t = 4.00$ s, the same equations give

$$y = -18.4 \text{ m}, \qquad v_y = -24.2 \text{ m/s}.$$

Thus, at time $t = 4.00$ s, the ball has passed its highest point and is 18.4 m *below* the origin (y is negative). It has a *downward* velocity (v_y is negative) with magnitude 24.2 m/s (greater than the initial velocity, as we should expect). Note that, to get these results, we don't need to find the highest point the ball reaches or the time at which it was reached. The equations of motion give the position and velocity at *any* time, whether the ball is on the way up or on the way down.

Part (b):   When the ball is 5.00 m above the origin, $y = +5.00$ m. Now we use our third equation to find the velocity v_y at this point:

$$v_y^2 = (15.0 \text{ m/s})^2 + 2(-9.80 \text{ m/s}^2)(5.00 \text{ m}) = 127 \text{ m}^2/\text{s}^2,$$
$$v_y = \pm 11.3 \text{ m/s}.$$

We get two values of v_y, one positive and one negative. That is, the ball passes the point $y = +5.00$ m *twice*, once on the way up and again on the way down. The velocity on the way up is $+11.3$ m/s, and on the way down it is -11.3 m/s.

▲ FIGURE 2.27

Part (c):   At the highest point, the ball's velocity is momentarily zero $(v_y = 0)$; it has been going up (positive v_y) and is about to start going down (negative v_y). From our third equation, we have

$$0 = (15.0 \text{ m/s})^2 - (19.6 \text{ m/s}^2)y,$$

and the maximum height (where $v_y = 0$) is $y = 11.5$ m.

We can now find the time t when the ball reaches its highest point from Equation 2.8, setting $v_y = 0$:

$$0 = 15.0 \text{ m/s} + (-9.80 \text{ m/s}^2)t,$$
$$t = 1.53 \text{ s}.$$

Alternative Solution: Alternatively, to find the maximum height, we may ask first *when* the maximum height is reached. That is, at what value of t is $v_y = 0$? As we just found, $v_y = 0$ when $t = 1.53$ s. Substituting this value of t back into the equation for y, we find that

$$y = (15 \text{ m/s})(1.53 \text{ s}) + \tfrac{1}{2}(-9.8 \text{ m/s}^2)(1.53 \text{ s})^2 = 11.5 \text{ m}.$$

REFLECT Although at the highest point the velocity is momentarily zero, the *acceleration* at that point is still -9.8 m/s^2. The ball stops for an instant, but its velocity is continuously changing, from positive values through zero to negative values.

Continued

The acceleration is constant throughout; it is *not* zero when $v_y = 0$!

Figure 2.28 shows graphs of position and velocity as functions of time for this problem. Note that the graph of v_y versus t has a constant negative slope. Thus, the acceleration is negative on the way up, at the highest point, and on the way down.

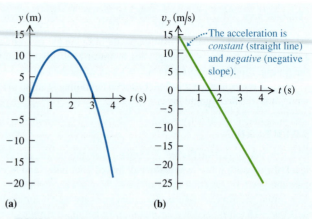

▲ **FIGURE 2.28** (a) Position and (b) velocity as functions of time for a ball thrown upward with an initial velocity of 15 m/s.

A pop fly

In a baseball game, a batter hits a pitched ball that goes straight up in the air above home plate. At the top of its motion, the ball is momentarily motionless. At this point,

A. the acceleration is zero because the ball is motionless at that instant.
B. the acceleration is zero because the motion is changing from slowing down to speeding up.
C. the acceleration is zero because at that instant the force from the impact with the bat is balanced by the pull of the earth.
D. the acceleration is 9.8 m/s² downward.

SOLUTION A nonzero acceleration means that an object is either speeding up or slowing down. If an object has no acceleration, its speed does not change. Since a ball at the top of its motion is about to move downward, it must have acceleration, even though it is motionless at that instant. This argument rules out A, B, and C; the ball's acceleration cannot be zero. But is D correct? When velocity and acceleration are in opposite directions, the velocity is decreasing in magnitude. When they are in the same direction, the velocity is increasing in magnitude. At the top, the velocity is about to increase in the downward direction (i.e., becomes more and more negative), and its direction becomes the same as that of the acceleration. So D is correct.

Tossing two stones

Suppose you throw two identical stones from the top of a tall building. You throw one directly upward with a speed of 10 m/s and the other directly downward with the same speed. When they hit the street below, how do their speeds compare? (Neglect air friction.)

A. The one thrown upward is traveling faster.
B. The one thrown downward is traveling faster.
C. Both are traveling at the same speed.

SOLUTION The stone thrown upward decreases its speed by 9.8 m/s every second as it goes upward and increases its speed by 9.8 m/s every second as it comes back down. Thus, when it returns to the point (at the top of the building) from which it was thrown, it has exactly its original speed; but it is moving downward instead of upward. Since it now has the same downward velocity as the stone that was originally thrown downward, the two stones must have the same velocity when they hit the ground.

*2.7 Relative Velocity along a Straight Line

We always describe the position and velocity of an object with reference to a particular coordinate system. When we speak of the velocity of a moving car, we usually mean its velocity with respect to an observer who is stationary on the earth. But when two observers measure the velocity of a moving object, they get different results if one observer is moving relative to the other. The velocity seen by a particular observer is called the velocity *relative* to that observer, or simply the **relative velocity.**

Figure 2.29 shows an example of the concept of relative velocity in action. In this example we'll assume that all the motions are along the same straight line, the x axis. A woman walks in a straight line with a velocity (x component) of

1.0 m/s along the aisle of a train that is moving along the same line with a velocity of 3.0 m/s. What is the woman's velocity? This seems like a simple enough question, but in reality it has no single answer. As seen by a passenger sitting in the train, she is moving at 1.0 m/s. A person on a bicycle standing beside the train sees the woman moving at 1.0 m/s + 3.0 m/s = 4.0 m/s. An observer in another train going in the opposite direction would give still another answer. The velocity is different for different observers. We have to specify which observer we mean, and we speak of the velocity *relative* to a particular observer. The woman's velocity relative to the train is 1.0 m/s, her velocity relative to the cyclist is 4.0 m/s, and so on. Each observer, equipped in principle with a meterstick and a stopwatch, forms what we call a **frame of reference.** Thus, a frame of reference is a coordinate system plus a timer.

Let's generalize this analysis. In Figure 2.29, we call the cyclist's frame of reference (at rest with respect to the ground) C and we call the frame of reference of the moving train T (Figure 2.29b). The woman's position at any time, relative to a reference point O_T in the moving train (i.e, in frame of reference T), is given by the distance $x_{W/T}$. Her position at any time, relative to a reference point O_C that is stationary on the ground (i.e, in the cyclist's frame C), is given by the distance $x_{W/C}$, and the position of the train's reference point O_T relative to the stationary one O_C is $x_{T/C}$. We choose the reference points so that at time $t = 0$ all these x's are zero. Then we can see from the figure that at any later time they are related by the equation

$$x_{W/C} = x_{W/T} + x_{T/C}. \qquad (2.18)$$

That is, the total distance from the origin of C to the woman at point W is the sum of the distance from the origin O_C of the cyclist's frame to the origin O_T of the train's frame, plus the distance from O_T to the position of the woman.

Because Equation 2.18 is true at any instant, it must also be true that the *rate of change* of $x_{W/C}$ is equal to the sum of the rates of change of $x_{W/T}$ and $x_{T/C}$. But the rate of change of $x_{W/C}$ is just the velocity of W with respect to C, which we'll denote as $v_{W/C}$, and similarly for $x_{W/T}$ and $x_{T/C}$. Thus, we arrive at the velocity relation

$$v_{W/C} = v_{W/T} + v_{T/C}. \qquad (2.19)$$

Remember that C is the cyclist's frame of reference, T is the frame of reference of the train, and point W represents the woman. Using the preceding notation, we have

$$v_{W/T} = 1.0 \text{ m/s}, \qquad v_{T/C} = 3.0 \text{ m/s}.$$

From Equation 2.19, the woman's velocity $v_{W/C}$ relative to the cyclist on the ground is

$$v_{W/C} = 1.0 \text{ m/s} + 3.0 \text{ m/s} = 4.0 \text{ m/s},$$

as we already knew.

In this example both velocities are toward the right, and we have implicitly taken that as the positive direction. If the woman walks toward the *left* relative to the train, then $v_{W/T} = -1.0$ m/s, and her velocity relative to the cyclist is 2.0 m/s. The sum in Equation 2.19 is always an *algebraic* sum, and any or all of the velocities may be negative.

When the woman looks out the window, the stationary cyclist on the ground appears to her to be moving backward; we can call the cyclist's velocity relative to the woman on the train $v_{C/W}$. Clearly, this is just the negative of $v_{W/C}$. In general, if A and B are any two points or frames of reference,

$$v_{A/B} = -v_{B/A}. \qquad (2.20)$$

(a)

(b)

▲ **FIGURE 2.29** (a) A woman walks in a moving train while observed by a cyclist on the ground outside. (b) The woman's position W, at the instant shown, in two frames of reference: that of the train (T) and that of the cyclist (C).

Note the order of the double subscripts on the velocities in our discussion; $v_{A/B}$ always means "the velocity of A (first subscript) relative to B (second subscript)." These subscripts obey an interesting kind of algebra, as Equation 2.19 shows. If we regard each one as a fraction, then the fraction on the left side is the *product* of the fractions on the right sides: For a point P relative to frames A and B, $P/A = (P/B)(B/A)$. This is a handy rule to use when you apply Equation 2.19. If there are *three* different frames of reference, A, B, and C, we can write immediately

$$v_{P/A} = v_{P/C} + v_{C/B} + v_{B/A},$$

and so on.

EXAMPLE 2.12   Relative velocity on the highway

Suppose you are driving north on a straight two-lane road at a constant 88 km/h (Figure 2.30). A truck traveling at a constant 104 km/h approaches you (in the other lane, fortunately). **(a)** What is the truck's velocity relative to you? **(b)** What is your velocity with respect to the truck?

SOLUTION

SET UP Let you be Y, the truck be T, the earth be E, and let the positive direction be north (Figure 2.30). Then $v_{Y/E} = +88$ km/h.

SOLVE **Part (a):** The truck is approaching you, so it must be moving south, giving $v_{T/E} = -104$ km/h. We want to find $v_{T/Y}$. Modifying Equation 2.19, we have

$$v_{T/E} = v_{T/Y} + v_{Y/E},$$
$$v_{T/Y} = v_{T/E} - v_{Y/E}$$
$$= -104 \text{ km/h} - 88 \text{ km/h} = -192 \text{ km/h}.$$

The truck is moving 192 km/h south relative to you.

Part (b): From Equation 2.25,

$$v_{Y/T} = -v_{T/Y} = -(-192 \text{ km/h}) = +192 \text{ km/h}.$$

You are moving 192 km/h north relative to the truck.

REFLECT How do the relative velocities of Example 2.9 change after you and the truck have passed? They don't change at all!

▲ **FIGURE 2.30** Velocities of you and the truck, relative to the ground.

The relative positions of the objects don't matter. The velocity of the truck relative to you is still -192 km/h, but it is now moving away from you instead of toward you.

Theory of Relativity

When we derived the relative-velocity relations, we assumed that all the observers use the same time scale. This assumption may seem so obvious that it isn't even worth mentioning, but it is precisely the point at which Einstein's special theory of relativity departs from the physics of Galileo and Newton. When any of the speeds approach the speed of light in vacuum, denoted by c, the velocity-addition equation has to be modified. It turns out that if the woman could walk down the aisle at $0.30c$ and the train could move at $0.90c$, then her speed relative to the ground would be not $1.20c$ but $0.94c$. No material object can travel faster than c; we'll return to the special theory of relativity later in the book.

SUMMARY

Displacement and Velocity

(Sections 2.1 and 2.2) When an object moves along a straight line, we describe its position with respect to an origin O by means of a coordinate such as x. If the object starts at position x_1 at time t_1 and arrives at position x_2 at time t_2, the object's **displacement** is a vector quantity whose x component is $\Delta x = x_2 - x_1$. The displacement doesn't depend on the details of how the object travels between x_1 and x_2.

The rate of change of position with respect to time is given by the **average velocity,** a vector quantity whose x component is

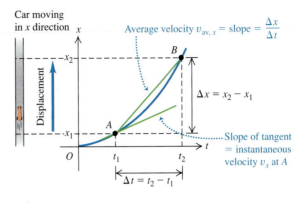

Car moving in x direction

$$v_{\text{av},x} = \frac{x_2 - x_1}{t_2 - t_1} = \frac{\Delta x}{\Delta t}. \qquad (2.3)$$

On a graph of x versus t, $v_{\text{av},x}$ is the slope of the line connecting the starting point (x_1, t_1) and the ending point (x_2, t_2). As the average velocity is calculated for progressively smaller intervals of time Δt, the average velocity approaches the **instantaneous velocity** v_x:
$v_x = \lim\limits_{\Delta t \to 0} (\Delta x / \Delta t)$ (Equation 2.4).

Acceleration

(Section 2.3) When the velocity of an object changes with time, we say that the object has an **acceleration.** Just as velocity describes the rate of change of *position* with time, acceleration is a vector quantity that describes rate of change of *velocity* with time. For an object with velocity v_{1x} at time t_1 and velocity v_{2x} at time t_2, the x component of average acceleration is

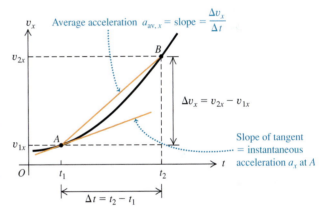

$$a_{\text{av},x} = \frac{v_{2x} - v_{1x}}{t_2 - t_1} = \frac{\Delta v}{\Delta t}. \qquad (2.5)$$

The average acceleration (x component) between two points can also be found on a graph of v_x versus t: $a_{\text{av},x}$ is the slope of the line connecting the first point (v_{1x} at time t_1) and the second point (v_{2x} at time t_2). As with velocity, when the average acceleration is calculated for smaller and smaller intervals of time Δt, the average acceleration approaches the **instantaneous acceleration** a_x.

Motion with Constant Acceleration

(Section 2.4) When an object moves with constant acceleration in a straight line, the following two equations describe its position and velocity as functions of time: $x = x_0 + v_{0x}t + \frac{1}{2}a_xt^2$ (Equation 2.12), and $v_x = v_{0x} + a_xt$ (Equation 2.8).

In these equations, x_0 and v_{0x} are, respectively, the position and velocity at an initial time $t = 0$, and x and v_x are, respectively, the position and velocity at any later time t. The final position x is the sum of three terms: the initial position x_0, plus the distance v_0t that the body would move if its velocity were constant, plus an additional distance $\frac{1}{2}at^2$ caused by the constant acceleration.

The following equation relates velocity, acceleration, and position without explicit reference to time: $v_x^2 = v_{0x}^2 + 2a_x(x - x_0)$ (Equation 2.13).

Three graphical views of constant-acceleration motion.

x versus *t* v_x versus *t* a_x versus *t*

Continued

Proportional Reasoning

(Section 2.5) Many problems have two variables that are related in a simple way. One variable may be a constant times the other, or a constant times the square of the other, or a similar simple relationship. In such problems, a change in the value of one variable is related in a simple way to the corresponding change in the value of the other. This relation can be expressed as a relation between the quotient of two values of one variable and the quotient of two values of the other, even when the constant proportionality factors are not known.

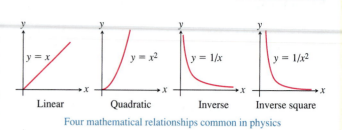

Four mathematical relationships common in physics

Freely Falling Objects

(Section 2.6) A freely falling object is an object that moves under the influence of a constant gravitational force. The term *free fall* includes objects that are initially at rest, as well as objects that have an initial upward or downward velocity. When the effects of air resistance are excluded, all bodies at a particular location fall with the same acceleration, regardless of their size or weight. The constant acceleration of freely falling objects is called the **acceleration due to gravity,** and we denote its magnitude with the letter g. At or near the earth's surface, the value of g is approximately 9.8 m/s².

The motion of an object tossed up and allowed to fall. (For clarity, we show a U-shaped path.) The object is in free fall throughout.

$a_y = -g$
$= -9.80 \text{ m/s}^2$

Relative Velocity along a Straight Line

(Section 2.7) When an object P moves relative to an object (or reference frame) B, and B moves relative to a second reference frame A, we denote the velocity of P relative to B by $v_{P/B}$, the velocity of P relative to A by $v_{P/A}$, and the velocity of B relative to A by $v_{B/A}$. These velocities are related by this modification of Equation 2.19:

$$v_{P/A} = v_{P/B} + v_{B/A}.$$

MP For instructor-assigned homework, go to www.masteringphysics.com

Conceptual Questions

1. Give an example or two in which the magnitude of the displacement of a moving object is (a) equal to the distance the object travels and (b) less than the distance the object travels. (c) Can the magnitude of the displacement ever be greater than the distance the object travels?

2. Does the speedometer of a car measure speed or velocity?

3. Under what conditions is average velocity equal to instantaneous velocity?

4. If an automobile is traveling north, can it have an acceleration toward the south? Under what circumstances?

5. True or false? (a) If an object's average speed is zero, its average velocity must also be zero. (b) If an object's average velocity is zero, its average speed must also be zero. Explain the reasoning behind your answers. If the statement is false, give several examples to show that it is false.

6. Is it possible for an object to be accelerating even though it has stopped moving? How? Illustrate your answer with a simple example.

7. If a tennis ball is hit upward with an initial velocity of 35 m/s, is it true that the ball's initial velocity is greater than its acceleration? Explain.

8. Under what conditions (constant speed, constant acceleration, etc.) is each of the following equations valid, or are they always valid? (a) $v_x = v_{0x} + a_x t$, (b) $v_{av,x} = \Delta x / \Delta t$, (c) $\Delta x = v_x t$, (d) $\Delta x = v_{av,x} t$, (e) $v_x^2 = v_{0x}^2 + 2a_x(x - x_0)$, (f) $x = x_0 + v_{0x} t + \frac{1}{2} a_x t^2$, (g) $v_{av,x} = (v_1 + v_2)/2$.

9. If the graph of the velocity of an object as a function of time is a straight line, what can you find out about the acceleration of this object? Consider cases in which the slope is positive, negative, and zero.

10. If the graph of the position of an object as a function of time is a straight line, what can you find out about the velocity of this object? Consider cases in which the slope is positive, negative, and zero.

11. The following table shows an object's position x as a function of time t:

x (in m)	6.50	6.75	7.00	7.25	7.50	7.75
t (in s)	2.00	4.00	6.00	8.00	10.0	12.0

(a) Just by looking at the table, what can you conclude about this object's velocity and acceleration? (b) To see if you are correct, calculate this object's average velocity and acceleration for a few time intervals. (c) How far did the object move between $t = 2.00$ s and $t = 12.0$ s?

12. The following table shows an object's velocity v as a function of time t:

v (in cm/s)	3.40	3.80	4.20	4.60	5.00	5.40
t (in s)	5.00	8.00	11.0	14.0	17.0	20.0

(a) Just by looking at the table, what can you conclude about this object's acceleration? (b) To see if you are correct, calculate the object's average acceleration for several time intervals.

13. True or false? If an object has a negative acceleration, it must be slowing down. Illustrate your answer with an example or two.

14. Figure 2.31 shows graphs of the positions of three different moving objects as a function of time. All three graphs pass through points A and B. (a) What can you conclude about the average velocities of these three objects between points A and B? Why? b) At point B, what characteristics of the motion do the three objects have in common? That is, are they in the same place, do they have the same velocity or speed, and do they have the same acceleration?

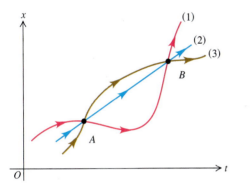

▲ **FIGURE 2.31** Question 14.

15. Figure 2.32 shows graphs of the velocities of three different moving objects as a function of time. All three graphs pass through points A and B. (a) What can you conclude about the average accelerations of these three objects between points A and B? Why? (b) At point A, what characteristics of the motion do the three objects have in common? That is, are they in the same place, do they have the same velocity or speed, and do they have the same acceleration?

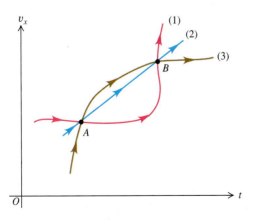

▲ **FIGURE 2.32** Question 15.

16. Figure 2.33 shows the graph of an object's position x as a function of time t. (a) Does this object ever reverse its direction of motion? If so, where? (b) Does the object ever return to its starting point? (c) Is the velocity of the object constant? (d) Is the object's speed ever zero? If so, where? (e) Does the object have any acceleration?

▲ **FIGURE 2.33** Question 16.

17. Figure 2.34 shows the graph of an object's velocity v_x as a function of time t. (a) Does this object ever reverse its direction of motion? b) Does the object ever return to its starting point? (c) Is the object's speed ever zero? If so, where? (d) Does the object have any acceleration?

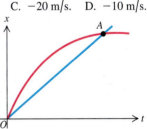

▲ **FIGURE 2.34** Question 17.

18. In a graph of an object's position as a function of time or velocity as a function of time, can the graph ever be (a) horizontal or (b) vertical? Explain your reasoning.

Multiple-Choice Problems

1. Which of the following statements about average speed is correct? (More than one statement may be correct.)
   A. The average speed is equal to the magnitude of the average velocity.
   B. The average speed can never be greater than the magnitude of the average velocity.
   C. The average speed can never be less than the magnitude of the average velocity.
   D. If the average speed is zero, then the average velocity must be zero.
   E. If the average velocity is zero, then the average speed must be zero.

2. A ball is thrown directly upwards with a velocity of $+20$ m/s. At the end of 4 s, its velocity will be closest to
   A. -50 m/s.   B. -30 m/s.   C. -20 m/s.   D. -10 m/s.

3. Two objects start at the same place at the same time and move along the same straight line. Figure 2.35 shows the position x as a function of time t for each object. At point A, what must be true about the motion of these objects? (More than one statement may be correct.)
   A. Both have the same speed.
   B. Both have the same velocity.
   C. Both are at the same position.
   D. Both have traveled the same distance.

▲ **FIGURE 2.35** Multiple-choice problem 3.

4. Based *only* on dimensional analysis, which formulas could *not* be correct? In each case, x is position, v is velocity, a

is acceleration, and t is time. (More than one choice may be correct.)

A. $v^2 = v_0^2 + 2at$
B. $x = v_0 + 1/2\, at^2$
C. $a = v^2/x$
D. $v = v_0 + 2at$

5. An object starts from rest and accelerates uniformly. If it moves 2 m during the first second, then, during the first 3 seconds, it will move

A. 6 m. B. 9 m. C. 10 m. D. 18 m.

6. If a car moving at 80 mph takes 400 ft to stop with uniform acceleration after its brakes are applied, how far will it take to stop under the same conditions if its initial velocity is 40 mph?

A. 20 ft B. 50 ft C. 100 ft D. 200 ft

7. Figure 2.36 shows the velocity of a jogger as a function of time. What statements must be true about the jogger's motion? (More than one statement may be correct.)

A. The jogger's speed is increasing.
B. The jogger's speed is decreasing.
C. The jogger's acceleration is increasing.
D. The jogger's acceleration is decreasing.

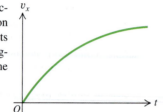

▲ **FIGURE 2.36** Multiple-choice problem 7.

8. A certain airport runway of length L allows planes to accelerate uniformly from rest to takeoff speed using the full length of the runway. Because of newly designed planes, the takeoff speed must be doubled, again using the full length of the runway and having the same acceleration as before. In terms of L, what must be the length of the new runway?

A. $4L$ B. $2L$ C. $L/2$ D. L^2

9. A redwood cone and an acorn fall from rest at the same instant and encounter no appreciable air resistance, but the redwood cone started from a height above the ground that was three times as high as that of the acorn. If the redwood cone takes time T to reach the ground, the time that the acorn takes is

A. $T/3$. B. $T/\sqrt{3}$. C. $T\sqrt{3}$. D. $3T$.

10. A frog leaps vertically into the air and encounters no appreciable air resistance. Which statement about the frog's motion is correct?

A. On the way up its acceleration is 9.8 m/s² upward, and on the way down its acceleration is 9.8 m/s² downward.
B. On the way up and on the way down its acceleration is 9.8 m/s² downward, and at the highest point its acceleration is zero.
C. On the way up, on the way down, and at the highest point its acceleration is 9.8 m/s² downward.
D. At the highest point, it reverses the direction of its acceleration.

11. You slam on the brakes of your car in a panic and skid a distance X on a straight, level road. If you had been traveling half as fast under the same road conditions, you would have skidded a distance

A. $\dfrac{X}{4}$. B. $\dfrac{X}{2}$. C. X. D. $\dfrac{X}{\sqrt{2}}$.

12. A cat runs in a straight line. Figure 2.37 shows a graph of the cat's position as a function of the following

statements about the cat's motion must be true? (There may be more than one correct choice.)

A. At point c, the cat has returned to the place where it started.
B. The cat's speed is zero at points a and c.
C. The cat's velocity is zero at point b.
D. The cat reverses the direction of its velocity at point b.

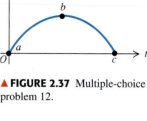

▲ **FIGURE 2.37** Multiple-choice problem 12.

13. A wildebeest is running in a straight line, which we shall call the x axis, with the positive direction to the right. Figure 2.38 shows this animal's velocity as a function of time. Which of the following statements about the animal's motion must be true? (There may be more than one correct choice.)

A. Its acceleration is increasing.
B. Its speed is decreasing from a to b and increasing from b to c.
C. It is moving to the right between a and c.
D. It is moving to the left between a and b and to the right between b and c.

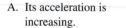

▲ **FIGURE 2.38** Multiple-choice problem 13.

14. Starting from rest, a car that is accelerating uniformly takes 15 m to reach a velocity v_x. Under the same driving conditions, how far would the car have to travel to reach a velocity of $2v_x$?

A. 15 m B. 20 m C. 30 m D. 60 m

15. A bullet is dropped into a river from a very high bridge. At the same time, another bullet is fired from a gun straight down towards the water. If air resistance is negligible, the acceleration of the bullets just before they strike the water

A. is greater for the dropped bullet.
B. is greater for the fired bullet.
C. is the same for both bullets.
D. depends on how high they started.

Problems

2.1 Displacement and Average Velocity

1. • An ant is crawling along a straight wire, which we shall call the x axis, from A to B to C to D (which overlaps A), as shown in Figure 2.39. O is the origin. Suppose you take measurements and find that AB is 50 cm, BC is 30 cm, and AO is 5 cm. (a) What is the ant's position at points A, B, C, and D? (b) Find the displacement of the ant and the distance it has moved over each of the following intervals: (i) from A to B, (ii) from B to C, (iii) from C to D, and (iv) from A to D.

▲ **FIGURE 2.39** Problem 1.

2. •• A person is walking briskly in a straight line, which we shall call the x axis. Figure 2.40 shows a graph of the person's position x along this axis as a function of time t. (a) What is the person's displacement during each of the following time intervals: (i) between $t = 1.0$ s and $t = 10.0$ s, (ii) between $t = 3.0$ s and $t = 10.0$ s, (iii) between $t = 2.0$ s and $t = 3.0$ s, and (iv) between $t = 2.0$ s and $t = 4.0$ s? (b) What distance did the person move from (i) $t = 0$ s to $t = 4.0$ s, (ii) $t = 2.0$ s to $t = 4.0$ s, and (iii) $t = 8.0$ s to $t = 10.0$ s?

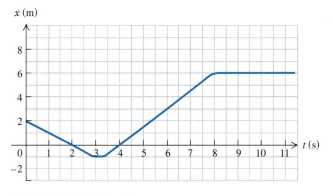

▲ **FIGURE 2.40** Problem 2.

3. • A dog runs from points A to B to C in 3.0 s. (See Figure 2.41.) Find the dog's average velocity and average speed over this 3-second interval.

▲ **FIGURE 2.41** Problem 3.

4. • **Hiking the Pacific Crest Trail.** The Pacific Crest Trail runs from the Mexican border to the Canadian border through California, Oregon, and Washington, covering 2650 miles of trail, but only about 1000 straight-line miles. If you hike this trail in 12 weeks, from Mexico to Canada, find your (a) average speed and (b) average velocity. (c) What is your average hiking speed if you hike only 8 hours per day?

5. •• Figure 2.42 shows the position of a moving object as a function of time. (a) Find the average velocity of this object from points A to B, B to C, and A to C. (b) For the intervals in part (a), would the average speed be less than, equal to, or greater than the values you found in that part? Explain your reasoning.

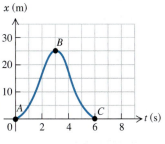

▲ **FIGURE 2.42** Problem 5.

6. •• An object moves along the x axis. Figure 2.43 shows a graph of its position x as a function of time. (a) Find the average velocity of the object from points A to B, B to C, and A to C. (b) For the intervals in part (a), would the average speed be less than,

equal to, or greater than the values you found in that part? Explain your reasoning.

7. •• A boulder starting from rest rolls down a hill in a straight line, which we shall call the x axis. A graph of its position x as a function of time t is shown in Figure 2.44. Find (a) the distance the boulder rolled between the end of the first second and the end of the third second and (b) the boulder's average speed during (i) the first second, (ii) the second second, (iii) the third second, (iv) the fourth second, and (v) the first 4 seconds.

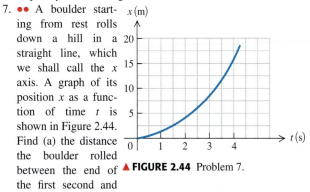

▲ **FIGURE 2.44** Problem 7.

8. •• Each graph in Figure 2.45 shows the position of a running cat, called Mousie, as a function of time. In each case, sketch a clear *qualitative* (no numbers) graph of Mousie's velocity as a function of time.

▲ **FIGURE 2.45** Problem 8.

9. • In 1954, Roger Bannister became the first human to run a mile in less than 4 minutes. Suppose that a runner on a straight track covers a distance of 1.00 mi in exactly 4.00 min. What is his average speed in (a) mi/h, (b) ft/s, and (c) m/s?

10. • **Hypersonic scramjet.** On March 27, 2004, the United States successfully tested the hypersonic X-43A scramjet, which flew at Mach 7 (seven times the speed of sound) for 11 seconds. (A scramjet gets its oxygen directly from the air, rather than from fuel.) (a) At this rate, how many minutes would it take such a scramjet to carry passengers the approximately 5000 km from San Francisco to New York? (Use 331 m/s for the speed of sound in air.) (b) How many kilometers did the scramjet travel during its 11 second test?

11. • **Plate tectonics.** The earth's crust is broken up into a series of more-or-less rigid plates that slide around due to motion of material in the mantle below. Although the speeds of these plates vary somewhat, they are typically about 5 cm/yr. Assume that this rate remains constant over time. (a) If you and your neighbor live on opposite sides of a plate boundary at which one plate is moving northward at 5.0 cm/yr with respect to the other plate, how far apart do your houses move in a century? (b) Los Angeles is presently 550 km south of San Francisco, but is on a plate moving northward relative to San Francisco. If the 5.0 cm/yr velocity continues, how many years will it take before Los Angeles has moved up to San Francisco?

12. • A runner covers one lap of a circular track 40.0 m in diameter in 62.5 s. (a) For that lap, what were her average speed and average velocity? (b) If she covered the first half-lap in 28.7 s, what were her average speed and average velocity for that half-lap?

▲ **FIGURE 2.43** Problem 6.

13. • **The smallest measured time interval.** In February 2004, Austrian physicists measured two events (having to do with the behavior of electrons) separated by the shortest time interval ever measured, 100 attoseconds. How far would light travel in this time interval? (See Table 1.1 and Appendix F.)

14. • **Ouch!** Nerve impulses travel at different speeds, depending **BIO** on the type of fiber through which they move. The impulses for touch travel at 76.2 m/s, while those registering pain move at 0.610 m/s. If a person stubs his toe, find (a) the time for each type of impulse to reach his brain, and (b) the time *delay* between the pain and touch impulses. Assume that his brain is 1.85 m from his toe and that the impulses travel directly from toe to brain.

15. • In air at 20°C, sound travels at a constant speed of 344 m/s. To answer some of the following questions, you will need to look up data in Appendix F: (a) The light year is defined as the distance light travels in 1 year. Use this information to determine how many meters there are in 1 light year. (b) How many meters does light travel in 1 nanosecond? How far does sound travel in this time? (c) When a solar flare occurs on our sun, how soon after its occurrence can we first observe it? (d) By bouncing laser beams off a reflector placed on our moon by the Apollo astronauts, astronomers can make very accurate measurements of the earth–moon distance. How long after it is sent does it take such a laser beam (which is just a light beam) to return to earth? (e) *Cassini at Saturn.* The *Cassini* spacecraft arrived at Saturn in July 2004. Photographs and other information were sent to earth by radio waves, which travel at the speed of light. How many hours did it take these waves to travel the 1.80 billion kilometers to earth? (This long time delay makes it necessary that robots on other planets travel slowly enough that nothing serious happens to them too quickly for Mission Control to send instructions for corrective action from earth.)

16. •• **Motions of the earth.** See Appendix F as needed in solving this problem. (a) How fast is a city on the earth's equator (such as Singapore) moving due to our planet's daily spin on its axis? (b) How fast is the earth moving due to its yearly motion around the sun?

17. •• **The freeway blues!** When you normally drive the freeway between Sacramento and San Francisco at an average speed of 105 km/hr (65 mph), the trip takes 1.0 hr and 20 min. On a Friday afternoon, however, heavy traffic slows you down to an average of 70 km/hr (43 mph) for the same distance. How much longer does the trip take on Friday than on the other days?

18. •• Two runners start simultaneously at opposite ends of a 200.0 m track and run toward each other. Runner A runs at a steady 8.0 m/s and runner B runs at a constant 7.0 m/s. When and where will these runners meet?

2.2 Instantaneous Velocity

19. •• A physics professor leaves her house and walks along the sidewalk toward campus. After 5 min, she realizes that it is raining and returns home. The distance from her house as a function of time is shown in Figure 2.46. At which of the labeled points is her velocity (a) zero? (b) constant and posi-

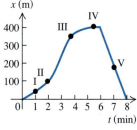

▲ **FIGURE 2.46** Problem 19.

tive? (c) constant and negative? (d) increasing in magnitude? and (e) decreasing in magnitude?

20. •• A test car travels in a straight line along the *x* axis. The graph in Figure 2.47 shows the car's position *x* as a function of time. Find its instantaneous velocity at points *A* through *G*.

▲ **FIGURE 2.47** Problem 20.

21. •• Figure 2.48 shows the position *x* of a crawling spider as a function of time. Use this graph to draw a *numerical* graph of the spider's velocity as a function of time over the same time interval.

▲ **FIGURE 2.48** Problem 21.

2.3 Average and Instantaneous Acceleration

22. •• The graph in Figure 2.49 shows the velocity of a motorcycle police officer plotted as a function of time. Find the instantaneous acceleration at times *t* = 3 s, at *t* = 7 s, and at *t* = 11 s.

23. •• A test driver at Incredible Motors, Inc., is testing a new model car having a speedometer calibrated to read m/s rather than mi/h. The following series of speedometer readings was obtained during a test run:

▲ **FIGURE 2.49** Problem 22.

Time (s)	0	2	4	6	8	10	12	14	16
Velocity (m/s)	0	0	2	5	10	15	20	22	22

(a) Compute the average acceleration during each 2 s interval. Is the acceleration constant? Is it constant during any part of the test run? (b) Make a velocity–time graph of the data shown, using scales of 1 cm = 1 s horizontally and 1 cm = 2 m/s vertically. Draw a smooth curve through the plotted points. By measuring the slope of your curve, find the magnitude of the instantaneous acceleration at times *t* = 9 s, 13 s, and 15 s.

24. • (a) The pilot of a jet fighter will black out at an acceleration greater than approximately 5*g* if it lasts for more than a few seconds. Express this acceleration in m/s² and ft/s². (b) The acceleration of the passenger during a car crash with an air bag is about 60*g* for a very short time. What is this acceleration in m/s² and ft/s²? (c) The acceleration of a falling body on our moon is 1.67 m/s². How many *g*'s is this? (d) If the acceleration of a test plane is 24.3 m/s², how many *g*'s is it?

25. •• For each graph of velocity as a function of time in Figure 2.50, sketch a qualitative graph of the acceleration as a function of time.

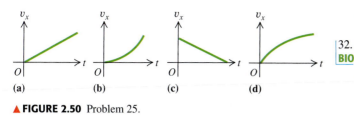

▲ FIGURE 2.50 Problem 25.

26. •• A little cat, Bella, walks along a straight line, which we shall call the x axis, with the positive direction to the right. As an observant scientist, you make measurements of her motion and construct a graph of the little feline's velocity as a function of time. (See Figure 2.51.) (a) Find Bella's velocity at $t = 4.0$ s and at $t = 7.0$ s. (b) What is her acceleration at $t = 3.0$ s? at $t = 6.0$ s? at $t = 7.0$ s? (c) Sketch a clear graph of Bella's acceleration as a function of time.

▲ FIGURE 2.51 Problem 26.

2.4 Motion with Constant Acceleration

27. • A car driving on the turnpike accelerates uniformly in a straight line from 88 ft/s (60 mph) to 110 ft/s (75 mph) in 3.50 s. (a) What is the car's acceleration? (b) How far does the car travel while it accelerates?

28. • **Animal motion.** Cheetahs, the fastest of the great cats, can reach 45 mph in 2.0 s starting from rest. Assuming that they have constant acceleration throughout that time, find (a) their acceleration (in ft/s² and m/s²) and (b) the distance (in m and ft) they travel during that time.

29. •• **The *Genesis* crash.** On Sept. 8, 2004, the returning capsule of the Genesis Mission (which collected particles of the solar wind) crashed to earth in the Utah desert when its parachute failed to open. The capsule, which was 162 cm in diameter, hit the ground at 311 km/h and penetrated the soil to 50% of its diameter. (a) What was its constant acceleration in m/s² and in g's, as the capsule penetrated the earth? (b) How long did it take the capsule to stop once it hit the ground?

30. •• **Blackout?** A jet fighter pilot wishes to accelerate from rest at 5g to reach Mach 3 (three times the speed of sound) as quickly as possible. Experimental tests reveal that he will black out if this acceleration lasts for more than 5.0 s. Use 331 m/s for the speed of sound. (a) Will the period of acceleration last long enough to cause him to black out? (b) What is the greatest speed he can reach with an acceleration of 5g before blacking out?

31. •• **Dizziness while standing up.** As you have probably noticed, people often feel dizzy if they suddenly stand up from a crouched position. (a) Make simple observations and measurements on yourself (or a cooperative friend) to calculate the acceleration (in m/s² and in g's) of your head when you stand up this way. Assume that it takes $\frac{1}{2}$ s to stand up and that you are speeding up for half that time and slowing down for the other half, with constant acceleration each way. (b) Do all parts

of your body have the acceleration you found in part (a) when you stand up? Why or why not?

32. • If a pilot accelerates at more than 4g, he begins to "gray out," but not completely lose consciousness. (a) What is the shortest time that a jet pilot starting from rest can take to reach Mach 4 (four times the speed of sound) without graying out? (b) How far would the plane travel during this period of acceleration? (Use 331 m/s for the speed of sound in cold air.)

33. • **Air-bag injuries.** During an auto accident, the vehicle's air bags deploy and slow down the passengers more gently than if they had hit the windshield or steering wheel. According to safety standards, the bags produce a maximum acceleration of 60 g, but lasting for only 36 ms (or less). How far (in meters) does a person travel in coming to a complete stop in 36 ms at a constant acceleration of 60 g?

34. •• Starting from rest, a boulder rolls down a hill with constant acceleration and travels 2.00 m during the first second. (a) How far does it travel during the second second? (b) How fast is it moving at the end of the first second? at the end of the second second?

35. • **Faster than a speeding bullet!** The Beretta Model 92S (the standard-issue U.S. army pistol) has a barrel 127 mm long. The bullets leave this barrel with a muzzle velocity of 335 m/s. (a) What is the acceleration of the bullet while it is in the barrel, assuming it to be constant? Express your answer in m/s² and in g's. (b) For how long is the bullet in the barrel?

36. •• An airplane travels 280 m down the runway before taking off. Assuming that it has constant acceleration, if it starts from rest and becomes airborne in 8.00 s, how fast (in m/s) is it moving at takeoff?

37. •• **Acceleration of a typical car.** (a) Use your own knowledge (or that of a helpful friend) to estimate how long it takes a typical car to accelerate from zero to 60 mph. Then use that estimate to calculate the acceleration (in ft/s² and in m/s²) of an ordinary car. b) How far (in feet and meters) does the car travel while it accelerates, assuming that the acceleration is uniform?

38. •• The "reaction time" of the average automobile driver is about 0.7 s. (The reaction time is the interval between the perception of a signal to stop and the application of the brakes.) If an automobile can slow down with an acceleration of 12.0 ft/s², compute the total distance covered in coming to a stop after a signal is observed (a) from an initial velocity of 15.0 mi/h (in a school zone) and (b) from an initial velocity of 55.0 mi/h.

39. •• According to recent typical test data, a Ford Focus travels 0.250 mi in 19.9 s, starting from rest. The same car, when braking from 60.0 mph on dry pavement, stops in 146 ft. Assume constant acceleration in each part of its motion, but not necessarily the same acceleration when slowing down as when speeding up. (a) Find this car's acceleration while braking and while speeding up. (b) If its acceleration is constant while speeding up, how fast (in mph) will the car be traveling after 0.250 mi of acceleration? (c) How long does it take the car to stop while braking from 60.0 mph?

40. •• A subway train starts from rest at a station and accelerates at a rate of 1.60 m/s² for 14.0 s. It runs at constant speed for 70.0 s and slows down at a rate of 3.50 m/s² until it stops at the next station. Find the *total* distance covered.

2.5 Proportional Reasoning

41. •• If the radius of a circle of area A and circumference C is doubled, find the new area and circumference of the circle in terms of A and C. (Consult Appendix A if necessary.)

42. •• In the redesign of a machine, a metal cubical part has each of its dimensions tripled. By what factor do its surface area and volume change?

43. •• Suppose you wish to reduce the volume of a sphere by a factor of 2. (Consult Appendix A if necessary.) (a) If its original radius was R, what is the reduced radius in terms of R? (b) By what factor does the sphere's surface area change?

44. •• Two rockets start from rest and accelerate to the same final speed, but one has twice the acceleration of the other. (a) If the high-acceleration rocket takes 50 s to reach the final speed, how long will it take the other rocket to reach that speed? b) If the high-acceleration rocket travels 250 m to reach its final speed, how far will the other rocket travel to do likewise?

45. •• Two rockets having the same acceleration start from rest, but rocket A travels for twice as much time as rocket B. (a) If rocket A goes a distance of 250 km, how far will rocket B go? (b) If rocket A reaches a speed of 350 m/s, what speed will rocket B reach?

46. •• Two cars having equal speeds hit their brakes at the same time, but car A has three times the acceleration as car B. (a) If car A travels a distance D before stopping, how far (in terms of D) will car B go before stopping? (b) If car B stops in time T, how long (in terms of T) will it take for car A to stop?

47. •• Airplane A, starting from rest with constant acceleration, requires a runway 500 m long to become airborne. Airplane B requires a takeoff speed twice as great as that of airplane A, but has the same acceleration, and both planes start from rest. (a) How long must the runway be for airplane B? (b) If airplane A takes time T to travel the length of its runway, how long (in terms of T) will airplane B take to travel the length of its runway?

2.6 Freely Falling Bodies

48. • (a) If a flea can jump straight up to a height of 22.0 cm, what is its initial speed (in m/s) as it leaves the ground, neglecting air resistance? (b) How long is it in the air? (c) What are the magnitude and direction of its acceleration while it is (i) moving upward? (ii) moving downward? (iii) at the highest point?

49. • A brick is released with no initial speed from the roof of a building and strikes the ground in 2.50 s, encountering no appreciable air drag. (a) How tall, in meters, is the building? (b) How fast is the brick moving just before it reaches the ground? (c) Sketch graphs of this falling brick's acceleration, velocity, and vertical position as functions of time.

50. • **Loss of power!** In December of 1989, a KLM Boeing 747 airplane carrying 231 passengers entered a cloud of ejecta from an Alaskan volcanic eruption. All four engines went out, and the plane fell from 27,900 ft to 13,300 ft before the engines could be restarted. It then landed safely in Anchorage. Neglecting any air resistance and aerodynamic lift, and assuming that the plane had no vertical motion when it lost power, (a) for how long did it fall before the engines were restarted, and (b) how fast was it falling at that instant? c) In reality, why would the plane not be falling nearly as fast?

51. •• A tennis ball on Mars, where the acceleration due to gravity is $0.379g$ and air resistance is negligible, is hit directly upward and returns to the same level 8.5 s later. (a) How high above its original point did the ball go? (b) How fast was it moving just after being hit? (c) Sketch clear graphs of the ball's vertical position, vertical velocity, and vertical acceleration as functions of time while it's in the Martian air.

52. • **Measuring g.** One way to measure g on another planet or moon by remote sensing is to measure how long it takes an object to fall a given distance. A lander vehicle on a distant planet records the fact that it takes 3.17 s for a ball to fall freely 11.26 m, starting from rest. (a) What is the acceleration due to gravity on that planet? Express your answer in m/s² and in earth g's. b) How fast is the ball moving just as it lands?

53. •• **That's a lot of hot air!** A hot-air balloonist, rising vertically with a constant speed of 5.00 m/s, releases a sandbag at the instant the balloon is 40.0 m above the ground. (See Figure 2.52.) After it is released, the sandbag encounters no appreciable air drag. (a) Compute the position and velocity of the sandbag at 0.250 s and 1.00 s after its release. (b) How many seconds after its release will the bag strike the ground? (c) How fast is it moving as it strikes the ground? (d) What is the greatest height above the ground that the sandbag reaches? (e) Sketch graphs of this bag's acceleration, velocity, and vertical position as functions of time.

$v = 5.00$ m/s

40.0 m to ground

▲ **FIGURE 2.52** Problem 53.

54. •• On Planet X, you drop a 25 kg stone from rest and measure its speed at various times. Then you use the data you obtained to construct a graph (see Figure 2.53) of its speed v as a function of time t. From the information in the graph, answer the following questions: (a) What is g on Planet X? (b) An astronaut drops a piece of equipment from rest out of the landing module, 3.5 m above the surface of Planet X. How long will it take this equipment to reach the ground, and how fast will it be moving when it gets there? (c) How fast would an astronaut have to project an object straight upward to reach a height of 18.0 m above the release point, and how long would it take to reach that height?

▲ **FIGURE 2.53** Problem 54.

55. •• **Astronauts on the moon.** Astronauts on our moon must function with an acceleration due to gravity of $0.170g$. (a) If an astronaut can throw a certain wrench 12.0 m vertically upward on earth, how high could he throw it on our moon if he gives it the same starting speed in both places? (b) How much *longer* would it be in motion (going up and coming down) on the moon than on earth?

56. • A student throws a water balloon vertically downward from the top of a building. The balloon leaves the thrower's hand

with a speed of 15.0 m/s. (a) What is its speed after falling freely for 2.00 s? (b) How far does it fall in 2.00 s? (c) What is the magnitude of its velocity after falling 10.0 m?

57. • A rock is thrown vertically upward with a speed of 12.0 m/s from the roof of a building that is 60.0 m above the ground. (a) In how many seconds after being thrown does the rock strike the ground? (b) What is the speed of the rock just before it strikes the ground? Assume free fall.

58. •• **Physiological effects of large acceleration.** The rocket-**BIO** driven sled *Sonic Wind No. 2,* used for investigating the physiological effects of large accelerations, runs on a straight, level track that is 1080 m long. Starting from rest, it can reach a speed of 1610 km/h in 1.80 s. (a) Compute the acceleration in m/s² and in *g*'s. (b) What is the distance covered in 1.80 s? (c) A magazine article states that, at the end of a certain run, the speed of the sled decreased from 1020 km/h to zero in 1.40 s and that, during this time, its passenger was subjected to more than 40*g*. Are these figures consistent?

59. •• Two stones are thrown vertically upward from the ground, one with three times the initial speed of the other. (a) If the faster stone takes 10 s to return to the ground, how long will it take the slower stone to return? (b) If the slower stone reaches a maximum height of *H,* how high (in terms of *H*) will the faster stone go? Assume free fall.

60. •• Two coconuts fall freely from rest at the same time, one from a tree twice as high as the other. (a) If the coconut from the taller tree reaches the ground with a speed *V,* what will be the speed (in terms of *V*) of the coconut from the other tree when it reaches the ground? (b) If the coconut from the shorter tree takes time *T* to reach the ground, how long (in terms of *T*) will it take the other coconut to reach the ground?

*2.7 Relative Velocity along a Straight Line

61. • A Toyota Prius driving north at 65 mph and a VW Passat driving south at 42 mph are on the same road heading toward each other (but in different lanes). What is the velocity of each car relative to the other (a) when they are 250 ft apart, just before they meet, and (b) when they are 525 ft apart, after they have passed each other?

62. • The wind is blowing from west to east at 35 mph, and an eagle in that wind is flying at 22 mph relative to the air. What is the velocity of this eagle relative to a person standing on the ground if the eagle is flying (a) from west to east relative to the air and (b) from east to west relative to the air?

63. •• A helicopter 8.50 m above the ground and descending at 3.50 m/s drops a package from rest (relative to the helicopter). Just as it hits the ground, find (a) the velocity of the package relative to the helicopter and (b) the velocity of the helicopter relative to the package. The package falls freely.

64. •• A jetliner has a cruising air speed of 600 mph relative to the air. How long does it take this plane to fly round-trip from San Francisco to Chicago, an east–west flight of 2,000 mi each way, (a) if there is no wind blowing and (b) if the wind is blowing at 150 mph from the west to the east?

65. •• City A lies directly west of city B. When there is no wind, an airliner makes the 5310 km round-trip flight between the two cities in 6.60 h of flying time while traveling at the same speed in both directions. When a strong, steady wind is blowing from west to east and the airliner has the same air speed as

before, the round-trip takes 6.70 h of flight time. How fast is the wind blowing?

General Problems

66. •• **Leaving the solar system.** In late 2002, the *Voyager 1* rocket sent back information to earth indicating that in a few years it would cross the edge of the solar system (called the *heliopause*), which scientists have now been able to calculate to be about 2.3×10^{10} km from the sun. As it crosses the heliopause, it will radio messages back to earth using radio waves, which travel at the speed of light. Assuming that the earth has a circular orbit, how long will it take the waves to reach us if our planet is at the point in its orbit that is closest to the spacecraft? Consult Appendix F as needed.

67. • **Life from space?** One rather controversial suggestion for **BIO** the origin of life on the earth is that the seeds of life arrived here from outer space in tiny spores—a theory called *panspermia.* Of course, any life in such spores would have to survive a long journey through the frigid near vacuum of outer space. If these spores originated at the distance of our nearest star, Alpha Centauri, and traveled at a constant 1000 km/s, how many years would it take for them to make the journey here? (Alpha Centauri is approximately $4\frac{1}{4}$ light years away, and the light year is the distance light travels in 1 year.)

68. •• At the instant the traffic light turns green, an automobile that has been waiting at an intersection starts ahead with a constant acceleration of 2.50 m/s². At the same instant, a truck, traveling with a constant speed of 15.0 m/s, overtakes and passes the automobile. (a) How far beyond its starting point does the automobile overtake the truck? (b) How fast is the automobile traveling when it overtakes the truck?

69. •• You leave for work early when there is little traffic, so your average speed is 60 mph. Coming home, however, your average speed is only 40 mph due to heavy traffic. (a) If you follow the same route both ways, what is your average speed for the round trip? (b) Did you expect the answer to be 50 mph? Why is it *not* 50 mph?

70. •• Two runners start simultaneously from the same point on a circular 200.0 m track and run in the same direction. One runs at a constant 6.20 m/s and the other at a constant 5.50 m/s. (a) When will the fast runner overtake (or "lap") the slower one, and (b) how far from the starting point will each one have run?

71. •• Two rocks are thrown directly upward with the same initial speeds, one on earth and one on our moon, where the acceleration due to gravity is one-sixth what it is on earth. (a) If the rock on the moon rises to a height *H,* how high, in terms of *H,* will the rock rise on the earth? (b) If the earth rock takes 4.0 s to reach its highest point, how long will it take the moon rock to do so?

72. • **Prevention of hip fractures.** Falls resulting in hip fractures **BIO** are a major cause of injury and even death to the elderly. Typically, the hip's speed at impact is about 2.0 m/s. If this can be reduced to 1.3 m/s or less, the hip will usually not fracture. One way to do this is by wearing elastic hip pads. (a) If a typical pad is 5.0 cm thick and compresses by 2.0 cm during the impact of a fall, what acceleration (in m/s² and in *g*'s) does the

hip undergo to reduce its speed to 1.3 m/s? (b) The acceleration you found in part (a) may seem like a rather large acceleration, but to fully assess its effects on the hip, calculate how long it lasts.

73. • **Are we martians?** It has been suggested, and not face-
BIO tiously, that life might have originated on Mars and been carried to Earth when a meteor hit Mars and blasted pieces of rock (perhaps containing primitive life) free of the surface. Astronomers know that many Martian rocks have come to Earth this way. (For information on one of these, search the Internet for "ALH 84001".) One objection to this idea is that microbes would have to undergo an enormous, lethal acceleration during the impact. Let us investigate how large such an acceleration might be. To escape Mars, rock fragments would have to reach its escape velocity of 5.0 km/s, and this would most likely happen over a distance of about 4.0 m during the impact. (a) What would be the acceleration, in m/s² and g's, of such a rock fragment? (b) How long would this acceleration last? (c) In tests, scientists have found that over 40% of *Bacillius subtilis* bacteria survived after an acceleration of 450,000g. In light of your answer to part (a), can we rule out the hypothesis that life might have been blasted from Mars to Earth?

74. •• **Testing reaction time.** A meterstick is held vertically above your hand, with the lower end between your thumb and first finger. On seeing the meter stick released, you grab it with those two fingers. You can calculate your reaction time from the distance the meterstick falls, read directly from the point where your fingers grabbed it. (a) Derive a relationship for your reaction time in terms of this measured distance d. (b) If the measured distance is 17.6 cm, what is the reaction time?

75. •• **Egg drop.** You are on the roof of the physics building of your school, 46.0 m above the ground. (See Figure 2.54.) Your physics professor, who is 1.80 m tall, is walking alongside the building at a constant speed of 1.20 m/s. If you wish to drop an egg on your professor's head, where should the professor be when you release the egg, assuming that the egg encounters no appreciable air drag.

▲ **FIGURE 2.54** Problem 75.

76. •• A 0.525 kg ball starts from rest and rolls down a hill with uniform acceleration, traveling 150 m during the second 10.0 s of its motion. How far did it roll during the first 5.0 s of motion?

77. •• **Space shuttle launch.** As part of the launch of the space shuttle, solid-rocket boosters (SRBs) first take it to an altitude of 45 km while they accelerate it to a speed of 4973 km/hr. The SRBs then separate from the shuttle and fall back to earth. Assume that the acceleration due to gravity is the same throughout their fall, and neglect air resistance. (a) How fast would the SRBs be moving when they reached the earth's surface if they were traveling upward when they released the space shuttle? (b) How long after they began to fall would it take the SRBs to reach the ground? (c) While the space shuttle

is being taken up, starting from rest, what is its acceleration (assumed constant), in m/s² and g's, and how long does it take to reach the 45 km altitude?

78. •• **Freeway ramps.** In designing a freeway on-ramp, you must make it long enough for cars to be able to accelerate and merge safely with traffic traveling at speeds of 70 mph. For an off-ramp, the cars must be able to come to a stop from 70 mph over the length of the ramp. Your traffic engineers provide the following data: Powerful cars can accelerate from rest to 60 mph in 5.0 s, while less powerful cars take twice as long to do this. When slowing down from 60 mph, a car with good tire treads will take 12.0 s to stop, whereas one with bald tires takes 20.0 s. In order to safely accommodate all the types of vehicles, what should be the minimum length (in meters) of on-ramps and off-ramps? Assume constant acceleration.

79. • **Fingernail growth.** According to data published by
BIO William B. Bean, on the basis of measurements of his own fingernails, his nails grew at 0.123 mm/day at age 32 and at 0.095 mm/day at age 67. Calculate the average acceleration of his fingernails over that period of his life in units of mm/day² and m/s².

80. •• You decide to take high-speed strobe light photos of your little dog Holly as she runs along. Figure 2.55 shows some of these photos. The strobe flashes at a uniform rate, which means that the time interval between adjacent images is the same in all the photos. For each case, sketch clear *qualitative* (no numbers) graphs of Holly's position as a function of time and her velocity as a function of time.

(a)

(b)

(c)

(d)

▲ **FIGURE 2.55** Problem 80.

81. •• A rocket blasts off vertically from rest on the launch pad with a constant upward acceleration of 2.50 m/s². At 20.0 s after blastoff, the engines suddenly fail, and the rocket begins free fall. (a) How high above the launch pad will the rocket eventually go? (b) Find the rocket's velocity and acceleration at its highest point. (c) How long after it was launched will the rocket fall back to the launch pad, and how fast will it be moving when it does so?

82. •• **Mouse at play, I.** A little mouse runs in a straight line, which we shall call the x axis. As an eager scientist, you record its position as a function of time and use the information you obtain to construct the graph plotted in Figure 2.56, which shows the mouse's position x as a function of time t. You have adopted the usual sign convention according to which quantities to the right are positive and those to the left are negative. Use the information on the graph to answer the following questions: (a) When is the mouse to the right of the origin? to the left of the origin? at the origin? (b) What are the magnitude and

direction of the mouse's initial velocity? (c) Does the mouse move with constant acceleration throughout the 10 seconds? (d) What is the mouse's maximum speed? In which direction is it moving with that speed? (e) When is the mouse moving to the right? moving to the left? not moving? (f) Through what total distance has the mouse moved during the first 3 s? during the first 10 s? (g) When is the mouse speeding up? slowing down? (h) Do the kinematics formulas $v_x = v_{0x} + a_x t$ and $x = x_0 + v_{0x}t + \frac{1}{2}a_x t^2$ apply to this mouse's motion throughout the 10 s? Why or why not?

▲ **FIGURE 2.56** Problem 82.

83. •• **Mouse at play, II.** On another day, you make more measurements on the little mouse in the previous problem and construct the graph of its velocity v as a function of time t shown in Figure 2.57, using the same sign convention as before. (a) What are the magnitude and direction of the mouse's initial velocity? (b) Find the mouse's greatest speed; in what direction is it moving at that speed? (c) When is the mouse moving to the right? moving to the left? not moving? (d) Find the mouse's largest acceleration; in which direction does it point? (e) When does the mouse change direction? (f) When is the mouse speeding up? slowing down? not moving? (g) Do the kinematics formulas $v_x = v_{0x} + a_x t$ and $x = x_0 + v_{0x}t + \frac{1}{2}a_x t^2$ apply to this mouse's motion throughout the 10 s? Why or why not?

▲ **FIGURE 2.57** Problem 83.

84. •• **Earthquake waves.** Earthquakes produce several types of shock waves. The best known are the P-waves (P for *primary* or *pressure*) and the S-waves (S for *secondary* or *shear*). In the earth's crust, P-waves travel at around 6.5 km/s while S-waves move at about 3.5 km/s. (The actual speeds vary with the type of material the waves are going through.) The time delay between the arrival of these two types of waves at a seismic recording station tells geologists how far away the earthquake that produced the waves occurred. (a) If the time delay at a seis-

mic station is 33 s, how far from that station did the earthquake occur? (b) One form of earthquake warning system detects the faster (but less damaging) P-waves and sounds an alarm when they first arrive, giving people a short time to seek cover before the more dangerous S-waves arrive. If an earthquake occurs 375 km away from such a warning device, how much time would people have to take cover between the alarm and the arrival of the S-waves?

85. •• **Landing on Mars.** In January 2004, the Mars Exploration Rover mission landed two vehicles—*Spirit* and *Opportunity*—on Mars. The spacecraft carrying the two vehicles approached Mars with a speed of 19,300 km/hr; then began a four-stage process to slow the craft down for the landing on the surface. **Stage I:** Atmospheric friction reduced the speed of the lander from 19,300 km/hr to 1600 km/hr in 4.0 min. **Stage II:** Starting from a height of 11,000 m above the surface, a parachute reduced the speed of the craft from 1600 km/hr to 321 km/hr while the vehicle traveled to 91 m above the surface. **Stage III:** Retro-rockets fired to reduce the speed to zero. **Stage IV:** The vehicle then descended in free fall, with $g = 3.71$ m/s², to hit the ground at 48 km/hr. Each stage occurred immediately after the preceding one. In our calculations, which are based on NASA's Jet Propulsion Laboratory data, we shall assume that the accelerations were all constant, which was not really the case. (a) Find the lander's acceleration during Stage I. Express your answer in m/s², earth *g*'s, and Mars *g*'s. (b) Find the lander's acceleration, in m/s², during Stage II. How long did Stage II last? (c) Neglecting air resistance, how high was the lander when Stage IV began, and how long did this stage last?

86. •• **Flying leap of the**
BIO flea. High-speed motion pictures (3500 frames/ second) of a jumping, 210-μg flea yielded the data used to plot the graph shown in Figure 2.58. (See "The Flying Leap of the Flea," by M. Rothschild, Y. Schlein, K. Parker, C. Neville, and S. Sternberg in the November 1973 *Scientific American.*) This flea was about 2 mm long and jumped at a nearly vertical takeoff angle. Use the graph to answer the following questions: (a) Is the acceleration of the flea ever zero? If so, when? Explain your reasoning. (b) Find the flea's acceleration at 0.5 ms, 1.0 ms, and 1.5 ms.

▲ **FIGURE 2.58** Problem 86.

87. •• **How high is the cliff?** Suppose you are climbing in the High Sierra when you suddenly find yourself at the edge of a fog-shrouded cliff. To find the height of this cliff, you drop a rock from the top and, 10.0 s later, hear the sound of it hitting the ground at the foot of the cliff. (a) Ignoring air resistance, how high is the cliff if the speed of sound is 330 m/s? (b) Suppose you had ignored the time it takes the sound to reach you. In that case, would you have overestimated or underestimated the height of the cliff? Explain your reasoning.

3 MOTION IN A PLANE

When you see a lizard jump, you probably don't think, "projectile!" However, except for the effects of air resistance and a couple of other minor factors, all objects that jump or are launched above the surface and then travel passively until they land move in exactly the same way and can be called projectiles. Projectile motion is a classic example of motion in a plane—the topic of this chapter.

A Navy F14 Tomcat jet fighter roars off from the deck of an aircraft carrier, moving 55 m/s relative to the deck. It quickly accelerates into the sky. The instruments in the cockpit tell the pilot the speed and altitude of the plane and warn of other airplanes nearby. Pilots must constantly be aware of the three-dimensional nature of their motion.

In the straight-line problems of Chapter 2, we could describe the position of a particle with a single coordinate. But to understand the curved flight of a baseball, the orbital motion of a satellite, or the path of the water from a fire hose, we need to extend our descriptions of motion to more than one dimension. We'll focus on motion in two dimensions—that is, in a plane—but the principles also apply to three-dimensional motion. For two-dimensional motion, the vector quantities displacement, velocity, and acceleration now have two components and lie in a plane rather than along a line. We'll also generalize the concept of relative velocity to motion in a plane, such as an airplane flying in a crosswind.

This chapter represents a merging of the vector language we learned in Chapter 1 with the kinematic language of Chapter 2. As before, we're concerned with *describing* motion, not with analyzing its causes. But the language you learn here will be an essential tool in later chapters when you use Newton's laws of motion to study the relation between force and motion.

3.1 Velocity in a Plane

To describe the *motion* of an object in a plane, we first need to be able to describe the object's *position*. (In this chapter, as in the preceding one, we assume that the objects we describe can be modeled as particles.) Often, it's useful to use a familiar *x-y* axis system (Figure 3.1a). For example, when a football player kicks a field goal, the ball (represented by point *P*) moves in a vertical plane. The ball's

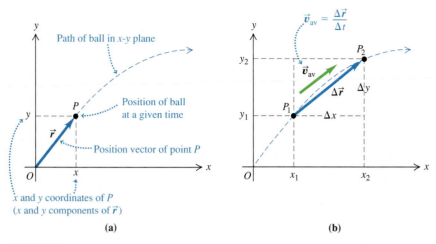

y

Path of ball in x-y plane

P

Position of ball
at a given time

$\vec{r}$

Position vector of point P

O   x

x and y coordinates of P
(x and y components of $\vec{r}$)

(a)

$\vec{v}_{av} = \dfrac{\Delta \vec{r}}{\Delta t}$

y

y_2

P_2

$\vec{v}_{av}$

$\Delta \vec{r}$ Δy

P_1

y_1 Δx

O x_1 x_2 x

(b)

▲ **FIGURE 3.1** Position vectors can specify the location and displacement of a point in an
x-y coordinate system. A position vector points from the origin to the point.

horizontal distance from the origin O at any time is x, and its vertical distance
above the ground at any time is y. The numbers x and and y are called the
coordinates of point P. The vector $\vec{r}$ from the origin O to point P is called the
position vector of point P, and the Cartesian coordinates x and y of point P are
the x and y components, respectively, of vector $\vec{r}$. (You may want to review
Section 1.8, "Components of Vectors.") The *distance* of point P from the origin is
the magnitude of vector $\vec{r}$:

$$r = |\vec{r}| = \sqrt{x^2 + y^2}.$$

Figure 3.1b shows the ball at two points in its curved path. At time t_1, it is at
point P_1 with position vector $\vec{r}_1$; at the later time t_2, it is at point P_2 with position
vector $\vec{r}_2$. The ball moves from P_1 to P_2 during the time interval $\Delta t = t_2 - t_1$. The
change in position (the displacement) during this interval is the vector
$\Delta \vec{r} = \vec{r}_2 - \vec{r}_1$. We define the **average velocity** $\vec{v}_{av}$ during the interval in the
same way we did in Chapter 2 for straight-line motion:

Definition of average velocity
The average velocity of a particle is the displacement $\Delta \vec{r}$, divided by the time
interval Δt:

$$\vec{v}_{av} = \frac{\vec{r}_2 - \vec{r}_1}{t_2 - t_1} = \frac{\Delta \vec{r}}{\Delta t}. \tag{3.1}$$

That is, the average velocity is a vector quantity having the same direction as $\Delta \vec{r}$
and a magnitude equal to the magnitude of $\Delta \vec{r}$, divided by the time interval Δt.
The magnitude of $\Delta \vec{r}$ is always the straight-line distance from P_1 to P_2, regardless
of the actual shape of the path taken by the object. Thus, the average velocity
would be the same for *any* path that would take the particle from P_1 to P_2 in the
same time interval Δt.

Figure 3.1b also shows that, during any displacement $\Delta \vec{r}$, Δx and Δy are the
components of the vector $\Delta \vec{r}$; it follows that the components $v_{av,x}$ and $v_{av,y}$ of the
average velocity vector are

$$v_{av,x} = \frac{\Delta x}{\Delta t} \quad \text{and} \quad v_{av,y} = \frac{\Delta y}{\Delta t}. \tag{3.2}$$

▲ **Not your parents' yo-yo.** The yo-yo may
seem like a child's toy, but looks can often be
deceiving. Knowledge of basic principles of
physics and engineering design has sparked
the creation of a new generation of high-
performance yo-yos. Some can be made to
spin at the end of the string for up to 14 minutes, the current world record set in 2003. In
the photo shown here, 1998 world champion
Jennifer Baybrook is demonstrating a classic
yo-yo trick. When the center of the spinning
yo-yo remains at the same position, its displacement and average velocity are zero.

We define the **instantaneous velocity** $\vec{v}$ as follows:

> **Definition of instantaneous velocity $\vec{v}$ in a plane**
> The instantaneous velocity is the limit of the average velocity as the time interval Δt approaches zero:
>
> $$\vec{v} = \lim_{\Delta t \to 0} \frac{\Delta \vec{r}}{\Delta t}. \tag{3.3}$$

The instantaneous velocity vector $\vec{v}$ is always tangent to the x-y path.

v_x and v_y are the x and y components of $\vec{v}$.

▲ **FIGURE 3.2** The two velocity components for motion in the x-y plane.

As $\Delta t \to 0$, points P_1 and P_2 move closer and closer together. In the limit, the vector $\Delta \vec{r}$ becomes *tangent* to the curve, as shown in Figure 3.2. The direction of $\Delta \vec{r}$ in the limit is also the direction of the instantaneous velocity $\vec{v}$. This analysis leads to an important conclusion:

> At every point along the path, the instantaneous velocity vector is tangent to the path.

During any displacement $\Delta \vec{r}$, the changes Δx and Δy in the coordinates x and y are the *components* of $\Delta \vec{r}$. It follows that the components v_x and v_y of the instantaneous velocity $\vec{v}$ are

$$v_x = \lim_{\Delta t \to 0} \frac{\Delta x}{\Delta t} \quad \text{and} \quad v_y = \lim_{\Delta t \to 0} \frac{\Delta y}{\Delta t}.$$

The instantaneous *speed* of the object is the *magnitude v* of the instantaneous velocity vector $\vec{v}$. This is given by the Pythagorean relation

$$|\vec{v}| = v = \sqrt{v_x^2 + v_y^2}. \quad \text{(speed of a particle in a plane)}$$

The direction of $\vec{v}$ is given by the angle θ in the figure. We see that when we measure θ in the usual way (counterclockwise from the $+x$ axis, as in Section 1.8),

$$\theta = \tan^{-1} \frac{v_y}{v_x}.$$

> **NOTE** ▶ In this text, we always use Greek letters for angles; we'll use θ (theta) for the directions of vectors measured counterclockwise from the $+x$ axis and ϕ (phi) for most other angles. ◀

Because velocity is a vector quantity, we may represent it either in terms of its components or in terms of its magnitude and direction, as described in Chapter 1. The *direction* of an object's instantaneous velocity at any point is *always* tangent to the path at that point. But in general, the position vector $\vec{r}$ does *not* have the same direction as the instantaneous velocity $\vec{v}$. (The direction of the position vector depends on where you place the origin, while the direction of $\vec{v}$ is determined by the shape of the path.)

EXAMPLE 3.1   A model car

Suppose you are operating a radio-controlled model car on a vacant tennis court. The surface of the court represents the x-y plane, and you place the origin at your own location. At time $t_1 = 2.00$ s the car has x and y coordinates $(4.0 \text{ m}, 2.0 \text{ m})$, and at time $t_2 = 2.50$ s it has coordinates $(7.0 \text{ m}, 6.0 \text{ m})$. For the time interval from t_1 to t_2, find **(a)** the components of the average velocity of the car and **(b)** the magnitude and direction of the average velocity.

Continued

SOLUTION

SET UP Figure 3.3 shows the sketch we draw. We see that $\Delta x = 7.0 \text{ m} - 4.0 \text{ m} = 3.0 \text{ m}$, $\Delta y = 6.0 \text{ m} - 2.0 \text{ m} = 4.0 \text{ m}$, and $\Delta t = 0.50 \text{ s}$.

SOLVE Part (a): To find the components of $\vec{v}_{av}$, we use their definitions (Equations 3.2):

$$v_{av,x} = \frac{\Delta x}{\Delta t} = \frac{3.0 \text{ m}}{0.50 \text{ s}} = 6.0 \text{ m/s},$$

$$v_{av,y} = \frac{\Delta y}{\Delta t} = \frac{4.0 \text{ m}}{0.50 \text{ s}} = 8.0 \text{ m/s}.$$

Part (b): The magnitude of $\vec{v}_{av}$ is obtained from the Pythagorean theorem:

$$|\vec{v}_{av}| = \sqrt{v_{av,x}^2 + v_{av,y}^2}$$
$$= \sqrt{(6.0 \text{ m/s})^2 + (8.0 \text{ m/s})^2} = 10.0 \text{ m/s}.$$

The direction of $\vec{v}_{av}$ is most easily described by its angle, measured counterclockwise from the positive x axis. Calling this angle θ, we have

$$\theta = \tan^{-1}\frac{v_{av,y}}{v_{av,x}} = \tan^{-1}\frac{8.0 \text{ m/s}}{6.0 \text{ m/s}} = 53°.$$

Alternative Solution: Alternatively, the magnitude of $\vec{v}_{av}$ is the distance between the points $(4.0 \text{ m}, 2.0 \text{ m})$ and $(7.0 \text{ m}, 6.0 \text{ m})$ (i.e., 5.0 m, found using Pythagoras's theorem), divided by the time interval (0.5 s):

$$|\vec{v}_{av}| = \frac{5.0 \text{ m}}{0.50 \text{ s}} = 10.0 \text{ m/s}.$$

$\vec{v}_{av}$ points from P_1 toward P_2. It doesn't matter how long you make it; its magnitude will be found mathematically.

▲ FIGURE 3.3 Our sketch for this problem.

Since the direction of $\vec{v}_{av}$ is the same as the direction of the displacement $\Delta\vec{r}$ between the two points, we can calculate it from Δx and Δy rather than $v_{av,x}$ and $v_{av,y}$:

$$\theta = \tan^{-1}\frac{\Delta y}{\Delta x} = \tan^{-1}\frac{4.0 \text{ m}}{3.0 \text{ m}} = 53°.$$

REFLECT Be sure you understand the relation between the two solutions to part (b). In the first, we calculated the magnitude and direction of $\vec{v}_{av}$ from the components of this vector quantity. In the alternative solution, we used the fact that the average velocity $\vec{v}_{av}$ and the displacement $\Delta\vec{r}$ have the same direction.

Practice Problem: Suppose you reverse the car's motion, so that it retraces its path in the opposite direction in the same time. Find the components of the average velocity of the car and the magnitude and direction of the average velocity. *Answers:* −6.0 m/s, −8.0 m/s, 10.0 m/s, 233°.

3.2 Acceleration in a Plane

Now let's consider the acceleration of an object moving on a curved path in a plane. In Figure 3.4, the vector $\vec{v}_1$ represents the particle's instantaneous velocity at point P_1 at time t_1, and the vector $\vec{v}_2$ represents the particle's instantaneous velocity at point P_2 at time t_2. In general, the two velocities differ in both magnitude and direction.

We define the **average acceleration** $\vec{a}_{av}$ of the particle as follows:

Definition of average acceleration $\vec{a}_{av}$

As an object undergoes a displacement during a time interval Δt, its average acceleration is its change in velocity, $\Delta\vec{v}$, divided by Δt:

$$\text{Average acceleration} = \vec{a}_{av} = \frac{\vec{v}_2 - \vec{v}_1}{t_2 - t_1} = \frac{\Delta\vec{v}}{\Delta t}. \tag{3.4}$$

Average acceleration is a vector quantity in the same direction as the vector $\Delta\vec{v}$. In Chapter 2, we stressed that acceleration is a quantitative description of the

To find the car's average acceleration between P_1 and P_2, we first find the change in velocity $\Delta\vec{v}$ by subtracting $\vec{v}_1$ from $\vec{v}_2$. (Notice that $\vec{v}_1 + \Delta\vec{v} = \vec{v}_2$.)

The average acceleration has the same direction as the change in velocity, $\Delta\vec{v}$.

(a)   (b)   (c)

▲ **FIGURE 3.4** Finding the average acceleration between two points in the x-y plane.

way an object's motion is *changing* with time. Figure 3.4b shows that the **final velocity $\vec{v}_2$ (at time t_2) is the vector sum of the original velocity $\vec{v}_1$ (at time t_1) and the change in velocity, $\Delta\vec{v}$, during the interval Δt.**

We define the **instantaneous acceleration** $\vec{a}$ at point P_1 as follows (Figure 3.5):

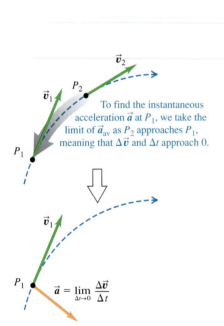

To find the instantaneous acceleration $\vec{a}$ at P_1, we take the limit of $\vec{a}_{av}$ as P_2 approaches P_1, meaning that $\Delta\vec{v}$ and Δt approach 0.

$\vec{a} = \lim\limits_{\Delta t \to 0} \dfrac{\Delta\vec{v}}{\Delta t}$

▲ **FIGURE 3.5** The instantaneous acceleration of a point in the x-y plane.

Definition of instantaneous acceleration $\vec{a}$

When the velocity of a particle changes by an amount $\Delta\vec{v}$ as the particle undergoes a displacement $\Delta\vec{r}$ during a time interval Δt, the instantaneous acceleration is the limit of the average acceleration as Δt approaches zero:

$$\text{Instantaneous acceleration} = \vec{a} = \lim\limits_{\Delta t \to 0} \dfrac{\Delta\vec{v}}{\Delta t}. \qquad (3.5)$$

The instantaneous acceleration vector at point P_1 in Figure 3.5 does *not* have the same direction as the instantaneous velocity vector $\vec{v}$ at that point; in general, there is no reason it should. (Recall from Chapter 2 that the velocity and acceleration components of a particle moving along a line could have opposite signs.) The construction in Figure 3.5 shows that the acceleration vector must always point toward the *concave* side of the curved path. **When a particle moves in a curved path, it *always* has nonzero acceleration, even when it moves with constant speed.** More generally, acceleration is associated with change of speed, change of direction of velocity, or both.

◀ **Can you spot the three accelerators?** Almost anyone will recognize the gas pedal as an accelerator—pressing it makes the car speed up. As a physics student, you probably also recognize the brake pedal as an accelerator—it slows the car. The third accelerator is the steering wheel, which changes the *direction* of the car's velocity.

(a) Components of average acceleration for the interval from P_1 to P_2.

(b) Components of instantaneous acceleration at P_1.

▲ **FIGURE 3.6** Components of average and instantaneous acceleration.

We often represent the acceleration of a particle in terms of the components of this vector quantity. Like Figure 3.2, Figure 3.6 shows the motion of a particle as described in a rectangular coordinate system. During a time interval Δt, the velocity of the particle changes by an amount $\Delta \vec{v}$, with components Δv_x and Δv_y. So we can represent the average acceleration $\vec{a}_{av}$ in terms of its x and y components:

$$a_{av,x} = \frac{\Delta v_x}{\Delta t}, \qquad a_{av,y} = \frac{\Delta v_y}{\Delta t}. \tag{3.6}$$

Similarly, the x and y components of instantaneous acceleration, a_x and a_y, are

$$a_x = \lim_{\Delta t \to 0} \frac{\Delta v_x}{\Delta t}, \qquad a_y = \lim_{\Delta t \to 0} \frac{\Delta v_y}{\Delta t}.$$

If we know the components a_x and a_y, we can find the magnitude and direction of the acceleration vector $\vec{a}$, just as we did with velocity:

$$|\vec{a}| = a = \sqrt{a_x^2 + a_y^2}, \qquad \theta = \tan^{-1} \frac{a_y}{a_x}. \tag{3.7}$$

The angle θ gives the direction of $\vec{a}$, measured counterclockwise from the $+x$ axis.

EXAMPLE 3.2 **The model car again**

Let's look again at the radio-controlled model car in Example 3.1. Suppose that at time $t_1 = 2.00$ s the car has components of velocity $v_x = 1.0$ m/s and $v_y = 3.0$ m/s and that at time $t_2 = 2.50$ s the components are $v_x = 4.0$ m/s and $v_y = 3.0$ m/s. Find **(a)** the components and **(b)** the magnitude and direction of the average acceleration during this interval.

SOLUTION

SET UP Figure 3.7 shows our sketch.

SOLVE Figure 3.6a outlines the relations we'll use.

Part (a): To find the components of average acceleration, we need the components of the change in velocity, Δv_x and Δv_y, and the time interval, which is $\Delta t = 0.50$ s. The change in v_x is $\Delta v_x = v_{2x} - v_{1x} = (4.0\ \text{m/s} - 1.0\ \text{m/s}) = 3.0\ \text{m/s}$, so the x component of average acceleration in the interval $\Delta t = 0.50$ s is

$$a_{\text{av},x} = \frac{\Delta v_x}{\Delta t} = \frac{3.0\ \text{m/s}}{0.50\ \text{s}} = 6.0\ \text{m/s}^2.$$

The change in v_y is zero, so $a_{\text{av},y}$ in this interval is also zero.

Part (b): The vector $\vec{a}_{\text{av}}$ has only an x component. The vector points in the $+x$ direction and has magnitude 6.0 m/s^2.

REFLECT We can always represent a vector quantity (such as displacement, velocity, or acceleration) either in terms of its components or in terms of its magnitude and direction.

▲ **FIGURE 3.7** Our sketch for this problem.

An acceleration parallel to an object's velocity changes the magnitude, but not the direction, of the velocity; the object moves in a straight line with changing speed.

(a)

An acceleration perpendicular to an object's velocity changes the direction, but not the magnitude, of the velocity; the object follows a curved path at constant speed.

(b)

▲ **FIGURE 3.8** Two special cases: acceleration (a) parallel and (b) perpendicular to an object's velocity.

Figure 3.8 shows two special cases. In Figure 3.8a, the acceleration vector $\vec{a}$ is *parallel* to the velocity vector $\vec{v}_1$. (In Fig. 3.8a, $\vec{a}$ points in the same direction as $\vec{v}$; it could alternatively point in the opposite direction.) Then, because $\vec{a}$ gives the rate of change of velocity, the *change* in $\vec{v}$ during a small time interval Δt is a vector $\Delta\vec{v}$ that has the same direction as $\vec{a}$ and hence the same direction as $\vec{v}_1$. As a result, the velocity $\vec{v}_2$ at the end of Δt, given by $\vec{v}_2 = \vec{v}_1 + \Delta\vec{v}$, is a vector having the *same direction* as $\vec{v}_1$ but somewhat greater (or smaller) magnitude.

In Figure 3.8b, the acceleration $\vec{a}$ is *perpendicular* to the velocity $\vec{v}$. In a small time interval Δt, the change $\Delta\vec{v}$ in the velocity vector $\vec{v}$ is a vector very nearly perpendicular to $\vec{v}_1$, as shown. Again, $\vec{v}_2 = \vec{v}_1 + \Delta\vec{v}$, but in this case $\vec{v}_1$ and $\vec{v}_2$ have different directions. As the time interval Δt approaches zero, the angle ϕ in the figure also approaches zero. In this limit, $\Delta\vec{v}$ becomes perpendicular to *both* $\vec{v}_1$ and $\vec{v}_2$, and the two vectors have the same magnitude.

We conclude that when $\vec{a}$ is *parallel* (or antiparallel) to $\vec{v}$, its effect is to change the magnitude of $\vec{v}$, but not its direction. When $\vec{a}$ is *perpendicular* to $\vec{v}$, its effect is to change the direction of $\vec{v}$, but not its magnitude. In general, $\vec{a}$ may have components *both* parallel and perpendicular to $\vec{v}_1$, but the preceding statements are still valid for the individual components. In particular, when an object travels along a curved path with constant speed, its acceleration is *not* zero, even though the magnitude of $\vec{v}$ does not change. In this case, the acceleration is always perpendicular to $\vec{v}$ at each point. For example, when a particle moves in a circle with constant speed, the acceleration at each instant is directed toward the center of the circle. We'll consider this special case in detail in Section 3.4.

3.3 Projectile Motion

A **projectile** is any object that is given an initial velocity and then follows a path determined entirely by the effects of gravitational acceleration and air resistance. A batted baseball, a thrown football, and a package dropped from an airplane are all examples of projectiles. The path followed by a projectile is called its *trajectory.*

To analyze this common type of motion, we'll start with an idealized model. We represent the projectile as a single particle with an acceleration (due to the earth's gravitational pull) that is constant in both magnitude and direction. We'll neglect the effects of air resistance and the curvature and rotation of the earth. Like all models, this one has limitations. The curvature of the earth has to be considered in the flight of long-range ballistic missiles, and air resistance is of crucial importance to a skydiver. Nevertheless, we can learn a lot by analyzing this simple model.

We first notice that projectile motion is always confined to a vertical plane determined by the direction of the initial velocity. We'll call this plane the *x-y coordinate plane,* with the x axis horizontal and the y axis directed vertically upward. Figure 3.9 shows a view of this plane from the side, along with a typical trajectory.

The key to analyzing projectile motion is the fact that *we can treat the x and y coordinates separately.* Why is this so? Anticipating a relation that we'll study in detail in Chapter 4, we note that the instantaneous acceleration of an object is proportional to (and in the same direction as) the net *force* acting on the object. Because of the assumptions made in our model, the only force acting on the projectile is the earth's gravitational attraction; we assume that this is constant in magnitude and always vertically downward in direction. Thus the vertical component of acceleration is the same as if the projectile moved only in the y direction, as it did in Section 2.6. Figure 3.10 shows two trajectories; the vertical displacements of the two objects at any time are the same, even though their horizontal displacements are different.

We conclude that the x component of acceleration, a_x, is zero and the y component a_y is constant and equal in magnitude to the acceleration of free fall:

$$a_x = 0; \qquad a_y = -g = -9.80 \text{ m/s}^2.$$

NOTE ▶ Remember that, by definition, g is always positive (because it is the magnitude of the acceleration vector due to gravity), but with our choice of coordinate directions, a_y is negative. ◀

So we can think of projectile motion as a combination of horizontal motion with constant velocity and vertical motion with constant acceleration. We can then express all the vector relationships in terms of separate equations for the horizontal and vertical components. The actual motion is a combination of of these separate motions. Figure 3.11 shows the horizontal and vertical components of motion for a projectile that starts at (or passes through) the origin of coordinates at time $t = 0$. As in Figure 3.10, the projectile is shown at equal time intervals.

The horizontal (x) and vertical (y) components of $\vec{a}$ for a projectile are

$$a_x = 0, \qquad a_y = -g.$$

We'll usually use $g = 9.80 \text{ m/s}^2$, but occasionally we'll use $g = 10 \text{ m/s}^2$ for approximate calculations.

Act|v
Physics ONLINE   3.1–3.7

- A projectile moves in a vertical plane that contains the intial velocity vector $\vec{v}_0$.
- Its trajectory depends only on $\vec{v}_0$ and on the acceleration due to gravity.

▲ **FIGURE 3.9** The trajectory of a projectile.

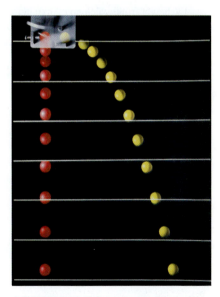

▲ **FIGURE 3.10** Independence of horizontal and vertical motion: At any given time, both balls have the same y position, velocity, and acceleration, despite having different x positions and velocities. Successive images are separated by equal time intervals.

At the top of the trajectory, the projectile has zero vertical velocity, but its vertical acceleration is still $-g$.

Vertically, the projectile exhibits constant-acceleration motion in response to the earth's gravitational pull. Thus, its velocity *changes* by equal amounts during equal time intervals.

$a_y = -g$

Horizontally, the projectile exhibits constant-velocity motion: Its horizontal acceleration is zero, so it moves equal x distances in equal time intervals.

▲ **FIGURE 3.11** Independence of horizontal and vertical motion. In the vertical direction, a projectile behaves like a freely falling object; in the horizontal direction, it moves with constant velocity.

Conceptual Analysis 3.1

Horizontal stone throw

If you throw a stone horizontally out over the surface of a lake, the time it is in the air (i.e., before it hits the water) is determined *only* by

A. the height from which you throw it.
B. the height from which you throw it and its initial speed.
C. its initial speed and the horizontal distance to the point where it splashes down.

SOLUTION As we've just learned, the horizontal and vertical components of a projectile's motion are independent. Therefore, the stone reaches the water at the same time as a rock that was dropped vertically from the same starting height. The time required for the stone to reach the water depends only on the height from which it is thrown, so answer A is the correct one. The *distance* the stone travels before splashing down, however, depends on both the height from which it is thrown and the speed with which it is thrown.

In projectile motion, the vertical and horizontal coordinates both vary with constant-acceleration motion. (The horizontal component of acceleration is constant at zero.) Therefore, we can use the same equations we derived in Section 2.4 for constant-acceleration motion. Here's a reminder of these relationships:

$$v_x = v_{0x} + a_x t, \quad \text{(velocity as a function of time)} \tag{2.8}$$
$$x = x_0 + v_{0x}t + \tfrac{1}{2}a_x t^2, \quad \text{(position as a function of time)} \tag{2.12}$$
$$v_x^2 = v_{0x}^2 + 2a_x(x - x_0). \quad \text{(velocity as a function of position)} \tag{2.13}$$

Our procedure will be to use this set of equations separately for each coordinate. That is, we use this set of equations for the x coordinate, and then we use a second set with all the x's replaced by y's for the y coordinate. Next, we have to choose the appropriate components of the constant acceleration $\vec{a}$ and the initial velocity $\vec{v}_0$. At time $t = 0$, the particle is at the point (x_0, y_0), and its velocity components have the initial values v_{0x} and v_{0y}. The components of acceleration are constant: $a_x = 0$, $a_y = -g$. When we put all the pieces together, here's what we get:

Equations for projectile motion (assuming that $a_x = 0$, $a_y = -g$)
Considering the x motion, we substitute $a_x = 0$ in Equations 2.8 and 2.12, obtaining

$$v_x = v_{0x}, \tag{3.8}$$
$$x = x_0 + v_{0x}t. \tag{3.9}$$

For the y motion, we substitute y for x, v_y for v_x, v_{0y} for v_{0x}, and $-g$ for a to get

$$v_y = v_{0y} - gt \tag{3.10}$$
$$y = y_0 + v_{0y}t - \tfrac{1}{2}gt^2 \tag{3.11}$$

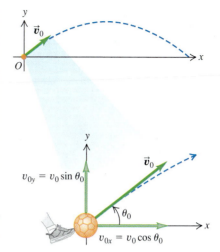

▲ **FIGURE 3.12** The initial velocity of a projectile, showing the components and the launch angle θ_0.

Usually it is simplest to take the initial position (at time $t = 0$) as the origin; in this case, $x_0 = y_0 = 0$. The initial position might be, for example, the position of a ball at the instant it leaves the thrower's hand or the position of a bullet at the instant it leaves the barrel of the gun.

As shown in Figure 3.11, the x component of acceleration for a projectile is zero, so v_x is constant, but v_y changes by equal amounts in equal times, corresponding to a constant y component of acceleration. At the highest point in the trajectory, $v_y = 0$. But a_y is still equal to $-g$ at this point. Make sure you understand why!

We can also represent the initial velocity $\vec{v}_0$ by its magnitude v_0 (the initial speed) and its angle θ_0 with the positive x axis, as shown in Figure 3.12. In terms of these quantities, the components v_{0x} and v_{0y} of initial velocity are

$$v_{0x} = v_0\cos\theta_0, \qquad v_{0y} = v_0\sin\theta_0.$$

Using these relations in Equations 3.8 through 3.11 and setting $x_0 = y_0 = 0$, we obtain the following alternative formulation for projectile motion:

Position and velocity of a projectile as functions of time t
$$x = (v_0\cos\theta_0)t \tag{3.12}$$
$$y = (v_0\sin\theta_0)t - \tfrac{1}{2}gt^2 \tag{3.13}$$
$$v_x = v_0\cos\theta_0 \tag{3.14}$$
$$v_y = v_0\sin\theta_0 - gt \tag{3.15}$$

We can get a lot of information from these equations. For example, the distance r of the projectile from the origin at any time (the magnitude of the position vector $\vec{r}$) is given by

$$r = \sqrt{x^2 + y^2}.$$

The projectile's speed v (the magnitude of its velocity) at any time is

$$v = \sqrt{v_x^2 + v_y^2}.$$

The *direction* of the velocity at any time, in terms of the angle θ it makes with the positive x axis, is given by

$$\theta = \tan^{-1}\frac{v_y}{v_x}.$$

The velocity vector $\vec{v}$ is tangent to the trajectory at each point. Note that v_x is constant, but that the *direction* of the velocity changes because v_y changes continuously.

The formulation just described gives us the coordinates and velocity components of a projectile as functions of time. The actual *shape* of the trajectory is a graph of y as a function of x. We can derive an equation for this relationship from Equations 3.12 and 3.13. First we solve Equation 3.12 for t, and then we

▲ **Which is accelerating the most?** If you answered "none of the above," you are correct. In the photo, one apple and one orange are moving up while the other two fruits are moving down. Despite their different positions and velocities, all four have the same rate of change of velocity. Like all freely falling objects near the earth's surface, they are accelerating downward at 9.8 m/s². The apple and orange moving up are losing upward velocity at exactly the same rate the other two fruits are gaining downward velocity. Even at the highest point of their path, where for an instant they move neither upward nor downward, they have the same acceleration, a rate of change in velocity of 9.8 m/s² toward the center of the earth.

▲ **FIGURE 3.13** Strobe photo of a bouncing ball; the images are separated by equal time intervals. The ball follows a parabolic trajectory after each bounce. It rises a little less after each bounce because it loses energy during each collision with the floor.

substitute the resulting expression for t into Equation 3.13 and simplify the result. We find that $t = x/(v_0 \cos\theta_0)$ and

$$y = v_0 \sin\theta_0 \left(\frac{x}{v_0 \cos\theta_0}\right) - \frac{1}{2}g\left(\frac{x}{v_0 \cos\theta_0}\right)^2,$$

$$y = (\tan\theta_0)x - \left(\frac{g}{2v_0{}^2 \cos^2\theta_0}\right)x^2.$$

Don't worry about the details of this equation; the important point is its general form. The quantities v_0, $\tan\theta_0$, $\cos\theta_0$, and g are all constants, so the equation is a relation between the variables x and y, with the general form

$$y = bx - cx^2,$$

where b and c are positive constants. This is the equation of a *parabola*. With projectile motion, for our simple model, the trajectory is always a parabola (Figure 3.13).

Horizontal paintball shot

A paintball is shot horizontally in the positive x direction. At time Δt after the ball is shot, it is 3 cm to the right and 3 cm below its starting point. Over the next interval Δt, the *changes* in horizontal and vertical position are

A. $\Delta x = 3$ cm, $\Delta y = -3$ cm;
B. $\Delta x = 3$ cm, $\Delta y = -9$ cm;
C. $\Delta x = 6$ cm, $\Delta y = -6$ cm.

SOLUTION The ball is a projectile, so we assume that its horizontal component of velocity is constant. Therefore, the changes

Δx in horizontal position during equal time intervals are equal. This result rules out choice C. Because the ball speeds up as it falls, the second Δy must be larger than the first, eliminating answer A. However, is answer B correct? With constant acceleration, the distance of fall from rest is proportional to t^2. This means that, as time increases from 1 to 2 to 3 in units of t, the distance fallen will be y, $4y$, and $9y$, or -3 cm, -12 cm, and -27 cm, in vertical height. The change in y from one time interval to the next is -3 cm, -9 cm $[= -12$ cm $- (-3$ cm$)]$, and -15 cm $[= -27$ cm $- (-12$ cm$)]$. The ratio of these numbers is $1:3:5$, the sequence of odd integers. Answer B is correct.

EXAMPLE 3.3 **Paintball gun**

The contestant in Figure 3.14 shoots a paintball horizontally at a speed of 75.0 m/s from a point 1.50 m above the ground. The ball misses its target and hits the ground. **(a)** For how many seconds is the ball in the air? **(b)** Find the maximum horizontal displacement (which we'll call the *range* of the ball). Ignore air resistance.

SOLUTION

SET UP We choose to place the origin of the coordinate system at ground level, directly below the end of the gun barrel, as shown in Figure 3.15. (This choice of position of the origin avoids having to deal with negative values of y, a modest convenience.) Then $x_0 = 0$ and $y_0 = 1.50$ m. The gun is fired horizon-

tally, so $v_{0x} = 75.0$ m/s and $v_{0y} = 0$. The final position of the ball, at ground level, is $y = 0$.

SOLVE Part (a): We're asked to find the total time the paintball is in the air. This is equal to the time it would take the paintball to fall vertically from its initial height to the ground. In each case, the vertical position is given as a function of time by Equation 3.11,

▲ **FIGURE 3.14**

▲ **FIGURE 3.15** Our sketch for this problem.

Continued

$y = y_0 + v_{0y}t - \frac{1}{2}gt^2$. In this problem, $y_0 = 1.5$ m, $y = 0$, and $v_{0y} = 0$, so that equation becomes simply

$$0 = y_0 - \tfrac{1}{2}gt^2.$$

We need to find the time t. Solving for t, and substituting numerical values, we obtain

$$t = \sqrt{\frac{2y_0}{g}} = \sqrt{\frac{2(1.50 \text{ m})}{9.80 \text{ m/s}^2}} = 0.553 \text{ s.}$$

Part (b): Now that we know the time t of the ball's flight through the air, we can find the range—that is, the horizontal distance x it travels during time t. We use Equation 3.9: $x = x_0 + v_{0x}t$. Setting $x_0 = 0$, we find that

$$x = x_0 + v_{0x}t = 0 + (75.0 \text{ m/s})(0.553 \text{ s}) = 41.5 \text{ m.}$$

REFLECT Actual ranges of paintballs are less than this, typically about 30 m. The difference is due primarily to air resistance, which decreases the horizontal component of velocity.

Practice Problem: If air resistance is neglected, what initial speed is required for a range of 20 m? *Answer:* 36.1 m/s.

PROBLEM-SOLVING STRATEGY 3.1   Projectile motion

The strategies that we used in Sections 2.4 and 2.6 for solving straight-line, constant-acceleration motion problems are equally useful for projectile motion.

SET UP

1. Define your coordinate system and make a sketch showing your axes. Usually, it is easiest to place the origin at the initial $(t = 0)$ position of the projectile, with the x axis horizontal and the y axis upward. Then $x_0 = 0$, $y_0 = 0$, $a_x = 0$, and $a_y = -g$.
2. List the known and unknown quantities. In some problems, the components (or magnitude and direction) of initial velocity will be given, and you can use Equations 3.12 through 3.15 to find the coordinates and velocity components at some later time. In other problems, you might be given two points on the trajectory and be asked to find the initial velocity. Be sure you know which quantities are given and which are to be found.
3. It often helps to state the problem in prose and then translate into symbols. For example, *when* does the particle arrive at a certain point (i.e, at what value of t)? *Where* is the particle when a velocity component has a certain value? (That is, what are the values of x and y when v_x or v_y has the specified value?)

SOLVE

4. At the highest point in a trajectory, $v_y = 0$. So the question "When does the projectile reach its highest point?" translates into "What is the value of t when $v_y = 0$?" Similarly, if $y_0 = 0$, then "When does the projectile return to its initial elevation?" translates into "What is the value of t when $y = 0$?" and so on.
5. Resist the temptation to break the trajectory into segments and analyze each one separately. You don't have to start all over, with a new axis system and a new time scale, when the projectile reaches its highest point. It is usually easier to set up Equations 3.8 through 3.11 (or Equations 3.12 through 3.15) at the start and use the same axes and time scale throughout the problem.

REFLECT

6. Try to make rough estimates as to what your answers should be, and then ask whether your calculations confirm your estimates. Ask, "Does this result make sense?"

▲ **Rocket scientist?** This African bombardier beetle may not be studying physics, but it is demonstrating the fundamental concept known as projectile motion. A chemical reaction inside the rocket bug produces the pressure that propels a hot liquid into the face of a would-be predator, allowing the bug to escape. Whether the projectile is a solid or a liquid, it is subject to the same laws of motion. If the beetle gets the angle θ_0 too wrong, it misses the predator and becomes a hot lunch.

EXAMPLE 3.4 **A home-run hit**

A home-run baseball is hit with an initial speed $v_0 = 37.0$ m/s at an initial angle $\theta_0 = 53.1°$. **(a)** Find the ball's position, and the magnitude and direction of its velocity, when $t = 2.00$ s. **(b)** Find the time when the ball reaches the highest point of its flight, and find its height h at that point. **(c)** Find the horizontal range R (the horizontal distance from the starting point to the point where the ball hits the ground).

SOLUTION

SET UP The ball is probably struck a meter or so above ground level, but we'll neglect this small distance and assume that it starts at ground level $(y_0 = 0)$. Figure 3.16 shows our sketch. We place the origin of coordinates at the starting point, so $x_0 = 0$. The components of initial velocity are

$$v_{0x} = v_0 \cos\theta_0 = (37.0 \text{ m/s})(0.600) = 22.2 \text{ m/s},$$
$$v_{0y} = v_0 \sin\theta_0 = (37.0 \text{ m/s})(0.800) = 29.6 \text{ m/s}.$$

SOLVE Part (a): We ignore the efffects of the air. We want to find x, y, v_x, and v_y at time $t = 2.00$ s. We substitute these values into Equations 3.8 through 3.11, along with the value $t = 2.00$ s. The coordinates at $t = 2.00$ s are

$$x = v_{0x}t = (22.2 \text{ m/s})(2.00 \text{ s}) = 44.4 \text{ m},$$
$$y = v_{0y}t - \tfrac{1}{2}gt^2$$
$$= (29.6 \text{ m/s})(2.00 \text{ s}) - \tfrac{1}{2}(9.80 \text{ m/s}^2)(2.00 \text{ s})^2 = 39.6 \text{ m}.$$

The components v_x and v_y of the velocity vector $\vec{v}$ at time $t = 2.00$ s are

$$v_x = v_{0x} = 22.2 \text{ m/s},$$
$$v_y = v_{0y} - gt = 29.6 \text{ m/s} + (-9.80 \text{ m/s}^2)(2.00 \text{ s})$$
$$= 10.0 \text{ m/s}.$$

The magnitude and direction of the velocity vector $\vec{v}$ at time $t = 2.00$ s are, respectively,

$$v = \sqrt{v_x^2 + v_y^2} = \sqrt{(22.2 \text{ m/s})^2 + (10.0 \text{ m/s})^2} = 24.3 \text{ m/s},$$
$$\theta = \tan^{-1}\frac{10.0 \text{ m/s}}{22.2 \text{ m/s}} = \tan^{-1}0.450 = 24.2°.$$

Part (b): At the highest point in the ball's path, the vertical velocity component v_y is zero. When does this happen? Call that time t_1; then, using $v_y = v_{0y} - gt$, we find that

$$v_y = 0 = 29.6 \text{ m/s} - (9.80 \text{ m/s}^2)t_1,$$
$$t_1 = 3.02 \text{ s}.$$

The height h at this time is the value of y when $t = 3.02$ s. We use Equation 3.11,

$$y = y_0 + v_{0y}t + \tfrac{1}{2}(-g)t^2,$$

to obtain

$$h = 0 + (29.6 \text{ m/s})(3.02 \text{ s}) + \tfrac{1}{2}(-9.80 \text{ m/s}^2)(3.02 \text{ s})^2$$
$$= 44.7 \text{ m}.$$

Alternatively, we can use the constant-acceleration formula

$$v_y^2 = v_{0y}^2 + 2a(y - y_0) = v_{0y}^2 + 2(-g)(y - y_0).$$

At the highest point, $v_y = 0$ and $y = h$. Substituting these in, along with $y_0 = 0$, we find that

$$0 = (29.6 \text{ m/s})^2 - 2(9.80 \text{ m/s}^2)h,$$
$$h = 44.7 \text{ m}.$$

This is roughly half the height of the Toronto Skydome above the playing field.

Part (c): To find the range R, we start by asking *when* the ball hits the ground. This occurs when $y = 0$. Call that time t_2; then, from Equation 3.11,

$$y = 0 = (29.6 \text{ m/s})t_2 + \tfrac{1}{2}(-9.80 \text{ m/s}^2)t_2^2.$$

This is a quadratic equation for t_2; it has two roots:

$$t_2 = 0 \qquad \text{and} \qquad t_2 = 6.04 \text{ s}.$$

There are two times at which $y = 0$: $t_2 = 0$ is the time the ball *leaves* the ground, and $t_2 = 6.04$ s is the time of its return. The latter is exactly twice the time taken to reach the highest point, so the time of descent equals the time of ascent. (This is *always* true if the starting and ending points are at the same elevation and air resistance is neglected. We'll prove it in Example 3.5.)

The range R is the value of x when the ball returns to the ground—that is, when $t = 6.04$ s:

$$R = v_{0x}t_2 = (22.2 \text{ m/s})(6.04 \text{ s}) = 134 \text{ m}.$$

▲ **FIGURE 3.16** Our sketch for this problem.

Continued

For comparison, the distance from home plate to center field at Pittsburgh's PNC Park is 399 ft (about 122 m). If we could neglect air resistance, the ball really would be a home run.

At the instant the ball returns to $y = 0$, its vertical component of velocity is

$$v_y = 29.6 \text{ m/s} + (-9.80 \text{ m/s}^2)(6.04 \text{ s}) = -29.6 \text{ m/s}.$$

That is, v_y has the same magnitude as the initial vertical velocity v_{0y}, but the opposite sign. Since v_x is constant, the angle $\theta = -53.1°$ (below the horizontal) at this point is the negative of the initial angle $\theta_0 = 53.1°$.

REFLECT The actual values of the maximum height h and the range R are substantially less than the values we've found, because

air resistance is *not* negligible. In fact, the range of a batted ball is substantially greater (on the order of 10 m for a home-run ball) in Denver than in Pittsburgh, because the density of air is almost 20% less in Denver.

Practice Problem: If the ball could continue to travel *below* its original level (through an appropriately shaped hole in the ground), then negative values of y corresponding to times greater than 6.04 s would be possible. Compute the ball's position and velocity 8.00 s after the start of its flight. *Answers:* $x = 178$ m, $y = -76.8$ m, $v_x = 22.2$ m/s, $v_y = -48.8$ m/s.

EXAMPLE 3.5   Range and maximum height of a home-run ball

For the situation of Example 3.4, derive general expressions for the maximum height h and the range R of a ball hit with an initial speed v_0 at an angle θ_0 above the horizontal (between 0 and 90°). For a given v_0, what value of θ_0 gives the maximum height? The maximum horizontal range?

SOLUTION

SET UP We can use the same coordinate system and diagram as for Example 3.4, so $y_0 = 0$.

SOLVE The basic relations are Equations 3.12 through 3.15. The solution will follow the same pattern as in Example 3.4, but now no numerical values are given. Thus the results won't be numbers, but rather symbolic expressions from which we can extract general relationships and proportionalities.

First, for a given θ_0, *when* does the projectile reach its highest point? At this point, $v_y = 0$, so, from Equation 3.15, the time t_1 at the highest point ($y = h$) is given by

$$v_y = v_0 \sin\theta_0 - gt_1 = 0, \qquad t_1 = \frac{v_0 \sin\theta_0}{g}.$$

Next, in terms of v_0 and θ_0, what is the value of y at this time? From Equations 3.10 and 3.13,

$$h = v_{0y}t - \tfrac{1}{2}gt^2 = v_0 \sin\theta_0 \left(\frac{v_0 \sin\theta_0}{g}\right) - \tfrac{1}{2}g\left(\frac{v_0 \sin\theta_0}{g}\right)^2,$$

$$h = \frac{v_0^2 \sin^2\theta_0}{2g}.$$

To derive a general expression for the range R, we again follow the procedure we used in Example 3.4. First we find an expression for the time t_2 when the projectile returns to its initial elevation. At that time, $y = 0$; from Equation 3.13,

$$t_2(v_0 \sin\theta_0 - \tfrac{1}{2}gt_2) = 0.$$

The two roots of this quadratic equation for t_2 are $t_2 = 0$ (the launch time) and $t_2 = 2v_0 \sin\theta_0/g$. The range R is the value of x at

the *second* time. Substituting this expression for t_2 into Equation 3.12, we find that

$$R = (v_0 \cos\theta_0)\frac{2v_0 \sin\theta_0}{g}.$$

We now use the trigonometric identity $2\sin\theta_0 \cos\theta_0 = \sin 2\theta_0$ to rewrite this equation as

$$R = \frac{v_0^2 \sin 2\theta_0}{g}.$$

REFLECT If we vary θ_0, the *maximum* value of h occurs when $\sin\theta_0 = 1$ and $\theta_0 = 90°$, in other words, when the ball is hit straight up. That's what we should expect. In that case, $h = v_0^2/2g$. If the ball is launched horizontally, then $\theta_0 = 0$, and the maximum height is zero! The maximum range R occurs when $\sin 2\theta_0$ has its greatest value, namely, unity. That occurs when $2\theta_0 = 90°$, or $\theta_0 = 45°$. This angle gives the maximum range for a given initial speed.

Note that both h and R are proportional to the *square* of the initial speed v_0; this relationship may be a little surprising. If we double the initial speed, the range and maximum height increase by a factor of four! We can also use the proportional-reasoning methods of Section 2.5, along with the equations for h and R just derived, to confirm that both of these quantities are proportional to v_0^2 and inversely proportional to g.

Practice Problem: Show that the range is the same when the launch angle is 30° as when it is 60° and that it is the same for any launch angle θ_0 as for the complementary angle $(90° - \theta_0)$. *Answer:* $\sin\phi = \sin(180° - \phi)$, so $\sin 2\theta_0 = \sin 2(90° - \theta_0)$.

◄ **Faster than a speeding bullet?** In a human cannonball act, the cannon must be angled so that the human projectile lands in the net. If the available space is short, this angle will be higher than 45°. Also, allowance must be made for the level of the net—it may be higher or lower than the level of the muzzle. Finally, a human cannonball is *not* an ideal projectile—air resistance has to be taken into account.

NOTE ▶ We don't recommend memorizing the equations for h and R. They are applicable only in the special circumstances that we have described. In particular, they are valid *only* when the launch and landing heights are equal. You may encounter problems to which these equations are *not* applicable. ◄

Figure 3.17 is based on a composite photograph of three trajectories of a ball projected from a spring gun at angles of $< 45°$, $45°$, and $> 45°$. The initial speed v_0 is approximately the same in all three cases. The horizontal ranges are nearly the same for the smallest and largest angles, and the range for $45°$ is greater than either.

Symmetry in Projectile Motion

Comparing the expressions for t_1 and t_2 in Example 3.5, we see that $t_2 = 2t_1$; that is, the total flight time is twice the time required to reach the highest point. It follows that the time required to reach the highest point equals the time required to fall from there back to the initial elevation, as we asserted in Example 3.4. More generally, Figure 3.11 shows that the path of the particle is symmetric about the highest point.

A 45° launch angle gives the greatest range; other angles fall shorter.

▲ **FIGURE 3.17** A firing angle of 45° gives the maximum horizontal range (based on a strobe photo).

Conceptual Analysis 3.3   **Throwing stones**

Two stones are launched from the top of a tall building. One stone is thrown in a direction 20° above the horizontal with a speed of 10 m/s; the other is thrown in a direction 20° below the horizontal with the same speed. How do their speeds compare just before they hit the ground below? (Neglect air friction.)

A. The one thrown upward is traveling faster.
B. The one thrown downward is traveling faster.
C. Both are traveling at the same speed.

SOLUTION We've just learned that the portion of a projectile's trajectory that lies above the initial height will be symmetric about its highest point. Thus, when the stone launched upward comes back to the level of the building's top, it is moving at 10 m/s in a direction 20° below the horizontal (symmetric to its launch velocity). At this point, it has the same speed and angle as the stone launched downward. The velocities of the two stones therefore match exactly at any position below the top of the building. So answer C is correct.

EXAMPLE 3.6   Kicking a field goal

For a field goal attempt, a football is kicked from a point on the ground that is a horizontal distance s from the goalpost. For the attempt to be successful, the ball must clear the crossbar, 10 ft (about 3.05 m) above the ground, as shown in Figure 3.18.

The ball leaves the kicker's foot with an initial speed of 20.0 m/s at an angle of 30° above the horizontal. What is the distance d between kicker and goalpost if the ball barely clears the crossbar?

The ball can pass over the goalposts on the way up or on the way down, so there are two possible values of x.

▲ **FIGURE 3.18** Kicking a field goal.

Continued

SOLUTION

SET UP We use our idealized model of projectile motion, in which we assume level ground, neglect effects of air resistance, and treat the football as a point particle. We place the origin of coordinates at the point where the ball is kicked. Then $x_0 = y_0 = 0$,

$v_{0x} = v_0 \cos 30.0° = (20.0 \text{ m/s})(0.866) = 17.3 \text{ m/s}$, and
$v_{0y} = v_0 \sin 30.0° = (20.0 \text{ m/s})(0.500) = 10.0 \text{ m/s}$.

SOLVE We first ask *when* (i.e., at what value of t) the ball is at a height of 3.05 m above the ground; then we find the value of x at that time. When that value of x is equal to the distance d, the ball is just barely passing over the crossbar.

To find the time t when $y = 3.05$ m, we use the equation $y = y_0 + v_{0y}t - \frac{1}{2}gt^2$. Substituting numerical values, we obtain

$$3.05 \text{ m} = (10.0 \text{ m/s})t - (4.90 \text{ m/s}^2)t^2.$$

This is a quadratic equation; to solve it, we first write it in standard form: $(4.90 \text{ m/s}^2)t^2 - (10.0 \text{ m/s})t + 3.05 \text{ m} = 0$. Then we use the quadratic formula. (See Appendix A if you need to review it.) We get

$$t = \frac{1}{2(4.9 \text{ m/s}^2)}$$
$$\times \left(10.0 \text{ m/s} \pm \sqrt{(10.0 \text{ m/s})^2 - 4(4.90 \text{ m/s}^2)(3.05 \text{ m})}\right)$$
$$= 0.373 \text{ s}, 1.67 \text{ s}.$$

There are two roots: $t = 0.373$ s and $t = 1.67$ s. The ball passes the height 3.05 m twice, once on the way up and once on the way down. We need to find the value of x at each of these times, using the equation for x as a function of time. Because $x_0 = 0$, we have simply $x = v_{0x}t$. For $t = 0.373$ s, we get $x = d_1 = (17.3 \text{ m/s})(0.373 \text{ s}) = 6.45$ m, and for $t = 1.67$ s, we get $x = d_2 = (17.3 \text{ m/s})(1.67 \text{ s}) = 28.9$ m. So if the goalpost is located between 6.45 m and 28.9 m from the initial point, the ball will pass over the crossbar; otherwise it will pass under it.

REFLECT The distance of 28.9 m is about 32 yards; field goal attempts are often successful at that distance. The ball passes the height $y = 10$ ft twice, once on the way up (when $t = 0.373$ s) and once on the way down (when $t = 1.67$ s). To verify this, we could calculate v_y at both times; when we do, we find that it is positive (upward) at $t = 0.373$ s and negative (downward) with the same magnitude at $t = 1.67$ s.

Practice Problem: If the kicker gives the ball the same initial speed and angle, but the ball is kicked from a point 25 m from the goalpost, what is the height of the ball above the crossbar as it crosses over the goalpost? *Answer:* 1.2 m.

EXAMPLE 3.7 **Robin Hood shoots a pear**

In a festival competition, the great archer Robin Hood is challenged to hit a falling pear with an arrow. At the sound of a horn, he is to shoot his arrow, and at the same instant the pear will be dropped from the top of a tall tower. As shown in Figure 3.19, Robin Hood aims *directly* at the initial position of the pear, seemingly making no allowance for the fact that the pear is dropping as the arrow moves toward it. His rivals assume that this is a mistake, but to their shock, he hits the pear. Show that if the arrow is aimed directly at the initial position of the pear, it will *always* hit the pear, regardless of the pear's initial location or initial speed (assuming that neither pear nor arrow hits the ground first).

▲ **FIGURE 3.19** Robin Hood's shot.

Continued

SOLUTION

SET UP To show that the arrow hits the pear, we have to prove that there is some time when the arrow and the pear have the same x and y coordinates. We place the origin at the point from which Robin Hood shoots the arrow. Figure 3.19 shows that, initially, the pear is a horizontal distance s and a vertical distance $h = s\tan\theta_0$ from this point. First, we derive an expression for the time when the x coordinates are the same. Then we ask whether the y coordinates are *also* the same at this time; if they are, the arrow hits the pear.

SOLVE The pear drops straight down, so for it, $x_{\text{pear}} = s$ at *all* times. For the arrow, x_{arrow} is given by Equation 3.12: $x_{\text{arrow}} = (v_0\cos\theta_0)t$. The time when the x coordinates of the arrow and pear are equal (i.e., $x_{\text{pear}} = x_{\text{arrow}}$) is given by $s = (v_0\cos\theta_0)t$, or

$$t = \frac{s}{v_0\cos\theta_0}.$$

Now we ask whether y_{arrow} and y_{pear} are also equal at this time; if they are, we have a hit. The pear is in one-dimensional free fall, and its position at *any* time t is given by Equation 3.11, that is, $y = y_0 + v_{0y}t - \frac{1}{2}gt^2$. The initial height is $y_0 = s\tan\theta_0$, the initial y component of velocity v_y is zero, and we find that

$$y_{\text{pear}} = s\tan\theta_0 - \frac{1}{2}gt^2.$$

For the arrow, we use Equation 3.13:

$$y_{\text{arrow}} = (v_0\sin\theta_0)t - \frac{1}{2}gt^2.$$

If the y coordinates are equal $(y_{\text{pear}} = y_{\text{arrow}})$ at the same time that $t = s/v_0\cos\theta_0$, the time when their x coordinates are equal, we have a hit. We see that this happens if $s\tan\theta_0 = (v_0\sin\theta_0)t$ at time $t = s/v_0\cos\theta_0$ (the time when the x coordinates are equal).

When we substitute this expression for t into the preceding equation, the right side becomes

$$(v_0\sin\theta_0)t = (v_0\sin\theta_0)\frac{s}{v_0\cos\theta_0} = s\tan\theta_0.$$

We see that the right side is indeed equal to the left side, showing that, at the time when the x coordinates of pear and arrow are equal, their y coordinates are also equal. Robin Hood wins the contest!

REFLECT We have established the fact that, at the time the x coordinates are equal, the y coordinates are also equal. Thus, an arrow aimed at the initial position of the pear *always* hits it, no matter what v_0 is. With no gravity $(g = 0)$, the pear would remain motionless, and the arrow would travel in a straight line to hit it. With gravity, both objects "fall" the same additional distance $\left(-\frac{1}{2}gt^2\right)$ below their $g = 0$ positions, and the arrow still hits the pear. We can see this explicitly in the expressions for the y positions of the two objects, where the effects of gravity are highlighted:

Arrow:
$$y_{\text{arrow}} = v_{0y}\,t - \tfrac{1}{2}gt^2$$
and
Pear:
$$y_{\text{pear}} = y_{0,\text{pear}} - \tfrac{1}{2}gt^2$$

Effect of gravity is the same for both.

Figure 3.20 shows a comparison of the situations with and without gravity.

Practice Problem: Suppose the pear is released from a height of 6.00 m above Robin's arrow, the arrow is shot at a speed of 30.0 m/s, and the distance between Robin Hood and the base of the tower is 15.0 m. Find the time at which the arrow hits the pear, the distance the pear has fallen, and the height of the arrow above its release point. *Answers:* 0.54 s, 1.4 m, and 4.6 m.

▲ FIGURE 3.20 An explanation of why an arrow that is aimed directly at a falling target always hits it (provided that neither the arrow nor the target hits the ground first).

We mentioned at the beginning of this section that air resistance isn't always negligible. When it has to be included, the calculations become a lot more complicated, because the air-resistance forces depend on velocity and the acceleration is no longer constant. Figure 3.21 shows a computer simulation of the trajectory of the baseball in Example 3.4 for 10 s of flight, with an air-resistance force proportional to the square of the particle's speed. We see that air resistance decreases the maximum height and range substantially, and the trajectory becomes asymmetric. In this case, the initial angle θ_0 that gives maximum range (for a given value of v_0) is less than 45°.

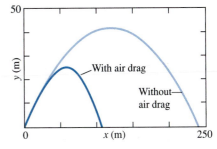

▲ **FIGURE 3.21** Computer-generated trajectories of a baseball with and without air resistance. Air resistance has a large cumulative effect on the flight of a baseball.

Quantitative Analysis 3.4

Shooting at a cliff

Suppose you shoot an arrow across a ravine at the vertical cliff opposite you, a distance d away, as shown in Figure 3.22. On your first try, you aim your arrow 15° above the horizontal, directly toward point A; it strikes the cliff a distance h below point A. On your next try, you aim the arrow 15° below the horizontal, toward point B, shooting it with the same speed. It will strike the cliff

A. the same distance h below point B.
B. less than distance h below point B.
C. more than distance h below point B.

SOLUTION If there were no gravitational force on the arrows, they would travel in straight lines, hitting the cliff at points A and B, respectively. The earth's gravitational attraction causes each arrow to fall below its straight-line path by an amount $\Delta y = -\frac{1}{2}gt^2$ for any time interval t. So, if the two arrows take the same time to reach the cliff, they will have fallen below their aiming points by the same amount $|\Delta y| = h$ when they strike, and answer A will be correct. Do they take the same time to reach the cliff? Remember that the time it takes a projectile to reach a given horizontal position x (the cliff, in this problem) depends on the projectile's horizontal component of velocity v_{0x}: $x - x_0 = v_{0x}t$ (where $x_0 = 0$ in this problem). Because the two arrows are shot at the same initial speed and at angles of 15° with respect to the horizontal, this component of velocity is the same for both. Therefore, the two arrows do in fact take the same time to reach the cliff and strike at equal distances below their aiming points.

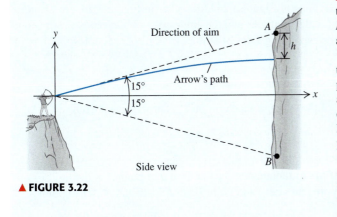

▲ **FIGURE 3.22**

3.4 Uniform Circular Motion

4.1

We discussed components of acceleration in Section 3.2. When a particle moves along a curved path, the direction of its velocity changes. Thus it *must* have a component of acceleration perpendicular to the path, even if its speed is constant.

When a particle moves in a circle with constant speed, the motion is called **uniform circular motion.** A car rounding a curve with a constant radius at constant speed, a satellite moving in a circular orbit, and an ice skater skating in a circle with constant speed are all examples of uniform circular motion. There is no component of acceleration parallel (tangent) to the path; otherwise, the speed would change (Figure 3.23). The component of acceleration perpendicular to the path, which causes the direction of the velocity to change, is related in a simple way to the speed v of the particle and the radius R of the circle. Our next project is to derive that relation.

First we note that this is a different problem from the projectile-motion situation in Section 3.3, in which the acceleration was always straight down and was constant in both magnitude and direction. Here the acceleration is perpendicular

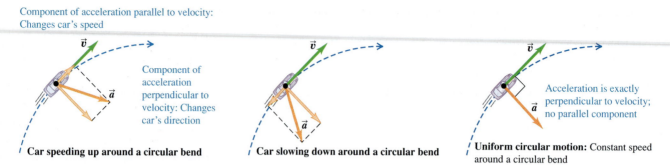

Component of acceleration parallel to velocity: Changes car's speed

Component of acceleration perpendicular to velocity: Changes car's direction

Car speeding up around a circular bend

Car slowing down around a circular bend

Acceleration is exactly perpendicular to velocity; no parallel component

Uniform circular motion: Constant speed around a circular bend

▲ **FIGURE 3.23** In uniform circular motion, an object moves at constant speed in a circular path, and its acceleration is perpendicular to its velocity.

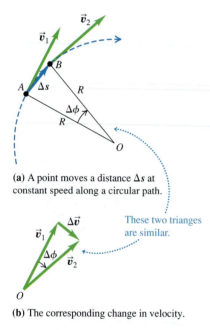

(a) A point moves a distance Δs at constant speed along a circular path.

These two triangles are similar.

(b) The corresponding change in velocity.

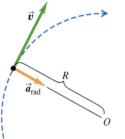

(c) The acceleration in uniform circular motion always points toward the center of the circle.

▲ **FIGURE 3.24** Finding the change in velocity $\vec{v}$ of an object moving in a circle at constant speed.

to the velocity at each instant; as the direction of the velocity changes, the direction of the acceleration also changes. As we will see, the acceleration vector at each point in the circular path is directed toward the *center* of the circle.

Figure 3.24a shows an object (represented by a dot) moving with constant speed in a circular path with radius R and center at O. The object moves from A to B, a distance Δs, in a time Δt. The vector change in velocity $\Delta\vec{v}$ during this time is shown in Figure 3.24b.

The two triangles, one in Figure 3.24a, the other in Figure 3.24b, are *similar,* because both are isosceles triangles and the angles $\Delta\phi$ are the same. From geometry, the ratios of corresponding sides of similar triangles are equal, so

$$\frac{|\Delta\vec{v}|}{v_1} = \frac{\Delta s}{R}, \quad \text{or} \quad |\Delta\vec{v}| = \frac{v_1}{R}\Delta s.$$

The magnitude a_{av} of the average acceleration $\vec{a}_{av}$ during Δt is therefore

$$a_{av} = \frac{|\Delta\vec{v}|}{\Delta t} = \frac{v_1}{R}\frac{\Delta s}{\Delta t}.$$

The magnitude a of the instantaneous acceleration $\vec{a}$ at point A is the limit of this expression as Δt approaches zero and point B gets closer and closer to point A:

$$a = \lim_{\Delta t \to 0}\frac{v_1}{R}\frac{\Delta s}{\Delta t} = \frac{v_1}{R}\lim_{\Delta t \to 0}\frac{\Delta s}{\Delta t}.$$

But the limit of $\Delta s/\Delta t$ is just the *speed* v_1 at point A. Also, A can be any point on the path, and the speed is the same at every point on the path. So we can drop the subscript and let v represent the speed at *any* point. Then we obtain the following relationship:

Acceleration in uniform circular motion
The acceleration of an object in uniform circular motion is *radial*, meaning that it always points toward the center of the circle and is perpendicular to the object's velocity $\vec{v}$. We denote it as $\vec{a}_{rad}$; its magnitude a_{rad} is given by

$$a_{rad} = \frac{v^2}{R}. \tag{3.16}$$

That is, the magnitude a_{rad} is proportional to the square of the speed $(a_{rad} \propto v^2)$ and inversely proportional to the radius $(a_{rad} \propto 1/R)$.

Because the acceleration of an object in uniform circular motion is always directed toward the center of the circle, it is sometimes called **centripetal acceleration.**

▶ **Where am I?** If you've ever used a global positioning system (GPS) unit for navigating or geocaching, you've used an application of uniform circular motion. This system uses a group of 24 satellites to pinpoint locations anywhere on the earth's surface or in the air, often to within as little as 3 meters. Although these satellites are moving at speeds of over 11,000 km/h, their orbits are precisely known, and their exact positions at any instant can be determined. In the field, distance readings taken simultaneously from several of the satellites to a GPS unit provide position vectors that are used to determine precise positions anywhere on the earth.

The word *centripetal* is derived from two Latin words meaning "seeking the center."

Figure 3.25 shows the directions of the velocity and acceleration vectors at several points for an object moving with uniform circular motion. Compare the motion shown in this figure with the projectile motion in Figure 3.11, in which the acceleration is always directed straight down and is *not* perpendicular to the path, except at the highest point in the trajectory.

It may seem odd that the centripetal acceleration is proportional to the *square* of the object's speed, rather simply proportional to the speed. Here's a way to make that relationship more plausible. Suppose that in Figure 3.24 we double the object's speed. This doubles the magnitude of the velocity vector, which would seem to double its rate of change when its direction changes. But note that the direction is also changing twice as rapidly, an effect that, by itself, would double the magnitude of the acceleration. So each of the two effects separately would double a_{rad}, and the combined effect is to increase a_{rad} by a factor of four when v is doubled. Hence we say that a_{rad} is proportional to v^2.

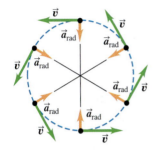

▲ **FIGURE 3.25** For an object in uniform circular motion, the velocity at each point is tangent to the circle, and the acceleration is directed toward the center of the circle.

EXAMPLE 3.8   **Fast car, flat curve**

The 2005 Corvette claims a "lateral acceleration" of 0.92 g, which is $(0.92)(9.8 \text{ m/s}^2) = 8.9 \text{ m/s}^2$. If this represents the maximum centripetal acceleration that can be attained without skidding out of the circular path, and if the car is traveling at a constant 45 m/s (about 101 mi/h), what is the minimum radius of curve the car can negotiate? (Assume that the curve is unbanked.)

SOLUTION

SET UP AND SOLVE Figure 3.26 shows our diagram. The solution is a straightforward application of Equation 3.16. We find that

$$R = \frac{v^2}{a_{rad}} = \frac{(45 \text{ m/s})^2}{8.9 \text{ m/s}^2} = 230 \text{ m} \qquad \left(\text{about } \tfrac{1}{7} \text{ mi}\right).$$

▲ **FIGURE 3.26** Our diagram for this problem.

REFLECT Don't try this at home! The acceleration given represents an absolute maximum with smooth, dry pavement and very grippy tires. If the curve is banked, the radius can be smaller, as we'll see in Chapter 5.

Practice Problem: A more reasonable maximum acceleration for varying pavement conditions is 5.0 m/s². Under these conditions, what is the maximum speed at which a car can negotiate a flat curve with radius 230 m? *Answer:* 34 m/s = 76 mi/h.

EXAMPLE 3.9 **A high-speed carnival ride**

The passengers in a carnival ride travel in a circle with radius 5.0 m (Figure 3.27). They make one complete circle in a time $T = 4.0$ s. What is their acceleration?

SOLUTION

SET UP Figure 3.28 shows our diagram.

SOLVE We again use Equation 3.16: $a = v^2/R$. To find the speed v, we use the fact that a passenger travels a distance equal to the circumference of the circle $(2\pi R)$ in the time T for one revolution:

$$v = \frac{2\pi R}{T} = \frac{2\pi(5.0\ \text{m})}{4.0\ \text{s}} = 7.9\ \text{m/s}.$$

The centripetal acceleration is

$$a_{rad} = \frac{v^2}{R} = \frac{(7.9\ \text{m/s})^2}{5.0\ \text{m}} = 12\ \text{m/s}^2.$$

REFLECT As in Example 3.8, the direction of $\vec{a}$ is always toward the center of the circle. The magnitude of $\vec{a}$ is greater than g, the acceleration due to gravity, so this is not a ride for the faint-hearted. (But some roller coasters subject their passengers to accelerations as great as $4g$.)

Practice Problem: If the ride increases in speed so that $T = 2.0$ s, what is a_{rad}? (This question can be answered by using proportional reasoning, without much arithmetic.) *Answer:* 49 m/s²

▶ **FIGURE 3.27**

▲ **FIGURE 3.28** Our diagram for this problem.

*3.5 Relative Velocity in a Plane

In Section 2.7, we introduced the concept of *relative velocity* for motion along a straight line. We can extend this concept to include motion in a plane by using vector addition to combine velocities. We suggest that you review Section 2.7 as a prelude to this discussion.

Suppose that the woman in Figure 2.29a is walking, not down the aisle of the railroad car, but from one side of the car to the other, with a speed of 1.0 m/s, as shown in Figure 3.29a. We can again describe the woman's position in two different frames of reference: that of the railroad car and that of the ground. Instead of coordinates x, we use position vectors $\vec{r}$. Let W represent the woman's position, C the frame of reference of the stationary ground observer (the cyclist), and T the frame of reference of the moving train. Then, as Figure 3.29b shows, the velocities are related by

$$\vec{v}_{W/C} = \vec{v}_{W/T} + \vec{v}_{T/C}.$$

(a)

(b) Relative velocities (seen from above)

▲ **FIGURE 3.29** (a) A woman walking across a railroad car. (b) Vector diagram for the velocity of the woman relative to the cyclist. Recall that vector addition is commutative.

Relative motion in a plane

When an object W is moving with velocity $\vec{v}_{W/T}$ relative to an object (or observer) T, and T is moving with velocity $\vec{v}_{T/C}$ with respect to an object (or observer) C, the velocity $\vec{v}_{W/C}$ of W with respect to C is given by

$$\vec{v}_{W/C} = \vec{v}_{W/T} + \vec{v}_{T/C}. \tag{3.17}$$

If the train's velocity relative to the cyclist has magnitude $v_{T/C} = 3.0$ m/s and the woman's velocity relative to the train has magnitude $v_{W/T} = 1.0$ m/s, then her velocity $\vec{v}_{W/C}$ relative to the cyclist is as shown in the vector diagram of Figure 3.29b. The Pythagorean theorem then gives us

$$v_{W/C} = \sqrt{(3.0 \text{ m/s})^2 + (1.0 \text{ m/s})^2} = \sqrt{10 \text{ m}^2/\text{s}^2} = 3.2 \text{ m/s}.$$

We can also see from the diagram that the *direction* of her velocity relative to the cyclist makes an angle ϕ with the train's velocity vector $\vec{v}_{T/C}$, where

$$\tan \phi = \frac{v_{W/T}}{v_{T/C}} = \frac{1.0 \text{ m/s}}{3.0 \text{ m/s}}, \qquad \phi = 18°.$$

As in Section 2.7, we have the general rule that if A and B are any two points or frames of reference, then

$$\vec{v}_{A/B} = -\vec{v}_{B/A}. \tag{3.18}$$

The velocity of the woman relative to the train is the negative of the velocity of the train relative to the woman, and so on.

PROBLEM-SOLVING STRATEGY 3.2   **Relative velocity**   (MP)

The strategy introduced in Section 2.7 is also useful here. The essential difference is that now the $\vec{v}$'s aren't all along the same line, so they have to be treated explicitly as vectors. For the double subscripts on the velocities, $\vec{v}_{A/B}$ always means "velocity of A relative to B." A useful rule for keeping the order of things straight is to regard each double subscript as a fraction. Then the fraction on the left side is the *product* of the fractions on the right sides: $P/A = (P/B)(B/A)$. This is helpful when you apply Equation 3.18. If there are *three* different frames of reference A, B, and C, you can write immediately

$$\vec{v}_{P/A} = \vec{v}_{P/C} + \vec{v}_{C/B} + \vec{v}_{B/A},$$

and so on. This is a *vector* equation, and you should always draw a vector diagram to show the addition of velocity vectors.

EXAMPLE 3.10   **Flying in a crosswind**

The compass of an airplane indicates that it is headed due north, and the airspeed indicator shows that the plane is moving through the air at 240 km/h. If there is a wind of 100 km/h from west to east, what is the velocity of the aircraft relative to the earth?

SOLUTION

SET UP Figure 3.30 shows the appropriate vector diagram. We choose subscript P to refer to the plane and subscript A to the moving air (which now plays the role of the railroad car in Figure 3.29). Subscript E refers to the earth. The information given is

$\vec{v}_{P/A} = 240$ km/h   due north,
$\vec{v}_{A/E} = 100$ km/h   due east,

and we want to find the magnitude and direction of $\vec{v}_{P/E}$.

Continued

SOLVE We adapt Equation 3.17 to the notation of this situation:

$$\vec{v}_{P/E} = \vec{v}_{P/A} + \vec{v}_{A/E}.$$

The three relative velocities and their relationship are shown in Figure 3.30. From this diagram, we find that

$$v_{P/E} = \sqrt{(240 \text{ km/h})^2 + (100 \text{ km/h})^2} = 260 \text{ km/h},$$

$$\alpha = \tan^{-1}\frac{100 \text{ km/h}}{240 \text{ km/h}} = 23° \text{ E of N}.$$

REFLECT The plane's velocity with respect to the air is straight north, but the air's motion relative to earth gives the plane's velocity with respect to earth a component toward the east.

Practice Problem: If the plane maintains its airspeed of 240 km/h, but the wind decreases, what is the wind speed if the plane's velocity with respect to earth is 15° east of north? *Answer:* 64 km/h

▲ **FIGURE 3.30** The plane is pointed north, but the wind blows east, giving the resultant velocity $\vec{v}_{P/E}$ relative to the earth.

EXAMPLE 3.11 Compensating for a crosswind

In what direction should the pilot in Example 3.10 head in order for the plane to travel due north? What will be her velocity relative to the earth then? (Assume that the wind velocity and the magnitude of her airspeed are the same as in Example 3.10.)

SOLUTION

SET UP Now the information given is

$$\vec{v}_{P/A} = 240 \text{ km/h} \quad \text{direction unknown,}$$
$$\vec{v}_{A/E} = 100 \text{ km/h} \quad \text{due east.}$$

Figure 3.31 shows the appropriate vector diagram. Be sure you understand why this is not the same diagram as that in Figure 3.30.

SOLVE We want to find $\vec{v}_{P/E}$; its magnitude is unknown, but we know that its direction is due north. Note that both this and the preceding example require us to determine two unknown quantities. In Example 3.10, these were the magnitude and direction of $\vec{v}_{P/E}$; in this example, the unknowns are the direction of $\vec{v}_{P/A}$ and the *magnitude* of $\vec{v}_{P/E}$.

The three relative velocities must still satisfy the vector equation

$$\vec{v}_{P/E} = \vec{v}_{P/A} + \vec{v}_{A/E}.$$

We find that

$$\beta = \sin^{-1}\frac{100 \text{ km/h}}{240 \text{ km/h}} = 25°,$$

$$v_{P/E} = \sqrt{(240 \text{ km/h})^2 - (100 \text{ km/h})^2} = 218 \text{ km/h}.$$

The pilot should head 25° west of north; her ground speed will then be 218 km/h.

REFLECT When a plane flies in a crosswind that is at right angles to the plane's velocity relative to the ground, its speed relative to

▲ **FIGURE 3.31** The pilot must point the plane in the direction of the vector $\vec{v}_{P/A}$ in order to travel due north relative to the earth.

the ground is always less than the airspeed; the trip takes longer than in calm air.

Practice Problem: Prove that if the wind speed is greater than or equal to 240 km/h, the plane can't fly straight north relative to the ground, no matter how hard it tries. Hurricanes often have wind speeds of greater than 240 km/h (about 150 mi/h).

SUMMARY

Position, Velocity, and Acceleration Vectors

(Sections 3.1 and 3.2) The position vector $\vec{r}$ of an object in a plane is the displacement vector from the origin to that object. Its components are the coordinates x and y. The average velocity $\vec{v}_{av}$ of the object during a time interval Δt is its displacement $\Delta \vec{r}$ (the change in the position vector $\vec{r}$), divided by Δt:

$$\vec{v}_{av} = \frac{\vec{r}_2 - \vec{r}_1}{t_2 - t_1} = \frac{\Delta \vec{r}}{\Delta t}. \tag{3.1}$$

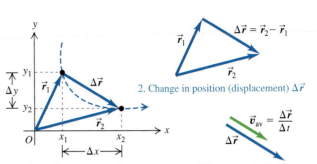

1. Position $\vec{r}$ in an x-y coordinate system

2. Change in position (displacement) $\Delta \vec{r}$

3. Average velocity $\vec{v}_{av}$ over a displacement

Because Δt is a scalar quantity, the direction of average velocity vector $\vec{v}_{av}$ is determined entirely by the direction of the vector displacement $\Delta \vec{r}$.

The instantaneous velocity $\vec{v}$ is $\vec{v} = \lim_{\Delta x \to 0} (\Delta \vec{r} / \Delta t)$; its components are $v_x = \lim_{\Delta t \to 0} (\Delta x / \Delta t)$ and $v_y = \lim_{\Delta t \to 0} (\Delta y / \Delta t)$.

The average acceleration $\vec{a}_{av}$ during the time interval Δt is the change in velocity, $\Delta \vec{v}$, divided by the time interval Δt:

$$\vec{a}_{av} = \frac{\vec{v}_2 - \vec{v}_1}{t_2 - t_1} = \frac{\Delta \vec{v}}{\Delta t}. \tag{3.4}$$

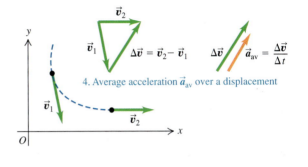

4. Average acceleration $\vec{a}_{av}$ over a displacement

Instantaneous acceleration $\vec{a}$ is $\vec{a} = \lim_{\Delta t \to 0} (\Delta \vec{v} / \Delta t)$; its components are $a_x = \lim_{\Delta t \to 0} (\Delta v_x / \Delta t)$, $a_y = \lim_{\Delta t \to 0} (\Delta v_y / \Delta t)$. An object has acceleration if *either* its speed or its direction of motion changes—that is, if either the magnitude or direction of its velocity changes.

Projectile Motion

(Section 3.3) **Projectile motion** occurs when an object is given an initial velocity and then follows a path determined entirely by the effect of a constant gravitational force. The path, called a **trajectory,** is a parabola in the x-y plane. The vertical motion of a projectile is independent of its horizontal motion.

In projectile motion, $a_x = 0$ (there is no horizontal component of acceleration) and $a_y = -g$ (a constant vertical component of acceleration due to a constant gravitational force). The coordinates and velocity components, as functions of time, are

$$x = (v_0 \cos \theta_0)t, \tag{3.12}$$

$$y = (v_0 \sin \theta_0)t - \frac{1}{2}gt^2, \tag{3.13}$$

$$v_x = v_0 \cos \theta_0, \tag{3.14}$$

$$v_y = v_0 \sin \theta_0 - gt. \tag{3.15}$$

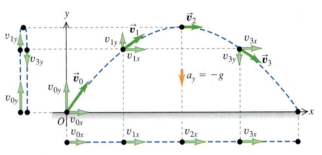

The vertical and horizontal components of a projectile's motion are independent.

Uniform Circular Motion

(Section 3.4) When a particle moves in a circular path with radius R and with constant speed v, it has an acceleration with magnitude

$$a_{rad} = \frac{v^2}{R} \tag{3.16}$$

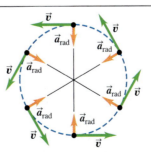

always directed toward the center of the circle and perpendicular to the instantaneous velocity v at each instant.

Continued

Relative Velocity

(Section 3.5) When an object P moves relative to another object (or reference frame) B, and B moves relative to a third object (or reference frame) A, we denote the velocity of P relative to B by $\vec{v}_{P/B}$, the velocity of P relative to A by $\vec{v}_{P/A}$, and the velocity of B relative to A by $\vec{v}_{B/A}$. These velocities are related by this variation of Equation 3.17:

$$\vec{v}_{P/A} = \vec{v}_{P/B} + \vec{v}_{B/A}.$$

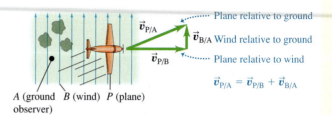

Plane relative to ground
$\vec{v}_{P/A}$
$\vec{v}_{B/A}$ Wind relative to ground
$\vec{v}_{P/B}$ .... Plane relative to wind

A (ground B (wind) P (plane)
observer)

$$\vec{v}_{P/A} = \vec{v}_{P/B} + \vec{v}_{B/A}$$

(MP) For instructor-assigned homework, go to www.masteringphysics.com

Conceptual Questions

1. A football is thrown in a parabolic path. Is there any point at which the acceleration is parallel to the velocity? Perpendicular to the velocity?

2. When a rifle is fired at a stationary distant target, the barrel is not lined up exactly with the target. Why not?

3. A physicist measures the acceleration of a falling body in an elevator traveling at a constant speed of 9.8 m/s. What result does she obtain if the elevator is traveling (a) upward and (b) downward?

4. Intrigued by her result in the previous question, the physicist now measures the acceleration of a falling body in an elevator accelerating at a constant 9.8 m/s^2. What result does she obtain if the elevator is accelerating (a) upward and (b) downward?

5. A package falls from an airplane in level flight at constant speed. If air resistance can be neglected, how does the motion of the package look to the pilot? To a person on the ground?

6. If an athlete can give himself the same initial speed regardless of the direction in which he jumps, how is his maximum vertical jump (high jump) related to his maximum horizontal jump (long jump)?

7. The maximum range of a projectile occurs when it is aimed at a 45° angle if air resistance is neglected. At what angle should you launch it so that it will achieve the maximum time in the air? What would be its range in that case?

8. If an artificial earth satellite is in an orbit around the earth's equator with a period of exactly 1 day, how does its motion look to an observer on the rotating earth if it orbits in the same direction as the earth turns? (Such an orbit is said to be *geosynchronous;* most communications satellites are placed in geosynchronous orbits.)

9. A projectile is fired at an angle above the horizontal from the edge of a vertical cliff. (a) Is its velocity ever only horizontal? If so, when? (b) Is its velocity ever only vertical? If so, why?

10. An archer shoots an arrow from the top of a vertical cliff at an angle θ above the horizontal. When the arrow reaches the level ground at the bottom of the cliff, will its speed depend on the angle θ at which it was shot?

11. An observer draws the path of a stone thrown into the air, as shown in the Figure 3.32. What is wrong with the path shown? (There are *two* things wrong with it; can you spot both of them?)

▲ **FIGURE 3.32** Problem 11.

12. A frisky grasshopper leaps into the air with an initial speed of 1.5 m/s at an angle of 60° above the level ground. The insect feels no air resistance. (a) Using the given information, what could you calculate regarding the grasshopper's motion? (Do not actually calculate it; just decide what things you *could* calculate.) (b) What information could you calculate if you knew only the grasshopper's initial speed, but not the angle at which it jumped?

13. You shoot an arrow upward at an angle above the horizontal, aiming directly at a target in a distant tree. As we saw in this chapter, if the target is released at the instant you shoot your arrow, you will hit it. Yet how can this be, since your arrow begins to fall the instant it leaves the bow?

14. Suppose a space capsule with an astronaut inside is launched from the top of a tower at some angle above the horizontal. (a) While the capsule is in free fall, what are the acceleration of the astronaut and the capsule? (b) If the astronaut measures his acceleration compared with that of the capsule, what value will he get? (c) In what sense can we say that the astronaut is "weightless" in the capsule? Is he "weightless" because the gravity of the earth has gone away?

15. A hunter shoots a bullet from the top of a cliff. What is wrong with the drawing of the bullet's path in Figure 3.33?

16. According to what we have seen about circular motion, the earth is accelerating toward the sun, yet it is not getting any closer to the sun. To many people, this situation would seem like a contradiction. Explain why it really is *not* a contradiction.

▲ **FIGURE 3.33** Problem 15.

Multiple-Choice Problems

1. A cannonball is fired toward a vertical building 400 m away with an initial velocity of 100 m/s at 36.9° above the horizontal. The ball will hit the building in
   A. 4.0 s.   B. 5.0 s.
   C. less than 4.0 s.   D. more than 5.0 s.

2. If the cannonball in the previous question is fired horizontally from a 150-m-high cliff, but still 400 m from the building, then the ball will hit the building in
   A. 4.0 s.   B. 5.0 s.
   C. less than 4.0 s.   D. more than 5.0 s.

3. A ball thrown horizontally from the top of a building hits the ground in 0.50 s. If it had been thrown with twice the speed in the same direction, it would have hit the ground in
   A. 4.0 s.   B. 1.0 s.   C. 0.50 s.
   D. 0.25 s.   E. 0.125 s.

4. Two balls are dropped from the top of the Leaning Tower of Pisa. The second ball is dropped a fraction of a second after the first ball. As they continue to accelerate to the ground, the distance between them will
   A. remain constant.
   B. decrease.
   C. increase.

5. Two balls are dropped at the same time from different heights. As they accelerate toward the ground, the distance between them will
   A. remain constant.
   B. decrease.
   C. increase.

6. A rock dropped from a small bridge encounters no air resistance and hits the pond below 1.0 s later. If it had been thrown horizontally with a speed of 10 m/s, then it would have hit the water
   A. more than 1.0 s later, since it has a greater distance to travel.
   B. 1.0 s later, since the vertical motion is not affected by the horizontal motion.
   C. less than 1.0 s later, since the higher speed would tend to get the ball to the ground more quickly.

7. An airplane flying at a constant horizontal velocity drops a package of supplies to a scientific mission in the Antarctic. If air resistance is negligibly small, the path of this package, *as observed by a person in the plane*, is
   A. a parabola.
   B. a straight line downward.
   C. a straight line pointing ahead of the plane.
   D. a straight line pointing behind the plane.

8. Your boat departs from the bank of a river that has a swift current parallel to its banks. If you want to cross this river in the shortest amount of time, you should direct your boat
   A. perpendicular to the current.
   B. upstream.
   C. downstream.
   D. so that it drifts with the current.

9. A car is driving toward a building at 10 mph. On the roof of the car, an insect is scurrying away from the building at 15 mph relative to the car's roof. To a person sitting in the building, the insect's velocity is
   A. 25 mph away from the building.
   B. 25 mph toward the building.
   C. 5 mph away from the building.
   D. 5 mph toward the building.

10. A ball is thrown horizontally from the top of a building and lands a distance d from the foot of the building after having been in the air for a time T and encountering no significant air resistance. If the building were twice as tall, the ball would have
    A. landed a distance $2d$ from the foot of the building.
    B. been in the air a time $2T$.
    C. been in the air a time $T\sqrt{2}$.
    D. reached the ground with twice the speed it did from the shorter building.

11. A ball is thrown horizontally from the top of a building and lands a distance d from the foot of the building after having been in the air for a time T and encountering no appreciable air resistance. If the ball had been thrown horizontally twice as fast, but all else were the same, it would have
    A. landed a distance $2d$ from the foot of the building.
    B. been in the air a time $2T$.
    C. been in the air a time $T\sqrt{2}$.
    D. reached the ground with twice the speed it did from the shorter building.

12. An object is thrown up at an angle of 35° above the horizontal and reaches a maximum height H. If the angle is now doubled to 70°, but nothing else is changed, its maximum height will be
    A. 1.64 H.   B. 2 H.   C. 2.68 H.   D. 4 H.

13. A golf ball is hit into the air, but not straight up, and encounters no significant air resistance. Which statements accurately describe its motion while it is in the air? (More than one choice may be correct.)
    A. On the way up it is accelerating upward, and on the way down it is accelerating downward.
    B. On the way up, both its horizontal and vertical velocity components are decreasing; on the way down, they are both increasing.
    C. Its vertical acceleration is zero at the highest point.
    D. Its horizontal velocity does not change once it is in the air, but its vertical velocity does change.

14. You shoot a bullet at a tasty apple high up in a tree some feet in front of you, hoping to knock it loose so you can catch it and eat it. In order to hit this apple, you should aim
    A. directly at it.
    B. above it.
    C. below it.

15. At the same time that rock A is dropped from rest from the top of a building, rock B is thrown horizontally away from the building, also starting at the top. Air resistance is not large enough to worry about. Which of the following statements are correct? (More than one choice may be correct.)
    A. Rock B hits the ground before rock A does.
    B. Both rocks have the same speed just as they reach the ground.
    C. Rock B has more acceleration than rock A.
    D. Both rocks reach the ground at the same time.

16. A stone is thrown horizontally with a speed of 15 m/s from the top of a vertical cliff at the edge of a lake. If the stone hits the water 2.0 s later, the height of the cliff is closest to
    A. 10 m.   B. 20 m.   C. 30 m.   D. 50 m.

17. An object traveling at constant speed V in a circle of radius R has an acceleration a. If *both* R and V are doubled, the new acceleration will be
    A. a.   B. $2a$.   C. $4a$.   D. $8a$.

Problems

3.1 Velocity in a Plane

3.2 Acceleration in a Plane

1. • A meteor streaking through the night sky is located with radar. At point A its coordinates are $(5.00 \text{ km}, 1.20 \text{ km})$, and 1.14 s later it has moved to point B with coordinates $(6.24 \text{ km}, 0.925 \text{ km})$. Find (a) the x and y components of its average velocity between A and B and (b) the magnitude and direction of its average velocity between these two points.

2. • At an air show, a jet plane has velocity components $v_x = 625 \text{ km/h}$ and $v_y = 415 \text{ km/h}$ at time 3.85 s and $v_x = 838 \text{ km/h}$ and $v_y = 365 \text{ km/h}$ at time 6.52 s. For this time interval, find (a) the x and y components of the plane's average acceleration and (b) the magnitude and direction of its average acceleration.

3. •• A dragonfly flies from point A to point B along the path shown in Figure 3.34 in 1.50 s. (a) Find the x and y components of its position vector at point A. (b) What are the magnitude and direction of its position vector at A? (c) Find the x and y components of the dragonfly's average velocity between A and B. (d) What are the magnitude and direction of its average velocity between these two points?

▲ **FIGURE 3.34** Problem 3.

4. • In the previous problem, if the dragonfly's velocity components at point A are $v_x = 6.20 \text{ m/s}$ and $v_y = 5.11 \text{ m/s}$ and at point B are $v_x = 4.05 \text{ m/s}$ and $v_y = 8.26 \text{ m/s}$, find (a) the x and y components of the dragonfly's average acceleration between A and B and (b) the magnitude and direction of its average acceleration between those points.

5. •• An athlete starts at point A and runs at a constant speed of 6.0 m/s around a round track 100 m in diameter, as shown in Figure 3.35. Find the x and y components of this runner's average velocity and average acceleration between points (a) A and B, (b) A and C, (c) C and D, and (d) A and A (a full lap). (e) Calculate the magnitude of the runner's average velocity between A and B. Is his average speed equal to the magnitude of his average velocity? Why or why not? (f) How can his velocity be changing if he is running at constant speed?

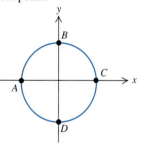

▲ **FIGURE 3.35** Problem 5.

3.3 Projectile Motion

6. • A stone is thrown horizontally at 30.0 m/s from the top of a very tall cliff. (a) Calculate its horizontal position and vertical

position at 2-s intervals for the first 10.0 s. (b) Plot your positions from part (a) to scale. Then connect your points with a smooth curve to show the trajectory of the stone.

7. • A marksman fires a . 22-caliber rifle horizontally at a target; the bullet has a muzzle velocity with magnitude 750 ft/s. How much does the bullet drop in flight if the target is (a) 50.0 yd away and (b) 150.0 yd away?

8. • A physics book slides off a horizontal tabletop with a speed of 1.10 m/s. It strikes the floor in 0.350 s. Ignore air resistance. Find (a) the height of the tabletop above the floor, (b) the horizontal distance from the edge of the table to the point where the book strikes the floor, and (c) the horizontal and vertical components of the book's velocity, and the magnitude and direction of its velocity, just before the book reaches the floor.

9. • A tennis ball rolls off the edge of a tabletop 0.750 m above the floor and strikes the floor at a point 1.40 m horizontally from the edge of the table. (a) Find the time of flight of the ball. (b) Find the magnitude of the initial velocity of the ball. (c) Find the magnitude and direction of the velocity of the ball just before it strikes the floor.

10. • A military helicopter on a training mission is flying horizontally at a speed of 60.0 m/s when it accidentally drops a bomb (fortunately, not armed) at an elevation of 300 m. You can ignore air resistance. (a) How much time is required for the bomb to reach the earth? (b) How far does it travel horizontally while falling? (c) Find the horizontal and vertical components of the bomb's velocity just before it strikes the earth. (d) Draw graphs of the horizontal distance vs. time and the vertical distance vs. time for the bomb's motion. (e) If the velocity of the helicopter remains constant, where is the helicopter when the bomb hits the ground?

11. • Two crickets, Chirpy and Milada, jump from the top of a vertical cliff. Chirpy jumps horizontally at 95.0 cm/s, while Milada simply drops and reaches the ground in 3.50 s. How far from the base of the cliff will Chirpy hit the ground?

12. •• A daring 510 N swimmer dives off a cliff with a running horizontal leap, as shown in Figure 3.36. What must her minimum speed be just as she leaves the top of the cliff so that she will miss the ledge at the bottom, which is 1.75 m wide and 9.00 m below the top of the cliff?

▲ **FIGURE 3.36** Problem 12.

13. •• **Leaping the river, I.** A 10,000 N car comes to a bridge during a storm and finds the bridge washed out. The 650 N driver must get to the other side, so he decides to try leaping it with his car. The side the car is on is 21.3 m above the river, while the opposite side is a mere 1.80 m above the river. The river itself is a raging torrent 61.0 m wide. (a) How fast should the car be traveling just as it leaves the cliff in order to clear the river and land safely on the opposite side? (b) What is the speed of the car just before it lands safely on the other side?

14. • A football is thrown with an initial upward velocity component of 15.0 m/s and a horizontal velocity component of 18.0 m/s. (a) How much time is required for the football to reach the highest point in its trajectory? (b) How high does it get above its release point? (c) How much time after it is thrown does it take to return to its original height? How does this time compare with what you calculated in part (b)? Is your

answer reasonable? (d) How far has the football traveled horizontally from its original position?

15. • A tennis player hits a ball at ground level, giving it an initial velocity of 24 m/s at 57° above the horizontal. (a) What are the horizontal and vertical components of the ball's initial velocity? (b) How high above the ground does the ball go? (c) How long does it take the ball to reach its maximum height? (d) What are the ball's velocity and acceleration at its highest point? (e) For how long a time is the ball in the air? (f) When this ball lands on the court, how far is it from the place where it was hit?

16. • (a) A baseball is hit by a batter at 51.0° above the horizontal with an initial speed of 65.2 m/s. What are the horizontal and vertical components of its initial velocity? Sketch this vector and its components to scale. (b) In a skeet shoot, a bullet is shot upward with an initial vertical velocity component of 818 m/s and an initial horizontal component of 511 m/s. Find the initial speed of the bullet and the angle it makes above the horizontal? Sketch this vector and its components to scale.

17. •• A major leaguer hits a baseball so that it leaves the bat at a speed of 30.0 m/s and at an angle of 36.9° above the horizontal. You can ignore air resistance. (a) At what two times is the baseball at a height of 10.0 m above the point at which it left the bat? (b) Calculate the horizontal and vertical components of the baseball's velocity at each of the two times you found in part (a). (c) What are the magnitude and direction of the baseball's velocity when it returns to the level at which it left the bat?

18. •• A balloon carrying a basket is descending at a constant velocity of 20.0 m/s. A person in the basket throws a stone with an initial velocity of 15.0 m/s horizontally perpendicular to the path of the descending balloon, and 4.00 s later this person sees the rock strike the ground. (See Figure 3.37.) (a) How high was the balloon when the rock was thrown out? (b) How far horizontally does the rock travel before it hits the ground? (c) At the instant the rock hits the ground, how far is it from the basket?

15.0 m/s

20.0 m/s

▲ **FIGURE 3.37**
Problem 18.

19. •• A batted baseball leaves the bat at an angle of 30.0° above the horizontal and is caught by an outfielder 375 ft from home plate at the same height from which it left the bat. (a) What was the initial speed of the ball? (b) How high does the ball rise above the point where it struck the bat?

20. •• A man stands on the roof of a 15.0-m-tall building and throws a rock with a velocity of magnitude 30.0 m/s at an angle of 33.0° above the horizontal. You can ignore air resistance. Calculate (a) the maximum height above the roof reached by the rock, (b) the magnitude of the velocity of the rock just before it strikes the ground, and (c) the horizontal distance from the base of the building to the point where the rock strikes the ground.

21. • **The champion jumper of the insect world.** The froghopper, *Philaenus spumarius*, holds the world record for insect jumps. When leaping at an angle of 58.0° above the horizontal, some of the tiny critters have reached a maximum height of 58.7 cm above the level ground. (See *Nature,* Vol. 424, 31 July 2003, p. 509.) (a) What was the takeoff speed for such a leap? (b) What horizontal distance did the froghopper cover for this world-record leap?

BIO

22. •• A grasshopper leaps into the air from the edge of a vertical cliff, as shown in Figure 3.38. Use information from the figure to find (a) the initial speed of the grasshopper and (b) the height of the cliff.

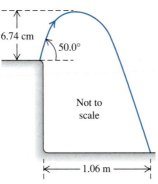

6.74 cm

50.0°

Not to scale

1.06 m

▲ **FIGURE 3.38** Problem 22.

23. •• Firemen are shooting a stream of water at a burning building. A high-pressure hose shoots out the water with a speed of 25.0 m/s as it leaves the hose nozzle. Once it leaves the hose, the water moves in projectile motion. The firemen adjust the angle of elevation of the hose until the water takes 3.00 s to reach a building 45.0 m away. You can ignore air resistance; assume that the end of the hose is at ground level. (a) Find the angle of elevation of the hose. (b) Find the speed and acceleration of the water at the highest point in its trajectory. (c) How high above the ground does the water strike the building, and how fast is it moving just before it hits the building?

24. •• Show that a projectile achieves its maximum range when it is fired at 45° above the horizontal if $y = y_0$.

25. •• A certain peewee soccer player can kick the ball with a maximum speed of 15.0 m/s. (a) At what angle should he kick it to achieve the maximum range? (b) What is the maximum range of the ball at that angle? (c) How high will the ball go?

26. •• A certain cannon with a fixed angle of projection has a range of 1500 m. What will be its range if you add more powder so that the initial speed of the cannonball is tripled?

27. • A cannon can be adjusted to various angles of elevation to launch shells at a target 1250 m away on level ground. What is the minimum muzzle velocity needed to reach this target? At what angle should the cannon launch the shells?

28. •• Two archers shoot arrows in the same direction from the same place with the same initial speeds but at different angles. One shoots at 45° above the horizontal, while the other shoots at 60.0°. If the arrow launched at 45° lands 225 m from the archer, how far apart are the two arrows when they land? (You can assume that the arrows start at essentially ground level.)

29. •• If a certain cannon can shoot a projectile a distance of 275 m when it is aimed at 66.0° above the horizontal, what is the maximum range the cannon could achieve with the same projectile, and at what angle should it be aimed to do this?

30. •• **Martian Olympics.** The world record for the discus throw is 74.08 m, set by Jürgen Schult in 1986. If he had been competing not on earth, but on Mars, where the acceleration due to gravity is 0.379 what it is on earth, and if he had thrown the discus in exactly the same way as on earth, what would be his Martian record for this throw? Assume that the discus is released essentially at ground level.

3.4 Uniform Circular Motion

31. • You swing a 2.2 kg stone in a circle of radius 75 cm. At what speed should you swing it so its centripetal acceleration will be 9.8 m/s²?

32. •• Consult Appendix F. Calculate the radial acceleration (in m/s² and g's) of an object (a) on the ground at the earth's equator and (b) at the equator of Jupiter (which takes 0.41 day to spin once), turning with the planet.

33. •• Consult Appendix F and assume circular orbits. (a) What is the magnitude of the orbital velocity, in m/s, of the earth around the sun? (b) What is the radial acceleration, in m/s, of the earth toward the sun? (c) Repeat parts (a) and (b) for the motion of the planet Mercury.

34. • A model of a helicopter rotor has four blades, each 3.40 m in length from the central shaft to the tip of the blade. The model is rotated in a wind tunnel at 550 rev/min. (a) What is the linear speed, in m/s, of the blade tip? (b) What is the radial acceleration of the blade tip, expressed as a multiple of the acceleration g due to gravity?

35. •• A wall clock has a second hand 15.0 cm long. What is the radial acceleration of the tip of this hand?

36. •• **Old Caruso records.** Suppose you discover your grandfather's collection of Caruso records from the early part of the 20th century. These disks played at 78 revolutions per minute (rpm) and were 9.0 in. in diameter. What was the radial acceleration of a point on the rim of such a record as you listened to the great tenor singing?

37. •• **Dizziness.** Our balance is maintained, at least in part, by **BIO** the endolymph fluid in the inner ear. Spinning displaces this fluid, causing dizziness. Suppose a dancer (or skater) is spinning at a very high 3.0 revolutions per second about a vertical axis through the center of his head. Although the distance varies from person to person, the inner ear is approximately 7.0 cm from the axis of spin. What is the radial acceleration (in m/s^2 and in g's) of the endolymph fluid?

38. • **Pilot blackout in a power dive.** A jet plane comes in for a **BIO** downward dive as shown in Figure 3.39. The bottom part of the path is a quarter circle having a radius of curvature of 350 m. According to medical tests, pilots lose consciousness at an acceleration of 5.5g. At what speed (in m/s and mph) will the pilot black out for this dive?

▲ **FIGURE 3.39** Problem 38.

3.5 Relative Velocity in a Plane

39. •• **Flying an airplane.** An airplane pilot wishes to fly directly westward. According to the weather bureau, a wind of 80 km/h is blowing toward the south. (a) If the speed of the plane relative to the air (called the "air speed") is measured by instruments in the plane to be 320 km/h, in which direction should the pilot head? (b) What is the speed of the plane over the ground (called the "ground speed")? Illustrate your solution with a vector diagram.

40. •• **Crossing the river, I.** A river flows due south with a speed of 2.0 m/s. A man steers a motorboat across the river; his velocity relative to the water is 4.2 m/s due east. The river is 800 m wide. (a) What is his velocity (magnitude and direction) relative to the earth? (b) How much time is required for the man to cross the river? (c) How far south of his starting point will he reach the opposite bank?

41. •• **Crossing the river, II.** (a) In which direction should the motorboat in the previous problem head in order to reach a point on the opposite bank directly east from the starting point? (The boat's speed relative to the water remains 4.2 m/s.) (b) What is

the velocity of the boat relative to the earth? (c) How much time is required to cross the river?

42. •• **Raindrops.** When a train's velocity is 12.0 m/s eastward, raindrops that are falling vertically with respect to the earth make traces that are inclined at 30.0° to the vertical on the windows of the train. (a) What is the horizontal component of a drop's velocity with respect to the earth? With respect to the train? (b) What is the magnitude of the velocity of the raindrop with respect to the earth? With respect to the train? (*Note:* You can see this effect yourself when driving in the rain or snow. If there isn't much wind, the rain or snow falls downward when the car is stopped—the faster you drive, the more the rain or snow appears to have a horizontal component of motion.)

43. •• **Bird migration.** Canadian geese migrate essentially along **BIO** a north–south direction for well over a thousand kilometers in some cases, traveling at speeds up to about 100 km/h. If one such bird is flying at 100 km/h relative to the air, but there is a 40 km/h wind blowing from west to east, (a) at what angle relative to the north–south direction should this bird head so that it will be traveling directly southward relative to the ground? (b) How long will it take the bird to cover a ground distance of 500 km from north to south? (*Note:* Even on cloudy nights, many birds can navigate using the earth's magnetic field to fix the north–south direction.)

General Problems

44. •• An airplane diving at an angle of 36.9° below the horizontal drops a bag of sand from an altitude of 1200 m. The bag is observed to strike the ground 6.00 s after its release. (a) What is the speed of the plane? (b) How far does the bag travel horizontally during its fall? (c) What are the horizontal and vertical components of its velocity just before it strikes the ground?

45. •• A player kicks a football at an angle of 40.0° with the horizontal, with an initial speed of 12.0 m/s. A second player standing at a distance of 30.0 m from the first (in the direction of the kick) starts running to meet the ball at the instant it is kicked. How fast must he run in order to catch the ball just before it hits the ground?

46. •• A jungle veterinarian with a blowgun loaded with a tranquilizer dart and a sly 1.5 kg monkey are each 25 m above the ground in trees 90 m apart. Just as the hunter shoots horizontally at the monkey, the monkey drops from the tree in a vain attempt to escape being hit. What must the minimum muzzle velocity of the dart have been for the hunter to hit the monkey before it reached the ground?

47. •• A movie stuntwoman drops from a helicopter that is 30.0 m above the ground and is moving with a constant velocity whose components are 10.0 m/s upward and 15.0 m/s horizontal and toward the south. You can ignore air resistance. Where on the ground (relative to the position of the helicopter when she drops) should the stuntwoman have placed the foam mats that break her fall?

48. •• **Fighting forest fires.** When fighting forest fires, airplanes work in support of ground crews by dropping water on the fires. A pilot is practicing by dropping a canister of red dye, hoping to hit a target on the ground below. If the plane is flying in a horizontal path 90.0 m above the ground and with a speed of 64.0 m/s (143 mi/h), at what horizontal distance from the

target should the pilot release the canister? Ignore air resistance.

49. •• **An errand of mercy.** An airplane is dropping bales of hay to cattle stranded in a blizzard on the Great Plains. The pilot releases the bales at 150 m above the level ground when the plane is flying at 75 m/s 55° above the horizontal. How far in front of the cattle should the pilot release the hay so that the bales will land at the point where the cattle are stranded?

50. •• A cart carrying a vertical missile launcher moves horizontally at a constant velocity of 30.0 m/s to the right. It launches a rocket vertically upward. The missile has an initial vertical velocity of 40.0 m/s relative to the cart. (a) How high does the rocket go? (b) How far does the cart travel while the rocket is in the air? (c) Where does the rocket land relative to the cart?

40.0 m/s

30.0 m/s

▲ **FIGURE 3.40** Problem 50.

51. •• **Don't do this!** A girl throws a water-filled balloon at an angle of 50.0° above the horizontal with a speed of 12.0 m/s. The horizontal component of the balloon's velocity is directed toward a car that is approaching the girl at a constant speed of 8.00 m/s. (See Figure 3.41.) If the balloon is to hit the car at the same height at which it leaves her hand, what is the maximum distance the car can be from the girl when the balloon is thrown? You can ignore air resistance.

$v = 12.0$ m/s

50.0°

$v = 8.00$ m/s

?

▲ **FIGURE 3.41** Problem 51.

52. •• **The longest home run.** According to the *Guinness Book of World Records,* the longest home run ever measured was hit by Roy "Dizzy" Carlyle in a minor-league game. The ball traveled 188 m (618 ft) before landing on the ground outside the ballpark. (a) Assuming that the ball's initial velocity was 45° above the horizontal, and ignoring air resistance, what did the initial speed of the ball need to be to produce such a home run if the ball was hit at a point 0.9 m (3.0 ft) above ground level? Assume that the ground was perfectly flat. (b) How far would the ball be above a fence 3.0 m (10 ft) in height if the fence were 116 m (380 ft) from home plate?

53. •• Your spaceship lands on an unknown planet. To determine the local value of g, you ask a steel-toed crew member to kick a stone, and you find that if she kicks it at 17.6 m/s at various angles, the maximum range she can achieve is 33.8 m. (a) What is g on this planet? (b) How long was the stone in the air? c) How high above the ground did the stone go?

54. •• A current of a river flows steadily from west to east at 1.00 m/s. A boat in the river travels at 3.00 m/s relative to the water. The river is 20.0 m wide with parallel banks. The boat leaves the shore at point A, and point B is directly across the river from that point. (a) At what angle with respect to the north–south direction should the boat head to go directly to point B? (b) If the boat heads as in part (a), how long will it take it to reach point B? (c) Suppose the boat's motor is low on gas, so that the person guiding it wants to get to the opposite bank as quickly as possible and does not care where the boat lands. In what direction should this person steer the boat, and where will it land relative to B?

55. •• A baseball thrown at an angle of 60.0° above the horizontal strikes a building 18.0 m away at a point 8.00 m above the point from which it is thrown. Ignore air resistance. (a) Find the magnitude of the initial velocity of the baseball (the velocity with which the baseball is thrown). (b) Find the magnitude and direction of the velocity of the baseball just before it strikes the building.

56. •• A boy 12.0 m above the ground in a tree throws a ball for his dog, who is standing right below the tree and starts running the instant the ball is thrown. If the boy throws the ball horizontally at 8.50 m/s, (a) how fast must the dog run to catch the ball just as it reaches the ground, and (b) how far from the tree will the dog catch the ball?

57. •• Suppose the boy in the previous problem throws the ball upward at 60.0° above the horizontal, but all else is the same. Repeat parts (a) and (b) of that problem.

58. •• A firefighting crew uses a water cannon that shoots water at 25.0 m/s at a fixed angle of 53.0° above the horizontal. The firefighters want to direct the water at a blaze that is 10.0 m above ground level. How far from the building should they position their cannon? There are *two* possibilities; can you get them both? (*Hint:* Start with a sketch showing the trajectory of the water.)

59. • A gun shoots a shell into the air with an initial velocity of 100.0 m/s, 60.0° above the horizontal on level ground. Sketch quantitative graphs of the shell's horizontal and vertical velocity components as functions of time for the complete motion.

60. ••• **Look out!** A snowball rolls off a barn roof that slopes downward at an angle of 40.0°. (See Figure 3.42.) The edge of the roof is 14.0 m above the ground, and the snowball has a speed of 7.00 m/s as it rolls off the roof. Ignore air resistance. How far from the edge of the barn does the snowball strike the ground if it doesn't strike anything else while falling?

$v_0 = 7.00$ m/s

40°

14.0 m

4.0 m

▲ **FIGURE 3.42** Problem 60.

61. •• **Record long jump.** The
BIO world's record for the women's long jump (formerly called the broad jump) is 7.52 m, set in 1988 by Galina Chistyakova. Assuming that she jumped at the angle for the maximum range, what was her takeoff speed in m/s and mph?

62. •• During a testing program, the path of a projectile is recorded (See Figure 3.43.) Use the information shown in the

figure to find (a) the initial speed of the projectile, (b) the angle at which the projectile is fired, and (c) the time during which this projectile is in the air.

▲ **FIGURE 3.43** Problem 62.

63. •• **A world record.** In the shot put, a standard track-and-
BIO field event, a 7.3 kg object (the shot) is thrown by releasing it at approximately 40° over a straight left leg. The world record for distance, set by Randy Barnes in 1990, is 23.11 m. Assuming that Barnes released the shot put at 40.0° from a height of 2.00 m above the ground, with what speed, in m/s and mph, did he release it?

64. •• A Ferris wheel with radius 14.0 m is turning about a horizontal axis through its center, as shown in Figure 3.44. The linear speed of a passenger on the rim is constant and equal to 7.00 m/s. What are the magnitude and direction of the passenger's acceleration as she passes through (a) the lowest point in her circular motion and (b) the highest point in her circular motion? (c) How much time does it take the Ferris wheel to make one revolution?

▲ **FIGURE 3.44** Problem 64.

65. ••• **Leaping the river, II.** A physics professor did daredevil stunts in his spare time. His last stunt was an attempt to jump across a river on a motorcycle. (See Figure 3.45.) The takeoff ramp was inclined at 53.0°, the river was 40.0 m wide, and the far bank was 15.0 m lower than the top of the ramp. The river itself was 100 m below the ramp. You can ignore air resistance. (a) What should his speed have been at the top of the ramp for him to have

▲ **FIGURE 3.45** Problem 65.

just made it to the edge of the far bank? (b) If his speed was only half the value found in (a), where did he land?

66. ••• In an action–adventure film, the hero is supposed to throw a grenade from his car, which is going 90 km/h, to his enemy's car, which is going 110 km/h. The enemy's car is 15.8 m in front of the hero's when he lets go of the grenade. If the hero throws the grenade so that its initial velocity relative to him is at an angle of 45° above the horizontal, what should the magnitude of the initial velocity be? The cars are traveling in the same direction on a level road. You can ignore air resistance. Find the magnitude of the velocity relative to the hero and relative to the earth.

67. •• A 76.0 kg boulder is rolling horizontally at the top of a vertical cliff that is 20.0 m above the surface of a lake, as shown in Figure 3.46. The top of the vertical face of a dam is located 100.0 m from the foot of the cliff, with the top of the dam level with the surface of the water in the lake. A level plain is 25.0 m below the top of the dam. (a) What must the minimum speed of the rock be just as it leaves the cliff so that it will travel to the plain without striking the dam? (b) How far from the foot of the dam does the rock hit the plain?

▲ **FIGURE 3.46** Problem 67.

68. •• A 0.17 kg ball is thrown upward with an initial speed of 20.0 m/s from the edge of a 45.0-m-high cliff. At the instant the ball is thrown, a woman starts running away from the base of the cliff with a constant speed of 6.00 m/s. The woman runs in a straight line on level ground, and air resistance acting on the ball can be ignored. At what angle above the horizontal should the ball be thrown so that the runner will catch it just before it hits the ground.

69. •• A shell is launched at 150 m/s 53° above the horizontal. When it has reached its highest point, it launches a projectile at a velocity of 100.0 m/s 30.0° above the horizontal relative to the *shell*. Find (a) the maximum height about the ground that the projectile reaches and (b) its distance from the place where the shell was fired to its landing place when it eventually falls back to the ground.

4 NEWTON'S LAWS OF MOTION

How can a tugboat push a cruise ship that's much heavier than the tug? Why is a long distance needed to stop the ship once it is in motion? Why does your foot hurt more when you kick a big rock than when you kick an empty cardboard box? Why is it harder to control a car on wet ice than on dry concrete? The answers to these and similar questions take us into the subject of **dynamics,** the relationship of motion to the forces associated with it. In the two preceding chapters we studied *kinematics,* the language for describing motion. Now we are ready to think about what makes objects move the way they do. In this chapter, we will use the kinematic quantities of displacement, velocity, and acceleration, along with two new concepts: *force* and *mass.*

All the principles of dynamics can be wrapped up in a neat package containing three statements called **Newton's laws of motion.** These laws, the cornerstone of mechanics, are based on experimental studies of moving objects. They are fundamental laws of nature; they cannot be deduced or proved from any other principles. They were clearly stated for the first time by Sir Isaac Newton (1642–1727), who published them in 1686 in his *Principia,* or *Mathematical Principles of Natural Philosophy.* Many other scientists before Newton contributed to the foundations of mechanics, especially Galileo Galilei (1564–1642), who died the same year Newton was born. Indeed, Newton himself said, "If I have been able to see a little farther than other men, it is because I have stood on the shoulders of giants."

One of these sparring foxes may prove stronger than the other. Yet the forces they exert on each other are always exactly equal in magnitude. In this chapter we'll learn why that is so.

4.1 Force

The concept of **force** gives us a quantitative description of the interaction between two objects or between an object and its environment (Figure 4.1). When you push on a car that is stuck in the snow, you exert a force on it. A locomotive exerts a force on the train it is pulling or pushing, a steel cable exerts a

• A force is a push or a pull.
• A force is an interaction between two objects or between an object and its environment.
• A force is a vector quantity, with magnitude and direction.

▲ **FIGURE 4.1** The concept of a force.

Normal force $\vec{n}$: When an object rests or pushes on a surface, the surface exerts a push on it that is directed perpendicular to the surface.

Friction force $\vec{f}$: In addition to the normal force, a surface may exert a frictional force on an object, directed parallel to the surface.

Tension force $\vec{T}$: A pulling force exerted on an object by a rope, cord, etc.

Weight $\vec{w}$: The pull of gravity on an object.

▲ **FIGURE 4.2** Some types of forces.

force on the beam it is lifting at a construction site, and so on. Each of these examples shows that force is a push or a pull acting on an object. In this chapter, we'll encounter several kinds of forces.

Types of Forces

When a force involves direct contact between two objects, we call it a **contact force.** When an object rests on a surface, there is always a component of force perpendicular to the surface; we call this component a **normal force,** denoted by $\vec{n}$ (Figure 4.2). There may also be a component of force parallel to the surface; we call this a **friction force,** denoted by $\vec{f}$. This force often (though not always) acts to resist sliding of the object on the surface.

When a rope or cord is attached to an object and pulled, the corresponding force applied to the object is referred to as a **tension,** denoted by $\vec{T}$.

A familiar force that we'll work with often is the gravitational attraction that the earth (or some other astronomical body) exerts on an object. This force is the object's **weight,** denoted by $\vec{w}$. You may be used to thinking of your weight as a property of your body, but actually it is a force exerted on you by the earth. The gravitational attraction of two objects acts even when the objects are not in contact. We'll discuss this concept at greater length in Section 4.4.

Measuring Force

Force is a vector quantity; to describe a force, we need to describe the direction in which it acts as well as its magnitude—the quantity that tells us "how much" or "how strongly" the force pushes or pulls. The SI unit of the magnitude of force is the *newton,* abbreviated N. (We haven't yet given a precise definition of the newton. The official definition is based on the standard kilogram; we'll get into that in Section 4.3.) The weight of a medium-sized apple is about 1 N; the pulling force of a diesel locomotive can be as much as 10^6 N.

When forces act on a solid object, they usually deform the object. For example, a coil spring stretches or compresses when forces act on its ends. This property forms the basis for a common instrument for *measuring* forces, called a *spring balance.* The instrument consists of a coil spring, enclosed in a case for protection, with a pointer attached to one end. When forces are applied to the ends of the spring, it stretches; the amount of stretch depends on the force. We can make a scale for the pointer and calibrate it by using a number of identical objects with weights of exactly 1 N each. When two, three, or more of these are suspended simultaneously from the balance, the total stretching force on each end of the spring is 2 N, 3 N, and so on, and we can label the corresponding positions of the pointer 2 N, 3 N, and so on. Then we can use our spring balance to measure the magnitude of an unknown force. We can also make a similar instrument that measures pushes instead of pulls.

Suppose we pull or push a box, as shown in Figure 4.3. As with other vector quantities, we can represent the force we exert on the box by a vector arrow. The arrow points in the direction of the force, and its length represents the magnitude

(a) A 10 N pull directed 30° above the horizontal

(b) A 10 N push directed 45° below the horizontal

▲ **FIGURE 4.3** Forces can be represented with vector arrows.

of the force. For example, we might scale the diagram so that an arrow 1 cm long represents a 5 N force.

Resultant of Forces

Experiment shows that when two forces $\vec{F}_1$ and $\vec{F}_2$ act at the same time on the same point of an object (Figure 4.4), the effect is the same as the effect of a single force equal to the vector sum of the original forces. This vector sum is often called the **resultant** of the forces or the *net force,* denoted by $\vec{R}$. That is, $\vec{R} = \vec{F}_1 + \vec{F}_2$. More generally, the effect of *any number* of forces applied at a point on an object is the same as the effect of a single force equal to the vector sum of the original forces. This important principle goes by the name **superposition of forces.**

The discovery that forces combine according to vector addition is of the utmost importance, and we'll use this fact many times throughout our study of physics. In particular, it allows us to represent a force by means of components, as we've done with displacement, velocity, and acceleration. (See Section 1.8 if you need a review.) In Figure 4.5a, for example, a force $\vec{F}$ acts on an object at a point that we'll designate as the origin of coordinates, O. The component vectors of $\vec{F}$ in the x and y directions are $\vec{F}_x$ and $\vec{F}_y$, and the corresponding components are F_x and F_y. As Figure 4.5b shows, if we apply two forces $\vec{F}_x$ and $\vec{F}_y$ to the object, the effect is exactly the same as applying the original force. **Any force can be replaced by its components, acting at the same point.**

In general, a force can have components in all three (x, y, and z) directions. It will usually be clear how to extend this discussion to three-dimensional situations, but we'll limit our discussion here to situations in which only x and y components are needed.

The x and y coordinate axes don't have to be vertical and horizontal. Figure 4.6 shows a stone block being pulled up a ramp by a force $\vec{F}$, represented by its components F_x and F_y with respect to axes parallel and perpendicular, respectively, to the sloping surface of the ramp. We draw a wiggly line through the force vector $\vec{F}$ to show that we have replaced it by its x and y components. Otherwise, the diagram would include the same force twice.

We'll often need to find the vector sum (resultant) of several forces acting on an object. We'll use the Greek letter Σ (capital sigma, equivalent to an S) as a shorthand notation for a sum. If the forces are labeled $\vec{F}_1$, $\vec{F}_2$, $\vec{F}_3$, and so on, we abbreviate the vector sum operation as

$$\vec{R} = \vec{F}_1 + \vec{F}_2 + \vec{F}_3 + \cdots = \Sigma\vec{F}, \quad \text{(resultant, or vector sum, of forces)} \quad (4.1)$$

where $\Sigma\vec{F}$ is read as "the vector sum of the forces" or "the net force." The component version of Equation 4.1 is the pair of component equations

$$R_x = \Sigma F_x, \qquad R_y = \Sigma F_y, \qquad \text{(components of vector sum of forces)} \quad (4.2)$$

Two forces $\vec{F}_1$ and $\vec{F}_2$ acting on a point have the same effect as a single force $\vec{R}$ equal to their vector sum (resultant).

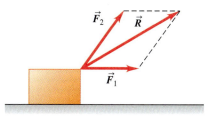

▲ **FIGURE 4.4** Superposition of forces.

(a) Component vectors: $\vec{F}_x$ and $\vec{F}_y$
Components: $F_x = F \cos\theta$ and $F_y = F \sin\theta$

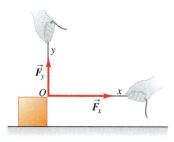

(b) Component vectors $\vec{F}_x$ and $\vec{F}_y$ together have the same effect as original force $\vec{F}$.

▲ **FIGURE 4.5** A force can be represented by its components.

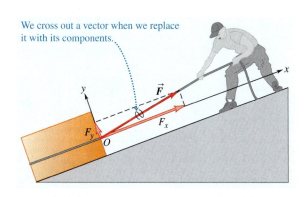

We cross out a vector when we replace it with its components.

▲ **FIGURE 4.6** The pull exerted by the mason can be replaced by components parallel and perpendicular to the direction of motion.

where $\sum F_x$ is the sum of the x components, and so on. Each component may be positive or negative; be careful with signs when you evaluate the sums in Equations 4.2.

Once we have the components R_x and R_y, we can find the magnitude and direction of the vector $\vec{R}$. The magnitude is

$$R = \sqrt{R_x^2 + R_y^2}, \qquad \text{(magnitude of vector sum of forces)}$$

and the angle θ between $\vec{R}$ and the x axis can be found from the relation $\tan\theta = R_y/R_x$. The components R_x and R_y may be positive or negative, and the angle θ may be in any of the four quadrants. As usual, we measure θ counterclockwise from the x axis. We've used this procedure in earlier chapters; in particular, you may want to review Section 1.8.

4.2 Newton's First Law

The fundamental role of a force is to change the state of motion of the object on which the force acts. The key word is "change." Newton's first law of motion, translated from the Latin of the *Principia* and put into modern language, is as follows:

> **Newton's first law**
> Every object continues either at rest or in constant motion in a straight line, unless it is forced to change that state by forces acting on it.

When *no* force acts on an object, or when the vector sum of forces on it is zero, the object either remains at rest or moves with constant velocity in a straight line. Once an object has been set in motion, no net force is needed to keep it moving. In other words, **an object acted on by no net force moves with constant velocity (which may be zero) and thus with zero acceleration.**

Everyday experience may seem to contradict this statement. Suppose you give a push to a hockey puck on a table, as shown in Figure 4.7a. After you stop pushing and take your hand away, the puck *does not* continue to move indefinitely; it slows down and stops. To keep it moving, you have to keep pushing. This is because, as the puck slides, the tabletop applies a frictional force to it in a direction *opposite* that of its motion.

But now imagine pushing the puck across the smooth ice of a skating rink (Figure 4.7b). Here, it will move a lot farther after you quit pushing before it stops. Put it on an air-hockey table, where it floats on a thin cushion of air, and it slides still farther (Figure 4.7c). The more slippery the surface, the less friction there is. The first law states that if we could eliminate friction completely, we would need *no forward force at all* to keep the puck moving with constant velocity once it had been started moving.

▲ **An object in motion.** Catapults are founded on Newton's first law. When the catapult arm is released from its cocked position, it accelerates rapidly, carrying the projectile with it. When the arm hits the crossbar, it comes to a sudden stop—but the projectile keeps going. Once in flight, the projectile experiences no forward force; it flies on because objects in motion tend to stay in motion. It *does* experience the downward force of gravity and a retarding force due to air resistance; these forces will end its flight if it doesn't hit a wall first. Today, a modern version of the catapult is used on aircraft carriers to help launch airplanes, which can reach speeds of 250 kilometers per hour in less than 3 seconds.

(a) Table: puck stops short   **(b)** Ice: puck slides farther   **(c)** Air-hockey table: puck slides even farther

▲ **FIGURE 4.7** An experimental approach to Newton's first law. As we reduce friction, the puck's motion comes closer and closer to constant velocity and the net force acting on the puck approaches zero, as predicted by Newton's first law.

▶ **Objects at rest?** This trick photo was taken an instant after a super-smooth table was very rapidly yanked out from underneath the dinner setting. The table was removed so rapidly that it exerted a force on the place setting only for a very short time. We can visualize the concept of inertia as described by Newton's first law. The objects at rest tend to stay at rest—but the force of gravity causes them to accelerate rapidly downward!

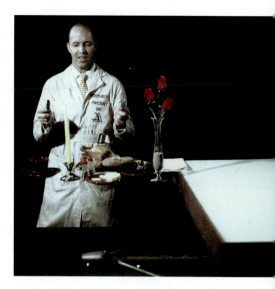

Inertia

The tendency of an object to remain at rest, or to keep moving once it is set in motion, results from a property called *inertia*. That's what you feel when you're behind home plate trying to catch a fastball pitch. That baseball really "wants" to keep moving. The tendency of an object at rest to remain at rest is also due to inertia. You may have seen a tablecloth yanked out from under the china without anything being broken. As the tablecloth slides, the force it exerts on the china isn't great enough to make the china move appreciably.

The quantitative measure of inertia is the physical quantity called **mass,** which we'll discuss in detail in the next section.

 Science or fiction?

In a 1950s TV science fiction show, the hero is cruising the vacuum of outer space when the engine of his space-ship dies and his ship drifts to a stop. Will rescue arrive before his air runs out? What do you think about the physics of this plot?

SOLUTION The engine creates a force that accelerates the ship by ejecting mass out of its stern. When the engine dies and this process stops, there is no force on the ship (assuming that the gravitational forces exerted by planets and stars are negligible). The ship doesn't come to a stop, but continues to move in a straight line with constant speed. Science fiction sometimes contains more fiction than science!

When a single force acts on an object, it changes the object's state of motion. An object that is initially at rest starts to move. If the object is initially moving, a force in the direction opposite that of the motion causes the object to slow down. (If the force is maintained, eventually the object stops and reverses direction.) Suppose a hockey puck rests on a horizontal surface with negligible friction, such as an air-hockey table or a slab of ice. If the puck is initially at rest and a single horizontal force $\vec{F}_1$ acts on it (Figure 4.8a), the puck starts to move. If the puck is in motion at the start, the force makes it speed up, slow down, or change direction, depending on the direction of the force.

Now suppose we apply a second force $\vec{F}_2$ (Figure 4.8b), equal in magnitude to $\vec{F}_1$, but opposite in direction. The two forces are negatives of each other ($\vec{F}_2 = -\vec{F}_1$), and their vector sum $\vec{R}$ is zero:

$$\vec{R} = \vec{F}_1 + \vec{F}_2 = 0.$$

We find that if the puck is at rest at the start, it remains at rest. If it is initially moving, it continues to move in the same direction with constant speed. These results show that, in Newton's first law, **zero resultant force is equivalent to no force at all.**

When an object is acted on by no forces or by several forces whose vector sum (resultant) is zero, we say that the object is in **equilibrium.** For an object in equilibrium,

$$\vec{R} = \Sigma\vec{F} = 0. \qquad \text{(equilibrium under zero resultant force)} \qquad (4.3)$$

For Equation 4.3 to be true, each component of $\vec{R}$ must be zero, so

$$\Sigma F_x = 0, \qquad \Sigma F_y = 0. \qquad \text{(object in equilibrium)} \qquad (4.4)$$

A puck on a frictionless surface accelerates when acted on by a single horizontal force.

(a)

An object acted on by forces whose vector sum is zero behaves as though no forces act on it.

$$\Sigma\vec{F} = 0$$
$$\vec{a} = 0$$

(b)

▲ **FIGURE 4.8** A puck responding to a nonzero net force (a) and to two forces whose vector sum is zero (b).

When Equations 4.4 are satisfied, the object is in equilibrium; that is, it has no acceleration. (We are assuming that the object can be modeled adequately as a particle. For an object with finite size, we also have to consider *where* on the object the forces are applied. We'll return to this point in Chapter 10.)

Conceptual Analysis 4.2

Air hockey

Your team decides to play leaf-blower ice hockey. You use your blower to apply a constant force that accelerates the puck in a straight line. An opponent skates up and uses her blower to apply an equally strong, constant force directed opposite to yours. Her force, acting together with yours, will cause the puck to

A. slow down and eventually stop.
B. stop immediately.
C. slow somewhat and then move with constant velocity.
D. continue to move, but with constant velocity.

SOLUTION The force from your blower alone causes the puck to accelerate. The force from your opponent's blower is equal in magnitude and opposite in direction to yours, so the vector sum of the two forces is zero. A puck that is acted upon by zero net force has no acceleration. Thus, the puck does not slow down or halt (which would be acceleration), but instead moves with constant velocity in accordance with Newton's first law. Thus, the answer is D.

Inertial Frames of Reference

In our discussions of relative velocity at the ends of Chapters 2 and 3, we stressed the concept of a *frame of reference*. This concept also plays a central role in Newton's laws of motion. Suppose you are sitting in an airplane as it accelerates down the runway during takeoff. You feel a forward force pushing on your back, but you don't start moving forward relative to the airplane. If you could stand in the aisle on roller skates, you would accelerate *backward* relative to the plane. In either case, it looks as though Newton's first law is not obeyed. Forward net force but no acceleration, or zero net force and backward acceleration. What's wrong?

The point is that the plane, accelerating with respect to the earth, is not a suitable frame of reference for Newton's first law. This law is valid in some frames of reference and not in others. A frame of reference in which Newton's first law *is* valid is called an **inertial frame of reference.** The earth is approximately an inertial frame of reference, but the airplane is not.

This may sound as though there's only one inertial frame of reference in the whole universe. On the contrary, if Newton's first law is obeyed in one particular reference frame, it is also valid in every other reference frame that moves with constant velocity relative to the first. All such frames are therefore inertial. For instance, Figure 4.9 shows three frames of reference: that of a person standing beside the runway, that of a truck driving at constant speed in a straight line, and that of the accelerating airplane. The stationary person's frame of reference is inertial. The truck moves with constant velocity relative to the person, so its frame of reference is also inertial. In both of these frames, Newton's first law is obeyed. However, the airplane, which is accelerating with respect to both of these observers, is in a non-inertial frame.

Thus, there is no single inertial frame of reference that is preferred over all others for formulating Newton's laws. If one frame is inertial, then every other frame moving relative to it with constant velocity is also inertial. Both the state of rest and the state of uniform motion (with constant velocity) can occur when the vector sum of forces acting on the object is zero. Because Newton's first law can be used to define what we mean by an inertial frame of reference, it is sometimes called the *law of inertia*.

The truck moves with constant velocity relative to the person on the ground. Newton's first law is obeyed in both frames, so they are **inertial**.

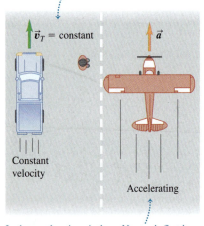

In the accelerating airplane, Newton's first law is not obeyed, so the frame of the airplane is **not inertial**.

▲ **FIGURE 4.9** Inertial and non-inertial frames of reference.

4.3 Mass and Newton's Second Law

2.1.3

Qualitatively, we've learned that when an object is acted on by a nonzero net force, it accelerates. We now want to know the relation of the acceleration to the force; this is what Newton's second law of motion is all about.

Let's look at several fundamental experiments. Consider a small object moving on a flat, level, frictionless surface. The object could be a puck on an air-hockey table, as we described in Section 4.2. Initially, it is moving to the right along the x axis of a coordinate system (Figure 4.10a). We apply a constant horizontal force $\vec{F}$ to the object, using the spring balance we described in Section 4.1, with the spring stretched a constant amount. We find that during the time the force is acting, the velocity of the object changes at a constant rate; that is, the object moves with *constant acceleration*. If we change the magnitude of the force, the acceleration changes in the same proportion. Doubling the force doubles the acceleration, halving the force halves the acceleration, and so on (Figures 4.10b and 4.10c). When we take away the force, the acceleration becomes zero and the object moves with constant velocity. We conclude that, for any given object, the acceleration is *directly proportional* to the force acting on it.

In another experiment (Figure 4.11), we give the object the same initial velocity as before. With no force, the velocity is constant (Figure 4.11a). With a constant force directed to the right (Figure 4.11b), the acceleration is constant and to the right. But when we reverse the direction of the force (Figure 4.11c), we find that the object moves more and more slowly to the right. (If we continue the experiment, the object stops and then moves toward the left with increasing speed.) The direction of the acceleration is toward the *left,* in the same direction as the force $\vec{F}$. We conclude that the *magnitude* of the acceleration is proportional to that of the force, and the *direction* of the acceleration is the same as that of the force, regardless of the direction of the velocity. If there is *no* force, the object has zero acceleration; no force is required to maintain motion with constant velocity.

A constant force $\vec{F}$ causes a constant acceleration $\vec{a}$.

(a)

Doubling the force doubles the acceleration.

(b)

Halving the force halves the acceleration.

(c)

▲ **FIGURE 4.10** Experiments demonstrating the direct proportion between an applied force and the resulting acceleration.

A puck moving with constant velocity: $\Sigma \vec{F} = 0$, $\vec{a} = 0$

(a)

A constant force in the direction of motion causes a constant acceleration in the same direction as the force.

(b)

A constant force opposite to the direction of motion causes a constant acceleration in the same direction as the force.

(c)

▲ **FIGURE 4.11** Experiments showing that an object's acceleration has the same direction as the net force acting on the object.

For a given object, the ratio of the magnitude F of the force to the magnitude a of the acceleration is constant. We call this ratio the inertial mass, or simply the **mass,** of the object and denote it as m. That is, $m = F/a$.

An equivalent statement is that when a force with magnitude F acts on an object with mass m, the magnitude a of the object's acceleration is

$$a = \frac{F}{m}. \tag{4.5}$$

The concept of mass is a familiar one. If you hit a table-tennis ball with a paddle and then hit a basketball with the same force, the basketball has a much smaller acceleration because it has a much greater mass. When a large force is needed to give an object a certain acceleration, the mass of the object is large. When only a small force is needed for the same acceleration, the mass is small. The greater the mass, the more the object "resists" being accelerated. Thus, mass is a quantitative measure of inertia, which we discussed in Section 4.2.

The SI unit of mass is the **kilogram.** We mentioned in Section 1.3 that the kilogram is officially defined to be the mass of a chunk of platinum–iridium alloy kept in a vault near Paris. We can use this standard kilogram, along with Equation 4.5, to define the fundamental SI unit of force, the **newton,** abbreviated N:

Definition of the newton

One newton is the amount of force that gives an acceleration of 1 meter per second squared to an object with a mass of 1 kilogram. That is,

$$1 \text{ N} = (1 \text{ kg})(1 \text{ m/s}^2).$$

We can use this definition to calibrate the spring balances and other instruments that we use to measure forces.

We can also use Equation 4.5 to compare a particular mass with the standard mass and thus to *measure* masses. Suppose we apply a constant force with magnitude F to an object having a known mass m_1 and we find an acceleration with magnitude a_1, as shown in Figure 4.12a. We then apply the *same* force to another object having an unknown mass m_2, and we find an acceleration with magnitude a_2 (Figure 4.12b). Then, according to Equation 4.5,

$$m_1 a_1 = m_2 a_2,$$

or

$$\frac{m_2}{m_1} = \frac{a_1}{a_2}. \tag{4.6}$$

The ratio of the masses is the inverse of the ratio of the accelerations. In principle, we could use this relation to measure an unknown mass m_2, but it is usually easier to determine an object's mass indirectly by measuring the object's weight. We'll return to this point in Section 4.4.

When two objects with masses m_1 and m_2 are fastened together, we find that the mass of the composite object is always $m_1 + m_2$ (Figure 4.12c). This additive property of mass may seem obvious, but it has to be verified experimentally. Ultimately, the mass of an object is related to the numbers of protons, electrons, and neutrons it contains. This wouldn't be a good way to *define* mass, because there is no practical way to count these particles. But the concept of mass is the most fundamental way to characterize the quantity of matter in an object.

A known force $\Sigma \vec{F}$ causes an object with mass m_1 to have an acceleration $\vec{a}_1$.

(a)

Applying the same force $\Sigma \vec{F}$ to a second object and noting the acceleration allows us to measure the mass.

(b)

When the two objects are fastened together, the same method shows that their composite mass is the sum of their individual masses.

(c)

▲ **FIGURE 4.12** For a constant force, the magnitude of acceleration is inversely proportional to the mass of an object. The mass of a composite object is the sum of the masses of its parts.

We need to generalize Equation 4.5 in two ways. First, the object doesn't necessarily have to move along a straight line; its path may be a curve. Its velocity, its acceleration, and the force acting on it can then all change directions, so they have to be treated as vector quantities. Second, there may be several forces $(\vec{F}_1, \vec{F}_2, \cdots)$ acting on the object. As discussed earlier, we can combine the forces by using vector addition; the effect of the forces acting together is the same as the effect of a single force equal to their vector sum, which we usually write as $\sum \vec{F}$ or $\vec{R}$.

Newton wrapped up all these relationships and experimental results in a single concise statement that we now call **Newton's second law of motion:**

Newton's second law of motion (vector form)

The vector sum (resultant) of all the forces acting on an object equals the object's mass times its acceleration (the rate of change of its velocity):

$$\sum \vec{F} = m\vec{a}. \tag{4.7}$$

The acceleration $\vec{a}$ has the same direction as the resultant force $\sum \vec{F}$.

Newton's second law is a fundamental law of nature, the basic relation between force and motion. Most of the remainder of this chapter and all of the next are devoted to learning how to apply this principle in various situations.

Equation 4.7 is a *vector* equation. We'll usually use it in component form:

Newton's second law of motion (component form)

For an object moving in a plane, each component of the total force equals the mass times the corresponding component of acceleration:

$$\sum F_x = ma_x, \qquad \sum F_y = ma_y. \tag{4.8}$$

Equations 4.7 and 4.8 are valid only when the mass m is *constant*. It's easy to think of systems whose masses change, such as a leaking tank truck, a rocket ship, or a moving railroad car being loaded with coal. Such systems are better handled by using the concept of momentum; we'll get to that in Chapter 8.

Like the first law, Newton's second law is valid only in inertial frames of reference. We'll usually assume that the earth is an adequate approximation to an inertial frame, even though it is not precisely inertial because of its rotation and orbital motion.

Remember that we defined the newton as $1\text{ N} = 1\text{ kg} \cdot \text{m/s}^2$. Notice that the newton *must* be defined this way for $\sum \vec{F} = m\vec{a}$ to be dimensionally consistent.

In this chapter, as we learn how to apply Newton's second law, we'll begin with problems involving only motion along a straight line, and we'll always take this line to be a coordinate axis, often the x axis. In these problems, $\vec{v}$ and $\vec{a}$ have components only along this axis. Individual forces may have components along directions other than the x axis, but the *sum* of those components will always be zero.

In Chapter 5, we'll consider more general problems in which v_y, a_y, and $\sum F_y$ need not be zero. We'll derive more general problem-solving strategies for applying Newton's laws of motion to these situations.

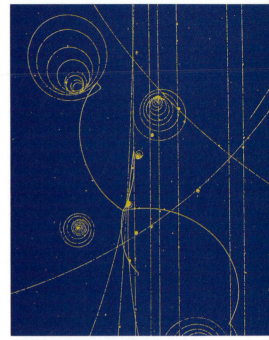

▲ **Too small to measure?** Bubble chamber images like the one shown here are used both to study characteristics of known subatomic particles and to search for new types of matter and antimatter particles. For example, the linked spiral tracks indicate the simultaneous creation of an electron–positron pair from a photon. Using such images, we can apply Newton's second law $(F = ma)$ or its relativistic generalization to determine the masses of particles so minute that they cannot be measured directly.

EXAMPLE 4.1 **A box on ice**

A worker with spikes on his shoes pulls with a constant horizontal force of magnitude 20 N on a box with mass 40 kg resting on the flat, frictionless surface of a frozen lake. What is the acceleration of the box?

SOLUTION

SET UP Figure 4.13 shows our sketch. We take the $+x$ axis in the direction of the horizontal force. "Frictionless" means that the ice doesn't supply any force that opposes the motion (such as the friction force mentioned in Section 4.1). Thus, the only horizontal force is the one due to the rope that the worker is pulling. Because the box has no vertical acceleration, we know that the sum of the vertical components of force is zero. However, two vertical forces do act on the box: the downward force of the earth's gravitational attraction and the upward normal force exerted by the ice on the box. For completeness, we show these two vertical forces in our sketch; their vector sum must be zero because $a_y = 0$.

SOLVE The acceleration is given by Newton's second law. There is only one horizontal component of force, so we have

$$\Sigma F_x = ma_x,$$
$$a_x = \frac{F_x}{m} = \frac{20 \text{ N}}{40 \text{ kg}} = \frac{20 \text{ kg} \cdot \text{m/s}^2}{40 \text{ kg}} = 0.5 \text{ m/s}^2.$$

The force is constant, so the acceleration is also constant. If we are given the initial position and velocity of the box, we can find

The box has no vertical acceleration, so the vertical components of the net force sum to zero. Nevertheless, for completeness, we show the vertical forces acting on the box.

▲ **FIGURE 4.13** Our sketch for this problem.

the position and velocity at any later time from the equations of motion with constant acceleration.

REFLECT Two vertical (y) components of force act on the box—its weight $\vec{w}$ and an upward normal force $\vec{n}$ exerted on the bottom of the box by the ice—but their vector sum is zero.

Practice Problem: If the box starts from rest, what is its speed after it has been pulled a distance of 0.36 m? *Answer:* 0.6 m/s.

EXAMPLE 4.2 **The ketchup slide**

A counter attendant in a diner shoves a ketchup bottle with mass 0.20 kg along a smooth, level lunch counter. The bottle leaves her hand with an initial velocity of 2.8 m/s. As it slides, it slows down because of the horizontal friction force exerted on it by the countertop. The bottle slides a distance of 1.0 m before coming to rest. What are the magnitude and direction of the friction force acting on it?

SOLUTION

SET UP Figure 4.14 shows our diagrams—one for the bottle's motion and one for the forces on the bottle. We place the origin at the point where the waitress releases the bottle and point the $+x$ axis in the direction the bottle moves. Because the bottle has no vertical acceleration, we know that the vertical forces on it (the weight $\vec{w}$ and the upward normal force $\vec{n}$) must sum to zero. The only horizontal force on the bottle is the friction force $\vec{f}$. Because the bottle is slowing down (a_x is negative in our coordinate system), we know that this force points in the $-x$ direction.

SOLVE We need to find the relation between v_x and a_x; to do this, we can use the constant-acceleration equation $v_x^2 - v_{0x}^2 = $

$2a_x(x - x_0)$ (Equation 2.13). The initial x component of velocity is $v_{0x} = 2.8$ m/s, and the final value is $v_x = 0$. Also, $x_0 = 0$ and $x = 1.0$ m. Once a_x is known, we can use the component form of Newton's second law, Equation 4.8 $(\Sigma F_x = ma_x)$, to find the magnitude f of the friction force. Because f is the only horizontal component of force, $\Sigma F_x = -f$. Using the numerical values in Equation 2.13, we first find the bottle's acceleration:

$$v_x^2 - v_0^2 = 2a_x(x - x_0),$$
$$0 - (2.8 \text{ m/s})^2 = 2a_x(1.0 \text{ m} - 0),$$
$$a_x = -3.9 \text{ m/s}^2.$$

We draw one diagram for the bottle's motion and one showing the forces on the bottle.

▲ **FIGURE 4.14** Our sketch for this problem.

Continued

We can now find the net force acting on the bottle.

$$\Sigma F_x = -f = ma_x$$
$$-f = (0.20 \text{ kg})(-3.9 \text{ m/s}^2) = -0.78 \text{ kg} \cdot \text{m/s}^2 = -0.78 \text{ N}.$$

Since the frictional force is the *only* horizontal force acting on the bottle, this answer gives us its magnitude (0.78 N) and also the fact that it acts in the $-x$ direction (which we already knew).

REFLECT Notice that we did most of the physics before doing any math. We knew that the vertical forces on the bottle summed to zero, and we knew the direction of the friction force. We did math only to find the magnitude of that force.

Practice Problem: Suppose the bottle travels 1.5 m before stopping, instead of 1.0 m. What is its initial velocity? *Answer:* 3.4 m/s.

EXAMPLE 4.3   **A TV picture tube**

In a color TV picture tube, an electric field exerts a net force with magnitude 1.60×10^{-13} N on an electron $(m = 9.11 \times 10^{-31} \text{ kg})$. What is the electron's acceleration?

SOLUTION

SET UP Figure 4.15 shows our simple diagram. The statement of the problem tells us that the *net force* on the electron is due to the electric field, so we consider only the electric-field force. (If other forces act on the electron, they are negligible or sum to zero.) The direction of the acceleration must be the same as that of the force; we designate this direction as the $+x$ direction.

SOLVE We use Newton's second law in component form, rearranging it slightly to solve for acceleration:

$$a_x = \frac{\Sigma F_x}{m} = \frac{1.60 \times 10^{-13} \text{ N}}{9.11 \times 10^{-31} \text{ kg}} = \frac{1.60 \times 10^{-13} \text{ kg} \cdot \text{m/s}^2}{9.11 \times 10^{-31} \text{ kg}}$$
$$= 1.76 \times 10^{17} \text{ m/s}^2.$$

▲ **FIGURE 4.15** Even for a simple problem, a quick sketch helps us to see the situation and avoid mistakes.

REFLECT Notice that the magnitudes of these quantities are far outside the range of everyday experience. Because the mass of the electron is miniscule, a tiny force produces a huge acceleration.

Practice Problem: If the electron starts from rest, what time is required for it to travel 0.20 m from its source to the screen of the picture tube? *Answer:* 1.51×10^{-9} s.

Quantitative Analysis 4.3   **Raising a toolbox**

Suppose you use a rope to hoist a box of tools vertically at a constant speed v. The rope exerts a constant upward force of magnitude F_{up} on the box, and gravity exerts a constant downward force (the weight of the box). No other forces act on the box. To raise the box twice as fast, the force of the rope on the box would have to have

A. the same magnitude F_{up}.
B. a magnitude of $2F_{up}$.

SOLUTION The key is that the box moves at constant velocity in both cases; it is in equilibrium. Thus, by Newton's first law, no *net* force acts on it; the vector sum of the upward and downward forces is zero. Since the downward force (the box's weight) is always the same, the upward force must be the same, too, regardless of the box's speed. Note that this is true only while the box is moving at constant speed, not during the initial acceleration from rest.

4.4 Mass and Weight

We've mentioned that the weight of an object is a force—the force of gravitational attraction of the earth (or whatever astronomical body the object is near, such as the moon or Mars). We'll study gravitational interactions in detail in Chapter 6, but we need some preliminary discussion now. The terms *mass* and *weight* are often misused and interchanged in everyday conversation. It's absolutely essential for you to understand clearly the distinctions between these two physical quantities.

Mass characterizes the *inertial* properties of an object. Mass is what keeps the china on the table when you yank the tablecloth out from under it. The greater the mass, the greater is the force needed to cause a given acceleration; this meaning is reflected in Newton's second law, $\Sigma \vec{F} = m\vec{a}$. Weight, on the other hand, is a *force* exerted on an object by the gravitational pull of the earth or some other astronomical body (Figure 4.16). Everyday experience shows us that objects that have large mass also have large weight. A cart loaded with bricks is hard to get started rolling because of its large *mass,* and it is also hard to lift off the ground

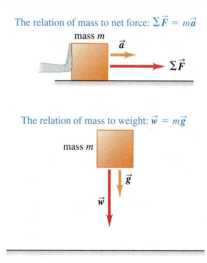

The relation of mass to net force: $\Sigma \vec{F} = m\vec{a}$

The relation of mass to weight: $\vec{w} = m\vec{g}$

▲ **FIGURE 4.16** The relation of mass to net force and to weight.

Mass = 1.00 kg

$w = 9.80 \text{ N}$ $g = 9.80 \text{ m/s}^2$

The mass of an object is constant, but its weight changes with location.

(a) On earth

Mass = 1.00 kg

$w = 1.62 \text{ N}$ $g = 1.62 \text{ m/s}^2$

(b) On the moon

▲ **FIGURE 4.17** Mass and weight for a 1 kg object on the earth and on the moon.

▲ **FIGURE 4.18** Astronaut Buzz Aldrin on the surface of the moon, trying to cope with his own inertia.

because of its large *weight*. On the moon, the cart would be just as hard to get rolling, but it would be easier to lift. So what exactly *is* the relationship between mass and weight?

The answer to this question, according to legend, came to Newton as he sat under an apple tree watching the apples fall. A freely falling object has an acceleration $\vec{a}$ with magnitude equal to g—that is, the acceleration due to gravity (also called the acceleration of free fall). Because of Newton's second law, this acceleration requires a force. If a 1 kg object falls with an acceleration of magnitude $g = 9.8 \text{ m/s}^2$, the required force $\vec{F}$ must have magnitude

$$F = ma = (1 \text{ kg})(9.8 \text{ m/s}^2) = 9.8 \text{ kg} \cdot \text{m/s}^2 = 9.8 \text{ N}.$$

But the force that makes the object accelerate downward is the gravitational pull of the earth—that is, the *weight* of the object. Any object near the surface of the earth that has a mass of 1 kg *must* have a weight with magnitude 9.8 N in order for it to have the acceleration we observe when it is in free fall. More generally, the relation of mass to weight must be as follows:

Relation of mass to weight
The weight of an object with mass m must have a magnitude w equal to the mass times the magnitude of acceleration due to gravity, g:

$$w = mg. \tag{4.9}$$

Because weight is a force, we can write this equation as a vector relation:

$$\vec{w} = m\vec{g}. \tag{4.10}$$

NOTE ▶ Remember that g is the *magnitude* of $\vec{g}$, the acceleration due to gravity, so, by definition, g is always a positive number, Thus, w, given by Equation 4.9, is the *magnitude* of the weight, and it, too, is always positive. In the discussion that follows, we'll sometimes call w "the weight" and F "the force," even though, strictly speaking, we should call w "the magnitude of the weight" and F "the magnitude of the force." ◀

We'll use the value $g = 9.80 \text{ m/s}^2$ for problems dealing with the earth. The value of g actually varies somewhat from point to point on the earth's surface, from about 9.78 to 9.82 m/s², because the earth is not perfectly spherical and because of effects due to its rotation, orbital motion, and composition. At a point where $g = 9.80 \text{ m/s}^2$, the weight of a standard kilogram is $w = 9.80 \text{ N}$. At a different point, where $g = 9.78 \text{ m/s}^2$, the weight is $w = 9.78 \text{ N}$, but the mass is still 1 kg. The weight of an object varies from one location to another; the mass does not. If we take a standard kilogram to the surface of the moon, where the acceleration of free fall is 1.62 m/s², the weight of the standard kilogram is 1.62 N, but its mass is still 1 kg (Figure 4.17). An 80 kg man has a weight on earth of $(80.0 \text{ kg})(9.80 \text{ m/s}^2) = 784 \text{ N}$, but on the moon his weight is only $(80.0 \text{ kg})(1.62 \text{ m/s}^2) = 130 \text{ N}$.

The following brief excerpt from Astronaut Buzz Aldrin's book *Men from Earth* offers some interesting insights into the distinction between mass and weight (Figure 4.18):

> Our portable life-support system backpacks looked simple, but they were hard to put on and tricky to operate. On earth the portable life-support system and space suit combination weighed 190 pounds, but on the moon it was only 30. Combined with my own body weight, that brought me to a total lunar-gravity weight of around 60 pounds.

▶ **Fore!** Alan Shepard is well known as the first American in space and was the fifth man on the moon, but he has another, lesser known distinction: Using the head of a six-iron on the handle of a lunar sample collector, he whacked this golf ball off into the distance, becoming the first and only lunar golfer. The mass of the ball was the same on the moon as on earth, but its weight was only one-sixth of its earth weight, increasing its flight distance substantially.

One of my tests was to jog away from the lunar module to see how maneuverable an astronaut was on the surface. I remembered what Isaac Newton had taught us two centuries before: Mass and weight are not the same. I weighed only 60 pounds, but my *mass* was the same as it was on Earth. Inertia was a problem. I had to plan ahead several steps to bring myself to a stop or to turn without falling.

NOTE ▶ As indicated by Buzz Aldrin's words, the pound is actually a unit of force, not mass. In fact, 1 pound is defined officially as exactly 4.448221615260 newtons. It's handy to remember that a pound is about 4.4 N and a newton is about 0.22 pound. Next time you want to order a "quarter-pounder," try asking for a "one-newtoner" and see what happens. ◀

Here's another useful fact: An object with a mass of 1 kg has a weight of about 2.2 lb at the earth's surface. In the British system, the unit of force is the *pound* (or pound-force), and the unit of mass is the *slug*. The unit of acceleration is 1 foot per second squared, so 1 pound = 1 slug $\cdot$ ft/s^2. In the cgs metric system (not used in this book), the unit of mass is the gram, equal to 10^{-3} kg, and the unit of distance is the centimeter, equal to 10^{-2} m. The corresponding unit of force is called the *dyne:* 1 dyne = 1 g $\cdot$ cm/s^2 = 10^{-5} N.

It's important to understand that the weight of an object, as given by Equation 4.10, acts on the object *all the time,* whether it is in free fall or not. When a 10-kg flowerpot hangs suspended from a chain, it is in equilibrium, and its acceleration is zero. But its 98 N weight is still pulling down on it. In this case the chain pulls up on the pot, applying a 98 N upward force. The *vector sum* of the two 98 N forces is zero, and the pot is in equilibrium.

Activ
ONLINE
Physics   2.9

EXAMPLE 4.4   **Quick stop of a heavy car**

A big luxury car weighing 1.96×10^4 N (about 4400 lb), traveling in the $+x$ direction, makes a fast stop; the x component of the net force acting on it is -1.50×10^4 N. What is its acceleration?

SOLUTION

SET UP Figure 4.19 shows our diagram. We draw the weight as a force with magnitude w. Because the car does not accelerate in the y direction, the road exerts an upward normal force of equal magnitude on the car; for completeness, we include that force in our diagram.

SOLVE To find the acceleration, we'll use Newton's second law, $\sum F_x = ma_x$. First, however, we need the car's mass. Since we know the car's weight, we can find its mass m from Equation 4.9, $w = mg$. We obtain

$$m = \frac{w}{g} = \frac{1.96 \times 10^4 \text{ N}}{9.80 \text{ m/s}^2} = \frac{1.96 \times 10^4 \text{ kg} \cdot \text{m/s}^2}{9.80 \text{ m/s}^2} = 2000 \text{ kg}.$$

▲ **FIGURE 4.19** Our diagram for this problem.

Continued

Then, $\sum F_x = ma_x$ gives

$$a_x = \frac{F_x}{m} = \frac{-1.50 \times 10^4 \text{ N}}{2000 \text{ kg}} = \frac{-1.50 \times 10^4 \text{ kg} \cdot \text{m/s}^2}{2000 \text{ kg}}$$
$$= -7.5 \text{ m/s}^2.$$

REFLECT This acceleration can be written as $-0.77g$. Note that -0.77 is also the ratio of -1.50×10^4 N to 1.96×10^4 N. An

acceleration of this magnitude is possible only on a dry paved road. Don't expect it on a wet or icy road!

Practice Problem: If passenger comfort requires that the acceleration should be no greater in magnitude than $0.10g$, what distance is required to stop the car if its speed is initially 30 m/s (roughly 60 mi/h)? What force is required? *Answers:* 459 m, 1960 N.

▲ **FIGURE 4.20** An equal-arm balance determines the mass of an object by comparing its weight to a known weight.

Usually, the easiest way to measure the mass of an object is to measure its weight, often by comparison with a standard weight. In accordance with Equation 4.10, two objects that have the same weight at a particular location also have the same mass. We can compare weights very precisely; the familiar equal-arm balance (Figure 4.20) can determine with great precision (to one part in 10^6) when the weights of two objects are equal and hence when their masses are equal. This method doesn't work, however, in the "zero-gravity" environment of outer space. Instead, we have to use Newton's second law directly: We apply a known force to the object, measure its acceleration, and compute the mass as the ratio of force to acceleration. This method, or a variation of it, is used to measure the masses of astronauts in orbiting space stations and also the masses of atomic and subatomic particles.

The concept of mass plays two rather different roles in mechanics. On the one hand, the weight of an object (the gravitational force acting on it) is proportional to its mass; we may therefore call the property related to gravitational interactions *gravitational mass*. On the other hand, we can call the inertial property that appears in Newton's second law the *inertial mass*. If these two quantities were different, the acceleration of free fall might well be different for different objects. However, extraordinarily precise experiments have established that, in fact, the two *are* the same, to a precision of better than one part in 10^{12}. Recent efforts to find departures from this equivalence, possibly showing evidence of a previously unknown force, have been inconclusive.

Finally, we remark that the SI units for mass and weight are often misused in everyday life. Incorrect expressions such as "This box weighs 6 kg" are nearly universal. What is meant is that the *mass* of the box, probably determined indirectly by *weighing,* is 6 kg. This usage is so common that there's probably no hope of straightening things out, but be sure you recognize that the term *weight* is often used when *mass* is meant. To keep your own thinking clear, be careful to avoid this kind of mistake! In SI units, weight (a force) is always measured in newtons, mass always in kilograms. (However, we'll often refer to the weight of an object when, strictly speaking, we mean the *magnitude* of its weight.)

4.5 Newton's Third Law

At the beginning of this chapter, we noted that force is a quantitative description of the interaction between two objects. A force acting on an object is always the result of that object's interaction with another object, so forces always come in pairs. As my hand pushes your shoulder, your shoulder pushes back on my hand. When you kick a football, the force your foot exerts on the ball launches it into its trajectory, but you also feel the force the ball exerts on your foot.

Experiments show that whenever two objects interact, the two forces they exert on each other are equal in magnitude and opposite in direction. This fact is called *Newton's third law.* In Figure 4.21, $\vec{F}_{\text{foot on ball}}$ is the force applied by the foot to the ball, and $\vec{F}_{\text{ball on foot}}$ is the force applied by the ball to the foot. The directions of the forces in this example correspond to a *repulsive* interaction,

▲ **FIGURE 4.21** An interacting ball and foot exert forces on each other that are equal in magnitude and opposite in direction.

▶ **An action shot.** This Olympic biathlon competitor knows her physics: Every action has an equal and opposite reaction. When she fires her rifle, the force propelling the bullet forward is matched by an equal and opposite force pushing against the rifle and her. If she had her skis pointed in the direction in which she is firing, she would be pushed backward on the slippery mat and maybe end up flat on her back. By keeping her back ski firmly planted sideways on the mat, she can avoid the possible consequences of ignoring Newton's third law.

tending to push the objects apart. However, interactions can also be *attractive,* such as the gravitational attraction of two masses or the electrical attraction of two particles with opposite charges.

Newton's third law

For two interacting objects A and B, the formal statement of Newton's third law is

$$\vec{F}_{A \text{ on } B} = -\vec{F}_{B \text{ on } A}. \tag{4.11}$$

Newton's own statement, translated from the Latin of the *Principia,* is

> To every action there is always opposed an equal reaction; or, the mutual actions of two objects upon each other are always equal, and directed to contrary parts.

NOTE ▶ In the preceding statement, "action" and "reaction" are the two opposite forces. This terminology is not meant to imply any cause-and-effect relationship: We can consider either force as the action and the other the reaction. We often say simply that the forces are "equal and opposite" meaning that they have equal magnitudes and opposite directions. ◀

EXAMPLE 4.5 Newton's apple on a table

An apple sits in equilibrium on a table. What forces act on the apple? What is the reaction force to each of the forces acting on it? What are the action–reaction pairs?

SOLUTION

SET UP First, in Figure 4.22a, we diagram the situation and the two forces that act on the apple. $\vec{F}_{\text{earth on apple}}$ is the weight of the apple—the downward gravitational force exerted *by* the earth *on* the apple. Similarly, $\vec{F}_{\text{table on apple}}$ is the upward normal force exerted *by* the table *on* the apple.

(a) The forces acting on the apple

(b) The action–reaction pair for the interaction between the apple and the earth

(c) The action–reaction pair for the interaction between the apple and the table

(d) Why the two forces acting on the apple don't form an action–reaction pair

▲ **FIGURE 4.22** The two forces in an action–reaction pair always act on different objects.

Continued

SOLVE The two forces acting on the apple are $\vec{F}_{\text{earth on apple}}$ and $\vec{F}_{\text{table on apple}}$. Because the apple is in equilibrium, it follows from Newton's first law that the vector sum of these two forces on the apple must be zero: $\vec{F}_{\text{earth on apple}} + \vec{F}_{\text{table on apple}} = 0$.

What is the reaction force for $\vec{F}_{\text{earth on apple}}$? As the earth pulls down on the apple, the apple exerts an equally strong upward pull $\vec{F}_{\text{apple on earth}}$ on the earth, as shown in Figure 4.22b. The two forces are

$$\vec{F}_{\text{apple on earth}} = -\vec{F}_{\text{earth on apple}}. \qquad \text{(action and reaction for earth and apple)}$$

These forces represent the mutual interaction between the apple and the earth; one force cannot exist without the other.

Also, as the table pushes up on the apple with force $\vec{F}_{\text{table on apple}}$, the corresponding reaction is the downward force $\vec{F}_{\text{apple on table}}$ exerted on the table by the apple (Figure 4.22c), and we have

$$\vec{F}_{\text{table on apple}} = -\vec{F}_{\text{apple on table}}. \qquad \text{(action and reaction for apple and table)}$$

The two forces acting on the apple are $\vec{F}_{\text{table on apple}}$ and $\vec{F}_{\text{earth on apple}}$. Are they an action–reaction pair? No, they aren't, despite the fact that they are "equal and opposite" (a consequence of Newton's *first* law, not the third). They do not represent the mutual interaction between two objects; they are two different forces acting on the same object. **The two forces in an action–reaction pair *never* act on the same object.** Figure 4.22d shows another way to look at this situation. Suppose we suddenly yank the table out from under the apple. The two forces $\vec{F}_{\text{table on apple}}$ and $\vec{F}_{\text{apple on table}}$ then become zero. But $\vec{F}_{\text{earth on apple}}$ and $\vec{F}_{\text{apple on earth}}$ are still there, and they *do* form an action–reaction pair. Thus, $\vec{F}_{\text{table on apple}}$ can't possibly be the negative of $\vec{F}_{\text{earth on apple}}$ with the table removed.

REFLECT Interaction forces always come in pairs; if you can't find both members of the pair, your diagrams aren't complete. Also, remember that the two forces in an action–reaction pair *never* act on the same object.

EXAMPLE 4.6 **Sliding a stone across the floor**

A stonemason drags a marble block across a floor by pulling on a rope attached to the block (Figure 4.23a). The block has just started to move, and it may not be in equilibrium. How are the various forces related? What are the action–reaction pairs?

SOLUTION

SET UP We have three interacting objects: the block, the rope, and the mason. First we draw separate diagrams showing the horizontal forces acting on each object (Figure 4.23b). Instead of writing out "block on rope," etc., we designate the block as B, the rope R, and the mason M.

SOLVE Vector $\vec{F}_{\text{M on R}}$ represents the force exerted *by the mason on the rope*. The reaction to $\vec{F}_{\text{M on R}}$ is the "equal and opposite" force $\vec{F}_{\text{R on M}}$ exerted *on the mason by the rope*. Vector $\vec{F}_{\text{R on B}}$ represents the force exerted on the block by the rope. The reaction to it is the equal and opposite force $\vec{F}_{\text{B on R}}$ exerted on the rope by the block. From Newton's third law,

$$\vec{F}_{\text{R on M}} = -\vec{F}_{\text{M on R}}$$

and

$$\vec{F}_{\text{B on R}} = -\vec{F}_{\text{R on B}}. \qquad \text{(action–reaction pairs)}$$

The forces $\vec{F}_{\text{M on R}}$ and $\vec{F}_{\text{B on R}}$ are *not* an action–reaction pair (Figure 4.23c). Both of these forces act on the *same* object (the rope); an action and its reaction *must* always act on *different* objects. Furthermore, the forces $\vec{F}_{\text{M on R}}$ and $\vec{F}_{\text{B on R}}$ are not necessarily equal in magnitude (Figure 4.23d). Applying Newton's second law to the rope (mass m_R, acceleration $\vec{a}_R$), we get

$$\vec{F}_{\text{M on R}} + \vec{F}_{\text{B on R}} = m_R \vec{a}_R.$$

If block and rope are accelerating to the right, the rope is not in equilibrium, and $\vec{F}_{\text{M on R}}$ must have greater magnitude than

(a) The block, the rope, and the mason

$\vec{F}_{\text{R on M}}$ $\vec{F}_{\text{M on R}}$

$\vec{F}_{\text{B on R}}$ $\vec{F}_{\text{R on B}}$
(b) The action–reaction pairs

These forces cannot be an action–reaction pair, because they act on the same object (the rope).

$\vec{F}_{\text{B on R}}$ $\vec{F}_{\text{M on R}}$
(c) *Not* an action–reaction pair

These forces are equal only if the rope is in equilibrium (or can be treated as massless).

$\vec{F}_{\text{R on B}}$ $\vec{F}_{\text{M on R}}$
(d) Not necessarily equal

▲ **FIGURE 4.23** Analyzing the forces involved when a stonemason pulls on a block.

Continued

$\vec{F}_{\text{B on R}}$. In the special case in which the rope is in equilibrium, the forces $\vec{F}_{\text{M on R}}$ and $\vec{F}_{\text{B on R}}$ are equal in magnitude, but this is an example of Newton's *first* law, not his *third*. Newton's third law holds whether the rope is accelerating or not. The action–reaction forces $\vec{F}_{\text{M on R}}$ and $\vec{F}_{\text{R on M}}$ are always equal in magnitude to *each other*, as are $\vec{F}_{\text{R on B}}$ and $\vec{F}_{\text{B on R}}$. But $\vec{F}_{\text{M on R}}$ is *not* equal in magnitude to $\vec{F}_{\text{B on R}}$ when the rope is accelerating.

REFLECT If you feel as though you're drowning in subscripts at this point, take heart. Go over this discussion again, comparing the symbols with the vector diagrams, until you're sure you see what's going on.

In the special case in which the rope is in equilibrium, or when we can consider it as massless, then the total force on the rope is zero, and $\vec{F}_{\text{B on R}}$ equals $-\vec{F}_{\text{M on R}}$ because of Newton's *first* or *second* law. Also, $\vec{F}_{\text{B on R}}$ always equals $-\vec{F}_{\text{R on B}}$ by Newton's *third* law, so in this special case, $\vec{F}_{\text{R on B}}$ also equals $\vec{F}_{\text{M on R}}$. We can then think of the rope as "transmitting" to the block, without change, the force that the stonemason exerts on it (Figure 4.23d). This is a useful point of view, but you have to remember that it is valid only when the rope has negligibly small mass or is in equilibrium.

▶ **Out of this world.** This photo shows the liftoff of a Delta Two rocket carrying the *Pathfinder* probe bound for the surface of Mars. A common misconception is that a rocket is propelled by the exhaust gases pushing against the earth. As we know from Newton's third law, the explosive force on the gases being rapidly expelled from the tail of the rocket is matched by an equal and opposite forward force on the rocket itself. It is this second force that pushes the rocket upward and allows it to continue accelerating toward Mars long after it is away from the ground. If the rocket's motion did depend on its gases pressing against the earth, it would be unable to maneuver in outer space and the *Pathfinder* could never reach the Red Planet.

An object, such as the rope in Figure 4.23, that has pulling forces applied at its ends is said to be in **tension,** as we mentioned in Section 4.1. The tension at any point is the magnitude of force acting at that point. In Figure 4.23c, the tension at the right-hand end of the rope is the magnitude of $\vec{F}_{\text{M on R}}$ (or of $\vec{F}_{\text{R on M}}$), and the tension at the left-hand end equals the magnitude of $\vec{F}_{\text{B on R}}$ (or of $\vec{F}_{\text{R on B}}$). If the rope is in equilibrium and if no forces act except at its ends, the tension is the same at both ends and throughout the rope. If the magnitudes of $\vec{F}_{\text{B on R}}$ and $\vec{F}_{\text{M on R}}$ are 50 N each, the tension in the rope is 50 N (*not* 100 N). Resist the temptation to add the two forces; remember that the total force $\vec{F}_{\text{B on R}} + \vec{F}_{\text{M on R}}$ on the rope in this case is zero!

NOTE ▶ Finally, we emphasize once more a fundamental truth: The two forces in an action–reaction pair *never* act on the same object. Remembering this simple fact can often help you avoid confusion about action–reaction pairs and Newton's third law. ◀

Conceptual Analysis 4.4

Giving a push

You use your car to push a friend's pickup truck that has broken down. To bring both of you to a stop, your friend applies the brakes in the truck. Then, in magnitude,

A. the force of the car on the truck is greater than the force of the truck on the car.

B. the force of the car on the truck is equal to the force of the truck on the car.

C. the force of the car on the truck is less than the force of the truck on the car.

SOLUTION Whenever two objects interact with each other, the interaction is described by an action–reaction pair. From Newton's third law, the two forces in this pair are always equal in magnitude and opposite in direction (even though in this case the car and truck may have different masses). So the answer is B. Also, Newton's third law is still obeyed when the objects are accelerating, as they are in this example. Unequal masses and accelerations of the objects don't alter the validity of the third law.

4.6 Free-Body Diagrams

Newton's three laws of motion are a beautifully wrapped package containing the basic principles we need to solve a wide variety of problems in mechanics. They are very simple in form, but the process of applying them to specific situations can pose real challenges.

Let's talk about some useful techniques. When you apply Newton's first or second law ($\sum \vec{F} = 0$ for an equilibrium situation or $\sum \vec{F} = m\vec{a}$ for a non-equilibrium situation), you *must* apply it to some specific object. It is absolutely essential to decide at the beginning what object you're talking about. This statement may sound trivial, but it isn't. Once you have chosen an object, then you have to identify all the forces acting on it. These are the forces that are included in $\sum \vec{F}$. As you may have noticed in Section 4.5, it is easy to get confused between the forces acting *on* an object and the forces exerted *by* that object *on* some other object. Only the forces acting *on* the object go into $\sum \vec{F}$.

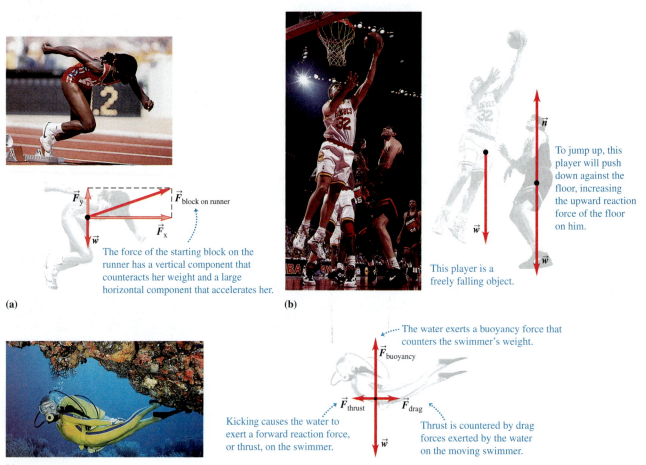

(a) The force of the starting block on the runner has a vertical component that counteracts her weight and a large horizontal component that accelerates her.

(b) This player is a freely falling object.

To jump up, this player will push down against the floor, increasing the upward reaction force of the floor on him.

(c) The water exerts a buoyancy force that counters the swimmer's weight.

Kicking causes the water to exert a forward reaction force, or thrust, on the swimmer.

Thrust is countered by drag forces exerted by the water on the moving swimmer.

▲ **FIGURE 4.24** Some examples of free-body diagrams.

To help identify the relevant forces, draw a **free-body diagram.** What's that? It is a diagram showing the chosen object by itself, "free" of its surroundings, with vectors drawn to show the forces applied to it by the various other objects that interact with it. We have already shown free-body diagrams in some previously worked-out examples. Be careful to include *all* the forces acting on the object, but be equally careful *not* to include any forces that the object exerts on any other object. In particular, the two forces in an action–reaction pair must *never* appear in the same free-body diagram, because they never act on the same object. Figure 4.24 shows some examples of free-body diagrams.

When you have a complete free-body diagram, you should be able to answer, for each force shown, the question "What other object is applying this force?" If you can't answer that question, you may be dealing with a nonexistent force. Sometimes you will have to take the problem apart and draw a separate free-body diagram for each part.

Conceptual Analysis 4.5

Dribble

A boy bounces a basketball straight down against the floor of the court. To answer the following question, it's helpful to draw a free-body diagram and consider the acceleration of the ball.

During the time the ball is in contact with the floor,

A. the force of the floor on the ball becomes much larger than the force of the ball on the floor.

B. the force of the ball on the floor plus the force of the floor on the ball equals the force of acceleration of the ball.

C. the force of the floor on the ball is equal to the force of gravity on the ball plus the force of inertia of the ball.

D. the force of the floor on the ball becomes much larger than the force of gravity on the ball.

SOLUTION First, there is no such thing as "force of acceleration" or "force of inertia." These are erroneous and misleading

concepts, so answers B and C should be eliminated immediately from consideration. During the very short time the ball is touching the floor, the upward force exerted by the floor quickly becomes greater in magnitude than the ball's weight. The ball continues to move downward, but with decreasing speed (and upward acceleration), stops for an instant, then begins to move upward with increasing speed (again upward acceleration). For upward acceleration, the upward force exerted by the floor on the ball must be greater in magnitude than the weight of the ball. Thus, answer D is correct. But Newton's third law requires the force of the floor on the ball and the force of the ball on the floor to be equal and opposite; therefore, answer A cannot be correct. Forces by the ball on other objects have no effect on the acceleration of the ball. The floor pushes up on the ball, and the earth pulls down on it. Because the direction of acceleration is upward as the ball slows, stops, and then accelerates upward, the larger force must be directed upward to produce this upward acceleration. The answer is D.

Quantitative Analysis 4.6

Relating graphs and free-body diagrams

An object moves along the x axis. Assuming that the positive coordinate is to the right and that the forces are constant, which of the following graphs of v_x as a function of time is consistent with the forces shown in the free-body diagram in Figure 4.25?

▶ **FIGURE 4.25**

SOLUTION The force diagram shows the larger force to the right, the positive direction. Hence, the acceleration must be to the right also; a_x is positive. This means that the object is either (a) moving toward the left (the negative direction) and slowing down or (b) moving toward the right and speeding up. None of the graphs show leftward, slowing motion. D shows rightward, slowing motion, while A shows a constant velocity. Both B and C show rightward and speeding-up motion, but only C has a constant slope (corresponding to constant acceleration). Since the forces are constant, the acceleration is constant also, as indicated by the straight line in answer C.

PROBLEM-SOLVING STRATEGY 4.1 **Newton's laws**

SET UP

1. Always define your coordinate system. A diagram showing the positive axis direction is essential. If you know the direction of the acceleration, it's often convenient to take that as your positive direction. If you will need to calculate displacements of the moving object, you also need to specify the location of the origin of your coordinate system.
2. Be consistent with signs. Once you define the x axis and its positive direction, velocity, acceleration, and force components in that direction are also positive.
3. In applying Newton's laws, always concentrate on a specific object. Draw a free-body diagram showing all the forces (magnitudes and directions) acting *on* this object, but *do not* include forces that the object exerts on any other object. The acceleration of the object is determined by the forces acting on it, not by the forces it exerts on something else. Represent the object as a dot or by a simple sketch; you don't have to be an artist.

SOLVE

4. Identify the known and unknown quantities, and give each unknown quantity an algebraic symbol. If you know the direction of a force at the start, use a symbol to represent the *magnitude* of the force (always a positive quantity). Keep in mind that the *component* of this force along a particular axis direction may still be either positive or negative.
5. Always check units for consistency. When appropriate, use the conversion $1\,\text{N} = 1\,\text{kg} \cdot \text{m/s}^2$.

REFLECT

6. Check to make sure that your forces obey Newton's third law. When you can guess the direction of the net force, make sure that its direction is the same as that of the acceleration, as required by Newton's second law.

In Chapter 5 we'll expand this strategy to deal with more complex problems, but it's important for you to use it consistently from the very start, to develop good habits in the systematic analysis of problems.

EXAMPLE 4.7 **Tension in a massless chain**

To improve the acoustics in an auditorium, a sound reflector with a mass of 200 kg is suspended by a chain from the ceiling. What is its weight? What force (magnitude and direction) does the chain exert on it? What is the tension in the chain? Assume that the mass of the chain itself is negligible.

SOLUTION

SET UP The reflector is in equilibrium, so we use Newton's first law, $\Sigma \vec{F} = 0$. We draw separate free-body diagrams for the reflector and the chain (Figure 4.26). We take the positive y axis to be upward, as shown. Each force has only a y component. We give symbolic labels to the magnitudes of the unknown forces, using T to represent the tension in the chain.

SOLVE The magnitude of the weight $\vec{w}$ of the reflector is given by Equation 4.9:

$$w = mg = (200\,\text{kg})(9.80\,\text{m/s}^2) = 1960\,\text{N}.$$

Armed with this number and Newton's first law, we can compute the unknown force magnitudes.

The weight $\vec{w}$ of the reflector is a force pointing in the negative y direction, so its y component is $-1960\,\text{N}$. The upward force $\vec{T}$ exerted on the reflector by the chain has unknown magnitude T. Because the reflector is in equilibrium, the sum of the y components of force on it must be zero:

$$\Sigma F_y = T + (-1960\,\text{N}) = 0, \qquad \text{so} \qquad T = 1960\,\text{N}.$$

The chain pulls *up* on the reflector with a force $\vec{T}$ of magnitude 1960 N. By Newton's third law, the reflector pulls *down* on the chain with a force of magnitude 1960 N.

Continued

The chain is also in equilibrium, so the vector sum of forces on it must equal zero. For this to be true, an upward force with magnitude 1960 N must act on it at its top end. The tension in the chain is $T = 1960$ N.

REFLECT Note that we have defined T to be the *magnitude* of a force, so it is always positive. But the y component of force acting on the chain at its lower end is $-T = -1960$ N. The tension is the same at every point in the chain; imagine cutting a link and then pulling the cut ends together. To hold them together requires a force with magnitude T on each cut end. If the chain isn't massless, the situation is different, as the next example shows.

Practice Problem: The weight of the reflector (the earth's gravitational pull) and the force the reflector exerts on the earth form an action–reaction pair. Determine the magnitude and direction of each of these forces. *Answers:* 1960 N down, 1960 N up.

(a) The reflector and chain

(b) Free-body diagrams for the reflector and the chain

▲ **FIGURE 4.26** The diagrams we draw for this problem.

EXAMPLE 4.8 **Tension in a chain with mass**

Suppose the mass of the chain in Example 4.7 is not negligible, but is 10.0 kg. Find the forces at the ends of the chain.

SOLUTION

SET UP Again we draw separate free-body diagrams for the reflector and the chain (Figure 4.27); each is in equilibrium. We take the y axis to be vertically upward. The weight w_C of the chain is $w_C = m_C g = (10.0\ \text{kg})(9.8\ \text{m/s}^2) = 98$ N. The free-body diagrams are different from those in Figure 4.26 because the magnitudes of the forces acting on the two ends of the chain are no longer equal. (Otherwise the chain couldn't be in equilibrium.) We label these two forces T_1 and T_2.

SOLVE Note that the two forces labeled T_2 form an action–reaction pair; that's how we know that they have the same magnitude. The equilibrium condition $\Sigma F_y = 0$ for the reflector is

$$T_2 + (-1960\ \text{N}) = 0, \quad \text{so} \quad T_2 = 1960\ \text{N}.$$

There are now three forces acting on the chain: its weight and the forces at the two ends. The equilibrium condition $\Sigma F_y = 0$ for the chain is

$$T_1 + (-T_2) + (-98\ \text{N}) = 0.$$

Note that the y component of T_1 is positive because it points in the $+y$ direction, but the y components of both T_2 and 98 N are negative. When we substitute the value $T_2 = 1960$ N and solve for T_1, we find that

$$T_1 = 2058\ \text{N}.$$

Alternative Solution: An alternative procedure is to draw a free-body diagram for the composite object consisting of the reflector and the chain together (Figure 4.27b). The two forces on this composite object are the upward force T_1 at the top of the chain and the total weight, with magnitude 1960 N + 98 N =

(a) Free-body diagrams for reflector and chain.

(b) Free-body diagram for reflector and chain treated as a unit.

▲ **FIGURE 4.27** Two alternative diagrams we could draw for this problem.

2058 N. Again, we find that $T_1 = 2058$ N. Note that we cannot find T_2 by this method; we still need a separate free-body diagram for one of the objects.

REFLECT When a composite object can be broken into two or more component parts, there are usually several alternative solutions. Often, the calculations can be simplified by a clever choice of subsystems. Also, solving a problem in two or more alternative ways provides a consistency check that's useful in finding errors.

Practice Problem: Solve the problem described in this example by using two free-body diagrams, one for the composite reflector–chain object, and one for the reflector alone.

EXAMPLE 4.9 **Weighing yourself in an elevator**

You stand on a bathroom scale that rests on the floor of an elevator. (Don't ask why!) Standing on the scale compresses internal springs and activates a dial that indicates your weight in newtons. When the elevator is at rest, the scale reads 600 N. Then the elevator begins to move upward with a constant acceleration $a_y = 2.00 \text{ m/s}^2$. **(a)** Determine your mass. **(b)** Determine the scale reading while the elevator is accelerating. **(c)** If you read the scale without realizing that the elevator is accelerating upward, what might you *think* your mass is?

SOLUTION

SET UP All the forces are vertical; we take the y axis to be vertically upward. We neglect the weight of the scale itself. When the scale is in equilibrium (not accelerating), the total force acting on it must be zero. When it reads 600 N, forces of magnitude 600 N (with opposite directions) are applied to its top and bottom surfaces. Using this analysis, we draw separate free-body diagrams for you and the scale (Figure 4.28).

SOLVE Part (a): At first, you, the scale, and the elevator are at rest in an inertial system; all three objects are in equilibrium. You push down on the scale with a force of magnitude 600 N, and (from Newton's third law) the scale applies an equal and opposite upward force to your feet. The only other force on you is your weight; you are in equilibrium, so the *total y* component of force on you is zero. Your weight is 600 N, and your mass is

$$m = \frac{w}{g} = \frac{600 \text{ N}}{9.80 \text{ m/s}^2} = 61.2 \text{ kg} \qquad \text{(about 135 lb).}$$

Part (b): When the system accelerates upward at 2.00 m/s^2, your weight is still 600 N, but now the upward force the scale applies to your feet is different because you are no longer in equilibrium. We'll call the magnitude of the upward force F (Figure 4.28b). We use Newton's second law to relate the acceleration to the net force:

$$F - 600 \text{ N} = ma = (61.2 \text{ kg})(2.00 \text{ m/s}^2)$$

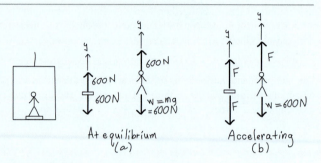

▲ **FIGURE 4.28** Our diagrams for this problem.

and

$$F = 722 \text{ N.}$$

Part (c): If you think your weight is 722 N, then you are likely to conclude that your mass is $m = w/g = (722 \text{ N})/(9.8 \text{ m/s}^2) = 73.7 \text{ kg}$, instead of the actual value of 61.2 kg.

REFLECT Relate what we've said here to your own feeling of being lighter or heavier in an elevator. Do these feelings occur only when the elevator is accelerating?

Practice Problem: Suppose the elevator is accelerating *downward* at 2.00 m/s^2. What does the scale read during the acceleration? *Answer:* 478 N.

SUMMARY

Force

(Section 4.1) Force, a vector quantity, is a quantitative measure of the mechanical interaction between two objects. When several forces act on an object, the effect is the same as when a single force, equal to the vector sum, or resultant, of the forces, acts on the object.

Two forces acting on a point have the same effect as a single force $\vec{R}$ equal to their vector sum.

A force may be treated as the vector sum of its component vectors.

Newton's First Law

(Section 4.2) Newton's first law states that when no force acts on an object or when the vector sum of all forces acting on it is zero, the object is in equilibrium. If the object is initially at rest, it remains at rest; if it is initially in motion, it continues to move with constant velocity. This law is valid only in inertial frames of reference.

If the vector sum of the forces acting on an object is zero, the object remains at rest or (as here) in motion with constant velocity.

Mass and Newton's Second Law

(Section 4.3) The inertial properties of an object are characterized by its *mass*. The acceleration of an object under the action of a given set of forces is directly proportional to the vector sum of the forces and inversely proportional to the mass of the object. This relationship is Newton's second law:

An object's acceleration depends on its mass and on the net force acting on it.

$$\Sigma\vec{F} = m\vec{a}, \qquad (4.7)$$

or, in component form, $\Sigma F_x = ma_x$ and $\Sigma F_y = ma_y$ (Equations 4.8).

Mass and Weight

(Section 4.4) The weight of an object is the gravitational force exerted on it by the earth (or whatever other object exerts the gravitational force). Weight is a force and is therefore a vector quantity. The magnitude of the weight of an object at any specific location is equal to the product of the mass m of the object and the magnitude of the acceleration due to gravity, g, at that location:

$$w = mg. \qquad (4.9)$$

The weight of an object depends on its location, but the mass is independent of location.

An object's weight depends on its mass and on the acceleration due to gravity at its location.

Newton's Third Law

(Section 4.5) Newton's third law states that "action equals reaction"; when two bodies interact, they exert forces on each other that, at each instant, are equal in magnitude and opposite in direction. The two forces in an action–reaction pair always act on two different bodies; they never act on the same object.

An action–reaction pair: $\vec{F}_{\text{ball on foot}} = -\vec{F}_{\text{foot on ball}}$. The two forces represent a *mutual interaction* of two objects, and each acts on a *different* object.

Free-Body Diagrams

(Section 4.6) In Newton's second law, only the forces acting on an object go into $\Sigma\vec{F}$. To help identify the relevant forces, draw a free-body diagram. Such a diagram shows the chosen object by itself, "free" of its surroundings, with vectors drawn to show the forces applied to it by the various other objects that interact with it. Be careful to include *all* the forces acting on the object, but be equally careful *not* to include any forces that the object exerts on any other object. In particular, the two forces in an action–reaction pair must *never* appear in the same free-body diagram, because they never act on the same object.

A free-body diagram of a man dragging a crate. The diagram shows *all* the forces acting on the man, and *only* forces acting on the man.

Man (treated as particle)

Conceptual Questions

1. When a car accelerates starting from rest, where is the force applied to the car in order to cause its acceleration? What object exerts this force on the car?

2. When a car stops suddenly, the passengers are "thrown forward" out of their seats (if they are not wearing seat belts). What causes this to happen? Are they really *thrown* forward?

3. For medical reasons, it is important for astronauts in outer space to determine their body mass at regular intervals. Devise a scheme for measuring body mass in a zero-gravity environment.

4. High-wire circus performers sometimes use a safety net to catch them if they fall. Since this net is not much above ground level, why does it provide a safer landing than if they had just landed on the ground?

5. A passenger in a bus notices that a ball which has been at rest in the aisle suddenly starts to roll toward the front of the bus. What can the passenger conclude about the motion of the bus from this observation?

6. If you hit the sidewalk with a hammer, the hammer bounces back at you. How does this process involve Newton's third law?

7. In a head-on collision between a compact hybrid car and a gas-guzzling SUV, which vehicle is acted upon by the greater force? So why are people in the smaller car more likely to get injured than those in the large one, assuming that both cars are equally strong?

8. Suppose you are in a car in a very dense fog and cannot see the meters on your dashboard or anything outside the car. (Maybe you should not be driving under these conditions!) (a) How can you tell if your car is speeding up or slowing down? (b) Can you tell if your car is at rest or is moving with uniform velocity?

9. If a woman in an elevator drops her briefcase, but it does not fall to the floor, what can she conclude about the elevator's motion?

10. You are in a spaceship far from any stars or planets when you notice that if you release an object, it accelerates toward your feet at 9.8 m/s². (a) What can you conclude about the motion of the spaceship? (b) What force, if any, do you feel on your feet from the floor? (c) Explain how your observations in parts (a) and (b) lead you to believe that gravity is present. (d) Is gravity *really* present in the spaceship? How has the ship generated artificial gravity?

11. When a car is hit from behind, people in that car can receive a whiplash injury to their necks. Use Newton's laws of motion to explain why this occurs.

12. If your hands are wet and no towel is handy, you can remove excess water by shaking them. Use Newton's laws to explain why doing this gets rid of the water.

13. It is possible to play catch with a softball in an airplane in level flight just as though the plane were at rest. Is this still possible when the plane is making a turn?

14. Newton's third law tells us that if you push a box with a 15 N force, it pushes back on you with a 15 N force. How can you ever accelerate this box if it always pushes back with the same force you exert on it?

15. If you drop a 10 lb rock and a 10 lb pillow from the same height with no air resistance, which one is moving faster when they reach the ground? So why would you rather be hit by the pillow than the rock?

16. Which "feels" a greater pull due to gravity, a heavy object or a light object? So why do heavy objects *not* accelerate faster than light objects?

17. If you step hard on the accelerator pedal of your car, your body feels "pushed back" in the seat. (a) Why do you feel this? Are you really pushed back? (b) Make a free-body diagram of your body under these circumstances.

Multiple-Choice Problems

1. A force F is required to push a crate along a rough horizontal floor at a constant speed V with friction present. What force is needed to push this crate along the same floor at a constant speed $3V$ if friction is the same as before?
   A. A constant force $3F$ is needed.
   B. A force that gradually increases from F to $3F$ is needed.
   C. A constant force F is needed.
   D. No force is needed, since the crate has no acceleration.

2. On a horizontal road, a small sedan is pulling a large station wagon that has run out of gas. While the sedan is speeding up to highway speeds,
   A. the sedan pulls harder on the station wagon than the station wagon pulls on the sedan; otherwise there would be no acceleration.
   B. the station wagon always pulls just as hard on the sedan as the sedan pulls on the station wagon, no matter what the acceleration is.
   C. it is not possible to know which car pulls harder on the other without knowing their masses.

3. You are standing on a spring scale in an elevator that is moving upward with a constant speed. The reading of this scale
   A. cannot be determined without knowing the speed of the elevator.
   B. is the same as when the elevator was at rest.
   C. is less than when the elevator was at rest.
   D. is greater than when the elevator was at rest.

4. A golfer tees off and hits the ball with a mighty swing. During the brief time the golf club is in contact with the ball,
   A. the ball pushes just as hard on the club as the club pushes on the ball.
   B. the push of the club on the ball is much greater than the push of the ball on the club, since the club makes the ball move.
   C. the push of the ball on the club would be equal to the push of the club on the ball only if the ball did not move.
   D. the club pushes harder on the ball than the ball does on the club because the club has a greater mass than the ball.

5. Three books are at rest on a horizontal table, as shown in Figure 4.29. The *net* force on the middle book is
   A. 5 N downward.
   B. 15 N upward.
   C. 15 N downward.
   D. 0 N.

▲ **FIGURE 4.29** Multiple-choice problem 5.

6. In outer space, where there is no gravity or air, an astronaut

pushes with an equal force of 12 N on a 2 N moon rock and on a 4 N moon rock.
A. Since both rocks are weightless, they will have the same acceleration.
B. The 4 N rock pushes back on the astronaut twice as hard as the 2 N rock.
C. Both rocks push back on the astronaut with 12 N.
D. Since both rocks are weightless, they do not push back on the astronaut.

7. A rocket in outer space (no gravity, no air) runs out of fuel at a time T when it has a speed V. Which graph or graphs below describe the rocket's motion after time T?

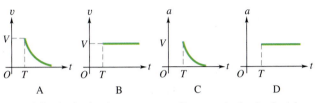

A   B   C   D

8. A 3 lb physics book rests on an ordinary scale that is placed on a horizontal table. The reaction force to the downward 3 lb force on the book is
A. an upward 3 lb force on the scale due to the table.
B. an upward 3 lb force on the book due to the scale.
C. an upward 3 lb force on the table due to the floor.
D. an upward 3 lb force on the earth due to the book.

9. A person pushes horizontally with constant force P on a 250 N box resting on a frictionless horizontal floor. Which of the following statements about this box is correct?
A. The box will accelerate no matter how small P is.
B. The box will not accelerate unless $P > 250$ N.
C. The box will move with constant velocity because P is constant.
D. Once the box is set moving, it will come to rest after P is removed.

10. Suppose the sun, including its gravity, suddenly disappeared. Which of the following statements best describes the subsequent motion of the earth?
A. The earth would continue moving in a straight line tangent to its original direction, but would gradually slow down.
B. The earth would speed up because the sun's gravity would not be able to slow it down.
C. The earth would continue moving in a straight line tangent to its original direction and would not change its speed.
D. The earth would move directly outward with constant speed away from the sun's original position.

11. Three weights hang by very light wires as shown in Figure 4.30. What must be true about the tensions in these wires? (There may be more than one correct choice.)
A. The tension in A is the greatest.
B. The tension in C is the greatest.
C. All three wires have the same tension because the system is in equilibrium.
D. The tension in C is the least.

▲ **FIGURE 4.30**
Multiple-choice problem 11.

12. A woman normally weighs 125 lb. If she is standing on a spring scale in an elevator that is traveling *downward,* but slowing up, the scale will read
A. more than 125 lb.
B. 125 lb.
C. less than 125 lb.
D. It is impossible to answer this question without knowing the acceleration of the elevator.

13. A worker pushes horizontally on a 2000 N refrigerator on a kitchen floor with a force of 25 N.
A. If the refrigerator moves forward, this person feels it pushing back with less than 25 N.
B. The person always feels a 25 N push from the refrigerator.
C. The person feels a 25 N push from the refrigerator only if it does not move.
D. The person feels a 2000 N push from the refrigerator.

14. Far from any gravity, an astronaut accidentally releases a metal wrench inside a spaceship that is traveling at a constant velocity of 250 km/s away from earth in outer space. What will be the subsequent behavior of that wrench as observed by the astronaut?
A. It will fall to the floor with constant velocity.
B. It will fall to the floor with constant acceleration.
C. It will fall to the back of the spaceship with constant velocity.
D. It will fall to the back of the spaceship with constant acceleration.
E. It will remain right where the astronaut released it.

15. A worker pulls horizontally on a crate on a rough horizontal floor, causing it to move forward with constant velocity. In Figure 4.31, force A is the pull of the worker and force B is the force of friction due to the floor. Which one of the following statements about these forces is correct?
A. $A < B$ B. $A = B$ C. $A > B$

▲ **FIGURE 4.31** Multiple-choice problem 15.

16. A person pushes two boxes with a horizontal 100 N force on a frictionless floor, as shown in Figure 4.32. Box A is heavier than box B. Which of the following statements about these boxes is correct?
A. Box A pushes on box B with a force of 100 N, and box B pushes on box A with a force of 100 N.
B. Box A pushes on box B harder than box B pushes on box A.
C. Boxes A and B push on each other with equal forces of less than 100 N.
D. The boxes will not begin to move unless the total weight of the two boxes is less than 100 N.

▲ **FIGURE 4.32** Multiple-choice problem 16.

Problems

4.1 Force

1. • A warehouse worker pushes a crate along the floor, as shown in Figure 4.33, by a force of 10 N that points downward at an angle of 45° below the horizontal. Find the horizontal and vertical components of the push.

2. • Two dogs pull horizontally on ropes attached to a post; the angle between the ropes is 60.0°. If dog A exerts a force of 270 N and dog B exerts a force of 300 N, find the magnitude of the resultant force and the angle it makes with dog A's rope.

▲ **FIGURE 4.33** Problem 1.

3. • A man is dragging a trunk up the loading ramp of a mover's truck. The ramp has a slope angle of 20.0°, and the man pulls upward with a force $\vec{F}$ of magnitude 375 N whose direction makes an angle of 30.0° with the ramp. (See Figure 4.34.) Find the horizontal and vertical components of the force $\vec{F}$.

▲ **FIGURE 4.34** Problem 3.

4. • **Jaw injury.** Due to a jaw injury, a patient must wear a strap (see Figure 4.35) that produces a net upward force of 5.00 N on his chin. The tension is the same throughout the strap. To what tension must the strap be adjusted to provide the necessary upward force?

▲ **FIGURE 4.35** Problem 4.

5. • Workmen are trying to free an SUV stuck in the mud. To extricate the vehicle, they use three horizontal ropes, producing the force vectors shown in Figure 4.36. (a) Find the x and y components of each of the three pulls. (b) Use the components to find the magnitude and direction of the resultant of the three pulls.

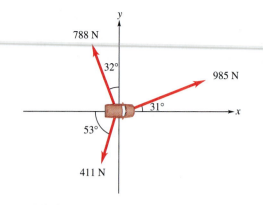

▲ **FIGURE 4.36** Problem 5.

4.3 Mass and Newton's Second Law

6. • A box rests on a frozen pond, which serves as a frictionless horizontal surface. If a fisherman applies a horizontal force with magnitude 48.0 N to the box and produces an acceleration of magnitude 3.00 m/s², what is the mass of the box?

7. • In outer space, a constant net force of magnitude 140 N is exerted on a 32.5 kg probe initially at rest. (a) What acceleration does this force produce? (b) How far does the probe travel in 10.0 s?

8. •• A 68.5 kg skater moving initially at 2.40 m/s on rough horizontal ice comes to rest uniformly in 3.52 s due to friction from the ice. What force does friction exert on the skater?

9. •• **Animal dynamics.** An adult 68 kg cheetah can accelerate from rest to 20.1 m/s (45 mph) in 2.0 s. Assuming constant acceleration, (a) find the net external force causing this acceleration. (b) Where does the force come from? That is, what exerts the force on the cheetah?

10. •• A hockey puck with mass 0.160 kg is at rest on the horizontal, frictionless surface of a rink. A player applies a force of 0.250 N to the puck, parallel to the surface of the ice, and continues to apply this force for 2.00 s. What are the position and speed of the puck at the end of that time?

11. •• A dock worker applies a constant horizontal force of 80.0 N to a block of ice on a smooth horizontal floor. The frictional force is negligible. The block starts from rest and moves 11.0 m in the first 5.00 s. What is the mass of the block of ice?

4.4 Mass and Weight

12. • (a) What is the mass of a book that weighs 3.20 N in the laboratory? (b) In the same lab, what is the weight of a dog whose mass is 14.0 kg?

13. • (a) What is the mass, in both kilograms and slugs, of a radio that weighs 6.00 lb on earth? (b) What is the weight, in both pounds and newtons, of a stereo speaker whose mass is 0.900 slug?

14. • (a) How many newtons does a 150 lb person weigh? (b) Should a veterinarian be skeptical if someone said that her adult collie weighed 40 N? (c) Should a nurse question a medical chart which showed that an average-looking patient had a mass of 200 kg?

15. • (a) An ordinary flea has a mass of 210 μg. How many newtons does it weigh? (b) The mass of a typical froghopper is 12.3 mg. How many newtons does it weigh? (c) A house cat

typically weighs 45 N. How many pounds does it weigh and what is its mass in kilograms?

16. • (a) Would 100 N be a reasonable weight for a typical adult **BIO** person? (b) Would 100 slugs be a reasonable mass for an adult? (c) How many pounds would a typical adult male weigh? (d) What would be a reasonable mass, in kilograms, for an ordinary adult female? (e) Would it be considered extraordinary if a newborn baby had a mass of 1.0 slug?

17. • Which is heavier, (a) a 1 kg stone or a 1 N stone, (b) a 1 slug stone or a 1 lb stone, (c) a 1 slug stone or a 1 N stone, (d) a 1 kg stone or a 1 slug stone, (e) a 1 kg stone or a 1 lb stone?

18. • **Interpreting a medical chart.** You, a resident physician, **BIO** are reading the medical chart of a normal adult female patient. Carelessly, one of the nurses has entered this woman's weight as a number without units. Another nurse has offered a suggestion for what the units might be. In each of the following cases, decide whether this nurse's suggestion is physically reasonable: (a) The number is 150, and the nurse suggests that the units are kilograms. (b) The number is 4.25, and the nurse suggests that the units are slugs. (c) The number is 65,000, and the nurse suggests that the units are grams.

19. • What does a 138 N rock weigh if it is accelerating (a) upward at 12 m/s², (b) downward at 3.5 m/s²? (c) What would be the answers to parts (a) and (b) if the rock had a mass of 138 kg? (d) What would be the answers to parts (a) and (b) if the rock were moving with a constant upward velocity of 23 m/s?

20. •• At the surface of Jupiter's moon Io, the acceleration due to gravity is 1.81 m/s². If a piece of ice weighs 44.0 N at the surface of the earth, (a) what is its mass on the earth's surface? (b) What are its mass and weight on the surface of Io?

21. •• A scientific instrument that weighs 85.2 N on the earth weighs 32.2 N at the surface of Mercury. (a) What is the acceleration due to gravity on Mercury? (b) What is the instrument's mass on earth and on Mercury?

22. •• **Planet X!** When venturing forth on Planet X, you throw a 5.24 kg rock upward at 13.0 m/s and find that it returns to the same level 1.51 s later. What does the rock weigh on Planet X?

23. •• The driver of a 1750 kg car traveling on a horizontal road at 110 km/h suddenly applies the brakes. Due to a slippery pavement, the friction of the road on the tires of the car, which is what slows down the car, is 25% of the weight of the car. (a) What is the acceleration of the car? (b) How many meters does it travel before stopping under these conditions?

4.5 Newton's Third Law

24. • You drag a heavy box along a rough horizontal floor by a horizontal rope. Identify the reaction force to each of the following forces: (a) the pull of the rope on the box, (b) the friction force on the box, (c) the normal force on the box, and (d) the weight of the box.

25. • Imagine that you are holding a book weighing 4 N at rest on the palm of your hand. Complete the following sentences: (a) A downward force of magnitude 4 N is exerted on the book by _____. (b) An upward force of magnitude _____ is exerted on _____ by the hand. (c) Is the upward force in part (b) the reaction to the downward force in part (a)? d) The reaction to the force in part (a) is a force of magnitude _____, exerted on _____ by

_____. Its direction is _____. (e) The reaction to the force in part (b) is a force of magnitude _____, exerted on _____ by _____. Its direction is _____. (f) The forces in parts (a) and (b) are "equal and opposite" because of Newton's _____ law. (g) The forces in parts (b) and (e) are "equal and opposite" because of Newton's _____ law.

26. • Suppose now that you exert an upward force of magnitude 5 N on the book in the previous problem. (a) Does the book remain in equilibrium? (b) Is the force exerted on the book by your hand equal and opposite to the force exerted on the book by the earth? (c) Is the force exerted on the book by the earth equal and opposite to the force exerted on the earth by the book? (d) Is the force exerted on the book by your hand equal and opposite to the force exerted on your hand by the book? Finally, suppose that you snatch your hand away while the book is moving upward. (e) How many forces then act on the book? (f) Is the book in equilibrium?

27. • A bottle is given a push along a frictionless tabletop and slides off the edge of the table. (a) What forces are exerted on the bottle while it is (i) being pushed, (ii) on the table, but free of the push, and (iii) falling from the table to the floor? (b) What is the reaction force to each force in part (a)?

4.6 Free-Body Diagrams

28. • A person throws a 2.5 lb stone into the air with an initial upward speed of 15 ft/s. Make a free-body diagram for this stone (a) after it is free of the person's hand and is traveling upward, (b) at its highest point, (c) when it is traveling downward, and (d) while it is being thrown upward, but is still in contact with the person's hand.

29. • The driver of a car traveling at 65 mph suddenly hits his brakes on a horizontal highway. (a) Make a free-body diagram of the car while it is slowing down. (b) Make a free-body diagram of a passenger in a car that is accelerating on a freeway entrance ramp.

30. • A tennis ball traveling horizontally at 22 m/s suddenly hits a vertical brick wall and bounces back with a horizontal velocity of 18 m/s. Make a free-body diagram of this ball (a) just before it hits the wall, (b) just after it has bounced free of the wall, and (c) while it is in contact with the wall.

31. • A 135 lb skater is coasting on a horizontal ice pond. Make a free-body diagram of this skater (a) if the pond is frictionless and (b) if the pond produces some friction on his skates.

32. • A 25 ton rocket is launched vertically upward by the thrust of its engines, increasing its speed by 0.50 m/s every second. Inside this rocket, a 126 lb astronaut stands vertically on the floor. Make a free-body diagram of (a) the rocket (which includes the astronaut inside) and (b) the astronaut.

33. • A person drags her 65 N suitcase along the rough horizontal floor by pulling upward at 30° above the horizontal with a 50 N force. Make a free-body diagram of this suitcase.

34. •• A factory worker pushes horizontally on a 250 N crate with a force of 75 N on a horizontal rough floor. A 135 N crate rests on top of the one being pushed and moves along with it. Make a free-body diagram of *each* crate if the friction force is less than the worker's push.

35. •• A dock worker pulls two boxes connected by a rope on a horizontal floor, as shown in Figure 4.37. All the ropes are

▲ **FIGURE 4.37** Problem 35.

horizontal, and there is some friction with the floor. Make a free-body diagram of each box.

36. •• A hospital orderly pushes horizontally on two boxes of equipment on a rough horizontal floor, as shown in Figure 4.38. Make a free-body diagram of each box.

▲ **FIGURE 4.38** Problem 36.

37. • A uniform 25.0 kg chain 2.00 m long supports a 50.0 kg chandelier in a large public building. Find the tension in (a) the bottom link of the chain, (b) the top link of the chain, and (c) the middle link of the chain.

38. • A 155 N rock is hoisted upward with an acceleration of 1.50 m/s^2 by a vertical chain of negligible weight. (a) Make a free-body diagram of the rock. (b) What is the tension in (i) the top link of the chain, (ii) the bottom link, and (iii) the middle link?

39. • A 275 N bucket is lifted with an acceleration of 2.50 m/s^2 by a 125 N uniform vertical chain. Start each of the following parts with a free-body diagram. Find the tension in (a) the top link of the chain, (b) the bottom link of the chain, and (c) the middle link of the chain.

40. •• **Human biomechanics.** World-class sprinters can spring **BIO** out of the starting blocks with an acceleration that is essentially horizontal and of magnitude 15 m/s^2. (a) How much horizontal force must a 55-kg sprinter exert on the starting blocks during a start to produce this acceleration? (b) What exerts the force that propels the sprinter, the blocks or the sprinter himself?

41. •• A 22-caliber rifle bullet of mass 1.80 g, traveling at 350 m/s, strikes a block of soft wood, which it penetrates to a depth of 0.130 m. The block of wood is clamped in place and doesn't move. Assume a constant retarding force. (a) Make a free-body diagram of the bullet while it is slowing down in the wood. (b) How much time is required for the bullet to stop? (c) What force, in newtons, does the wood exert on the bullet?

42. •• **Human biomechanics.** The fastest pitched baseball was **BIO** measured at 46 m/s. Typically, a baseball has a mass of 145 g. If the pitcher exerted his force (assumed to be horizontal and constant) over a distance of 1.0 m, (a) what force did he produce on the ball during this record-setting pitch? (b) Make free-body diagrams of the ball during the pitch and just *after* it has left the pitcher's hand.

43. •• You walk into an elevator, step onto a scale, and push the "up" button. You also recall that your normal weight is 625 N. Start each of the following parts with a free-body diagram. (a) If the elevator has an acceleration of magnitude 2.50 m/s^2, what does the scale read? (b) If you start holding a 3.85 kg package by a light vertical string, what will be the tension in this string once the elevator begins accelerating?

44. •• In the previous problem, suppose you had pushed the "down" button instead, but everything else was the same. (a) What does the scale read? (b) What is the tension in the string supporting the package? (Don't forget the free-body diagrams!)

45. •• **The space shuttle.** During the first stage of its launch, a space shuttle goes from rest to 4973 km/h while rising a vertical distance of 45 km. Assume constant acceleration and no variation in g over this distance. (a) What is the acceleration of the shuttle? (b) If a 55.0 kg astronaut is standing on a scale inside the shuttle during this launch, how hard will the scale push on her? Start with a free-body diagram of the astronaut. (c) If this astronaut did not realize that the shuttle had left the launch pad, what would she think were her weight and mass?

46. • In the previous problem, suppose a tool having a normal earth weight of 125 N was hanging by a very light wire from the ceiling of the shuttle. (a) Make a free-body diagram of this tool. (b) Find the tension in the wire.

General Problems

47. •• An 11,000 N test car travels 44.5 m before stopping from an initial speed of 28.7 m/s on dry horizontal pavement with its wheels locked. (a) Make a free-body diagram of this car while it is slowing down. (b) What external force causes it to slow down? (c) Assuming constant acceleration, find the magnitude of the force in part (b).

48. •• A rifle shoots a 4.20 g bullet out of its barrel. The bullet has a muzzle velocity of 965 m/s just as it leaves the barrel. Assuming a constant horizontal acceleration over a distance of 45.0 cm starting from rest, with no friction between the bullet and the barrel, (a) what force does the rifle exert on the bullet while it is in the barrel? (b) Draw a free-body diagram of the bullet (i) while it is in the barrel and (ii) just *after* it has left the barrel. (c) How many g's of acceleration does the rifle give this bullet? (d) For how long a time is the bullet in the barrel?

49. •• **Insect dynamics.** The froghopper (*Philaenus spumarius*), **BIO** the champion leaper of the insect world, has a mass of 12.3 mg and leaves the ground (in the most energetic jumps) at 4.0 m/s from a vertical start. The jump itself lasts a mere 1.0 ms before the insect is clear of the ground. Assuming constant acceleration, (a) make a free-body diagram of this mighty leaper while the jump is taking place, (b) find the force that the ground exerts on the froghopper during its jump, and (c) express the force in part (b) in terms of the froghopper's weight.

50. •• **Mars landing.** During the first stage of its 2004 landing, the *Mars Explorer Rover* rocket reduced its speed from 19,300 km/h to 1600 km/h in 4.0 min. The acceleration due to

gravity on Mars is 3.71 m/s^2, which you can assume to be constant over the distances involved. (a) What were the magnitude and direction of the Mars lander's acceleration during the first stage, assuming the acceleration to be constant? (b) If a 2.50 kg instrument were being weighed on a spring scale inside the lander, what would this scale read? Start with a free-body diagram. (c) Express the scale reading in part (b) in terms of this instrument's normal weight (i) on Mars and (ii) on the earth. (d) If there were an astronaut inside the lander who did not know that it was accelerating, what would he think were the instrument's weight and mass?

51. •• **A standing vertical jump.** Basketball player Darrell Griffith is on record as attaining a standing vertical jump of 1.2 m (4 ft). (This means that he moved upward by 1.2 m after his feet left the floor.) Griffith weighed 890 N (200 lb). (a) What was his speed as he left the floor? (b) If the time of the part of the jump before his feet left the floor was 0.300 s, what were the magnitude and direction of his acceleration (assuming it to be constant) while he was pushing against the floor? (c) Draw a free-body diagram of Griffith during the jump. (d) Use Newton's laws and the results of part (b) to calculate the force he applied to the ground during his jump.
BIO

52. •• You leave the doctor's office after your annual checkup and recall that you weighed 683 N in her office. You then get into an elevator that, conveniently, has a scale. Find the magnitude and direction of the elevator's acceleration if the scale reads (a) 725 N, (b) 595 N.

53. •• **Human biomechanics.** The fastest served tennis ball, served by "Big Bill" Tilden in 1931, was measured at 73.14 m/s. The mass of a tennis ball is 57 g, and the ball is typically in contact with the tennis racquet for 30.0 ms, with the ball starting from rest. Assuming constant acceleration, (a) what force did Big Bill's tennis racquet exert on the tennis ball if he hit it essentially horizontally? (b) Make free-body diagrams of the tennis ball during the serve and just after it has moved free of the racquet.
BIO

54. •• **Extraterrestrial physics.** You have landed on an unknown planet, Newtonia, and want to know what objects will weigh there. You find that when a certain tool is pushed on a frictionless horizontal surface by a 12.0 N force, it moves 16.0 m in the first 2.00 s, starting from rest. You next observe that if you release this tool from rest at 10.0 m above the ground, it takes 2.58 s to reach the ground. What does the tool weigh on Newtonia and what would it weigh on Earth?

55. •• **Lunar blast-off.** An astronaut who is weighing himself inside of a rocket blasting off from the moon with an upward acceleration of 1.25 m/s^2 records a scale reading of 188 N. The acceleration due to gravity on the moon is 1.67 m/s^2. Start with a free-body diagram of the astronaut. (a) What is the mass of this astronaut? (b) What would he weigh standing on the surface of (i) the earth, (ii) the moon?

56. •• **Jumping to the ground.** A 75.0 kg man steps off a platform 3.10 m above the ground. He keeps his legs straight as he falls, but at the moment his feet touch the ground his knees begin to bend, and, treated as a particle, he moves an additional 0.60 m before coming to rest. (a) What is his speed at the instant his feet touch the ground? (b) Treating him as a particle, what are the magnitude and direction of his acceleration as he slows down if the acceleration is constant? (c) Draw a free-body diagram of this man as he is slowing down. (c) Use Newton's laws and the results of part (b) to calculate the force the ground exerts on him while he is slowing down. Express this force in newtons and also as a multiple of the man's weight. (d) What are the magnitude and direction of the reaction force to the force you found in part (c)?

57. •• A parachutist relies on air resistance (mainly on her parachute) to decrease her downward velocity. She and her parachute have a mass of 55.0 kg, and air resistance exerts an upward force of 620 N on her and her parachute. (a) What is the weight of the parachutist (including the parachute)? (b) Draw a free-body diagram of the parachutist Use the diagram to calculate the net force on the parachutist (including the parachute). Is the net force upward or downward? (c) What is the acceleration (magnitude and direction) of the parachutist?

58. •• An electron (mass $= 9.11 \times 10^{-31}$ kg) leaves one end of a TV picture tube with zero initial speed and travels in a straight line to the accelerating grid, which is 1.80 cm away. It reaches the grid with a speed of 3.00×10^6 m/s. If the accelerating force is constant, compute (a) the acceleration of the electron, (b) the time it takes the electron to reach the grid, and (c) the net force that is accelerating the electron, in newtons. (You can ignore the gravitational force on the electron.)

APPLICATIONS OF NEWTON'S LAWS

5

If you had hooves, would you want to go rock-hopping? In fact, like the soles of hiking boots, the design of this goat's hooves allows them to stick, not slip, on rocky surfaces. In this chapter we'll learn about the interactions that give good traction.

Newton's three laws of motion, the foundation of classical mechanics, can be stated very simply, as we have seen. But applying these laws to situations such as a locomotive, a suspension bridge, a car rounding a banked curve, or a toboggan sliding down a hill requires some analytical skills and some problem-solving technique. In this chapter we introduce no new principles, but we'll try to help you develop some of the problem-solving skills you'll need to analyze such situations.

We begin with equilibrium problems, concentrating on systems at rest. Then we generalize our problem-solving techniques to include systems that are not in equilibrium, for which we need to deal precisely with the relationships between forces and motion. We'll learn how to describe and analyze the contact force that acts on an object when it rests or slides on a surface, as well as the elastic forces that are present when a solid object is deformed. Finally, we take a brief look at the fundamental nature of force and the kinds of forces found in the physical universe.

5.1 Equilibrium of a Particle

We learned in Chapter 4 that an object is in **equilibrium** when it is at rest or moving with constant velocity in an inertial frame of reference. A hanging lamp, a rope-and-pulley setup for hoisting heavy loads, a suspension bridge—all these are examples of equilibrium situations. In this section, we consider only the equilibrium of an object that can be modeled as a particle. (Later, in Chapter 10, we'll consider the additional principles needed when an object can't be represented adequately as a particle.) The essential physical principle is Newton's first law: **When an object is at rest or is moving with constant velocity in an inertial**

frame of reference, the vector sum of all the forces acting on it must be zero.
That is, as discussed in Chapter 4, we have the following principle:

Necessary condition for equilibrium of an object
For an object to be in equilibrium, the vector sum of the forces acting on it
must be zero:

$$\sum \vec{F} = 0. \tag{4.3}$$

This condition is sufficient only if the object can be treated as a particle,
which we assume in the next principle and throughout the remainder of the
chapter.

We'll usually use Equation 4.3 in component form:

Equilibrium conditions in component form
An object is in equilibrium if the sum of the components of force in each axis
direction is zero:

$$\sum F_x = 0, \qquad \sum F_y = 0. \tag{4.4}$$

This chapter is about solving problems. We strongly recommend that you
study carefully the strategies that follow, look for their applications in the
worked-out examples, and then try to apply them when you solve problems.

PROBLEM-SOLVING STRATEGY 5.1 **Solving problems involving an object in equilibrium** (MP)

SET UP
1. Draw a simple sketch of the apparatus or structure, showing all relevant
   dimensions and angles.
2. Identify the object or objects in equilibrium that you will consider.
3. Draw a free-body diagram for each object identified in step 2.
   a. Assuming that the object can be modeled as a particle, you can represent
      it by a large dot. Do not include other objects (such as a surface the object
      may be resting on or a rope pulling on it) in your free-body diagram.
   b. Identify all the ways in which other things interact with the object,
      either by touching it or via a noncontact force such as gravity. Draw a
      force vector to represent each force *acting on the object.* Do not include
      forces exerted *by* the object. For each force, make sure that you can
      answer the question "What other object interacts with the chosen object
      to cause that force?" If you can't answer that question, you may be
      imagining a force that isn't there.
   c. Label each force with a symbol representing the *magnitude* of the force
      (*w* for the object's weight; *n* for a normal force; *T* for a tension force,
      etc.); indicate the directions with appropriate angles. (If the object's
      mass is given, use $w = mg$ to find its weight.)
4. Choose a set of coordinate axes, and represent each force acting on the
   object in terms of its components along those axes. Cross out each force
   that has been replaced by its components, so that you don't count it twice.
   You can often simplify the problem by using a particular choice of coordinate axes. For example, when an object rests or slides on a plane surface, it
   is usually simplest to take the axes in the directions parallel and perpendicular to this surface, even when the plane is tilted.

Continued

▲ **Easy does it!** This crane is unloading a
50 ton, 8.2 meter mirror for the European
Southern Observatory in Antofagasta, Chile.
It is one of four such mirrors that make up an
instrument known as the Very Large Telescope, one of the world's biggest, most
advanced optical telescopes. The crane
moves the mirror steadily, so that it remains
nearly in equilibrium—the vector sum of the
forces on it is almost zero. However, that
does not ensure the mirror's safety, because it
is not a particle. The forces acting on different *parts* of it are not the same. Warping or
deforming would be disastrous. The mirror is
heavy in part because it is heavily reinforced.

5. For each object, set the algebraic sum of all x components of force equal to zero. In a separate equation, set the algebraic sum of all y components equal to zero. (Never add x and y components in a single equation.) You can then solve these equations for up to two unknown quantities, which may be force magnitudes, components, or angles.

6. If you are dealing with two or more objects that interact with each other, use Newton's third law to relate the forces they exert on each other. You need to find as many independent equations as the number of unknown quantities. Then solve these equations to obtain the values of the unknowns. This part is algebra, not physics, but it's an essential step.

7. Whenever possible, look at your results and ask whether they make sense. When the result is a symbolic expression or formula, try to think of special cases (particular values or extreme cases for the various quantities) for which you can guess what the results ought to be. Check to see that your formula works in these particular cases. Think about what the problem has taught you that you can apply to other problems in the future.

EXAMPLE 5.1 One-dimensional equilibrium

A gymnast has just begun climbing up a rope hanging from a gymnasium ceiling. She stops, suspended from the lower end of the rope by her hands. Her weight is 500 N, and the weight of the rope is 100 N. Analyze the forces on the gymnast and on the rope.

SOLUTION

SET UP First we sketch the situation (Figure 5.1a). Then we draw two free-body diagrams, one for the gymnast and the other for the rope (Figures 5.1b and c). (We'll explain Figure 5.1d below.) The forces acting on the gymnast are her weight (magnitude 500 N) and the upward force (magnitude T_1) exerted on her by the rope. We *don't* include the downward force she exerts on the rope, because it isn't a force that acts *on* her. We take the y axis to be directed vertically upward, the x axis horizontally. There are no x components of force; that's why we call this a one-dimensional problem.

SOLVE The gymnast is motionless, so we know that she is in equilibrium. Since we know her weight, we can use Equation 4.4, $\Sigma F_y = 0$, to find the magnitude of the upward tension T_1 on her. This force pulls in the positive y direction. Her weight acts in the negative y direction, so its y component is the *negative* of the magnitude—that is, -500 N. Thus,

$$\Sigma F_y = 0,$$
$$T_1 + (-500 \text{ N}) = 0, \quad \text{(equilibrium of gymnast)}$$
$$T_1 = 500 \text{ N}.$$

The two forces acting on the gymnast are *not* an action–reaction pair, because they act on the same object.

Next we need to consider the forces acting on the rope (Figure 5.1c). Newton's third law tells us that the gymnast exerts a force on the rope that is equal and opposite to the force it exerts on her. In other words, she pulls down on the rope with a force

These are action–reaction pairs

(a) (b) (c) (d)

▲ **FIGURE 5.1** Our diagrams for this problem. We sketch the situation (a), plus free-body diagrams for the gymnast (b) and rope (c). (d) A partial free-body diagram for the ceiling. (See "Reflect.")

whose magnitude T_1 is 500 N. As you probably expect, this force equals the gymnast's weight.

The other forces on the rope are its own weight (magnitude 100 N) and the upward force (magnitude T_2) exerted on its upper end by the ceiling. The equilibrium condition $\Sigma F_y = 0$ for the rope gives

$$\Sigma F_y = T_2 + (-100 \text{ N}) + (-500 \text{ N}) = 0, \quad \text{(equilibrium}$$
$$T_2 = 600 \text{ N}. \qquad\qquad\qquad\qquad \text{of rope)}$$

Continued

REFLECT The tension is 100 N greater at the top of the rope (where it must support the weights of both the rope and the gymnast) than at the bottom (where it supports only the gymnast).

Figure 5.1d is a partial free-body diagram of the ceiling, showing that the rope exerts a downward force with magnitude T_2

on the ceiling. From Newton's third law, the magnitude of this force is also 600 N.

Practice Problem: Determine the tension at the midpoint of the rope. *Answer:* 550 N.

The strength of the rope in Example 5.1 probably isn't a major concern. The breaking strength of a string, rope, or cable is described by the maximum tension it can withstand without breaking. A few typical breaking strengths are shown in Table 5.1.

TABLE 5.1 Approximate breaking strengths

Thin white string	50 N
$\frac{1}{4}''$ nylon clothesline rope	4000 N
11 mm Perlon mountaineering rope	3×10^4 N
$1\frac{1}{4}''$ manila climbing rope	6×10^4 N
$\frac{1}{4}''$ steel cable	6×10^4 N

EXAMPLE 5.2   Two-dimensional equilibrium

In Figure 5.2a, a car engine with weight w hangs from a chain that is linked at point O to two other chains, one fastened to the ceiling and the other to the wall. Find the tension in each of the three chains, assuming that w is given and the weights of the chains themselves are negligible.

(a)

▶ **FIGURE 5.2**

(b) Free-body diagram of engine

(c) Free-body diagram of ring O

SOLUTION

SET UP Figure 5.2b is our free-body diagram for the engine. Without further ceremony, we can conclude that $T_1 = w$. (Because we neglect the weights of the chains, the tension is the same throughout the length of each chain.) The horizontal and slanted chains do not exert forces on the engine itself, because they are not attached to it, but they do exert forces on the ring (point O), where three chains join. So let's consider the *ring* as a particle in equilibrium; the weight of the ring itself is negligible.

In our free-body diagram for the ring (Figure 5.2c), T_1, T_2, and T_3 are the *magnitudes* of the forces; their directions are shown by the vectors in the diagram. We add an x-y coordinate system and resolve the force with magnitude T_3 into its x and y components. Note that the downward force with magnitude T_1 of the chain acting on the ring and the upward force with magnitude T_1 of the chain acting on the engine are not an action–reaction pair.

SOLVE We now apply the equilibrium conditions *for the ring,* writing separate equations for the x and y components. (Note that

x and y components are *never* added together in a single equation.) We find that

$$\sum F_x = 0, \qquad T_3 \cos 60° + (-T_2) = 0,$$
$$\sum F_y = 0, \qquad T_3 \sin 60° + (-T_1) = 0.$$

Because $T_1 = w$, we can rewrite the second equation as

$$T_3 = \frac{T_1}{\sin 60°} = \frac{w}{\sin 60°} = 1.155w.$$

We can now use this result in the first equation:

$$T_2 = T_3 \cos 60° = (1.155w) \cos 60° = 0.577w.$$

So we can express all three tensions as multiples of the weight w of the engine, which we assume is known. To summarize, we have

$$T_1 = w,$$
$$T_2 = 0.577w,$$
$$T_3 = 1.155w.$$

If the engine's weight is $w = 2200$ N (about 500 lb), then

$$T_1 = 2200 \text{ N},$$
$$T_2 = (0.577)(2200 \text{ N}) = 1270 \text{ N},$$
$$T_3 = (1.155)(2200 \text{ N}) = 2540 \text{ N}.$$

Continued

SOLVE There is only one x component of force, so

$$\Sigma F_x = w\sin\alpha.$$

From $\Sigma F_x = ma_x$, we have

$$w\sin\alpha = ma_x,$$

and since $w = mg$, the acceleration is

$$a_x = g\sin\alpha.$$

The y-component equation gives $\Sigma F_y = n + (-mg\cos\alpha)$. We know that the y component of acceleration is zero, because there is no motion in the y direction. So $\Sigma F_y = 0$ and $n = mg\cos\alpha$.

REFLECT The mass m does not appear in the expression for a_x; this means that *any* toboggan, regardless of its mass or number of passengers, slides down a frictionless hill with an acceleration of $g\sin\alpha$. In particular, when $\alpha = 0$ (a flat surface with no slope at all), the acceleration is $a_x = 0$, as we should expect. When the surface is vertical, $\alpha = 90°$ and $a_x = g$ (free fall).

Note that the magnitude n of the normal force exerted on the toboggan by the surface of the hill $(n = mg\cos\alpha)$ is *propor-*

(a) The situation   **(b)** Free-body diagram for toboggan

▲ **FIGURE 5.8** Our diagrams for this problem.

tional to the magnitude mg of the toboggan's weight; the two are *not* equal, except in the special case where $\alpha = 0$.

Practice Problem: At what angle does the hill slope if the acceleration is $g/2$? *Answer:* 30°.

EXAMPLE 5.7   **An air track in a physics lab**

Figure 5.9 shows a glider with mass m_1 that moves on a level, frictionless air track in a physics lab. It is connected by a string passing over a small frictionless pulley to a hanging weight with total mass m_2. The string is light and flexible, and it doesn't stretch. Find the acceleration of each object and the tension in the string.

SOLUTION

SET UP The two objects have different motions, so we need to draw a separate free-body diagram and coordinate system for each, as shown in Figure 5.9b and c. We are free to use different coordinate axes for the two objects; in this case, it's convenient to take the $+x$ direction to the right for the glider and the $+y$ direction downward for the hanging weight. Then the glider has only an x component of acceleration a_{1x} (i.e., $a_{1y} = 0$), and the weight hanger has only a y component a_{2y} (i.e., $a_{2x} = 0$). There is no fric-

tion in the pulley, and we consider the string to be massless, so the tension T in the string is the same throughout; it applies a force with magnitude T to each object. The weights are $m_1 g$ and $m_2 g$.

SOLVE We apply Newton's second law, in component form, to each object in turn.

For the glider on the track, Newton's second law gives

$$\Sigma F_x = T = m_1 a_{1x}$$
$$\Sigma F_y = n + (-m_1 g) = m_1 a_{1y} = 0,$$

(a) Apparatus

(b) Free-body diagram for glider

(c) Free-body diagram for weight

▲ **FIGURE 5.9**

Continued

EXAMPLE 5.5   **A simple accelerometer**

You tape one end of a piece of string to the ceiling light of your car and hang a key with mass m to the other end (Figure 5.7). A protractor taped to the light allows you to measure the angle the string makes with the vertical. Your friend drives the car while you make measurements. When the car has a constant acceleration with magnitude a toward the right, the string hangs at rest (relative to the car), making an angle β with the vertical. **(a)** Derive an expression for the acceleration a in terms of the mass m and the measured angle β. **(b)** In particular, what is a when $\beta = 45°$? When $\beta = 0$?

(a) Low-tech accelerometer

(b) Free-body diagram for the key

▲ **FIGURE 5.7**

SOLUTION

SET UP Our free-body diagram is shown in Figure 5.7b. The forces acting on the key are its weight $w = mg$ and the string tension T. We direct the x axis to the right (in the direction of the acceleration) and the y axis vertically upward.

SOLVE Part (a): This problem may look like an equilibrium problem, but it isn't. The string and the key are at rest with respect to the car, but car, string, and key are all accelerating in the $+x$ direction. Thus, there must be a horizontal component of force acting on the key. Therefore, we use Newton's second law in component form: $\Sigma F_x = ma_x$ and $\Sigma F_y = ma_y$.

We find the components of the string tension, as shown in Figure 5.7b. The sum of the horizontal components of force is

$$\Sigma F_x = T\sin\beta,$$

and the sum of the vertical components is

$$\Sigma F_y = T\cos\beta + (-mg).$$

The x component of acceleration is the acceleration a_x of the car, string, and key, and the y component of acceleration is zero, so

$$\Sigma F_x = T\sin\beta = ma_x,$$
$$\Sigma F_y = T\cos\beta + (-mg) = ma_y = 0.$$

Rearranging terms, we obtain

$$T\sin\beta = ma_x, \qquad T\cos\beta = mg.$$

When we divide the first equation by the second, we get

$$a_x = g\tan\beta.$$

The acceleration a_x is thus proportional to the tangent of the angle β.

Part (b): When $\beta = 0$, the key hangs vertically and the acceleration is zero; when $\beta = 45°$, $a_x = g$, and so on.

REFLECT We note that β can never be 90°, because that would require an infinite acceleration. We note also that the relation between a_x and β doesn't depend on the mass of the key, but it *does* depend on the acceleration due to gravity.

Practice Problem: What is the angle β if the acceleration is $g/2$? *Answer:* 26.6°.

EXAMPLE 5.6   **Acceleration down a hill**

A toboggan loaded with vacationing students (total weight w) slides down a long, snow-covered slope. The hill slopes at a constant angle α, and the toboggan is so well waxed that there is virtually no friction at all. Find the toboggan's acceleration and the magnitude n of the normal force the hill exerts on the toboggan.

SOLUTION

SET UP As a reminder of the importance of drawing sketches, we'll show the diagrams we draw in pencil, rather than in printed style (Figure 5.8). The only forces acting on the toboggan are its weight w and the normal force n (Figure 5.8b). The direction of the weight is straight down, but the direction of the normal force is perpendicular to the surface of the hill, at an angle α with the vertical. We take axes parallel and perpendicular to the surface of the hill and resolve the weight into x and y components.

Continued

SOLVE There is only one x component of force, so

$$\sum F_x = w\sin\alpha.$$

From $\sum F_x = ma_x$, we have

$$w\sin\alpha = ma_x,$$

and since $w = mg$, the acceleration is

$$a_x = g\sin\alpha.$$

The y-component equation gives $\sum F_y = n + (-mg\cos\alpha)$. We know that the y component of acceleration is zero, because there is no motion in the y direction. So $\sum F_y = 0$ and $n = mg\cos\alpha$.

REFLECT The mass m does not appear in the expression for a_x; this means that *any* toboggan, regardless of its mass or number of passengers, slides down a frictionless hill with an acceleration of $g\sin\alpha$. In particular, when $\alpha = 0$ (a flat surface with no slope at all), the acceleration is $a_x = 0$, as we should expect. When the surface is vertical, $\alpha = 90°$ and $a_x = g$ (free fall).

Note that the magnitude n of the normal force exerted on the toboggan by the surface of the hill $(n = mg\cos\alpha)$ is propor-

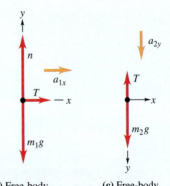

(a) The situation   (b) Free-body diagram for toboggan

▲ **FIGURE 5.8** Our diagrams for this problem.

tional to the magnitude mg of the toboggan's weight; the two are *not* equal, except in the special case where $\alpha = 0$.

Practice Problem: At what angle does the hill slope if the acceleration is $g/2$? *Answer:* $30°$.

EXAMPLE 5.7 **An air track in a physics lab**

Figure 5.9 shows a glider with mass m_1 that moves on a level, frictionless air track in a physics lab. It is connected by a string passing over a small frictionless pulley to a hanging weight with total mass m_2. The string is light and flexible, and it doesn't stretch. Find the acceleration of each object and the tension in the string.

SOLUTION

SET UP The two objects have different motions, so we need to draw a separate free-body diagram and coordinate system for each, as shown in Figure 5.9b and c. We are free to use different coordinate axes for the two objects; in this case, it's convenient to take the $+x$ direction to the right for the glider and the $+y$ direction downward for the hanging weight. Then the glider has only an x component of acceleration a_{1x} (i.e., $a_{1y} = 0$), and the weight hanger has only a y component a_{2y} (i.e., $a_{2x} = 0$). There is no fric-

tion in the pulley, and we consider the string to be massless, so the tension T in the string is the same throughout; it applies a force with magnitude T to each object. The weights are $m_1 g$ and $m_2 g$.

SOLVE We apply Newton's second law, in component form, to each object in turn.

For the glider on the track, Newton's second law gives

$$\sum F_x = T = m_1 a_{1x}$$
$$\sum F_y = n + (-m_1 g) = m_1 a_{1y} = 0,$$

(a) Apparatus

▲ **FIGURE 5.9**

(b) Free-body diagram for glider   (c) Free-body diagram for weight

Continued

▲ **Gravity-defying liquid?** Although this container is on a level tabletop, the liquid inside forms a slant. How can that be? You may have guessed that the photo shows a demonstration of a simple liquid-filled accelerometer. As the container is accelerated to the left, the surface of the liquid forms an angle with the horizontal. The tangent of the angle is proportional to the acceleration. Can you verify that if the container is 19.6 cm wide, the height of the liquid at the right end (in cm) above its level when the apparatus is at rest will give the acceleration of the container itself, in meters per second squared?

The following problem-solving strategy is similar to our strategy for solving equilibrium problems, presented in Section 5.1:

PROBLEM-SOLVING STRATEGY 5.2 Using Newton's second law

SET UP

1. Draw a sketch of the physical situation, and identify the moving object or objects to which you will apply Newton's second law.

2. Draw a free-body diagram for each chosen object, showing all the forces acting *on* that object, as described in the strategy for Newton's first law (Problem-Solving Strategy 5.1). Label the magnitudes of unknown forces with algebraic symbols. Usually, one of the forces will be the object's weight; it is generally best to label this as mg. If a numerical value of mass is given, you can compute the corresponding weight.

3. Show your coordinate axes explicitly in each free-body diagram, and then determine components of forces with reference to these axes. If you know the direction of the acceleration, it is usually best to take that direction as one of the axes. When you represent a force in terms of its components, cross out the original force so as not to include it twice. When there are two or more objects, you can use a separate axis system for each object; you don't have to use the same axis system for all the objects. But in the equations for each object, the signs of the components *must* be consistent with the axes you have chosen for that object.

SOLVE

4. Write the equations for Newton's second law in component form: $\sum F_x = ma_x$ and $\sum F_y = ma_y$ (Equations 4.8). Be careful not to add x and y components in the same equation.

5. If more than one object is involved, repeat step 4 for each object. In addition, the motions of the bodies may be related. For example, the objects may be connected by a rope. Express these relations in algebraic form as relations between the accelerations of the various bodies. Then solve the equations to find the required unknowns.

REFLECT

6. Check particular cases or extreme values of quantities, when possible, and compare the results for these particular cases with your intuitive expectations. Ask yourself, "Does this result make sense?" Think about what the problem has taught you that you can apply to other problems in the future.

 A two-cart train

The carts in Figure 5.6 are speeding up as they are pulled to the right with increasing speed across a frictionless surface. The ropes have negligible mass. We can conclude that

A. The pull of rope 1 on cart *A* has greater magnitude than the pull of rope 1 on cart *B*.
B. The pull of rope 2 on cart *B* has greater magnitude than the pull of rope 1 on cart *B*.
C. The pull of rope 1 on cart *A* has greater magnitude than the pull of rope 2 on cart *B*.

SOLUTION Answer B is correct: For cart *B* to accelerate, there must be a net force to the right. Answer A cannot be right; if the

▲ **FIGURE 5.6**

rope is massless, the forces acting on its two ends must add to zero. Nor can answer C be right: The two carts have the same acceleration; therefore, the tension in rope 2 must be great enough to give this acceleration to both carts, while the tension in rope 1 is just great enough to give cart *A* the same acceleration.

SOLUTION

SET UP Figure 5.5a shows an idealized model for the system. We draw two free-body diagrams, one for the dirt and bucket (Figure 5.5b) and one for the granite block on its cart (Figure 5.5c). In drawing the coordinate axes for each object, we're at liberty to orient them differently for the two objects; the choices shown are the most convenient ones. (But we must *not* change the orientation of the objects themselves.) We represent the weight of the granite block in terms of its components in the chosen axis system. The tension T in the cable is the same throughout, because we are assuming that the cable's weight is negligible. (The pulley changes the *directions* of the cable forces, but if it is frictionless and massless, it can't change their *magnitudes*.)

SOLVE Each object is in equilibrium. Applying $\sum F_y = 0$ to the bucket (Figure 5.5b), we find that

$$T + (-w_2) = 0, \qquad T = w_2.$$

Applying $\sum F_x$ to the cart (Figure 5.5c), we get

$$T + (-w_1 \sin 15°) = 0, \qquad T = w_1 \sin 15°.$$

Equating the two expressions for T yields

$$w_2 = w_1 \sin 15° = 0.26 w_1.$$

REFLECT If the weight w_2 of the dirt and bucket totals 26% of the weight w_1 of the granite block and cart, the system can move in either direction with constant speed. In the real world, where friction tends to hold back the motion, would w_2 need to be more or less than $0.26w_1$ for the granite block to move up with constant speed?

Practice Problem: Determine the total normal force n that the tracks apply to the wheels of the granite cart, as a fraction of w_1. *Answer:* $n = w_1 \cos 15° = 0.97 w_1$.

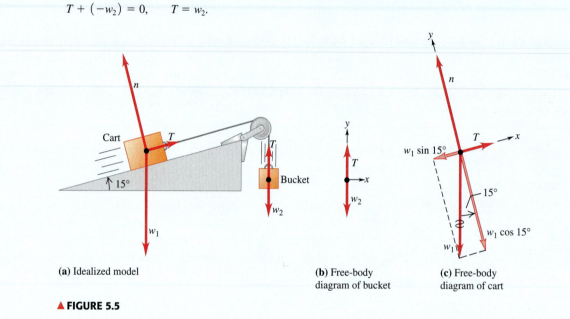

(a) Idealized model

(b) Free-body diagram of bucket

(c) Free-body diagram of cart

▲ **FIGURE 5.5**

5.2 Applications of Newton's Second Law

2.1.5, 2.2–2.4, 2.11

We're now ready to discuss problems in **dynamics,** showing applications of Newton's second law to systems that are *not* in equilibrium. Here's a restatement of that law:

Newton's second law

An object's acceleration equals the vector sum of the forces acting on it, divided by its mass. In vector form, we rewrite this statement as

$$\sum \vec{F} = m\vec{a}. \tag{4.7}$$

However, we'll usually use this relation in its component form:

$$\sum F_x = ma_x, \qquad \sum F_y = ma_y. \tag{4.8}$$

REFLECT The tension is 100 N greater at the top of the rope (where it must support the weights of both the rope and the gymnast) than at the bottom (where it supports only the gymnast).

Figure 5.1d is a partial free-body diagram of the ceiling, showing that the rope exerts a downward force with magnitude T_2

on the ceiling. From Newton's third law, the magnitude of this force is also 600 N.

Practice Problem: Determine the tension at the midpoint of the rope. *Answer:* 550 N.

The strength of the rope in Example 5.1 probably isn't a major concern. The breaking strength of a string, rope, or cable is described by the maximum tension it can withstand without breaking. A few typical breaking strengths are shown in Table 5.1.

TABLE 5.1 Approximate breaking strengths

Thin white string	50 N
$\frac{1}{4}''$ nylon clothesline rope	4000 N
11 mm Perlon mountaineering rope	3×10^4 N
$1\frac{1}{4}''$ manila climbing rope	6×10^4 N
$\frac{1}{4}''$ steel cable	6×10^4 N

EXAMPLE 5.2 Two-dimensional equilibrium

In Figure 5.2a, a car engine with weight w hangs from a chain that is linked at point O to two other chains, one fastened to the ceiling and the other to the wall. Find the tension in each of the three chains, assuming that w is given and the weights of the chains themselves are negligible.

(a)

▶ **FIGURE 5.2**

(b) Free-body diagram of engine

(c) Free-body diagram of ring O

SOLUTION

SET UP Figure 5.2b is our free-body diagram for the engine. Without further ceremony, we can conclude that $T_1 = w$. (Because we neglect the weights of the chains, the tension is the same throughout the length of each chain.) The horizontal and slanted chains do not exert forces on the engine itself, because they are not attached to it, but they do exert forces on the ring (point O), where three chains join. So let's consider the *ring* as a particle in equilibrium; the weight of the ring itself is negligible.

In our free-body diagram for the ring (Figure 5.2c), T_1, T_2, and T_3 are the *magnitudes* of the forces; their directions are shown by the vectors in the diagram. We add an *x-y* coordinate system and resolve the force with magnitude T_3 into its x and y components. Note that the downward force with magnitude T_1 of the chain acting on the ring and the upward force with magnitude T_1 of the chain acting on the engine are not an action–reaction pair.

SOLVE We now apply the equilibrium conditions *for the ring,* writing separate equations for the x and y components. (Note that

x and y components are *never* added together in a single equation.) We find that

$$\Sigma F_x = 0, \qquad T_3 \cos 60° + (-T_2) = 0,$$
$$\Sigma F_y = 0, \qquad T_3 \sin 60° + (-T_1) = 0.$$

Because $T_1 = w$, we can rewrite the second equation as

$$T_3 = \frac{T_1}{\sin 60°} = \frac{w}{\sin 60°} = 1.155w.$$

We can now use this result in the first equation:

$$T_2 = T_3 \cos 60° = (1.155w) \cos 60° = 0.577w.$$

So we can express all three tensions as multiples of the weight w of the engine, which we assume is known. To summarize, we have

$$T_1 = w,$$
$$T_2 = 0.577w,$$
$$T_3 = 1.155w.$$

If the engine's weight is $w = 2200$ N (about 500 lb), then

$$T_1 = 2200 \text{ N},$$
$$T_2 = (0.577)(2200 \text{ N}) = 1270 \text{ N},$$
$$T_3 = (1.155)(2200 \text{ N}) = 2540 \text{ N}.$$

Continued

REFLECT Each of the three tensions is proportional to the weight w; if we double w, all three tensions double. Note that T_3 is greater than the weight of the engine. If this seems strange, observe that T_3 must be large enough for its vertical component to be equal in magnitude to w, so T_3 itself must have a magnitude *larger* than w.

Practice Problem: If we change the angle of the upper chain from 60° to 45°, determine the new expressions for the three tensions. *Answers:* $T_1 = w$, $T_2 = w\cos 45°/\sin 45° = w$, $T_3 = w/\sin 45° = \sqrt{2}\, w$.

EXAMPLE 5.3   Car on a ramp

A car with a weight of 1.76×10^4 N rests on the ramp of a trailer (Figure 5.3a). The car's brakes and transmission lock are released; only the cable prevents the car from rolling backward off the trailer. The ramp makes an angle of 26.0° with the horizontal. Find the tension in the cable and the force with which the ramp pushes on the car's tires.

We replace the weight by its components.

▶ **FIGURE 5.3**   **(a)** Car on ramp   **(b)** Free-body diagram for car

---

SOLUTION

SET UP Figure 5.3b shows our free-body diagram for the car. The three forces exerted on the car are its weight (magnitude w), the tension in the cable (magnitude T), and the normal force with magnitude n exerted by the ramp. (Because we treat the car as a particle, we can lump the normal forces on the four wheels together as a single force.) We orient our coordinate axes parallel and perpendicular to the ramp, and we replace the weight force by its components.

SOLVE The car is in equilibrium, so we first find the components of each force in our axis system and then apply Newton's first law. To find the components of the weight, we note that the angle α between the ramp and the horizontal is equal to the angle α between the weight vector and the normal to the ramp, as shown. The angle α is *not* measured in the usual way, counterclockwise from the $+x$ axis. To find the components of the weight $(w_x$ and $w_y)$, we use the right triangles in Figure 5.3b. We find that $w_x = -w\sin\alpha$ and $w_y = -w\cos\alpha$. The equilibrium conditions then give us

$$\sum F_x = 0, \qquad T + (-w\sin\alpha) = 0,$$
$$\sum F_y = 0, \qquad n + (-w\cos\alpha) = 0.$$

Be sure you understand how the signs are related to our choice of coordinate axis directions. Remember that, by defini-

tion, T, w, and n are *magnitudes* of vectors and are therefore positive.

Solving these equations for T and n, we find that

$$T = w\sin\alpha,$$
$$n = w\cos\alpha.$$

Finally, inserting the numerical values $w = 1.76 \times 10^4$ N and $\alpha = 26°$, we obtain

$$T = (1.76 \times 10^4 \text{ N})(\sin 26°) = 7.72 \times 10^3 \text{ N},$$
$$n = (1.76 \times 10^4 \text{ N})(\cos 26°) = 1.58 \times 10^3 \text{ N}.$$

REFLECT To check some special cases, note that if the angle α is zero, then $\sin\alpha = 0$ and $\cos\alpha = 1$. In this case, the ramp is horizontal; no cable tension T is needed to hold the car, and the magnitude of the total normal force n is equal to the car's weight. If the angle is 90° (the ramp is vertical), then $\sin\alpha = 1$ and $\cos\alpha = 0$. In that case, the cable tension T equals the weight w and the normal force n is zero.

We also note that these results would still be correct if the car were on a ramp on a car transport trailer traveling down a straight highway at a constant speed of 65 mi/h. Do you see why?

Practice Problem: What ramp angle would be needed in order for the cable tension to equal one-half of the car's weight? *Answer:* 30°.

EXAMPLE 5.4   Lifting granite and dumping dirt

Blocks of granite, each with weight w_1, are being hauled up a 15° slope out of a quarry (Figure 5.4). For environmental reasons, dirt is also being dumped into the quarry to fill up old holes. You have been asked to find a way to use this dirt to move the granite out more easily. You design a system that lets the dirt (weight w_2, including the weight of the bucket) that drops vertically into the quarry pull out a granite block on a cart with steel wheels (total weight w_1), rolling on steel rails. Ignoring the weight of the cable and friction in the pulley and wheels, determine how the weights w_1 and w_2 must be related for the system to move with constant speed.

▲ **FIGURE 5.4**

Continued

and for the hanging weight,

$$\sum F_y = m_2 g + (-T) = m_2 a_{2y}.$$

Now, because the string doesn't stretch, the two objects must move equal distances in equal times, and their *speeds* at any instant must be equal. When the speeds change, they change by equal amounts in a given time, so the accelerations of the two bodies must have the same magnitude a. We can express this relation as

$$a_{1x} = a_{2y} = a.$$

(The directions of the two accelerations are different, of course.) The two Newton's-second-law equations are then

$$T = m_1 a,$$
$$m_2 g + (-T) = m_2 a.$$

We'd like to get separate expressions for T and a, in terms of the masses and g.

An easy way to get an expression for a is to replace $-T$ in the second equation by $-m_1 a$ and rearrange the result; when we do so, we obtain $m_2 g + (-m_1 a) = m_2 a$, $m_2 g = (m_1 + m_2)a$, and, finally,

$$a = \frac{m_2}{m_1 + m_2} g.$$

Then, to get an expression for T, we substitute this expression for a back into the first equation. The result is

$$T = \frac{m_1 m_2}{m_1 + m_2} g = \frac{m_1}{m_1 + m_2} m_2 g.$$

REFLECT It's always a good idea to check general symbolic results such as this for particular cases where we can guess what the answer ought to be. For example, if the mass of the glider is zero $(m_1 = 0)$, we expect that the hanging weight (mass m_2) would fall freely with acceleration g and there would be no tension in the string. When we substitute $m_1 = 0$ into the preceding expressions for T and a, they do give $T = 0$ and $a = g$, as expected. Also, if $m_2 = 0$, there is nothing to create tension in the string or accelerate either mass. For this case, the equations give $T = 0$ and $a = 0$. Thus, in these two special cases, the results agree with our intuitive expectations.

We also note that, in general, the tension T is *not* equal to the weight $m_2 g$ of the hanging mass m_2, but is *less* by a factor of $m_1/(m_1 + m_2)$. If T *were* equal to $m_2 g$, then m_2 would be in equilibrium, but it isn't.

5.3 Contact Forces and Friction

We've seen several problems in which an object rests or slides on a surface that exerts forces on the object. At the beginning of Chapter 4, we introduced the terms *normal force* and *friction force* to describe these forces. Whenever two objects interact by direct contact (touching) of their surfaces, we call the interaction forces *contact forces*. Normal and friction forces are both contact forces. Friction is important in many aspects of everyday life, for both facilitating and preventing the slipping of an object in contact with a surface. For example, the oil in a car engine facilitates sliding between moving parts, but friction between the tires and the road prevents slipping. Similarly, air drag decreases automotive fuel economy, but makes parachutes work. Without friction, nails would pull out, light bulbs and bottle caps would unscrew effortlessly, and riding a bicycle would be hopeless. A "frictionless surface" is a useful concept in idealized models of mechanical systems in which the friction forces are negligibly small. In the real world, such an idealization is unattainable, although driving a car on wet ice comes fairly close!

Let's consider an object sliding across a surface. When you try to slide a heavy box of books across the floor, the box doesn't move at all until you reach a certain critical force. Then the box starts moving, and you can usually keep it moving with less force than you needed to get it started. If you take some of the books out, you need less force than before to get it started or keep it moving. What general statements can we make about this behavior?

First, when an object rests or slides on a surface, we can always represent the contact force exerted by the surface on the object in terms of components of force perpendicular and parallel to the surface (Figure 5.10). We call the perpendicular component the *normal force,* denoted by $\vec{n}$. (*Normal* is a synonym for *perpendicular.*) The component parallel to the surface is the *friction force,* denoted

Act|v ONLINE Phys|cs   2.1.1, 2.1.4, 2.5–2.8, 2.10

The frictional and normal forces are really components of a single contact force.

▲ **FIGURE 5.10** The frictional and normal forces for a block sliding on a rough surface.

▲ Friction can be fun. As this rock climber shows, frictional forces can be important. Without them, a climber could not move or maintain an equilibrium position. Notice how the climber is demonstrating one of the key concepts of frictional forces: The frictional force is proportional to the normal force. Therefore, even in a narrow crack, a good climber tries to contact the rock at an angle as close as feasible to 90°. This maximizes the normal force and therefore also maximizes the frictional force.

by $\vec{f}$. By definition, $\vec{n}$ and $\vec{f}$ are always perpendicular to each other. When an object is sliding with respect to a surface, the associated friction force is called a *kinetic-friction* force, with magnitude f_k. When there is no relative motion, we speak of a *static-friction* force, with magnitude f_s. We'll discuss these two possibilities separately.

When one object is moving relative to a surface, the *direction* of the kinetic-friction force on the object is always opposite to the direction of motion of that object relative to the surface. For example, when a book slides from left to right along a tabletop, the friction force on it acts to the left, as in Figure 5.10. According to Newton's third law, the book simultaneously applies a force to the table that is equal in magnitude, but directed to the right; in effect, the book tries to drag the table along with it.

The *magnitude* f_k of a kinetic-friction force usually increases when the normal force magnitude n increases. Thus, more force is needed to slide a box full of books across the floor than to slide the same box when it is empty. This principle is also used in automotive braking systems: The harder the brake pads are squeezed against the rotating brake disks, the greater is the braking effect. In some cases, the magnitude of the sliding friction force f_k is found to be approximately *proportional* to the magnitude n of the normal force. In such cases, we call the ratio f_k/n the **coefficient of kinetic friction,** denoted as μ_k:

Relation between kinetic-friction force and normal force
When the magnitude of the sliding friction force f_k is roughly proportional to the magnitude n of the normal force, the two are related by a constant μ_k called the coefficient of kinetic friction:

$$f_k = \mu_k n. \tag{5.1}$$

Because μ_k is the ratio of two force magnitudes, it has no units.

The more slippery the surface, the smaller the coefficient of friction is. Because it is a quotient of two force magnitudes, μ_k is a pure number, without units.

NOTE ▶ The friction force and the normal force are always perpendicular, so Equation 5.1 is *not* a vector equation, but a relation between the *magnitudes* of the two forces. ◀

The numerical value of the coefficient of kinetic friction for any two surfaces depends on the materials and the surfaces. For Teflon on steel, μ_k is about 0.04. For rubber tires on rough dry concrete (or sneakers on a dry gym floor), μ_k can be as large as 1.0 to 1.2. For two smooth metal surfaces, it is typically 0.4 to 0.8.

Although these numbers are given to two significant figures, they are only approximate values; indeed, Equation 5.1 is just an *approximate* representation of a complex phenomenon. On a microscopic level, friction and normal forces result from the intermolecular forces (fundamentally electrical in nature) between two rough surfaces at high points where they come into contact. Figure 5.11 suggests the nature of the interaction. The actual area of contact is usually much smaller than the total surface area. When two smooth surfaces of the same metal are brought together, these forces can cause a "cold weld"; a similar effect occurs

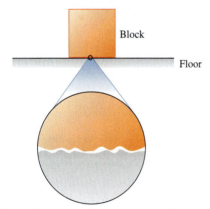

Block

Floor

On a microscopic level, even smooth surfaces are rough; they tend to catch and cling.

▲ FIGURE 5.11 The origin of frictional forces.

with aluminum pistons in an unlubricated aluminum cylinder. Indeed, the success of lubricating oils depends on the fact that they maintain a film between the surfaces that prevents them from coming into actual contact. Friction forces can also depend on the *velocity* of the object relative to the surface. We'll ignore that complication for now in order to concentrate on the simplest cases.

Friction forces may also act when there is *no* relative motion between the surfaces of contact. If you try to slide that box of books across the floor, the box may not move at all if you don't push hard enough, because the floor exerts an equal and opposite friction force on the box. This force is called a **static-friction force** $\vec{f}_s$. In Figure 5.12a, the box is at rest, in equilibrium, under the action of its weight $\vec{w}$ and the upward normal force $\vec{n}$, which is equal in magnitude to the weight and exerted on the box by the floor. Now we tie a rope to the box (Figure 5.12b) and gradually increase the tension T in the rope. At first the box remains at rest, because, as T increases, the force of static friction f_s also increases (staying equal in magnitude to T).

At some point, however, T becomes greater than the maximum friction force f_s that the surface can exert; the box then "breaks loose" and starts to slide. Figure 5.12c shows the force diagram when T is at this critical value, and Figure 5.12d is the case when T exceeds this value and the box begins to move. Figure 5.12e shows how the friction force varies if we start with no applied force ($T = 0$) and gradually increase the force until the object starts to slide. Note that the force f_k of kinetic friction is somewhat less than the maximum force $f_{s,\,max}$ of static friction: Less force is needed to keep the box sliding with constant speed than to start it moving initially.

For a given pair of surfaces, the maximum value of f_s depends on the normal force. In some cases, the maximum value of f_s is approximately *proportional* to n;

▲ **Friction can be a problem.** If you're trying to saw stone, friction is not necessarily a good thing. If this saw blade were not lubricated, friction would make it hard to draw the saw through the cut, and the heat from friction could warp or melt the blade. Therefore, the blade of this "wet saw" in a commercial stone quarry is continuously showered with water to minimize frictional forces and carry away heat. Even so, a cut like this will take time to complete.

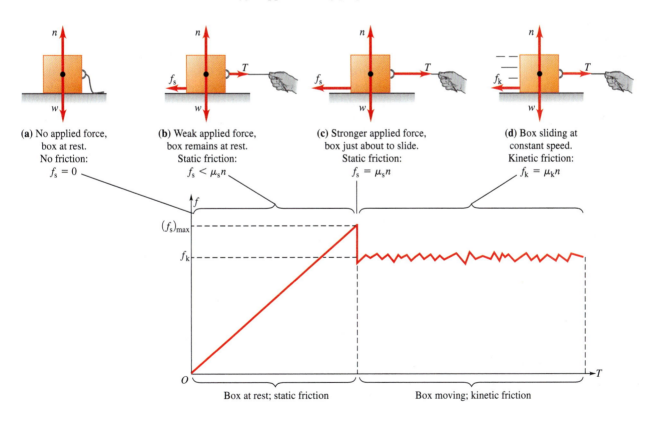

(a) No applied force, box at rest.
No friction:
$f_s = 0$

(b) Weak applied force, box remains at rest.
Static friction:
$f_s < \mu_s n$

(c) Stronger applied force, box just about to slide.
Static friction:
$f_s = \mu_s n$

(d) Box sliding at constant speed.
Kinetic friction:
$f_k = \mu_k n$

Box at rest; static friction

Box moving; kinetic friction

(e)

▲ **FIGURE 5.12** Static and kinetic friction for a box subjected to a gradually increasing pulling force.

we call the proportionality factor μ_s the **coefficient of static friction.** In a particular situation, the actual force of static friction can have any magnitude between zero (when there is no other force parallel to the surface) and a maximum value $f_{s,max}$ given by $f_{s,max} = \mu_s n$. Like μ_k, μ_s has no unit.

Relation between normal force and maximum static-friction force

When the maximum magnitude of the static-friction force can be represented as proportional to the magnitude of the normal force, the two are related by a constant μ_s called the coefficient of static friction:

$$f_s \leq \mu_s n. \qquad (5.2)$$

The equality sign holds only when the applied force T, parallel to the surface, has reached the critical value at which motion is about to start (Figure 5.12c). When T is *less* than this value (Figure 5.12b), the inequality sign holds. In that case, we have to use the equilibrium conditions $\sum \vec{F} = 0$ to find f_s. For any given pair of surfaces, the coefficient of kinetic friction is usually *less* than the coefficient of static friction. As a result, when sliding starts, the friction force usually *decreases*, as Figure 5.12e shows.

In some situations, the surfaces will alternately stick (static friction is operative) and slip (kinetic friction arises); this alternation is what causes the horrible squeak made by chalk held at the wrong angle while you're writing on the blackboard. Another slip-and-stick phenomenon is the squeaky noise your windshield-wiper blades make when the glass is nearly dry; still another is the outraged shriek of tires sliding on asphalt pavement. A more positive example is the sound produced by the motion of a violin bow against the string.

Liquids and gases also show frictional effects. Friction between two solid surfaces separated by a layer of liquid or gas is determined primarily by the *viscosity* of the fluid. In a car engine, the pistons are separated from the cylinder walls by a thin layer of oil. When an object slides on a layer of gas, friction can be made very small. In the familiar linear air track (like the one in Example 5.7), the gliders are supported on a layer of air. The frictional force is velocity dependent, but at typical speeds the effective coefficient of friction is on the order of 0.001. A device similar to the air track is the frictionless air table, on which pucks are supported by an array of small air jets about 2 cm apart.

For a wheeled vehicle, we can define a **coefficient of rolling friction,** μ_r, which is the horizontal force needed for constant speed on a flat surface, divided by the upward normal force exerted by the surface. Typical values of μ_r are 0.002 to 0.003 for steel wheels on steel rails and 0.01 to 0.02 for rubber tires on concrete. These values are one reason that railroad trains are, in general, much more fuel efficient than highway trucks.

Quantitative Analysis 5.2   A friction experiment

A block is pulled along a horizontal surface (with friction) by a constant force with magnitude F_x, and the acceleration a_x is measured. The experiment is repeated several times, with different values of F_x, and a graph of acceleration as a function of force is plotted. For the various trials, which of the graphs of acceleration versus force shown at right is most nearly correct?

SOLUTION No motion occurs unless the force F_x exceeds the maximum static-friction force; when it does, the block starts to

move under the action of F_x and the smaller kinetic-friction force. Only answer A shows no acceleration at small values of the applied force.

Conceptual Analysis 5.3

Turning things over

You are pushing the heavy plastic block in Figure 5.13 across the room with constant velocity. You decide to turn the block on end, reducing the surface area in contact with the floor by half. In this new orientation, to push this same block across the same floor with the same speed as before, the magnitude of force that you must apply is

A. twice as great as before.
B. the same as before.
C. half as great as before.

SOLUTION For many surfaces, dry sliding friction depends only on the normal force with which the object presses against the sur-

▲ **FIGURE 5.13**

face, in this case a force equal to the weight of the block. The frictional force does not depend on the area of contact. Since the frictional force is the same in both orientations, the applied force needed is the same. The correct answer is B.

EXAMPLE 5.8 ## Delivering the goods

A delivery company has just unloaded a 500 N crate full of home exercise equipment in your level driveway. You find that to get it started moving toward your garage, you have to pull with a horizontal force of magnitude 230 N. Once it "breaks loose" and starts to move, you can keep it moving at constant velocity with only 200 N of force. What are the coefficients of static and kinetic friction?

SOLUTION

SET UP As shown in Figure 5.14, the forces acting on the crate are its weight (magnitude w), the force applied by the rope (magnitude T), and the normal and frictional components (magnitudes n and f, respectively) of the contact force the driveway surface exerts on the crate. We draw free-body diagrams for the crate at the instant it starts to move (when the static frictional force is maximum) and while it is in motion.

SOLVE Whether the crate is moving or not, the friction force opposes your pull because it tends to prevent the crate from sliding relative to the surface. An instant before the crate starts to move, the static-friction force has its maximum possible value, $f_{s,\text{max}} = \mu_s n$. The state of rest and the state of motion with constant velocity are both equilibrium conditions. Remember that w, n, and f are the *magnitudes* of the forces; some of the components have negative signs. For example, the magnitude of the weight is 500 N, but its y component is -500 N. We write Newton's second law in component form, $\Sigma F_x = 0$ and $\Sigma F_y = 0$, for the crate. Then

$$\Sigma F_y = n + (-w) = n - 500\,\text{N} = 0, \qquad n = 500\,\text{N},$$
$$\Sigma F_x = T + (-f_s) = 230\,\text{N} - f_s = 0, \qquad f_s = 230\,\text{N},$$
$$f_{s,\text{max}} = \mu_s n \qquad \text{(motion about to start)},$$
$$\mu_s = \frac{f_{s,\text{max}}}{n} = \frac{230\,\text{N}}{500\,\text{N}} = 0.46.$$

After the crate starts to move, the friction force becomes that of kinetic friction (Figure 5.14c). The crate moves with constant velocity, so it is still in equilibrium. Thus, the vector sum of the forces is still zero, and we have

$$\Sigma F_y = n + (-w) = n - 500\,\text{N} = 0, \qquad n = 500\,\text{N},$$
$$\Sigma F_x = T + (-f_k) = 200\,\text{N} - f_k = 0, \qquad f_k = 200\,\text{N},$$
$$f_k = \mu_k n \qquad \text{(moving)}.$$

The coefficient of kinetic friction is

$$\mu_k = \frac{f_k}{n} = \frac{200\,\text{N}}{500\,\text{N}} = 0.40.$$

REFLECT There is no vertical motion, so $a_y = 0$ and $n = w$. It is easier to keep the crate moving than to start it moving from rest, because $\mu_k < \mu_s$. Note, however, that just as the crate begins to move, the acceleration is nonzero while the velocity changes from zero to its final, constant value.

Practice Problem: On a different part of the driveway, $\mu_s = 0.30$ and $\mu_k = 0.25$. What horizontal force is required to start the crate moving? What force is required to keep it sliding at constant velocity? *Answers:* 150 N, 125 N.

▶ **FIGURE 5.14** **(a)**

(b) Crate just as it starts to move

(c) Crate moving at constant speed

EXAMPLE 5.9 Not pulling hard enough

What is the friction force if the crate in Example 5.8 is at rest on the surface and a horizontal force of 50 N is applied to it?

SOLUTION

SET UP AND SOLVE The setup is the same as for Example 5.8. From the equilibrium conditions, we have

$$\Sigma F_x = T + (-f_s) = 50 \text{ N} - f_s = 0,$$
$$f_s = 50 \text{ N}.$$

REFLECT In this case, $f_s < \mu_s n$. The frictional force can prevent motion for any horizontal force less than 230 N.

Quantitative Analysis 5.4   Pushing too hard

A baggage handler applies a constant horizontal force with magnitude F to push a box across a rough horizontal surface with a very small constant acceleration, starting from rest. Then he pushes a second box, identical to the first, with a force twice as great in magnitude. How does the acceleration of the second box compare with that of the first?

A. It is more than double the first acceleration.
B. It is exactly double the first acceleration.
C. It is less than double the first acceleration.

SOLUTION From Newton's second law, $F - f_k = ma_x$. In the first case, the acceleration is small, so F is only a little greater than f_k, and the net horizontal component of force $(F - f_k)$ is much smaller than F. Therefore, if F is doubled, the net horizontal force is much larger than before. Thus the acceleration is also much larger than before. Answer A is correct.

EXAMPLE 5.10 Moving the exercise equipment again

Suppose you try to move the crate full of exercise equipment in Example 5.8 by pulling upward on the rope at an angle of 30° above the horizontal. How hard do you have to pull to keep the crate moving with constant velocity? Is this easier or harder than pulling horizontally? Recall that $w = 500$ N and $\mu_k = 0.40$ for this crate.

(a)

(b) Free-body diagram for moving crate

▲ FIGURE 5.15

SOLUTION

SET UP Figure 5.15 shows the situation and our free-body diagram. We use the same coordinate system as in Example 5.8. The magnitude f_k of the friction force is still equal to $\mu_k n$, but now the magnitude n of the normal force is *not* equal in magnitude to the weight of the crate. Instead, the force exerted by the rope has an additional vertical component that tends to lift the crate off the floor; this component makes n less than w.

SOLVE The crate is moving with constant velocity, so it is still in equilibrium. Applying $\Sigma \vec{F} = 0$ in component form, we find that

$$\Sigma F_x = T\cos 30° + (-f_k) = T\cos 30° - 0.40n = 0,$$
$$\Sigma F_y = T\sin 30° + n + (-500 \text{ N}) = 0.$$

These are two simultaneous equations for the two unknown quantities T and n. To solve them, we can eliminate one unknown and

Continued

solve for the other. There are many ways to do this. Here is one way: Rearrange the second equation to the form

$$n = 500\,\text{N} - T\sin 30°.$$

Then substitute this expression for n back into the first equation:

$$T\cos 30° - 0.40(500\,\text{N} - T\sin 30°) = 0.$$

Finally, solve this equation for T, and then substitute the result back into either of the original equations to obtain n. The results are

$$T = 188\,\text{N}, \qquad n = 406\,\text{N}.$$

REFLECT The normal-force magnitude n is *less* than the weight $(w = 500\,\text{N})$ of the box, and the tension required is a little less than the force needed (200 N) when you pulled horizontally.

Practice Problem: Try pulling at 22°; you'll find that you need even less force. (In fact, this angle gives the smallest possible value of T.) *Answers:* $T = 186\,\text{N}, n = 430\,\text{N}$.

EXAMPLE 5.11 **Toboggan ride with friction**

Let's go back to the toboggan we studied in Example 5.6. The wax has worn off, and there is now a coefficient of kinetic friction μ_k. The slope has just the right angle to make the toboggan slide with constant velocity. Derive an expression for the slope angle in terms of w and μ_k.

SOLUTION

SET UP Figure 5.16 shows our sketch and free-body diagram. The slope angle is α. The forces on the toboggan are identified by their magnitudes: its weight (w) and the normal (n) and frictional (f_k) components of the contact force exerted on it by the sloping surface. We take axes perpendicular and parallel to the surface and represent the weight in terms of its components in these two directions as shown.

SOLVE The toboggan is moving with constant velocity and is therefore in equilibrium. The equilibrium conditions are

$$\sum F_x = w\sin\alpha + (-f_k) = w\sin\alpha - \mu_k n = 0,$$
$$\sum F_y = n + (-w\cos\alpha) = 0.$$

Rearranging terms, we get

$$\mu_k n = w\sin\alpha, \qquad n = w\cos\alpha.$$

Note that the normal force n is less than the weight w. When we divide the first of these equations by the second, we find that

$$\mu_k = \frac{\sin\alpha}{\cos\alpha} = \tan\alpha.$$

▲ **FIGURE 5.16** Our diagrams for this problem.

REFLECT The normal force is *not* equal in magnitude to the weight; it is always smaller. The weight w doesn't appear in the expression for μ_k; *any* toboggan, regardless of its weight, slides down an incline with constant speed if the tangent of the slope angle of the hill equals the coefficient of kinetic friction. The greater the coefficient of friction, the steeper the slope has to be for the toboggan to slide with constant velocity. This behavior is just what we should expect.

EXAMPLE 5.12 **A steeper hill**

Suppose the toboggan in Example 5.11 goes down a steeper hill. The coefficient of friction is the same, but this time the toboggan accelerates. Derive an expression for the acceleration in terms of g, α, μ_k, and w.

SOLUTION

SET UP Our free-body diagram (Figure 5.17) is almost the same as for Example 5.11, but the toboggan is no longer in equilibrium: a_y is still zero, but a_x is not.

SOLVE We apply Newton's second law in component form. From $\sum F_x = ma_x$ and $\sum F_y = ma_y$, we get the two equations

$$\sum F_x = mg\sin\alpha + (-f_k) = ma_x,$$
$$\sum F_y = n + (-mg\cos\alpha) = 0.$$

From the second equation, we find that $n = mg\cos\alpha$; then, from Equation 5.1 $(f_k = \mu_k n)$, we get $f_k = \mu_k n = \mu_k mg\cos\alpha$.

▲ **FIGURE 5.17** Our diagrams for the toboggan on a steeper hill.

Continued

That is, the magnitude of the friction force equals μ_k times the component of the weight normal to the surface. We substitute this expression for f_k back into the x-component equation. The result is

$$mg\sin\alpha + (-\mu_k mg\cos\alpha) = ma_x,$$
$$a_x = g(\sin\alpha - \mu_k\cos\alpha).$$

REFLECT Does this result make sense? Let's check some special cases. First, if the hill is *vertical*, $\alpha = 90°$; then $\sin\alpha = 1$, $\cos\alpha = 0$, and $a_x = g$. This is free fall, just what we would expect. Second, on a hill with angle α with *no* friction, $\mu_k = 0$. Then $a_x = g\sin\alpha$. The situation is the same as in Example 5.6,

and we get the same result; that's encouraging! Next, suppose that $a_x = 0$. Then there is just enough friction to make the toboggan move with constant velocity. In that case, $a_x = 0$, and it follows that

$$\sin\alpha = \mu_k\cos\alpha \quad \text{and} \quad \mu_k = \tan\alpha.$$

This agrees with our result from Example 5.11; good! Finally, note that there may be *so much* friction that $\mu_k\cos\alpha$ is actually greater than $\sin\alpha$. In that case, a_x is negative. If we give the toboggan an initial downhill push, it will slow down and eventually stop.

We have pretty much beaten the toboggan problem to death, but there is an important lesson to be learned. We started out with a simple problem and then extended it to more and more general situations. Our most general result includes all the previous ones as special cases, and that's a nice, neat package! Don't memorize this package; it is useful only for this one set of problems. But do try to understand how we obtained it and what it means.

One final variation that you may want to try out is the case in which we give the toboggan an initial push *up* the hill. The direction of the friction force is now reversed, so the acceleration is different from the downhill value. It turns out that the expression for a_x is the same as before, except that the minus sign becomes a plus sign.

EXAMPLE 5.13 **Fluid friction**

When an object moves through a fluid (such as water or air), it exerts a force on the fluid to push it out of the way. By Newton's third law, the fluid pushes back on the object, in a direction opposite to the object's velocity relative to the fluid, always opposing the object's motion and usually increasing with speed. In high-speed motion through air, the resisting force is approximately proportional to the square of the object's speed v; it's called a *drag force,* or simply *drag.* We can represent its magnitude F_D by

$$F_D = Dv^2,$$

where D is a proportionality constant that depends on the shape and size of the object and the density of air.

When an object falls vertically through air, the drag force opposing the object's motion increases, and the downward acceleration decreases. Eventually, the object reaches a *terminal velocity:* its acceleration approaches zero and the velocity becomes nearly constant. Derive an expression for the terminal velocity magnitude v_T in terms of D and the weight mg of the object.

SOLUTION

SET UP As shown in Figure 5.18, we take the positive y direction to be downward, and we neglect any force associated with buoyancy in the fluid. The net vertical component of force is $mg - Dv^2$.

SOLVE Newton's second law gives

$$mg - Dv_y^2 = ma_y.$$

When the object has reached terminal velocity v_T, the acceleration a_y is zero, and

$$mg - Dv_T^2 = 0, \quad \text{or} \quad v_T = \sqrt{\frac{mg}{D}}.$$

REFLECT For a skydiver in the spread-eagled position, the value of the constant D is found experimentally to be about 0.25 kg/m.

Before terminal velocity: Object accelerating; drag force less than weight.

$Dv^2 < mg$

$Dv^2 = mg$

At terminal velocity: Object in equilibrium; drag force equals weight.

▲ FIGURE 5.18 An object falling through air, before and after reaching its terminal velocity.

Continued

(Does this number have the correct units?) If the skydiver's mass is 80 kg, the terminal velocity magnitude is

$$v_T = \sqrt{\frac{mg}{D}} = \sqrt{\frac{(80 \text{ kg})(9.8 \text{ m/s}^2)}{0.25 \text{ kg/m}}} = 56 \text{ m/s}.$$

This terminal velocity magnitude is about 125 mi/h. Does this seem reasonable?

Practice Problem: For an average-sized cat, the constant D is approximately one-fourth that for a human, or about $D = 0.062$ kg/m. Find the terminal velocity magnitude of a 4.5 kg cat. *Answer:* 27 m/s.

Skydivers everywhere

As we just saw, objects falling through the air at high speeds are acted upon by a drag force proportional in magnitude to v^2. A falling object speeds up until the magnitude of the force from air drag equals the magnitude of the object's weight. If a 120 lb woman using a parachute falls with terminal velocity v, a 240 lb man using an identical chute will fall with terminal velocity

A. v. B. $\sqrt{2}v$. C. $2v$.

SOLUTION Since both people use the same chute, the constant D is the same for both. The mass of the man is twice the mass of the woman, so he requires twice the drag force to produce zero acceleration. The drag force is proportional to v^2; hence, it doubles if the velocity increases by a factor of $\sqrt{2}$. The correct answer is B.

Rolling vehicles also experience air drag, which usually increases proportionally to the square of the speed. Air drag is often negligible at low speeds, but at highway speeds it is comparable to or greater than rolling friction.

 2.1.2

5.4 Elastic Forces

In Section 4.1, when we introduced the concept of *force,* we mentioned that when forces are applied to a solid object, they usually deform the object. In particular, we discussed the use of a coil spring in a device called a spring balance that can be used to measure the magnitudes of forces.

Let's look at the relation of force to deformation in a little more detail. Figure 5.19 shows a coil spring with one end attached to an anchor point and the other end attached to an object that can slide without friction along the x axis. The coordinate x describes the position of the right end of the spring. When $x = 0$, the spring is neither stretched nor compressed. When the object is moved a distance x to the right, the spring is stretched by an amount x. It then exerts a force with magnitude F_{spr} on the object and an "equal and opposite" force on the anchor point. When the string is stretched more, greater forces are required. For many common materials, such as steel coil springs, experiments show that stretching the spring an amount $2x$ requires forces with magnitude $2F_{spr}$; that is, the magnitude of force required is *directly proportional* to the amount of stretch.

If the spring has spaces between its coils, as in the figure, then it can be compressed as well as stretched (Figure 5.19d). Again, experiments show that the amount of compression is directly proportional to the magnitude of the force. In both stretching and compressing, the sign of the x coordinate of the right end of the spring is always opposite the sign of the x component of force the spring applies to the object at its right end. When x is positive, the spring is stretched and applies a force that pulls to the left (the negative x direction) on the object. When x is negative, the spring is compressed and pushes to the right (the positive x direction) on the object.

This proportionality of force to stretching and compressing can be summarized in a simple equation called *Hooke's law* (after Robert Hooke, a contemporary of Newton):

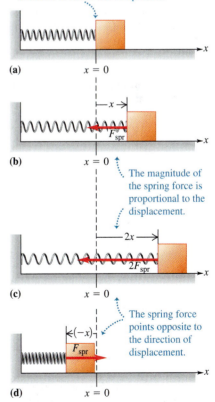

▲ FIGURE 5.19 Some experiments exploring spring forces.

Elastic behavior of springs (Hooke's law)

For springs, the spring force F_{spr} is approximately proportional to the distance x by which the spring is stretched or compressed:

$$F_{spr} = -kx. \tag{5.3}$$

In this equation, k is a positive proportionality constant called the **force constant,** or sometimes the *spring constant,* of the spring. If force is measured in newtons and x in meters, the units of k are N/m. The negative sign indicates that the spring force on the object is always opposite to the displacement.

A very stiff spring requires a large force for a little deformation, corresponding to a large value of the constant k; a weak spring, made with thin wire, requires only a small force for the same deformation, corresponding to a smaller value of k.

Although this relationship is called Hooke's *law,* it is only an approximate relation. Most metallic springs obey it quite well for deformations that are small compared with the overall length of the spring, but rubber bands don't obey it even for small deformations. So it would be safer to call it "Hooke's rule of thumb" (without intending any disparagement of Hooke, one of the great pioneers of late 17th-century science).

EXAMPLE 5.14 Fishy business

A spring balance used to weigh fish is built with a spring that stretches 1.00 cm when a 12.0 N weight is placed in the pan. When the 12.0 N weight is replaced with a 1.50 kg fish, what distance does the spring stretch?

SOLUTION

SET UP Figure 5.20a and b show how the spring responds to the 12.0 N weight and to the 1.50 kg fish. The spring and fish are in equilibrium. We draw a free-body diagram for the fish (Figure 5.20c), showing the downward force of gravity and the upward force exerted by the stretched spring. We point the x axis vertically downward, so x is zero with no fish and positive when the fish is attached and the spring stretches.

SOLVE We want to use Hooke's law $(F_{spr} = -kx)$ to relate the stretch of the spring to the force, but first we need to find the force constant k. The problem states that forces of magnitude 12.0 N are required to stretch the spring 1.00 cm $(= 1.00 \times 10^{-2}\,\text{m})$, so

$$k = -\frac{-12.0\,\text{N}}{1.00 \times 10^{-2}\,\text{m}} = 1200\,\text{N/m}.$$

The weight of the 1.50 kg fish is $w = mg = (1.50\,\text{kg}) \cdot (9.80\,\text{m/s}^2) = 14.7\,\text{N}$. The equilibrium condition for the fish is

$$\Sigma F_x = 0, \quad mg + F_{spr} = 0,$$
$$14.7\,\text{N} - (1200\,\text{N/m})x = 0,$$

and finally, $x = 0.0123\,\text{m} = 1.23\,\text{cm}$.

REFLECT The weight of the fish is greater than the amount of force needed to stretch the spring 1.00 cm, so we expect the fish to stretch the spring more than 1.00 cm. We've used the fact that x can stand for any length change of a Hooke's law spring and F_{spr} for the corresponding change in the component of the spring force.

Practice Problem: If, instead of the fish, we place a 3.00 kg rock in the pan, how much does the spring stretch? *Answer:* Twice as much, 2.45 cm.

(a) The scale stretched by a known weight

(b) The scale stretched by a known mass

(c) Free-body diagram for the fish

▶ **FIGURE 5.20** Weighing a fish.

EXAMPLE 5.15 **An innerspring mattress**

You have just bought an innerspring mattress that contains coil springs in a rectangular array 20 coils wide and 40 coils long. You estimate that when you lie on the mattress, your weight is supported by about 200 springs (about one-fourth of the total number of springs in the mattress). Lacking further funds for a foundation spring, you lay the mattress directly on the floor. You observe that the springs compress about 2.6 cm when you lie on the mattress. Assuming that your weight of 800 N is supported equally by 200 springs, find the force constant of each spring.

SOLUTION

SET UP You are the object in equilibrium, so start with a free-body diagram of yourself (Figure 5.21). Observe that the spring forces are *additive,* in the sense that the total upward force they exert on your body is just 200 times the force of each individual spring. Your body is in equilibrium under the action of the total spring force and your weight.

SOLVE For equilibrium, the total upward force of all the supporting springs must be 800 N, so $(200)k(2.6 \times 10^{-2} \, \text{m}) = 800 \, \text{N}$, and

$$k = 154 \, \text{N/m} = 1.54 \, \text{N/cm}.$$

REFLECT To borrow a term from electric circuit analysis, the springs are *in parallel;* the deformation is the same for each, and the total force is the sum of the individual spring forces. Of course, the assumption that all the deformations are the same is probably not realistic.

▲ **FIGURE 5.21** Free-body diagram of yourself on the mattress.

Practice Problem: Suppose you lay a thin, lightweight sheet of plywood on top of the mattress, so that your weight is spread over all 800 springs. How much does each spring compress? *Answer:* 0.65 cm.

5.5 Forces in Nature

The historical development of our understanding of the forces (or interactions) found in nature has traditionally placed them into four distinct classes (Figure 5.22). Two are familiar in everyday experience. The other two involve fundamental particle interactions that we cannot observe with the unaided senses.

Of the two familiar classes, **gravitational interactions** were the first to be studied in detail. The *weight* of an object results from the earth's gravitational pull acting on it. The sun's gravitational attraction for the earth keeps the earth in its nearly circular orbit around the sun. Newton recognized that the motions of the planets around the sun and the free fall of objects on earth are both the result of gravitational forces. In the next chapter, we'll study gravitational interactions in greater detail and we'll analyze their vital role in the motions of planets and satellites.

The second familiar class of forces, **electromagnetic interactions,** includes electric and magnetic forces. When you run a comb through your hair, you can then use the comb to pick up bits of paper or fluff; this interaction is the result of an *electric* charge on the comb, which also causes the infamous "static cling." *Magnetic* forces occur in interactions between magnets or between a magnet and a piece of iron. These forces may seem to form a different category, separate from electric forces, but magnetic interactions are actually the result of electric charges in motion. In an electromagnet, an electric current in a coil of wire causes magnetic interactions. One of the great achievements of 19th-century physics was the *unification* of theories of electric and magnetic interactions into a single theoretical framework. We'll study these interactions in detail in the second half of this book.

Gravitational and electromagnetic interactions differ enormously in their strength. The electrical repulsion between two protons at a given distance is

(a)

(b)

(c)

(d)

◄**FIGURE 5.22** Instances of the four fundamental forces. (a) Gravitational interactions hold the earth and moon in orbit around each other. (b) Electromagnetic interactions hold together the atoms of a DNA molecule. (c) The strong nuclear interaction is involved in the nuclear reactions that release energy in stars, such as our sun. (d) The weak nuclear interaction plays a role in the release of energy in supernovae, which partly involves the decay of unstable nuclei. (The arrow in the left image indicates the star that has become a supernova in the right image.)

stronger than their gravitational attraction by a factor on the order of 10^{35}. Gravitational forces play no significant role in atomic or molecular structure. But in bodies of astronomical size, positive and negative charge are usually present in nearly equal amounts, and the resulting electrical interactions nearly cancel out. Gravitational interactions are the dominant influence in the motion of planets and also in the internal structure of stars.

The other two classes of interactions are less familiar. One, the **strong interaction,** is responsible for holding the nucleus of an atom together. Nuclei contain electrically neutral and positively charged particles. The charged particles repel each other, and a nucleus could not be stable if it were not for the presence of an *attractive* force of a different kind that counteracts the repulsive electrical interactions. In this context, the strong interaction is also called the *nuclear force*. It has a much shorter range than electrical interactions, but within its range it is much stronger. The strong interaction is also responsible for the creation of unstable particles in high-energy particle collisions.

Finally, there is the **weak interaction.** This force plays no direct role in the behavior of ordinary matter, but it is of vital importance in the behavior of fundamental particles. The weak interaction is responsible for beta decay (one kind of nuclear radiation), as well as the decay of many unstable particles produced in high-energy collisions of fundamental particles. It also plays a significant role in the evolution of stars.

During the 1970s, a unified theory of the electromagnetic and weak interactions was developed. This interaction is now called the *electroweak interaction*. In a sense, it reduces the number of classes of forces from four to three. Similar attempts have been made to understand all strong, electromagnetic, and weak interactions on the basis of a single unified theory called *quantum chromodynamics* (QCD), or a *grand unified theory* (GUT), in which only two forces are postulated. The most promising of the GUT theories make use of vibrating entities called *strings,* whose description requires a space with many more dimensions than our familiar three-dimensional space.

Finally, the ultimate goal is to include gravitational forces in the unification, to produce a *theory of everything* (TOE). Theories of this nature are intimately related to the very early history of the universe, following the Big Bang. Such theories are still highly speculative and raise many unanswered questions. The entire field is in much ferment today. Recent research has had the remarkable effect of connecting our understanding of the *smallest* objects in the universe—that is, fundamental particles—with our understanding of the *largest* objects—the universe itself and its evolution in time since the Big Bang.

SUMMARY

Equilibrium of a Particle

(Section 5.1) When an object is in equilibrium, the vector sum of the forces acting on it must be zero: $\sum \vec{F} = 0$. (Equation 4.3). In component form,

$$\sum F_x = 0, \qquad \sum F_y = 0. \qquad (4.4)$$

Free-body diagrams are useful in identifying the forces acting on the object being considered. Newton's third law is also frequently needed in equilibrium problems. The two forces in an action–reaction pair never act on the same object.

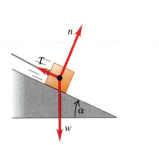

An object moving at constant velocity down a frictionless ramp is in equilibrium: $\sum \vec{F} = 0$.

A free-body diagram and coordinate system for the object. The weight vector is replaced by its components.

Applications of Newton's Second Law

(Section 5.2) When the vector sum of the forces on an object is not zero, the object has an acceleration determined by Newton's second law, $\sum \vec{F} = m\vec{a}$ (Equation 4.7). In component form,

$$\sum F_x = ma_x, \qquad \sum F_y = ma_y. \qquad (4.8)$$

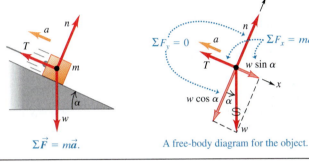

$\sum \vec{F} = m\vec{a}$.

A free-body diagram for the object.

Contact Forces and Friction

(Section 5.3) The contact force between two objects can always be represented in terms of a normal component n perpendicular to the surface of interaction and a frictional component f parallel to the surface. When sliding occurs, the kinetic-friction force f_k is often approximately proportional to n. Then the proportionality constant is μ_k, the coefficient of kinetic friction: $f_k = \mu_k n$ (Equation 5.1).

When there is no relative motion, the maximum possible friction force is approximately proportional to the normal force, and the proportionality constant is μ_s, the coefficient of static friction. The governing equation is $f_s \leq \mu_s n$ (Equation 5.2).

The actual static-friction force may be anything from zero to the maximum value given by the equality in Equation 5.2, depending on the situation. Usually, μ_k is less than μ_s for a given pair of surfaces.

The static-friction force remains equal in magnitude to the tension force until its maximum value $(f_s)_{max}$ is exceeded.

Elastic Forces

(Section 5.4) When forces act on a solid object, the object usually deforms. In some cases, such as a stretched or compressed spring, the deformation is approximately proportional to the magnitude of the applied force. This proportionality is called Hooke's law:

$$F_{spr} = -kx. \qquad (5.3)$$

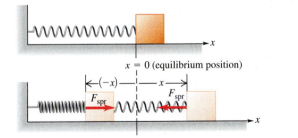

When stretched or compressed from equilibrium, the spring exerts a force $\vec{F}_{spr}$ whose magnitude is approximately proportional to the displacement.

Forces in Nature

(Section 5.5) Historically, forces have been classified as strong, electromagnetic, weak, and gravitational. Present-day research includes intensive efforts to create a unified description of forces in all these categories.

Conceptual Questions

1. Can a body be in equilibrium when only one force acts on it?
2. A clothesline is hung between two poles, and then a shirt is hung near the center of the line. No matter how tightly the line is stretched, it always sags a little at the center. Show why.
3. How can pushing *down* on a bicycle pedal make the bicycle move *forward?*
4. Is it physically possible for the coefficient of friction ever to be greater than one? What would this mean?
5. Why is it so much more difficult to walk on icy pavement than dry pavement?
6. A car accelerates gradually to the right with power on the two rear wheels. What is the direction of the friction force on these wheels? Show why. Is it static or kinetic friction?
7. Without doing any calculations, decide whether the tension T in Figure 5.23 will be equal to, greater than, or less than the weight of the suspended object.
8. A box slides up an incline, comes to rest, and then slides down again, accelerating in both directions.

▲ **FIGURE 5.23** Question 7.

Answer the following questions, using only a free-body diagram and *without* doing any calculations: (a) If there is no friction on the incline, how will the box's acceleration going up compare in magnitude *and* direction with its acceleration going down? (b) If there is kinetic friction on the incline, how will the box's acceleration going up compare in magnitude *and* direction with its acceleration going down? (c) What will be the box's acceleration at its highest point?
9. For the objects shown in Figure 5.24, will the tension in the wire be greater than, equal to, or less than the weight W? Decide *without* doing any calculations.

▲ **FIGURE 5.24** Question 9.

10. A woman is pushing horizontally on two boxes on a factory floor, as shown in Figure 5.25. Which is greater, the force the woman exerts on the 10 lb box or the force the 10 lb box exerts on the 250 lb box? Decide without doing any calculations.

▲ **FIGURE 5.25** Question 10.

11. In a world *without* friction, could you (a) walk on a horizontal sidewalk, (b) climb a ladder, (c) climb a vertical pole, (d) jump into the air, (e) ride your bike, and (f) drive around a curve on a flat roadway? Explain your reasoning.
12. How could you measure the acceleration of a spaceship by using only simple instruments (such as springs, strings, and rulers) located *within* the ship?
13. You often hear people say, "Friction always opposes motion." Is this statement true? Can you think of any counterexamples? In what sense *is* the statement true?
14. (a) Show that, in terms of the fundamental quantities, the units of the force constant k for a spring reduce to kg/s^2. (b) Why is

it physically more sensible to express k in N/m instead of in its fundamental units of kg/s^2?
15. List some elastic biological materials.
16. True or false? The minus sign in Hooke's law ($F_{spr} = -kx$) means that the spring's force always points in the negative direction. If the statement is false, what *does* the minus sign mean?

Multiple-Choice Problems

1. A horizontal force accelerates a box across a rough horizontal floor with friction present, producing an acceleration a. If the force is now tripled, but all other conditions remain the same, the acceleration will become
   A. greater than $3a$.
   B. equal to $3a$.
   C. less than $3a$.
2. A child of mass M using a parachute reaches a terminal velocity V, with the air resistance directly proportional to the square of the child's velocity. If an adult of mass $3M$ uses the same parachute under exactly the same conditions, his terminal velocity will be closest to
   A. $3V$.
   B. $9V$.
   C. $\dfrac{V}{\sqrt{3}}$.
   D. $V\sqrt{3}$.

3. An artist wearing spiked shoes pushes two crates across her frictionless horizontal studio floor. (See Figure 5.26.) If she exerts a horizontal 36 N force on the smaller crate, then the smaller crate exerts a force on the larger crate that is closest to

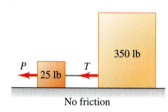

▲ **FIGURE 5.26** Multiple-choice problem 3.

   A. 36 N. B. 30 N. C. 200 N. D. 240 N.
4. A horizontal pull P pulls two wagons over a horizontal frictionless floor, as shown in Figure 5.27. The tension in the light horizontal rope connecting the wagons is

▲ **FIGURE 5.27** Multiple-choice problem 4.

   A. equal to P, by Newton's third law.
   B. equal to 2000 N.
   C. greater than P.
   D. less than P.
5. A horizontal pull P drags two boxes connected by a horizontal rope having tension T, as shown in Figure 5.28. The floor is horizontal and frictionless. Decide which of the following statements is true *without* doing any calculations:

▲ **FIGURE 5.28** Multiple-choice problem 5.

   A. $P > T$ B. $P = T$ C. $P < T$
   D. We need more information to decide which is greater.

6. A crate slides up an inclined ramp and then slides down the ramp after momentarily stopping near the top. This crate is acted upon by friction on the ramp and accelerates both ways. Which statement about this crate's acceleration is correct?
   A. The acceleration going up the ramp is greater than the acceleration going down.
   B. The acceleration going down the ramp is greater than the acceleration going up.
   C. The acceleration is the same in both directions.

7. A spring having a force constant of 15.0 N/cm and an unstretched length of 20.0 cm is pulled so that it is 23.0 cm long. The force required to stretch it this much is
   A. 45 N.   B. 300 N.   C. 322.5 N.   D. 345 N.

8. A weightless spring scale is attached to two equal weights as shown in Figure 5.29. The reading in the scale will be
   A. 0.   B. W.
   C. 2W.

▲ **FIGURE 5.29** Multiple-choice problem 8.

9. Two objects are connected by a light wire as shown in Figure 5.30, with the wire pulling horizontally on the 400 N object. After this system is released from rest, the tension in the wire will be
   A. less than 300 N.
   B. 300 N.
   C. 200 N.
   D. 100 N.

$\mu_s = \frac{1}{2}, \ \mu_k = \frac{1}{4}$

▲ **FIGURE 5.30** Multiple-choice problem 9.

10. A 100 N weight is supported by two weightless wires A and B as shown in Figure 5.31. What can you conclude about the tensions in these wires?
    A. The tensions are equal to 50 N each.
    B. The tensions are equal, but less than 50 N each.
    C. The tensions are equal, but greater than 50 N each.
    D. The tensions are equal to 100 N each.

11. The two blocks in Figure 5.32 are in balance, and there is no friction on the surface of the incline. If a slight vibration occurs, what will M do after that?
    A. It will accelerate up the ramp.
    B. It will accelerate down the ramp.
    C. It will not accelerate.

▲ **FIGURE 5.32** Multiple-choice problem 11.

▲ **FIGURE 5.31** Multiple-choice problem 10.

▲ **FIGURE 5.33** Multiple-choice problem 12.

12. The system shown in Figure 5.33 is released from rest, there is no friction between B and the tabletop, and all of the objects move together. What must be true about the friction force on A?
    A. It is zero.
    B. It acts to the right on A.
    C. It acts to the left on A.
    D. We cannot tell whether there is any friction force on A because we do not know the coefficients of friction between A and B.

13. In the system shown in Figure 5.34, $M > m$, the surface of the bench is horizontal and frictionless, and the connecting string pulls horizontally on m. As more and more weight is gradually added to m, which of the following statements best describes the behavior of the system after it is released?
    A. The acceleration remains the same in all cases, since there is no friction and the pull of gravity on M is the same.
    B. The acceleration becomes zero when enough weight is added so that $m = M$.
    C. The velocity becomes zero when $m = M$.
    D. None of the preceding statements is correct.

▲ **FIGURE 5.34** Multiple-choice problem 13.

Problems

5.1 Equilibrium of a Particle

1. • A 15.0 N bucket is to be raised at a constant speed of 50.0 cm/s by a rope. According to the information in Table 5.1, how many kilograms of cement can be put into this bucket without breaking the rope if it is made of (a) thin white string, (b) $\frac{1}{4}$ in. nylon clothesline, (c) $1\frac{1}{4}$ in. manila climbing rope?

2. • In a museum exhibit, three equal weights are hung with identical wires, as shown in Figure 5.35. Each wire can support a tension of no more than 75.0 N without breaking. Start each of the following parts with an appropriate free-body diagram. (a) What is the maximum value that W can be without breaking any wires? (b) Under these conditions, what is the tension in each wire?

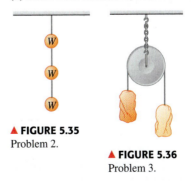

▲ **FIGURE 5.35** Problem 2.

▲ **FIGURE 5.36** Problem 3.

3. • Two 25.0 N weights are suspended at opposite ends of a rope that passes over a light, frictionless pulley. The pulley is attached to a chain that is fastened to the ceiling. (See Figure 5.36.) Start solving this problem by making a free-body diagram of each weight. (a) What is the tension in the rope? (b) What is the tension in the chain?

4. • Two weights are hanging as shown in Figure 5.37. (a) Draw a free-body diagram of each weight. (b) Find the tension in cable *A*. (c) Find the tension in cables *B* and *C*.

▲ **FIGURE 5.37** Problem 4.

5. • An adventurous archaeologist crosses between two rock cliffs by slowly going hand over hand along a rope stretched between the cliffs. He stops to rest at the middle of the rope (Figure 5.38). The rope will break if the tension in it exceeds 2.50×10^4 N. Our hero's mass is 90.0 kg. (a) If the angle θ is 10.0°, find the tension in the rope. Start with a free-body diagram of the archaeologist. (b) What is the smallest value the angle θ can have if the rope is not to break?

▲ **FIGURE 5.38** Problem 5.

6. • A uniform chain of weight *W* hangs with some slack as shown in Figure 5.39, making an angle of 21° below the horizontal at its ends. (a) Draw a free-body diagram of the chain. (b) What is the tension (in terms of *W*) in the chain at the points where it is attached to the walls?

▲ **FIGURE 5.39** Problem 6.

7. •• **Tension in a muscle.** Muscles are attached to bones by
   BIO means of tendons. The maximum force that a muscle can exert is directly proportional to its cross-sectional area *A* at the widest point. We can express this relationship mathematically as $F_{max} = \sigma A$, where σ (sigma) is a proportionality constant. Surprisingly, σ is about the same for the muscles of all animals and has the numerical value of 3.0×10^5 in SI units. (a) What are the SI units of σ in terms of newtons and meters and also in terms of the fundamental quantities (kg, m, s)? (b) In one set of experiments, the average maximum force that the gastrocnemius muscle in the back of the lower leg could exert was measured to be 755 N for healthy males in their midtwenties. What does this result tell us was the average cross-sectional area, in cm², of that muscle for the people in the study?

8. •• **Muscles and tendons.** The gastrocnemius muscle, in the
   BIO back of the leg, has two portions, known as the medial and lateral heads. Assume that they attach to the Achilles tendon as shown in Figure 5.40. The cross-sectional area of each of these two muscles is typically 30 cm² for many adults. What is the maximum tension they can produce in the Achilles tendon? (See the previous problem for some useful information.)

▲ **FIGURE 5.40** Problem 8.

9. • **Traction apparatus.** In order to
   BIO prevent muscle contraction from misaligning bones during healing (which can cause a permanent limp), injured or broken legs must be supported horizontally and at the same time kept under tension (traction) directed along the leg. One version of a device to accomplish this aim, the Russell traction apparatus, is shown in Figure 5.41. This system allows the apparatus to support the full weight of the injured leg and at the same time provide the traction along the leg. If the leg to be supported weighs 47.0 N, (a) what must be the weight of *W* and (b) what traction force does this system produce along the leg?

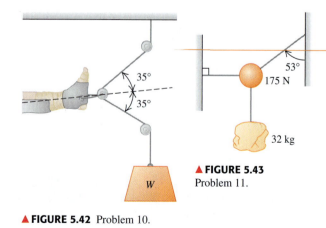

▲ **FIGURE 5.41** Problem 9.

10. • **A broken thigh bone.** When the thigh is fractured, the
    BIO patient's leg must be kept under traction. One method of doing so is a variation on the Russell traction apparatus. (See Figure 5.42.) If the physical therapist specifies that the traction force directed along the leg must be 25 N, what must *W* be?

▲ **FIGURE 5.42** Problem 10.

▲ **FIGURE 5.43** Problem 11.

11. •• Two artifacts in a museum display are hung from vertical walls by very light wires, as shown in Figure 5.43. (a) Draw a

free-body diagram of each artifact. (b) Find the tension in each of the three wires. (c) Would the answers be different if each wire were twice as long, but the angles were unchanged? Why or why not?

12. •• In a rescue, the 73 kg police officer is suspended by two cables, as shown in Figure 5.44. (a) Sketch a free-body diagram of him. (b) Find the tension in each cable.

▲ **FIGURE 5.44** Problem 12.

13. •• A tetherball leans against the smooth, frictionless post to which it is attached. (See Figure 5.45.) The string is attached to the ball such that a line along the string passes through the center of the ball. If the string is 1.40 m long and the ball has a radius of 0.110 m with mass 0.270 kg, (a) make a free-body diagram of the ball. (b) What is the tension in the rope? (c) What is the force the pole exerts on the ball?

▲ **FIGURE 5.45** Problem 13.

14. •• Find the tension in each cord in Figure 5.46 if the weight of the suspended object is 250 N.

(a)   **(b)**

▲ **FIGURE 5.46** Problem 14.

15. •• Two blocks, each with weight w, are held in place on a frictionless incline as shown in Figure 5.47. In terms of w and the angle α of the incline, calculate the tension in (a) the rope connecting the blocks and (b) the rope that connects block A to the wall. (c) Calculate the magnitude of the force that the incline exerts on each block. (d) Interpret your answers for the cases $\alpha = 0$ and $\alpha = 90°$.

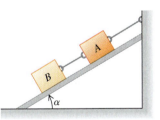

▲ **FIGURE 5.47** Problem 15.

16. •• A man pushes on a piano of mass 180 kg so that it slides at a constant velocity of 12.0 cm/s *down* a ramp that is inclined at 11.0° above the horizontal. No appreciable friction is acting on the piano. Calculate the magnitude and direction of this push (a) if the man pushes parallel to the incline, (b) if the man pushes the piano *up* the plane instead, also at 12.0 cm/s parallel to the incline, and (c) if the man pushes horizontally, but still with a speed of 12.0 cm/s.

5.2 Applications of Newton's Second Law

17. •• **Air-bag safety.** According to safety standards for air bags, **BIO** the maximum acceleration during a car crash should not exceed 60g and should last for no more than 36 ms. (a) In such a case, what force does the air bag exert on a 75 kg person? Start with a free-body diagram. (b) Express the force in part (a) in terms of the person's weight.

18. •• **Forces during chin-ups.** People who do chin-ups raise **BIO** their chin just over a bar (the chinning bar), supporting themselves only by their arms. Typically, the body below the arms is raised by about 30 cm in a time of 1.0 s, starting from rest. Assume that the entire body of a 680 N person who is chinning is raised this distance and that half the 1.0 s is spent accelerating upward and the other half accelerating downward, uniformly in both cases. Make a free-body diagram of the person's body, and then apply it to find the force his arms must exert on him during the accelerating part of the chin-up.

19. •• **Force on a tennis ball.** The record speed for a tennis ball that is served is 73.14 m/s. During a serve, the ball typically starts from rest and is in contact with the tennis racquet for 30 ms. Assuming constant acceleration, what was the average force exerted on the tennis ball during this record serve, expressed in terms of the ball's weight W?

20. •• A 75,600 N spaceship comes in for a vertical landing. From an initial speed of 1.00 km/s, it comes to rest in 2.00 min with uniform acceleration. (a) Make a free-body diagram of this ship as it is coming in. (b) What braking force must its rockets provide? Ignore air resistance.

21. •• **Force during a jump.** An average person can reach a **BIO** maximum height of about 60 cm when jumping straight up from a crouched position. During the jump itself, the person's body from the knees up typically rises a distance of around 50 cm. To keep the calculations simple and yet get a reasonable result, assume that the *entire body* rises this much during the jump. (a) With what initial speed does the person leave the ground to reach a height of 60 cm? (b) Make a free-body diagram of the person during the jump. (c) In terms of this jumper's weight W, what force does the ground exert on him or her during the jump?

22. •• A short train (an engine plus four cars) is accelerating at 1.10 m/s². If the mass of each car is 38,000 kg, and if each car has negligible frictional forces acting on it, what are (a) the force of the engine on the first car, (b) the force of the first car on the second car, (c) the force of the second car on the third car, and (d) the force of the third car on the fourth car? In solving this problem, note the importance of selecting the correct set of cars to isolate as your object.

23. •• A large fish hangs from a spring balance supported from the roof of an elevator. (a) If the elevator has an upward acceleration of 2.45 m/s² and the balance reads 60.0 N, what is the true weight of the fish? (b) Under what circumstances will the balance read 35.0 N? (c) What will the balance read if the elevator cable breaks?

24. •• **Runway design.** A transport plane takes off from a level landing field with two gliders in tow, one behind the other. The mass of each glider is 700 kg, and the total resistance (air drag plus friction with the runway) on each may be assumed constant and equal to 2500 N. The tension in the towrope between the transport plane and the first glider is not to

exceed 12,000 N. (a) If a speed of 40 m/s is required for take-off, what minimum length of runway is needed? (b) What is the tension in the towrope between the two gliders while they are accelerating for the takeoff?

25. •• The TGV, France's high-speed train, pulls out of the Lyons station and is accelerating uniformly to its cruising speed. Inside one of the cars, a 3.00 N digital camera is hanging from the luggage compartment by a light, flexible strap that makes a 12.0° angle with the vertical. (a) Make a free-body diagram of this camera. (b) Apply Newton's second law to the camera, and find the acceleration of the train and the tension in the strap.

26. •• Which way and by what angle does the accelero-meter in Figure 5.48 deflect under the following condi-tions? (a) The cart is mov-ing toward the right with speed increasing at 3.0 m/s². (b) The cart is moving to-ward the left with speed de-creasing at 4.5 m/s². (c) The cart is moving toward the left with a constant speed of 4.0 m/s.

▲ **FIGURE 5.48** Problem 26.

27. • A skier approaches the base of an icy hill with a speed of 12.5 m/s. The hill slopes upward at 24° above the horizontal. Ignoring all friction forces, find the acceleration of this skier (a) when she is going up the hill, (b) when she has reached her highest point, and (c) after she has started sliding down the hill. In each case, start with a free-body diagram of the skier.

28. • At a construction site, a 22.0 kg bucket of concrete is connected over a very light frictionless pulley to a 375 N box on the roof of a building. (See Figure 5.49.) There is no appre-ciable friction on the box, since it is on roller bearings. The box starts from rest. (a) Make free-body dia-grams of the bucket and the box. (b) Find the acceleration of the bucket. (c) How fast is the bucket moving after it has fallen 1.50 m (assuming that the box has not yet reached the edge of the roof)?

▲ **FIGURE 5.49** Problem 28.

29. •• Two boxes are connected by a light string that passes over a light, frictionless pulley. One box rests on a frictionless ramp that rises at 30.0° above the hori-zontal (see Figure 5.50), and the system is released from rest. (a) Make free-body diagrams of each box. (b) Which way will the 50.0 kg box move, up the plane or down the plane? Or will it even move at all? Show why or why not. (c) Find the acceleration of each box.

▲ **FIGURE 5.50** Problem 29.

5.3 Frictional Forces

30. • An 80 N box initially at rest is pulled by a horizontal rope on a horizontal table. The coefficients of kinetic and static fric-tion between the box and the table are $\frac{1}{4}$ and $\frac{1}{2}$, respectively. What is the friction force on this box if the pull is (a) 0 N, (b) 25 N, (c) 39 N, (d) 41 N, (e) 150 N?

31. • A box of bananas weighing 40.0 N rests on a horizontal sur-face. The coefficient of static friction between the box and the surface is 0.40, and the coefficient of kinetic friction is 0.20. (a) If no horizontal force is applied to the box and the box is at rest, how large is the friction force exerted on the box? (b) What is the magnitude of the friction force if a monkey applies a hor-izontal force of 6.0 N to the box and the box is initially at rest? (c) What minimum horizontal force must the monkey apply to start the box in motion? (d) What minimum horizontal force must the monkey apply to keep the box moving at constant velocity once it has been started?

32. • **Friction at the hip joint.** Fig-ure 5.51 shows the bone structure at the hip joint. The bones are nor-mally not in direct contact, but instead are covered with cartilage to reduce friction. The space between them is filled with water-like synovial fluid, which further decreases friction. Due to this fluid, the coefficient of kinetic friction between the bones can range from 0.0050 to 0.020. (The wide range of values is due to the fact that motion such as running causes more fluid to squirt between the bones, thereby reduc-ing friction when they strike each other.) Typically, approxi-mately 65% of a person's weight is above the hip—we'll call this the *upper weight*. (a) Show that when a person is simply standing upright, each hip supports half of his upper weight. (b) When a person is walking, each hip now supports up to 2.5 times his upper weight, depending on how fast he is walk-ing. (Recall that when you walk, your weight shifts from one leg to the other and your body comes down fairly hard on each leg.) For a 65 kg person, what is the maximum kinetic friction force at the hip joint if μ_k has its minimum value of 0.0050? (c) As a person gets older, the aging process, as well as osteoarthritis, can alter the composition of the synovial fluid. In the worst case, this fluid could disappear, leaving bone-on-bone contact with a coefficient of kinetic friction of 0.30. What would be the greatest friction force for the walking person in part (b)? The increased friction causes pain and, in addition, wears down the joint even more.

▲ **FIGURE 5.51** Problem 32.

33. • At a construction site, a pallet of bricks is to be suspended by attaching a rope to it and con-necting the other end to a cou-ple of heavy crates on the roof of a building, as shown in Figure 5.52. The rope pulls hor-izontally on the lower crate, and the coefficient of static friction between the lower crate and the roof is 0.666. (a) What is the weight of the heaviest pallet of bricks that can be supported this way? Start with appropriate free-body diagrams. (b) What is the friction force on the upper crate under the conditions of part (a)?

▲ **FIGURE 5.52** Problem 33.

34. •• Two crates connected by a rope of negligible mass lie on a horizontal surface. (See Figure 5.53.) Crate A has mass m_A and

crate B has mass m_B. The coefficient of kinetic friction between each crate and the surface is μ_k. The crates are pulled to the right at a constant velocity of 3.20 cm/s by a horizontal force $\vec{F}$. In terms of m_A, m_B, and μ_k, calculate (a) the magnitude of the force $\vec{F}$ and (b) the tension in the rope connecting the blocks. Include the free-body diagram or diagrams you used to determine each answer.

▲ **FIGURE 5.53** Problem 34.

35. •• A hockey puck leaves a player's stick with a speed of 9.9 m/s and slides 32.0 m before coming to rest. Find the coefficient of friction between the puck and the ice.

36. •• **Stopping distance of a car.** (a) If the coefficient of kinetic friction between tires and dry pavement is 0.80, what is the shortest distance in which you can stop an automobile by locking the brakes when traveling at 29.1 m/s (about 65 mi/h)? (b) On wet pavement, the coefficient of kinetic friction may be only 0.25. How fast should you drive on wet pavement in order to be able to stop in the same distance as in part (a)? (*Note:* Locking the brakes is *not* the safest way to stop.)

37. •• A car with locked wheels stops in a distance D on a dry pavement. If the pavement is icy, so that the coefficient of kinetic friction is one-eighth of what it was for dry pavement, how far (in terms of D) will this car travel before stopping if it started with the same initial velocity in both cases?

38. •• A coefficient of kinetic friction, μ, is needed to stop a car in a distance D on dry pavement with the wheels locked if the car starts from speed V_0. What coefficient of kinetic friction (in terms of μ) is needed to stop this car in the same distance if it starts from an initial speed of $3V_0$?

39. •• A stockroom worker pushes a box with mass 11.2 kg on a horizontal surface with a constant speed of 3.50 m/s. The coefficients of kinetic and static friction between the box and the surface are 0.200 and 0.450, respectively. (a) What horizontal force must the worker apply to maintain the motion of the box? (b) If the worker stops pushing, what will be the acceleration of the box?

40. •• The coefficients of static and kinetic friction between a 476 N crate and the warehouse floor are 0.615 and 0.420, respectively. A worker gradually increases his horizontal push against this crate until it just begins to move and from then on maintains that same maximum push. What is the acceleration of the crate after it has begun to move? Start with a free-body diagram of the crate.

41. •• **Measuring the coefficients of friction.** One straightforward way to measure the coefficients of friction between a box and a wooden surface is illustrated in Figure 5.54. The sheet of wood can be raised by pivoting it about one edge. It is first raised to an angle θ_1 (which is measured) for which the box just begins to slide downward. The sheet is then immediately low-

▲ **FIGURE 5.54** Problem 41.

ered to an angle θ_2 (which is also measured) for which the box slides with constant speed down the sheet. Apply Newton's second law to the box in both cases to find the coefficients of kinetic and static friction between it and the wooden sheet in terms of the measured angles θ_1 and θ_2.

42. With its wheels locked, a van slides down a hill inclined at 40.0° to the horizontal. Find the acceleration of this van a) if the hill is icy and frictionless, and b) if the coefficient of kinetic friction is 0.20.

43. • **The Trendelberg position.** In emergencies with major BIO blood loss, the doctor will order the patient placed in the Trendelberg position, which is to raise the foot of the bed to get maximum blood flow to the brain. If the coefficient of static friction between the typical patient and the bedsheets is 1.2, what is the maximum angle at which the bed can be tilted with respect to the floor before the patient begins to slide?

44. •• **Injuries to the spinal column.** In treating spinal injuries, BIO it is often necessary to provide some tension along the spinal column to stretch the backbone. One device for doing this is the Stryker frame, illustrated in part (a) of Figure 5.55. A weight W is attached to the patient (sometimes around a neck collar, as shown in part (b) of the figure), and friction between the person's body and the bed prevents sliding. (a) If the coefficient of static friction between a 78.5 kg patient's body and the bed is 0.75, what is the maximum traction force along the spinal column that W can provide without causing the patient to slide? (b) Under the conditions of maximum traction, what is the tension in each cable attached to the neck collar?

(a)

W

(b)

▲ **FIGURE 5.55** Problem 44.

45. •• A winch is used to drag a 375 N crate up a ramp at a constant speed of 75 cm/s by means of a rope that pulls parallel to the surface of the ramp. The rope slopes upward at 33° above the horizontal, and the coefficient of kinetic friction between the ramp and the crate is 0.25. (a) What is the tension in the rope? (b) If the rope were suddenly to snap, what would be the acceleration of the crate immediately after the rope broke?

46. •• A toboggan approaches a snowy hill moving at 11.0 m/s. The coefficients of static and kinetic friction between the snow and the toboggan are 0.40 and 0.30, respectively, and the hill slopes upward at 40.0° above the horizontal. Find the acceleration of the toboggan (a) as it is going up the hill and

(b) after it has reached its highest point and is sliding down the hill.

47. •• A truck is dragging a load of mass M with the use of a rope that makes an angle of ϕ above the horizontal ground. The coefficient of kinetic friction between the load and the ground is μ, and the load (and truck) have an acceleration a. (a) Find the tension in the rope in terms of M, a, μ, g, and ϕ. (b) Evaluate your answer in part (a) in the following special cases to see if you get a reasonable result: (i) There is no friction between the load and the ground; (ii) the rope pulls horizontally on the load.

48. •• A person pushes on a stationary 125 N box with 75 N at 30° below the horizontal, as shown in Figure 5.56. The coefficient of static friction between the box and the horizontal floor is 0.80. (a) Make a free-body diagram of the box. (b) What is the normal force on the box? (c) What is the friction force on the box? (d) What is the largest the friction force could be? (e) The person now replaces his push with a 75 N pull at 30° above the horizontal. Find the normal force on the box in this case.

▲ **FIGURE 5.56** Problem 48.

49. • An atmospheric drag force with magnitude $F_D = Dv^2$, where v is speed, acts on a falling 300 mg raindrop that reaches a terminal velocity of 11 m/s. (a) Show that the SI units of D are kg/m. (b) Find the value of D.

50. • If we model the air resistance on a falling person as being proportional to the square of that person's speed, in certain circumstances the proportionality constant between the air resistance and the square of the speed is equal to 0.10 kg/m. (a) What would be the terminal velocity of a 60.0 kg person? (b) What would be the air resistance when the person's speed is half the terminal velocity?

51. •• If the air resistance is proportional to the square of the speed for an object of weight W, what is the air resistance (in terms of W) when this object's speed is equal to (a) its terminal velocity, (b) one-half its terminal velocity, and (c) one-third its terminal velocity?

52. •• If the air resistance is proportional to the square of the speed for a sphere of weight W, and that sphere has a terminal velocity V_T, what is the terminal velocity (in terms of V_T) for an equal-diameter sphere of weight (a) $2W$, (b) $3W$, and (c) $4W$?

53. •• An object is dropped from rest and encounters air resistance that is proportional to the square of its speed. Sketch qualitative graphs (no numbers) showing (a) the air resistance on this object as a function of its speed, (b) the *net* force on the object as a function of its speed, (c) the *net* force on the object as a function of time, (d) the speed of the object as a function of time, and (e) the acceleration of the object as a function of time.

5.4 Elastic Forces

54. • You find that if you hang a 1.25 kg weight from a vertical spring, it stretches 3.75 cm. (a) What is the force constant of this spring in N/m? (b) How much mass should you hang from the spring so it will stretch by 8.13 cm from its original, unstretched length?

55. • An unstretched spring is 12.00 cm long. When you hang an 875 g weight from it, it stretches to a length of 14.40 cm. (a) What is the force constant (in N/m) of this spring? (b) What total mass must you hang from the spring to stretch it to a total length of 17.72 cm?

56. • **Heart repair.** A surgeon is using material from a donated **BIO** heart to repair a patient's damaged aorta and needs to know the elastic characteristics of this aortal material. Tests performed on a 16.0 cm strip of the donated aorta reveal that it stretches 3.75 cm when a 1.50 N pull is exerted on it. (a) What is the force constant of this strip of aortal material? (b) If the maximum distance it will be able to stretch when it replaces the aorta in the damaged heart is 1.14 cm, what is the greatest force it will be able to exert there?

57. • **Postal scale.** In a simple postal scale, used to weigh letters, a flat pan is supported by an ordinary spring (inside the device), as shown in Figure 5.57. When you place a letter on the pan, it causes the pan to move downward against the spring, while a pointer reads the weight of the letter. You observe that with nothing on it, the pan is at equilib-rium 45.0 mm above the body of the scale. When you place a 1.0 oz letter on the scale, the pan moves down to 42.0 mm above the body of the scale. Recall that there are 16 oz in a pound, and consult Appendix E. (a) Find the force constant of this spring, in N/cm. (b) By how much from its equilibrium position would a 3.5 oz letter depress the pan?

▲ **FIGURE 5.57** Problem 57.

58. •• A student measures the force required to stretch a spring by various amounts and makes the graph shown in Figure 5.58, which plots this force as a function of the distance the spring has stretched. (a) Does this spring obey Hooke's law? How do you know? (b) What is the force constant of the spring, in N/m? (c) What force would be needed to stretch the spring a distance of 17 cm from its unstretched length, assuming that it continues to obey Hooke's law?

▲ **FIGURE 5.58** Problem 58.

59. •• A student hangs various masses from a spring and records the resulting distance the spring has stretched. She then uses her data to construct the graph shown in Figure 5.59, which plots the mass hung from the spring as a function of the distance the mass caused the spring to stretch beyond its unstretched length. (a) Does this spring obey Hooke's law? How do you know? (b) What is the force constant of the spring, in N/m? (c) By how much will the spring have stretched if you hang a 2.35 kg mass from it, assuming that it continues to obey Hooke's law?

▲ **FIGURE 5.59** Problem 59.

60. • Three identical 6.40 kg masses are hung by three identical springs, as shown in Figure 5.60. Each spring has a force constant of 7.80 kN/m and was 12.0 cm long before any masses were attached to it. (a) Make a free-body diagram of each mass. (b) How long is each spring when hanging as shown? (*Hint:* First isolate only the bottom mass. Then treat the bottom two masses as a system. Finally, treat all three masses as a system.)

▲ **FIGURE 5.60** Problem 60.

61. • A light spring having a force constant of 125 N/m is used to pull a 9.50 kg sled on a horizontal frictionless ice rink. If the sled has an acceleration of 2.00 m/s², by how much does the spring stretch if it pulls on the sled (a) horizontally, (b) at 30.0° above the horizontal?

62. •• In the previous problem, what would the answers in both cases be if there were friction and the coefficient of kinetic friction between the sled and the ice were 0.200?

General Problems

63. •• **Prevention of hip injuries.** People (especially the elderly) **BIO** who are prone to falling can wear hip pads to cushion the impact on their hip from a fall. Experiments have shown that if the speed at impact can be reduced to 1.3 m/s or less, the hip will usually not fracture. Let us investigate the worst-case scenario, in which a 55 kg person completely loses her footing (such as on icy pavement) and falls a distance of 1.0 m, the distance from her hip to the ground. We shall assume that the person's entire body has the same acceleration, which, in reality, would not quite be true. (a) With what speed does her hip reach the ground? (b) A typical hip pad can reduce the person's speed to 1.3 m/s over a distance of 2.0 cm. Find the acceleration (assumed to be constant) of this person's hip while she is slowing down and the force the pad exerts on it. (c) The force in part (b) is very large. To see if it is likely to cause injury, calculate how long it lasts.

64. •• **Modeling elastic hip pads.** In the previous problem, we **BIO** assumed constant acceleration (and hence a constant force) due to the hip pad. But of course, such a pad would most likely be somewhat elastic. Assuming that the force you found in the previous problem was the maximum force over the period of impact with the ground, and that the hip pad is elastic enough to obey Hooke's law, calculate the force constant of this pad, using appropriate data from the previous problem.

65. •• **Springs in parallel.** Figure 5.61 shows two springs connected in *parallel*. This combination can be thought of as being equivalent to a *single* spring having an effective force

▲ **FIGURE 5.61** Problem 65.

constant k_{eff}. Obviously, the effective force constant must be related to the force constants k_1 and k_2 of the individual springs. We will assume that the springs have no significant mass. Suppose we stretch the combination a total distance x from its equilibrium position. (a) Show that both springs must stretch by the same distance x. (A simple sketch should make this clear.) (b) Show that the force F required to stretch the

combination is the *sum* of the forces exerted by all the springs and is given by $F = k_1x + k_2x = (k_1 + k_2)x$. (c) Show that the effective force constant obeys the equation $F = k_{eff}x$ and is given by the formula $k_{eff} = k_1 + k_2$. (d) If you connect a spring of force constant 25 N/cm in parallel with one of force constant 45 N/cm, what is the force constant of the *single* spring that will be equivalent to this combination?

66. ••• **Springs in series.** Two (or more) springs are in *series* if they are connected one after the other, as shown in Figure 5.62. A combination of two springs

▲ **FIGURE 5.62** Problem 66.

can be thought of as being equivalent to a *single* spring having an effective force constant k_{eff} that must be related to the force constants k_1 and k_2 of the individual springs. We will assume that the springs have no significant mass. Suppose we stretch this combination a total distance x from its equilibrium position, causing spring 1 to stretch by x_1 and spring 2 to stretch by x_2. (a) Show that $x = x_1 + x_2$. (A simple sketch should make this clear.) (b) Use Newton's laws to show that each spring exerts the *same* amount of force F and that this force is the same as the combination exerts. (c) Use Hooke's law to show that $F = k_1x_1$, $F = k_2x_2$, and $F = k_{eff}x$. (d) Show that the effective force constant obeys the formula $1/k_{eff} = 1/k_1 + 1/k_2$. (*Hint:* Start with the result from part (a), and then substitute for x, x_1, and x_2, using the results from part (c).) (e) If springs of force constants 25.0 N/cm and 50.0 N/cm are connected in series, what is the effective force constant of this combination? If you wanted to replace the combination with a single equivalent spring, what should be its force constant?

67. • **Mountaineering.** Figure 5.63 shows a technique called *rappelling*, used by mountaineers for descending vertical rock faces. The climber sits in a rope seat, and the rope slides through a friction device attached to the seat. Suppose that the rock is perfectly smooth (i.e., there is no friction) and that the climber's feet push horizontally onto the rock. If the climber's weight is 600.0 N, find (a) the tension in the rope and (b) the force the climber's feet exert on the rock face. Start with a free-body diagram of the climber.

▲ **FIGURE 5.63** Problem 67.

68. •• Two identical, perfectly smooth 71.2 N bowling balls 21.7 cm in diameter are hung together from the same hook in the ceiling by means of two thin, light wires, as shown in Figure 5.64, find (a) the tension in each wire and (b) the force the balls exert on each other.

▲ **FIGURE 5.64** Problem 68.

69. •• **Stay awake!** An astro- **BIO** naut is inside a 2.25 × 10⁶ kg rocket that is blasting off vertically from the launch pad. You want this rocket to reach the speed of sound (331 m/s) as

quickly as possible, but you also do not want the astronaut to black out. Medical tests have shown that astronauts are in danger of blacking out for an acceleration greater than $4g$. (a) What is the maximum thrust the engines of the rocket can have to just barely avoid blackout? Start with a free-body diagram of the rocket. (b) What force, in terms of her weight W, does the rocket exert on the astronaut? Start with a free-body diagram of the astronaut. (c) What is the shortest time it can take the rocket to reach the speed of sound?

70. •• **Neck injuries.** When a
BIO patient's injured neck is healing, it is often desirable to prevent the weight of the head from pushing down on the neck. This can be accomplished with the system of pulleys shown in Figure 5.65. The pulleys are all small and extremely light in weight and have no appreciable friction. Typically, a person's head makes

▲ **FIGURE 5.65** Problem 70.

up 7.0% of his or her body weight. (a) If the head of a 72 kg person is to be supported completely by the apparatus shown, what should the mass of W be? Start with a free-body diagram of the head. (b) Show how this system, besides supporting the head, tends to keep the neck stationary and upright. (*Hint:* If the neck moves a small distance from the vertical, show that the system tends to return it to the vertical position.)

71. •• Block A in Figure 5.66
weighs 60.0 N. The coefficient of static friction between the block and the surface on which it rests is 0.25. The weight w is 12.0 N and the system remains at rest. (a) Find the friction force exerted on block A. (b) Find the maximum weight w for which the system will remain at rest.

▲ **FIGURE 5.66** Problem 71.

72. •• **Launch of the space shuttle.** At launch, the Space Shuttle weighs $4\frac{1}{2}$ million pounds (2.04 million kilograms). As the vehicle starts from rest on the launch pad, the booster rockets and engines accelerate it to 161 km/h in just 8.0 s. (a) What combined thrust do the booster rockets and engine exert during this period of liftoff, assuming constant acceleration? Start with a free-body diagram. (b) If a 725 N astronaut is strapped in a seat inside the shuttle, what force must this seat exert on him during liftoff? Start with a free-body diagram of the astronaut.

73. •• A student attaches a series of weights to a tendon and
BIO measures the *total length* of the tendon for each weight. He then uses the data he has gathered to construct the graph shown in Figure 5.67, giving the weight as a function of the length of the tendon. (a) Does this tendon obey Hooke's law? How do you know? (b) What is the force constant (in N/m) for the tendon? (c) What weight should you hang from the tendon to make it stretch by 8.0 cm from its unstretched length?

▲ **FIGURE 5.67** Problem 73.

74. •• **The flying leap of a**
BIO **flea.** High-speed motion pictures (3500 frames/second) of a jumping 210 μg flea yielded the data to plot the flea's acceleration as a function of time as shown in Figure 5.68. (See "The Flying Leap of the Flea," by M. Rothschild et al., in the

▲ **FIGURE 5.68** Problem 74.

November 1973 issue of *Scientific American*.) This flea was about 2 mm long and jumped at a nearly vertical takeoff angle. Use measurements made on the graph to answer the following questions: (a) Find the *initial* net external force on the flea. How does it compare with the flea's weight? (b) Find the *maximum* net external force on this jumping flea. When does the maximum force occur?

75. •• **Mars Exploration Rover landings.** In January 2004 the Mars Exploration Rover spacecraft landed on the surface of the Red Planet, where the acceleration due to gravity is 0.379 what it is on earth. The descent of this 827 kg vehicle occurred in several stages, three of which are outlined here. In Stage I, friction with the Martian atmosphere reduced the speed from 19,300 km/h to 1600 km/h in a 4.0 min interval. In Stage II, a parachute reduced the speed from 1600 km/h to 321 km/h in 94 s, and in Stage III, which lasted 2.5 s, retrorockets fired to reduce the speed from 321 km/h to zero. As part of your solution to this problem, make a free-body diagram of the rocket during each stage. Assuming constant acceleration, find the force exerted on the spacecraft (a) by the atmosphere during Stage I, (b) by the parachute during Stage II, and (c) by the retrorockets during Stage III.

76. •• Block A in Figure 5.69 weighs 1.20 N and block B weighs 3.60 N. The coefficient of kinetic friction between all surfaces is 0.300. Find the magnitude of the horizontal force $\vec{F}$ necessary to drag block B to the left at a constant speed of 2.50 cm/s (a) if A rests on B and moves with it (Figure 5.69a); (b) if A is held at rest by a string (Figure 5.69b). (c) In part (a), what is the friction force on block A?

(a)   (b)

▲ **FIGURE 5.69** Problem 76.

77. •• **Crash of the Genesis Mission.** You are assigned the task of designing an accelerometer to be used inside a rocket ship in outer space. Your equipment consists of a very light spring that is 15.0 cm long when no forces act to stretch or compress it, plus a 1.10 kg weight. One end of this spring will be

attached to a friction-free tabletop, while the 1.10 kg weight is attached to the other end, as shown in Figure 5.70. (Such a spring-type accelerometer system was actually used in the ill-fated Genesis Mission, which collected particles of the solar wind. Unfortunately, because it was installed *backward,* it did not measure the acceleration correctly during the craft's descent to earth. As a result, the parachute failed to open and the capsule crashed on Sept. 8, 2004.) (a) What should be the force constant of the spring so that it will stretch by 1.10 cm when the rocket accelerates forward at 2.50 m/s²? Start with a free-body diagram of the weight. (b) What is the acceleration (magnitude *and* direction) of the rocket if the spring is *compressed* by 2.30 cm?

▲ **FIGURE 5.70** Problem 77.

78. •• A 15.0 kg ball hangs by a string from the roof of a 20.0 kg box that is attached to a 10.0 kg rock over a very light frictionless pulley, as shown in Figure 5.71. There is no appreciable friction between the box and the table it rests on. (a) Make a free-body diagram of the ball as the system is mov-

▲ **FIGURE 5.71** Problem 78.

ing. (b) What angle does the string inside the box make with the vertical while motion is occurring? (c) If you could vary the weight of the rock, what is the *maximum* angle the string could make with the vertical?

79. •• A pickup truck is carrying a toolbox, but the rear gate of the truck is missing, so the box will slide out if it is set moving. The coefficients of kinetic and static friction between the box and the bed of the truck are 0.355 and 0.650, respectively. Starting from rest, what is the shortest time this truck could accelerate uniformly to 30.0 m/s (≈ 60 mph) without causing the box to slide. Include a free-body diagram of the toolbox as part of your solution. (*Hint:* First use Newton's second law to find the maximum acceleration that static friction can give the box, and then solve for the time required to reach 30.0 m/s.)

80. •• **Accident analysis.** You have been called to testify as an expert witness in a trial involving an automobile accident. The speed limit on the highway where the accident occurred was 40 mph. The driver of the car slammed on his brakes, locking his wheels, and left skid marks as the car skidded to a halt. You measure the length of these skid marks to be 219 ft, 9 in., and determine that the coefficient of kinetic friction between the wheels and the pavement at the time of the accident was 0.40. How fast was this car traveling (to the nearest number of

mph) just before the driver hit his brakes? Was he guilty of speeding?

81. • Without a parachute, a 75 kg person reaches a terminal velocity of about 60 m/s (≈ 135 mph — alas!). With a parachute, the terminal velocity is reduced to about 6 m/s (≈ 13 mph). If the air resistance is proportional to the square of the person's speed, (a) find the constant of proportionality between the air resistance and the square of the speed both with and without the parachute. (b) What would be the terminal velocity of a 62 kg person both with and without a parachute if the proportionality constant is the same?

82. • **A fractured tibia.** While

BIO a fractured tibia (the larger of the two major lower leg bones in mammals) is healing, it must be held horizontal and kept under some tension so that the bones will heal properly to prevent a permanent limp. One way to do this is to support the leg by using a variation of the Russell traction apparatus. (See Figure 5.72.) The lower leg (including the foot) of a particular

▲ **FIGURE 5.72** Problem 82.

patient weighs 51.5 N, all of which must be supported by the traction apparatus. (a) What must be the mass of *W*, shown in the figure? (b) What traction force does the apparatus provide along the direction of the leg?

83. • You push with a horizontal force of 50 N against a 20 N box, pressing it against a rough vertical wall to hold it in place. The coefficients of kinetic and static friction between this box and the wall are 0.20 and 0.50, respectively. (a) Make a free-body diagram of this box. (b) What is the friction force on the box? (c) How hard would you have to press for the box to slide downward with a uniform speed of 10.5 cm/s?

84. •• Some sliding rocks approach the base of a hill with a speed of 12 m/s. The hill rises at 36° above the horizontal and has coefficients of kinetic and static friction of 0.45 and 0.65, respectively, with these rocks. Start each part of your solution to this problem with a free-body diagram. (a) Find the acceleration of the rocks as they slide up the hill. (b) Once a rock reaches its highest point, will it stay there or slide down the hill? If it stays there, show why. If it slides down, find its acceleration on the way down.

85. • A 2.0 kg box and a 3.0 kg box on a perfectly smooth horizontal floor have a spring of force constant 250 N/m compressed between them. If the initial compression of the spring is 6.0 cm, find the acceleration of each box the instant after they are released. Be sure to include free-body diagrams of each box as part of your solution.

86. •• At night while it is dark, a driver inadvertently parks his car on a drawbridge. Some time later, the bridge must be raised to allow a boat to pass through. The coefficients of friction between the bridge and the car's tires are $\mu_s = 0.750$ and $\mu_k = 0.550$. Start each part of your solution to this problem with a free-body diagram of the car. (a) At what angle will the car just start to slide? (b) If the bridge attendant sees the car

suddenly start to slide and immediately turns off the bridge's motor, what will be the car's acceleration after it has begun to move?

87. •• A block is placed against the vertical front of a cart as shown in Figure 5.73. What acceleration must the cart have in order that block A does not fall? The coefficient of static friction between the block and the cart is μ_s.

▲ **FIGURE 5.73** Problem 87.

88. •• **The monkey and her bananas.** A 20 kg monkey has a firm hold on a light rope that passes over a frictionless pulley and is attached to a 20 kg bunch of bananas (Figure 5.74). The monkey looks up, sees the bananas, and starts to climb the rope to get them. (a) As the monkey climbs, do the bananas move up, move down, or remain at rest? (b) As the monkey climbs, does the distance between the monkey and the bananas decrease, increase, or remain constant? (c) The monkey releases her hold on the rope. What happens to the distance between the monkey and the bananas while she is falling? (d) Before reaching the ground, the monkey grabs the rope to stop her fall. What do the bananas do?

20 kg

20 kg

▲ **FIGURE 5.74** Problem 88.

CIRCULAR MOTION AND GRAVITATION

6

In Chapter 5, we learned how to apply Newton's laws to a variety of mechanics problems. In this chapter, we'll continue our study of dynamics, concentrating especially on *circular motion*. Objects move in circular paths in a wide variety of situations, such as cars on racetracks, rotating machine parts, and the motions of planets and satellites, so it's worthwhile to study this special class of motions in detail. We also return to *gravitational* interactions for a detailed study of Newton's law of gravitation. This law plays a central role in planet and satellite motion, and it also provides a fuller understanding of the concept of weight than does the formula $w = mg$ by itself.

Why do these skaters lean deeply into their turn? They do it so that the force of the ice on their skates has a large component directed inward toward the center of the turn. In this chapter, we will learn why turning motions require inward-directed forces.

6.1 Force in Circular Motion

We explored the *kinematics* of circular motion in Section 3.4; we suggest that you review that section now to help you understand what is to come. Here's a brief summary of what we learned. When a particle moves along any curved path, the direction of its velocity must change. Thus, it *must* have a component of acceleration perpendicular to its path, even if its speed is constant.

In particular, when a particle moves in a circular path with constant speed, there is *no* component of acceleration parallel to the instantaneous velocity (tangent to the path); otherwise the speed would change. Motion with constant speed in a circular path (either a complete circle or a fraction of a circle) is called *uniform circular motion*. In this motion, the particle's acceleration at each instant is directed toward the center of the circle (perpendicular to the instantaneous velocity), as shown in Figure 6.1. As we found in Chapter 3, the magnitude a_{rad} of

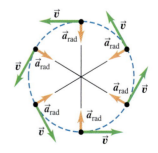

▲ **FIGURE 6.1** The kinematics of uniform circular motion.

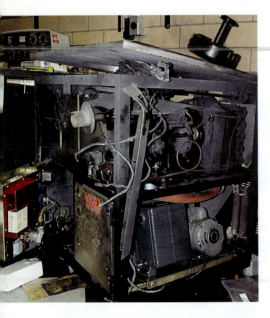

◄ **If all else fails, read the instructions!** The instrument shown used to be an ultracentrifuge—a washing-machine-sized device used in medical and biochemical laboratories to purify and analyze biological specimens, particularly those in which a liquid contains suspended solid particles with density different from that of the liquid. Inside a vacuum chamber, a precisely balanced rotor containing the specimens can be spun at over 1000 revolutions per second, with centripetal accelerations of up to 100,000g. Different components of the specimen have different densities and tend to separate, with the denser components migrating to the larger path radii, so centrifugation can separate the components. However, if the rotor somehow breaks, its massive machined parts, moving in accordance with Newton's first law, fly off tangentially with enormous speeds. That is why ultracentrifuges are kept in containment structures. Fortunately, no one was present when this one blew out.

the acceleration is constant and is given in terms of the speed v and the radius R of the circle by the following equation:

Acceleration in uniform circular motion

When an object moves at constant speed around a circle (or an arc of a circle) the magnitude of its acceleration (a_{rad}) is proportional to the square of its speed v and inversely proportional to the radius R of the circle:

$$a_{rad} = \frac{v^2}{R}. \tag{3.16}$$

4.1, 4.5 **Activ ONLINE Physics**

The subscript "rad" is a reminder that at each point the direction of the acceleration is radially inward toward the center of the circle, perpendicular to the instantaneous velocity. We explained in Section 3.4 why this acceleration is sometimes called *centripetal acceleration*.

We can also express the centripetal acceleration a_{rad} in terms of the **period** T, the time for one revolution. The speed v is equal to the distance $(2\pi R)$ the particle travels in one revolution (i.e., the circumference of the circle), divided by the time T, so

$$v = \frac{2\pi R}{T}. \quad \text{(relation of period to speed)} \tag{6.1}$$

Expressed in terms of the period,

$$a_{rad} = \frac{4\pi^2 R}{T^2}. \tag{6.2}$$

NOTE ► In earlier chapters, we've used T to denote tension in a rope or string. Here we use T to denote the period of a periodic motion, including uniform circular motion. From here on, we'll usually denote tension by F_T. ◄

A ball whirls on a string attached to a rotating peg in the center of a frictionless table (viewed from above). Suddenly, the string breaks, releasing the radial force on the ball.

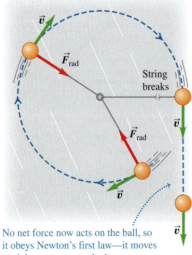

No net force now acts on the ball, so it obeys Newton's first law—it moves straight at constant velocity.

▲ **FIGURE 6.2** An object moves in a circle because of a centripetal net force.

Like all other motions of an object that can be modeled as a particle, circular motion is governed by Newton's second law. The object's acceleration toward the center of the circle must be caused by a force, or several forces, such that their vector sum $\sum \vec{F}$ is a vector that is always directed toward the center, with constant magnitude. The magnitude of the radial acceleration is given by $a_{rad} = v^2/R$, so the magnitude of the net inward radial force F_{net} on an object with mass m must be equal to the object's mass m, multiplied by this acceleration:

$$F_{net} = m\frac{v^2}{R}. \quad \text{(relation of net force to acceleration)} \tag{6.3}$$

Here's a familiar example: We fasten a small object, such as a ball, to a string and whirl it in a horizontal circle (Figure 6.2). To keep the ball moving in a circle,

▶ **Slip slidin' away.** When a car rounds a curve on a level surface, the centripetal force that keeps it moving in a circle is provided by the friction force of the road on the tires. For a bobsledder racing on a frozen track, friction is minimal, and level turns are impossible. Therefore, the curves are steeply and precisely banked. The normal force of the track presses on the sled, providing the necessary horizontal centripetal force. This force allows sharp, nearly frictionless turns at speeds of over 120 km/hr and helped Jill Bakken and Vonetta Flowers win the gold medal at the 2002 Winter Olympics—the first USA bobsledding medal since 1956.

the string has to pull constantly toward the center. If the string breaks, then the inward force no longer acts, and the ball moves off in a direction tangent to the circle—not radially outward.

When several forces act on an object in uniform circular motion, their *vector sum* must be a vector with magnitude given by Equation 6.3 and direction always toward the center of the circle. The net force magnitude in Equation 6.3 is sometimes called *centripetal force*. This term tends to imply that such a force is somehow different from ordinary forces, and it really isn't. The term *centripetal* refers to the fact that, in uniform circular motion, the direction of the net force that causes the acceleration toward the center must also point toward the center. In the equation $\sum \vec{F} = m\vec{a}$, the sum of the forces must include only the real physical forces—pushes or pulls exerted by strings, rods, gravitation, and so on. The quantity $m(v^2/R)$ does *not* appear in $\sum \vec{F}$, but rather in the $m\vec{a}$ side of the equation.

 Conceptual Analysis 6.1

Two cars on a curving road

A small car with mass m and a large car with mass $2m$ drive around a highway curve of radius R with the same speed v. As they travel around the curve, their accelerations are

A. equal.
B. along the direction of motion.
C. in the ratio of 2 to 1.
D. zero.

SOLUTION Equation 3.16 gives the acceleration of an object moving with uniform speed v in a circular path of radius R. The acceleration depends only on the speed and the radius. Both cars have the *same* speed and radius, so both must have the same acceleration. The correct answer is A. Because their masses are different, different forces are required for the two cars, even though their accelerations are the same. Answers B and D are certainly not right: The acceleration is not zero (otherwise the cars would move in a straight line), nor is it along the direction of motion (otherwise the speed would increase or decrease).

Conceptual Analysis 6.2

Skateboarder takes the hills

The following pictures show a skateboarder (seen from the side) moving along a straight or curved track.

Which picture is consistent with the free-body diagram shown in Figure 6.3?

SOLUTION Force $\vec{F}$ is the net normal force of the track on the skateboard wheels. Force $\vec{w}$ has a larger magnitude than force $\vec{F}$. The net force is directed downward, so the acceleration must also

▲ **FIGURE 6.3**

be downward. In A, there is no vertical component of acceleration, so this choice cannot be correct. In B, the acceleration is upward, toward the center of the circular path. This would require a net upward force, not downward. The center of the circular path in C is downward from the ball. The acceleration is downward (toward the center), requiring a net downward force, as in Figure 6.3. The correct picture is C.

The strategies for dynamics problems outlined at the beginning of Section 5.2 are equally applicable here, and we suggest that you reread them before studying the examples that follow.

NOTE ▶ A serious peril in circular-motion problems is the temptation to regard $m(v^2/R)$ as a *force,* as though the object's circular motion somehow generates an extra force in addition to the real physical forces exerted by strings, contact with other bodies, gravitation, or whatever. *Resist this temptation!* The quantity $m(v^2/R)$ is *not* a force; it corresponds to the $m\vec{a}$ side of $\Sigma\vec{F} = m\vec{a}$ and *must not* appear in $\Sigma\vec{F}$. It may help to draw the free-body diagram with colored pencils, using one color for the forces and a different color for the acceleration. Then, in the $\Sigma\vec{F} = m\vec{a}$ equations, write the force terms in the force color and the $m(v^2/R)$ term in the acceleration color. This may sound silly, but if it helps, do it! ◀

EXAMPLE 6.1 Model airplane on a string

Suppose you fly a propeller-driven model airplane on a 5.00 m string in a horizontal circle. The airplane, which has a mass of 0.500 kg, flies level and at constant speed and makes one revolution every 4.00 seconds. How hard must you pull on the string to keep the plane flying in a circle?

SOLUTION

SET UP Figure 6.4 shows our sketches. For the free-body diagram, we assume that the string has negligible mass, so that the force you exert on it equals the tension force it exerts on the plane (which keeps the plane moving in a circle). The plane flies horizontally, so its weight must be countered by an upward lift force from its wings. Thus, the net force is the tension from the string. (The plane also encounters drag from the air and thrust from its propeller, neither of which is shown in the plane of our free-body diagram. However, since the plane travels at constant speed, these forces also sum to zero.)

SOLVE We first find the airplane's centripetal acceleration and then use Newton's second law to find the tension force F_T. We begin by calculating the plane's speed v, using Equation 6.1 and the period T and radius R given:

$$v = \frac{2\pi R}{T} = \frac{2(3.14)(5.00\text{ m})}{(4.00\text{ s})}$$
$$= 7.85\text{ m/s}, \quad (\text{speed of airplane in circular path})$$

We now use this value with Equation 3.16 to calculate the centripetal acceleration:

$$a_{\text{rad}} = \frac{v^2}{R} = \frac{(7.85\text{ m/s})^2}{(5.00\text{ m})} = 12.3\text{ m/s}^2. \quad \begin{array}{l}(\text{acceleration in}\\ \text{circular motion})\end{array}$$

Alternatively, we could use Equation 6.2 to find a_{rad}:

$$a_{\text{rad}} = \frac{4\pi^2 R}{T^2} = \frac{4\pi^2(5.00\text{ m})}{(4.00\text{ s})^2} = 12.3\text{ m/s}^2.$$

(a) Sketch (from above)

(b) Free-body diagram of plane (from in front or behind)

▲ **FIGURE 6.4** Our diagrams for this problem.

Finally, we use Newton's second law to calculate the radial force necessary to produce this centripetal acceleration:

$$\Sigma F_x = F_T = ma_{\text{rad}} = (0.500\text{ kg})(12.3\text{ m/s}^2) = 6.15\text{ N}.$$

This is the magnitude of force exerted by the string on the airplane; it is also the magnitude of force you have to exert on the string to keep the airplane flying in its circular path.

REFLECT The free-body diagram shows that the force on an object moving in a circle at constant speed is inward (toward the center of the circle), *not* outward.

Practice Problem: What if the string you are using is rated for no more than 50 N (approx 10 lb). How fast could you fly your model plane before the string breaks? *Answer:* 22.4 m/s.

EXAMPLE 6.2   **At the end of the tether**

A tetherball is attached to a swivel in the ceiling by a light cord of length L. When the ball is hit by a paddle, it swings in a horizontal circle with constant speed v, and the cord makes a constant angle β with the vertical direction. The ball goes through one revolution in time T. Assuming that T, the mass m, and the length L of rope are known, derive algebraic expressions for the tension F_T in the cord and the angle β.

SOLUTION

SET UP Figure 6.5 shows our diagrams. Two forces act on the ball: its weight $\vec{w}$ and the tension force $\vec{F}_T$ exerted by the cord. In our free-body diagram, we point the x axis toward the center of the circle (in the direction of the centripetal acceleration a_{rad}), and we replace the tension force by its x and y components: $F_x = F_T \sin\beta$ and $F_y = F_T \cos\beta$, respectively. The y components of force sum to zero, so the net force on the ball is the x component of tension, which acts toward the center of the ball's circular path.

SOLVE Because the period T is known, we express a_{rad} in terms of T and the radius R of the circle, using Equation 6.2: $a_{\text{rad}} = 4\pi^2 R/T^2$. (Note that the radius of the circular path is $L\sin\beta$, not L.)

To find F_T, we use Newton's second law for the x component of net force:

$$\Sigma F_x = ma_x = ma_{\text{rad}}, \qquad F_T\sin\beta = m\frac{4\pi^2 R}{T^2}.$$

Next, we substitute the expression for the radius R of the circle ($R = L\sin\beta$) into the preceding equation:

$$F_T\sin\beta = m\frac{4\pi^2(L\sin\beta)}{T^2}.$$

The factor $\sin\beta$ divides out, and we get

$$F_T = m\frac{4\pi^2 L}{T^2}.$$

We're halfway home; the foregoing equation gives the rope tension F_T in terms of known quantities. To obtain an expression for the angle β, we use Newton's second law for the y component of net force. (Remember that this component must be zero ($\Sigma F_y = 0$), because there is no y component of acceleration.) Newton's second law yields

$$\Sigma F_y = F_T\cos\beta + (-mg) = 0.$$

We substitute our expression for F_T into this equation to get

$$m\frac{4\pi^2 L}{T^2}\cos\beta + (-mg) = 0, \qquad \cos\beta = \frac{gT^2}{4\pi^2 L}.$$

So we've succeeded in expressing the tension F_T and the cosine of the angle β in terms of known quantities.

REFLECT For a given length L, $\cos\beta$ decreases and β increases as T becomes smaller and the ball makes more revolutions per second. The angle can never be 90°, however; that would require that $T = 0$, $F_T = \infty$, and $v = \infty$. The relationship between T and β doesn't contain the *mass* of the ball, but the force magnitude F_T is directly proportional to m. When β is very small, F_T is approximately equal to the ball's weight, $\cos\beta$ is approximately unity, and the expressions we found above give the approximate expression $T = 2\pi\sqrt{(L/g)}$.

Practice Problem: What is the speed v of the ball if $T = 2.0$ s and $L = 2.0$ m? *Answer:* 5.5 m/s.

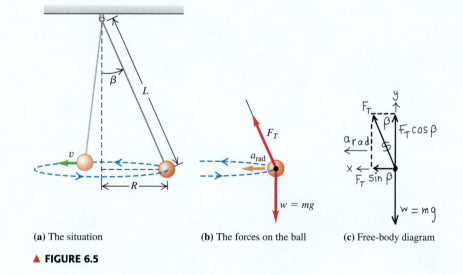

(a) The situation   (b) The forces on the ball   (c) Free-body diagram

▲ **FIGURE 6.5**

NOTE ▶ You may be tempted to add an extra outward force to the forces in Figure 6.5b, to "keep the object out there" at angle β or to "keep it in equilibrium." You may have heard the term *centrifugal force;* "centrifugal means" "fleeing from the center." Resist that temptation! First, the object *doesn't* stay "out there"; it is in constant motion around its circular path. Its velocity is constantly changing in direction—it accelerates—so it is *not* in equilibrium. Second, if there *were* an additional outward ("centrifugal") force to balance the inward force, there would then be *no* net inward force to cause the circular motion, and the object would move in a straight line, not a circle. In an inertial frame of reference, there is no such thing as centrifugal force, and we promise not to mention this term again. ◄

EXAMPLE 6.3 Rounding a flat curve

A car rounds a flat, unbanked curve with radius R. **(a)** If the coefficient of static friction between tires and road is μ_s, derive an expression for the maximum speed v_{max} at which the driver can take the curve without sliding. **(b)** What is the maximum speed if $R = 250$ m and $\mu_s = 0.90$?

SOLUTION

SET UP Figure 6.6 shows the situation, plus a free-body diagram for the car. As in the preceding example, we point the x axis toward the center. Note that the friction between a rolling wheel and the pavement is *static* friction, because the portion of the wheel in contact with the pavement doesn't slide relative to the pavement. (If the wheel slides or skids, however, the friction force is kinetic.) This friction force f_s is responsible for the car's centripetal acceleration $a_{rad} = v^2/R$; it points toward the center of the circle, in the x direction. In the y direction, the car's weight and the normal force on the car sum to zero.

SOLVE Part **(a):** The component equations from Newton's second law are

$$f_s = m\frac{v^2}{R}, \qquad n + (-mg) = 0.$$

In the first equation, f_s is the force *needed* to keep the car moving in its circular path at a given speed v; this force increases with v. But the maximum friction force *available* is $f_s = \mu_s n = \mu_s mg$; this limitation determines the car's maximum speed v_{max}. When we equate the maximum friction force available to the force mv^2/R required for the circular motion, we find that

$$\mu_s mg = m\frac{v_{max}^2}{R} \qquad \text{and} \qquad v_{max} = \sqrt{\mu_s gR}.$$

Part (b): If $\mu_s = 0.90$ and $R = 250$ m, then

$$v_{max} = \sqrt{(0.90)(9.8 \text{ m/s}^2)(250 \text{ m})} = 47 \text{ m/s},$$

or about 105 mi/h.

REFLECT If the car travels around the curve at less than v_{max}, f_s is less than $\mu_s n$, but it is still true that $f_s = mv^2/R$. If the car is moving at more than v_{max}, not enough friction is available to provide the needed centripetal acceleration. Then the car skids. Because the kinetic friction acting on skidding tires is less than the static friction acting before the car skids, a car always skids toward the outside of the curve.

It's possible to bank a curve so that at one certain speed no friction at all is needed. Then a car moving at just the right speed can round the curve even on wet ice with Teflon® tires. Airplanes *always* bank at this angle when making turns, and bobsled racing depends on the same idea. We'll explore the banking of curves in Example 6.4.

Practice Problem: What is the friction force on a 1200 kg car if it rounds a curve with radius 150 m at a speed of 25 m/s? What minimum coefficient of friction is needed?

Answers: 5000 N, 0.43.

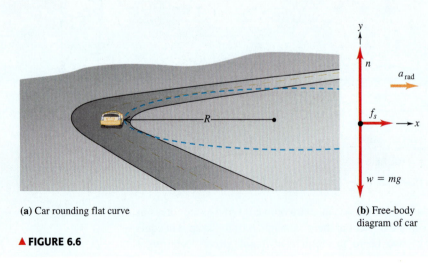

(a) Car rounding flat curve

(b) Free-body diagram of car

▲ **FIGURE 6.6**

Quantitative Analysis 6.3

Speeding up on the curves

A frictional force f_s provides the centripetal force as a car goes around an unbanked curve of radius R at speed v. If the driver speeds up on this curve until the speed of the car is tripled to $3v$, and if the car still follows the curved path, the frictional force must now be

A. $3f_s$.   B. $\dfrac{1}{3}f_s$.   C. $9f_s$.   D. $\dfrac{1}{9}f_s$.

SOLUTION The centripetal acceleration, and therefore the frictional force needed, is proportional to v^2. When the speed increases by a factor of 3, the force needed increases by a factor of $3^2 = 9$. Thus, C is the correct answer. Note that both m and R are constant. If this isn't clear, you may want to review Example 6.3.

EXAMPLE 6.4   Rounding a banked curve

An engineer proposes to rebuild the curve in Example 6.3, banking it so that, at a certain speed v, *no* friction at all is needed for the car to make the curve. At what angle β should it be banked if $v = 25$ m/s (56 mi/h)?

SOLUTION

SET UP Figure 6.7 shows the free-body diagram for a car following a horizontal, circular path around the curve at the designated speed. We use the same coordinate system as in Example 6.3. The car's centripetal acceleration is now due to the horizontal component of the normal force exerted by the banked pavement. No friction force is needed.

SOLVE The horizontal component of $\vec{n}$ must now cause the acceleration v^2/R; there is no vertical component of acceleration. The component equations from Newton's second law are

$$n\sin\beta = \frac{mv^2}{R}, \qquad n\cos\beta + (-mg) = 0.$$

Dividing $n\sin\beta$ by $n\cos\beta$, we find that

$$\tan\beta = \frac{v^2}{gR}.$$

As in Example 6.3, $R = 250$ m. For the specified speed $v = 25$ m/s,

$$\beta = \tan^{-1}\frac{(25 \text{ m/s})^2}{(9.8 \text{ m/s}^2)(250 \text{ m})} = 14°$$

REFLECT The banking angle depends on the speed as well as the radius, but *not* on the mass of the vehicle. (Mass does not appear in the equation.) That's why it's possible to make banked curves that work for both cars and trucks, provided that the vehicles do not drive too fast. Highway designers assume friction will be available under good driving conditions and bank curves at angles less than β.

Practice Problem: In this example, what is the magnitude of the normal force on the 1200 kg car as it rounds the curve? *Answer:* 12,000 N.

(a) Car rounding banked curve

(b) Free-body diagram of car

▲ **FIGURE 6.7**

6.2 Motion in a Vertical Circle

4.2–4.4 In all the examples in Section 6.1, the object moved in a horizontal circle. Motion in a *vertical* circle is no different in principle, but the weight of the object has to be treated carefully. The next example shows what we mean.

EXAMPLE 6.5   Dynamics of a Ferris wheel ride

A passenger on a Ferris wheel moves in a vertical circle of radius R with constant speed v. **(a)** Assuming that the seat remains upright during the motion, derive expressions for the magnitude of the upward force the seat exerts on the passenger at the top and bottom of the circle if the passenger's mass is m. **(b)** What are these forces if the passenger's mass is 60.0 kg, the radius of the circle is $R = 8.00$ m, and the wheel makes one revolution in 10.0 s? How do they compare with the passenger's actual weight?

SOLUTION

SET UP Figure 6.8 shows the Ferris wheel, with free-body diagrams for the passenger at the top and at the bottom. All the vector quantities (forces and accelerations) have only vertical components. We take the positive y direction as upward in both cases. We use n_T and n_B to denote the magnitude of force the seat applies to the passenger at the top and bottom of the wheel, respectively.

SOLVE Part (a): To derive expressions for the magnitudes n_T and n_B, we use Newton's second law for the y component of net force: $\sum F_y = ma_y$. Notice that the sign of a_y is negative at the top of the wheel, but positive at the bottom, although its magnitude is v^2/R at both places. Also, the y component of weight (magnitude mg) is negative, but the y components of both n_T and n_B are positive.

Thus, at the top of the Ferris wheel,

$$n_{T,y} + w_y = ma_y, \quad n_T + (-mg) = m\left(-\frac{v^2}{R}\right),$$

$$\text{or} \quad n_T = m\left(g - \frac{v^2}{R}\right) = mg\left(1 - \frac{v^2}{gR}\right).$$

This means that, at the top of the Ferris wheel, the upward force the seat applies to the passenger is *smaller* in magnitude than the passenger's weight.

At the bottom of the circle (Figure 6.8c) the acceleration is upward, and Newton's second law gives

$$n_B + (-mg) = +m\frac{v^2}{R}, \quad \text{or}$$

$$n_B = m\left(g + \frac{v^2}{R}\right) = mg\left(1 + \frac{v^2}{gR}\right).$$

At this point, the upward force provided by the seat is always *greater than* the passenger's weight. You feel the seat pushing up on you more firmly than when you are at rest.

Part (b): We want to calculate n_T and n_B for a 60.0 kg passenger riding a Ferris wheel with radius $R = 8.00$ m and a period of 10.0 s. The speed v is the circumference $2\pi R$, divided by the time T for one revolution:

$$v = \frac{2\pi R}{T} = \frac{2\pi(8.00 \text{ m})}{10.0 \text{ s}} = 5.03 \text{ m/s}.$$

(a)

(b) Passenger at top of circle

(c) Passenger at bottom of circle

▲ **FIGURE 6.8** A passenger on a Ferris wheel.

The magnitude of the radial acceleration is

$$a_{\text{rad}} = \frac{v^2}{R} = \frac{(5.03 \text{ m/s})^2}{(8.00 \text{ m})} = 3.16 \text{ m/s}^2.$$

The two forces (the apparent weights at top and bottom) are

$$n_T = (60.0 \text{ kg})(9.80 \text{ m/s}^2 - 3.16 \text{ m/s}^2) = 398 \text{ N}$$
$$n_B = (60.0 \text{ kg})(9.80 \text{ m/s}^2 + 3.16 \text{ m/s}^2) = 778 \text{ N}.$$

The passenger's weight is 588 N, and n_T and n_B are, respectively, about 30% less than and greater than the weight.

REFLECT If the Ferris wheel turned so fast that v^2/R were equal to g, the seat would apply *no* force to the passenger at the top of the ride. If the wheel went still faster, n_T would become negative, so that a *downward* force would be needed to keep the passenger in the seat. We could supply a seat belt, or we could glue the passenger to the seat.

Some military aircraft are capable of an apparent gravitational acceleration of 9g when pulling out of a dive. (That is, $g + v^2/R = 9g$.) However, even wearing special flight suits, human pilots black out quickly at such accelerations.

NOTE ▶ When we tie a string to an object and whirl it in a vertical circle, the preceding analysis isn't directly applicable. The speed v isn't constant in this case, because, at every point except the top and bottom, there is a component of force (and therefore of acceleration) tangent to the circle. Even worse, we can't use the constant-acceleration formulas to relate the speeds at various points, since *neither* the magnitude nor the direction of the acceleration is constant. The speed relations we need are best obtained by using energy relations. We'll consider such problems in Chapter 7. ◀

A stone-age toy

A stone of mass m is attached to a strong string and whirled in a vertical circle of radius R. At the lowest point of the path, the tension in the string is six times the stone's weight. The stone's speed at this point is given by

A. $5\sqrt{gR}$ B. $\sqrt{gR}$ C. $\sqrt{5gR}$

SOLUTION At the lowest point of the circle, the forces acting on the stone are its weight (downward, with magnitude mg) and the string tension force (upward, with magnitude $6mg$). The net upward force has magnitude $5mg$ and must equal the mass m times the magnitude of the centripetal acceleration v^2/R. Thus, $5mg = mv^2/R$, and it follows that $v = \sqrt{5gR}$. The correct answer is C.

A very slippery ramp

A box slides down a circular, frictionless ramp, as shown in Figure 6.9. The forces on the box at the instant it reaches point A, and their relative magnitudes, are

A. the upward push of the ramp, which is greater than the inertial force ma of the box.
B. the upward push of the ramp, which equals the downward pull of the earth.
C. the upward push of the ramp, which is greater than the downward pull of the earth.

SOLUTION The quantity ma is not a force; there is no such thing as an inertial force. Answer A is wrong both quantitatively and

▲ **FIGURE 6.9**

conceptually. If B were correct, the net force on the box would be zero and it would have to move in a straight line, not a circle. For circular motion at point A, there must be a net upward force; the correct answer is C.

Walking and Circular Motion

The swinging motion of your legs when you walk can be modeled approximately as circular motion, and this model can be used to find the maximum speed a person of a given leg length can walk. Humans keep the weight-bearing leg straight while walking. Consequently, as shown in Figure 6.10, each hip in turn moves in a circular arc with a radius R equal to the length of the leg and with the weight-bearing foot at the center of the circle. In the simplest model, we imagine the person's entire mass M to be concentrated near the hip. In this model, when a person walks with speed v, the force required to keep the hips in circular motion is

$$F_{\text{rad}} = \frac{Mv^2}{R}.$$

Gravity provides this force, so the maximum available force is the person's weight Mg. Thus, in this simple model, the maximum speed v_{max} a person can walk is given by

$$Mg = \frac{M(v_{\text{max}})^2}{R}, \quad \text{or} \quad v_{\text{max}} = \sqrt{gR}.$$

The average adult leg length is about 1 m long; assuming this length, we get

$$v_{\text{max}} = \sqrt{(9.8\,\text{m/s}^2)(1.0\,\text{m})} = 3.1 \text{ m/s, or } 7.0 \text{ mi/h}.$$

▲ **FIGURE 6.10** A simple model of human walking.

We assume that the person's mass is all located at the hip.

In each stride, the hip follows a circular arc around the planted foot.

Path of hip

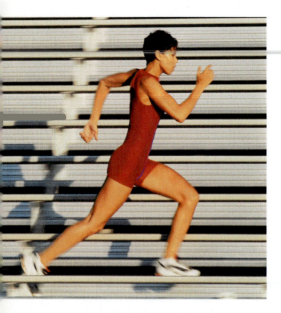

This number is quite realistic. Adults can walk at speeds up to about 2.7 m/s, although usual walking speeds are below 2.0 m/s. Race walkers use a special motion that flattens the arc followed by the hip and allows them to walk at up to 4.0 m/s.

6.3 Newton's Law of Gravitation

About 300 years ago, Newton discovered that gravitation—the force that makes an apple fall out of a tree—also keeps the planets in their nearly circular orbits around the sun. As we remarked in Section 5.5, gravitation is one of the four classes of forces found in nature, and it was the earliest one of the four to be studied extensively.

Our most familiar encounter with the gravitational force is the *weight* of an object—the force that attracts it toward the earth (or toward whatever astronomical body it is near, such as a moon, planet, or star). Newton discovered the **law of gravitation** during his study of the motions of planets around the sun, and he published it in 1686.

▲ **An earth-moving experience?** In walking, a person has at least one foot on the ground at all times. When we model walking as a circular motion of the body, pivoting about the grounded foot, we find that physics imposes a speed limit of about 3 m/s for normal walking (for a foot-to-hip distance of about 1 m). However, this limit does not hold in running, in which the feet are off the ground for part of each stride. In either case—walking or running—you use your leg muscles to press backwards on the earth. The reaction force pushes forward to propel you forward. As Newton's third law tells us, the forward acceleration of a runner times the runner's mass equals the backward acceleration of the earth times its mass. So if you want to move the earth, just go for a run!

Newton's law of gravitation
Newton's law of gravitation may be stated as follows:

Every particle of matter in the universe attracts every other particle with a force that is directly proportional to the product of the masses of the particles and inversely proportional to the square of the distance between them.

For two particles with masses m_1 and m_2, separated by a distance r (Figure 6.11), Newton's law of gravitation can be expressed as

$$F_g = G\frac{m_1 m_2}{r^2}, \tag{6.4}$$

where F_g is the magnitude of the gravitational force on either particle and G is a fundamental physical constant called the **gravitational constant.** Gravitational forces are always attractive; gravitation always pulls objects toward each other.

Gravitational forces between two particles always obey Newton's third law; they always act along the line joining the two particles, and they form an action–reaction pair. Even when the masses of the particles are different, the two interaction forces have equal magnitude. The attractive force that your body exerts on the earth has the same magnitude as the force it exerts on you.

We've stated the law of gravitation in terms of the interaction forces between two *particles*. It turns out that the interaction between any two objects having *spherically symmetric* mass distributions (such as solid spheres or spherical shells) is the same as though all the mass of each were concentrated at its center, as in Figure 6.12. In effect, we can replace each spherically symmetric object with a particle at its center. Thus, if we model the earth as a solid sphere with mass m_E, then the force exerted by it on a particle or a spherically symmetric object with mass m at a distance r between the two centers is

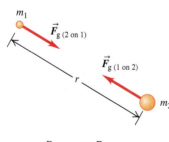

$$F_{g\,(1\ on\ 2)} = F_{g\,(2\ on\ 1)}$$

▲ **FIGURE 6.11** Two particles exert attractive gravitational forces of equal magnitude on each other, even if their masses are quite different.

$$F_g = G\frac{mm_E}{r^2}, \tag{6.5}$$

provided that the object lies outside the earth. A force of the same magnitude is exerted *on* the earth by the object.

NOTE ▶ Notice that *r* is the distance between the *centers* of the two objects, not between their surfaces. ◀

At points *inside* the earth, the situation is different. If we could drill a hole to the center of the earth and measure the gravitational force on a particle at various depths, we would find that the force *decreases* as we approach the center, rather than increasing as $1/r^2$. As the object entered the interior of the earth (or another spherical object), some of the earth's mass would be on the side of the object opposite from the center and would pull in the opposite direction. Exactly at the center, the gravitational force on the object would be zero.

To determine the value of the gravitational constant *G*, we have to *measure* the gravitational force between two objects with known masses m_1 and m_2 at a known distance *r*. For bodies of reasonable size, the force is extremely small, but it can be measured with an instrument called a *torsion balance*, used by Sir Henry Cavendish in 1798 to determine *G*.

The Cavendish balance consists of a light, rigid rod shaped like an inverted T (Figure 6.13) and supported by a very thin vertical quartz fiber. Two small spheres, each of mass m_1, are mounted at the ends of the horizontal arms of the T. When we bring two large spheres, each of mass m_2, to the positions shown, the attractive gravitational forces twist the T through a small angle. To measure this angle, we shine a beam of light on a mirror fastened to the T; the reflected beam strikes a scale, and as the T twists, the beam moves along the scale.

After calibrating the instrument, we can measure gravitational forces and thus determine *G*. The currently accepted value (in SI units) is

$$G = 6.674 \times 10^{-11} \, \text{N} \cdot \text{m}^2/\text{kg}^2.$$

Because $1 \, \text{N} = 1 \, \text{kg} \cdot \text{m}/\text{s}^2$, the units of *G* can also be expressed (in fundamental SI units) as $\text{m}^3/(\text{kg} \cdot \text{s}^2)$.

Gravitational forces combine vectorially. If each of two masses exerts a force on a third, the *total* force on the third mass is the vector sum of the individual forces due to the first two. That is, gravitational forces obey the principle of superposition, introduced in Section 4.1.

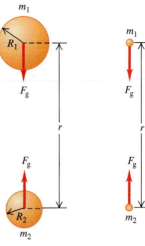

(a) Two spherically symmetric masses m_1 and m_2

(b) Two particles with masses m_1 and m_2

▲ **FIGURE 6.12** Spherically symmetric objects interact gravitationally as though all the mass of each were concentrated at its center.

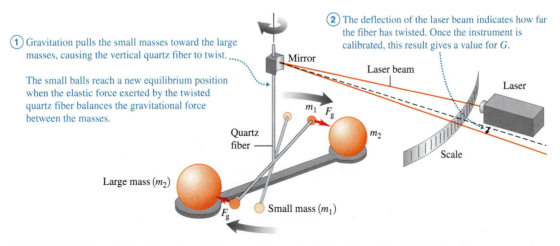

① Gravitation pulls the small masses toward the large masses, causing the vertical quartz fiber to twist.

The small balls reach a new equilibrium position when the elastic force exerted by the twisted quartz fiber balances the gravitational force between the masses.

② The deflection of the laser beam indicates how far the fiber has twisted. Once the instrument is calibrated, this result gives a value for *G*.

Mirror

Laser beam

Laser

Quartz fiber

m_1 F_g

m_2

Scale

Large mass (m_2)

F_g Small mass (m_1)

▲ **FIGURE 6.13** The principle of the Cavendish balance. The angle of deflection is exaggerated for clarity.

EXAMPLE 6.6 **Gravitational forces in a Cavendish balance**

The mass m_1 of one of the small spheres of a Cavendish balance is 10.0 g (=0.0100 kg), the mass m_2 of one of the large spheres is 0.500 kg, and the center-to-center distance between each large sphere and the nearer small one is 0.0500 m. Find the magnitude of the gravitational force F_g on each sphere due to the nearest other sphere.

SOLUTION

SET UP AND SOLVE Figure 6.14 shows our sketch. Assuming that the spheres have spherically symmetric mass distributions, we can apply Newton's law of gravitation, taking the distance r to be the distance between centers of the spheres. The magnitude of each force is

$$F_g = G\frac{m_1 m_2}{r^2}$$

$$= (6.67 \times 10^{-11} \text{ N} \cdot \text{m}^2/\text{kg}^2)\frac{(0.0100 \text{ kg})(0.500 \text{ kg})}{(0.0500 \text{ m})^2}$$

$$= 1.33 \times 10^{-10} \text{ N}.$$

▲ **FIGURE 6.14** Our sketch for this problem.

REFLECT Gravitational forces between objects of familiar sizes are extremely small. Also, gravitational forces obey Newton's third law: The force that mass m_1 exerts on mass m_2 is equal in magnitude to the force that m_2 exerts on m_1, even though their masses are very different.

Practice Problem: What is the force magnitude F_g if the separation between centers of the spheres is doubled to 0.100 m? *Answer:* One-fourth as much: 3.34×10^{-11} N.

EXAMPLE 6.7 **Accelerations of Cavendish spheres**

Suppose one large and one small sphere in Example 6.6 are detached from the apparatus and placed 0.0500 m (between centers) from each other at a point in space far removed from all other objects. What is the magnitude of the acceleration of each sphere relative to an inertial system?

SOLUTION

SET UP AND SOLVE The force on each sphere has the same magnitude that we found in Example 6.6. From Newton's second law, the acceleration magnitude a_1 of the smaller sphere is

$$a_1 = \frac{F_g}{m_1} = \frac{1.33 \times 10^{-10} \text{ N}}{0.0100 \text{ kg}} = 1.33 \times 10^{-8} \text{ m/s}^2.$$

The acceleration magnitude a_2 of the larger sphere is

$$a_2 = \frac{F_g}{m_2} = \frac{1.33 \times 10^{-10} \text{ N}}{0.500 \text{ kg}} = 2.66 \times 10^{-10} \text{ m/s}^2.$$

REFLECT Although the forces on the objects are equal in magnitude, the two accelerations are *not* equal in magnitude. Also, they are not constant, because the gravitational forces increase in magnitude as the spheres start to move toward each other.

6.4 Weight

In Section 4.4, we tentatively defined your *weight* as the attractive gravitational force exerted on you by the earth. We can now broaden our definition:

> **The weight of an object is the *total* gravitational force exerted on the object by all other objects in the universe.**

When the object is near the surface of the earth, we can neglect all other gravitational forces and consider the weight as just the gravitational force exerted on the object by the earth. At the surface of the *moon* we can consider an object's weight to be the gravitational force exerted on it by the moon, and so on.

If we again model the earth as a spherically symmetric object with radius R_E and mass m_E, then the weight w of a small object of mass m at the earth's surface (a distance R_E from its center) is

$$w = F_g = \frac{Gm m_E}{R_E^2}. \tag{6.6}$$

But we also know from Section 4.4 that the weight w of an object is its mass m times the acceleration g of free fall at the location of the object: $w = mg$; weight is the force that causes the acceleration of free fall. Thus, Equation 6.6 must be equal to mg:

$$mg = \frac{Gmm_E}{R_E^2}.$$

Dividing by m, we find

$$g = \frac{Gm_E}{R_E^2}. \tag{6.7}$$

Because this result does not contain m, the acceleration due to gravity g is independent of the mass m of the object. We already knew that, but we can now see how it follows from the law of gravitation.

Furthermore, we can *measure* all the quantities in Equation 6.7 except for m_E, so this relation allows us to compute the mass of the earth. We first solve Equation 6.7 for m_E, obtaining

$$m_E = \frac{gR_E^2}{G}.$$

Taking $R_E = 6380$ km $= 6.38 \times 10^6$ m and $g = 9.80$ m/s^2, we find that

$$m_E = 5.98 \times 10^{24} \text{ kg}.$$

Once Cavendish had measured G, he could compute the mass of the earth! He described his measurement of G with the grandiose phrase "weighing the earth." That's not really what he did; he certainly didn't hang our planet from a spring balance. But after he had determined G, he carried out the preceding calculation and determined the mass (not the weight) of the earth.

The weight of an object decreases inversely with the square of its distance from the earth's center. At a radial distance $r = 2R_E$ from earth's center, the weight is one-quarter of its value at the earth's surface. Figure 6.15 shows how weight varies with height above the earth for an astronaut who weighs 700 N on earth.

▲ **Falling with style.** This is a gravity map of the earth. Protrusions represent areas of stronger gravity (because of nonuniform mass distribution), and dips show areas of weaker gravity. For example, the Andes represent an area of strong gravity because of the extra mass of the mountain range. The map was made by the Gravity Recovery and Climate Experiment (GRACE) project. To measure gravity, GRACE employs a pair of satellites that orbit the earth in formation while precisely monitoring the distance between them. For instance, as the pair approaches a mountain range, the lead satellite will speed up in response to the mountains' gravitational pull, increasing the distance between the two satellites. As the satellites straddle the mountains, the pull of the extra mass then shrinks the distance between them, and as they pass the mountains, the distance increases again.

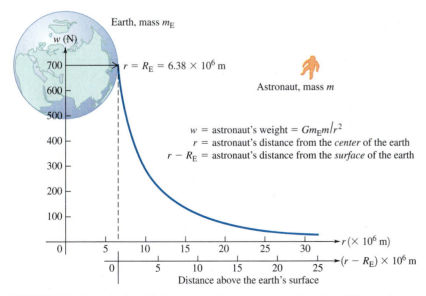

▲ **FIGURE 6.15** A graph of weight (gravitational interaction) as a function of distance from the earth's surface.

EXAMPLE 6.8 **Density of the earth**

Using the values of m_E and R_E quoted above, determine the average *density* (mass per unit volume) of the earth.

SOLUTION

SET UP The volume, assuming a spherical earth is

$$V = \frac{4}{3}\pi R_E^3 = \frac{4}{3}\pi(6.38 \times 10^6 \text{ m})^3 = 1.09 \times 10^{21} \text{ m}^3.$$

SOLVE The average density ρ of the earth is the total mass divided by the total volume:

$$\rho = \frac{M}{V} = \frac{5.98 \times 10^{24} \text{ kg}}{1.09 \times 10^{21} \text{ m}^3} = 5500 \text{ kg/m}^3 = 5.50 \text{ g/cm}^3.$$

REFLECT For comparison, the density of water is $1.00 \text{ g/cm}^3 = 1000 \text{ kg/m}^3$. The density of igneous rock near the earth's surface, such as basalt, is about $3 \text{ g/cm}^3 = 3000 \text{ kg/m}^3$. So the interior of the earth must be much more dense than the surface. In fact, the maximum density at the center, where the pressure is enormous, is thought to be nearly 15 g/cm^3. Figure 6.16 is a graph of density as a function of distance from the earth's center.

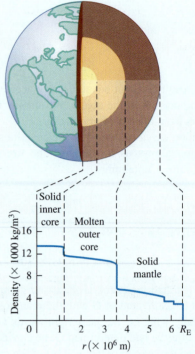

▶ **FIGURE 6.16** The density of the earth decreases with increasing distance from its center. The "steps" in the graph represent major changes in composition or in phase (solid versus liquid).

EXAMPLE 6.9 **Gravity on Mars**

You're involved in the design of a mission carrying humans to the surface of the planet Mars, which has a radius $R_{Mars} = 3.38 \times 10^6$ m and a mass $m_{Mars} = 6.42 \times 10^{23}$ kg. The earth weight of the Mars lander is 39,200 N. Calculate the weight F_g of the Mars lander and the acceleration due to Mars's gravity, g_{Mars}, **(a)** at the surface of Mars, and **(b)** at 6.00×10^6 m above the surface of Mars (corresponding to the orbit of the Martian moon Phobos).

SOLUTION

SET UP Figure 6.17 diagrams the problem. Notice that the altitude given is 6.00×10^6 m above the *surface* of Mars. To find the gravitational forces, we need to translate that altitude to the distance from the *center* of Mars: $r = 6.00 \times 10^6$ m + 3.38×10^6 m = 9.38×10^6 m.

SOLVE **Part (a):** In Equations 6.6 and 6.7 we replace m_E with m_{Mars} and R_E with R_{Mars}. The value of G is the same everywhere; it is a fundamental physical constant. The mass m of the lander is its *earth* weight w, divided by the acceleration due to gravity, g, on the earth:

$$m = \frac{w}{g} = \frac{3.92 \times 10^4 \text{ N}}{9.80 \text{ m/s}^2} = 4.00 \times 10^3 \text{ kg}.$$

The mass is the same whether the lander is on the earth, on Mars, or in between. From Equation 6.6,

▲ **FIGURE 6.17**

Continued

$$F_g = \frac{Gmm_{Mars}}{r^2}$$
$$= \frac{(6.67 \times 10^{-11}\ \text{N} \cdot \text{m}^2/\text{kg}^2)(4.00 \times 10^3\ \text{kg})(6.42 \times 10^{23}\ \text{kg})}{(3.38 \times 10^6\ \text{m})^2}$$
$$= 1.50 \times 10^4\ \text{N}.$$

The acceleration due to the gravity of Mars at its surface is

$$g_{Mars} = \frac{F_g}{m} = \frac{1.50 \times 10^4\ \text{N}}{4.00 \times 10^3\ \text{kg}} = 3.75\ \text{m/s}^2.$$

We can also obtain g_{Mars} directly from Equation 6.7:

$$g_{Mars} = \frac{Gm_{Mars}}{R_{Mars}^2}$$
$$= \frac{(6.67 \times 10^{-11}\ \text{N} \cdot \text{m}^2/\text{kg}^2)(6.42 \times 10^{23}\ \text{kg})}{(3.38 \times 10^6\ \text{m})^2}$$
$$= 3.75\ \text{m/s}^2.$$

Part (b): To find F_g and g at a point 6.0×10^6 m above the surface of Mars, we repeat the preceding calculations, replacing $R_{Mars} = 3.38 \times 10^6$ m with $r = 9.38 \times 10^6$ m. At that altitude, both F_g and g are smaller than they are at the surface, by a factor of

$$\left(\frac{3.38 \times 10^6\ \text{m}}{9.38 \times 10^6\ \text{m}}\right)^2 = 0.130,$$

and we find that $F_g = 1.95 \times 10^3$ N and $g = 0.487\ \text{m/s}^2$. The latter is also the acceleration of Phobos in its orbit due to Mars's gravity, even though Phobos has far more mass than our lander.

REFLECT On the surface of Mars, F_g and g are roughly 40% as large as they are on the surface of the earth. At a point in the orbit of Phobos, they are 13% as large as they are on the surface of Mars.

6.5 Satellite Motion

Satellites orbiting the earth are a familiar fact of contemporary life. We know that they differ only in scale, not in principle, from the motion of our moon around the earth or the motion of the moons of Jupiter. But we still have to deal with questions such as "What holds that thing up there anyway?" So let's see how we can use Newton's laws and the law of gravitation for a detailed analysis of satellite motion.

To begin, think back to the discussion of projectile motion in Section 3.3. In Example 3.3, we fired a paintball horizontally from some distance above the ground; it followed a parabolic path until it struck the ground. In a similar situation, a motorcycle rider rides horizontally off the edge of a cliff, launching himself into a parabolic path that ends on the flat ground at the base of the cliff (Figure 6.18).

If he survives and repeats the experiment with an increased launch speed, he will land farther from the starting point. We can imagine him launching himself with great enough speed that the earth's curvature becomes significant. As he falls, the earth curves away beneath him. If he is going fast enough, and if his launch point is high enough that he clears the mountaintops, he may be able to go right on around the earth without ever landing.

Figure 6.19 shows a variation on this theme. We launch a projectile from point A in a direction tangent to the earth's surface (i.e., horizontally). Trajectories

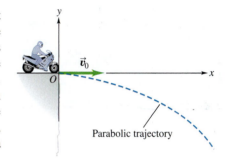

▲ **FIGURE 6.18** The trajectory of a biker launching himself horizontally from a cliff.

 4.6

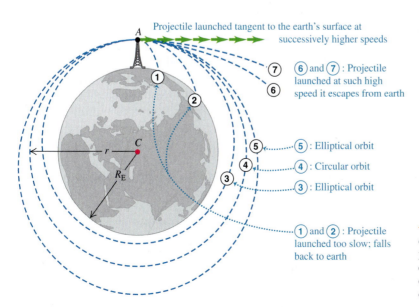

Projectile launched tangent to the earth's surface at successively higher speeds

(7)
(6) and (7): Projectile launched at such high speed it escapes from earth

(5): Elliptical orbit
(4): Circular orbit
(3): Elliptical orbit

(1) and (2): Projectile launched too slow; falls back to earth

◀ **FIGURE 6.19** An orbit is not fundamentally different from familiar trajectories on earth. If you launch a projectile slowly, it falls back to earth. If you launch it fast enough, the earth curves away from it as it falls, and it goes into orbit.

◀ **It's a bird—it's a plane.** No, it's actually a very souped-up motorcycle. This 1974 photo shows the "Skycycle" upon which Evel Knievel attempted to jump the 500-meter-wide Snake River Canyon near Twin Falls, Idaho, in the northwestern United States. As you know, the greater the initial velocity in a jump like this, the greater is the distance that can be traveled before landing. Powered by a steam-driven rocket engine, Knievel was able to reach a launch speed of over 550 km/hr; he landed less than 50 meters short of his target. If only he could have started off at 40,200 km/hr (the escape velocity for an object on earth's surface), he could have cleared not only the canyon, but also Canada, the Arctic Ocean, and the earth itself!

1 through 7 show the effect of increasing the initial speed. Trajectory 3 just misses the earth, and the projectile has become an earth satellite. If there is no retarding force (such as air resistance), its speed when it returns to point *A* is the same as its initial speed, and it repeats its motion indefinitely.

Trajectories 1 through 5 are ellipses or segments of ellipses; trajectory 4 is a circle (a special case of an ellipse). Trajectories 6 and 7 are not closed orbits; in these trajectories, the projectile never returns to its starting point, but travels farther and farther away from the earth.

A circular orbit is the simplest case and is the only one we'll analyze in detail. Artificial satellites often have nearly circular orbits, and the orbits of most of the planets around the sun are also nearly circular. As we learned in Section 3.4, a particle in uniform circular motion with speed v and radius r has an acceleration with magnitude $a_{rad} = v^2/r$, always directed toward the center of the circle. For a satellite with mass m, the *force* that provides this acceleration is the gravitational attraction of the earth (mass m_E), as shown in Figure 6.20. If the radius of the circular orbit, measured from the *center* of the earth, is r, then the gravitational force is given by the law of gravitation: $F_g = Gmm_E/r^2$.

The principle governing the motion of the satellite is Newton's second law; the force is F_g, and the acceleration is v^2/r, so the equation $\sum \vec{F} = m\vec{a}$ becomes

$$\frac{Gmm_E}{r^2} = \frac{mv^2}{r}.$$

Solving this equation for v, we find that

$$v = \sqrt{\frac{Gm_E}{r}}. \tag{6.8}$$

Equation 6.8 shows that we can't choose the radius r of the orbit and the speed v of the satellite independently; if we choose a value of r, then v is determined. Equation 6.8 also shows that the satellite's motion *does not* depend on its mass m, because m doesn't appear in the equation. If we could cut a satellite in half without changing its speed, each half would continue on with the original motion.

We can also derive a relation between the radius r of the orbit and the period T of the satellite—the time for one revolution. The speed v is equal to the distance $2\pi r$ (the circumference of the orbit) traveled in one revolution, divided by the time T for one revolution. Thus,

$$v = \frac{2\pi r}{T}. \tag{6.9}$$

To get an expression for T, we solve Equation 6.9 for T and combine the resulting equation with Equation 6.8:

$$T = \frac{2\pi r}{v} = 2\pi r\sqrt{\frac{r}{Gm_E}} = \frac{2\pi r^{3/2}}{\sqrt{Gm_E}}. \tag{6.10}$$

▲ **FIGURE 6.20** The force F_g due to the earth's gravitational attraction provides the centripetal force that keeps a satellite in orbit.

Equations 6.8 and 6.10 show that larger orbits correspond to slower speeds and longer periods.

Conceptual Analysis 6.6

Orbital speed of a satellite

A satellite in a circular orbit travels at constant speed because

A. the net force acting on it is zero.
B. the pull of gravity is balanced by the centrifugal force.
C. there is no component of force along its direction of motion.

SOLUTION The net force is not zero; if it were, the satellite would travel in a straight line, not a circle. Thus, A can't be right. There is no such thing as a balancing centrifugal force; if the pull of gravity were balanced by some mythical outward force, the satellite would move in a mythical straight line! So B is wrong, too. The net force on the satellite is the pull of the earth's gravity on the satellite. This pull is always directed toward the center of the orbit, and it provides the centripetal acceleration to maintain the satellite in circular motion. The net force is perpendicular to the satellite's velocity and therefore acts only to change the direction of the velocity. It has no component along the direction of the satellite's motion; if it did, the speed of the satellite would change. The correct answer is C.

Conceptual Analysis 6.7

Why doesn't the moon fall?

The moon is pulled directly toward the earth by the earth's gravity, yet it does not fall to the earth because

A. the net force on it is zero.
B. the pull of earth's gravity is balanced by the centrifugal force.
C. the moon pulls back on the earth with an equal and opposite force.
D. . . . but it *is* constantly falling!

SOLUTION The correct answer is D. Recall our earlier discussion about the daredevil motorcyclist going off the cliff. If he goes fast enough, the earth curves away beneath him. At one very high speed, he falls at just the right rate to stay on a circular path. This same argument applies to the moon. Without gravity, it would shoot away from earth in a straight line. The moon does fall, but just enough to keep it on a circular path around the earth. Concerning answer A, the net force is certainly *not* zero. With respect to answer B, a balancing centrifugal force is a mythical "beast," like the unicorn and the free lunch. Answer C tries to bring in an additional force that doesn't act *on* the moon. It is a misuse of Newton's second law!

EXAMPLE 6.10   **A weather satellite**

Suppose we want to place a weather satellite into a circular orbit 300 km above the earth's surface. What speed, period, and radial acceleration must it have? The earth's radius is 6380 km = 6.38×10^6 m, and its mass is 5.98×10^{24} kg. (See Appendix F.)

SOLUTION

SET UP AND SOLVE Figure 6.21 shows our sketch. The radius of the satellite's orbit is

r = 6380 km + 300 km = 6680 km = 6.68×10^6 m.

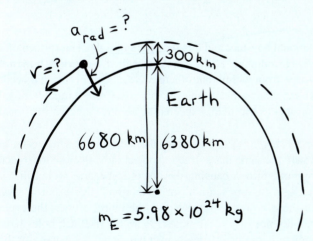

▲ **FIGURE 6.21** Our sketch for this problem.

From Equation 6.8,

$$\frac{Gmm_E}{r^2} = \frac{mv^2}{r},$$

$$v = \sqrt{\frac{Gm_E}{r}} = \sqrt{\frac{(6.67 \times 10^{-11}\,\text{N} \cdot \text{m}^2/\text{kg}^2)(5.98 \times 10^{24}\,\text{kg})}{6.68 \times 10^6\,\text{m}}}$$

$$= 7730\,\text{m/s}.$$

From Equation 6.10,

$$T = \frac{2\pi r}{v} = \frac{2\pi(6.68 \times 10^6\,\text{m})}{7730\,\text{m/s}}$$

$$= 5430\,\text{s} = 90.5\,\text{min}.$$

The radial acceleration is

$$a_{\text{rad}} = \frac{v^2}{r} = \frac{(7730\,\text{m/s})^2}{6.68 \times 10^6\,\text{m}}$$

$$= 8.95\,\text{m/s}^2.$$

Continued

REFLECT The radial acceleration of the satellite is somewhat less than the value of the free-fall acceleration $g = 9.8 \text{ m/s}^2$ at the earth's surface; it is equal to the value of g at a height of 300 km above the earth's surface. The value of T we obtained is only a little larger than the smallest possible period for an earth satellite (corresponding to the smallest possible orbit radius, i.e., the radius of earth itself).

Practice Problem: Find the speed and orbit radius for an earth satellite with a period of 1 day (86,400 s). *Answer:* 3.07×10^3 m/s, 4.23×10^7 m (from the center of the earth).

Masses of Astronomical Objects

We've talked mostly about artificial earth satellites, but we can apply the same analysis to the circular motion of *any* object acted upon by a gravitational force from a stationary object. Other familiar examples are our moon, the moons of other planets, and the planets orbiting the sun in nearly circular paths. The rings of Saturn (Figure 6.22), Jupiter, and Neptune are composed of small pieces of matter traveling in circular orbits around those planets.

Observations of satellite motions have been used to determine the masses of the planets in our solar system and of many other astronomical objects. For example, Jupiter has over 30 moons; the orbit radii and periods of many of them have been measured by astronomical observations. The appropriate relationship is Equation 6.10; we replace m_E with m_{Jupiter} and then solve for m_{Jupiter}:

$$T^2 = \frac{4\pi^2 r^3}{G m_{\text{Jupiter}}}, \qquad m_{\text{Jupiter}} = \frac{4\pi^2 r^3}{G T^2}.$$

If the orbit radius r and period T of a satellite of Jupiter can be measured, we can calculate the mass of Jupiter.

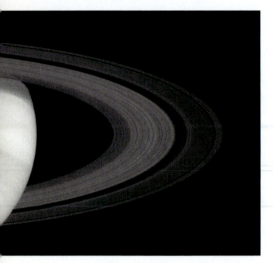

▲ **FIGURE 6.22** Saturn's rings consist of myriad separate particles orbiting the planet independently.

Black Holes

A more dramatic example of the sort of analysis just described is the discovery of **black holes**—aggregations of matter that are so massive and so dense that nothing (not even light) can escape from their gravitational field. In 1916, Karl Schwarzschild predicted, on the basis of Einstein's general theory of relativity, that if an aggregation of matter with total mass M has a radius less than a critical value R_S, called the **Schwarzschild radius,** then nothing (not even light) can escape from its gravitational field. The value of R_S is given by

$$R_S = \frac{2GM}{c^2},$$

where G is the gravitational constant and c is the speed of light. The surface of a sphere with radius R_S surrounding a black hole is called the **event horizon;** because light can't escape from within that sphere, we can't see events that occur inside. All we can know about a black hole is its mass (from its gravitational field), its charge (from its electric field, expected to be zero), and its rotational characteristics.

At points far from a black hole, its gravitational effects are the same as those of any normal object with the same mass. But any object moving close to a black hole is acted upon by huge forces, causing the object to become so hot that it emits not just visible light (as in "red-hot" or "white-hot" light), but x rays. Astronomers look for these x rays (emitted *before* the object crosses the event horizon) to signal the presence of a black hole (Figure 6.23). Black holes have also been observed indirectly by the effects their gravitational fields have on the motions of nearby astronomical objects.

(a)   (b)

▲ **FIGURE 6.23** (a) When a spherical object with mass M has a radius R greater than the Schwarzschild radius R_S, matter and energy can escape from its gravitational attraction. (b) When the radius is less than R_S, the object is a black hole. No matter or energy at a distance less than R_S from its center (the event horizon) can escape, because the escape speed would need to be greater than the speed of light.

The concept of a black hole is one of the most interesting and startling products of modern gravitational theory. Experimental and theoretical studies of black holes are a vital and exciting area of research in contemporary physics.

Weightlessness

What does it mean to say that an astronaut orbiting the earth in a spacecraft is *weightless?* The earth's gravitation still acts on the spacecraft and its occupants, as it must to provide the centripetal acceleration that keeps the craft in orbit. Yet, to the occupants, the environment *seems* to have no gravity. How can we understand this apparent paradox?

To answer this question, let's return to Example 4.10, a person standing in an accelerating elevator. We learned there that if the person stands on a spring scale, the scale doesn't read the true weight of the person during the acceleration. Now let's consider an implausible, though instructive, extreme. Suppose the elevator cables have all been broken and all the safety brakes have failed, so that both the elevator and its contents are in free fall, with a downward acceleration of magnitude $g = 9.8 \text{ m/s}^2$. What does the spring scale read now? The scale can't exert any upward force on the person; otherwise her acceleration would be less than g. So the scale must read zero, and the passenger *seems* to be weightless, even though the earth's gravitation still acts on her and her actual weight hasn't changed. If, in the excitement of the moment, she lets go of her purse, it doesn't fall to the floor, because it is already accelerating downward with the same acceleration as the elevator!

The same discussion is applicable to astronauts in a spacecraft orbiting the earth (Figure 6.24). The earth's gravity acts on both the spacecraft and its occupants, giving them the same acceleration. Thus, when an object is released inside the spacecraft, it doesn't fall relative to the craft, so it *appears* to be weightless.

The physiological effects of prolonged apparent weightlessness afford an interesting medical problem that is being actively explored. Gravity plays an important role in distributing blood in the body; one reaction to apparent weightlessness is a decrease in blood volume through increased excretion of water. In some cases, astronauts returning to earth have experienced temporary impairment of their sense of balance, a greater tendency toward motion sickness, and decalcification of their bones.

▲ **FIGURE 6.24** Astronauts appear to be weightless as they orbit the earth, because their acceleration is the same as that of their spacecraft. They still interact gravitationally with the earth, however, and thus have weight in the true sense; this weight is the force that holds them in orbit.

Historical Footnote

We close this chapter with a bit of historical perspective about the role of gravitation and orbital motion in the evolution of scientific thought. The study of planetary motion played a pivotal role in the early development of physics. Johannes Kepler (1571–1630) spent several painstaking years analyzing the motions of the planets, basing his work on remarkably precise measurements made by the Danish astronomer Tycho Brahe (1546–1601) *without the aid of a telescope.* (The telescope was invented in 1608.) Kepler discovered that the orbits of the planets are (nearly circular) ellipses and that the period of a planet in its orbit is proportional to the three-halves power of the radius of the orbit, as Equation 6.10 shows.

But it remained for Isaac Newton (1642–1727) to show, with his laws of motion and law of gravitation, that this celestial behavior of the planets could be understood on the basis of the very same physical principles he had developed to analyze *terrestrial* motion. Newton recognized that the falling apple (Section 4.4) was pulled to the earth by gravitational attraction. But to arrive at the $1/r^2$ form of the law of gravitation, he had to do something much subtler than this qualitative observation: He had to take Brahe's observations of planetary motions, as systematized by Kepler, and show that Kepler's rules demanded a $1/r^2$ force law.

From our historical perspective more than 300 years later, there is absolutely no doubt that this **Newtonian synthesis,** as it has come to be called, is one of the greatest achievements in the entire history of science, certainly comparable in significance to the development of quantum mechanics, the theory of relativity, and the understanding of DNA in the 20th century. It was an astonishing leap in understanding, made by a giant intellect!

SUMMARY

Circular Motion Dynamics

(Sections 6.1 and 6.2) For an object in uniform circular motion, the acceleration vector $\vec{a}_{rad}$ is directed toward the center of the circle and has constant magnitude $a_{rad} = v^2/R$ (Equation 3.16). The period T is the time required for the object to make one complete circle; the magnitude of the acceleration vector can also be written $a_{rad} = 4\pi^2 R/T^2$ (Equation 6.2). Provided that the object can be treated as a particle, circular motion (like other motions) is governed by Newton's second law, $\Sigma \vec{F} = m\vec{a}$. Because the net force vector points in the same direction as the acceleration vector, an object in uniform circular motion is acted upon by a net force directed toward the center of the circle, with magnitude $F_{net} = m(v^2/R)$ (Equation 6.3).

Newton's Law of Gravitation

(Section 6.3) Two particles with masses m_1 and m_2, a distance r apart, attract each other gravitationally with forces of magnitude

$$F_g = G\frac{m_1 m_2}{r^2}. \qquad (6.4)$$

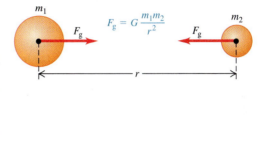

These forces form an action–reaction pair in accordance with Newton's third law. If the objects cannot be treated as particles, but are spherically symmetric, this law is still valid; then, r is the distance between their centers. The gravitational interaction of a spherically symmetric object, from any point outside the object, is just the same as though all its mass were concentrated at the object's center.

Weight

(Section 6.4) The weight w of a body is the total gravitational force exerted on it by all other bodies in the universe. Near the surface of the earth, an object's weight is very nearly equal to the gravitational force exerted by the earth alone. If the earth's mass is m_E, the weight of an object of mass m is

$$w = F_g = \frac{Gmm_E}{R_E^2} \qquad (6.6)$$

and the acceleration due to gravity g is

$$g = \frac{Gm_E}{R_E^2}. \qquad (6.7)$$

Satellite Motion

(Section 6.5) When a satellite moves in a circular orbit, the centripetal acceleration is provided by the gravitational attraction of the astronomical body it orbits. If the satellite orbits the earth in an orbit of radius r, its speed v and period T are, respectively,

$$v = \sqrt{\frac{Gm_E}{r}}, \qquad (6.8)$$

$$T = \frac{2\pi r}{v} = 2\pi r\sqrt{\frac{r}{Gm_E}} = \frac{2\pi r^{3/2}}{\sqrt{Gm_E}}. \qquad (6.10)$$

A black hole is an aggregation of matter that is so dense that nothing can escape its gravitational attraction. A nonrotating spherical distribution of mass is a black hole if its total mass M is contained within a radius of less than $R_s = 2GM/c^2$ (the Schwarzschild radius), where c is the speed of light.

Conceptual Questions

1. True or false? Satellites traveling in circular orbits at constant speed around the earth do not fall to the ground because they are in equilibrium. Explain your reasoning.
2. In discussing the Cavendish balance, a student claimed that the reason the small pivoted masses move toward the larger stationary masses, rather than the larger toward the smaller, is that the larger masses exert a stronger gravitational pull than the smaller ones. Is this explanation correct? If not, what is the correct one?
3. A student wrote, "The reason an apple falls downward to meet the earth instead of the earth falling upward to meet the apple is that the earth is much more massive than the apple and therefore exerts a much greater pull than the apple does." Is this explanation correct? If not, what is the correct one?
4. In discussions of satellites by laymen, one often hears questions such as "What keeps the satellite moving in its orbit?" and "What keeps the satellite up?" How do you answer these questions? Are your answers also applicable to the moon?
5. Suppose you are sealed inside a lab on the planet Vulcan. After some time, you notice that objects do not fall to the floor when released. Without looking outside the lab, could you determine whether you and the lab are in free fall or whether the Vulcans have somehow found a way to turn off the force of gravity?
6. During an actual interview for a college teaching position in physics, several candidates said that the earth does not fall into the sun because the gravitational pull from the outer planets prevents it from doing so. If you were on the interview committee, would you hire any of these candidates? Explain your reasoning.
7. If two planets have the same mass, will they *necessarily* produce the same gravitational pull on 1.0 kg objects that are (a) at their surfaces; (b) the same center-to-center distance from both planets (but above their surfaces)? Explain.
8. True or false? Astronauts in satellites orbiting around the earth are weightless because the earth's gravity is so weak up there that it is negligible. Explain.
9. True or false? If a rock is acted upon by a gravitational force F from the earth when it is a distance d above the surface of our planet, it will be acted upon by a force $F/4$ if it is raised to twice the height $(2d)$ above the surface. Explain your reasoning.
10. On an icy road, you approach a curve that has the banking angle calculated for 55 mph. Your passenger suggests you slow down below 55 mph, just to be on the safe side, but you say that you should maintain your speed at 55 mph. (a) Who is correct, you or your passenger? (b) What would happen if you were to slow down (or speed up)? (c) Would your passenger's suggestion be a good one on an *unbanked* road?
11. You approach a curve posted at 45 mph. Your car has old, bald tires, so you decide to reduce your speed below 45 mph. Is this a good idea (a) if the highway is unbanked? (b) if the highway is at the banking angle for 45 mph? Explain your reasoning.
12. The moon is accelerating toward the earth. Does this mean that it is getting closer to our planet? Explain your reasoning.
13. A passenger in a car rounding a sharp curve feels "thrown" toward the outside of the curve. (a) What causes this to happen? Is the person really *thrown* away from the center of the curve? (b) Make a free-body diagram of the person.
14. How does a lettuce spinner remove water from lettuce?
15. What is *wrong* with this statement? "A satellite stays in orbit because the outward centrifugal force just balances the inward centripetal force." Make a free-body diagram of the satellite.

Multiple-Choice Problems

1. Objects in orbiting satellites are apparently weightless because
   A. they are too far from earth to feel its gravity.
   B. earth's gravitational pull is balanced by the outward centrifugal force.
   C. earth's gravitational pull is balanced by the centripetal force.
   D. both they and the satellite are in free fall toward the earth.
2. If the earth had twice its present mass, its orbital period around the sun (at our present distance from the sun) would be
   A. $\sqrt{2}$ years.   B. 1 year.
   C. $\dfrac{1}{\sqrt{2}}$ year.   D. $\frac{1}{2}$ year.
3. If the sun had twice its present mass, the earth's orbital period around the sun (at our present distance from the sun) would be
   A. 2 years.   B. $\sqrt{2}$ years.
   C. $\dfrac{1}{\sqrt{2}}$ year.   D. $\frac{1}{2}$ year.
4. A stone of mass m is attached to a strong string and whirled in a vertical circle of radius R. At the exact top of the path, the tension in the string is three times the stone's weight. At this point, the stone's speed is
   A. $2\sqrt{gR}$.   B. $\sqrt{2gR}$.
   C. $3\sqrt{gR}$.   D. $\sqrt{3gR}$.
5. A frictional force f provides the centripetal force as a car goes around an unbanked curve of radius R at speed V. Later, the car encounters a similar curve, except of radius $2R$, and the driver continues around this curve at the same speed V. In order to make this second curve, the frictional force on the car must be equal to
   A. $2f$.   B. f.   C. $\frac{1}{2}f$.   D. $\frac{1}{4}f$.
6. In the 1960s, during the Cold War, the Soviet Union put a rocket into a nearly circular orbit around the earth. One U.S. senator expressed concern that a nuclear bomb could be dropped on our nation if it were released when the rocket was over the United States. If such a bomb were, in fact, released when the rocket was directly over the United States, where would it land?
   A. Directly below, on the United States.
   B. It would follow a curved path and most likely land somewhere in the ocean.
   C. It would not hit the United States, because it would remain in orbit with the rocket.
   D. It would move in a straight line out into space.
7. Two masses m and $2m$ are each forced to go around a curve of radius R at the same constant speed. If, as they move around this curve, the smaller mass is acted upon by a net force F, then the larger one is acted upon by a net force of
   A. $\frac{1}{2}F$.   B. F.   C. $2F$.   D. $4F$.

8. A weight W is swung in a vertical circle at constant speed at the end of a rigid bar that pivots about the opposite end (like the spoke of a wheel). If the tension in this bar is equal to $2W$ when the weight is at its lowest point, then the tension when the weight is at the highest point will be
   A. 0.   B. W.
   C. $2W$.   D. $3W$.

9. If a planet had twice the earth's radius, but only half its mass, the acceleration due to gravity at its surface would be
   A. G.   B. $\frac{1}{2}g$.
   C. $\frac{1}{4}g$.   D. $\frac{1}{8}g$.

10. When a mass goes in a horizontal circle with speed V at the end of a string of length L on a frictionless table, the tension in the string is T. If the speed of this mass were doubled, but all else remained the same, the tension would be
    A. $2T$.   B. $4T$.
    C. $T\sqrt{2}$.   D. $\dfrac{T}{\sqrt{2}}$.

11. In the previous problem, if *both* the speed and the length were doubled, the tension in the string would be
    A. T.   B. $2T$.
    C. $4T$.   D. $T\sqrt{2}$.

12. Two 1.0 kg point masses a distance D apart each exert a gravitational attraction F on the other one. If 1.0 kg is now added to each mass, the gravitational attraction exerted by each would be
    A. $2F$.   B. $3F$.   C. $4F$.

13. Two massless bags contain identical bricks, each brick having a mass M. Initially, each bag contains four bricks, and the bags mutually exert a gravitational attraction F_1 on each other. You now take two bricks from one bag and add them to the other bag, causing the bags to attract each other with a force F_2. What is the closest expression for F_2 in terms of F_1?
    A. $F_2 = \frac{3}{4}F_1$.
    B. $F_2 = \frac{1}{2}F_1$.
    C. $F_2 = \frac{1}{4}F_1$.
    D. $F_2 = F_1$ because neither the total mass nor the distance between the bags has changed.

14. When two point masses are a distance D apart, each exerts a gravitational attraction F on the other mass. To reduce this force to $\frac{1}{3}F$, you would have to separate the masses to a distance of
    A. $D\sqrt{3}$.   B. $3D$.
    C. $9D$.   D. $\frac{1}{3}D$.

15. If a planet is ever discovered orbiting midway between the earth and the sun, its orbital period will be closest to
    A. 2.0 years.   B. 0.50 year.
    C. 0.35 year.   D. 0.25 year.

Problems

6.1 Force in Circular Motion

1. • A racing car drives at *constant speed* around the horizontal track shown in Figure 6.25. At points A, B, and C, draw a vector showing the magnitude and direction of the net force on this car. Make sure that the lengths of your arrows represent the relative magnitudes of the three forces.

▲ **FIGURE 6.25** Problem 1.

2. • A stone with a mass of 0.80 kg is attached to one end of a string 0.90 m long. The string will break if its tension exceeds 60.0 N. The stone is whirled in a horizontal circle on a frictionless tabletop; the other end of the string remains fixed. (a) Make a free-body diagram of the stone. (b) Find the maximum speed the stone can attain without breaking the string.

3. •• **Force on a skater's wrist.** A 52 kg ice skater spins about a
   BIO vertical axis through her body with her arms horizontally outstretched, making 2.0 turns each second. The distance from one hand to the other is 1.50 m. Biometric measurements indicate that each hand typically makes up about 1.25% of body weight. (a) Draw a free-body diagram of one of her hands. (b) What horizontal force must her wrist exert on her hand? (c) Express the force in part (b) as a multiple of the weight of her hand.

4. • A flat (unbanked) curve on a highway has a radius of 220 m. A car rounds the curve at a speed of 25.0 m/s. (a) Make a free-body diagram of the car as it rounds this curve. (b) What is the minimum coefficient of friction that will prevent sliding?

5. •• The "Giant Swing" at a county fair consists of a vertical central shaft with a number of horizontal arms attached at its upper end. (See Figure 6.26.) Each arm supports a seat suspended from a 5.00-m-long rod, the upper end of which is

▲ **FIGURE 6.26** Problem 5.

fastened to the arm at a point 3.00 m from the central shaft. (a) Make a free-body diagram of the seat, including the person in it. (b) Find the time of one revolution of the swing if the rod supporting the seat makes an angle of 30.0° with the vertical. (c) Does the angle depend on the weight of the passenger for a given rate of revolution?

6. • Suppose that the motor running the "Giant Swing" in the previous problem were to malfunction, making the system spin faster and faster. (a) Would it be possible for it to spin fast enough to make the seats swing out so that the rods supporting them become horizontal? (b) What would have to be the tension in the rods in that case?

7. • Using only astronomical data from Appendix F, calculate (a) the speed of the planet Venus in its essentially circular orbit around the sun and (b) the gravitational force that the sun must be exerting on Venus. Start with a free-body diagram of Venus.

8. • A highway curve with radius 900.0 ft is to be banked so that a car traveling 55.0 mph will not skid sideways even in the absence of friction. (a) Make a free-body diagram of this car. (b) At what angle should the curve be banked?

9. •• **The Indy 500.** The Indianapolis Speedway (home of the Indy 500) consists of a 2.5 mile track having four turns, each 0.25 mile long and banked at 9°12′. What is the no-friction-needed speed (in m/s and mph) for these turns? (Do you think drivers actually take the turns at that speed?)

6.2 Motion in a Vertical Circle

10. • A bowling ball weighing 71.2 N is attached to the ceiling by a 3.80 m rope. The ball is pulled to one side and released; it then swings back and forth like a pendulum. As the rope swings through its lowest point, the speed of the bowling ball is measured at 4.20 m/s. At that instant, find (a) the magnitude and direction of the acceleration of the bowling ball and (b) the tension in the rope. Be sure to start with a free-body diagram.

11. •• The Cosmoclock 21 Ferris wheel in Yokohama City, Japan, has a diameter of 100 m. Its name comes from its 60 arms, each of which can function as a second hand (so that it makes one revolution every 60.0 s). (a) Find the speed of the passengers when the Ferris wheel is rotating at this rate. (b) A passenger weighs 882 N at the weight-guessing booth on the ground. What is his apparent weight at the highest and at the lowest point on the Ferris wheel? (c) What would be the time for one revolution if the passenger's apparent weight at the highest point were zero? (d) What then would be the passenger's apparent weight at the lowest point?

12. •• A 50.0 kg stunt pilot who has been diving her airplane vertically pulls out of the dive by changing her course to a circle in a vertical plane. (a) If the plane's speed at the lowest point of the circle is 95.0 m/s, what should the minimum radius of the circle be in order for the centripetal acceleration at this point not to exceed 4.00g? (b) What is the apparent weight of the pilot at the lowest point of the pullout?

13. •• **Effect on blood of walking.** While a person is walking, his arms swing through approximately a 45° angle in $\frac{1}{2}$ s. As a reasonable approximation, we can assume that the arm moves with constant speed during each swing. A typical arm is 70.0 cm long, measured from the shoulder joint. (a) What is the acceleration of a 1.0 gram drop of blood in the fingertips at the bottom of the swing? (b) Make a free-body diagram of the drop of blood in part (a). (c) Find the force that the blood vessel must exert on the drop of blood in part (b). Which way

does this force point? (d) What force would the blood vessel exert if the arm were not swinging?

14. • **Stay dry!** You tie a cord to a pail of water, and you swing the pail in a vertical circle of radius 0.600 m. What minimum speed must you give the pail at the highest point of the circle if no water is to spill from it? Start with a free-body diagram of the water at its highest point.

15. • **Walking on the moon.** The first person to walk on the moon, where the acceleration due to gravity is 1.67 m/s², was Neil Armstrong in 1969. If his leg was 95 cm long, (a) what was his maximum walking speed on the moon? (b) Compare your result from part (a) with his maximum walking speed on earth.

6.3 Newton's Law of Gravitation

16. • If two tiny identical spheres attract each other with a force of 3.0 nN when they are 25 cm apart, what is the mass of each sphere?

17. • What gravitational force do the two protons in the helium nucleus exert on each other? Their separation is approximately 1.0 fm. (Consult Appendix F and Table 1-1.)

18. • **Rendezvous in space!** A couple of astronauts agree to rendezvous in space after hours. Their plan is to let gravity bring them together. One of them has a mass of 65 kg and the other a mass of 72 kg, and they start from rest 20.0 m apart. (a) Make a free-body diagram of each astronaut, and use it to find his or her initial acceleration. As a rough approximation, we can model the astronauts as uniform spheres. (b) If the astronauts' acceleration remained constant, how many days would they have to wait before reaching each other? (Careful! They *both* have acceleration toward each other.) (c) Would their acceleration, in fact, remain constant? If not, would it increase or decrease? Why?

19. • What is the ratio of the gravitational pull of the sun on the moon to that of the earth on the moon? (Assume that the distance of the moon from the sun is approximately the same as the distance of the earth from the sun.) Use the data in Appendix F. Is it more accurate to say that the moon orbits the earth or that the moon orbits the sun? Why?

20. • A 2150 kg satellite used in a cellular telephone network is in a circular orbit at a height of 780 km above the *surface* of the earth. What is the gravitational force on the satellite? What fraction is this force of the satellite's weight at the surface of the earth?

21. • **Sedna.** On March 16, 2004, astronomers discovered Sedna, the most distant object in the solar system. It orbits our sun in a highly elliptical orbit in which its distance from the sun varies from about 10 billion kilometers to 130 billion kilometers. (a) Sketch Sedna's orbit to scale. (b) Calculate the ratio of the greatest gravitational force to the smallest gravitational force our sun exerts on Sedna.

22. •• Find the magnitude and direction of the net gravitational force on mass *A* due to masses *B* and *C* in Figure 6.27. Each mass is 2.00 kg.

▲ **FIGURE 6.27** Problem 22.

23. •• A small mass M and a small mass $3M$ are 1.00 m apart. Where should you put a third small mass so that the net gravitational force on it due to the other two masses is zero?

24. •• Each mass in Figure 6.28 is 3.00 kg. Find the magnitude and direction of the net gravitational force on mass A due to the other masses.

(a) Equilateral triangle of side 10 cm   (b) Square of side 10 cm

▲ **FIGURE 6.28** Problem 24.

25. •• Two unequal point masses attract each other with a force F when they are located a distance d apart. What force (in terms of F) will they exert on each other if (a) the mass of one of them is tripled, but the distance does not change; (b) both masses are tripled; (c) the masses stay the same, but the distance between them is doubled; (d) both masses are doubled *and* the distance between them is cut in half? (e) How far apart (in terms of d) should these masses be so that the original force will be reduced by one-half?

6.4 Weight

26. • How many kilometers would you have to go above the *surface* of the earth for your weight to decrease to half of what it was at the surface?

27. •• Your spaceship lands on an unknown planet. To determine the characteristics of this planet, you drop a 1.30 kg wrench from 5.00 m above the ground and measure that it hits the ground 0.811 s later. You also do enough surveying to determine that the circumference of the planet is 62,400 km. (a) What is the mass of the planet, in kilograms? (b) Express the planet's mass in terms of the earth's mass.

28. •• If an object's weight is W on the earth, what would be its weight (in terms of W) if the earth had (a) twice its present mass, but was the same size, (b) half its present radius, but the same mass, (c) half its present radius and half its present mass, (d) twice its present radius and twice its present mass?

29. •• **Huygens probe on Titan.** In January 2005 the *Huygens* probe landed on Saturn's moon Titan, the only satellite in the solar system having a thick atmosphere. Titan's diameter is 5150 km, and its mass is 1.35×10^{23} kg. The probe weighed 3120 N on the earth. What did it weigh on the surface of Titan?

30. •• The mass of the moon is about $1/81$ the mass of the earth, its radius is $\frac{1}{4}$ that of the earth, and the acceleration due to gravity at the earth's surface is 9.80 m/s^2. Without looking up either body's mass, use this information to compute the acceleration due to gravity on the moon's surface.

31. •• Neutron stars, such as the one at the center of the Crab Nebula, have about the same mass as our sun, but a *much* smaller diameter. If you weigh 675 N on the earth, what would you weigh on the surface of a neutron star that has the same mass as our sun and a diameter of 20.0 km?

32. •• Mathematical models of planet formation show a wide range of possible sizes for the planets. (a) Find the mass of a planet three times the earth's diameter, but having the same average density of 5.5 g/cm^3. (b) What is the acceleration due to gravity at the surface of this planet? Express your answer in m/s^2 and in g's. (c) If an astronaut weighed 650 N at the earth's surface, what would he weigh at the surface of the planet in question?

6.5 Satellite Motion

33. • An earth satellite moves in a circular orbit with an orbital speed of 6200 m/s. (a) Find the time of one revolution of the satellite. (b) Find the radial acceleration of the satellite in its orbit. (c) Make a free-body diagram of the satellite.

34. • What is the period of revolution of a satellite with mass m that orbits the earth in a circular path of radius 7880 km (about 1500 km above the surface of the earth)?

35. • What must be the orbital speed of a satellite in a circular orbit 780 km above the surface of the earth?

36. •• **Planets beyond the solar system.** On October 15, 2001, a planet was discovered orbiting around the star HD68988. Its orbital distance was measured to be 10.5 million kilometers from the center of the star, and its orbital period was estimated at 6.3 days. What is the mass of HD68988? Express your answer in kilograms and in terms of our sun's mass. (Consult Appendix F.)

37. •• **Communications satellites.** Communications satellites are used to bounce radio waves from the earth's surface to send messages around the curvature of the earth. In order to be available all the time, they must remain above the same point on the earth's surface and must move in a circle above the equator. (a) How long must it take for a communications satellite to make one complete orbit around the earth? (Such an orbit is said to be *geosynchronous*.) (b) Make a free-body diagram of the satellite in orbit. (c) Apply Newton's second law to the satellite and find its altitude above the earth's *surface*. (d) Draw the orbit of a communications satellite to scale on a sketch of the earth.

38. •• **Lunar colonies.** When we eventually build colonies on the moon, we will probably need communications satellites. (See previous problem.) (a) Using data from Appendix F, as well as the fact that the moon spins on its axis once every 27.3 days, calculate the height above the lunar *surface* at which these satellites should be placed in orbit. Start with a free-body diagram of such a satellite. (b) Draw the orbit you just found to scale on a sketch of the moon.

39. •• Assuming that the earth's orbit around the sun is circular, use the appropriate information about the earth in Appendix F to calculate the mass of the sun.

40. •• **Apparent weightlessness in a satellite.** You have probably seen films of astronauts floating freely in orbiting satellites. People often think the astronauts are weightless because they are free of the gravity of the earth. Let us see if that explanation is correct. (a) Typically, such satellites orbit around 400 km above the *surface* of the earth. If an astronaut weighs 750 N on the ground, what will he weigh if he is 400 km above the surface? (b) Draw the orbit of the satellite in part (a) to scale on a sketch of the earth. (c) In light of your answers to parts (a) and (b), are the astronauts weightless because gravity is so weak? Why are they apparently weightless?

41. •• Suppose the earth were shrunk until it became a black hole. (a) What would be the radius of its event horizon? Consult Appendix F. (b) If you weigh 750 N on the present-day earth, what would you weigh at the surface of the event horizon of the shrunken earth, assuming that you could stand there?

42. •• **Baseball on Deimos!** Deimos, a moon of Mars, is about 12 km in diameter, with a mass of 2.0×10^{15} kg. Suppose you are stranded alone on Deimos and want to play a one-person game of baseball. You would be the pitcher, and you would be the batter! With what speed would you have to throw a baseball so that it would go into orbit and return to you so you could hit it? Do you think you could actually throw it at that speed?

General Problems

43. •• **International Space Station.** The International Space Station, launched in November 1998, makes 15.65 revolutions around the earth each day in a circular orbit. (a) Draw a free-body diagram of this satellite. (b) Apply Newton's second law to the space station and find its height (in kilometers) above the earth's surface. (Consult Appendix F.)

44. •• **Artificial gravity.** One way to create artificial gravity in a space station is to spin it. If a cylindrical space station 275 m in diameter is to spin about its central axis, at how many revolutions per minute (rpm) must it turn so that the outermost points have an acceleration equal to g?

45. •• **Hip wear on the moon.** (a) Use data from Appendix F to calculate the acceleration due to gravity on the moon. (b) Calculate the friction force on a walking 65 kg astronaut carrying a 43 kg instrument pack on the moon if the coefficient of kinetic friction at her hip joint is 0.0050. (If necessary, see problem 32 in Chapter 5 and recall that approximately 65% of the body weight is above the hip.) (c) What would be the friction force on earth for this astronaut?

46. •• **Volcanoes on Io.** Jupiter's moon Io has active volcanoes (in fact, it is the most volcanically active body in the solar system) that eject material as high as 500 km (or even higher) above the surface. Io has a mass of 8.94×10^{22} kg and a radius of 1815 km. Ignore any variation in gravity over the 500 km range of the debris. How high would this material go on earth if it were ejected with the same speed as on Io?

47. •• You are driving with a friend who is sitting to your right on the passenger side of the front seat of your car. You would like to be closer to your friend, so you decide to use physics to achieve your romantic goal by making a quick turn. (a) Which way (to the left or to the right) should you turn the car to get your friend to slide toward you? (b) If the coefficient of static friction between your friend and the car seat is 0.55 and you keep driving at a constant speed of 15 m/s, what is the maximum radius you could make your turn and still have your friend slide your way?

48. •• **Mission to Titan.** On December 25, 2004, the *Huygens* probe separated from the *Cassini* spacecraft orbiting Saturn and began a 22-day journey to Saturn's giant moon Titan (see Figure 6.29), on whose surface it landed. Besides the data in Appendix F, it is useful to know that Titan is 1.22×10^6 km from the center of Saturn and has a mass of 1.35×10^{23} kg and a diameter of 5150 km. At what

▲ **FIGURE 6.29** Problem 48.

distance from Titan should the gravitational pull of Titan just balance the gravitational pull of Saturn?

49. •• On the ride "Spindletop" at the amusement park Six Flags Over Texas, people stood against the inner wall of a hollow vertical cylinder with radius 2.5 m. The cylinder started to rotate, and when it reached a constant rotation rate of 0.60 rev/s, the floor on which the people were standing dropped about 0.5 m. The people remained pinned against the wall. (a) Draw a free-body diagram for a person on this ride after the floor has dropped. (b) What minimum coefficient of static friction is required if the person on the ride is not to slide downward to the new position of the floor? (c) Does your answer in part (b) depend on the mass of the passenger? (*Note:* When the ride is over, the cylinder is slowly brought to rest. As it slows down, people slide down the walls to the floor.)

50. •• **Physical training.** As part of a training program, an athlete **BIO** runs while holding 8.0 kg weights in each hand. As he runs, the weights swing through a 30.0° arc in $\frac{1}{3}$ s at essentially constant speed. His hands are 72 cm from his shoulder joint, and they are light enough that we can neglect their weight compared with that of the 8.0 kg weight he is carrying. (a) Make a free-body diagram of one of the 8.0 kg weights at the bottom of its swing. (b) What force does the runner's hand exert on each weight at the bottom of the swing?

51. •• The asteroid Toro has a radius of about 5.0 km. Consult Appendix F as necessary. (a) Assuming that the density of Toro is the same as that of the earth (5.5 g/cm^3), find its total mass and find the acceleration due to gravity at its surface. (b) Suppose an object is to be placed in a circular orbit around Toro, with a radius just slightly larger than the asteroid's radius. What is the speed of the object? Could you launch yourself into orbit around Toro by running?

52. •• **The Planet Vulcan.** Suppose that a planet were discovered between the sun and Mercury with a circular orbit of radius equal to two-thirds the average radius of Mercury's orbit. (Such a planet was once postulated, in part to explain the precession of Mercury's orbit. It was even given the name Vulcan, although we now have no evidence that it actually exists. Mercury's precession has been explained by general relativity.) What would be the orbital period of such a planet? (Consult Appendix F for pertinent information.)

53. •• Your starship, the *Aimless Wanderer*, lands on the mysterious planet Mongo. As chief scientist–engineer, you make the following measurements: A 2.50 kg stone thrown upward from the ground at 12.0 m/s returns to the ground in 8.00 s; the circumference of Mongo at the equator is 2.00×10^5 km; and there is no appreciable atmosphere on Mongo. The starship commander, Captain Confusion, asks for the following information: (a) What is the mass of Mongo? (b) If the *Aimless Wanderer* goes into a circular orbit 30,000 km above the surface of Mongo, how many hours will it take the ship to complete one orbit?

54. •• **Exploring Europa.** Europa, a satellite of Jupiter, is **BIO** believed to have an ocean of liquid water (with the possibility of life) beneath its icy surface. (See Figure 6.30.) Europa is 3130 km in diameter and has a mass of 4.78×10^{22} kg. In the future, we will surely want to send astronauts to investigate Europa. In planning such a future mission, what is the fastest that such an astronaut could walk on the surface of Europa if her legs are 1.0 m long?

▲ FIGURE 6.30 Problem 54.   **▲ FIGURE 6.31** Problem 56.

55. •• **Living on Sedna.** Sedna, the most distant known object in the solar system, was discovered on March 16, 2004. It has a diameter of about 1700 km and is probably similar to Pluto in many ways, which would give it a density of 2.1 g/cm³. Assuming that it is spherical, what would a 675 N (earth weight) astronaut weigh at the surface of Sedna?

56. •• **Catch a piece of a comet.** The *Stardust* spacecraft was designed to visit a comet and bring samples of its material back to the earth. The craft is 1.7 m across and has a mass of 385 kg. In January 2004, from a distance of 237 km, it took the photograph of the nucleus of comet Wild2, shown in Figure 6.31. The distance across this nucleus is 5 km, and we can model it as an approximate sphere. Since astronomers think that comets have a composition similar to that of Pluto, we can assume a density the same as Pluto's, which is 2.1 g/cm³. The samples taken will be returned to earth on Jan. 15, 2006. (a) What gravitational force did the comet exert on the spacecraft when it took the photo in the figure? (b) Compare this force with the force that the earth's gravity exerted on it when the spacecraft was on the launch pad.

57. •• The 4.00 kg block in the figure is attached to a vertical rod by means of two strings. When the system rotates about the axis of the rod, the strings are extended as shown in Figure 6.32 and the tension in the upper string is 80.0 N. (a) What is the tension in the lower cord? Start with a free-body diagram of the block. (b) What is the speed of the block?

▲ FIGURE 6.32 Problem 57.

1.25 m, 2.00 m, 4.00 kg, 1.25 m

58. •• As your bus rounds a flat curve at constant speed, a package with mass 0.500 kg, suspended from the luggage compartment of the bus by a string 45.0 cm long, is found to hang at rest relative to the bus, with the string making an angle of 30.0° with the vertical. In this position, the package is 50.0 m from the center of curvature of the curve. What is the speed of the bus?

59. •• **An Earth-like planet?** In August 2004, a team of European astronomers discovered the smallest-known (up to that time) planet orbiting another star. (Well over 100 other "extrasolar" planets have been discovered.) This planet has a mass of 14 times the mass of the earth (known by measuring its effect on its star's speed) and orbits around the star μ Arae. If the planet is similar to the earth, it could have the same average density, 5.5 g/cm³. Under these circumstances, (a) what would

be the radius of the planet? (Consult Appendix F.) (b) What would be the acceleration of a freely falling object at its surface? Express your answer in m/s² and in g's.

60. •• **Artificial gravity in space stations.** One problem for humans living in outer space is that they are apparently weightless. One way around this problem is to design a cylindrical space station that spins about an axis through its center at a constant rate. (See Figure 6.33.) This spin creates "artificial gravity" at the outside rim of the station. (a) If the diameter of the space station is 800.0 m, how fast must the rim be moving in order for the "artificial gravity" acceleration to be g at the outer rim? (b) If the space station is a waiting area for travelers going to Mars, it might be desirable to simulate the acceleration due to gravity on the Martian surface. How fast must the rim move in this case? (c) Make a free-body diagram of an astronaut at the outer rim.

800.0 m

▲ FIGURE 6.33 Problem 60.

61. **A Visit to Santa.** You decide to visit Santa Claus at the North Pole to put in a good word about your splendid behavior throughout the year. While there, you notice that the elf Sneezy, when hanging from a rope, produces a tension of 475.0 N in the rope. If Sneezy hangs from a similar rope while delivering presents at the earth's equator, what will the tension in it be? (Recall that the earth is rotating about an axis through its North and South Poles.) Consult Appendix F and start with a free-body diagram of Sneezy at the equator.

62. •• **Astrology, anyone?** One of the tenets of the pseudoscience (i.e., "false science") of astrology is that, in some mysterious way, the positions of the planets at the time of a person's birth somehow influence the characteristics of that person. To see if this proposition seems plausible, let us compare the gravitational influence of Mars when it is closest to earth with the gravitational influence of the medical doctor who delivers a baby. For a rough calculation, we shall assume that the doctor is 50 cm from the baby (she is likely to be even closer at delivery), has a mass of 75 kg, and can be modeled as a uniform sphere. (a) Using the data from Appendix F, draw the positions of the earth and Mars when Mars is closest to the earth. How far is Mars from the earth at that time? (b) Calculate the ratio of the gravitational force the doctor exerts on the baby to the gravitational force that Mars exerts on the baby. (c) If there is any influence, which is greater, that of Mars or that of the doctor?

WORK AND ENERGY

For an instant, this skateboarder hangs in the air. As he descends, gravity increases his speed. In this chapter we'll learn to analyze such sequences in terms of a new quantity, energy.

In the preceding three chapters, we've developed an understanding of mechanics as embodied in Newton's three laws of motion. In principle, these laws provide a complete description of the relation between the motion of an object and the forces that act on it. But some problems aren't as simple as they look. Suppose you try to find the speed of a toy glider launched by a compressed spring that applies a varying force. You apply Newton's laws and all the problem-solving techniques that we've learned, but you find that the acceleration isn't constant and the simple methods we've learned can't be implemented directly. As we'll see, there are powerful alternative methods for dealing with such problems.

In this chapter, we'll introduce a new concept—*energy*—that is one of the most important unifying concepts in all of physical science. Its importance stems from the principle of *conservation of energy*. We'll concentrate on mechanical energy, which is associated with the motions and positions of mechanical systems. In the opening section of the chapter, we'll tour the main ideas associated with energy on a qualitative level. Then we'll develop the concepts of work and kinetic energy (energy of motion) and the relationship between them. In the remainder of the chapter, we'll learn how to apply these concepts to the analysis of problems.

7.1 An Overview of Energy

The concept of **energy** appears throughout every area of physics, yet it's not easy to define just what energy is. This concept is the cornerstone of a fundamental law of nature called **conservation of energy,** which states that the total energy in any isolated system is constant, no matter what happens within the system. (Later in the chapter, we'll explain what an *isolated system* is.) Energy can be converted from one form to another, but it cannot be created or destroyed.

Conservation laws, including conservation of mass, energy, momentum, angular momentum, electric charge, and other quantities, play vital roles in every area of physics and provide unifying threads that run through the whole fabric of the subject. Every conservation law says that the total amount of some physical quantity in every isolated system is constant.

An example is the conservation of mass in chemical reactions. The total mass of the material participating in a chemical reaction is always the same (within the limits of experimental precision) before and after the reaction. This generalization is called the principle of *conservation of mass,* and it is obeyed in all chemical reactions.

Something analogous happens in collisions between objects. For a particle with mass m moving with speed v, we define a quantity $\frac{1}{2}mv^2$ called the **kinetic energy** of the particle. When two hard, springy objects, such as steel ball bearings, collide, we find that the individual speeds change, but that the total kinetic energy (the sum of the $\frac{1}{2}mv^2$ quantities for the two balls) is very nearly the same after the collision as before. When it is *exactly* the same, we say that kinetic energy is *conserved.* We haven't really said what kinetic energy *is,* only that this product of half the mass and the square of the speed is useful in representing a conservation principle in a particular class of interactions.

When two soft, deformable objects (such as two balls of putty or chewing gum) collide, we find that kinetic energy is *not* conserved, but the bodies become warmer. It turns out that there is a definite relationship between the rise in temperature and the loss of kinetic energy. We can define a new quantity, *internal energy,* that increases with temperature in a definite way such that the *sum* of the kinetic energy and the internal energy *is* conserved in these collisions. We can also define additional forms of energy that enable us to extend the principle of conservation of energy to broader classes of phenomena.

Energy is transformed from one form to another, but it is not created or destroyed. There is energy associated with heat, elastic deformations, electric and magnetic fields, and, according to the theory of relativity, even with mass itself. Newtonian mechanics has its limitations; it doesn't work for very fast motion, for which we have to use the theory of relativity, or for atomic or subatomic systems, for which we need quantum mechanics. But conservation of energy holds even in these realms. It is a *universal* conservation principle; no exception has ever been found. Studying conservation of energy is like studying a snowflake under a microscope, or the finer and finer details of a fractal pattern, or the structure of a Bach fugue. The more closely you look, the richer the subject becomes.

Figure 7.1 conveys a sense of energy transfer and transformation. A little of the sun's nuclear energy is successively transformed into other forms and eventually appears as energy you spend when exercising. This energy is not created spontaneously, and it is not "used up"; instead, it is transformed from one form to another.

Forms of Mechanical Energy

In this chapter, we'll be concerned only with **mechanical energy**—the energy associated with motion, position, and deformation of objects. We'll find that, in some interactions, mechanical energy is conserved; in others, there is a conversion of mechanical energy to or from other forms. In Chapters 15 and 16, we'll study in detail the relation of mechanical energy to heat; in later chapters, we'll define still other forms of energy.

As we mentioned at the beginning of this chapter, the energy associated with motion of an object is called kinetic energy. For an object with constant mass, kinetic energy depends only on its speed v and mass m. When a moving object

Nuclear energy in the sun's core …

Becomes energy of the sun's hot gas …

Becomes energy of sunlight …

Which is converted by plants to the chemical energy of grains and other foods …

Which you may consume as calories …

Which can be used to lift weights …

And the story goes on.

▲ **FIGURE 7.1** A typical sequence of energy transfers and transformations—one that sustains life on earth.

▲ **FIGURE 7.2** Elastic potential energy stored in a stretched rubber band.

The gravitational potential energy is larger when the skateboarder is at this higher position.

Gravitational potential energy in the process of becoming kinetic energy

▲**FIGURE 7.3** Transformation of gravitational potential energy to kinetic energy.

TABLE 7.1   The analogy between energy and money

How money is like energy:

- It can take multiple forms (coins, bills, checks, bank accounts).
- You can transform it (e.g., by cashing a check) or transfer it to others.
- These transfers and transformations do not change its total amount.
- It can be stored or spent.

How money is not like energy:

- Money can be created or destroyed, whereas energy cannot be.

such as a kicked football or a speeding car interacts with another object, obvious changes (such as broken windows or bent fenders) result, and associated with these changes are transfers of kinetic energy to other forms of energy.

The other class of mechanical energy we'll consider is energy that is not directly associated with motion, but rather a quantity that is *stored* as a result of the position or elastic deformation of an object. Consider a stretched rubber band (Figure 7.2). You have to expend energy to stretch it, and as soon as it is released, physical changes occur; for instance, it may fly across the room. An unstretched rubber band lacks this capability. The act of stretching the rubber band stores energy in it, and releasing the rubber band allows this stored energy to be transformed to other types of energy, such as kinetic energy. We call this stored energy **potential energy.** Energy that is stored in an elastic object when you stretch, compress, twist, or otherwise deform it is called **elastic potential energy.**

Another example of potential energy is provided by the skateboarder in Figure 7.3. When he descends from the top edge of the quarter-pipe, he speeds up and gains kinetic energy. While he momentarily stops at the top of the opposite edge, he has no kinetic energy. As soon as he begins his descent, he gains kinetic energy as the gravitational force (his weight) pulls him downward. Thus, his initial elevated position represents a form of *stored energy;* we call it **gravitational potential energy.** Whenever an object moves vertically while a gravitational force (its weight) acts on it, the gravitational potential energy changes. The greater the change in height, the greater is the change in gravitational potential energy.

Kinetic energy, elastic potential energy, and gravitational potential energy are all forms of mechanical energy.

Energy and Money

Earlier, we remarked that even physicists have a hard time defining what energy *is*. You may now feel that same difficulty. What *is* this entity that goes from object to object and from one form to another? An analogy that you're probably familiar with is *money*. Money takes many forms, such as a coin, a bill, and an electronic number in a bank's computer. You can store money, or you can spend it to buy things. Even though money is real, it is also in a sense a pure abstraction. Energy, similarly, is both an abstract idea and a very real quantity that is involved in changes and transformations of physical systems. Table 7.1 sums up this analogy between money and energy.

Conservation of Energy

In discussing energy relations, we'll often use the concept of a **system.** A system usually consists of one or more objects that can interact, move, and undergo deformations. In general, a system can interact with its surroundings. In the special case where a system has *no* interaction with its surroundings, we call it an **isolated system.** As we mentioned earlier, the principle of conservation of energy states that **the total energy in any isolated system is constant, no matter what happens within the system.** Energy cannot be created or destroyed. This statement is believed to be an *absolute* conservation law; no exception has ever been observed. It is one of the core principles of physics.

Here's another example of energy relations: Suppose we use a slingshot to shoot a rock straight upward (Figure 7.4). For the present, we'll ignore air resistance. Initially, the rock sits in the pouch of the stretched sling (Figure 7.4a). At this time, the sling's stretched elastic bands hold elastic potential energy. When the pouch is released, the sling propels the rock upward. The sequence in Figure 7.4b begins where the rock has just lost contact with the pouch. Most of the elastic potential energy that was stored in the sling has now become kinetic energy of the rock. As the rock rises, it slows; the gravitational potential energy of the system increases as the rock's kinetic energy decreases. The total energy of the system is constant, but there is a transformation from kinetic energy to gravitational potential energy. At the highest point in the rock's path, it comes to rest momentarily and has zero kinetic energy. At this point, all of the energy is gravitational potential energy. As the rock falls, the gravitational potential energy again becomes kinetic energy. Every change in the system represents a transformation or transfer of energy, but *the total* mechanical energy (kinetic plus potential) remains the same.

Dissipation of Mechanical Energy

Real-world systems often include interactions that allow mechanical energy to be transformed into *non*mechanical types of energy. In the case of the slingshot, for instance, we ignored air drag, which would remove kinetic energy from the system without any compensating increase in potential energy. And when the rock hits the ground, all its kinetic energy disappears, and we have a rock sitting on the ground. What became of this lost mechanical energy?

Most of the mechanical energy of this system goes into slightly warming the rock, the air through which it passes, and the ground the rock strikes. To understand this transformation, think about a brick kicked across the floor. As the brick slides, friction eventually brings it to a halt. On a microscopic level, the brick consists of molecules vibrating randomly, held together by a web of springlike bonds (Figure 7.5). *The hotter an object, the more strongly its molecules vibrate.* This random, atomic-scale vibration is a form of energy called **internal energy.** On a microscopic scale, internal energy consists of the kinetic and potential energies of individual molecules, but it is useful to distinguish it from energy of position and motion of macroscopic (large-scale) objects.

When two objects slide against each other, they catch and tug on each other. These interactions cause the surface molecules of each object to vibrate more strongly. As shown in Figure 7.6, when friction slows a sliding block, the block's kinetic energy is transformed into internal energy of random vibrations of molecules in the block, the floor, and the surrounding air.

In our slingshot example, the rock may lose kinetic energy to air drag (a form of friction). Figure 7.7 shows the effect of air drag on a tennis ball. As the ball passes through air, some of its kinetic energy is transferred to the air, increasing the random motion of the air molecules. Thus, air drag converts some of an object's kinetic energy to internal energy of both the air and the surface of the moving object.

Any force, such as friction, that turns mechanical energy into nonmechanical forms of energy, is called a **dissipative** force, because it dissipates (reduces) the mechanical energy in a system, converting it to other forms of energy.

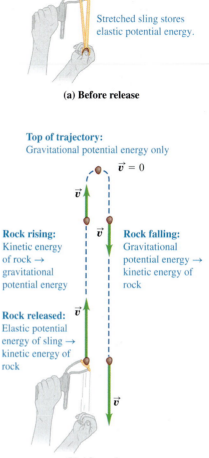

(a) Before release

Stretched sling stores elastic potential energy.

Top of trajectory: Gravitational potential energy only

$\vec{v} = 0$

Rock rising: Kinetic energy of rock → gravitational potential energy

Rock falling: Gravitational potential energy → kinetic energy of rock

Rock released: Elastic potential energy of sling → kinetic energy of rock

(b) After release

▲ **FIGURE 7.4** Energy is conserved as it is first transferred from a slingshot to a rock and then transformed between kinetic energy and gravitational potential energy during the rock's flight.

▶ **Efficient locomotion through springs.** The hopping gait of kangaroos is exceptionally energy efficient. Much of this efficiency comes from the fact that kangaroo's hind legs are, in effect, big pogo sticks. The massive tendons you see in the photo are elastic, like stiff rubber bands. At the end of each hop, the impact stretches these tendons, transforming energy of motion into elastic potential energy. This stored energy helps to launch the animal on its next hop, thus transforming back to kinetic energy. Because most of the kinetic energy from each hop is saved and reused, the kangaroo's muscles need to add only a little kinetic energy at the start of each hop.

Typical solid material —

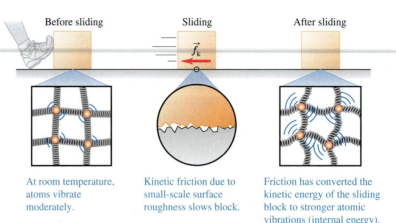

Before sliding

Sliding

After sliding

$\vec{f}_k$

At room temperature, atoms vibrate moderately.

Kinetic friction due to small-scale surface roughness slows block.

Friction has converted the kinetic energy of the sliding block to stronger atomic vibrations (internal energy).

▲ **FIGURE 7.6** How friction converts kinetic energy to internal energy. The "atomic-scale" view in the square insets represents a far higher level of magnification than the small-scale roughness in the middle inset.

The atoms and molecules of a solid can be thought of as particles vibrating randomly on springlike bonds. This random vibration is an example of **internal energy**. The stronger the vibration, the hotter is the object.

▲ **FIGURE 7.5** A simple model of internal energy in a solid.

NOTE ▶ When we speak of "dissipation of mechanical energy," we really mean conversion of mechanical energy into other forms. Physicists and engineers sometimes say that a system "loses" mechanical energy. The energy isn't really lost; mechanical energy is transformed into nonmechanical energy, but the total energy (mechanical and nonmechanical) doesn't change. ◀

Let's summarize the key points we've established in this section:

- Energy can take various forms. In this chapter, we'll concentrate on kinetic energy, gravitational potential energy, and elastic potential energy, all of which are forms of mechanical energy.
- The total energy (mechanical plus nonmechanical) of an isolated system is *always* conserved. It can be transferred between objects or transformed into different forms, but its total amount remains the same.
- Mechanical energy can be dissipated to nonmechanical forms of energy. For instance, friction dissipates kinetic energy, converting it to internal energy.

Undisturbed air ahead of the ball. The lines are thin smoke streams.

In the ball's wake, the air's motion is stronger and more random.

▲ **FIGURE 7.7** The motion of air in the wake of a tennis ball. This photo is from a wind-tunnel study of the aerodynamics of tennis balls at typical court speeds of over 100 mi/hr. The wind tunnel blows air past a fixed ball, but the effects are exactly the same as for a ball moving through still air. The lines in the air are due to thin smoke streams that are used to make the air's motion visible.

7.2 Work

In everyday usage, *work* is any activity that requires muscular or mental exertion. Physicists have a much more specific definition, involving a force acting on an object while the object undergoes a displacement. The importance of the concept of work stems from the fact that, in any motion of a particle, the change in *kinetic energy* of the particle equals the total work done by the forces acting on it. We'll develop this relationship in Section 7.3; but first, let's learn how to calculate work in a variety of situations.

The simplest case is straight-line motion of an object acted on by a constant force $\vec{F}$. When the displacement $\vec{s}$ and force $\vec{F}$ have the same direction (Figure 7.8), we define the work W done by the force as the product of the magnitudes of these two quantities ($W = Fs$). More generally, if the force makes an angle ϕ with the displacement (Figure 7.9), then the component of the force along the direction of the displacement is $F_\parallel = F\cos\phi$ (where the subscript $\parallel$ means *parallel,* indicating that this component is parallel to the direction of displacement). We can now define work as the product of the *component* of force in the direction of displacement and the magnitude s of the displacement.

$\vec{F}$

x

$\vec{s}$

▲ **FIGURE 7.8** Work is the product of the magnitudes of a displacement $\vec{s}$ and a constant force $\vec{F}$ in the direction of $\vec{s}$.

$F_\perp$ does *no* work on the car.

$F_\perp = F\sin\phi$

$\vec{F}$

$F_\parallel$ does work on the car.

ϕ

$F_\parallel = F\cos\phi$

$\vec{s}$

▲ **FIGURE 7.9** The work done by a constant force $\vec{F}$ during a straight-line displacement $\vec{s}$ is $(F\cos\phi)s$.

Definition of work

When an object undergoes a displacement $\vec{s}$ with magnitude s along a straight line, while a constant force $\vec{F}$ with magnitude F, making an angle ϕ with $\vec{s}$ (Figure 7.9), acts on the object, the **work** done by the force on the object is

$$W = F_\parallel s = (F\cos\phi)s. \tag{7.1}$$

Unit: joule (J). In SI units, the unit of force is the newton, the unit of distance is the meter, and their product is the *newton-meter* $(\text{N} \cdot \text{m})$. This combination appears so often in mechanics that we give it a special name, the **joule** (abbreviated J and pronounced "jewel"). It was named in honor of the English physicist James Prescott Joule:

1 joule = 1 newton-meter   or   1 J = 1 N · m.

In the British system, the unit of force is the pound (lb), the unit of distance is the foot, and the unit of work is the *foot-pound* $(\text{ft} \cdot \text{lb})$. The following conversions are useful:

1 J = 0.7376 ft · lb,   1 ft · lb = 1.356 J.

▲ **Low and Sleek.** Many engineering problems boil down to reducing dissipative forces. For instance, a standard bicycle places the rider in a position that catches a lot of wind, creating significant air drag. On a recumbent bicycle, the rider's low profile causes much less air drag. The real-life difference is so great that, in 1933, a second-string racer rode a recumbent at nearly 30 miles an hour, smashing by 10% a record almost 20 years old. After that, recumbent bicycles were banned from racing. A *fairing*—an aerodynamic shell—further reduces air drag and thus increases speed even more; faired recumbent bicycles can travel 36 mph and can break 65 mph for short distances.

EXAMPLE 7.1 Pushing a stalled car

Steve is trying to impress Elaine with his new car, but the engine dies in the middle of an intersection. While Elaine steers, Steve pushes the car 19 m to clear the intersection. If he pushes with a constant force with magnitude 210 N (about 47 lb), how much work does he do on the car **(a)** if he pushes in the direction the car is heading and **(b)** if he pushes at 30° to that direction?

SOLUTION

SET UP AND SOLVE From Equation 7.1, $W = F\cos\phi\, s$.

Part (a): When Steve pushes in the direction the car is headed, $\phi = 0$, $\cos\phi = 1$, and

$W = (F\cos\phi)s = (210\,\text{N})(1)(19\,\text{m}) = 4.0 \times 10^3\,\text{J}.$

Part (b): In this case, $\phi = 30°$, $\cos\phi = 0.866$, and

$W = (F\cos\phi)s = (210\,\text{N})(0.866)(19\,\text{m}) = 3.5 \times 10^3\,\text{J}.$

REFLECT In part (a), Steve pushed the car in the direction he wanted it to go. In (b), he pushed at an angle of 30° to that direction. Only the component of force in the direction of the car's motion, $F\cos\phi$ is effective in moving the car.

Practice Problem: What force would be required for Steve to do as much work when he pushes at $\phi = 30°$ as when he pushed in the $\phi = 0$ direction? *Answer:* 240 N.

It's important to understand that work is a *scalar* quantity, even though it is calculated by using two vector quantities (force and displacement). A 5 N force toward the east acting on an object that moves 6 m to the east does exactly the same 30 J of work as a 5 N force toward the north acting on an object that moves 6 m to the north. Work can be positive or negative. When the force has a component in the *same direction* as the displacement (ϕ between zero and 90°), $\cos\phi$ in

5.1

The force has a component in the direction of displacement:
- The work on the object is positive. (The object speeds up.)
- $W = F_\parallel s = (F\cos\phi)s$

The force has a component opposite to the direction of displacement:
- The work on the object is negative. (The object slows down.)
- $W = F_\parallel s = (F\cos\phi)s$
- Mathematically, $W < 0$ because $F\cos\phi$ is negative for $90° < \phi < 270°$.

The force is perpendicular to the direction of displacement:
- The force does *no* work on the object.
- More generally, if a force acting on an object has a component $F_\perp$ perpendicular to the object's displacement, that component does no work on the object.

▲ **FIGURE 7.10** Three cases in which a single constant force does work on an object.

Equation 7.1 is positive, and the work W is *positive* (Figure 7.10a). When the force has a component *opposite* to the displacement (ϕ between 90° and 270°), $\cos\phi$ is negative, and the work is *negative* (Figure 7.10b). When the force is *perpendicular* to the displacement, $\phi = 90°$, and the work done by the force is *zero* (Figure 7.10c).

Conceptual Analysis 7.1

Work and orbital motion

A communications satellite moves in a circular orbit at constant speed in response to gravity, as shown in Figure 7.11. Which of the following statements is correct?

A. The earth does positive work on the satellite.
B. The earth does negative work on the satellite.
C. The earth does no work on the satellite.
D. Once a coordinate system is specified, the work changes sign every half orbit, so that the average work is zero.

▲ **FIGURE 7.11** A satellite in a circular orbit.

SOLUTION In circular gravitational orbits, the force on the orbiting object is always perpendicular to the object's velocity, as indicated in the figure. The displacement of the object is always along the direction of the velocity, so the force is always perpendicular to the displacement. Therefore, $F_\parallel = 0$, and the work is zero for any displacement along the orbit. This result still might seem confusing, since your intuition may correctly guess that orbiting objects have energy. But remember that *work is the transfer of energy that changes an object's speed.* Since the speed of an object is constant in uniform circular motion, $W = 0$, and all answers other than choice C can be rejected. As we'll see later, energy is required to set an object in orbital motion, and the orbital system holds onto this energy, but no additional energy needs to be supplied to maintain the object in its orbit. Our solar system has been executing orbital motion for about 5 billion years and does not require an energy source to maintain its orbits.

We always speak of work done *by* a specific force *on* a particular object. Always be sure to specify exactly what force is doing the work you are talking about. When a spring is stretched, the work done on the spring by the stretching force is positive. When an object is lifted, the work done on the object by the lifting force is positive. However, the work done by the *gravitational* force on an object being lifted is *negative* because the (downward) gravitational force is opposite to the (upward) displacement. You might think it is "hard work" to hold this book out at arm's length for five minutes, but you aren't actually doing any work at all on the book, because there is no displacement. Even when you walk with constant velocity on a level floor while carrying the book, you do no work on it, because the (vertical) supporting force you exert on the book has no component in the direction of the (horizontal) motion. In this case, in Equation 7.1, $\phi = 90°$ and $\cos\phi = 0$. When an object slides along a surface, the work done by the normal force acting on the object is zero; and when an object moves in a circle, the work done by the centripetal force on the object is also zero. (See Figure 7.11.).

How do we calculate work when several forces act on an object? One way is to use Equation 7.1 to compute the work done by each separate force. Then, because work is a scalar quantity, the *total* work W_{total} done on the object by all the forces is the algebraic sum of the quantities of work done by the individual forces. An alternative route to finding the total work is to compute the vector sum (resultant) of the forces and then use this vector sum as $\vec{F}$ in Equation 7.1.

EXAMPLE 7.2 **Sliding down a ramp**

A package with mass m is unloaded from a truck with an inclined ramp, as shown in Figure 7.12. The ramp has rollers that eliminate friction, and the truck unloads the package from an initial height h. The ramp is inclined at an angle β. Find an algebraic expression in terms of these quantities for the work done on the package during its trip down the ramp.

▲ **FIGURE 7.12** A package sliding down a friction-less ramp.

SOLUTION

SET UP Figure 7.13 shows our sketches. We diagram the situation, indicating the package's displacement $\vec{s}$ and the height h. Then we draw a free-body diagram for the package, pointing the x axis in the direction of the displacement. Only the weight has a component parallel to the direction of displacement, so only this force does work on the package. The normal force $\vec{n}$ is perpendicular to the displacement, so it does no work on the package.

SOLVE We solve for the work done on the package by the x (parallel) component of weight. Notice, however, that the angle we are given, β, is *not* the angle between the direction of displacement and the weight force (ϕ in Figure 7.13b). To use Equation 7.1 directly, we could define $\phi = 90 - \beta$. Instead, we choose to use β directly, modifying the trigonometry to fit. Because weight is the only force doing work on the package, the work done on the package is

$$W = (F\sin\beta)s$$
$$= (mg\sin\beta)s.$$

The statement of the problem gives the height h rather than the distance s measured along the ramp, but we can solve for h by recognizing from the geometry in Figure 7.13 that $s\sin\beta = h$. Therefore,

$$W = (mg\sin\beta)s = mgh.$$

REFLECT Because we are neglecting friction, the only force that does work on the package is its weight mg. We've found that the work W is the product of the weight mg and the vertical distance h through which the package falls. In Section 7.5, we'll restate this result in terms of potential energy, which we haven't yet defined precisely. We'll find that the work done on the package is the negative of the change in the potential energy. When the force of gravity does a positive amount of work $W = mgh$ on the package, the potential energy must decrease by the same amount. The work done on the package by gravity depends only on the change in the package's vertical position h.

(a) Sketch of situation (b) Free-body diagram of package

▲ **FIGURE 7.13** Our sketches for this problem.

EXAMPLE 7.3 **Work done by several forces**

Farmer Johnson hitches his tractor to a sled loaded with firewood and pulls it a distance of 20.0 m along level frozen ground (Figure 7.14a). The total weight of sled and load is 14,700 N. The tractor exerts a constant force $\vec{F}_T$ with magnitude 5000 N at an angle of $\phi = 36.9°$ above the horizontal, as shown. A constant 3500 N friction force opposes the motion. Find the work done on the sled by each force individually and the total work done on the sled by all the forces.

SOLUTION

SET UP Figure 7.14b shows a free-body diagram and a coordinate system, identifying all the forces acting on the sled. As in the preceding example, we point the x axis in the direction of displacement.

SOLVE The work W_w done by the weight is zero because its direction is perpendicular to the displacement. (The angle between the two directions is 90°, and the cosine of the angle is zero.) For the same reason, the work W_n done by the normal force $\vec{n}$ (which, incidentally, is *not* equal in magnitude to the weight) is also zero. So $W_w = W_n = 0$.

That leaves F_T and f. From Equation 7.1, the work W_T done by the tractor is (with $\cos \phi = \cos 36.9° = 0.800$)

$$W_T = (F_T \cos \phi)s$$
$$= (5000 \text{ N})(0.800)(20.0 \text{ m}) = 80,000 \text{ N} \cdot \text{m} = 80.0 \text{ kJ}.$$

The friction force f is opposite to the displacement, so, for this force, $\phi = 180°$ and $\cos \phi = -1$. The work W_f done by the friction force is

$$W_f = fs \cos 180° = -(3500 \text{ N})(20.0 \text{ m})$$
$$= -70,000 \text{ N} \cdot \text{m} = -70.0 \text{ kJ}.$$

The total work W_{total} done by all of the forces on the sled is the algebraic sum (*not* the vector sum) of the work done by the individual forces:

$$W_{total} = W_T + W_w + W_n + W_f$$
$$= 80.0 \text{ kJ} + 0 + 0 + (-70.0 \text{ kJ}) = 10.0 \text{ kJ}.$$

Alternative Solution: In the alternative approach, we first find the vector sum (resultant) of the forces and then use it to compute the total work. The vector sum is best found by using components. From Figure 7.14b,

$$\Sigma F_x = (5000 \text{ N}) \cos 36.9° - 3500 \text{ N} = 500 \text{ N},$$
$$\Sigma F_y = (5000 \text{ N}) \sin 36.9° + n + (-14,700 \text{ N}).$$

We don't really need the second equation; we know that the y component of force is perpendicular to the displacement, so it does no work. Besides, there is no y component of acceleration, so ΣF_y has to be zero anyway. The work done by the total x component is therefore the total work:

$$W_{total} = (500 \text{ N})(20.0 \text{ m}) = 10,000 \text{ J} = 10.0 \text{ kJ}.$$

This is the same result that we found by computing the work of each force separately.

REFLECT Be sure you understand why the two solution methods are equivalent and give the same result.

Practice Problem: Suppose the tractor pulls horizontally on the sled instead of at an angle of 36.9°. As a result, the magnitude of the friction force increases to 4400 N. What is the total work done on the sled? *Answer:* 1.20×10^4 J.

(a)

(b) Free-body diagram of sled

▲ **FIGURE 7.14** (a) A tractor pulls a sled. (b) Our sketch for this problem.

7.3 Work and Kinetic Energy

Now we're ready to develop the relation between the work done on an object and that object's change in kinetic energy. This important relationship is called the *work–energy theorem* (more precisely, the work–kinetic energy theorem).

Let's consider a particle with mass m moving along the x axis under the action of a constant net force with magnitude F_{total} directed along the x axis. The particle's acceleration is constant and is given by Newton's second law, $F_{total} = ma$. Suppose the particle's speed increases from v_i to v_f while the particle undergoes a displacement s from point x_i to x_f. Using the constant-acceleration equation (Equation 2.13) and replacing v_{0x} by v_i, v_x by v_f, and $(x - x_0)$ by s, we have

$$v_f^2 = v_i^2 + 2as,$$
$$a = \frac{v_f^2 - v_i^2}{2s}.$$

When we multiply the last equation by m and replace ma with F_{total}, we obtain

$$F_{total} = ma = m\frac{v_f^2 - v_i^2}{2s}$$

and

$$F_{total}s = \tfrac{1}{2}mv_f^2 - \tfrac{1}{2}mv_i^2. \tag{7.2}$$

The product $F_{total}s$ is the work done by the net force F_{total} and thus is equal to the total work W_{total} done by all the forces. In Section 7.1, we defined the quantity $\tfrac{1}{2}mv^2$ as kinetic energy. We'll denote this quantity as K. Then

$$K = \tfrac{1}{2}mv^2. \tag{7.3}$$

The first term on the right side of Equation 7.2 is the final kinetic energy of the particle, $K_f = \tfrac{1}{2}mv_f^2$ (after the displacement). The second term is the initial kinetic energy, $K_i = \tfrac{1}{2}mv_i^2$, and the difference between these terms is the *change* in the particle's kinetic energy during the displacement s. So Equation 7.2 relates the particle's change in kinetic energy to the work done by the forces that act on the particle.

Work–energy theorem

The kinetic energy K of a particle with mass m moving with speed v is $K = \tfrac{1}{2}mv^2$. During any displacement of the particle, the work done by the net external force on it is equal to its change in kinetic energy, or

$$W_{total} = K_f - K_i = \Delta K. \tag{7.4}$$

This theorem is the foundation for most of what follows in this chapter.

Kinetic energy, like work, is a scalar quantity. It can never be negative, although work can be either positive or negative. The kinetic energy of a moving particle depends only on its speed (the magnitude of its velocity), not on the direction of its motion. A car (viewed as a particle) has the same kinetic energy when going north at 5 m/s as when going east at 5 m/s. The *change* in kinetic energy during any displacement is determined by the total work W_{total} done by all the forces acting on the particle. When W_{total} is *positive,* the particle speeds up during the displacement, K_f is greater than K_i, and the kinetic energy *increases.* When W_{total} is *negative,* the kinetic energy and speed *decrease;* and when $W_{total} = 0$, K is *constant.*

In SI units, m is measured in kilograms and v in meters per second, so the quantity $\tfrac{1}{2}mv^2$ (kinetic energy) has the units $kg \cdot m^2/s^2$. From Equation 7.2 or Equation 7.4, kinetic energy must have the same units as work, which we saw is measured in joules (newton-meters). To confirm that these units are the same, we recall from Newton's second law that $1\ N = 1\ kg \cdot m/s^2$, so

$$1\ J = 1\ N \cdot m = 1(kg \cdot m/s^2) \cdot m = 1\ kg \cdot m^2/s^2.$$

The joule is the SI unit of both work and kinetic energy and, indeed, as we will see later, of all kinds of energy. In the British system,

$$1 \text{ ft} \cdot \text{lb} = 1 \text{ ft} \cdot \text{slug} \cdot \text{ft}/\text{s}^2 = 1 \text{ slug} \cdot \text{ft}^2/\text{s}^2.$$

NOTE ▶ In calculating W_{total} for Equation 7.4, remember what we learned in Section 7.2: First, only the component of net force parallel to the displacement does work on the particle; second, W_{total} can be calculated either as the work done by the net force or as the algebraic sum of the amounts of work done by the individual forces. ◄

Conceptual Analysis 7.2

Work and kinetic energy

Two blocks of ice, one twice as heavy as the other, are at rest on a frozen lake. A person pushes each block a distance of 5 m with a constant force (the same magnitude of force for each block). Assume that friction may be neglected. The kinetic energy of the light block after the push is

A. smaller than that of the heavy block.
B. equal to that of the heavy block.
C. larger than that of the heavy block.

SOLUTION Three forces act on each block: its weight, the normal force exerted by the surface, and the push applied by the person. The weight and the normal force are perpendicular to the displacement, so they do no work on the block. Only the person's push does work on each block. Both this force and the displacement are the same for the two blocks, so the amounts of work done on them are equal. The work–energy theorem, $W_{total} = K_f - K_i = \Delta K$, says that the change in each block's kinetic energy equals the net work done on it. Both blocks have the same initial kinetic energy ($K_i = 0$) and have equal amounts of work done on them. Therefore, they must have equal final kinetic energies K_f. Answer B is correct.

PROBLEM-SOLVING STRATEGY 7.1 **Work and kinetic energy**

SET UP

1. Draw a free-body diagram; make sure you show all the forces that act on the object. List the forces; represent any unknown forces by algebraic symbols.
2. List the initial and final kinetic energies K_i and K_f. If a quantity such as v_i or v_f is unknown, express it in terms of an algebraic symbol. When you calculate kinetic energies, make sure you use the *mass* of the object, not its *weight*.

SOLVE

3. Calculate the total work done on the object. You can do this in either of two ways: by calculating the work done by each individual force and taking the algebraic sum (usually the easiest method) or by finding the net force and then calculating the work it does on the object. Be sure to check signs. When a force has a component in the same direction as the displacement, its work is positive; when the direction is opposite to the displacement, the work is negative. When force and displacement are perpendicular, the work is zero.
4. Use the relationship $W_{total} = K_f - K_i = \Delta K$; insert the results from the preceding steps and solve for whatever unknown is required.

REFLECT

5. Remember that kinetic energy can never be negative. If you come up with a negative K, you've made a mistake. Maybe you interchanged subscripts i and f or made a sign error in one of the calculations of work.

EXAMPLE 7.4 **Using work and energy to calculate speed**

Let's revisit the sled from Example 7.3. The free-body diagram is shown again in Figure 7.15. We found that the total work done on the sled by all the forces is 10,000 J = 10.0 kJ, so the kinetic energy of the sled must increase by 10.0 kJ. The mass of the sled is $m = (14,700 \text{ N})/(9.80 \text{ m/s}^2) = 1500 \text{ kg}$. Suppose the sled's initial speed v_i is 2.00 m/s. What is its final speed?

Continued

SOLUTION

SET UP Steps 1 and 2 of the problem-solving strategy were done in Example 7.3, where we found that $W_{total} = 10.0$ kJ. The initial kinetic energy K_i is

$$K_i = \tfrac{1}{2}mv_i^2$$
$$= \tfrac{1}{2}(1500 \text{ kg})(2.00 \text{ m/s})^2 = 3000 \text{ kg} \cdot \text{m}^2/\text{s}^2 = 3000 \text{ J}.$$

The final kinetic energy K_f is

$$K_f = \tfrac{1}{2}(1500 \text{ kg})v_f^2,$$

where v_f is the unknown final speed that we want to find.

SOLVE Equation 7.4 gives

$$K_f = K_i + W_{total},$$
$$\tfrac{1}{2}(1500 \text{ kg})v_f^2 = 3000 \text{ J} + 10,000 \text{ J} = 13,000 \text{ J}.$$

Solving for v_f, we find

$$v_f = 4.16 \text{ m/s}.$$

REFLECT This problem can also be done without the work–energy theorem. We can find the acceleration from $F = ma$ and then use the equations of motion with constant acceleration to find v_f. (Recall from Example 7.3 that the sled moves through a displacement of 20.0 m.) We have

$$a = \frac{F}{m} = \frac{4000 \text{ N} - 3500 \text{ N}}{1500 \text{ kg}} = 0.333 \text{ m/s}^2,$$

and

$$v_f^2 = v_i^2 + 2as = (2.0 \text{ m/s})^2 + 2(0.333 \text{ m/s}^2)(20 \text{ m})$$
$$= 17.3 \text{ m}^2/\text{s}^2,$$
$$v_f = 4.16 \text{ m/s}.$$

▲ **FIGURE 7.15** The free-body diagram from Example 7.3.

The work–energy approach lets us avoid the intermediate step of finding the acceleration. You'll find several other examples and problems in this chapter and the next that *can* be done without using energy considerations, but that are easier when energy methods are used. Also, when a problem can be done by two different methods, doing it both ways is always a good way to check your work.

Practice Problem: If the tractor pulls horizontally and the friction force again has magnitude 4400 N, find the magnitude of the force the tractor must exert to make the sled move with constant speed. Verify that in this case the kinetic energy of the sled doesn't change. *Answer:* 4400 N.

EXAMPLE 7.5   Forces on a hammerhead

In a pile driver, a steel hammerhead with mass 200 kg is lifted 3.00 m above the top of a vertical I-beam being driven into the ground (Figure 7.16a). The hammer is then dropped, driving the I-beam 7.40 cm farther into the ground. The vertical rails that guide the hammerhead exert a constant 60.0 N friction force on it. Use the work–energy theorem to find **(a)** the speed of the hammerhead just as it hits the I-beam and **(b)** the average force the hammerhead exerts on the I-beam.

SOLUTION

SET UP Figures 7.16b and 7.16c are free-body diagrams for the hammerhead during two intervals: first, while it falls (from point 1 to point 2 in Figure 7.16a) and second, while it pushes the I-beam (from point 2 to point 3). Because the displacement is vertical, any horizontal forces that may be present do no work. Therefore, our free-body diagrams show only the vertical forces on the hammerhead.

SOLVE The forces on the hammerhead during the 3.00 m drop are its weight, with magnitude $mg = (200 \text{ kg})(9.80 \text{ m/s}^2) = 1960$ N and the upward friction force, with magnitude 60.0 N. The net

downward force on the hammerhead has magnitude 1900 N, and the total work done on it during the 3.00 m drop is

$$W_{total} = (1900 \text{ N})(3.00 \text{ m}) = 5700 \text{ J}.$$

Part (a): In place of our usual subscripts i and f, we'll use 1 and 2, referring to points 1 and 2 in Figure 7.16. The hammerhead is initially at rest (point 1), so its initial kinetic energy K_1 is zero. Equation 7.4 gives

$$W_{total} = K_2 - K_1,$$
$$5700 \text{ J} = \tfrac{1}{2}(200 \text{ kg})v_2^2 - 0,$$
$$v_2 = 7.55 \text{ m/s}.$$

Continued

This is the hammerhead's speed at point 2, just as it hits the beam.

Part (b): We now consider the interval from point 2 to point 3, during which the hammerhead pushes the I-beam through a downward displacement of 7.40 cm. As shown in Figure 7.16c, the hammerhead now also is acted upon by an upward normal force $\vec{n}$ (which we assume is constant). At point 3, where the hammerhead comes to rest, its kinetic energy K_3 is again zero. The work W_n done by the normal force is

$$W_n = (F\cos\phi)s$$
$$= (n\cos 180°)(0.0740 \text{ m}) = n(-1)(0.0740 \text{ m}).$$

The total work done on the hammerhead during its displacement of 0.0740 m is the sum of the work done by the weight, the friction force, and the normal force. We already know that the vector sum of the weight and friction forces has a magnitude of 1900 N, so we sum the work done by that resultant force and by the normal force:

$$W_{\text{total}} = (1900 \text{ N})(0.0740 \text{ m}) + n(0.0740 \text{ m})(-1).$$

The total work is equal to the change in kinetic energy, $K_3 - K_2 = 0 - 5700$ J, so we have

$$(1900 \text{ N} - n)(0.0740 \text{ m}) = 0 - 5700 \text{ J},$$
$$n = 79{,}000 \text{ N}.$$

The force *on* the I-beam is the equal, but opposite, *downward* reaction force of 79,000 N (about 9 tons).

REFLECT The total change in the hammerhead's kinetic energy during the whole process is zero; a relatively small force does positive work over a large distance, and then a much larger force does negative work over a much smaller distance. The same thing happens if you speed your car up gradually and then drive it into a brick wall. The very large force needed to reduce the kinetic energy to zero over a short distance is what does the damage to your car—and possibly to you!

Practice Problem: Suppose the pile is driven 15.0 cm instead of 7.4 cm. What force (assumed constant) is exerted on it? *Answer:* 39,900 N.

(a)

(b) Free-body diagram for falling hammerhead

(c) Free-body diagram for hammerhead pushing I-beam

▲ **FIGURE 7.16**

NOTE ▶ Because we used Newton's laws in deriving the work–kinetic energy theorem, we must use the theorem only in an inertial frame of reference. The speeds we use to compute the kinetic energies and the distances we use to compute work *must* be measured in an inertial frame. But the work–energy theorem is valid in *all* inertial frames. For a given situation, the work and kinetic energies will be different in different frames of reference because the speed of an object is different in different frames. ◀

7.4 Work Done by a Varying Force

In Section 7.2, we defined work done by a *constant* force. But what happens when you stretch a spring? The more you stretch it, the harder you have to pull, so the force is *not* constant as the spring is stretched. You can think of many other situations in which a force that varies, in both magnitude and direction, acts on an

▶ **Nature's rubber bands.** Biologists used to believe that tendons and ligaments were simple straps, without significant elasticity. We now know that they are often elastic, like very stiff rubber bands, and that their elasticity is central to their function in the body. The photo shows the microscopic basis of tendon and ligament elasticity. The fibers you see consist of collagen, a tough, fibrous protein that is the main constituent of tendon and ligament tissue. Notice that the collagen fibers are wavy. As the tissue stretches, these wavy fibers straighten out; then they pull back to their equilibrium wavy configuration when released.

object moving along a curved path. We need to be able to compute the work done by the force in these more general situations.

To add only one complication at a time, let's consider straight-line motion under the influence of a force that is directed along the line, but that may change in magnitude as the object moves. For example, imagine a train on a straight track, with the engineer constantly changing the locomotive's throttle setting or applying the brakes. Suppose a particle moves along the x axis from point x_i to point x_f, as shown in Figure 7.17a. Figure 7.17b is a graph of the x component of force as a function of the particle's coordinate x. To find the work done by this force, we divide the total displacement into small segments Δx_1, Δx_2, and so on (Figure 7.17c). We approximate the work done by the force during segment Δx_1 as the average force F_{1x} in that segment, multiplied by its length Δx_1. We do this for each segment and then add the results for all the segments. The work done by the force in the total displacement from x_i to x_f is approximately

$$W = F_{1x} \Delta x_1 + F_{2x} \Delta x_2 + F_{3x} \Delta x_3 + \cdots.$$

We see that $F_{1x} \Delta x_1$ represents the *area* of the first vertical strip in Figure 7.17c, $F_{2x} \Delta x_2$ the area of the second, and so on. The sum represents the area under the curve of Figure 7.17b between x_i and x_f. **On a graph of force as a function of position, the total work done by the force is represented by the area under the curve between the initial and final positions.**

Now let's apply this analysis to a stretched spring. To keep a spring stretched an amount x beyond its unstretched length, we have to apply a force with magnitude F at each end (Figure 7.18). As we learned in Chapter 5, if the elongation is not too great, the spring obeys Hooke's law; that is, F is directly proportional to x, or

$$F = kx, \tag{7.5}$$

where k is a constant called the force constant (or spring constant) of the spring. Equation 7.5 shows that the units of k are force divided by distance. In SI, the units are N/m.

Suppose we apply forces with equal magnitude and opposite direction to the ends of the spring and gradually increase the forces, starting from zero. We hold the left end stationary; the force at this end does no work on the spring. The force at the moving end *does* do work. Figure 7.19 is a graph of the x component of force, F_x, as a function of x (the elongation of the spring). The total work done on the spring by the force F_x when the elongation goes from zero to a maximum value X is represented by the area under the graph (the shaded triangle in the figure). The area is equal to half the product of the base (X) and altitude (kX), or

$$W = \tfrac{1}{2}(X)(kX) = \tfrac{1}{2}kX^2. \tag{7.6}$$

This result also says that the work is equal to the *average* force $kX/2$, multiplied by the total displacement X. Thus, the total work is proportional to the *square* of the final elongation X. When the elongation is doubled, the total work needed increases by a factor of four.

The spring also exerts a force on the hand, which moves during the stretching process. The displacement of the hand is the same as that of the

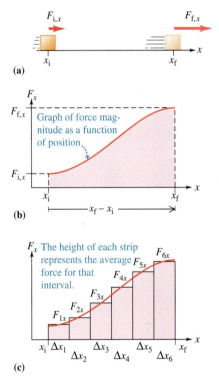

Particle moving from x_i to x_f in response to a changing force in the x direction

(a)

F_x

Graph of force magnitude as a function of position.

(b)

F_x The height of each strip represents the average force for that interval.

(c)

▲ **FIGURE 7.17** Graphs of force as a function of displacement for a particle moving in response to a varying force.

▲ **FIGURE 7.18** The force needed to stretch an ideal spring is proportional to the elongation: $F_x = kx$ (Hooke's law).

The area under the curve represents the work done on the spring as the spring is stretched from $x = 0$ to a maximum value X:

$$W = \tfrac{1}{2}kX^2$$

▲ **FIGURE 7.19** The work done in stretching a spring is equal to the area of the shaded triangle.

moving end of the spring, but the force on it is opposite in direction to the force on the spring, because the two forces form an action–reaction pair. Thus, the work done *on* the hand *by* the spring is the negative of the work done on the spring, namely, $-\tfrac{1}{2}kX^2$. In problems involving work and its relation to kinetic energy, we will nearly always want to find the work done *by* a force *on* the object under study, and we have to be careful to write work quantities with the correct sign.

Now, suppose the spring is stretched a distance x_i at the start. Then the work we have to do on it to stretch it to a greater elongation x_f is

$$W = \tfrac{1}{2}kx_f^2 - \tfrac{1}{2}kx_i^2. \tag{7.7}$$

If the spring has spaces between the coils when it is unstretched, then it can be compressed as well as stretched, and Hooke's law holds for compression as well as stretching. In this case, F and x in Equation 7.5 are both negative, the force again has the same direction as the displacement, and the work done by F is again positive. So the total work is still given by Equation 7.6 or 7.7, even when X or either or both of x_i and x_f are negative.

Quantitative Analysis 7.3 **Stretching a spring**

A spring is stretched from $x = 0$ to $x = 2a$, as shown in Figure 7.20a. Is more energy required to stretch the spring through the first half of this displacement (from $x = 0$ to $x = a$) or through the second half (from $x = a$ to $x = 2a$)?

SOLUTION Hooke's law $(F_x = kx)$ tells us that the force required to stretch a spring increases with increasing elongation. Thus, more energy is required to stretch the spring through the second half of its displacement. The graph in Figure 7.20b shows how much more. As we've seen, the area under a graph of force versus displacement for an object represents the work done by the force on the object. In this case, the area under the curve for the second half of the displacement can be divided into three triangles, each of which has an area equal to that under the curve for the first half. Thus, three times as much energy is needed to stretch the spring through the second half of the displacement than through the first half.

(a) Stretching a spring through two equal halves of a total displacement $2a$

This half of the area can be divided into three triangles, each equal in area to the triangle under the first half of the curve.

(b) Force-versus-distance curve for the two halves of the displacement

▲ **FIGURE 7.20**

EXAMPLE 7.6 **Work done on a spring scale**

A woman weighing 600 N steps on a bathroom scale containing a heavy spring (Figure 7.21). The spring compresses by 1.0 cm under her weight. Find the force constant of the spring and the total work done on it during the compression.

Because of our choice of axis, both the force component and displacement are negative. The work on the spring is positive.

▶ **FIGURE 7.21** Compressing the spring of a bathroom scale.

Continued

SOLUTION

SET UP AND SOLVE If positive values of x correspond to elongation, then $x = -0.010$ m when $F_x = -600$ N. We need to use Equation 7.5 (Hooke's law) to find the force constant k and then use Equation 7.6 to find the work W done on the spring. We have

$$k = \frac{F_x}{x} = \frac{-600 \text{ N}}{-0.010 \text{ m}} = 6.0 \times 10^4 \text{ N/m,}$$
$$W = \tfrac{1}{2}kX^2 = \tfrac{1}{2}(6.0 \times 10^4 \text{ N/m})(-0.010 \text{ m})^2$$
$$= 3.0 \text{ N} \cdot \text{m} = 3.0 \text{ J.}$$

REFLECT The force of gravity is the woman's weight, a constant 600 N. As she steps on the scale, the force pushing down on the top of the spring varies from 0 to 600 N, with an average value of 300 N, as it is compressed 0.010 m. The total work done on the spring is the average force (300 N) multiplied by the displacement (0.010 m), or 3.0 J.

Practice Problem: Suppose we want to modify the scale to permit a weight of 900 N when the spring is compressed 1.00 cm. What should the force constant of the spring be? *Answer:* 9.0×10^4 N/m.

7.5 Potential Energy

An object gains or loses kinetic energy because it interacts with other objects that exert forces on it. We've learned that, during any interaction, the change in a particle's kinetic energy is equal to the total work done on the particle by the forces that act on it during the interaction.

But there are many situations in which it seems as though kinetic energy has been *stored* in a system, to be recovered later. It's like a savings account in a bank: You deposit money, and then you can draw it out later. When we raise the steel hammerhead of Example 7.5 into the air, we're storing energy in the system, energy that is later converted into kinetic energy as the hammer is released and falls back down. Or consider the humble pogo stick, in which a spring is compressed as you jump on the stick and then rebounds, launching you into the air. Or a mousetrap, in which the spring stores energy that is released when the trigger is tripped. And so on.

All these examples point to the idea of an energy associated with the *position* of bodies in a system. In some cases, changes in this energy may accompany opposite changes in kinetic energy in such a way that the *total* energy remains constant, or is *conserved*. Energy associated with position is called potential energy, and forces that can be associated with a potential energy are called **conservative forces.** A system in which the total mechanical energy, kinetic and potential, is constant, is called a **conservative system.** As we'll see, there is potential energy associated with an object's weight and its height above the ground. There is also potential energy associated with *elastic* deformations of an object, such as stretching or compressing a spring (Figure 7.21).

Another way to look at potential energy is that "potential" refers to the potential for a force to do work on an object. When the pile-driver hammer is raised, the earth's gravitational force (the hammer's weight) gains the *opportunity* to do work on the hammer as it falls. When we set a mousetrap, we give it the opportunity to do work on whatever is in its way when the spring snaps back. So potential energy is associated with the opportunity, or potential, to do work.

The kinetic energy of a falling object increases as it drops because a force (the earth's gravity, or, in other words, the object's weight) is doing positive work on it. Remember, $W_{\text{total}} = \Delta K$. Another way to say this is that the kinetic energy increases because the potential energy decreases. When the force we are considering (such as the pile-driver's weight) does positive work, the potential energy must decrease. So we can think of potential energy as a shorthand way to calculate the work done by some of the forces in a system.

Gravitational Potential Energy

To begin our detailed study of potential energy, let's apply the work–energy theorem to the work done on an object when it moves under the action of the earth's

▲ **Energy-efficient transport.** In Indonesia and other countries, some women are known to carry loads of up to 70% of their body weight in baskets on their heads. Westerners who attempt to carry a load in this way expend almost twice as much energy as people who do it normally. This puzzling difference prompted an additional study, which found that, when Westerners walk, they have more up-and-down motion than do women accustomed to carrying baskets. For larger vertical motion, more work is done by gravity on the load; thus, more energy is required to raise the load a higher distance against the force of gravity.

(a)

(b)

▲ **FIGURE 7.22** The work done by the gravitational force w as an object moves downward or upward changes the gravitational potential energy.

gravitational force (again, the object's weight). This will lead directly to the concept of *gravitational potential energy*—energy associated with the *position* of the object relative to the earth.

Let's consider an object with mass m that moves along the (vertical) y axis (Figure 7.22). The forces acting on the object are its weight, with magnitude $w = mg$, and possibly some other forces; we call the resultant of all the other forces $\vec{F}_{\text{other}}$. We'll assume that the object stays close enough to earth's surface that the weight is constant. We want to find the work done by the weight when the object drops from a height y_i above the origin to a smaller height y_f (Figure 7.22a). The weight and displacement are in the same direction, so the work W_{grav} done on the object by its weight is positive and is given by

$$W_{\text{grav}} = Fs = mg(y_i - y_f) = mgy_i - mgy_f. \tag{7.8}$$

This expression also gives the correct work when the object moves upward and y_f is greater than y_i (Figure 7.22b). In that case, the quantity $(y_i - y_f)$ is negative, and W_{grav} is negative because the weight and displacement are opposite in direction.

Equation 7.8 shows that we can express W_{grav} in terms of the values of the quantity mgy at the beginning and at the end of the displacement. This quantity, the product of the weight mg and the height y above the origin of coordinates, is called the gravitational potential energy and is denoted by U_{grav}.

Definition of gravitational potential energy

When an object with mass m is a vertical distance y above the origin of coordinates, in a uniform gravitational field g, the gravitational potential energy U_{grav} of the system is

$$U_{\text{grav}} = mgy. \tag{7.9}$$

Like work and all forms of energy, gravitational potential energy is measured in joules.

In Figure 7.22, the initial value of U_{grav} is $U_{\text{grav,i}} = mgy_i$, and its final value is $U_{\text{grav,f}} = mgy_f$. We can express the work W_{grav} done by the gravitational force during the displacement from y_i to y_f as

$$W_{\text{grav}} = U_{\text{grav,i}} - U_{\text{grav,f}} = -\Delta U_{\text{grav}}. \tag{7.10}$$

The negative sign in front of ΔU_{grav} is essential. Remember that ΔU_{grav} always means the final value minus the initial value. When the object moves down, y decreases, the gravitational force does *positive* work, and the potential energy *decreases* (Figure 7.22a). It's like drawing some money out of the bank (decreasing U) and spending it (doing positive work). When the object moves *up* (Figure 7.22b), the work done by the gravitational force is *negative,* and the potential energy *increases*—you put money into the bank.

> **NOTE** ▶ We use the subscript "grav" to distinguish gravitational potential energy from other forms of potential energy we'll introduce later. But in problems where the *only* potential energy is gravitational, we'll sometimes drop this subscript to simplify the notation. ◀

Here's a simple example of the usefulness of the concept of potential energy. An object moves along a straight vertical line. Suppose the object's weight is the *only* force acting on it, so that $\vec{F}_{\text{other}} = 0$. The object may be in free fall, or perhaps we throw it upward. Let its speed at point y_i be v_i and its speed at y_f be v_f. The work–energy theorem, Equation 7.4, says that $W_{\text{total}} = K_f - K_i$, and in this case, $W_{\text{total}} = W_{\text{grav}} = U_i - U_f$. Putting these equations together, we get

$$U_i - U_f = K_f - K_i,$$

which we can rewrite as

$$K_i + U_i = K_f + U_f,$$

or

$$\tfrac{1}{2}mv_i^2 + mgy_i = \tfrac{1}{2}mv_f^2 + mgy_f. \qquad (7.11)$$

We now define $K + U$ to be the **total mechanical energy** (kinetic plus potential) of the system; let's call it E. Then $E_i = (K_i + U_i)$ is the total energy when the object is at position y_i, and $E_f = (K_f + U_f)$ is the total energy at y_f. Equation 7.11 says that when the object's weight is the only force doing work on it, $E_i = E_f$. That is, E is constant; it has the same value at y_i and at all points during the motion. When $\vec{F}_{other} = 0$, the total mechanical energy is constant or conserved. This is our first example of the principle of **conservation of energy.**

When we throw a ball straight upward, it slows down on the way up as kinetic energy is converted to potential energy. On the way back down, potential energy is converted back to kinetic energy, and the ball speeds up. But the total energy, kinetic plus potential, is the same at every point in the motion. (We're assuming, of course, that air resistance and other frictional effects are negligible.)

EXAMPLE 7.7 **Height of a baseball from energy conservation**

You throw a 0.150 kg baseball straight up in the air, giving it an initial upward velocity with magnitude 20.0 m/s. Use conservation of energy to find how high it goes, ignoring air resistance.

SOLUTION

SET UP The only force doing work on the ball after it leaves your hand is its weight, and we can use Equation 7.11. We place the origin at the starting (initial) point, (point i), where the ball leaves your hand; then $y_i = 0$ (Figure 7.23). At this point, $v_i = 20.0$ m/s. We want to find the height at the final point (point f), where the ball stops and begins to fall back to earth. At this point, $v_f = 0$ and y_f is unknown.

SOLVE Equation 7.11 says that $K_i + U_i = K_f + U_f$, or

$$\tfrac{1}{2}mv_i^2 + mgy_i = \tfrac{1}{2}mv_f^2 + mgy_f,$$
$$\tfrac{1}{2}(0.150 \text{ kg})(20.0 \text{ m/s})^2 + (0.150 \text{ kg})(9.80 \text{ m/s}^2)(0)$$
$$= \tfrac{1}{2}(0.150 \text{ kg})(0)^2 + (0.150 \text{ kg})(9.80 \text{ m/s}^2)y_f,$$
$$y_f = 20.4 \text{ m.}$$

The mass divides out, as we should expect; we learned in Chapter 2 that the motion of an object in free fall doesn't depend on its mass.

REFLECT We could have substituted the values $y_i = 0$ and $v_f = 0$ in Equation 7.11 and then solved algebraically for y_f to get

$$y_f = \frac{v_i^2}{2g}.$$

$v_f = 0$ y_f Final point

After the ball leaves your hand, the only force acting on it is its weight.

$v_i = 20.0$ m/s
$m = 0.150$ kg

$y_i = 0$ Initial point

▲ **FIGURE 7.23**

We could also have derived this result by using the methods of Section 2.6, without energy considerations.

Practice Problem: You throw the same baseball up from the surface of the moon (where the acceleration due to gravity is 1.62 m/s^2) with the same speed as before. Find how high the ball goes. *Answer:* 123 m.

An important point about gravitational potential energy is that it doesn't matter where we put the origin of coordinates. If we shift the origin for y, both y_i and y_f change, but the *difference* $(y_f - y_i)$ does not. It follows that, although the potential energies U_i and U_f depend on where we place the origin, their difference $(U_f - U_i)$ does not. The physically significant quantity is not the value of U at a particular point, but only the *difference* in U between two points. We can define U

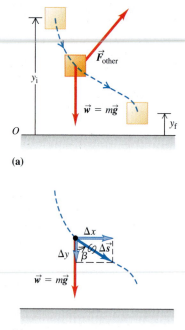

(a)

(b)

▲ **FIGURE 7.24** (a) A displacement along a curved path. (b) The work done by the gravitational force w depends only on the vertical component of the displacement Δy.

to be zero at any point we choose (in this case, at the origin); the difference in the value of U between any two points is independent of this choice.

In the preceding examples, the object moved along a straight vertical line. What happens when the path is slanted or curved, as in Figure 7.24a? The forces include the gravitational force $w = mg$ and possibly an additional force $\vec{F}_{\text{other}}$. The work done by the gravitational force during the displacement of the object is still given by Equation 7.10:

$$W_{\text{grav}} = U_i - U_f = mgy_i - mgy_f. \tag{7.12}$$

To prove that this equation is valid, we divide the path into small segments Δs; a typical segment is shown in Figure 7.24b. The work done in this segment by the gravitational force is the magnitude of the force, multiplied by the vertical component of the displacement, $\Delta y = -\Delta s \cos\beta$. (The negative sign is needed because Δs is positive, while Δy is negative.) As the figure shows, the angle between the force and displacement vectors is β. The work done during the displacement is therefore $mg\,\Delta s \cos\beta$. But $\Delta s \cos\beta$ is equal to Δy, so the work done by w is

$$mg\,\Delta s \cos\beta = -mg\,\Delta y.$$

The work is the same as though the object had been displaced vertically a distance Δy. This is true for every segment, so the *total* work done by the gravitational force depends only on the *total* vertical displacement $(y_f - y_i)$. The total work is $-mg(y_f - y_i)$; this work is independent of any horizontal motion that may occur.

We haven't spoken about the gravitational potential energy *of an object* moving in the earth's gravitational field because the energy belongs not just to the object, but rather to the *system* consisting of the object and the earth. The earth has much more mass than the objects we've been considering. However, when the masses of the objects are more comparable, it is more obvious that the gravitational potential energy cannot be given to one of them.

Elastic Potential Energy

When a railroad car runs into a spring bumper at the end of the track, the spring is compressed as the car is brought to a stop. If there is no friction, the bumper springs back, and the car rolls away in the opposite direction. During the interaction with the spring, the car's kinetic energy is "stored" in the elastic deformation of the spring. Something similar happens in a spring gun. Work is done on the spring by the force that compresses it; that work is stored in the spring until you pull the trigger and the spring gives kinetic energy to the projectile.

This is the same pattern that we saw with the pile driver: Do work on the system to store energy; then this energy can later be converted to kinetic energy. We can apply the concept of elastic potential energy to the storage process. We proceed just as we did for gravitational potential energy. We begin with the work done by the force that the spring exerts on an object (which we will call the **spring force**) and then combine this work with the work–energy theorem.

In Section 7.4, we discussed work associated with stretching or compressing a spring. Figure 7.25 shows the spring from Figure 7.18, with its left end held stationary and its right end attached to an object with mass m that can move along the x axis. The object is at $x = 0$ when the spring is neither stretched nor compressed (Figure 7.25a). An external force $\vec{F}_{\text{ext}}$ acts on the object to make it undergo a displacement (Figure 7.25b), while the spring force $\vec{F}_{\text{spring}}$ pulls on it in the other direction. How much work does the spring force do on the object?

(a)

(b)

(c)

(d)

▲ **FIGURE 7.25** A block and spring on a horizontal surface. Both the spring force $\vec{F}_{\text{spring}}$ and the external force $\vec{F}_{\text{ext}}$ do work on the block.

We found in Section 7.4 that the work we must do *on* the spring to stretch it from an elongation x_i to a greater elongation x_f is $\frac{1}{2}kx_f^2 - \frac{1}{2}kx_i^2$, where k is the force constant of the spring. Now we need to find the work done *by* the spring *on* the object. From Newton's third law, the two quantities of work are just negatives of each other. Changing the signs in the expression on the right-hand side of Equation 7.7, we find that, in a displacement from x_i to x_f, the spring does an amount of work W_{el} given by

$$W_{el} = \tfrac{1}{2}kx_i^2 - \tfrac{1}{2}kx_f^2,$$

where the subscript "el" stands for *elastic*. When x_f is greater than x_i (Figure 7.25c), this quantity is negative because the object moves in the $+x$ direction while the spring pulls on it in the $-x$ direction. If the spring can be compressed as well as stretched, then x_i, x_f, or both may be negative (Figure 7.25d), and the expression for W_{el} is still valid.

Following the same procedure as for gravitational work, we define **elastic potential energy** as follows:

Definition of elastic potential energy

When a spring that obeys Hooke's law, $F = kx$, is stretched or compressed a distance x from its undistorted state, the associated potential energy U_{el} is given by

$$U_{el} = \tfrac{1}{2}kx^2. \tag{7.13}$$

The units of k are N/m, so the units of U_{el} are J. (Remember that $1\ \text{J} = 1\ \text{N} \cdot \text{m}$.) The joule is the unit used for *all* energy and work quantities.

> **NOTE** ▶ In the expression $U_{el} = \frac{1}{2}kx^2$, x *must* be the displacement of the spring from its *unstretched* length (because we have used $F = kx$ to derive the expression). ◀

We can use Equation 7.13 to express the work W_{el} done on the object by the spring force in terms of the change in potential energy:

$$W_{el} = \tfrac{1}{2}kx_i^2 - \tfrac{1}{2}kx_f^2 = U_{el,i} - U_{el,f} = -\Delta U_{el}. \tag{7.14}$$

When x increases, W_{el} is *negative* and the stored energy U_{el} *increases;* when x decreases, W_{el} is *positive* and U_{el} *decreases.* If the spring can be compressed as well as stretched, then x is negative for compression. But, as Equation 7.13 shows, U_{el} is positive for both positive and negative x, and Equations 7.13 and 7.14 are valid in both cases. When $x = 0$, $U_{el} = 0$, and the spring is neither stretched nor compressed.

The work–energy theorem says that $W_{total} = K_f - K_i$, no matter what kind of forces are acting. If the spring force is the *only* force that does work on the object, then

$$W_{total} = W_{el} = U_i - U_f.$$

The work–energy theorem then gives us

$$K_i + U_{el,i} = K_f + U_{el,f} \quad \text{and} \quad \tfrac{1}{2}mv_i^2 + \tfrac{1}{2}kx_i^2 = \tfrac{1}{2}mv_f^2 + \tfrac{1}{2}kx_f^2 \tag{7.15}$$

In this case, the total energy $E = K + U_{el}$ is *conserved.*

▲ **Climbing El Capitan.** One of the world's most famous climbing rocks is the 884 m El Capitan in Yosemite National Park. The red line shows a common climbing route, which involves an overnight stay on a ledge. For a typical 75 kg male climber, the change in gravitational potential energy from the bottom to the top of El Capitan is about 6.5×10^5 J. That sounds like a lot, but in fact, it's less than the energy you get from eating a typical candy bar! The work that results in the net change in gravitational potential energy represents just a small part of the total energy expended on such a climb.

EXAMPLE 7.8   **Potential energy on an air track**

A glider with mass $m = 0.200$ kg sits on a frictionless, horizontal air track, connected to a spring of negligible mass with force constant $k = 5.00$ N/m. You pull on the glider, stretching the spring 0.100 m, and then release it with no initial velocity. The glider begins to move back toward its equilibrium position $(x = 0)$. What is its speed when $x = 0.0800$ m?

SOLUTION

SET UP Figure 7.26 shows our diagram. We mark the $x = 0$ position at which the spring is relaxed, and we show the initial and final positions we will use. As the glider starts to move, potential energy is converted into kinetic energy. The spring force is the only force doing work on the glider, so $W_{other} = 0$, the total mechanical energy is constant, and we may use Equation 7.15. The energy quantities are

$$K_i = \tfrac{1}{2}(0.200 \text{ kg})(0)^2 = 0,$$
$$U_i = \tfrac{1}{2}(5.00 \text{ N/m})(0.100 \text{ m})^2 = 0.0250 \text{ J},$$
$$K_f = \tfrac{1}{2}(0.200 \text{ kg})v_f^2,$$
$$U_f = \tfrac{1}{2}(5.00 \text{ N/m})(0.0800 \text{ m})^2 = 0.0160 \text{ J}.$$

SOLVE From Equation 7.15,

$$\tfrac{1}{2}mv_i^2 + \tfrac{1}{2}kx_i^2 = \tfrac{1}{2}mv_f^2 + \tfrac{1}{2}kx_f^2,$$
$$0 + 0.0250 \text{ J} = \tfrac{1}{2}(0.200 \text{ kg})v_f^2 + 0.0160 \text{ J},$$
$$v_f = \pm 0.300 \text{ m/s}.$$

REFLECT The quadratic equation for v_f has two roots. The object doesn't stop at $x = 0$, but overshoots; when it returns to $x = 0$, the direction of its motion is reversed. Note that this problem

▲ **FIGURE 7.26** Our sketch for this problem. We show the initial and final states we will use in solving the problem.

cannot be solved by using the equations of motion with constant acceleration, because the spring force varies with position. The energy method, in contrast, offers a simple and elegant solution.

Practice Problem: What is the value of x when the object's speed is 0.15 m/s? *Answer:* ± 0.095 m.

7.6 Conservation of Energy

In the examples of the preceding section, we classified the forces acting on an object as gravitational, elastic, and "other." The general form of the work–energy theorem is

$$\Delta K = K_f - K_i = W_{total} = W_{grav} + W_{el} + W_{other}.$$

We've learned that the work done by the gravitational and elastic forces can be represented in terms of changes in their associated potential energy U_{grav} and U_{el}:

$$W_{grav} = U_{grav,i} - U_{grav,f} = -\Delta U_{grav} \quad \text{and} \quad W_{el} = U_{el,i} - U_{el,f} = -\Delta U_{el}.$$

When we substitute these expressions into the general work–energy theorem, we find that

$$K_f - K_i = U_{grav,i} - U_{grav,f} + U_{el,i} - U_{el,f} + W_{other},$$

or

$$K_f + U_{grav,f} + U_{el,f} = K_i + U_{grav,i} + U_{el,i} + W_{other}. \tag{7.16}$$

This equation bristles with subscripts and may seem complicated. But when we look at the individual terms, we recognize the quantity $K + U_{grav} + U_{el}$, with subscript i (initial) or f (final), as representing the total mechanical energy of the system. Therefore, Equation 7.16 states that the total mechanical energy of a system at the end (f) of any process equals the total mechanical energy at the beginning (i), plus the work W_{other} done by the forces *other than* gravitational and

▲ **Catapult legs.** To jump, a grasshopper must straighten its hind legs faster than its leg muscles can contract. It does so by using a catapult mechanism. The black swelling on the first joint of each jumping leg marks a spot where the insect's exoskeleton has been modified into a pair of stiff springs shaped like flattened C's. Before a jump, the limb muscles build up elastic potential energy by compressing these springs while the joint is flexed. To jump, the animal releases the springs, which cause the legs to snap straight. Such mechanisms rely on conservation of mechanical energy.

elastic forces. If we abbreviate the total potential energy as $U = U_{grav} + U_{el}$, we can say, more simply, that

$$K_f + U_f = K_i + U_i + W_{other}.$$

If there are no forces other than gravitational and elastic forces, or if the vector sum of all other forces is zero, then $\vec{F}_{other} = 0$, $W_{other} = 0$, and *all* the work can be represented in terms of changes in potential energy. In this special case, the *total* mechanical energy, $E = K + U_{grav} + U_{el}$, is constant, or *conserved*. Earlier, we mentioned that such a system is called a *conservative system* because mechanical energy is conserved. In this section, we'll discuss several examples of conservative systems.

5.2–5.4

Conceptual Analysis 7.4

Mass-and-pulley system

Two unequal masses are connected by a massless cord passing over a frictionless pulley as shown in Figure 7.27. Considering the two masses as a system, which of the following statements is true about the gravitational potential energy U_{grav} and kinetic energy K after the masses are released from rest?

A. U_{grav} increases and K increases.
B. U_{grav} decreases and K increases.
C. Both U_{grav} and K remain constant.

SOLUTION The total kinetic energy K of the system is the sum of the two objects' individual kinetic energies, and the total gravitational potential energy U_{grav} is the sum of the individual gravitational potential energies.

Because both objects start from rest and end up moving, the total kinetic energy of the system increases. (Remember that kinetic energy depends on speed, not velocity, so the *direction* of motion has no effect on the kinetic energy.)

Now let's consider the change in gravitational potential energy. The downward motion of the heavy block decreases the

Before release   **After release**

▲ **FIGURE 7.27**

U_{grav} associated with this block. The upward motion of the light block increases the associated U_{grav}. However, since U_{grav} depends directly on mass, the decrease due to the heavy block dominates, so the total gravitational potential energy decreases. Thus, choice B is correct.

Quantitative Analysis 7.5

Total mechanical energy

In Figure 7.28, two blocks with masses m_A and m_B, where $m_A > m_B$, are attached to a thin string that passes over a frictionless pulley. The larger mass is resting on a spring that is compressed a distance s from its equilibrium position. The spring's compression is maintained by a trigger mechanism. What is the total mechanical energy for this system?

A. $m_A g h_A + m_B g h_B + \frac{1}{2} k h_A^2$
B. $m_A g h_A + m_B g h_B + \frac{1}{2} k s^2$
C. $m_A g h_A - m_B g h_B + \frac{1}{2} k s^2$

SOLUTION The total mechanical energy E is the sum of the energies for the individual parts of the system and is given by $E = K + U$, where $K = \frac{1}{2} m_B v_B^2 + \frac{1}{2} m_A v_A^2$ and $U = U_{grav} + U_{el}$. Using the tabletop for the reference level as shown in Figure 7.28, we find that $U_{grav} = m_A g h_A + m_B g h_B$. The spring is compressed a distance s, so $U_{el} = \frac{1}{2} k s^2$. With the trigger in place,

The spring is compressed a distance s from its uncompressed length.

▲ **FIGURE 7.28**

neither block is moving, and $K = 0$. Thus, $E = U_{grav} + U_{el} = m_A g h_A + m_B g h_B + \frac{1}{2} k s^2$ (choice B).

PROBLEM-SOLVING STRATEGY 7.2 **Conservation of energy with conservative forces**

SET UP

1. Identify the system you will analyze, and decide on the initial and final states (positions and velocities) you will use in solving the problem. Use the subscript i for the initial state and f for the final state. Draw one or more sketches showing the initial and final states.
2. Define your coordinate system, particularly the zero points for gravitational and elastic potential energies (the point at which $y = 0$ in the case of gravitational potential energy or at which the spring or other elastic object is relaxed in the case of elastic potential energy). For gravitational potential energy, Equation 7.9 assumes that the positive direction for y is upward; we suggest that you use this choice consistently.
3. List the initial and final kinetic and potential energies—that is, K_i, K_f, U_i, and U_f. Some of these will be known and some unknown. Use algebraic symbols for any unknown coordinates or velocities. In general, U includes both gravitational and elastic potential energy.

SOLVE

4. Write expressions for the total initial mechanical energy and for the total final mechanical energy, equate them, and solve to find whatever unknown quantity is required.

REFLECT

5. Check to make sure there are no forces other than gravitational and elastic forces that do work on the system. If there are additional forces, W_{other} is not zero, and you need to use the method we'll discuss in the next section (Problem-Solving Strategy 7.3).

EXAMPLE 7.9 Maximum height of a home-run ball

In Example 3.5 (Section 3.3) we derived an expression for the maximum height h of a projectile launched with initial speed v_0 at initial angle θ_0 (neglecting air resistance):

$$h = \frac{v_0^2 \sin^2 \theta_0}{2g}.$$

Derive this expression now by using energy considerations.

SOLUTION

SET UP There are no nonconservative forces; the work done by gravity is accounted for in the potential-energy terms. As shown in Figure 7.29, we choose the launch point as the initial point and the highest point on the trajectory as the final point. We place $y = 0$ at the launch level; then $U_i = 0$ and $U_f = mgh$, where h is unknown. We can express the kinetic energy at each point in terms of the components of velocity, using the fact that, at each point, $v^2 = v_x^2 + v_y^2$:

$$K_i = \tfrac{1}{2}m(v_{i,x}^2 + v_{i,y}^2)$$
$$K_f = \tfrac{1}{2}m(v_{f,x}^2 + v_{f,y}^2)$$

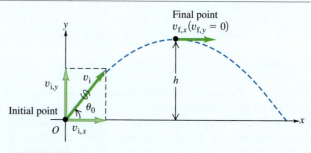

▲ **FIGURE 7.29**

Continued

SOLVE Conservation of energy gives $K_i + U_i = K_f + U_f$, so

$$\tfrac{1}{2}m\left(v_{i,x}^2 + v_{i,y}^2\right) + 0 = \tfrac{1}{2}m\left(v_{f,x}^2 + v_{f,y}^2\right) + mgh.$$

To simplify this equation, we multiply through by $2/m$ to obtain

$$v_{i,x}^2 + v_{i,y}^2 = v_{f,x}^2 + v_{f,y}^2 + 2gh.$$

Now for the *coup de grace:* We recall that, in projectile motion, the x component of acceleration is zero, so the x component of velocity is constant, and $v_{i,x} = v_{f,x}$. Also, because the final point is the highest point, the vertical component of velocity is zero at that point: $v_{f,y} = 0$. Subtracting the v_x^2 terms from both sides, we get

$$v_{i,y}^2 = 2gh.$$

But $v_{i,y}$ is just the y component of initial velocity, which is equal to $v_0 \sin\theta_0$. Making this substitution and solving for h, we find that

$$h = \frac{v_0^2 \sin^2\theta_0}{2g}.$$

REFLECT This result agrees with our result from Example 3.5. The energy approach has the advantage that we don't have to solve for the time when the maximum height is reached.

Practice Problem: Use the energy method to show that, for a given initial speed, the maximum height is greatest when $\theta_0 = 90°$.

EXAMPLE 7.10 Calculating speed along a vertical circle

Your cousin Throckmorton skateboards down a quarter-pipe with radius $R = 3.0$ m (Figure 7.30). The total mass of Throcky and the skateboard is 25.0 kg. If he starts from rest and there is no friction, derive an algebraic expression for his speed at the bottom of the ramp. Evaluate this expression with the values given. (Throcky's center of mass moves in a circle with radius somewhat smaller than R; neglect this small difference.)

SOLUTION

SET UP This is a conservative system. We can't use the equations of motion with constant acceleration; the acceleration isn't constant, because the slope decreases as Throcky descends. However, if there is no friction, the only force other than his weight is the normal force $\vec{n}$ exerted by the ramp (Figure 7.30b). The work done by this force is zero because, at each point, it is perpendicular to his velocity at that point. Thus, $W_{other} = 0$, and mechanical energy is conserved. We take his starting point as the initial point and the lowest point in the pipe as the final point. Then $y_i = R$ and $y_f = 0$. Throcky starts from rest at the top, so $v_i = 0$. The various energy quantities are

$$K_i = 0, \qquad K_f = \tfrac{1}{2}mv_f^2,$$
$$U_i = mgR, \qquad U_f = 0.$$

SOLVE From conservation of energy,

$$K_i + U_i = K_f + U_f,$$
$$0 + mgR = \tfrac{1}{2}mv_f^2 + 0,$$
$$v_f = \sqrt{2gR} = \sqrt{2\left(9.80\ \text{m/s}^2\right)\left(3.00\ \text{m}\right)} = 7.67\ \text{m/s}.$$

REFLECT Throcky's speed at the bottom is the same as if he had fallen vertically through a height R, and it is independent of his mass.

Practice Problem: Find Throcky's speed at the bottom of the pipe if he is given a push at the top edge, so that he has an initial downward speed of 2.00 m/s. *Answer:* 7.93 m/s.

Initial point
$v_i = 0$
$m = 25.0$ kg
$R = 3.0$ m

At each point, the normal force acts perpendicular to the direction of displacement, so only Throcky's weight does work on him.

v_f
Final point

$n = 0$
w
n
w

(a)

(b)

▲ **FIGURE 7.30** (a) Motion showing initial and final points. (b) Free-body diagrams for initial and final points.

EXAMPLE 7.11 **Elevator safety (or not)**

In a "worst-case" design scenario, a 2000 kg elevator with broken cables is falling at 8.00 m/s when it first contacts a cushioning spring at the bottom of the shaft. The spring is supposed to stop the elevator, compressing 3.00 m as it does so (Figure 7.31). As an energy consultant, you are asked to determine what the force constant of the spring should be. Ignore air resistance and friction in the elevator guides.

SOLUTION

SET UP AND SOLVE We take the initial point as the elevator's position when it first contacts the spring $(y_i = 3.00 \text{ m})$ and the final point as its position when the spring is fully compressed $(y_f = 0)$. The elevator's initial speed is $v_i = 8.00 \text{ m/s}$, so

$$K_i = \tfrac{1}{2}mv_i^2 = \tfrac{1}{2}(2000 \text{ kg})(8.00 \text{ m/s})^2 = 64{,}000 \text{ J}.$$

The elevator stops at the final point; thus, $K_f = 0$. The elastic potential energy at the initial point is zero because the spring isn't yet compressed. The initial gravitational potential energy is

$$U_i = mgy_i = (2000 \text{ kg})(9.80 \text{ m/s}^2)(3.00 \text{ m}) = 58{,}800 \text{ J}.$$

At the final point, the gravitational potential energy is zero (because $y_f = 0$) and the elastic potential energy is

$$U_f = \tfrac{1}{2}kx^2 = \tfrac{1}{2}k(-3.00 \text{ m})^2,$$

where the force constant k is to be determined.
Inserting all these values in Equation 7.16, we find that

$$K_i + U_i = K_f + U_f,$$
$$64{,}000 \text{ J} + 58{,}800 \text{ J} = 0 + \tfrac{1}{2}k(-3.00 \text{ m})^2,$$
$$k = 2.73 \times 10^4 \text{ N/m}.$$

REFLECT You still have to explain to the client that the elevator won't stay at the bottom of the shaft, but will bounce back up and

▲ **FIGURE 7.31**

then return to hit the spring again and again until enough energy has been removed by friction for it to stop.

Practice Problem: If the mass of the elevator (with four fewer passengers than before) is 1600 kg, what should the spring constant be for a maximum compression of 3.00 m? *Answer:* $2.18 \times 10^4 \text{ N/m}$.

7.7 Conservative and Nonconservative Forces

5.5–5.7

Activ ONLINE Physics

In the preceding section, we discussed several problems involving work done on an object by conservative forces. In these problems, the work could be described completely in terms of changes in mechanical energy, and the *total* mechanical energy (kinetic plus potential) was conserved. We also hinted at methods for dealing with problems involving forces that do work W_{other} that can't be described in terms of a potential energy. We called these forces $\vec{F}_{\text{other}}$. Let's now return to this more general class of problem.

The key to dealing with problems involving nonconservative forces is Equation 7.16:

$$K_f + U_{\text{grav,f}} + U_{\text{el,f}} = K_i + U_{\text{grav,i}} + U_{\text{el,i}} + W_{\text{other}}. \tag{7.16}$$

Translated into words, this equation says that the total mechanical energy $(K + U_{\text{grav}} + U_{\text{el}})$ at the end of any process equals the total mechanical energy at the beginning, plus the work done by "other" forces whose work is not (or cannot be) included in the potential-energy terms. In such systems, mechanical energy is *not* conserved, but the initial and final values of total mechanical energy are related simply to the work done by the "other" forces.

Following are several examples of this more general class of problems and of the application of Equation 7.16. Then we'll close this section with a more general discussion of the nature of conservative and nonconservative forces.

The strategy outlined in Section 7.6 is equally useful here. In the list of kinetic and potential energies in Step 3, you should include both gravitational and elastic potential energies when appropriate. Remember that every force that does work must be represented *either* in U or in W_{other}, but *never* in both places. The work done by the gravitational and elastic forces is accounted for by the potential energies; the work of the other forces, W_{other}, has to be included separately. In some cases there will be "other" forces that do no work, as we mentioned in Section 7.2. Remember that, in the expression $U = \frac{1}{2}kx^2$, the coordinate x must be the displacement of the spring from its *unstretched* length (because we have used $F = -kx$ to derive U).

EXAMPLE 7.12   **Work and energy on an air track**

For the system of Example 7.8, suppose the glider is initially at rest at $x = 0$, with the spring unstretched. Then you apply a constant force $\vec{F}$ with magnitude 0.610 N to the glider. What is the glider's speed when it has moved to $x = 0.100$ m?

SOLUTION

SET UP Figure 7.32 shows our sketch. Mechanical energy is not conserved, because of the work W_{other} done by the force $\vec{F}$, but we can still use the energy relation of Equation 7.16. Let the initial point be $x = 0$ and the final point be $x = 0.100$ m. The energy quantities are

$$K_i = 0, \quad K_f = \tfrac{1}{2}(0.200 \text{ kg})v_f^2,$$
$$U_i = 0, \quad U_f = \tfrac{1}{2}(5.00 \text{ N/m})(0.100 \text{ m})^2 = 0.0250 \text{ J},$$
$$W_{other} = (0.610 \text{ N})(0.100 \text{ m}) = 0.0610 \text{ J}.$$

SOLVE Putting the pieces into Equation 7.16, we obtain

$$K_f + U_f = K_i + U_i + W_{other},$$
$$\tfrac{1}{2}(0.200 \text{ kg})v_f^2 + 0.0250 \text{ J} = 0 + 0 + 0.0610 \text{ J},$$
$$v_f = 0.600 \text{ m/s}.$$

REFLECT The total mechanical energy of the system changes by an amount equal to the work W_{other} done by the applied force. Even

▲ **FIGURE 7.32** Our sketch for this problem.

though mechanical energy isn't conserved, energy considerations simplify this problem greatly.

Practice Problem: If the 0.610 N force is removed when the glider reaches the 0.100 m point, at what distance from the starting point does the glider come to rest? *Answer:* 0.156 m.

EXAMPLE 7.13   **Throcky on the half-pipe again**

Suppose the ramp in Example 7.10 is not frictionless and that Throcky's speed at the bottom is only 7.00 m/s. What work was done by the frictional force acting on him?

SOLUTION

SET UP We choose the same initial and final points and reference level as in Example 7.10 (Figure 7.30). In this case, $W_{other} = W_f$. The energy quantities are

$$K_i = 0,$$
$$U_i = mgR = (25.0 \text{ kg})(9.80 \text{ m/s}^2)(3.00 \text{ m}) = 735 \text{ J},$$
$$K_f = \tfrac{1}{2}mv_f^2 = \tfrac{1}{2}(25.0 \text{ kg})(7.00 \text{ m/s})^2 = 613 \text{ J},$$
$$U_f = 0.$$

SOLVE From Equation 7.16,

$$W_{other} = K_f + U_f - K_i - U_i$$
$$= 613 \text{ J} + 0 - 0 - 735 \text{ J} = -122 \text{ J}.$$

The work done by the friction force is -122 J, and the total mechanical energy *decreases* by 122 J.

REFLECT W_{other} has to be negative because, at each point, the friction force is opposite in direction to Throcky's velocity. In this problem, as in several others in this chapter, Throcky's motion is

Continued

determined by Newton's second law, $\sum \vec{F} = m\vec{a}$. But it would be very difficult to apply that law here because the acceleration is continuously changing, in both magnitude and direction, as Throcky skates down. The energy approach, in contrast, relates the motions at the top and bottom of the ramp without involving the details of what happens in between. This simplification is typical of many problems that are easy if we use energy considerations, but very complex if we try to use Newton's laws directly.

The work W_f done by the nonconservative friction forces is -122 J. As Throcky rolls down, the wheels, the bearings, and the ramp all get a little warmer. The same temperature changes could have been produced by adding 122 J of heat to these objects. Their *internal* energy increases by 122 J; the sum of this energy and the final mechanical energy equals the initial mechanical energy, and the total energy of the system (including nonmechanical forms of energy) is conserved.

Practice Problem: If Throcky's speed at the bottom of the quarter-pipe is exactly half of what it would be without friction, how much work does the friction force do? *Answer:* -551 J.

EXAMPLE 7.14   Loading a crate onto a truck

A crate full of machine parts sits on the floor; the total mass is 8.0 kg. The crate must be raised to the floor of a truck by sliding it up a ramp 2.5 m long, inclined at 30°. The shop foreman, giving no thought to the force of friction, calculates that he can get the crate up the ramp by giving it an initial speed of 5.0 m/s at the bottom and letting it go. Unfortunately, friction is *not* negligible; the crate slides 1.6 m up the ramp, stops, and slides back down. Figure 7.33 shows the situation. **(a)** Assuming that the friction force acting on the crate is constant, find its magnitude. **(b)** How fast is the crate moving when it reaches the bottom of the ramp?

SOLUTION

SET UP We have three critical points: ground level (point 1 in Figure 7.33a), the point where the crate stops on the ramp (point 2), and the point where it reaches the ground again (point 3 in Figure 7.33b). (We count points 1 and 3 separately because the crate's velocity is different on the return trip.) For part (a), point 1 is the initial point and point 2 is the final point; for part (b), point 1 is the initial point and point 3 is the final point.

SOLVE Part (a): For this part of the problem, the final point is $(1.6 \text{ m})(\sin 30°) = 0.80$ m above the floor. If we take $U = 0$ at floor level, we have $y_1 = 0$, $y_2 = 0.80$ m. The energy quantities are

$$K_1 = \tfrac{1}{2}(8.0 \text{ kg})(5.0 \text{ m/s})^2 = 100 \text{ J}, \qquad K_2 = 0,$$
$$U_1 = 0, \qquad U_2 = (8.0 \text{ kg})(9.8 \text{ m/s}^2)(0.80 \text{ m}) = 62.7 \text{ J},$$
$$W_{\text{other}} = -fs = -f(1.6 \text{ m}),$$

where f is the magnitude of the unknown friction force. Using Equation 7.16, we find that

$$K_1 + U_1 + W_{\text{other}} = K_2 + U_2,$$
$$100 \text{ J} + 0 - f(1.6 \text{ m}) = 0 + 62.7 \text{ J},$$
$$f = 23 \text{ N}.$$

Part (b): This time we use points 1 and 3 as our initial and final points, respectively. The friction force reverses direction for the return trip, so the frictional work is negative for both halves of the trip, and the total work done by friction is twice the previous amount. The total gravitational work for the round-trip is zero, so the total work is

$$W_{\text{other}} = W_f = -2(1.6 \text{ m})(23.3 \text{ N}) = -74.6 \text{ J}.$$

The other energy quantities are

$$K_1 = 100 \text{ J}, \qquad U_1 = U_3 = 0, \qquad K_3 = \tfrac{1}{2}(8.0 \text{ kg})v_3^2,$$

▲ FIGURE 7.33

Continued

where v_3 is the unknown final speed. Substituting these values into Equation 7.16, we get

$$100\,\text{J} + 0 + (-74.6\,\text{J}) = \tfrac{1}{2}(8.0\,\text{kg})v_3^2 + 0,$$
$$v_3 = 2.5\,\text{m/s}.$$

REFLECT The crate's speed and kinetic energy when it returns to the bottom of the ramp are less than when it left that point; mechanical energy is lost to friction. We could have applied Equation 7.16 to points 2 and 3, considering the second half of the trip by itself.

Practice Problem: Follow the suggestion to apply Equation 7.16 to points 2 and 3 to verify that you get the same result for v_3 as before.

Nonconservative Forces

In our discussions of potential energy, we've talked about "storing" kinetic energy by converting it to potential energy. When you throw a ball up in the air, it slows down as kinetic energy is converted into potential energy. On the way down, the conversion is reversed, and potential energy is converted completely back to kinetic energy (if air resistance is neglected.).

Similarly, when a glider moving on a frictionless, horizontal air track runs into a spring bumper at the end of the track, the spring compresses and the glider stops. But then the glider bounces back with the same speed and kinetic energy that it had before the collision. Again, there is a two-way conversion from kinetic to potential energy and back.

A force that permits two-way conversion between kinetic and potential energies is called a **conservative force.** The work of a conservative force is always *reversible:* Anything that we deposit in the energy "bank" can later be withdrawn without loss. In some cases (including gravitational forces), an object may move from an initial to a final point by various paths (Figure 7.34), but if the force is conservative, the work done by the force is the same for all of these paths. If an object moves around a *closed* path, ending at the same point where it started, the *total* work done by the gravitational force is always zero.

The work done by a conservative force has these properties:

1. It can always be expressed as the difference between the initial and final values of a *potential-energy* function.
2. It is reversible.
3. It is independent of the path of the object and depends only on the starting and ending points.
4. When the starting and ending points are the same, the total work is zero.

The work done by the gravitational force is the same for all three paths, because this force is conservative.

Initial position

Final position

◀ **FIGURE 7.34** The work done by a conservative force is independent of the path taken.

When all the work done on an object is done by conservative forces, the total mechanical energy $E = K + U$ is constant.

Not all forces are conservative. Consider the friction force acting on the crate sliding on a ramp in Example 7.14. There is no potential-energy function for this force. When the object slides up and then back down to the starting point, the total work done on it by the friction force is *not* zero. When the direction of motion reverses, so does the friction force, and it does *negative* work in *both* directions. When a car with its brakes locked skids across the pavement with decreasing speed (and decreasing kinetic energy), the lost kinetic energy cannot be recovered by reversing the motion (or, for that matter, in any other way), and mechanical energy is *not* conserved.

Such a force is called a **nonconservative force** or a **dissipative force.** To describe the associated energy relations, we have to introduce additional kinds of energy and a more general energy-conservation principle. When an object slides on a rough surface, such as tires on pavement or a box dropped on a conveyer belt, the surfaces become hotter; the energy associated with this change in the state of the materials is called *internal energy.* In later chapters, we'll study the relation of internal energy to temperature changes, heat, and work. This is the heart of the area of physics called *thermodynamics.*

7.8 Power

Time considerations aren't involved directly in the definition of work. If you lift a barbell weighing 400 N through a vertical distance of 0.5 m at constant velocity, you do 200 J of work on it, whether it takes you 1 second, 1 hour, or 1 year to do it. Often, though, we need to know how quickly work is done. The time rate at which work is done or energy is transferred is called **power.** Like work and energy, power is a scalar quantity. We define **average power** as follows:

▲ **Measuring energy burned.** Animals (including humans) obtain energy from food by "burning" the food with oxygen from the air. Therefore, to measure how fast food energy is used during a given activity, scientists measure the rate at which the animal consumes oxygen. Here, the oxygen consumption of a moving llama is being measured.

> **Definition of average power P_{av}**
>
> When a quantity of work ΔW is done during a time interval Δt, the average power P_{av}, or work per unit time, is defined as
>
> $$P_{av} = \frac{\Delta W}{\Delta t}. \tag{7.17}$$
>
> **Unit:** watt (W), where 1 watt is defined as 1 joule per second (J/s).

The rate at which work is done isn't necessarily constant. Even when it varies, however, we can define the **instantaneous power** P as the limit of this quotient as Δt approaches zero:

$$P = \lim_{\Delta t \to 0} \frac{\Delta W}{\Delta t}.$$

For many applications, power is measured in kilowatts or megawatts $(1\ MW = 10^6\ W)$. In the British system, in which work is expressed in foot-pounds, the unit of power is the foot-pound per second. A larger unit called the *horsepower* (hp) is also used:

$$1\ hp = 550\ ft \cdot lb/s = 33,000\ ft \cdot lb/min.$$

That is, a 1 hp motor running at full load does 33,000 ft · lb of work every minute. A useful conversion factor is

$$1\ hp = 746\ W = 0.746\ kW.$$

Note that 1 horsepower equals about $\frac{3}{4}$ of a kilowatt, a useful figure to remember.

The watt is a familiar unit of *electrical* power; a 100 W lightbulb converts 100 J of electrical energy into light and heat each second. But there is nothing inherently electrical about the watt; a lightbulb could be rated in horsepower, and some automobile manufacturers rate their engines in kilowatts as well as horsepower.

Power units can be used to define new units of work or energy. The *kilowatt-hour* (kWh) is the usual commercial unit of electrical energy. One kilowatt-hour is the total work done in 1 hour (3600 s) when the power is 1 kilowatt (10^3 J/s), so

$$1 \text{ kWh} = (10^3 \text{ J/s})(3600 \text{ s}) = 3.6 \times 10^6 \text{ J} = 3.6 \text{ MJ}.$$

The kilowatt-hour is a unit of *work* or *energy,* not power.

When a force acts on a moving object, it does work on the object (unless the force and velocity are always perpendicular). The corresponding power can be expressed in terms of force and velocity. Suppose a force $\vec{F}$ acts on an object while it undergoes a vector displacement $\Delta\vec{s}$. If $F_\parallel$ is the component of $\vec{F}$ tangent to the path (parallel to $\Delta\vec{s}$), then the work is $\Delta W = F_\parallel \, \Delta s$, where Δs is the magnitude of the displacement $\Delta\vec{s}$, and the average power is

$$P_{av} = \frac{F_\parallel \, \Delta s}{\Delta t} = F_\parallel \frac{\Delta s}{\Delta t} = F_\parallel v_{av}.$$

Instantaneous power P is the limit of P_{av} as $\Delta t \to 0$:

$$P = F_\parallel v, \tag{7.18}$$

where v is the magnitude of the instantaneous velocity.

It's a curious fact of modern life that although energy is an abstract physical quantity, it is bought and sold. We don't buy a newton of force or a meter per second of velocity, but a kilowatt-hour of electrical energy usually costs from 2 to 10 cents, depending on one's location and the amount purchased.

EXAMPLE 7.15 **Power in a jet engine**

A jet airplane engine develops a thrust (a forward force on the plane) of 15,000 N (roughly 3000 lb). When the plane is flying at 300 m/s (roughly 670 mi/h), what horsepower does the engine develop?

SOLUTION

SET UP AND SOLVE From Equation 7.18,

$$P = Fv = (1.50 \times 10^4 \text{ N})(300 \text{ m/s}) = 4.50 \times 10^6 \text{ W}$$
$$= (4.50 \times 10^6 \text{ W}) \left(\frac{1 \text{ hp}}{746 \text{ W}} \right) = 6030 \text{ hp}.$$

REFLECT This power is comparable to the power developed by a Diesel railroad locomotive. The airplane travels 10 times as fast as the locomotive, with a much smaller cargo weight.

Practice Problem: Suppose the airplane carries 150 passengers with an average mass of 55 kg each. After disembarking, all these passengers get on a freight elevator, which itself has a mass of 750 kg. How fast can the elevator's 6000 hp motor lift the loaded elevator? (That is, at what speed is 6000 hp just enough to keep the elevator rising?) *Answer:* 51 m/s.

EXAMPLE 7.16 **A marathon stair climb**

As part of a charity fund-raising drive, a Chicago marathon runner with mass 50.0 kg runs up the stairs to the top of the Sears Tower, the tallest building in Chicago (443 m), in 15.0 minutes (Figure 7.35). What is her average power output in watts? In kilowatts? In horsepower?

Continued

▲ **FIGURE 7.35** Climbing the Sears Tower.

SOLUTION

SET UP AND SOLVE The runner's total work W is her weight mg, multiplied by the height h she climbs:

$$W = mgh = (50.0 \text{ kg})(9.80 \text{ m/s}^2)(443 \text{ m}) = 2.17 \times 10^5 \text{ J}.$$

The time is 15 min = 900 s, so the average power is

$$P_{av} = \frac{2.17 \times 10^5 \text{ J}}{900 \text{ s}} = 241 \text{ W} = 0.241 \text{ kW} = 0.323 \text{ hp}.$$

Alternative Solution: The average vertical component of velocity is $(443 \text{ m})/(900 \text{ s}) = 0.492 \text{ m/s}$, so the average power is

$$P_{av} = Fv_{av} = (mg)v_{av}$$
$$= (50.0 \text{ kg})(9.80 \text{ m/s}^2)(0.492 \text{ m/s}) = 241 \text{ W}.$$

REFLECT A horse can supply considerably more than 1 hp for short periods of time.

Practice Problem: If all the runner's work output could be collected and sold at the rate of 10 cents per kilowatt-hour, what would be the cash value of the work? *Answer:* 0.603 cents.

SUMMARY

Overview of Energy

(Section 7.1) Energy is one of the most important unifying concepts in all of physical science. Its importance stems from the principle of conservation of energy. Energy is exchanged and transformed during interactions of systems, but the total energy in a closed system is constant. This chapter is concerned with mechanical energy of three types: kinetic energy, associated with the motion of objects that have mass; gravitational potential energy, associated with gravitational interactions; and elastic potential energy, associated with elastic deformations of objects. Potential energy can be viewed as a stored quantity that represents the potential for doing work.

Work

(Section 7.2) When a force acts on an object that undergoes a displacement, the force does work on the object and transfers energy to it. For a constant force, $W = F_\parallel s$ (Equation 7.1), where $F_\parallel$ is the component of force parallel to the object's displacement (of magnitude s). This component can be positive, negative, or zero. Work is a scalar quantity, not a vector. If $F_\parallel$ points opposite to the displacement, then $W < 0$. When several forces act on an object, the total work done by all the forces is the sum of the amounts of work done by the individual forces.

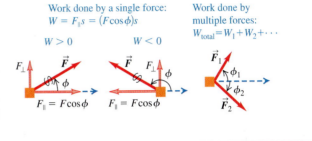

Work done by a single force:
$$W = F_\parallel s = (F\cos\phi)s$$

$W > 0$ $W < 0$

$F_\parallel = F\cos\phi$ $F_\parallel = F\cos\phi$

Work done by multiple forces:
$$W_{total} = W_1 + W_2 + \cdots$$

Work and Kinetic Energy

(Section 7.3) The kinetic energy K of an object is defined in terms of the object's mass m and speed v as $K = \frac{1}{2}mv^2$. When forces act on an object, the change in its kinetic energy is equal to the total work done by all the forces acting on it: $W_{total} = K_f - K_i = \Delta K$ (Equation 7.4). When W is positive, the object speeds up; when W is negative, it slows down.

$v = 2.0$ m/s $v = 1.0$ m/s

Honda, mass 1300 kg   Mercedes, mass 2600 kg

$K = \frac{1}{2}mv^2 = 2600$ J $K = \frac{1}{2}mv^2 = 1300$ J

Work Done by a Varying Force

(Section 7.4) When an object moves under the action of a varying force parallel to the displacement, the work done by the force is represented graphically as the area under a graph of the force as a function of displacement. If the magnitude of force F required to stretch a spring a distance x beyond its natural length is proportional to x, then $F = kx$, where k is a constant for the spring, called its force constant or spring constant. The total work W needed to stretch the spring from $x = 0$ to $x = X$ is $W = \frac{1}{2}kX^2$.

Potential Energy

(Section 7.5) Potential energy can be thought of as *stored* energy. For an object with mass m at a height y above a chosen origin (where $y = 0$), the gravitational potential energy is $U_{grav} = mgy$ (Equation 7.9). When a spring is stretched or compressed a distance x from its uncompressed length, the spring stores elastic potential energy $U_{el} = \frac{1}{2}kx^2$ (Equation 7.13). Potential energy is associated only with conservative forces, not with nonconservative forces such as friction.

$U_{grav,i} = mgy_i$

$F = mg$

$U_{grav,f} = mgy_f$

$x = 0$

Gravitational potential energy:
For an object at vertical position y,
$$U_{grav} = mgy$$
For a change in vertical position,
$$\Delta U_{grav} = U_{grav,f} - U_{grav,i}$$

Elastic potential energy: For a spring stretched or compressed by a distance x from equilibrium,
$$U_{el} = \frac{1}{2}kx^2$$

Continued

Conservation of Energy

(Sections 7.6 and 7.7) When only conservative forces act on an object, the total mechanical energy (kinetic plus potential) is constant; that is, $K_i + U_i = K_f + U_f$, where U may include both gravitational and elastic potential energies. If some of the forces are nonconservative, we label their work as W_{other}. The change in total energy (kinetic plus potential) of an object during any motion is equal to the work W_{other} done by the nonconservative forces: $K_i + U_i + W_{other} = K_f + U_f$ (Equation 7.16). Nonconservative forces include friction forces, which usually act to decrease the total mechanical energy of a system.

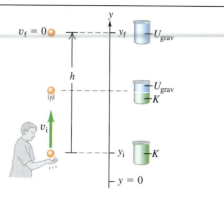

Power

(Section 7.8) Power is the time rate of doing work or the rate at which energy is transferred or transformed. For mechanical systems, power is the time rate at which work is done by or on an object or a system. When an amount of work ΔW is done during a time interval Δt, the average power is $P_{av} = \frac{\Delta W}{\Delta t}$ (Equation 7.17).

MP For instructor-assigned homework, go to www.masteringphysics.com

Conceptual Questions

1. How does friction produce internal energy? Explain what is happening at the molecular level to produce this form of energy.
2. True or false? If hydrogen molecules and oxygen molecules have the same kinetic energy, then they have the same speed. Explain your answer.
3. What is wrong with the following statement? "If a stone is thrown into the air at an angle θ above the horizontal, the y-component of its kinetic energy is converted to potential energy at its highest point." Explain your reasoning.
4. An elevator is hoisted by its cables at constant speed. Is the *total* work done on the elevator positive, negative, or zero? Explain your reasoning.
5. A rope tied to an object is pulled, causing the object to accelerate. According to Newton's third law, the object pulls back on the rope with an equal and opposite force. Is the total net work done on the object then zero? If so, how can the object's kinetic energy change?
6. If a projectile is fired upward at various angles above the horizontal, it has the same initial kinetic energy in each case. Why does it *not* then rise to the same maximum height in each case?
7. When you use a jack to lift a car, the force you exert on the jack is much less than the weight of the car. Does this mean that less work is done on the car than if the car were lifted directly?
8. Using simple observations, how can you tell that (a) sound has energy and (b) light has energy? (*Hint: Can you find ways in which sound and light produce more familiar forms of energy, such as kinetic energy or thermal energy?*)
9. A compressed spring is clamped in its compressed position and is then dissolved in acid. What becomes of the spring's potential energy?

10. You bounce on a trampoline, going a little higher with each bounce. Explain how you increase your total mechanical energy.
11. When you jump from the ground into the air, where does your kinetic energy come from? What force does work on you to lift you into the air? Could you jump if you were floating in outer space?
12. Hydroelectric energy comes from gravity pulling down water through dams in rivers. Explain how such energy is really just a form of solar energy by tracing how the sun's energy is able to get the water from the ocean to the reservoir behind the dam.
13. Does the kinetic energy of a car change more when the car speeds up from 10 mph to 15 mph or from 15 mph to 20 mph?
14. True or false? If a force is in the negative direction, then the work it does is negative. Explain your reasoning.
15. You often hear that the energy we use on the earth comes from the sun. Explain how this is true. For example, how does the kinetic energy of a running person come from the sun?
16. On your electrical "power" bill, you are charged for kilowatt-hours (kWh). Is this really a power bill? What kind of quantity is the kilowatt-hour?

Multiple-Choice Problems

1. A spiral spring is compressed so as to add U units of potential energy to it. When this spring is instead stretched two-thirds of the distance it was compressed, its remaining potential energy in the same units will be (see Section 2.5 for a review of proportional reasoning)
   A. $2U/3$ B. $4U/9$ C. $U/3$ D. $U/9$
2. A block slides a distance d down a frictionless plane and then comes to a stop after sliding a distance s across a rough horizontal plane, as shown in the accompanying figure. What frac-

tion of the distance s does the block slide before its speed is reduced to one-third of the maximum speed it had at the bottom of the ramp?

A. $s/3$ B. $2s/3$ C. $s/9$ D. $8s/9$

▲ **FIGURE 7.36** Multiple-choice problem 2.

3. You slam on the brakes of your car in a panic and skid a distance d on a straight and level road. If you had been traveling twice as fast, what distance would the car have skidded under the same conditions?

A. $4d$ B. $2d$ C. $\sqrt{2}d$ D. $d/2$

4. You wish to accelerate your car from rest at a constant acceleration. Assume that there is negligible air drag. To create a constant acceleration, the car's engine must

A. maintain a constant power output.
B. develop ever-decreasing power.
C. develop ever-increasing power.

5. Consider two frictionless inclined planes with the same vertical height. Plane 1 makes an angle of 30° with the horizontal, and plane 2 makes an angle of 60° with the horizontal. Mass m_1 is placed at the top of plane 1, and mass m_2 is placed at the top of plane 2. Both masses are released at the same time. At the bottom, which mass is going faster?

A. m_1
B. m_2
C. Neither; they both have the same speed at the bottom.

6. A brick is dropped from the top of a building through the air (friction is present) to the ground below. How does the brick's kinetic energy (K) just before striking the ground compare with the gravitational potential energy (U_{grav}) at the top of the building? Set $y = 0$ at the ground level.

A. K is equal to U_{grav}.
B. K is greater than U_{grav}.
C. K is less than U_{grav}.

7. Which of the following statements about work is or are true? (More than one statement may be true.)

A. Negative net work done on an object always reduces the object's kinetic energy.
B. If the work done on an object by a force is zero, then either the force or the displacement must have zero magnitude.
C. If a force acts downward, it does negative work.
D. The formula $W = Fd\cos\theta$ can be used only if the force is constant over the distance d.

8. A 10 kg stone and a 100 kg stone are released from rest at the same height above the ground. There is no appreciable air drag. Which of the following statements is or are true? (More than one statement may be true.)

A. Both stones have the same initial gravitational potential energy.
B. Both stones will have the same acceleration as they fall.
C. Both stones will have the same speed when they reach the ground.

D. Both stones will have the same kinetic energy when they reach the ground.
E. Both stones will reach the ground at the same time.

9. Two *identical* objects are pressed against two different springs so that each spring stores 50 J of potential energy. The objects are then released from rest. One spring is quite stiff (hard to compress), while the other one is quite flexible (easy to compress). Which of the following statements is or are true? (More than one statement may be true.)

A. Both objects will have the same maximum speed after being released.
B. The object pressed against the stiff spring will gain more kinetic energy than the other object.
C. Both springs are initially compressed by the same amount.
D. The stiff spring has a larger spring constant than the flexible spring.
E. The flexible spring must have been compressed more than the stiff spring.

10. For each of two objects with *different* masses, the gravitational potential energy is 100 J. They are released from rest and fall to the ground. Which of the following statements is or are true? (More than one statement may be true.)

A. Both objects are released from the same height.
B. Both objects will have the same kinetic energy when they reach the ground.
C. Both objects will have the same speed when they reach the ground.
D. Both objects will accelerate toward the ground at the same rate.
E. Both objects will reach the ground at the same time.

11. Two objects with *different* masses are launched vertically into the air by identical springs. The two springs are compressed by the same amount before launching. Which of the following statements is or are true? (More than one statement may be true.)

A. Both masses reach the same maximum height.
B. Both masses leave the springs with the same energy.
C. Both masses leave the springs with the same speed.
D. Both masses leave the springs with the same kinetic energy.
E. The lighter mass will gain more gravitational potential energy than the heavier mass.

12. Two objects with *unequal* masses are released from rest from the *same height*. They slide without friction down a slope and then encounter a rough horizontal region, as shown in the accompanying figure. The coefficient of kinetic friction in the rough region is the same for both masses. Which of the following statements is or are true? (More than one statement may be true.)

A. Both masses start out with the same gravitational potential energy.
B. Both objects have the same speed when they reach the base of the slope.

▲ **FIGURE 7.37** Multiple-choice problem 12.

C. Both masses have the same kinetic energy at the bottom of the slope.

D. Both masses travel the same distance on the rough horizontal surface before stopping.

E. Both masses will generate the same amount of thermal energy due to friction on the rough surface.

13. A 1 g grasshopper and a 0.1 g cricket leap vertically into the air with the same initial speed in the absence of air drag. Which of the following statements must be true? (More than one statement may be true.)

A. The grasshopper goes 10 times as high as the cricket.

B. Both will reach the same height.

C. At the highest point, both will have the same amount of gravitational potential energy relative to the ground.

D. At the highest point, the gravitational potential energy for the grasshopper will be 10 times as great as that for the cricket.

E. The grasshopper and the cricket have the same initial kinetic energy.

14. Two balls having *different* masses reach the same height when shot into the air from the ground. If there is no air drag, which of the following statements must be true? (More than one statement may be true.)

A. Both balls left the ground with the same speed.

B. Both balls left the ground with the same kinetic energy.

C. Both balls will have the same gravitational potential energy at the highest point.

D. The heavier ball must have left the ground with a greater speed than the lighter ball.

E. Both balls have no acceleration at their highest point.

15. The stone in the accompanying figure can be carried from the bottom to the top of a cliff by various paths. Which path requires more work?

A. *AC*

B. *ABC*

C. The work is the same for both paths.

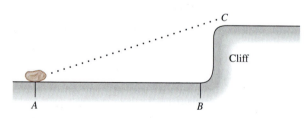

▲ **FIGURE 7.38** Multiple-choice problem 15.

Problems

7.2 Work

1. • A fisherman reels in 12.0 m of line while landing a fish, using a constant forward pull of 25.0 N. How much work does the tension in the line do on the fish?

2. • A tennis player hits a 58.0 g tennis ball so that it goes straight up and reaches a maximum height of 6.17 m. How much work does gravity do on the ball on the way up? On the way down?

3. • A boat with a horizontal tow rope pulls a water skier. She skis off to the side, so the rope makes an angle of 15.0° with the forward direction of motion. If the tension in the rope is

180 N, how much work does the rope do on the skier during a forward displacement of 300.0 m?

4. • A constant horizontal pull of 8.50 N drags a box along a horizontal floor through a distance of 17.4 m. (a) How much work does the pull do on the box? (b) Suppose that the same pull is exerted at an angle above the horizontal. If this pull now does 65.0 J of work on the box while pulling it through the same distance, what angle does the force make with the horizontal?

5. • You push your physics book 1.50 m along a horizontal tabletop with a horizontal push of 2.40 N while the opposing force of friction is 0.600 N. How much work does each of the following forces do on the book? (a) your 2.40 N push, (b) the friction force, (c) the normal force from the table, and (d) gravity? (e) What is the net work done on the book?

6. • A 128.0 N carton is pulled up a frictionless baggage ramp inclined at 30.0° above the horizontal by a rope exerting a 72.0 N pull parallel to the ramp's surface. If the carton travels 5.20 m along the surface of the ramp, calculate the work done on it by (a) the rope, (b) gravity, and (c) the normal force of the ramp. (d) What is the net work done on the carton? (e) Suppose that the rope is angled at 50.0° above the horizontal, instead of being parallel to the ramp's surface. How much work does the rope do on the carton in this case?

7. • A factory worker moves a 30.0 kg crate a distance of 4.5 m along a level floor at constant velocity by pushing horizontally on it. The coefficient of kinetic friction between the crate and the floor is 0.25. (a) What magnitude of force must the worker apply? (b) How much work is done on the crate by the worker's push? (c) How much work is done on the crate by friction? (d) How much work is done by the normal force? By gravity? (e) What is the net work done on the crate?

8. •• An 8.00 kg package in a mail-sorting room slides 2.00 m down a chute that is inclined at 53.0° below the horizontal. The coefficient of kinetic friction between the package and the chute's surface is 0.40. Calculate the work done on the package by (a) friction (b) gravity, and (c) the normal force. (d) What is the net work done on the package?

9. •• A 715 N person walks up three flights of stairs, covering a total vertical distance of 10.5 m. (a) If, as is typical, only 20% of the caloric (food) energy is converted to work by the muscles, how many joules and food calories of energy did the person use? (One food calorie = 4186 J.) (b) What happened to the other 80% of the food energy?

10. • Assume that the earth and the moon have circular orbits (which is almost true) and that the periods of their orbits are 365 days and 28 days, respectively. (a) How much work does the earth do on the moon in one day? (b) How much work does the sun do on the earth in one month?

11. •• A boxed 10.0 kg computer monitor is dragged by friction 5.50 m up along the moving surface of a conveyor belt inclined at an angle of 36.9° above the horizontal. If the monitor's speed is a constant 2.10 cm/s, how much work is done on the monitor by (a) friction, (b) gravity, and (c) the normal force of the conveyor belt?

7.3 Work and Kinetic Energy

12. • It takes 4.186 J of energy to raise the temperature of 1.0 g of water by 1.0°C. (a) How fast would a 2.0 g cricket have to jump to have that much kinetic energy? (b) How fast would a 4.0 g cricket have to jump to have the same amount of kinetic energy?

13. • A bullet is fired into a large stationary absorber and comes to rest. Temperature measurements of the absorber show that the bullet lost 1960 J of kinetic energy, and high-speed photos of the bullet show that it was moving at 965 m/s just as it struck the absorber. What is the mass of the bullet?

14. •• **Animal energy.** Adult cheetahs, the fastest of the great
BIO cats, have a mass of about 70 kg and have been clocked at up to 72 mph (32 m/s). (a) How many joules of kinetic energy does such a swift cheetah have? (b) By what factor would its kinetic energy change if its speed were doubled?

15. •• A racing dog is initially running at 10.0 m/s, but is slowing down. (a) How fast is the dog moving when its kinetic energy has been reduced by half? (b) By what fraction has its kinetic energy been reduced when its speed has been reduced by half?

16. •• If a running house cat has 10.0 J of kinetic energy at speed v, (a) At what speed (in terms of v) will she have 20.0 J of kinetic energy? (b) What would her kinetic energy be if she ran half as fast as the speed in part (a)?

17. • A 0.145 kg baseball leaves a pitcher's hand at a speed of 32.0 m/s. If air drag is negligible, how much work has the pitcher done on the ball by throwing it?

18. ••• A 1.50 kg book is sliding along a rough horizontal surface. At point A it is moving at 3.21 m/s, and at point B it has slowed to 1.25 m/s. (a) How much work was done on the book between A and B? (b) If -0.750 J of work is done on the book from B to C, how fast is it moving at point C? (c) How fast would it be moving at C if $+0.750$ J of work were done on it from B to C?

19. •• **Stopping distance of a car.** The driver of an 1800 kg car (including passengers) traveling at 23.0 m/s slams on the brakes, locking the wheels on the dry pavement. The coefficient of kinetic friction between rubber and dry concrete is typically 0.700. (a) Use the work–energy principle to calculate how far the car will travel before stopping. (b) How far would the car travel if it were going twice as fast? (c) What happened to the car's original kinetic energy?

20. • **Everyday kinetic energies.** Make reasonable estimates of the quantities necessary to calculate the following kinetic energies: (a) Approximately how many joules of kinetic energy does a walking adult have? What about a jogging adult? (b) Approximately how many joules of kinetic energy does a large car going at freeway speeds have? (c) If you drop an object with mass 1 kg (weight about 2 lb) from shoulder height, approximately how many joules of kinetic energy will the object have when it reaches the ground?

21. •• You throw a 20 N rock into the air from ground level and observe that, when it is 15.0 m high, it is traveling upward at 25.0 m/s. Use the work–energy principle to find (a) the rock's speed just as it left the ground and (b) the maximum height the rock will reach.

22. • A 0.420 kg soccer ball is initially moving at 2.00 m/s. A soccer player kicks the ball, exerting a constant 40.0 N force in the same direction as the ball's motion. Over what distance must her foot be in contact with the ball to increase the ball's speed to 6.00 m/s?

23. •• A 61 kg skier on level snow coasts 184 m to a stop from a speed of 12.0 m/s. (a) Use the work–energy principle to find the coefficient of kinetic friction between the skis and the snow. (b) Suppose a 75 kg skier with twice the starting speed coasted the same distance before stopping. Find the coefficient of kinetic friction between that skier's skis and the snow.

24. • **Other metric energy units.** Besides the joule, several other units of energy are commonly used in the metric system. One of these is the *calorie,* which is defined as the amount of heat energy required to raise the temperature of 1.0 g of water by 1.0°C; 1.00 cal is equal to 4.186 J. *(Note: Do not confuse this calorie with the food calorie, which is a thousand of the calories defined here.)* Another unit is the *erg;* just as the joule is defined as kg · m²/s², the erg is defined as g · cm²/s². A third energy unit is the *kilowatt-hour* (kWh), which is the energy produced when 1.0 kilowatt of power (1 kW = 1000 J/s) acts for an hour. (a) By converting units, show that 1 J = 10^7 ergs. (b) How many joules and how many calories are there in 1.00 kWh? (c) If a 0.250 mg flea jumps at 2.0 m/s, how many ergs of kinetic energy does it have? (d) How many kWh and how many ergs are required to raise the temperature of 1.0 g of water by 1.0°C?

7.4 Work Done by a Varying Force

25. • To stretch a certain spring by 2.5 cm from its equilibrium position requires 8.0 J of work. (a) What is the force constant of this spring? (b) What was the maximum force required to stretch it by that distance?

26. •• A spring is 17.0 cm long when it is lying on a table. One end is then attached to a hook and the other end is pulled by a force that increases to 25.0 N, causing the spring to stretch to a length of 19.2 cm. (a) What is the force constant of this spring? (b) How much work was required to stretch the spring from 17.0 cm to 19.2 cm? (c) How long will the spring be if the 25 N force is replaced by a 50 N force?

27. •• A spring of force constant 300.0 N/m and unstretched length 0.240 m is stretched by two forces, pulling in opposite directions at opposite ends of the spring, that increase to 15.0 N. How long will the spring now be, and how much work was required to stretch it that distance?

28. •• An unstretched spring has a force constant of 1200 N/m. How large a force and how much work are required to stretch the spring: (a) by 1.0 m from its unstretched length, and (b) by 1.0 m beyond the length reached in part (a)?

29. •• The graph in the accompanying figure shows the magnitude of the force exerted by a given spring as a function of the distance x the spring is stretched. How much work is needed to stretch this spring: (a) a distance of 5.0 cm, starting with it unstretched, and (b) from $x = 2.0$ cm to $x = 7.0$ cm?

▲ **FIGURE 7.39** Problem 29.

7.5 Potential Energy

30. • A 575 N woman climbs a staircase that rises at 53° above
BIO the horizontal and is 4.75 m long. Her speed is a constant
45 cm/s. (a) Is the given weight a reasonable one for an adult
woman? (b) How much has the gravitational potential energy
increased by her climbing the stairs? (c) How much work has
gravity done on her as she climbed the stairs?

31. • **How high can we jump?** The maximum height a typical
BIO human can jump from a crouched start is about 60 cm. By how
much does the gravitational potential energy increase for a 72 kg
person in such a jump? Where does this energy come from?

32. •• **Interplanetary potential energy.** For a hammer dropped
on earth, the initial gravitational potential energy is 60.0 J.
(a) What would be the initial gravitational potential energy for
the hammer on the moon (where the acceleration due to gravity is 1.67 m/s² if it is released from the same height in both
places? (b) From what height (compared with the height on
earth) would you have to drop the hammer on Mars (where the
acceleration due to gravity is 3.7 m/s²) to produce the same
initial amount of potential energy that it had on earth?

33. •• The accompanying figure shows a graph of the gravitational potential energy for an object as a function of its height
above the ground, at which $y = 0$. Use information obtained
from this graph to find the object's mass.

▲ **FIGURE 7.40** Problem 33.

34. • A force of magnitude 800.0 N stretches a certain spring by
0.200 m from its equilibrium position. (a) What is the force
constant of this spring? (b) How much elastic potential energy
is stored in the spring when it is: (i) stretched 0.300 m from its
equilibrium position and (ii) compressed by 0.300 m from its
equilibrium position? (c) How much work was done in stretching the spring by the original 0.200 m?

35. • **Tendons.** Tendons are strong elastic fibers that attach mus-
BIO cles to bones. To a reasonable approximation, they obey
Hooke's law. In laboratory tests on a particular tendon, it was
found that, when a 250 g object was hung from it, the tendon
stretched 1.23 cm. (a) Find the force constant of this tendon in
N/m. (b) Because of its thickness, the maximum tension this
tendon can support without rupturing is 138 N. By how much
can the tendon stretch without rupturing, and how much
energy is stored in it at that point?

36. ••• A certain spring stores 10.0 J of potential energy when it is
stretched by 2.00 cm from its equilibrium position. (a) How
much potential energy would the spring store if it were
stretched an additional 2.00 cm? (b) How much potential
energy would it store if it were compressed by 2.00 cm from its
equilibrium position? (c) How far from the equilibrium position
would you have to stretch the string to store 20.0 J of potential
energy? (d) What is the force constant of this spring?

37. • In designing a machine part, you need a spring that is 8.50 cm
long when no forces act on it and that will store 15.0 J of
energy when it is compressed by 1.20 cm from its equilibrium
position. (a) What should be the force constant of this spring?
(b) Can the spring store 850 J by compression?

38. •• Measurements of the magnitude of the restoring force F of
a 15.0-cm-long spring as a function of the distance x it is
stretched from its equilibrium position yield the graph shown
in the accompanying figure. Use numerical information from
this graph to answer the following questions. (a) Does this
spring obey Hooke's law? How do you know? (b) What is the
force constant of this spring? (c) How much force is needed to
stretch this spring 8.0 cm from its equilibrium position, and
how much energy is stored in the spring at that point?

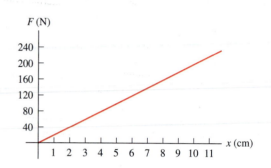

▲ **FIGURE 7.41** Problem 38.

39. •• **Food calories.** The *food calorie,* equal to 4186 J, is a
BIO measure of how much energy is released when food is metabolized by the body. A certain brand of fruit-and-cereal bar contains 140 food calories per bar. (a) If a 65 kg hiker eats one of
these bars, how high a mountain must he climb to "work off"
the calories, assuming that all the food energy goes only into
increasing gravitational potential energy? (b) If, as is typical,
only 20% of the food calories go into mechanical energy, what
would be the answer to part (a)? *(Note: In this and all other
problems, we are assuming that 100% of the food calories that
are eaten are absorbed and used by the body. This is actually
not true. A person's "metabolic efficiency" is the percentage of
calories eaten that are actually used; the rest are eliminated
by the body. Metabolic efficiency varies considerably from
person to person.)*

40. •• **A good workout.** You overindulged on a delicious dessert,
BIO so you plan to work off the extra calories at the gym. To
accomplish this, you decide to do a series of arm raises holding a 5.0 kg weight in one hand. The distance from your elbow
to the weight is 35 cm, and in each arm raise you start with
your arm horizontal and pivot it until it is vertical. Assume that
the weight of your arm is small enough compared with the
weight you are lifting that you can ignore it. As is typical, your
muscles are 20% efficient in converting the food energy they
use up into mechanical energy, with the rest going into heat. If
your dessert contained 350 food calories, how many arm raises
must you do to work off these calories? Is it realistic to do
them all in one session?

41. •• **An exercise program.** A 75 kg person is put on an exer-
BIO cise program by a physical therapist, the goal being to burn up
500 food calories in each daily session. Recall that human
muscles are about 20% efficient in converting the energy they

use up into mechanical energy. The exercise program consists of a set of consecutive high jumps, each one 50 cm into the air (which is pretty good for a human) and lasting 2.0 s, on the average. How many jumps should the person do per session, and how much time should be set aside for each session? Do you think that this is a physically reasonable exercise session?

7.6 Conservation of Energy

42. • Tall Pacific Coast redwood trees (*Sequoia sempervirens*) can reach heights of about 100 m. If air drag is negligibly small, how fast is a sequoia cone moving when it reaches the ground if it dropped from the top of a 100 m tree?

43. • The total height of Yosemite Falls is 2425 ft. (a) How many more joules of gravitational potential energy are there for each kilogram of water at the top of this waterfall compared with each kilogram of water at the foot of the falls? (b) Find the kinetic energy and speed of each kilogram of water as it reaches the base of the waterfall, assuming that there are no losses due to friction with the air or rocks and that the mass of water had negligible vertical speed at the top. How fast (in m/s and mph) would a 70 kg person have to run to have that much kinetic energy? (c) How high would Yosemite Falls have to be so that each kilogram of water at the base had twice the kinetic energy you found in part (b); twice the speed you found in part (b)?

44. • **The speed of hailstones.** Although the altitude may vary considerably, hailstones sometimes originate around 500 m (about 1500 ft) above the ground. (a) Neglecting air drag, how fast will these hailstones be moving when they reach the ground, assuming that they started from rest? Express your answer in m/s and in mph. (b) From your own experience, are hailstones actually falling that fast when they reach the ground? Why not? What has happened to most of the initial potential energy?

45. •• Pebbles of weight w are launched from the edge of a vertical cliff of height h at speed v_0. How fast (in terms of the quantities just given) will these pebbles be moving when they reach the ground if they are launched (a) straight up, (b) straight down, (c) horizontally away from the cliff, and (d) at an angle θ above the horizontal? (e) How would the answers to the previous parts change if the pebbles weighed twice as much?

46. • **Volcanoes on Io.** Io, a satellite of Jupiter, is the most volcanically active moon or planet in the solar system. It has volcanoes that send plumes of matter over 500 km high (see the accompanying figure). Due to the satellite's small mass, the acceleration due to gravity on Io is only 1.81 m/s², and Io has no appreciable atmosphere. Assume that there is no variation in gravity over the distance traveled. (a) What must be the speed of material just as it leaves the volcano to reach an altitude of 500 km? (b) If the gravitational potential energy is zero at the surface, what is the potential energy for a 25 kg fragment at its maximum height on Io? How much would this gravitational potential energy be if it were at the same height above earth?

▲ **FIGURE 7.42** Problem 46.

47. •• **Human energy vs. insect energy.** For its size, the common flea is one of the most accomplished jumpers in the animal world. A 2.0-mm-long, 0.50 mg critter can reach a height of 20 cm in a single leap. (a) Neglecting air drag, what is the takeoff speed of such a flea? (b) Calculate the kinetic energy of this flea at takeoff and its kinetic energy per kilogram of mass. (c) If a 65 kg, 2.0-m-tall human could jump to the same height compared with his length as the flea jumps compared with its length, how high could he jump, and what takeoff speed would he need? (d) In fact, most humans can jump no more than 60 cm from a crouched start. What is the kinetic energy per kilogram of mass at takeoff for such a 65 kg person? (e) Where does the flea store the energy that allows it to make such a sudden leap?

48. •• A 25 kg child plays on a swing having support ropes that are 2.20 m long. A friend pulls her back until the ropes are 42° from the vertical and releases her from rest. (a) What is the potential energy for the child just as she is released, compared with the potential energy at the bottom of the swing? (b) How fast will she be moving at the bottom of the swing? (c) How much work does the tension in the ropes do as the child swings from the initial position to the bottom?

49. •• Two stones of different masses are thrown straight upward, one on earth and one on the moon (where gravity produces an acceleration of 1.67 m/s²). Both reach the *same height*. If the stone on the moon had an initial speed v, what was the initial speed of the stone on earth, in terms of v?

50. •• A slingshot obeying Hooke's law is used to launch pebbles vertically into the air. You observe that if you pull a pebble back 2.0 cm against the elastic band, the pebble goes 6.0 m high. (a) Assuming that air drag is negligible, how high will the pebble go if you pull it back 4.0 cm instead? (b) How far must you pull it back so it will reach 12 m? (c) If you pull a pebble that is twice as heavy back 2.0 cm, how high will it go?

51. •• When a piece of wood is pressed against a spring and compresses the spring by 5.0 cm, the wood gains a maximum kinetic energy K when it is released. How much kinetic energy (in terms of K) would the piece of wood gain if the spring were compressed 10.0 cm instead?

52. • A 1.5 kg box moves back and forth on a horizontal frictionless surface between two different springs, as shown in the accompanying figure. The box is initially pressed against the stronger spring, compressing it 4.0 cm, and then is released from rest. (a) By how much will the box compress the weaker spring? (b) What is the maximum speed the box will reach?

▲ **FIGURE 7.43** Problem 52.

53. •• A 12.0 N package of whole wheat flour is suddenly placed on the pan of a scale such as you find in grocery stores. The pan is supported from below by a vertical spring of force constant 325 N/m. If the pan has negligible weight, find the maximum distance the spring will be compressed if no energy is dissipated by friction.

54. •• A basket of negligible weight hangs from a vertical spring scale of force constant 1500 N/m. (a) If you suddenly put a

3.0 kg adobe brick in the basket, find the maximum distance that the spring will stretch. (b) If, instead, you release the brick from 1.0 m above the basket, by how much will the spring stretch at its maximum elongation?

7.7 Conservative and Nonconservative Forces

55. • A 1.50 kg brick is sliding along on a rough horizontal surface at 13.0 m/s. If the brick stops in 4.80 s, how much mechanical energy is lost, and what happens to this energy?

56. • A fun-loving 11.4 kg otter slides up a hill and then back down to the same place. If she starts up at 5.75 m/s and returns at 3.75 m/s, how much mechanical energy did she lose on the hill, and what happened to that energy?

57. • A 12.0 g plastic ball is dropped from a height of 2.50 m and is moving at 3.20 m/s just before it hits the floor. How much mechanical energy was lost during the ball's fall?

58. • **Old Faithful.** Old Faithful, the most famous geyser in Yellowstone National Park, shoots water approximately 61 m into the air. The water has been measured to leave the geyser at a speed of 50 m/s. (a) How many joules of mechanical energy are lost by each kilogram of water on the way up? (b) What happens to the "lost" energy? Is it really *lost*? To what other forms of energy is it converted?

59. • While a roofer is working on a roof that slants at 36° above the horizontal, he accidentally nudges his 85.0 N toolbox, causing it to start sliding downward, starting from rest. If it starts 4.25 m from the lower edge of the roof, how fast will the toolbox be moving just as it reaches the edge of the roof if the kinetic friction force on it is 22.0 N?

60. •• A 1.1 kg mass hangs from a spring of force constant 400.0 N/m. The mass is then pulled down 13.0 cm from the equilibrium position and released. At the end of five complete cycles of vibration, the mass reaches only 10.0 cm from the equilibrium position. (a) How much mechanical energy is lost during these five cycles? (b) What percentage of the mechanical energy is lost during the five cycles?

61. •• A loaded 375 kg toboggan is traveling on smooth horizontal snow at 4.5 m/s when it suddenly comes to a rough region. The region is 7.0 m long and reduces the toboggan's speed by 1.5 m/s. (a) What average friction force did the rough region exert on the toboggan? (b) By what percent did the rough region reduce the toboggan's (i) kinetic energy and (ii) speed?

62. •• A 62.0 kg skier is moving at 6.50 m/s on a frictionless, horizontal snow-covered plateau when she encounters a rough patch 3.50 m long. The coefficient of kinetic friction between this patch and her skis is 0.300. After crossing the rough patch and returning to friction-free snow, she skis down an icy, frictionless hill 2.50 m high. (a) How fast is the skier moving when she gets to the bottom of the hill? (b) How much internal energy was generated in crossing the rough patch?

7.8 Power

63. • (a) How many joules of energy does a 100 watt lightbulb use every hour? (b) How fast would a 70 kg person have to run to have that amount of kinetic energy? Is it possible for a person to run that fast? (c) How high a tree would a 70 kg person

have to climb to increase his gravitational potential energy relative to the ground by that amount? Are there any trees that tall?

64. • The engine of a motorboat delivers 30.0 kW to the propeller while the boat is moving at 15.0 m/s. What would be the tension in the towline if the boat were being towed at the same speed?

65. •• At 7.35 cents per kilowatt-hour, (a) what does it cost to operate a 10.0 hp motor for 8.00 hr? (b) What does it cost to leave a 75 W light burning 24 hours a day?

66. • A tandem (two-person) bicycle team must overcome a force of 165 N to maintain a speed of 9.00 m/s. Find the power required per rider, assuming that each contributes equally.

67. •• A ski tow operates on a 15.0° slope of length 300 m. The rope moves at 12.0 km/h and provides power for 50 riders at one time, with an average mass per rider of 70.0 kg. Calculate the power required to operate the tow.

68. •• **U.S. power use.** The total consumption of electrical energy in the United States is about 1.0×10^{19} joules per year. (a) Express this rate in watts and kilowatts. (b) If the U.S. population is about 260 million people, what is the average rate of electrical energy consumption per person?

69. •• **Solar energy.** The sun transfers energy to the earth by radiation at a rate of approximately 1.0 kW per square meter of surface. (a) If this energy could be collected and converted to electrical energy with 25% efficiency, how large an area (in square kilometers) would be required to collect the electrical energy used by the United States? (See the previous problem.) (b) If the solar collectors were arranged in a square array, what would be the length of its sides in kilometers and in miles? Does an array of these dimensions seem technologically feasible?

70. •• A 20.0 kg rock slides on a rough horizontal surface at 8.00 m/s and eventually stops due to friction. The coefficient of kinetic friction between the rock and the surface is 0.200. What average thermal power is produced as the rock stops?

71. •• **Horsepower.** In the English system of units, power is expressed as *horsepower* (hp) instead of watts, where 1.00 hp = 746 W. Horsepower is often used for motors and automobiles. (a) What should be the power rating in horsepower of a 100 W lightbulb? (b) How many watts does a 75 hp motor produce? (c) Electrical resistors are rated in watts to indicate how much power they can tolerate without burning up. If a resistor is rated at 2.00 W, what should be its rating in horsepower? (d) Our sun radiates 3.92×10^{26} J of energy each second. What is its horsepower rating? (e) How many kilowatt-hours of energy is produced when you run a 25 hp motor for 90 minutes?

72. •• **Maximum sustainable human power.** The maximum **BIO** *sustainable* mechanical power a human can produce is about $\frac{1}{3}$ hp. How many food calories can a human burn up in an hour by exercising at this rate? (Remember that only 20% of the food energy used goes into mechanical energy.)

73. •• **Should you walk or run?** It is 5.0 km from your home to **BIO** the physics lab. As part of your physical fitness program, you could run that distance at 10 km/hr (which uses up energy at the rate of 700 W), or you could walk it leisurely at 3.0 km/hr (which uses energy at 290 W). Which choice would burn up more energy, and how much energy (in joules) would it burn? Why is it that the more intense exercise actually burns up less energy than the less intense one?

74. •• **Human power.** Time yourself while running up a flight of steps, and compute your maximum power in horsepower. Are you stronger than a horse?

75. •• **The power of the human heart.** The human heart is a **BIO** powerful and extremely reliable pump. Each day it takes in and discharges about 7500 L of blood. Assume that the work done by the heart is equal to the work required to lift that amount of blood a height equal to that of the average American female, approximately 1.63 m. The density of blood is 1050 kg/m³. (a) How much work does the heart do in a day? (b) What is the heart's power output in watts? (c) In fact, the heart puts out more power than you found in part (b). Why? What other forms of energy does it give the blood?

76. ••• **Hydroelectric power.** The Grand Coulee Dam is 1270 m wide and 170 m high. The electrical power output from the generators at the base of the dam is approximately 2000 MW. (a) How many cubic meters per second of water must flow from the top of the dam to produce this amount of power if all the initial gravitational potential energy is converted to electrical energy? (Each cubic meter of water has a mass of 1000 kg.) (b) What would be the answer to part (a) if the conversion process to electrical energy were only 92% efficient?

General Problems

77. • **Bumper guards.** You are asked to design spring bumpers for the walls of a parking garage. A freely rolling 1200 kg car moving at 0.65 m/s is to compress the spring no more than 7.0 cm before stopping. (a) What should be the force constant of the spring, and what is the maximum amount of energy that gets stored in it? (b) If the springs that are actually delivered have the proper force constant but can become compressed by only 5.0 cm, what is the maximum speed of the given car for which they will provide adequate protection?

78. •• **Human terminal velocity.** By landing properly and on soft ground (and by being lucky!), humans have survived falls from airplanes when, for example, a parachute failed to open, with astonishingly little injury. Without a parachute, a typical human eventually reaches a terminal velocity of about 62 m/s. Suppose the fall is from an airplane 1000 m high. (a) How fast would a person be falling when he reached the ground if there were no air drag? (b) If a 70 kg person reaches the ground traveling at the terminal velocity of 62 m/s, how much mechanical energy was lost during the fall? What happened to that energy?

79. •• A 0.800 kg ball is tied to the end of a string 1.60 m long and swung in a vertical circle. (a) Starting anywhere in the path, calculate the net work done on this ball during one complete cycle by (i) the tension in the string and (ii) gravity. (b) Repeat part (a) for motion along the semicircle from the lowest to the highest point on the path.

80. •• **Mountain climbing!** A 75.0 kg mountain climber is holding his 60.0 kg partner over a cliff when he suddenly steps on frictionless ice at the horizontal top of the cliff, as shown in the accompanying figure. The rope has negligible mass and is held horizontally by the climber. There is no appreciable friction at the icy edge of the cliff. Use energy methods to calculate the speed of the climbers after the lower one has descended 1.50 m starting from rest.

75.0 kg

60.0 kg

▲ **FIGURE 7.44** Problem 80.

81. •• **More mountain climbing!** What would be the speed of the climbers in the previous problem after they had moved 1.50 m if there were friction between the upper climber and the ice with a coefficient of kinetic friction of 0.250?

82. •• Suppose the worker in Problem 7 pushes downward at an angle of 30° below the horizontal. (a) What magnitude of force must the worker apply to move the crate at constant velocity? (b) How much work is done on the crate by this force when the crate is pushed a distance of 4.5 m? (c) How much work is done on the crate by friction during the displacement of the crate? (d) How much work is done by the normal force of the floor? By gravity? (e) What is the net work done on the crate?

83. •• A 50 g object and a 500 g object are launched by pressing them against identical springs and compressing both springs by the same amount. (a) Which spring has more initial potential energy? (b) Which object gains more kinetic energy after being released? (c) Which object gains more speed after being released? (d) Which object is acted upon by a greater initial force from the spring? (e) Which object has a greater acceleration the instant after it is released? In each case, explain the reasoning behind your answer.

84. •• On an essentially frictionless horizontal ice-skating rink, a skater moving at 3.0 m/s encounters a rough patch that reduces her speed by 45% due to a friction force that is 25% of her weight. Use the work–energy principle to find the length of the rough patch.

85. ••• **Pendulum.** A small 0.12 kg metal ball is tied to a very light (essentially massless) string 0.80 m long to form a pendulum that is then set swinging by releasing the ball from rest when the string makes a 45° angle with the vertical. Air drag and other forms of friction are negligible. What is the speed of the ball when the string passes through its vertical position, and what is the tension in the string at that instant?

86. •• **Pendulum.** A pendulum consists of a small 4.5 N metal weight attached to a very light 1.75 m string. The weight is released from rest when the string makes an angle of 62.0° with the vertical. At the end of the first swing, the string reaches an angle of only 56.5°. (a) How much mechanical energy has the pendulum lost during this swing? (b) Where did the energy go? Explain physically how it could have been converted to other forms of energy.

87. •• A pump is required to lift 750 liters of water per minute from a well 14.0 m deep and eject it with a speed of 18.0 m/s. How much work per minute does the pump do?

88. •• A 350 kg roller coaster starts from rest at point A and slides down the frictionless loop-the-loop shown in the accompanying figure. (a) How fast is this roller coaster moving at point B? (b) How hard does it press against the track at point B?

▲ **FIGURE 7.45** Problem 88.

89. ••• **Automobile air-bag safety.** An automobile air bag cushions the force on the driver in a head-on collision by absorbing her energy before she hits the steering wheel. Such a bag can be modeled as an elastic force, similar to that produced by a spring. (a) Use energy conservation to show that the effective force constant k of the air bag is $k = mv_0^2/x_{max}^2$, where m is the mass of the driver, v_0 is the speed of the car (and driver) at the instant of the accident, and x_{max} is the maximum distance the bag gets compressed, which, in a severe accident, would be the distance from the driver's body to the steering wheel. (b) Show that the maximum force the air bag would exert on the driver is $F_{max} = mv_0^2/x_{max}$. (c) Now let's put in some realistic numbers. Experimental tests have shown that injury occurs when a force *density* greater than 5.0×10^5 N/m² acts on human tissue. (The *total* force is this force density times the area over which it acts.) As the accompanying figure shows, the force of the air bag acts mostly on the upper front half of the driver's body, over an area of about 2500 cm². (Check your own body to see if this is reasonable.) Use this value to calculate the total force on the driver's body at the threshold of injury. (d) Use your results to calculate the effective force constant k of the air bag and the maximum speed for which the bag will prevent injury to a 65 kg driver if she is 30 cm from the steering wheel at the instant of impact. Express the speed in m/s and mph. (e) How could you design a safer air bag for higher speed collisions? What things could you alter to do this? Would it be safe to make a stiffer air bag by inflating it more? Explain your reasoning.

▲ **FIGURE 7.46** Problem 89.

90. •• On a frictionless horizontal laboratory floor, a 15.0 N scientific instrument is attached to a light (that is, essentially massless) spring having a force constant of 75 N/cm. The other end of the spring is attached to the wall. (a) If the instrument is pulled 1.20 cm from its equilibrium position and released from rest, find its maximum *speed* and its maximum *acceleration*.

(b) Do the maximum speed and acceleration occur at the same time? If not, when in the motion does each of them occur?

91. ••• **Bone fractures.** The maximum energy that a bone can absorb without breaking depends on its characteristics, such as its cross-sectional area and its elasticity. For healthy human leg bones of approximately 6.0 cm² cross-sectional area, this energy has been experimentally measured to be about 200 J. (a) From approximately what maximum height could a 60 kg person jump and land rigidly upright on both feet without breaking his legs? (b) You are probably surprised at how small the answer to part (a) is. People obviously jump from much greater heights without breaking their legs. How can that be? What else absorbs the energy when they jump from greater heights? *(Hint: How did the person in part (a) land? How do people normally land when they jump from greater heights?)* (c) In light of your answers to parts (a) and (b), what might be some of the reasons that older people are much more prone than younger ones to bone fractures from simple falls (such as a fall in the shower)?

92. •• **Whiplash injuries.** When a car is hit from behind, its passengers undergo sudden forward acceleration, which can cause a severe neck injury, known as *whiplash*. During normal acceleration, the neck muscles play a large role in accelerating the head so that the bones are not injured. But during a very sudden acceleration the muscles do not react immediately, because they are flexible, so most of the accelerating force is provided by the neck bones. Experimental tests have shown that these bones will fracture if they absorb more than 8.0 J of energy. (See the discussion in the previous problem.) (a) If a car waiting at a stoplight is rear-ended in a collision that lasts for 10.0 ms, what is the greatest speed this car and its driver can reach without breaking neck bones if his head has a mass of 5.0 kg (which is about right for a 70 kg person)? Express your answer in m/s and mph. (b) What is the acceleration of the passengers during the collision in part (a), and how large a force is acting to accelerate their heads? Express the acceleration in m/s² and in g's.

93. •• A 250 g object on a frictionless, horizontal lab table is pushed against a spring of force constant 35 N/cm and then released. Just before the object is released, the spring is compressed 12.0 cm. How fast is the object moving when it has gained half of the spring's original stored energy?

94. •• In the accompanying figure, a 5.0 N ball is fastened to two identical springs that pull in opposite directions and that can slide on a frictionless horizontal surface. The ball is initially stationary and is then moved 3.0 cm to the right and released from rest. (a) Find the magnitude and direction of the net force on the ball just after it is released. (b) What is the potential energy of the system just after the ball is released? (c) Find the maximum speed of the ball.

k = 12 N/cm   Ball   k = 12 N/cm

Frictionless surface

▲ **FIGURE 7.47** Problem 94.

95. •• **Automobile accident analysis.** In an auto accident, a car hit a pedestrian and the driver then slammed on the brakes to stop the car. During the subsequent trial, the driver's lawyer

claimed that the driver was obeying the posted 35 mph speed limit, but that the limit was too high to enable him to see and react to the pedestrian in time. You have been called as the state's expert witness. In your investigation of the accident site, you make the following measurements: The skid marks made while the brakes were applied were 280 ft long, and the tread on the tires produced a coefficient of kinetic friction of 0.30 with the road. (a) In your testimony in court, will you say that the driver was obeying the posted speed limit? You must be able to back up your answer with clear numerical reasoning during cross-examination. (b) If the driver's speeding ticket is $10 for each mile per hour he was driving above the posted speed limit, would he have to pay a ticket, and if so, how much would it be?

96. ••• **Bouncing ball.** A rubber ball is dropped from an initial height h. After each bounce, the ball returns to 75% of its previous height. What percent of the maximum potential energy, maximum kinetic energy, and maximum speed is lost as a result of the first bounce?

97. •• **Riding a loop-the-loop.** A car in an amusement park ride travels without friction along the track shown in the accompanying figure, starting from rest at point A. If the loop the car is currently on has a radius of 20.0 m, find the mini-

▲ **FIGURE 7.48** Problem 97.

mum height h so that the car will not fall off the track at the top of the circular part of the loop.

98. •• A 2.0 kg piece of wood slides on the surface shown in the accompanying figure. All parts of the surface are frictionless, except for a 30-

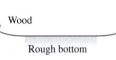

▲ **FIGURE 7.49** Problem 98.

m-long rough segment at the bottom, where the coefficient of kinetic friction with the wood is 0.20. The wood starts from rest 4.0 m above the bottom. (a) Where will the wood eventually come to rest? (b) How much work is done by friction by the time the wood stops?

99. •• A 68 kg skier approaches the foot of a hill with a speed of 15 m/s. The surface of this hill slopes up at 40.0° above the horizontal and has coefficients of static and kinetic friction of 0.75 and 0.25, respectively, with the skis. (a) Use energy conservation to find the maximum height above the foot of the hill that the skier will reach. (b) Will the skier remain at rest once she stops, or will she begin to slide down the hill? Prove your answer.

100. •• **Energy requirements of the body.** A 70 kg human uses **BIO** energy at the rate of 80 J/s, on average, for just resting and sleeping. When the person is engaged in more strenuous activities, the rate can be much higher. (a) If the individual did nothing but rest, how many food calories per day would she or he have to eat to make up for those used up? (b) In what forms is energy used when a person is resting or sleeping? In other words, what happens to those 80 J/s? *(Hint: What kinds of energy, mechanical and otherwise, do our body components have?)* (c) If an average person rested and did other low-level activity for 16 hours (which consumes 80 J/s) and did light activity on the job for 8 hours (which consumes 200 J/s), how many calories would she or he have to consume per day to make up for the energy used up?

101. •• From the top edge of a horizontal plateau, a 175.0 N bag of mountain-climbing gear is launched horizontally by pressing it against a spring of force constant 385.0 N/cm. Just before the launch, the spring is compressed 10.0 cm from its equilibrium position. Once the bag is free of the spring, it goes over a vertical cliff 3.45 m high and lands in the snow below. How far from the foot of the cliff does the bag land, and how fast is it moving when it gets there?

102. •• Two paint buckets are connected by a lightweight rope passing over a pulley of negligible mass and friction. (a) As shown in the accompanying figure, the system is released from rest with the 12.0 kg bucket 2.00 m above the floor. Use energy conservation to find the speed with which this bucket strikes the floor. (b) Suppose the pulley had appreciable mass but no bearing friction. Would the bucket's speed be greater than, less than, or the same as you found in part (a)? Explain your reasoning in terms of energy.

▲ **FIGURE 7.50**
Problem 102.

103. •• (a) Use data from Appendix F to calculate the kinetic energy of the earth as it moves around the sun and the kinetic energy of the moon as it moves around the earth. (b) Express these kinetic energies in units of megatons of TNT. (One ton of TNT releases 4.184×10^9 J of energy.)

104. ••• A ball is thrown upward with an initial velocity of 15 m/s at an angle of 60.0° above the horizontal. Use energy conservation to find the ball's greatest height above the ground.

105. •• **Gasoline energy.** When it is burned, 1 gallon of gasoline produces 1.3×10^8 J of energy. A 1500 kg car accelerates from rest to 37 m/s in 10.0 s. The engine of this car is only 15% efficient (which is typical), meaning that only 15% of the combustion energy goes into accelerating the car. The rest goes into things like heating up the engine and exhaust gas. (a) How many gallons of gasoline does the car use during its acceleration? (b) How many such accelerations will it take to burn 1 gallon of gasoline?

106. ••• **Mass extinctions.** One of the greatest mass extinctions occurred about 65 million years ago, when, along with many other life-forms, the dinosaurs went extinct. Most geologists and paleontologists agree that this event was caused when a large asteroid hit the earth. Scientists estimate that this asteroid was about 10 km in diameter and that it would have been traveling at least as fast as 11 km/s. The density of asteroid material is about 3.5 g/cm³, on the average. (a) What would be the approximate mass of the asteroid, assuming it to be spherical? (b) How much kinetic energy would the asteroid have delivered to the earth? (c) In order to put the amount of energy you found in part (b) in perspective, consider the following: One of the largest nuclear weapons ever tested by the U. S. (the Castle/Bravo bomb) was a 15 megaton bomb, meaning that it released the energy of 15 million tons of TNT. One ton of TNT releases 4.184×10^9 J. How many Castle/Bravo bombs would it take to produce the kinetic energy of the asteroid that did in the dinosaurs?

107. •• **Avoiding mass extinctions.** It has been suggested that we can protect the earth from devastating asteroidal impacts such as the one discussed in the previous problem by using nuclear devices to alter the orbits of such asteroids around the sun so that they will miss our planet. If this is done very far from earth, it is necessary to move them only a few centimeters to spare the earth a mass extinction. How much energy would it take to move the asteroid that has been implicated in the dinosaur extinction by a few centimeters? (See the previous problem.) To make the calculation reasonable, assume that we need to exert a force on the asteroid that will accelerate it uniformly from rest through a distance of 5.0 cm in 0.50 s. The energy we must give to the asteroid is the added kinetic energy from this motion. To see if it is feasible to do this, how many 1.0 megaton bombs would it take to accomplish the task?

108. •• In an experiment, a ball is dropped from various heights and its kinetic energy is measured just as it reaches the floor. A graph of the kinetic energy of the ball as a function of the height h from which it is dropped is shown in the accompanying figure. Use information obtained from the graph to answer the following questions: (a) How many newtons does the ball weigh? (b) From what height should the ball be dropped so it will be moving at 4.0 m/s when it reaches the floor? (c) Sketch a clear graph of the gravitational potential energy as a function of h.

▲ **FIGURE 7.51** Problem 108.

109. •• A graph of the potential energy stored in a tendon as a
BIO function of the *square* of the distance x it has stretched from its equilibrium position is shown in the accompanying figure. (a) Does the tendon obey Hooke's law? Explain your reasoning. (b) What is the force constant of the tendon? (c) How far must the tendon be stretched from its equilibrium position to store 10.0 J of energy? (d) What force is necessary to hold the tendon in place in part (c)? (e) Sketch a clear graph of the potential energy stored in the tendon as a function of x.

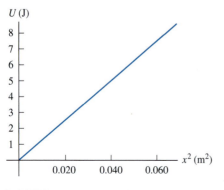

▲ **FIGURE 7.52** Problem 109.

110. •• The accompanying figure shows the kinetic energy of an object as a function of the *square* of its speed. (a) What is the mass of the object? (b) If the object is moving at 3.0 m/s, what is its kinetic energy? (c) How fast must the object move to have a kinetic energy of 5.0 J? (d) Sketch a graph of the object's kinetic energy as a function of its speed.

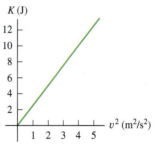

▲ **FIGURE 7.53** Problem 110.

111. •• A sled with rider having a combined mass of 125 kg travels over the perfectly smooth icy hill shown in the accompanying figure. How far does the sled land from the foot of the cliff?

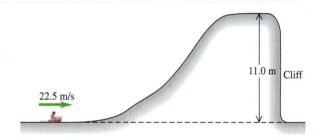

▲ **FIGURE 7.54** Problem 111.

8 MOMENTUM

When an 18-wheeler collides head-on with a compact car, why are the occupants of the car much more likely to be injured than those of the truck? How do you decide how to aim the cue ball in pool so as to knock the eight ball into the pocket? How can a rocket engine accelerate a space shuttle in outer space, where there's nothing to push against?

To answer these and similar questions, we need two new concepts—momentum and impulse—and a new conservation law: conservation of momentum. This law is every bit as important as conservation of energy, and its validity extends far beyond the bounds of classical mechanics, to include relativistic mechanics (the mechanics of the very fast) and quantum mechanics (the mechanics of the very small). Within classical mechanics, it enables us to analyze many situations that would be difficult to handle if we used Newton's laws directly. Among these situations are collision problems, in which two colliding objects exert large forces on each other for a short time.

The tugboat and the container ship have the same velocity, but if they accidentally collided with a dock, the container ship would do far more damage because of its greater mass. In this chapter we consider the combination of mass multiplied by velocity, which we call *momentum.*

8.1 Momentum

When a particle with mass m moves with velocity $\vec{v}$, we define its **momentum** $\vec{p}$ as follows:

Definition of momentum

The momentum of a particle, denoted by $\vec{p}$, is the product of its mass m and its velocity $\vec{v}$:

$$\vec{p} = m\vec{v}. \tag{8.1}$$

Unit: $\text{kg} \cdot \text{m/s}$ (This combination has no special name.)

Momentum $\vec{p}$ is a vector quantity; a particle's momentum has the same direction as its velocity $\vec{v}$.

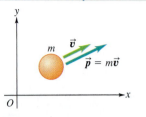

▲ **FIGURE 8.1** Momentum is a vector quantity.

Because velocity is a vector quantity, momentum is also a vector quantity. (See Figure 8.1.) Momentum has a magnitude (mv, mass times speed) and a direction (the same as that of the velocity vector). The momentum of a car driving north at 20 m/s is different from the momentum of the same car driving east at the same speed (even though both cars have the same kinetic energy). A fastball thrown by a major-league pitcher has greater momentum than the same ball thrown by a child, because the speed is greater. An 18-wheeler going 55 mi/h has greater momentum than a Saturn automobile going the same speed, because the truck's mass is greater.

Conceptual Analysis 8.1

Momentum and kinetic energy

Two objects have the same momentum but different masses. Which of the following statements about them is correct?

A. The one with less mass has more kinetic energy.
B. Both objects have the same kinetic energy.
C. The one with more mass has more kinetic energy.

SOLUTION Momentum is defined as $\vec{p} = m\vec{v}$, so if two objects have the same magnitude of momentum $p = mv$, the one with

the smaller mass m must have the greater speed v. However, kinetic energy depends on the *square* of speed: $K = \frac{1}{2}mv^2$. The kinetic energy can be expressed as

$$K = \tfrac{1}{2}mv^2 = \tfrac{1}{2}m\left(\frac{p}{m}\right)^2 = \frac{p^2}{2m}.$$

Solving for p, we get $p = \sqrt{2mK}$. Thus, if two objects have the same magnitude of momentum, p, the one with smaller mass m must have greater kinetic energy K. So choice A is right.

Coup

Contrecoup

▲ **Contrecoup injury.** The large mass of the human brain makes us susceptible to a type of head trauma known as a contrecoup brain injury (*contrecoup* is French for "across from the blow"). A blow to the head accelerates both the skull and brain. The brain's large mass gives it considerable momentum. When the skull stops moving, the brain runs into it. Depending on how suddenly the skull slows down, this second, contrecoup blow to the brain can cause as much or more injury as the initial blow. Animals with less massive brains rarely suffer this type of injury.

We'll often express the momentum of a particle in terms of its components. It follows from Equation 8.1 that if the particle has velocity components v_x, v_y, and v_z, its components of momentum, p_x, p_y, and p_z, are given by

$$p_x = mv_x$$
$$p_y = mv_y \qquad \text{(components of momentum)} \qquad (8.2)$$
$$p_z = mv_z$$

These three component equations are equivalent to Equation 8.1. In most of the problems in this chapter, the velocities will lie in the x-y plane and $\vec{v}$ will have only x and y components, but all the component relations are easily generalized to three-dimensional situations in which three components of velocity are needed.

The importance of momentum can be traced to its close relation to Newton's second law, $\Sigma\vec{F} = m\vec{a}$. We assume for now that the mass m of the particle is constant. (Later we'll learn how to deal with systems in which the mass changes.) When m is constant, we can express Newton's second law for a particle in terms of momentum. First, the instantaneous acceleration $\vec{a}$ of the particle is defined as

$$\vec{a} = \lim_{\Delta t \to 0} \frac{\Delta \vec{v}}{\Delta t},$$

so Newton's second law can be written as

$$\Sigma\vec{F} = m \lim_{\Delta t \to 0} \frac{\Delta \vec{v}}{\Delta t}.$$

Now if m is constant, the right side of this expression is just the instantaneous rate change of momentum of the particle. To show this, we note that if m is constant, $m\,\Delta\vec{v}$ is the change of momentum during the interval Δt:

$$m\,\Delta\vec{v} = m(\vec{v}_2 - \vec{v}_1) = m\vec{v}_2 - m\vec{v}_1 = \vec{p}_2 - \vec{p}_1 = \Delta\vec{p},$$

so we obtain

Newton's second law in terms of momentum
The vector sum of forces acting on a particle equals the rate of change of momentum of the particle with respect to time:

$$\Sigma \vec{F} = \lim_{\Delta t \to 0} \frac{\Delta \vec{p}}{\Delta t}. \qquad (8.3)$$

This, not $\Sigma \vec{F} = m\vec{a}$, is the modern equivalent of Newton's original statement of his second law. It is actually more general than our original form of the second law, because it includes the possibility of a change in momentum resulting from a change in mass as well as from a change in velocity. Note that both forms of the second law are valid only in inertial frames of reference.

Total Momentum
We define the *total momentum* of two or more particles as the vector sum of the momenta (plural of momentum) of the particles. Thus, if two particles A and B have momenta $\vec{p}_A$ and $\vec{p}_B$, their total momentum $\vec{P}$ is the vector sum

$$\vec{P} = \vec{p}_A + \vec{p}_B.$$

We can extend this definition directly to any number of particles.

Definition of total momentum
The total momentum $\vec{P}$ of any number of particles is equal to the vector sum of the momenta of the individual particles:

$$\vec{P} = \vec{p}_A + \vec{p}_B + \vec{p}_C + \cdots.$$
$$\text{(total momentum of a system of particles)} \qquad (8.4)$$

We'll often use Equation 8.4 in component form. If $p_{A,x}$, $p_{A,y}$, and $p_{A,z}$ are the components of momentum of particle A, $p_{B,x}$, $p_{B,y}$, and $p_{B,z}$ the components for particle B, and so on, then Equation 8.4 is equivalent to the component equations

$$P_x = p_{A,x} + p_{B,x} + \cdots,$$
$$P_y = p_{A,y} + p_{B,y} + \cdots, \qquad \text{(components of total momentum)} \qquad (8.5)$$
$$P_z = p_{A,z} + p_{B,z} + \cdots.$$

Momentum is sometimes called *linear momentum* to distinguish it from *angular momentum,* which plays an important role in rotational motion. We won't usually use the prefix *linear,* except where there is danger of confusion with angular momentum.

NOTE ▸ It's absolutely essential to remember that momentum is a vector quantity; Equations 8.1 through 8.5 are *vector* equations. (Equations 8.2 and 8.5 express a vector relationship in terms of components of the vectors.) We'll often add momentum vectors by the use of components, so everything that you've learned about components of vectors will be useful with momentum. ◂

EXAMPLE 8.1 **Preliminary analysis of a collision**

A small compact car with a mass of 1000 kg is traveling north on Morewood Avenue with a speed of 15 m/s. At the intersection of Morewood and Fifth Avenues, it collides with a truck with a mass of 2000 kg that is traveling east on Fifth Avenue at 10 m/s. Treating each vehicle as a particle, find the total momentum (magnitude and direction) just before the collision.

SOLUTION

SET UP Because momentum is a vector quantity, we need coordinate axes. We draw a sketch (Figure 8.2a), labeling the car A and the truck B.

SOLVE We need to find (1) the components of momentum of each vehicle, (2) the components of total momentum, and then (3) the magnitude and direction of the total momentum vector (as sketched in Figure 8.2b). The components of momentum of the two vehicles are

$$p_{A,x} = m_A v_{A,x} = (1000 \text{ kg})(0) = 0,$$
$$p_{A,y} = m_A v_{A,y} = (1000 \text{ kg})(15 \text{ m/s}) = 1.5 \times 10^4 \text{ kg} \cdot \text{m/s},$$
$$p_{B,x} = m_B v_{B,x} = (2000 \text{ kg})(10 \text{ m/s}) = 2.0 \times 10^4 \text{ kg} \cdot \text{m/s},$$
$$p_{B,y} = m_B v_{B,y} = (1000 \text{ kg})(0) = 0$$

There are no z components of velocity or momentum.

From Equations 8.5, the components of the total momentum $\vec{P}$ are

$$P_x = m_A v_{A,x} + m_B v_{B,x} = 0 + 2.0 \times 10^4 \text{ kg} \cdot \text{m/s}$$
$$= 2.0 \times 10^4 \text{ kg} \cdot \text{m/s},$$
$$P_y = m_A v_{A,y} + m_B v_{B,y} = 1.5 \times 10^4 \text{ kg} \cdot \text{m/s} + 0$$
$$= 1.5 \times 10^4 \text{ kg} \cdot \text{m/s}.$$

The total momentum $\vec{P}$ is a vector quantity with these components. Its magnitude is

$$P = \sqrt{(2.0 \times 10^4 \text{ kg} \cdot \text{m/s})^2 + (1.5 \times 10^4 \text{ kg} \cdot \text{m/s})^2}$$
$$= 2.5 \times 10^4 \text{ kg} \cdot \text{m/s}.$$

(a)   (b)

▲ **FIGURE 8.2** Our sketches for this problem.

Its direction is given by the angle θ in Figure 8.2b, where

$$\tan\theta = \frac{1.5 \times 10^4 \text{ kg} \cdot \text{m/s}}{2.0 \times 10^4 \text{ kg} \cdot \text{m/s}} = \frac{3}{4}, \qquad \theta = 36.9°.$$

REFLECT It is essential to treat momentum as a vector. When we add the momenta of the two objects we must do vector addition, using the method of components. Each vehicle has momentum in only one coordinate direction so has only one nonzero component of momentum, but the total momentum of the system has both x and y components.

Practice Problem: If the car is moving at 15 m/s, how fast must the truck move for the total momentum vector to make a 45° angle with the $+x$ and $+y$ axes? *Answer:* 7.5 m/s.

8.2 Conservation of Momentum

The concept of momentum is particularly important in situations in which two or more objects interact. Let's consider first an idealized system consisting of two objects that interact with each other, but not with anything else—for example, two astronauts who touch each other as they float freely in the zero-gravity environment of outer space (Figure 8.3). Think of the astronauts as particles. Each particle exerts a force on the other; according to Newton's third law, the two forces are always equal in magnitude and opposite in direction. From Newton's second law, as reformulated in Equation 8.3, the vector sum of forces acting on each particle equals the rate of change of that particle's momentum. This means that, at any instant, the two rates of change of momentum are equal in magnitude and opposite in direction, so the rate of change of the *total* momentum is zero, and the total momentum is constant. We say that total momentum is *conserved.*

Let's focus our attention on a definite collection of particles that we'll call a **system.** For instance, the two astronauts in Figure 8.3 could be taken as a system. For any system, the various particles exert forces on each other. We'll call these **internal forces.** In addition, forces may be exerted on any part of the system by

The forces exerted by the astronauts on each other form an action–reaction pair.

▲ **FIGURE 8.3** The internal forces the astronauts exert on each other don't change the total momentum of the two astronauts.

▶ **Strike!** A strike in bowling demonstrates conservation of momentum. The system consists of the ball and pins. Assuming that friction is negligible, the external forces acting on it—weight and normal forces—sum to zero, so the system can be regarded as isolated. Before the strike, the system's momentum is all in the moving ball (because the pins are stationary). Afterward, it is divided among the ball and the scattering pins—but the vector sum of the momenta of the ball and pins equals the momentum of the ball before impact.

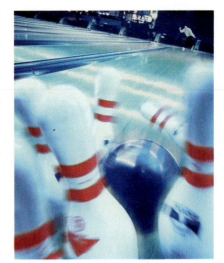

objects *outside* the system; we call these **external forces.** A system that is acted upon by *no* external forces is called an **isolated system.** We have defined the total momentum of the system, *P*, as the vector sum of the momenta of the individual particles:

$$\vec{P} = \vec{p}_A + \vec{p}_B + \vec{p}_C + \cdots. \qquad \text{(total momentum of a system)}$$

The essential point to be made is that **internal forces cannot change the total momentum of a system.**

Here's why: Suppose particle A exerts a force $\vec{F}_{A\,\text{on}\,B}$ on particle B. Then, from Newton's third law, particle B must simultaneously exert a force $\vec{F}_{B\,\text{on}\,A}$ on particle A that is equal in magnitude and opposite in direction: $\vec{F}_{A\,\text{on}\,B} = -\vec{F}_{B\,\text{on}\,A}$. Each force by itself would cause the total momentum of the system to change, according to Equation 8.3. But because the two forces are negatives of each other, the two rates of change of momentum are also negatives of each other, and the *total* rate of change of momentum from this interaction is zero. Similarly, the changes in momentum caused by *all* the internal forces cancel out in pairs, and the rate of change of the total momentum $\vec{P}$ with respect to time due to internal forces is always zero. Internal forces can change the momenta of individual particles, but not the total momentum of the system.

If the internal forces cannot change the total momentum, and if there are no external forces, then the total momentum cannot change. We conclude that **the total momentum of an isolated system is constant.** Furthermore, if there are external forces, but their vector sum is zero, the total momentum is again constant.

Conservation of momentum
The total momentum of a system is constant whenever the vector sum of the external forces on the system is zero. In particular, the total momentum of an isolated system is constant.

Activ
Physics   6.6, 6.7

NOTE ▶ We have used Newton's second law to derive the principle of conservation of momentum, so we have to be careful to use this principle only in inertial frames of reference. ◀

In some ways, the principle of conservation of momentum is more general than the principle of conservation of mechanical energy. For example, it is valid *even when the internal forces are not conservative;* by contrast, mechanical energy is conserved *only when the internal forces are conservative.* In this chapter, we'll analyze some situations in which both momentum and mechanical energy are conserved and others in which only momentum is conserved. These two principles play a fundamental role in all areas of physics, and we'll encounter them throughout our study.

PROBLEM-SOLVING STRATEGY 8.1 **Conservation of momentum**

Momentum is a vector quantity; you *must* use vector addition to compute the total momentum of a system. Using components is usually the simplest method.

SET UP

1. Define the system you are analyzing. Choose a coordinate system, specifying the positive direction for each axis. Often, it is easiest to choose the x axis as having the direction of one of the initial velocities. Make sure that you are using an inertial frame of reference.

2. Treat each object as a particle. Sketch "before" and "after" diagrams, including your coordinate system. Add vectors on each diagram to represent all known velocities. Label the vectors with magnitudes, angles, components, or whatever information is given, and give each unknown magnitude, angle, or component an algebraic symbol. It's often helpful to use multiple subscripts on velocity and momentum symbols to ensure complete identification. For example, the initial value (i) of the x component of velocity of object A can be written as $v_{A,i,x}$.

SOLVE

3. Compute the x and y components of momentum of each particle, both before and after the interaction, using the relations $p_x = mv_x$ and $p_y = mv_y$. Some of the components will be expressed in terms of symbols representing unknown quantities. Even when all the velocities lie along a line (such as the x axis), the components of velocity and momentum along this line can be positive or negative, so be careful with signs!

4. Determine whether both the x and the y components of total momentum are conserved, and why or why not. If they are conserved, write a relation that equates the total *initial* x component of momentum to the total *final* x component of momentum. Write another equation for the y components. These two equations express conservation of momentum in component form. In some problems, only one component of momentum is conserved. If the sum of the x components of the external forces is zero, then the x component of total momentum is conserved, and so on.

5. Solve the equations you wrote in step 4 to determine whatever quantities the problem asks for. In some problems, you'll have to convert from the x and y components of a velocity to its magnitude and direction, and in others you'll need to make the opposite conversion from magnitude and direction to x and y components.

   Remember that the x and y components of velocity or momentum are *never* added together in the same equation.

REFLECT

6. As with all problem solving, especially when the results are expressed in symbols rather than numbers, try to think of particular cases in which you can guess what the results of your analysis should be. What happens when two masses are equal? When one mass is zero? Is the result what you would expect?

EXAMPLE 8.2 **Astronaut rescue**

An astronaut finds herself floating in space 100 m from her ship when her safety cable becomes unlatched. She and the ship are motionless relative to each other. The astronaut's mass (including space suit) is 100 kg; she has a 1.0 kg wrench and only a 20 minute air supply. Thinking back to her physics classes, she devises

Continued

a plan to use conservation of momentum to get back to the ship safely by throwing the wrench away from her. In what direction should she throw the wrench? What is the magnitude of her recoil velocity if she throws the wrench at 10 m/s? Will her recoil velocity be enough to get her back to the spacecraft before she runs out of air?

SOLUTION

SET UP We choose a system consisting of the astronaut plus the wrench. No external forces act on this system, so the total momentum is conserved. We draw diagrams showing the situation just before and just after she throws the wrench; we point the x axis to the right (Figure 8.4). We use the subscripts i and f (initial and final) to label the situations before and after the wrench is thrown, and we use subscripts A and W (astronaut and wrench) to identify the parts of the system.

SOLVE The astronaut needs to acquire a velocity *toward* the spaceship. Because the total momentum of herself and the wrench is zero, she should throw the wrench directly *away* from the ship.

All the vector quantities lie along the x axis, so we're concerned only with x components. We write an equation expressing the equality of the initial and final values of the total x component of momentum:

$$m_A(v_{A,i,x}) + m_W(v_{W,i,x}) = m_A(v_{A,f,x}) + m_W(v_{W,f,x})$$

In this case, the initial velocity of each object is zero, so the left side of the equation is zero. That is, $m_A(v_{A,f,x}) + m_W(v_{W,f,x}) = 0$. Solving for $v_{A,f,x}$, the astronaut's x component of velocity after she throws the wrench, we get

$$v_{A,f,x} = \frac{-m_W(v_{W,f,x})}{m_A} = \frac{-(1.0 \text{ kg})(10.0 \text{ m/s})}{(100 \text{ kg})} = -0.10 \text{ m/s.}$$

▲ **FIGURE 8.4** Our sketches for this problem.

The negative sign indicates that the astronaut is moving toward the ship, opposite to our chosen +x direction.

To find the total time required for the astronaut to travel 100 m (at constant velocity) to reach the ship, we use x = vt, or

$$t = \frac{100 \text{ m}}{0.10 \text{ m/s}} = 1.00 \times 10^3 \text{ s} = 16 \text{ min } 40 \text{ s.}$$

REFLECT With a 20 minute air supply, she makes it back to the ship safely, with 3 min 20 s, to spare.

Practice Problem: If the astronaut has only a 10 minute air supply left, how fast must she throw the wrench so that she makes it back to the spaceship in time? *Answer:* 17 m/s.

EXAMPLE 8.3   Recoil of a rifle

A marksman holds a 3.00 kg rifle loosely, allowing it to recoil freely when fired, and fires a bullet of mass 5.00 g horizontally with a speed $v_B = 300$ m/s. What is the recoil speed v_R of the rifle? What are the final kinetic energies of the bullet and the rifle?

SOLUTION

SET UP We consider an idealized model in which the horizontal forces the marksman exerts on the rifle are negligible. We also neglect the momentum of the expanding gases. Then we can consider the rifle and bullet as an isolated system. (The net vertical force is zero.) The total momentum $\vec{P}$ of the system is zero both before and after the marksman fires the rifle. We take the positive x axis to be the direction in which the rifle is aimed; Figure 8.5 shows our sketch.

SOLVE Before the bullet is fired, the x component of the total momentum is zero. After the bullet is fired, the x component of its momentum is $(5.00 \times 10^{-3} \text{ kg})(300 \text{ m/s})$ and that of the rifle is $(3.00 \text{ kg})v_{R,f,x}$. Conservation of the x component of total momentum, P_x, before and after the firing, gives us

$$P_{i,x} = P_{f,x} = 0 = (5.00 \times 10^{-3} \text{ kg})(300 \text{ m/s})$$
$$+ (3.00 \text{ kg})(v_{R,f,x}) \text{ (zero total momentum),}$$
$$v_{R,f,x} = -0.500 \text{ m/s.)}$$

▲ **FIGURE 8.5** Our sketches for this problem.

The negative sign means that the recoil of the rifle is in the direction opposite that of the bullet. If the butt of a rifle were to hit your shoulder traveling at this speed, you would probably feel the "kick."

Continued

The final kinetic energy of the bullet is

$$K_{\text{bullet}} = \tfrac{1}{2}(5.00 \times 10^{-3}\,\text{kg})(300\,\text{m/s})^2 = 225\,\text{J},$$

and the final kinetic energy of the rifle is

$$K_{\text{rifle}} = \tfrac{1}{2}(3.00\,\text{kg})(0.500\,\text{m/s})^2 = 0.375\,\text{J}.$$

REFLECT The bullet acquires much greater kinetic energy than the rifle does because the bullet moves much farther than the rifle during the interaction, so the interaction force on the bullet does more work than the force on the rifle (even though the two forces are equal and opposite). In fact, the ratio of the two kinetic energies, 600 : 1, is equal to the inverse ratio of the masses. Note that because the bullet has much less mass than the rifle, it has much greater acceleration during the firing.

Practice Problem: The same rifle fires a bullet with mass 10.0 g with the same speed as before. For the same idealized model, find the ratio of the final kinetic energies of the bullet and rifle. *Answer:* 450 J/1.5 J, or a ratio of 300 : 1, independent of the muzzle velocity of the bullet.

EXAMPLE 8.4   A head-on collision

Two gliders move toward each other on a linear air track (Figure 8.6), which we assume is frictionless. Glider A has a mass of 0.50 kg, and glider B has a mass of 0.30 kg; both gliders move with an initial speed of 2.0 m/s. After they collide, glider B moves away with a final velocity whose x component is $+2.0$ m/s (Figure 8.6c). What is the final velocity of A?

SOLUTION

SET UP We take the x axis as lying along the air track, with the positive direction to the right. All the velocities and momenta have only x components. Our system consists of the two gliders. There are no external horizontal forces, so the x component of total momentum is the same before and after the collision.

SOLVE Let the final x component of velocity of A be $v_{A,\text{f},x}$. Then we write an expression for the total x component of momentum before the collision (subscript i) and one for after the collision (subscript f):

$$P_{\text{i},x} = (0.50\,\text{kg})(2.0\,\text{m/s}) + (0.30\,\text{kg})(-2.0\,\text{m/s}),$$
$$P_{\text{f},x} = (0.50\,\text{kg})(v_{A,\text{f},x}) + (0.30\,\text{kg})(+2.0\,\text{m/s}).$$

From conservation of the x component of momentum, these two quantities must be equal. When we solve the resulting equation for $v_{A,\text{f},x}$, we get

$$v_{A,\text{f},x} = -0.40\,\text{m/s}. \qquad \text{(final x velocity of glider A)}$$

REFLECT The two initial velocities are equal in magnitude, but the two final velocities are not. Although the total momentum is the same before and after the collision, it is distributed differently after the collision than before.

▶ **FIGURE 8.6**   (c) After collision

Practice Problem: Suppose the initial x component of velocity of glider A is changed to 3.0 m/s, with all other values remaining the same as before. Find the velocity of glider A after the collision. *Answer:* 0.60 m/s.

EXAMPLE 8.5   Collision in a horizontal plane

Figure 8.7 shows two chunks of ice sliding on the surface of a frictionless frozen pond. Chunk A, with mass $m_A = 5.0$ kg, moves with initial velocity $v_{A,\text{i}} = 2.0$ m/s parallel to the x axis. It collides with chunk B, which has mass $m_B = 3.0$ kg and is initially at rest. After the collision, the velocity of A is found to be $v_{A,\text{f}} = 1.0$ m/s in a direction at an angle $\alpha = 30°$ with the initial direction. What is the final velocity of B (magnitude and direction)?

SOLUTION

SET UP The velocities are not all along a single line, so we have to use both x and y components of momentum for each chunk of ice. There are no horizontal external forces, so the total horizontal momentum of the system is the same before and after the collision. Conservation of momentum requires that the sum of the x components before the collision must equal their sum after the collision, and similarly for the y components. We must

Continued

write a separate equation for each component. We draw in the coordinate axes as shown in Figure 8.7. We also express the final velocities in terms of their components.

SOLVE We start by writing expressions for the total x component of momentum before and after the collision. For the x components, we have

$$m_A(v_{A,i,x}) + m_B(v_{B,i,x})$$
$$= (5.0\,\text{kg})(2.0\,\text{m/s}) + (3.0\,\text{kg})(0), \quad \text{(before)}$$
$$m_A(v_{A,f,x}) + m_B(v_{B,f,x})$$
$$= (5.0\,\text{kg})(1.0\,\text{m/s})(\cos 30°) + (3.0\,\text{kg})(v_{B,f,x}). \quad \text{(after)}$$

Equating these two expressions and solving for $v_{B,f,x}$, we find that

$$v_{B,f,x} = 1.89\,\text{m/s}. \quad (x\text{ component of final velocity of }B)$$

Conservation of the y component of total momentum gives

$$m_A(v_{A,i,y}) + m_B(v_{B,i,y})$$
$$= (5.0\,\text{kg})(0) + (3.0\,\text{kg})(0), \quad \text{(before)}$$
$$m_A(v_{A,f,y}) + m_B(v_{B,f,y})$$
$$= (5.0\,\text{kg})(1.0\,\text{m/s})(\sin 30°) + (3.0\,\text{kg})(v_{B,f,y}). \quad \text{(after)}$$

Equating these two expressions and solving for $v_{B,f,y}$, we obtain

$$v_{B,f,y} = -0.83\,\text{m/s}. \quad (y\text{ component of final velocity of }B)$$

We now have the x and y components of the final velocity $\vec{v}_{B,f}$ of chunk B. The magnitude of $\vec{v}_{B,f}$ is

$$|\vec{v}_{B,f}| = \sqrt{(1.89\,\text{m/s})^2 + (-0.83\,\text{m/s})^2} \quad \text{(final }speed\text{ of }B)$$
$$= 2.1\,\text{m/s},$$

▲ FIGURE 8.7

and the angle β of its direction from the positive x axis is

$$\beta = \tan^{-1}\frac{-0.83\,\text{m/s}}{1.89\,\text{m/s}} = -24°.$$

REFLECT It's essential to treat velocity and momentum as vector quantities, representing them in terms of components. You can then use these components to find the magnitudes and directions of unknown vector quantities.

Practice Problem: If chunk B has an initial velocity of magnitude 2.0 m/s in the $+y$ direction instead of being initially at rest, find its final velocity (magnitude and direction). *Answer:* 2.2 m/s, 32°.

Exploding projectile

A model rocket travels as a projectile in a parabolic path after its first stage burns out. At the top of its trajectory, where its velocity points horizontally to the right, a small explosion separates it into two sections with equal masses. One section falls straight down, with no horizontal motion. What is the direction of the motion of the other part just after the explosion?

A. Up and to the left
B. Straight up
C. Up and to the right

SOLUTION We consider the two rocket sections as a system. During the explosion, internal forces dominate, and the external forces of gravity and air drag can be neglected. Therefore, we can assume that, during the short time of the explosion, the total momentum is conserved. Figure 8.8 illustrates our reasoning. Before the explosion, the rocket's momentum points horizontally to the right. The *total* momentum of the system must be the same just after the explosion as just before. We're told that one section

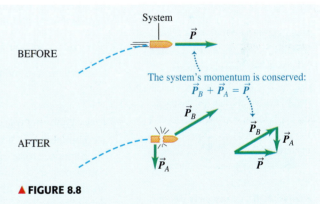

▲ FIGURE 8.8

moves straight down. Therefore, the other section must move up in order for the system as a whole to still have zero vertical momentum. This section must also move to the right, so that the system retains its original horizontal momentum. Thus, the correct choice is C.

8.3 Inelastic Collisions

In everyday speech, *collision* is likely to mean some sort of automotive disaster. We'll use it in that sense, but we'll also broaden the meaning to include any strong interaction between two objects that lasts a relatively short time. So we

Activ ONLINE *Physics* 6.8

(a) Before collision

Kinetic energy is stored as potential energy in compressed springs.

(b) Elastic collision

The system of the two gliders has the same kinetic energy after the collision as before it.

(c) After collision

▲ **FIGURE 8.9** An elastic collision.

(a) Before collision

The gliders stick together

(b) Completely inelastic collision

The system of the two gliders has less kinetic energy after the collision than before it.

(c) After collision

▲ **FIGURE 8.10** A completely inelastic collision.

include not only car accidents, but also balls hitting each other on a billiard table, the slowing of neutrons in a nuclear reactor by encounters with nuclei, and the impact of a meteor on the Arizona desert.

If the interaction forces are much larger than any external forces, we can model the system as an *isolated* system, neglecting the external forces entirely. Two cars colliding at an icy intersection provide a good example. Even two cars colliding on dry pavement can be treated as an isolated system during the collision if, as happens all too often, the interaction forces between the cars are much larger than the external forces, such as friction forces of pavement against tires.

If the interaction forces between the objects are conservative, the total kinetic energy of the system is the same after the collision as before. Such a collision is called an **elastic collision.** A collision between two steel balls or two billiard balls is very nearly elastic, and collisions between subatomic particles are often, though not always, elastic. Figure 8.9 shows a model of an elastic collision. When the objects collide, the springs are momentarily compressed, and some of the original kinetic energy is converted to elastic potential energy. Then the objects bounce apart, the springs expand, and the potential energy is reconverted to kinetic energy.

A collision in which the total kinetic energy after the collision is *less* than that before the collision is called an **inelastic collision.** In one kind of inelastic collision, the colliding objects stick together and move as one object after the collision. In Figure 8.10, we've replaced the springs in Figure 8.9 with strips of Velcro®, causing the gliders to have a completely inelastic collision. A paintball striking a window shade, a bullet embedding itself in a block of wood, and two cars colliding and locking their fenders are additional examples of completely inelastic collisions.

Let's do a general analysis of a completely inelastic collision. Imagine two objects (*A* and *B*) that move along a straight line, which we'll designate as the *x* axis. Because they stick together after the collision, their final velocities must be equal, and the final total momentum is $\vec{P}_f = (m_A + m_B)\vec{v}_f$. We'll use $v_{f,x}$ to denote the *x* component of the common final velocity $\vec{v}_f$. We have

$$\vec{v}_{A,f} = \vec{v}_{B,f} = \vec{v}_f, \qquad v_{A,f,x} = v_{B,f,x} = v_{f,x}. \qquad \text{(equal final velocities)}$$

Conservation of momentum gives the relation

$$m_A(v_{A,i,x}) + m_B(v_{B,i,x}) = (m_A + m_B)(v_{f,x}). \qquad (8.6)$$

If we know the masses and initial velocities of the objects, we can compute the *x* component $v_{f,x}$ of the common final velocity $\vec{v}_f$.

Suppose, for example, that an object with mass m_A and initial velocity with component $v_{A,i,x}$ along the $+x$ axis collides inelastically with an object with mass m_B that is initially at rest ($v_{B,i,x} = 0$). From Equation 8.6, the common *x* component of velocity $v_{f,x}$ of the two objects after the collision is

$$v_{f,x} = \frac{m_A}{m_A + m_B}(v_{A,i,x}).$$

(common final velocity in completely inelastic collision) (8.7)

Let's verify that the total kinetic energy after this completely inelastic collision is less than before the collision. Using the above expression for $v_{f,x}$, we find that the kinetic energies K_i and K_f before and after the collision are, respectively,

$$K_i = \tfrac{1}{2}m_A(v_{A,i,x})^2,$$

$$K_f = \tfrac{1}{2}(m_A + m_B)(v_{f,x})^2 = \tfrac{1}{2}(m_A + m_B)\left(\frac{m_A}{m_A + m_B}\right)^2(v_{A,i,x})^2.$$

Dividing the second of these equations by the first, we find that the ratio of final to initial kinetic energy is

$$\frac{K_f}{K_i} = \frac{m_A}{m_A + m_B}. \tag{8.8}$$

Because $m_A + m_B$ is always greater than m_A, the right side of this equation is always less than 1. Therefore, as expected, the final kinetic energy of the system is less than the initial kinetic energy.

When two objects with equal mass have a completely inelastic collision, the final kinetic energy is one-half the initial value. Even when the initial velocity of m_B is not zero, it is not hard to verify that the kinetic energy after a completely inelastic collision is always less than before.

NOTE ▶ We don't recommend memorizing the preceding equations. We derived them only to prove that kinetic energy is always lost in a completely inelastic collision. ◀

▲ **Get outta my way!** Since momentum is the product of mass and velocity, even slow-moving objects can have substantial momentum if they are massive enough.

Quantitative Analysis 8.3

Energy in an inelastic collision

An iron block B with mass m_B slides with speed v_B across a frictionless horizontal plane (Figure 8.11). It collides with and sticks to a magnet M with mass m_M. The magnet is attached to a spring with spring constant k. We can find the speed V of the two blocks immediately after the collision by applying conservation of momentum and solving: $(m_B + m_M)V = m_B v_B$. The masses stop when the spring is compressed an amount x_{max}. Which of the following equations would you use to find x_{max}?

A. $\frac{1}{2}m_B V^2 = \frac{1}{2}kx_{max}^2$
B. $\frac{1}{2}m_B v_B^2 = \frac{1}{2}kx_{max}^2$
C. $\frac{1}{2}(m_M + m_B)V^2 = \frac{1}{2}kx_{max}^2$

SOLUTION Because the two masses stick together, mechanical energy is not conserved. Therefore, choice B, which equates the

initial kinetic energy of the iron block and the final potential energy of the compressed spring, can't be correct. However, once the masses have collided and stuck, mechanical energy is conserved while the masses compress the spring. Thus, the correct choice is C, which equates the kinetic energy of the blocks just after the collision with the final elastic potential energy of the spring. We have to find the speed V of the combined masses $(m_M + m_B)$ and then apply conservation of energy to the compression of the spring.

▲ **FIGURE 8.11**

EXAMPLE 8.6 **Inelastic collision on an air track**

We perform a collision experiment using the Velcro®-equipped gliders of Figure 8.10. As in Example 8.4, glider A has a mass of 0.50 kg and glider B has a mass of 0.30 kg; both move with initial speeds of 2.0 m/s. Find the final velocity of the joined gliders, and compare the initial and final kinetic energies.

SOLUTION

SET UP Figure 8.12 shows our sketches for this problem. As in Example 8.4, we point the x axis in the direction of motion. All the velocity and momentum vectors lie along the x axis.

SOLVE We need to write expressions for the total x component of momentum before and after the collision and equate them. From conservation of the x component of momentum, we have

$$(0.50 \text{ kg})(2.0 \text{ m/s}) + (0.30 \text{ kg})(-2.0 \text{ m/s})$$
$$= (0.50 \text{ kg} + 0.30 \text{ kg})(v_{f,x})$$
$$v_{f,x} = 0.50 \text{ m/s}.$$

Because $v_{f,x}$ is positive, the gliders move together to the right (the $+x$ direction) after the collision. Before the collision, the kinetic energy of glider A is

$$K_{A,i} = \frac{1}{2}m_A(v_{A,i,x})^2 = \frac{1}{2}(0.50 \text{ kg})(2.0 \text{ m/s})^2 = 1.0 \text{ J},$$

▲ **FIGURE 8.12** Our sketches for this problem.

and that of glider B is

$$K_{B,i} = \frac{1}{2}m_B(v_{B,i,x})^2 = \frac{1}{2}(0.30 \text{ kg})(-2.0 \text{ m/s})^2 = 0.60 \text{ J}.$$

Note that the initial kinetic energy of glider B is positive, even though the x components of its initial velocity, $v_{B,i,x}$, and momentum, $m_B(v_{B,i,x})$, are both negative. (Remember that

Continued

kinetic energy is a scalar, not a vector component, and that it can never be negative.)

The total kinetic energy before the collision is 1.6 J. The kinetic energy after the collision is

$$\tfrac{1}{2}(m_A + m_B)(v_{f,x})^2 = \tfrac{1}{2}(0.50 \text{ kg} + 0.30 \text{ kg})(0.50 \text{ m/s})^2$$
$$= 0.10 \text{ J}.$$

REFLECT The final kinetic energy is only $\tfrac{1}{16}$ of the original, and $\tfrac{15}{16}$ is "lost" in the collision. Of course, it isn't really lost; it is converted from mechanical energy to various other forms of energy. For instance, if there were a wad of chewing gum between the gliders, it would squash irreversibly on impact and become warmer. If the gliders coupled together like two freight cars, the energy would go into elastic waves that would eventually dissipate. If there were a spring between the gliders that compressed as they locked together, then the energy would be stored as potential energy in the spring. In all of these cases, the *total* energy of the system *is* conserved, even though *kinetic* energy is not. However, in an isolated system, momentum is *always* conserved, whether the collision is elastic or not.

Practice Problem: If glider A has twice the mass of glider B, determine the ratio of final to initial kinetic energy. *Answer:* $\tfrac{1}{9}$.

EXAMPLE 8.7   The ballistic pendulum

How fast is a speeding bullet? Figure 8.13 shows a simple form of ballistic pendulum, a system for measuring the speed of a bullet. The bullet, with mass m_B, is fired into a block of wood with mass m_W suspended like a pendulum. The bullet makes a completely inelastic collision with the block, becoming embedded in it. After the impact of the bullet, the block swings up to a maximum height h. Given values of h, m_B, and m_W, how can we find the initial speed v of the bullet? What becomes of its initial kinetic energy?

SOLUTION

SET UP We analyze this event in two stages: first, the embedding of the bullet in the block, and second, the subsequent swinging of the block on its strings. During the first stage, the bullet embeds itself in the block so quickly that the block doesn't have time to swing appreciably away from its initial position. So, during the impact, the supporting strings remain very nearly vertical, there is negligible external horizontal force acting on the system, and the horizontal component of momentum is conserved. In the second stage, after the collision, the block and bullet move as a unit. The only forces are the weight (a conservative force) and the string tensions (which do no work). As the pendulum swings upward and to the right, mechanical energy is conserved.

To keep the notation simple, we'll denote the x component of the bullet's velocity just before impact as v and the x component of the velocity of block plus bullet just after the impact as V.

SOLVE Figure 8.13 shows the situation just before impact, the situation just after impact, and the block (with the embedded bullet) at the highest point of its path. Conservation of momentum just before impact and just after gives us

$$m_B v = (m_B + m_W)V,$$
$$v = \frac{m_B + m_W}{m_B}V.$$

The kinetic energy of the system just after the collision is $K = \tfrac{1}{2}(m_B + m_W)V^2$. The pendulum comes to rest (for an instant) at a height h, where its kinetic energy $\tfrac{1}{2}(m_B + m_W)V^2$ has all become potential energy $(m_B + m_W)gh$; then it swings back down. Energy conservation gives

$$\tfrac{1}{2}(m_B + m_W)V^2 = (m_B + m_W)gh.$$

Assuming that h can be measured, we solve this equation for V:

$$V = \sqrt{2gh}. \quad \text{(velocity of block and bullet just after impact)}$$

BEFORE COLLISION

AFTER COLLISION

TOP OF SWING

▲ **FIGURE 8.13** Using a ballistic pendulum to find a bullet's speed.

Now we substitute this result into the momentum equation to find v:

$$v = \frac{m_B + m_W}{m_B}\sqrt{2gh}. \quad \text{(speed of bullet just before impact)}$$

By measuring m_B, m_W, and h, we can compute the original velocity v of the bullet. For example, if $m_B = 5.00 \text{ g} = 0.00500 \text{ kg}$, $m_W = 2.00 \text{ kg}$, and $h = 3.00 \text{ cm} = 0.0300 \text{ m}$, then

$$v = \frac{2.00 \text{ kg} + 0.00500 \text{ kg}}{0.00500 \text{ kg}}\sqrt{2(9.80 \text{ m/s}^2)(0.0300 \text{ m})}$$
$$= 307 \text{ m/s}.$$

Continued

The x component V of velocity of the block just after impact is

$$V = \sqrt{2gh} = \sqrt{2(9.80 \text{ m/s}^2)(0.0300 \text{ m})}$$
$$= 0.767 \text{ m/s}.$$

Once we have the needed velocities, we can compute the kinetic energies just before and just after impact. The total kinetic energy just before impact is $K_i = \frac{1}{2}m_B v^2 = \frac{1}{2}(0.00500 \text{ kg}) \cdot (307 \text{ m/s})^2 = 236$ J. We find that just after impact, it is $K_f = \frac{1}{2}(m_B + m_W)V^2 = \frac{1}{2}(2.005 \text{ kg}) \cdot (0.767 \text{ m/s})^2 = 0.590$ J. Only a small fraction of the initial kinetic energy remains.

REFLECT When an object collides inelastically with a stationary object having much greater mass, nearly all of the first object's

kinetic energy is lost. In this problem, the wood splinters, and the bullet and wood become hotter as mechanical energy is converted to internal energy.

Practice Problem: Suppose the mass of the bullet, the mass of the block, and the height of the block's swing have the same values as above. If the bullet goes all the way through the block and emerges with half its initial velocity, what was its initial speed?

Answer: $v = \dfrac{2m_W}{m_B}\sqrt{2gh} = 615$ m/s.

EXAMPLE 8.8   **Collision analysis, continued**

In Example 8.1, we considered the impending collision of a small car with a larger truck. It's now 2 seconds later, and the collision has occurred. Fortunately, all occupants were wearing seat belts, and there were no injuries; but the two vehicles became thoroughly tangled and moved away from the point of impact as one mass. The insurance adjuster has asked you to help find the velocity of the wreckage just after impact.

SOLUTION

SET UP Figure 8.14 shows our sketches. The "before" diagram is the same as the one for Example 8.1. We worked out the initial momentum components in that example. We suggest you review that calculation before proceeding. To find out what happens *after* the collision, we'll assume that we can treat the vehicles as an isolated system during the collision. This approach may seem implausible; the pavement certainly exerts substantial friction forces on the tires. But the interaction forces between the vehicles during the collision are much larger—so much larger, in fact, that they crumple the vehicles. So it's reasonable to neglect the friction forces and consider the two vehicles together as an isolated system during the impact.

SOLVE The total momentum $\vec{P}$ of the vehicles just after the collision is the same as we calculated in Example 8.1: 2.5×10^4 kg · m/s in a direction 36.9° north from straight east. Assuming that no parts fall off the wreckage, the total mass of wreckage is $M = 3000$ kg. Calling the final velocity $\vec{V}$, we have $\vec{P} = M\vec{V}$. The direction of the velocity $\vec{V}$ is the same as that of the momentum $\vec{P}$, and its magnitude is

$$V = \frac{P}{M} = \frac{2.5 \times 10^4 \text{ kg} \cdot \text{m/s}}{3000 \text{ kg}} = 8.3 \text{ m/s}. \quad \text{(final speed)}$$

This is an inelastic collision, so we expect the total kinetic energy to be less after the collision than before. When you make the calculations, you'll find that the initial kinetic energy is 2.1×10^5 J and the final kinetic energy is 1.0×10^5 J. More than half of the initial kinetic energy is converted to other forms of energy.

REFLECT If you were tempted to find the final velocity by taking the vector sum of the initial velocities, go back two squares and ask yourself why you would expect that to work. Is there a law of conservation of velocities? *Absolutely not;* the conserved quantity is the total *momentum* of the system.

▲ **FIGURE 8.14** Our sketches for this problem.

Let's look again at the matter of neglecting the friction of tires against pavement and treating the two vehicles as an isolated system. Here are some numbers: The mass of the truck is 2000 kg, so its weight is about 20,000 N. If the coefficient of friction is 0.5, the friction force is somewhere around 10,000 N. That sounds like a large force. But suppose the truck runs into a brick wall while going 10 m/s. Its kinetic energy just before impact is $\frac{1}{2}(2000 \text{ kg})(10 \text{ m/s})^2 = 1.0 \times 10^5$ J, so the force applied by the wall must do -1.0×10^5 J of work on the truck to stop (and crumple) it. The truck may crumple 0.2 m or so; for the stopping force to do -1.0×10^5 J of work in 0.2 m, the force must have a magnitude of 5.0×10^5 N, or 50 times as great as the friction force. You'll see now why it's not so unreasonable to neglect the friction forces on both vehicles and assume that during the collision they form an isolated system.

Practice Problem: Suppose the vehicles are both moving at 10 m/s, the 2000 kg truck heading east and the 1000 kg car heading north. Find the velocity (magnitude and direction) of the wreckage. *Answer:* 7.5 m/s, 27° N of E.

8.4 Elastic Collisions

In Section 8.3, we defined an elastic collision in an isolated system to be a collision in which kinetic energy (as well as momentum) is conserved. Elastic collisions occur when the interaction forces between the objects are conservative. When two steel balls collide, they squash a little near the surface of contact, but then they spring back. Some of the kinetic energy is stored temporarily as elastic potential energy, but by the end of the collision it is reconverted to kinetic energy.

Let's look at an elastic collision between two objects A and B. We start with a head-on collision, in which all the velocities lie along the same line; we choose this line to be the x axis. Each momentum and velocity then has only an x component. (Later we'll consider collisions in two dimensions.) We'll simplify our notation, calling the x components of velocity before the collision $v_{A,i}$ and $v_{B,i}$ and those after the collision $v_{A,f}$ and $v_{B,f}$. From conservation of kinetic energy, we have

$$\tfrac{1}{2}m_A v_{A,i}^2 + \tfrac{1}{2}m_B v_{B,i}^2 = \tfrac{1}{2}m_A v_{A,f}^2 + \tfrac{1}{2}m_B v_{B,f}^2,$$

and conservation of momentum gives

$$m_A v_{A,i} + m_B v_{B,i} = m_A v_{A,f} + m_B v_{B,f}.$$

If the masses m_A and m_B and the initial velocities (i.e., x components) $v_{A,i}$ and $v_{B,i}$ are known, these two equations can be solved simultaneously to find the two final velocities $v_{A,f}$ and $v_{B,f}$.

The general solution is a little complicated, so we'll concentrate on the particular case in which object B is at rest before the collision. Think of it as a target for m_A to hit. Then the equations for conservation of kinetic energy and momentum are, respectively,

$$\tfrac{1}{2}m_A v_{A,i}^2 = \tfrac{1}{2}m_A v_{A,f}^2 + \tfrac{1}{2}m_B v_{B,f}^2 \tag{8.9}$$

and

$$m_A v_{A,i} = m_A v_{A,f} + m_B v_{B,f}. \tag{8.10}$$

6.2–6.5, 6.9, 6.10

These are a pair of simultaneous equations that can be solved for the two final velocities $v_{A,f}$ and $v_{B,f}$ in terms of the masses and the initial velocity $v_{A,i}$. This involves some fairly strenuous algebra; we'll omit the details and go straight to the beautifully simple final results. We find that

$$v_{A,f} = \frac{m_A - m_B}{m_A + m_B} v_{A,i}, \tag{8.11}$$

$$v_{B,f} = \frac{2m_A}{m_A + m_B} v_{A,i}. \tag{8.12}$$

Let's interpret these results by looking at several particular cases. Suppose object A is a Ping-Pong ball and B is a bowling ball (Figure 8.15a). We expect A to bounce back after the collision with a velocity nearly equal to its original

▲ **Light sail.** All current spaceships use rockets of one sort or another. A disadvantage of a rocket is that the craft must carry its own fuel. One alternative is to use a light sail—an enormous sheet of reflective material. In 1873, James Clerk Maxwell showed that light reflected by a mirror applies a slight pressure to the mirror. Thus, in principle, light bouncing off a reflective sail could propel a spacecraft. The more perfectly reflective the sail, the greater its efficiency; for maximum momentum transfer we want the light to bounce off the sail rather than being absorbed.

(a) Ping-Pong ball strikes bowling ball | **(b) Bowling ball strikes Ping-Pong ball**

BEFORE

$v_{A,i}$ A B x — $v_{A,i}$ A B x

AFTER

$v_{A,f} \approx -v_{A,i}$ $v_{B,f}$ A B x — $v_{A,f}$ $v_{B,f}$ A B x

▶ **FIGURE 8.15** Collisions between a Ping-Pong ball and a bowling ball, one or the other of which is initially at rest.

value, but in the opposite direction, and we expect B's final velocity to be much smaller in magnitude. That's just what the equations predict: When m_A is much smaller than m_B, the fraction in the expression for $v_{A,f}$ in Equation 8.11 is approximately equal to -1, so $v_{A,f}$ is approximately equal to $-v_{A,i}$. Also, when m_A is much smaller than m_B, the fraction in Equation 8.12 is much smaller than 1, so $v_{B,f}$ (the final velocity of the bowling ball) is much less than $v_{A,i}$.

Figure 8.15b shows the opposite case, in which A is the bowling ball, B is the Ping-Pong ball, and m_A is much larger than m_B. What do you expect to happen in this case? Check your predictions against Equations 8.11 and 8.12.

Another interesting case occurs when the masses are equal, as in the case of the billiard balls in Figure 8.16. If $m_A = m_B$, then Equations 8.11 and 8.12 give $v_{A,f} = 0$ and $v_{B,f} = v_{A,i}$. That is, the object that was moving stops dead; it gives all of its momentum and kinetic energy to the object that was initially at rest. This behavior is familiar to all pool players and marble shooters.

Now comes a surprise bonus. From Equations 8.11 and 8.12, we can find the x component of the velocity of B *relative to* A after the collision (that is, $v_{B,f} - v_{A,f}$), by simply subtracting Equation 8.12 from Equation 8.11. The result is astonishingly simple:

$$v_{B,f} - v_{A,f} = v_{A,i}. \qquad \text{(relative velocity before and after collision)} \quad (8.13)$$

Now, $v_{B,f} - v_{A,f}$ is the velocity of B relative to A *after* the collision, and $v_{A,i}$ is the negative of the velocity of B relative to A *before* the collision. Thus, **the relative velocity has the same magnitude, but opposite sign, before and after the collision.**

We have proved this result only for straight-line collisions in which one object is initially at rest, but it turns out that a similar *vector* relationship is a general property of *all* elastic collisions, even when both objects are moving initially and the velocities do not all lie along the same line. That is,

$$\vec{v}_{B,f} - \vec{v}_{A,f} = -(\vec{v}_{B,i} - \vec{v}_{A,i}).$$

This result provides an alternative and equivalent definition of an elastic collision: **In an elastic collision, the relative velocity of the two objects has the same magnitude before and after the collision, and the two relative velocities have opposite directions.** Whenever this condition is satisfied, the total kinetic energy is also conserved.

When a moving object A has a 1-D elastic collision with an equal-mass, motionless object B…

…all of A's momentum and kinetic energy are transferred to B.

▲ FIGURE 8.16 An elastic collision between two objects of equal mass, one of which is initially at rest.

EXAMPLE 8.9   **Elastic collision on an air track**

Let's carry out another collision between the air-track gliders of Examples 8.4 and 8.6. This time, we equip the gliders with spring bumpers so that the collision will be elastic. As before, glider A has a mass of 0.50 kg, glider B has a mass of 0.30 kg, and each moves with an initial speed of 2.0 m/s as they approach each other. What are the velocities of A and B after the collision?

SOLUTION

SET UP We draw "before" and "after" sketches, using the same coordinate system as in Example 8.4 (Figure 8.17). The masses and initial velocities of the gliders are the same as in Examples 8.4 and 8.6, so the initial total kinetic energy (1.6 J) is also the same as in those examples.

SOLVE We can't use Equations 8.11 and 8.12 because in this instance neither object is at rest before the collision. But we can use conservation of momentum, along with the relative-velocity relation we've just discussed, to obtain two simultaneous equations for the two final velocities. Because we're dealing with a one-dimensional problem, we'll drop the x subscripts on the

▲ FIGURE 8.17 Our sketches for this problem.

velocities, while keeping in mind that they are all x components of velocities.

Continued

From conservation of momentum,

$$m_A v_{A,i} + m_B v_{B,i} = m_A v_{A,f} + m_B v_{B,f},$$
$$(0.50 \text{ kg})(2.0 \text{ m/s}) + (0.30 \text{ kg})(-2.0 \text{ m/s})$$
$$= (0.50 \text{ kg})v_{A,f} + (0.30 \text{ kg})v_{B,f},$$
$$0.50v_{A,f} + 0.30v_{B,f} = 0.40 \text{ m/s}.$$

(In the last equation we've divided through by the unit "kg.") From the relative-velocity relation for an elastic collision,

$$v_{B,f} - v_{A,f} = -(v_{B,i} - v_{A,i})$$
$$= -(-2.0 \text{ m/s} - 2.0 \text{ m/s}) = 4.0 \text{ m/s}.$$

Solving these equations simultaneously, we obtain

$$v_{A,f} = -1.0 \text{ m/s}, \qquad v_{B,f} = 3.0 \text{ m/s}.$$
(final x components of velocity)

REFLECT Both gliders reverse their directions of motion; A moves to the left at 1.0 m/s and B moves to the right at 3.0 m/s. This result is different from the result of Example 8.4; but that collision was *not* an elastic one, so we shouldn't expect the results to be the same. In this case, the total kinetic energy after the collision is

$$K_f = \tfrac{1}{2}(0.50 \text{ kg})(-1.0 \text{ m/s})^2 + \tfrac{1}{2}(0.30 \text{ kg})(3.0 \text{ m/s})^2$$
$$= 1.6 \text{ J}.$$

This equals the total kinetic energy before the collision, as expected.

Practice Problem: Suppose we interchange the two gliders, making $m_A = 0.30$ kg and $m_B = 0.50$ kg. (We also turn them around, so the springs still meet.) If the initial speeds are the same as before, find the two final velocities. *Answers:* -3.0 m/s, 1.0 m/s.

EXAMPLE 8.10 Moderator in a nuclear reactor

High-speed neutrons are produced in a nuclear reactor during nuclear fission processes. Before a neutron can trigger additional fissions, it has to be slowed down by collisions with nuclei of a material called the *moderator.* In some reactors (including the one involved in the Chernobyl accident), the moderator consists of carbon in the form of graphite. The masses of nuclei and subatomic particles are measured in units called *atomic mass units,* abbreviated u, where $1 \text{ u} = 1.66 \times 10^{-27}$ kg. Suppose a neutron (mass 1.0 u) traveling at 2.6×10^7 m/s makes an elastic head-on collision with a carbon nucleus (mass 12 u) that is initially at rest. What are the velocities after the collision?

SOLUTION

SET UP Figure 8.18 shows our sketches. We use subscripts n and C to denote the neutron and carbon nucleus, respectively.

SOLVE Because we have a head-on elastic collision, all velocity and momentum vectors lie along the x axis, and we can use Equations 8.10 and 8.13, with $m_n = 1.0$ u, $m_C = 12$ u, and $v_{n,i} = 2.6 \times 10^7$ m/s. We'll get two simultaneous equations that we'll need to solve for v_n and v_C.

First, conservation of the x component of momentum gives

$$m_n(v_{n,i}) + m_C(v_{C,i}) = m_n(v_{n,f}) + m_C(v_{C,f}),$$
$$(1.0 \text{ u})(2.6 \times 10^7 \text{ m/s}) + (12.0 \text{ u})(0)$$
$$= (1.0 \text{ u})v_{n,f} + (12.0 \text{ u})v_{C,f}.$$

Second, the relative-velocity relation yields

$$v_{n,i} - v_{C,i} = -(v_{n,f} - v_{C,f}),$$
$$2.6 \times 10^7 \text{ m/s} = v_{C,f} - v_{n,f}.$$

These are two simultaneous equations for $v_{n,f}$ and $v_{C,f}$. We'll let you do the algebra; the results are

$$v_{n,f} = -2.2 \times 10^7 \text{ m/s},$$
$$v_{C,f} = 0.40 \times 10^7 \text{ m/s}.$$
(final x velocities)

▲ **FIGURE 8.18** Our sketches for this problem.

REFLECT The neutron ends up with $\tfrac{11}{13}$ of its original speed, and the speed of the recoiling carbon nucleus is $\tfrac{2}{13}$ of the neutron's original speed. Kinetic energy is proportional to speed squared, so the neutron's final kinetic energy is $\left(\tfrac{11}{13}\right)^2$, or about 0.72 of its original value. If the neutron makes a second such collision, its kinetic energy is $(0.72)^2$, or about half its original value, and so on. After many such collisions, the neutron's kinetic energy is reduced to a small fraction (1/100 or less) of its initial value.

Practice Problem: If the neutron's kinetic energy is reduced to $\tfrac{9}{16}$ of its initial value in a single collision, what is the mass of the moderator nucleus? *Answer:* 7.0 u.

When an elastic collision between two objects isn't head-on, the velocities don't all lie along a single line. If they all lie in a plane, each final velocity has two unknown components, and there are four unknowns in all. Conservation of energy and conservation of the x and y components of momentum give only three equations. To determine the final velocities, we need additional information, such as the direction or magnitude of one of the final velocities.

EXAMPLE 8.11 **An off-center elastic collision on an air table**

Two pucks collide on a frictionless air-hockey table. The pucks have equal masses $m = 0.20$ kg. Puck A has an initial velocity of 4.0 m/s in the positive x direction and a final velocity of 2.0 m/s at an angle of 60° to the +x axis. Puck B is initially at rest. Find the final velocity of puck B (magnitude and direction). Is the collision elastic?

SOLUTION

SET UP Figure 8.19 shows "before" and "after" diagrams. We take the x axis as the horizontal and the positive direction to the right.

SOLVE We need to write two equations, one for conservation of the x component of momentum and one for the y component. We denote the unknown components of the final velocity of B as $v_{B,\mathrm{f},x}$ and $v_{B,\mathrm{f},y}$. The x and y components of momentum of A after the collision are, respectively,

$$m_A(v_{A,\mathrm{f},x}) = (0.20 \text{ kg})(2.0 \text{ m/s})\cos 60°$$

and

$$m_A(v_{A,\mathrm{f},y}) = (0.20 \text{ kg})(2.0 \text{ m/s})\sin 60°.$$

The x and y components of momentum of B after the collision are, respectively,

$$m_B(v_{B,\mathrm{f},x}) = (0.20 \text{ kg})(v_{B,\mathrm{f},x})$$

and

$$m_B(v_{B,\mathrm{f},y}) = (0.20 \text{ kg})(v_{B,\mathrm{f},y}).$$

Conservation of the x component of total momentum gives

$$m_A(v_{A,\mathrm{i},x}) + m_B(v_{B,\mathrm{i},x}) = m_A(v_{A,\mathrm{f},x}) + m_B(v_{B,\mathrm{f},x}),$$
$$(0.20 \text{ kg})(4.0 \text{ m/s}) + 0 = (0.20 \text{ kg})(2.0 \text{ m/s})\cos 60°$$
$$+ (0.20 \text{ kg})v_{B,\mathrm{f},x},$$

and

$$v_{B,\mathrm{f},x} = 3.0 \text{ m/s}. \qquad \text{(final } x \text{ component of velocity of } B\text{)}$$

Conservation of the y component of total momentum gives the equations

$$m_A(v_{A,\mathrm{i},y}) + m_B(v_{B,\mathrm{i},y}) = m_A(v_{A,\mathrm{f},y}) + m_B(v_{B,\mathrm{f},y}),$$
$$0 = (0.20 \text{ kg})(2.0 \text{ m/s})\sin 60° + (0.20 \text{ kg})v_{B,\mathrm{f},y},$$

and

$$v_{B,\mathrm{f},y} = -\sqrt{3} \text{ m/s} = -1.73 \text{ m/s}.$$
$$\text{(final } y \text{ component of velocity of } B\text{)}$$

The magnitude $v_{B,\mathrm{f}}$ of the final velocity of B is

$$v_{B,\mathrm{f}} = \sqrt{v_{B,\mathrm{f},x}{}^2 + v_{B,\mathrm{f},y}{}^2} = \sqrt{(3.0 \text{ m/s})^2 + (-\sqrt{3} \text{ m/s})^2}$$
$$= 2\sqrt{3} \text{ m/s} = 3.5 \text{ m/s}.$$

Its direction (an angle θ measured from the +x axis) is

$$\theta = \tan^{-1}\frac{v_{B,\mathrm{f},y}}{v_{B,\mathrm{f},x}} = \tan^{-1}\left(\frac{-\sqrt{3} \text{ m/s}}{3.0 \text{ m/s}}\right) = -30°.$$

▲ **FIGURE 8.19**

Is kinetic energy conserved? The initial kinetic energy of A (equal to the initial *total* kinetic energy) is

$$K_{A,\mathrm{i}} = K_\mathrm{i} = \tfrac{1}{2}m_A(v_{A,\mathrm{i}})^2 = \tfrac{1}{2}(0.20 \text{ kg})(4.0 \text{ m/s})^2 = 1.6 \text{ J}.$$

The final total kinetic energy of A and B together is

$$K_\mathrm{f} = \tfrac{1}{2}m_A(v_{A,\mathrm{f}})^2 + \tfrac{1}{2}m_B(v_{B,\mathrm{f}})^2$$
$$= \tfrac{1}{2}(0.20 \text{ kg})(2.0 \text{ m/s})^2 + \tfrac{1}{2}(0.20 \text{ kg})(2\sqrt{3} \text{ m/s})^2$$
$$= 1.6 \text{ J}.$$

The total initial and final kinetic energies are equal, so the collision is elastic.

REFLECT We used a separate equation for conservation of each component of momentum. The x and y components of momentum are *never* added together in a conservation-of-momentum equation. Because the masses are equal, we could have simplified the calculations by dividing the factor m out of each momentum equation. The two final velocities are perpendicular. In fact, it can be shown that in *every* elastic collision between two objects with equal mass, when one object is initially at rest, the two final velocities are *always* perpendicular (except when the collision is head-on and one final velocity is zero). Every good billiards player is familiar with this fact.

Practice Problem: Suppose the final direction of puck A's velocity is at 30° to the +x axis instead of 60°. Find the final velocity (magnitude and direction) of puck B. *Answers:* 2.5 m/s, −24°.

We've classified collisions according to energy considerations. A collision in which kinetic energy is conserved is called *elastic*. A collision in which the total kinetic energy decreases is called *inelastic*. There are also cases in which the final

▲ FIGURE 8.20 A racquet hitting a tennis ball. Typically, the ball is in contact with the racket for approximately 0.01 s. The ball flattens noticeably on both sides, and the frame of the racket vibrates during and after the impact.

kinetic energy is *greater* than the initial kinetic energy. A recoiling rifle, discussed in Example 8.3, is an example.

> **NOTE** ► We emphasize again that we can sometimes use conservation of momentum even when external forces act on the system. If the vector sum of the external forces is zero, momentum is conserved. Also, if the internal forces between colliding objects are much stronger than the net external force acting on the system, we may use an idealized model that neglects the external forces during the actual collision. ◄

8.5 Impulse

When a force acts on an object, the object's change in momentum depends on the force and on the time interval during which it acts. We've seen several examples of interactions in which large forces act during a short time of impact. A recoiling rifle, exploding projectiles, a tennis ball struck by a racket (Figure 8.20)—all are examples of such interactions. To analyze these events in detail, we'll find it useful to define a quantity called **impulse:**

6.1 Activ Physics

Definition of impulse

When a constant force $\vec{F}$ acts on an object, the impulse of the force, denoted by $\vec{J}$, is the force multiplied by the time interval during which it acts:

$$\vec{J} = \vec{F}(t_f - t_i) = \vec{F}\,\Delta t. \qquad (8.14)$$

Notice that impulse is a vector quantity; its direction is the same as that of the force $\vec{F}$.

Unit: Force times time $(\text{N} \cdot \text{s})$. Because $1\,\text{N} = 1\,\text{kg} \cdot \text{m/s}^2$, an alternative set of units for impulse is $\text{kg} \cdot \text{m/s}$; thus, the units of impulse are the same as those of momentum.

To see what impulse is good for, let's go back to Newton's second law, as we restated it in terms of momentum in Equation 8.4, namely,

$$\vec{F} = \lim_{\Delta t \to 0} \frac{\Delta \vec{p}}{\Delta t},$$

where $\vec{F}$ represents the vector sum (resultant) of forces acting on an object. If $\vec{F}$ doesn't vary with time, we can simplify this equation to

$$\vec{F} = \frac{\Delta \vec{p}}{\Delta t}, \quad \text{or} \quad \Delta \vec{p} = \vec{F}\,\Delta t.$$

Combining this result with Equation 8.14, we get the following relation, called the **impulse–momentum theorem:**

▲ Long legs for leaping. Why are this frog's legs so long? Short legs could supply an equal magnitude of force. The answer hinges on the fact that muscles are limited in the force they can develop and the speed with which they can contract. The longer the frog's legs, the greater is the time interval during which the legs can deliver their force, and thus the greater is the total impulse delivered. Since impulse represents a change in momentum, longer legs result in a larger change in momentum, imparting a greater velocity to a frog of a given mass.

Relation of impulse to change in momentum:
The impulse–momentum theorem

When a constant force $\vec{F}$ acts on an object during a time interval $\Delta t = t_f - t_i$, the change in the object's momentum is equal to the impulse of the force acting on the object, or

$$\Delta \vec{p} = \vec{F}\,\Delta t = \vec{F}(t_f - t_i) = \vec{J}. \qquad (8.15)$$

Unit: mass times velocity $(\text{kg} \cdot \text{m/s})$

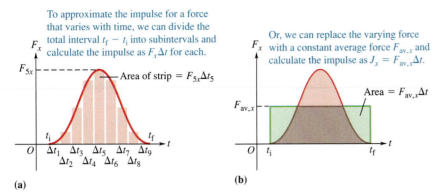

To approximate the impulse for a force that varies with time, we can divide the total interval $t_f - t_i$ into subintervals and calculate the impulse as $F_x \Delta t$ for each.

Area of strip = $F_{5x}\Delta t_5$

Or, we can replace the varying force with a constant average force $F_{av,x}$ and calculate the impulse as $J_x = F_{av,x}\Delta t$.

Area = $F_{av,x}\Delta t$

(a)

(b)

▲ **FIGURE 8.21** Determining the impulse of a force that varies with time.

As noted, impulse and momentum are both vector quantities, and Equations 8.14 and 8.15 are vector equations. In specific problems, it's often easiest to use these equations in component form:

$$J_x = F_x \Delta t = p_{f,x} - p_{i,x} = mv_{f,x} - mv_{i,x},$$
$$J_y = F_y \Delta t = p_{f,y} - p_{i,y} = mv_{f,y} - mv_{i,y}. \qquad (8.16)$$

Now, what if the force isn't constant? Suppose, for example, that the x component of force varies, as shown in Figure 8.21. Then we can divide the total time interval $t_f - t_i$ into small subintervals, as in Figure 8.21a, apply Equation 8.15 to each, and add all the $\vec{F} \Delta t$ quantities. Thus, the impulse–momentum relation $\vec{J} = \vec{p}_f - \vec{p}_i$ is valid even when the force $\vec{F}$ varies with time. Figure 8.21a also shows that the impulse of the force is the area under the graph of force versus time.

As shown in Figure 8.21b, we can also define an average force $\vec{F}_{av}$ such that even when $\vec{F}$ isn't constant, its impulse $\vec{J}$ is given by

$$\vec{J} = \vec{F}_{av}(t_f - t_i). \qquad (8.17)$$

Conceptual Analysis 8.4

Soften the blow

A baseball player catching a fastball lets his hand move backward (in the direction of the ball's motion) during the catch. This maneuver reduces the force of impact on his hand principally because:

A. the speed of impact is lessened.
B. the time of impact is increased.
C. the impulse is reduced.

SOLUTION Whether the hand moves or not, $\Delta\vec{p}$, and therefore the impulse $\vec{J}$, is roughly the same, because the speed of the ball is much larger than any motion of the hand. However, for the same impulse, the relation $\vec{J} = \vec{F}_{av}\Delta t$ shows that if we increase the time interval Δt of the interaction, we decrease the average force. The correct answer is B.

EXAMPLE 8.12   A ball hits a wall

Suppose you throw a ball with mass 0.40 kg against a brick wall (Figure 8.22). It hits the wall moving horizontally to the left at 30 m/s and rebounds horizontally to the right at 20 m/s. Find the impulse of the force exerted on the ball by the wall. If the ball is in contact with the wall for 0.010 s, find the average force on the ball during the impact.

BEFORE $v_{i,x} = -30$ m/s

AFTER $v_{f,x} = 20$ m/s

$m = 0.40$ kg

▲ **FIGURE 8.22** Impulse imparted to a wall by a ball that hits the wall and rebounds.

Continued

SOLUTION

SET UP We take the x axis as horizontal and the positive direction to the right.

SOLVE We need to find the x component of momentum just before and just after impact, find the *change* in momentum, and then equate this change to the impulse. Then we divide by the time interval to find the average force on the ball.

The initial x component of momentum of the ball is

$$p_{i,x} = mv_{i,x} = (0.40\text{ kg})(-30\text{ m/s}) = -12\text{ kg}\cdot\text{m/s}.$$

The final x component of momentum is

$$p_{f,x} = mv_{f,x} = +(0.40\text{ kg})(20\text{ m/s}) = 8.0\text{ kg}\cdot\text{m/s}.$$

The change in the x component of momentum is

$$\Delta p_x = p_{f,x} - p_{i,x} = mv_{f,x} - mv_{i,x}$$
$$= 8.0\text{ kg}\cdot\text{m/s} - (-12\text{ kg}\cdot\text{m/s}) = 20\text{ kg}\cdot\text{m/s}.$$

(Note the signs carefully. The initial x component of momentum is negative, and we are subtracting it from the final value to find the change Δp_x.)

According to Equation 8.17, the preceding result equals the x component of impulse of the force exerted on the ball by the wall, so $J_x = 20\text{ kg}\cdot\text{m/s} = 20\text{ N}\cdot\text{s}$.

If the force acts for 0.010 s, then, from $J_x = F_{av,x}\Delta t$,

$$F_{av,x} = \frac{J_x}{\Delta t} = \frac{20\text{ N}\cdot\text{s}}{0.010\text{ s}} = 2000\text{ N}.$$

Curve A: Force with short duration and high peak

$F_{av,x}(t_f - t_i)$ is the same for both curves, so they deliver the same impulse.

Curve B: Force with longer duration and lower peak

▲ **FIGURE 8.23** Forces that differ in duration and peak magnitude may deliver the same impulse.

REFLECT The force exerted by the wall on the ball isn't constant; its variation with time may be similar to a varying force described by one of the curves in Figure 8.23. The force is zero before impact, rises to a maximum, and then decreases to zero when the ball loses contact with the wall. If the ball is relatively rigid, like a baseball or a golf ball, the time of collision is small and the maximum force is large, as in curve A of the figure. If the ball is softer, like a tennis ball, the collision time is larger and the maximum force is less, as in curve B. Either way, the area under the curve represents the same impulse: $J_x = F_{av,x}\Delta t$.

Practice Problem: Suppose you have a pitching machine that throws five balls per second, with the same mass and initial and final velocities as given in this example. Find the average force exerted on the wall by this stream of balls. *Answer:* 100 N.

EXAMPLE 8.13 **Kicking a soccer ball**

Let's consider the soccer ball in Figure 8.24a. The ball has mass 0.40 kg. Initially it moves horizontally to the left at 20 m/s, but then it is kicked and given a velocity with magnitude 30 m/s and direction 45° upward and to the right. Find the impulse of the force and the average force on the ball, assuming a collision time $\Delta t = 0.010$ s.

SOLUTION

SET UP The velocities aren't along the same line, so we must treat momentum and impulse as vector quantities, using their x and y components. As shown in Figure 8.24a, we point the x axis to the right and the y axis upward. We find the following initial and final velocity components:

$$v_{i,x} = -20\text{ m/s}, \qquad v_{i,y} = 0,$$
$$v_{f,x} = v_{f,y} = \cos45°(v_f) = (0.707)(30\text{ m/s}) = 21\text{ m/s}.$$

(a) Before-and-after diagram

(b) Average force on the ball

▲ **FIGURE 8.24**

Continued

SOLVE The x component of the impulse is equal to the x component of the change in momentum, and the same is true for the y components:

$$J_x = m(v_{f,x} - v_{i,x}) = (0.40 \text{ kg})[21 \text{ m/s} - (-20 \text{ m/s})]$$
$$= 16.4 \text{ kg} \cdot \text{m/s},$$
$$J_y = m(v_{f,y} - v_{i,y}) = (0.40 \text{ kg})(21 \text{ m/s} - 0) = 8.4 \text{ kg} \cdot \text{m/s}.$$

The components of average force on the ball (Figure 8.24b) are

$$F_{av,x} = \frac{J_x}{\Delta t} = 1640 \text{ N}, \qquad F_{av,y} = \frac{J_y}{\Delta t} = 840 \text{ N}.$$

The magnitude and direction of the average force are, respectively,

$$F_{av} = \sqrt{(1640 \text{ N})^2 + (840 \text{ N})^2} = 1.8 \times 10^3 \text{ N},$$
$$\theta = \tan^{-1}\frac{840 \text{ N}}{1640 \text{ N}} = 27°,$$

where θ is measured counterclockwise from the $+x$ axis.

REFLECT The direction of the ball's final velocity is not the same as that of the average force acting on it. Indeed, there's no reason it should be. The average magnitude of force on the ball is about 400 lb; that's roughly three times as much force as though you just stood on the ball!

Practice Problem: Suppose the ball is moving at 30° downward from the horizontal before it is kicked. If all the numerical values are the same as before, find the magnitude and direction of the average force on the ball. *Answer:* 2.0×10^3 N, 39°.

NOTE ▶ The relation between impulse and change in momentum, $\Delta \vec{p} = \vec{F}\,\Delta t = \vec{J}$ (Equation 8.15), has a superficial resemblance to the work–kinetic energy theorem that we developed in Chapter 7, namely, $W_{total} = K_f - K_i$ (Equation 7.4). However, there are important differences. First, impulse is a product of a force and a *time* interval, while work is a product of a force and a *distance* and depends on the angle between the force and displacement vectors. Second, impulse and momentum are vector quantities, and work and kinetic energy are scalars. Even in straight-line motion, in which only one component of a vector is involved, force, velocity, and momentum may have components along this line that are either positive or negative. ◀

8.6 Center of Mass

We can restate the principle of conservation of momentum in a useful way with the help of the concept of **center of mass,** which we define as follows:

Definition of center of mass

Suppose we have several particles A, B, etc., with masses m_A, m_B, ... Let the coordinates of A be (x_A, y_A), let those of B be (x_B, y_B), and so on. We define the center of mass of the system as the point having coordinates (x_{cm}, y_{cm}) given by

$$x_{cm} = \frac{m_A x_A + m_B x_B + m_C x_C + \cdots}{m_A + m_B + m_C + \cdots},$$
$$y_{cm} = \frac{m_A y_A + m_B y_B + m_C y_C + \cdots}{m_A + m_B + m_C + \cdots}. \qquad (8.18)$$

In statistical language, the center of mass is a *mass-weighted average* position of the particles.

For a solid object, which we often model as having a continuous distribution of matter, locating the center of mass often frequently requires calculus. However, symmetry considerations can be helpful. For example, whenever a homogeneous solid object has a geometric center, such as a billiard ball, an ice cube, or a can of frozen orange juice, the center of mass is at the geometric center (Figure 8.25). Also, whenever an object has an axis of symmetry, such as a wheel or a pulley, the center of mass always lies on that axis. Note, however, that the center of mass isn't always within the object. For example, the center of mass of a doughnut is right in the middle of the hole.

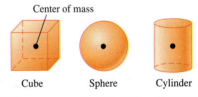

Center of mass

Cube   Sphere   Cylinder

If a homogeneous object has a geometric center, that is where the center of mass is located.

Axis of symmetry

Disk   Donut

If an object has an axis of symmetry, the center of mass lies along it. As in the case of the donut, the center of mass may not be within the object.

▲ **FIGURE 8.25** Location of the center of mass for some symmetric objects.

When the particles in a system move, the center of mass may also move. Equations 8.18 give the coordinates (x_{cm}, y_{cm}) of the center of mass in terms of the coordinates of the particles. The rates of change of these quantities (the components of the velocity of the center of mass) are related to the components of the velocity of the particles in the same way. Therefore, we immediately find the following relation:

Velocity of center of mass

The velocity $\vec{v}_{cm}$ of the center of mass of a collection of particles is the mass-weighted average of the velocities of the individual particles:

$$\vec{v}_{cm} = \frac{m_A \vec{v}_A + m_B \vec{v}_B + m_C \vec{v}_C + \cdots}{m_A + m_B + m_C + \cdots}. \tag{8.19}$$

In terms of components,

$$v_{cm,x} = \frac{m_A v_{A,x} + m_B v_{B,x} + m_C v_{C,x} + \cdots}{m_A + m_B + m_C + \cdots},$$

$$v_{cm,y} = \frac{m_A v_{A,y} + m_B v_{B,y} + m_C v_{C,y} + \cdots}{m_A + m_B + m_C + \cdots}. \tag{8.20}$$

We denote the total mass $m_A + m_B + \cdots$ by M; we can then rewrite Equation 8.19 as

$$M\vec{v}_{cm} = m_A \vec{v}_A + m_B \vec{v}_B + m_C \vec{v}_C + \cdots.$$

The right side is the total momentum of the system, so we have $\vec{P} = M\vec{v}_{cm}$.

Total momentum $\vec{P}$ in terms of center of mass

For a system of particles, the total momentum $\vec{P}$ is the total mass $M = m_A + m_B + \cdots$ times the velocity $\vec{v}_{cm}$ of the center of mass:

$$M\vec{v}_{cm} = m_A \vec{v}_A + m_B \vec{v}_B + m_C \vec{v}_C + \cdots = \vec{P} \tag{8.21}$$

It follows that, for an *isolated* system, in which the total momentum is constant, the velocity of the center of mass is also constant.

EXAMPLE 8.14 Quarreling pets

A 2.0 kg cat and a 3.0 kg dog are moving toward each other along the x axis, heading for a fight. At a particular instant, the cat is 1.0 m to the right of the origin and is moving in the $+x$ direction with speed 3.0 m/s, and the dog is 2.0 m to the right of the origin, moving in the $-x$ direction with speed 1.0 m/s. Find the position and velocity of the center of mass of the two-pet system, and also find the total momentum of the system.

SOLUTION

SET UP Figure 8.26 shows our sketch. We represent the pets' motion as x components of velocity, being careful with signs.

SOLVE To find the center of mass of the two-pet system, we use Equation 8.18:

$$x_{cm} = \frac{m_{cat}(x_{cat}) + m_{dog}(x_{dog})}{m_{cat} + m_{dog}}$$

$$= \frac{(2.0\ \text{kg})(1.0\ \text{m}) + (3.0\ \text{kg})(2.0\ \text{m})}{2.0\ \text{kg} + 3.0\ \text{kg}} = 1.6\ \text{m}.$$

▲ **FIGURE 8.26** Our sketch for this problem.

Continued

To find the velocity of the center of mass, we use Equation 8.20:

$$v_{cm,x} = \frac{m_{cat}v_{cat,x} + m_{dog}v_{dog,x}}{m_{cat} + m_{dog}}$$

$$= \frac{(2.0 \text{ kg})(3.0 \text{ m/s}) + (3.0 \text{ kg})(-1.0 \text{ m/s})}{2.0 \text{ kg} + 3.0 \text{ kg}}$$

$$= 0.60 \text{ m/s}.$$

The total x component of momentum is the sum of the x components of momenta of the two animals:

$$P_x = m_{cat}(v_{cat,x}) + m_{dog}(v_{dog,x})$$

$$= (2.0 \text{ kg})(3.0 \text{ m/s}) + (3.0 \text{ kg})(-1.0 \text{ m/s})$$

$$= 3.0 \text{ kg} \cdot \text{m/s}.$$

Alternatively, the total momentum is the total mass M, times the velocity of the center of mass:

$$P_x = Mv_{cm,x} = (5.0 \text{ kg})(0.60 \text{ m/s}) = 3.0 \text{ kg} \cdot \text{m/s}.$$

REFLECT As always, remember that an object moving in the $-x$ direction has a negative x component of velocity. The total momentum of the system is equal to the momentum of a single particle with mass equal to the total mass of the system and with velocity equal to the velocity of the center of mass of the system.

Practice Problem: At the instant described, the cat decides to avoid combat. It quickly turns around and runs in the $-x$ direction with speed 2.0 m/s. Find the position and velocity of the center of mass, and the total momentum of the system, at this instant. *Answers:* $x_{cm} = 1.6$ m, $v_{cm} = -1.4$ m/s, $P_x = -7.0$ kg $\cdot$ m/s.

8.7 Motion of the Center of Mass

In Section 8.6, we defined the center of mass of a system of particles as an average position of the particles, weighted according to their masses. We found that the total momentum of the system is related simply to the total mass and the velocity of the center of mass. Now our final step is to look at the relationship between the acceleration of the center of mass and the forces acting on the system. Again we'll find a simple and elegant relation.

Equations 8.20 and 8.21 give the velocity of the center of mass in terms of the velocities of the individual particles. Proceeding one additional step, we take the rate of change of each term in these equations to show that the accelerations are related in the same way. Let $\vec{a}_{cm}$ be the acceleration of the center of mass (the rate of change of $\vec{v}_{cm}$ with respect to time); then

$$M\vec{a}_{cm} = m_A\vec{a}_A + m_B\vec{a}_B + m_C\vec{a}_C + \cdots \quad (8.22)$$

Now, $m_A\vec{a}_A$ is equal to the vector sum of forces on particle A, and so on, so the right side of Equation 8.22 is equal to the vector sum $\Sigma\vec{F}$ of *all* the forces acting on *all* the particles. Just as we did in Section 8.2, we may classify each force as *internal* or *external*. The sum of forces on all the particles is then

$$\Sigma\vec{F} = \Sigma\vec{F}_{ext} + \Sigma\vec{F}_{int} = M\vec{a}_{cm}.$$

Because of Newton's third law, the internal forces all cancel in pairs, and $\Sigma\vec{F}_{int} = 0$. Only the sum of the external forces is left, and we have the following result:

▲ **Please don't sneeze!** To the physics students in the audience, these acrobats are demonstrating the concept of the center of mass of a system. Individually, each of them has his or her own separate mass. However, while moving together, they can be considered as one large mass centered at the mass-weighted average position of all the acrobats. As long as this center of mass is positioned directly above the bicycle, they can keep up their precarious balancing act.

Acceleration of center of mass

When an object or a collection of particles is acted on by external forces, the center of mass moves just as though all the mass were concentrated at that point and were acted on by a resultant force equal to the sum of the external forces on the system. Stated symbolically, this relationship is

$$\Sigma\vec{F}_{ext} = M\vec{a}_{cm}. \quad (8.23)$$

Let's look at some applications of this result. Suppose the center of mass of an adjustable wrench lies partway down the handle. Figure 8.27 shows what happens when we send the wrench spinning across a smooth tabletop. The overall motion appears complicated, but the center of mass (marked by a white dot) follows a straight line, as though all the mass were concentrated at that point. As

▲ FIGURE 8.27 The center of mass of this wrench is marked with a white dot. The total external force acting on the wrench is small. As the wrench spins on a smooth horizontal surface, the center of mass moves in a straight line.

another example, suppose an explosive shell traveling in a parabolic trajectory (neglecting air resistance) explodes in flight, splitting into two fragments with equal mass (Figure 8.28a). The fragments follow new parabolic paths, but the center of mass of the shell continues on the original parabolic trajectory, just as though all the mass were still concentrated at that point. Exploding fireworks are a spectacular example of this principle (Figure 8.28b).

The property of the center of mass we've just discussed will be important when we analyze the motion of extended rigid objects in Chapter 10. The center of mass also plays an important role in the motion of astronomical objects. The earth and the moon revolve in orbits centered on their center of mass, as do the two stars in a binary system.

Finally, we note again that, for an isolated system, $\sum \vec{F}_{\text{ext}} = 0$. In this case, Equation 8.23 shows that the acceleration $\vec{a}_{\text{cm}}$ of the center of mass is zero, so its velocity $\vec{v}_{\text{cm}}$ is constant, and from Equation 8.21, the total momentum $\vec{P}$ is also constant. This conclusion reaffirms our statement in Section 8.2 that the total momentum of an isolated system is constant.

*8.8 Rocket Propulsion

Momentum considerations are particularly useful when we have to analyze a system in which the masses of parts of the system change with time. In such cases, we can't use Newton's second law ($\sum \vec{F} = m\vec{a}$) directly, because m changes. Rocket propulsion offers a typical and interesting example of this kind of analysis. A rocket is propelled forward by the rearward ejection of burned fuel that initially was in the rocket. The forward force on the rocket is the reaction to the backward force on the ejected material. The total mass of the system is constant, but the mass of the rocket itself decreases as material is ejected. As a simple example, we consider a rocket fired in outer space, where there is no gravitational field and no air resistance (so that the system is isolated). We choose our x axis to be along the rocket's direction of motion.

NOTE ▶ Be especially careful with signs in this discussion. Negative signs may appear where you don't expect them; be sure you understand why they have to be where they are. ◀

Figure 8.29 shows the rocket at a time t after firing, when its mass is m and the x component of its velocity relative to our coordinate system is v. The x component of the total momentum P at this instant is $P = mv$. In a short time interval

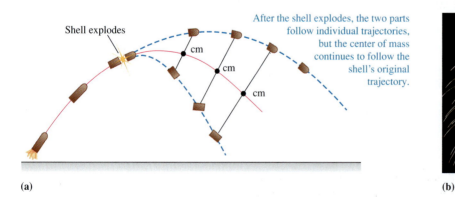

Shell explodes

After the shell explodes, the two parts follow individual trajectories, but the center of mass continues to follow the shell's original trajectory.

cm
cm
cm

(a)

(b)

▲ FIGURE 8.28 (a) A projectile explodes in flight. If air resistance can be ignored, the fragments follow individual parabolic trajectories, but the center of mass continues on the same trajectory the projectile was following before it exploded. (b) A firework represents an exploding projectile.

At time $t + \Delta t$, the rocket has mass $m + \Delta m$ (where Δm is inherently *negative*) and x component of velocity $v + \Delta v$. The burned fuel has x component of velocity $v' = v - v_{\text{ex}}$ and mass $-\Delta m$. (The minus sign is needed to make $-\Delta m$ *positive*, because Δm is negative.)

At time t, the rocket has mass m and x component of velocity v.

+x direction

Rocket
v

m

Burned fuel
$v' = v - v_{\text{ex}}$

$-\Delta m$

Rocket
$v + \Delta v$

$m + \Delta m$

(a) (b)

▲ **FIGURE 8.29** A rocket moving in gravity-free outer space.

Δt, the mass of the rocket changes by an amount Δm. This is an inherently negative quantity, because the rocket's mass m *decreases* with time as fuel is burned. During Δt, a positive mass $(-\Delta m)$ of burned fuel is ejected from the rocket. Let v_{ex} be the exhaust speed of this material relative to the rocket. Then the x component of the velocity v' of the fuel relative to our coordinate system is

$$v' = v - v_{\text{ex}},$$

and the x component of momentum of the mass $-\Delta m$ is

$$(-\Delta m)v' = (-\Delta m)(v - v_{\text{ex}}).$$

At the end of the time interval Δt, the mass of the rocket (including the unburned fuel) has decreased to $m + \Delta m$, and the rocket's velocity has increased to $v + \Delta v$ (Figure 8.29). (Remember that Δm is negative.) The rocket's momentum at this time is

$$(m + \Delta m)(v + \Delta v).$$

Thus, the total x component of the momentum of the rocket plus the ejected fuel at time $t + \Delta t$ is

$$P = (m + \Delta m)(v + \Delta v) + (-\Delta m)(v - v_{\text{ex}}).$$

According to our initial assumption, the rocket and fuel are an isolated system. Hence, momentum is conserved; the total momentum P of the system must be the same at time t and at time $t + \Delta t$:

$$mv = (m + \Delta m)(v + \Delta v) + (-\Delta m)(v - v_{\text{ex}}).$$

This equation can be simplified to

$$m\,\Delta v = -\Delta m v_{\text{ex}} - \Delta m\,\Delta v.$$

We can neglect the term $\Delta m\,\Delta v$ because it is a product of two small quantities and thus is much smaller than the other terms. Dropping that term, dividing by Δt, and rearranging terms, we find that

$$m\frac{\Delta v}{\Delta t} = -v_{\text{ex}}\frac{\Delta m}{\Delta t}. \tag{8.24}$$

Because $\Delta v/\Delta t$ is the x component of acceleration of the rocket, the left side of this equation (mass times acceleration) equals the x component of the resultant force F, or *thrust*, on the rocket, so

$$F = -v_{\text{ex}}\frac{\Delta m}{\Delta t}. \qquad \text{(thrust of rocket)} \tag{8.25}$$

▲ **A jet-propelled . . . jellyfish?** These jellyfish move by using the same physical principles of propulsion that we see in interplanetary rockets. By forcing water out of their bells in one direction, they are able to move in the opposite direction.

The thrust is proportional both to the relative speed v_{ex} of the ejected fuel and to the (positive) mass of fuel ejected per unit time, $-\Delta m/\Delta t$. (Remember that $\Delta m/\Delta t$ is negative because it is the rate of change of the rocket's mass.)

The x component of acceleration a of the rocket is

$$a = \frac{\Delta v}{\Delta t} = -\frac{v_{ex}}{m}\frac{\Delta m}{\Delta t}. \qquad \text{(acceleration of rocket)} \qquad (8.26)$$

The rocket's mass m decreases continuously while the fuel is being consumed. If v_{ex} and $\Delta m/\Delta t$ are constant, the acceleration increases until all the fuel is gone.

EXAMPLE 8.15 Launch of a rocket

A rocket floats next to an interplanetary space station far from any planet. It ignites its engine. In the first second of its flight, it ejects $\frac{1}{60}$ of its mass with a relative velocity magnitude of 2400 m/s. Find its acceleration.

SOLUTION

SET UP AND SOLVE We are given that $\Delta m = -m/60$ and $\Delta t = 1.0$ s. We use the same coordinate system as in Figure 8.29, with the $+x$ axis to the right.

The acceleration is given by Equation 8.26:

$$a = -\frac{v_{ex}}{m}\frac{\Delta m}{\Delta t}$$
$$= -\frac{2400 \text{ m/s}}{m}\left(\frac{-m/60}{1.0 \text{ s}}\right) = 40 \text{ m/s}^2.$$

REFLECT At the start of the flight, when the velocity of the rocket is zero, the ejected exhaust is moving to the left, relative to our coordinate system, at 2400 m/s. At the end of the first sec-

ond, the rocket is moving at 40 m/s. The speed of the exhaust relative to our system is 2360 m/s. We could now compute the acceleration at $t = 1.0$ s (using the decreased rocket mass), find the velocity at $t = 2.0$ s, and so on, stepping through the calculation one second at a time until all the fuel is used up. As the mass decreases, the acceleration in successive 1 s intervals increases.

Detailed calculation shows that, after about 22 s, the rocket's velocity in our coordinate system passes 2400 m/s. The exhaust ejected after this time therefore moves *forward,* not backward, in our system. The final velocity acquired by the rocket can be greater in magnitude (and is often *much* greater) than the relative speed v_{ex}.

Practice Problem: Find the rocket's velocities 2.0 s and 3.0 s after launch. *Answers:* 81 m/s, 122 m/s.

In the early days of rocket propulsion, people who didn't understand conservation of momentum thought that a rocket couldn't function in outer space because it wouldn't have anything to "push against." On the contrary, rockets work *best* in outer space! Figure 8.30 shows a dramatic example of rocket propulsion. The rocket is *not* "pushing against the ground" to get into the air.

▲ **FIGURE 8.30** Launch of the Titan 4B Centaur, a dramatic example of rocket propulsion.

SUMMARY

Momentum

(Section 8.1) The momentum $\vec{p}$ of a particle with mass m moving with velocity $\vec{v}$ is defined as the vector quantity $\vec{p} = m\vec{v}$ (Equation 8.1). Newton's second law can be restated as follows: The rate of change of momentum of a particle equals the vector sum of the forces acting on it:

$$\sum \vec{F} = \lim_{\Delta t \to 0} \frac{\Delta \vec{p}}{\Delta t}. \qquad (8.3)$$

The total momentum $\vec{P}$ of a system of particles is the vector sum of the momenta of the individual particles:

$$\vec{P} = \vec{p}_A + \vec{p}_B + \cdots = m_A \vec{v}_A + m_B \vec{v}_B + \cdots. \quad (8.4, 8.5)$$

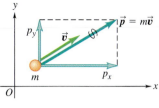

Momentum is a vector quantity; it has the same direction as the object's velocity and can be represented by components.

Conservation of Momentum

(Section 8.2) An internal force is a force exerted by one part of a system on another part of the same system; an external force is a force exerted on part or all of a system by something outside the system. An isolated system is a system that experiences either no external forces or external forces whose vector sum is zero. The total momentum of an isolated system is constant: $\vec{P}_i = \vec{P}_f$. Each component of momentum is conserved separately.

When the astronaut throws the wrench, the total momentum $\vec{P}$ of the system is conserved, although the individual momenta $\vec{p}_A$ and $\vec{p}_W$ are not.

Collisions

(Sections 8.3 and 8.4) Collisions can be classified according to energy relations and final velocities. In an elastic collision between two objects, kinetic energy is conserved and the initial and final relative velocities have the same magnitude. In an inelastic two-object collision, the final kinetic energy is less than the initial kinetic energy; if the two objects have the same final velocity (for instance, if they stick together), the collision is completely inelastic.

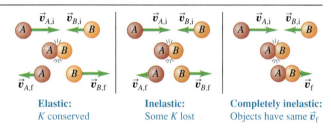

Impulse

(Section 8.5) The impulse $\vec{J}$ of a constant force $\vec{F}$ acting over a time interval Δt from t_i to t_f is the vector quantity $\vec{J} = \vec{F}(t_f - t_i) = \vec{F} \Delta t$ (Equation 8.14). The change in momentum of a particle during any time interval equals the impulse of the total force acting on the particle: $\Delta \vec{p} = \vec{F} \Delta t = \vec{F}(t_f - t_i) = \vec{J}$ (Equation 8.15).

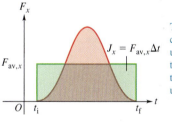

The impulse $\vec{J}$ of a force over a certain time interval is the area under the graph of force versus time. If the force varies with time, the impulse may be calculated by using the average force.

Center of Mass

(Sections 8.6 and 8.7) The coordinates x_{cm} and y_{cm} of the center of mass of a system of particles are defined as

$$x_{cm} = \frac{m_A x_A + m_B x_B + m_C x_C + \cdots}{m_A + m_B + m_C + \cdots},$$

$$y_{cm} = \frac{m_A y_A + m_B y_B + m_C y_C + \cdots}{m_A + m_B + m_C + \cdots}. \qquad (8.18)$$

The total momentum $\vec{P}$ of the system equals the total mass M, multiplied by the velocity $\vec{v}_{cm}$ of the center of mass:

$$M\vec{v}_{cm} = m_A \vec{v}_A + m_B \vec{v}_B + m_C \vec{v}_C + \cdots = \vec{P} \qquad (8.21)$$

The center of mass of a system moves as though all the mass were concentrated at the center of mass: $\sum \vec{F}_{ext} = M\vec{a}_{cm}$ (Equation 8.23).

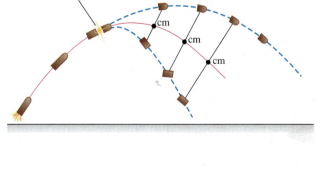

After the shell explodes, the center of mass continues to follow the shell's original trajectory.

Shell explodes

Continued

Rocket Propulsion

(Section 8.8) In rocket propulsion, the mass of the rocket changes as the fuel is burned. Analysis of the momentum relations must include the momentum carried away by the fuel, as well as the momentum of the rocket itself.

(MP) For instructor-assigned homework, go to www.masteringphysics.com

Conceptual Questions

1. The objects shown in Figure 8.31 move together. Identify internal and external forces for each of the following systems: (a) The system consists of only block A. (b) The system consists of only block B. (c) The system consists of both blocks A and B.

▲ **FIGURE 8.31** Question 1.

2. Gliders A and B are headed directly toward each other on an air track and collide head-on. Identify the internal and external forces on each glider during the collision. What are the internal and external forces if the system consists of *both* gliders?

3. Example 8.3, as well as some of the problems in this chapter, describe how, when an object explodes into two fragments, the lighter one gets more kinetic energy than the heavier one. How can this be so, since both fragments are acted upon by the same force for the same amount of time during the explosion? (*Hint:* Does the force act over the same *distance* on each fragment?)

4. Is the momentum of a satellite in a circular orbit conserved? What about its kinetic energy? Explain your reasoning.

5. Golfers, tennis players, and baseball batters are told to "follow through" with their swing. Why? What does a follow-through enable them to do?

6. When a catcher in a baseball game catches a fast ball, he does not hold his arms rigid, but relaxes them so that the mitt moves several inches while the ball is being caught. Why is this important?

7. You are shooting cannonballs from a cannon. To achieve the maximum range of the ball, would you be better off fastening the cannon to the ground or letting it be free to recoil, or wouldn't it matter? Explain your reasoning.

8. When rockets were first suggested, some people scoffed that they would not work in space because there is nothing out there for them to push against. So why *do* they work in space, since there really is nothing out there for them to push against?

9. (a) If the momentum of a *single* object is equal to zero, must its kinetic energy also be zero? (b) If the momentum of a *pair* of objects is equal to zero, must the kinetic energy of those objects also be zero? (c) If the kinetic energy of a pair of objects is equal to zero, must the momentum of those objects also be zero? Explain your reasoning in each case.

10. (a) When a large car collides with a small car, which one undergoes the greater change in momentum, the large one or the small one? Or is it the same for both? (b) In light of your answer to part (a), why are the occupants of the small car more likely to be hurt than those of the large car, assuming that both cars are equally sturdy?

11. When rain falls from the sky, what becomes of the momentum of the raindrops as they hit the ground? Is your answer also valid for Newton's famous apple?

12. In old-time Western movies, people often fell forward when shot from the front by a rifle. In more "realistic" modern films, such people often fly backwards through the air. Given that a typical mass of a rifle bullet is about 4 grams and the speed of such a bullet is about 970 m/s, which (if any) of these two reactions to being shot is realistic? Back up your answer with a reasonable numerical calculation.

13. A machine gun is fired at a steel plate. Is the impulse imparted to the plate from the impact of the bullets greater if the bullets bounce off or if they are squashed and stick to the plate?

14. How do Mexican jumping beans work? Do they violate conservation of momentum? conservation of energy?

15. At the highest point in its parabolic trajectory, a shell explodes into two fragments. Is it possible for *both* fragments to fall straight down after the explosion? Why or why not?

16. If the movie "supergorilla" King Kong beats his chest on a frozen frictionless lake, will he go backward? Why?

Multiple-Choice Problems

1. A small car collides head-on with a large SUV. Which of the following statements concerning this collision are correct? (There may be more than one correct choice.)
   A. Both vehicles are acted upon by the same magnitude of average force during the collision.
   B. The small car is acted upon by a greater magnitude of average force than the SUV.
   C. The small car undergoes a greater change in momentum than the SUV.
   D. Both vehicles undergo the same change in magnitude of momentum.

2. A ball of mass 0.18 kg moving with speed 11.3 m/s collides head-on with an identical stationary ball. (Notice that we do not know the type of collision.) Which of the following quantities can be calculated from this information alone?
   A. The force each ball exerts on the other.
   B. The velocity of each ball after the collision.
   C. Total kinetic energy of both balls after the collision.
   D. Total momentum of both balls after the collision.

3. A proton with a speed of 50,000 km/s makes an *elastic* head-on collision with a stationary carbon nucleus. We can look up

the masses of both particles. Which of the following quantities can be calculated from only the known information? (There may be more than one correct choice.)
A. The velocity of the proton and carbon nucleus after the collision.
B. The kinetic energy of each of the particles after the collision.
C. The momentum of each of the particles after the collision.

4. In which of the following collisions would you expect the kinetic energy to be conserved? (There may be more than one correct choice.)
A. A bullet passes through a block of wood.
B. Two bull elk charge each other and lock horns.
C. Two asteroids collide by a glancing blow, but do not actually hit each other, and their only interaction is through gravity.
D. Two cars with springlike bumpers collide at fairly low speeds.

5. A rifle of mass M is initially at rest, but is free to recoil. It fires a bullet of mass m with a velocity $+v$ relative to the ground. After the rifle is fired, its velocity relative to the ground is
A. $-\sqrt{m/M}v$.
B. $-mv/(m+M)$.
C. $-mv/M$.
D. $-v$.

6. Two carts, one twice as heavy as the other, are at rest on a horizontal frictionless track. A person pushes each cart with the same force for 5 s. If the kinetic energy of the *lighter* cart after the push is K, the kinetic energy of the heavier cart is
A. $\frac{1}{4}K$.
B. $\frac{1}{2}K$.
C. K.
D. $2K$.
E. $4K$.

7. For the carts in the previous problem, if the magnitude of the momentum of the *lighter* cart after the push is P, the magnitude of the momentum of the heavier cart is
A. $\frac{1}{4}P$.
B. $\frac{1}{2}P$.
C. P.
D. $2P$.
E. $4P$.

8. Two masses, M and $5M$, are at rest on a horizontal frictionless table with a compressed spring of negligible mass between them. When the spring is released (there may be more than one correct choice),
A. the two masses receive equal magnitudes of momentum.
B. the two masses receive equal amounts of kinetic energy from the spring.
C. the heavier mass gains more kinetic energy than the lighter mass.
D. the lighter mass gains more kinetic energy than the heavier mass.

9. Cart A, of mass 1 kg, approaches and collides with cart B, which has a mass of 4 kg and is initially at rest. (See Figure 8.32.) When the springs have reached their maximum compression,
A. cart A has come to rest relative to the ground.
B. both carts have the same velocity.
C. both carts have the same momentum.
D. all the initial kinetic energy of cart A has been converted to elastic potential energy.

▲ **FIGURE 8.32** Multiple-choice problem 9.

10. A glider airplane is coasting horizontally when a very heavy object suddenly falls out of it. As a result of dropping this object, the glider's speed will
A. increase.
B. decrease.
C. remain the same as it was.

11. Which of the following statements is true for an *inelastic* collision? (There may be more than one correct choice.)
A. Both momentum and kinetic energy are conserved.
B. Momentum is conserved, but kinetic energy is not conserved.
C. Kinetic energy is conserved, but momentum is not conserved.
D. The amount of momentum lost by one object is the same as the amount gained by the other object.
E. The amount of kinetic energy lost by one object is the same as the amount gained by the other object.

12. Which of the following statements is true for an *elastic* collision? (There may be more than one correct choice.)
A. Both momentum and kinetic energy are conserved.
B. Momentum is conserved, but kinetic energy is not conserved.
C. Kinetic energy is conserved, but momentum is not conserved.
D. The amount of momentum lost by one object is the same as the amount gained by the other object.
E. The amount of kinetic energy lost by one object is the same as the amount gained by the other object.

13. Two lumps of clay having equal masses and speeds, but traveling in opposite directions on a frictionless horizontal surface, collide and stick together. Which of the following statements about this system of lumps must be true? (There may be more than one correct choice.)
A. The momentum of the system is conserved during the collision.
B. The kinetic energy of the system is conserved during the collision.
C. The two masses lose all their kinetic energy during the collision.
D. The velocity of the center of mass of the system is the same after the collision as it was before the collision.

14. A heavy rifle initially at rest fires a light bullet. Which of the following statements about these objects is true? (There may be more than one correct choice.)
A. The bullet and rifle both gain the same magnitude of momentum.
B. The bullet and rifle are both acted upon by the same average force during the firing.
C. The bullet and rifle both have the same acceleration during the firing.
D. The bullet and the rifle gain the same amount of kinetic energy.

15. You drop an egg from rest with no air resistance. As it falls,
A. only its momentum is conserved.
B. only its kinetic energy is conserved.
C. both its momentum and its mechanical energy are conserved.
D. its mechanical energy is conserved, but its momentum is not conserved.

Problems

8.1 Momentum

1. • For each case in Figure 8.33, the system consists of the masses shown with the indicated velocities. Find the net momentum of each system.

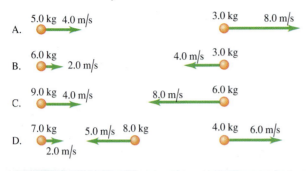

▲ **FIGURE 8.33** Problem 1.

2. • For each case in Figure 8.34, the system consists of the masses shown with the indicated velocities. Find the x and y components of the net momentum of each system.

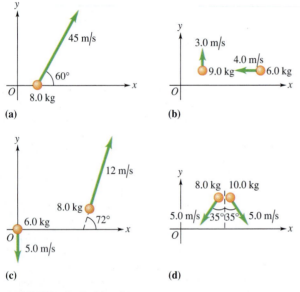

▲ **FIGURE 8.34** Problem 2.

3. • Three objects A, B, and C are moving as shown in Figure 8.35. Find the x and y components of the net momentum of the particles if we define the system to consist of (a) A and C, (b) B and C, (c) all three objects.

▲ **FIGURE 8.35** Problem 3.

4. • A 1200 kg car is moving on the freeway at 65 mph. (a) Find the magnitude of its momentum and its kinetic energy in SI units. (b) If a 2400 kg SUV has the same speed as the 1200 kg car, how much momentum and kinetic energy does it have?

5. • The speed of the fastest-pitched baseball was 45 m/s, and the ball's mass was 145 g. (a) What was the magnitude of the momentum of this ball, and how many joules of kinetic energy did it have? (b) How fast would a 57 gram ball have to travel to have the same amount of (i) kinetic energy, and (ii) momentum?

6. •• **Some useful relationships.** The following relationships between the momentum and kinetic energy of an object can be very useful for calculations: If an object of mass m has momentum of magnitude p and kinetic energy K, show that (a) $K = (p^2/2m)$, and (b) $p = \sqrt{2mK}$. (c) Find the momentum of a 1.15 kg ball that has 15.0 J of kinetic energy. (d) Find the kinetic energy of a 3.50 kg cat that has 0.220 kg · m/s of momentum.

7. •• The magnitude of the momentum of a cat is p. What would be the magnitude of the momentum (in terms of p) of a dog having three times the mass of the cat if it had (a) the same speed as the cat, and (b) the same kinetic energy as the cat?

8.2 Conservation of Momentum

8. • Two figure skaters, one weighing 625 N and the other 725 N, push off against each other on frictionless ice. (a) If the heavier skater travels at 1.50 m/s, how fast will the lighter one travel? (b) How much kinetic energy is "created" during the skaters' maneuver, and where does this energy come from?

9. • **Recoil speed of the earth.** In principle, any time someone jumps up, the earth moves in the opposite direction. To see why we are unaware of this motion, calculate the recoil speed of the earth when a 75 kg person jumps upward at a speed of 2.0 m/s. Consult Appendix F as needed.

10. • On a frictionless air track, a 0.150 kg glider moving at 1.20 m/s to the right collides with and sticks to a stationary 0.250 kg glider. (a) What is the net momentum of this two-glider system before the collision? (b) What must be the net momentum of this system after the collision? Why? (c) Use your answers in parts (a) and (b) to find the speed of the gliders after the collision. (d) Is kinetic energy conserved during the collision?

11. • **Baseball.** A regulation 145 g baseball can be hit at speeds of 100 mph. If a line drive is hit essentially horizontally at this speed and is caught by a 65 kg player who has leapt directly upward into the air, what horizontal speed (in cm/s) does he acquire by catching the ball?

12. • You are standing on a sheet of ice that covers the football stadium parking lot in Buffalo; there is negligible friction between your feet and the ice. A friend throws you a 0.400 kg ball that is traveling horizontally at 10.0 m/s. Your mass is 70.0 kg. (a) If you catch the ball, with what speed do you and the ball move afterwards? (b) If the ball hits you and bounces off your chest, so that afterwards it is moving horizontally at 8.00 m/s in the opposite direction, what is your speed after the collision?

13. •• On a frictionless, horizontal air table, puck A (with mass 0.250 kg) is moving toward puck B (with mass 0.350 kg), which is initially at rest. After the collision, puck A has a velocity of 0.120 m/s to the left, and puck B has a velocity of 0.650 m/s to the right. (a) What was the speed of puck A before

the collision? (b) Calculate the change in the total kinetic energy of the system that occurs during the collision.

14. •• Block *A* in Figure 8.36 has mass 1.00 kg, and block *B* has mass 3.00 kg. The blocks are forced together, compressing a spring *S* between them; then the system is released from rest on a level, frictionless surface. The spring, which has negligible mass, is not fastened to either block and drops to the surface after it has expanded. Block *B* acquires a speed of 1.20 m/s. (a) What is the final speed of block *A*? (b) How much potential energy was stored in the compressed spring?

▲ **FIGURE 8.36** Problem 14.

15. •• A railroad handcar is moving along straight, frictionless tracks with negligible air resistance. In the cases that follow, the car initially has a total mass (car and contents) of 200.0 kg and is traveling east with a velocity of magnitude 5.00 m/s. Find the *final velocity* of the handcar in each case, assuming that it does not leave the tracks. (a) A 25.0 kg mass is thrown sideways out of the car with a velocity of magnitude 2.00 m/s relative to the car's initial velocity. (b) A 25.0 kg mass is thrown backward out of the car with a velocity of 5.00 m/s relative to the initial motion of the car. (c) A 25.0 kg mass is thrown into the car with a velocity of 6.00 m/s relative to the ground and opposite in direction to the initial velocity of the car. (d) A 25.0 kg mass is thrown directly upward at 5.00 m/s relative to the handcar.

16. •• **Changing mass.** An open-topped freight car with mass 24,000 kg is coasting without friction along a level track. It is raining very hard, and the rain is falling vertically downward. Originally, the car is empty and moving with a speed of 4.00 m/s. (a) What is the speed of the car after it has collected 3000 kg of rainwater? (b) Since the rain is falling *downward,* how is it able to affect the *horizontal* motion of the car?

17. •• A 4.25 g bullet traveling horizontally with a velocity of magnitude 375 m/s is fired into a wooden block with mass 1.12 kg, initially at rest on a level frictionless surface. The bullet passes *through* the block and emerges with its speed reduced to 122 m/s. How fast is the block moving just after the bullet emerges from it?

18. •• A ball with a mass of 0.600 kg is initially at rest. It is struck by a second ball having a mass of 0.400 kg, initially moving with a velocity of 0.250 m/s toward the right along the *x* axis. After the collision, the 0.400 kg ball has a velocity of 0.200 m/s at an angle of 36.9° above the *x* axis in the first quadrant. Both balls move on a frictionless, horizontal surface. (a) What are the magnitude and direction of the velocity of the 0.600 kg ball after the collision? (b) What is the change in the total kinetic energy of the two balls as a result of the collision?

19. •• **Combining conservation laws.** A 5.00 kg chunk of ice is sliding at 12.0 m/s on the floor of an ice-covered valley when it collides with and sticks to another 5.00 kg chunk of ice that is initially at rest. (See Figure 8.37.) Since the valley is icy, there is no friction. After the collision, how high above the valley floor will the combined chunks go? (*Hint:* Break this problem into

two parts—the collision and the behavior after the collision—and apply the appropriate conservation law to each part.)

▲ **FIGURE 8.37** Problem 19.

20. •• **Combining conservation laws.** A 15.0 kg block is attached to a very light horizontal spring of force constant 500.0 N/m and is resting on a frictionless horizontal table. (See Figure 8.38.) Suddenly it is struck by a 3.00 kg stone traveling horizontally at 8.00 m/s to the right, whereupon the stone rebounds at 2.00 m/s horizontally to the left. Find the maximum distance that the block will compress the spring after the collision. (*Hint:* Break this problem into two parts—the collision and the behavior after the collision—and apply the appropriate conservation law to each part.)

▲ **FIGURE 8.38** Problem 20.

8.3 Inelastic Collisions

21. • Three identical boxcars are coupled together and are moving at a constant speed of 20.0 m/s on a level track. They collide with another identical boxcar that is initially at rest and couple to it, so that the four cars roll on as a unit. Friction is small enough to be neglected. (a) What is the speed of the four cars? (b) What percentage of the kinetic energy of the boxcars is dissipated in the collision? What happened to this energy?

22. • On a highly polished, essentially frictionless lunch counter, a 0.500 kg submarine sandwich moving 3.00 m/s to the left collides with an 0.250 kg grilled cheese sandwich moving 1.20 m/s to the right. (a) If the two sandwiches stick together, what is their final velocity? (b) How much mechanical energy dissipates in the collision? Where did this energy go?

23. Two frisky grasshoppers collide in midair at the top of their respective trajectories and grab onto each other, holding tight thereafter. One is a robust 250 g beast initially moving south at 20.0 cm/s, while the other is a svelte 150 g creature initially moving north at 60.0 cm/s. Calculate the decrease in kinetic energy that results from the collision. What happened to the "lost" kinetic energy?

24. •• **That pesky kid next door!** Your neighbor's pesky kid insists on throwing 25.0 g rocks at your new 2.25 kg light fixture hanging by a 26.0 cm wire from the ceiling of your porch. If each rock strikes the fixture traveling at 10.0 m/s horizontally and rebounds at 2.00 m/s backwards, how high above the lowest point does the impact make your light fixture swing?

25. •• A 5.00 g bullet is fired horizontally into a 1.20 kg wooden block resting on a horizontal surface. The coefficient of kinetic friction between block and surface is 0.20. The bullet remains embedded in the block, which is observed to slide 0.230 m along the surface before stopping. What was the initial speed of the bullet?

26. •• The morning after a winter ice storm in Dallas, a 1400 kg automobile going west on Chestnut Street at 35.0 km/h collides with a 2800 kg truck going south *across* Chestnut Street at 50.0 km/h. If they become coupled on collision, what are the magnitude and direction of their velocity after colliding? You can ignore forces between the vehicles and the icy road.

27. •• A hungry 11.5 kg predator fish is coasting from west to east at 75.0 cm/s when it suddenly swallows a 1.25 kg fish swimming from north to south at 3.60 m/s. Find the magnitude and direction of the velocity of the large fish just after it snapped up this meal. Neglect any effects due to the drag of the water.

28. •• **Bird defense.** To protect their young in the nest, peregrine
BIO falcons will fly into birds of prey (such as ravens) at high speed. In one such episode, a 600 gram falcon flying at 20.0 m/s ran into a 1.5 kg raven flying at 9.0 m/s. The falcon hit the raven at right angles to its original path and bounced back with a speed of 5.0 m/s. (These figures were estimated by one of the authors (WRA) as he watched this attack occur in northern New Mexico.) By what angle did the falcon change the raven's direction of motion?

29. •• **Accident analysis.** Two cars collide at an intersection. Car *A*, with a mass of 2000 kg, is going from west to east, while car *B*, of mass 1500 kg, is going from north to south at 15 m/s. As a result of this collision, the two cars become enmeshed and move as one afterwards. In your role as an expert witness, you inspect the scene and determine that, after the collision, the enmeshed cars moved at an angle of 65° south of east from the point of impact. (a) How fast were the enmeshed cars moving just after the collision? (b) How fast was car *A* going just before the collision?

30. •• A hockey puck *B* rests on frictionless, level ice and is struck by a second puck *A*, which was originally traveling at 40.0 m/s and which is deflected 30.0° from its original direction. (See Figure 8.39.) Puck *B* acquires a velocity at a 45.0° angle to the original direction of *A*. The pucks have the same mass. (a) Compute the speed of each puck after the collision. (b) What fraction of the original kinetic energy of puck *A* dissipates during the collision?

▲ **FIGURE 8.39** Problem 30.

8.4 Elastic Collisions

31. • A 0.300 kg glider is moving to the right on a frictionless, horizontal air track with a speed of 0.80 m/s when it makes a head-on collision with a stationary 0.150 kg glider. (a) Find the magnitude and direction of the final velocity of each glider if the collision is elastic. (b) Find the final kinetic energy of each glider.

32. • **That pesky kid next door again!** That neighbor's pesky kid (see Problem 24) now has new missiles that make elastic collisions. If all else is the same as in Problem 24 (except, of course, the recoil velocity of the missiles), how high will the light fixture go after it is hit by one of these new missiles?

33. •• **Nuclear collisions.** Collisions between atomic and subatomic particles are often perfectly elastic. In one such colli-

sion, a proton traveling to the right at 258 km/s collides head-on and elastically with a stationary alpha particle (a helium nucleus, having mass 6.65×10^{-27} kg). Consult Appendix F as needed. (a) Find the magnitude and direction of the velocity of each particle after the collision. (b) How much kinetic energy does the proton lose during the collision? (c) How can the collision be elastic if the proton loses kinetic energy?

34. •• On an air track, a 400.0 g glider moving to the right at 2.00 m/s collides elastically with a 500.0 g glider moving in the opposite direction at 3.00 m/s. Find the velocity of each glider after the collision.

35. •• Suppose that a bowling ball traveling with speed *V* collides elastically with a stationary table-tennis ball. What do Equations (8.11) and (8.12) give for the velocity of each ball after the collision? Derive algebraic expressions.

36. •• Two identical objects traveling in opposite directions with the same speed *V* make a head-on collision. Find the speed of each object after the collision if (a) they stick together and (b) if the collision is perfectly elastic.

8.5 Impulse

37. • A catcher catches a 145 g baseball traveling horizontally at 36.0 m/s. (a) How large an impulse does the ball give to the catcher? (b) If the ball takes 20 ms to stop once it is in contact with the catcher's glove, what average force did the ball exert on the catcher?

38. • A block of ice with a mass of 2.50 kg is moving on a frictionless, horizontal surface. At $t = 0$, the block is moving to the right with a velocity of magnitude 8.00 m/s. Calculate the magnitude and direction of the velocity of the block after each of the following forces has been applied for 5.00 s: (a) a force of 5.00 N directed to the right; (b) a force of 7.00 N directed to the left.

39. •• **Biomechanics.** The mass of a regulation tennis ball is
BIO 57 g (although it can vary slightly), and tests have shown that the ball is in contact with the tennis racket for 30 ms. (This number can also vary, depending on the racket and swing.) We shall assume a 30.0 ms contact time throughout this problem. The fastest-known served tennis ball was served by "Big Bill" Tilden in 1931, and its speed was measured to be 73.14 m/s. (a) What impulse and what force did Big Bill exert on the tennis ball in his record serve? (b) If Big Bill's opponent returned his serve with a speed of 55 m/s, what force and what impulse did he exert on the ball, assuming only horizontal motion?

40. •• To warm up for a match, a tennis player hits the 57.0 g ball vertically with her racket. If the ball is stationary just before it is hit and goes 5.50 m high, what impulse did she impart to it?

41. •• A 150 gram baseball is hit toward the left by a bat. The magnitude of the force the bat exerts on the ball as a function of time is shown in Figure 8.40. (a) Find the magnitude and

▲ **FIGURE 8.40** Problem 41.

direction of the impulse that the bat imparts to the ball. (b) Find the magnitude and direction of the ball's velocity just after it is hit by the bat if the ball is initially (i) at rest, and (ii) moving to the right at 30.0 m/s.

42. •• A 250 gram ball is moving horizontally to the right at 175 m/s when it is hit toward the left by a metal club. The graph in Figure 8.41 shows the magnitude of the force this club exerts on the ball as a function of time. Find the magnitude and direction of the ball's velocity just after it is hit by the club.

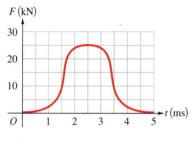

▲ **FIGURE 8.41** Problem 42.

43. •• **Bone fracture.** Experimental tests have shown that bone **BIO** will rupture if it is subjected to a force density of 1.0×10^8 N/m². Suppose a 70.0 kg person carelessly roller-skates into an overhead metal beam that hits his forehead and completely stops his forward motion. If the area of contact with the person's forehead is 1.5 cm², what is the greatest speed with which he can hit the wall without breaking any bone if his head is in contact with the beam for 10.0 ms?

44. •• A bat strikes a 0.145 kg baseball. Just before impact, the ball is traveling horizontally to the right at 50.0 m/s, and it leaves the bat traveling to the left at an angle of 30° above horizontal with a speed of 65.0 m/s. (a) What are the horizontal and vertical components of the impulse the bat imparts to the ball? (b) If the ball and bat are in contact for 1.75 ms, find the horizontal and vertical components of the average force on the ball.

8.7 Motion of the Center of Mass

45. • **Carbon monoxide molecule.** Find the center of mass of the carbon monoxide molecule (CO), given that carbon has a mass of 12 u, oxygen has a mass of 16 u, and the two atoms are 0.111 nm apart.

46. • Two small-sized objects are placed on a uniform 9.00 kg plastic beam 3.00 m long, as shown in Figure 8.42. Find the location of the center of mass of this system by setting $x = 0$ at (a) the left end of the beam and (b) the right end of the beam. (c) Do you get the same result both ways?

▲ **FIGURE 8.42** Problem 46.

47. •• **Detecting planets around other stars.** Over 100 planets have so far been detected beyond our solar system. This is accomplished by looking for the effect the planet has on the star. The star is not truly stationary; instead, it and its planets orbit around the center of mass of the system. Astronomers can

measure this wobble in the position of a star. (a) For a star with the mass and size of our sun and having a planet with five times the mass of Jupiter, where would the center of mass of this system be located, relative to the center of the star, if the distance from the star to the planet was the same as the distance from Jupiter to our sun? (Consult Appendix F.) (b) If the planet had earth's mass, where would the center of mass of the system be located if the planet was just as far from the star as the earth is from the sun? (c) In view of your results in parts (a) and (b), why is it much easier to detect stars having large planets rather than small ones?

48. • Three odd-shaped blocks of chocolate have the following masses and center-of-mass coordinates: (1) 0.300 kg, $(0.200 \text{ m}, 0.300 \text{ m})$; (2) 0.400 kg, $(0.100 \text{ m}, -0.400 \text{ m})$; (3) 0.200 kg, $(-0.300 \text{ m}, 0.600 \text{ m})$. Find the coordinates of the center of mass of the system of three chocolate blocks.

49. •• Weights of 10 N, 20 N, 30 N, and 40 N are at the corners of a square as shown in Figure 8.43. The weights are connected together by four identical uniform plastic rods, each 1.0 m long. (a) Find the location of the center of mass of this system if the weights of the four plastic rods are negligibly small. (b) Suppose now that the plastic rods have weights comparable to those at the corners of the square. Will the center of mass of this system be different from what you found in part (a)? If it will be unchanged, explain why. If it will be changed, which way will it be shifted (up or down, right or left) compared with what you found in part (a)?

▲ **FIGURE 8.43** Problem 49.

50. •• **Changing your center of mass.** To keep the calculations **BIO** fairly simple, but still reasonable, we shall model a human leg that is 92.0 cm long (measured from the hip joint) by assuming that the upper leg and the lower leg (which includes the foot) have equal lengths and that each of them is uniform. For a 70.0 kg person, the mass of the upper leg would be 8.60 kg, while that of the lower leg (including the foot) would be 5.25 kg. Find the location of the center of mass of this leg, relative to the hip joint, if it is (a) stretched out horizontally and (b) bent at the knee to form a right angle with the upper leg remaining horizontal.

51. • A 1200 kg station wagon is moving along a straight highway at 12.0 m/s. Another car, with mass 1800 kg and speed 20.0 m/s, has its center of mass 40.0 m ahead of the center of mass of the station wagon. (See Figure 8.44.) (a) Find the position of the center of mass of the system consisting of the two automobiles. (b) Find the magnitude of the total momentum of the system from the given data. (c) Find the speed of the center of mass of the system. (d) Find the total momentum of the system, using the speed of the center of mass. Compare your result with that of part (b).

▲ **FIGURE 8.44** Problem 51.

52. •• **Walking in a boat.** A 45.0 kg woman stands up in a 60.0 kg canoe of length 5.00 m. She walks from a point 1.00 m from one end to a point 1.00 m from the other end. (See Figure 8.45.) If the resistance of the water is negligible, how far does the canoe move during this process?

Start ⟷ Finish
1.00 m | 3.00 m | 1.00 m

▲ **FIGURE 8.45** Problem 52.

*8.8 Rocket Propulsion

53. • A small rocket burns 0.0500 kg of fuel per second, ejecting it as a gas with a velocity of magnitude 1600 m/s relative to the rocket. (a) What is the thrust of the rocket? (b) Would the rocket operate in outer space, where there is no atmosphere? If so, how would you steer it? Could you brake it?

54. • A rocket is fired in deep space, where gravity is negligible. If the rocket has an initial mass of 6000 kg and ejects gas at a relative velocity of magnitude 2000 m/s, how much gas must it eject in the first second to have an initial acceleration of 25.0 m/s^2.

55. • A rocket is fired in deep space, where gravity is negligible. In the first second, it ejects 1/160 of its mass as exhaust gas and has an acceleration of 15.0 m/s^2. What is the speed of the exhaust gas relative to the rocket?

56. •• In outer space, where gravity is negligible, a 75,000 kg rocket (including 50,000 kg of fuel) expels this fuel at a steady rate of 135 kg/s with a speed of 1200 m/s relative to the rocket. (a) Find the thrust of the rocket. (b) What are the initial acceleration and the maximum acceleration of the rocket? (c) After the fuel runs out, what happens to this rocket's acceleration? Does it (i) remain the same as it was just as the fuel ran out, (ii) suddenly become zero, or (iii) gradually drop to zero? Explain your reasoning. (d) After the fuel runs out, what happens to the rocket's speed? Does it (i) remain the same as it was just as the fuel ran out, (ii) suddenly become zero, or (iii) gradually drop to zero? Explain your reasoning.

57. •• **Launch of the space shuttle.** At liftoff from the launch pad, the space shuttle's initial mass is 2.04 million kilograms and its rockets provide a total thrust of 35 million newtons. During the first minute of flight, it consumes 230,000 kg of fuel. (a) Find the initial acceleration of the space shuttle. (b) At what rate do the rockets consume fuel, assuming the rate to be constant? (c) At what speed relative to the shuttle is fuel expelled?

General Problems

58. •• Find the average recoil force on a machine gun firing 120 shots per minute. The mass of each bullet is 10.0 g, and the muzzle speed is 600 m/s.

59. •• A station wagon traveling west collides with a pickup truck traveling north. They stick together as a result of the col-

lision. The station wagon has a mass of 1400 kg, and the pickup truck has a mass of 900 kg. A police officer estimates from the skid marks that, immediately after the collision, the combined object was traveling at 12.0 m/s in a direction 37.0° west of north. Calculate the speeds of the station wagon and pickup just before the collision.

60. •• A 5.00 kg ornament is hanging by a 1.50 m wire when it is suddenly hit by a 3.00 kg missile traveling horizontally at 12.0 m/s. The missile embeds itself in the ornament during the collision. What is the tension in the wire immediately after the collision?

61. •• A stone with a mass of 0.100 kg rests on a frictionless, horizontal surface. A bullet of mass 2.50 g traveling horizontally at 500 m/s strikes the stone and rebounds horizontally at right angles to its original direction with a speed of 300 m/s. (a) Compute the magnitude and direction of the velocity of the stone after it is struck. (b) Is the collision perfectly elastic?

62. •• A steel ball with a mass of 40.0 g is dropped from a height of 2.00 m onto a horizontal steel slab. The ball rebounds to a height of 1.60 m. (a) Calculate the impulse delivered to the ball during the impact. (b) If the ball is in contact with the slab for 2.00 ms, find the average force on the ball during the impact.

63. •• A neutron with a mass of 1.67×10^{-27} kg and moving with a speed of 45.0 km/s makes a head-on collision with a boron nucleus with a mass of 1.66×10^{-26} kg. The boron nucleus is originally at rest. (a) If the collision is completely inelastic, so that the neutron and boron nucleus stick together, what is the final kinetic energy of the system, expressed as a fraction of the original kinetic energy? (b) If the collision is perfectly elastic, what fraction of the neutron's original kinetic energy is transferred to the boron nucleus?

64. •• **Tennis, anyone?** Tennis players sometimes leap into the air to return a volley. (a) If a 57 g tennis ball is traveling horizontally at 72 m/s (which does occur), and a 61 kg tennis player leaps vertically upward and hits the ball, causing it to travel at 45 m/s in the reverse direction, how fast will her center of mass be moving horizontally just after hitting the ball? (b) If, as is reasonable, her racket is in contact with the ball for 30.0 ms, what force does her racket exert on the ball? What force does the ball exert on the racket?

65. •• The results of a one-dimensional elastic collision between two objects, where object B is initially at rest, are given by Equations 8.11 and 8.12. It was shown in Section 8.4 that when m_A is much less than m_B, these equations give $v_{A,f} \approx -v_{A,i}$ and $v_{B,f} \approx 0$, and that when $m_A = m_B$, the equations give $v_{A,f} = 0$ and $v_{B,f} = v_{A,i}$. Make a similar analysis for the following special cases: (a) $m_A = 2m_B$ and (b) $m_B = 2m_A$.

66. •• Two cars, one a compact with a mass of 1200 kg and the other a large gas-guzzler with mass 3000 kg, collide head-on at typical freeway speeds. (a) Which car has a greater change in the magnitude of its momentum? Which car has a greater change in velocity? Calculate the change in the velocity of the small car in terms of the change in velocity, ΔV, of the large car. (b) Which car's occupants would you expect to sustain greater injuries, assuming equally sturdy cars? Explain.

67. •• Two identical 1.50 kg masses are pressed against opposite ends of a light spring of force constant 1.75 N/cm, compressing the spring by 20.0 cm from its normal length. Find the speed of each mass when it has moved free of the spring on a frictionless horizontal lab table.

68. •• A rifle bullet with mass 8.00 g strikes and embeds itself in a block with a mass of 0.992 kg that rests on a frictionless, horizontal surface and is attached to a coil spring. (See Figure 8.46.) The impact compresses the spring 15.0 cm. Calibration of the spring shows that a force of 0.750 N is required to compress the spring 0.250 cm. (a) Find the magnitude of the block's velocity just after impact. (b) What was the initial speed of the bullet?

▲ **FIGURE 8.46** Problem 68.

69. •• A 5.00 g bullet traveling horizontally at 450 m/s is shot *through* a 1.00 kg wood block suspended on a string 2.00 m long. If the center of mass of the block rises a distance of 0.450 cm, find the speed of the bullet as it emerges from the block.

70. •• **Neutron decay.** A neutron that is at rest decays (breaks up) into a proton and an electron. Energy is released in the decay and appears as kinetic energy of the proton and electron. The mass of a proton is 1836 times the mass of an electron. What fraction of the total energy released goes into the kinetic energy of the proton?

71. •• Jonathan and Jane are sitting in a sleigh that is at rest on frictionless ice. Jonathan's weight is 800 N, Jane's weight is 600 N, and that of the sleigh is 1000 N. They see a poisonous spider on the floor of the sleigh and immediately jump off. Jonathan jumps to the left with a velocity (relative to the ice) of 5.00 m/s at 30.0° above the horizontal, and Jane jumps to the right at 7.00 m/s at 36.9° above the horizontal (relative to the ice). Calculate the sleigh's horizontal velocity (magnitude and direction) after they jump out.

72. •• **A sports exhibit.** You are designing an athletics exhibit containing a baseball bat that will be suspended horizontally by a single thin wire attached to it midway between its ends. Although shapes, sizes, and weights vary a bit, a typical baseball bat is 34.0 in. long, weighs 8.60 N, and has its center of mass three-fourths of the way from the end of the handle. In your exhibit, you glue a 150 g baseball to the thick end of the bat. In order that the bat hang horizontally, where should you attach a small 15.0 N weight so that the center of mass of this system will be at the point where the support wire is attached to the bat?

73. •• **Animal propulsion.** Squids and octopuses propel themselves by expelling water. They do this by taking the water into a cavity and then suddenly contracting the cavity, forcing the water to shoot out of an opening. A 6.50 kg squid (including the water in its cavity) that is at rest suddenly sees a dangerous predator. (a) If this squid has 1.75 kg of water in its cavity, at what speed must it expel the water to suddenly achieve a speed of 2.50 m/s to escape the predator? Neglect any drag effects of the surrounding water. (b) How much kinetic energy does the squid create for this escape maneuver?

74. •• The objects in Figure 8.47 are constructed of uniform wire bent into the shapes shown. Find the position of the center of mass of each one.

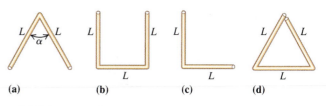

▲ **FIGURE 8.47** Problem 74.

75. •• **Origin of the moon.** Astronomers believe that our moon originated when a Mars-sized body collided with the earth over 4.5 billion years ago, knocking off matter that condensed to form the moon. To get some idea of how such a collision would affect the earth, assume that the collision occurred head-on (with the two bodies traveling in opposite directions), that the Mars-sized body merged completely with the earth and was originally the same mass as Mars, and that the earth's orbital speed was the same as it is now. Assume further that the speed of the colliding body was equal to the earth's escape velocity of 11 km/s (although it could have been greater). (a) By how much (in m/s) did such a collision change the earth's speed? Consult Appendix F. (b) How much thermal energy would such a collision create? (c) To how many megaton bombs is the energy in part (b) equivalent? (One ton of TNT releases 4.184×10^9 J of energy.)

76. •• You are standing on a concrete slab that in turn is resting on a frozen lake. Assume that there is no friction between the slab and the ice. The slab has a weight five times your weight. If you begin walking forward at 2.00 m/s relative to the ice, with what speed, relative to the ice, does the slab move?

77. •• **Forensic science.** Forensic scientists can measure the muzzle velocity of a gun by firing a bullet horizontally into a large hanging block that absorbs the bullet and swings upward. (See Figure 8.48.) The measured maximum angle of swing can be used to calculate the speed of the bullet. In one such test, a rifle fired a 4.20 g bullet into a 2.50 kg block hanging by a thin wire 75.0 cm long, causing the block to swing upward to a maximum angle of 34.7° from the vertical. What was the original speed of this bullet?

75.0 cm

4.20 g   2.50 kg

▲ **FIGURE 8.48** Problem 77.

78. •• **Automobile accident analysis.** You are called as an expert witness to analyze the following auto accident: Car B, of mass 1900 kg, was stopped at a red light when it was hit from behind by car A, of mass 1500 kg. The cars locked bumpers during the collision and slid to a stop with brakes locked on all wheels. Measurements of the skid marks left by the tires showed them to be 7.15 m long. The coefficient of kinetic friction between the tires and the road was 0.65. (a) What was the speed of car A just before the collision? (b) If the speed limit was 35 mph, was car A speeding, and if so, by how many mph was it *exceeding* the speed limit?

79. •• Three coupled railroad cars roll along and couple with a fourth car, which is initially at rest. The four cars roll along and couple with a fifth car initially at rest. The process continues until the speed of the final collection of railroad cars is one-fifth

the speed of the initial three railroad cars. All the cars are identical. Ignoring friction, how many cars are in the final collection?

80. •• **Molotov cocktail.** Suppose that a "Molotov cocktail" contains enough gasoline to release 1.37×10^8 J of energy when it is burned. The vessel holding the gasoline is originally at rest and has a mass of 10.0 kg. It breaks into two pieces, one four times heavier than the other. Assume that all the energy released by the gasoline goes only into the kinetic energy of these pieces. (In reality, the "cocktail" breaks into many fragments and a great deal of heat is produced by burning gases.) (a) What is the ratio of the speed of the lighter piece to that of the heavier piece? (b) Calculate the speed of each piece just after the explosion. (c) Find the ratio of the kinetic energy of the smaller piece to that of the larger piece.

81. •• **The structure of the atom.** During 1910–1911, Sir Ernest Rutherford performed a series of experiments to determine the structure of the atom. He aimed a beam of alpha particles (helium nuclei, of mass 6.65×10^{-27} kg) at an extremely thin sheet of gold foil. Most of the alphas went right through with little deflection, but a small percentage bounced directly back. These results told him that the atom must be mostly empty space with an extremely small nucleus. The alpha particles that bounced back must have made a head-on collision with this nucleus. A typical speed for the alpha particles before the collision was 1.25×10^7 m/s, and the gold atom has a mass of 3.27×10^{-25} kg. Assuming (quite reasonably) elastic collisions, what would be the speed after the collision of a gold atom if an alpha particle makes a direct hit on the nucleus?

82. •• **Rocket failure!** Just as it has reached an upward speed of 5.0 m/s during a vertical launch, a rocket explodes into two pieces. Photographs of the explosion reveal that the lower piece, with a mass one-fourth that of the upper piece, was moving downward at 3.0 m/s the instant after the explosion. (a) Find the speed of the upper piece just after the explosion. (b) How high does the upper piece go above the point where the explosion occurred?

83. •• In a common physics demonstration, two identical carts having rigid metal surfaces and equal speeds collide with each other. Each cart has a piece of Velcro® at one end and a spring at the other end. For each collision shown in the figure, find the magnitude and direction of the velocity of each cart after the collision. Are both collisions elastic? What causes one of them to be inelastic, and what happens to the "lost" kinetic energy?

84. •• **Sharing of the energy released by an explosion.** An object at rest explodes into two fragments of masses m_1 and m_2 having kinetic energies K_1 and K_2, respectively. (a) Show that the ratio of the kinetic energies of these fragments is $K_1/K_2 = m_2/m_1$. (b) Which fragment gets more kinetic energy from the explosion, the heavier one or the lighter one? (c) Under what circumstances will the two fragments share the liberated energy equally?

85. •• A 7.0 kg shell at rest explodes into two fragments, one with a mass of 2.0 kg and the other with a mass of 5.0 kg. If the heavier fragment gains 100 J of kinetic energy from the explosion, how much kinetic energy does the lighter one gain?

86. •• **Radioactive beta decay.** *Beta decay* is a radioactive decay in which a neutron in the nucleus of an atom breaks apart (decays) to form a proton, an electron, and a neutrino. The electron is also known as a *beta particle*. The proton remains in the nucleus, while the electron and neutrino shoot out. Before the discovery of the neutrino, it was assumed that only the electron was emitted. Assuming (incorrectly) that there is no neutrino, and that the neutron is initially at rest inside the nucleus, find (a) the ratio of the speed of the electron to the speed of the proton just after the decay and (b) the ratio of the kinetic energy of the electron to that of the proton just after the decay. Look up the necessary masses in Appendix F. (c) Use the results from parts (a) and (b) to explain why it is the electron, and not the proton, that shoots out of the nucleus. (*Note:* Electrons actually emerge with a range of speeds; this observation provided the first experimental evidence that an additional particle (the neutrino) must also be emitted.)

87. •• A 15.0 g acorn falls from rest from the top of a 35.0-m-high oak tree. When it is halfway to the ground, a 135 g bird gliding horizontally at 75.0 cm/s scoops it up with its beak. Find (a) the horizontal and vertical components of the bird's velocity, and (b) the speed of the bird and the angle its velocity makes with the vertical, just after the bird scoops up the acorn.

88. •• **Accident analysis.** A 1500 kg sedan goes through a wide intersection traveling from north to south when it is hit by a 2200 kg SUV traveling from east to west. The two cars become enmeshed due to the impact and slide as one thereafter. On-the-scene measurements show that the coefficient of kinetic friction between the tires of these cars and the pavement is 0.75, and the cars slide to a halt at a point 5.39 m west and 6.43 m south of the impact point. How fast was each car traveling just before the collision?

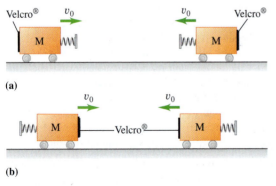

(a)

(b)

▲ **FIGURE 8.49** Problem 83.

ROTATIONAL MOTION

In previous chapters, we would have considered these cyclists as so many particles in motion up the road. However, while each bicycle moves along the road, its wheels move in circles. In this chapter we start to look at objects that cannot be treated as particles. In particular, we will look at the motion of objects that *rotate*.

What do a Ferris wheel, a circular saw blade, and a ceiling fan have in common? None of these objects can be represented adequately as a moving *point;* each is a rigid object that *rotates* about an axis that is stationary in some inertial frame of reference. Rotation occurs on all size scales, from the motion of electrons in atoms to the motion of hurricanes, to the motions of entire galaxies.

In this chapter and the next, we'll consider the motion of objects that have a definite and unchanging size and shape; we'll neglect any stretching, twisting, and squeezing caused by the forces acting on the object. We call this idealized model a **rigid body.** (We could call it a rigid *object,* but physicists usually call it a rigid body.) We'll begin with kinematic language for describing rotational motion. Next, we'll look at the kinetic energy of rotation—the key to applying energy methods to rotational motion. Then we develop principles of rotational dynamics, analogous to Newton's laws for particles, to relate the forces on an object to its rotational motion.

9.1 Angular Velocity and Angular Acceleration

Let's think first about a rigid body that rotates about a stationary axis. (We'll also use the term *fixed axis.*) Both terms refer to an axis that is at rest in some inertial frame of reference and doesn't change direction relative to that frame. The body might be the shaft of a motor, a chunk of roast beef on a barbecue skewer, or a merry-go-round. Figure 9.1 shows a rigid body rotating about a stationary axis passing through point O (which may be the origin of a coordinate system) and perpendicular to the plane of the diagram. Line OP is fixed in the body and rotates with it. The angle θ that this line makes with the $+x$ axis describes the

Generic rigid body rotating counterclockwise around an axis at the origin

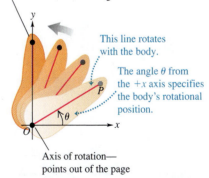

This line rotates with the body.

The angle θ from the $+x$ axis specifies the body's rotational position.

Axis of rotation— points out of the page

▲ **FIGURE 9.1** A rigid body rotating about an axis pointing out of the paper.

One radian is the angle at which the arc *s* has the same length as the radius *r*.

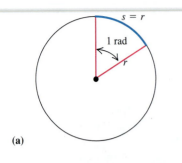

(a)

An angle θ in radians is the ratio of the arc length *s* to the radius *r*.

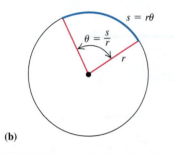

(b)

▲ **FIGURE 9.2** An angle θ in radians is defined as the ratio of the arc length *s* to the radius *r*.

Angular displacement $\Delta\theta$ of a rotating rigid body over a time interval Δt:

(a)

(b)

▲ **FIGURE 9.3** (a) Angular displacement $\Delta\theta$ of a rotating body. (b) Every part of a rigid body has the same angular velocity.

rotational position of the body and serves as a *coordinate* for the body's rotational position. Thus, θ is analogous to x, which we used as the coordinate to specify position in our treatment of straight-line motion of a particle.

We usually measure the angle θ in **radians.** As is shown in Figure 9.2a, 1 radian (denoted 1 rad) is defined as the angle subtended at the center of a circle by an arc with a length equal to the radius of the circle. In Figure 9.2b, an angle θ is subtended by an arc of length s on a circle of radius r; θ (in radians) is equal to s divided by r:

$$\theta = \frac{s}{r}, \quad \text{or} \quad s = r\theta. \tag{9.1}$$

An angle measured in radians is the quotient of two lengths, so it is a pure number, without dimensions. If $s = 1.5$ m and $r = 1.0$ m, then $\theta = 1.5$, but we'll often write this as 1.5 rad to distinguish it from an angle measured in degrees or revolutions.

The circumference of a circle is 2π times the radius, so there are 2π (about 6.283) radians in one complete revolution $(360°)$. Therefore,

$$1 \text{ rad} = \frac{360°}{2\pi} = 57.3°.$$

Similarly, $180° = \pi$ rad, $90° = \pi/2$ rad, and so on.

We'll often encounter angles greater than 360°; for a body in constant rotation, the angle θ may increase or decrease continuously.

Angular Velocity

Just as we described straight-line motion in terms of the rate of change of the coordinate x, we can describe rotational motion of a rigid body in terms of the rate of change of θ. In Figure 9.3a, a reference line OP in a rotating body makes an angle θ_1 with the $+x$ axis at time t_1. At a later time t_2, the angle has changed to θ_2. We define the **average angular velocity** ω_{av} of the body as follows:

> **Definition of average angular velocity**
>
> When a rigid body rotates through an angular displacement $\Delta\theta = \theta_2 - \theta_1$ in a time interval $\Delta t = t_2 - t_1$, the average angular velocity ω_{av} is defined as the ratio of the angular displacement to the time interval:
>
> $$\omega_{av} = \frac{\theta_2 - \theta_1}{t_2 - t_1} = \frac{\Delta\theta}{\Delta t}. \tag{9.2}$$
>
> Unit: rad/s

We can then define the **instantaneous angular velocity** ω as the limit of ω_{av} as Δt approaches zero:

$$\omega = \lim_{\Delta t \to 0} \frac{\Delta\theta}{\Delta t}. \tag{9.3}$$

Because the body is rigid, all lines in it rotate through the same angle in the same time (Figure 9.3b). Thus, **at any given instant, every part of a rigid body has the same angular velocity.** If the angle θ is measured in radians, the unit of angular velocity is 1 radian per second (1 rad/s). Other units, such as the revolution per minute (rev/min or rpm), are often used. Two useful conversions are

$$1 \text{ rev/s} = 2\pi \text{ rad/s} \quad \text{and} \quad 1 \text{ rev/min} = 1 \text{ rpm} = \frac{2\pi}{60} \text{ rad/s}. \quad (9.4)$$

Conceptual Analysis 9.1

Merry-go-round

A boy and a girl ride a turning merry-go-round. The boy is at the outer edge; the girl is near the axis of rotation. How do their angular velocities compare?

A. The boy has the greater angular velocity.
B. The girl has the greater angular velocity.
C. Both children have the same angular velocity.

▲ **FIGURE 9.4**

SOLUTION An object's *angular* velocity, as opposed to its (straight-line) velocity, is determined by the change in angle of a line drawn from the axis of rotation to the object during any given unit of time (Figure 9.4). Both children have fixed posi- tions on the same rotating object; they rotate through the same angle $\Delta\theta$ in the same time interval Δt. Their angular velocity is the same as that of the merry-go-round. Answer C is correct.

Angular Acceleration

When the angular velocity of a rigid body changes, the body has an angular acceleration. If ω_1 and ω_2 are the instantaneous angular velocities at times t_1 and t_2, respectively (Figure 9.5), we define the **average angular acceleration** α_{av} as follows:

Definition of average angular acceleration

The average angular acceleration α_{av} of a rotating rigid body is the change in angular velocity, $\Delta\omega$, divided by the time interval Δt:

$$\alpha_{av} = \frac{\omega_2 - \omega_1}{t_2 - t_1} = \frac{\Delta\omega}{\Delta t}. \quad (9.5)$$

Unit: rad/s^2

The average angular acceleration is the change in angular velocity divided by the time interval:

$$\alpha_{av} = \frac{\omega_2 - \omega_1}{t_2 - t_1} = \frac{\Delta\omega}{\Delta t}$$

At t_1 At t_2

▲ **FIGURE 9.5** The meaning of angular acceleration.

The **instantaneous angular acceleration** α is the limit of α_{av} as $\Delta t \to 0$:

$$\alpha = \lim_{\Delta t \to 0} \frac{\Delta\omega}{\Delta t}. \quad (9.6)$$

▶ **A boring tool?** The old-fashioned hand drill uses the principle of relative angular velocity to allow a carpenter to bore holes in very hard woods. Each part of the large wheel connected to the drill's handle has the same angular velocity. However, the large size of this wheel accommodates a large number of gear teeth compared with the few teeth that fit on the small wheel turning the drill bit. When these wheels are coupled together, a relatively small angular velocity of the handle can cause a much greater angular velocity of the drill bit, allowing it to penetrate dense woods with speed and precision.

EXAMPLE 9.1 **Rotation of a compact disk**

A compact disk (CD) rotates at high speed while a laser reads data encoded in a spiral pattern. The disk has radius $R = 6.0$ cm $= 0.060$ m; when data are being read, it spins at 7200 rev/min. What is the CD's angular velocity ω in radians per second? How much time is required for it to rotate through 90°? If it starts from rest and reaches full speed in 4.0 s, what is its average angular acceleration?

SOLUTION

SET UP We make a sketch, showing the data (Figure 9.6). We need to be careful to use consistent units; we'll choose radians, meters, and seconds.

SOLVE To convert the disk's angular velocity ω to radians per second, we multiply by $(1 \text{ min}/60 \text{ s})$ and by $(2\pi \text{ rad}/1 \text{ rev})$:

$$\omega = \frac{7200 \text{ rev}}{1 \text{ min}} = \frac{7200 \text{ rev}}{1 \text{ min}} \left(\frac{1 \text{ min}}{60 \text{ s}}\right)\left(\frac{2\pi \text{ rad}}{1 \text{ rev}}\right) = 754 \text{ rad/s}.$$

From the definition of angular velocity ($\omega = \Delta\theta/\Delta t$), we find the time Δt for the disk to turn through 90° ($\pi/2 \text{ rad}$):

$$\Delta t = \frac{\Delta\theta}{\omega} = \frac{\pi/2 \text{ rad}}{754 \text{ rad/s}} = 0.0021 \text{ s} = 2.1 \text{ ms}.$$

From the definition of angular acceleration ($\alpha_{av} = \Delta\omega/\Delta t$), if the disk reaches a final angular velocity of 754 rad/s in 4.0 s (starting from rest), the average angular acceleration is

$$\alpha_{av} = \frac{\Delta\omega}{\Delta t} = \frac{754 \text{ rad/s}}{4.0 \text{ s}} = 189 \text{ rad/s}^2.$$

REFLECT A typical circular (table or radial-arm) saw found in woodworking shops runs at 3600 rev/min and reaches full

▲ **FIGURE 9.6** Our sketch for this problem.

speed about 1 s after it is turned on. The radius of a typical blade is 12 cm. Note, however, that the radius is not needed for the angular acceleration calculation. The angular acceleration is about twice that for the CD.

Practice Problem: An old-fashioned vinyl record is designed to turn at 33 rev/min. Find the angular velocity and period (the time for one revolution) of this record. *Answers:* $\omega = 3.5$ rad/s, $T = 1.8$ s.

You've probably noticed that we're using Greek letters for angular kinematic quantities: θ for angular position, ω for angular velocity, and α for angular acceleration. These are analogous to x for position, v_x for the x component of velocity, and a_x for the x component of acceleration, respectively, in straight-line motion. In each case, velocity is the rate of change of position, and acceleration is the rate of change of velocity.

We've used the word *velocity* rather loosely in our discussion of angular quantities; we haven't said anything about vector aspects of these quantities. We'll return to this point in Chapter 10. But in the preceding discussion, the angular quantities *do* have algebraic signs. When an object rotates about an axis that is perpendicular to the plane of the drawing, it's customary to take the counterclockwise sense of rotation as positive and the clockwise sense as negative (Figure 9.7). For example, if the compact disk in Example 9.1 were to reverse its sense of rotation from 800 rad/s counterclockwise (positive) to 600 rad/s clockwise (negative) in 4.0 s, the average angular acceleration would be

$$\alpha_{av} = \frac{\omega_2 - \omega_1}{t_2 - t_1} = \frac{(-600 \text{ rad/s}) - (800 \text{ rad/s})}{4.0 \text{ s}} = -350 \text{ rad/s}^2.$$

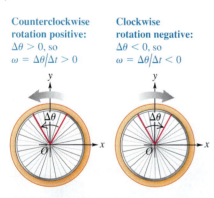

Counterclockwise rotation positive:
$\Delta\theta > 0$, so
$\omega = \Delta\theta/\Delta t > 0$

Clockwise rotation negative:
$\Delta\theta < 0$, so
$\omega = \Delta\theta/\Delta t < 0$

▲ **FIGURE 9.7** The convention for the sign of angular velocity.

7.7

9.2 Rotation with Constant Angular Acceleration

In Chapter 2, we found that analyzing straight-line motion is particularly simple when the acceleration is constant. This is also true of rotational motion: When the angular acceleration is constant, we can derive equations for angular velocity and angular position using exactly the same procedure that we used in Section 2.4. In fact, the equations that we are about to derive are identical to Equations 2.8, 2.12, and 2.13 if we replace x with θ, v_x with ω, and a_x with α. We suggest that you review Section 2.4 before continuing.

Let's proceed to derive relationships among the various angular quantities, assuming a constant angular acceleration α. We define θ_0 to be the angular position at time $t = 0$, θ the angular position at any later time t, ω_0 the angular velocity at time $t = 0$, and ω the angular velocity at any later time t. The angular acceleration α is constant and equal to the average value for any interval. Using Equation 9.5 with the interval from 0 to t, we find that

$$\alpha = \frac{\omega - \omega_0}{t - 0}, \qquad \text{or}$$
$$\omega = \omega_0 + \alpha t. \qquad \text{(angular velocity as function of time)} \qquad (9.7)$$

The product αt is the total change in ω between $t = 0$ and the later time t; the angular velocity ω at time t is the sum of the initial value ω_0 and this total change.

With constant angular acceleration, the angular velocity changes at a uniform rate, so its average value ω_{av} between 0 and t is the average of the initial and final values:

$$\omega_{av} = \frac{\omega_0 + \omega}{2}. \qquad (9.8)$$

We also know that ω_{av} is the total angular displacement $(\theta - \theta_0)$ divided by the time interval $(t - 0)$:

$$\omega_{av} = \frac{\theta - \theta_0}{t - 0}. \qquad (9.9)$$

When we equate Equations 9.8 and 9.9 and multiply the result by t, we get

$$\theta - \theta_0 = \tfrac{1}{2}(\omega_0 + \omega)t. \qquad (9.10)$$

Note that this relation doesn't contain the angular acceleration α.

To obtain a relation between θ and t that doesn't contain ω, we substitute Equation 9.7 into Equation 9.10:

$$\theta - \theta_0 = \tfrac{1}{2}(\omega_0 + \omega_0 + \alpha t)t,$$
$$\theta = \theta_0 + \omega_0 t + \tfrac{1}{2}\alpha t^2. \qquad (9.11)$$
$$\text{(angular position with constant angular acceleration)}$$

That is, if at the initial time $t = 0$, the body is at angular position θ_0 and has angular velocity ω_0, then its angular position θ at any later time t is the sum of three terms: its initial angular position θ_0, plus the rotation $\omega_0 t$ it would have if the angular velocity were constant, plus an additional rotation $\tfrac{1}{2}\alpha t^2$ caused by the changing angular velocity.

Following the same procedure as in Section 2.4, we can combine Equations 9.7 and 9.11 to obtain a relation between θ and ω that doesn't contain t. We invite you to work out the details, following the same procedure we used to get Equation 2.13. In fact, because of the perfect analogy between straight-line and rotational quantities, we can simply take Equation 2.13 and replace each straight-line quantity by its rotational analog; we get

$$\omega^2 = \omega_0^2 + 2\alpha(\theta - \theta_0). \qquad (9.12)$$
$$\text{(angular velocity in terms of angular displacement)}$$

Keep in mind that all of these results are valid *only* when the angular acceleration α is constant; be careful not to try to apply them to problems in which α is

TABLE 9.1   Comparison of linear and angular motion with constant acceleration

Straight-line motion with constant linear acceleration		Fixed-axis rotation with constant angular acceleration	
$a = \text{constant}$		$\alpha = \text{constant}$	
$v = v_0 + at$	(2.8)	$\omega = \omega_0 + \alpha t$	(9.7)
$x = x_0 + v_0 t + \frac{1}{2}at^2$	(2.12)	$\theta = \theta_0 + \omega_0 t + \frac{1}{2}\alpha t^2$	(9.11)
$v^2 = v_0^2 + 2a(x - x_0)$	(2.13)	$\omega^2 = \omega_0^2 + 2\alpha(\theta - \theta_0)$	(9.12)
$x - x_0 = \frac{1}{2}(v + v_0)t$	(2.14)	$\theta - \theta_0 = \frac{1}{2}(\omega + \omega_0)t$	(9.10)

not constant. Table 9.1 compares Equations 9.7, 9.10, 9.11, and 9.12, for fixed-axis rotation with constant angular acceleration, to the analogous equations for straight-line motion with constant acceleration.

EXAMPLE 9.2   Rotation of a bicycle wheel

The angular velocity of the rear wheel of a stationary exercise bike is 4.00 rad/s at time $t = 0$, and its angular acceleration is constant and equal to 2.00 rad/s^2. A particular spoke coincides with the $+x$ axis at time $t = 0$ (Figure 9.8). What angle does this spoke make with the $+x$ axis at time $t = 3.00$ s? What is the wheel's angular velocity at this time?

At $t = 0$:
$\alpha = 2.00$ rad/s^2
$\omega_0 = 4.00$ rad/s
$\theta_0 = 0$ for chosen spoke

▲ FIGURE 9.8

SOLUTION

SET UP We take $\theta = 0$ at the position where the chosen spoke is horizontal, and we take the counterclockwise sense of rotation to be positive. The initial conditions are $\theta_0 = 0$, $\omega_0 = 4.00$ rad/s, and $\alpha = 2.00$ rad/s^2.

SOLVE We can use Equations 9.11 and 9.7 to find θ and ω at any time. The angle θ is given as a function of time by Equation 9.11:

$$\theta = \theta_0 + \omega_0 t + \frac{1}{2}\alpha t^2$$
$$= 0 + (4.00 \text{ rad/s})(3.00 \text{ s}) + \frac{1}{2}(2.00 \text{ rad/s}^2)(3.00 \text{ s})^2$$
$$= 21.0 \text{ rad} = 21.0 \text{ rad}\left(\frac{1 \text{ rev}}{2\pi \text{ rad}}\right) = 3.34 \text{ rev}.$$

The wheel has turned through three complete revolutions plus an additional 0.34 rev, or $(0.34 \text{ rev})(2\pi \text{ rad/rev}) = 2.14 \text{ rad} = 123°$. Thus, the chosen spoke is at an angle of 123° with the $+x$ axis.

The wheel's angular velocity ω is given as a function of time by Equation 9.7, $\omega = \omega_0 + \alpha t$. At time $t = 3.0$ s,

$$\omega = 4.00 \text{ rad/s} + (2.00 \text{ rad/s}^2)(3.00 \text{ s}) = 10.0 \text{ rad/s}.$$

Alternatively, from Equation 9.12, we get

$$\omega^2 = \omega_0^2 + 2\alpha(\theta - \theta_0)$$
$$= (4.00 \text{ rad/s})^2 + 2(2.00 \text{ rad/s}^2)(21.0 \text{ rad}) = 100 \text{ rad}^2/\text{s}^2,$$
$$\omega = 10.0 \text{ rad/s} = 1.59 \text{ rev/s}.$$

REFLECT Note the step-by-step similarity between these equations and the kinematic relations for straight-line motion.

Practice Problem: Suppose we double the angular acceleration. What would be the new values for θ and ω? *Answers:* $\theta = 30.0$ rad, $\omega = 16.0$ rad/s.

9.3 Relationship between Linear and Angular Quantities

In order to develop the principles of dynamics for rigid bodies, we need to be able to find the velocity and acceleration of a particular point in a rotating rigid body. For example, to find the kinetic energy of a rotating object, we have to start from $K = \frac{1}{2}mv^2$ for a particle. That requires knowing v for a particle in a rigid body. And in Chapter 10 we'll need to be able to find the acceleration of a point in a rigid body in order to work out general relations between force and motion for rotation, starting from $\Sigma \vec{F} = m\vec{a}$.

So it's worthwhile to develop general relations between the angular velocity and acceleration of a rigid body rotating about a fixed axis, on the one hand, and the velocity and acceleration of a specific point in the body, on the other. We'll sometimes use the terms *linear velocity* and *linear acceleration* for the familiar quantities that we defined in Chapters 2 and 3, to make sure we distinguish clearly between these and the *angular* quantities introduced in this chapter.

When a rigid body rotates about a fixed axis, every particle in the body moves in a circular path that is centered on the axis and lies in a plane perpendicular to the axis. The speed of a particle is directly proportional to the body's angular velocity; the faster the body rotates, the greater is the speed of each particle. In Figure 9.9, point P is a constant distance r away from the axis of rotation, and it moves in a circle of radius r. At any time, the angle θ (in radians) and the arc length s are related by the formula

$$s = r\theta.$$

When the angle θ increases by a small amount $\Delta\theta$ during a time interval Δt, the particle moves through an arc length $\Delta s = r\,\Delta\theta$. Thus the average speed of the particle is given by

$$v_{av} = \frac{\Delta s}{\Delta t} = r\frac{\Delta\theta}{\Delta t} = r\omega_{av}.$$

In the limit as $\Delta t \to 0$, this equation becomes

$$v = r\omega. \tag{9.13}$$

We'll continue to use the term *speed* to mean the magnitude of a particle's linear velocity; the *direction* of the particle's linear velocity is tangent to its circular path at each point.

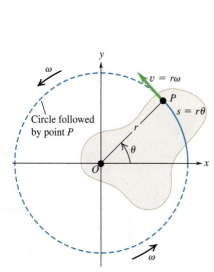

▲ **FIGURE 9.9** The distance s traversed by a point P on a rigid body equals $r\theta$ if θ is measured in radians.

 Quantitative Analysis 9.2

Rotating disk

A disk rotates about an axis perpendicular to its plane. Point B on the disk is three times farther from the axis than point A. If the speed of point B is v, what is the speed of point A?

A. $3v$ B. $\frac{1}{3}v$ C. v

SOLUTION Speed in this case means, the magnitude of *linear* velocity, not the magnitude of *angular* velocity. Because the disk is a rigid object, all points on the disk rotate with the same angular velocity ω. The speed of a point is directly proportional to its distance r from the axis of rotation: $v = r\omega$. Because point A is one-third the distance from the axis as point B, its speed is $v/3$ (choice B).

We can represent the acceleration $\vec{a}$ of a particle in terms of its radial and tangential components (Figure 9.10). By definition, the radial component a_{rad} at each point is along a radial line from the particle to the center of its circular path. The tangential component a_{tan} is tangent to the path at each point (and thus parallel or antiparallel to the velocity at each point). Because the particles in a rotating rigid body move in circular paths, every particle *must* have a radial component of acceleration. When the body undergoes angular acceleration, every particle must also have a tangential component of acceleration.

To find the **tangential component of acceleration,** a_{tan}, we note that if the angular velocity ω changes by an amount $\Delta\omega$, the particle's speed changes by an amount Δv given by

$$\Delta v = r\,\Delta\omega.$$

◀ **Not so fast.** This is a velocipede, one of the earliest bicycles produced. When invented in the 1800s, it was more of a curiosity than a practical means of transportation. Because the pedals attach directly to the front wheel, the wheel turns only once for each revolution of the pedals. Therefore, the only way to achieve a reasonable forward speed at a feasible rate of pedaling is to use a huge front wheel. These bicycles are difficult to mount and quite dangerous. Bicycles did not become widely used for transportation until the development of the chain-and-sprocket mechanism, which allowed each turn of the pedals to rotate a smaller wheel more than once.

This corresponds to a component of acceleration a_{tan} tangent to the particle's circular path. If these changes take place in a small time interval Δt, then

$$(a_{tan})_{av} = \frac{\Delta v}{\Delta t} = r\frac{\Delta\omega}{\Delta t},$$

and in the limit as $\Delta t \to 0$,

$$a_{tan} = r\alpha, \tag{9.14}$$

where a_{tan} is the **tangential component of instantaneous acceleration.** This component is parallel to the instantaneous velocity at each point; it acts to change the *magnitude* of velocity of the particle (i.e., its speed). It is equal to the rate of change of speed. This component of a particle's acceleration is always tangent to the circular path of the particle.

The **radial component of acceleration**, a_{rad}, of the particle is associated with change in *direction* of the particle's velocity. In Section 3.4, we worked out the relation $a_{rad} = v^2/r$ for a particle moving in a circle with radius r. We can express this in terms of ω by using Equation 9.13:

$$a_{rad} = \frac{v^2}{r} = \omega^2 r. \tag{9.15}$$

This is true at each instant, even when ω and v are not constant.

The vector sum of the radial and tangential components of acceleration of a particle in a rotating body is the linear acceleration $\vec{a}$ (Figure 9.10). We use the modifier *linear* to emphasize that $\vec{a}$ is the rate of change of velocity $\vec{v}$, *not* the rate of change of angular velocity. The radial and tangential components are always perpendicular, so the magnitude of $\vec{a}$ is given by

$$|\vec{a}| = a = \sqrt{a_{rad}^2 + a_{tan}^2}.$$

NOTE ▶ Remember that Equation 9.1 ($s = r\theta$) is valid *only* when θ is measured in radians. The same is true of any equation derived from that relation, including Equations 9.13, 9.14, and 9.15. When you use these equations, you *must* express the angular quantities in radians, not revolutions or degrees. ◀

Radial and tangential acceleration components:
• a_{rad} is point P's centripetal acceleration.
• a_{tan} means that P's rotation is speeding up (the body has angular acceleration).

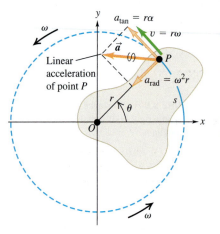

▲ **FIGURE 9.10** The components of acceleration for a point P on a rigid body whose angular rotation is speeding up.

 Conceptual Analysis 9.3

Angular and centripetal acceleration

A disk spins with increasing angular velocity. Point B on the disk is twice as far from the axis of rotation as point A is. Which of the following statements is or are correct?

A. The angular acceleration of A is greater than that of B.
B. The radial acceleration of A is greater than that of B.
C. A and B have the same angular acceleration.
D. A and B have the same radial acceleration.

SOLUTION The disk's angular velocity is increasing, so the disk has an angular acceleration. All points on the disk rotate through the same angle in a given time interval and thus have the same angular velocity and angular acceleration. Therefore, choice A is incorrect and C is correct. The radial acceleration of each point is $a_{rad} = \omega^2 r$. Point B is farther from the axis than point A is, so its radial acceleration is greater than that of A, and answers B and D are incorrect. The only correct choice is C.

EXAMPLE 9.3 **Throwing a discus**

A discus thrower turns with angular acceleration $\alpha = 50 \text{ rad/s}^2$, moving the discus in a circle of radius 0.80 m (Figure 9.11). Find the radial and tangential components of acceleration of the discus (modeled as a point) and the magnitude of its acceleration at the instant when the angular velocity is 10 rad/s.

▲ **FIGURE 9.11**

SOLUTION

SET UP As shown in Figure 9.12, we model the thrower's arm as a rigid body, so r is constant. (This may not be completely realistic.) We model the discus as a particle moving in a circular path.

SOLVE The components of acceleration are given by Equations 9.14 and 9.15:

$$a_{\text{rad}} = \omega^2 r = (10 \text{ rad/s})^2 (0.80 \text{ m}) = 80 \text{ m/s}^2,$$
$$a_{\text{tan}} = r\alpha = (0.80 \text{ m})(50 \text{ rad/s}^2) = 40 \text{ m/s}^2.$$

The magnitude of the acceleration vector is

$$a = \sqrt{a_{\text{rad}}^2 + a_{\text{tan}}^2} = 89 \text{ m/s}^2.$$

REFLECT The magnitude of the acceleration is about nine times the acceleration due to gravity; the corresponding force supplied by the thrower's arm must be about nine times the weight of the discus. Note that we have dropped the unit *radian* from our final results; we can do this because a radian is a dimensionless quantity.

▲ **FIGURE 9.12** Our sketch for this problem.

Practice Problem: What is the direction of the acceleration vector of the discus if the angular acceleration is 25 rad/s²? *Answer:* 76° from a radial line toward the center of the circle.

EXAMPLE 9.4 **Designing a propeller**

You are asked to design an airplane propeller to turn at 1500 rev/min. The forward airspeed of the plane is to be 90 m/s, and the speed of the tips of the propeller blades through the air must not exceed 300 m/s, the speed of sound in very cold air (Figure 9.13). Determine the maximum radius of the propeller.

▲ **FIGURE 9.13**

SOLUTION

SET UP Figure 9.14 shows how we sketch this problem. The velocity of each propeller tip is the vector sum of the velocity $\vec{v}_{\text{plane}}$ of the plane through the air (magnitude 90 m/s) and the tangential velocity $\vec{v}_{\text{tan}}$ of the tip relative to the plane (magnitude $v_{\text{tan}} = r\omega$, where r is to be determined).

SOLVE First we convert the angular velocity ω to rad/s:

$$\omega = 1500 \text{ rpm} = \left(\frac{1500 \text{ rev}}{1 \text{ min}}\right)\left(\frac{2\pi \text{ rad}}{1 \text{ rev}}\right)\left(\frac{1 \text{ min}}{60 \text{ s}}\right) = 157 \text{ rad/s}.$$

The tangential velocity $v_{\text{tan}} = r\omega$ of the propeller tip is perpendicular to the forward velocity v_{plane} of the plane through the air

Continued

(Figure 9.14). The magnitude of the vector sum of these velocities is

$$v_{tip} = \sqrt{v_{plane}^2 + v_{tan}^2} = \sqrt{v_{plane}^2 + (r\omega)^2}$$
$$= \sqrt{(90 \text{ m/s})^2 + (157 \text{ rad/s})^2 r^2}.$$

To find the desired propeller radius (at which $v_{tip} = 300$ m/s), we solve this equation for r:

$$(90 \text{ m/s})^2 + (157 \text{ rad/s})^2 r^2 = (300 \text{ m/s})^2,$$
$$r = \frac{1}{157 \text{ rad/s}}\sqrt{(300 \text{ m/s})^2 - (90 \text{ m/s})^2}$$
$$= 1.82 \text{ m}.$$

REFLECT If the radius r is greater than 1.82 m, the airspeed at the propeller tips is greater than 300 m/s, meaning that it is supersonic in cold air.

We can find the radial acceleration of a propeller tip with our calculated radius, using Equation 9.15:

$$a_{rad} = \omega^2 r$$
$$= (157 \text{ rad/s})^2(1.82 \text{ m}) = 4.49 \times 10^4 \text{ m/s}^2.$$

From $\Sigma \vec{F} = m\vec{a}$, the propeller must provide a centripetal force of magnitude 4.49×10^4 N (about 10,000 pounds) for each

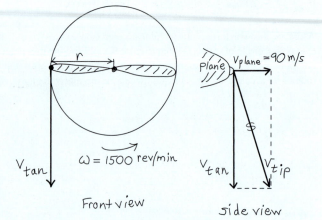

▲ **FIGURE 9.14** Our sketches for this problem.

kilogram of tip! The propeller has to be made out of tough material.

Practice Problem: If the plane's forward airspeed is 180 m/s and $\omega = 3000$ rev/min, what is the maximum propeller radius? *Answer:* 0.764 m.

EXAMPLE 9.5 **Bicycle gears**

How are the angular speeds of the two bicycle sprockets in Figure 9.15 related to their respective numbers of teeth, N_A and N_B?

SOLUTION

SET UP AND SOLVE The chain does not slip or stretch; therefore, it moves at the same tangential speed v on both sprockets. We use the relation $v = r\omega$ for each sprocket and equate the two tangential speeds:

$$v = r_A\omega_A = r_B\omega_B, \quad \text{or} \quad \frac{\omega_B}{\omega_A} = \frac{r_A}{r_B}.$$

The angular speed of each sprocket is inversely proportional to its radius.

This relationship holds as well for pulleys connected by a belt, provided that the belt doesn't slip. Also, for chain sprockets, the spacing of the teeth must be the same on both sprockets for the chain to mesh properly with both. Let N_A and N_B be the numbers of teeth on the two sprockets; then

$$\frac{2\pi r_A}{N_A} = \frac{2\pi r_B}{N_B}, \quad \text{or} \quad \frac{r_A}{r_B} = \frac{N_A}{N_B}.$$

Combining this equation with the previous one, we get

$$\frac{\omega_B}{\omega_A} = \frac{N_A}{N_B}.$$

REFLECT The angular speed of each sprocket is inversely proportional to its number of teeth. On an 18-speed bike, you get the highest angular speed ω_B of the rear wheel for a given pedaling

▲ **FIGURE 9.15**

rate ω_A using the larger-radius front sprocket and the smallest-radius rear sprocket, giving the maximum front-to-back-teeth ratio N_A/N_B.

Practice Problem: If the front sprocket has four times as many teeth as the rear sprocket and the rear wheel radius is 0.33 m, how fast is the bike moving when the pedaling rate is $\omega_A = 0.80$ rev/s? *Answer:* 6.6 m/s.

9.4 Kinetic Energy of Rotation and Moment of Inertia

A rotating rigid body consists of mass in motion, so it has kinetic energy. We can express this kinetic energy in terms of the body's angular velocity and a new quantity called moment of inertia, that we'll define shortly. To develop this relationship, we think of the body as made up of a lot of particles, with masses m_A, m_B, m_C, . . . , at distances r_A, r_B, r_C, . . . , from the axis of rotation. The particles don't necessarily all lie in the same plane, so we specify that each r is the perpendicular distance from the particle to the axis.

When a rigid body rotates about a fixed axis, the speed v of a typical particle is given by Equation 9.13, $v = r\omega$, where ω is the body's angular velocity in radians per second. Particle A has a perpendicular distance r_A from the axis of rotation and has a speed v_A given by $v_A = r_A\omega$. Different particles have different values of r and v, but ω is the same for all. (Otherwise the body wouldn't be rigid.) The kinetic energy K_A of particle A can be expressed as

$$K_A = \tfrac{1}{2}m_A v_A^2 = \tfrac{1}{2}m_A(r_A^2\omega^2).$$

The total kinetic energy K of the body is the sum of the kinetic energies of all its particles:

$$\begin{aligned}
K &= \tfrac{1}{2}m_A v_A^2 + \tfrac{1}{2}m_B v_B^2 + \tfrac{1}{2}m_C v_C^2 + \cdots \\
&= \tfrac{1}{2}m_A(r_A^2\omega^2) + \tfrac{1}{2}m_B(r_B^2\omega^2) + \tfrac{1}{2}m_C(r_C^2\omega^2) + \cdots \\
&= \tfrac{1}{2}(m_A r_A^2 + m_B r_B^2 + m_C r_C^2 + \cdots)\omega^2.
\end{aligned}$$

The quantity in parentheses in the last line, obtained by multiplying the mass of each particle by the square of its distance from the axis of rotation and adding all the products together, is called the **moment of inertia** of the body, denoted by I:

ActivPhysics ONLINE 7.7

Definition of moment of inertia

A body's moment of inertia, I, describes how its mass is distributed in relation to an axis of rotation:

$$I = m_A r_A^2 + m_B r_B^2 + m_C r_C^2 + \cdots. \tag{9.16}$$

Unit: $\text{kg} \cdot \text{m}^2$

In terms of moment of inertia I, the kinetic energy K of a rotating rigid body is

$$K = \tfrac{1}{2}I\omega^2. \tag{9.17}$$

This is analogous to the expression $K = \tfrac{1}{2}mv^2$ for the kinetic energy of a particle; thus moment of inertia is analogous to mass, and angular velocity ω is analogous to speed v. This kinetic energy is not a new form of energy; it's the same physical quantity that we expressed as $\tfrac{1}{2}mv^2$ for a single particle. But Equation 9.17 is much easier to use when we have to find the kinetic energy of a rotating body.

▶ **Faster, not heavier.** One way to store energy is in a rotating disk, called a flywheel. Traditional flywheels, like the one shown here, are massive, carefully machined steel disks. The danger of such flywheels is that if the disk breaks, the parts fly off like cannonballs. As we've learned, however, the flywheel's kinetic energy is proportional to the *square* of its angular velocity: $K = \tfrac{1}{2}I\omega^2$. Therefore, a flywheel's angular velocity is more important than its mass (or moment of inertia) for storing energy. Engineers are now developing lightweight composite flywheels that rotate at very high speed. These flywheels break by unraveling, not by fragmenting into projectiles, so they pose less danger than traditional flywheels. Future generations of hybrid autos may use such flywheels in place of batteries to store energy.

NOTE ▶ As in our previous discussion, ω *must* be measured in radians per second, not revolutions or degrees per second. ◀

EXAMPLE 9.6   An abstract sculpture

An artist is designing a part for a kinetic sculpture. The part consists of three massive disks connected by light supporting rods (Figure 9.16) that can be considered massless. Find the moment of inertia about an axis passing through disks B and C and the moment of inertia about an axis that passes through disk A and is perpendicular to the plane of that disk. If the object rotates about the axis through disk A with angular velocity 4.0 rad/s, find its kinetic energy.

▲ **FIGURE 9.16**

SOLUTION

SET UP For each calculation, we need to find the perpendicular distance from each disk to the axis of rotation. We'll model each disk as a point. For the axis passing through disks B and C, their distance from that axis is zero. Similarly, the distance of disk A from the axis passing through it is zero.

SOLVE The moment of inertia is defined as $I = m_A r_A^2 + m_B r_B^2 + m_C r_C^2$, where each r is measured from the chosen axis of rotation. For axis BC, disks B and C both lie *on* the axis ($r_B = r_C = 0$), so neither contributes to the moment of inertia. Only disk A contributes; $m_A = 0.30$ kg, $r_A = 0.40$ m, and we find that

$$I_{BC} = m_A r_A^2 = (0.30 \text{ kg})(0.40 \text{ m})^2 = 0.048 \text{ kg} \cdot \text{m}^2.$$

For the axis through point A perpendicular to the plane of the diagram, disk A lies on the axis, so $r_A = 0$. The masses are the same as before, but now

$$r_B = 0.50 \text{ m} \quad \text{and} \quad r_C = 0.40 \text{ m}.$$

The moment of inertia for this axis is

$$\begin{aligned}
I_A &= m_B r_B^2 + m_C r_C^2 \\
&= (0.10 \text{ kg})(0.50 \text{ m})^2 + (0.20 \text{ kg})(0.40 \text{ m})^2 \\
&= 0.057 \text{ kg} \cdot \text{m}^2.
\end{aligned}$$

If the object rotates about this axis with angular velocity $\omega = 4.0$ rad/s, its kinetic energy is

$$K = \tfrac{1}{2} I_A \omega^2 = \tfrac{1}{2}(0.057 \text{ kg} \cdot \text{m}^2)(4.0 \text{ rad/s})^2 = 0.46 \text{ J}.$$

REFLECT The moment of inertia of an object depends on the location of the axis. We can't just say, "The moment of inertia of this body is 0.048 kg · m²." We have to say, "The moment of inertia of this object *with respect to axis BC* is 0.048 kg · m²." Note that whenever a particle lies on the axis of rotation, $r = 0$, so that particle does not contribute to the moment of inertia.

Practice Problem: Find the moment of inertia and the corresponding rotational kinetic energy if the sculpture rotates with angular velocity $\omega = 4.0$ rad/s about an axis through point B, perpendicular to the plane of the diagram. *Answers:* 0.093 kg · m², 0.74 J.

In Example 9.6, we represented the body as several point masses and we evaluated the sum in Equation 9.16 directly. When the body is a continuous distribution of matter, such as a solid cylinder or plate, we need methods of integral calculus to evaluate the sum. Table 9.2 gives moments of inertia for several familiar shapes in terms of the masses and dimensions. In the formulas in the table, note that dimensions measured parallel to the axis of rotation never appear in the expressions. For example, two solid cylinders with the same mass and radius have equal moments of inertia about their axes, even if their lengths are different.

NOTE ▶ You may be tempted to try to compute the moment of inertia of a body by assuming that all of its mass is concentrated at the center of mass and then multiplying the total mass by the square of the distance from the center of mass to the axis. Resist that temptation; it doesn't work! For example, when a uniform thin rod with length L and mass M rotates about an axis through one end and perpendicular to the rod, the moment of inertia is $I = ML^2/3$. (Table 9.2b). If we took the mass as concentrated at the center of the rod, a distance $L/2$ from the axis, we would obtain the *incorrect* result $I = M(L/2)^2 = ML^2/4$. ◀

TABLE 9.2   Moments of inertia for various bodies

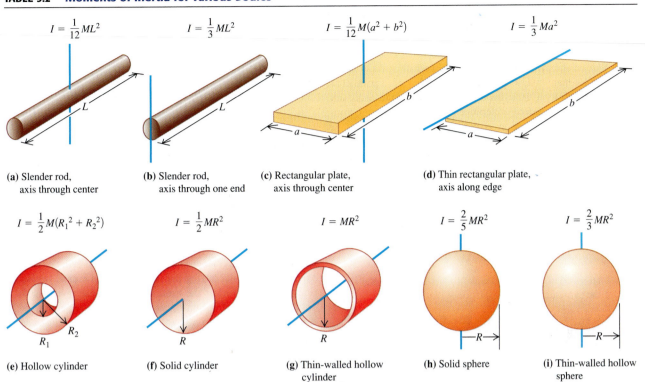

$I = \frac{1}{12}ML^2$	$I = \frac{1}{3}ML^2$	$I = \frac{1}{12}M(a^2 + b^2)$	$I = \frac{1}{3}Ma^2$
(a) Slender rod, axis through center	**(b)** Slender rod, axis through one end	**(c)** Rectangular plate, axis through center	**(d)** Thin rectangular plate, axis along edge

$I = \frac{1}{2}M(R_1{}^2 + R_2{}^2)$	$I = \frac{1}{2}MR^2$	$I = MR^2$	$I = \frac{2}{5}MR^2$	$I = \frac{2}{3}MR^2$
(e) Hollow cylinder	**(f)** Solid cylinder	**(g)** Thin-walled hollow cylinder	**(h)** Solid sphere	**(i)** Thin-walled hollow sphere

Now that we know how to calculate the kinetic energy of a rotating rigid body, we can apply the energy principles of Chapter 7 to rotational motion. Here are some points of strategy and some examples.

PROBLEM-SOLVING STRATEGY 9.1   Rotational energy

We suggest that you review the problem-solving strategies outlined in Sections 7.3, 7.6, and 7.7; they are equally useful here. The only new idea is that the kinetic energy K is expressed in terms of the moment of inertia I and angular velocity ω of the body instead of its mass m and speed v. You can use work–energy relations and conservation of energy to find relations involving the position and motion of a rotating body.

The kinematic relations of Section 9.3, particularly Equations 9.13 and 9.14, are often useful, especially when a rotating cylindrical body functions as any sort of pulley. Examples 9.7 and 9.8 illustrate this point; in both, the angular velocity ω and the tangential component of velocity v_{tan} at the surface of the cylinder are related by $v_{tan} = r\omega$.

EXAMPLE 9.7   A cable unwinding from a winch

A light, flexible, nonstretching cable is wrapped several times around a winch drum—a solid cylinder with mass 50 kg and diameter 0.12 m that rotates about a stationary horizontal axis that turns in frictionless bearings (Figure 9.17). The free end of the cable is pulled with a constant force of magnitude 9.0 N for a distance of 2.0 m. It unwinds without slipping, turning the cylinder as it does so. If the cylinder is initially at rest, find its final angular velocity ω and the final speed v of the cable.

▲ **FIGURE 9.17**

Continued

SOLUTION

SET UP Figure 9.18 shows how we sketch this problem.

SOLVE No energy is lost in friction, so the final kinetic energy $K = \frac{1}{2}I\omega^2$ of the cylinder is equal to the work $W = Fs$ done by the force (of magnitude F, pulling through a distance s parallel to the force) acting on the cylinder. We need to use the mass and diameter of the cylinder to determine its moment of inertia, from Table 9.2. The work done on the cylinder by the force is

$$W = Fs = (9.0\ \text{N})(2.0\ \text{m}) = 18\ \text{J}.$$

From Table 9.2f, the moment of inertia for a solid cylinder is

$$I = \tfrac{1}{2}MR^2 = \tfrac{1}{2}(50\ \text{kg})(0.060\ \text{m})^2 = 0.090\ \text{kg}\cdot\text{m}^2.$$

The work–energy theorem $(W = \Delta K)$ from Chapter 7 then gives

$$18\ \text{J} = \tfrac{1}{2}(0.090\ \text{kg}\cdot\text{m}^2)\omega^2,$$
$$\omega = 20\ \text{rad/s}.$$

The final speed of the cable is equal to the final tangential speed v_{tan} of the cylinder, given by Equation 9.13:

$$v_{\text{tan}} = R\omega = (0.060\ \text{m})(20\ \text{rad/s}) = 1.2\ \text{m/s}.$$

▲ **FIGURE 9.18** Our sketch for this problem.

REFLECT The speed of the cable at each instant equals the tangential component of velocity of the cylinder because there is no slipping between cable and cylinder; if there were slipping, the winch wouldn't work.

Practice Problem: Suppose we replace the solid cylinder with a thin-walled cylinder having the same mass and radius. (a) How does the final speed of the cable differ from our result for the solid cylinder? (b) Does this mean that energy is not conserved? *Answers:* (a) $v_{\text{tan}} = 0.85\ \text{m/s}$; (b) no; kinetic energy is the same.

EXAMPLE 9.8 **Conservation of energy in a well**

In an old-fashioned well, a bucket is suspended over the well shaft by a winch and rope (Figure 9.19). The winch includes a solid cylinder with mass M and radius R and rotates without friction about a horizontal axis. The bucket (mass m) must descend a height h to reach the water; it is suspended by a rope of negligible mass that wraps around the winch. If the winch handle falls off, releasing the bucket to fall to the water, rotating the cylinder as it falls, find the speed v of the bucket and the angular velocity ω of the cylinder just before the bucket hits the water.

▶ **FIGURE 9.19**

SOLUTION

SET UP This problem is similar to Example 9.7, but it isn't identical, because both the rotating cylinder and the falling bucket have kinetic energy. Figure 9.20 shows our sketches. Since we will use conservation of energy, we draw before and after diagrams. We take the potential energy of the bucket–earth system as zero $(U = 0)$ when the bucket is at the water level. Then the bucket's initial potential energy is $U_i = mgh$ and the final value U_f is zero. The initial kinetic energy K_i is also zero. Just before impact, the bucket (mass m) has kinetic energy $\frac{1}{2}mv^2$ and the

rotating cylinder has kinetic energy $\frac{1}{2}I\omega^2$. The speed v of the dropping bucket at any time is proportional to the angular velocity ω of the cylinder at that time: $v = r\omega$ (assuming that the rope unwinds without slipping). There are no nonconservative forces, so the initial and final total energies are equal.

SOLVE Conservation of energy tells us that $K_i + U_i = K_f + U_f$. (The cable does no net work; at the bucket end the force and displacement are in the same direction, and at the winch end they are in opposite directions. So the *total* work done by the two ends of the cable is zero.)

Continued

Just before the bucket hits the water, both it and the cylinder have kinetic energy. The total kinetic energy K_f at that time is

$$K_f = \tfrac{1}{2}mv^2 + \tfrac{1}{2}I\omega^2.$$

From Table 9.2, we find that the moment of inertia of the cylinder is $I = \tfrac{1}{2}MR^2$. Also, v and ω are related by $v = R\omega$, because the speed of mass m must equal the tangential speed of the outer surface of the cylinder. Using these relations and equating the initial and final total energies, we find that

$$K_i + U_i = K_f + U_f,$$

$$0 + mgh = \tfrac{1}{2}mv^2 + \tfrac{1}{2}\left(\tfrac{1}{2}MR^2\right)\left(\frac{v}{R}\right)^2 = \tfrac{1}{2}\left(m + \tfrac{1}{2}M\right)v^2,$$

$$v = \sqrt{\frac{2gh}{1 + M/2m}}.$$

The final angular velocity ω is obtained from $\omega = v/R$.

REFLECT We can check some particular cases. When M is much larger than m (i.e., a very heavy cylinder and a tiny bucket), v is very small, as we would expect. When M is much *smaller* than m (i.e., a very light cylinder and a heavy bucket), there isn't much to hold the bucket back, and its final speed is nearly equal to the speed of a body in free fall with initial height h, namely, $\sqrt{2gh}$. Does it surprise you that v doesn't depend on the radius of the cylinder?

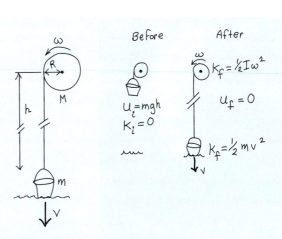

▲ **FIGURE 9.20** Our sketches for this problem.

Practice Problem: If the winch has the form of a thin cylindrical shell with mass M and radius R, derive expressions for the speed of the bucket and the angular velocity of the cylinder just before the bucket hits the water. *Answer:*

$$v = \sqrt{\frac{2gh}{1 + M/m}}.$$

Potential Energy of a Rigid Body

Later we'll need to know how to calculate the potential energy of a rigid body. In a uniform gravitational field, the gravitational potential energy is the same as though all the mass were concentrated at the center of mass of the body. Suppose we take the y axis vertically upward and define the potential energy to be zero at $y = 0$. Then, for an object with total mass M, the potential energy U is simply

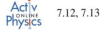

7.12, 7.13

$$U = Mgy_{cm}, \tag{9.18}$$

where y_{cm} is the vertical coordinate of the center of mass. As always, we need to define the origin of coordinates, where $y_{cm} = 0$ and $U = 0$.

To prove Equation 9.18, we again represent the body as a collection of mass elements m_A, m_B, m_C, $\cdots$. The weight of element m_A is $m_A g$, its potential energy is $m_A g y_A$, and the *total* potential energy is

$$U = m_A g y_A + m_B g y_B + m_C g y_C + \cdots.$$

But from Equations 8.18, which define the coordinates of the center of mass,

$$m_A y_A + m_B y_B + m_C y_C + \cdots = (m_A + m_B + m_C + \cdots)y_{cm} = My_{cm},$$

where $M = m_A + m_B + m_C + \cdots$ is the total mass. Combining this with the earlier expression for U, we obtain

$$U = Mgy_{cm},$$

in agreement with Equation 9.18.

9.5 Rotation about a Moving Axis

In the examples of rigid-body motion we've talked about so far, the axis of rotation has been stationary. Now let's consider some situations in which the axis moves. Familiar examples include a ball rolling down a hill or a yo-yo dropping

◄ **Spinning through space.** The moon rotates around its axis while orbiting the earth. Thus, it is an example of a body that rotates about a moving axis; its kinetic energy is the sum of its rotational energy and the translational energy of motion of its center of mass. But the earth also rotates on its axis, and the earth–moon system rotates while orbiting the sun, which itself moves as part of the Milky Way galaxy, which rotates while moving through space. Although these systems are not rigid bodies, in each case their kinetic energy has both rotational and translational terms.

This simple baton toss can be represented as a combination of **rotation** and **translation:**

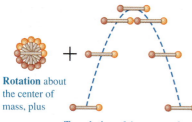

Rotation about the center of mass, plus

Translation of the center of mass

▲ **FIGURE 9.21** The motion of a rigid body can always be represented as a combination of rotation about the center of mass and translation of the center of mass.

as the string unwinds. We can apply energy considerations to such problems, but we need two additional principles:

1. **Every possible motion of a rigid body can be represented as a combination of motion of the center of mass and rotation about an axis through the center of mass.**
2. **The total kinetic energy can always be represented as the sum of a part associated with motion of the center of mass, treated as a point, plus a part associated with rotation about an axis through the center of mass.**

Figure 9.21 illustrates the first of these principles. We'll often use the terms *translational* and *rotational* motion to refer to motion of the center of mass and rotational motion, respectively.

Suppose the rigid body has mass M and moment of inertia I_{cm} about the axis through the center of mass. If the center of mass has translational motion with velocity of magnitude v_{cm}, and the object rotates with angular velocity ω about this axis, the total kinetic energy K_{total} is given by

$$K_{total} = \tfrac{1}{2}Mv_{cm}^2 + \tfrac{1}{2}I_{cm}\omega^2. \tag{9.19}$$

We'll omit detailed derivation of this relationship and simply remark that it looks reasonable and that it can be proved rigorously. We'll often refer to the two terms in Equation 9.19 as *translational kinetic energy* ($K_{trans} = \tfrac{1}{2}Mv_{cm}^2$, associated with motion of the center of mass) and *rotational kinetic energy* ($K_{rot} = \tfrac{1}{2}I_{cm}\omega^2$, associated with rotation about an axis through the center of mass). With the help of Equation 9.19, we can apply conservation of energy to many problems involving rigid bodies whose axis of rotation moves. We'll continue to assume, however, that the *direction* of the axis of rotation doesn't change.

NOTE ▶ When applying Equation 9.19, we *must* use the moment of inertia about the axis through the center of mass; otherwise this relationship isn't applicable.

Conceptual Analysis 9.4

Racing canned food

A can of dog food (with fairly solid contents) and a can of chicken broth are released simultaneously to roll down an inclined plane. The two cans have the same diameter and the same mass. Which can (if either) reaches the bottom of the plane first?

A. The dog food.
B. The chicken broth.
C. They arrive simultaneously.

SOLUTION Because the equal masses roll down from the same height, the decrease in gravitational potential energy U_{grav} is the same for both cans. This energy is converted to kinetic energy; some of it becomes *translational* kinetic energy K_{trans} (energy of motion of the center of mass), and some becomes *rotational* kinetic energy K_{rot}. Conservation of energy gives $U_{grav,i} = K_{trans,f} + K_{rot,f}$. Because both cans have the same $U_{grav,i}$, the can with the smaller $K_{rot,f}$ will have the larger $K_{trans,f}$, and therefore the larger value of $\tfrac{1}{2}mv^2$ and of v. The can with the larger v wins the race. Both cans have the same mass, but much of the fluid chicken broth does not rotate—mostly just the can rotates—and this results in a smaller K_{rot} for the chicken broth, a larger K_{trans}, and therefore a larger v. Choice B is correct; the chicken broth wins the race to the bottom of the slope. (We've neglected the fact that some mechanical energy may be dissipated by the internal motion of the viscous chicken broth.)

EXAMPLE 9.9   A primitive yo-yo

Figure 9.22 shows a primitive (and not very practical) yo-yo in the form of a solid disk with radius R and total mass M. It is released from rest, the supporting hand is stationary, and the string unwinds without slipping. Find an expression for the speed v_{cm} of the center of mass of the solid cylinder after it has dropped a distance h.

▲ **FIGURE 9.22**

SOLUTION

SET UP We take the potential energy to be zero at a distance h below the starting point. Then the initial and final potential energies are $U_i = Mgh$ and $U_f = 0$. The initial kinetic energy K_i is zero, and the final kinetic energy K_f is given by Equation 9.19:

$$K_f = \tfrac{1}{2}Mv_{cm}^2 + \tfrac{1}{2}I_{cm}\omega^2.$$

There are no nonconservative forces, so the total energy is conserved:

$$K_i + U_i = K_f + U_f.$$

SOLVE From conservation of energy,

$$0 + Mgh = \tfrac{1}{2}Mv_{cm}^2 + \tfrac{1}{2}I_{cm}\omega^2.$$

Both v_{cm} and ω are unknown; but if we assume that the string unwinds without slipping, these two quantities are *proportional*. When the cylinder has rotated through one complete revolution $(2\pi$ radians$)$, the string has unwound a distance equal to the circumference of the cylinder $(2\pi R)$. Thus the distance traveled during any time interval Δt is R times the *angular* displace-

ment during that interval. It follows that $v_{cm} = R\omega$. Also, from Table 9.2, $I_{cm} = \tfrac{1}{2}MR^2$, so conservation of energy gives

$$Mgh = \tfrac{1}{2}Mv_{cm}^2 + \tfrac{1}{2}\left(\tfrac{1}{2}MR^2\right)\left(\frac{v_{cm}}{R}\right)^2 = \tfrac{3}{4}Mv_{cm}^2$$

and

$$v_{cm} = \sqrt{\tfrac{4}{3}gh}.$$

REFLECT If the object had fallen freely from a height h, its final speed would be $v_{cm} = \sqrt{2gh}$. The actual speed is less than this, because the same total energy has to be shared by the translational (center-of-mass) motion and the rotational motion. Note that both the mass and radius of the object cancel out, so the results would be the same for a long, skinny solid cylinder and a thin solid disk (but not for a cylindrical shell or a doughnut-shaped disk).

Practice Problem: Carry out the same analysis for a thin-walled cylinder. *Answer:* $v_{cm} = \sqrt{gh}$.

EXAMPLE 9.10   Race of the rolling objects

In a lecture demonstration, an instructor "races" various round objects by releasing them from rest at the top of an inclined plane and then rolling them down the plane (Figure 9.23). The students guess (and sometimes bet on) which object will win. Suppose a thin-walled hollow cylinder (Table 9.2g) and a solid cylinder (Table 9.2f) race. Which one would you bet on to win the race?

▲ **FIGURE 9.23**

SOLUTION

SET UP We use conservation of energy, ignoring rolling friction and air drag. If the objects roll without slipping, then no work is done by friction and the total energy is conserved. Each object starts from rest at the top of an incline with height h, so $K_i = 0$, $U_i = mgh$, and $U_f = 0$ for each. From Equation 9.19,

$$K_f = \tfrac{1}{2}mv_{cm}^2 + \tfrac{1}{2}I_{cm}\omega^2.$$

Both v_{cm} and ω are unknown; but if we assume that the objects roll without slipping, these two quantities are *proportional*. When an object with radius R has rotated through one complete revolution $(2\pi$ radians$)$, it has rolled a distance equal to its circumference $(2\pi R)$. Thus the distance traveled during any time interval Δt is R times the *angular* displacement during that interval, and it follows that $v_{cm} = R\omega$. (The geometry of this situation is identical to that in Example 9.9, in which the speed of the center-of-mass of the yo-yo is proportional to its angular velocity.)

Continued

SOLVE For the thin-walled cylindrical shell, Table 9.2g gives $I_{shell} = MR^2$. Conservation of energy then results in

$$0 + Mgh = \tfrac{1}{2}Mv_{cm}^2 + \tfrac{1}{2}I_{shell}\omega^2 = \tfrac{1}{2}Mv_{cm}^2 + \tfrac{1}{2}(MR^2)(v_{cm}/R)^2$$
$$= \tfrac{1}{2}Mv_{cm}^2 + \tfrac{1}{2}Mv_{cm}^2 = Mv_{cm}^2,$$
$$v_{cm} = \sqrt{gh}.$$

For the solid cylinder, Table 9.2f gives $I_{solid} = \tfrac{1}{2}MR^2$, and the corresponding equations are

$$0 + Mgh = \tfrac{1}{2}Mv_{cm}^2 + \tfrac{1}{2}I_{solid}\omega^2 = \tfrac{1}{2}Mv_{cm}^2 + \tfrac{1}{2}(\tfrac{1}{2}MR^2)(v_{cm}/R)^2$$
$$= \tfrac{1}{2}Mv_{cm}^2 + \tfrac{1}{4}Mv_{cm}^2 = \tfrac{3}{4}Mv_{cm}^2,$$
$$v_{cm} = \sqrt{\tfrac{4}{3}gh}.$$

We see that the solid cylinder's speed at the bottom of the hill is greater than that of the hollow cylinder by a factor of $\sqrt{\tfrac{4}{3}}$, so the solid cylinder wins the race.

We can generalize this result in an elegant way. We note that the moments of inertia of all the round objects in Table 9.2 (about axes through their centers of mass) can be expressed as $I_{cm} = \beta MR^2$, where β is a pure number between 0 and 1 that depends on the shape of the body. For a thin-walled hollow cylinder, $\beta = 1$; for a solid cylinder, $\beta = \tfrac{1}{2}$; and so on. From conservation of energy,

$$0 + Mgh = \tfrac{1}{2}Mv_{cm}^2 + \tfrac{1}{2}I\omega^2 = \tfrac{1}{2}Mv_{cm}^2 + \tfrac{1}{2}(\beta MR^2)(v_{cm}/R)^2$$
$$= \tfrac{1}{2}(1 + \beta)Mv_{cm}^2,$$
$$v_{cm} = \sqrt{\frac{2gh}{1 + \beta}}.$$

REFLECT This is a fairly amazing result; the final speed of the center of mass doesn't depend on either the mass M of the body or its radius R. All uniform solid cylinders have the same speed at the bottom, even if their masses and radii are different, because they have the same β. All solid spheres have the same speed, and so on. The smaller the value of β, the faster the body is moving at the bottom (and at any point on the way down). Small-β bodies always beat large-β bodies because they have less kinetic energy tied up in rotation and have more available for translation. For the hollow cylinder ($\beta = 1$), the translational and rotational energies at any point are equal, but for the solid cylinder ($\beta = \tfrac{1}{2}$), the rotational energy at any point is half the translational energy. Reading the values of β from Table 9.2, we see that the order of finish is as follows: any solid sphere, any solid cylinder, any thin spherical shell, and any thin cylindrical shell.

Practice Problem: (a) Find the ratio of the final speeds for a solid sphere and a solid cylinder. (b) Why aren't the expressions for moments of inertia of these two objects the same? *Answers:* (a) 1.035; (b) the sphere has a greater fraction of its mass close to the axis than the cylinder has.

SUMMARY

Angular Velocity and Angular Acceleration

(Section 9.1) When a rigid body rotates about a stationary axis, its position is described by an angular coordinate θ. When an object turns through an angle $\Delta\theta$ in a time interval Δt, the average angular velocity ω_{av} is defined as $\omega_{av} = \Delta\theta/\Delta t$ (Equation 9.2). The instantaneous angular velocity ω is

$$\omega = \lim_{\Delta t \to 0} \frac{\Delta\theta}{\Delta t}. \qquad (9.3)$$

If the angular velocity changes by an amount $\Delta\omega$ in a time interval Δt, the average angular acceleration α_{av} is defined as $\alpha_{av} = \Delta\omega/\Delta t$ (Equation 9.5), and the instantaneous angular velocity α is

$$\alpha = \lim_{\Delta t \to 0} \frac{\Delta\omega}{\Delta t}. \qquad (9.6)$$

Angular velocity ω: Rate of change of angular position:

$$\omega_{av} = \frac{\Delta\theta}{\Delta t}$$

Angular acceleration α: Rate of change of angular velocity:

$$\alpha_{av} = \frac{\Delta\omega}{\Delta t}$$

Rotation with Constant Angular Acceleration

(Section 9.2) When a body rotates with constant angular acceleration, the angular position, velocity, and acceleration are related by the equations: $\omega = \omega_0 + \alpha t$ (Equation 9.7), $\theta - \theta_0 = \frac{1}{2}(\omega_0 + \omega)t$ (Equation 9.10), $\theta = \theta_0 + \omega_0 t + \frac{1}{2}\alpha t^2$ (Equation 9.11), and $\omega^2 = \omega_0^2 + 2\alpha(\theta - \theta_0)$ (Equation 9.12), where θ_0 and ω_0 are the initial values of the angular position and angular velocity, respectively, of the body. These expressions are analogous to the equations for linear motion found in Chapter 2.

Relationship between Linear and Angular Quantities

(Section 9.3) A particle in a rotating rigid body at a distance r from the axis of rotation has a tangential speed v given by $v = r\omega$ (Equation 9.13). The particle's acceleration $\vec{a}$ has a tangential component $a_{tan} = r\alpha$ (Equation 9.14) and a radial component

$$a_{rad} = \frac{v^2}{r} = \omega^2 r. \qquad (9.15)$$

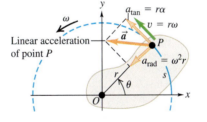

Kinetic Energy of Rotation and Moment of Inertia

(Section 9.4) The moment of inertia I of a body with respect to a given axis is defined as $I = m_A r_A^2 + m_B r_B^2 + m_C r_C^2 + \cdots$ (Equation 9.16) where r_A is the distance of mass element m_A from the axis of rotation, and so on. The kinetic energy of a rigid body rotating about a stationary axis is given by $K = \frac{1}{2}I\omega^2$ (Equation 9.17). In a uniform gravitational field, the gravitational potential energy of a rigid body with center of mass at a distance y_{cm} above the reference level (where $U = 0$) is $U = Mgy_{cm}$ (Equation 9.18).

Rotation about a Moving Axis

(Section 9.5) When a rigid body undergoes both motion of its center of mass and rotation about an axis through the center of mass, the total kinetic energy is given by

$$K_{total} = \frac{1}{2}Mv_{cm}^2 + \frac{1}{2}I_{cm}\omega^2. \qquad (9.19)$$

(MP) For instructor-assigned homework, go to www.masteringphysics.com

Conceptual Questions

1. What is the difference between the tangential acceleration and the radial acceleration of a point on a rotating object?
2. A flywheel rotates with constant angular velocity. Does a point on its rim have tangential acceleration? radial acceleration? Are these accelerations constant in magnitude? in direction?
3. A flywheel rotates with constant angular acceleration. Does a point on its rim have tangential acceleration? radial acceleration? Are these accelerations constant in magnitude? in direction?
4. How might you experimentally determine a moment of inertia of an *irregularly* shaped body by using materials from a typical introductory physics laboratory (such as pulleys, turntables, timers, etc.)?
5. A uniform ring of mass M and radius R and a point mass M a distance R from the axis of the ring both rotate about that axis, which is perpendicular to the ring at its center. Both objects have the same formula for their moment of inertia, $I = MR^2$, about this axis. (a) Is there a good physical reason that they have the same formula? (b) If the ring were replaced by a solid uniform disk of mass M and radius R, would the disk and point mass then have the same moment-of-inertia formula? Why or why not?
6. To maximize the moment of inertia of a flywheel while minimizing its weight, what shape should the flywheel have?
7. According to experienced riders, you make a bike less tiring to ride if you reduce its weight in the wheels rather than in the frame. Why is this so?
8. A solid ball, a solid cylinder, and a hollow cylinder roll down a slope. Which one reaches the bottom first? last? Does it matter whether the radii are the same? What about the masses?
9. Experienced cooks can tell whether an egg is raw or hard boiled by rolling it down a slope (and taking care to catch it at the bottom). How is this possible? Which type of egg should reach the bottom of the slope first?
10. Part of the kinetic energy of a moving automobile is in the rotational motion of its wheels. When the brakes are applied hard on an icy street, the wheels lock and the car starts to slide. What becomes of the rotational kinetic energy?
11. In what ways is the moment of inertia *similar* to mass, and in what ways is it *different* from mass?
12. A client has come to you with two metal balls of the same size and mass. He thinks that one might be solid and the other might be hollow inside. By rolling both balls down a slope, how could you tell which one is hollow and which is solid?
13. In what ways does a jogger's body have *rotational* kinetic energy?
14. As a car of mass M travels with speed V, its kinetic energy is $\frac{1}{2}MV^2$. But this is not the whole story. What additional contributions are there to this car's kinetic energy from *internal* motion, both translational and rotational?
15. If a ball rolls down an *irregularly* shaped hill without slipping, it is very easy to find its speed at the bottom by using conservation of energy. Why could we not just as easily use Newton's second law to find the speed?

Multiple-Choice Problems

1. When a wheel turns through one complete rotation, the angle (in *radians*) that it has turned through is closest to
   A. 57.   B. 6.   C. 360.
2. Two points are on a disk that rotates about an axis perpendicular to the plane of the disk at its center. Point B is 3 times as far from the axis as point A. If the linear speed of point B is V, then the linear speed of point A is
   A. $9V$.   B. $3V$.   C. V.
   D. $\dfrac{V}{3}$.   E. $\dfrac{V}{9}$.
3. For the two points A and B in the previous question, if the angular speed of point B is ω, then the angular speed of point A is
   A. 9ω.   B. 3ω.   C. ω.
   D. $\dfrac{\omega}{3}$.   E. $\dfrac{\omega}{9}$.
4. You are designing a flywheel to store large amounts of kinetic energy. Which one of the following uniform shapes will be the *most* effective for storing the greatest amount of kinetic energy if all the objects have the same mass and same angular velocity?
   A. A solid sphere of diameter D rotating about a diameter.
   B. A solid cylinder of diameter D rotating about an axis perpendicular to each face through its center.
   C. A thin-walled hollow cylinder of diameter D rotating about an axis perpendicular to the plane of the circular face at its center.
   D. A solid thin bar of length D rotating about an axis perpendicular to it at its center.
5. Four uniform objects having the same mass and diameter are released simultaneously from rest at the same distance above the bottom of a hill and roll down without slipping. The objects are a solid sphere, a solid cylinder, a hollow cylinder, and a thin-walled hollow cylinder, as illustrated in Table 9.2. Which of these objects will be the first one to reach the bottom of the hill?
   A. The solid sphere
   B. The solid cylinder
   C. The hollow cylinder
   D. The thin-walled hollow cylinder
6. Which of the objects in question 5 will be the last one to reach the bottom of the hill?
   A. The solid sphere
   B. The solid cylinder
   C. The hollow cylinder
   D. The thin-walled hollow cylinder
7. For the objects in question 5, which of the following statements are correct? (There may be more than one correct choice.)
   A. All these objects have the same forward speed at the bottom of the hill.
   B. All these objects have the same kinetic energy at the bottom of the hill.
   C. All these objects have the same rotational kinetic energy at the bottom of the hill.
   D. All these objects have the same angular velocity at the bottom of the hill.

8. Two uniform solid spheres of the same size, but different mass, are released from rest simultaneously at the same height on a hill and roll to the bottom without slipping. Which of the following statements about these spheres are true? (There may be more than one correct choice.)
   A. Both spheres reach the bottom at the same time.
   B. The heavier sphere reaches the bottom ahead of the lighter one.
   C. Both spheres arrive at the bottom with the same forward speed.
   D. Both spheres arrive at the bottom with the same total kinetic energy.

9. A disk starts from rest and has a constant angular acceleration. If it takes time T to make its first revolution, in time $2T$ (starting from rest) the disk will make
   A. $\sqrt{2}$ revolutions.
   B. 2 revolutions.
   C. 4 revolutions.
   D. 8 revolutions.

10. Two unequal masses m and $2m$ are attached to a thin bar of negligible mass that rotates about an axis perpendicular to the bar. When m is a distance $2d$ from the axis and $2m$ is a distance d from the axis, the moment of inertia of this combination is I. If the masses are now interchanged, the moment of inertia will be
   A. $\frac{2}{3}I$.   B. I.   C. $\frac{3}{2}I$.
   D. $2I$.   E. $4I$.

11. A thin uniform bar has a moment of inertia I about an axis perpendicular to it through its center. If *both* the mass and length of this bar are doubled, its moment of inertia about the same axis will be
   A. $2I$.   B. $4I$.
   C. $8I$.   D. $16I$.

12. Two small objects of equal weight are attached to the ends of a thin weightless bar that spins about an axis perpendicular to the bar at its center. Each mass is a distance d from the axis of rotation. The system spins at a rate so that its kinetic energy is K. If *both* masses are now moved closer in so that each is $d/2$ from the rotation axis, while the angular velocity does not change, the kinetic energy of the system will be
   A. $\frac{1}{4}K$.   B. $\frac{1}{2}K$.
   C. $2K$.   D. $4K$.

13. A disk starts from rest and rotates with constant angular acceleration. If the angular velocity is ω at the end of the first two revolutions, then at the end of the first eight revolutions it will be
   A. $\sqrt{2}\omega$.   B. 2ω.
   C. 4ω.   D. 16ω.

14. A wheel starts spinning from rest with uniform angular acceleration. If its angular speed at the end of the first 3 s is ω, then at the end of the first 6 s its angular speed will be
   A. 2ω.   B. 4ω.
   C. 6ω.   D. 9ω.

15. A solid sphere and a hollow sphere, both uniform and having the same mass and radius, are released from rest at the same height on a ramp. If they roll down the ramp without slipping, which one will have the *greater* forward velocity at the bottom of the ramp?
   A. The solid sphere
   B. The hollow sphere
   C. Both will have the same forward velocity.

16. A uniform ball rolls without slipping toward a hill with a forward speed V. In which case will this ball go farther up the hill?
   A. There is enough friction on the hill to prevent slipping of the ball.
   B. The hill is frictionless.
   C. The ball will reach the same height in both cases, since it has the same initial kinetic energy in each case.

Problems

9.1 Angular Velocity and Angular Acceleration

1. • A flexible straight wire 75.0 cm long is bent into the arc of a circle of radius 2.50 m. What angle (in radians and degrees) will this arc subtend at the center of the circle?

2. • (a) What angle in radians is subtended by an arc 1.50 m in length on the circumference of a circle of radius 2.50 m? What is this angle in degrees? (b) An arc 14.0 cm in length on the circumference of a circle subtends an angle of 128°. What is the radius of the circle? (c) The angle between two radii of a circle with radius 1.50 m is 0.700 rad. What length of arc is intercepted on the circumference of the circle by the two radii?

3. • (a) Calculate the angular velocity (in rad/s) of the second, minute, and hour hands on a wall clock. (b) What is the period of each of these hands?

4. • The once-popular LP (long-play) records were 12 in. in diameter and turned at a constant $33\frac{1}{3}$ rpm. Find (a) the angular speed of the LP in rad/s and (b) its period in seconds.

5. • If a wheel 212 cm in diameter takes 2.25 s for each revolution, find its (a) period and (b) angular speed in rad/s.

6. • Find the angular velocity, in rad/s, of (a) the earth due to its daily spin on its axis, (b) the earth due to its yearly motion around the sun, and (c) our moon due to its monthly motion around the earth. Consult Appendix F as needed.

7. • Through what angle (in degrees and radians) does the earth move around the sun from the morning of Mozart's birthday (Jan. 27) to the morning of Einstein's birthday (March 14), assuming it is not a leap year?

8. • **Communications satellites.** Communications satellites are placed in orbits so that they always remain above the same point of the earth's surface. (a) What must be the period of such a satellite? (b) What is its angular velocity in rad/s?

9. • An airplane propeller is rotating at 1900 rpm. (a) Compute the propeller's angular velocity in rad/s. (b) How many seconds does it take for the propeller to turn through 35°? (c) If the propeller were turning at 18 rad/s, at how many rpm would it be turning? (d) What is the period (in seconds) of this propeller?

10. •• A wall clock on Planet X has two hands that are aligned at midnight and turn in the same direction at uniform rates, one at 0.0425 rad/s and the other at 0.0163 rad/s. At how many seconds after midnight are these hands (a) first aligned and (b) next aligned?

9.2 Rotation with Constant Angular Acceleration

11. • A turntable that spins at a constant 78.0 rpm takes 3.50 s to reach this angular speed after it is turned on. Find (a) its angular acceleration (in rad/s^2), assuming it to be constant, and (b) the number of degrees it turns through while speeding up.

12. • When the power is turned off on a turntable spinning at 78.0 rpm, you find that it takes 10.5 revolutions for it to stop while slowing down at a uniform rate. (a) What is the angular acceleration (in rad/s^2) of this turntable? (b) How long does it take to stop after the power is turned off?

13. • **DVDs.** The angular speed of digital video discs (DVDs) varies with whether the inner or outer part of the disc is being read. (CDs function in the same way.) Over a 133 min playing time, the angular speed varies from 570 rpm to 1600 rpm. Assuming it to be constant, what is the angular acceleration (in rad/s^2) of such a DVD? (*Note:* Much faster systems will soon be on the market.)

14. • A circular saw blade 0.200 m in diameter starts from rest. In 6.00 s, it reaches an angular velocity of 140 rad/s with constant angular acceleration. Find the angular acceleration and the angle through which the blade has turned in this time.

15. • A wheel turns with a constant angular acceleration of 0.640 rad/s^2. (a) How much time does it take to reach an angular velocity of 8.00 rad/s, starting from rest? (b) Through how many revolutions does the wheel turn in this interval?

16. • An electric fan is turned off, and its angular velocity decreases uniformly from 500.0 rev/min to 200.0 rev/min in 4.00 s. (a) Find the angular acceleration in rev/s^2 and the number of revolutions made by the motor in the 4.00 s interval. (b) How many more seconds are required for the fan to come to rest if the angular acceleration remains constant at the value calculated in part (a)?

17. •• A flywheel in a motor is spinning at 500.0 rpm when a power failure suddenly occurs. The flywheel has mass 40.0 kg and diameter 75.0 cm. The power is off for 30.0 s, and during this time the flywheel slows down uniformly due to friction in its axle bearings. During the time the power is off, the flywheel makes 200.0 complete revolutions. (a) At what rate is the flywheel spinning when the power comes back on? (b) How long after the beginning of the power failure would it have taken the flywheel to stop if the power had not come back on, and how many revolutions would the wheel have made during this time?

18. •• A flywheel having constant angular acceleration requires 4.00 s to rotate through 162 rad. Its angular velocity at the end of this time is 108 rad/s. Find (a) the angular velocity at the beginning of the 4.00 s interval; (b) the angular acceleration of the flywheel.

19. •• Emilie's potter's wheel rotates with a constant 2.25 rad/s^2 angular acceleration. After 4.00 s, the wheel has rotated through an angle of 60.0 rad. What was the angular velocity of the wheel at the beginning of the 4.00 s interval?

20. •• Derive Eq. 9.12 by combining Eqs. 9.7 and 9.11 to eliminate *t*.

9.3 Relationship between Linear and Angular Quantities

21. • When an electric drill bit 13.0 mm in diameter is turning at 1250 rpm to drill a hole in a wooden board, how fast is the sur-

face of the bit moving against the wood at the inner surface of the hole?

22. • (a) A cylinder 0.150 m in diameter rotates in a lathe at 620 rpm. What is the tangential speed of the surface of the cylinder? (b) The proper tangential speed for machining cast iron is about 0.600 m/s. At how many revolutions per minute should a piece of stock 0.0800 m in diameter be rotated in a lathe to produce this tangential speed?

23. • A wheel rotates with a constant angular velocity of 6.00 rad/s. (a) Compute the radial acceleration of a point 0.500 m from the axis, using the relation $a_{rad} = \omega^2 r$. (b) Find the tangential speed of the point, and compute its radial acceleration from the relation $a_{rad} = v^2/r$.

24. • **Ultracentrifuge.** Find the required angular speed (in rpm) of an ultracentrifuge for the radial acceleration of a point 2.50 cm from the axis to equal 400,000g.

25. •• **Exercise!** An exercise bike that you peddle in place has a bicycle chain connecting the wheel you peddle to the large wheel in front, as shown in Figure 9.24. For the wheel *diameters* shown, how many rpm must you produce to turn the large wheel at 75 rpm?

▲ **FIGURE 9.24** Problem 25.

26. •• A flywheel with a radius of 0.300 m starts from rest and accelerates with a constant angular acceleration of 0.600 rad/s^2. Compute the magnitude of the tangential acceleration, the radial acceleration, and the resultant acceleration of a point on its rim (a) at the start, (b) after it has turned through 60.0°, and (c) after it has turned through 120.0°.

27. •• **Cassette tape.** When a cassette tape is playing, spinning tape guides drive the tape, by friction, at a constant speed of $1\frac{7}{8}$ ips (inches per second) over the playing heads, forcing the tape off of and onto the take-up reels. (See Figure 9.25.) Measurements of a standard cassette and tape deck show that the tape guides are 2.0 mm in diameter, while the inner and

▲ **FIGURE 9.25** Problem 27.

outer diameters of the take-up reels are $\frac{7}{8}''$ and $2''$, respectively. (a) Find the angular speed of the tape guides in rad/s. (b) What is the angular speed of the take-up reels when they are (i) full of tape and (ii) empty? (c) How many meters of tape are there on a 90 minute cassette (45 min each way)?

28. •• **Dental hygiene.** Electric toothbrushes can be effective in removing dental plaque. One model consists of a head 1.1 cm in diameter that rotates back and forth through a 70.0° angle 7600 times per minute. The rim of the head contains a thin row of bristles. (See Figure 9.26.) (a) What is the average angular speed in each direction of the rotating head, in rad/s? (b) What is the average linear speed in each direction of the bristles against the teeth? (c) Using your own observations, what is the approximate speed of the bristles against your teeth when you brush by hand with an *ordinary* toothbrush?

BIO

◄ **FIGURE 9.26** Problem 28.

29. •• **Rotary toothbrush.** Assuming that the toothbrush in the previous problem has constant angular acceleration in each of the directions it turns, find (a) the angular acceleration (in rad/s²) of the rotating head and (b) the tangential acceleration (in m/s²) of the bristles.

9.4 Kinetic Energy of Rotation and Moment of Inertia

30. • Each part in Figure 9.27 contains two uniform objects of the same mass and general size, but having different distributions of that mass. Which one of each pair has the *greater* moment of inertia about the dashed-line axis shown? Do not attempt any calculations, but just explain your reasoning, using simple physical arguments.

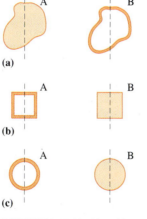

▲ **FIGURE 9.27** Problem 30.

31. • Three small blocks, each with mass m, are clamped at the ends and at the center of a light rod of length L. Compute the moment of inertia of the system about an axis perpendicular to the rod and passing through a point one-fourth of the length from one end. You can ignore the moment of inertia of the light rod.

32. • Use the formulas of Table 9.2 to find the moment of inertia about each of the following axes for a rod that is 0.300 cm in diameter and 1.50 m long, with a mass of 0.0420 kg: (a) about an axis perpendicular to the rod and passing through its center; (b) about an axis perpendicular to the rod and passing through one end; and (c) about an axis along the length of the rod.

33. •• Four small 0.200 kg spheres, each of which you can regard as a point mass, are arranged in a square 0.400 m on a side and connected by light rods. (See Figure 9.28.) Find the moment of inertia of the system about an axis (a) through the center of the square, perpendicular to its plane at point O; (b) along the line AB; and (c) along the line CD.

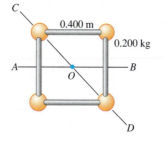

▲ **FIGURE 9.28** Problem 33.

34. •• **Compound objects.** Moment of inertia is a scalar. Therefore, if several objects are connected together, the moment of inertia of this compound object is simply the scalar (algebraic) sum of the moments of inertia of each of the component objects. Use this principle to answer each of the following questions about the moment of inertia of compound objects: (a) A thin uniform 2.50 kg bar 1.50 m long has a small 1.25 kg mass glued to each end. What is the moment of inertia of this object about an axis perpendicular to the bar through its center? (b) What is the moment of inertia of the object in part (a) about an axis perpendicular to the bar at one end? (c) A 725 g metal wire is bent into the shape of a hoop 60.0 cm in diameter. Six wire spokes, each of mass 112 g, are added from the center of the hoop to the rim. What is the moment of inertia of this object about an axis perpendicular to it through its center?

35. •• **Compound objects.** (See the previous problem.) (a) A solid uniform wooden cylinder has mass m and radius R. To make this object suitable for a machine part, you need to increase its moment of inertia about an axis though its center perpendicular to its faces. To do this, you add a very thin layer of an extremely dense metal to the outside of the cylinder, so that the radius of the cylinder will not change appreciably. What mass of metal (in terms of m) must you add to double the cylinder's moment of inertia? (b) A uniform solid wooden sphere of mass M and radius R is spinning about an axis through its center. In order to meet weight specifications, its mass needs to be increased without changing its size. This is done by adding a very thin uniform coating of a dense metal foil to the outer surface of the sphere. Such a coating will not appreciably change the diameter of the sphere. If you add enough of this foil to double the sphere's mass, what is the ratio of its new moment of inertia to the moment of inertia of the original wooden sphere without the foil?

36. •• A wagon wheel is constructed as shown in Figure 9.29. The radius of the wheel is 0.300 m, and the rim has a mass of 1.40 kg. Each of the wheel's eight spokes, which come out from the center and are 0.300 m long, has a mass of 0.280 kg. What is the moment of inertia of the wheel about an axis through its center and perpendicular to the plane of the wheel?

▲ **FIGURE 9.29** Problem 36.

37. •• In redesigning a machine, you need to replace a uniform 5.55 N solid spherical part with a

uniform solid disk of the same diameter without changing the moment of inertia of the part. If the original spherical part spun around an axis through its center and the replacement disk must spin about the same axis perpendicular to it at its center, what must be the weight of the disk?

38. • A grinding wheel in the shape of a solid disk is 0.200 m in diameter and has a mass of 3.00 kg. The wheel is rotating at 2200 rpm about an axis through its center. (a) What is its kinetic energy? (b) How far would it have to drop in free fall to acquire the same amount of kinetic energy?

39. •• The flywheel of a gasoline engine is required to give up 500 J of kinetic energy while its angular velocity decreases from 650 rev/min to 520 rev/min. What moment of inertia is required?

40. •• **Tidal energy.** In March 2004, a British company successfully tested a power system to tap the energy of ocean tides. The energy will be stored in an underwater turbine consisting of two metal blades, each 15 m long. The movement of the water due to the tides will give kinetic energy to the turbine blades, causing them to spin. In the calculations that follow, ignore any frictional drag due to the seawater. If we model each of these two blades as a thin uniform steel bar 15 m long and 25.0 cm in diameter, at what rate (in rad/s and rpm) must they spin for the turbine to store 1.0 MJ of energy? The density of steel is 7800 kg/m³. (Recall that density is equal to an object's mass divided by its volume.)

41. •• **Storing energy in flywheels.** It has been suggested that we should use our power plants to generate energy in the off-hours (such as late at night) and store it for use during the day. One idea put forward is to store the energy in large flywheels. Suppose we want to build such a flywheel in the shape of a hollow cylinder of inner radius 0.500 m and outer radius 1.50 m, using concrete of density 2.20 × 10³ kg/m³. (a) If, for stability, such a heavy flywheel is limited to 1.75 second for each revolution and has negligible friction at its axle, what must be its length to store 2.5 MJ of energy in its rotational motion? (b) Suppose that by strengthening the frame you could safely double the flywheel's rate of spin. What length of flywheel would you need in that case? (Solve this part *without* reworking the entire problem!)

42. •• A light string is wrapped around the outer rim of a solid uniform cylinder of diameter 75.0 cm that can rotate without friction about an axle through its center. A 3.00 kg stone is tied to the free end of the string, as shown in Figure 9.30. When the

3.00 kg

▲ **FIGURE 9.30** Problem 42.

system is released from rest, you determine that the stone reaches a speed of 3.50 m/s after having fallen 2.50 m. What is the mass of the cylinder?

43. •• A solid uniform 3.25 kg cylinder, 65.0 cm in diameter and 12.4 cm long, is connected to a 1.50 kg weight over two massless frictionless pulleys as shown in Figure 9.31. The cylinder is free to rotate about an axle through its center perpendicular to its circular faces, and the system is released from rest. (a) How far must the 1.50 kg weight fall before it reaches a speed of 2.50 m/s? (b) How fast is the cylinder turning at this instant?

3.25 kg

1.50 kg

▲ **FIGURE 9.31** Problem 43.

44. •• What does the moment of inertia approach in the following limiting cases for the objects in Table 9.2? In each case, explain why the answer you get for the limit is physically reasonable. (a) $L \to 0$ for objects (a) and (b). (b) $a \to 0$ for object (c). (c) $b \to 0$ for object (d). (d) $R_1 \to 0$ for object (e). (e) $R_2 \to R_1$ for object (e). (f) $R \to 0$ for objects (h) and (i).

9.5 Rotation about a Moving Axis

45. • **Gymnastics.** We can roughly model a gymnastic tumbler **BIO** as a uniform solid cylinder of mass 75 kg and diameter 1.0 m. If this tumbler rolls forward at 0.50 rev/s, (a) how much total kinetic energy does he have and (b) what percent of his total kinetic energy is rotational?

46. •• A bicycle racer is going downhill at 11.0 m/s when, to his horror, one of his 2.25 kg wheels comes off when he is 75.0 m above the foot of the hill. We can model the wheel as a thin-walled cylinder 85.0 cm in diameter and neglect the small mass of the spokes. (a) How fast is the wheel moving when it reaches the foot of the hill if it rolled without slipping all the way down? (b) How much total kinetic energy does the wheel have when it reaches the bottom of the hill?

47. •• **The spin of a baseball.** In baseball, the rules specify that the ball is 23.0 cm in circumference with a mass of 145 g. (These numbers can vary slightly.) If a pitcher throws a fastball at 38.0 m/s, its spin typically can be 25.0 rev/s. We can reasonably model the ball as a uniform solid sphere. (a) How much total kinetic energy has the pitcher given this ball? (b) What percentage of the ball's total kinetic energy is rotational? (c) If the baseball were *rolling* without slipping, instead of having the indicated spin, what percentage of its total kinetic energy would be rotational? (d) What would be the percentage in part (b) if the ball had the structure of a tennis ball of instead of a baseball? (*Hint:* How can you reasonably model a tennis ball?)

48. •• A solid uniform sphere and a uniform spherical shell, both having the same mass and radius, roll without slipping down a hill that rises at an angle θ above the horizontal. Both spheres start from rest at the same vertical height h. (a) How fast is each sphere moving when it reaches the bottom of the hill? (b) Which sphere will reach the bottom first, the hollow one or the solid one?

49. •• A size-5 soccer ball of diameter 22.6 cm and mass 426 g rolls up a hill without slipping, reaching a maximum height of 5.00 m above the base of the hill. We can model this ball as a thin-walled hollow sphere. (a) At what rate was it rotating at the base of the hill? (b) How much rotational kinetic energy did it then have?

50. •• A solid uniform marble and a block of ice, each with the same mass, start from rest at the same height H above the bottom of a hill and move down it. The marble rolls without slipping, but the ice slides without friction. (a) Find the speed of each of these objects when it reaches the bottom of the hill. (b) Which object is moving faster at the bottom, the ice or the marble? (c) Which object has more kinetic energy at the bottom, the ice or the marble?

51. •• A solid uniform cylinder and a solid uniform sphere, each with the same mass and diameter, approach a hill rolling with a forward speed of 6.50 m/s. Both of them roll up the hill without slipping. (a) Find the maximum height that each of the centers will reach. (b) Why do they reach different heights? Didn't both of them have the same speed at the bottom of the hill? (c) Would your answers to part (a) be different if these two objects (i) did not have the same masses or (ii) did not have the same diameters? What makes you say this?

52. •• A string is wrapped several times around the rim of a small hoop with a radius of 0.0800 m and a mass of 0.180 kg. If the free end of the string is held in place and the hoop is released from rest (see Figure 9.32), calculate the angular speed of the rotating hoop after it has descended 0.750 m.

0.0800 m

▲ **FIGURE 9.32** Problem 52.

53. •• A thin light string is wrapped around the outer rim of a uniform hollow cylinder of mass 4.75 kg having inner and outer radii as shown in Figure 9.33. The cylinder is then released from rest. (a) How far must the cylinder fall before its center is moving at 6.66 m/s? (b) If you just dropped this cylinder without any string, how fast would its center be moving when it had fallen the distance in part (a)? (c) Why do you get two different answers? The cylinder falls the same distance in both cases.

54. •• A uniform hollow ball (like a soccer ball) is released from rest at the top of a hill of height H. Find its forward linear speed (in terms of H) at the base of this hill if (a) there is no friction on

20.0 cm

35.0 cm

▲ **FIGURE 9.33** Problem 53.

the hill and (b) the hill is rough enough so that the ball rolls without slipping.

General Problems

55. •• A 7300 N elevator is to be given an acceleration of $0.150g$ by connecting it to a cable of negligible weight wrapped around a turning cylindrical shaft. If the shaft's diameter can be no larger than 16.0 cm due to space limitations, what must be its minimum angular acceleration to provide the required acceleration of the elevator?

56. •• (a) If your car has 28-inch-diameter tires that do not slip on the pavement, how many revolutions per second do these tires make when you are driving at a freeway speed of 65 mph? (b) For the tires in part (a), how fast (in mph) is each of the following points moving relative to the highway surface: (i) the center of the tire, (ii) the top of the tire, and (iii) the bottom of the tire?

57. •• **Odometer.** The odometer (mileage gauge) of a car tells you the number of miles you have driven, but it doesn't count the miles directly. Instead, it counts the number of revolutions of your car's wheels and converts this quantity to mileage, assuming a standard size tire and that your tires do not slip on the pavement. (a) A typical midsize car has tires 24 inches in diameter. How many revolutions of the wheels must the odometer count in order to show a mileage of 0.10 mile? (b) What will the odometer read when the tires have made 5,000 revolutions? (c) Suppose you put oversize 28-inch-diameter tires on your car. How many miles will you really have driven when your odometer reads 500 miles?

58. •• **Speedometer.** Your car's speedometer works in much the same way as its odometer (see the previous problem), except that it converts the angular speed of the wheels to a linear speed of the car, assuming standard-size tires and no slipping on the pavement. (a) If your car has standard 24-inch-diameter tires, how fast are your wheels turning when you are driving at a freeway speed of 55 mph? (b) How fast are you going when your wheels are turning at 500 rpm? (c) If you put on under-size 20-inch-diameter tires, what will the speedometer read when you are actually traveling at 50 mph?

59. •• A meterstick with a mass of 0.160 kg is pivoted without friction about a horizontal axis perpendicular to it at one end. The stick is released from rest in a horizontal position. As it swings through the vertical, calculate (a) the change in gravitational potential energy that has occurred, (b) the angular speed of the stick, and (c) the linear speed of the end of the stick opposite the axis. (d) Compare the answer in part (c) with the speed of a particle that has fallen 1.00 m, starting from rest.

60. •• A passenger bus in Zurich, Switzerland, derived its motive power from the energy stored in a large flywheel. Whenever the bus was stopped at a station, the wheel was brought up to speed with the use of an electric motor that could then be attached to the electric power lines. The flywheel was a solid cylinder with a mass of 1000 kg and a diameter of 1.80 m; its top angular speed was 3000 rev/min. At this angular speed, what was the kinetic energy of the flywheel?

61. •• **Kinetic energy of the earth.** Consult Appendix F as necessary. Assuming that the earth is of uniform density inside, find the kinetic energy of the earth (a) due to its yearly motion around the sun and (b) due to its daily spin on its axis.

(c) What percent of the earth's total kinetic energy is contained in its axial spin motion?

62. •• **Compact discs.** When a compact disc (CD) is playing, the angular speed of the turntable is adjusted so that the laser beam, which reads the digital information encoded in the surface of the disc, maintains a constant *tangential* speed. The laser begins tracking at the inside of the disc and spirals outward as

▲ **FIGURE 9.34** Problem 62.

the disc plays, while the angular speed of the disc varies between 500 rpm and 200 rpm. A certain CD (see Figure 9.34) plays for 74 minutes and has a playing area of outer diameter 12.1 cm (which is also essentially the outside diameter of the disc). (a) What is the tangential speed of the laser beam? (b) What is the diameter of the inside of the playing area of this CD? (c) What is the angular acceleration of the CD while it is playing, assuming it to be constant?

63. •• If today Mars is 45° ahead of earth in its orbit around the sun (see Figure 9.35), when will the two planets first be aligned along a straight line from the sun, assuming circular orbits? (*Note:* All the planets orbit the sun in the same direction, and the year on Mars is 1.9 earth years.)

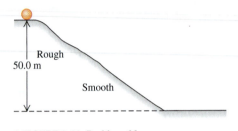

▲ **FIGURE 9.35** Problem 63.

64. •• A basketball (which can be closely modeled as a hollow spherical shell) rolls down a mountainside into a valley and then up the opposite side, starting from rest at a height H_0 above the bottom. In Figure 9.36, the rough part of the terrain prevents slipping while the smooth part has no friction. (a) How high, in terms of H_0, will it go up the other side? (b) Why doesn't the ball return to height H_0? Has it lost any of its original potential energy?

▲ **FIGURE 9.36** Problem 64.

65. •• **Human rotational energy.** A dancer is spinning at 72 rpm about an axis through her center with her arms outstretched, as shown in Figure 9.37. From biomedical measurements, the typical distribution of mass in a human body is as follows:

Head: 7.0%
Arms: 13% (for both)
Trunk and legs: 80.0%

Suppose you are this dancer. Using this information plus length measurements on your own body, calculate (a) your moment of inertia about your spin axis and (b) your rotational kinetic energy. Use the figures in Table 9.2 to model reasonable approximations for the pertinent parts of your body.

▲ **FIGURE 9.37** Problem 65.

66. •• A solid uniform spherical boulder rolls down the hill as shown in Figure 9.38, starting from rest when it is 50.0 m above the bottom. The upper half of the hill is free of ice, so the boulder rolls without slipping. But the lower half is covered with perfectly smooth ice. How fast is the boulder moving when it reaches the bottom of the hill?

▲ **FIGURE 9.38** Problem 66.

67. ••• At what times of day do the minute and hour hands of a wall clock point in opposite directions?

68. •• In redesigning a piece of equipment, you need to replace a solid spherical part of mass M with a hollow spherical shell of the same size. If both parts must spin at the same rate about an axis through their center, and the new part must have the same kinetic energy as the old one, what must be the mass of the new part in terms of M?

69. •• A solid uniform spherical stone starts moving from rest at the top of a hill. At the bottom of the hill the ground curves upward, launching the stone vertically a distance H below its start. How high will the stone go (a) if there is no friction on the hill and (b) if there is enough friction on the hill for the stone to roll without slipping? (c) Why do you get two different answers even though the stone starts with the same gravitational potential energy in both cases?

70. •• A solid, uniform ball rolls without slipping up a hill, as shown in Figure 9.39. At the top of the hill, it is moving

▲ **FIGURE 9.39** Problem 70.

horizontally; then it goes over the vertical cliff. (a) How far from the foot of the cliff does the ball land, and how fast is it moving just before it lands? (b) Notice that when the ball lands, it has a larger translational speed than it had at the bottom of the hill. Does this mean that the ball somehow *gained* energy by going up the hill? Explain!

71. •• **The kinetic energy of walking.** If a person of mass M
BIO simply moved forward with speed V, his kinetic energy
would be $\frac{1}{2}MV^2$. However, in addition to possessing a forward motion, various parts of his body (such as the arms and
legs) undergo rotation. Therefore, his total kinetic energy is
the sum of the energy from his forward motion plus the rotational kinetic energy of his arms and legs. The purpose of this
problem is to see how much this rotational motion contributes
to the person's kinetic energy. Biomedical measurements
show that the arms and hands together typically make up
13% of a person's mass, while the legs and feet together
account for 37%. For a rough (but reasonable) calculation, we
can model the arms and legs as thin uniform bars pivoting
about the shoulder and hip, respectively. In a brisk walk, the
arms and legs each move through an angle of about $\pm 30°$ (a
total of 60°) from the vertical in approximately 1 second. We
shall assume that they are held straight, rather than being
bent, which is not quite true. Let us consider a 75 kg person
walking at 5.0 km/h, having arms 70 cm long and legs 90 cm
long. (a) What is the average angular velocity of his arms and
legs? (b) Using the average angular velocity from part (a),

calculate the amount of rotational kinetic energy in this person's arms and legs as he walks. (c) What is the total kinetic
energy due to both his forward motion and his rotation?
(d) What percentage of his kinetic energy is due to the rotation of his legs and arms?

72. •• **The kinetic energy of running.** Using the previous prob-
BIO lem as a guide, apply it to a person running at 12 km/h, with
his arms and legs each swinging through $\pm 30°$ in $\frac{1}{2}$ s. As
before, assume that the arms
and legs are kept straight.

73. •• A uniform marble rolls
without slipping down the path
shown in Figure 9.40, starting
from rest. (a) Find the minimum height h required for the
marble not to fall into the pit.
(b) The moment of inertia of
the marble depends on its
radius. Explain why the answer
to part (a) does not depend on
the radius of the marble.

▲ **FIGURE 9.40** Problem 73.

DYNAMICS OF ROTATIONAL MOTION

This roaring menace exemplifies conservation of *angular momentum*—the rotational analog of linear momentum. Like dust devils (their little sisters), tornadoes form from masses of air that have some net rotation. If the center of the mass warms and rises, it pulls in the surrounding air. As this air moves inward, its angular velocity increases . . . as you see.

When you use a wrench to loosen lug nuts when you change a flat tire, the whole wheel starts to turn unless you find a way to hold it still. What is it about the force you apply to the handle of the wrench that makes the wheel turn? More generally, what is it that gives a rotating body an *angular* acceleration? A force is a push or a pull, but to produce rotational motion, we need a twisting or turning action.

In this chapter we'll define a physical quantity, *torque*, that describes the twisting or turning effort of a force. We'll incorporate this quantity into a fundamental dynamic relationship for rotational motion. We also need to look at work and power in rotational motion to understand such problems as how energy is transmitted by a rotating shaft (e.g., a drive shaft or an axle in a car or the shaft of a rotating turbine in a jet engine). Next, we'll develop a new conservation principle, *conservation of angular momentum*, that is useful in analyzing rotational motion, but that has much broader significance as well. We'll explore the relevance of torque for problems involving *equilibrium* of a rigid body. Then we'll conclude this chapter by studying briefly how gyroscopes work. Rotational motion can have some interesting surprises, as you may know if you've ever played with a toy gyroscope.

10.1 Torque

7.1

What is it about a force that determines how effective it is in causing or changing a rotational motion? The magnitude and direction of the force certainly play a role, but the point at which the force is applied is also important. When you try to swing a heavy door open, it's a lot easier if you push near the knob than if you push close to the hinges. The farther from the axis of rotation you push, the more effective the push is. In Figure 10.1, a wrench is being used to loosen a tight bolt. Note that force $\vec{F}_b$, applied at the end of the handle, is more effective than force $\vec{F}_a$, applied near the bolt, even though the two forces have equal magnitude. Force $\vec{F}_c$, directed along the length of the handle, does no good at all.

The quantitative measure of the tendency of a force to cause or change a body's rotational motion is called **torque.** Figure 10.2 shows a body that can rotate about an axis that passes through point O and is perpendicular to the plane of the figure. The body is acted on by a force $\vec{F}_1$ in the plane of the figure. The tendency of $\vec{F}_1$ to cause a rotation about point O depends on the magnitude F_1 of the force. It also depends on the perpendicular distance l_1 between the line of action of the force (i.e., the line along which the force vector lies) and O. The distance l_1 plays the role of the wrench handle, and we call it the **moment arm** (or *lever arm*) of force $\vec{F}_1$ about O. The twisting effort is proportional to both F_1 and l_1. We define the **torque,** or **moment,** of the force $\vec{F}_1$ with respect to point O as the product $F_1 l_1$. We use the Greek letter τ ("tau") to denote torque:

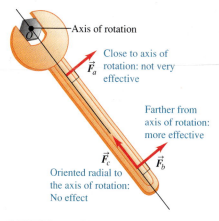

▲ FIGURE 10.1 These three equal forces are *not* equally effective at loosening the nut.

Definition of torque

Torque is a quantitative measure of the tendency of a force to cause or change rotational motion around a chosen axis. Torque is the product of the magnitude of the force and the moment arm, which is the perpendicular distance between the axis and the line of action of the force:

$$\tau = Fl \qquad (10.1)$$

Unit: newton-meter (N · m)

NOTE ▶ The SI unit of torque is the newton-meter. In our discussion of work and energy, we called this combination the *joule*. But torque is *not* work or energy, and torque should be expressed in newton-meters, not joules. ◀

Figure 10.3 shows two additional forces acting on the body shown in Figure 10.2. The moment arm of $\vec{F}_2$ is the perpendicular distance l_2, just as the moment arm of $\vec{F}_1$ is the perpendicular distance l_1. Force $\vec{F}_3$ has a line of action that passes *through* the reference point O, so the moment arm for $\vec{F}_3$ is zero, and its torque with respect to point O is zero. Note that torque is always defined with reference to a specific point that could serve as an axis of rotation. Often (but not always), we take this point as the origin of our coordinate system. If we change the position of that point, the torque of each force usually also changes.

Force $\vec{F}_1$ in Figure 10.3 tends to cause *counterclockwise* rotation about O, and $\vec{F}_2$ tends to cause *clockwise* rotation. To distinguish between these two possibilities, we'll use the convention that **counterclockwise torques are positive and clockwise torques are negative.** With this convention, the torque τ_1 of $\vec{F}_1$ about O is

$$\tau_1 = +F_1 l_1$$

and the torque τ_2 of $\vec{F}_2$ is

$$\tau_2 = -F_2 l_2.$$

Note that this choice of signs is consistent with our choice for angular position, velocity, and acceleration in Section 9.1. Thus, we'll sometimes refer to counterclockwise rotation as the **positive sense of rotation.**

Figure 10.4 shows a force $\vec{F}$ applied at a point P. The vector $\vec{r}$ represents the position of P with respect to the chosen axis through O. There are several alternative ways to calculate the torque of this force. We can find the moment arm l and use $\tau = Fl$. Or we can determine the angle ϕ between the directions of vectors $\vec{F}$ and $\vec{r}$; the moment arm is $r\sin\phi$, so $\tau = rF\sin\phi$. Finally, we can represent $\vec{F}$ in

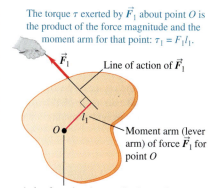

The torque τ exerted by $\vec{F}_1$ about point O is the product of the force magnitude and the moment arm for that point: $\tau_1 = F_1 l_1$.

▲ FIGURE 10.2 The torque of a force about a point is the product of the magnitude of the force and the moment arm.

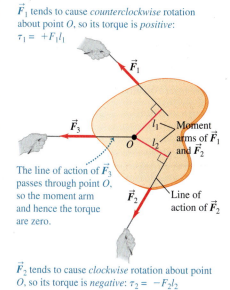

$\vec{F}_1$ tends to cause *counterclockwise* rotation about point O, so its torque is *positive*: $\tau_1 = +F_1 l_1$

$\vec{F}_2$ tends to cause *clockwise* rotation about point O, so its torque is *negative*: $\tau_2 = -F_2 l_2$

▲ FIGURE 10.3 The sign of a torque depends on whether it tends to cause clockwise or counterclockwise rotation about the chosen point. A force whose line of action passes through the chosen point has no torque.

Three ways to calculate torque:
$\tau = Fl = rF\sin\phi = F_{tan}r$

▲ **FIGURE 10.4** The magnitude of the torque caused by a force $\vec{F}$ depends only on the tangential component of the force: $\tau = rF\sin\phi$.

terms of a radial component F_{rad} along the direction of $\vec{r}$ (the radial line from O to P) and a tangential component F_{tan} at right angles, perpendicular to $\vec{r}$. (We call F_{tan} a tangential component because when the object rotates, the point P at which the force acts moves in a circle, and this component is tangent to that circle.) Then $F_{tan} = F\sin\phi$, and

$$\tau = F_{tan}r = r(F\sin\phi) = Fl. \tag{10.2}$$

The component F_{rad} has no torque with respect to O, because its moment arm with respect to that point is zero.

NOTE ▶ Equations 10.1 and 10.2 give the *magnitude* of torque. When we use the sign conventions we've described (counterclockwise positive, clockwise negative), we have to be sure to attach the correct sign to each torque. ◀

EXAMPLE 10.1 **A weekend plumber**

An amateur plumber, unable to loosen a pipe fitting, slips a piece of scrap pipe (a "cheater") over the handle of his wrench. He then applies his full weight of 900 N to the end of the cheater by standing on it. The distance from the center of the fitting to the point where the weight acts is 0.80 m, and the wrench handle and cheater make an angle of 19° with the horizontal (Figure 10.5a). Find the magnitude and direction of the torque of his weight about the center of the pipe fitting.

SOLUTION

SET UP Figure 10.5b diagrams the position of the force exerted by the plumber in relation to the axis of rotation at point O.

SOLVE We have a choice of several methods for solving this problem. From Figure 10.5b, the angle ϕ between the vectors $\vec{r}$ and $\vec{F}$ is 109°, and the moment arm l is

$$l = (0.80\text{ m})(\sin 109°) = (0.80\text{ m})(\sin 71°)$$
$$= 0.76\text{ m}.$$

We can find the magnitude of the torque from either Equation 10.1 or Equation 10.2. From Equation 10.1,

$$\tau = Fl = (900\text{ N})(0.76\text{ m}) = 680\text{ N} \cdot \text{m}.$$

Or, from Equation 10.2,

$$\tau = rF\sin\phi = (0.80\text{ m})(900\text{ N})(\sin 109°) = 680\text{ N} \cdot \text{m}.$$

ALTERNATIVE SOLUTION Alternatively, we can start with the components of $\vec{F}$. From Figure 10.6b, we see that the component of force $\vec{F}$ perpendicular to $\vec{r}$ (which we call F_{tan}, as explained earlier) is

$$F_{tan} = F(\cos 19°) = (900\text{ N})(\cos 19°) = 850\text{ N}.$$

Then the torque is

$$\tau = F_{tan}r = (850\text{ N})(0.80\text{ m}) = 680\text{ N} \cdot \text{m}.$$

REFLECT The force tends to produce a counterclockwise rotation about O, so with the convention described above, this torque is $+680\text{ N} \cdot \text{m}$, *not* $-680\text{ N} \cdot \text{m}$. Also, please don't try to use this plumbing technique at home; you're very likely to break a pipe.

Practice Problem: If the pipe fitting under consideration can withstand a maximum torque of $1000\text{ N} \cdot \text{m}$ without breaking, what is the maximum moment arm at which our amateur plumber can safely apply his full weight? *Answer:* 1.12 m.

(a) Diagram of situation

(b) Free-body diagram

▲ **FIGURE 10.5**

► **Don't fall for it.** To stay balanced while walking the tightrope, this acrobat must keep her center of mass directly above the rope. If the center of mass shifts to one side, gravity will exert a torque on the acrobat, tending to cause a rotation about the rope—a fall. To stay balanced, the acrobat must create a countertorque having equal magnitude and opposite sign. That is why tightrope walkers carry a long pole. Because the torque due to a force is the product of the magnitude of the force and the moment arm, the gravitational forces on the ends of the pole exert significant torques. Thus, the acrobat controls the net torque acting on her center of gravity by manipulating the pole. Also, the acrobat holds the pole low, moving her center of gravity closer to the rope.

Often, one of the important forces acting on a body is its weight. This force is not concentrated at a single point, but is distributed over the entire body. Nevertheless, it turns out that **in a uniform gravitational field, the total torque on a body due to its weight is the same as though all the weight were concentrated at the** *center of mass* **of the body.** We'll derive this relationship later in this chapter and use it for several problems.

10.2 Torque and Angular Acceleration

We're now ready to develop the fundamental dynamical relation for rotational motion of a rigid body. We'll show that the angular acceleration of a rotating body is directly proportional to the sum of the torques with respect to the axis of rotation. The proportionality factor is the moment of inertia.

To develop this relationship, we again imagine a body as being made up of a large number of particles. Figure 10.6 shows a particular particle, labeled A, that has mass m_A and is located a perpendicular distance r_A from the axis of rotation of the body. The *total force* $\vec{F}_A$ acting on this particle has a component $F_{A,\text{rad}}$ along the radial direction and a component $F_{A,\text{tan}}$ tangent to the circle of radius r_A in which the particle moves as the body rotates. (The force $\vec{F}_A$ may also have a component parallel to the axis of rotation, but this component has no torque with respect to the axis and therefore can be ignored in the analysis that follows.) Newton's second law for the tangential components is

$$F_{A,\text{tan}} = m_A a_{A,\text{tan}}. \tag{10.3}$$

We can express $a_{A,\text{tan}}$ in terms of the angular acceleration α, using Equation 9.14: $a_{A,\text{tan}} = r_A \alpha$. Using this relation and multiplying both sides of Equation 10.3 by r_A we obtain

$$F_{A,\text{tan}} r_A = m_A r_A (r_A \alpha) = (m_A r_A^2) \alpha. \tag{10.4}$$

Now, $F_{A,\text{tan}} r_A$ is just the torque τ_A of the force F_A with respect to the axis through point O. Also, $m_A r_A^2$ is the moment of inertia of particle A about this axis. The component $F_{A,\text{rad}}$ acts along a line passing through the axis of rotation and so has no torque with respect to the axis. Hence, we can rewrite Equation 10.4 as

$$\tau_A = I_A \alpha = (m_A r_A^2) \alpha.$$

We can write an equation like this for every particle in the body and then add all the equations together:

$$\tau_A + \tau_B + \tau_C + \cdots = (m_A r_A^2 + m_B r_B^2 + m_C r_C^2 + \cdots) \alpha$$

The left side of this equation is the sum of *all* the torques acting on *all* the particles. We'll call this sum simply $\Sigma \tau$. The right side of the equation is the total moment of inertia (Equation 9.16), namely,

$$I = m_A r_A^2 + m_B r_B^2 + m_C r_C^2 + \cdots,$$

multiplied by the angular acceleration α, which is the same for every particle in the body. Thus, for the entire body, we have the following relationship:

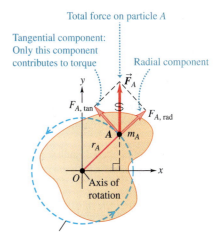

▲ **FIGURE 10.6** The components of the net force acting on one of the particles of a rigid body.

7.8–7.10

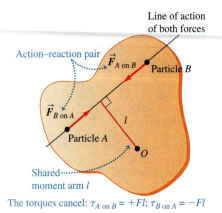

Line of action of both forces

Action–reaction pair $\vec{F}_{A\,\text{on}\,B}$ Particle B

$\vec{F}_{B\,\text{on}\,A}$ l

Particle A

O

Shared moment arm l

The torques cancel: $\tau_{A\,\text{on}\,B} = +Fl$; $\tau_{B\,\text{on}\,A} = -Fl$

▲ **FIGURE 10.7** Why internal forces do not contribute to net torque.

Relation of torque to angular acceleration

The net torque (about a chosen axis) of all the forces acting on a rigid body equals the body's moment of inertia (about that axis), multiplied by its angular acceleration:

$$\sum \tau = I\alpha. \qquad (10.5)$$

This equation is the rotational analog of Newton's second law, $\sum \vec{F} = m\vec{a}$. It is the dynamic relationship we need to relate the rotational motion of a rigid body to the forces acting on it.

Now let's think a little more about the forces. The force $\vec{F}$ on each particle is the vector sum of the external and internal forces acting on it, as we defined these in Section 8.2. The internal forces that any pair of particles exert on each other are an action–reaction pair. According to Newton's third law, they have equal magnitude and opposite direction (Figure 10.7). Assuming that they act along the line joining the two particles, their *moment arms* with respect to any axis are also equal, so the *torques* for each such pair add to zero. Indeed, **the torques due to all the internal forces add to zero,** so the sum of the torques on a body includes only the torques of the *external* forces acting on the body.

Conceptual Analysis 10.1

Net torque on a pulley

Figure 10.8 shows two blocks with equal mass suspended by a cord over a pulley whose mass is half the mass of each block. Block B is given an initial push downward, after which it moves downward with constant velocity. There is no friction in the pulley axle, and the cord's weight can be ignored. While B is moving down,

A. the left cord pulls on the pulley with greater force than the right cord.
B. the left and right cords pull with equal force on the pulley.
C. the right cord pulls with greater force on the pulley than the left cord.

SOLUTION After the initial push, each block moves with constant velocity and so is in equilibrium. The tension in each side of the cord is equal to the weight of one block, so the tensions on the two sides of the cord are equal. The torques applied to the pulley

▲ **FIGURE 10.8**

by the two sides of the cord are equal in magnitude but opposite in sign. Therefore, the net torque on the pulley is zero, and its angular acceleration is zero. The two blocks move with constant velocity, and the pulley turns with constant angular velocity. If either answer A or answer C were correct, the pulley would have a nonzero angular acceleration. Answer B is correct.

Quantitative Analysis 10.2

Rotating masses

Two heavy masses are mounted on a light rod that can be rotated by a string wrapped around a central cylinder of negligible mass, forming a winch (Figure 10.9). A force F is applied to the string to turn the system. With respect to the variables given in the figure, the equation for the angular acceleration α is

A. $rF/2mR^2$.
B. $RF/2mr^2$.
C. $rF/3mR^2$.
D. $RF/3mr^2$.

SOLUTION From Equation 10.5, $\alpha = (\sum \tau)/I$. The only torque with respect to the axis of rotation is supplied by the string force

(magnitude F), which is always tangent to the surface of the small cylinder. The moment arm of the force is the radius r of the cylinder, so the torque is $\tau = rF$. The moment of inertia I is the sum of the mR^2 terms for each mass. Because both m and $2m$ are at distance R from the axis of rotation, the total moment of inertia is $3mR^2$. Combining the results for torque and moment of inertia, we get $rF/3mR^2$ (answer C).

Mass $= 2m$ F Light rod Mass $= m$ r R

▲ **FIGURE 10.9**

PROBLEM-SOLVING STRATEGY 10.1   **Rotational dynamics**

Our strategy for solving problems in rotational dynamics is similar to Problem-Solving Strategy 5.2 on the use of Newton's second law.

SET UP

1. Sketch the situation and select a body or bodies to analyze. You will apply $\sum \vec{F} = m\vec{a}$ or $\sum \tau = I\alpha$, or sometimes both, to each object.
2. Draw a free-body diagram for each body. Because we're now dealing with extended bodies rather than objects that can be treated as particles, your diagram must show the shape of the body accurately, with all dimensions and angles that you'll need for calculations of torque. A body may have translational motion, rotational motion, or both. As always, include all the forces that act on each body (and no others), including the body's weight (taken to act at the center of mass).
3. Choose coordinate axes for each body. Remember that, by convention, the positive sense of rotation is counterclockwise; this is the positive sense for angular position, angular velocity, angular acceleration, and torque.
4. If more than one object is involved, carry out the preceding steps for each object. There may be geometrical relations between the motions of two or more objects or between the translational and rotational motions of the same object. Express these in algebraic form, usually as relations between two linear accelerations or between a linear acceleration and an angular acceleration.

SOLVE

5. Write a separate equation of motion ($\sum \vec{F} = m\vec{a}$ or $\sum \tau = I\alpha$, or both) for each body, including separate equations for the x and y components of forces if necessary. Then solve the equations to find the unknown quantities. This may involve solving a set of simultaneous equations.

REFLECT

6. Check particular cases or extreme values of quantities when possible, and compare the results for these particular cases or values with your intuitive expectations. Ask yourself whether the result makes sense.

EXAMPLE 10.2   Unwinding a winch (again)

Figure 10.10a shows the same situation that we analyzed in Example 9.7. A cable is wrapped several times around a uniform solid cylinder with diameter 0.12 m and mass 50 kg that can rotate freely about its axis. The cable is pulled by a force with magnitude 9.0 N. Assuming that the cable unwinds without stretching or slipping, find the magnitude of its acceleration.

▶ **FIGURE 10.10**   (a)   (b)

Continued

SOLUTION

SET UP We draw a free-body diagram for the cylinder (Figure 10.10b). Because the force acts tangent to the outside of the cylinder, its moment arm relative to the axis of rotation is the cylinder's radius.

SOLVE The torque is $\tau = Fl = (9.0 \text{ N})(0.060 \text{ m}) = 0.54 \text{ N} \cdot \text{m}$. The moment of inertia is

$$I = \tfrac{1}{2}MR^2 = \tfrac{1}{2}(50 \text{ kg})(0.060 \text{ m})^2 = 0.090 \text{ kg} \cdot \text{m}^2.$$

The angular acceleration α is given by Equation 10.5:

$$\alpha = \frac{\tau}{I} = \frac{0.54 \text{ N} \cdot \text{m}}{0.090 \text{ kg} \cdot \text{m}^2} = 6.0 \text{ rad/s}^2.$$

The magnitude a of the acceleration of the cable is given by Equation 9.14:

$$a = R\alpha = (0.060 \text{ m})(6.0 \text{ rad/s}^2)$$
$$= 0.36 \text{ m/s}^2.$$

REFLECT In the equation $\alpha = \tau/I$, check the units to make sure they are consistent.

Practice Problem: Use the preceding results, together with an equation from Chapter 2, to determine the speed of the cable after it has been pulled 2.0 m. Compare your result with Example 9.7, in which we found this speed by using work and energy considerations. *Answer:* 1.2 m/s.

EXAMPLE 10.3 **Dynamics of a bucket in a well**

Let's go back to the old-fashioned well in Example 9.8. Find the acceleration of the bucket (mass m) and the angular acceleration of the winch cylinder.

SOLUTION

SET UP We start by sketching the situation, using the information from Example 9.8 (Figure 10.11a). As before, the winch cylinder has mass M and radius R; the bucket has mass m and falls a distance h. We must treat the two objects separately, so we draw a free-body diagram for each (Figure 10.11b). We take the positive direction of the y coordinate for the bucket to be downward; the positive sense of rotation for the winch is counterclockwise. We assume that the rope is massless and that it unwinds without slipping.

SOLVE Newton's second law applied to the bucket (mass m) gives

$$\sum F_y = mg - T = ma_y.$$

The forces on the cylinder are its weight Mg, the upward normal force n exerted by the axle, and the rope tension T. The first two forces act along lines through the axis of rotation and thus have no torque with respect to that axis. The moment arm of the force T on the cylinder is R, and the torque is $\tau = TR$. Applying Equation 10.5 and the expression for the moment of inertia of a solid cylinder (Table 9.2) to the winch cylinder, we find that

$$\sum \tau = I\alpha \quad \text{and} \quad TR = \tfrac{1}{2}MR^2\alpha.$$

As in Example 10.2, the angular acceleration α of the cylinder is proportional to the magnitude of acceleration a_y of the unwinding rope: $a_y = R\alpha$. We use this equation to replace $(R\alpha)$ with a_y in the cylinder equation, and then we divide by R. The result is

$$T = \tfrac{1}{2}Ma_y.$$

Now we substitute this expression for T into the equation of motion for the bucket (mass m):

$$mg - \tfrac{1}{2}Ma_y = ma_y.$$

(a) Diagram of situation   **(b)** Free-body diagrams

▲ **FIGURE 10.11** Our sketches for this problem.

When we solve this equation for a_y, we get

$$a_y = \frac{g}{1 + M/2m}.$$

Combining this result with the kinematic equation $a_y = R\alpha$, we obtain the angular acceleration α:

$$\alpha = \frac{g/R}{1 + M/2m}.$$

Continued

Finally, we can substitute the equation for a_y back into the equation $\Sigma \vec{F} = m\vec{a}$ for m to get an expression for the tension T in the rope:

$$T = mg - ma_y = mg - m\frac{g}{1 + M/2m} \quad \text{and} \quad T = \frac{mg}{1 + 2m/M}.$$

REFLECT First, note that the tension in the rope is *less than* the weight mg of the bucket; if the two forces were equal (in magnitude), the bucket wouldn't accelerate downward.

We can check two particular cases. When M is much larger than m (a massive winch and a little bucket), the ratio m/M is much smaller than unity. Then the tension is nearly equal to mg, and the acceleration a_y is correspondingly much *less* than g. When M is zero, $T = 0$ and $a = g$; the bucket then falls freely. If

it starts from rest at a height h above the water, its speed v when it strikes the water is given by $v^2 = 2a_y h$; thus,

$$v = \sqrt{2a_y h} = \sqrt{\frac{2gh}{1 + M/2m}}.$$

This is the same result that we obtained from energy considerations in Example 9.8. But note that there we couldn't find the tension in the rope or the accelerations of the winch cylinder and bucket using energy considerations.

Practice Problem: (a) What is the relation between m and M if the bucket's acceleration is half the acceleration of free fall? (b) In this case, what is the rope tension T? *Answer:* (a) $m = M/2$; (b) $T = mg/2 = Mg/4$.

NOTE ▶ In problems such as Example 10.3, in which an object is suspended by a rope, you may be tempted to assume at the start that the tension in the rope is equal to the object's weight. If the object is in equilibrium, this may be true, but when the object accelerates, the tension is usually *not* equal to the object's weight. Be careful! ◀

Rotation about a Moving Axis

In Section 9.5, we discussed the kinetic energy of a rigid body rotating about a moving axis. We can extend our analysis of the dynamics of rotational motion to some cases in which the axis of rotation moves. In these cases, the body has both translational and rotational motion. As we noted in Section 9.5, every possible motion of a rigid body can be represented as a combination of translational motion of the center of mass and rotation about an axis through the center of mass. A rolling wheel or ball and a yo-yo unwinding at the end of a string are familiar examples of such motion.

Activ ONLINE Physics   7.11

The key to this more general analysis, which we won't derive in detail, is that Equation 10.5 ($\Sigma \tau = I\alpha$) is valid *even when the axis of rotation moves* if the following two conditions are met: (1) The axis must be an axis of symmetry and must pass through the center of mass of the body; (2) the axis must not change direction. Note that the moving axis is not necessarily at rest in an inertial frame of reference. The moment of inertia must be computed with respect to the moving axis through the center of mass; to emphasize this point, we'll denote it as I_{cm}.

PROBLEM-SOLVING STRATEGY 10.2 **Rotation about a moving axis** (MP)

The problem-solving strategy outlined in Section 10.2 is equally useful here. There is one new wrinkle: When a rigid body undergoes translational and rotational motion at the same time, we need two separate equations of motion *for the same body*. (The situation is reminiscent of our analysis of projectile motion in Chapter 3, where we used separate equations for the x and y coordinates of a projectile.)

For a rigid body, one of the equations of motion is based on $\Sigma \vec{F} = m\vec{a}$ for the translational motion of the center of mass of the body. We showed in Equation 8.23 that for a body with total mass M, the acceleration $\vec{a}_{cm}$ of the center of mass is the same as that of a point mass M acted on by all the forces that act on the actual body. The other equation of motion is based on $\Sigma \tau = I_{cm}\alpha$ for the rotational motion of the body about the axis through the center of mass with moment of inertia I_{cm}. In addition, there is often a geometric relation between the linear and angular accelerations, such as when a wheel rolls without slipping or a string rotates a pulley while passing over it.

EXAMPLE 10.4 **Dynamics of a primitive yo-yo**

Let's consider again the yo-yo we analyzed in Example 9.9. As shown in Figure 10.12a, the yo-yo consists of a solid disk with radius R and mass M. In our previous analysis, we used energy considerations to find the yo-yo's speed after it had dropped a certain distance. Now let's find the acceleration of the yo-yo and the tension in the string (which we can't do by using energy considerations alone).

SOLUTION

SET UP We start with a free-body diagram, including a coordinate system (Figure 10.12b). If the string unwinds without slipping, the linear displacement of the center of mass of the cylindrical yo-yo in any time interval equals R times its angular displacement. This gives us the kinematic relations $v_{cm,y} = R\omega$ and $a_{cm,y} = R\alpha$. (If this scenario isn't obvious, imagine moving along with the center of mass of the cylinder and watching the string unwind. From that point of view, the kinematic situation is just the same as in Examples 10.2 and 10.3.)

SOLVE The equation for the translational motion of the center of mass is

$$\sum F_y = Mg - T = Ma_{cm,y}.$$

The moment of inertia for an axis through the center of mass is $I_{cm} = \frac{1}{2}MR^2$, and the equation for rotational motion about the axis through the center of mass is

$$\sum \tau = TR = I_{cm}\alpha = \frac{1}{2}MR^2\alpha.$$

We can now combine this equation with the relation $a_{cm,y} = R\alpha$ to eliminate α, obtaining $TR = \frac{1}{2}MRa_{cm,y}$, or $T = \frac{1}{2}Ma_{cm,y}$. Finally, we combine this result with the equation for the center-of-mass motion ($\sum F_y = Mg - T = Ma_{cm,y}$) to obtain expressions for T and $a_{cm,y}$. The results are amazingly simple:

$$a_{cm,y} = \frac{2}{3}g, \qquad T = \frac{1}{3}Mg.$$

(a) The yo-yo   **(b)** Our free-body diagram

▲ FIGURE 10.12

REFLECT The acceleration and tension are both proportional to g, as we should expect. The acceleration is independent of M and R, and the mass cancels out of the dynamic equations. For a yo-yo in the form of a solid disk, the acceleration is exactly two-thirds the acceleration of free fall.

Practice Problem: If the solid cylinder is replaced by a thin cylindrical shell with the same mass and radius as before, find $a_{cm,y}$ and T. *Answer:* $a_{cm,y} = g/2, T = Mg/2$.

EXAMPLE 10.5 **A rolling bowling ball**

A bowling ball rolls without slipping down the return ramp at the side of the alley (Figure 10.13a). The ramp is inclined at an angle β to the horizontal. What is the ball's acceleration? What is the friction force acting on the ball? Treat the ball as a uniform solid sphere, ignoring the finger holes.

SOLUTION

SET UP Again, let's start with a free-body diagram, with the positive coordinate directions indicated (Figure 10.13b). Referring back to Table 9.2, we see that the moment of inertia of a solid sphere about an axis through its center of mass is $I_{cm} = \frac{2}{5}MR^2$. Because the ball rolls without slipping, the acceleration $a_{cm,x}$ of the center of mass is proportional to the ball's angular acceleration α ($a_{cm,x} = R\alpha$). We've represented the forces in terms of their components; it's most convenient to take the axes as parallel and perpendicular to the sloping ramp. The contact force of the ramp on the ball is represented in terms of its normal (n) and frictional (f_s) components. Note that f_s is a *static* friction force, because the ball doesn't slip on the ramp.

SOLVE The equations of motion for translational motion and for rotation about the axis through the center of mass are:

$$\text{Translation: } \sum F_x = Mg\sin\beta - f_s = Ma_{cm,x},$$
$$\text{Rotation: } \sum \tau = f_s R = I_{cm}\alpha = \left(\frac{2}{5}MR^2\right)\alpha.$$

We eliminate α from the second equation by using the kinematic relation $a_{cm} = R\alpha$. Then we express I_{cm} in terms of M and R and divide through by R:

$$f_s R = I_{cm}\alpha = \left(\frac{2}{5}MR^2\right)\left(\frac{a_{cm,x}}{R}\right) \quad \text{and} \quad f_s = \frac{2}{5}Ma_{cm,x}.$$

Next, we insert this expression for f_s into the first equation above and solve for $a_{cm,x}$:

$$Mg\sin\beta - \frac{2}{5}Ma_{cm,x} = Ma_{cm,x},$$
$$a_{cm,x} = \frac{5}{7}g\sin\beta.$$

Continued

Finally, we substitute the right-hand side of this result back into the expression for f_s to obtain

$$f_s = \tfrac{2}{7}Mg\sin\beta.$$

REFLECT The acceleration is $\tfrac{5}{7}$ as large as it would be if the ball could *slide* without friction down the slope, like the toboggan in Example 5.12 (Section 5.2). That is why the friction force f_s is a *static* friction force; it is needed to prevent slipping and to give the ball its angular acceleration. We can derive an expression for the minimum coefficient of static friction μ_s needed to prevent slipping. The magnitude of the normal force is $n = Mg\cos\beta$. To prevent slipping, the coefficient of friction must be at least as great as

$$\mu_s = \frac{\tfrac{2}{7}Mg\sin\beta}{Mg\cos\beta} = \tfrac{2}{7}\tan\beta.$$

If the plane is tilted only a little, β and $\tan\beta$ are small, and only a small value of μ_s is needed to prevent slipping. But as the angle increases, the required value of μ_s also increases, as we would expect intuitively.

Finally, suppose μ_s is *not* large enough to prevent slipping. Then we have a whole new ball game, so to speak. Our basic dynamic equations are still valid, but now the ball slides and rotates at the same time. There is no longer a definite relation between $a_{cm,x}$ and α, and the friction force is now a *kinetic* friction force, given by $f_k = \mu_k n = \mu_k Mg\cos\beta$. The acceleration of the center of mass is then

$$a_{cm,x} = g(\sin\beta - \mu_k\cos\beta).$$

This is the same result that we found in Example 5.12 (Section 5.3), in which we hoped that the toboggan would slide, and not roll, down the hill.

Practice Problem: Suppose we replace the bowling ball with a solid cylinder. Then the minimum coefficient of static friction needed to prevent slipping is $\mu_s = k\tan\beta$, where k is a dimensionless constant (equal to $\tfrac{2}{7}$ for the bowling ball). Determine the value of k for the cylinder. *Answer:* $k = \tfrac{1}{3}$.

(a)   **(b)**

▲ **FIGURE 10.13**

10.3 Work and Power in Rotational Motion

When you pedal a bicycle, you apply forces to a rotating body and do work on it. Similar things happen in many real-life situations, such as a rotating motor shaft driving a power tool or a car engine propelling the vehicle. We can express this work in terms of torque and angular displacement.

Suppose a tangential force with constant magnitude F_{tan} acts at the rim of a merry-go-round platform with radius R (Figure 10.14) while the platform rotates through an angle $\Delta\theta$ about a fixed axis during a small time interval Δt. The displacement of the point at which the force acts is Δs. By definition, the work ΔW done by the force F_{tan} is $\Delta W = F_{tan}\Delta s$. If θ is measured in radians, $\Delta s = R\Delta\theta$, and it follows that

$$\Delta W = F_{tan}R\,\Delta\theta.$$

Now, $F_{tan}R$ is the *torque* τ due to the force F_{tan}, so

$$\Delta W = \tau\,\Delta\theta. \tag{10.6}$$

If the torque is *constant* while the angle changes by a finite amount $\Delta\theta = \theta_2 - \theta_1$, then the work done on the body by the torque is as follows:

◄ **A two-oxpower engine?** Long before the invention of electricity and 1000 horsepower racing engines, people relied on animals to provide power for daily chores such as lifting water from a well. For rotational motion, like that used to turn this well lift, power is proportional to torque, and torque is the product of the force applied times the distance from the center of rotation. So to produce the maximum power to operate this well, while walking at a comfortable speed, these animals are applying their force a large distance away from the center. This maximizes the torque applied and increases the power available for lifting the water from the bottom of the well.

Work done by a constant torque

The work done on a body by a constant torque equals the product of the torque and the angular displacement of the body:

$$W = \tau(\theta_2 - \theta_1) = \tau \, \Delta\theta. \qquad (10.7)$$

This equation is the rotational analog of Equation 7.1, $W = F_{\parallel}s$, for the work done by a constant force with component $F_{\parallel}$ in the direction of displacement.

Unit: If τ is expressed in newton-meters $(\text{N} \cdot \text{m})$ and θ in radians, the work is in joules.

Child applies tangential force

$\vec{F}_{\text{tan}}$

(a)

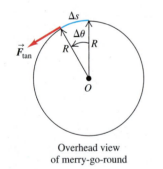

Δs

$\Delta\theta$

$\vec{F}_{\text{tan}}$

R R

O

Overhead view of merry-go-round

(b)

▲ **FIGURE 10.14** The work done by a tangential force acting on a body.

The force in Figure 10.14b has no radial component. If there were such a component, it would do no work, because the displacement of the point of application has no radial component. A radial component of force would also make no contribution to the torque about the axis of rotation, so Equations 10.6 and 10.7 are correct for any force, even if it does have a radial component. The same argument applies to an *axial* component of force—that is, a component parallel to the axis of rotation.

What about the *power* associated with work done by a torque acting on a rotating body? When we divide both sides of Equation 10.7 by the time interval Δt during which the angular displacement occurs, we find that

$$\frac{\Delta W}{\Delta t} = \tau \frac{\Delta\theta}{\Delta t}.$$

But $\Delta W / \Delta t$ is the rate of doing work, or *power P*, and $\Delta\theta / \Delta t$ is the body's angular velocity ω, so we obtain the following relation for power in rotational motion:

$$P = \tau\omega. \qquad (10.8)$$

When a torque τ (with respect to the axis of rotation) acts on a body that rotates with angular velocity ω, its power (rate of doing work) is the product of torque and angular velocity. This is the analog of the relation $P = Fv$ that we developed in Chapter 7 for particle motion.

NOTE ▶ In the relations just derived, angular displacements *must* be expressed in radians and angular velocities in radians per second. ◄

EXAMPLE 10.6   Power of an electric motor

An electric motor exerts a constant torque of $\tau = 10\,\text{N} \cdot \text{m}$ on a grindstone mounted on its shaft; the moment of inertia of the grindstone is $I = 2.0\,\text{kg} \cdot \text{m}^2$. If the system starts from rest, find the work done by the motor in 8.0 s and the kinetic energy at the end of this time. What was the average power delivered by the motor?

Continued

SOLUTION

SET UP AND SOLVE We want to use Equation 10.7 ($W = \tau\,\Delta\theta$) to find the total work done and then divide that by the time interval $\Delta t = 8.0$ s to find the average power (work per unit time). But first we need to find the total angle $\Delta\theta$ (in radians) through which the grindstone turns. The angular acceleration α is constant, so we can use $\tau = I\alpha$ to find α and then apply the formulas developed in Chapter 9 for constant angular acceleration.

The angular acceleration is

$$\alpha = \frac{\tau}{I} = \frac{10\ \text{N} \cdot \text{m}}{2.0\ \text{kg} \cdot \text{m}^2} = 5.0\ \text{rad/s}^2.$$

For constant angular acceleration,

$$\theta = \theta_0 + \omega_0 t + \tfrac{1}{2}\alpha t^2 = 0 + 0 + \tfrac{1}{2}(5.0\ \text{rad/s}^2)(8\ \text{s})^2 = 160\ \text{rad}.$$

The total work is

$$W = \tau\,\Delta\theta = (10\ \text{N} \cdot \text{m})(160\ \text{rad}) = 1600\ \text{J}.$$

Finally, the average power is the total work divided by the time interval:

$$P_{av} = \frac{W}{\Delta t} = \frac{1600\ \text{J}}{8.0\ \text{s}} = 200\ \text{J/s} = 200\ \text{W}.$$

REFLECT We can check the energy relations. The angular velocity of the grindstone after 8.0 s is

$$\omega = \alpha t = (5.0\ \text{rad/s}^2)(8.0\ \text{s}) = 40\ \text{rad/s}.$$

The grindstone's kinetic energy at this time is

$$K = \tfrac{1}{2}I\omega^2 = \tfrac{1}{2}(2.0\ \text{kg} \cdot \text{m}^2)(40\ \text{rad/s})^2 = 1600\ \text{J}.$$

This amount equals the total work done, as of course it must. Note that the power is *not* constant during this process. The torque is constant, but as the angular velocity increases, so does the rate of doing work. The instantaneous power, $\tau\omega$, increases linearly with time, from zero, when $\omega = 0$, to 400 W, with an average value of 200 W.

Practice Problem: In this problem, suppose we use a larger motor that applies a constant torque of $20\ \text{N} \cdot \text{m}$. Find the total work done in 8.0 s and the average power during this period. *Answer:* 6400 J, 800 W.

10.4 Angular Momentum

An Olympic ice skater with outstretched arms sets herself spinning about a vertical axis. When she pulls her arms in to her sides, she spins faster. When an Olympic diver goes off the high board in a "layout" position and then pulls his knees in toward his chest into a "tuck" position, he spins faster, even though there is no appreciable external torque acting on him. Both of these familiar phenomena, and many others (Figure 10.15), can be understood on the basis of a quantity called *angular momentum*, which we'll introduce in this section.

Every rotational quantity that we've seen so far in this chapter and the previous one is the analog of some quantity related to the motion of a particle. Angular momentum is the analog of the linear momentum ($\vec{p} = m\vec{v}$) of a particle. We define angular momentum as follows:

Definition of angular momentum

When a rigid body with moment of inertia I (with respect to a specified symmetry axis) rotates with angular velocity ω about that axis, the **angular momentum** of the body with respect to the axis is the product of the moment of inertia I about the axis and the angular velocity ω. We denote angular momentum by L:

$$L = I\omega. \tag{10.9}$$

The sign of angular momentum depends on the sign of ω; thus, according to our usual convention, it is positive for counterclockwise rotation and negative for clockwise rotation.

Unit: $\text{kg} \cdot \text{m}^2/\text{s}$

▲ **FIGURE 10.15** As this diver goes into a tuck, her rotation speeds up, because angular momentum is conserved.

▲ **Gearing down.** Nanoengineering involves the construction of submicroscopic machines, often built through the manipulation of individual atoms. Engineers have recently made tiny gears from carbon "nanotubes" with interlocking teeth made of organic molecules precisely placed on the tube surfaces. The operation of these gears is based on the same physical principles of torque and angular momentum as are applied to their macroscopic counterparts. To turn the gears, a laser shines tangentially onto the atoms at the end of the cylinder, creating a torque. This torque can cause a gear to rotate up to several thousand times per nanosecond.

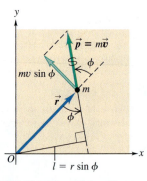

▲ **FIGURE 10.16** A particle with mass m rotating in the x-y plane. The angular momentum of the particle has magnitude $L = mvl$.

The basic dynamic principle for rotational motion (Equation 10.5, $\sum \tau = I\alpha$) can be restated in terms of angular momentum. If the axis doesn't move within the rotating object, then I is constant. In that case,

$$I\alpha = I\frac{\Delta\omega}{\Delta t} = \frac{\Delta(I\omega)}{\Delta t} = \frac{\Delta L}{\Delta t},$$

and Equation 10.5 can be rewritten as follows:

> **Torque and rate of change of angular momentum**
> The rate of change of angular momentum of a rigid body with respect to any axis equals the sum of the torques of the forces acting on it with respect to that axis:
>
> $$\sum \tau = \frac{\Delta L}{\Delta t}. \tag{10.10}$$

We'll use this result soon when we discuss a conservation principle for angular momentum.

We can also define angular momentum for a single particle. In Figure 10.16, a particle moves in the x-y plane; its radial and tangential components of velocity are shown. The instantaneous velocity and linear momentum of the particle lie along a line at a perpendicular distance l from the axis through point O. We define the angular momentum of this particle as

$$L = mvl. \tag{10.11}$$

In the figure, the directions of $\vec{v}$ and $\vec{p}$ correspond to a counterclockwise (positive) sense of rotation. The distance l serves as a moment arm for the velocity, analogous to the moment arm (or lever arm) of a force in the definition of torque.

Equation 10.11 is consistent with our original definition of angular momentum of a rigid body. Suppose the object consists of a collection of particles with masses $m_A, m_B, m_C, \ldots$ at distances $r_A, r_B, r_C, \ldots$ from the axis through O. For each particle, the angle ϕ in Figure 10.16 is $90°$, so the moment arm l for particle A is its distance r_A from the axis of rotation. When the object rotates with angular velocity ω, the magnitude v_A of the velocity of particle A is $v_A = \omega r_A$, and the angular momentum L_A of this particle is

$$L_A = m_A v_A r_A = m_A(\omega r_A) r_A = m_A r_A^2 \omega.$$

If the object is rigid, *all* the particles must have the same angular velocity ω; the total angular momentum of all the particles is then

$$L = (m_A r_A^2 + m_B r_B^2 + m_C r_C^2 + \cdots)\omega = I\omega,$$

in agreement with our previous definition of the angular momentum of a rigid body.

> **NOTE** ▶ As with all angular quantities, angular momentum is defined with reference to a particular axis of rotation. It is essential to specify this axis and use it consistently when applying the principles we've just discussed. ◀

Equation 10.10 will be particularly useful when we develop the principle of conservation of angular momentum in the next section. We've discussed changes in angular momentum that occur when the angular velocity ω of a body changes, but there are also cases in which ω is constant and I changes because of a change of shape or rearrangement of component parts of a body. In cases where I isn't constant, Equation 10.5 ($\sum \tau = I\alpha$) isn't valid. But the angular momentum is still given at each instant by $L = I\omega$, and the rate of change of angular momentum is still given by Equation 10.10. The next section includes some examples in which we have to take this more general view.

We've discussed angular momentum in the context of macroscopic bodies, but it is vitally important in physics at all scales, from nuclear to galactic. Angular momentum plays an essential role in classifying the quantum states of nuclei, atoms, and molecules and in describing their interactions. Angular momentum considerations are also an important tool in analyzing the motions of stars, galaxies, and nebulae. Along with mass, energy, and momentum, angular momentum is one of the unifying threads woven through the entire fabric of physical science.

EXAMPLE 10.7　A kinetic sculpture

A part of a mobile suspended from the ceiling of an airport terminal building consists of two metal spheres, each with mass 2.0 kg, connected by a uniform metal rod with mass 3.0 kg and length $s = 4.0$ m. The assembly is suspended at its midpoint by a wire and rotates in a horizontal plane, making 3.0 revolutions per minute. Find the angular momentum and kinetic energy of the assembly.

SOLUTION

SET UP Figure 10.17 shows our sketch. We draw the assembly as viewed from above (or below), in its plane of rotation.

SOLVE First, we need to find the moment of inertia of the assembly about an axis through its midpoint; we'll assume that each sphere can be treated as a point. Then the angular momentum L is given by $L = I\omega$, and the kinetic energy is $K = \frac{1}{2}I\omega^2$.

The moment of inertia of each sphere (treated as a point) is

$$I_{sphere} = m\left(\frac{s}{2}\right)^2 = (2.0 \text{ kg})(2.0 \text{ m})^2 = 8.0 \text{ kg} \cdot \text{m}^2.$$

From Table 9.2, the moment of inertia of a rod about an axis through its midpoint and perpendicular to its length is

$$I_{rod} = \tfrac{1}{12}Ms^2 = \tfrac{1}{12}(3.0 \text{ kg})(4.0 \text{ m})^2 = 4.0 \text{ kg} \cdot \text{m}^2.$$

So the total moment of inertia of the assembly is

$$I_{total} = 2(8.0 \text{ kg} \cdot \text{m}^2) + 4.0 \text{ kg} \cdot \text{m}^2 = 20 \text{ kg} \cdot \text{m}^2.$$

The angular velocity is given in revolutions per minute; we must convert it to radians per second:

$$\omega = 3.0 \text{ rev/min} = \left(\frac{3.0 \text{ rev}}{1 \text{ min}}\right)\left(\frac{1 \text{ min}}{60 \text{ s}}\right)\left(\frac{2\pi \text{ rad}}{1 \text{ rev}}\right) = 0.31 \text{ rad/s}.$$

▲ **FIGURE 10.17**

Now we can calculate the angular momentum of the assembly:

$$L = I\omega = (20 \text{ kg} \cdot \text{m}^2)(0.31 \text{ rad/s}) = 6.2 \text{ kg} \cdot \text{m}^2/\text{s}.$$

The kinetic energy is

$$K = \tfrac{1}{2}I\omega^2 = \tfrac{1}{2}(20 \text{ kg} \cdot \text{m}^2)(0.31 \text{ rad/s})^2$$
$$= 0.96 \text{ kg} \cdot \text{m}^2/\text{s}^2 = 0.96 \text{ J}.$$

REFLECT The mass of the rod is comparable to that of the spheres, but it contributes less to the total moment of inertia because most of its mass is closer to the axis of rotation than are the masses of the spheres.

Practice Problem: How long would an equal-mass rod have to be in order for its contribution to the total moment of inertia to equal that of the two spheres together? *Answer:* 8.0 m.

10.5 Conservation of Angular Momentum

We've seen that angular momentum can be used in an alternative statement of the basic dynamic principle for rotational motion. Angular momentum also forms the basis for a very important conservation principle: the principle of **conservation of angular momentum.** Like conservation of energy and conservation of linear momentum, this principle appears to be a universal conservation law, valid at all scales, from atomic and nuclear systems to the motions of galaxies.

Activ
ONLINE
Physics　7.14

The principle is based on the concept of an **isolated system,** introduced in Section 8.2. We generalize this term to mean a system in which the total external force is zero *and* the total external torque is zero. Then our new conservation principle states simply that **the total angular momentum of an isolated system is constant.**

◀ **The day the day got shorter.** The earthquake that caused the devastating tsunami of December 26, 2004, represented a rupture along a 1200 km stretch of the fault where the India plate of the earth's crust dives under the Burma plate, allowing the India plate to move downward by about 15 m. This downward shift of mass reduced our planet's moment of inertia slightly. Its angular momentum about its axis of rotation is very nearly constant; to conserve this angular momentum, the speed of rotation increased, shortening the length of the day. Scientists estimated that the quake shortened the length of the day by 2.7 microseconds.

The proof of this principle follows directly from Equation 10.10 ($\sum \tau = \Delta L / \Delta t$). When a system has several parts, the internal forces that the parts exert on each other cause changes in the angular momenta of the parts, but the *total* angular momentum of the system doesn't change. Here's an example: When two bodies A and B interact with each other but not with anything else, A and B together form an *isolated system*. Suppose body A exerts a force $\vec{F}_{A \text{ on } B}$ on body B; the corresponding torque (with respect to whatever axis we choose) is $\tau_{A \text{ on } B}$. According to Equation 10.10, this torque is equal to the rate of change of angular momentum of B:

$$\tau_{A \text{ on } B} = \frac{\Delta L_B}{\Delta t}.$$

At the same time, body B exerts a force $\vec{F}_{B \text{ on } A}$ on body A, with a corresponding torque $\tau_{B \text{ on } A}$, and

$$\tau_{B \text{ on } A} = \frac{\Delta L_A}{\Delta t}.$$

From Newton's third law, $\vec{F}_{B \text{ on } A} = -\vec{F}_{A \text{ on } B}$. Furthermore, if the forces act along the same line, their moment arms with respect to the chosen axis are equal. Figure 10.7 demonstrated this point; we repeat it here as Figure 10.18. Thus, the torques of these two forces are equal and opposite, and $\tau_{B \text{ on } A} = -\tau_{A \text{ on } B}$. So when we add the preceding two equations, we find that

$$\frac{\Delta L_A}{\Delta t} + \frac{\Delta L_B}{\Delta t} = 0,$$

or, because $L_A + L_B$ is the *total* angular momentum L of the system,

$$\frac{\Delta L}{\Delta t} = 0. \tag{10.12}$$

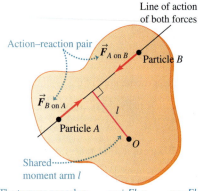

▲ **FIGURE 10.18** Why internal forces cannot change the total angular momentum of a system.

That is, the total angular momentum of the system is constant; we also say that it is *conserved*. The torques of the internal forces can transfer angular momentum from one interacting object to another, but they can't change the *total* angular momentum of the system.

Conservation of angular momentum
When the sum of the torques of all the external forces acting on a system is zero, the total angular momentum of the system is constant (conserved).

An ice skater performing a pirouette on the toe of one skate takes advantage of this principle. Figure 10.19 shows the skater at the start of her pirouette, with her arms extended and with a counterclockwise angular momentum. As she pulls in her arms, she reduces her moment of inertia I. Because her angular momentum $L = I\omega$ must remain constant as I decreases, her angular velocity ω increases; she spins faster. That is,

$$I_i \omega_i = I_f \omega_f. \tag{10.13}$$

▲ **FIGURE 10.19** As this skater reduces her moment of inertia by pulling in her arms, she spins faster, conserving angular momentum.

A diver going into a tuck uses the same principle. Only by reducing his moment of inertia is he able to rotate multiple times before hitting the water. Notice that the skater and the diver can both be treated as isolated systems. The net external forces and torques on the skater are slight. Gravity has a major effect on the diver's translational motion, but once he is in the air it exerts no net torque on him. Thus, in terms of angular momentum, he is isolated.

EXAMPLE 10.8 Two rotating disks interacting

Figure 10.20 shows two disks, one an engine flywheel, the other a clutch plate attached to a transmission shaft. Their moments of inertia are I_A and I_B; initially, they are rotating with constant angular velocities ω_A and ω_B, respectively. We then push the disks together with forces acting along the axis, so as not to apply any torque on either disk. The disks rub against each other and eventually reach a common final angular velocity ω_f. Derive an expression for ω_f.

▶ **FIGURE 10.20**

SOLUTION

SET UP The two disks are an isolated system. The only torque acting on either disk is the torque applied by the other disk; there are no external torques. Thus the total angular momentum of the system is the same before and after they are pushed together. At the end, they rotate together as one body with total moment of inertia $I_f = I_A + I_B$ and angular velocity ω_f.

SOLVE Conservation of angular momentum gives

$$I_A\omega_A + I_B\omega_B = (I_A + I_B)\omega_f,$$
$$\omega_f = \frac{I_A\omega_A + I_B\omega_B}{I_A + I_B}.$$

REFLECT This is the analog of a completely inelastic collision of two particles, which we analyzed in Section 8.3. The final kinetic energy is always less than the initial value. This can be proved in general, using the above expression for ω_f.

Practice Problem: Suppose $I_B = 2I_A$. How must ω_A and ω_B be related if the entire system comes to rest after the interaction? *Answer:* $\omega_A = -2\omega_B$.

Quantitative Analysis 10.3 Mass on a string: I

In Figure 10.21, a block slides in a circular path on a horizontal frictionless plane under the action of a string that passes through a hole in the plane and is held vertically underneath it. By pulling on the lower end of the string, we reduce the radius to half of its original value. If the initial speed of the block is v_i, then the speed of the block after the string is shortened is

A. $\frac{1}{2}v_i$.   B. $2v_i$.   C. $4v_i$.

SOLUTION From Equation 10.11 the angular momentum of the block about a vertical axis through the hole is mvr. The force from the string pulls directly toward the axis. Therefore, it exerts no torque with respect to this axis, and it cannot change the block's angular momentum. Thus the angular momentum mvr of

▲ **FIGURE 10.21**

the block must be constant. If r is reduced by half, then v must double to keep the angular momentum constant (answer B).

Quantitative Analysis 10.4

Mass on a string: II

Let's consider again the whirling block shown in Figure 10.21. By letting additional string pass through the hole in the plane, we increase the radius to twice its original value. If the initial tension in the string is T, then the tension in the string after the radius is increased is

A. $\frac{1}{2}T$.

B. $\frac{1}{4}T$.

C. $\frac{1}{8}T$.

SOLUTION From Quantitative Analysis 10.3, we see that in this situation the angular momentum of the block doesn't change: if r is doubled, then v must decrease by half. The tension T provides the needed centripetal force, according to the relationship $T = mv^2/r$. In the situation presented here, r doubles and v is reduced to half its original value. Thus, in the expression for T, the denominator doubles and the numerator is reduced to one-fourth its initial value, for an overall reduction of T to one-eighth of its initial value (answer C).

EXAMPLE 10.9 Anyone can be a ballerina

An acrobatic physics professor stands at the center of a turntable, holding his arms extended horizontally, with a 5.0 kg dumbbell in each hand (Figure 10.22). He is set rotating about a vertical axis, making one revolution in 2.0 s. His moment of inertia (without the dumbbells) is $3.0 \text{ kg} \cdot \text{m}^2$ when his arms are outstretched, and drops to $2.2 \text{ kg} \cdot \text{m}^2$ when his arms are pulled in close to his chest. The dumbbells are 1.0 m from the axis initially and 0.20 m from it at the end. Find the professor's new angular velocity if he pulls the dumbbells close to his chest, and compare the final total kinetic energy with the initial value.

▶ **FIGURE 10.22**   BEFORE   AFTER

SOLUTION

SET UP If we neglect friction in the turntable, there are no external torques with respect to the vertical axis, and the angular momentum about this axis is constant. That is,

$$I_i \omega_i = I_f \omega_f,$$

where I_i and ω_i are the initial total moment of inertia and angular velocity, respectively, and I_f and ω_f are the final values.

SOLVE In each case, $I = I_{prof} + I_{dumb}$; thus,

$$I_i = 3.0 \text{ kg} \cdot \text{m}^2 + 2(5.0 \text{ kg})(1.0 \text{ m})^2 = 13 \text{ kg} \cdot \text{m}^2$$
$$I_f = 2.2 \text{ kg} \cdot \text{m}^2 + 2(5.0 \text{ kg})(0.20 \text{ m})^2 = 2.6 \text{ kg} \cdot \text{m}^2$$
$$\omega_i = 2\pi \frac{1 \text{ rev}}{2.0 \text{ s}} = \pi \text{ rad/s}.$$

From conservation of angular momentum,

$$(13 \text{ kg} \cdot \text{m}^2)(\pi \text{ rad/s}) = (2.6 \text{ kg} \cdot \text{m}^2)\omega_f,$$
$$\omega_f = 5.0\pi \text{ rad/s} = 2.5 \text{ rev/s}.$$

That is, the angular velocity increases by a factor of five.

The initial kinetic energy is

$$K_i = \frac{1}{2}I_i\omega_i^2 = \frac{1}{2}(13 \text{ kg} \cdot \text{m}^2)(\pi \text{ rad/s})^2$$
$$= 64 \text{ J}.$$

The final kinetic energy is

$$K_f = \frac{1}{2}I_f\omega_f^2 = \frac{1}{2}(2.6 \text{ kg} \cdot \text{m}^2)(5.0\pi \text{ rad/s})^2$$
$$= 320 \text{ J}.$$

REFLECT Where did the "extra" 256 J of kinetic energy come from?

Practice Problem: Suppose the professor drops the dumbbells and then pulls his arms close to his chest. What is his final angular velocity? *Answer:* 0.68 rev/s.

EXAMPLE 10.10 Angular momentum in a crime bust

A uniform door 1.0 m wide with a mass of 15 kg is hinged at one side so that it can rotate without friction about a vertical axis. The door is unlatched. A police detective fires a bullet with a mass of 10 g and a speed of 400 m/s into the exact center of the door in a direction perpendicular to the plane of the door. Find the angular velocity of the door just after the bullet embeds itself in it. Is kinetic energy conserved?

Continued

SOLUTION

SET UP We consider the door and bullet together as a system. We denote the mass of the bullet as m, the mass of the door as M, and the door's width as s. Figure 10.23 shows our sketch. There is no external torque about the axis defined by the hinges, so angular momentum about this axis is conserved. We find the initial angular momentum of the bullet from Equation 10.11 ($L = mvl$). This quantity is equal to the final total angular momentum $I_{total}\omega_f$, where $I_{total} = I_{door} + I_{bullet}$. From Table 9.2, $I_{door} = Ms^2/3$. (Table 9.2 uses L for the length of the body, measured perpendicular to the axis; we substitute s here to avoid confusion with angular momentum L.)

SOLVE We compute all moments of inertia and angular momenta with respect to the axis defined by the door's hinges. The initial angular momentum of the bullet is

$$L_{bullet} = m_{bullet}v_{bullet}l = (0.010\ \text{kg})(400\ \text{m/s})(0.50\ \text{m})$$
$$= 2.0\ \text{kg} \cdot \text{m}^2/\text{s}.$$

The moment of inertia of the door is

$$I_{door} = \frac{Ms^2}{3} = \frac{(15\ \text{kg})(1.0\ \text{m})^2}{3} = 5.0\ \text{kg} \cdot \text{m}^2.$$

The moment of inertia of the bullet (with respect to the axis along the hinges) is

$$I_{bullet} = ml^2 = (0.010\ \text{kg})(0.50\ \text{m})^2 = 0.0025\ \text{kg} \cdot \text{m}^2.$$

Conservation of angular momentum requires that $m_{bullet}v_{bullet}l = I_{total}\omega_f$, so we can solve for the final angular velocity ω_f:

$$2.0\ \text{kg} \cdot \text{m}^2/\text{s} = (5.0\ \text{kg} \cdot \text{m}^2 + 0.0025\ \text{kg} \cdot \text{m}^2)\omega_f,$$
$$\omega_f = 0.40\ \text{rad/s}.$$

The initial kinetic energy of the bullet is

$$K_i = \tfrac{1}{2}mv^2 = \tfrac{1}{2}(0.010\ \text{kg})(400\ \text{m/s})^2$$
$$= 800\ \text{J}.$$

▲ **FIGURE 10.23**

The final total kinetic energy of the door and bullet is

$$K_f = \tfrac{1}{2}I\omega^2 = \tfrac{1}{2}(5.0025\ \text{kg} \cdot \text{m}^2)(0.40\ \text{rad/s})^2$$
$$= 0.40\ \text{J}.$$

REFLECT Kinetic energy is *not* conserved. The final kinetic energy is only $\frac{1}{2000}$ of the initial value. The collision of bullet and door is inelastic because nonconservative forces act during the impact. Thus, we do not expect kinetic energy to be conserved.

Practice Problem: Suppose the bullet goes through the door and emerges with a speed of 100 m/s. Find the final angular velocity of the door just after the bullet goes through it. *Answer:* 0.30 rad/s.

10.6 Equilibrium of a Rigid Body

Here's an experiment to try: Face a wall, with your toes just touching the wall. Now try standing on tiptoe. What happens? You start falling over backward. Why? There is a net torque on you, and you are no longer in equilibrium. The need to consider torque occurs with a suspension bridge, a ladder leaning against a wall, or a crane hoisting a bucket full of concrete.

A body that can be modeled as a particle is in equilibrium whenever the vector sum of the forces acting on it is zero. But for the problems that we've just described, that condition isn't enough. Many bodies can't be adequately modeled as particles. The vector sum of the forces on such a body must still be zero, but an additional requirement must be satisfied to ensure that the body has no tendency to *rotate*. This requirement is based on the principles of rotational dynamics developed in this chapter. For a rigid body in equilibrium, the sum of the *torques* about any axis must be zero. We can compute the torque due to the weight of a body using the concept of center of mass from Section 8.6 and the related concept of center of gravity, which we'll introduce in this section.

Conditions for Equilibrium

We learned in Section 5.1 that a particle acted on by several forces is in equilibrium (in an inertial frame of reference) if the vector sum of the forces acting on the particle is zero ($\sum \vec{F} = 0$). This is often called the **first condition for equilibrium.** In terms of x and y components,

$$\sum F_x = 0, \qquad \sum F_y = 0. \tag{10.14}$$

For a rigid body, there is a **second condition for equilibrium** that must be met if the body is not to rotate:

Second condition for equilibrium
The sum of the torques due to all forces acting on the body, with respect to any specified axis, must be zero:

$$\sum \tau = 0. \quad \text{(about any axis)} \tag{10.15}$$

The second condition for equilibrium is based on the dynamics of rotational motion in exactly the same way that the first condition is based on Newton's first law. A rigid body at rest has zero angular momentum ($L = 0$). For it to *remain* at rest, the *rate of change* of angular momentum $\Delta L / \Delta t$ must also be zero. From Equation 10.10, this means that the sum of the torques ($\sum \tau$) of all the forces acting on the object must be zero. Furthermore, because every point in the body is at rest in an inertial frame, any axis can be used as a reference line. Therefore, the sum of the torques about *any* axis must be zero. The object doesn't actually have to be pivoted about an axis through the chosen point. If a rigid body is in equilibrium, it can't have any tendency to begin to rotate about *any* axis. Thus, the sum of the torques must be zero, *no matter what axis is chosen.* (But don't compute some of the torques with respect to one axis and others with respect to a different axis; choose one axis and use it consistently.)

Although the choice of axis is arbitrary, once we choose it we must use the same axis to calculate all of the torques. An important element of the strategy for problems involving torques is to pick the axis or axes so as to simplify the calculations as much as possible.

Torque Due to Gravitational Force

In most equilibrium problems, one of the forces acting on the object is its weight. We need to be able to calculate the torque of this force. The weight doesn't act at a single point; rather, it is distributed over the entire body. But when the acceleration due to gravity is the same at every point in the body, we can always calculate the torque due to the body's weight by assuming that the entire force of gravity is concentrated at the center of mass of the object, which we defined in Equation 8.18. We stated this principle, without detailed proof, in Section 10.1. Because of it, the center of mass of an object is sometimes called its *center of gravity* (cg). Note, however, that the center of mass is defined independently of any gravitational effect.

We can often use symmetry considerations to locate the center of gravity of a body. **The center of gravity of a homogeneous sphere, cube, circular disk, or rectangular plate is at its geometric center. The center of gravity of a right circular cylinder or cone is on the axis of symmetry, and so on.**

The center of gravity has several other important properties. First, when a body is in equilibrium in a gravitational field, supported or suspended at a single point, the center of gravity is always at or directly above or below the point of suspension. If it were anywhere else, the weight would have a torque with respect to that point, and the body could not be in rotational equilibrium.

This fact can be used to determine experimentally the location of the center of gravity of an irregular body (Figure 10.24). Try the following experiment: Cut an

Where do you place the string so that this cutout will hang horizontally?

1) Hold the cutout by any point on its edge and allow it to hang freely. A vertical line drawn from your hand passes through the center of gravity.

2) Repeat the process, holding the cutout at a different point. The spot where your two lines cross is the center of gravity.

Center of gravity

When suspended from the center of gravity, the cutout hangs level.

▲ **FIGURE 10.24** How to find the center of gravity of a flat object.

irregular shape out of cardboard, and then grasp it gently between your thumb and forefinger. The body rotates until its center of gravity is directly below the point you're grasping. Draw a vertical line through this point; the center of gravity must lie along this line. Repeat this procedure for a different suspension point; the intersection of the two lines must be the center of gravity. Pick a third point; the three lines must intersect at a single point. Once you've located the intersection point, poke a small hole in the body at that point and insert a pointed pen or pencil to confirm that the body balances there.

A force applied to a rigid body at its center of gravity doesn't tend to cause the body to rotate about an axis through that point. A force applied at any other point can cause both rotational and translational motion. We used this fact implicitly in the examples of Section 10.2.

▲ **An accident waiting to happen?** If these plates were not spinning rapidly, it would be nearly impossible to balance them on the ends of their sticks. When they are spinning, each stick exerts frictional forces on the underside of its plate; these forces tend to move the point of contact of the stick toward the center of the plate. Once centered, each spinning plate behaves like a gyroscope flywheel with its axis vertical and its center of mass directly above the point of support. Although the plates aren't in equilibrium (because they are slowing down), they can maintain their spinning motion for a considerable time.

PROBLEM-SOLVING STRATEGY 10.3 **Equilibrium of a rigid body**

The principles of rigid-body equilibrium are few and simple: The vector sum of the forces on the object must be zero, and the sum of the torques about any axis must be zero. The more challenging part is applying these principles to specific problems. Careful and systematic problem-solving methods always pay off. The following strategy is similar to the suggestions in Section 5.1 for equilibrium of a particle.

SET UP

1. Sketch the physical situation, including dimensions.
2. Choose some appropriate body as the body in equilibrium and draw a free-body diagram, showing the forces acting *on* this body and no others. Follow all the rules and sign conventions we've discussed previously. *Do not* include forces exerted *by* this body on other bodies. Be careful to show correctly the point at which each force acts; this is crucial for correct torque calculations.
3. Draw coordinate axes, and represent the forces in terms of their components with respect to these axes.

SOLVE

4. Write equations expressing the equilibrium conditions. Remember that $\sum F_x = 0$, $\sum F_y = 0$, and $\sum \tau = 0$ are always separate equations; *never* add x and y components in a single equation.
5. In choosing an axis of rotation for computing torques, note that if a force has a line of action that goes *through* a particular rotation axis, the torque of the force with respect to that axis is zero. You can often eliminate unknown forces or components from the torque equation by a clever choice of axis. Also remember that when a force is represented in terms of its components, you can compute the torque of that force by finding the torque of each component separately, each with its appropriate moment arm and sign, and adding the results. This approach is often easier than determining the moment arm of the original force.

REFLECT

6. You always need as many equations as you have unknowns. Depending on the number of unknowns, you may need to compute torques with respect to two or more rotation axes to obtain enough equations. There often are several equally good sets of force and torque equations for a particular problem; there is usually no single "right" combination of equations. When you have as many independent equations as unknowns, you can solve the equations simultaneously. We'll illustrate this point in some of the examples that follow by using various sets of equations.

EXAMPLE 10.11 Playing on a seesaw

You and a friend play on a seesaw. Your mass is 90 kg, and your friend's mass is 60 kg. The seesaw board is 3.0 m long and has negligible mass. Where should the pivot be placed so that the seesaw will balance when you sit on the left end and your friend sits on the right end?

SOLUTION

SET UP Figure 10.25 shows our sketches. First we sketch the physical situation, and then we make a free-body diagram, placing the pivot at a distance x from the left end. Note that each weight is the corresponding mass multiplied by g, so g will divide out of the final result. Remember that counterclockwise torques are positive and clockwise torques are negative. For the seesaw to be in equilibrium, the sum of the torques about any axis must be zero. We choose to take torques about the pivot axis; then the normal force acting at the pivot doesn't enter into the analysis. The moment arms are x for you and $(3.0 \text{ m} - x)$ for your friend.

SOLVE Your torque is $\tau_{\text{you}} = +(90 \text{ kg})gx$. Your friend is $3.0 \text{ m} - x$ from the pivot, and the corresponding torque is $\tau_{\text{friend}} = -(60 \text{ kg})g(3.0 \text{ m} - x)$. For equilibrium, the sum of these torques must be zero:

$$\tau_{\text{you}} + \tau_{\text{friend}} = 0$$
$$+(90 \text{ kg})gx - (60 \text{ kg})g(3.0 \text{ m} - x) = 0.$$

We divide through by g and solve for x, obtaining $x = 1.2 \text{ m}$.

REFLECT If we put the pivot at the center of the board ($x = 1.5 \text{ m}$), we would have equal moment arms but unequal weights, so it's clear that the pivot must be to the *left* of center.

(a) Sketch of physical situation

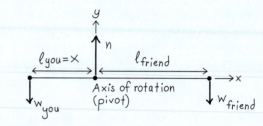

(b) Free-body diagram

▲ FIGURE 10.25

Practice Problem: If the board has a mass of 20 kg, where should the pivot be placed for balance? *Answer:* 1.24 m from the left end.

EXAMPLE 10.12 A heroic rescue

Sir Lancelot is trying to rescue the Lady Elayne from the Black Castle by climbing a uniform ladder that is 5.0 m long and weighs 180 N. Lancelot, who weighs 800 N, stops a third of the way up the ladder (Figure 10.26a). The bottom of the ladder rests on a horizontal stone ledge and leans across the castle's moat in equilibrium against a vertical wall that is frictionless because of a thick layer of moss. The ladder makes an angle of 53° with the horizontal, conveniently forming a 3–4–5 right triangle. **(a)** Find the normal and friction forces on the ladder at its base. **(b)** Find the minimum coefficient of static friction needed to prevent slipping. **(c)** Find the magnitude and direction of the contact force on the ladder at the base.

SOLUTION

SET UP Figure 10.26b shows a free-body diagram for the ladder. Since it is described as "uniform," we can assume that its center of gravity is at its center, halfway between the base and the wall. Lancelot's weight pushes down on the ladder at a point one-third of the way from the base toward the wall. The contact force n_1 at the top of the ladder is horizontal and to the left, because the wall is frictionless. The components of the contact force at the base are the upward normal force n_2 and the friction force f_s, which must point to the right to prevent slipping.

SOLVE **Part (a)** The first condition for equilibrium, in component form, gives

$$\Sigma F_x = f_s + (-n_1) = 0,$$
$$\Sigma F_y = n_2 + (-800 \text{ N}) + (-180 \text{ N}) = 0.$$

These are two equations for the three unknowns n_1, n_2, and f_s. The first equation tells us that the two horizontal forces must be equal and opposite, and the second equation gives $n_2 = 980 \text{ N}$. That is, the ledge pushes up with a force of 980 N to balance the total (downward) weight ($800 \text{ N} + 180 \text{ N}$).

Continued

We don't yet have enough equations, but now we can use the second condition for equilibrium. We can take torques about any point we choose. The smart choice is the point that will give us the fewest terms and fewest unknowns in the torque equation. With this thought in mind, we choose point B, at the base of the ladder. The two forces n_2 and f_s have no torque about that point. From Figure 10.26b, we see that the moment arm for the ladder's weight is 1.5 m, the moment arm for Lancelot's weight is 1.0 m, and the moment arm for n is 4.0 m. The torque equation for point B is thus

$$\Sigma \tau_B = n_1(4.0 \text{ m}) - (180 \text{ N})(1.5 \text{ m})$$
$$- (800 \text{ N})(1.0 \text{ m}) + n_2(0) + f_s(0) = 0.$$

Solving for n_1, we get

$$n_1 = 268 \text{ N}.$$

Now we substitute this result back into the equation $\Sigma F_x = 0$ to get

$$f_s = 268 \text{ N}.$$

Part (b) The static friction force f_s cannot exceed $\mu_s n_2$, so the *minimum* coefficient of static friction to prevent slipping is

$$(\mu_s)_{\min} = \frac{f_s}{n_2} = \frac{268 \text{ N}}{980 \text{ N}} = 0.27.$$

Part (c) The components of the contact force at the base are the static friction force $f_s = 286 \text{ N}$ and the normal force $n_2 = 980 \text{ N}$; the magnitude of $\vec{F}_B$ is

$$F_B = \sqrt{(268 \text{ N})^2 + (980 \text{ N})^2} = 1020 \text{ N},$$

and its direction (Figure 10.26c) is

$$\theta = \tan^{-1} \frac{980 \text{ N}}{268 \text{ N}} = 75°.$$

REFLECT First, the contact force $\vec{F}_B$ at an angle of 75° is *not* directed along the length of the ladder, which is at an angle of 53° If it were, the sum of torques with respect to the point where Lancelot stands couldn't be zero.

Second, as Lancelot climbs higher on the ladder, the moment arm and torque of his weight about B increase, thereby increasing the values of n_1, f_s, and $(\mu_s)_{\min}$. At the top, his moment arm would be nearly 3 m, giving a minimum coefficient of static friction of nearly 0.7. An aluminum ladder on a wood floor wouldn't have a value of μ_s this large, so present-day aluminum ladders are usually equipped with nonslip rubber feet.

Third, a larger ladder angle (i.e., a more upright ladder) would decrease the moment arms of the weights of the ladder and Lancelot with respect to B and would increase the moment arm of n_1, all of which would decrease the required friction force. Some manufacturers recommend that their ladders be used at an angle of 75°. (Why not 90°?)

Practice Problem: Carry out an alternative procedure for obtaining the results asked for in Parts (a), (b), and (c) by taking torques about an axis at the top of the ladder; check to see that your results agree with the previous ones.

(a) (b) (c)

▲ **FIGURE 10.26**

EXAMPLE 10.13 **Equilibrium and pumping iron**

Figure 10.27a shows a human arm lifting a dumbbell. The forearm is in equilibrium under the action of the weight w of the dumbbell, the tension T in the tendon connected to the biceps muscle at point A, and the forces exerted on the forearm by the upper arm at the elbow joint. For clarity, the tendon force has been displaced away from the elbow farther than its actual position. The weight w and the angle θ are given. Find the tension T in the tendon and the two components of force (E_x and E_y) at the elbow (three unknown quantities in all). Neglect the weight of the forearm itself. Evaluate your results for $w = 50 \text{ N}$, $d = 0.10 \text{ m}$, $l = 0.50 \text{ m}$, and $\theta = 80°$.

Continued

SOLUTION

SET UP As the body in equilibrium, we choose the forearm plus dumbbell (the colored elements in Figure 10.27a). Figure 10.27b shows our free-body diagram. We apply a coordinate system and draw the three forces on the forearm, representing the tension force and the forces on the elbow in terms of components along the x and y directions. Note that we don't yet know the sign of the elbow force component E_y (although we drew it as positive for convenience); it could come out either way. Study this free-body diagram; be sure you understand how these forces allow you to lift things.

SOLVE First we use the components T_x and T_y of the tension force, along with the given angle θ, to represent the unknown magnitude:

$$T_x = T\cos\theta \qquad T_y = T\sin\theta.$$

Next we note that if we take torques about the elbow joint (point E), the resulting torque equation does not contain E_x, E_y, or T_x because the lines of action of all these forces pass through this point. The torque equation is then simply

$$\sum \tau_E = lw - dT_y = 0.$$

From this equation, we find that

$$T_y = \frac{lw}{d} \qquad \text{and} \qquad T = \frac{lw}{d\sin\theta}.$$

To find E_x and E_y, we could now use the first condition for equilibrium: $\sum F_x = 0$ and $\sum F_y = 0$. Instead, for added practice in using torques, we take torques about the point A where the tendon is attached:

$$(l - d)w + dE_y = 0 \qquad \text{and} \qquad E_y = -\frac{(l-d)w}{d}.$$

The negative sign shows that our initial guess for the direction of E_y was wrong; it is actually vertically *downward*.

Finally, we take torques about point B in the figure and remember to use the shortest perpendicular distance to the vector $\vec{w}$ to simplify our calculations.

$$\sum \tau_B = lw - hE_x = 0 \qquad \text{and} \qquad E_x = \frac{lw}{h}.$$

Evaluating our expressions for $w = 50$ N, $d = 0.10$ m, $l = 0.50$ m, and $\theta = 80°$, we get $\tan\theta = h/d$, and we find $h = d\tan\theta = (0.10 \text{ m})(5.67) = 0.57$ m. We then have

$$T = \frac{(0.50 \text{ m})(50 \text{ N})}{(0.10 \text{ m})(0.98)} = 250 \text{ N},$$

$$E_y = -\frac{(0.50 \text{ m} - 0.10 \text{ m})(50 \text{ N})}{0.10 \text{ m}} = -200 \text{ N},$$

$$E_x = \frac{(0.50 \text{ m})(50 \text{ N})}{0.57 \text{ m}} = 44 \text{ N}.$$

The magnitude of the force at the elbow is

$$E = \sqrt{E_x^2 + E_y^2} = 200 \text{ N}.$$

As we mentioned earlier, we have not explicitly used the first condition for equilibrium, that the vector sum of the forces be zero. To check our answer, we can compute $\sum F_x$ and $\sum F_y$ to verify that they really *are* zero. Such checks help verify internal consistency. Checking, we obtain

$$\sum F_x = E_x - T_x = 44 \text{ N} - (250 \text{ N})\cos 80° = 0,$$
$$\sum F_y = E_y + T_y - w$$
$$= -200 \text{ N} + (250 \text{ N})\sin 80° - 50 \text{ N} = 0.$$

REFLECT Notice how much we have simplified these calculations by using a little ingenuity in choosing the point for calculating torques so as to eliminate one or more of the unknown quantities. In the last step, the force T has no torque about point B; thus, when the torques of T_x and T_y are computed separately, they must add to zero.

Practice Problem: Double the weight of the dumbbell. What is the new tension T in the tendon connected to the biceps muscle at point B? *Answer:* $T = 510$ N.

Tendon actually inserts close to elbow—moved here for clarity

Body in equilibrium (dumbbell plus forearm)

We don't know the sign of this component; we draw it positive for convenience.

(a)

(b)

▲ **FIGURE 10.27**

*10.7 Vector Nature of Angular Quantities

Rotational quantities associated with an axis of rotation, such as angular velocity, angular momentum, and torque, can be represented as *vector* quantities. For a body rotating about a fixed axis that is an axis of symmetry, the directions of these vector quantities are along the axis of rotation, in a direction given by the **right-hand rule,** illustrated in Figure 10.28. If you curl the fingers of your *right* hand in the direction the object rotates, then your thumb points in the direction of the vector angular velocity $\vec{\omega}$ and angular momentum $\vec{L}$. In the case of a torque, you curl the fingers of your right hand in the direction the torque would turn the body if acting on its own; then your thumb points in the torque's direction.

So far, we've dealt with rotating bodies whose axis of rotation, whether stationary or moving, has a fixed direction that is perpendicular to the planes in which the particles of the body revolve. (We've oriented our coordinate systems so that the particles of the body move parallel to the *x-y* plane and the axis of rotation is perpendicular to that plane.) When the axis of rotation can change direction, the situation becomes much richer in the variety of physical phenomena (some quite unexpected) that can occur. For example, if you try to balance a stationary top on its point, it falls over; but when it's spinning, it balances easily. Why? And why are bicycles "tippy" when moving slowly but stable when moving fast? General answers to questions such as these are quite complex, but we can go a little way into understanding this behavior.

For a symmetric body turning about its axis of symmetry, the magnitude of the angular momentum is $L = I\omega$ (Equation 10.9). The corresponding relationship between *vector* angular momentum and *vector* angular velocity is

$$\vec{L} = I\vec{\omega}, \tag{10.16}$$

where I is the moment of inertia about the axis of rotation. Thus, for rotation about an axis of symmetry, the angular velocity and angular momentum vectors have the same direction. Furthermore, we can define a vector torque that is related to the rate of change of vector angular momentum with respect to time by a vector equation analogous to Equation 10.10:

$$\sum \vec{\tau} = \frac{\Delta \vec{L}}{\Delta t}, \quad \text{or} \quad \Delta \vec{L} = \sum \vec{\tau} \, \Delta t. \tag{10.17}$$

In the problems we've worked out so far, $\sum \vec{\tau}$ and $\vec{L}$ have always had the same direction, so only one component of each vector quantity is different from zero. But Equation 10.17 is valid even when $\sum \vec{\tau}$ and $\vec{L}$ have different directions. Then the *direction* of the axis of rotation may change, as with a spinning top, and we have to consider the vector nature of the various angular quantities carefully.

An example of a three-dimensional application of Equation 10.17 is the gyroscope. Figure 10.29 shows a typical toy gyroscope. We set the flywheel spinning by wrapping a string around its shaft and pulling. When the shaft is supported at only one end, as shown in the figure, one possible motion is a steady circular motion of the axis in a horizontal plane, combined with the spinning motion of the flywheel about the axis. This phenomenon is quite unexpected when you see it for the first time; intuition suggests that the free end of the axis should simply drop if it isn't supported. Indeed, if the flywheel isn't spinning, that *is* what happens. The vector nature of angular momentum is the key to understanding the horizontal motion of the axis when the wheel is spinning.

Suppose we take a stationary gyroscope and lift the flywheel until its axis is horizontal, as shown in Figure 10.30. Then when we let it go, two forces act on the flywheel: its weight $\vec{w}$, acting downward at the center of mass, and the normal force $\vec{n}$ at the pivot point O. The weight has a moment arm r; the resulting torque, whose direction is given by the right-hand rule, causes the free end of the flywheel

Angular velocity and angular momentum: Curl the fingers of your right hand in the direction of rotation. Your thumb then points in the direction of angular velocity and momentum.

You must use your right hand!

Torque: Curl the fingers of your right hand in the direction the torque would cause the body to rotate. Your thumb points in the torque's direction.

Right-hand screws are threaded so that they move in the direction of the torque applied to them.

▲ **FIGURE 10.28** The right-hand rule for angular quantities.

When the flywheel and its axis are stationary, they will fall to the table surface. When the flywheel spins, it and its axis "float" in the air while moving in a circle about the pivot.

▲ **FIGURE 10.29** A typical toy gyroscope.

When the flywheel is not rotating, its weight creates a torque around the pivot, causing it to fall along a circular path until its axis rests on the table surface.

In falling, the flywheel rotates about the pivot and thus has an angular momentum $\vec{L}$. The *direction* of $\vec{L}$ stays constant.

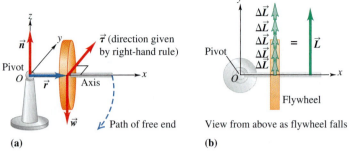

(a)   (b)

▲ **FIGURE 10.30** What happens when we lift and release a gyroscope that is not rotating.

axis to fall along a path forming a circle in a vertical plane, centered on the pivot, until it hits the table. In doing so, the torque gives the flywheel angular momentum according to Equation 10.17: $\Delta\vec{L} = \sum\vec{\tau}\,\Delta t$. Because the axis of rotation is stationary, the directions of both the torque and the angular momentum are constant. Indeed, if we divide the motion into time intervals Δt (Figure 10.30b), we see that the successive $\Delta\vec{L}$'s are all parallel. These $\Delta\vec{L}$'s add to give a horizontal angular momentum that is constant in *direction* but continuously increases in *magnitude.*

Now let's start over; this time we lift the flywheel and start it rotating before we let it go (Figure 10.31). Now the initial angular momentum $\vec{L}$ of the flywheel (before we let it go) is *along* the flywheel's axis of rotation. Once we let go, the flywheel is acted upon by a torque due to the weight and normal forces, as before. Again, we divide the motion into time intervals Δt (Figure 10.31b). Each $\Delta\vec{L}$ is perpendicular to the flywheel's axis. This causes the *direction* of $\vec{L}$ to change, but not its *magnitude.* The center of mass of the flywheel moves in a horizontal circle. The normal force magnitude n is then equal to the flywheel's weight w, and the corresponding torque is $\tau = rw$. (The situation is analogous to a particle moving in uniform circular motion, where the centripetal force causes changes $\Delta\vec{p}$ in linear momentum that are always perpendicular to the linear momentum $\vec{p}$ that already exists, changing the direction of $\vec{p}$, but not its magnitude.)

In Figure 10.31a, at the instant shown, the gyroscope has a definite nonzero angular momentum described by the vector $\vec{L}_i$. The *change* $\Delta\vec{L}$ in angular momentum in a short time interval Δt following this instant is given by Equation 10.17:

When the flywheel is rotating, the system starts with an angular momentum $\vec{L}_i$ parallel to the flywheel's axis of rotation.

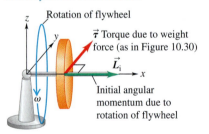

(a)

Now the effect of the torque is to cause the angular momentum to precess around the pivot. The gyroscope circles around its pivot without falling.

(b)

▲ **FIGURE 10.31** What happens when we set a gyroscope rotating before releasing it.

$$\Delta\vec{L} = \vec{\tau}\,\Delta t.$$

The direction of $\Delta\vec{L}$ is the same as that of $\vec{\tau}$. After a time Δt, the angular momentum is $\vec{L} + \Delta\vec{L}$. As the vector diagram shows, this means that the gyroscope axis has turned through a small angle $\Delta\phi$ given by $\Delta\phi = |\Delta\vec{L}|/|\vec{L}|$. We see that such a motion of the axis, called **precession,** is required by the torque–angular momentum relationship.

The rate at which the axis moves, $\Delta\phi/\Delta t$, is called the *precession angular velocity.* Denoting this quantity by Ω, we find that

$$\Omega = \frac{\Delta\phi}{\Delta t} = \frac{|\Delta\vec{L}|/|\vec{L}|}{\Delta t} = \frac{\tau}{L} = \frac{wr}{I\omega}. \tag{10.18}$$

Thus, the precession angular velocity is *inversely* proportional to the angular velocity of spin about the axis. A rapidly spinning gyroscope precesses slowly; as the flywheel slows down, the precession angular velocity *increases.*

EXAMPLE 10.14 A laboratory gyroscope

Figure 10.32 shows a top view of a gyroscope wheel in the form of a solid cylinder, driven by an electric motor. The pivot is at O, and the mass of the axle and motor are negligible. Is the precession clockwise or counterclockwise, as seen from above? If the gyroscope takes 4.0 s for one revolution of precession, what is the wheel's angular velocity?

(a) Top view of spinning cylindrical gyroscope wheel

(b) Vector diagram

▲ **FIGURE 10.32**

SOLUTION

SET UP The right-hand rule shows that $\vec{\omega}$ and $\vec{L}$ are to the left (Figure 10.32b). The weight $\vec{w}$ points into the page, the torque $\vec{\tau}$ is toward the top of the page, with magnitude rw (where r is the distance from the pivot point O to the center of mass of the cylinder), and $\Delta\vec{L}/\Delta t$ is also toward the top of the page. Adding a small $\Delta\vec{L}$ to the $\vec{L}$ that we have at the start changes the direction of $\vec{L}$ as shown, so the precession is clockwise as seen from above.

Be careful not to mix up ω and Ω. The precession angular velocity Ω is given as $\Omega = (1 \text{ rev})/(4.0 \text{ s}) = (2\pi \text{ rad})/(4.0 \text{ s}) = \pi/2 \text{ rad/s}$. The weight is equal to mg, and the moment of inertia of a solid cylinder with radius R is $I = \frac{1}{2}mR^2$.

SOLVE As shown in the "Set Up" discussion, the precession is clockwise as seen from above. Solving Equation 10.18 for ω, we find that

$$\omega = \frac{wr}{I\Omega} = \frac{mgr}{(mR^2/2)\Omega}$$

$$= \frac{2(9.8 \text{ m/s}^2)(2.0 \times 10^{-2} \text{ m})}{(3.0 \times 10^{-2} \text{ m})^2(\pi/2 \text{ rad/s})} = 280 \text{ rad/s} = 2700 \text{ rev/min}.$$

REFLECT The mass of the flywheel divides out and does not appear in the final result. If we double the mass, the torque causing the precession doubles, but the moment of inertia also doubles, and the two effects cancel.

As the gyroscope precesses, the center of mass moves in a circle with radius r in a horizontal plane. Its vertical component of acceleration is zero, so the pivot must exert an upward normal force $\vec{n}$ just equal in magnitude to the weight. The circular motion of the center of mass with angular velocity Ω requires a force $\vec{F}$ directed toward the center of the circle, with magnitude $F = m\Omega^2 r$. This force must also be supplied by the pivot.

The preceding analysis of the gyroscope gives us a glimpse into the richness of the dynamics of rotational motion, which can involve some complex phenomena.

SUMMARY

Torque

(Section 10.1) When a force F acts on a body, the torque τ of that force with respect to a point O is given by $\tau = Fl = rF\sin\phi$ (Equations 10.1 and 10.2). We use the sign convention that a torque tending to cause counterclockwise rotation is positive, while one tending to cause clockwise rotation is negative.

$$F_{rad} = F\cos\phi$$
$$F_{tan} = F\sin\phi$$
$$l = r\sin\phi$$
$$= \text{moment arm}$$
$$\tau = Fl$$
$$= rF\sin\phi$$
$$= F_{tan}r$$

Torque and Angular Acceleration

(Section 10.2) The angular acceleration α of a rigid body rotating about a stationary axis is related to the total torque $\Sigma\tau$ and the moment of inertia I of the body by $\Sigma\tau = I\alpha$ (Equation 10.5). This relation is also valid for a body with a moving axis of rotation, provided that the rotation axis is an axis of symmetry that passes through the center of mass and does not change direction.

$$\Sigma\tau = I\alpha$$

Work and Power

(Section 10.3) When a constant torque τ acts on a rigid body that undergoes an angular displacement $\Delta\theta$ from θ_1 to θ_2, the work W done by the torque is $W = \tau(\theta_2 - \theta_1) = \tau\,\Delta\theta$ (Equation 10.7). When the object rotates with angular velocity ω, the power P (rate at which the torque does work) is $P = \tau\omega$ (Equation 10.8).

Angular Momentum

(Section 10.4) The angular momentum L, with respect to an axis through a point O, of a particle with mass m and velocity $\vec{v}$ is $L = mvl$ (Equation 10.11). When a rigid body with moment of inertia I rotates with angular velocity ω about a stationary axis, the angular momentum with respect to that axis is $L = I\omega$ (Equation 10.9).

In terms of torque τ and angular momentum L, the basic dynamic relation for rotational motion can be restated as

$$\Sigma\tau = \frac{\Delta L}{\Delta t}. \qquad (10.10)$$

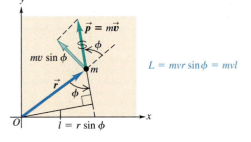

$$L = mvr\sin\phi = mvl$$

Conservation of Angular Momentum

(Section 10.5) If a system consists of bodies that interact with each other but not with anything else, or if the total torque associated with the external forces is zero, then the total angular momentum of the system is constant (conserved): $\vec{L}_i = \vec{L}_f$.

Equilibrium of a Rigid Body

(Section 10.6) The two conditions for equilibrium of a rigid body are $\Sigma\vec{F} = 0$ (Equation 10.14) and $\Sigma\tau = 0$ (Equation 10.15). The former ensures that the center of mass of the body has no linear acceleration a, and the latter ensures that it has no angular acceleration α about any axis.

Continued

Vector Nature of Angular Quantities

(Section 10.7) Vector angular velocity $\vec{\omega}$ is a vector quantity whose direction is that of the axis of rotation and whose magnitude is the (scalar) angular velocity. The sense of the vector $\vec{\omega}$ is given by the right-hand rule. When a body rotates about an axis of symmetry, the vector angular momentum $\vec{L}$ is given by $\vec{L} = I\vec{\omega}$.

In terms of vector torque $\vec{\tau}$ and angular momentum $\vec{L}$, the basic dynamic relation for rotational motion can be restated as

$$\Sigma\vec{\tau} = \frac{\Delta\vec{L}}{\Delta t}. \qquad (10.17)$$

MP For instructor-assigned homework, go to www.masteringphysics.com

Conceptual Questions

1. When tightening a bolt, mechanics sometimes extend the length of a wrench handle by slipping a section of pipe over the handle. Why could this procedure easily damage the bolt?
2. Must there necessarily be matter at the center of mass of an object? Illustrate your answer with several common examples.
3. Two identical uniform 12 inch bricks are placed one atop the other and pushed past the edge of a table. (See Figure 10.33.) What is the greatest that x can be?
4. A uniform 10 cm × 20 cm box is placed on a ramp that rises at an angle θ above the horizontal. (See Figure 10.34.) Assuming that there is enough friction to prevent this box from sliding, what is the largest that θ can be without tipping it over?
5. (a) Can you change the location of your body's center of mass? How? (b) Can your change your body's moment of inertia? How?
6. True or false? There must be equal amounts of matter on either side of the center of mass. Justify your answer with a clear example.
7. When a tall, heavy object, such as a refrigerator, is pushed across a rough floor, what things determine whether it slides or tips?
8. (a) If the forces on an object balance, do the torques necessarily balance? (b) If the torques on an object balance, do the forces necessarily balance? Illustrate your answers with clear examples.

▲ **FIGURE 10.33** Question 3.

▲ **FIGURE 10.34** Question 4.

9. Why is a tapered water glass with a narrow base easier to tip over than one with straight sides? Does it matter whether the glass is full or empty?
10. True or false? In picking an axis about which to compute torques in rotational equilibrium, it is nearly always best to choose an axis through the center of mass of the object. Explain your reasoning.
11. People sometimes prop open a door by wedging an object in the space between the vertical hinged side of the door and the frame. Explain why this often results in the hinge screws being ripped out.
12. In Example 10.12, the ladder was able to remain stable even though the wall was frictionless. Could it have remained stable if the floor were frictionless instead of the wall? Why?
13. In terms of torques, discuss the action of a claw hammer in pulling out nails.
14. Why is it easier to hold a 10 kg body in your hand at your side than to hold it with your arm extended horizontally?
15. If two spinning objects have the same angular momentum, will they necessarily have the same rotational kinetic energy? If they have the same rotational kinetic energy, will they necessarily have the same angular momentum?

Multiple-Choice Problems

1. You are designing a wheel that must have a fixed mass and diameter, but that can have its mass distributed in various uniform ways. If the torque you exert on it is also fixed, which of the wheels shown will have the *smallest* angular acceleration about an axis perpendicular to it at its center?

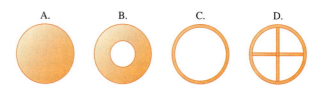

A.   B.   C.   D.

2. Two equal masses *m* are connected by a very light string over a frictionless pulley of mass *m*/2. (See Figure 10.35.) The system has been given a push to get it moving as shown, but that push is no longer acting. In which segment of the string is the tension greater?

   A. The tension in *A* is greater.
   B. The tension in *B* is greater.
   C. The two tensions are the same.

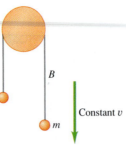

▲ **FIGURE 10.35** Multiple-choice problem 2.

3. The irregular object shown in Figure 10.36 is dropped from rest on the moon, where there is no air. Its center of mass is as shown in the figure. What will it do after it is dropped?

   A. It will start rotating clockwise about its center of mass.
   B. It will start rotating counterclockwise about its center of mass.
   C. It will rotate until point *A* is directly below its center of mass, and then it will stop turning.
   D. It will rotate until point *A* is directly above its center of mass, and then it will stop turning.
   E. It will not rotate.

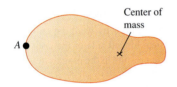

▲ **FIGURE 10.36** Multiple-choice problem 3.

4. A student is sitting on a frictionless rotating stool with her arms outstretched holding equal heavy weights in each hand. If she suddenly lets go of the weights, her angular speed will

   A. increase
   B. stay the same
   C. decrease.

5. If the torques on an object balance, then it follows that this object (there could be more than one correct choice)

   A. cannot be rotating.
   B. cannot have any angular acceleration.
   C. cannot be moving.
   D. cannot be accelerating.

6. If the forces on an object balance, then it follows that this object (there could be more than one correct choice)

   A. cannot be rotating.
   B. cannot have any angular acceleration.
   C. cannot be moving.
   D. cannot be accelerating.

7. A solid uniform ball and a solid uniform cylinder with the same mass and diameter are released from rest and roll without slipping down a hill. Which one will have a *greater linear* acceleration on the hill?

   A. the sphere.
   B. the cylinder.
   C. They will both have the same acceleration.

8. A uniform beam is suspended horizontally as shown in Figure 10.37. It is attached to the wall by a small hinge. The force that the hinge exerts *on the beam* has components

   A. upward and to the right.
   B. upward and to the left.
   C. downward and to the right.
   D. downward and to the left.

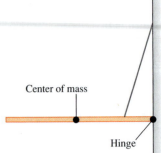

▲ **FIGURE 10.37** Multiple-choice problem 8.

9. A uniform bar is hanging by a hook from the ceiling when it is suddenly struck by a mass traveling horizontally. The mass sticks to the bar. Which quantities are conserved during the collision?

   A. Only linear momentum is conserved.
   B. Only kinetic energy is conserved.
   C. Only angular momentum is conserved.
   D. Both angular momentum and linear momentum are conserved.

10. A person pushes vertically downward with force *P* on a lever of length *L* that is inclined at an angle θ above the horizontal as shown in Figure 10.38. The torque that the person's push produces about point *A* is

    A. $PL \sin\theta$.
    B. $PL \cos\theta$.
    C. PL.

▲ **FIGURE 10.38** Multiple-choice problem 10.

11. String is wrapped around the outer rim of a solid uniform cylinder that is free to rotate about a frictionless axle through its center. When the string is pulled with a force *P* tangent to the rim, it gives the cylinder an angular acceleration α. If the cylinder had *twice* the radius, but everything else was the same, the angular acceleration would be

    A. 4α.   B. 2α.
    C. $\alpha/2$.   D. $\alpha/4$.

12. A weight *W* swings from a hook in the ceiling by a light string of length *L*, as shown in Figure 10.39. *T* is the tension in the string. When the string makes an angle θ with the vertical, the *net* torque about the hook is

    A. *WL*.
    B. $(W - T)L$.
    C. *TL*.
    D. $WL \sin\theta$.
    E. $WL \cos\theta$.

▲ **FIGURE 10.39** Multiple-choice problem 12.

13. A ball of mass 0.20 kg is whirled in a horizontal circle at the end of a light string 75 cm long at a speed of 3.0 m/s. If the string is lengthened to 1.5 m while the ball is being twirled, then the speed of the ball will now be

    A. 12 m/s.   B. 6.0 m/s.   C. 1.5 m/s.   D. 0.75 m/s.

14. If the tension in the string in the previous question was T before the string was lengthened, then the tension in the string after it is lengthened is
    A. $8T$. B. $4T$. C. T.
    D. $T/4$. E. $T/8$.

15. A uniform metal meterstick is balanced as shown in Figure 10.40 with a 1.0 kg rock attached to the left end of the stick. (Pay attention to the scale of the diagram.) What is the mass of the meterstick?
    A. 0.60 kg. B. 1.0 kg. C. 2.0 kg. D. 3.0 kg.

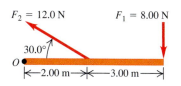

▲ **FIGURE 10.40** Multiple-choice problem 15.

Problems

10.1 Torque

1. • Calculate the torque (magnitude and direction) about point O due to the force $\vec{F}$ in each of the situations sketched in Figure 10.41. In each case, the force $\vec{F}$ and the rod both lie in the plane of the page, the rod has length 4.00 m, and the force has magnitude 10.0 N.

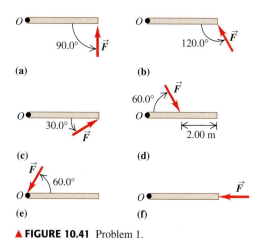

▲ **FIGURE 10.41** Problem 1.

2. • Calculate the net torque about point O for the two forces applied as in Figure 10.42. The rod and both forces are in the plane of the page.

▲ **FIGURE 10.42** Problem 2.

3. • Forces $F_1 = 7.50$ N and $F_2 = 5.30$ N are applied tangentially to a wheel with radius 0.330 m, as shown in Figure 10.43. What is the net torque on the wheel due to these two forces for an axis perpendicular to the wheel and passing through its center?

▲ **FIGURE 10.43** Problem 3.

4. • In Figure 10.44, forces $\vec{A}$, $\vec{B}$, $\vec{C}$, and $\vec{D}$, each have magnitude 50 N and act at the same point on the object. (a) What torque (magnitude and direction) does each of these forces exert on the object about point P? (b) What is the total torque about point P?

5. •• A square metal plate 0.180 m on each side is pivoted about an axis through point O at its center and perpendicular to the plate. (See Figure 10.45.) Calculate the net torque about this axis due to the three forces shown in the figure if the magnitudes of the forces are $F_1 = 18.0$ N, $F_2 = 26.0$ N, and $F_3 = 14.0$ N. The plate and all forces are in the plane of the page.

▲ **FIGURE 10.44** Problem 4.

▲ **FIGURE 10.45** Problem 5.

10.2 Torque and Angular Acceleration

6. • A cord is wrapped around the rim of a wheel 0.250 m in radius, and a steady pull of 40.0 N is exerted on the cord. The wheel is mounted on frictionless bearings on a horizontal shaft through its center. The moment of inertia of the wheel about this shaft is 5.00 kg · m². Compute the angular acceleration of the wheel.

7. • A certain type of propeller blade can be modeled as a thin uniform bar 2.50 m long and of mass 24.0 kg that is free to rotate about a frictionless axle perpendicular to the bar at its midpoint. If a technician strikes this blade with a mallet 1.15 m from the center with a 35.0 N force perpendicular to the blade, find the maximum angular acceleration the blade could achieve.

8. •• A 750 gram grinding wheel 25.0 cm in diameter is in the shape of a uniform solid disk. (We can ignore the small hole at the center.) When it is in use, it turns at a constant 220 rpm about an axle perpendicular to its face through its center. When the power switch is turned off, you observe that the wheel stops in 45.0 s with constant angular acceleration due to friction at the axle. What torque does friction exert while this wheel is slowing down?

9. •• A grindstone in the shape of a solid disk with diameter 0.520 m and a mass of 50.0 kg is rotating at 850 rev/min. You press an ax against the rim with a normal force of 160 N (see Figure 10.46), and the grindstone comes to rest in 7.50 s. Find the coefficient of kinetic friction between the ax and the grindstone. There is negligible friction in the bearings.

▲ **FIGURE 10.46** Problem 9.

10. •• A 15.0 kg bucket of water is suspended by a rope of negligible weight that is wrapped around a solid cylinder 0.300 m in diameter and with mass 12.0 kg. The cylinder pivots on a frictionless axle through its center. The bucket is released from rest at the top of a well and falls 10.0 m to the water. (a) What is the tension in the rope while the bucket is falling? (b) What is the time of fall? (c) While the bucket is falling, what is the force exerted on the cylinder by the axle?

11. •• A 2.00 kg stone is tied to a thin, light wire wrapped around the outer edge of the uniform 10.0 kg cylindrical pulley shown in Figure 10.47. The inner diameter of the pulley is 60.0 cm, while the outer diameter is 1.00 m. The system is released from rest, and there is no friction at the axle of the pulley. Find (a) the acceleration of the stone, (b) the tension in the wire, and (c) the angular acceleration of the pulley.

▲ **FIGURE 10.47** Problem 11.

12. •• A light rope is wrapped several times around a large wheel with a radius of 0.400 m. The wheel rotates in frictionless bearings about a stationary horizontal axis, as shown in Figure 10.48. The free end of the rope is tied to a suitcase with a mass of 15.0 kg. The suitcase is released from rest at a height of 4.00 m above the ground. The suitcase has a speed of 3.50 m/s when it reaches the ground. Calculate (a) the angular velocity of the wheel when the suitcase reaches the ground and (b) the moment of inertia of the wheel.

13. •• A 22,500 N elevator is to be accelerated upward by connecting it to a counterweight using a light (but strong!)

4.00 m

▲ **FIGURE 10.48** Problem 12.

cable passing over a solid uniform disk-shaped pulley. There is no appreciable friction at the axle of the pulley, but its mass is 875 kg and it is 1.50 m in diameter. (a) How heavy should the counterweight be so that it will accelerate the elevator upward through 6.75 m in the first 3.00 s, starting from rest? (b) Under these conditions, what is the tension in the cable on each side of the pulley?

14. •• A thin, light string is wrapped around the rim of a 4.00 kg solid uniform disk that is 30.0 cm in diameter. A person pulls on the string with a constant force of 100.0 N tangent to the disk, as shown in Figure 10.49. *The disk is not attached to anything and is free to move and turn.* (a) Find the angular acceleration of the disk about its center of mass and the linear acceleration of its center of mass. (b) If the disk is replaced by a hollow thin-walled cylinder of the same mass and diameter, what will be the accelerations in part (a)?

▲ **FIGURE 10.49** Problem 14.

15. •• A 12.5 kg hollow spherical ball 35.2 cm in diameter is supported by first wrapping thin wire around its outer rim and then fastening the opposite ends of the wire to the ceiling, as shown in Figure 10.50. Suddenly, one end of the wire pulls out of the ceiling, and the ball falls, unwrapping the wire without slipping. (a) What is the acceleration of the center of the ball? (b) Find the tension in the remaining wire. (c) What is the angular acceleration of the ball?

▲ **FIGURE 10.50** Problem 15.

16. •• A hollow spherical shell with mass 2.00 kg rolls without slipping down a 38.0° slope. (a) Find the acceleration of the shell and the friction force on it. Is the friction kinetic or static friction? Why? (b) How would your answers to part (a) change if the mass were doubled to 4.00 kg?

17. •• As a logging truck rounds a bend in the road, some logs come loose and begin to roll without slipping down the mountainside. The mountain slopes upward at 48.0° above the horizontal, and we can model the logs as solid uniform cylinders of mass 575 kg and diameter 1.20 m. (a) Find the acceleration of the logs as they roll down the mountain. (b) What is the friction force on the rolling logs? Is it kinetic or static friction?

10.3 Work and Power in Rotational Motion

18. • What is the power output in horsepower of an electric motor turning at 4800 rev/min and developing a torque of 4.30 N · m?

19. • A playground merry-go-round has a radius of 4.40 m and a moment of inertia of 245 kg · m² and turns with negligible friction about a vertical axle through its center. (a) A child applies a 25.0 N force tangentially to the edge of the merry-go-round for 20.0 s. If the merry-go-round is initially at rest, what is its angular velocity after this 20.0 s interval? (b) How much work did the child do on the merry-go-round? (c) What is the average power supplied by the child?

20. • The flywheel of a motor has a mass of 300.0 kg and a moment of inertia of 580 kg · m². The motor develops a constant torque of 2000.0 N · m, and the flywheel starts from rest. (a) What is the angular acceleration of the flywheel? (b) What is its angular velocity after it makes 4.00 revolutions? (c) How much work is done by the motor during the first 4.00 revolutions?

21. •• (a) Compute the torque developed by an industrial motor whose output is 150 kW at an angular speed of 4000.0 rev/min. (b) A drum with negligible mass and 0.400 m in diameter is attached to the motor shaft, and the power output of the motor is used to raise a weight hanging from a rope wrapped around the drum. How heavy a weight can the motor lift at constant speed? (c) At what constant speed will the weight rise?

10.4 Angular Momentum

22. • Calculate the angular momentum and kinetic energy of a solid uniform sphere with a radius of 0.120 m and a mass of 14.0 kg if it is rotating at 6.00 rad/s about an axis through its center.

23. • Find the magnitude of the angular momentum of the second hand on a clock about an axis through the center of the clock face. The clock hand has a length of 15.0 cm and a mass of 6.00 g. Take the second hand to be a slender rod rotating with constant angular velocity about one end.

24. • A small 0.300 kg bird is flying horizontally at 3.50 m/s toward a 0.750 kg thin bar hanging vertically from a hook at its upper end, as shown in Figure 10.51. (a) When the bird is far from the bar, what are the magnitude and direction (clockwise or counterclockwise) of its angular momentum about a horizontal axis perpendicular to the plane of the figure and passing through (i) point A, (ii) point B, and (iii) point C? (b) Repeat part (a) when the bird is just ready to hit the bar, but is still flying horizontally.

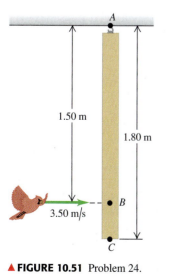

▲ **FIGURE 10.51** Problem 24.

25. • A small 4.0 kg brick is released from rest 2.5 m above a horizontal seesaw on a fulcrum at its center, as shown in Figure 10.52. Find the angular momentum of this brick about a horizontal axis through the fulcrum and perpendicular to the plane of the figure (a) the instant the brick is released and (b) the instant before it strikes the seesaw.

▲ **FIGURE 10.52** Problem 25.

26. • A woman with mass 50.0 kg is standing on the rim of a large disk that is rotating at 0.50 rev/s about an axis perpendicular to it through its center. The disk has a mass of 110 kg and a radius of 4.0 m. Calculate the magnitude of the total angular momentum of the woman-plus-disk system, assuming that you can treat the woman as a point.

27. •• A certain drawbridge can be modeled as a uniform 15,000 N bar, 12.0 m long, pivoted about its lower end. When this bridge is raised to an angle of 60.0° above the horizontal, the cable holding it suddenly breaks, allowing the bridge to fall. At the instant after the cable breaks, (a) what is the torque on this bridge about the pivot and (b) at what rate is its angular momentum changing?

10.5 Conservation of Angular Momentum

28. • On an old-fashioned rotating piano stool, a woman sits holding a pair of dumbbells at a distance of 0.60 m from the axis of rotation of the stool. She is given an angular velocity of 3.00 rad/s, after which she pulls the dumbbells in until they are only 0.20 m distant from the axis. The woman's moment of inertia about the axis of rotation is 5.00 kg · m² and may be considered constant. Each dumbbell has a mass of 5.00 kg and may be considered a point mass. Neglect friction. (a) What is the initial angular momentum of the system? (b) What is the angular velocity of the system after the dumbbells are pulled in toward the axis? (c) Compute the kinetic energy of the system before and after the dumbbells are pulled in. Account for the difference, if any.

29. • **The spinning figure skater.** The outstretched hands and arms of a figure skater preparing for a spin can be considered a slender rod pivoting about an axis through its center. (See Figure 10.53.) When the skater's hands and arms are brought in and wrapped around his body to execute the spin, the hands and arms can be considered a thin-walled hollow cylinder. His hands and arms have a combined mass of 8.0 kg. When outstretched, they span 1.8 m; when wrapped, they form a cylinder of radius 25 cm. The moment of inertia about the axis of rotation of the remainder of his body is constant and equal to 0.40 kg · m². If the skater's original angular speed is 0.40 rev/s, what is his final angular speed?

▲ **FIGURE 10.53** Problem 29.

30. •• A small block on a frictionless horizontal surface has a mass of 0.0250 kg. It is attached to a massless cord passing through a hole in the surface. (See Figure 10.54.) The block is originally revolving at a

▲ **FIGURE 10.54** Problem 30.

distance of 0.300 m from the hole with an angular speed of 1.75 rad/s. The cord is then pulled from below, shortening the radius of the circle in which the block revolves to 0.150 m. You may treat the block as a particle. (a) Is angular momentum conserved? Why or why not? (b) What is the new angular speed? (c) Find the change in kinetic energy of the block. (d) How much work was done in pulling the cord?

31. •• A uniform 4.5 kg square solid wooden gate 1.5 m on each side hangs vertically from a frictionless pivot at the center of its upper edge. A 1.1 kg raven flying horizontally at 5.0 m/s flies into this door at its center and bounces back at 2.0 m/s in the opposite direction. (a) What is the angular speed of the gate just after it is struck by the unfortunate raven? (b) During the collision, why is the angular momentum conserved, but not the linear momentum?

32. •• **What a catch!** An 85 kg baseball player who has leapt vertically into the air to catch a line drive catches the ball as it is headed horizontally directly into his glove. The ball has a mass of 145 g and is headed perpendicular to his arm at 52 m/s just before he catches it. Just after he catches the ball with his arm extended horizontally, what is the player's angular speed about a vertical axis through his head and feet, assuming that he was stationary at the instant he caught it? To make the calculations reasonable, you can model the player's body as a uniform solid cylinder of mass 73 kg and diameter 35 cm and his arms as thin 6.0 kg rods, each 70 cm long, pivoting around a vertical axis through his center.

33. •• A large turntable rotates about a fixed vertical axis, making one revolution in 6.00 s. The moment of inertia of the turntable about this axis is 1200 kg · m². A child of mass 40.0 kg, initially standing at the center of the turntable, runs out along a radius. What is the angular speed of the turntable when the child is 2.00 m from the center, assuming that you can treat the child as a particle?

34. •• A large wooden turntable in the shape of a flat disk has a radius of 2.00 m and a total mass of 120 kg. The turntable is initially rotating at 3.00 rad/s about a vertical axis through its center. Suddenly, a 70.0 kg parachutist makes a soft landing on the turntable at a point on its outer edge. Find the angular speed of the turntable after the parachutist lands. (Assume that you can treat the parachutist as a particle.)

10.6 Equilibrium of a Rigid Body

35. • Which of the objects shown in Figure 10.55 are in only translational equilibrium, only rotational equilibrium (about the axis *A*), both translational and rotational equilibrium (about *A*), or neither equilibrium?

36. • (a) In each of the objects indicated in Figure 10.56, what magnitude of force *F* (if any) is needed to put the object into rotational equilibrium about the axis *A* shown? (b) After you have found the *F* required to put the object into rotational equilibrium, find out which (if any) of these objects is also in translational equilibrium.

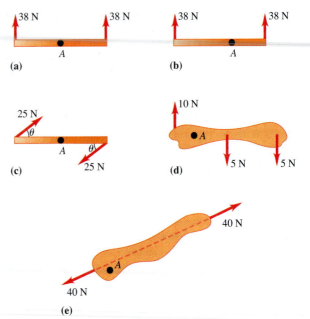

▲ **FIGURE 10.55** Problem 35.

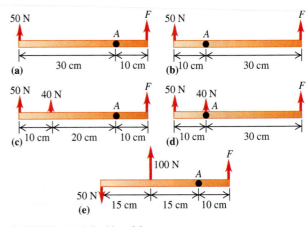

▲ **FIGURE 10.56** Problem 36.

37. •• **BIO** **Supporting a broken leg.** A therapist tells a 74 kg patient with a broken leg that he must have his leg in a cast suspended horizontally. For minimum discomfort, the leg should be supported by a vertical strap attached at the center

▲ **FIGURE 10.57** Problem 37.

of mass of the leg–cast system. (See Figure 10.57.) In order to comply with these instructions, the patient consults a table of typical mass distributions and finds that both upper legs (thighs) together typically account for 21.5% of body weight and the center of mass of each thigh is 18.0 cm from the hip joint. The patient also reads that the two lower legs (including the feet) are 14.0% of body weight, with a center of mass 69.0 cm from the hip joint. The cast has a mass of 5.50 kg, and its center of mass is 78.0 cm from the hip joint. How far from the hip joint should the supporting strap be attached to the cast?

38. •• Two people are carrying a uniform wooden board that is 3.00 m long and weighs 160 N. If one person applies an

upward force equal to 60 N at one end, at what point and with what force does the other person lift? Start with a free-body diagram of the board.

39. •• **Push-ups.** To strengthen his arm and chest muscles, an
BIO 82 kg athlete 2.0 m tall is doing a series of push-ups as shown in Figure 10.58. His center of mass is 1.15 m from the bottom of his feet, and the centers of his palms are 30.0 cm from the top of his head. Find the force that the floor exerts on each of his feet and on each hand, assuming that both feet exert the same force and both palms do likewise. Begin with a free-body diagram of the athlete.

▲ **FIGURE 10.58** Problem 39.

40. •• Two people carry a heavy electric motor by placing it on a light board 2.00 m long. One person lifts at one end with a force of 400.0 N, and the other lifts at the opposite end with a force of 600.0 N. (a) Start by making a free-body diagram of the motor. (b) What is the weight of the motor? (c) Where along the board is its center of gravity located?

41. •• Suppose that you can lift no more than 450 N (about 100 lb) unaided. (a) How much can you lift using a 2.0-m-long wheelbarrow? Assume that the wheelbarrow weighs 80 N and that its center of gravity is 0.70 m from the wheel. In addition, assume that the load carried in the wheelbarrow is also 0.70 m from the wheel. Start with a free-body diagram of the wheelbarrow. (b) Where does the force come from to enable you to lift more than 450 N when you use the wheelbarrow?

42. •• You take your dog Clea to the vet, and the doctor decides he must locate the little beast's center of gravity. It would be awkward to hang the pooch from the ceiling, so the vet must devise another method. He places Clea's front feet on one scale and her hind feet on another. The front scale reads 157 N while the rear scale reads 89 N. The vet next measures Clea and finds that her hind feet are 0.95 m behind her front feet. How much does Clea weigh and where is her center of gravity? Start by making a free-body diagram of the dog.

43. •• The horizontal beam in Figure 10.59 weighs 150 N, and its center of gravity is at its center. First make a free-body diagram of the beam. Then find (a) the tension in the cable and (b) the horizontal and vertical components of the force exerted on the beam at the wall.

44. •• The boom in Figure 10.60 weighs 2600 N and is attached to a frictionless pivot at its lower end. It is not uniform; the distance of its center of gravity from the pivot is 35% of its length. Find (a) the tension in the guy wire and (b) the horizontal and vertical components of the force exerted on the boom at its lower end. Start with a free-body diagram of the boom.

▲ **FIGURE 10.59** Problem 43.

▲ **FIGURE 10.60** Problem 44.

45. • A uniform 250 N ladder rests against a perfectly smooth wall, making a 35° angle with the wall. (a) Draw a free-body diagram of the ladder. (b) Find the normal forces that the wall and the floor exert on the ladder. (c) What is the friction force on the ladder at the floor?

46. •• A uniform ladder 7.0 m long weighing 450 N rests with one end on the ground and the other end against a perfectly smooth vertical wall. The ladder rises at 60.0° above the horizontal floor. A 750 N painter finds that she can climb 2.75 m up the ladder, measured along its length, before it begins to slip. (a) Make a free-body diagram of the ladder. (b) What force does the wall exert on the ladder? (c) Find the friction force and normal force that the floor exerts on the ladder.

47. •• A 9.0 m uniform beam is hinged to a vertical wall and held horizontally by a 5.0 m cable attached to the wall 4.0 m above the hinge, as shown in Figure 10.61. The metal of this cable has a test strength of 1.00 kN, which means that it will break if the tension in it exceeds that amount. (a) Draw a free-body diagram of the beam. (b) What is the heaviest beam that the cable can support with the given configuration? (c) Find the horizontal and vertical components of the force the hinge exerts on the beam.

▲ **FIGURE 10.61** Problem 47.

48. •• A uniform beam 4.0 m long and weighing 2500 N carries a 3500 N weight 1.50 m from the far end, as shown in Figure 10.62. It is supported horizontally by a hinge at the wall and a metal wire at the far end. (a) Make a free-body diagram of the beam. (b) How strong does the wire have to be? That is, what is the minimum tension it must be able to support without breaking? (c) What are the horizontal and vertical components of the force that the hinge exerts on the beam?

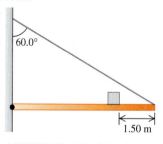

▲ **FIGURE 10.62** Problem 48.

49. •• **Leg raises.** In a simplified version of the musculature
BIO action in leg raises, the abdominal muscles pull on the femur (thigh bone) to raise the leg by pivoting it about one end, as

shown in Figure 10.63. When you are lying horizontally, these muscles make an angle of approximately 5° with the femur, and if you raise your legs, the muscles remain approximately horizontal, so the angle θ increases. We shall assume for simplicity that these muscles attach to the

▲ **FIGURE 10.63** Problem 49.

femur in only one place, 10 cm from the hip joint (although, in reality, the situation is more complicated). For a certain 80 kg person having a leg 90 cm long, the mass of the leg is 15 kg and its center of mass is 44 cm from his hip joint as measured along the leg. If the person raises his leg to 60° above the horizontal, the angle between the abdominal muscles and his femur would also be about 60°. (a) With his leg raised to 60°, find the tension in the abdominal muscle on each leg. As usual, begin your solution with a free-body diagram. (b) When is the tension in this muscle greater, when the leg is raised to 60° or when the person just starts to raise it off the ground? Why? (Try this yourself to check your answer.) (c) If the abdominal muscles attached to the femur were perfectly horizontal when a person was lying down, could the person raise his leg? Why or why not?

50. •• **Out on a limb!** Large trees manage to support some very heavy branches with nothing more than wood fibers inside the tree trunk. The tree in part (a) of Figure 10.64 is supporting a 60 kg (about 130 lb) horizontal branch whose center of mass is 1.75 m from the vertical centerline of the trunk. The trunk is 65 cm in diameter at the level of the branch. The only place the forces (and torques) necessary to hold up this heavy branch can come from is inside the trunk. To get an idea of how large these forces need to be, we can model this tree as a horizontal bar supported by a cable (the wood fibers), as in part (b) of the figure. (a) Make a free-body diagram of the branch. (b) Find the tension in the fiber.

52. •• **Pumping iron.** A
BIO 72.0 kg weight lifter is doing arm raises using a 7.50 kg weight in her hand. Her arm pivots around the elbow joint, starting 40.0° below the horizontal. (See Figure 10.65.) Biometric measurements have shown that both forearms and the hands together account for 6.00% of a person's weight. Since the upper arm is held vertically, the

▲ **FIGURE 10.65** Problem 52.

biceps muscle always acts vertically and is attached to the bones of the forearm 5.50 cm from the elbow joint. The center of mass of this person's forearm–hand combination is 16.0 cm from the elbow joint, along the bones of the forearm, and the weight is held 38.0 cm from the elbow joint. (a) Make a free-body diagram of the forearm. (b) What force does the biceps muscle exert on the forearm? (c) Find the magnitude and direction of the force that the elbow joint exerts on the forearm. (d) As the weight lifter raises her arm toward a horizontal position, will the force in the biceps muscle increase, decrease, or stay the same? Why?

53. •• **The deltoid muscle.** The deltoid muscle is the main mus-
BIO cle that allows you to raise your arm or even hold it out. It is connected to the humerus of the upper arm. (See part (a) of Figure 10.66.) The person shown is holding his arm out horizontally with a 2.50 kg weight in his hand. This weight is 60.0 cm from the shoulder joint. His forearm (including his hand) has a mass of 2.44 kg and is 34.0 cm long; its center of mass is 43 cm from the shoulder joint, measured along the arm. His upper arm is 26.0 cm long and has a mass of 2.63 kg; its center of mass is 13.0 cm from the shoulder joint. The deltoid muscle is attached to the humerus 15.0 cm from the shoulder joint and makes a 14.0° angle with the humerus. (See part (b) of the figure.) (a) Make a free-body diagram of the arm. (b) What is the tension in the deltoid muscle?

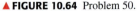

▲ **FIGURE 10.64** Problem 50.

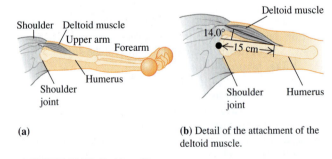

(a)

(b) Detail of the attachment of the deltoid muscle.

▲ **FIGURE 10.66** Problem 53.

51. •• A door 1.00 m wide and 2.00 m high weighs 280 N and is supported by two hinges, one 0.50 m from the top and the other 0.50 m from the bottom. Each hinge supports half the total weight of the door. Assuming that the door's center of mass is at its geometric center, find the horizontal components of force exerted on the door by each hinge. Begin by making a free-body diagram of the door.

54. •• **More deltoid muscle.** Suppose the person in the previous
BIO problem raises his forearm vertically by pivoting it through 90° at the elbow. Find the tension in the deltoid muscle in this case.

*10.7 Vector Nature of Angular Quantities

55. • **A gyro stabilizer.** The stabilizing gyroscope of a ship is a solid disk with a mass of 60,000 kg and a radius of 2.00 m; it

rotates about a vertical axis with an angular speed of 500 rev/min. Find the torque needed to cause the axis to precess in a vertical fore-and-aft plane at the rate of 1.00°/s.

56. • The rotor (flywheel) of a toy gyroscope has a mass of 0.140 kg. Its moment of inertia about its axis is 1.20×10^{-4} kg·m². The mass of the frame is 0.0250 kg. The gyroscope is supported on a single pivot (see Figure 10.67) with its center of mass a horizontal distance of 4.00 cm from the pivot. The gyroscope is precessing in a horizontal plane at the rate of 1 revolution in 2.20 s. (a) Find the upward force exerted by the pivot. (b) Find the angular speed with which the rotor is spinning about its axis, expressed in rev/min. (c) Copy the diagram and draw vectors to show the angular momentum of the rotor and the torque acting on it.

▲ **FIGURE 10.67** Problem 56.

57. • **Stabilization of the Hubble Space Telescope.** The Hubble Space Telescope is stabilized to within an angle of about 2 millionths of a degree by means of a series of gyroscopes that spin at 19,200 rpm. Although the structure of these gyroscopes is actually quite complex, we can model each of the gyroscopes as a thin-walled cylinder of mass 2.0 kg and diameter 5.0 cm, spinning about its central axis. How large a torque would it take to cause these gyroscopes to precess through an angle of 1.0×10^{-6} degree during a 5.0 hour exposure of a galaxy?

58. •• **Precession of the earth.** The earth's axis of spin precesses just like that of a top or a gyroscope. (This is why the North Star moves away from the north over many centuries.) The cause is the torque on the earth due to the gravitational pull of the moon and the sun on the earth's equatorial bulge. The time for a complete cycle of this precession is 26,000 years. How much combined torque do the sun and moon exert on the earth to cause the observed precession? (See Appendix F.)

General Problems

59. •• **Back pains during pregnancy.** Women often suffer from
BIO back pains during pregnancy. Let us investigate the cause of these pains, assuming that the woman's mass is 60 kg before pregnancy. Typically, women gain about 10 kg during pregnancy, due to the weight of the fetus, placenta, amniotic fluid, etc. To make the calculations easy, but still realistic, we shall model the unpregnant woman as a uniform cylinder of diameter 30 cm. We can model the added mass due to the fetus as a 10 kg sphere 25 cm in diameter and centered about 5 cm *outside* the woman's original front surface. (a) By how much does her pregnancy change the horizontal location of the woman's center of mass? (b) How does the change in part (a) affect the way the pregnant woman must stand and walk? In other words, what must she do to her posture to make up for her shifted center of mass? (c) Can you now explain why she might have backaches?

60. •• You are asked to design the decorative mobile shown in Figure 10.68. The strings and rods have negligible weight, and the rods are to hang horizontally. (a) Draw a free-body diagram for each rod. (b) Find the weights of the balls A, B, and C. Find the tensions S_1, S_2, and S_3 in the strings. (c) What can you say about the horizontal location of the mobile's center of gravity? Explain.

▲ **FIGURE 10.68** Problem 60.

61. •• A lawn roller whose diameter is 1.00 m weighs 520 N. What is the minimum horizontal force necessary to pull the roller over a brick 0.100 m high when the force is applied (a) at the center of the roller and (b) at the top of the roller? In each case, show a clear free-body diagram of the roller.

62. •• **A good workout.** You
BIO are doing exercises on a Nautilus machine in a gym to strengthen your deltoid (shoulder) muscles. Your arms are raised vertically and can pivot around the shoulder joint, and you grasp the cable of the machine in your hand 64.0 cm from your shoulder joint. The deltoid muscle is attached to the humerus 15.0 cm from the shoulder joint and makes a 12.0° angle with that bone. (See Figure 10.69.) If you have set the tension in the cable of the machine to 36.0 N on each arm, what is the tension in each deltoid muscle if you simply hold your outstretched arms in place? (*Hint:* Start by making a clear free-body diagram of your arm.)

▲ **FIGURE 10.69** Problem 62.

63. •• A pickup truck has a wheelbase of 3.00 m. Ordinarily, 10,780 N rests on the front wheels and 8820 N on the rear wheels when the truck is parked on a level road. (a) A box weighing 3600 N is now placed on the tailgate, 1.00 m behind the rear axle. How much total weight now rests on the front wheels? On the rear wheels? (b) How much weight would need to be placed on the tailgate to make the front wheels come off the ground?

64. •• A uniform drawbridge must be held at a 37° angle above the horizontal to allow ships to pass underneath. The

drawbridge weighs 45,000 N, is 14.0 m long, and pivots about a hinge at its lower end. A cable is connected 3.5 m from the hinge, as measured along the bridge, and pulls horizontally on the bridge to hold it in place. (a) What is the tension in the cable? (b) Find the magnitude and direction of the force the hinge exerts on the bridge. (c) If the cable suddenly breaks, what is the initial angular acceleration of the bridge?

65. •• **Tarzan and Jane in the 21st century.** Tarzan has foolishly gotten himself into another scrape with the animals and must be rescued once again by Jane. The 60.0 kg Jane starts from rest at a height of 5.00 m in the trees and swings down to the ground using a thin, but very rigid, 30.0 kg vine 8.00 m long. She arrives just in time to snatch the 72.0 kg Tarzan from the jaws of an angry hippopotamus. What is Jane's (and the vine's) angular speed (a) just before she grabs Tarzan and (b) just after she grabs him? (c) How high will Tarzan and Jane go on their first swing after this daring rescue?

66. •• A uniform 250 kg beam is supported by a cable connected to the ceiling, as shown in Figure 10.70. The lower end of the beam rests on the floor. (a) What is the tension in the cable? (b) What is the minimum coefficient of static friction between the beam and the floor required for the beam to remain in this position?

▲ **FIGURE 10.70** Problem 66.

67. •• **Atwood's machine.** Figure 10.71 illustrates an Atwood's machine. Find the linear accelerations of blocks *A* and *B*, the angular acceleration of the wheel *C*, and the tension in each side of the cord if there is no slipping between the cord and the surface of the wheel. Let the masses of blocks *A* and *B* be 4.00 kg and 2.00 kg, respectively, the moment of inertia of the wheel about its axis be $0.300 \text{ kg} \cdot \text{m}^2$, and the radius of the wheel be 0.120 m.

▲ **FIGURE 10.71** Problem 67.

68. •• **Neck muscles.** A student bends her **BIO** head at 40.0° from the vertical while intently reading her physics book, pivoting the head around the upper vertebra (point *P* in Figure 10.72). Her head has a mass of 4.50 kg (which is typical), and its center of mass is 11.0 cm from the pivot point *P*. Her neck muscles are 1.50 cm from point *P*, as measured *perpendicular* to these muscles. The neck itself and the vertebrae are held vertical. (a) Draw a free-body diagram of the student's head. (b) Find the tension in her neck muscles.

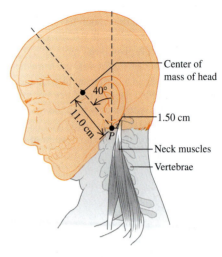

▲ **FIGURE 10.72** Problem 68.

69. •• A uniform drawbridge 8.00 m long is attached to the roadway by a frictionless hinge at one end and can be raised by a cable attached to the other end. The bridge is at rest suspended at 60.0° above the horizontal when the cable suddenly breaks. Start with a free-body diagram of the bridge. (a) Find the angular acceleration of the drawbridge just after the cable breaks. (b) Could you use the equation $\omega = \omega_0 + \alpha t$ to calculate the angular speed of the drawbridge at a later time? Explain. (c) What is the angular speed of the drawbridge as it **BIO** becomes horizontal?

70. •• **Russell traction apparatus.** The device shown in Figure 10.73 is one version of a Russell traction apparatus. It has two functions: to support the injured leg horizontally and at the same time provide a horizontal traction force on it. This can be done by adjusting the weight *W* and the angle *θ*. For this patient, his leg (including his foot) is 95.0 cm long (measured from the hip joint) and has a mass of 14.2 kg. Its center of mass is 41.0 cm from the hip joint. A support strap is attached to the patient's ankle 13.0 cm from the bottom of his foot. (a) What weight *W* is needed to support the leg horizontally? (b) If the therapist specifies that the traction force must be

▲ **FIGURE 10.73** Problem 70.

11

ELASTICITY AND PERIODIC MOTION

In preceding chapters, we've often used idealized models to represent objects as particles or rigid bodies. A rigid body doesn't bend, stretch, or squash when forces act on it. But the rigid body is an idealized model; all real materials do deform to some extent. In this chapter we'll introduce concepts and principles that help us predict the deformations that occur when forces are applied to a real (not perfectly rigid) body. Elastic properties of materials are tremendously important. You want the wings of an airplane to be able to bend a little, but you don't want them to break off. The steel frame of an earthquake-resistant building has to be able to flex, but not too much. Many of the necessities of everyday life, from rubber bands to suspension bridges, depend on the elastic properties of materials.

Next we'll study a class of problems, including some that involve elastic behavior, in which an object repeats the same motion over and over again in a cyclic pattern. Any such motion is called a *periodic motion* or an *oscillation.* Many familiar examples of oscillating objects come to mind: the pendulum of a grandfather's clock, the vibrating strings of a musical instrument, the pistons in a gasoline engine, a child playing on a swing. Less obvious oscillatory phenomena are the vibrations of the quartz crystal in a watch, the electromagnetic waves of radio and television transmission, and the vibrations of atoms in the crystal structure of a solid material. Periodic motion plays a vital role in many areas of physics, and studying it will give us an important foundation for later work in several areas.

One topic we'll cover in this chapter is the motion of pendulums such as this swing. We'll learn that the frequency of a swing—how often it moves back and forth per unit of time—depends on the length of the ropes or chains suspending it but not on the mass of the rider. If a child uses this swing next, its frequency will be the same.

11.1 Stress, Strain, and Elastic Deformations

The rigid body is a useful idealized model, but the stretching, squeezing, and twisting of real objects when forces are applied are often too important to ignore. Figure 11.1 shows examples of these types of forces. For each case, we'll study

Tensile stress: Opposed forces stretch the bone.

Shear stress: Opposed forces twist the bone.

Compressive stress: Opposed forces compress the bone.

Volume stress: Water pressure squeezes the swimmer.

▲ **FIGURE 11.1** Four types of stress that we will study.

the relation between forces and deformations. We'll introduce a quantity called **stress** that characterizes the strength of the forces associated with the stretch, squeeze, or twist, usually on a "force per unit area" basis. Another quantity, **strain,** describes the deformation that occurs. When the stress and strain are small enough, we often find that the two are directly proportional. The harder you pull on something, the more it stretches; and the more you squeeze it, the more it compresses. The general pattern that emerges can be formulated as

$$\frac{\text{Stress}}{\text{Strain}} = \text{Constant.} \qquad (11.1)$$

The proportionality between stress and strain (under certain conditions) is called **Hooke's law,** after Robert Hooke (1635–1703), a contemporary of Newton. We saw a special case of Hooke's law in Sections 5.4 and 7.4: The elongation of a spring is approximately proportional to the stretching forces involved. The constant in Equation 11.1 is often called an *elastic modulus.*

Tensile and Compressive Stress and Strain

The simplest elastic behavior to understand is the stretching of a bar, rod, or wire when its ends are pulled. Figure 11.2a shows a bar with uniform cross-sectional area A, with equal and opposite forces with magnitude $F_\perp$ pulling at its ends. We say that the bar is in **tension.** We've already talked a lot about tensions in ropes and strings; it's the same concept here. Figure 11.2b shows a cross section through the bar; the part to the right of the section pulls on the part to the left with a force with magnitude $F_\perp$ and vice versa. The force is distributed uniformly over the section, as shown by the short arrows in the figure. (This is always the case if the forces at the *ends* are uniformly distributed.)

We define the **tensile stress** at the cross section as the ratio of the force magnitude $F_\perp$ to the cross-sectional area A:

$$\text{Tensile stress} = \frac{F_\perp}{A}. \qquad (11.2)$$

The SI unit of stress is the newton per square meter (N/m^2). This unit is also called the **pascal** (abbreviated Pa):

$$1 \text{ pascal} = 1 \text{ Pa} = 1 \text{ N}/\text{m}^2.$$

In the British system, the logical unit of stress would be the pound per square foot, but the pound per square inch $(\text{lb}/\text{in.}^2, \text{ or psi})$ is more commonly used.

The units of stress are the same as those of *pressure,* which we'll encounter often in later chapters. Steel cables are commonly required to withstand tensile stresses on the order of 10^8 Pa (about 150,000 psi).

Cross-sectional area A

$F_\perp$ ⟷ $F_\perp$

(a) A bar in tension

We assume that the tension force is distributed evenly over any cross section through the bar.

$F_\perp$ ⟷ $F_\perp$

(b) Force on a cross section through the bar

▲ **FIGURE 11.2** Tensile stress.

Cross-sectional area A

$F_\perp$ → ← $F_\perp$

(a) A bar in compression

$F_\perp$ → ← $F_\perp$

(b) Force on a cross section through the bar

▲ **FIGURE 11.3** Compressive stress.

Cross-sectional area A

l_0 Δl

$F_\perp$ Stretched $F_\perp$

$l = l_0 + \Delta l$

Tensile stress $= \dfrac{F_\perp}{A}$ Tensile strain $= \dfrac{\Delta l}{l_0}$

▲ **FIGURE 11.4** Tensile strain.

▶ **Bridging the gap.** The modern cable-stayed bridge is not only beautiful, but also a study in tension and compression. In this type of bridge, the weight of the roadway is carried by sets of diagonal cables attached to tall towers. The cables are in tension, while the roadway and the towers are in compression. Because the cables are oriented at angles to the vertical, they experience very high tensile stress and are thus quite stiff, making this a desirable type of bridge for windy conditions. In addition, the cables act as guy wires to stabilize the towers in the direction parallel to the roadway. This photo shows the Millau Viaduct in France while it was under construction. It is currently the world's tallest bridge.

When the forces on the ends of a bar are pushes rather than pulls (Figure 11.3a), the bar is in **compression,** and the stress is a **compressive stress.** At the cross section shown, each side pushes, rather than pulls, on the other.

The fractional change in length (the stretch) of an object under a tensile stress is called the **tensile strain.** Figure 11.4 shows a bar with unstretched length l_0 that stretches to a length $l = l_0 + \Delta l$ when equal and opposite forces with magnitude $F_\perp$ are applied to its ends. The elongation Δl, measured along the same line as l_0, doesn't occur only at the ends; every part of the bar stretches in the same proportion. The tensile strain is defined as the ratio of the elongation Δl to the original length l_0:

$$\text{Tensile strain} = \frac{l - l_0}{l_0} = \frac{\Delta l}{l_0}. \tag{11.3}$$

Tensile strain is the amount of stretch per unit length. It is a ratio of two lengths, always measured in the same units, so strain is a pure (dimensionless) number with no units. The **compressive strain** of a bar in compression is defined in the same way as tensile strain, but Δl has the opposite direction (Figure 11.5). In this case, it is often convenient to treat Δl as a negative quantity.

Experiments have shown that, for a sufficiently small tensile or compressive stress, stress and strain are proportional, as stated by Hooke's law, Equation 11.1. The corresponding proportionality constant, called **Young's modulus** (denoted by Y), is given by

$$Y = \frac{\text{Tensile stress}}{\text{Tensile strain}} \quad \text{or} \quad \frac{\text{Compressive stress}}{\text{Compressive strain}},$$

or

$$Y = \frac{F_\perp/A}{\Delta l/l_0} = \frac{l_0}{A}\frac{F_\perp}{\Delta l}. \tag{11.4}$$

Strain is a pure number, so the units of Young's modulus are the same as those of stress: force per unit area. Young's modulus is a property of a specific material, rather than of any particular object made of that material. A material with a large value of Y is relatively *unstretchable;* a large stress is required for a given strain. For example, steel has a much larger value of Y than rubber. Table 11.1 lists values of Y for a few representative materials.

When you stretch a wire or a rubber band, it gets *thinner* as well as longer. When Hooke's law holds, the fractional decrease in width is found to be proportional to the tensile strain, typically 0.2 to 0.4 times the tensile strain. Similarly, a material under compressive stress bulges at the sides, and again the fractional change in width is proportional to the compressive strain. For many materials, though not all, Young's modulus has the same values for both tensile and compressive stress.

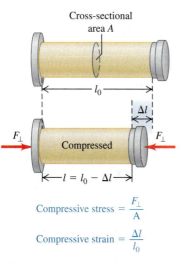

Cross-sectional area A

$$\text{Compressive stress} = \frac{F_\perp}{A}$$

$$\text{Compressive strain} = \frac{\Delta l}{l_0}$$

▲ **FIGURE 11.5** Compressive strain.

TABLE 11.1 Young's modulus

Material	Y (Pa)
Aluminum	0.70×10^{11}
Brass	0.91×10^{11}
Copper	1.1×10^{11}
Glass	0.55×10^{11}
Iron	1.9×10^{11}
Steel	2.0×10^{11}
Tungsten	3.6×10^{11}

EXAMPLE 11.1 **A stretching elevator cable**

A small elevator with a mass of 550 kg hangs from a steel cable that is 3.0 m long when not loaded. The wires making up the cable have a total cross-sectional area of 0.20 cm², and with a 550 kg load, the cable stretches 0.40 cm beyond its unloaded length. Determine the cable's stress and strain. Assuming that the cable is equivalent to a rod with the same cross-sectional area, determine the value of Young's modulus for the cable's steel.

SOLUTION

SET UP AND SOLVE Figure 11.6 shows our diagram. The tension in the cable is $F_\perp = mg = (550 \text{ kg})(9.8 \text{ m/s}^2)$. We use the definitions of tensile stress and strain, and Young's modulus, given by Equations 11.2, 11.3, and 11.4:

$$\text{Stress} = \frac{F_\perp}{A} = \frac{(550 \text{ kg})(9.8 \text{ m/s}^2)}{2.0 \times 10^{-5} \text{ m}^2} = 2.7 \times 10^8 \text{ Pa},$$

$$\text{Strain} = \frac{\Delta l}{l_0} = \frac{0.0040 \text{ m}}{3.0 \text{ m}} = 0.00133,$$

$$Y = \frac{\text{Stress}}{\text{Strain}} = \frac{2.7 \times 10^8 \text{ Pa}}{0.00133} = 2.0 \times 10^{11} \text{ Pa}.$$

REFLECT The cable stretches by about 0.1% of its original length.

Practice Problem: If we want the elongation of the cable to be no greater than 0.001 m, what cross-sectional area must the cable have? *Answer:* 0.80 cm².

▲ **FIGURE 11.6** Our sketch for this problem.

▲ **Hooke, line, and sinker.** In addition to weighing a northern pike, this biologist is also demonstrating the relationship between stress and strain. Within reasonable limits, the spring inside the scale obeys Hooke's law: The displacement of the end of the spring (strain) is proportional to the force applied at the end by the weight of the fish (stress). Because the spring constant (force divided by elongation) does not vary, you can measure the displacement of the end of the spring and determine the mass of the fish.

Modeling an Elastic Material as a Spring

Young's modulus characterizes the elastic properties of a material under tension or compression in a way that is independent of the size or shape of the particular object. To find the relation of force to elongation of any specific rod, cable, or spring, we solve Equation 11.4 for the magnitude $F_\perp$ of the force at each end causing the elongation; we obtain

$$F_\perp = \frac{YA}{l_0} \Delta l.$$

Now let $k = YA/l_0$, call the elongation x instead of Δl, and call the force magnitude F_x instead of $F_\perp$; then we have

$$F_x = kx.$$

We recognize k as the force constant (or spring constant) for a spring; we encountered it in Sections 5.4 and 7.4. When Hooke's law is obeyed, the force F_x needed (on each end) to stretch a spring a distance x beyond its undistorted length is directly proportional to x, and the ratio of F_x to x is the force constant k. Similarly, the shortening of an object in compression is directly proportional to the compressing force. Hooke's law was originally stated in this form; it was reformulated in terms of stress and strain much later by other physicists.

Volume Stress and Strain

When you dive under water, the water exerts nearly uniform pressure everywhere on your surface and squeezes you to a slightly smaller volume (Figure 11.1). This situation is different from tensile and compressive stresses and strains. The stress is now a uniform pressure on all sides, and the resulting deformation is a change in volume. We use the terms **volume stress** and **volume strain** to describe these quantities. Another familiar example is the compression of a gas under pressure, such as the air in a car's tires. We'll use the terms *volume stress* and *pressure* interchangeably.

The **pressure** in a fluid, denoted by p, is the force $F_\perp$ per unit area A transmitted across any cross section of the fluid, against a wall of its container, or against a surface of an immersed object:

$$p = \frac{F_\perp}{A}. \qquad (11.5)$$

When a solid object is immersed in a fluid and both are at rest, **the forces that the fluid exerts on the surface of the object are always perpendicular to the surface at each point.** If they were not, the fluid would move relative to the object.

When we apply pressure to the surface of a fluid in a container, such as the cylinder and piston shown in Figure 11.7, the pressure is transmitted through the fluid and also acts on the surface of any object immersed in the fluid. This principle is called **Pascal's law.** If pressure differences due to differences in depth within the fluid can be neglected, the pressure is the same at every point in the fluid and at every point on the surface of any submerged object.

Pressure has the same units as stress; commonly used units include 1 Pa (or $1\ \mathrm{N/m^2}$) and $1\ \mathrm{lb/in.^2}$ (or 1 psi). Also in common use is the **atmosphere,** abbreviated atm. One atmosphere is defined to be the average pressure of the earth's atmosphere at sea level:

$$1\ \text{atmosphere} = 1\ \text{atm} = 1.013 \times 10^5\ \text{Pa} = 14.7\ \mathrm{lb/in^2}.$$

Pressure is a scalar quantity, not a vector quantity; it has no direction.

We've noted that pressure plays the role of volume stress in a volume deformation. The corresponding strain, called **volume strain,** is defined as the fractional change in volume (Figure 11.8)—that is, the ratio of the change in volume, ΔV, to the original volume V_0:

$$\text{Volume strain} = \frac{\Delta V}{V_0}. \qquad (11.6)$$

Volume strain is change in volume per unit volume. Like tensile or compressive strain, it is a pure number, without units.

When Hooke's law is obeyed, the volume strain is *proportional* to the volume stress (change in pressure). The corresponding constant ratio of stress to strain is called the **bulk modulus,** denoted by B. When the pressure on an object changes by a small amount Δp, from p_0 to $p_0 + \Delta p$, and the resulting volume strain is $\Delta V/V_0$, Hooke's law takes the form

$$B = -\frac{\Delta p}{\Delta V/V_0}. \qquad (11.7)$$

The force applied to the piston is distributed over the surface of the object.

At each point on the object, the force applied by the fluid is perpendicular to the object's surface.

▲ **FIGURE 11.7** Volume stress.

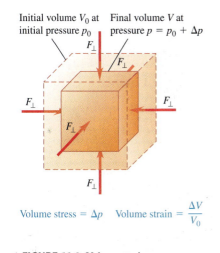

Initial volume V_0 at initial pressure p_0 Final volume V at pressure $p = p_0 + \Delta p$

Volume stress $= \Delta p$ Volume strain $= \dfrac{\Delta V}{V_0}$

▲ **FIGURE 11.8** Volume strain.

▶ **A high-pressure lifestyle.** Fish living deep in the ocean are adapted to the very high pressure caused by the weight of the water above them. At a depth of 500 m, where fish such as this hatchetfish live, the pressure is roughly 50 atmospheres. Many fishes regulate their buoyancy by means of a gas-filled organ called a swim bladder. Gases have a very low bulk modulus, meaning that, for a relatively small change in stress (force due to water pressure), there is a very large strain (change in volume). If such a deep-sea fish is brought rapidly to the surface, it can actually explode as the gas in the swim bladder expands faster than it can be released.

TABLE 11.2 Bulk modulus

Material	B (Pa)
Aluminum	0.70×10^{11}
Brass	0.61×10^{11}
Copper	1.4×10^{11}
Glass	0.37×10^{11}
Iron	1.0×10^{11}
Steel	1.6×10^{11}
Tungsten	2.0×10^{11}

We include a minus sign in this equation because an *increase* in pressure always causes a *decrease* in volume. In other words, when Δp is positive, ΔV is negative. The negative sign in Equation 11.7 makes B itself a positive quantity.

Table 11.2 lists values of the bulk modulus for several solid materials. Values for liquids are usually considerably smaller, typically between 1×10^9 Pa and 5×10^9 Pa. (I.e., in general, liquids are more easily compressed than solids). For small pressure changes in a solid or a liquid, we consider B to be constant. The bulk modulus of a *gas*, however, depends on the initial pressure p_0. The units of B—force per unit area, or pascals—are the same as those of pressure (and of tensile or compressive stress).

EXAMPLE 11.2 Squeezing water

The bulk modulus of water is 2.2×10^9 Pa $(= 2.2 \times 10^9 \text{ N/m}^2)$. By how much does a cubic meter of water decrease in volume when it is taken from the surface of the ocean down to a depth of 1.0 km, where the pressure is 9.8×10^6 Pa greater than at the surface?

SOLUTION

SET UP AND SOLVE From Equation 11.7, the bulk modulus is

$$B = -\frac{\Delta p}{\Delta V / V_0}.$$

We solve this equation for ΔV:

$$\Delta V = -\frac{\Delta p V_0}{B} = -\frac{(9.8 \times 10^6 \text{ Pa})(1.0 \text{ m}^3)}{(2.2 \times 10^9 \text{ N/m}^2)}$$
$$= -4.5 \times 10^{-3} \text{ m}^3 = -4500 \text{ cm}^3.$$

REFLECT The negative sign indicates that the volume has decreased while the pressure has increased. Although the pressure at a 1 km depth is roughly 100 times that at the surface, the fractional change in volume is only about 0.5%.

Practice Problem: A fluid with an initial volume of 0.35 m³ is subjected to a pressure decrease of 3.2×10^3 Pa. The volume is then found to have increased by 0.20 cm³. What is the bulk modulus of the fluid? *Answer: $B = 5.6 \times 10^9$ Pa.*

A block subjected to shear stress from two directions

▲ **FIGURE 11.9** Shear stress.

Shear Stress and Strain

Another kind of stress–strain situation shown in Figure 11.1 is called shear. The block in Figure 11.9 is under **shear stress,** which we define as the force $F_\parallel$ tangent to a material surface, divided by the area A of the surface on which the force acts:

$$\text{Shear stress} = \frac{F_\parallel}{A}. \tag{11.8}$$

Shear stress, like the other two types of stress, is a force per unit area. For systems in equilibrium, shear stress can exist only in *solid* materials; a fluid would simply flow in response to the tangential force.

Figure 11.10 shows an object deformed by shear. We define **shear strain** as the ratio of the displacement x to the transverse dimension h; that is,

$$\text{Shear strain} = \frac{x}{h} = \tan \phi, \tag{11.9}$$

with x and h defined as in Figure 11.10. In real-life situations, x is nearly always much smaller than h, $\tan \phi$ is very nearly equal to ϕ, and the strain is simply the angle ϕ, measured in radians. Like all strains, shear strain is a dimensionless number because it is a ratio of two lengths.

If the forces are small enough so that Hooke's law is obeyed, the shear strain is *proportional* to the shear stress. The corresponding proportionality constant (ratio of shear stress to shear strain), is called the **shear modulus,** denoted by S:

$$S = \frac{\text{Shear stress}}{\text{Shear strain}} = \frac{F_\parallel/A}{x/h} = \frac{h}{A}\frac{F_\parallel}{x} = \frac{F_\parallel/A}{\phi}. \tag{11.10}$$

Shear stress $= \dfrac{F_\parallel}{A}$ Shear strain $= \dfrac{x}{h}$

▲ **FIGURE 11.10** Shear strain.

For a given material, S is usually a third to a half as large as Y. A few representative values of S for common materials are listed in Table 11.3.

NOTE ▶ Keep in mind that only a *solid* material has a shear modulus. A liquid or gas flows freely under the action of a shear stress, so a fluid at rest cannot sustain such a stress. ◀

TABLE 11.3 Shear modulus

Material	S (Pa)
Aluminum	0.30×10^{11}
Brass	0.36×10^{11}
Copper	0.42×10^{11}
Glass	0.23×10^{11}
Iron	0.70×10^{11}
Steel	0.84×10^{11}
Tungsten	1.5×10^{11}

EXAMPLE 11.3 Minor earthquake damage

Suppose the brass baseplate of an outdoor sculpture experiences shear forces as a result of a mild earthquake. The plate is a square, 0.80 m on a side and 0.50 cm thick. How large a force $F_{\parallel}$ must be exerted on each of its edges if the displacement x in Figure 11.10b is 0.016 cm? The shear modulus of brass is listed in Table 11.3.

SOLUTION

SET UP Figure 11.11 shows our sketch. The shear stress at each edge of the plate is the force divided by the area of the edge:

$$\text{Shear stress} = \frac{F_{\parallel}}{A} = \frac{F_{\parallel}}{(0.80 \text{ m})(0.0050 \text{ m})} = (250 \text{ m}^{-2})F_{\parallel}.$$

The shear strain is

$$\text{Shear strain} = \frac{x}{h} = \frac{1.6 \times 10^{-4} \text{ m}}{0.80 \text{ m}} = 2.0 \times 10^{-4}.$$

SOLVE From Table 11.3, the shear modulus S is

$$S = \frac{\text{Shear stress}}{\text{Shear strain}} = 0.36 \times 10^{11} \text{ Pa} = \frac{(250 \text{ m}^{-2})F_{\parallel}}{2.0 \times 10^{-4}}.$$

Solving for $F_{\parallel}$, we obtain

$$F_{\parallel} = 2.9 \times 10^4 \text{ N}.$$

▲ **FIGURE 11.11** Our sketch for this problem.

REFLECT This force is nearly 7000 lb, or roughly twice the weight of a medium-size car.

Practice Problem: We replace the plate with another brass plate that has the same horizontal dimensions (0.80 m on a side), but a different thickness. If the shear forces have magnitude 1.2×10^5 N and the shear strain is the same as before, what is the plate's thickness? *Answer:* 2.1 cm.

Elasticity and Plasticity

Hooke's law, the proportionality between stress and strain in elastic deformations, has a limited range of validity. We know that if you pull, squeeze, or twist *anything* hard enough, it will bend or break. Just what *are* the limitations of Hooke's law?

Let's look at tensile stress and strain again. Suppose we gradually increase the tensile stress on an object, measure the corresponding strain, and plot a graph of stress as a function of strain. Figure 11.12 shows a typical stress–strain graph for a metal such as copper or soft iron subjected to tensile stress. The strain is shown as the *percent* elongation ($\Delta l/l_0 \times 100\%$).

The first part of the graph (to point A) is a straight line. During this phase, the object (say, a piece of copper wire) obeys Hooke's law: stress is proportional to strain, and the proportionality constant is Young's modulus. At point A, the plot ceases to be a straight line; strain is no longer exactly proportional to stress. However, up to point B, the wire still returns to its original, unstrained length if you release the stress. We call this reversible behavior an **elastic deformation**. (Note that an object can behave elastically without following Hooke's law.) This is the behavior you see when you pluck a guitar string; when it finishes vibrating, its length is unchanged.

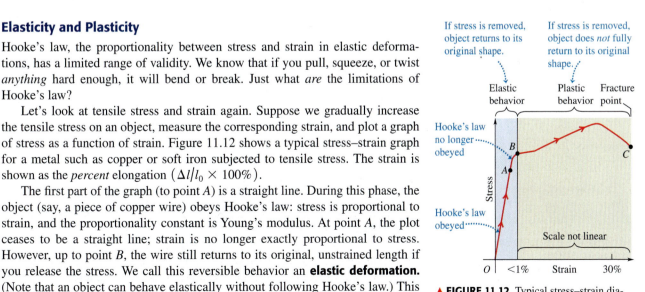

▲ **FIGURE 11.12** Typical stress–strain diagram for a ductile metal under tension.

◀ **As strong as silk.** This fancifully colorized scanning electron micrograph shows silk fibers emerging from the spinning glands on a spider's abdomen. Spider silk has a unique combination of high strength and high elasticity. It can have a tensile strength of up to 17×10^8 Pa, comparable to some of the strongest high-tensile steels we can produce. Considering that its density is only about 20% that of steel, spider's silk has sometimes been called "five times stronger" than steel. It is also quite elastic, having a Young's elastic modulus of only 3×10^8 Pa, less than 1% that of steel. Therefore, in addition to being very strong, spider silk can stretch to at least twice its length before breaking, allowing it to absorb large amounts of energy from flying insects. It has even been proposed that a web made from pencil-thick spider's silk would be able to stop a jet airplane in flight!

At greater stresses, the object does *not* fully return to its original shape when the stress is removed; it has undergone some degree of permanent deformation. If you subject a copper wire to a stress in this range, then, when you release the stress, the wire springs back somewhat, but not all the way back to its original length. We say that the wire undergoes **plastic deformation.** Finally, at point *C*, the wire breaks.

For some materials, a large amount of plastic deformation takes place between the elastic limit and the fracture (breaking) point. Such a material is said to be *ductile*. But if fracture occurs soon after the elastic limit is passed, the material is said to be *brittle*. A soft iron wire that can undergo considerable permanent stretch without breaking is ductile; a steel piano string that breaks soon after its elastic limit is reached is brittle.

The stress required to cause actual fracture of a material is called the **breaking stress** or (in the case of tensile stress) the **tensile strength.** Two materials, such as two types of steel, may have very similar values of Young's modulus but vastly different breaking stresses. Table 11.4 gives a few typical values of breaking stress for several materials in tension. The conversion factor 6.9×10^8 Pa = 100,000 psi will help put these numbers in perspective. For example, if the breaking stress of a particular steel is 6.9×10^8 Pa, then a bar or cable with a 1 in.^{2} cross section has a breaking strength of 100,000 lb.

TABLE 11.4 Breaking stresses of materials

Material	Breaking stress (N/m^2 or Pa)
Aluminum	2.2×10^8
Arterial wall	2.0×10^6
Bone	$1-2 \times 10^8$
Brass	4.7×10^8
Collagen	1.0×10^8
Glass	10×10^8
Iron	3.0×10^8
Phosphor bronze	5.6×10^8
Steel	11.0×10^8
Wood	$1-2 \times 10^8$

11.2 Periodic Motion

An object such as a vibrating guitar string or the swinging pendulum of a grandfather clock repeats the same motion over and over. We refer to such motion as **periodic motion** or **oscillation.** A mechanical system that undergoes periodic motion always has a stable equilibrium position. When it is moved away from this position and released, a force comes into play to pull it back toward equilibrium. But by the time it gets there, it has picked up some kinetic energy, so it overshoots, stopping somewhere on the other side, and is again pulled back toward equilibrium. If this cycle repeats over and over, we say that the motion is periodic.

Simple Harmonic Motion

One of the simplest systems that can have periodic motion is shown in Figure 11.13. A glider with mass *m* moves along the *x* axis on a frictionless horizontal air track. It is attached to a spring that can be either stretched or compressed. The spring obeys Hooke's law and has force constant *k*. (You may want to review the definition of the force constant in Sections 5.4 and 11.1.) The left end of the spring is held stationary. The spring force is the only horizontal force acting on the object. (We neglect the very small friction force on the air track.) The two vertical forces (the normal and weight forces) always add to zero.

It is simplest to define our coordinate system so that the origin *O* is at the equilibrium position, where the spring is neither stretched nor compressed. Then *x* is the displacement of the object from equilibrium and is also the change in length of the spring. The *x* component of acceleration is given by $a_x = F_x/m$.

Spring with force constant k

Equilibrium position (spring relaxed)

▲ **FIGURE 11.13** A system for demonstrating periodic motion.

Figure 11.14 shows complete free-body diagrams for three different positions of the object:

1. **x is negative** (Figure 11.14a). The object is to the left of O, so the spring is compressed. The spring pushes toward the right (toward the equilibrium point) on the object, so the acceleration is also toward the right. Thus, F_x and a_x are both positive. (The object may be *moving* toward either the left or right, however.)

2. **$x = 0$** (Figure 11.14b). The object is at O, the equilibrium position. The spring is neither stretched nor compressed; it exerts no force on the object. The acceleration is zero, and the object is instantaneously moving with constant velocity toward either the right or left.

3. **x is positive** (Figure 11.14c). The object is to the right of O, so the spring is stretched. The spring pulls toward the left (toward the equilibrium point) on the object, so the acceleration is also toward the left. Thus, F_x and a_x are both negative. (The object may be *moving* toward either the left or right, however.)

The force acting on the object tends always to restore it to the equilibrium position, and we call it a **restoring force. On either side of the equilibrium position, F_x and x always have opposite signs.** In Section 5.4, we represented the force acting *on* a stretched spring as $F_x = kx$. The force the spring exerts *on the object* is the negative of this, so the x component of force F_x acting on the body is

$$F_x = -kx. \tag{11.11}$$

This equation gives the correct magnitude and sign of the force, whether x is positive, negative, or zero. The force constant k is always positive and has units of N/m. A useful alternative set of units for k is kg/s^2.

The x component of acceleration, a_x, of the body at any point is determined by $\Sigma \vec{F} = m\vec{a}$, with the x component of force given by Equation 11.11:

$$a_x = \frac{F_x}{m} = -\frac{k}{m}x. \tag{11.12}$$

The acceleration is *not* constant, so don't even think of using the constant-acceleration equations from Chapter 2! Figure 11.15 shows a complete cycle of simple harmonic motion. If we displace the object to the right a distance A (so that $x = A$) and release it, its initial acceleration, from Equation 11.12, is $-kA/m$. As it approaches the equilibrium position, its acceleration decreases in magnitude, but its speed increases. It overshoots the equilibrium position and comes to a stop on the other side; we'll show later that the stopping point is at $x = -A$. Then it accelerates to the right, overshoots equilibrium again, and stops at the starting point $x = A$, ready to repeat the whole process. If there is no friction or other force to remove mechanical energy from the system, this motion repeats forever.

The motion that we've just described—periodic motion under the action of a restoring force that is *directly proportional* to the displacement from equilibrium, as given by Equation 11.11—is called **simple harmonic motion,** abbreviated **SHM.** Many periodic motions, such as the vibration of the quartz crystal in a watch, vibrations of molecules, the motion of a tuning fork, and the electric current in an alternating-current circuit, are approximately simple harmonic motion. However, not *all* periodic motions are simple harmonic.

Here are several terms that we'll use in discussing periodic motions:

Definitions of quantities that describe periodic motion

- The **amplitude** of the motion, denoted by A, is the maximum magnitude of displacement from equilibrium—that is, the maximum value of $|x|$. It is always positive. The total overall range of the motion is $2A$.

$x < 0$: glider displaced to the left from the equilibrium position.

$F_x > 0$, so $a_x > 0$: Compressed spring pushes glider toward equilibrium position.

(a)

$x = 0$: The relaxed spring exerts no force on the glider, so the glider has zero acceleration.

(b)

$x > 0$: glider displaced to the right from the equilibrium position.

$F_x < 0$, so $a_x < 0$: stretched spring pulls glider toward equilibrium position.

(c)

▲ **FIGURE 11.14** A model for periodic motion. If the spring obeys Hooke's law, the motion of the glider is simple harmonic motion.

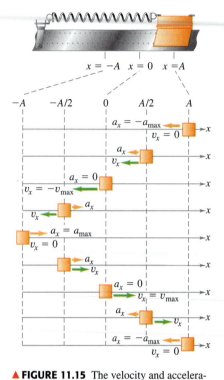

▲ **FIGURE 11.15** The velocity and acceleration of the glider at different points in one cycle of harmonic motion. The maximum acceleration is $a_{max} = kA/m$ and the maximum speed is v_{max}.

• A **cycle** is one complete round trip—for example, from A to $-A$ and back to A, or from O to A, back through O to $-A$, and back to O. Note that motion from one side to the other (say, from $-A$ to A) is a half-cycle, not a whole cycle.

• The **period**, T, is the time for one whole cycle. It is always positive; the SI unit is the second, but it is sometimes expressed as "seconds per cycle."

• The **frequency**, f, is the number of cycles in a unit of time. It is always positive; the SI unit of frequency is the hertz, defined as follows:

$$1 \text{ hertz} = 1 \text{ Hz} = 1 \text{ cycle/s} = 1 \text{ s}^{-1}.$$

This unit is named in honor of Heinrich Hertz, one of the pioneers investigating electromagnetic waves during the late 19th century.

• The **angular frequency**, ω, is 2π times the frequency:

$$\omega = 2\pi f.$$

We'll learn later why ω is a useful quantity. It represents the rate of change of an angular quantity (not necessarily related to a rotational motion) that is always measured in radians, so its units are rad/s.

From the definitions of period T and frequency f, we see that each is the reciprocal of the other:

$$f = \frac{1}{T}, \qquad T = \frac{1}{f}. \tag{11.13}$$

Also, from the definition of ω,

$$\omega = 2\pi f = \frac{2\pi}{T}. \tag{11.14}$$

EXAMPLE 11.4 Ultrasound for medical imaging

An ultrasonic transducer (a kind of ultrasonic loudspeaker) used for medical diagnosis is oscillating at a frequency of 6.7 MHz $(6.7 \times 10^6 \text{ Hz})$ (Figure 11.16). How much time does each oscillation take, and what is the angular frequency?

▶ **FIGURE 11.16** Ultrasonic vibrations for medical diagnosis are produced by an electronic transducer.

SOLUTION

SET UP We first identify the frequency: $f = 6.7 \times 10^6 \text{ Hz} = 6.7 \times 10^6 \text{ s}^{-1}$.

SOLVE The period T is given by Equation 11.13 and the angular frequency by Equation 11.14:

$$T = \frac{1}{f} = \frac{1}{6.7 \times 10^6 \text{ Hz}} = 1.5 \times 10^{-7} \text{ s} = 0.15 \ \mu\text{s},$$
$$\omega = 2\pi f = 2\pi(6.7 \times 10^6 \text{ Hz}) = 4.2 \times 10^7 \text{ rad/s}.$$

REFLECT The transducer's rapid vibration corresponds to large values of f and ω and small values of T. The reverse would be true for a slow oscillator, such as the pendulum of a large grandfather clock.

Not all periodic motion is simple harmonic. **Only in SHM is the restoring force *directly proportional* to the displacement.** In more complex types of periodic motion, the force may depend on the displacement in a more complicated way. However, many periodic motions are *approximately* simple harmonic if the amplitude is small enough that the force is approximately proportional to the displacement. Thus, we can use SHM as an approximate model for many different periodic motions, such as the motion of a pendulum and the vibrations of atoms in molecules and solids.

11.3 Energy in Simple Harmonic Motion

In this section and the next, we'll analyze the spring–mass model of SHM that we've just described. What questions shall we ask? Given the mass m of the object and the force constant k of the spring, we'd like to be able to predict the period T and the frequency f. We also want to know how fast the object is moving at each point in its motion. That is, we want to know its x component of velocity, v_x, and its x component of acceleration a_x, as functions of position x (the x component of displacement from the equilibrium position). Best of all would be to have expressions for x, v_x, and a_x as functions of *time*, so that we can find where the object is and how it is moving at any specified time. In the next few pages we'll work all these things out.

 9.3, 9.5

We'll approach these questions first by using energy considerations and then by using $\Sigma \vec{F} = m\vec{a}$ along with a geometric construction called the circle of reference. Let's start with energy. We've already noted that the spring force is the only horizontal force on the object. It is a *conservative* force, and the vertical forces do no work, so the total mechanical energy of the system is conserved. We'll also assume that the mass of the spring itself is negligible.

The kinetic energy of the object is $K = \frac{1}{2}mv_x^2$, and the potential energy of the spring is $U = \frac{1}{2}kx^2$, just as we found in Section 7.4. (You may want to review that section.) The equation for the conservation of mechanical energy is $K + U = E =$ constant, or

$$E = \tfrac{1}{2}mv_x^2 + \tfrac{1}{2}kx^2 = \text{constant.} \qquad (11.15)$$

The total mechanical energy E is also directly related to the amplitude A of the motion. When the object reaches the point $x = A$ or $x = -A$ (its maximum displacement from equilibrium), it stops momentarily as it turns back toward the equilibrium position. That is, when $x = \pm A$, $v_x = 0$. At this point, the energy is entirely potential energy and $E = \frac{1}{2}kA^2$. Because E is constant, this quantity also equals E at any other point; combining the preceding expression for E with Equation 11.15, we get

$$E = \tfrac{1}{2}kA^2 = \tfrac{1}{2}mv_x^2 + \tfrac{1}{2}kx^2. \qquad (11.16)$$

Solving Equation 11.16 for v_x, we find the following relationship:

Velocity of an object in SHM as a function of position
From the basic energy relation in Equation 11.16,

$$v_x = \pm\sqrt{\frac{k}{m}}\sqrt{A^2 - x^2}. \qquad (11.17)$$

We can use this equation to find the magnitude of the velocity (but not its sign) for any given position x. For example, when $x = \pm A/2$,

$$v_x = \pm\sqrt{\frac{k}{m}}\sqrt{A^2 - \left(\pm\frac{A}{2}\right)^2} = \pm\sqrt{\frac{3}{4}}\sqrt{\frac{k}{m}}A.$$

▲ **FIGURE 11.17** In simple harmonic motion, the total energy E is constant, continually transforming from potential energy U to kinetic energy K and back again.

(a) The potential energy U and total energy E of an object in SHM as a function of x position.

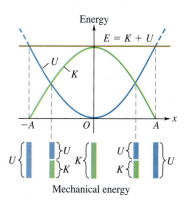

(b) The same graph as in **(a)**, showing kinetic energy K as well.

▲ **FIGURE 11.18** Kinetic, potential, and total energies as functions of position for SHM. At each value of x, the sum of K and U equals the constant total energy E.

Equation 11.17 also shows that the *maximum* speed v_{max} occurs at $x = 0$ and is given by

$$v_{max} = \sqrt{\frac{k}{m}}A. \tag{11.18}$$

Figure 11.17 is a pictorial display of the energy quantities at several x positions, and Figure 11.18 is a graphical display of Equation 11.15. Mechanical energy (kinetic, potential, and total) is plotted vertically, and the coordinate x is plotted horizontally. The parabolic curve in Figure 11.18a represents the potential energy $U = \frac{1}{2}kx^2$. The horizontal line represents the constant total energy E (which doesn't vary with x). This line intersects the potential-energy curve at $x = -A$ and $x = A$, where the energy is entirely potential.

Suppose we start on the horizontal axis at some value of x between $-A$ and A. The vertical distance from the x axis to the parabola is U, and since $E = K + U$, the remaining vertical distance up to the horizontal line is K. Figure 11.18b shows both K and U as functions of x. As the object oscillates between $-A$ and A, the mechanical energy is continuously transformed from potential to kinetic to potential and back. At $x = \pm A$, $E = U$ and $K = 0$.

We see again why A is the maximum displacement. If we tried to make x greater than A (or less than $-A$), U would be greater than E, and K would have to be negative. As we learned in Chapter 7, K can never be negative, so x can't be greater than A or less than $-A$. (In quantum mechanics, it *is* possible in some circumstances for a particle to traverse regions where classically it would have negative kinetic energy. This concept is important in alpha decay of nuclei and in the tunneling electron microscope, but it plays no role in the mechanics of macroscopic objects.)

Quantitative Analysis 11.1 **Energy of a spring**

A mass attached to a spring oscillates with SHM. If the maximum displacement from equilibrium is A and the total mechanical energy of the system is E, what is the system's kinetic energy when the position of the mass is half its maximum displacement?

A. $\frac{1}{2}E$. B. $\frac{3}{4}E$. C. E.

SOLUTION The total mechanical energy E of an oscillator is the sum of its kinetic and potential energies: $E = K + U$. But $U = \frac{1}{2}kx^2$. If $x = A$, then $U = E$ and $K = 0$. At $x = \frac{1}{2}A$, $U = \frac{1}{4}E$ and $K = E - U = \frac{3}{4}E$.

EXAMPLE 11.5 **Simple harmonic motion on an air track**

$F = 6.0$ N

$x = 0$ $x = 0.030$ m

(a)

$m = 0.50$ kg

$x = 0$ $x = 0.040$ m

(b)

▲ **FIGURE 11.19**

A spring is mounted horizontally on an air track (Figure 11.19a), with the left end held stationary. We attach a spring balance to the free end of the spring, pull toward the right, and measure the elongation. We determine that the stretching force is proportional to the displacement and that a force of 6.0 N causes an elongation of 0.030 m. We remove the spring balance and attach a 0.50 kg object to the end, pull it a distance of 0.040 m, release it, and watch it oscillate in SHM (Figure 11.19b). Find the following quantities:

(a) the force constant of the spring.
(b) the maximum and minimum velocities attained by the vibrating object.
(c) the maximum and minimum acceleration.
(d) the velocity and acceleration when the object has moved halfway to the center from its initial position.
(e) the kinetic energy, the potential energy, and the total energy in the halfway position.

SOLUTION

SET UP AND SOLVE For this glider, the amplitude is $A = 0.040$ m.

Part (a): When $x = 0.030$ m, the force the spring exerts on the object is $F_x = -6.0$ N. From Equation 11.11, the force constant k is

$$k = -\frac{F_x}{x} = -\frac{-6.0 \text{ N}}{0.030 \text{ m}} = 200 \text{ N/m}.$$

Part (b): From Equation 11.18, the maximum velocity occurs at the equilibrium position, $x = 0$:

$$v_{max} = \sqrt{\frac{k}{m}}A = \sqrt{\frac{200 \text{ N/m}}{0.50 \text{ kg}}}(0.040 \text{ m}) = 0.80 \text{ m/s}.$$

The minimum (most negative) velocity also occurs at $x = 0$ and is the negative of the maximum value. The minimum *magnitude* of velocity, occurring at $x = \pm A$, is zero.

Part (c): The acceleration for any x is given by Equation 11.12:

$$a_x = -\frac{k}{m}x.$$

The maximum (most positive) acceleration a_{max} occurs at the most negative value of x, that is, $x = -A$; therefore,

$$a_{max} = -\frac{k}{m}(-A) = -\frac{200 \text{ N/m}}{0.50 \text{ kg}}(-0.040 \text{ m}) = 16.0 \text{ m/s}^2.$$

The minimum (most negative) acceleration is -16.0 m/s^2, occurring at $x = +A = +0.040$ m.

Part (d): The velocity v_x at any position x is given by Equation 11.17:

$$v_x = \pm\sqrt{\frac{k}{m}}\sqrt{A^2 - x^2}.$$

At the halfway point, $x = A/2 = 0.020$ m. We find that

$$v_x = -\sqrt{\frac{200 \text{ N/m}}{0.50 \text{ kg}}}\sqrt{(0.040 \text{ m})^2 - (0.020 \text{ m})^2} = -0.69 \text{ m/s}.$$

We've chosen the negative square root because the object is moving in the negative x direction, from $x = A$ toward $x = 0$. From Equation 11.12,

$$a_x = -\frac{k}{m}x = -\frac{200 \text{ N/m}}{0.50 \text{ kg}}(0.020 \text{ m}) = -8.0 \text{ m/s}^2.$$

Part (e): The energy quantities are the terms in Equation 11.16. From (d), when $x = A/2 = (0.040 \text{ m})/2$, $v_x = \pm0.69$ m/s. At this point, the kinetic energy is

$$K = \tfrac{1}{2}mv_x^2 = \tfrac{1}{2}(0.50 \text{ kg})(0.69 \text{ m/s})^2 = 0.12 \text{ J},$$

the potential energy is

$$U = \tfrac{1}{2}kx^2 = \tfrac{1}{2}(200 \text{ N/m})(0.020 \text{ m})^2 = 0.040 \text{ J},$$

and the total energy is $E = K + U = 0.12 \text{ J} + 0.040 \text{ J} = 0.16 \text{ J}$. Alternatively,

$$E = \tfrac{1}{2}kA^2 = \tfrac{1}{2}(200 \text{ N/m})(0.040 \text{ m})^2 = 0.16 \text{ J}.$$

The conditions at $x = 0$, $\pm A/2$, and $\pm A$ are shown in Figure 11.15.

REFLECT The equations we've used in this solution enable us to find relations among position, velocity, acceleration, and force. But they don't help us to find directly how these quantities vary with time. In the next section, we'll work out relations that enable us to do just that and also to relate the period and frequency of the motion to the mass and force constant of the system.

11.4 Equations of Simple Harmonic Motion

9.4, 9.6–9.9

Simple harmonic motion is closely related to uniform circular motion, which we've studied several times. By examining this relationship, we can gain additional insight into both kinds of motion. In this section we'll derive equations for the position, velocity, and acceleration of an object undergoing SHM, as functions of time. We'll also show how the period and frequency of the motion are determined by the mass m and force constant k of the system.

Circle of Reference

Our analysis is based on a geometric representation called the **circle of reference.** The basic idea is shown in Figure 11.20 First, imagine the apparatus shown in Figure 11.20a. We glue a small ball to the rim of a rotating turntable on a flat horizontal tabletop (viewed from above in the figure). Behind the turntable, we set up a vertical screen. Then we illuminate the turntable from in front by a flat, horizontal beam of light placed at the level of the turntable. As the ball rotates, its shadow appears on the screen. And, while the ball moves in uniform circular motion, we find that **the shadow moves from side to side in SHM!**

Figure 11.20b shows the circle of reference—an abstract representation of the phenomenon in Figure 11.20a. Point Q (representing the ball) moves counterclockwise around a circle whose radius is equal to the amplitude A of the shadow's simple harmonic motion. The constant angular velocity ω of the ball (measured in rad/s) is equal to the angular frequency of the shadow's SHM. Thus, ω is the rate of change of the angle ϕ with time: $\omega = \Delta\phi/\Delta t$.

The vector from the origin O to point Q (which we can denote as OQ) is the position vector of point Q relative to O. This vector has constant magnitude A, and at time t it is at an angle ϕ (measured counterclockwise from the positive x axis). As Q moves, vector OQ rotates counterclockwise with constant angular velocity $\omega = \Delta\phi/\Delta t$. As we'll soon see, the x component of this vector represents the actual motion of the object under study.

Now let's prove that the horizontal component of the vector OQ represents the actual motion of the shadow. In Figure 11.20b, point P represents the ball's

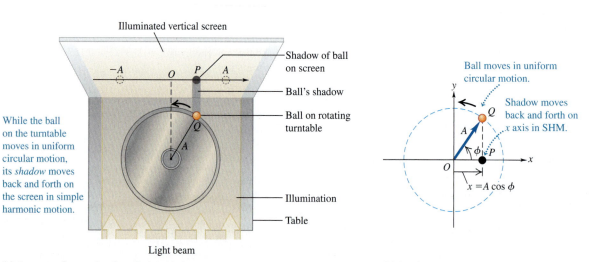

(a) Apparatus for creating the reference circle

(b) An abstract representation of the motion in (a).

▲ **FIGURE 11.20** The circle of reference relates simple harmonic motion to uniform circular motion.

shadow; it lies on the diameter of the circle that coincides with the x axis, directly below point Q, just as the shadow in Figure 11.20a is always directly in line with the ball. We call Q the *reference point,* the circle itself the *circle of reference,* and P the *projection* of Q onto the diameter. As Q revolves, P moves back and forth along the diameter, staying always directly below (or above) Q.

The position of P with respect to the origin O at any time t is the coordinate x; from Figure 11.20a,

$$x = A \cos \phi.$$

If point Q is at the extreme right end of the diameter at time $t = 0$, then $\phi = 0$ when $t = 0$. Because ω is constant, ϕ increases uniformly with time; that is,

$$\phi = \omega t,$$

and

$$x = A \cos \omega t. \tag{11.19}$$

Now ω, the angular velocity of Q (in radians per second) is related to f, the number of complete revolutions of Q per second. There are 2π radians in one complete revolution, so $\omega = 2\pi f$. Furthermore, the point P makes one complete back-and-forth vibration (one cycle) for each revolution of Q. Hence f is also the number of vibrations per second or the *frequency* of vibration of point P. Thus we can also write Equation 11.19 as

$$x = A \cos 2\pi f t. \tag{11.20}$$

We can find the instantaneous velocity of P with the help of Fig. 11.21a. The reference point Q moves with a tangential speed $v_Q = v_\parallel$ given by Equation 9.13:

$$v_\parallel = \omega A = 2\pi f A.$$

Point P is always directly below or above the reference point, so the velocity v_x of P at each instant must equal the x component of the velocity of Q. That is, from Figure 11.21a,

$$v_x = -v_\parallel \sin \phi = -\omega A \sin \phi,$$

and it follows that

$$v_x = -\omega A \sin \omega t = -2\pi f A \sin 2\pi f t. \tag{11.21}$$

The minus sign is needed because, at the instant shown, the direction of the velocity is toward the left. When Q is below the horizontal diameter, the velocity of P is toward the right, but $\sin \phi$ is negative at such points. So the minus sign is needed in both cases, and Equation 11.21 gives the velocity of point P at any time.

We can also find the acceleration of point P. Because P is always directly below or above Q, its x component of acceleration must equal the x component of the acceleration of Q. Point Q moves in a circular path with constant angular velocity ω, and its acceleration is toward the center of the circle, with magnitude $a_Q = a_{\text{rad}}$ given by Equation 9.15:

$$a_{\text{rad}} = \omega^2 A = 4\pi^2 f^2 A.$$

From Figure 11.21b, the x component of this acceleration is

$$a_x = -a_{\text{rad}} \cos \phi;$$

or

$$a_x = -\omega^2 A \cos \omega t = -4\pi^2 f^2 A \cos 2\pi f t. \tag{11.22}$$

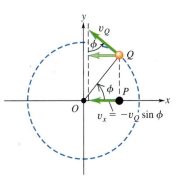

(a) Using the reference circle to determine the velocity of point P.

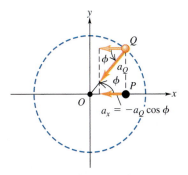

(b) Using the reference circle to determine the acceleration of point P.

▲ **FIGURE 11.21** The velocity and acceleration of point P are the horizontal components of the velocity and acceleration, respectively, of point Q.

The minus sign is needed because, at the instant shown, the acceleration is toward the left. When Q is to the left of the center, the acceleration of P is toward the right, but since $\cos \phi$ is negative at such points, the minus sign is still needed. Therefore, Equation 11.22 gives the acceleration of P at any time.

Now comes the reward for our lengthy analysis—the crucial step in showing that the motion of P is simple harmonic. We combine Equations 11.19 and 11.22, obtaining

$$a_x = -\omega^2 x. \tag{11.23}$$

Because ω is constant, **the acceleration a_x at each instant equals a negative constant times the displacement x at that instant.** But this is just the essential feature of simple harmonic motion, as given by Equation 11.12: Force and acceleration are proportional to the negative of the displacement from equilibrium. This shows that **the motion of P is indeed simple harmonic.**

 Quantitative Analysis 11.2

Using equations of motion

An object undergoing simple harmonic motion along the x axis obeys the equation $x = 12.0 \cos 0.25t$, where x is in cm and t is in seconds. Which of the following choices correctly gives the position, velocity, and acceleration of the object at the moment it is released (i.e., at time $t = 0$)?

A. $x = +12$ cm, $v_x = 0.00$ cm/s, $a_x = -0.75$ cm/s^2.
B. $x = 0.00$ cm, $v_x = 3.0$ cm/s, $a_x = 0.00$ cm/s^2.
C. $x = -12$ cm, $v_x = 0.00$ cm/s, $a_x = -0.75$ cm/s^2.
D. $x = 0.00$ cm, $v_x = -3.0$ cm/s, $a_x = 0.00$ cm/s^2.

SOLUTION At the initial time $t = 0$, the object has its maximum positive displacement, so at that instant $x = 12$ cm. The object is released from rest (i.e., with zero initial velocity), so $v_x = 0$. Only answer A is consistent with these two results. To confirm this choice, we can find the value of a_x at time $t = 0$. From Equation 11.19, $\omega = 0.25$ s^{-1}, and from Equation 11.22 at time $t = 0$, $a_x = -\omega^2 A = -(0.25$ s$^{-1})^2(12$ cm$) = -0.75$ cm/s^2 (also consistent with answer A). So answer A is correct.

▲ **Hanging in the balance.** Scientists recently used a single carbon nanotube to create a device to measure the mass of incredibly tiny objects, such as a tiny graphite particle with a mass of only 22 femtograms $(22 \times 10^{-15}$ g$)$. Although submicroscopic, this "nanobalance" was shown to obey the same physical laws as a macroscopic mass oscillating on the end of an elastic beam—in particular, the period and frequency of oscillation depend on the mass at the end. The nanotube's resonant frequency of oscillation in response to an applied voltage was measured with and without the tiny graphite particle attached at the end. This procedure allowed the scientists to determine the particle's mass, and the value agreed well with the calculated mass for a graphite particle of that size. Thus, someday soon it may be possible to determine directly the mass of individual cells and even virus particles.

Frequency and Period of an Object in Simple Harmonic Motion

We're now ready to find how the frequency f and angular frequency ω of simple harmonic motion are related to the physical properties of the system (the spring constant k and the mass m). To make Equations 11.12 and 11.23 agree completely, we must choose an angular velocity ω for the reference point Q such that

$$\omega^2 = \frac{k}{m}, \quad \text{or} \quad \omega = \sqrt{\frac{k}{m}}. \tag{11.24}$$

With this choice, the frequency of motion of Q is equal to that of the simple harmonic motion of the actual particle P:

Frequency and period of SHM in terms of mass m and force constant k

$$f = \frac{\omega}{2\pi} = \frac{1}{2\pi}\sqrt{\frac{k}{m}}. \tag{11.25}$$

The period T of the motion (the time for one cycle) is the reciprocal of the frequency: $T = 1/f$. From Equation 11.25,

$$T = \frac{1}{f} = 2\pi\sqrt{\frac{m}{k}}. \tag{11.26}$$

The general form of Equations 11.25 and 11.26 can be understood intuitively. When m is large, a given displacement (and force) causes a relatively small acceleration, and we expect the motion to be slow and ponderous, corresponding to small f and large T. A large value of k means a very stiff spring, corresponding to a relatively large restoring force for a given displacement, resulting in large f and small T.

It may be surprising that these equations *do not* contain the amplitude A of the motion. Suppose we give our spring–mass system some initial displacement, release it, and measure its frequency. Then we stop it, give it a *different* initial displacement, and release it again. We find that the two frequencies are the same. To be sure, the maximum displacement, maximum speed, and maximum acceleration are all different in the two cases, but *not* the frequency. When the amplitude is increased, the mass has a greater distance to travel during each cycle, but the force and acceleration are also greater, on the average. In SHM, these two effects exactly cancel.

NOTE ▶ The preceding paragraph sums up one of the most important characteristics of simple harmonic motion: **The frequency of the motion does not depend on its amplitude.** For instance, a tuning fork vibrates with the same frequency, regardless of how hard you hit it (i.e., regardless of the amplitude of its vibration). As we'll learn in the next chapter, the pitch of a musical tone is determined primarily by the frequency of vibration. Thus, tuning forks always produce the same note. Indeed, if it were not for this property of simple harmonic motion, it would be impossible to play most musical instruments in tune. ◀

Quantitative Analysis 11.3

Frequency of a spring–mass system

An object with mass $m = 4\ \text{kg}$ is attached to a spring and vibrates in simple harmonic motion with frequency f. When this object is replaced by one with mass 1 kg, the new object vibrates at a frequency of

A. f.
B. $2f$.
C. $4f$.
D. $\frac{1}{2}f$.

SOLUTION Equation 11.25 states that the frequency is related to the inverse square root of the mass. If the mass is reduced, then the frequency must increase, so B and C are possible answers. (This also makes sense physically, since the same force applied to a lighter mass produces a greater acceleration at any given point.) When the mass changes from 4 kg to 1 kg, the square root of the mass changes from 2 to 1 and its reciprocal from 1 to 2. So B is the correct answer.

We can simplify many of the relationships in simple harmonic motion by using the angular frequency $\omega = 2\pi f$ rather than the frequency f. In terms of ω, we can rewrite Equations 11.12 and 11.17 respectively as

$$a_x = -\frac{k}{m}x = -\omega^2 x,$$
$$v_x = \pm\omega\sqrt{A^2 - x^2}. \tag{11.27}$$

In these and most of the other equations of simple harmonic motion, using ω instead of f lets us avoid a lot of factors of 2π. By convention, the hertz is *not* used as a unit of angular frequency; the usual unit for ω is the radian per second, or simply s^{-1}.

Equations for position, velocity, and acceleration of a simple harmonic oscillator as functions of time

Here's a summary of our results for the position x, velocity v_x, and acceleration a_x of a simple harmonic oscillator as functions of time:

$$x = A\cos\omega t = A\cos(2\pi ft), \tag{11.19, 11.20}$$
$$v_x = -\omega A\sin\omega t = -2\pi fA\sin(2\pi ft), \tag{11.21}$$
$$a_x = -\omega^2 A\cos\omega t = -(2\pi f)^2 A\cos(2\pi ft). \tag{11.22}$$

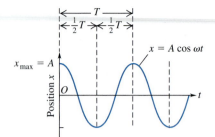

$x_{\text{max}} = A$

$x = A \cos \omega t$

(a) Position as a function of time

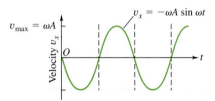

$v_{\text{max}} = \omega A$

$v_x = -\omega A \sin \omega t$

(b) Velocity as a function of time

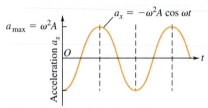

$a_{\text{max}} = \omega^2 A$

$a_x = -\omega^2 A \cos \omega t$

(c) Acceleration as a function of time

▲ **FIGURE 11.22** Graphs of position, velocity, and acceleration as functions of time for a particle in simple harmonic motion.

The strip chart pen moves in SHM on the spring while writing on the strip chart. The shadow of the peg follows the pen's motion exactly.

Pen trace

Strip chart pen mounted on spring

Light beam

Peg on rotating turntable

▲ **FIGURE 11.23** The strip chart pen, moving in simple harmonic motion, draws a curve of position as a function of time (the same curve as in Figure 11.22a). Meanwhile, the shadow of the peg on the turntable matches the motion of the pen.

Figure 11.22 shows graphs of these equations—for the position, velocity, and acceleration—as functions of time. We invite you to check that v_x at any time is the slope of the curve of x versus t and that a_x at any time is the slope of the curve of v_x versus t. We can plot a graph of x as a function of t with the help of an apparatus shown schematically in Figure 11.23.

Throughout this discussion, we've assumed that the initial position x_0 of the particle (at time $t = 0$) is its maximum positive displacement A (i.e., $x_0 = A$), but our analysis can be adapted to different starting conditions. Different initial positions correspond to different initial positions of the reference point Q. For example, if at time $t = 0$ the radial line OQ makes an angle ϕ_0 with the positive x axis, then the angle ϕ at time t is given, not by $\phi = \omega t$ as before, but by

$$\phi = \phi_0 + \omega t.$$

The object's position is then given as a function of time by

$$x = A \cos(\omega t + \phi_0).$$

With appropriate choices of the two quantities A and ϕ_0, this more general expression can be used to describe motion with any initial position and initial velocity. As before, the period and frequency are independent of the amplitude.

PROBLEM-SOLVING STRATEGY 11.1 **Simple harmonic motion** (MP)

SET UP

1. Be careful to distinguish between quantities that represent basic physical properties of the system and quantities that describe a particular motion that occurs when the system is set in motion in a specific way. The physical properties include the mass m, the force constant k, and the quantities derived from these, including the period T, the frequency f, and the angular frequency $\omega = 2\pi f$. In some problems, m or k, or both, can be determined from other information given about the system. Quantities that describe a particular motion include the amplitude A, the maximum velocity v_{max}, and any quantity that represents the position, velocity, or acceleration at a particular time.

SOLVE

2. If the problem involves a relation among position, velocity, and acceleration without reference to time, it is usually easier to use Equations 11.12 or 11.17 than to use the general expression for position as a function of time, Equation 11.19 or 11.20.

3. When detailed information about positions, velocities, and accelerations at various times is required, then Equations 11.20 through 11.22 must be used.

4. The energy equation, Equation 11.16, which includes the relation $E = \frac{1}{2}kA^2$, sometimes provides a convenient alternative to relations between velocity and position, especially when energy quantities are also required.

REFLECT

5. Try changing a value of one of the given quantities, and check whether the resulting changes in your answers make sense. Are they in the direction you would expect? Remember always to check for consistency of units in your results.

EXAMPLE 11.6 SHM on an air track, II: physical properties

Consider the oscillating air-track glider from Example 11.5 (Figure 11.24). As in that example, the force constant of the spring is $k = 200$ N/m and the glider mass is $m = 0.50$ kg. Find the angular frequency, frequency, and period of the glider's motion.

▲ **FIGURE 11.24**

SOLUTION

SET UP AND SOLVE All the necessary relations are contained in Equations 11.24 through 11.26. From Equation 11.24,

$$\omega = \sqrt{\frac{k}{m}} = \sqrt{\frac{200 \text{ N/m}}{0.50 \text{ kg}}} = \sqrt{\frac{200 \, (\text{kg} \cdot \text{m/s}^2)/\text{m}}{0.50 \text{ kg}}} = 20 \text{ s}^{-1},$$

and from Equation 11.25,

$$f = \frac{\omega}{2\pi} = 3.2 \text{ Hz}, \qquad T = \frac{1}{f} = 0.31 \text{ s}.$$

REFLECT The angular frequency is not directly proportional to the force constant, as one might naively guess. To double the value of ω, we would have to increase k by a factor of four.

Practice Problem: Suppose we could "tune" this system by varying the mass; what mass would be required for a period of 1.0 s? *Answer:* 5.1 kg.

EXAMPLE 11.7 SHM on an air track, III: position vs. time

Suppose the object in Example 11.6 is released from rest at $x = 0.040$ m. How much time is required for it to move halfway to the center from the initial position?

SOLUTION

SET UP We can use the circle of reference, as shown in Figure 11.25. We need to find the angle ϕ of the radial line OQ when the glider has moved from the initial position $x = A$ to the later position $x = A/2$. Then we need to find the time required for ϕ to change by the corresponding amount.

SOLVE From Figure 11.25, we see that $x = A/2$ when $\cos\phi = 1/2$ and $\phi = 60° = \pi/3$. Also, $\phi = \omega t$, so we find that

$$t = \frac{\phi}{\omega} = \frac{\pi/3}{20 \text{ s}^{-1}} = 0.052 \text{ s}.$$

REFLECT The radial line OQ rotates through an angle of $\pi/3$ (1/6 revolution) in 0.052 s, corresponding to a time equal to the period, $T = 0.31$ s, needed for a full revolution. Note that we *must* express the angular quantity ϕ in radians.

▲ **FIGURE 11.25**

Practice Problem: How much time is required for the glider to move from $x = A/2$ to $x = 0$? *Answer:* 0.026 s.

11.5 The Simple Pendulum

A **simple pendulum** is an idealized model consisting of a point mass suspended by a weightless, unstretchable string in a uniform gravitational field. When the mass is pulled to one side of its straight-down equilibrium position and released, it oscillates about the equilibrium position. Familiar situations such as a wrecking ball on a crane's cable, the plumb bob on a surveyor's transit, and a child on a swing can be modeled as simple pendulums. We can now analyze the motion of such systems, asking in particular whether it is simple harmonic.

9.10–9.11

The path of the object (modeled as a point mass) is an arc of a circle with radius L equal to the length of the string (Figure 11.26). We use as our coordinate the distance x measured along the arc. If the motion is simple harmonic, the restoring force must be directly proportional to x, or (because $x = L\theta$) to θ. Is it?

In Figure 11.26, we represent the forces on the mass in terms of tangential and radial components. The restoring force F at each point is the component of force tangent to the circular path at that point:

$$F = -mg\sin\theta. \tag{11.28}$$

The restoring force is therefore proportional *not* to θ, but to $\sin\theta$, so the motion is *not* simple harmonic. However, *if the angle θ is small,* $\sin\theta$ is very nearly equal to θ (in radians). For example, when $\theta = 0.1$ rad (about 6°), $\sin\theta = 0.0998$, a difference of only 0.2%. With this approximation, Equation 11.28 becomes

$$F = -mg\theta = -mg\frac{x}{L}, \quad \text{or}$$

$$F = -\frac{mg}{L}x. \tag{11.29}$$

(a) A real pendulum

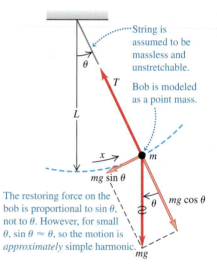

String is assumed to be massless and unstretchable.

Bob is modeled as a point mass.

The restoring force on the bob is proportional to sin θ, not to θ. However, for small θ, sin θ ≈ θ, so the motion is *approximately* simple harmonic.

(b) An idealized simple pendulum

▲ **FIGURE 11.26** The simple pendulum, an idealized model of a real pendulum.

The restoring force F is then proportional to the coordinate x *for small displacements,* and the constant mg/L represents the force constant k. From Equation 11.24, the angular frequency ω of a simple pendulum with small amplitude is given by the following expressions:

Frequency and period of simple pendulum with length L:

$$\omega = \sqrt{\frac{k}{m}} = \sqrt{\frac{mg/L}{m}} = \sqrt{\frac{g}{L}}. \tag{11.30}$$

The corresponding frequency and period relations are

$$f = \frac{\omega}{2\pi} = \frac{1}{2\pi}\sqrt{\frac{g}{L}}, \tag{11.31}$$

$$T = \frac{2\pi}{\omega} = \frac{1}{f} = 2\pi\sqrt{\frac{L}{g}}. \tag{11.32}$$

Note that these expressions don't contain the *mass* of the particle. This is because the restoring force, a component of the particle's weight, is proportional to m. Thus, the mass appears on *both* sides of $\sum\vec{F} = m\vec{a}$ and cancels out. **For small oscillations, the period of a pendulum for a given value of g is independent of its mass and is determined entirely by its length.**

Galileo invented an elegant argument four centuries ago to show that the period should be independent of the mass. Make a simple pendulum, said Galileo, measure its period, and then split the pendulum down the middle, string and all. Because of the symmetry, neither half could have been pushing or pulling on the other before it was split. So splitting it can't change the motion, and each half must swing with the same period as the original. Therefore, the period cannot depend on the mass!

The dependence of the angular frequency, the frequency, and the period on L and g in Equations 11.30 through 11.32, respectively, is just what we should expect on the basis of everyday experience. A long pendulum has a longer period than a shorter one. Increasing g increases the restoring force, causing the frequency to increase and the period to decrease.

▶ **As the world turns.** In 1848, Jean-Bernard-Léon Foucault used a very long pendulum, now known as a Foucault pendulum, to demonstrate the rotation of the Earth itself. Newton's first law tells us that a pendulum tends to oscillate in a single plane in space unless a force deflects it. However, the plane of rotation of a Foucault pendulum seems to *rotate* in space: If the pendulum starts out swinging north–south, later in the day it will be swinging east–west. Is Newton wrong? No; the pendulum's plane of motion does not change, but the surface of the *earth* rotates beneath it. We humans see the pendulum as rotating because we mistake the earth's surface for an inertial frame of reference.

The simple pendulum is also a precise and convenient method for measuring the acceleration due to gravity (g), since L and T can be measured easily. Such measurements are often used in geophysics. Local deposits of ore or oil affect the local value of g because their density differs from that of their surroundings. Precise measurements of g over an area being surveyed often furnish valuable information about the nature of the underlying deposits.

NOTE ▶ We emphasize again that **the motion of a pendulum is only** *approximately* **simple harmonic.** For very small displacements, the approximation is quite precise. For example, when the angular amplitude is 15°, the actual period differs from the prediction of our approximate analysis by less than 0.5%. Indeed, the usefulness of the pendulum in clocks depends on the fact that, for small amplitudes, the motion is very nearly independent of amplitude. ◀

Changing the length of a pendulum

A pendulum with a string of length L swings with a period T. If the string is made twice as long, the pendulum's period will be about

A. T.
B. $\sqrt{2}T$.
C. 2T.

SOLUTION By now you should be able to work problems like this in your head quickly with thinking like the following: Since T is proportional to $\sqrt{L}$ (see Equation 11.32), if L is changed to 2L, then T changes to $\sqrt{2}T$. Thus, the answer is B. In more detail, Equation 11.23 can also be written as

$$\frac{T_{\text{new}}}{T_{\text{old}}} = \frac{\sqrt{L_{\text{new}}}}{\sqrt{L_{\text{old}}}} = \frac{\sqrt{2L_{\text{old}}}}{\sqrt{L_{\text{old}}}} = \sqrt{2}.$$

EXAMPLE 11.8 Period and frequency of a simple pendulum

Find the period and frequency of a simple pendulum 1.000 m long in Pittsburgh, where $g = 9.801$ m/s².

SOLUTION

SET UP AND SOLVE From Equation 11.32,

$$T = 2\pi\sqrt{\frac{1.000 \text{ m}}{9.801 \text{ m/s}^2}} = 2.007 \text{ s}$$

and

$$f = \frac{1}{T} = 0.4983 \text{ Hz}.$$

REFLECT The period is almost exactly 2 s; at one time there was a proposal to define the second as half the period of a 1-meter pendulum.

EXAMPLE 11.9 The lost Martian

A Martian who frequently gets lost in the solar system keeps a ball on a string so that he can always figure out what planet he happens to be on. On Mars, where the acceleration due to gravity is $g_{\text{Mars}} = 0.38g_{\text{earth}}$, the ball oscillates with a period of 1.5 s when it is swung like a pendulum bob (Figure 11.27). During one journey, the Martian finds himself on a planet where the ball oscillates with a period of 0.92 s. What planet is he on?

Continued

SOLUTION

SET UP Each planet has a different value of the gravitational acceleration g near its surface. The Martian can measure g at his location, and from this he can determine what planet he's on. First we use the information about Mars to find the length L of the string that the Martian is swinging. Then we use that length to find the acceleration due to gravity on the unknown planet.

SOLVE First we use the Mars data to determine L. We solve Equation 11.32 for L:

$$T_{Mars} = 2\pi\sqrt{\frac{L}{g_{Mars}}} \quad \text{and}$$

$$L = \frac{T^2 g_{Mars}}{4\pi^2} = \frac{T^2(0.38g_{earth})}{4\pi^2} = \frac{(1.5\ s)^2(0.38 \times 9.8\ m/s^2)}{4\pi^2}$$
$$= 0.21\ m.$$

Now we use this value of L with $T = 0.92\ s$ to solve for the acceleration due to gravity on the unknown planet, g_{planet}:

$$g_{planet} = \frac{4\pi^2 L}{T^2} = \frac{4\pi^2(0.21\ m)}{(0.92\ s)^2} = 9.8\ m/s^2.$$

The Martian is surprised to find that he is on planet earth!

REFLECT In principle, the Martian can use this method to measure the acceleration due to gravity of any planet or satellite while traveling around the universe.

On Mars:
Period = 1.5 s
$g_{Mars} = 0.38g_{Earth}$

Unknown planet:
Period = 0.92 s
$g = ?$

▲ **FIGURE 11.27**

Practice Problem: The acceleration due to gravity near the surface of the moon is about $1.6\ m/s^2$. If the Martian arrives there and swings the same pendulum bob, what will be the period of the pendulum? *Answer: $T = 2.3\ s$.*

11.6 Damped and Forced Oscillations

The idealized oscillating systems that we've discussed thus far are frictionless. There are no nonconservative forces, the total mechanical energy is constant, and a system set into motion continues oscillating forever with no decrease in amplitude.

Real-world systems always have some friction, however, and oscillations do die out with time unless we provide some means for replacing the mechanical energy lost to friction. A pendulum clock continues to run because the potential energy stored in the spring or a hanging weight system replaces the mechanical energy lost because of friction in the pendulum and the gears. But the spring eventually runs down, or the weights reach the bottom of their travel. Then no more energy is available, and the pendulum swings decrease in amplitude and stop.

◄ **Don't get hammered.** The oscillation of this construction worker's jackhammer is very effective at breaking up hard surfaces, such as concrete and asphalt. However, the repetitive motion can also damage the nerves and blood vessels in the hands, leading to the pain, tingling, and numbness characteristic of Raynaud's syndrome, or "white finger." It is not just the mechanical pounding on the tissue that causes the damage, but also the frequency of the vibration itself, which can set up damaging resonances in the human body. As little as five minutes of exposure to vibrations of 60 Hz can damage small arteries, and slower vibrations of 2 to 4 Hz can cause whole-body resonance as they are transmitted through the human skeleton. Occupational safety experts are designing new equipment and protective gear to minimize vibration-induced injury for workers using oscillating equipment.

The decrease in amplitude caused by dissipative forces is called **damping,** and the corresponding motion is called **damped oscillation.** The suspension system of an automobile is a familiar example of damped oscillations. The shock absorbers (Figure 11.28) provide a velocity-dependent damping force. The direction of the force always opposes the car's up-and-down motion, so that when the car goes over a bump, it doesn't continue bouncing forever. For optimal passenger comfort, the system should have enough damping that it bounces only once or twice after each bump. As the shocks get old and worn, the damping decreases and the bouncing is more persistent. Not only is this nauseating, but it is bad for steering, because the front wheels have less positive contact with the ground. Thus, damping is an advantage in this kind of system. But in a system such as a clock or an electrical oscillating system in a radio transmitter, it is often desirable to have as little damping as possible.

Figure 11.29 shows graphs of position x as a function of time for a damped oscillator—one graph for a relatively small damping force, the other for greater damping.

What happens when an additional periodically varying force is applied to an oscillating system? A factory floor supported by a slightly flexible steel framework may begin to vibrate when an oscillating machine rests on it. Or consider your little brother on a playground swing. You can keep him swinging with constant amplitude by giving him a little push once each cycle. More generally, we can maintain a constant-amplitude oscillation in a damped harmonic oscillator by applying a force that varies with time in a periodic or cyclic way, with a definite period and frequency. We call this additional force a **driving force.**

We denote the angular frequency of the driving force by ω_d. This angular frequency doesn't have to equal the angular frequency ω with which the system would naturally oscillate without a driving force. When a periodically varying driving force is present, the mass can undergo a periodic motion *with the same angular frequency ω_d as that of the driving force.* We call this motion a **forced oscillation,** or a *driven oscillation;* it is different from the motion that occurs when the system is simply set into motion and then left alone to oscillate with its natural frequency ω. The frequency of a forced oscillation is that of the driving force, not the system's natural frequency.

When the angular frequency of the driving force is nearly *equal* to the natural angular frequency $\omega = \sqrt{k/m}$ of the system, we are forcing the system to vibrate with a frequency that is close to the frequency it would have even with no driving force. In this case, we expect the amplitude of the resulting oscillation to be larger than it is when the two frequencies ω and ω_d are very different. This expectation is borne out by more detailed analysis and by experimental observation.

If we vary the frequency ω_d of the driving force, the amplitude of the resulting forced oscillation varies in an interesting way (Figure 11.30). When there is very little damping, the amplitude goes through a sharp peak as the driving angular frequency ω_d nears the natural oscillation angular frequency ω. When the damping is increased, the peak becomes broader and smaller in height and shifts toward lower frequencies.

The fact that there is an amplitude peak at driving frequencies close to the natural frequency of the system is called **resonance.** Physics is full of examples of resonance; building up the oscillations of a child on a swing by pushing with a frequency equal to the swing's natural frequency is one. A vibrating rattle in a car that occurs only at a certain engine speed or wheel-rotation speed is an all-too-familiar example. You may have heard of the dangers of a band marching in step

▲ FIGURE 11.28 A shock absorber used in a car. The top part, connected to the piston, is attached to the car's frame; the bottom part, connected to the lower cylinder, is connected to the axle. The viscous fluid causes a damping force that depends on the relative velocity of the two ends of the unit. The device helps control wheel bounce and jounce.

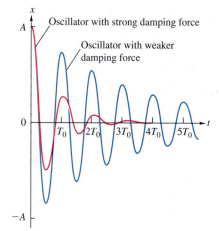

▲ FIGURE 11.29 Graph showing damped harmonic oscillation for two oscillators, one strongly damped and one more weakly damped.

Each curve shows the amplitude for an oscillator subjected to a driving force at various angular frequencies.

Successive curves from blue to gold represent successively greater damping forces.

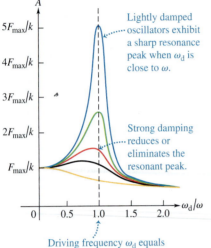

Lightly damped oscillators exhibit a sharp resonance peak when ω_d is close to ω.

Strong damping reduces or eliminates the resonant peak.

Driving frequency ω_d equals angular frequency ω of oscillator.

▲ **FIGURE 11.30** Graph of the amplitude A of the forced oscillation of a damped harmonic oscillator as a function of the angular frequency ω_d of the driving force. (The latter is plotted on the horizontal axis as the ratio of ω_d to the angular frequency $\omega = \sqrt{k/m}$ of an undamped oscillator.)

across a bridge. If the frequency of their steps is close to a natural vibration frequency of the bridge, dangerously large oscillations can build up. Inexpensive loudspeakers often have an annoying buzz or boom when a musical note happens to coincide with the resonant frequency of the speaker cone.

Finally, we mention the famous collapse of the Tacoma Narrows suspension bridge in 1940; nearly everyone has seen the film of this catastrophe (Figure 11.31). This is usually cited as an example of resonance, but there's some doubt as to whether it should be called that. The wind didn't have to vary *periodically* with a frequency close to a natural frequency of the bridge. The air flow past the bridge is turbulent, and vortices are formed with a regular frequency that depends on the flow speed. It is conceivable that this frequency may have resonated with a natural frequency of the bridge. But the cause may well have been something more subtle called a *self-excited oscillation,* in which the aerodynamic forces caused by a *steady* wind blowing on the bridge tended to displace it farther from equilibrium at times when it was already moving away from equilibrium.

It is as though we had a velocity-dependent damping force, but with the direction reversed. In that case, the force always has the *same* direction as the velocity and becomes an *anti-damping* force. Instead of draining mechanical energy away from the system, this force pumps energy into the system, building up the oscillations to destructive amplitudes. A similar phenomenon is the flapping of a flag in a wind.

The Tacoma Narrows bridge has been rebuilt, and engineers have now learned how to stabilize suspension bridges, both structurally and aerodynamically, to prevent such disasters.

▲ **FIGURE 11.31** The Tacoma Narrows Bridge collapsed four months and six days after it was opened for traffic. The main span was 2800 ft long and 39 ft wide, with 8-ft-high steel stiffening girders on both sides. The maximum amplitude of the twisting vibrations was 35°; the frequency was about 0.2 Hz.

SUMMARY

Stress, Strain, and Elastic Deformation

(Section 11.1) Forces that tend to stretch, squeeze, or twist an object constitute **stress.** The resulting deformation is called **strain.** Particularly for small deformations, stress and strain may be directly proportional: Stress/Strain = constant (Equation 11.1). We call this relationship **Hooke's law.**

Tensile and compressive stresses stretch and compress an object, respectively. Tensile stress is tensile force per unit area, $F_\perp/A$ (Equation 11.2). Tensile strain is the fractional change in length, $\Delta l/l_0$ (Equation 11.3).

Pressure or **volume stress** is force per unit area: $p = (F_\perp/A)$ (Equation 11.5). The force is a uniform force around an object and acts to increase or decrease its volume. The resulting deformation is volume **strain,** $\Delta V/V_0$ (Equation 11.6).

Shear stress is tangent force per unit area: $F_\parallel/A$ (Equation 11.8). The resulting deformation is **shear strain.**

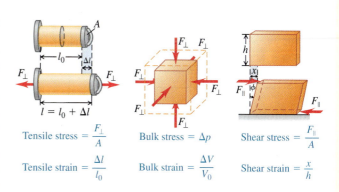

Tensile stress $= \dfrac{F_\perp}{A}$ Bulk stress $= \Delta p$ Shear stress $= \dfrac{F_\parallel}{A}$

Tensile strain $= \dfrac{\Delta l}{l_0}$ Bulk strain $= \dfrac{\Delta V}{V_0}$ Shear strain $= \dfrac{x}{h}$

Elasticity and Plasticity

(Section 11.1) For small stresses, the strain of many materials is elastic; when the stress is removed, an object returns to its original size and shape. For stresses beyond a particular value, the deformation becomes **plastic:** when the stress is removed, the object does not return to its original shape. At a high enough stress, the object breaks.

Periodic Motion

(Section 11.2) Periodic motion is motion that repeats itself in a definite cycle. Periodic motion occurs whenever an object has a stable equilibrium position and is subject to a restoring force that acts when the object is displaced from equilibrium. When the restoring force is directly proportional to the displacement ($F_x = -kx$), which is often the case for small displacements, the resulting motion is called **simple harmonic motion.**

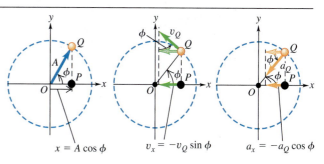

Energy in Simple Harmonic Motion

(Section 11.3) In simple harmonic motion, the total mechanical energy is constant: $E = \frac{1}{2}mv_x^2 + \frac{1}{2}kx^2 = \text{constant}$ (Equation 11.15). At points of maximum displacement, where $x = A$ and $v_x = 0$, all of the energy is in the form of elastic potential energy, so the (constant) total mechanical energy can be expressed as $E = \frac{1}{2}kA^2$ (Equation 11.16).

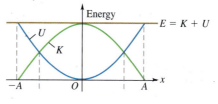

Equations of Simple Harmonic Motion

(Section 11.4) We obtain equations describing simple harmonic motion by using the **circle of reference.** We consider a point that moves counterclockwise with constant angular velocity ω around a circle of radius A. By evaluating the x components of the point's position, velocity, and acceleration, we find that

$$x = A\cos\omega t = A\cos(2\pi ft), \quad (11.19,\ 11.20)$$
$$v_x = -\omega A\sin\omega t = -2\pi f A\sin(2\pi ft), \quad (11.21)$$
$$a_x = -\omega^2 A\cos\omega t = -(2\pi f)^2 A\cos(2\pi ft). \quad (11.22)$$

$x = A\cos\phi$ $v_x = -v_Q\sin\phi$ $a_x = -a_Q\cos\phi$

Continued

The Simple Pendulum

(Section 11.5) A **simple pendulum** is an idealized model consisting of a point mass suspended from a string with length L. For small amplitudes, the motion is nearly simple harmonic and the angular frequency is nearly independent of the amplitude and the object's mass: $\omega = \sqrt{g/L}$ (Equation 11.30). For larger displacements, the frequency depends on the amplitude.

Damped and Forced Oscillations

(Section 11.6) Real-world systems always have some friction (damping); oscillations die out with time, unless the lost mechanical energy is replaced.

When a periodically varying force is added to a harmonic oscillator, the resulting motion is called a **forced oscillation.** The system can then oscillate with a frequency equal to that of the driving force ω_d, not the system's natural oscillation frequency $\omega = \sqrt{k/m}$. The amplitude peaks as ω_d nears the natural frequency ω; this phenomenon is called **resonance.**

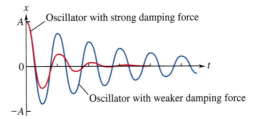

Oscillator with strong damping force

Oscillator with weaker damping force

(MP) For instructor-assigned homework, go to www.masteringphysics.com

Conceptual Questions

1. Think of several examples in everyday life of motion that is at least approximately simple harmonic. In what respects does each differ from SHM?

2. The analysis of simple harmonic motion in this chapter neglected the mass of the spring. How would the spring's mass affect the period and frequency of the motion? Explain your reasoning.

3. In any periodic motion, unavoidable friction always causes the amplitude to decrease with time. Does friction also affect the *period* of the motion? Give a qualitative argument to support your answer. (*Hint:* Does the friction affect the kinetic energy? If so, how does this affect the speed, and therefore the period, of a cycle?)

4. A mass attached by a light spring to the ceiling of an elevator oscillates vertically while the elevator ascends with constant acceleration. Is the period greater than, less than, or the same as when the elevator is at rest? Why?

5. A pendulum is mounted in an elevator that moves upward with constant acceleration. Is the period greater than, less than, or the same as when the elevator is at rest? Why?

6. At what point in the motion of a simple pendulum is (a) the tension in the string greatest, (b) the string tension least, (c) the radial acceleration greatest, (d) the angular acceleration least, (e) the speed greatest?

7. Looking at the molecular structure of matter, discuss why gases are generally more compressible than liquids and solids.

8. If a mass–spring system and a simple pendulum are vibrating "in sync" on earth, would they still vibrate "in sync" on Mars, where the pull of gravity is weaker than on our planet? If so, why? If not, which one would have a higher frequency on Mars?

9. Which could you use as a timekeeping device in an orbiting satellite, a pendulum or a mass on a spring? Or could you use them both? Why?

10. What happens to the original energy as a damped pendulum (or spring) "runs down"? Explain *how* this energy gets dissipated.

11. Distinguish clearly between the angular frequency (ω) and the angular velocity (also ω) of a pendulum. Which of the two quantities is constant?

12. It is easy to get mixed up and think that the angular frequency ω of a pendulum is equal to $\sqrt{L/g}$ instead of $\sqrt{g/L}$. How can you use dimensional analysis to find out which version is the correct formula? Would such an analysis help to identify missing (or extra) factors of 2π? Why?

13. On the basis of your own simple observations, do you think that concrete behaves the same under *tensile* stress as it does under *compressive* stress? Discuss your reasoning.

14. Would you expect a rubber band to have a larger or a smaller force constant than that of an iron wire? Why? How would you think that Young's modulus for these two materials would compare?

15. Would you expect Styrofoam™ to have a larger or a smaller bulk modulus than that of wood? Why?

Multiple-Choice Questions

1. A spring–mass system is undergoing simple harmonic motion of amplitude 2.0 cm and angular frequency 10.0 s^{-1}. The acceleration of the mass as it passes through the equilibrium position is
   A. 0.00 m/s^2.   B. 0.20 m/s^2.
   C. 2.0 m/s^2.   D. 31.4 m/s^2.

2. In a design for a piece of medical apparatus, you need a material that is easily compressed when a pressure is applied to it.
   A. This material should have a large bulk modulus.
   B. This material should have a small bulk modulus.
   C. The bulk modulus is not relevant to this situation.

3. If the force F in Figure 11.32 is constant over the area A, the pressure on that area is
   A. 2.50 Pa.
   B. 4.33 Pa.
   C. 5.00 Pa.

$F = 10.0$ N
$60.0°$
$A = 2.00$ m^2

▲ **FIGURE 11.32** Multiple-choice problem 3.

4. In the previous question, the shear stress on A due to the force F is
   A. 2.50 Pa.
   B. 4.33 Pa.
   C. 5.00 Pa.

5. When a mass attached to a spring is released from rest 3.0 cm from its equilibrium position, it oscillates with frequency f. If this mass were instead released from rest 6.0 cm from its equilibrium position, it would oscillate with frequency
   A. $2f$.
   B. $\sqrt{2}f$
   C. f.
   D. $f/2$

6. As the bob on a pendulum swings down toward its lowest point, its angular frequency ω
   A. increases.
   B. decreases.
   C. does not change.

7. Suppose you increase the amplitude of oscillation of a mass vibrating on a spring. Which of the following statements about this mass are correct? (There may be more than one correct choice.)
   A. Its maximum speed increases.
   B. Its period of oscillation increases.
   C. Its maximum acceleration increases.
   D. Its maximum kinetic energy increases.

8. An object of mass M suspended by a spring vibrates with period T. If this object is replaced by one of mass $4M$, the new object vibrates with a period
   A. T.
   B. $2T$.
   C. $4T$.
   D. $16T$.

9. When two wires of identical dimensions are used to hang 25 kg weights, wire A is observed to stretch twice as much as wire B. From this observation, you can make the following conclusions about the Young's moduli of these wires:
   A. $Y_A = 4Y_B$.
   B. $Y_A = 2Y_B$.
   C. $Y_A = \frac{1}{2}Y_B$.
   D. $Y_A = \frac{1}{4}Y_B$.

10. A mass on a spring oscillates with a period T. If both the mass and the force constant of the spring are doubled, the new period will be
    A. $4T$.
    B. $\sqrt{2}T$.
    C. T.
    D. $T/\sqrt{2}$.
    E. $T/4$.

11. A pendulum oscillates with a period T. If both the mass of the bob and the length of the pendulum are doubled, the new period will be
    A. $4T$.
    B. $\sqrt{2}T$.
    C. T.
    D. $T/\sqrt{2}$.
    E. $T/4$.

12. When a weight is hung from a cylindrical wire of diameter D, it produces a tensile stress X in the wire. If the same weight is hung from a wire having twice the diameter as the first one, the tensile stress in this wire will be
    A. $X/\sqrt{2}$.
    B. $X/2$.
    C. $X/4$.
    D. $2X$.
    E. $4X$.

13. An object with mass M suspended by a spring vibrates with frequency f. When a second object is attached to the first, the system now vibrates with frequency $f/2$. The mass of the second object is
    A. $4M$.
    B. $3M$.
    C. $2M$.
    D. M.

14. A pendulum on earth swings with angular frequency ω. On an unknown planet, it swings with angular frequency $\omega/2$. The acceleration due to gravity on this planet is
    A. $4g$.
    B. $2g$.
    C. $g/2$.
    D. $g/4$.

15. A mass oscillates with simple harmonic motion of amplitude A. The kinetic energy of the mass will equal the potential energy of the spring when the position is
    A. $x = 0$.
    B. $x = A/2$.
    C. $x = A/\sqrt{2}$.
    D. $x = A/4$.

Problems

11.1 Stress, Strain, and Elastic Deformations

1. • A thin, light wire 75.0 cm long having a circular cross section 0.550 mm in diameter has a 25.0 kg weight attached to it, causing it to stretch by 1.10 mm. (a) What is the stress in this wire? (b) What is the strain of the wire? (c) Find Young's modulus for the material of the wire.

2. • A metal rod that is 4.00 m long and 0.50 cm^2 in cross-sectional area is found to stretch 0.20 cm under a tension of 5000 N. What is Young's modulus for this metal?

3. • A vertical solid steel post 25 cm in diameter and 2.50 m long is required to support a load of 8000 kg. You may ignore the weight of the post. What are (a) the stress in the post, (b) the strain in the post, and (c) the change in the post's length when the load is applied?

4. • A 5.0 kg mass is hung by a vertical steel wire 0.500 m long and 6.0×10^{-3} cm^2 in cross-sectional area. Hanging from the bottom of this mass is a similar steel wire, from which in turn hangs a 10.0 kg mass. For each wire, compute (a) the tensile strain and (b) the elongation.

5. • **Biceps muscle.** A relaxed biceps muscle requires a force of **BIO** 25.0 N for an elongation of 3.0 cm; under maximum tension, the same muscle requires a force of 500 N for the same elongation. Find Young's modulus for the muscle tissue under each of these conditions if the muscle can be modeled as a uniform cylinder with an initial length of 0.200 m and a cross-sectional area of 50.0 cm^2.

6. • **Stress on a mountaineer's rope.** A nylon rope used by mountaineers elongates 1.10 m under the weight of a 65.0 kg climber. If the rope is 45.0 m in length and 7.0 mm in diameter, what is Young's modulus for this nylon?

7. • A steel wire 2.00 m long with circular cross section must stretch no more than 0.25 cm when a 400.0 N weight is hung from one of its ends. What minimum diameter must this wire have?

8. • **Achilles tendon.** The Achilles tendon, which connects the **BIO** calf muscles to the heel, is the thickest and strongest tendon in the body. In extreme activities, such as sprinting, it can be subjected to forces as high as 13 times a person's weight. According to one set of experiments, the average area of the Achilles tendon is 78.1 mm^2, its average length is 25 cm, and its average Young's modulus is 1474 MPa. (a) How much tensile

stress is required to stretch this muscle by 5.0% of its length? (b) If we model the tendon as a spring, what is its force constant? (c) If a 75 kg sprinter exerts a force of 13 times his weight on his Achilles tendon, by how much will it stretch?

9. •• **Artificial tendons.** The largest Young's modulus measured
BIO for any biological material is 30 GPa, for the S-layer of cell walls. Suppose that in the future we are able to use this material to construct an artificial Achilles tendon (see previous problem) for an athlete who has damaged his. The artificial Achilles tendon should be just as long as the original one so that it can connect at the proper places. (a) If the artificial tendon has a circular cross section, what should be its diameter be so that it will have the same force constant as the natural Achilles tendon? (b) How does this diameter compare with that of a natural Achilles tendon?

10. •• **Human hair.** According to one set of measurements, the
BIO tensile strength of hair is 196 MPa, which produces a maximum strain of 0.40 in the hair. The thickness of hair varies considerably, but let's use a diameter of 50 μm. (a) What is the magnitude of the force giving this tensile stress? (b) If the length of a strand of the hair is 12 cm at its breaking point, what was its unstressed length?

11. •• **The effect of jogging on the knees.** High-impact activi-
BIO ties such as jogging can cause considerable damage to the cartilage at the knee joints. Peak loads on each knee can be eight times body weight during jogging. The bones at the knee are separated by cartilage called the medial and lateral meniscus. Although it varies considerably, the force at impact acts over approximately 10 cm^2 of this cartilage. Human cartilage has a Young's modulus of about 24 MPa (although that also varies). (a) By what percent does the peak load impact of jogging compress the knee cartilage of a 75 kg person? (b) What would be the percentage for a lower-impact activity, such as power walking, for which the peak load is about four times body weight?

12. • A specimen of oil having an initial volume of 600 cm^3 is subjected to a pressure increase of 3.6×10^6 Pa, and the volume is found to decrease by 0.45 cm^3. What is the bulk modulus (in Pa) of the material?

13. • In the Challenger Deep of the Marianas Trench, the depth of seawater is 10.9 km and the pressure is 1.16×10^8 Pa (about 1150 atmospheres). (a) If a cubic meter of water is taken to this depth from the surface (where the normal atmospheric pressure is about 1.0×10^5 Pa), what is the change in its volume? Assume that the bulk modulus for seawater is the same as for freshwater $(2.2 \times 10^9$ Pa$)$. (b) At the surface, seawater has a density of 1.03×10^3 kg/m^3. What is the density of seawater at the depth of the Challenger Deep?

14. • **Effect of diving on blood.** It is reasonable to assume that
BIO the bulk modulus of blood is about the same as that of water (2.2 GPa). As one goes deeper and deeper in the ocean, the pressure *increases* by 1.0×10^4 Pa for every meter below the surface. (a) If a diver goes down 33 m (a bit over 100 ft) in the ocean, by how much does each cubic centimeter of her blood change in volume? (b) How deep must a diver go so that each drop of blood compresses to half its volume at the surface? Is the ocean deep enough to have this effect on the diver?

15. • **Oil on Venus.** The bulk modulus for oil is 5.0 GPa. If you take 5.00 L of oil from the earth to Venus, where the surface pressure is 92 atmospheres, how much will its volume change,

assuming that it is in a flexible (and hence compressible) container? (Ignore the temperature change.)

16. •• **Compression of human bone.** The bulk modulus for bone
BIO is 15 GPa. (a) If a diver-in-training is put into a pressurized suit, by how much would the pressure have to be raised (in atmospheres) above atmospheric pressure to compress her bones by 0.10% of their original volume? (b) Given that the pressure in the ocean increases by 1.0×10^4 Pa for every meter of depth below the surface, how deep would this diver have to go for her bones to compress by 0.10%? Does it seem that bone compression is a problem she needs to be concerned with when diving?

17. • In Figure 11.33, suppose the object is a square steel plate, 10.0 cm on a side and 1.00 cm thick. Find the magnitude of force required on each of the four sides to cause a shear strain of 0.0400.

▲ **FIGURE 11.33** Problem 17.

18. • In lab tests on a 9.25 cm cube of a certain material, a force of 1375 N directed at 8.50° to the cube, as shown in Figure 11.34, causes the cube to deform through an angle of 1.24°. What is the shear modulus of the material?

▲ **FIGURE 11.34** Problem 18.

▲ **FIGURE 11.35** Problem 19.

19. • **Downhill hiking.** During vigorous downhill hiking, the
BIO force on the knee cartilage (the medial and lateral meniscus) can be up to eight times body weight. Depending on the angle of descent, this force can cause a large shear force on the cartilage and deform it. The cartilage has an area of about 10 cm^2 and a shear modulus of 12 MPa. If the hiker plus his pack have a combined mass of 110 kg (not unreasonable), and if the maximum force at impact is 8 times his body weight (which, of course, includes the weight of his pack) at an angle of 12° with the cartilage (see Figure 11.35), through what angle (in degrees) will his knee cartilage be deformed? (Recall that the bone below the cartilage pushes upward with the same force as the downward force.)

20. • A steel wire has the following properties:

Length = 5.00 m
Cross-sectional area = 0.040 cm^2
Young's modulus = 2.0×10^{11} Pa
Shear modulus = 0.84×10^{11} Pa
Proportional limit = 3.60×10^8 Pa
Breaking stress = 11.0×10^8 Pa

The wire is fastened at its upper end and hangs vertically. (a) How great a weight can be hung from the wire without exceeding the proportional limit? (b) How much does the wire stretch under this load? (c) What is the maximum weight that can be supported?

21. •• A steel cable with cross-sectional area of 3.00 cm² has an elastic limit of 2.40×10^8 Pa. Find the maximum upward acceleration that can be given to a 1200 kg elevator supported by the cable if the stress is not to exceed one-third of the elastic limit.

22. •• **Weight lifting.** The legs of a weight lifter must ultimately **BIO** support the weights he has lifted. A human tibia (shinbone) has a circular cross section of approximately 3.6 cm outer diameter and 2.5 cm inner diameter. (The hollow portion contains marrow.) If a 90 kg lifter stands on both legs, what is the heaviest weight he can lift without breaking his legs, assuming that the breaking stress of the bone is 200 MPa?

11.2 Periodic Motion

23. • (a) **Music.** When a person sings, his or her vocal cords **BIO** vibrate in a repetitive pattern having the same frequency of the note that is sung. If someone sings the note B flat that has a frequency of 466 Hz, how much time does it take the person's vocal cords to vibrate through one complete cycle, and what is the angular frequency of the cords? (b) **Hearing.** When sound waves strike the eardrum, this membrane vibrates with the same frequency as the sound. The highest pitch that typical humans can hear has a period of 50.0 μs. What are the frequency and angular frequency of the vibrating eardrum for this sound? (c) **Vision.** When light having vibrations with angular frequency ranging from 2.7×10^{15} rad/s to 4.7×10^{15} rad/s strikes the retina of the eye, it stimulates the receptor cells there and is perceived as visible light. What are the limits of the period and frequency of this light? (d) **Ultrasound.** High-frequency sound waves (ultrasound) are used to probe the interior of the body, much as x rays do. To detect a small objects such as tumors, a frequency of around 5.0 MHz is used. What are the period and angular frequency of the molecular vibrations caused by this pulse of sound?

24. • Find the period, frequency, and angular frequency of (a) the second hand and (b) the minute hand of a wall clock.

25. • If an object on a horizontal frictionless surface is attached to a spring, displaced, and then released, it oscillates. Suppose it is displaced 0.120 m from its equilibrium position and released with zero initial speed. After 0.800 s, its displacement is found to be 0.120 m on the opposite side and it has passed the equilibrium position once during this interval. Find (a) the amplitude, (b) the period, and (c) the frequency of the motion.

26. • The graph shown in Figure 11.36 closely approximates the displacement x of a tuning fork as a function of time t as it is

▲ **FIGURE 11.36** Problem 26.

playing a single note. What are (a) the amplitude, (b) period , (c) frequency, and (d) angular frequency of this fork's motion?

27. • **The human voice.** The voiceprint shown in Figure 11.37 **BIO** represents the displacement of a vocal cord of a bass singer singing a single note. This motion is *not* simple harmonic motion, but it *is* periodic. What are (a) the period of vibration of this vocal cord, (b) its frequency of vibration, and (c) its angular frequency?

▲ **FIGURE 11.37** Problem 27.

11.3 Energy in Simple Harmonic Motion

28. • A 0.500 kg glider on an air track is attached to the end of an ideal spring with force constant 450 N/m; it undergoes simple harmonic motion with an amplitude of 0.040 m. Compute (a) the maximum speed of the glider, (b) the speed of the glider when it is at $x = -0.015$ m, (c) the magnitude of the maximum acceleration of the glider, (d) the acceleration of the glider at $x = -0.015$ m, and (e) the total mechanical energy of the glider at any point in its motion.

29. • A 0.150 kg toy is undergoing SHM on the end of a horizontal spring with force constant 300.0 N/m. When the object is 0.0120 m from its equilibrium position, it is observed to have a speed of 0.300 m/s. Find (a) the total energy of the object at any point in its motion, (b) the amplitude of the motion, and (c) the maximum speed attained by the object during its motion.

30. • A 2.00 kg frictionless block is attached to an ideal spring with force constant 315 N/m. Initially the spring is neither stretched nor compressed, but the block is moving in the negative direction at 12.0 m/s. Find (a) the amplitude of the motion, (b) the maximum acceleration of the block, and (c) the maximum force the spring exerts on the block.

31. • Repeat the previous problem, but assume that initially the block has velocity −4.00 m/s and displacement +0.200 m.

32. • A tuning fork has the tip of each of its two prongs vibrating in simple harmonic motion with a frequency of 392 Hz and an amplitude of 0.600 mm, while a housefly with mass 0.0270 g is holding onto the tip of one of the prongs. What are (a) the maximum speed of the tip of a prong and (b) the fly's maximum kinetic energy?

33. •• A mass is oscillating with amplitude A at the end of a spring. How far (in terms of A) is this mass from the equilibrium position of the spring when the elastic potential energy equals the kinetic energy?

34. •• (a) If a vibrating system has total energy E_0, what will its total energy be (in terms of E_0) if you double the amplitude of vibration? (b) If you want to triple the total energy of a vibrating system with amplitude A_0, what should its new amplitude be (in terms of A_0)?

11.4 Equations of Simple Harmonic Motion

35. • A 2.40 kg ball is attached to an unknown spring and allowed to oscillate. Figure 11.38 shows a graph of the ball's position x

as a function of time t. For this motion, what are (a) the period, (b) the frequency, (c) the angular frequency, and (d) the amplitude? (e) What is the force constant of the spring?

▲ **FIGURE 11.38** Problem 35.

36. • A proud deep-sea fisherman hangs a 65.0 kg fish from an ideal spring having negligible mass. The fish stretches the spring 0.120 m. (a) What is the force constant of the spring? (b) What is the period of oscillation of the fish if it is pulled down 3.50 cm and released?

37. • For the oscillating ball of Problem 35, what are (a) its maximum speed and (b) its maximum acceleration? (c) When does each of these maxima occur?

38. • An object is undergoing simple harmonic motion with period 0.600 s. Initially, the object is at $x = 0$ and has velocity in the positive direction. Use the circle of reference to calculate the time it takes the object to go from $x = 0$ to $x = A/4$.

39. •• A harmonic oscillator is made by using a 0.600 kg frictionless block and an ideal spring of unknown force constant. The oscillator is found to have a period of 0.150 s. Find the force constant of the spring.

40. •• **Weighing astronauts.** In order to study the long-term **BIO** effects of weightlessness, astronauts in space must be weighed (or at least "massed"). One way in which this is done is to seat them in a chair of known mass attached to a spring of known force constant and measure the period of the oscillations of this system. If the 35.4 kg chair alone oscillates with a period of 1.25 s, and the period with the astronaut sitting in the chair is 2.23 s, find (a) the force constant of the spring and (b) the mass of the astronaut.

41. •• A mass m is attached to a spring of force constant 75 N/m and allowed to oscillate. Figure 11.39 shows a graph of its velocity v_x as a function of time t. Find (a) the period, (b) the frequency, and (c) the angular frequency of this motion. (d) What is the amplitude (in cm), and at what times does the mass reach this position? (e) Find the maximum acceleration of the mass and the times at which it occurs. (f) What is the mass m?

▲ **FIGURE 11.39** Problem 41.

42. •• An object of unknown mass is attached to an ideal spring with force constant 120 N/m and is found to vibrate with a frequency of 6.00 Hz. Find (a) the period, (b) the angular frequency, and (c) the mass of this object.

43. •• **Weighing a virus.** In February 2004, scientists at Purdue **BIO** University used a highly sensitive technique to measure the mass of a vaccinia virus (the kind used in smallpox vaccine). The procedure involved measuring the frequency of oscillation of a tiny sliver of silicon (just 30 nm long) with a laser, first without the virus and then after the virus had attached itself to

the silicon. The difference in mass caused a change in the frequency. We can model such a process as a mass on a spring. (a) Show that the ratio of the frequency with the virus attached (f_{S+V}) to the frequency without the virus (f_S) is given by the formula

$$\frac{f_{S+V}}{f_S} = \frac{1}{\sqrt{1 + \dfrac{m_V}{m_S}}},$$

where m_V is the mass of the virus and m_S is the mass of the silicon sliver. Notice that it is *not* necessary to know or measure the force constant of the spring. (b) In some data, the silicon sliver has a mass of 2.10×10^{-16} g and a frequency of 2.00×10^{15} Hz without the virus and 2.87×10^{14} Hz with the virus. What is the mass of the virus, in grams and femtograms?

11.5 The Simple Pendulum

44. • A science museum has asked you to design a simple pendulum that will make 25.0 complete swings in 85.0 s. What length should you specify for this pendulum?

45. • A simple pendulum in a science museum entry hall is 3.50 m long, has a 1.25 kg bob at its lower end, and swings with an amplitude of 11.0°. How much time does the pendulum take to swing from its extreme right side to its extreme left side?

46. • You want to construct a simple pendulum with a 3.25 kg bob that will take 1.13 s to swing from a maximum angle of 9.5° to its lowest point after being released from rest. How long should this pendulum be?

47. •• **A pendulum on Mars.** A certain simple pendulum has a period on earth of 1.60 s. What is its period on the surface of Mars, where the acceleration due to gravity is 3.71 m/s²?

48. •• In the laboratory, a student studies a pendulum by graphing the angle θ that the string makes with the vertical as a function of time t, obtaining the graph shown in Figure 11.40. (a) What are the period, frequency, angular frequency, and amplitude of the pendulum's motion? (b) How long is the pendulum? (c) Is it possible to determine the mass of the bob?

▲ **FIGURE 11.40** Problem 48.

49. •• (a) If a pendulum has period T and you double its length, what is its new period in terms of T? (b) If a pendulum has a length L and you want to triple its frequency, what should be its length in terms of L? (c) Suppose a pendulum has a length L and period T on earth. If you take it to a planet where the acceleration of freely falling objects is ten times what it is on earth, what should you do to the length to keep the period the same as on earth? (d) If you do *not* change the pendulum's length in part (c), what is its period on that planet in terms of T? (e) If a pendulum has a period T and you triple the mass of its bob, what happens to the period (in terms of T)?

11.6 Damped and Forced Oscillations

50. • A 1.35 kg object is attached to a horizontal spring of force constant 2.5 N/cm and is started oscillating by pulling it 6.0 cm from its equilibrium position and releasing it so that it is free to oscillate on a frictionless horizontal air track. You observe that after eight cycles its maximum displacement from equilibrium is only 3.5 cm. (a) How much energy has this system lost to damping during these eight cycles? (b) Where did the "lost" energy go? Explain physically how the system could have lost energy.

51. • A 2.50 kg rock is attached at the end of a thin, very light rope 1.45 m long and is started swinging by releasing it when the rope makes an 11° angle with the vertical. You record the observation that it rises only to an angle of 4.5° with the vertical after $10\frac{1}{2}$ swings. (a) How much energy has this system lost during that time? (b) What happened to the "lost" energy? Explain *how* it could have been "lost."

52. •• A mass is vibrating at the end of a spring of force constant 225 N/m. Figure 11.41 shows a graph of its position x as a function of time t. (a) At what times is the mass not moving? (b) How much energy did this system originally contain? (c) How much energy did the system lose between $t = 1.0$ s and $t = 4.0$ s? Where did this energy go?

▲ **FIGURE 11.41** Problem 52.

53. •• A small 1.15 kg tool is swinging at the end of a very light 63.5 cm wire. A graph of the angle θ this wire makes with the vertical as a function of time t is shown in Figure 11.42. (a) At what times is the tool not moving? (b) How much energy did this system initially contain? (c) How much energy did the system lose between $t = 0.80$ s and $t = 2.4$ s? What happened to the energy?

▲ **FIGURE 11.42** Problem 53.

General Problems

54. • What is the maximum kinetic energy of the vibrating ball in Problem 35, and when does it occur?

55. •• **SHM in a car engine.** The motion of the piston of an automobile engine is approximately simple harmonic. (a) If the stroke (twice the amplitude) of an engine is 0.100 m and the engine runs at 3500 rpm, compute the acceleration of the piston at the endpoint of its stroke. (b) If the piston has mass 0.450 kg, what net force must be exerted on it at this point? (c) What are the speed and kinetic energy of the piston at the midpoint of its stroke?

56. •• Four passengers with a combined mass of 250 kg compress the springs of a car with worn-out shock absorbers by 4.00 cm when they enter it. Model the car and passengers as a single body on a single ideal spring. If the loaded car has a period of vibration of 1.08 s, what is the period of vibration of the empty car?

57. •• An astronaut notices that a pendulum which took 2.50 s for a complete cycle of swing when the rocket was waiting on the launch pad takes 1.25 s for the same cycle of swing during liftoff. What is the acceleration of the rocket? (*Hint:* Inside the rocket, it appears that g has increased.)

58. •• An object suspended from a spring vibrates with simple harmonic motion. At an instant when the displacement of the object is equal to one-half the amplitude, what fraction of the total energy of the system is kinetic and what fraction is potential?

59. •• On the planet Newtonia, a simple pendulum having a bob with a mass of 1.25 kg and a length of 185.0 cm takes 1.42 s, when released from rest, to swing through an angle of 12.5°, where it again has zero speed. The circumference of Newtonia is measured to be 51,400 km. What is the mass of the planet Newtonia?

60. •• A 5.00 kg partridge is suspended from a pear tree by an ideal spring of negligible mass. When the partridge is pulled down 0.100 m below its equilibrium position and released, it vibrates with a period of 4.20 s. (a) What is its speed as it passes through the equilibrium position? (b) What is its acceleration when it is 0.050 m above the equilibrium position?

61. •• A block with mass M rests on a frictionless surface and is connected to a horizontal spring of force constant k, the other end of which is attached to a wall (Figure 11.43). A second block with mass m rests on top of the first block. The coefficient of static friction between the blocks is μ_s. Find the maximum amplitude of oscillation such that the top block will not slip on the bottom block.

▲ **FIGURE 11.43** Problem 61.

62. ••• **Tarzan to the rescue!** Tarzan spies a 35 kg chimpanzee in severe danger, so he swings to the rescue. He adjusts his strong, but very light, vine so that he will first come to rest 4.0 s after beginning his swing, at which time his vine makes a 12° angle with the vertical. (a) How long is Tarzan's vine, assuming that he swings at the bottom end of it? (b) What are the frequency and amplitude (in degrees) of Tarzan's swing? (c) Just as he passes through the lowest point in his swing, Tarzan nabs the chimp from the ground and sweeps him out of the jaws of danger. If Tarzan's mass is 65 kg, find the frequency and amplitude (in degrees) of the swing with Tarzan holding onto the grateful chimp.

63. •• A 15.0 kg mass fastened to the end of a steel wire with an unstretched length of 0.50 m is whirled in a vertical circle with angular velocity 2.00 rev/s at the bottom of the circle. The cross-sectional area of the wire is 0.010 cm². Calculate the elongation of the wire when the mass is at the lowest point of the path. (See Table 11.1.)

64. •• A metal wire 3.50 m long and 0.70 mm in diameter was given the following test: A load weighing 20 N was originally hung from the wire to keep it taut. The position of the lower end of the wire was read on a scale as more load was added. (a) Graph the values shown in the table that follows, plotting the increase in length horizontally and the added load vertically. (b) Calculate the value of Young's modulus. (c) If the proportional limit occurred at a scale reading of 3.34 cm, what was the stress at this point?

Added Load (N)	Scale Reading (cm)
0	3.02
10	3.07
20	3.12
30	3.17
40	3.22
50	3.27
60	3.32
70	4.27

65. •• **Stress on the shinbone.** The compressive strength of our
BIO bones is important in everyday life. Young's modulus for bone is
approximately 14 GPa. Bone can take only about a 1.0% change
in its length before fracturing. If Hooke's law were to hold up
to fracture: (a) What is the maximum force that can be applied
to a bone whose minimum cross-sectional area is 3.0 cm². (This
is approximately the cross-sectional area of a tibia, or shinbone,
at its narrowest point.) (b) Estimate the maximum height from
which a 70 kg man can jump and not fracture the tibia. Take the
time between when he first touches the floor and when he has
stopped to be 0.030 s, and assume that the stress is distributed
equally between his legs.

66. •• Suppose the time for a chemical process to take place on
earth is 10.0 swings of a certain standard pendulum. If this
process takes the same amount of time on our moon, where the
objects fall toward its surface with an acceleration of 1.67 m/s²,
how many swings of the same pendulum will it take for that
process on the moon?

67. •• A brass rod with a length of 1.40 m and a cross-sectional
area of 2.00 cm² is fastened end to end to a steel rod with
length L and cross-sectional area 1.00 cm². The compound rod
is subjected to equal and opposite pulls of magnitude 1.00×10^4 N at its ends. (a) Find the length L of the steel rod if the
elongations of the two rods are equal. (b) What is the stress in
each rod? (c) What is the strain in each rod? (See Table 11.1.)

68. •• **Tendon-stretching exer-**
cises. As part of an exercise
program, a 75 kg person does
toe raises in which he raises
his entire body weight on the
ball of one foot, as shown in
Figure 11.44. The Achilles
tendon pulls straight upward
on the heel bone of his foot.
This tendon is 25 cm long and
has a cross-sectional area of
78 mm² and a Young's modulus of 1470 MPa. (a) Make a
free-body diagram of the person's foot (everything below
the ankle joint). You can neglect the weight of the foot.

Achilles tendon

Tibia

Ankle joint

|← 4.6 →|← 12.5 →|
cm   cm

▲ **FIGURE 11.44** Problem 68.

(b) What force does the Achilles tendon exert on the heel during
this exercise? Express your answer in newtons and in multiples
of his weight. (c) By how many millimeters does the exercise
stretch his Achilles tendon?

69. •• An amusement park ride
consists of airplane-shaped
cars attached to steel rods
(Figure 11.45). Each rod has a
length of 15.0 m and a cross-
sectional area of 8.00 cm², and
each car plus two people
seated in it has a total weight
of 1900 N. The rods are free to
swing up from the vertical as
the angular speed of the ride
increases. (a) How much is the
rod stretched when the ride is
at rest? (b) When operating,
the ride has a maximum angu-
lar speed of 8.00 rev/min. How much is the rod stretched then?

▲ **FIGURE 11.45** Problem 69.

70. •• A 100 kg mass suspended from a wire whose unstretched
length is 4.00 m is found to stretch the wire by 6.0 mm. The
wire has a uniform cross-sectional area of 0.10 cm². (a) If the
load is pulled down a small additional distance and released,
find the frequency at which it vibrates. (b) Compute Young's
modulus for the wire.

71. •• **Density of water on Venus.** The pressure at the surface of
Venus is 92 times what it is at the earth's surface. (a) What
would be the density of fresh water on Venus? Express your
answer in kg/m³ and as a percent of the density of water on the
earth, and neglect any effects due to the high temperature on
Venus. The bulk modulus of water is 2.2 GPa. (b) Is this difference in density large enough to have noticeable effects?

72. •• **Rapunzel, Rapunzel, let down your golden hair.** In the
Grimms' fairy tale *Rapunzel,* she lets down her golden hair to a
length of 20 yards (we'll use 20 m, which is not much different)
so that the prince can climb up to her room. Human hair has a
Young's modulus of about 490 MPa, and we can assume that
Rapunzel's hair can be squeezed into a rope about 2.0 cm in
cross-sectional diameter. The prince is described as young and
handsome, so we can estimate a mass of 60 kg for him. (a) Just
after the prince has started to climb at constant speed, while he
is still near the bottom of the hair, by how many centimeters
does he stretch Rapunzel's hair? (b) What is the mass of the
heaviest prince that could climb up, given that the maximum
tensile stress hair can support is 196 MPa? (Assume that
Hooke's law holds up to the breaking point of the hair, even
though that would not actually be the case.)

73. •• A moonshiner produces pure ethanol (ethyl alcohol, having a bulk modulus of 9.09×10^8 Pa) late at night and stores
it in a stainless-steel tank in the form of a cylinder 0.300 m in
diameter with a tight-fitting piston at the top. The total volume
of the tank is 250 L (0.250 m^3). In an attempt to squeeze a
little more into the tank, he piles 1420 kg of lead bricks on top
of the piston. What additional volume does this create inside
the tank, assuming that the wall of the tank is perfectly rigid?

12 MECHANICAL WAVES AND SOUND

When you go to the beach to enjoy the ocean surf, you're experiencing a wave motion. Ripples on a pond, musical sounds, sounds we *can't* hear, the wiggles of a Slinky® stretched out on the floor—all these are *wave* phenomena. Waves can occur whenever a system has an equilibrium position and when a disturbance away from that position can travel, or *propagate,* from one region of the system to another. Sound, light, ocean waves, radio and television transmission, and earthquakes are all wave phenomena. Waves occur in all branches of physical and biological science, and the concept of waves is one of the most important unifying threads running through the entire fabric of the natural sciences.

Why do male elephant seals have swollen noses? The nose serves as a resonating chamber, modifying the seal's voice. For the same reason tree frogs, grouse, and various other animals inflate special throat sacs while calling.

12.1 Mechanical Waves

This chapter is about mechanical waves. Every type of mechanical wave is associated with some material or substance called the **medium** for that type. (In Chapter 23, we'll study electromagnetic waves, such as radio and light waves, which do not require a medium and thus are not mechanical waves.) As the wave travels through the medium, the particles that make up the medium undergo displacements of various kinds, depending on the nature of the wave. Figure 12.1 shows waves produced by drops falling on a water surface. The speed of travel of a wave depends on the mechanical properties of the medium. Some waves are *periodic,* meaning that the particles of the medium undergo periodic motion during wave propagation. If the motion of each particle is simple harmonic (i.e., a sinusoidal function of time), the wave is called a *sinusoidal* wave.

Figure 12.2 shows three examples of mechanical waves. In Figure 12.2a, the medium is a stretched rope. (It could also be a spring or Slinky®.) If we give the left end a small up-and-down wiggle, the resulting pulse travels down the

▲ **FIGURE 12.1** A series of drops falling vertically into water produces a wave pattern that moves radially outward from its source. The wave crests and troughs are concentric circles.

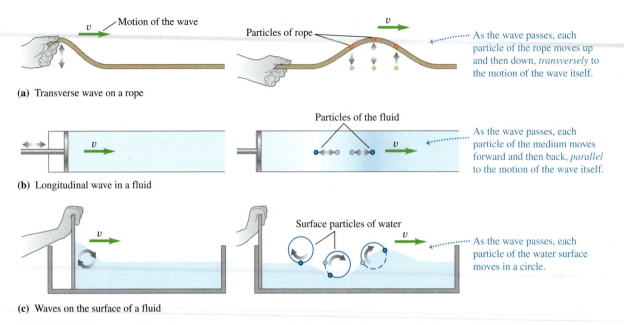

(a) Transverse wave on a rope

Particles of rope

As the wave passes, each particle of the rope moves up and then down, *transversely* to the motion of the wave itself.

Motion of the wave

Particles of the fluid

As the wave passes, each particle of the medium moves forward and then back, *parallel* to the motion of the wave itself.

(b) Longitudinal wave in a fluid

Surface particles of water

As the wave passes, each particle of the water surface moves in a circle.

(c) Waves on the surface of a fluid

▲ **FIGURE 12.2** Examples of (a) a transverse wave on a rope, (b) a longitudinal wave in a cylinder containing a gas or liquid, and (c) a surface wave with transverse and longitudinal components.

length of the rope. Successive sections of rope undergo the same up-and-down motion that we gave to the end, but at successively later times. Because the displacements of particles of the medium are perpendicular (transverse) to the direction of travel of the wave along the medium, this type of wave is called a **transverse wave.**

In Figure 12.2b, the medium is a liquid or gas in a tube with a rigid wall at the right end and a movable piston at the left end. If we give the piston a back-and-forth motion, a displacement and a pressure fluctuation travel down the length of the medium. This time, the particles of the medium move back and forth parallel to the wave's direction of travel; we call this type of wave a **longitudinal wave.**

Longitudinal waves are familiar to you as sound. Your ears are designed to detect longitudinal waves carried by air, but sound waves can also be carried by liquids such as water (you can hear under water) and by solid objects such as walls.

In Figure 12.2c, the medium is water in a trough. When we move the flat board at the left end back and forth, a disturbance travels down the length of the trough. In this case, the displacements of the water particles are found to have *both* longitudinal and transverse components. The familiar waves of oceans and lakes are of this type; they are most often generated by wind moving over the water surface.

Earthquake waves have both longitudinal and transverse displacements. The longitudinal components travel faster and so give advance warning of the arrival of the more destructive transverse components—as much as 60 seconds at a distance of 200 miles from the source.

All the waves in Figure 12.2 have several characteristics in common. For each, there is an equilibrium state. For the stretched rope, it is the state in which the rope is at rest, stretched out along a straight line (if we neglect the sag due to gravity). For the fluid in a tube, it is a state of rest with uniform pressure, and for the water in a trough it is a smooth, level water surface. In each case, the wave motion is a disturbance from the equilibrium state that travels from one region of the medium to another. In each case, there are forces that tend to restore the system to its equilibrium position when it is displaced, just as the force of gravity tends to pull a pendulum toward its straight-down equilibrium position when it is displaced.

In each of these situations, the medium as a whole does not travel through space; its individual particles undergo back-and-forth motions around their equi-

▶ **Two-minute warning.** Earthquakes are caused by large-scale movements of the Earth's crust; these movements generate both transverse and longitudinal waves in the crust. Using monitoring instruments known as seismographs, scientists can record these waves and detect the presence and location of distant earthquakes. The low-amplitude longitudinal waves travel faster than the more destructive transverse waves and arrive at a seismograph station sooner— several minutes sooner for an earthquake 1000 km away. Thus, prompt detection of the longitudinal waves from an earthquake can provide an early warning of the arrival of the destructive transverse waves. Often, even a minute or two of advance notice can be critical to safeguard life and property.

librium positions. What *does* travel is the pattern of the wave disturbance. To set any of these systems in motion, we have to put in energy by doing mechanical work on the system. The wave motion transports this energy from one region of the medium to another. **Waves transport energy, but not matter, from one region to another.** In each case, the disturbance is found to travel, or *propagate,* with a definite speed through the medium. This speed is called the speed of propagation or simply the **wave speed.** It is determined by the mechanical properties of the medium. We'll use the symbol v for wave speed.

Conceptual Analysis 12.1

Making waves

You and a friend hold the ends of a Slinky® that lies straight between you on a table. You create a wave by suddenly moving your hand toward and then away from your friend. The resulting wave

A. is purely transverse.
B. is purely longitudinal.
C. has both transverse and longitudinal components.

SOLUTION As the wave travels toward your friend, successive particles in the Slinky® undergo the same to-and-fro motion that you gave to the end. Since this motion is parallel to the direction in which the wave itself travels, the wave is longitudinal. (However, you could also cause the Slinky® to carry transverse waves by moving its end transversely.)

12.2 Periodic Mechanical Waves

The easiest kind of wave to demonstrate is a transverse wave on a stretched rope or flexible cable. Suppose we tie one end of a long, flexible rope to a stationary object and pull on the other end, stretching the rope out horizontally. In Figure 12.2a, we saw what happens when we give the end a single up-and-down shake. The resulting wiggle, or *wave pulse,* travels down the length of the rope. The tension in the rope restores the rope's straight-line shape once the wiggle has passed. (We are neglecting any sag in the rope due to the rope's weight.) Later we'll discuss what happens when the wiggle reaches the far end of the rope.

A more interesting situation develops when we give the free end of the rope a repetitive, or *periodic,* motion. In particular, suppose we use the setup in Figure 12.3 to move the end up and down with simple harmonic motion having

 10.1

The SHM of the spring and mass generates a sinusoidal wave in the rope. Each particle in the rope exhibits the same harmonic motion as the spring and mass; the amplitude of the wave is the amplitude of this motion.

▲ **FIGURE 12.3** The simple harmonic motion of the spring–mass system produces a sinusoidal transverse wave on the rope.

The rope is shown at time intervals of $\frac{1}{8}$ period for a total of one period T. The highlighting shows the motion of one wave.

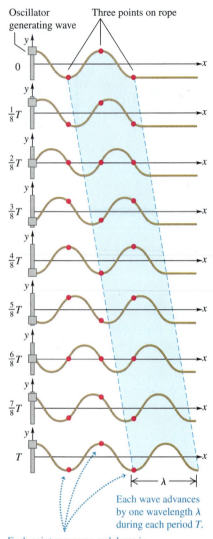

Each wave advances by one wavelength λ during each period T.

Each point moves up and down in place. Particles one wavelength apart move in phase with each other.

▲ **FIGURE 12.4** A sinusoidal transverse wave shown at intervals of one-eighth of a period.

amplitude A, frequency f, and period T. As usual, $f = 1/T = \omega/2\pi$, where ω is the angular frequency. A *continuous succession* of transverse sinusoidal waves then advances along the rope.

Figure 12.4 shows the shape of a part of the rope near the left end, at intervals of one-eighth of a period, for a total time of one period. The waveform advances steadily toward the right, while any one point on the rope oscillates up and down about its equilibrium position with simple harmonic motion. Be very careful to distinguish between the motion of a *waveform* (the shape of the displaced rope at any time), which moves with constant speed v *along* the rope, and the motion of *a particle of the rope,* which is simple harmonic and transverse (perpendicular) to the length of the rope. The **amplitude** A of the wave is defined as the amplitude of the transverse simple harmonic (sinusoidal) motion of a particle of the medium; it corresponds to the amplitude of the harmonic oscillation that creates the wave. As Figure 12.3 shows, for a periodic transverse wave, the amplitude is the distance from the equilibrium position to a peak or trough.

The shape of the rope at any instant is a repeating pattern—a series of identical shapes. For a periodic wave, the length of one complete wave pattern is the distance between any two points at corresponding positions on successive repetitions in the wave shape. We call this the **wavelength** of the wave, denoted by λ. The waveform travels with constant speed v and advances a distance of one wavelength λ in a time interval of one period T. We can relate these quantities as follows:

> **Relation among the speed, wavelength, period, and frequency of a transverse wave**
>
> The wave advances a distance of one wavelength λ during one period T, so the wave speed v is given by $v = \lambda/T$. Because frequency $f = 1/T$, the wave speed also equals the product of wavelength and frequency:
>
> $$v = \lambda f = \frac{\lambda}{T}. \tag{12.1}$$
>
> Note the familiar pattern: Speed equals distance divided by time.

To understand the mechanics of a *longitudinal* wave such as a sound wave in air, we consider a long tube filled with air, with a plunger at the left end, as shown in Figure 12.5. The cone of a loudspeaker is simply a sophisticated version of a plunger like this. If we push the plunger in, we compress the air near it, increasing the pressure in this region. The air in the region then pushes against the neighboring region of air, and so on, forming a wave pulse that moves along the tube.

◄ **Surf's up!** Thanks to the study of physics and the marvels of engineering, this surfer can enjoy a wild ride in a pool hundreds of miles from the ocean. This surf pool takes advantage of the physics of wave generation by repetitive motion to produce realistic "ocean" waves. The waves are generated by giant water cannons that fire repetitively at one end of the pool. By altering the shape of the cannon outlet and the pool floor and by changing the timing of the impulses, waves of different heights (up to 3 m), shapes, and angles can be generated. By studying a combination of oceanography and physics, engineers have even been able to duplicate the waves found in specific surfing hot spots such as California, Hawaii, and Indonesia.

The pressure fluctuations play the role of the restoring force, tending to restore the air to equilibrium and uniform pressure.

Now, suppose we move the plunger back and forth with simple harmonic motion along a line parallel to the direction of the tube. This motion forms regions where the pressure and density are alternately greater and less than the equilibrium values. We call a region of increased pressure a *compression*. A region of reduced pressure is an *expansion* (or *rarefaction*).

Figure 12.6 shows the waves in our apparatus at intervals of one-eighth of a period. The compressions and expansions move to the right with constant speed v. The motion of the individual particles of the medium (air) is simple harmonic, parallel to the direction of propagation. As we found for transverse waves, the amplitude A of a longitudinal wave is the amplitude of the periodic motion of the particles of the medium. That is, A represents the maximum displacement of a particle of the medium from its equilibrium position.

Earlier we mentioned that your ears detect longitudinal waves as sound. For a musical tone, you detect the amplitude of sound waves as loudness and their frequency as pitch—the higher pitched a sound, the greater its frequency. The wavelength is the distance between two successive compressions or two successive expansions. The same fundamental equation that we found for periodic transverse waves, $v = \lambda f$, also holds for periodic longitudinal waves and, indeed, for *all* types of periodic waves.

Forward motion of the plunger creates a compression (a zone of high pressure); backward motion creates an expansion (a zone of low pressure).

The wavelength λ is the distance between corresponding points on successive cycles.

▲ **FIGURE 12.5** A piston creating a sinusoidal longitudinal wave in a tube.

Quantitative Analysis 12.2

Distance from a sound source

A World War I infantryman sees the flash of a fired artillery gun; 20 s later he hears the gun's sound. The speed of sound in air is about a fifth of a mile per second. Which of the following is a reasonable estimate for the distance to the gun?

A. 1 mi.
B. 2 mi.
C. 4 mi.

SOLUTION The speed of *light* in air is roughly a million times as great as the speed of *sound* in air. Thus, in this example, the time between the creation of the flash and seeing it from a distance of several miles is negligible. In air, sound travels a fifth of a mile each second, or one mile in five seconds. It would take 20 seconds to travel 4 miles. A useful rule of thumb is that each mile gives a time delay of 5 seconds. If you see a lightning flash, and if you hear the accompanying thunder 10 seconds later, the flash was about 2 miles away.

EXAMPLE 12.1 **Frequencies of musical notes**

What is the wavelength of a sound wave in air at 20°C if the frequency is $f = 262$ Hz (the approximate frequency of the note "middle C" on the piano)? Assume that the speed of sound in air is 344 m/s.

SOLUTION

SET UP AND SOLVE The relation of wavelength λ to frequency f is given by Equation 12.1:

$$\lambda = \frac{v}{f} = \frac{344 \text{ m/s}}{262 \text{ s}^{-1}} = 1.31 \text{ m.}$$

REFLECT The "high C" sung by coloratura sopranos is two octaves above middle C (a factor of four in frequency), or about

1050 Hz. The corresponding wavelength is $(1.31 \text{ m})/4 = 0.327$ m.

Practice Problem: The frequency of the lowest note on large pipe organs is about 16 Hz. What is the corresponding wavelength? *Answer:* 21 m.

12.3 Wave Speeds

The speed of propagation of a wave depends on the mechanical properties of the medium. For transverse waves on a rope, these are the rope's tension and mass. Intuition suggests that increasing the tension should increase the restoring forces

10.2

Longitudinal waves shown at intervals of $\frac{1}{8}T$ for one period T.

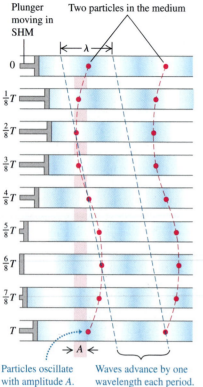

Plunger moving in SHM

Two particles in the medium

0

$\frac{1}{8}T$

$\frac{2}{8}T$

$\frac{3}{8}T$

$\frac{4}{8}T$

$\frac{5}{8}T$

$\frac{6}{8}T$

$\frac{7}{8}T$

T

$\rightarrow A \leftarrow$

Particles oscillate with amplitude A.

Waves advance by one wavelength each period.

▲ **FIGURE 12.6** A sinusoidal longitudinal wave shown at intervals of one-eighth of a period.

that tend to straighten the rope when it is disturbed and thus increase the wave speed. We might also guess that increasing the rope's mass should make the motion more sluggish and decrease the speed.

Both of these expectations are confirmed by more detailed analysis. The inertial property of the rope is best described not just by its total mass m (which depends on its length L), but on the mass *per unit length,* which we'll denote by μ. That is, $\mu = m/L$. We denote the tension in the rope by F_T. Analysis then shows that the wave speed v is given by the following expression:

Speed of a transverse wave
The speed of a transverse wave in a rope under tension is proportional to the square root of the tension, divided by the mass per unit length:

$$v = \sqrt{\frac{F_T}{\mu}}. \qquad (12.2)$$

This result confirms our prediction that the wave speed v should increase when the tension F_T increases, but decrease when the mass per unit length μ increases.

NOTE ▶ The wave speed v is *directly* proportional, *not* to the tension F_T, but rather to the *square root* of F_T. Similarly, it is inversely proportional, not to the mass per unit length, μ, but to the square root of that quantity. ◀

Conceptual Analysis 12.3

Waves on a string

An oscillator creates periodic waves on a stretched rope. Which of the following parameters *cannot* be changed by altering the motion of the oscillator?

A. Wave frequency.
B. Wave speed.
C. Wavelength.

SOLUTION As we've just seen, the speed of a wave depends on the properties of the medium alone. Thus, at least choice B is correct. The frequency of the wave is determined only by the frequency of the oscillator, so choice A is *not* correct. What about wavelength (choice C)? Remember that wavelength equals wave speed divided by frequency: $\lambda = v/f$. Thus, wavelength depends partly on the medium and partly on the oscillator, so choice C, too, is incorrect.

Quantitative Analysis 12.4

A vibrating string

An oscillator creates periodic waves on a stretched string. If the oscillator frequency doubles, what happens to the wavelength and wave speed?

A. Wavelength doubles; wave speed is unchanged.
B. Wavelength is unchanged; wave speed doubles.
C. Wavelength is halved; wave speed is unchanged.

SOLUTION The speed of a wave depends only on the properties of the medium, so changing the frequency of the oscillator does not change the wave speed. Wavelength depends on frequency and wave speed: $\lambda = v/f$. As this equation shows, doubling the frequency will *halve* the wavelength, so C is the right answer. This conclusion makes intuitive sense: If you double the frequency without changing the wave speed, you must fit twice as many waves into a given length of string, so the waves must be half as long.

EXAMPLE 12.2 **Mineral samples in a mine shaft**

One end of a nylon rope is tied to a stationary support at the top of a vertical mine shaft that is 80.0 m deep (Figure 12.7). The rope is stretched taut by a box of mineral samples with mass 20.0 kg suspended from the lower end. The mass of the rope is 2.00 kg. The geologist at the bottom of the mine signals to his colleague at the top by jerking the rope sideways. What is the speed of a transverse wave on the rope? If a point on the rope is given a transverse simple harmonic motion with a frequency of 20 Hz, what is the wavelength of the wave?

SOLUTION

SET UP We can calculate the wave speed v from the tension F_T and the mass per unit length, $\mu = m/L$. The tension at the bottom of the rope is equal to the weight of the 20.0 kg load:

$$F_T = (20.0 \text{ kg})(9.80 \text{ m/s}^2)$$
$$= 196 \text{ N},$$

and the mass per unit length is

$$\mu = \frac{m}{L} = \frac{2.00 \text{ kg}}{80.0 \text{ m}} = 0.0250 \text{ kg/m}.$$

SOLVE The wave speed is given by Equation 12.2:

$$v = \sqrt{\frac{F_T}{\mu}} = \sqrt{\frac{196 \text{ N}}{0.0250 \text{ kg/m}}} = 88.5 \text{ m/s}.$$

From Equation 12.1,

$$\lambda = \frac{v}{f} = \frac{88.5 \text{ m/s}}{20.0 \text{ s}^{-1}} = 4.43 \text{ m}.$$

REFLECT We have neglected the 10% increase in tension in the rope between bottom and top due to the rope's own weight. Can you verify that the wave speed at the top is 92.9 m/s?

$m_{\text{rope}} = 2.00 \text{ kg}$

80.0 m

$m_{\text{samples}} = 20.0 \text{ kg}$

▶ **FIGURE 12.7**

Practice Problem: Another box of samples is hoisted by the same rope. If the rope is shaken with the same frequency as before, and the wavelength is found to be 8.85 m, what is the mass of this box of samples? *Answer:* 80.0 kg.

A transverse wave traveling along a rope carries *energy* from one region of the rope to another. If the wave is traveling from left to right, then the part of the rope to the left of a given point exerts a transverse force on the part to the right of the point as the point undergoes vertical displacements. Thus, the left part does *work* on the right part and transfers energy to it. A detailed calculation of the rate of doing work (power) shows that, for a sinusoidal wave with amplitude A and frequency f, the rate of energy transfer is proportional to the *square* of the amplitude and to the square of the frequency. (We'll return to this discussion later, in the context of sound waves.)

Longitudinal waves can occur in solid, liquid, and gaseous materials. In all cases, the wave speed is determined by the mechanical characteristics of the material. Ordinarily, the wave speed is proportional to the square root of an elastic factor (such as the bulk or shear modulus) and inversely proportional to the square root of the density of the material. Table 12.1 lists the speed of sound in several familiar materials. Notice that the speed of sound in a medium depends on temperature; in both air and water, the speed increases with increasing temperature.

TABLE 12.1   Speed of sound in various materials

Material	Speed of sound (m/s)
Gases	
Air (20°C)	344
(25°C)	347
(30°C)	350
Helium (20°C)	999
Hydrogen (20°C)	1330
Liquids	
Liquid helium (4 K)	211
Water (0°C)	1402
Water (100°C)	1543
Mercury (20°C)	1451
Solids	
Polystyrene	1840
Bone	3445
Brass	3480
Pyrex™ glass	5170
Steel	5000
Beryllium	12,870

*12.4 Mathematical Description of a Wave

We've described several characteristics of periodic waves, using the concepts of wave speed, period, frequency, and wavelength. Sometimes, though, we need a more detailed description of the positions and motions of individual particles of the medium at particular times during wave propagation. As a specific example, let's look again at waves on a stretched string. If we ignore the sag of the string

▲ **FIGURE 12.8** Coordinate system for a mathematical description of transverse waves on a string.

due to gravity, the equilibrium position of the string is along a straight line. We take this to be the x axis of a coordinate system. Waves on a string are *transverse:* During wave motion, a particle with equilibrium position x is displaced some distance y in the direction perpendicular to the x axis (Figure 12.8). The value of y depends on which particle we are talking about (i.e, on x) and also on the time t when we look at it. Thus, y is a *function* of x and t: $y = f(x, t)$. If we know this function for a particular wave motion, we can use it to find the displacement (from equilibrium) of any particle at any time.

Let's consider the application of the concept we've just described to a sinusoidal wave on a string. Suppose the left end of the string is at $x = 0$. We give this end a transverse displacement y that varies sinusoidally with time:

$$y = A \sin \omega t = A \sin 2\pi f t. \tag{12.3}$$

The resulting wave disturbance travels with speed v from $x = 0$ to all the points to the right of the origin (with positive values of x). Every such point undergoes simple harmonic motion with the same amplitude and frequency as the endpoint $(x = 0)$, but the motion of each point has a time delay x/v equal to the time required for a point on the wave shape to travel from $x = 0$ to the point x. Thus, the motion of point x at time t is the same as the motion of point $x = 0$ at the earlier time $t - x/v$. Therefore, we can find the displacement of any point x at any time t simply by replacing t in Equation 12.3 by $(t - x/v)$. We obtain

$$y(x, t) = A \sin \omega \left(t - \frac{x}{v} \right) = A \sin 2\pi f \left(t - \frac{x}{v} \right). \tag{12.4}$$

The notation $y(x, t)$ is a reminder that the displacement y is a function of both the equilibrium location x of the point and the time t. If we know the amplitude, frequency, and wave speed, we can use this equation to find the displacement y of *any* point on the string (i.e., any value of x) by substituting the appropriate values.

We can rewrite Equation 12.4 in several useful ways, presenting the same relationship in different forms. Here's one of the most useful forms expressing the wave properties in terms of the period $T = 1/f$ and the wavelength $\lambda = v/f$:

$$y(x, t) = A \sin 2\pi \left(\frac{t}{T} - \frac{x}{\lambda} \right). \tag{12.5}$$

If we use Equation 12.5 to plot y as a function of x for time $t = 0$, the curve shows the *shape* of the string at $t = 0$.

(a)

If we use Equation 12.5 to plot y as a function of t for position $x = 0$, the curve shows the *displacement y* of the particle at that coordinate as a function of time.

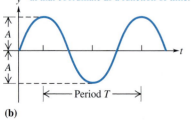

(b)

▲ **FIGURE 12.9** Two ways to graph Equation 12.5.

At any specific instant of time t, Equation 12.4 or 12.5 gives the displacement y of a particle from its equilibrium position as a function of the *coordinate x* of the particle. If the wave is a transverse wave on a string, the equation represents the *shape* of the string at that instant, as if we had taken a stop-action photograph of the string. In particular, at time $t = 0$, Equation 12.5 becomes

$$y(x, 0) = A \sin 2\pi \left(0 - \frac{x}{\lambda} \right) = A \sin 2\pi \left(-\frac{x}{\lambda} \right).$$

This equation, which gives the shape of the string at time $t = 0$, is plotted in Figure 12.9a.

One period later, at time $t = T$, Equation 12.5 becomes

$$y(x, T) = A \sin 2\pi \left(1 - \frac{x}{\lambda} \right) = A \sin 2\pi \left(-\frac{x}{\lambda} \right).$$

(We've used the formula for the sine of the difference of two quantities.) This is the same expression as that for time $t = 0$, confirming the fact that the shape of the string varies periodically with period T, as we should expect. After a time T (and therefore also after 2T, 3T, and so on), the string instantaneously has the same shape that it had at time $t = 0$.

We can show that Equation 12.5 represents a periodic wave having a repeating pattern with wavelength λ. To do this, we replace x by $x + \lambda$ in Equation 12.5

and again use the formula for the sine of the difference of two quantities. The result is that, at any time, point x has the same displacement as point $x + \lambda$, confirming that the wave shape is a repeating pattern with wavelength λ.

At any specific *coordinate x*, Equation 12.4 or Equation 12.5 gives the displacement y of the particle at that coordinate as a function of *time*. That is, it describes the motion of that particle. In particular, at the position $x = 0$,

$$y = A \sin \omega t = A \sin 2\pi \frac{t}{T}.$$

This equation is consistent with our original assumption that the motion at $x = 0$ is simple harmonic. The curve of the equation is plotted in Figure 12.9b; it is *not* a picture of the shape of the string, but rather a graph of the position y of a particle as a function of time.

12.5 Reflections and Superposition

In our study of mechanical waves thus far, we haven't been concerned with what happens when a wave arrives at an end or boundary of its medium. But there are many wave phenomena in which boundaries play a significant role. When you yell at a flat wall some distance away, the sound wave is reflected from the rigid surface, and an echo comes back. When you send a wave pulse down the length of a rope whose far end is tied to a rigid support, a reflected pulse comes back to you. In both cases, the initial and reflected waves overlap in the same region of the medium. Figure 12.10 is a multiflash photograph showing the reflection of a pulse at a stationary end of a stretched spring. Both the displacement and the direction of propagation of the reflected pattern are opposite to those of the initial pulse.

Figure 12.11 shows reflection of a wave pulse from an end that is held stationary and from one that is free to move transversely. In Figure 12.11a, a wave

▲ **FIGURE 12.10** Successive strobe images of a stretched spring. The photos show a wave pulse traveling to the right, reflecting at the fixed end of the spring, and traveling back to the left.

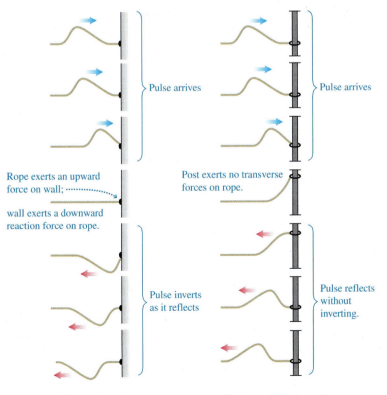

Pulse arrives

Pulse arrives

Rope exerts an upward force on wall;

Post exerts no transverse forces on rope.

wall exerts a downward reaction force on rope.

Pulse inverts as it reflects

Pulse reflects without inverting.

(a) Wave reflects from a fixed end   **(b)** Wave reflects from a free end

▲ **FIGURE 12.11** Reflection of a wave pulse (a) at a fixed end of a string and (b) at a free end.

As the pulses overlap, the displacement of the string at any point is the vector sum of the displacements due to the individual pulses.

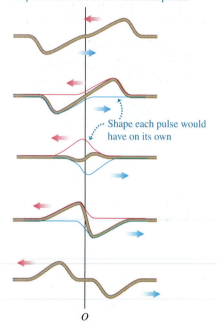

Shape each pulse would have on its own

O

▲ **FIGURE 12.12** An encounter between two waves traveling in opposite directions, one inverted with respect to the other.

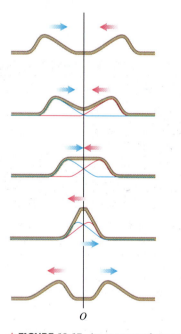

O

▲ **FIGURE 12.13** An encounter between two identical waves traveling in opposite directions.

10.4–10.6 Activ Physics ONLINE

pulse arrives at an end of the rope that is fastened to a rigid support so that the end point of the rope can't move. The arriving wave exerts a force on the support; the reaction to this force, exerted *by* the support *on* the rope, "kicks back" on the rope and sets up a *reflected* pulse or wave traveling in the reverse direction, inverted with respect to the incoming pulse. We would see the same result for a sinusoidal wave arriving at a fixed end.

The opposite extreme (Figure 12.11b) is an end that is perfectly free to move in the direction transverse to the length of the rope. For example, the rope might be tied to a light ring that slides on a smooth rod perpendicular to the length of the rope. The ring and rod maintain the tension, but exert no transverse force. When a wave arrives at a free end, where there is no transverse force, the end "overshoots," and again a reflected wave is set up, this time *not* inverted. The conditions at the end of the rope, such as the presence of a rigid support or the complete absence of a transverse force, are called **boundary conditions.**

The formation of the reflected pulse is similar to the overlap of two pulses traveling in opposite directions. Figure 12.12 shows two pulses with the same shape, but one inverted with respect to the other, traveling in opposite directions. As the pulses overlap and pass each other, the total displacement of any point of the string is the *vector sum* of the displacements at that point in the individual pulses. At points along the vertical line in the middle of the figure, the total displacement is zero at all times. Thus, the motion of the left half of the string would be the same if we cut the string at point O, threw away the right side, and held the end at O stationary. The two pulses on the left side then correspond to the incident and reflected pulses, combining so that the total displacement at the end of the string is *always* zero. For this to occur, the reflected pulse must be inverted relative to the incident pulse.

Figure 12.13 shows two pulses with the same shape, traveling in opposite directions, but *not* inverted relative to each other. The displacement at the midpoint is not zero, but the slope of the string at that point is always zero. In this case, the motion of the left half of the string would be the same if we cut the string at point O and anchored the end with a sliding ring (Figure 12.11b) to maintain tension without exerting any transverse force. This situation corresponds to the reflection of a pulse at a free end of a string at the point in question. In this case, the reflected pulse is *not* inverted.

In each case, the actual displacement of any point on the rope is the vector sum of the displacements corresponding to the two separate pulses at that point. This is an example of the **principle of superposition,** which states that **whenever two waves overlap, the actual displacement of any point on the string, at any time, is obtained by vector addition of the following two displacements: the displacement the point would have if only the first wave were present and the displacement it would have with only the second wave present.** This principle holds for the overlap of sinusoidal waves as well as for individual wave pulses. Later in the chapter, we'll see that the principle applies to both longitudinal and transverse waves and also to the addition of three or more waves.

12.6 Standing Waves and Normal Modes

Now let's look in more detail at what happens when a *sinusoidal* transverse wave is reflected by a stationary point on a string (such as a fixed end of a string). When the original wave combines with the reflected wave, the resulting motion no longer looks like two waves traveling in opposite directions. Instead, the string appears to be subdivided into a number of segments, as in the time-exposure photographs of Figure 12.14. Figure 12.14e shows the shape of the string in Figure 12.14b at two different instants. Let's compare this behavior with that of the waves we studied earlier in the chapter. (We'll refer to those as *traveling waves,* because when there are no reflections, they travel in one direction through the

(a) String is one-half wavelength long.

(b) String is one wavelength long.

(c) String is one and a half wavelengths long.

(d) String is two wavelengths long.

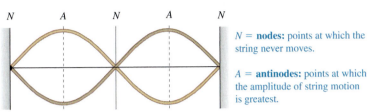

(e) The shape of the string in **(b)** at two different instants.

N = **nodes:** points at which the string never moves.

A = **antinodes:** points at which the amplitude of string motion is greatest.

▲ **FIGURE 12.14** (a–d) Standing waves in a stretched string (time exposure). (e) A standing wave, with nodes at the center and at the ends.

medium.) In a traveling wave, the amplitude is constant and the waveform moves with a speed equal to the wave speed. In the kind of wave we are examining here, the waveform remains in the same position along the string, and its amplitude fluctuates. There are particular points called **nodes** (labeled N in Figure 12.14e) that never move at all. Midway between the nodes are points called **antinodes** (labeled A in the figure), where the amplitude of motion is greatest. Because the wave pattern doesn't appear to be moving in either direction along the string, it is called a **standing wave.**

A standing wave, unlike a traveling wave, *does not* transfer energy from one end to the other. The two waves that form a standing wave would individually carry equal amounts of power in opposite directions. There is a local flow of energy from each node to the adjacent antinodes and back, but the *average* rate of energy transfer is zero at every point.

Figure 12.15 shows how we can use the superposition principle to understand the formation of a sinusoidal standing wave. The figure shows the waveform at instants one-sixteenth of a period apart. The thin red curves show a wave traveling to the left. The thin blue curves show a wave with the same propagation speed, wavelength, and amplitude, traveling to the right. (It could be a reflection of the red wave.) The brown curves show the resultant waveform—the actual shape a string would have at each given instant—obtained by applying the principle of superposition. At each point, the actual displacement of the string (the position of the brown curve) represents the vector sum of the displacements due to the two separate waves (i.e., the values of y for the two separate waves). The resultant (total) displacement at each node (marked N) is always zero. Midway between the nodes, the antinodes (marked A) have the greatest amplitude of displacement. We can see from the figure that **the distance between successive nodes or between successive antinodes is one half-wavelength, or $\lambda/2$.**

Normal Modes

We've mentioned that an echo of a sound wave can be produced by reflection at a rigid wall. Now suppose we have two parallel walls. If we stand between the walls and produce a sharp sound pulse (for example, by clapping our hands), the result is a series of regularly spaced echoes caused by repeated back-and-forth

▲ **Just passing through.** These two sets of ripples on water demonstrate the principle of superposition of mechanical waves. Notice how the two set of waves pass through each other without changing each other's overall shape or speed. At each point of intersection of individual waves, the vertical motion of the water is the vector sum of the motions of the two waves. Where the waves intersect exactly in step, they reinforce each other, resulting in a crest or trough height that is the sum of the heights of the individual waves. Where they intersect exactly out of step, they cancel each other and there is no vertical displacement of the water. This principle also holds true for a series of waves that are reflected from a boundary and return to interact with themselves.

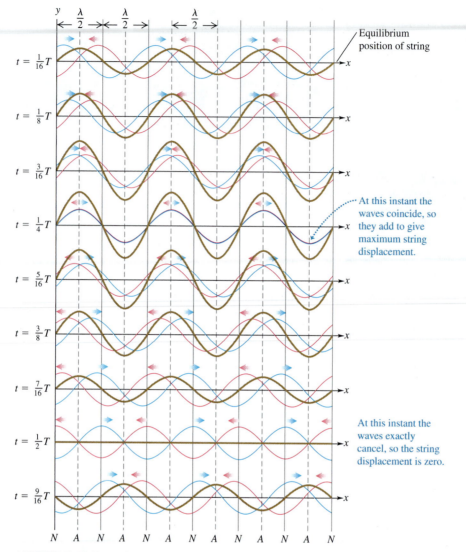

$t = \frac{1}{16}T$

$t = \frac{1}{8}T$

$t = \frac{3}{16}T$

$t = \frac{1}{4}T$

$t = \frac{5}{16}T$

$t = \frac{3}{8}T$

$t = \frac{7}{16}T$

$t = \frac{1}{2}T$

$t = \frac{9}{16}T$

Equilibrium position of string

At this instant the waves coincide, so they add to give maximum string displacement.

At this instant the waves exactly cancel, so the string displacement is zero.

▲ **FIGURE 12.15** Formation of a standing wave. A wave traveling to the left (red) combines with an identical wave traveling to the right (blue) to form a standing wave on a string (brown). We see successive instants at intervals of $1/16$ of a period.

reflection between the walls. In room acoustics, this phenomenon is called "flutter echo"; it is the bane of acoustical engineers.

The analogous situation with transverse waves on a string is a string with some definite length L, rigidly held at *both* ends. If we produce a sinusoidal wave on a guitar string, the wave is reflected and re-reflected from the ends. The waves combine to form a standing wave like one of the waves shown in Figure 12.14. Both ends must be nodes, and adjacent nodes are one half-wavelength $(\lambda/2)$ apart. The length L of the string, therefore, has to be some integer multiple of $\lambda/2$ (i.e., $(\lambda/2), 2(\lambda/2), 3(\lambda/2), \dots$), that is, an integer number of half-wavelengths:

$$L = n\frac{\lambda}{2} \qquad (n = 1, 2, 3, \dots).$$

A standing wave can exist on a string with length L, held stationary at both ends, only when its wavelength satisfies the preceding equation. When we solve the equation for λ and label the possible values of λ as λ_n, we obtain the following expression:

Wavelengths for standing waves on a string

On a string that is fixed at both ends, the only possible standing waves have wavelengths λ_n that are related to the string length L by the formula

$$\lambda_n = \frac{2L}{n} \qquad (n = 1, 2, 3, \dots).$$ (12.6)

When the wavelength is *not* equal to one of these values, no standing wave is possible.

Corresponding to this series of possible wavelengths is a series of possible frequencies f_n, each related to its corresponding wavelength by $f_n = v/\lambda_n$. The smallest frequency, f_1, corresponds to the largest wavelength (when $n = 1$), $\lambda = 2L$:

$$f_1 = \frac{v}{2L} \qquad \text{(string, held at both ends)}.$$

This frequency is called the **fundamental frequency.** The other frequencies are $f_2 = 2v/2L$, $f_3 = 3v/2L$, and so on. These are all integer multiples of f_1, such as $2f_1$, $3f_1$, $4f_1$, and so on, and we can express *all* the frequencies as follows:

Frequencies for standing waves on a string

On a string of length L that is held stationary at both ends, standing waves can have only frequencies f_n that are related to L and the wave speed v by the formula

$$f_n = n\frac{v}{2L} = nf_1, \qquad (n = 1, 2, 3, \dots).$$ (12.7)

These frequencies, all integer multiples of f_1, are called **harmonics,** and the series is called a **harmonic series.** Musicians sometimes call f_2, f_3, and so on **overtones;** f_2 is the second harmonic or the first overtone, f_3 is the third harmonic or the second overtone, and so on. (You can think of overtones as the first, second, third, etc., "tones over" the fundamental frequency.)

A **normal mode** is a motion in which all particles of the string move sinusoidally (i.e., with simple harmonic motion) with the same frequency. Each of the frequencies given by Equation 12.7 corresponds to a possible normal-mode pattern. There are infinitely many normal modes, each with its characteristic frequency and vibration pattern. Figure 12.16 shows the four lowest-frequency

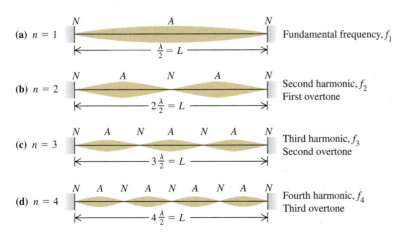

◀ FIGURE 12.16 The first four normal modes of a string fixed at both ends.

normal-mode patterns and their associated frequencies and wavelengths. We can contrast this situation with a simpler vibrating system, the harmonic oscillator, which has only one normal mode and one characteristic frequency.

If we displace a string so that its shape is the same as one of the normal-mode patterns and then release it, it vibrates with the frequency of that mode. But when a piano string is struck or a guitar string is plucked, not only is the fundamental frequency present in the resulting vibration, but also many overtones. This motion is therefore a combination, or *superposition,* of many normal modes. Several frequencies and motions are present simultaneously, and the displacement of any point on the string is the vector sum (or superposition) of displacements associated with the individual modes.

As we've seen, the fundamental frequency of a vibrating string is $f_1 = v/2L$. The wave speed v is determined by Equation 12.2, $v = \sqrt{F_T/\mu}$. Combining these equations, we obtain the following expression:

Fundamental frequency of a vibrating string
The fundamental frequency f_1 of a vibrating string with length L, held at both ends, is

$$f_1 = \frac{1}{2L}\sqrt{\frac{F_T}{\mu}}, \tag{12.8}$$

where the string tension is F_T and the mass per unit length is μ.

All string instruments are "tuned" to the correct frequencies by varying the tension F_T. An increase in tension increases the wave speed v and thus also increases the frequency (and the pitch) for a string of any fixed length L. The inverse dependence of frequency on length L is illustrated by the long strings of the bass (low-frequency) section of the piano or the string bass, compared with the shorter strings of the piano treble or the violin (Figure 12.17). One reason for winding the bass strings of a piano with wire is to increase the mass per unit length μ so as to obtain the desired low frequency without resorting to a string that is inconveniently long or inflexible. In playing the violin or guitar, the usual means of varying the pitch is to press the strings against the fingerboard with the fingers to change the length L of the vibrating portion of the string. As Equation 12.8 shows, decreasing L increases f_1.

▲ **FIGURE 12.17** The ranges of a bass, cello, viola, and violin compared with that of a concert grand piano. In all cases, longer strings give lower notes.

PROBLEM-SOLVING STRATEGY 12.1   **Standing waves and normal modes**

In all wave problems, it's useful to distinguish between the purely kinematic quantities, such as the wave speed v, wavelength λ, and frequency f, and the dynamic quantities involving the properties of the medium, including F_T and μ. You can compute the wave speed if you know either λ and f or F_T and μ. Try to determine whether the properties of the medium are involved in the problem at hand or whether the problem is only kinematic in nature.

To visualize nodes and antinodes in standing waves, it's always helpful to draw a diagram. For a string, you can draw the shape at one instant and label the nodes N and the antinodes A. For longitudinal waves (discussed in the next section), it's not so easy to draw the shape, but you can still label the nodes and antinodes. The distance between two adjacent nodes or two adjacent antinodes is always $\lambda/2$, and the distance between a node and the adjacent antinode is always $\lambda/4$. For a string held at both ends, the fundamental mode has nodes only at the ends and one antinode in the middle.

Changing the fundamental frequency

In the apparatus shown in Figure 12.18, the wire is tensioned by the weight of the hanging block. If the vibrating portion of the wire has a fundamental frequency f when the block has mass m, what should the block's mass be in order to give a fundamental frequency of $2f$?

A. $\sqrt{2}\,m$
B. $2m$
C. $4m$

SOLUTION The frequency is related to the tension in the wire by Equation 12.8:

$$f_1 = \frac{1}{2L}\sqrt{\frac{F_T}{\mu}}.$$

▲ **FIGURE 12.18**

This equation says that the fundamental frequency is directly proportional to the square root of the tension F_T in the wire. We can assume that the tension is equal to the block's weight and thus is directly proportional to its mass. Thus, f_1 is directly proportional to the square root of the block's mass. In that case, to double the frequency, you must increase the mass by a factor of four—so C is the correct answer.

EXAMPLE 12.3   **A giant bass viol**

In an effort to get your name in the *Guinness Book of World Records,* you set out to build a bass viol with strings that have a length of 5.00 m between fixed points. One of the strings has a mass per unit length of 40.0 g/m and a fundamental frequency of 20.0 Hz. **(a)** Calculate the tension in this string. **(b)** Calculate the frequency and wavelength of the second harmonic. **(c)** Calculate the frequency and wavelength of the second overtone.

SOLUTION

SET UP Figure 12.19 shows our diagram. Remember that the second overtone is the third harmonic. (Refer to Figure 12.16 if you're confused.)

SOLVE Part (a): To find the tension F_T in the string, we first solve Equation 12.8 for F_T:

$$F_T = 4\mu L^2 f_1^2.$$

We are given that $\mu = 4.00 \times 10^{-2}$ kg/m, $L = 5.00$ m, and $f_1 = 20.0$ s^{-1}. Substituting these values, we find that

$$F_T = 4(4.00 \times 10^{-2}\ \text{kg/m})(5.00\ \text{m})^2(20.0\ \text{s}^{-1})^2 = 1600\ \text{N}.$$

N   A   N   A   N

$\longleftarrow$ $L = 5.00$ m $\longrightarrow$

Second harmonic ($n = 2$)

N   A   N   A   N   A   N

Second overtone ($n = 3$)

▲ **FIGURE 12.19** Our sketch for this problem.

Continued

(In a real bass viol, the tension in each string is typically a few hundred newtons.)

Part (b): From Equation 12.7, the second harmonic frequency $(n = 2)$ is

$$f_2 = 2f_1 = 2(20.0 \text{ Hz}) = 40.0 \text{ Hz}.$$

From Equation 12.6, the wavelength of the second harmonic is

$$\lambda_2 = \frac{2L}{2} = 5.00 \text{ m}.$$

Part (c): The second overtone is the "second tone over" (above) the fundamental; that is, $n = 3$, and

$$f_3 = 3f_1 = 3(20.0 \text{ Hz}) = 60.0 \text{ Hz}.$$

The wavelength is

$$\lambda_3 = \frac{2L}{3} = 3.33 \text{ m}.$$

REFLECT The 20.0 Hz fundamental frequency for this string is approximately the frequency of the E below the lowest C on the piano and is roughly at the threshold for human hearing. The second and third harmonics have higher frequencies and would thus be easier to hear.

Practice Problem: With the same values of μ and F_T, what length of string would be needed for a fundamental frequency of 33.0 Hz (the lowest C on the piano)? *Answer:* 3.03 m.

12.7 Longitudinal Standing Waves

When longitudinal waves propagate in a fluid (such as air or water) contained in a pipe with finite length, the waves are reflected from the ends in the same way that transverse waves on a string are reflected at its ends. The superposition of the waves traveling in opposite directions again forms a standing wave.

When reflection takes place at a *closed* end (an end with a rigid barrier or plug), the displacement of the particles at this end must always be zero. Just as with a stationary end of a string, there is no displacement at the end, and the end is a *node.* If the pipe is closed at both ends, then each end is a node; there may also be nodes at intermediate positions within the pipe. If an end of a pipe is *open* and the pipe is narrow in comparison with the wavelength (which is true for most wind instruments, including some organ pipes), the open end is an *antinode*—a point at which the displacement of the medium is maximal. (If this doesn't seem right, recall that a free end of a stretched string, like that in Figure 12.11b, is also a displacement antinode.) Thus, longitudinal waves in a column of fluid are reflected at the closed and open ends of a pipe in the same way that transverse waves in a string are reflected at stationary and free ends, respectively. A closed end is always a node, and an open end is always an antinode.

A standing longitudinal wave in a pipe always has alternating nodes and antinodes. The pressure variations in the pipe also have an alternating pattern. It turns out that the antinodes (points of maximum displacement) correspond to points where there is *no* pressure variation. We can call these *pressure nodes.* To distinguish the two kinds of nodes, we sometimes speak of *displacement nodes* and *pressure nodes,* and similarly for the antinodes. A displacement node is always a pressure antinode, and a displacement antinode is always a pressure node. The relationship will become clearer in the next section, where we discuss normal modes for longitudinal waves.

We can demonstrate longitudinal standing waves in a column of gas, and also measure the wave speed, with an apparatus called a Kundt's tube (Figure 12.20). A horizontal glass tube a meter or so long is closed at one end and at the other end has a flexible diaphragm that can transmit vibrations. As our sound source, we use a small loudspeaker, driven by a sinusoidal oscillator whose frequency we can vary. We place a small amount of light powder or cork dust inside the pipe and distribute it uniformly along the bottom side of the pipe. As we vary the frequency of the sound, we pass through frequencies at which the amplitude of the standing waves becomes large enough for the moving gas to sweep the cork dust along the pipe at all points where the gas is in motion. The powder therefore col-

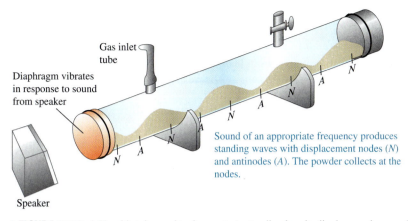

Sound of an appropriate frequency produces standing waves with displacement nodes (*N*) and antinodes (*A*). The powder collects at the nodes.

▲ **FIGURE 12.20** A Kundt's tube used to demonstrate standing longitudinal waves in a gas. The dust collects at the displacement nodes, where the displacement of gas due to the standing wave is minimal.

lects at the displacement nodes (where the gas is not moving). Adjacent nodes are separated by a distance equal to $\lambda/2$, and we can measure this distance. We read the frequency f from the oscillator dial, and we can then calculate the speed v of the waves from the relation $v = \lambda f$.

EXAMPLE 12.4 **Speed of sound in hydrogen**

At a frequency of 25 kHz, the distance from a closed end of a tube of hydrogen gas to the nearest displacement node of a standing wave is 0.026 m. Calculate the wave speed.

SOLUTION

SET UP AND SOLVE Figure 12.21 shows our sketch. This is a common way to represent a longitudinal standing wave in a tube. While the curves *look* like the real shape of a transverse standing wave on a string, for a longitudinal wave they don't show directly what the medium is doing. Rather, you can think of them as a graph of displacement (on the vertical axis) versus position (on the horizontal axis). As our sketch shows, the closed end of the tube is a displacement node. The statement of the problem tells us that the next displacement node is 0.026 m away. Adjacent nodes are always a half-wavelength apart, so we have $\lambda/2 = 0.026$ m and $\lambda = 0.052$ m. Then the wave speed is

$$v = \lambda f = (0.052 \text{ m})(25,000 \text{ s}^{-1}) = 1300 \text{ m/s}.$$

▲ **FIGURE 12.21** Our sketch for this problem.

REFLECT This result is close to the value given in Table 12.1 for the speed of sound in hydrogen at 20°C (1330 m/s). Either value is about four times the speed of sound in air at 20°C.

Practice Problem: If the hydrogen in the tube is replaced by air at 20°C, what frequency would be needed to produce standing waves with the same wavelength? *Answer:* 6600 Hz.

Normal Modes

Many musical instruments, including organ pipes and all the woodwind and brass instruments, use longitudinal standing waves (normal modes) in vibrating air columns to produce musical tones. Organ pipes are one of the simplest examples. Air is supplied by a blower, at a pressure typically on the order of 10^3 Pa, or 10^{-2} atm (above normal atmospheric pressure), to the bottom end of the pipe (Figure 12.22). A stream of air is directed against the mouth of each pipe, as shown in the figure. The column of air in the pipe is set into vibration, and there is a series of possible normal modes, just as with a stretched string. The mouth always acts as an open end; thus, it is a displacement antinode. The top of a pipe may be either open or closed. Figure 12.23 shows three normal modes in a schematic organ pipe open at the top end. (The pipes are shown on their sides.)

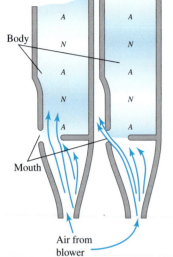

Vibrations from turbulent airflow set up standing waves in the pipe.

▲ **FIGURE 12.22** A cross section of an organ pipe. Vibrations from the turbulent air flow set up standing waves in the pipe.

Let's consider the general problem of normal modes in an air column. The pipe may be a flute, a clarinet, an organ pipe, or any other wind instrument. In Figure 12.23, both ends of the pipe are open, so both are displacement antinodes. An organ pipe that is open at both ends is called an *open pipe*. The fundamental frequency f_1 corresponds to a standing-wave pattern with a displacement antinode at each end and a displacement node in the middle (Figure 12.23a). The distance between adjacent nodes is always equal to one half-wavelength, and in this case that is equal to the length L of the pipe: $\lambda/2 = L$. The corresponding frequency, obtained from the relation $f = v/\lambda$, is

$$f_1 = \frac{v}{2L} \qquad \text{(open pipe).} \qquad (12.9)$$

The other two parts of Figure 12.23 show the second and third harmonics (first and second overtones); their vibration patterns have two and three displacement nodes, respectively. For these patterns, the length L of the pipe is equal to two or three half-wavelengths, so $\lambda/2$ is equal to $L/2$ and $L/3$, respectively, and the frequencies are twice and three times the fundamental frequency, respectively (i.e., $f_2 = 2f_1$ and $f_3 = 3f_1$). For *every* normal mode, the length L must be an integer number of half-wavelengths, and the possible wavelengths λ_n are given by

$$L = n\frac{\lambda_n}{2}, \qquad \text{or} \qquad \lambda_n = \frac{2L}{n} \qquad (n = 1, 2, 3, \dots).$$

The corresponding frequencies f_n are given by $f_n = v/\lambda_n$, so all the normal-mode frequencies for a pipe that is open at both ends are given by

$$f_n = n\frac{v}{2L} = nf_1 \qquad (n = 1, 2, 3, \dots). \qquad \text{(open pipe).} \qquad (12.10)$$

The value $n = 1$ corresponds to the fundamental frequency, $f_1 = v/2L$, $n = 2$ to the second harmonic (or first overtone), and so on.

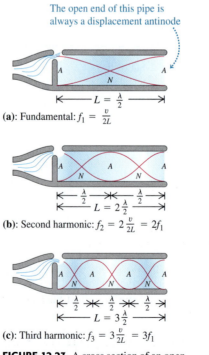

The open end of this pipe is always a displacement antinode

$L = \frac{\lambda}{2}$

(a): Fundamental: $f_1 = \frac{v}{2L}$

$\frac{\lambda}{2}$ $\frac{\lambda}{2}$
$L = 2\frac{\lambda}{2}$

(b): Second harmonic: $f_2 = 2\frac{v}{2L} = 2f_1$

$\frac{\lambda}{2}$ $\frac{\lambda}{2}$ $\frac{\lambda}{2}$
$L = 3\frac{\lambda}{2}$

(c): Third harmonic: $f_3 = 3\frac{v}{2L} = 3f_1$

▲ **FIGURE 12.23** A cross section of an open pipe, showing the first three normal modes as well as the displacement nodes and antinodes.

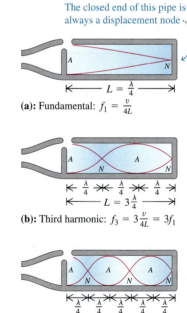

The closed end of this pipe is always a displacement node

$L = \frac{\lambda}{4}$

(a): Fundamental: $f_1 = \frac{v}{4L}$

$\frac{\lambda}{4}$ $\frac{\lambda}{4}$ $\frac{\lambda}{4}$
$L = 3\frac{\lambda}{4}$

(b): Third harmonic: $f_3 = 3\frac{v}{4L} = 3f_1$

$\frac{\lambda}{4}$ $\frac{\lambda}{4}$ $\frac{\lambda}{4}$ $\frac{\lambda}{4}$ $\frac{\lambda}{4}$
$L = 5\frac{\lambda}{4}$

(c): Fifth harmonic: $f_5 = 5\frac{v}{4L} = 5f_1$

▲ **FIGURE 12.24** A cross section of a stopped pipe, showing the first three normal modes as well as the displacement nodes and antinodes. Only odd harmonics are possible.

Figure 12.24 shows a pipe open at the left (mouth) end but closed at the right end. We call this a *stopped pipe*. The left (open) end is an antinode, but the right (closed) end is a node. The distance between a node and the adjacent antinode is always one quarter-wavelength. Figure 12.24a shows the fundamental frequency; the length of the pipe is a quarter-wavelength $(L = \lambda_1/4)$. The fundamental frequency is $f_1 = v/\lambda_1$, or

$$f_1 = \frac{v}{4L} \qquad \text{(stopped pipe).} \qquad (12.11)$$

This is one-half the fundamental frequency for an *open* pipe of the same length. In musical language, the *pitch* of a stopped pipe is one octave lower (a factor of two in frequency) than that of an open pipe of the same length. Figure 12.24b shows the next mode, for which the length of the pipe is *three-quarters* of a wavelength, corresponding to a frequency $3f_1$. In Figure 12.24c, $L = 5\lambda/4$ and the frequency is $5f_1$. The possible wavelengths are given by

$$L = n\frac{\lambda_n}{4} \qquad \text{or} \qquad \lambda_n = \frac{4L}{n} \qquad (n = 1, 3, 5, \dots).$$

The normal-mode frequencies are given by $f_n = v/\lambda_n$, or

$$f_n = n\frac{v}{4L} = nf_1 \qquad (n = 1, 3, 5, \dots), \qquad \text{(stopped pipe),} \qquad (12.12)$$

with the fundamental frequency f_1 given by Equation 12.11. We see that the second, fourth, and, indeed, all *even* harmonics are missing. In a pipe that is closed at one end, the fundamental frequency is $f_1 = v/4L$, and only the odd harmonics in the series $(3f_1, 5f_1, 7f_1, \dots)$ are possible.

EXAMPLE 12.5 Harmonics of an organ pipe

On a day when the speed of sound is 345 m/s, the fundamental frequency of an open organ pipe is 690 Hz. If the second *harmonic* of this pipe has the same wavelength as the second *overtone* of a stopped pipe, what is the length of each pipe?

SOLUTION

SET UP Figure 12.25 shows our sketch. Note that the frequency of the second harmonic of the open pipe is twice its fundamental frequency, but the second overtone of the stopped pipe has a frequency five times that of the fundamental. Do you see why?

SOLVE For an open pipe, $f_1 = v/2L$, so the length of the open pipe is

$$L_{\text{open}} = \frac{v}{2f_1} = \frac{345 \text{ m/s}}{2(690 \text{ s}^{-1})} = 0.250 \text{ m}.$$

The second harmonic of the open pipe has a frequency of

$$f_2 = 2f_1 = 2(690 \text{ Hz}) = 1380 \text{ Hz}.$$

If the wavelengths are the same, the frequencies are the same, so the frequency of the second overtone of the stopped pipe is also 1380 Hz. The first overtone of a stopped pipe is at $3f_1$, and the second at $5f_1 = 5(v/4L)$. If this equals 1380 Hz, then

$$1380 \text{ Hz} = 5\left(\frac{345 \text{ m/s}}{4L_{\text{stopped}}}\right) \qquad \text{and} \qquad L_{\text{stopped}} = 0.313 \text{ m}.$$

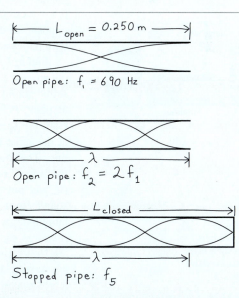

▲ **FIGURE 12.25** Our sketch for this problem.

REFLECT A final possibility is a pipe that is closed at *both* ends and therefore has nodes at both ends. This pipe wouldn't be of much use as a musical instrument, because there would be no way for the vibrations to get out of it.

Practice Problem: An open pipe and a stopped pipe have the same length. Does any harmonic of the open pipe have the same frequency as any harmonic of the stopped pipe? *Answer:* No.

▲ **Boning up on physics.** You don't need a physicist's knowledge of standing waves to learn how to make a flute. This photo shows 9000-year-old bone flutes from Jiahu, China. The bone flute is one of the earliest known musical instruments. Blowing into the hollow bone causes a longitudinal wave to form in the internal air space. The wave produces a note with a fundamental frequency corresponding to a standing wave with a displacement antinode at each end of the flute. By placing their fingers over holes carved into the bone, these early musicians could change the effective length of the flute, thus varying the frequency of the waves produced and allowing them to play notes of different pitch.

In an actual organ pipe, several modes are always present at once. The situation is analogous to a string that is struck or plucked, producing several modes at the same time. In each case, the motion is a *superposition* of various modes. The extent to which modes higher than the fundamental mode are present depends on the cross section of the pipe, the proportion of the length to width, the shape of the mouth, and other, more subtle factors. The harmonic content of the tone is an important factor in determining its tone quality, or timbre. A very narrow pipe produces a tone that is rich in higher harmonics, which we hear as a thin and "stringy" tone; a fatter pipe produces mostly the fundamental mode, heard as a softer, more flutelike tone.

In this section we've talked mostly about organ pipes, but our discussion is also applicable to other wind instruments. The flute and the recorder are directly analogous. The most significant difference is that those instruments have holes along the pipe. Opening and closing the holes with the fingers changes the effective length L of the air column and thus changes the pitch. Any individual organ pipe, by comparison, plays only a single note. The flute and recorder behave as *open* pipes, but the clarinet acts as a *stopped* pipe (closed at the reed end, open at the bell).

Equations 12.9 and 12.11 show that the frequencies of any such instrument are proportional to the speed of sound v in the air column inside the instrument. In all gases (including air), v increases when the temperature increases. Thus, the pitch of all wind instruments rises with increasing temperature. An organ that has some of its pipes at one temperature and others at a different temperature is bound to sound out of tune.

12.8 Interference

Wave phenomena that occur when two or more periodic waves with the same frequency overlap in the same region of space are grouped under the heading of *interference.* As we have seen, standing waves are a simple example of an interference effect. Two waves with the same frequency and amplitude, traveling in opposite direction in a medium, combine to produce a standing-wave pattern, with nodes and antinodes that do not move.

Figure 12.26 shows an example of interference involving waves that spread out in space. Two speakers, driven by the same amplifier, emit identical sinusoidal sound waves with the same constant frequency. We place a microphone at point P in the figure, equidistant from the speakers. Wave crests emitted from the speakers at the same time travel equal distances and arrive at point P at the same time. The amplitudes add according to the principle of superposition. The total wave amplitude at P is twice the amplitude from each individual wave, and we can measure this combined amplitude with the microphone. (If you put your ear where the microphone is, the sound is *louder* than the sound from either speaker alone.) When interference causes an increase in amplitude, we call it **constructive interference,** and we say that the two waves *reinforce* each other.

Now let's move the microphone to point Q, where the distances from the two speakers to the microphone differ by a half-wavelength. Then the two waves arrive a half-cycle out of step; a positive crest from one speaker arrives at the same time as a negative crest from the other, and the net amplitude measured by the microphone at Q is much *smaller* than when only one speaker is present. When interference causes a decrease in amplitude, we call it **destructive interference** or *cancellation.*

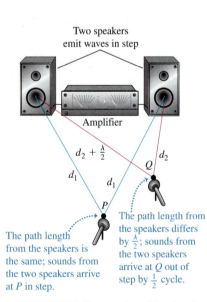

Two speakers emit waves in step

Amplifier

$d_2 + \frac{\lambda}{2}$ d_2

Q

d_1 d_1

P

The path length from the speakers is the same; sounds from the two speakers arrive at P in step.

The path length from the speakers differs by $\frac{\lambda}{2}$; sounds from the two speakers arrive at Q out of step by $\frac{1}{2}$ cycle.

▲ **FIGURE 12.26** Two speakers driven by the same amplifier produce sound waves that interfere. The waves are in step as they emerge from the speakers; they interfere constructively at point P, destructively at point Q.

EXAMPLE 12.6 **Interference from two loudspeakers**

Two small loudspeakers A and B (Figure 12.27) are driven by the same amplifier and emit pure sinusoidal waves; crests from the speakers are emitted simultaneously ("in step"). If the speed of sound is 350 m/s, for what frequencies does maximum constructive interference occur at point P? For what frequencies does destructive interference (cancellation) occur at point P?

▶ **FIGURE 12.27**

SOLUTION

SET UP First we need to find the difference in path lengths from points A and B to point P. Maximum constructive interference occurs when the path difference d is an integer number of wavelengths; maximum destructive interference occurs when the path difference is a half-integer number of wavelengths. Once the wavelengths are known, the corresponding frequencies can be found from $f = v/\lambda$.

SOLVE The distance from speaker A to point P is $[(2.00 \text{ m})^2 + (4.00 \text{ m})^2]^{1/2} = 4.47$ m, and the distance from speaker B to point P is $[(1.00 \text{ m})^2 + (4.00 \text{ m})^2]^{1/2} = 4.12$ m. The path difference is $d = 4.47$ m $- 4.12$ m $= 0.35$ m.

Maximum constructive interference occurs when the path difference d is an integer multiple of λ: $d = 0, v/f, 2v/f, \ldots = nv/f$ ($n = 0, 1, 2, \ldots$). So the possible frequencies for maximum constructive interference are

$$f_n = n\frac{v}{d} = n\frac{350 \text{ m/s}}{0.35 \text{ m}} \qquad (n = 1, 2, 3, \ldots)$$
$$= 1000 \text{ Hz}, 2000 \text{ Hz}, 3000 \text{ Hz}, \ldots$$

Maximum destructive interference (cancellation) occurs when the path difference for the two waves is a half-integer number of wavelengths:

$$d = \lambda/2, 3\lambda/2, 5\lambda/2, \ldots, \qquad \text{or}$$
$$d = v/2f, 3v/2f, 5v/2f, \ldots$$

The possible frequencies for destructive interference are

$$f_n = n\frac{v}{2d} = n\frac{350 \text{ m/s}}{2(0.35 \text{ m})} \qquad (n = 1, 3, 5, \ldots)$$
$$= 500 \text{ Hz}, 1500 \text{ Hz}, 2500 \text{ Hz}, \ldots$$

REFLECT As we increase the frequency, the sound at point P alternates between large and small amplitudes; the maxima and minima occur at the frequencies we have found. It would be hard to notice this effect in an ordinary room because of multiple reflections from the walls, floor, and ceiling. Such an experiment is best done in an anechoic chamber (Figure 12.28)—a room with walls that are almost completely nonreflecting for sound.

▲ **FIGURE 12.28** An anechoic chamber.

12.9 Sound and Hearing

Sound can travel in gases (such as air), liquids (such as water), and solid materials. The simplest sound waves are sinusoidal waves, which have definite frequency, amplitude, and wavelength. The human ear is sensitive to waves in the frequency range from about 20 to 20,000 Hz, but we also use the term *sound* for similar waves with frequencies above **(ultrasonic)** and below **(infrasonic)** the range of human hearing.

Sound waves may also be described in terms of variations of *pressure* at various points. In a sinusoidal sound wave in air, the pressure fluctuates above and below atmospheric pressure p_a with a sinusoidal variation having the same frequency as the motions of the air particles. The *maximum* variation in pressure above and below atmospheric pressure is called the *pressure amplitude,* denoted by p_{max}. Microphones and similar devices usually sense pressure variations, not displacements.

▲ **Not so loud!** The human ear is a marvelous instrument for detecting the vibrations caused by sound waves. This highly magnified photo shows the tiny hairs inside the cochlea of the inner ear that sense these vibrations. (Technically, these hairs are the stereocilia of cochlear hair cells.) When these microscopic hairs bend, the hair cells send nerve signals to the brain, and we perceive those signals as different sounds. Between the threshold of hearing and the sound of a raging rock concert, these hairs are sensitive to sounds ranging in power over 14 orders of magnitude. They can sense very faint, low-power sounds, but can be damaged by prolonged exposure to loud, high-power sounds. Therefore, it's important to minimize one's exposure to sources of very loud sound waves and to wear proper ear protection if exposure is unavoidable.

Amplitude

Measurements of sound waves show that, in the loudest sounds the human ear can tolerate without pain, the maximum pressure variations are on the order of $p_{max} = 30$ Pa above and below atmospheric pressure p_a (nominally, 1.013×10^5 Pa at sea level). If the frequency is 1000 Hz, the corresponding amplitude A (maximum displacement) is about $A = 0.012$ mm.

Thus, the displacement amplitude of even the loudest sound is *extremely* small. The maximum pressure variation in the *faintest* audible sound, of frequency 1000 Hz, is only about 3×10^{-5} Pa. The corresponding displacement amplitude is about 10^{-11} m. For comparison, the wavelength of yellow light is 6×10^{-7} m, and the diameter of a molecule is about 10^{-10} m. The ear is an extremely sensitive organ!

The Human Ear

Figure 12.29 shows the anatomy of the human ear. When a sound wave enters the auditory canal, it causes the eardrum to vibrate. The vibration is transmitted to the three small bones called the incus, the malleus, and the stapes. This motion is in turn transmitted to the fluid-filled *cochlea* of the inner ear. The motion of the cochlear fluid is then imparted to specialized hair cells in the cochlea, and the resulting nerve impulses are transmitted to the brain.

12.10 Sound Intensity

Like all other waves, sound waves transfer energy from one region to another. We define the **intensity** of a wave, denoted by I, as *the time-averaged rate at which energy is transported by the wave, per unit area,* across a surface perpendicular to the direction of propagation. That is, the intensity I is the average *power* transported per unit area. The intensity of the faintest sound wave that can be heard by a person with normal hearing is about 10^{-12} W/m², or 10^{-16} W/cm².

The average *total* power (energy per unit time) carried across a surface by a sound wave equals the product of the intensity (power per unit area) at the surface and the surface area (assuming that the intensity over the surface is uniform). The average total sound power emitted by a person speaking in an ordinary conversational tone is about 10^{-5} W, and a loud shout corresponds to about 3×10^{-2} W. If all the residents of New York City were to talk at the same time, the total sound power would be about 100 W, equivalent to the electric power requirement of a medium-sized light bulb! Yet the power required to fill a large auditorium with loud sound is considerable. The intensity at an individual point is proportional to the square of the amplitude of the sound wave and also proportional to the frequency of the wave.

▲ **FIGURE 12.29** The structure of the human ear. The eardrum and the bones of the middle ear transmit sound waves into the cochlea, where the information is coded into nerve impulses.

EXAMPLE 12.7 **An auditorium sound system**

For a sound system for a 2000-seat auditorium, suppose we want the sound intensity over the surface of a hemisphere 20 m in radius to be 1.0 W/m^2. What acoustic power output would be needed from an array of speakers at the center of the sphere?

SOLUTION

SET UP AND SOLVE The total power needed is the intensity (power per unit area) times the area of the hemisphere. The area of the hemispherical surface is $\frac{1}{2}(4\pi R^2) = \frac{1}{2}(4\pi)(20 \text{ m})^2$, or about 2500 m^2. The total acoustic power needed is

$$(1.0 \text{ W/m}^2)(2500 \text{ m}^2) = 2500 \text{ W} = 2.5 \text{ kW}.$$

REFLECT The efficiency of loudspeakers in converting electrical energy into sound is not very high (typically a few percent for ordinary speakers and up to 25% for horn-type speakers). The

electrical power input to the speakers would need to be considerably larger than 2.5 kW.

However, 1.0 W/m^2 is *very* loud sound, at the threshold of pain and definitely in the range where permanent hearing damage is likely.

Practice Problem: In a smaller auditorium, we want the sound intensity over the surface of a hemisphere 10 m in radius to be 1.0 W/m^2. If the speakers have an efficiency of 20% (i.e., 20% of the electrical energy is converted into sound), what total electrical power input is required? *Answer:* 3.1 kW.

If a source of sound can be considered as a point, the intensity at a distance r from the source is inversely proportional to r^2. This relationship follows directly from energy conservation: If the power output of the source is P, then the average intensity I_1 through a sphere with radius r_1 and surface area $4\pi r_1^2$ is

$$I_1 = \frac{P}{4\pi r_1^2}.$$

The average intensity I_2 through a sphere with a different radius r_2 is given by a similar expression. If no energy is absorbed between the two spheres, the power P must be the same for both, and we have

$$4\pi r_1^2 I_1 = 4\pi r_2^2 I_2$$
$$\frac{I_1}{I_2} = \frac{r_2^2}{r_1^2}. \qquad (12.13)$$

The intensity I at any distance r is therefore inversely proportional to r^2. This inverse-square relationship also holds for various other energy-flow situations involving a point source, such as light emitted by a point source.

Decibels

Because the ear is sensitive over such a broad range of intensities, a *logarithmic* intensity scale is usually used. The **intensity level** (or *sound level*) β of a sound wave is defined by the equation

$$\beta = (10 \text{ dB})\log\frac{I}{I_0}. \qquad (12.14)$$

In this equation, I_0 is a reference intensity chosen to be 10^{-12} W/m^2, and "log" denotes the logarithm to the base 10, not the natural logarithm (ln). The units of β are **decibels,** abbreviated dB. A sound wave with an intensity I equal to I_0 $(=10^{-12} \text{ W/m}^2)$ has an intensity level of 0 dB. This level corresponds roughly to the faintest sound that can be heard by a person with normal hearing, although that depends on the frequency of the sound. The intensity at the pain threshold, about 1 W/m^2, corresponds to an intensity level of 120 dB.

Table 12.2 gives the intensity levels in decibels of several familiar noises. It is taken from a survey made by the New York City Noise Abatement Commission.

TABLE 12.2 Noise levels due to various sources (representative values)

Type of noise	Sound level, dB	Intensity, W/m^2
Rock concert	140	100
Threshold of pain	120	1
Riveter	95	3.2×10^{-3}
Elevated train	90	10^{-3}
Busy street traffic	70	10^{-5}
Ordinary conversation	65	3.2×10^{-6}
Quiet automobile	50	10^{-7}
Quiet radio in home	40	10^{-8}
Average whisper	20	10^{-10}
Rustle of leaves	10	10^{-11}
Threshold of hearing	0	10^{-12}

PROBLEM-SOLVING STRATEGY 12.2 Sound intensity

Quite a few quantities are involved in characterizing the amplitude and intensity of a sound wave, and it's easy to get lost in the maze of relationships. It helps to put them into categories: The amplitude is described by A or p_{max}; the frequency f is related to the wavelength λ and the wave speed v, which in turn is determined by the properties of the medium. Take a hard look at the problem at hand, identifying which of these quantities are given and which you have to find; then start looking for relationships that take you where you want to go.

In using Equation 12.14 for the sound intensity level, remember that I and I_0 must be in the same units, usually W/m^2. If they aren't, convert!

EXAMPLE 12.8 Temporary deafness

A 10-minute exposure to 120 dB sound typically shifts your threshold of hearing temporarily from 0 dB up to 28 dB. Studies have shown that, on average, 10 years of exposure to 92 dB sound causes a *permanent* shift of up to 28 dB. What intensities correspond to 28 dB and 92 dB?

SOLUTION

SET UP AND SOLVE We rearrange Equation 12.14, dividing both sides by 10 dB and then taking inverse logarithms of both sides:

$$I = I_0 10^{(\beta/10\text{dB})}.$$

When $\beta = 28$ dB,

$$I = (10^{-12} \text{ W/m}^2) 10^{(28\text{dB}/10\text{dB})} = (10^{-12} \text{ W/m}^2)(10^{2.8})$$
$$= 6.3 \times 10^{-10} \text{ W/m}^2.$$

When $\beta = 92$ dB,

$$I = (10^{-12} \text{ W/m}^2) 10^{(92\text{dB}/10\text{dB})} = (10^{-12} \text{ W/m}^2)(10^{9.2})$$
$$= 1.6 \times 10^{-3} \text{ W/m}^2.$$

REFLECT If your answers are a factor of 10 too large, you may have entered 10×10^{-12} in your calculator instead of 1×10^{-12}. Be careful! Also, note that the human ear is sensitive to an extremely broad range of intensities.

EXAMPLE 12.9 A bird sings in a meadow

Consider an idealized model with a point source emitting a sound with constant power with an intensity inversely proportional to the square of the distance from the bird (Figure 12.30). By how many dB does the sound intensity level drop when you move to a point twice as far away from the bird?

Continued

SOLUTION

SET UP AND SOLVE We label the two points 1 and 2 (Figure 12.30), and we use Equation 12.14 twice. The difference in sound intensity level, $\beta_2 - \beta_1$, is given by

$$\beta_2 - \beta_1 = (10\,\text{dB})\left(\log\frac{I_2}{I_0} - \log\frac{I_1}{I_0}\right)$$
$$= (10\,\text{dB})[(\log I_2 - \log I_0) - (\log I_1 - \log I_0)]$$
$$= (10\,\text{dB})\log\frac{I_2}{I_1}.$$

Now we use Equation 12.13, inverted: $I_2/I_1 = r_1^2/r_2^2$. Then

$$\beta_2 - \beta_1 = (10\,\text{dB})\log\frac{r_1^2}{r_2^2} = (10\,\text{dB})\log\frac{r_1^2}{(2r_1)^2}$$
$$= (10\,\text{dB})\log\frac{1}{4} = -6.0\,\text{dB}.$$

A decrease in intensity of a factor of four corresponds to a 6 dB decrease in sound intensity level.

REFLECT The decibel scale is logarithmic; a factor of two in intensity corresponds to a 3 dB difference in sound intensity level,

▲ **FIGURE 12.30** When you double your distance from a point source of sound, how much does the sound intensity level drop?

a factor of eight to a 9 dB difference, and so on. In this problem, if two birds are singing, the sound intensity level increases by 3 dB.

Practice Problem: If the listener moves to a point four times the original distance from the bird, how many birds would have to sing in order to produce the same intensity level at this point as in the initial problem? *Answer:* 16 birds.

We invite you to prove that an increase in intensity of a factor of two corresponds to about a 3 dB increase in intensity level. This change is barely perceptible to the human ear. An increase of 8 to 10 dB in intensity level is usually interpreted by the ear as a doubling of loudness.

12.11 Beats

In several earlier sections, we've talked about *interference* effects that occur when two different waves with the same frequency overlap in the same region of space. Now let's look at the superposition of two waves with equal amplitude but slightly different frequencies. This phenomenon occurs, for example, when two guitar strings with slightly different frequencies are sounded together or when two organ pipes that are supposed to sound exactly the same pitch are slightly "out of tune." What you hear from two sound waves with slightly different frequencies is a slow pulsing or beating sound called **beats.**

Consider a particular point in space where the two waves overlap. The displacements of the individual waves at this point are plotted as functions of time in Figure 12.31a. The total length of the time axis represents about 1 s, and the frequencies are 16 Hz and 18 Hz. Applying the principle of superposition, we add the two displacements at each instant of time to find the total displacement at that time, obtaining the graph in Figure 12.31b. At certain times, the two waves are "in step": Their maxima coincide, and their amplitudes add. But as time goes on, they become more and more out of step because of their slightly different frequencies. Eventually, a maximum of one wave coincides with a maximum in the opposite direction for the other wave. The two waves then cancel each other, and the total amplitude is zero.

The resulting wave looks like a single sinusoidal wave with a varying amplitude that goes from a maximum to zero and back, as Figure 12.31b shows. In this

Activ Physics 10.7

The two waves interfere constructively when they are in step and destructively when they are a half-cycle out of step. The resultant wave waxes and wanes in intensity, forming beats.

▲ **FIGURE 12.31** When two waves with slightly different frequency interfere, the resultant wave fluctuates in amplitude. We hear these fluctuations as beats. (a) Two interacting waves; (b) the resultant wave formed by superposition of the two original waves.

example, the amplitude goes through two maxima and two minima in 1 s; thus, the frequency of this amplitude variation is 2 Hz. The resulting variations in amplitude (loudness) are beats, and the frequency with which the amplitude varies is called the **beat frequency.** In this example the beat frequency is the *difference* of the two frequencies. If the beat frequency is a few hertz, we hear it as a waver or pulsation in the tone.

We can show that the beat frequency is *always* the difference of the two frequencies f_1 and f_2. Suppose f_1 is larger than f_2; then the corresponding periods are T_1 and T_2, with $T_1 < T_2$. If the two waves start out in step at time $t = 0$, they will be in step again at a time T_{beat} such that the first wave has gone through exactly one more cycle than the second. Let n be the number of cycles of the first wave in time T_{beat}; then the number of cycles of the second wave in the same time is $(n - 1)$, and we have the relations

$$T_{beat} = nT_1 \quad \text{and} \quad T_{beat} = (n - 1)T_2.$$

We solve the second equation for n and substitute the result back into the first equation (to eliminate n), obtaining

$$T_{beat} = \frac{T_1 T_2}{T_2 - T_1}.$$

Now, T_{beat} is just the *period* of the beat, and its reciprocal is the beat *frequency* $f_{beat} = 1/T_{beat}$. So

$$f_{beat} = \frac{T_2 - T_1}{T_1 T_2} = \frac{1}{T_1} - \frac{1}{T_2},$$

and finally,

$$f_{beat} = f_1 - f_2. \tag{12.15}$$

Beats between two tones can be heard up to a beat frequency of 6 or 7 Hz. Two piano strings or two organ pipes differing in frequency by 2 or 3 Hz sound wavery and "out of tune," although some organ stops contain two sets of pipes deliberately tuned to beat frequencies of about 1 to 2 Hz for a gently undulating effect. Listening for beats (or their absence) is an important technique in tuning all musical instruments.

At higher frequency differences, we no longer hear individual beats, and the sensation merges into one of *consonance* or *dissonance,* depending on the frequency ratio of the two tones. In some cases the ear perceives a tone called a *difference tone,* with a pitch equal to the beat frequency of the two tones.

In multiengine aircraft, the engines have to be synchronized so that the sounds don't cause annoying beats, which are heard as loud throbbing sounds. On some planes this is done electronically; on others the pilot does it by ear, just like tuning a piano.

12.12 The Doppler Effect

You've probably noticed that when a car approaches you with its horn sounding, the pitch seems to drop as the car passes. This phenomenon is called the **Doppler effect.** When a source of sound and a listener are in motion relative to each other, the frequency of the sound heard by the listener is not the same as the source frequency. We can work out a relation between the frequency shift and the source and listener velocities.

To keep things simple, we'll consider only the special case in which the velocities of both source and listener lie along the line joining them. We'll take this line to be the x axis, with the positive direction to the right, and we'll assume that the source S is to the right (at greater x) of the listener L. We assume that this coordinate system is at rest with respect to the air. Let v_S and v_L be the x components of velocity of source and listener, respectively, with respect to this coordinate system. Thus, the direction from the listener L to the source S is the positive direction for both v_S and v_L. The speed of sound v is always considered positive, but v_S and v_L can be either positive or negative because they are components of velocity, a vector quantity. If $v_L > 0$, the listener is moving to the right; if $v_L < 0$, the listener is moving to the left. The same rules apply to v_S.

Moving Listener

Let's think first about a listener L moving with velocity v_L toward a stationary source S (Figure 12.32). The source emits a sound wave with frequency f_S and wavelength $\lambda = v/f_S$. The figure shows several wave crests, separated by equal

▲ **Found at sea.** Another important application of the physics of wave formation and propagation is sonar, which was used to find the long-lost steam ship Portland shown above, which sank in 1898. Sonar (SOund Navigation And Ranging) works by transmitting an ultrasonic pulse of sound waves through air or water and sensing the waves reflected from objects in the path of these waves. The frequency of the sound transmitted is about 50 kHz, well above the upper limit of the human ear, which is about 20 kHz. When the sound waves reach an object, they are reflected in various ways, depending on the position, shape, orientation, and surface characteristics of the object. The images from this shipwreck clearly show the side-by-side smokestacks and the diamond-shaped metal walking beam that provided power to the ship's side paddle wheels.

Activ Physics 10.8–10.9

▲ **FIGURE 12.32** A listener moving toward a stationary sound source hears a frequency that is higher than the source frequency because the relative velocity of listener and wave is greater than the wave speed v.

distances λ. The waves approaching the moving listener have a speed of propagation of $v + v_L$ *relative to the listener,* so the frequency f_L with which the wave crests arrive at the listener's position (the frequency the listener hears) is

$$f_L = \frac{v + v_L}{\lambda} = \frac{v + v_L}{v/f_S} = \frac{v + v_L}{v} f_S. \quad (12.16)$$

So a listener moving toward a source $(v_L > 0)$ hears a sound that has a greater frequency (higher pitch) than a stationary listener hears. A listener moving away from the source $(v_L < 0)$ hears a sound that has a lesser frequency (lower pitch).

Moving Source

Now suppose the source is also moving, with velocity v_S (Figure 12.33). The wave speed relative to the air is still v; it is determined by the properties of the wave medium and is not changed by the motion of the source. But the wavelength is no longer equal to v/f_S. Here's why: The time for the emission of one cycle of the wave is the period $T = 1/f_S$. During this time, the wave travels a distance $vT = v/f_S$ and the displacement of the source is $v_S T = v_S/f_S$ (where v_s may be either positive or negative). The wavelength is the distance between successive wave crests and is determined by the *relative* displacement of source and wave. As Figure 12.33 shows, this is different in front of and behind the source. In the region to the right of the source in the figure, the wavelength is

$$\lambda = \frac{v}{f_S} - \frac{v_S}{f_S} = \frac{v - v_S}{f_S}. \quad (12.17)$$

In the region to the left of the source, the wavelength is

$$\lambda = \frac{v + v_S}{f_S}. \quad (12.18)$$

When v_S is positive (as it is in Figure 12.33), the waves are compressed in front of the source and stretched out behind it.

To find the frequency heard by the listener, we substitute Equation 12.18 into the first form of Equation 12.16 to obtain

$$f_L = \frac{v + v_L}{\lambda} = (v + v_L)\frac{f_S}{v + v_S},$$

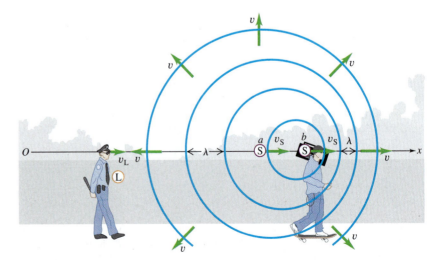

▲ **FIGURE 12.33** Wave crests emitted by a moving source are crowded together in front of the source and stretched out behind it.

which we can rewrite as follows:

Doppler effect when both listener and source may be moving

For a listener L and source S moving along the line joining them, the frequency f_L heard by the listener is related to the frequency f_S produced by the source as follows:

$$f_L = \frac{v + v_L}{v + v_S} f_S. \tag{12.19}$$

In this equation, v is the speed of sound and v_L and v_S are the x components of velocity of the listener and source, respectively.

Equation 12.19 includes all possibilities for the motion of source and listener (relative to the medium) along the line joining them. If the source happens to be at rest in the medium, v_S is zero; if the listener is at rest in the medium, v_L is zero. When both source and listener are at rest or have the same velocity relative to the medium, then $v_L = v_S$ and $f_L = f_S$. Whenever the source's or listener's velocity is in the negative x direction (opposite to the direction from listener toward source), the corresponding component of velocity (v_L or v_S) in Equation 12.19 is negative. But the wave speed v is always positive.

PROBLEM-SOLVING STRATEGY 12.3 **Doppler effect** (MP)

SET UP

1. Establish a coordinate system. Define the positive direction to be the direction from listener to source, and make sure that you know the signs of all the relevant velocities. A velocity in the direction from listener to source has a positive x component; a velocity in the opposite direction has a negative x component. Also, the velocities must all be measured relative to the air in which the sound is traveling.
2. Use consistent notation to identify the various quantities: subscript S for source, L for listener.

SOLVE

3. When a wave is reflected from a surface, either stationary or moving, the analysis can be carried out in two steps. In the first, the surface plays the role of listener; the frequency with which the wave crests arrive at the surface is f_L. Then think of the surface as a new source, emitting waves with this same frequency f_L. Finally, determine what frequency is heard by a listener detecting these new waves.

REFLECT

4. Ask whether your final result makes sense. If the source and listener are moving toward each other, f_L is always greater than f_S; if they are moving apart, f_L is always less than f_S. If source and listener have zero relative velocity, then $f_S = f_L$.

EXAMPLE 12.10 **Police car chasing a speeder**

A police siren emits a sinusoidal wave with frequency $f_S = 300$ Hz. The speed of sound is 340 m/s. **(a)** Find the wavelength of the waves if the siren is at rest in the air. **(b)** If the siren is moving with velocity $v_S = 30.0$ m/s, find the wavelengths of the waves ahead of and behind the source.

Continued

SOLUTION

SET UP (a) When the siren is at rest, $\lambda = v/f_S$. Figure 12.34 shows the situation for part (b). For the moving siren, we use Equations 12.17 and 12.18 with $v_S = 30.0$ m/s.

SOLVE Part (a): When the source is at rest,

$$\lambda = \frac{v}{f_S} = \frac{340 \text{ m/s}}{300 \text{ Hz}} = 1.13 \text{ m.}$$

Part (b): We use Equations 12.17 and 12.18. In front of the siren,

$$\lambda = \frac{v - v_S}{f_S} = \frac{340 \text{ m/s} - 30.0 \text{ m/s}}{300 \text{ Hz}} = 1.03 \text{ m.}$$

Behind the siren,

$$\lambda = \frac{v + v_S}{f_S} = \frac{340 \text{ m/s} + 30.0 \text{ m/s}}{300 \text{ Hz}} = 1.23 \text{ m.}$$

▲ **FIGURE 12.34** Wavelengths ahead of and behind the police siren when the siren is moving relative to the air.

REFLECT The wavelength is smaller in front of the moving siren, and greater behind it, than when the siren is at rest.

Practice Problem: If the siren speeds up until the wavelength in front of it is 1.00 m, what is its speed? *Answer:* 40.0 m/s.

EXAMPLE 12.11 A bystander observes the chase

If the listener is at rest and the siren is moving away from the listener at 30.0 m/s, what frequency does the listener hear?

SOLUTION

SET UP Figure 12.35 shows our diagram. We use Equation 12.19, with $v_L = 0$ and $v_S = 30.0$ m/s.:

SOLVE From Equation 12.19,

$$f_L = \frac{v + v_L}{v + v_S} f_S = \frac{340 \text{ m/s} + 0}{340 \text{ m/s} + 30.0 \text{ m/s}} (300 \text{ Hz}) = 276 \text{ Hz.}$$

REFLECT As the siren recedes, the listener hears sound of smaller frequency than when the siren is at rest.

▲ **FIGURE 12.35** Our sketch for this problem.

Practice Problem: What frequency does the policeman hear? Answer: 300 Hz.

EXAMPLE 12.12 Driving past the stationary police car

If the siren is at rest and the listener is in a car moving away from the siren at 30 m/s, what frequency does the listener hear?

SOLUTION

SET UP Figure 12.36 shows our sketch. The positive direction is still from the listener toward the source, so this time $v_L = -30.0$ m/s and $v_S = 0$.

SOLVE From Equation 12.19,

$$f_L = \frac{v + v_L}{v + v_S} f_S$$

$$= \frac{340 \text{ m/s} + (-30.0 \text{ m/s})}{340 \text{ m/s} + 0} (300 \text{ Hz}) = 274 \text{ Hz.}$$

▲ **FIGURE 12.36** Our sketch for this problem.

REFLECT The listener again hears sound of smaller frequency than when he and the siren are at rest, but not by the same amount as when the siren is moving.

EXAMPLE 12.13 **Following the police car**

If the siren is moving away from the listener with a speed of 45.0 m/s relative to the air, and the listener is moving in the same direction as the siren with a speed of 15.0 m/s relative to the air, what frequency does the listener hear?

SOLUTION

SET UP Figure 12.37 shows our sketch. In this case, $v_L =$ 15.0 m/s and $v_s =$ 45.0 m/s. (Both velocities are positive because both velocity vectors point in the +x direction, from listener to source.)

$v_L = 15 \, m/s$ $v_s = 45 \, m/s$

○─(L)────────────(S)──→×

▲ **FIGURE 12.37** Our sketch for this problem.

SOLVE From Equation 12.17,

$$f_L = \frac{v + v_L}{v + v_s} f_S = \frac{340 \text{ m/s} + 15.0 \text{ m/s}}{340 \text{ m/s} + 45.0 \text{ m/s}} (300 \text{ Hz}) = 277 \text{ Hz}.$$

REFLECT When the source and listener are moving apart, the frequency f_L heard by the listener is always *less than* the frequency f_S emitted by the source. This is the case in all of the last three examples. Note that the *relative velocity* of source and listener (30.0 m/s) is the same in all three, but the Doppler shifts are all different because the velocities relative to the air are different.

Doppler Effect for Light

In our discussion thus far, the velocities v_L and v_S have always been measured *relative to the air* or whatever medium we are considering. There is also a Doppler effect for electromagnetic waves in empty space, such as light waves or radio waves. According to the special theory of relativity, the speed of light c is the same in all inertial frames of reference. When a source emits radiation with frequency f_S, a listener moving away from the source with speed v observes a smaller frequency f_L given by

$$f_L = \sqrt{\frac{c - v}{c + v}} f_S.$$

When the listener is moving directly toward the source, v is negative and f_L is *greater* than f_S.

A familiar application of the Doppler effect with radio waves is the radar device used in police cars to check other cars' speeds. The electromagnetic wave emitted by the device is reflected from a moving car, which then acts as a moving source, and the wave reflected back to the device is Doppler shifted in frequency. The transmitted and reflected signals are combined to produce beats, and the speed can be computed from the frequency of the beats.

The Doppler effect for light is of fundamental importance in astronomy. Light emitted by elements in stars of distant galaxies shows shifts toward longer wavelength and smaller frequency, compared with light from the same elements on earth. These shifts are Doppler shifts caused by the receding motion of the galaxies containing the stars. Because the shift is nearly always toward the longer wavelength (red end) of the visible spectrum, it is called a *red shift*. These observations provide solid evidence for the "big bang" theory, which describes a universe that has been expanding for about 14 billion years.

12.13 Applications of Acoustics

The importance of acoustic principles goes far beyond human hearing. Several animals use sound for navigation. Bats depend primarily on sound rather than sight for guidance during flight. That's how they can fly in the total darkness of a cave. They emit short pulses of ultrasonic sound, typically 30 to 150 kHz; the returning echoes give the bats information about the location and size of obstacles and potential prey such as flying insects.

Dolphins use an analogous system for underwater navigation. The frequencies are again ultrasonic, about 100 kHz. With such a system, the animal can

▲ **Take cover!** Meteorologists studying severe weather use radar (RAdio Detection And Ranging) and take advantage of the Doppler effect to monitor the occurrence and movement of thunderstorms, hurricanes, and tornadoes. Doppler radar towers transmit radio-frequency waves and can detect rain, hail, and snow by recording the waves reflected by these types of atmospheric moisture. Doppler radar also compares the frequencies of the transmitted and reflected waves to determine the movement of the moisture. Waves reflected from moisture moving toward the tower have a higher frequency than that of the transmitted wavelength, and the frequency of waves reflected from receding moisture is lower. Thus, knowledge of the physics of wave propagation allows us to receive advance warning of severe weather and can prevent unnecessary damage and injury.

sense objects of about the size of the wavelength of the sound (1.4 cm) or larger. The corresponding human-designed systems, used for submarine navigation, depth measurements, finding the locations of fish or wrecked ships, and so on, are called **sonar.** Sonar systems using the Doppler effect can measure the motion, as well as position, of submerged objects.

Analysis of elastic waves in the earth provides important information about its structure. The interior of the earth may be pictured crudely as being made of concentric spherical shells around a solid inner core. Mechanical properties such as density and elastic moduli are different in different shells. Waves produced by explosions or earthquakes are reflected and refracted at the interfaces between these shells, and analysis of these waves helps geologists measure the dimensions and properties of the shells. Local anomalies such as oil deposits can also be detected by studying wave propagation.

Acoustic phenomena have many important medical applications. Shock waves are used to break up kidney stones and gallstones without invasive surgery, by means of a technique with the impressive name *extracorporeal shock-wave lithotripsy.* A shock wave is produced outside the body and is then focused by a reflector or acoustic lens so that as much of its energy as possible converges on the stone. When the resulting stresses in the stone exceed its tensile strength, it breaks into small pieces and can be eliminated. This technique requires accurate determination of the location of the stone.

Ultrasonic imaging (the reflection of ultrasonic waves from regions in the interior of the body) is used for prenatal examinations, the detection of anomalous conditions such as tumors, and the study of heart-valve action, to name a few applications. Ultrasound is more sensitive than x rays in distinguishing various kinds of tissues, and it does not have the radiation hazards associated with x rays. At much higher power levels, ultrasound appears to have promise as a selective destroyer of pathological tissue in the treatment of arthritis and certain cancers. The sound is always produced by first generating an electrical wave and then using this wave to drive a loudspeakerlike device called a **transducer** that converts electrical waves to sound. Techniques have been developed in which transducers move over, or *scan,* the region of interest and a computer-reconstructed image is produced. An example of such an image is shown in Figure 12.38.

Acoustic principles have many important applications to environmental problems, such as noise control. The design of quiet mass-transit vehicles, for example, involves detailed study of the generation and propagation of sound in the motors, wheels, and supporting structures. Excessive noise levels often lead to permanent hearing impairment; studies have shown that many young rock musicians have hearing that is typical of persons 65 years of age. Prolonged listening to music at high intensity levels (100 to 120 dB) can lead to permanent hearing loss. Stereo headsets used at high volume levels pose similar threats to hearing. Be careful!

▲ **FIGURE 12.38** An ultrasound image of an unborn fetus.

*12.14 Musical Tones

Several aspects of musical sound are directly related to the physical characteristics of sound waves. The **pitch** of a musical tone is the quality that lets us classify it as "high" or "low." Middle C on the piano has a frequency of 262 Hz. The musical interval of an *octave* corresponds to a factor of two in frequency. The C note an octave above middle C has a frequency of $2 \times 262\,\text{Hz} = 524\,\text{Hz}$, and the "high C" sung by coloratura sopranos, two octaves above middle C, has a frequency of $4 \times 262\,\text{Hz}$, or 1048 Hz. The ear can be fooled, however: When a listener hears two sinusoidal tones with the same frequency but different intensities, the louder one usually seems to be slightly lower in pitch.

Musical tones usually contain many frequencies. A plucked, bowed, or struck string or the column of air in a wind instrument vibrates with a fundamental frequency and many harmonics at the same time. Two tones may have the same fundamental frequency (and thus the same pitch) but may sound different because of the presence of different intensities of the various harmonics. The difference is called *tone color, quality,* or **timbre,** often described in subjective terms such as reedy, golden, round, mellow, or tinny. A tone that is rich in harmonics usually sounds thin and "stringy" or "reedy," and a tone containing mostly a fundamental is more mellow and flutelike.

Another factor in determining tone quality is the behavior at the beginning and end of a tone. A piano tone begins percussively with a thump and then dies away gradually. A harpsichord tone, in addition to having different harmonic content, begins much more quickly and incisively with a click, and the higher harmonics begin before the lower ones. The ending of the tone, when the key is released, is also much more incisive on the harpsichord than the piano. Similar effects are present with other musical instruments; with wind and string instruments, the player has considerable control over the attack and decay of the tone, and these characteristics help to define the unique characteristics of each instrument.

When combinations of musical tones are heard together or in succession, even a listener with no musical training hears a relationship among them; they sound comfortable together, or they clash. Musicians use the terms *consonant* and *dissonant* to describe these effects. A *consonant interval* is a combination of two tones that sound comfortable or pleasing together. The most consonant interval is the *octave,* consisting of two tones with a frequency ratio of $2:1$. An example is middle C on the piano and the next C above it. Another set of consonant tones is obtained by playing C, E, and G. These form what is called a *major triad,* and the frequencies are in the ratio $4:5:6$. The interval from C to G, with a frequency ratio of $3:2$, is a perfect fifth; C to E, with $5:4$, is a major third; and so on. These combinations sound good together because they have many harmonics in common. For example, for the interval of the octave, every harmonic in the harmonic series of the lower-frequency tone is also present in the harmonic series of the upper tone. For other intervals, the overlap of harmonics is only partial, but it is there.

If we want to be able to play major triads starting on various tones on a keyboard instrument such as the piano or organ, complications arise. Either we add a lot of extra keys in each octave to get the exact frequencies we need, or else we compromise a little on the frequencies. The most common compromise in piano tuning is called *equal temperament,* in which every pair of adjacent keys (white and black) is tuned to the same frequency ratio of $2^{1/12}$. This interval is called a *semitone* or a *halftone;* a succession of 12 of these intervals then forms an exact $2:1$ octave. The perfect fifth is seven semitones; the corresponding frequency ratio is $2^{7/12} = 1.4983$. This ratio is close to the ideal one of $3:2$, or 1.5000, but a sensitive ear can hear the difference.

Thus, a piano tuned in equal temperament is not quite in tune, in terms of the ideal ratios, in *any* key, but it is equally good (or bad) in all keys. An alternative would be to tune the white keys to form ideal intervals. Doing this would make the instrument sound better for music in the key of C, but music in some other keys would sound worse in comparison with music played in equal temperament. So an instrument that is intended to be used for compositions in all keys is usually tuned to equal temperament.

In the Baroque period, however, keys with more than three sharps or flats were seldom used, and various compromise temperaments were invented to favor the commonly used keys. Organs and harpsichords that are intended primarily for music of this period are often tuned to one of these unequal temperaments. The great J. S. Bach favored such temperaments rather than equal temperament. His composition "The Well-Tempered Clavier" contains preludes and fugues in all the major and minor keys, but it is important not to misconstrue *well tempered* as meaning *equally tempered!*

SUMMARY

Mechanical Waves

(Sections 12.1–12.4) A mechanical wave is any disturbance from an equilibrium condition that propagates from one region of space to another through some material called the medium. In a periodic wave, the motion of each particle of the medium is periodic; the period T, frequency f, wavelength λ, and wave speed v are related by $v = \lambda f = \lambda/T$. For a string with mass per unit length μ and tension F_T, the speed of transverse waves is

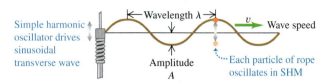

$$v = \sqrt{\frac{F_T}{\mu}}. \qquad (12.2)$$

Superposition, Standing Waves, and Normal Modes

(Sections 12.5–12.6) The **principle of superposition** states that when two waves overlap, the resulting displacement at any point is obtained by vector addition of the displacements that would be caused by the two individual waves. When a sinusoidal wave is reflected at a stationary or free end, the original and reflected wave combine to make a **standing wave.** At the **nodes** of a standing wave, the displacement is always zero; the **antinodes** are the points of maximum displacement. Fixed string ends are nodes; ends that are free to move transversely are antinodes.

Standing waves on a string of length L can have only certain specific frequencies. When both ends are held stationary, the allowed frequencies f_n are

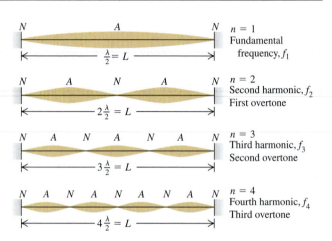

$$f_n = n\frac{v}{2L} = nf_1, \qquad (n = 1, 2, 3, \dots) \qquad (12.7)$$

A **normal mode** is a motion in which all particles on the string move sinusoidally with one of the frequencies f_n. Each value of f_n corresponds to a different normal mode.

Longitudinal Standing Waves

(Section 12.7) When a longitudinal wave propagates in a fluid in a pipe with a finite length, the waves reflect and form a standing wave. The closed end of a pipe is a *node,* and the open end is an *antinode.* For an open pipe of length L, the lowest frequency with antinodes at both ends is the fundamental frequency $f_1 = v/2L$ (Equation 12.9), and the harmonics are integer multiples of this fundamental frequency: $f_n = nf_1$. If a pipe is closed at one end, the fundamental frequency is $f_1 = v/4L$ (Equation 12.11) and the harmonics are

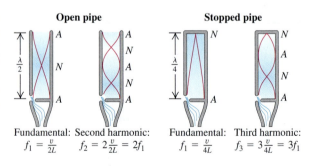

$$f_n = n\frac{v}{4L} = nf_1, \qquad (n = 1, 3, 5, \dots) \qquad (12.12)$$

Interference

(Section 12.8) Wave phenomena that occur when two or more waves overlap in the same region of space are grouped under the heading *interference.* According to the principle of superposition, if two periodic waves are *in step* at a point, then their amplitudes add together. This phenomenon is called **constructive interference.** If the waves are a half-cycle *out of step* at a point, the resulting amplitude is smaller and the phenomenon is called **destructive interference.**

Continued

Sound, Intensity, and Beats

(Sections 12.9–12.11) A *logarithmic* intensity scale is usually used to measure the **intensity level** β of a sound wave:

$$\beta = (10 \text{ dB}) \log \frac{I}{I_0}. \qquad (12.14)$$

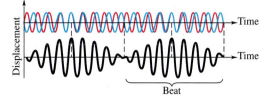

In this equation, I_0 is a reference intensity chosen to be 10^{-12} W/m^2, and the units of β are **decibels,** abbreviated dB. When two sound waves of slightly different frequency interfere, alternating constructive and destructive interference produces **beats.** The beat frequency is $f_{\text{beat}} = f_1 - f_2$ (Equation 12.15).

The Doppler Effect

(Section 12.12) The **Doppler effect** is the frequency shift that occurs when a listener is in motion relative to a source of sound. The source and listener frequencies f_S and f_L and their velocity components v_S and v_L are related by

$$f_L = \frac{v + v_L}{v + v_S} f_S. \qquad (12.19)$$

Applications of Acoustics

(Section 12.13) The importance of acoustic principles goes far beyond human hearing. Bats locate insects, and dolphins navigate, using ultrasonic waves. We study properties of the earth by measuring the reflected and refracted elastic waves passing through its interior. Ultrasonic shock waves are used to break up kidney stones or gallstones without invasive surgery. Ultrasonic imaging is used to view a fetus or tumor without the dangerous radiation associated with x-ray imaging.

*Musical Tones

(Section 12.14) Several aspects of musical sound are directly related to the physical characteristics of sound waves. Musical tones usually contain many frequencies. A plucked, bowed, or struck string or the column of air in a wind instrument vibrates with a fundamental frequency and many harmonics at the same time. Two tones may have the same fundamental frequency (and thus the same pitch), but sound different because of the presence of different intensities of the various harmonics.

MP For instructor-assigned homework, go to www.masteringphysics.com

Conceptual Questions

1. What kinds of energy are associated with waves on a stretched string? How could such energy be detected experimentally?
2. In what forms does a sound wave carry its energy, and how does it transfer it to your eardrum?
3. Sci-fi movies sometimes show the explosion of a star accompanied by a great surge of noise. What is wrong with that picture?
4. Which of the characteristics of a sound wave (amplitude or frequency) is most closely related to musical pitch? To loudness?
5. Musical notes produced by different instruments (such as a flute and an oboe) may have the same pitch and loudness and yet sound different. What is the difference, in physical terms?
6. Energy can be transferred along a string by wave motion. However, in a standing wave, no energy can ever be transferred past a node. Why not?
7. Some opera singers, such as Enrico Caruso, have been reputed to be able to break a glass by singing the appropriate note. What physical phenomenon could account for such a feat? (In fact, this is a legend and is not known ever to have occurred.)

8. Lane dividers on highways sometimes have regularly spaced ridges or ripples. When the tires of a moving car roll along such a divider, a musical note is produced. Why? Could this phenomenon be used to measure the car's speed? How?

9. Two tuning forks have identical frequencies, but one is stationary while the other is mounted on a rotating record turntable. Describe the sound that a listener hears from these forks.

10. (a) Does a sound level of zero decibels mean that there is no sound? (b) Is there any physical meaning to a sound having a negative intensity level? What is it? (c) Does a sound intensity of zero mean that there is no sound? (d) Is there any physical meaning to a sound having a negative intensity? Why?

11. Players of stringed instruments tune them by tightening the string. Why does this work? How does a piano tuner tune the instrument?

12. You are standing several meters from the railroad tracks with a train approaching, sounding its whistle. (a) As the train gets closer and closer, what happens to the loudness of the sound. Why? (b) As the train gets closer and closer, the pitch you hear from the whistle gets lower and lower. Why? (c) Would both observations in parts (a) and (b) hold true if you were standing *on* the tracks? Why?

13. As you pour water into a soda bottle, the sound you hear gets higher and higher in pitch. Why?

14. TV weather forecasters often refer to *Doppler radar* in predicting advancing storms. How do you think Doppler radar works?

15. If a tree falls in the forest with no one around to hear it, does it make a sound? Explain.

Multiple-Choice Questions

1. A hiker sees a lightning flash; 15 s later he hears the sound of the thunder. Recalling from his study of physics that the speed of sound in air is approximately $\frac{1}{3}$ km/s, he estimates that the distance to where the lightning flash occurred is approximately
   A. 5 km. B. 10 km. C. 15 km. D. 45 km.

2. A segment *A* of wire stretched tightly between two posts a distance *L* apart vibrates in its fundamental mode with frequency *f*. A segment *B* of an identical wire is stretched with the same tension, but between two different posts. You observe that the frequency of the second harmonic of wire *B* is the same as the fundamental frequency of wire *A*. The length of wire *B* must be
   A. *L*. B. 2*L*. C. 4*L*.

3. Two pulses of exactly the same size and shape are traveling toward each other along a stretched rope. They differ only in that one is upright while the other is inverted. Superposition tells us that when the pulses meet each other, they will cancel each other exactly at that instant and the rope will show no evidence of a pulse. What happens *afterwards?*
   A. Each pulse continues as though it had never met the other one.
   B. The rope remains straight, since the pulses have cancelled each other.
   C. The pulses rebound from each other, each going back in the direction from which it came.

4. An organ pipe open at one end, but closed at the other, is vibrating in its fundamental mode, producing sound of frequency 1000 Hz. If you now open the closed end, the new fundamental frequency will be
   A. 2000 Hz. B. 1000 Hz. C. 500 Hz. D. 250 Hz.

5. A person listening to a siren from a stationary police car observes the frequency and wavelength of that sound. This person now moves rapidly toward the police car.
   A. The wavelength of the sound the person observes is shorter than it was, but the frequency does not change.
   B. The frequency of the sound the person observes is higher than it was, but the wavelength does not change.
   C. The wavelength of the sound the person observes is shorter than it was, and the frequency is higher than it was.

6. A person listening to a siren from a stationary police car observes the frequency and wavelength of that sound. The car now drives rapidly toward the person.
   A. The wavelength of the sound the person observes will be shorter than it was, but the frequency will not be changed.
   B. The frequency of the sound the person observes will be higher than it was, but the wavelength will not be changed.
   C. The wavelength of the sound the person observes will be shorter than it was, and the frequency will also be higher than it was.

7. A string of length 0.600 m is vibrating at 100.0 Hz in its second harmonic and producing sound that moves at 340 m/s. What is true about the frequency and wavelength of this sound? (There may be more than one correct choice.)
   A. The wavelength of the sound is 0.600 m.
   B. The wavelength of the sound is 3.40 m.
   C. The frequency of the sound is 100.0 Hz.
   D. The frequency of the sound is 567 Hz.

8. When a 15 kg mass is hung vertically from a thin, light wire, pulses take time *t* to travel the full length of the wire. If an additional 15 kg mass is added to the first one without changing the length of the wire, the time taken for pulses to travel the length of the wire will be
   A. 2*t*. B. $\sqrt{2}t$. C. *t*/2. D. $t/\sqrt{2}$.

9. An omnidirectional loudspeaker produces sound waves uniformly in all directions. The total power received by a sphere of radius 2.0 m centered on the speaker is 100 W. A sphere of radius 4.0 m will receive a total power of
   A. 100 W. B. 50 W. C. 25 W.

10. An organ pipe open at both ends is resonating in its fundamental mode at frequency *f*. If you close both ends, the fundamental frequency will now be
    A. 2*f*. B. *f*. C. *f*/2. D. *f*/4.

11. You are standing between two stereo speakers that are emitting sound of wavelength 10.0 cm in step with each other. They are very far apart compared with that wavelength. If you start in the middle and walk a distance *x* directly toward one speaker, you observe that the sound from these speakers first cancels when *x* is equal to
    A. 20.0 cm. B. 10.0 cm. C. 5.0 cm. D. 2.5 cm.

12. A sound that is below the threshold of human hearing has
    A. a negative intensity level (in dB).
    B. a negative intensity (in W/m^2).
    C. an intensity level of zero.
    D. an intensity level less than 1 dB, but greater than 0.

13. A string tied at both ends vibrates at a frequency of 500 Hz in its first *overtone*. In its fourth *harmonic,* it vibrates at
    A. 125 Hz. B. 250 Hz. C. 1000 Hz. D. 2000 Hz.

14. A thin, light string supports a weight *W* hanging from the ceiling. In this situation, the string produces a note of frequency *f* when vibrating in its fundamental mode. In order to cause this

string to produce a note one octave higher in its fundamental mode without stretching it, we must change the weight to

A. 4*W*.   B. 2*W*.   C. $\sqrt{2}W$.
D. *W*/2.   E. *W*/4.

15. String *A* weighs twice as much as string *B*. Both strings are thin and light and have the same length. If you hang equal weights at the bottom of each of these strings, the ratio of the speed of waves on string *A* to the speed of waves on string *B* will be

A. $v_A/v_B = 2$.
B. $v_A/v_B = \sqrt{2}$.
C. $v_A/v_B = 1/\sqrt{2}$.
D. $v_A/v_B = \frac{1}{2}$.

Problems

Unless otherwise indicated, assume that the speed of sound in air is 344 m/s.

12.2 Periodic Mechanical Waves

1. • (a) **Audible wavelengths.** The range of audible frequencies
BIO is from about 20 Hz to 20,000 Hz. What is range of the wavelengths of audible sound in air? (b) **Visible light.** The range of visible light extends from 400 nm to 700 nm. What is the range of visible frequencies of light? (c) **Brain surgery.** Surgeons can remove brain tumors by using a cavitron ultrasonic surgical aspirator, which produces sound waves of frequency 23 kHz. What is the wavelength of these waves in air? (d) **Sound in the body.** What would be the wavelength of the sound in part (c) in bodily fluids in which the speed of sound is 1480 m/s, but the frequency is unchanged?

2. • **The electromagnetic spectrum.** Electromagnetic waves, which include light, consist of vibrations of electric and magnetic fields, and they all travel at the speed of light. (a) **FM radio.** Find the wavelength of an FM radio station signal broadcasting at a frequency of 104.5 MHz. (b) **X rays.** X rays have a wavelength of about 0.10 nm. What is their frequency? (c) **The Big Bang.** Microwaves with a wavelength of 1.1 mm, left over from soon after the big bang, have been detected. What is their frequency? (d) **Sunburn.** Sunburn (and skin cancer) are caused by ultraviolet light waves having a frequency of around 10^{16} Hz. What is their wavelength? (e) **SETI.** It has been suggested that extraterrestrial civilizations (if they exist) might try to communicate by using electromagnetic waves having the same frequency as that given off by the spin flip of the electron in hydrogen, which is 1.43 GHz. To what wavelength should we tune our telescopes in order to search for such signals? (f) **Microwave ovens.** Microwave ovens cook food with electromagnetic waves of frequency around 2.45 GHz. What wavelength do these waves have?

3. • If an earthquake wave having a wavelength of 13 km causes the ground to vibrate 10.0 times each minute, what is the speed of the wave?

4. •• A fisherman notices that his boat is moving up and down periodically, owing to waves on the surface of the water. It takes 2.5 s for the boat to travel from its highest point to its lowest, a total distance of 0.62 m. The fisherman sees that the wave crests are spaced 6.0 m apart. (a) How fast are the waves traveling? (b) What is the amplitude of each wave? (c) If the total vertical distance traveled by the boat were 0.30 m, but the

other data remained the same, how would the answers to parts (a) and (b) be affected?

12.3 Wave Speeds

5. • A steel wire 4.00 m long has a mass of 0.0600 kg and is stretched with a tension of 1000 N. What is the speed of propagation of a transverse wave on the wire?

6. • With what tension must a rope with length 2.50 m and mass 0.120 kg be stretched for transverse waves of frequency 40.0 Hz to have a wavelength of 0.750 m?

7. • One end of a horizontal rope is attached to a prong of an electrically driven tuning fork that vibrates at 120 Hz. The other end passes over a pulley and supports a 1.50 kg mass. The linear mass density of the rope is 0.0550 kg/m. (a) What is the speed of a transverse wave on the rope? (b) What is the wavelength? (c) How would your answers to parts (a) and (b) change if the mass were increased to 3.00 kg?

8. •• (a) If the amplitude in a sound wave is doubled, by what factor does the intensity of the wave increase? (b) By what factor must the amplitude of a sound wave be increased in order to increase the intensity by a factor of 9?

9. •• When a mass *M* hangs from a vertical wire of length *L*, waves travel on this wire with a speed *V*. What will be the speed of these waves (in terms of *V*) if (a) we double *M* without stretching the wire? (b) we replace the wire with an identical one, except twice as long? (c) we replace the wire with one of the same length, but three times as heavy? (d) we stretch the wire to twice its original length? (e) we increase *M* by a factor of 10, which stretches the wire to double its original length?

*12.4 Mathematical Description of a Wave

10. • A certain transverse wave is described by the equation

$$y(x, t) = (6.50 \text{ mm}) \sin 2\pi \left(\frac{t}{0.0360 \text{ s}} - \frac{x}{0.280 \text{ m}} \right).$$

Determine this wave's (a) amplitude, (b) wavelength, (c) frequency, (d) speed of propagation, and (e) direction of propagation.

11. • Transverse waves on a string have wave speed 8.00 m/s, amplitude 0.0700 m, and wavelength 0.320 m. These waves travel in the *x* direction, and at *t* = 0 the *x* = 0 end of the string is at *y* = 0 and moving downward. (a) Find the frequency, period, and wave number of these waves. (b) Write the equation for *y*(*x*, *t*) describing these waves. (c) Find the transverse displacement of a point on the string at *x* = 0.360 m at time *t* = 0.150 s.

12. • The equation describing a transverse wave on a string is

$$y(x, t) = (1.50 \text{ mm}) \sin[(157 \text{ s}^{-1})t - (41.9 \text{ m}^{-1})x].$$

Find (a) the wavelength, frequency, and amplitude of this wave, (b) the speed and direction of motion of the wave, and (c) the transverse displacement of a point on the string when *t* = 0.100 s and at a position *x* = 0.135 m.

13. •• Transverse waves are traveling on a long string that is under a tension of 4.00 N. The equation describing these waves is

$$y(x, t) = (1.25 \text{ cm}) \sin[(415 \text{ s}^{-1})t - (44.9 \text{ m}^{-1})x].$$

Find the linear mass density of this string.

12.5 Reflections and Superposition
12.6 Standing Waves and Normal Modes

14. • **Mapping the ocean floor.** The ocean floor is mapped by sending sound waves (sonar) downward and measuring the time it takes for their echo to return. From this information, the ocean depth can be calculated if one knows that sound travels at 1531 m/s in seawater. If a ship sends out sonar pulses and records their echo 3.27 s later, how deep is the ocean floor at that point, assuming that the speed of sound is the same at all depths?

15. • In Figure 12.39, each pulse is traveling on a string at 1 cm/s, and each square represents 1 cm. Draw the shape of the string at the end of 6 s, 7 s, and 8 s.

16. • A 1.50-m-long rope is stretched between two supports with a tension that makes the speed of transverse waves 48.0 m/s. What are the wavelength and frequency of (a) the fundamental tone? (b) the second overtone? (c) the fourth harmonic?

▲ **FIGURE 12.39** Problem 15.

17. • A piano tuner stretches a steel piano wire with a tension of 800 N. The wire is 0.400 m long and has a mass of 3.00 g. (a) What is the frequency of its fundamental mode of vibration? (b) What is the number of the highest harmonic that could be heard by a person who is capable of hearing frequencies up to 10,000 Hz?

18. • A wire with mass 40.0 g is stretched so that its ends are tied down at points 80.0 cm apart. The wire vibrates in its fundamental mode with frequency 60.0 Hz and with an amplitude of 0.300 cm at the antinodes. (a) What is the speed of propagation of transverse waves in the wire? (b) Compute the tension in the wire.

19. •• The portion of string between the bridge and upper end of the fingerboard (the part of the string that is free to vibrate) of a certain musical instrument is 60.0 cm long and has a mass of 2.00 g. The string sounds an A_4 note (440 Hz) when played. (a) Where must the player put a finger (at what distance x from the bridge) to play a D_5 note (587 Hz)? (See Figure 12.40.) For both notes, the string vibrates in its fundamental mode. (b) Without retuning, is it possible to play a G_4 note (392 Hz) on this string? Why or why not?

Finger board

60.0 cm

Bridge

▲ **FIGURE 12.40** Problem 19.

20. •• **Voiceprints.** In this chapter, we have been concentrating on sinusoidal waves. But most waves in the real world are far more complicated. However, many complicated waves can be created by adding together sine waves of varying amplitude and frequency. When a singer, for example, sings a note, the pitch we hear is the fundamental frequency at which his or her larynx is vibrating. But the larynx also vibrates in other frequencies (the overtones) at the same time. So the sound we hear is a superposition of the fundamental frequency plus all the overtones. This set of all the frequencies (with their respective amplitudes) is called the person's *voiceprint*. (a) To see how this works, carefully graph a sine wave of frequency 440 Hz (concert A), with time on the horizontal axis and displacement on the vertical axis. Let the amplitude be 1 unit. On the same set of axes, graph the first overtone of 880 Hz, but with an amplitude of $\frac{1}{2}$ unit. (b) Now add the two waves to find their superposition. Notice that the shape is no longer a sine wave.

21. •• **Voiceprints.** Suppose a singer singing F# (370 Hz, the fundamental frequency) has one overtone of frequency 740 Hz with half the amplitude of the fundamental and another overtone of frequency 1110 Hz having one-third the amplitude of the fundamental. Using the previous problem as a guide, graph the superposition of these three waves to show the complex sound wave produced by this singer.

22. •• One end of a horizontal string is tied to a wall, and the other end is tied to an object with weight W that hangs over a pulley to hold the string taut. The object is large enough that the string never moves at the pulley. Under these conditions, the string vibrates with wavelength λ and frequency f in its first harmonic. (a) If we add enough weight to double W without appreciably stretching the string, what will be the wavelength and frequency (in terms of λ and f) of the string's first harmonic vibration? (b) If we do not change W, but move the pulley so that the vibrating part of the string is half as long, what will be the wavelength and frequency (in terms of λ and f) of the string in its first harmonic? (c) If we now double W (without appreciably stretching the string) and at the same time move the pulley so that the vibrating part of the string is twice as long as it originally was, what are the wavelength and frequency (in terms of λ and f) of the string in its first harmonic?

12.7 Longitudinal Standing Waves

23. • Standing sound waves are produced in a pipe that is 1.20 m long. For the fundamental frequency and the first two overtones, determine the locations along the pipe (measured from the left end) of the displacement nodes if (a) the pipe is open at both ends; (b) the pipe is closed at the left end and open at the right end.

24. • Find the fundamental frequency and the frequency of the first three overtones of a pipe 45.0 cm long (a) if the pipe is open at both ends; (b) if the pipe is closed at one end. (c) For each of the preceding cases, what is the number of the highest harmonic that may be heard by a person who can hear frequencies from 20 Hz to 20,000 Hz?

25. • The longest pipe found in most medium-size pipe organs is 4.88 m (16 ft) long. What is the frequency of the note corresponding to the fundamental mode if the pipe is (a) open at both ends, (b) open at one end and closed at the other?

26. • The frequency of the note F_4 is 349 Hz. If an organ pipe is open at one end and closed at the other, what length must it have for its fundamental mode to produce this note at 20° C?

27. • **The role of the mouth in sound.** The production of sound during speech or singing is a complicated process. Let's con-

centrate on the mouth. A typical depth for the human mouth is about 8.0 cm, although this number can vary. (Check it against your own mouth.) We can model the mouth as an organ pipe that is open at the back of the throat. What are the wavelengths and frequencies of the first four harmonics you can produce if your mouth is (a) open, (b) closed? Use $v = 354$ m/s.

28. •• (a) Derive the formula for the wavelengths of the harmonics for a hollow pipe of length L that is closed at both ends. (b) Compare this result with the case of a pipe that is open at both ends.

29. •• **The vocal tract.** Many opera singers (and some pop
BIO singers) have a range of about $2\frac{1}{2}$ octaves or even greater. Suppose a soprano's range extends from A below middle C (frequency 220 Hz) up to E^b above high C (frequency 1244 Hz). Although the vocal tract is quite complicated, we can model it as a resonating air column, like an organ pipe, that is open at the top and closed at the bottom. The column extends from the mouth down to the diaphragm in the chest cavity, and we can also assume that the lowest note is the fundamental. How long is this column of air if $v = 354$ m/s? Does your result seem reasonable, on the basis of observations of your own body?

30. •• **Singing in the shower!** We all sound like great singers in the shower, due to standing waves. Assume that your shower is 2.45 m (about 8 ft) tall and can be modeled as an organ pipe. (a) What will we have at the floor and ceiling, displacement nodes or antinodes? (b) What are the wavelength and frequency of the fundamental harmonic for standing waves in this shower? (See the answer to Problem 28.) (c) What are the wavelength and frequency of the first two overtones for this shower?

31. •• **French horn.** The French horn, one of the most beautiful-sounding instruments in the orchestra, consists of about 3.7 m (roughly 12 ft) of thin tubing, rolled into a spiral shape (although sizes do vary). The player blows into the mouthpiece, which can be treated as a closed end, and places his hand in the opposite end, which has a large flared opening. In brass instruments, the fundamental note is not normally playable. Instead the *first overtone* is the lowest playable note. (a) If the player's hand keeps the large end open, what is the frequency of the lowest *playable* note? (b) If the player now closes the large end with his hand, what is the frequency of the lowest playable note? See the answer to Problem 28. (*Note:* The physics of the French horn is much more complex than is indicated here. The player's hand in the open end also changes the effective length of the tube, which then affects the frequency of the sound.)

▲ **FIGURE 12.41** Problem 31.

32. •• An organ pipe has two successive harmonics with frequencies 1372 and 1764 Hz. (a) Is this an open or a stopped pipe? Explain. (b) What two harmonics are these? (c) What is the length of the pipe?

12.8 Interference

33. • Two small speakers A and B are driven in step at 725 Hz by the same audio oscillator. These speakers both start out 4.50 m from the listener, but speaker A is slowly moved away. (See Figure 12.42.) (a) At what distance d will the sound from the speakers first produce destructive interference at the location of the listener? (b) If A keeps moving, at what distance d will the speakers next produce destructive interference at the listener? (c) After A starts moving away, at what distance will the speakers first produce constructive interference at the listener?

▲ **FIGURE 12.42** Problem 33.

34. •• In a certain home sound system, two small speakers are located so that one is 45.0 cm closer to the listener than the other. For what frequencies of audible sound will these speakers produce (a) destructive interference at the listener, (b) constructive interference at the listener? In each case, find only the three lowest audible frequencies.

35. •• Two small stereo speakers are driven in step by the same variable-frequency oscillator. Their sound is picked up by a microphone arranged as shown in Figure 12.43. For what frequencies does their sound at the speakers produce (a) constructive interference, (b) destructive interference?

▲ **FIGURE 12.43** Problem 35.

12.9 Sound and Hearing

36. • **Human hearing.** The
BIO human outer ear contains a more-or-less cylindrical cavity called the *auditory canal* that behaves like a resonant tube to aid in the hearing process. One end terminates at the eardrum (tympanic membrane), while the other opens to the outside. (See Figure 12.44.) Typically, this canal is approximately 2.4 cm long. (a) At what frequencies would it resonate in its first two harmonics? (b) What are the corresponding sound wavelengths in part (a)?

▲ **FIGURE 12.44** Problem 36.

37. • **Ultrasound and infrasound.** (a) **Whale communica-**
BIO **tion.** Blue whales apparently communicate with each other using sound of frequency 17 Hz, which can be heard nearly 1000 km away in the ocean. What is the wavelength

of such a sound in seawater, where the speed of sound is 1531 m/s? (b) **Dolphin clicks.** One type of sound that dolphins emit is a sharp click of wavelength 1.5 cm in the ocean. What is the frequency of such clicks? (c) **Dog whistles.** One brand of dog whistles claims a frequency of 25 kHz for its product. What is the wavelength of this sound? (d) **Bats.** While bats emit a wide variety of sounds, one type emits pulses of sound having a frequency between 39 kHz and 78 kHz. What is the range of wavelengths of this sound? (e) **Sonograms.** Ultrasound is used to view the interior of the body, much as x rays are utilized. For sharp imagery, the wavelength of the sound should be around one-fourth (or less) the size of the objects to be viewed. Approximately what frequency of sound is needed to produce a clear image of a tumor that is 1.0 mm across if the speed of sound in the tissue is 1550 m/s?

38. •• A 75.0 cm wire of mass 5.625 g is tied at both ends and adjusted to a tension of 35.0 N. When it is vibrating in its second overtone, find (a) the frequency and wavelength at which it is vibrating and (b) the frequency and wavelength of the sound waves it is producing.

39. •• Suppose sound goes from one medium into another, such as from air into water. (a) Make a good physical argument to show that the frequency of the sound does *not* change, whereas the wavelength *does*. (b) Find the wavelength of a sound wave in water (where its speed is 1498 m/s) if it has a wavelength of 2.50 m in air.

12.10 Sound Intensity

40. • A small omnidirectional stereo speaker produces waves in all directions that have an intensity of 6.50 W/m² at a distance of 2.50 m from the speaker. (a) At what rate does this speaker produce energy? (b) What is the intensity of this sound 7.00 m from the speaker? (c) What is the *total* amount of energy received each second by the walls (including windows and doors) of the room in which this speaker is located?

41. • Find the intensity (in W/m²) of (a) a 55.0 dB sound, (b) a 92.0 dB sound, (c) a −2.0 dB sound.

42. • Find the noise level (in dB) of a sound having an intensity of (a) 0.000127 W/m², (b) 6.53×10^{-10} W/cm², (c) 1.5×10^{-14} W/m².

43. •• **The dreaded leaf blowers!** The Sacramento City Council recently adopted a law to reduce the allowed sound intensity level of the much-despised leaf blowers from their current level of 95.0 dB to 70.0 dB. Under the new law, what is the ratio of the allowed intensity to the previously allowed intensity?

44. •• You live on a busy street, but as a music lover, you want to reduce the traffic noise. (a) If you install special sound-reflecting windows that reduce the sound intensity level (in dB) by 30 dB, by what fraction have you lowered the sound intensity (in W/m²)? (b) If, instead, you reduce the intensity by half, what change (in dB) do you make in the sound intensity level?

45. •• **Eavesdropping!** You are trying to overhear a juicy conversation, but from your distance of 15.0 m, it sounds like only an average whisper of 20.0 dB. So you decide to move closer to give the conversation a sound level of 60.0 dB instead. How close should you come?

46. •• **Energy delivered to the ear.** Sound is detected when a **BIO** sound wave causes the tympanic membrane (the eardrum) to

vibrate. (See Figure 12.29). Typically, the diameter of this membrane is about 8.4 mm in humans. (a) How much energy is delivered to the eardrum each second when someone whispers (20 dB) a secret in your ear? (b) To comprehend how sensitive the ear is to very small amounts of energy, calculate how fast a typical 2.0 mg mosquito would have to fly (in mm/s) to have this amount of kinetic energy.

47. •• **Human hearing.** A fan at a rock concert is 30 m from the **BIO** stage, and at this point the sound intensity level is 110 dB. (a) How much energy is transferred to her eardrums each second? (See the previous problem.) (b) How fast would a 2.0 mg mosquito have to fly to have this much kinetic energy? Compare the mosquito's speed with that found for the whisper in part (a) of the previous problem.

48. •• At point A, 3.0 m from a small source of sound that is emitting uniformly in all directions, the intensity level is 53 dB. (a) What is the intensity of the sound at A? (b) How far from the source must you go so that the intensity is one-fourth of what it was at A? (c) How far must you go so that the sound level is one-fourth of what it was at A? (d) Does intensity obey the inverse square law? What about intensity level?

49. •• (a) If two sounds differ by 5.00 dB, find the ratio of the intensity of the louder sound to that of the softer one. (b) If one sound is 100 times as intense as another, by how much do they differ in sound intensity level (in decibels)? (c) If you increase the volume of your stereo so that the intensity doubles, by how much does the sound intensity level increase?

12.11 Beats

50. • A trumpet player is tuning his instrument by playing an A note simultaneously with the first-chair trumpeter, who has perfect pitch. The first-chair player's note is exactly 440 Hz, and 2.8 beats per second are heard. What are the two possible frequencies of the other player's note?

51. • **Musical dissonance.** When you play two adjacent semitone notes (such as D and D#), the resulting tone sounds harsh, or *dissonant,* to most people. (Try this exercise on a piano by simultaneously playing a white key and the adjacent black key.) The dissonance comes in part from a beat having a frequency a little too high for us to hear the individual beats. Nevertheless, it is perceptible to us as a harsh sound. What would be the beat frequency when D (frequency 294 Hz) and D# (frequency 311 Hz) are played simultaneously?

52. • Two tuning forks are producing sounds of wavelength 34.40 cm and 33.94 cm simultaneously. How many beats do you hear each second?

53. •• **Adjusting airplane motors.** The motors that drive airplane propellers are, in some cases, tuned by using beats. The whirring motor produces a sound wave having the same frequency as the propeller. (a) If one single-bladed propeller is turning at 575 rpm and you hear a 2.0 Hz beat when you run the second propeller, what are the two possible frequencies (in rpm) of the second propeller? (b) Suppose you increase the speed of the second propeller slightly and find that the beat frequency changes to 2.1 Hz. In part (a), which of the two answers was the correct one for the frequency of the second single-bladed propeller? How do you know?

54. •• **Tuning a violin.** A violinist is tuning her instrument to concert A (440 Hz). She plays the note while listening to an electronically generated tone of exactly that frequency and hears a

beat of frequency 3 Hz, which increases to 4 Hz when she tightens her violin string slightly. (a) What was the frequency of her violin when she heard the 3-Hz beat? (b) To get her violin perfectly tuned to concert A, should she tighten or loosen her string from what it was when she heard the 3-Hz beat?

12.12 The Doppler Effect

55. • A railroad train is traveling at 25.0 m/s in still air. The frequency of the note emitted by the locomotive whistle is 400 Hz. What is the wavelength of the sound waves (a) in front of the locomotive? (b) behind the locomotive? What is the frequency of the sound heard by a stationary listener (c) in front of the locomotive? (d) behind the locomotive?

56. • Two train whistles, A and B, each have a frequency of 392 Hz. A is stationary and B is moving toward the right (away from A) at a speed of 35.0 m/s. A listener is between the two whistles and is moving toward the right with a speed of 15.0 m/s. (See Figure 12.45.) (a) What is the frequency from A as heard by the listener? (b) What is the frequency from B as heard by the listener? (c) What is the beat frequency detected by the listener?

▲ **FIGURE 12.45** Problem 56.

57. • On the planet Arrakis, a male ornithoid is flying toward his stationary mate at 25.0 m/s while singing at a frequency of 1200 Hz. If the female hears a tone of 1240 Hz, what is the speed of sound in the atmosphere of Arrakis?

58. • Two swift canaries fly towards each other, each moving at 15.0 m/s relative to the ground, each warbling a note of frequency 1750 Hz. (a) What frequency note does each bird hear from the other one? (b) What wavelength will each canary measure for the note from the other one?

59. •• **Wagnerian opera.** A man marries a great Wagnerian soprano, but alas, he discovers that he cannot stand Wagnerian opera. In order to save his eardrums, the unhappy man decides that he must silence his larklike wife for good. His plan is to tie her to the front of his car and send car and soprano speeding towards a brick wall. This soprano, however is quite shrewd, having studied physics in her student days at the music conservatory. She realizes that the wall has a resonant frequency of 600 Hz, which means that if a continuous sound wave of that frequency hits the wall, it will fall down, and she will be saved to sing again. The car is heading toward the wall at a high speed of 30 m/s. (a) At what frequency must the soprano sing so that the wall will crumble? (b) What frequency will the soprano hear reflected from the wall just before it crumbles?

60. •• The siren of a fire engine that is driving northward at 30.0 m/s emits a sound of frequency 2000 Hz. A truck in front of this fire engine is moving northward at 20.0 m/s. (a) What is the frequency of the siren's sound that the fire engine's driver hears reflected from the back of the truck? (b) What wavelength would this driver measure for these reflected sound waves?

61. •• A stationary police car emits a sound of frequency 1200 Hz that bounces off of a car on the highway and returns with a frequency of 1250 Hz. The police car is right next to the highway, so the moving car is traveling directly toward or away from it. (a) How fast was the moving car going? Was it moving towards or away from the police car? (b) What frequency would the police car have received if it had been traveling toward the other car at 20.0 m/s?

62. •• In each of the following cases, what is the frequency of sound measured by the listener if the source is emitting a sound of frequency f_s? (a) The source moves toward the stationary listener at the speed of sound. (b) The listener moves toward the stationary source at the speed of sound. (c) The listener moves away from the stationary source at the speed of sound.

63. ••• **Supersonic Doppler effect.** Suppose a listener is approaching a stationary speaker at *twice* the speed of sound. (a) What frequency will the listener hear? (b) What frequency in terms of f will the listener hear if the speaker is emitting sound of frequency f after he has *passed* the speaker? Interpret your answer physically. (c) If the speaker is playing Alban Berg's violin concerto, what will the listener hear after passing the speaker?

64. •• **Moving source vs. moving listener.** (a) A sound source producing 1.00 kHz waves moves toward a stationary listener at one-half the speed of sound. What frequency will the listener hear? (b) Suppose instead that the source is stationary and the listener moves toward the source at one-half the speed of sound. What frequency does the listener hear? How does your answer compare with that in part (a)? Did you expect to get the same answer in both cases? Explain on physical grounds why the two answers differ.

65. •• The sun (and the earth with it) are traveling at 2.0×10^4 km/s toward a star that is 45 light years away. (A light year is the distance light travels in one year.) If an astronomer on earth measures light of wavelength 523.4 nm from this star, what frequency and wavelength would an observer at rest with respect to the star measure for the light it emits?

General Problems

66. •• One end of a 14.0-m-long wire having a total mass of 0.800 kg is fastened to a fixed support in the ceiling, and a 7.50 kg object is hung from the other end. If the wire is struck a transverse blow at one end, how much time does the pulse take to reach the other end?

67. •• **Ultrasound in medicine.** A 2.00 MHz sound wave travels through a pregnant woman's abdomen and is reflected from the fetal heart wall of her unborn baby. The heart wall is moving toward the sound receiver as the heart beats. The reflected sound is then mixed with the transmitted sound, and 85 beats per second are detected. The speed of sound in body tissue is 1500 m/s. Calculate the speed of the fetal heart wall at the instant this measurement is made.

68. •• A very noisy chain saw operated by a tree surgeon emits a total acoustic power of 20.0 W uniformly in all directions. At what distance from the source is the sound level equal to (a) 100 dB, (b) 60 dB?

69. •• A vibrating string 50.0 cm long is under a tension of 1.00 N. The results from five successive stroboscopic pictures are shown in Figure 12.46. The strobe rate is set at 36,000 flashes per minute, and observations reveal that the

maximum displacement occurred at flashes 1 and 5, with no other maxima in between. (a) Find the period, frequency, and wavelength of the traveling waves on this string. (b) In what normal mode (harmonic) is the string vibrating? (c) What is the speed of the traveling waves on the string? (d) What is the mass of this string?

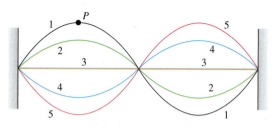

▲ **FIGURE 12.46** Problem 69.

70. •• A baby's mouth is 30.0 cm from her father's ear and 1.50 m from her mother's ear. What is the difference between the sound intensity levels (in dB) heard by the father and by the mother?

71. •• **Tuning a cello.** A cellist tunes the C-string of her instrument to a fundamental frequency of 65.4 Hz. The vibrating portion of the string is 0.600 m long and has a mass of 14.4 g. (a) With what tension must she stretch that portion of the string? (b) What percentage increase in tension is needed to increase the frequency from 65.4 Hz to 73.4 Hz, corresponding to a rise in pitch from C to D?

72. •• In its first overtone, an organ pipe that is open at one end and closed at the other end produces the note concert A, of 440 Hz. (a) Find the frequency and wavelength of the fundamental mode. (b) What will the fundamental frequency be if (i) the open end is now closed (see Problem 2.8); (ii) both ends are now open?

73. •• A bat flies toward a wall, emitting a steady sound of frequency 2000 Hz. The bat hears its own sound, plus the sound reflected by the wall. How fast should the bat fly in order to hear a beat frequency of 10.0 Hz? (*Hint:* Break this problem into two parts, first with the bat as the source and the wall as the listener and then with the wall as the source and the bat as the listener.)

74. •• **Music.** You are designing a two-string instrument with metal string 35.0 cm long, as shown in Figure 12.47. Both strings are under the *same tension.* String S_1 has a mass of 8.00 g and produces the note middle C (frequency 262 Hz) in its fundamental mode. (a) What should be the tension in the string? (b) What should be the mass of string S_2 so that it will produce A# (frequency 466 Hz) as its fundamental? (c) To extend the range of your instrument, you include a fret located just under the strings, but not normally touching them. How far from the upper end should you put this fret so that when you press

▲ **FIGURE 12.47** Problem 74.

S_1 tightly against it, this string will produce C# (frequency 277 Hz) in its fundamental? That is, what is x in the figure? (d) If you press S_2 against the fret, what frequency of sound will it produce in its fundamental?

75. •• The sound source of a ship's sonar system operates at a frequency of 22.0 kHz. The speed of sound in water (assumed to be at a uniform 20° C) is 1482 m/s. (a) What is the wavelength of the waves emitted by the source? (b) What is the difference in frequency between the directly radiated waves and the waves reflected from a whale traveling straight toward the ship at 4.95 m/s? The ship is at rest in the water.

76. •• **The range of human hearing.** A young person with normal hearing can hear sounds ranging from 20 Hz to 20 kHz. How many octaves can such a person hear? (Recall that if two tones differ by an octave, the higher frequency is twice the lower frequency.)

77. •• A swimming duck paddles the water with its feet once every 1.6 s, producing surface waves with that period. The duck is moving at constant speed in a pond in which the speed of surface waves is 0.32 m/s and the crests of the waves ahead of the duck are spaced 0.12 m apart. (a) What is this little quacker's speed? (b) How far apart are the crests behind the duck?

78. •• A person leaning over a 125-m-deep well accidentally drops a siren emitting sound of frequency 2500 Hz. Just before this siren hits the bottom of the well, find the frequency and wavelength of the sound the person hears (a) coming directly from the siren, (b) reflected off the bottom of the well. (c) What beat frequency does this person perceive?

79. •• Two identical parallel wires, A and B, are vibrating in their second *overtone.* A bumblebee flying between them from B toward A at 8.0 m/s perpendicular to the wires hears a 15 Hz beat. What frequency of sound is each wire producing?

80. •• A flexible stick can oscillate in a standing-wave pattern, much as a string does. (a) Are the ends of the stick displacement nodes or antinodes? Why? (If in doubt, use a handy stick at home or in the laboratory and try it out.) (b) A flexible stick 3.00 m long is free to wiggle. Using the conditions from part (a), find the wavelengths of the first five harmonics for this stick.

81. •• A turntable 1.50 m in diameter rotates at 75 rpm. Two speakers, each giving off sound of wavelength 31.3 cm, are attached to the rim of the table at opposite ends of a diameter. A listener stands in front of the turntable. (a) What is the greatest beat frequency the listener will receive from this system? (b) Will the listener be able to distinguish individual beats?

82. •• **Musical scale.** The frequency ratio of a semitone interval on the equally tempered scale is $2^{1/12}$. (a) Show that this ratio is 1.059. (b) Find the speed of an automobile passing a listener at rest in still air if the pitch of the car's horn drops a semitone between the times when the car is coming directly toward him and when it is moving directly away from him.

83. •• Two identical 4.50 g wires, each 1.40 m long and supporting a 100 kg weight, hang next to each other. How much mass should you add to one of these weights so that, in their fundamental harmonics, these wires produce a 5.0 Hz beat? Assume that the wires are strong enough that they do not stretch with the added weight.

13 FLUID MECHANICS

Fluids play a vital role in many aspects of everyday life. We drink them, breathe them, and swim in them; they circulate through our bodies, they control our weather, airplanes fly through them, and ships float in them. A fluid is any substance that can flow; we use the term for both liquids and gases. Usually, gases are easily compressed while liquids are quite incompressible. We'll see some of the consequences of this difference.

We begin our study with *fluid statics,* the study of fluids at rest (in equilibrium). Like the analysis of other equilibrium situations, the study of fluid statics is based on Newton's first and third laws. The key concepts include density, pressure, buoyancy, and surface tension. *Fluid dynamics* is the study of fluids in motion. Fluid dynamics is much more complex and indeed is one of the most complex branches of mechanics. Fortunately, we can analyze many important situations with simple idealized models and familiar principles such as Newton's laws and conservation of energy. Even so, we will barely scratch the surface of this broad and interesting topic.

To sail well, the crews must understand how their boats interact with two fluids, the water and the air.

13.1 Density

A block of Styrofoam™ can have the same mass as a steel nail, but a much greater volume. To express this difference, we need the concept of *density.* The **density** of a material is defined as its mass per unit volume (Figure 13.1). Because density is defined as *mass divided by volume,* all objects made of a given material have the same density, irrespective of their size.

Different mass, same density
Because the wrench and nail are both made of steel, they have the same density (mass per unit volume)

Steel wrench   Steel nail

▲ **FIGURE 13.1** Density is mass per unit volume.

▲ Layers of liquids. This coffee concoction was made by using liquids of differing densities and a steady hand. The liquid with the highest specific gravity (density relative to water) was poured first and the lighter liquid was carefully poured on top of the previous, more dense layer. As you know, any liquid will float on top of another liquid with a greater density, as long as no mixing occurs.

Definition of density

We use the Greek letter ρ (rho) for density. If a mass m of material has volume V, its density is

$$\rho = \frac{m}{V}. \tag{13.1}$$

Units: The SI unit of density is the kilogram per cubic meter (1 kg/m^3). The cgs unit, the gram per cubic centimeter (1 g/cm^3), is also widely used. (Notice that $1 \text{ g/cm}^3 = 1000 \text{ kg/m}^3$.)

A homogeneous material such as ice or iron has the same density throughout. Table 13.1 gives the densities of several common solids and liquids at ordinary temperatures. Note the wide range of magnitudes. The densest material found on earth is the metal osmium ($22{,}500 \text{ kg/m}^3$, or 22.5 g/cm^3). The density of air at sea level is about 1.2 kg/m^3 (0.0012 g/cm^3), but the density of white-dwarf stars is on the order of 10^{10} kg/m^3, and that of neutron stars is on the order of 10^{18} kg/m^3!

The **specific gravity** of a material is the ratio of its density to the density of water; it is a pure (unitless) number. For example, the specific gravity of aluminum is 2.7; this means that the density of aluminum is 2.7 times as great as that of water. ("Specific gravity" is a poor term, since it has nothing to do with gravity; "relative density" would be better.)

Density measurements are an important analytical technique. For example, an auto mechanic can determine the freezing point of antifreeze by measuring its density. Antifreeze used in car engines is usually a solution of ethylene glycol (density $1.12 \times 10^3 \text{ kg/m}^3$) in water. The glycol concentration determines the freezing point of the solution; it can be found from a simple density measurement, performed routinely in service stations with the aid of a *hydrometer*. The auto mechanic measures density with this instrument by observing the level at which a calibrated body floats in a sample of the solution. (The hydrometer is discussed in Section 13.3.)

TABLE 13.1 Densities of Some Common Substances

Material	Density (kg/m^3)*	Material	Density (kg/m^3)*
Gases		Concrete	2×10^3
Air (1 atm, 20° C)	1.20	Aluminum	2.7×10^3
		Iron, steel	7.8×10^3
Liquids		Brass	8.6×10^3
Benzene	0.90×10^3	Copper	8.9×10^3
Ethanol	0.81×10^3	Silver	10.5×10^3
Water	1.00×10^3	Lead	11.3×10^3
Seawater	1.03×10^3	Gold	19.3×10^3
Blood	1.06×10^3	Platinum	21.4×10^3
Solids		Mercury	13.6×10^3
Glycerin	1.26×10^3	White-dwarf star	10^{10}
Ice	0.92×10^3	Neutron star	10^{18}

*To obtain the densities in grams per cubic centimeter, simply divide by 10^3.

 Conceptual Analysis 13.1

Changing density?

If you cut a block of modeling clay in half, the density of each half is _____ the density of the original block.

A. twice B. the same as C. half

SOLUTION Because the clay in the block is a homogeneous material, its density (mass per unit volume) is the same for pieces of any size. Thus, B is the right answer.

The weight of a roomful of air

Find the mass of air, and its weight, in a living room with a 4.0 m × 5.0 m floor and a ceiling 3.0 m high. What would be the mass and weight of an equal volume of water?

SOLUTION

SET UP AND SOLVE Even for a problem like this, a simple sketch such as the one in Figure 13.2 helps to prevent mistakes. First we'll find the volume of the room; then we'll use the density of air to find the mass of air it contains. The room's volume is $V = l \times w \times h = (4.0\text{ m})(5.0\text{ m})(3.0\text{ m}) = 60\text{ m}^3$.

From Table 13.1, air has a density of $\rho = 1.2\text{ kg/m}^3$. From Equation 13.1, $\rho = m/V$, so the mass of air in the room is $m = \rho V = (1.2\text{ kg/m}^3)(60\text{ m}^3) = 72\text{ kg}$. The weight of the air is $w = mg = (72\text{ kg})(9.8\text{ m/s}^2) = 710\text{ N}$.

From Table 13.1, the density of water is $\rho = 1.0 \times 10^3\text{ kg/m}^3$. Thus, the mass of a volume of water that would fill the room is $m = \rho V = (1000\text{ kg/m}^3)(60\text{ m}^3) = 6.0 \times 10^4\text{ kg}$. The weight is $w = (6.0 \times 10^4\text{ kg})(9.8\text{ m/s}^2) = 5.9 \times 10^5\text{ N}$.

▲ **FIGURE 13.2** Our sketch for this problem.

REFLECT The weight of the air is about 160 lb. Does it surprise you that a roomful of air weighs this much? But the weight of the same volume of water is about 1.3×10^5 lb, or 66 tons! This much weight would certainly collapse the floor of an ordinary house. (We'll learn later why the weight of the room's air doesn't stress the floor.)

Practice Problem: What volume of water would have a mass equal to the mass of air in the room? *Answer:* $7.2 \times 10^{-2}\text{ m}^3$, or 72 L.

13.2 Pressure in a Fluid

When a fluid (either a liquid or a gas) is at rest, it exerts a force perpendicular to any surface in contact with it, such as the wall of a container or the surface of a body immersed in it. To see that this must be so, imagine a surface located *within* the fluid (Figure 13.3a). The fluid on either side of this surface exerts forces on it. Because the fluid is at rest, we know that the forces acting on the two sides must be equal in magnitude and opposite in direction (otherwise the surface would accelerate and the fluid would not remain at rest), and they must be oriented perpendicular to the surface. Similarly, any surface of an object immersed in the fluid is acted upon by a force perpendicular to the surface.

Pressure is force per unit area. We define the **pressure** p at a point in a fluid as the ratio of the normal force $F_\perp$ on a small area A around that point to the area.

Definition of pressure

The pressure p on a plane surface of area A is the magnitude $F_\perp$ of the force exerted on that surface, divided by the area:

$$p = \frac{F_\perp}{A}, \qquad F_\perp = pA. \qquad \text{(if p is the same at all points on the surface)} \qquad (13.2)$$

Units: The SI unit of pressure is N/m^2. As we noted in Chapter 11, this unit is given a special name: the pascal (Pa). That is, $1\text{ N/m}^2 = 1\text{ Pa}$. Two related units, used principally in meteorology, are the *bar,* equal to 10^5 Pa, and the *millibar,* equal to 100 Pa. The British unit pounds per square inch (lb/in.^2, or psi) is still in common use in the United States. Another unit of pressure is the *atmosphere,* defined next. Later in this chapter, we'll encounter additional units used in specific situations.

The force exerted by the fluid on any surface must be perpendicular to the surface, otherwise it would have a component of shear that would cause the surface to accelerate.

Arbitrary surface in fluid

(a) Why forces due to fluid pressure must act normal to a surface.

Although these two surfaces differ in area and orientation, the pressure on them (force divided by area) is the same.

Note that pressure is a scalar—it has no direction.

(b) Pressure equals force divided by area.

▲ **FIGURE 13.3** The forces due to pressure on arbitrary surfaces within a fluid.

Atmospheric pressure p_{atm} is the pressure of the earth's atmosphere—the pressure in the sea of air in which we live. This pressure varies with weather changes and with elevation. The average atmospheric pressure at sea level is used as a unit of pressure called the **atmosphere** (atm), defined as

$$1 \text{ atm} = 1.013 \times 10^5 \text{ Pa} = 14.7 \text{ psi} = 1.013 \text{ bars} = 1013 \text{ millibars}.$$

EXAMPLE 13.2   **The force of a roomful of air**

In the room described in Example 13.1, what is the total force on the floor due to the air above the surface if the air pressure is 1.00 atm?

SOLUTION

SET UP The total force on the floor has magnitude equal to the pressure multiplied by the area. We're given 1.00 atm of pressure—that is, $p = 1.013 \times 10^5$ Pa.

SOLVE The floor area is $A = (4.0 \text{ m})(5.0 \text{ m}) = 20 \text{ m}^2$. From Equation 13.3, the magnitude $F_{\perp}$ of the total force is

$$F_{\perp} = pA = (1.013 \times 10^5 \text{ Pa})(20 \text{ m}^2)$$
$$= 2.0 \times 10^6 \text{ N} \ (= 4.5 \times 10^5 \text{ lb} = 225 \text{ tons}).$$

REFLECT This force is equal to the total weight of all the air in a column directly above the floor. It is more than enough force to

collapse the floor. So why doesn't it collapse? Because there is an upward force on the underside of the floor. If we neglect the thickness of the floor, this upward force is exactly equal in magnitude to the downward force on the top surface, and the total force due to air pressure is zero.

Practice Problem: If the room has a window with dimensions 0.50 m × 1.0 m, what is the total force on the window due to the air inside? Why doesn't this force push the window out? *Answer:* 5.1×10^4 N; there is equal pressure on the outside surface.

Pascal's Law

If the weight of the fluid can be neglected, the pressure in a fluid at rest is the same throughout. We used that assumption in our discussion of bulk stress and strain in Section 11.3. But often the fluid's weight is *not* negligible. The reason atmospheric pressure is greater at sea level than on a high mountain is that there is more air above you at sea level and greater weight pushing down on you. And when you dive into deep water, your ears tell you that the pressure increases rapidly with increasing depth below the surface.

We can derive a general relation between the pressure p at any point in a fluid in a gravitational field and the elevation h of that point relative to some reference level (where $h = 0$ and the pressure is p_0). We define h to be positive for points above the reference level. If the fluid is in equilibrium, every portion of it is in equilibrium. Consider the rectangular volume element shown in Figure 13.4. The bottom surface of the element is at $h = 0$, and the top surface is a distance h above that. The area of each of these surfaces is A. The height of the element is h, its volume is $V = hA$, its mass is $m = \rho V = \rho hA$, and its weight has magnitude $w = mg = \rho ghA$.

Let the pressure at the bottom surface of the volume element be p_0; then the total upward force on this surface (due to the fluid underneath pushing up) has magnitude $p_0 A$. The pressure at the top surface is p, and the total downward force on the top surface (due to the fluid above pushing down) has magnitude pA. The fluid in this volume is in equilibrium, so the total vertical component of force, including the weight of the fluid in the volume element and the forces at the bottom and top surfaces, must be zero. This condition gives

$$p_0 A - pA - \rho ghA = 0.$$

We can divide out the area A and rearrange terms, obtaining the following relation:

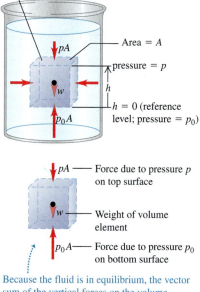

Arbitrary volume element of fluid (forces on front and back sides not shown)

Area = A

pressure = p

h

$h = 0$ (reference level; pressure = p_0)

pA —— Force due to pressure p on top surface

w —— Weight of volume element

$p_0 A$ —— Force due to pressure p_0 on bottom surface

Because the fluid is in equilibrium, the vector sum of the vertical forces on the volume element must be zero:
$$p_0 A - pA - w = 0$$

▲ **FIGURE 13.4** The forces on an arbitrary volume element in a fluid.

Variation of pressure with height in a fluid

If the pressure at a point in a fluid is p_0, then, at a point in the fluid at a distance h above this point, the pressure is $p_0 - \rho g h$; that is,

$$p = p_0 - \rho g h. \qquad \text{(variation of pressure with height)} \qquad (13.3)$$

When h is positive, p is less than p_0; when h is negative (i.e., a point deeper in the fluid than the reference level $h = 0$), p is greater than p_0, as we would expect. Pressure increases with depth: When we decrease h, we increase p.

Let's apply this equation to a liquid in an open container, as shown in Figure 13.5. Again, we let p_0 be the pressure at $h = 0$ (a distance h below the surface). At the surface of the liquid, the pressure is atmospheric pressure, so $p = p_{\text{atm}}$. We're interested in the pressure p_0 at a depth h below the surface. In Equation 13.3, we substitute p_{atm} for p; we obtain $p_{\text{atm}} - p_0 = -\rho g h$, or

$$p_0 = p_{\text{atm}} + \rho g h. \qquad (13.4)$$

The pressure p_0 at a depth h below the surface is greater than the pressure p_{atm} at the surface by an amount $\rho g h$. It also follows from Equation 13.4 that if the pressure at the top surface is increased in any way—say, by inserting a piston on the top surface and pressing down on it—the pressure p_0 at any depth must increase by exactly the same amount. This fact was recognized in 1653 by the French scientist Blaise Pascal (1623–1662) and is called **Pascal's law:**

Pascal's law

Pressure applied to an enclosed fluid is transmitted undiminished to every portion of the fluid and the walls of the containing vessel. The pressure depends only on depth; the shape of the container does not matter.

For instance, notice that the liquid in Figure 13.6 rises to the same height in all of the arms, regardless of their shape. This is the level at which $p = p_{\text{atm}}$. At any level below the surface, the pressure is the same in all four arms.

The hydraulic jack shown schematically in Figure 13.7 illustrates Pascal's law. A piston with a small cross-sectional area A_1 exerts a force with magnitude F_1 on the surface of a liquid such as oil. The pressure $p = F_1/A_1$ is transmitted through the connecting pipe to a larger piston with area A_2. In this case, the two pistons are at the same height, so they experience the same pressure p:

$$p = \frac{F_1}{A_1} = \frac{F_2}{A_2} \qquad \text{and} \qquad F_2 = \frac{A_2}{A_1}F_1. \qquad (13.5)$$

Therefore, the hydraulic jack is a force-multiplying device with a multiplication factor equal to the ratio (A_2/A_1) of the areas of the two pistons. Dentists' chairs, car lifts and jacks, some elevators, and hydraulic brakes all use this principle.

Fluid with density p

At a given level, the pressure p equals the external pressure (here, p_{atm}) plus the pressure due to the weight of the overlying liquid ($\rho g h$, where h is the distance below the surface):
$p_0 = p_{\text{atm}} + \rho g h$

▲ **FIGURE 13.5** The pressure at a depth h in a liquid is greater than the surface pressure by $\rho g h$.

▲ **FIGURE 13.6** The pressure in a fluid is the same at all points having the same elevation, regardless of the container's shape.

③ Acting on a piston with a large area, the pressure creates a force that can support a car.

① A small force is applied to a piston with a small area.

② At any given height, the pressure p is the same everywhere in the fluid (Pascal's law).

▲ **FIGURE 13.7** The principle of the hydraulic lift, an application of Pascal's law.

EXAMPLE 13.3   The hydraulic lift: an application of Pascal's law

Suppose the hydraulic lift shown in Figure 13.7 has a small cylindrical piston with radius 5.0 cm and a larger piston with radius 20 cm. The mass of a car placed on the larger piston platform is 1000 kg. **(a)** Assuming that the two pistons are at the same height, what force must be applied to the small piston to lift the car? **(b)** How far must the small piston move down to lift the car through a height of 0.10 m?

Continued

SOLUTION

SET UP A downward external force with magnitude F_1 is applied on the smaller piston, and a downward force with magnitude F_2 equal to the weight of the car is applied on the larger piston. The weight of the car is $F_2 = w = mg = (1000 \text{ kg})(9.8 \text{ m/s}^2) = 9800 \text{ N}$.

SOLVE Part (a): From Pascal's law, the pressure at any given level is the same throughout the hydraulic fluid. Since the pistons are at the same level, we can use Equation 13.5. The downward force on the smaller piston needed to lift the car is

$$F_1 = \frac{A_1}{A_2}F_2 = \frac{\pi r_1^2}{\pi r_2^2}F_2 = \frac{\pi(0.050 \text{ m})^2}{\pi(0.20 \text{ m})^2}(9800 \text{ N}) = 610 \text{ N}.$$

So a force of 610 N can lift a car weighing 9800 N.

Part (b): If the small piston moves a distance d_1, the volume of fluid displaced is $V_1 = d_1 A_1$. Because the total volume of fluid is constant, V_1 must equal the volume V_2 displaced by the large piston. It follows that $d_1 A_1 = d_2 A_2$. If the car is hoisted a distance $d_2 = 0.10 \text{ m}$, the small piston moves a distance d_1 given by

$$d_1 = \frac{\pi r_2^2}{\pi r_1^2}d_2 = \frac{\pi(0.20 \text{ m})^2}{\pi(0.05 \text{ m})^2}(0.10 \text{ m}) = 1.6 \text{ m}.$$

ALTERNATIVE SOLUTION Part (b) may also be solved by using conservation of energy. If we neglect friction, the amount of work done by the applied force must equal the work done to lift the car. Thus,

$$W_1 = W_2 \quad \text{or} \quad F_1 d_1 = F_2 d_2,$$
$$(610 \text{ N})(d_1) = (9800 \text{ N})(0.10 \text{ m}),$$
$$d_1 = 1.6 \text{ m}.$$

REFLECT The hydraulic lift is a force-multiplying device. The multiplication factor is the ratio of the areas of the pistons. It seems as though we get something for nothing. But the much larger weight is lifted through a much smaller distance, and the two quantities of work are the same in magnitude. The device multiplies force, but it can't multiply *energy*.

Practice Problem: Engineers are designing a hydraulic lift that can be used to repair trucks with a mass of 5000 kg. What ratio of piston areas would you suggest for the design if the maximum available external force is to be 3000 N? *Answer:* $A_2/A_1 = 16.3$.

Atmospheric pressure

Atmospheric pressure is about 1.013×10^5 Pa at sea level. This means that

A. the weight of a column of air 1 square meter in cross section extending up to the top of the atmosphere is about 1.013×10^5 N.
B. the weight of 1 cubic meter of air at sea level is about 1.013×10^5 N.
C. the density of air at sea level is about 1.013×10^5 times the density of water at sea level.

SOLUTION As we've just learned, the pressure at a given level in a fluid (such as air) is caused by the weight of the overlying fluid, plus any external pressure applied to the fluid. In the case of earth's atmosphere, there is no external pressure, because the atmosphere is open to outer space at the top. Remember also that pressure is force divided by area. In the case of the atmosphere, the force is the weight of the overlying air. If atmospheric pressure is 1.013×10^5 Pa, then the air exerts a weight force of 1.013×10^5 N per square meter. Thus, choice A is correct and choices B and C are not.

The assumption that the density ρ of a fluid is constant is often reasonable for liquids, which are relatively incompressible, but it is realistic for gases only over short vertical distances. When we calculated the weight of air in a room of known volume, it was reasonable to assume that the density of the air was the same throughout the room. To justify this assumption, we note that, in a room with a ceiling height of 3.0 m filled with air of density 1.2 kg/m³, the difference in pressure between floor and ceiling, given by Equation 13.3, is

---

◀ **A close look at pressure.** Fluid pressure in the human body is highly regulated, not just in the veins and arteries, but within the eye as well. This instrument, called a *tonometer,* is being used to measure the pressure of the fluid inside the eyeball as a means of diagnosing glaucoma, an eye disease characterized by a loss of vision from damage to the retina and the optic nerve. Glaucoma is often caused by excessive pressure within the eyeball. As Pascal's law states, if the weight of a fluid at rest can be neglected, the pressure in the fluid at rest is the same at all points. Therefore, using a tonometer to measure the pressure in the front of the eyeball, doctors can determine the pressure against the optic nerve at the back and diagnose whether excess pressure is the cause of vision problems.

$$\rho g h = (1.2 \text{ kg/m}^3)(9.8 \text{ m/s}^2)(3.0 \text{ m}) = 35 \text{ Pa},$$

or about 0.00035 atm, a very small difference. The resulting difference in density between floor and ceiling is correspondingly very small. But between sea level and the summit of Mount Everest (8850 m), the density of air changes by a factor of nearly three. In such situations, it wouldn't be correct to use Equation 13.3 $(p - p_0 = -\rho g h)$.

At great enough pressures, even liquids are compressed appreciably. The deepest point in the oceans is the Marianas Trench, which is 10,920 m deep. If the density of seawater were constant, the pressure at this depth would be 1.10×10^8 Pa (about 1000 atm or 16,000 lb/in.^{2}). But because seawater is compressed to greater density under high pressures, the actual pressure at this depth is 1.16×10^8 Pa (nearly 17,000 lb/in.^{2}).

If the pressure inside a car tire is equal to atmospheric pressure, the tire is flat. The pressure has to be *greater than* atmospheric to support the car, and the significant quantity is the *difference* between the inside and outside pressures. When we say that the pressure in a car tire is "32 pounds" (actually, 32 lb/in.^{2} = 32 psi, equal to 220 kPa, or 2.2×10^5 Pa), we mean that it is *greater* than atmospheric pressure (14.7 lb/in.^{2}, or 1.01×10^5 Pa) by that amount.

The *total* pressure in the tire is 47 lb/in.^{2}, or 320 kPa. The excess pressure above atmospheric pressure is usually called the **gauge pressure,** and the total pressure is called the **absolute pressure.** Engineers use the abbreviations psig and psia for "pounds per square inch gauge" and "pounds per square inch absolute," respectively. If the pressure is *less than* atmospheric, as in a partial vacuum, the gauge pressure is negative.

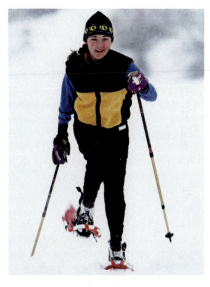

▲ **On top of the situation.** Snowshoes have been used for centuries to allow travel on foot in deep snow, long before we had defined pressure as force divided by area. If you try to walk in fresh snow without snowshoes, your feet sink in because you exert too much pressure for the snow to support. Snowshoes reduce the pressure you exert by distributing your weight over a larger area, allowing you to walk atop the snow without sinking in significantly.

Conceptual Analysis 13.3

An open U-tube

The equilibrium state of two nonmixing liquids in an open U-tube is shown in Figure 13.8. At which level(s) must the pressure be the same in both sides of this tube?

A. h_1.
B. h_2.
C. h_3.
D. The pressure at h_1 must equal the pressure at h_2.

SOLUTION The two liquids rise to different heights in the tube because the brown liquid is denser than the blue liquid. At level h_1, if the pressure in the two sides of the tube were *different,* the liquids would respond by moving. Since the liquids are in equilibrium (motionless), the pressure at h_1 is the same on both sides of the tube—so A is correct. (This argument also tells us that D is not correct.) At h_3, the pressure on both sides of the tube is atmospheric, so C is also correct. At h_2, the pressure on the left

▲ **FIGURE 13.8**

side is atmospheric, but the pressure on the right side equals the atmospheric pressure *plus* the pressure due to the weight of the blue liquid above h_2. Thus, B is not correct.

EXAMPLE 13.4 **Finding absolute and gauge pressures**

A solar water-heating system uses solar panels on the roof, 12.0 m above the storage tank. The pressure at the level of the panels is 1 atmosphere. What is the absolute pressure at the top of the tank? The gauge pressure?

SOLUTION

SET UP Figure 13.9 shows our sketch.

SOLVE To find the absolute pressure p_{tank} at the tank, 12 m below the panels, we use Equation 13.4, with $p_0 = p_{\text{tank}}$:

$$\begin{aligned} p_{\text{tank}} &= p_{\text{atm}} + \rho g h \\ &= (1.01 \times 10^5 \text{ Pa}) \\ &\quad + (1.00 \times 10^3 \text{ kg/m}^3)(9.80 \text{ m/s}^2)(12.0 \text{ m}) \\ &= 2.19 \times 10^5 \text{ Pa}. \end{aligned}$$

Continued

The gauge pressure is the amount by which p_{tank} exceeds atmospheric pressure—that is, $p_{tank} - p_{atm}$:

$$p_{tank} - p_{atm} = (2.19 - 1.01) \times 10^5 \, \text{Pa} = 1.18 \times 10^5 \, \text{Pa}$$
$$= 1.16 \, \text{atm} = 17.1 \, \text{lb/in}^2 = 17.1 \, \text{psig}.$$

REFLECT If the tank has a pressure gauge, it is usually calibrated to read gauge pressure rather than absolute pressure. As we have mentioned, the variation in *atmospheric* pressure over this height is negligibly small.

Practice Problem: At what distance below the panels is the gauge pressure equal to 1 atmosphere? *Answer:* 10.3 m.

▲ **FIGURE 13.9** Our sketch for this problem.

(a) Open-tube manometer

The pressure at level $h = 0$ is the same on both sides of the tube.

The top of the tube contains near-vacuum

The level to which the mercury rises depends on the atmospheric pressure exerted on the mercury in the dish.

(b) Mercury barometer

▲ **FIGURE 13.10** Two types of pressure gauges.

Pressure Gauges

The simplest pressure gauge is the **open-tube manometer,** shown in Figure 13.10a. The U-shaped tube contains a liquid; one end of the tube is connected to the container in which the pressure is to be measured, and the other end is open to the atmosphere at pressure p_{atm}. According to Pascal's law, the pressures on the two sides of the tube at the level labeled $h = 0$ must be equal. On the left side, the pressure at this height is p_0, and on the right side (from Equation 13.4), it is $p_{atm} + \rho g h$. Equating these two expressions, we find that

$$p_0 = p_{atm} + \rho g h \qquad \text{and} \qquad p_{gauge} = \rho g h. \qquad (13.6)$$

In Equation 13.6, the pressure p_0 is the absolute pressure; the difference $p - p_{atm}$ between absolute and atmospheric pressure is the gauge pressure. Thus, the gauge pressure is proportional to the difference in height h of the liquid columns on the two sides.

Another common pressure gauge is the **mercury barometer;** it consists of a long glass tube, closed at one end, that has been filled with mercury and then inverted in a dish of mercury, as shown in Figure 13.10b. The space above the mercury column contains only mercury vapor; the pressure of the vapor is negligibly small, so the pressure above the mercury column is practically zero. From Equation 13.3, $(p = p_0 - \rho g h)$, with $p = 0$ and $p_0 = p_{atm}$,

$$p_{atm} = \rho g h.$$

NOTE ▶ The *shape* and *diameter* of the tubes in the open-tube manometer and mercury barometer don't matter. As we found in deriving Pascal's law, the fact that pressure is defined as force *per unit area* means that it is independent of area. ◀

Pressures are sometimes described in terms of the height of the corresponding mercury column as so many "inches of mercury" or "millimeters of mercury" (abbreviated mm Hg). Thus, the mercury barometer reads atmospheric pressure in mm Hg directly from the height of the mercury column. A pressure of 1 mm Hg is sometimes called 1 torr, after Evangelista Torricelli, inventor of the mercury barometer. The mm Hg and the torr depend on the density of mercury, which varies with temperature, and on the value of g, which varies with location, so the pascal is the preferred unit of pressure. As we noted earlier in this section, two related units are the *bar,* defined as 10^5 Pa, and the *millibar,* defined as 10^{-3} bar, or 10^2 Pa. Atmospheric pressures are on the order of 1000 millibars; the National Weather Service usually reports atmospheric pressures in this unit. The conversions are as follows:

$$1.013 \times 10^5 \, \text{Pa} = 1.013 \, \text{bars} = 1013 \, \text{millibars} = 1 \, \text{atm}.$$

Quantitative Analysis 13.4

Two-liquid barometer

The barometer in Figure 13.11 contains two liquids, A and B, differing in density. According to this device, the barometric pressure is

A. $\rho_A g h_A$.
B. $\rho_B g h_B$.
C. $\rho_A g h_A + \rho_B g h_B$.
D. $g(h_A + h_B)(\rho_A + \rho_B)/2$.

SOLUTION In the open dish, the surface of the liquid is at atmospheric pressure. Therefore, by Pascal's law, the liquid at that level inside the tube must also be at atmospheric pressure. But the pressure at this level in the tube *also* equals the pressure due to the weights of the overlying liquids. This pressure is given by the sum in choice C. Therefore, C gives the atmospheric (barometric) pressure.

▲ **FIGURE 13.11**

EXAMPLE 13.5 **Atmospheric pressure**

Compute the atmospheric pressure p_{atm} on a day when the height of mercury in a barometer is 76.0 cm.

SOLUTION

SET UP Figure 13.12 shows our sketch; from Table 13.1, the density of mercury is $\rho = 13.6 \times 10^3 \text{ kg/m}^3$. We assume that the pressure in the volume above the mercury column is zero.

SOLVE We use Equation 13.3 with $p = 0$, $p_0 = p_{atm}$:

$$p_{atm} = \rho g h = (13.6 \times 10^3 \text{ kg/m}^3)(9.80 \text{ m/s}^2)(0.760 \text{ m})$$
$$= 101,300 \text{ N/m}^2 = 1.013 \times 10^5 \text{ Pa} = 1.013 \text{ bars}.$$

REFLECT This is about 14.7 lb/in.². With weather variations, atmospheric pressure typically varies from about 0.97 bar to 1.03 bars; in the eye of a hurricane, it can be as little as 0.90 bar.

Practice Problem: On a very stormy day, the pressure is 0.950 bar. What is the height of mercury in a barometer? *Answer:* 71.3 cm (pressure 713 torr).

▲ **FIGURE 13.12** Our sketch for this problem.

Measuring Blood Pressure

Blood-pressure measurements are an important diagnostic tool in medicine. Blood-pressure readings, such as 130/80, refer to the maximum and minimum gauge pressures in the arteries, measured in mm Hg or torr. Blood pressure varies with height; the standard reference point is the upper arm, level with the heart.

In a commonly used blood-pressure gauge, known as a *sphygmomanometer,* an inflatable band, called a *cuff,* is placed around the upper arm, at heart level, as shown in Figure 13.13. The band is inflated by squeezing a flexible bulb, increasing the pressure on the arm. A stethoscope is used to detect the pulse at the elbow. When the pressure in the cuff exceeds the blood pressure, an artery under the cuff collapses and the pulse is no longer detectable. The pressure itself is measured with a mercury manometer or a mechanical pressure gauge.

To measure blood pressure, you listen through the stethoscope for arterial flow while letting the cuff deflate. Flow starts when the pressure in the deflating cuff reaches the arterial pressure.

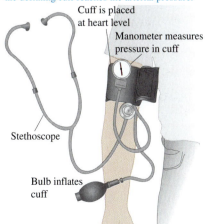

Cuff is placed at heart level

Manometer measures pressure in cuff

Stethoscope

Bulb inflates cuff

▶ **FIGURE 13.13** Measuring blood pressure with a pressure cuff and a stethoscope. (In practice, one measures two pressures: the *systolic* pressure, at which blood first starts to spurt discontinuously through the compressed vessel, and the lower *diastolic* pressure, at which blood flows continuously.)

EXAMPLE 13.6 **Feeling light-headed?**

Suppose you have a healthy systolic (maximum) blood pressure of 1.30×10^4 Pa (about 100 mm Hg), measured at the level of your heart. **(a)** If the density of blood is 1.06×10^3 kg/m^3, find the blood pressure at a point in your head, 35.0 cm above your heart. **(b)** Find the difference in blood pressure between your head and your feet when you are sitting down, a distance of 1.10 m. (Ignore the fact that the blood is in motion and is not in equilibrium.)

SOLUTION

SET UP Figure 13.14 shows our sketch. We put the reference level $h = 0$ at the level of the heart, where the pressure is p_0. Notice that h_2, the distance to the foot, is *negative*.

SOLVE We use Equation 13.3, $p - p_0 = -\rho g h$, for the variation in pressure with height.

Part (a): Let p_1 be the pressure at the level of the head; p_0 is the pressure at the level of the heart, and the height h_1 is 35.0 cm = 0.350 m. From Equation 13.3,

$$p_1 = p_0 - \rho g h_1$$
$$= 1.30 \times 10^4 \text{ Pa}$$
$$\quad - (1.06 \times 10^3 \text{ kg/m}^3)(9.80 \text{ m/s}^2)(0.350 \text{ m})$$
$$= 9.4 \times 10^3 \text{ Pa.}$$

As expected, we get a blood pressure for the head that is lower than that at heart level. (If our result had been *greater* than the blood pressure at heart level, we would know we had made a mistake.)

Part (b): This time, p_2 is the pressure at the level of the foot, and the height is $h_2 = -1.10$ m. Then

$$p_2 = p_0 - \rho g h_2$$
$$= 1.30 \times 10^4 \text{ Pa}$$
$$\quad - (1.06 \times 10^3 \text{ kg/m}^3)(9.80 \text{ m/s}^2)(-1.10 \text{ m})$$
$$= 2.44 \times 10^4 \text{ Pa.}$$

▲ **FIGURE 13.14** Our sketch for this problem.

As expected, the blood pressure at foot level is greater than that at heart level.

REFLECT Notice that we didn't need to know anything about the shape or volume of the blood vessels—just the relative heights of head, heart, and feet. If you lie down, then your head and feet are at the same level as your heart, and the differences we calculated disappear. Also, our results are somewhat simplistic because Pascal's law is valid only for fluids in equilibrium. As we will see later in the chapter, the viscosity of circulating blood has effects on its local pressure, in addition to the pressure differences due to relative height.

Practice Problem: When a person 1.70 m tall stands up, what is the difference in blood pressure between head and feet? *Answer:* 1.8×10^4 Pa.

13.3 Archimedes's Principle: Buoyancy

Buoyancy is a familiar phenomenon: An object immersed in water seems to weigh less than when it is in air. When the object is less dense than the fluid, it floats. Rafts inflated with air float in water, and a helium-filled balloon floats in air. Buoyancy is described by Archimedes's principle:

> **Archimedes's principle**
> When an object is completely or partially immersed in a fluid, the fluid exerts an upward force on the object equal to the weight of the fluid that is displaced by the object.

To derive this principle, we consider an arbitrary volume element of fluid at rest (in equilibrium), as shown in Figure 13.15a. The forces labeled $\vec{F}_\perp$ represent the forces exerted on the surface of the element by the surrounding fluid—that is, the forces due to the pressure of the fluid.

Because the entire beaker of fluid is in equilibrium, the sum of all the y components of force acting on the chosen element of fluid must be zero. Therefore, the sum of the y components of the surface forces must be an upward force equal in magnitude to the weight mg of the fluid inside the surface. Also, the sum of

Arbitrary element of fluid in equilibrium

The forces on the fluid element due to pressure must sum to a buoyancy force equal in magnitude to the element's weight.

(a)

Fluid element replaced with solid object of the same size and shape.

The forces due to pressure are the same, so the object must be acted upon by the same buoyancy force as the fluid element, *regardless of the object's weight.*

(b)

▲ **FIGURE 13.15** The origin of the buoyancy force. (a) The forces on a volume element of fluid in equilibrium. (b) The fluid element is replaced with a solid object having the same shape and size.

the torques of these forces must be zero, so the line of action of the resultant y component of surface forces must pass through the center of gravity of this portion of fluid.

Now, suppose that we remove the chosen element of fluid and replace it with a solid object having exactly the same shape (Figure 13.15b). The pressure at each point on the surface of this object is exactly the same as before, so the total upward force exerted on the object by the surrounding fluid is also the same, again equal in magnitude to the weight mg of the fluid that formerly occupied this spot. We call this upward force the **buoyant force** on the solid object.

NOTE ▶ Notice that the object *need not have the same weight as the fluid it replaces.* If the object's weight is greater than that of the displaced fluid, the object sinks; if less, then it rises. Thus, objects that are denser than the surrounding fluid sink; those that are less dense rise. ◀

Notice also that the center of gravity of the object need not coincide with that of the fluid that's replaced. As we just explained, the line of action of the buoyant force passes through the center of gravity of the replaced portion of fluid. If the *object's* center of gravity does not lie along this line (as in Figure 13.16), the buoyant force exerts a torque on the object.

As a helium balloon loses helium, it passes through a condition in which it neither floats nor sinks, but is in equilibrium with the surrounding air. At this point, the balloon's weight must be the same as the weight of the air it displaces. That is, the average density of a balloon floating in equilibrium must be the same as that of the surrounding air. Similarly, when a submerged submarine is in equilibrium, its weight must equal the weight of the water it displaces.

An object whose average density is less than that of a liquid can float partially submerged at the free upper surface of the liquid. The greater the density of the liquid, the less far the object is submerged. When you swim in seawater (density 1030 kg/m^3), your body floats higher than in fresh water (1000 kg/m^3). Unlikely as it may seem, lead floats in mercury. Very flat surfaced "float glass" is made by floating glass on molten tin and then letting it cool.

Another familiar example is the hydrometer, shown in Figure 13.17a. The calibrated float sinks into the fluid until the weight of the fluid it displaces is exactly equal to its own weight. The hydrometer floats *higher* in denser liquids than in less dense liquids. It is weighted at its bottom end so that the upright position is stable, and a scale in the top stem permits direct density readings.

The cg of this object does not coincide with the cg of the displaced fluid.

BEFORE

Thus, the buoyant force exerts a torque about the object's cg, causing the object to rotate.

Because the object's weight is greater in magnitude than the buoyant force, the object also sinks.

AFTER

▲ **FIGURE 13.16** A case in which the buoyancy force does not act through the center of gravity of an immersed object.

The depth to which the weighted scale sinks tells you the density of the fluid.

(a) A simple hydrometer

(b) Using a hydrometer to measure the density of battery acid or antifreeze

▲ **FIGURE 13.17** Hydrometers, for measuring the density of a fluid.

Figure 13.17b shows a hydrometer that is commonly used to measure the density of battery acid or antifreeze. The bottom of the tube is immersed in the liquid; the bulb is squeezed to expel air and is then released, like a giant medicine dropper. The liquid rises into the outer tube, and the hydrometer floats in this sample of the liquid.

Floating lead

A lead ball floats in liquid mercury and sinks in water. Which statement is true about the buoyant force acting on the lead ball?

A. It is greater when the ball is floating in the mercury.
B. It is greater when the ball is totally submerged in the water.
C. It is the same in both cases.

SOLUTION The ball's behavior depends on the difference in magnitude between its weight and the buoyant force. The ball's weight mg is the same in both experiments. The ball floats partially submerged in mercury, so the buoyant force equals the magnitude of the ball's weight. (It would be greater if the ball were completely submerged.) In water the ball sinks, so the buoyant force is less in magnitude than the ball's weight. Thus, A is correct: Mercury exerts a greater buoyant force on the ball than water does.

Buoyant Ping-Pong™ ball

A Ping-Pong™ ball is held submerged in a bucket of water by a string attached to the bucket's bottom. What happens to the tension in the string as water is added to the bucket, increasing the distance between the ball and the surface?

A. The tension does not change.
B. The tension increases.
C. The tension decreases.

SOLUTION The buoyant force is equal in magnitude to the weight of the water displaced by the Ping-Pong™ ball. As water is added to the bucket, the *pressure* at the level of the ball increases. We'll assume that water is nearly incompressible, so this pressure change is too small to cause a significant change in the *density* of water. Therefore, the weight of the displaced water remains the same, and so does the buoyant force. Thus, the tension doesn't change. (If the fluid were a compressible gas rather than water, changing the pressure might indeed have a significant effect on the buoyancy force.)

EXAMPLE 13.7 **Raising sunken treasure**

A 15.0 kg solid-gold statue is being raised from a sunken treasure ship, as shown in Figure 13.18a. **(a)** Find the tension in the hoisting cable when the statue is completely immersed. **(b)** Find the tension when the statue is completely out of the water.

SOLUTION

SET UP When immersed in water, the statue is acted upon by an upward buoyant force with magnitude F_B. From Archimedes's principle, this force is equal in magnitude to the weight of water displaced. Figure 13.18b shows a free-body diagram for the statue, including its weight, the tension T, and the upward buoyant force F_B.

SOLVE Part (a): To find F_B, we first find the volume of the statue, using its mass and the density of gold from Table 13.1:

$$V = \frac{m_{\text{statue}}}{\rho_{\text{gold}}} = \frac{15.0 \text{ kg}}{19.3 \times 10^3 \text{ kg/m}^3} = 7.77 \times 10^{-4} \text{ m}^3.$$

Continued

The weight of an equal volume of water is

$$m_{water}g = \rho_{water}Vg$$
$$= (1.00 \times 10^3 \text{ kg/m}^3)(7.77 \times 10^{-4} \text{ m}^3)(9.80 \text{ m/s}^2)$$
$$= 7.61 \text{ N}.$$

This weight is equal to the magnitude F_B of the buoyant force. In equilibrium, the tension in the cable equals the weight of the statue minus the magnitude of the buoyant force. Taking the positive y direction as upward, we find that

$$T + F_B - w = 0,$$
$$T + 7.61 \text{ N} - 147 \text{ N} = 0,$$
$$T = 139 \text{ N}.$$

We note that this tension is less than the weight of the statue.

Part (b): To find the tension when the statue is in air, we neglect the very small buoyant force of *air* (as we have done in earlier chapters). The tension when the block is in air is just equal to its weight:

$$m_{statue}g = (15.0 \text{ kg})(9.80 \text{ m/s}^2) = 147 \text{ N}.$$

REFLECT The tensions calculated here are for a statue at rest or being hoisted at *constant* speed. Here is a shortcut leading to the same result for the buoyant force: The density of water is less than that of gold by a factor of

$$\frac{1.00 \times 10^3 \text{ kg/m}^3}{19.3 \times 10^3 \text{ kg/m}^3} = \frac{1}{19.3} = 0.0518.$$

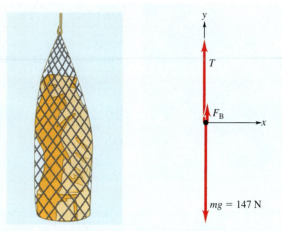

(a) Immersed statue in equilibrium   (b) Free-body diagram of statue

▲ **FIGURE 13.18**

That is, the weight of a given volume of water is 0.0518 times that of an equal volume of gold, and the weight of the displaced water is $(1.00/19.3)(147 \text{ N}) = 7.62 \text{ N}$.

Practice Problem: A brass statue with a mass of 0.500 kg and a density of $8.00 \times 10^3 \text{ kg/m}^3$ is suspended from a string. What is the tension in the string when the statue is completely immersed in water? *Answer: T = 4.29 N.*

Conceptual Analysis 13.7

Weighing in water

Suppose you place a beaker of water on a scale, weigh it, and then immerse the statue from Example 13.7 in the water, suspending it so that it is under water, but does not touch the bottom of the beaker (Figure 13.19). Does the scale reading increase, decrease, or stay the same?

A. Increase.
B. Decrease.
C. Stay the same.

SOLUTION Consider the water and the statue together as a system; its total weight does not change when the statue is immersed. Thus, the total supporting force—the vector sum of the tension $\vec{T}$ and the upward force $\vec{F}$ of the scale on the container (equal to the reading on the scale)—is the same in both cases. But T decreases when the statue is immersed, so the scale reading F must *increase* by the same amount. Thus, A is correct. Alternatively, we can see that the scale force *must* increase because, when the statue is immersed, the water level

▲ **FIGURE 13.19**

in the container rises, increasing the pressure of water on the bottom of the container.

*13.4 Surface Tension and Capillarity

What do the following observations (Figure 13.20) have in common? A liquid emerges from the tip of a pipette or medicine dropper as a succession of drops, not as a continuous stream. A paper clip, if placed carefully on a water surface, makes a small depression in the surface and rests there without sinking, even

(a)   **(b)**   **(c)**

▲ **FIGURE 13.20** Three examples of surface tension. (a) Surface tension causes the drops at the ends of these pipettes to adopt a near-spherical shape. (b) A paperclip rests on water, supported by surface tension. (c) water striders spend their life walking on water.

(a)

(b)

▲ **FIGURE 13.21** A flexible loop of thread in a wire ring that has been dipped in a soap solution (a) before and (b) after puncturing the film inside the loop.

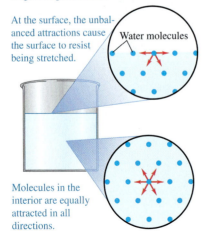

Molecules in a liquid are attracted by neighboring molecules.

At the surface, the unbalanced attractions cause the surface to resist being stretched.

Water molecules

Molecules in the interior are equally attracted in all directions.

▲ **FIGURE 13.22** The physical origin of surface tension.

though its density is several times that of water. Some insects can walk on the surface of water; their feet make indentations in the surface, but do not penetrate it. When a small, clean glass tube is dipped into water, the water rises in the tube, but when the tube is dipped in mercury, the mercury is depressed.

In all these situations, the surface of the liquid seems to be under *tension.* Here's another example: We attach a loop of thread to a wire ring, as shown in Figure 13.21a. We dip the ring and thread into a soap solution and remove them, forming a thin film of liquid in which the thread "floats" freely. When we puncture the film inside the loop, the thread springs out into a circular shape (Figure 13.21b) as the tension of the liquid surface pulls radially outward on it.

Why does the surface of a liquid behave this way? The key is that water molecules attract each other. (That's what makes liquid water cohere.) Figure 13.22 compares the forces of attraction on a water molecule on the surface with those on a molecule below the surface. Below the surface, a molecule is equally attracted in all directions. At the surface, a molecule is attracted to the molecules around and below it, but not to the overlying air. If you place a paper clip on the water surface, these forces cause the surface to resist being stretched; the resulting tension supports the clip.

A drop of liquid in free fall in vacuum is always spherical in shape (*not* teardrop shaped), because a surface under tension tends to have the minimum possible area. A sphere has a smaller surface area for a given volume than any other geometric shape has. Figure 13.23 is a beautiful example of the formation of spherical droplets in a very complex phenomenon: the impact of a drop on a liquid surface.

Figure 13.24 shows another example of surface tension. A piece of wire is bent into a U shape, and a second piece of wire slides on the arms of the U. When the apparatus is dipped into a soap solution and removed, the upward surface tension force may be greater in magnitude than the weight of the wire. If it is, the slider is pulled up toward the top of the inverted U by the upward surface tension force. To hold the slider in equilibrium, there must be a total downward force with a magnitude greater than the weight of the wire. When we apply a large enough downward force, we can pull the slider down, increasing the area of the film. Molecules move from the interior of the liquid (which is many molecules thick, even in a thin film) into the surface layers, which are not stretched like a rubber sheet. Instead, more surface is created by molecules moving from the bulk liquid.

Let *l* be the length of the wire slider. The film has two surfaces, so the surface force acts along a total length 2*l*. The **surface tension** γ in the film is defined as *the ratio of the magnitude F of the surface force to the length d* (perpendicular to the force) *along which the force acts:*

Definition of surface tension (γ)

Surface tension is a *force per unit length:*

$$\gamma = \frac{F}{d}.$$ (13.7)

Units: The SI unit of surface tension is the newton per meter (N/m), but the cgs unit, the dyne per centimeter (dyn/cm), is more commonly used: $1\ \text{dyn/cm} = 10^{-3}\ \text{N/m}$.

▲ **FIGURE 13.23** Aftermath of a drop splashing on a liquid surface.

In the case of the sliding wire, $d = 2l$ and

$$\gamma = \frac{F}{2l}.$$

Typical values of γ for familiar liquids are in the range from 20 to 100 dyn/cm. Surface tension for a particular liquid usually decreases as temperature increases.

Surface tension tends to pull the surface of a soap bubble inward, collapsing it. Excess pressure inside the bubble is needed to maintain its spherical shape. Detailed analysis shows that the excess pressure $p - p_{\text{atm}}$ inside a soap bubble with radius R, due to surface tension, is

$$p - p_{\text{atm}} = \frac{4\gamma}{R}. \quad \text{(bubble)}$$ (13.8)

For a liquid drop, which has only *one* surface film, the difference between the pressure of the liquid and that of the outside air is half that for a soap bubble:

$$p - p_{\text{atm}} = \frac{2\gamma}{R} \quad \text{(liquid drop).}$$ (13.9)

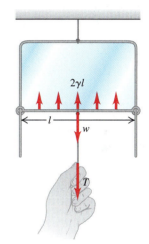

▲ **FIGURE 13.24** The horizontal slide wire is in equilibrium under the action of the upward surface-tension force $2\gamma l$ and downward pull $w + T$.

EXAMPLE 13.8 A drop of mercury

Mercury has an unusually large surface tension, about 465 dyn/cm. Calculate the excess pressure inside a drop of mercury 4.00 mm in diameter.

SOLUTION

SET UP AND SOLVE We first convert the surface tension γ to SI units:

$$\gamma = 465\ \text{dyn/cm} = 465 \times 10^{-3}\ \text{N/m}.$$

Now we have, from Equation 13.9,

$$p - p_{\text{atm}} = \frac{2\gamma}{R} = \frac{(2)(465 \times 10^{-3}\ \text{N/m})}{0.00200\ \text{m}}$$
$$= 465\ \text{Pa}$$
$$= 0.00459\ \text{atm}.$$

REFLECT The excess pressure (the difference between the inside and outside pressures) is a very small fraction of atmospheric pressure.

Practice Problem: What would the diameter of the drop be if the inside pressure were 2 atm? *Answer:* 0.009 mm.

When a gas–liquid interface meets a solid surface, such as the wall of a container (Figure 13.25), surface tension causes the interface to curve upward in a concave shape or curve downward in a convex shape, near the line where it meets the solid surface. The interface is concave if the fluid *wets* the solid surface—

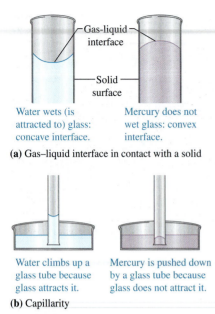

Water wets (is attracted to) glass: concave interface.

Mercury does not wet glass: convex interface.

(a) Gas–liquid interface in contact with a solid

Water climbs up a glass tube because glass attracts it.

Mercury is pushed down by a glass tube because glass does not attract it.

(b) Capillarity

▲ **FIGURE 13.25** Two effects of surface tension when a gas–liquid interface meets a solid surface that the liquid either wets or does not wet.

that is, if the surface attracts the fluid at a molecular level. It is convex if the solid does not attract the fluid (allowing surface tension to pull the fluid toward a spherical shape). As you can see from Figure 13.25a, water wets glass and forms a concave interface; mercury does not wet glass, and it forms a convex interface.

If you push a thin glass tube into water, the attraction of the glass actually causes the water to climb a certain distance up into the tube, as shown in Figure 13.25b. Conversely, if you push a glass tube into mercury, surface tension makes it difficult for the mercury to enter the tube, so the tube pushes the mercury down. These two phenomena, called **capillarity,** are responsible for the absorption of water by paper towels, the rise of melted wax in a candle wick, and many other everyday phenomena.

Related to surface tension is the phenomenon of *negative pressure.* The stress in a liquid is ordinarily *compressive,* but in some circumstances liquids can sustain *tensile* stresses. Consider a cylindrical tube that is closed at one end and has a tight-fitting piston at the other. We fill the tube completely with a liquid that wets and adheres to both the inner surface of the tube and the piston face; the molecules of liquid adhere to all the surfaces. If the surfaces are very clean and the liquid very pure, then, when we pull the piston face, we observe a *tensile* stress and a slight *increase* in volume; we are *stretching* the liquid! Adhesive forces prevent it from pulling away from the walls of the container.

With water, tensile stresses as large as 300 atm have been observed in the laboratory. This situation is highly unstable: A liquid under tension tends to break up into many small droplets. In tall trees, however, negative pressures are a regular occurrence. Negative pressure is believed to be an important mechanism for the transport of water and nutrients from the roots to the leaves in the small xylem tubes (diameter on the order of 0.1 mm) in the tree's outer wood.

13.5 Fluid Flow

We're now ready to consider *motion* of a fluid. Fluid flow can be extremely complex, as shown by the flow of a river in flood or the swirling flames of a campfire. Despite this complexity, some situations can be represented by relatively simple idealized models. An **ideal fluid** is a fluid that is *incompressible* (i.e., that has constant density) and has no internal friction or viscosity. The assumption of incompressibility is usually a good approximation for liquids, and we may also treat a gas as incompressible whenever the pressure differences from one region to another are not too great. Internal friction in a fluid causes shear stresses when two adjacent layers of fluid move relative to each other, such as when the fluid flows inside a tube or around an obstacle. In some cases, these shear forces are negligible in comparison with forces arising from gravitation and pressure differences.

The path of an individual element of a moving fluid is called a **flow line.** If the overall flow pattern does not change with time, the flow is called **steady flow.** In steady flow, every element passing through a given point follows the same flow line. In this case the "map" of the fluid velocities at various points in space remains constant, although the velocity of a particular particle of the fluid changes in both magnitude and direction during its motion.

Figure 13.26 shows groups of flow lines for motion of a fluid flowing from left to right around a number of obstacles. The photographs were made by injecting dye into water flowing between two closely spaced glass plates. These patterns are typical of **laminar flow,** in which adjacent layers of fluid slide smoothly past each other. At sufficiently high flow rates or when boundary surfaces cause abrupt changes in velocity, the flow becomes irregular and chaotic; this is called **turbulent flow.** Smoke rising from a candle or an incense stick typically exhibits laminar flow near the bottom and then breaks up into chaotic swirls as the flow

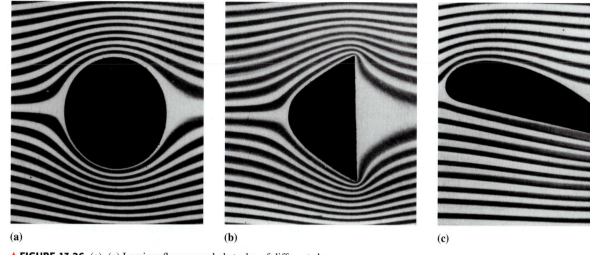

(a)   **(b)**   **(c)**

▲ **FIGURE 13.26** (a)–(c) Laminar flow around obstacles of different shapes.

becomes turbulent. (Figure 13.27). In turbulent flow, *there is no steady-state pattern;* the flow pattern continuously changes.

Conservation of mass in fluid flow gives us an important relationship called the **continuity equation.** The essence of this relation is contained in the familiar maxim "Still waters run deep." If the flow rate of a river with constant width is the same everywhere along a certain length, the water must run faster where it is shallow than where it is deep. As another example, the stream of water from a faucet tapers down in width because the water speeds up as it falls and a smaller diameter is needed to carry the same volume flow rate as at the top.

We can turn these observations into a quantitative relation. We'll consider only incompressible fluids, for which the density is constant. Figure 13.28 shows a fluid flowing through a gradually narrowing tube. We'll look at two points along the tube at which the cross-sectional areas are, respectively, A_1 and A_2 and the speeds of fluid flow are v_1 and v_2. During a small time interval Δt, the fluid at A_1 moves a distance $v_1 \Delta t$. The volume of fluid ΔV_1 that flows into the tube across A_1 during this interval is the fluid in the cylindrical element with base A_1 and height $v_1 \Delta t$; that is, $\Delta V_1 = A_1 v_1 \Delta t$.

If the density of the fluid is ρ, the mass Δm_1 that flows into the tube across A_1 during time Δt is the density ρ multiplied by the volume ΔV_1; that is, $\Delta m_1 = \rho \, \Delta V_1 = \rho A_1 v_1 \Delta t$. Similarly, the mass Δm_2 that flows out across A_2 in the same time is $\Delta m_2 = \rho A_2 v_2 \Delta t$. In steady flow the total mass in the tube is constant, so these two masses must be equal: $\Delta m_1 = \Delta m_2$, and

$$\rho A_1 v_1 \Delta t = \rho A_2 v_2 \Delta t, \qquad \text{or} \qquad A_1 v_1 = A_2 v_2.$$

Thus, we find the following:

Continuity equation

This equation expresses conservation of mass for an incompressible fluid flowing in a tube or some other channel. It says that the amount (either mass or volume) of fluid flowing through a cross section of the tube in a given time interval must be the same for all cross sections, or

$$\frac{\Delta V}{\Delta t} = A_1 v_1 = A_2 v_2. \tag{13.10}$$

The product Av is the **volume flow rate** $(\Delta V / \Delta t = Av)$, the time rate at which a given volume crosses any section of the tube. Similarly, the product $\Delta m / \Delta t = \rho Av$ is the **mass flow rate,** the time rate at which a given mass crosses a section of the tube.

▲ **FIGURE 13.27** Smoke rising from incense shows laminar flow near the bottom and turbulent flow farther up.

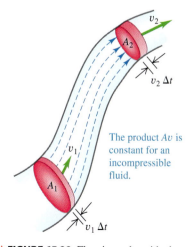

The product Av is constant for an incompressible fluid.

▲ **FIGURE 13.28** Flow in a tube with changing cross-sectional area.

◀ **Meandering along.** In a relatively straight, slow-moving waterway, the movement of the water approximates laminar flow; adjacent layers of water slide smoothly past each other with little mixing. As the flow approaches a bend in the river, it becomes slightly turbulent, and water on the outside of the bend travels faster than water on the inside. The turbulence causes erosion of the outside riverbank due to the higher flow rate and results in the deposition of suspended sediment on the inside riverbank as the water there slows. These combined processes lead to an ever-widening series of bends and turns, a phenomenon known as *meandering* that is characteristic of rivers on flat plains. So, if you're traveling by boat on this mature river, the shortest distance between two points may not be a straight line!

Equation 13.10 shows that the volume flow rate and the mass flow rate are constant along any given tube. When the cross section of the tube decreases, the speed of flow increases. The shallow part of a river has a smaller cross section and a faster current than the deep part, but the volume flow rates are the same in both. The stream from the faucet narrows as it gains speed during its fall, but $\Delta V / \Delta t$ is the same everywhere along the stream. If a water pipe with a 2 cm diameter is connected to a pipe with a 1 cm diameter, the flow speed is four times as great in the 1 cm part as in the 2 cm part (because the cross-sectional area is proportional to the square of the diameter).

We derived the continuity equation for a steady flow in a physically distinct tube, pipe, or channel. However, a larger steady flow pattern can be thought of as a bundle of side-by-side tubes with imaginary boundaries separating adjacent tubes. If there is no mixing across boundaries of the individual tubes, then the fluid in each tube behaves according to Equation 13.10. For instance, if a river has slowly moving water near the banks and swifter water in the middle, with little mixing between the two, the continuity equation can be applied separately to the faster-moving central portion and to a more slowly moving channel near the bank. In the discussion that follows, we'll use the term **flow tube** to describe the flow patterns in a fluid, even when the tube isn't bounded by a real physical wall.

Conceptual Analysis 13.8

Flow through a tube

Water flows steadily through a horizontal pipe that has a narrowed section. What happens to the volume flow rate as the water passes through the narrow section?

A. It decreases because the speed of the fluid decreases.
B. It remains constant.
C. It increases because the speed of the fluid increases.

SOLUTION As we've just seen, when an incompressible fluid such as water flows steadily through a pipe, the *same amount* of water must pass through each portion of the pipe in any given amount of time. This is equivalent to saying that the volume flow rate, $\Delta V / \Delta t$, is constant (choice B). For the product Av to be constant, the flow speed v must increase when the cross-sectional area A decreases. Thus, narrowing the pipe increases the flow speed.

13.6 Bernoulli's Equation

According to the continuity equation, the speed of fluid flow can vary along the paths of the fluid particles. The pressure can also vary; it depends on height, as in the static situation, and it also depends on the speed of flow. We can now use the concepts introduced in Section 13.5, along with the work–energy theorem, to derive an important relationship called **Bernoulli's equation** that relates the pressure, flow speed, and height for flow in an ideal fluid.

The dependence of pressure on fluid speed follows from Equation 13.10. When an incompressible fluid flows along a flow tube with varying cross section, the flow speed *must* change. Therefore, each element of fluid must have an acceleration, and the force that causes this acceleration has to be applied by the surrounding fluid. When an element of the fluid speeds up, we know that it is moving from a region of higher pressure to one of lower pressure; the pressure difference provides the net forward force needed to accelerate it. So when the cross section of a flow tube changes, the pressure *must* vary along the tube, even when there is no difference in elevation. If the elevation also changes, this causes an additional pressure difference.

To derive the Bernoulli equation, we use the work–energy theorem, which we studied in Chapter 7. We'll use the general form stated at the beginning of Section 7.6. Let's review that relationship; it is

$$\Delta K + \Delta U = W_{\text{other}},$$

where ΔK is the change in kinetic energy of an object during the motion we're considering, ΔU is the change in its potential energy (in this case, gravitational potential energy ΔU_{grav}), and W_{other} is the work done by the forces whose work is not included in ΔU_{grav}. We'll compute each of these three pieces for a system consisting of a segment of fluid in a flow tube; then we'll combine the pieces according to the work–energy theorem.

In Figure 13.29, we consider as our system the segment of fluid that lies between the two cross sections a and c at some initial time. The speed at the upstream end is v_1, and the pressure there is p_1. In a small time interval Δt, the fluid initially at a moves to b, a distance $\Delta s_1 = v_1 \Delta t$, where v_1 is the speed at this end of the tube. In the same time interval, the fluid initially at c moves to d, a distance $\Delta s_2 = v_2 \Delta t$. The cross-sectional areas at the two ends are A_1 and A_2, as shown. Because of the continuity relation, the volume ΔV of fluid passing *any* cross section during time Δt is the same at both ends: $\Delta V = A_1 \Delta s_1 = A_2 \Delta s_2$.

Note that the fluid between cross sections a and b is part of our system at the beginning of Δt, but not at the end, and that the fluid between cross sections c and d are part of our system at the end of Δt, but not at the beginning.

To apply the work–energy theorem, let's first compute W_{other}, which is the work done on this segment of fluid during Δt by the fluid adjacent to it. The pressure on the segment at cross section a is p_1; the total force exerted on this cross section by the adjacent fluid has magnitude $p_1 A_1$, and the displacement of the segment during the interval Δt is Δs_1. Thus, the work done on the segment by the force at cross section a during time Δt (force times displacement) has magnitude $p_1 A_1 \Delta s_1$. Similarly, the magnitude of the work done on the segment at cross section c is $p_2 A_2 \Delta s_2$. Therefore, the net work W_{other} done on the segment by the adjacent fluid during this displacement is

$$W_{\text{other}} = p_1 A_1 \Delta s_1 - p_2 A_2 \Delta s_2$$
$$= (p_1 - p_2) \Delta V.$$

We need the negative sign in the second term because the force at c is opposite in direction to the displacement.

Next, let's find the change in gravitational potential energy during time Δt. The gravitational potential energy of the mass between a and b at the beginning of Δt is $\Delta m \, gy_1 = \rho \, \Delta V \, gy_1$, where y is the height of the mass above some reference level at which $y = 0$. At the end of the interval Δt, this mass has left our system, and there's a corresponding decrease in the potential energy of the system. But during the same interval, the mass between c and d has been added to the system, bringing with it a potential-energy increase $\Delta m \, gy_2 = \rho \, \Delta V \, gy_2$. Thus, the *net* change in potential energy ΔU_{grav} during Δt is

$$\Delta U_{\text{grav}} = \rho \, \Delta V \, g(y_2 - y_1).$$

Finally, we compute the change ΔK in kinetic energy of our system during Δt. At the beginning of Δt, the fluid between a and b has volume $A_1 \Delta s_1$, mass $\rho A_1 \Delta s_1$, and kinetic energy $\frac{1}{2} m v_1^2 = \frac{1}{2} \rho (A_1 \Delta s_1) v_1^2 = \frac{1}{2} \rho \, \Delta V v_1^2$. At the end of Δt, this fluid is no longer in the system, but the fluid between c and d is now included; it brings in kinetic energy $\frac{1}{2} \rho (A_2 \Delta s_2) v_2^2 = \frac{1}{2} \rho \, \Delta V v_2^2$. The net *change* in kinetic energy ΔK during time Δt is the difference of these quantities:

$$\Delta K = \frac{1}{2} \rho \, \Delta V (v_2^2 - v_1^2).$$

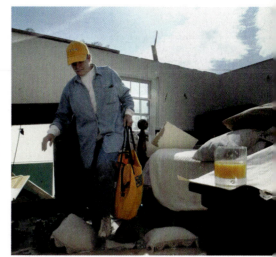

▲ **Raising the roof.** In severe weather accompanied by high winds, the roofs of houses may be blown completely off. At first you might think that the direct force of the wind pushed this roof off. In fact, the wind *pulled* the roof off—or, alternatively, the pressure inside the house blew it off. The wind that flowed up and over the house was forced to take a longer path than wind that did not meet the house. Therefore, it flowed faster. Bernoulli's principle tells us that the pressure in this fast-moving air was lower than the pressure elsewhere—such as inside the house. After a severe storm, you will often see that the windows of houses are blown out rather than in.

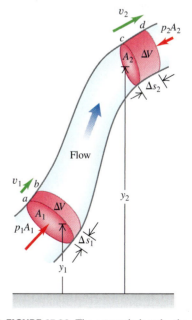

▲ **FIGURE 13.29** The net work done by the pressure equals the change in the kinetic energy plus the change in the gravitational potential energy.

(Note that there is no net change in kinetic energy of the fluid between cross sections *b* and *c*: There is just as much of our system contained between these sections at the end of the interval as at the beginning, and the flow velocity at any point doesn't change.)

Now we combine all these pieces in the work–energy theorem:

$$\Delta K + \Delta U_{grav} = W_{other},$$

$$\tfrac{1}{2}\rho\,\Delta V(v_2^2 - v_1^2) + \rho\,\Delta V\,g(y_2 - y_1) = (p_1 - p_2)\,\Delta V,$$

or

$$p_1 - p_2 = \tfrac{1}{2}\rho(v_2^2 - v_1^2) + \rho g(y_2 - y_1). \tag{13.11}$$

This is **Bernoulli's equation.** We may interpret it in terms of pressures. The second term on the right is the pressure difference between any two points in the fluid, caused by the weight of the fluid and the difference in elevation of the two ends. The first term on the right is the additional pressure difference associated with the change in speed of the fluid.

Equation 13.11 can also be written as follows:

Bernoulli's equation: pressure, flow speed, and height in a fluid

$$p_1 + \rho g y_1 + \tfrac{1}{2}\rho v_1^2 = p_2 + \rho g y_2 + \tfrac{1}{2}\rho v_2^2. \tag{13.12}$$

The subscripts 1 and 2 refer to *any* two points along the flow tube, so Bernoulli's equation may also be written as

$$p + \rho g y + \tfrac{1}{2}\rho v^2 = \text{constant}. \tag{13.13}$$

PROBLEM-SOLVING STRATEGY 13.1   **Bernoulli's equation**   (MP)

Bernoulli's equation is derived from the work–energy relationship, so it isn't surprising that much of the problem-solving strategy suggested in Section 7.6 is equally applicable here.

SET UP

1. Always begin by identifying points 1 and 2 clearly, with reference to Bernoulli's equation.
2. Write down (or show on a sketch) the known and unknown quantities in Equation 13.12. The variables are p_1, p_2, v_1, v_2, y_1, and y_2, and the constants are ρ and g. What is given? What do you need to determine? Be sure that your pressures are either all gauge pressures or all absolute pressures; don't mix them. Be careful about consistency of units. In SI units, pressure is expressed in pascals, density in kilograms per cubic meter, and speed in meters per second.

SOLVE

3. In some problems you'll need to use the continuity equation, Equation 13.10, to get a relation between the two speeds in terms of cross-sectional areas of pipes or containers. Or perhaps you will know both speeds and will need to determine one of the areas.
4. The volume flow rate $\Delta V/\Delta t$ across any area A is given by $\Delta V/\Delta t = Av$, and the corresponding mass flow rate $\Delta m/\Delta t$ is $\Delta m/\Delta t = \rho A v$. These relations sometimes come in handy.

REFLECT

5. Always try to estimate comparative magnitudes of your results. Are they what you expected? Do they agree with commonsense predictions or estimates?

EXAMPLE 13.9   **Water pressure in the home**

Water enters a house through a pipe with an inside diameter of 2.0 cm at a gauge pressure of 4.0×10^5 Pa (about 4 atm, or 60 lb/in^2). The cold-water pipe leading to the second-floor bathroom 5.0 m above is 1.0 cm in diameter (Figure 13.30). Find the flow speed and gauge pressure in the bathroom when the flow speed at the inlet pipe is 2.0 m/s. How much time would be required to fill a 100 L bathtub?

SOLUTION

SET UP Let point 1 be at the inlet pipe and point 2 at the bathroom. The speed v_2 of the water at the bathroom is obtained from the continuity equation, Equation 13.10. We take $y_1 = 0$ at the inlet and $y_2 = 5.0$ m at the bathroom. We are given p_1 and v_1; we can find p_2 from Bernoulli's equation, Equation 13.12. To find the time to fill the bathtub, we use the volume flow-rate relation $\Delta V / \Delta t = Av$. The bathtub's volume is $100 \, \text{L} = 100 \times 10^{-3} \, \text{m}^3$.

SOLVE From the continuity equation, the flow speed v_2 in the bathroom is

$$v_2 = \frac{A_1}{A_2}v_1 = \frac{\pi(1.0 \text{ cm})^2}{\pi(0.50 \text{ cm})^2}(2.0 \text{ m/s}) = 8.0 \text{ m/s}.$$

From Bernoulli's equation, the gauge pressure p_2 in the bathroom is

$$
\begin{aligned}
p_2 &= p_1 - \tfrac{1}{2}\rho(v_2^2 - v_1^2) - \rho g(y_2 - y_1) \\
&= 4.0 \times 10^5 \text{ Pa} \\
&\quad - \tfrac{1}{2}(1.0 \times 10^3 \text{ kg/m}^3)(64 \text{ m}^2/\text{s}^2 - 4.0 \text{ m}^2/\text{s}^2) \\
&\quad - (1.0 \times 10^3 \text{ kg/m}^3)(9.8 \text{ m/s}^2)(5.0 \text{ m}) \\
&= 3.2 \times 10^5 \text{ Pa} \\
&= 3.2 \text{ atm} = 47 \text{ lb/in}^2. \quad \text{(gauge pressure).}
\end{aligned}
$$

The volume flow rate is

$$
\begin{aligned}
\Delta V / \Delta t &= A_2 v_2 = \pi(0.50 \times 10^{-2} \text{ m})^2(8.0 \text{ m/s}) \\
&= 6.3 \times 10^{-4} \text{ m}^3/\text{s} = 0.63 \text{ L/s.}
\end{aligned}
$$

The time needed to fill the tub is $100 \, \text{L} / (0.63 \, \text{L/s}) = 160$ s.

▲ **FIGURE 13.30** What is the water pressure in the second-story bathroom of this house?

To second floor (1 cm pipe)

5.0 m

Water meter

Hot-water tank

From water supply (2 cm pipe)

REFLECT Note that when the water is turned off, the second term on the right of the pressure equation vanishes, and the pressure rises to 3.5×10^5 Pa. In fact, when the fluid is not moving, Bernoulli's equation (Equation 13.12) reduces to the pressure relation that we derived for a fluid at rest, Equation 13.3.

13.7 Applications of Bernoulli's Equation

The sections that follow discuss several practical applications of Bernoulli's equation.

Speed of Efflux; Torricelli's Theorem

Figure 13.31 shows a gasoline storage tank with cross-sectional area A_1 filled to a depth h with a liquid of density ρ. The space above the gasoline is vented to the atmosphere, so it contains air at atmospheric pressure p_{atm}, and the gasoline flows out through a short pipe with cross-sectional area A_2. How fast does the gasoline run out?

To answer this question, we consider the entire volume of moving liquid as a single flow tube; v_1 and v_2 are the speeds at points 1 and 2, respectively. The pressure at both points is atmospheric pressure p_{atm}, so the pressure differential is zero. We apply Bernoulli's equation to points 1 and 2 and take $y_2 = 0$ at the bottom of the tank.

When we set $y_1 = h$, Bernoulli's equation becomes

$$p_{\text{atm}} + \tfrac{1}{2}\rho v_1^2 + \rho g h = p_{\text{atm}} + \tfrac{1}{2}\rho v_2^2.$$

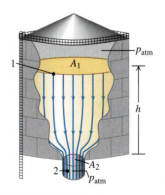

▲ **FIGURE 13.31** How fast does the gasoline run out of this storage tank?

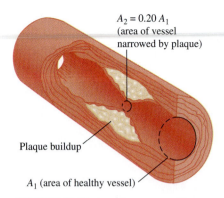

$A_2 = 0.20\,A_1$
(area of vessel
narrowed by plaque)

Plaque buildup

A_1 (area of healthy vessel)

▲ **FIGURE 13.32** An artery narrowed by plaque in arteriosclerosis.

Difference in height results from reduced pressure in throat.

h

A_1 v_1 p_1 1 2 A_2 p_2 v_2

▲ **FIGURE 13.33** The Venturi meter.

The air going over the wing takes a longer path than the air going under the wing, so its speed is higher and its pressure consequently lower.

$\vec{p}_i$ $\vec{p}_f$

$\vec{p}_i$

$\Delta\vec{p}$ (air)

$\vec{p}_f$

Alternatively, the wing's shape imparts a net downward momentum to the air; the reaction force on the airplane is upward.

▲ **FIGURE 13.34** How the flow of air around an airplane wing generates lift.

But A_2 is much smaller than A_1; therefore, v_1^2 is much smaller than v_2^2 and can be neglected. What remains is

$$\rho g h = \tfrac{1}{2}\rho v_2^2, \qquad \text{or} \qquad v_2 = \sqrt{2gh}.$$

This expression should look familiar. Recall from Chapter 7 that when an object of mass m falls through a height h, conservation of mechanical energy requires that $mgh = \tfrac{1}{2}mv^2$, or $v = \sqrt{2gh}$. Thus, the speed of efflux from an opening at a distance h below the top surface of a liquid is the same as the speed a body would acquire in falling freely through a height h. This equivalence should not be surprising, since we used conservation of energy to derive Bernoulli's equation. Each small portion of fluid acts like a particle with mass m.

Collapse of a Blood Vessel

Over 200,000 people die each year from arteriosclerosis. One aspect of this disease is a narrowing of blood vessels due to the buildup of plaque on the vessel wall. The disease is considered critical when a portion of vessel becomes 80% blocked. We can find the drop in pressure when blood flowing at 50 cm/s enters such a region.

In Figure 13.32, the cross-sectional area of the healthy portion of the blood vessel is A_1 while the cross-sectional area of the narrowing is A_2. Eighty percent blockage means that 20% of the original area remains, so $A_2 = 0.20A_1$. We first use the continuity equation to find the speed v_2 in the narrow part of the vessel:

$$A_1 v_1 = A_2 v_2 \qquad \text{and} \qquad v_2 = \frac{A_1}{A_2}v_1 = \frac{A_1}{0.2A_1}(0.50 \text{ m/s}) = 2.5 \text{ m/s}.$$

Then we use Bernoulli's equation, taking $y_2 = y_1$, to find the drop in blood pressure in the narrow region. The density of blood is about $1.06 \times 10^3 \text{ kg/m}^3$.

For the numerical values given, the drop in blood pressure is

$$p_1 - p_2 = \tfrac{1}{2}(1.06 \times 10^3 \text{ kg/m}^3)[(2.5 \text{ m/s})^2 - (0.50 \text{ m/s})^2]$$
$$= 3.2 \times 10^3 \text{ Pa}.$$

A pressure drop of this magnitude inside the narrow region can act to collapse the blood vessel. Thus, blood flow can stop abruptly even before plaque has entirely closed off the vessel.

The Venturi Meter

The Venturi meter, shown in Figure 13.33, is used to measure flow speed in a pipe. The narrow part of the pipe is called the *throat*. Because A_1 is greater than A_2, v_2 is greater than v_1, and the pressure p_2 in the throat is less than p_1. Thus, the difference in height h of the fluid in the two vertical tubes is directly related to v_1. By applying Bernoulli's equation to the wide (point 1) and narrow (point 2) parts, we can derive a relation between h and v_1. We'll omit the details of the calculation; the result is

$$v_1 = \sqrt{\frac{2gh}{(A_1/A_2)^2 - 1}}.$$

This same concept is used in some gasoline engines, in which gasoline is sprayed from a nozzle or an injector into a low-pressure region produced in a Venturi throat.

Lift on an Airplane Wing

Figure 13.34 shows flow lines around a cross section of an airplane wing. The lines crowd together above the wing, corresponding to increased flow speed and reduced pressure in this region, just as in the Venturi throat. Because the upward force on the underside of the wing is greater than the downward force on the top side, there is a net upward force, or *lift.* (This highly simplified discussion ignores the effect of turbulent flow and the formation of vortices; a more complete discussion would take these into account.)

We can also understand the lift force on the basis of momentum changes. Figure 13.34 shows that there is a net *downward* change in the vertical component of momentum of the air flowing past the wing, corresponding to the downward force the wing exerts on it. The reaction force *on* the wing is *upward,* as we concluded in the previous paragraph.

The Curveball

Does a curveball *really* curve? Yes, it certainly does. Figure 13.35 shows a ball moving through air from left to right. To an observer moving with the center of the ball, the air stream appears to move from right to left, as shown by the flow lines in the figure. Because of the large speeds that are ordinarily involved (up to 100 mi/h for a baseball or a served tennis ball), there is a region of turbulent flow behind the ball.

Figure 13.35b shows a spinning ball with "top spin," viewed from the side. When the ball is spinning, the viscosity of air causes layers of air near the ball's surface to be pulled around in the direction of spin. Therefore, the speed of the air relative to the ball's surface is smaller at the top of the ball than at the bottom (Also, the region of turbulence becomes asymmetric; turbulence occurs farther forward on the top side than on the bottom.) The difference in the speed of the air between the top and bottom of the ball causes a pressure difference: The average pressure at the top of the ball becomes greater than that at the bottom. The corresponding net downward force deflects the ball downward, as shown. This could be a side view of a tennis ball (Figure 13.35d) moving from left to right with "top spin." In a baseball curve pitch, the ball spins about a nearly vertical axis, and the actual deflection is mostly sideways. In that case, Figure 13.35c is a *top view* of the situation. Note that a curveball thrown by a left-handed pitcher curves *toward* a right-handed batter, making it harder to hit than the same ball thrown to a left-handed batter (in which case the ball would curve *away from* the batter).

A similar effect occurs with golf balls, which always have "backspin" from impact with the slanted face of the golf club. The resulting pressure difference

v_{ball}

(a) Motion of air relative to a nonspinning ball

This side of the ball moves opposite to the air flow.

This side moves in the direction of the air flow.

(b) Motion of a spinning ball

A moving ball drags the adjacent air with it. So, when air moves past a spinning ball:

On one side the ball **slows the air**, creating a region of **high pressure**.

On the other side the ball **speeds the air**, creating a region of **low pressure**.

The resultant force points in the direction of the low-pressure side.

(c) Force generated when a spinning ball moves through air

(d) Spin pushing a tennis ball downward

(e) Spin causing a curveball to be deflected sideways

▲ **FIGURE 13.35** How spin on a ball creates forces that cause the ball to follow a nonparabolic trajectory.

▲ **FIGURE 13.36** Strobe photo of a golf ball being struck by a club. The picture was taken at 1000 flashes per second. The ball rotates about once in eight pictures, corresponding to an angular velocity of 125 rev/s, or 7500 rpm.

▲ **FIGURE 13.37** Velocity profile for a viscous fluid in a cylindrical pipe.

between the top and bottom of the ball causes a "lift" force that keeps the ball in the air considerably longer than would be possible without spin. From the tee, a well-hit drive appears to float, or even curve *upward,* during the initial portion of its flight. This is a real effect, not an illusion. The dimples on the ball play an essential role: Because of effects associated with the viscosity of air, a ball without dimples has a much shorter trajectory than a dimpled ball, given the same initial velocity and spin. One manufacturer even claims that the *shape* of the dimples is significant: Polygonal dimples are alleged to be more effective than round ones. Figure 13.36 shows the backspin of a golf ball just after it is struck by a club.

*13.8 Real Fluids: Viscosity and Turbulence

Viscosity is internal friction in a fluid; viscous forces oppose the motion of one portion of a fluid relative to another. Viscosity is the reason that paddling a canoe through calm water requires effort, but it is also the reason the paddle works. Viscosity plays a vital role in the flow of fluids in pipes, the flow of blood, the lubrication of engine parts, and many other areas of practical importance. An ideal fluid, the model we used to derive the Bernoulli equation, has no viscosity, but in real-life fluids, especially liquids, effects associated with viscosity are often significant.

A viscous fluid always tends to cling to a solid surface that is in contact with it. There is always a thin *boundary layer* of fluid near the surface in which the fluid is nearly at rest with respect to the surface. That's why dust particles can cling to a fan blade even when it is rotating rapidly and why you can't get all the mud off your car by just squirting a hose at it.

Viscosity plays an important role in the flow of fluids through pipes. Let's think first about a fluid with zero viscosity, so that we can apply Bernoulli's equation, Equation 13.12. For a pipe of uniform cross section, if the two ends are at the same height (so that $y_1 = y_2$) and have the same flow speed ($v_1 = v_2$) and the fluid has zero acceleration, then the Bernoulli equation states that the pressure is the same at the two ends. But if viscosity is taken into account, the pressure must be greater at the upstream end than at the downstream end. To see why, let's consider the velocity profile for flow of a viscous fluid in a cylindrical pipe (Figure 13.37). The flow velocity is different at different points of a cross section. The outermost layer of fluid clings to the walls, so the speed is zero at the pipe walls. The walls exert a backward drag on this layer, which in turn drags backward on the next layer inward, and so on. The flow speed is greatest along the axis of the pipe.

The motion is like that of many coaxial telescoping tubes sliding relative to one another, with the central tube moving fastest and the outermost tube at rest. The viscous forces between the tubes resist this motion, so, for the fluid to keep moving, the pressure p_1 at the back end has to be greater than the pressure p_2 at the front end. The strength of the viscous resisting forces is characterized by a quantity called the *coefficient of viscosity,* or simply the *viscosity,* denoted by η (Greek eta). Very viscous fluids, such as molasses, have large values of η; gases have much smaller values, and water is in between. The coefficient of viscosity is strongly dependent on temperature, decreasing with increasing temperature for liquids, but increasing with temperature for gases.

Detailed analysis of the flow pattern of a viscous fluid in a cylindrical pipe shows that the volume flow rate $\Delta V/\Delta t$ is proportional to the pressure difference $p_1 - p_2$ between the ends and inversely proportional to the length L of the pipe. That is, the volume flow rate is proportional to the pressure change *per unit length,* which is called the *pressure gradient.* The volume flow rate is also proportional to the *fourth power* of the pipe's radius R. The specific relationship, called **Poiseuille's law,** is

$$\frac{\Delta V}{\Delta t} = \frac{\pi R^4}{8\eta} \frac{p_1 - p_2}{L}.$$

If the radius R is doubled, the volume flow rate increases by a factor of 16. This relation is familiar to physicians in connection with hypodermic needles. Needle size is much more important than thumb pressure in determining the flow rate from the needle; doubling the needle diameter has the same effect as increasing the thumb force by a factor of 16. Similarly, blood flow in arteries and veins can be controlled over a wide range by relatively small changes in diameter, an important temperature-control mechanism in warm-blooded animals. Relatively slight narrowing of arteries due to arteriosclerosis can result in elevated blood pressure and added strain on the heart muscle.

One more useful relation in viscous fluid flow is the expression for the magnitude F of force exerted on a sphere of radius r that moves with speed v through a fluid with viscosity η. When v is small enough that there is no turbulence, the relationship is simple:

$$F = 6\pi\eta rv.$$

This relation is called **Stokes's law.** We've encountered a similar velocity-dependent force before, in Example 5.13 (Section 5.3).

A sphere falling in a viscous fluid reaches a *terminal speed* v_t for which the total force, including the weight of the sphere and the viscous retarding force, is zero, and the sphere no longer accelerates. (We neglect the effect of buoyancy of the sphere in the fluid.) Let ρ be the density of the sphere; then the weight of the sphere is $\frac{4}{3}\pi r^3\rho g$. When the sphere reaches terminal speed, the total force on it is zero:

$$6\pi\eta rv_t - \tfrac{4}{3}\pi r^3\rho g = 0,$$

or

$$v_t = \tfrac{2}{9}\frac{r^2 g\rho}{\eta}.$$

The Stokes's-law force is what keeps clouds in the air. The terminal speed for a water droplet of radius 10^{-5} m is on the order of 1 mm/s. At higher speeds the flow often becomes turbulent, and Stokes's law is no longer valid. In air, the drag force at highway speeds is approximately proportional to v^2. We've discussed the applications of Stokes's law to skydiving (Example 5.13, Section 5.3) and to the air drag of a moving automobile (Section 7.9). Raindrops have terminal speeds of a few meters per second because of air drag; otherwise, they would smash everything in their path!

As we've mentioned previously, flow can be either laminar, with layers of fluid slipping smoothly past each other, or turbulent—irregular, complex, and ever changing. Figure 13.27 showed rising smoke changing from laminar to turbulent flow. Figure 13.38 compares laminar and turbulent flow in streams of water.

The transition from laminar to turbulent flow is often very sudden. A flow pattern that is stable at low speeds suddenly becomes unstable when a critical speed is reached. Irregularities in the flow pattern can be caused by roughness in a pipe wall, variations in density of the fluid, and many other factors. At small

Laminar flow   Turbulent flow

▲ **FIGURE 13.38** Laminar and turbulent flow in a stream of water.

flow speeds, these disturbances are damped out and the flow pattern tends to maintain its laminar nature. But when the critical speed is reached, the disturbances no longer damp out; instead, they grow until they destroy the entire laminar-flow pattern.

Turbulence poses some profound questions for theoretical physics. The motion of any particular particle in a fluid is presumably determined by Newton's laws. If we know the motion of the fluid at some initial time, shouldn't we be able to predict the motion at any later time? After all, when we launch a projectile, we can compute the entire trajectory if we know the initial position and velocity. How is it that a system that obeys well-defined and supposedly deterministic physical laws can have unpredictable, chaotic behavior?

There is no simple answer to these questions. Indeed, the study of chaotic behavior in deterministic systems is a highly active field of research in theoretical physics. The development of supercomputers in recent years has enabled scientists to carry out computer simulations of the behavior of physical systems on a scale that would have been hopeless only a few years ago. The results of such simulations have often guided new developments in the theory of chaotic behavior. A particularly significant result of these studies has been the discovery of common characteristics in the behavior of widely divergent kinds of systems, including turbulent fluid flow, population fluctuations in ecosystems, the growth of crystals, the shapes of coastlines, and many others.

SUMMARY

Density and Pressure in a Fluid

(Sections 13.1 and 13.2) **Density** is mass per unit volume. If a mass m of material has volume V, its density ρ is $\rho = m/V$ (Equation 13.1). **Specific gravity** is the ratio of the density of a material to the density of water.

  Pressure is force per unit area. Assuming that the pressure is constant over the area in question, we express pressure as $p = F_\perp/A$ (Equation 13.2). **Pascal's law** states that the pressure applied to the surface of an enclosed fluid is transmitted undiminished to every portion of the fluid. The total pressure at any level in a fluid is the external pressure plus the pressure due to the weight of the overlying fluid. The pressure p at a height h above or below a reference level where $h = 0$, relative to the pressure p_0 at the reference level, is $p - p_0 = -\rho g h$ (where ρ is the density of the fluid) (Equation 13.3).

  Absolute pressure is the total pressure in a fluid; **gauge pressure** is the difference between absolute pressure and atmospheric pressure. The SI unit of pressure is the pascal (Pa), where $1\ \text{Pa} = 1\ \text{N/m}^2$. Additional units of pressure are the bar $(1\ \text{bar} = 10^5\ \text{Pa})$, the torr $[1\ \text{torr} = 1$ millimeter of mercury $(\text{mm Hg})]$, and the atmosphere (atm) $(1\ \text{atm} = 1.013 \times 10^5\ \text{Pa} = 760\ \text{torrs} = 1.013\ \text{bar})$

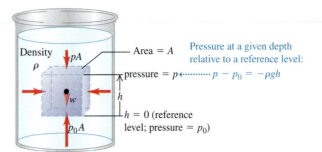

Density
ρ

Area $= A$

pressure $= p$

$p_0 A$

h

$h = 0$ (reference level; pressure $= p_0$)

Pressure at a given depth relative to a reference level:
$p - p_0 = -\rho g h$

Archimedes's Principle: Buoyancy

(Section 13.3) **Archimedes's principle** states that when an object is immersed in a fluid, the fluid exerts an upward buoyant force on the object equal in magnitude to the weight of the fluid the object displaces. Thus, an object denser than the surrounding fluid sinks; one less dense than the surrounding fluid floats.

The pressure on any volume element of a fluid produces a buoyancy force $\vec{F}_B$ that exactly cancels the element's weight.

$\vec{F}_B$

cg

$\vec{w}_{\text{fluid}}$

$\vec{F}_B$

$\vec{w}_{\text{object}}$

The buoyancy force on a solid object is equal in magnitude to the weight of the displaced fluid.

Surface Tension and Capillarity

(Section 13.4) A boundary surface between a liquid and a gas behaves like a surface under tension (**surface tension**). Where a liquid–gas interface meets a solid surface, the interface is concave if the liquid is attracted to (wets) the solid and convex if not. In the related phenomenon of **capillarity**, a liquid climbs up a narrow tube if it wets the tube's material, but is pushed down by the tube if it does not.

Why liquids exhibit surface tension

Surface molecules— asymmetric attraction

Interior molecules— symmetric attraction

Fluid Flow, Bernoulli's Equation

(Sections 13.5–13.7) An ideal fluid is an incompressible fluid with no viscosity. A flow line is the path of a fluid particle. In **laminar flow**, layers of fluid slide smoothly past each other. In **turbulent flow**, there is disorder and a constantly changing flow pattern.

  Conservation of mass for an incompressible fluid is expressed by the **equation of continuity:** For a liquid flowing in a tube with varying cross section, the flow speeds v_1 and v_2 at two cross sections with areas A_1 and A_2, respectively, are related by $A_1 v_1 = A_2 v_2$ (Equation 13.10). The product Av is the **volume flow rate**, $\Delta V/\Delta t$, the rate at which volume crosses a section of the tube: $\Delta V/\Delta t = Av$.

  Bernoulli's equation relates the pressure p, flow speed v, and elevation y in an ideal fluid. For any two points, indicated by subscripts 1 and 2, $p_1 + \rho g y_1 + \frac{1}{2}\rho v_1^2 = p_2 + \rho g y_2 + \frac{1}{2}\rho v_2^2$ (Equation 13.12). This equation states that faster flow is associated with lower pressure. That fact underlies the working of Venturi meters and is also responsible for the lift on airplane wings and for the nonparabolic trajectories of spinning baseballs and golf balls.

Lift due to Bernoulli's principle: Air travels farther and therefore faster over the top than the bottom of the wing; the result is lower pressure over the top of the wing.

Continued

Real Fluids: Viscosity and Turbulence

(Section 13.8) Real fluids have viscosity. Consequently, the boundary layer fluid in contact with a stationary wall or surface is nearly at rest, whereas flow speeds peak in the center of a pipe or channel. Flow is typically laminar at low speeds; at higher speeds, flow tends to become turbulent.

 For instructor-assigned homework, go to www.masteringphysics.com

Conceptual Questions

1. A clear plastic hose is attached to the narrow end of a funnel, and its free end is bent around to point upward (Figure 13.39). When water is poured into the funnel, it rises in the hose to the same level as in the funnel, despite the fact that the funnel has a lot more water in it than the hose. Why does it do this? Where does the force come from to support the weight of the extra water in the funnel?

▲ **FIGURE 13.39** Question 1.

2. In describing the size of a large ship, one uses the expression "It displaces 20,000 tons." What does this expression mean? Can the weight of the ship be obtained from this information?

3. A popular, though expensive, sport is hot-air ballooning, in which a large nylon balloon is filled with air heated by a gas burner at the bottom. Why must the air be heated? How does the balloonist control the balloon's ascent and descent?

4. A rigid lighter-than-air balloon filled with helium cannot continue to rise indefinitely. Why not? What determines the maximum height it can attain?

5. Suppose the door of a room makes an airtight, but frictionless, fit in its frame. Do you think you could open the door if the air pressure on one side were standard atmospheric pressure and that on the other side differed from standard by 1%? Back up your answer with a simple but reasonable calculation.

6. When a smooth-flowing stream of water comes out of a faucet, it narrows as it falls. Why does it do this?

7. Why does air escaping from the open end of a small pipe make a lot more noise than air escaping at the same volume rate from a large pipe?

8. A very smooth wooden block is pressed against the bottom of a container of water so that no water remains under the block. Will this block rise to the surface when it is released? Why? (*Hint:* Can the water exert a force on the bottom of the block?)

9. A marble is in a little box that is floating in a beaker of water. The marble is then removed from the box and dropped into the water, sinking to the bottom. What happens to the water level in the beaker when you do this? Does it go up, go down, or stay the same? Why? (It might help to draw a figure.)

10. A beaker of water rests on a scale. You slowly lower a piece of metal into the water, using a string attached to the metal, but you do not allow the metal to touch the walls or bottom of the beaker. (a) What happens to the reading on the scale when you do this? (b) How does the scale "know" that the metal is in the water, since the metal never touches either the beaker or the scale? (It might help to draw a figure.)

11. If a rocketship traveling through the vacuum of space is hit by a small asteroid, it could lose its air through the hole caused by the collision. Many people would describe this situation by saying that the air was *sucked out* by the vacuum. Is this a good *physical* explanation of what is happening? Does the vacuum actually suck out the air? What does make the air go out?

12. If you walk along a coastal seaport, you often see recently caught fish that are enormously bloated. These are fish that live very deep in the sea. What caused them to be so bloated? Were they that way deep down where they normally live?

13. Submarines can remain at equilibrium at various depths in the ocean, and they are made of rigid metal to withstand great pressures. (a) What must be the average density of a submarine? (b) Devise a simple way that a submarine could cause itself to go up (or down) without using its propellers.

14. You ask the service attendant at an auto garage to check the air in a soft tire, and he says "13 lb." (a) Does he actually mean that? What does that "13 lb" really mean in proper units? (b) The "13 lb" is below atmospheric pressure, so how can it keep the tire partially inflated, let alone support your car? What pressure must that "13 lb" be, gauge or absolute?

15. A helium-filled balloon is tied to a light string inside of a car at rest. The other end of the string is attached to the floor of the car, so the balloon pulls the string vertical. You now accelerate forward. Which way does the balloon move, forward or backward, or does it not move? Justify your reasoning with reference to buoyancy. (If you have a chance, try this experiment yourself—but with someone else doing the driving!)

Multiple-Choice Questions

1. Which has a greater buoyant force on it, a 25 cm^3 piece of wood floating with part of its volume above water or a 25 cm^3 piece of submerged iron?
   A. The floating wood.
   B. The submerged iron.
   C. They have the same buoyant force on them.
   D. It is impossible to tell without knowing their weights.

2. A rectangular crate of weight W is floating in water with two-thirds of its volume above water. If you now want to push down on it to hold it lower in the water, so that only one-third

of its volume is above water, the downward force needed to do this is

   A. *W*.   B. 2*W*.   C. *W*/2.   D. *W*/3.

3. A mass of sunken lead is resting against the bottom in a glass of water. You take this lead, put it in a small boat of negligible mass, and float the boat in the water. Which of the following statements are true? (There may be more than one correct choice.)

   A. The sunken lead displaces a volume of water equal to the lead's own volume.

   B. The floating lead displaces a volume of water equal to the lead's own volume.

   C. The sunken lead displaces a volume of water whose weight equals the lead's weight.

   D. The floating lead displaces a volume of water whose weight equals the lead's weight.

4. Two equal-sized buckets are filled to the brim with water, but one of them has a piece of wood floating in it. Which bucket of water weighs more?

   A. The bucket with the wood.

   B. The bucket without the wood.

   C. They weigh the same amount.

5. Two equal *mass* pieces of metal are sitting side by side at the bottom of a deep lake. One piece is aluminum and the other is lead. Which piece has the greater buoyant force acting on it?

   A. The aluminum.

   B. The lead.

   C. They both have the same buoyant force acting on them.

6. If a 5 lb force is required to keep a block of wood 1 ft beneath the surface of water, the force needed to keep it 2 ft beneath the surface is

   A. 2.5 lb.   B. 5 lb.   C. 10 lb.

7. A horizontal pipe with water flowing through it has a circular cross section that varies in diameter. The diameter at the wide section is 3 times that of the diameter at the narrow section. If the rate of flow of the water in the narrow section is 9.0 L/min, the rate of flow of the water in the wide section is

   A. 1.0 L/min.   B. 3.0 L/min.   C. 9.0 L/min.

   D. 18 L/min.   E. 36 L/min.

8. A horizontal cylindrical pipe has a part with a diameter half that of the rest of the pipe. If *V* is the speed of the fluid in the wider section of pipe, then the speed of the fluid in the narrower section is

   A. *V*/4.   B. *V*/2.   C. 2*V*.   D. 4*V*.

9. If the *absolute* pressure at a depth *d* in a lake is *P*, the absolute pressure at a depth 2*d* will be

   A. 2*P*.   B. *P*.

   C. Greater than 2*P*.   D. Less than 2*P*.

10. If the *gauge* pressure at a depth *d* in a lake is *P*, the gauge pressure at a depth 2*d* will be

   A. 2*P*.   B. *P*.

   C. Greater than 2*P*.   D. Less than 2*P*.

11. There is a great deal of ice floating on the oceans near the North Pole. If this ice were to melt due to global warming, what would happen to the level of the oceans?

   A. The level would rise.

   B. The level would fall.

   C. The level would stay the same.

12. A rigid metal object is dropped into a lake and sinks to the bottom. The density of the water in this lake is the same every-

where. As the object sinks deeper and deeper below the surface, the buoyant force on it

   A. gets greater and greater.

   B. gets less and less.

   C. does not change.

   D. is equal to the weight of this object.

13. A spherical object has a density ρ. If it is compressed under high pressure to half of its original diameter, its density will now be

   A. $\rho/8$.   B. $\rho/4$.   C. 2ρ.

   D. 4ρ.   E. 8ρ.

14. When placed in water of density 1 g/cm³, an object floats with one-third of its volume above the surface of the water. When placed in oil, this object also floats, but with none of its volume above the surface. The density of the oil is

   A. $\frac{1}{3}$ g/cm³.   B. $\frac{2}{3}$ g/cm³.   C. $\frac{3}{2}$ g/cm³.

15. A solid uniform metal sphere of radius *R* has a density of 8.0 g/cm³. If you carefully scrape away the outer part so that the radius of the resulting sphere is now *R*/2, its density will be

   A. 8.0 g/cm³.   B. 4.0 g/cm³.

   C. 2.0 g/cm³.   D. 1.0 g/cm³.

Problems

13.1 Density

1. • You purchase a rectangular piece of metal that has dimensions 5.0 mm × 15.0 mm × 30.0 mm and mass 0.0158 kg. The seller tells you that the metal is gold. To check this, you compute the average density of the piece. What value do you get? Were you cheated?

2. • A kidnapper demands a 40.0 kg cube of platinum as a ransom. What is the length of a side?

3. • On a part-time job, you are asked to bring a cylindrical iron rod of length 85.8 cm and diameter 2.85 cm from a storage room to a machinist. Will you need a cart? (To answer, calculate the weight of the rod.)

4. • By how many newtons do you increase the weight of your car when you fill up your 11.5 gal gas tank with gasoline? A gallon is equal to 3.788 L and the density of gasoline is 737 kg/m³.

5. •• **How big is a million dollars?** At the time this problem was written, the price of gold was $426.60 per ounce, while that of platinum was $879.00 an ounce. The "ounce" in this case is the *troy ounce,* which is equal to 31.1035 g. (The more familiar *avoirdupois ounce* is equal to 28.35 g.) The density of gold is 19.3 g/cm³ and that of platinum is 21.4 g/cm³. (a) If you find a spherical gold nugget worth 1.00 million dollars, what would be its *diameter?* (b) How much would a platinum nugget of this size be worth?

6. •• A cube 5.0 cm on each side is made of a metal alloy. After you drill a cylindrical hole 2.0 cm in diameter all the way through and perpendicular to one face, you find that the cube weighs 7.50 N. (a) What is the density of this metal? (b) What did the cube weigh before you drilled the hole in it?

7. •• A cube of compressible material (such as Styrofoam™ or balsa wood) has a density ρ and sides of length *L*. (a) If you keep its mass the same, but compress each side to half its length, what will be its new density, in terms of ρ? (b) If you keep the mass and shape the same, what would the length of each side have to be (in terms of *L*) so that the density of the cube was three times its original value?

35. •• A hollow plastic sphere is held below the surface of a fresh-water lake by a cord anchored to the bottom of the lake. The sphere has a volume of 0.650 m³ and the tension in the cord is 900 N. (a) Calculate the buoyant force exerted by the water on the sphere. (b) What is the mass of the sphere? (c) The cord breaks and the sphere rises to the surface. When the sphere comes to rest, what fraction of its volume will be submerged?

36. •• You construct an ocean-going barge out of 250,000 kg of iron. The shape of your barge is a rectangular bottom measuring 18.0 m × 15.0 m and having vertical sides. (a) What is the minimum height the sides must be so that your barge will float in the ocean? (b) Suppose you make the sides 75% higher than the minimum necessary. What is the mass of the heaviest load you could carry in the ocean without sinking? (c) If your barge goes up the Mississippi River, which is fresh water, how much *extra* mass can you carry without sinking?

37. •• **The tip of the iceberg.** Icebergs consist of freshwater ice and float in the ocean with only about 10% of their volume above water (the "tip of the iceberg," so to speak). This percentage can vary, depending on the condition of the ice. Assume that the ice has the density given in Table 13.1, although, in reality, this can vary considerably, depending on the condition of the ice and the amount of impurities in it. (a) What does this 10% observation tell us is the density of seawater? (b) What percentage of the icebergs' volume would be above water if they were floating in a large freshwater lake such as Lake Superior?

*13.4 Surface Tension and Capillarity

38. • At 20° C, the surface tension of water is 72.8 dynes/cm. Find the excess pressure inside of (a) an ordinary-size water drop of radius 1.50 mm and (b) a fog droplet of radius 0.0100 mm.

39. • Find the gauge pressure in pascals inside a soap bubble 7.00 cm in diameter. The surface tension of this soap is 25.0 dynes/cm.

40. • What radius must a water drop have for the difference between the inside and outside pressures to be 0.0200 atm? The surface tension of water is 72.8 dynes/cm.

41. •• At 20° C, the surface tension of water is 72.8 dynes/cm and that of carbon tetrachloride (CCl_4) is 26.8 dynes/cm. If the gauge pressure is the same in two drops of these liquids, what is the ratio of the *volume* of the water drop to that of the CCl_4 drop?

13.5 Fluid Flow

42. • At a point where an irrigation canal having a rectangular cross section is 18.5 m wide and 3.75 m deep, the water flows at 2.50 cm/s. At a point downstream, but on the same level, the canal is 16.5 m wide, but the water flows at 11.0 cm/s. How deep is the canal at this point?

43. • Water is flowing in a pipe with a varying cross-sectional area, and at all points the water completely fills the pipe. At point 1, the cross-sectional area of the pipe is 0.070 m² and the magnitude of the fluid velocity is 3.50 m/s. What is the fluid speed at points in the pipe where the cross-sectional area is (a) 0.105 m², (b) 0.047 m²?

44. • Water is flowing in a cylindrical pipe of varying circular cross-sectional area, and at all points the water completely fills the pipe. (a) At one point in the pipe, the radius is 0.150 m. What is the speed of the water at this point if the volume flow rate in the pipe is 1.20 m³/s? (b) At a second point in the pipe, the water speed is 3.80 m/s. What is the radius of the pipe at this point?

45. • **Home repair.** You need to extend a 2.50-inch-diameter pipe, but you have only a 1.00-inch-diameter pipe on hand. You make a fitting to connect these pipes end to end. If the water is flowing at 6.00 cm/s in the wide pipe, how fast will it be flowing through the narrow one?

46. •• A fluid is flowing through a rubber hose. (a) If you squeeze the hose in one place to half its original diameter, what happens to the speed of the fluid at that place? (b) What would you have to do to the hose's cross-sectional area to make the fluid's speed five times slower than at the rest of the hose? (c) What would you have to do to the diameter of the hose to make the fluid's speed five times faster than at the rest of the hose?

13.6 Bernoulli's Equation
13.7 Applications of Bernoulli's Equation

47. • A small circular hole 6.00 mm in diameter is cut in the side of a large water tank, 14.0 m below the water level in the tank. The top of the tank is open to the air. Find the speed at which the water shoots out of the tank.

48. • A sealed tank containing seawater to a height of 11.0 m also contains air above the water at a gauge pressure of 3.00 atm. Water flows out from the bottom through a small hole. Calculate the speed with which the water comes out of the tank.

49. • What gauge pressure is required in the city water mains for a stream from a fire hose connected to the mains to reach a vertical height of 15.0 m? (Assume that the mains have a much larger diameter than that of the fire hose.)

50. • At one point in a pipeline, the water's speed is 3.00 m/s and the gauge pressure is 4.00×10^4 Pa. Find the gauge pressure at a second point in the line 11.0 m lower than the first if the pipe diameter at the second point is twice that at the first.

51. •• **Lift on an airplane.** Air streams horizontally past a small airplane's wings such that the speed is 70.0 m/s over the top surface and 60.0 m/s past the bottom surface. If the plane has a mass of 1340 kg and a wing area of 16.2 m², what is the net vertical force (including the effects of gravity) on the airplane? The density of the air is 1.20 kg/m³.

52. •• **Old pipes!** You have bought an old house to restore, and you find that a portion of one of the horizontal water pipes is corroded inside, blocking 40% of the area. The water coming into this region is moving at 8.5 cm/s just before the blocked segment of pipe. (a) What is the speed of the water as it goes through the partially blocked segment? (b) By how many pascals does the pressure in the blocked segment decrease compared with the pressure in the normal pipe?

53. •• Water discharges from a horizontal cylindrical pipe at the rate of 465 cm³/s. At a point in the pipe where the radius is 2.05 cm, the absolute pressure is 1.60×10^5 Pa. What is the pipe's radius at a constriction if the pressure there is reduced to 1.20×10^5 Pa?

54. •• **Artery blockage.** A medical technician is trying to determine what percentage of a patient's artery is blocked by plaque. To do this, she measures the blood pressure just before the region of blockage and finds that it is 1.20×10^4 Pa, while in the region of blockage it is 1.15×10^4 Pa. Furthermore, she knows that blood flowing through the normal artery just before the point of blockage is traveling at 30.0 cm/s, and the specific gravity of this

of its volume is above water, the downward force needed to do this is

   A. W.   B. $2W$.   C. $W/2$.   D. $W/3$.

3. A mass of sunken lead is resting against the bottom in a glass of water. You take this lead, put it in a small boat of negligible mass, and float the boat in the water. Which of the following statements are true? (There may be more than one correct choice.)

   A. The sunken lead displaces a volume of water equal to the lead's own volume.

   B. The floating lead displaces a volume of water equal to the lead's own volume.

   C. The sunken lead displaces a volume of water whose weight equals the lead's weight.

   D. The floating lead displaces a volume of water whose weight equals the lead's weight.

4. Two equal-sized buckets are filled to the brim with water, but one of them has a piece of wood floating in it. Which bucket of water weighs more?

   A. The bucket with the wood.

   B. The bucket without the wood.

   C. They weigh the same amount.

5. Two equal *mass* pieces of metal are sitting side by side at the bottom of a deep lake. One piece is aluminum and the other is lead. Which piece has the greater buoyant force acting on it?

   A. The aluminum.

   B. The lead.

   C. They both have the same buoyant force acting on them.

6. If a 5 lb force is required to keep a block of wood 1 ft beneath the surface of water, the force needed to keep it 2 ft beneath the surface is

   A. 2.5 lb.   B. 5 lb.   C. 10 lb.

7. A horizontal pipe with water flowing through it has a circular cross section that varies in diameter. The diameter at the wide section is 3 times that of the diameter at the narrow section. If the rate of flow of the water in the narrow section is 9.0 L/min, the rate of flow of the water in the wide section is

   A. 1.0 L/min.   B. 3.0 L/min.   C. 9.0 L/min.

   D. 18 L/min.   E. 36 L/min.

8. A horizontal cylindrical pipe has a part with a diameter half that of the rest of the pipe. If V is the speed of the fluid in the wider section of pipe, then the speed of the fluid in the narrower section is

   A. $V/4$.   B. $V/2$.   C. $2V$.   D. $4V$.

9. If the *absolute* pressure at a depth d in a lake is P, the absolute pressure at a depth $2d$ will be

   A. $2P$.   B. P.

   C. Greater than $2P$.   D. Less than $2P$.

10. If the *gauge* pressure at a depth d in a lake is P, the gauge pressure at a depth $2d$ will be

   A. $2P$.   B. P.

   C. Greater than $2P$.   D. Less than $2P$.

11. There is a great deal of ice floating on the oceans near the North Pole. If this ice were to melt due to global warming, what would happen to the level of the oceans?

   A. The level would rise.

   B. The level would fall.

   C. The level would stay the same.

12. A rigid metal object is dropped into a lake and sinks to the bottom. The density of the water in this lake is the same every-where. As the object sinks deeper and deeper below the surface, the buoyant force on it

   A. gets greater and greater.

   B. gets less and less.

   C. does not change.

   D. is equal to the weight of this object.

13. A spherical object has a density ρ. If it is compressed under high pressure to half of its original diameter, its density will now be

   A. $\rho/8$.   B. $\rho/4$.   C. 2ρ.

   D. 4ρ.   E. 8ρ.

14. When placed in water of density 1 g/cm^3, an object floats with one-third of its volume above the surface of the water. When placed in oil, this object also floats, but with none of its volume above the surface. The density of the oil is

   A. $\frac{1}{3}$ g/cm^3.   B. $\frac{2}{3}$ g/cm^3.   C. $\frac{3}{2}$ g/cm^3.

15. A solid uniform metal sphere of radius R has a density of 8.0 g/cm^3. If you carefully scrape away the outer part so that the radius of the resulting sphere is now $R/2$, its density will be

   A. 8.0 g/cm^3.   B. 4.0 g/cm^3.

   C. 2.0 g/cm^3.   D. 1.0 g/cm^3.

Problems

13.1 Density

1. ● You purchase a rectangular piece of metal that has dimensions 5.0 mm × 15.0 mm × 30.0 mm and mass 0.0158 kg. The seller tells you that the metal is gold. To check this, you compute the average density of the piece. What value do you get? Were you cheated?

2. ● A kidnapper demands a 40.0 kg cube of platinum as a ransom. What is the length of a side?

3. ● On a part-time job, you are asked to bring a cylindrical iron rod of length 85.8 cm and diameter 2.85 cm from a storage room to a machinist. Will you need a cart? (To answer, calculate the weight of the rod.)

4. ● By how many newtons do you increase the weight of your car when you fill up your 11.5 gal gas tank with gasoline? A gallon is equal to 3.788 L and the density of gasoline is 737 kg/m^3.

5. ●● **How big is a million dollars?** At the time this problem was written, the price of gold was \$426.60 per ounce, while that of platinum was \$879.00 an ounce. The "ounce" in this case is the *troy ounce*, which is equal to 31.1035 g. (The more familiar *avoirdupois ounce* is equal to 28.35 g.) The density of gold is 19.3 g/cm^3 and that of platinum is 21.4 g/cm^3. (a) If you find a spherical gold nugget worth 1.00 million dollars, what would be its *diameter?* (b) How much would a platinum nugget of this size be worth?

6. ●● A cube 5.0 cm on each side is made of a metal alloy. After you drill a cylindrical hole 2.0 cm in diameter all the way through and perpendicular to one face, you find that the cube weighs 7.50 N. (a) What is the density of this metal? (b) What did the cube weigh before you drilled the hole in it?

7. ●● A cube of compressible material (such as Styrofoam™ or balsa wood) has a density ρ and sides of length L. (a) If you keep its mass the same, but compress each side to half its length, what will be its new density, in terms of ρ? (b) If you keep the mass and shape the same, what would the length of each side have to be (in terms of L) so that the density of the cube was three times its original value?

8. •• **Density of mixtures.** Use Table 13.1 to find the density of each of the following mixtures, assuming that the liquids retain their original volumes (i.e., one does not dissolve in the other): (a) You mix 200 cm³ of glycerin with 300 cm³ of water. (b) You mix 200 g of glycerin with 300 g of water.

9. •• **Density of mixtures.** Suppose you mix two liquids having densities ρ_1 and ρ_2 and they retain their original volumes (i.e., one does not dissolve in the other). (a) If the liquids you mix have equal mass, will the density of the mixture be equal to the average of the densities? If so, prove it; if not, what will it be? (b) If the liquids you mix have equal volume, will the density of the mixture be equal to the average of the densities? If so, prove it; if not, what will it be?

13.2 Pressure in a Fluid

10. • **Blood pressure.** Systemic blood pressure is defined as the ratio of two pressures, both expressed in millimeters of mercury. Normal blood pressure is about $\frac{120 \text{ mm}}{80 \text{ mm}}$, which is usually just stated as $\frac{120}{80}$. (See also Problem 24.) What would normal systemic blood pressure be if, instead of millimeters of mercury, we expressed pressure in each of the following units, but continued to use the same ratio format? (a) atmospheres, (b) torr, (c) Pa, (d) N/m², (e) psi.

11. • **Blood.** (a) **Mass of blood.** The human body typically contains 5 L of blood of density 1060 kg/m³. How many kilograms of blood are in the body? (b) The average blood pressure is 13,000 Pa at the heart. What average force does the blood exert on each square centimeter of the heart? (c) **Red blood cells.** Red blood cells have a specific gravity of 5.0 and a diameter of about 7.5 μm. If they are spherical in shape (which is not quite true), what is the mass of such a cell?

12. • **Landing on Venus.** One of the great difficulties in landing on Venus is dealing with the crushing pressure of the atmosphere, which is 92 times the earth's atmospheric pressure. (a) If you are designing a lander for Venus in the shape of a hemisphere 2.5 m in diameter, how many newtons of inward force must it be prepared to withstand due to the Venusian atmosphere? (Don't forget about the bottom!) (b) How much force would the lander have to withstand on the earth?

13. • You are designing a diving bell to withstand the pressure of seawater at a depth of 250 m. (a) What is the gauge pressure at this depth? (You can ignore the small changes in the density of the water with depth.) (b) At the 250 m depth, what is the net force due to the water outside and the air inside the bell on a circular glass window 30.0 cm in diameter if the pressure inside the diving bell equals the pressure at the surface of the water? (You may ignore the small variation in pressure over the surface of the window.)

14. • **Glaucoma.** Under normal circumstances, the vitreous humor, a jelly-like substance in the main part of the eye, exerts a pressure of up to 24 mm of mercury that maintains the shape of the eye. If blockage of the drainage duct for aqueous humor causes this pressure to increase to about 50 mm of mercury, the condition is called *glaucoma*. What is the *increase* in the total force (in newtons) on the walls of the eye if the pressure increases from 24 mm to 50 mm of mercury? We can quite accurately model the eye as a sphere 2.5 cm in diameter.

15. • **Origin of life?** Deep in the oceans, hot thermal vents release dark smoke into the water and are therefore called *black smokers*. These vents range in depth from about 1.5 km to 3.2 km. Some biologists propose that life may have originated around such vents around 4 billion years ago, drawing its energy from the heat of the vents. What range of gauge pressures would organisms have had to withstand at the depths of these vents? (In fact, black smokers still teem with life even today.)

16. • What gauge pressure must a pump produce to pump water from the bottom of the Grand Canyon (elevation 730 m) to Indian Gardens (elevation 1370 m)? Express your result in pascals and in atmospheres.

17. • **Intravenous feeding.** A hospital patient is being fed intravenously with a liquid of density 1060 kg/m³. (See Figure 13.40.) The container of liquid is raised 1.20 m above the patient's arm where the fluid enters his veins. What is the pressure this fluid exerts on his veins, expressed in millimeters of mercury?

1.20 m

▲ **FIGURE 13.40** Problem 17.

18. • **Oceans on Mars.** Findings during 2004 from the Mars rover *Opportunity* at the Meridiani Planum landing site revealed that Mars once may have had an ocean 0.50 km deep. The acceleration due to gravity on Mars is 0.379g, and we shall assume (unrealistically) the oceans consisted of fresh water. (a) What would have been the gauge pressure (in Pa) at the bottom of this Martian ocean? (b) What is the gauge pressure (in Pa) at the same depth in the earth's saltwater oceans?

19. •• (a) How high a column of water will a pressure of 1.0 torr support? (b) If a "mercury barometer" has water substituted for the mercury, how high would the column of water be at 1.0 atm of pressure? Do you now see why it is much more convenient to use mercury instead of water in a barometer?

20. • **Standing on your head.** (a) When you stand on your head, what is the *difference* in pressure of the blood in your brain compared with the pressure when you stand on your feet if you are 1.85 m tall? The density of blood is 1060 kg/m³. (b) What effect does the increased pressure have on the blood vessels in your brain?

21. •• You are designing a machine for a space exploration vehicle. It contains an enclosed column of oil that is 1.50 m tall, and you need the pressure difference between the top and the bottom of this column to be 0.125 atm. (a) What must be the density of the oil? (b) If the vehicle is taken to Mars, where the acceleration due to gravity is 0.379g, what will be the pressure difference (in earth atmospheres) between the top and bottom of the oil column?

22. •• **Ear damage from diving.** If the force on the tympanic membrane (eardrum) increases by about 1.5 N above the force from atmospheric pressure, the membrane can be damaged. When you go scuba diving in the ocean, below what depth could damage to your eardrum start to occur? The eardrum is typically 8.2 mm in diameter. (Consult Table 13.1.)

23. •• A barrel contains a 0.120 m layer of oil of density 600 kg/m³ floating on water that is 0.250 m deep. (a) What is the gauge pressure at the oil–water interface? (b) What is the gauge pressure at the bottom of the barrel?

24. •• **Blood pressure.** Systemic blood pressure is expressed as the ratio of the *systolic* pressure (when the heart first ejects

blood into the arteries) to the *diastolic* pressure (when the heart is relaxed):

$$\text{systemic blood pressure} = \frac{\text{systolic pressure}}{\text{diastolic pressure}}$$

Both pressures are measured at the level of the heart and are expressed in millimeters of mercury (or torr), although the units are not written. Normal systemic blood pressure is $\frac{120}{80}$. (a) What are the maximum and minimum forces (in newtons) that the blood exerts against each square centimeter of the heart for a person with normal blood pressure? (b) As pointed out in the text, blood pressure is normally measured on the upper arm at the same height as the heart. Due to therapy for an injury, a patient's upper arm is extended 30.0 cm above his heart. In that position, what should be his systemic blood pressure reading, expressed in the standard way, if he has normal blood pressure? The density of blood is 1060 kg/m^3.

25. •• **Blood pressure on the moon.** When we eventually establish lunar colonies, people living there will need to have their blood pressure taken. Assume that we continue to express the systemic blood pressure as we now do on earth (see previous problem) and that the density of blood does not change. Suppose also that normal blood pressure on the moon is still $\frac{120}{80}$ (which may not actually be true). If a lunar colonizer has her blood pressure taken at her upper arm when it is raised 25 cm above her heart, what will be her systemic blood pressure reading, expressed in the standard way, if she has normal blood pressure? The acceleration due to gravity on the moon is 1.67 m/s^2.

26. • The piston of a hydraulic automobile lift is 0.30 m in diameter. What gauge pressure, in pascals, is required to lift a car with a mass of 1200 kg? Now express this pressure in atmospheres.

27. •• **Hydraulic lift.** You are designing a hydraulic lift for an automobile garage. It will consist of two oil-filled cylindrical pipes of different diameters. A worker pushes down on a piston at one end, raising the car on a platform at the other end. (See Figure 13.41.) To handle a full range of jobs, you must be able to lift cars up to 3000 kg, plus the 500 kg platform on which they are parked. To avoid injury to your workers, the maximum amount of force a worker should need to exert is 100 N. (a) What should be the diameter of the pipe under the platform? (b) If the worker pushes down with a stroke 50 cm long, by how much will he raise the car at the other end?

▲ **FIGURE 13.41** Problem 27.

28. •• A narrow U-shaped glass tube with open ends is filled with 25.0 cm of oil (of specific gravity 0.80) and 25.0 cm of water on opposite sides, with a barrier separating the liquids. (See Figure 13.42.) (a) Assume that the two liquids do not mix, and find the final height of the columns of liquid in each side of the tube after the barrier is removed. (b) For the following cases, arrive at your answer by simple physical reasoning, not by calculations: (i) What would be the height on each side if the oil and water had equal densities? (ii) What would the heights be if the oil's density were much less than that of water?

▲ **FIGURE 13.42** Problem 28.

13.3 Archimedes's Principle: Buoyancy

29. • A solid aluminum ingot weighs 89 N in air. (a) What is its volume? (See Table 13.1.) (b) The ingot is suspended from a rope and totally immersed in water. What is the tension in the rope (the *apparent* weight of the ingot in water)?

30. •• **Fish navigation.** (a) As you can tell by watching them in an aquarium, fish are able to remain at any depth in water with no effort. What does this ability tell you about their density? (b) Fish are able to inflate themselves using a sac (called the *swim bladder*) located under their spinal column. These sacs can be filled with an oxygen–nitrogen mixture that comes from the blood. If a 2.75 kg fish in fresh water inflates itself and increases its volume by 10%, find the *net* force that the *water* exerts on it. (c) What is the net *external* force on it? Does the fish go up or down when it inflates itself?

31. •• When an open-faced boat has a mass of 5750 kg, including its cargo and passengers, it floats with the water just up to the top of its gunwales (sides) on a freshwater lake. (a) What is the volume of this boat? (b) The captain decides that it is too dangerous to float with his boat on the verge of sinking, so he decides to throw some cargo overboard so that 20% of the boat's volume will be above water. How much mass should he throw out?

32. •• An ore sample weighs 17.50 N in air. When the sample is suspended by a light cord and totally immersed in water, the tension in the cord is 11.20 N. Find the total volume and the density of the sample.

33. •• A slab of ice floats on a freshwater lake. What minimum volume must the slab have for a 45.0 kg woman to be able to stand on it without getting her feet wet?

34. •• A cubical block of wood 10.0 cm on a side floats at the interface between oil and water with its lower surface 1.50 cm below the interface. (See Figure 13.43.) The density of the oil is 790 kg/m^3. (a) What is the gauge pressure at the upper face of the block? (b) What is the gauge pressure at the lower face of the block? (c) What are the mass and density of the block?

▲ **FIGURE 13.43** Problem 34.

35. •• A hollow plastic sphere is held below the surface of a fresh-water lake by a cord anchored to the bottom of the lake. The sphere has a volume of 0.650 m³ and the tension in the cord is 900 N. (a) Calculate the buoyant force exerted by the water on the sphere. (b) What is the mass of the sphere? (c) The cord breaks and the sphere rises to the surface. When the sphere comes to rest, what fraction of its volume will be submerged?

36. •• You construct an ocean-going barge out of 250,000 kg of iron. The shape of your barge is a rectangular bottom measuring 18.0 m × 15.0 m and having vertical sides. (a) What is the minimum height the sides must be so that your barge will float in the ocean? (b) Suppose you make the sides 75% higher than the minimum necessary. What is the mass of the heaviest load you could carry in the ocean without sinking? (c) If your barge goes up the Mississippi River, which is fresh water, how much *extra* mass can you carry without sinking?

37. •• **The tip of the iceberg.** Icebergs consist of freshwater ice and float in the ocean with only about 10% of their volume above water (the "tip of the iceberg," so to speak). This percentage can vary, depending on the condition of the ice. Assume that the ice has the density given in Table 13.1, although, in reality, this can vary considerably, depending on the condition of the ice and the amount of impurities in it. (a) What does this 10% observation tell us is the density of seawater? (b) What percentage of the icebergs' volume would be above water if they were floating in a large freshwater lake such as Lake Superior?

*13.4 Surface Tension and Capillarity

38. • At 20° C, the surface tension of water is 72.8 dynes/cm. Find the excess pressure inside of (a) an ordinary-size water drop of radius 1.50 mm and (b) a fog droplet of radius 0.0100 mm.

39. • Find the gauge pressure in pascals inside a soap bubble 7.00 cm in diameter. The surface tension of this soap is 25.0 dynes/cm.

40. • What radius must a water drop have for the difference between the inside and outside pressures to be 0.0200 atm? The surface tension of water is 72.8 dynes/cm.

41. •• At 20° C, the surface tension of water is 72.8 dynes/cm and that of carbon tetrachloride (CCl_4) is 26.8 dynes/cm. If the gauge pressure is the same in two drops of these liquids, what is the ratio of the *volume* of the water drop to that of the CCl_4 drop?

13.5 Fluid Flow

42. • At a point where an irrigation canal having a rectangular cross section is 18.5 m wide and 3.75 m deep, the water flows at 2.50 cm/s. At a point downstream, but on the same level, the canal is 16.5 m wide, but the water flows at 11.0 cm/s. How deep is the canal at this point?

43. • Water is flowing in a pipe with a varying cross-sectional area, and at all points the water completely fills the pipe. At point 1, the cross-sectional area of the pipe is 0.070 m² and the magnitude of the fluid velocity is 3.50 m/s. What is the fluid speed at points in the pipe where the cross-sectional area is (a) 0.105 m², (b) 0.047 m²?

44. • Water is flowing in a cylindrical pipe of varying circular cross-sectional area, and at all points the water completely fills the pipe. (a) At one point in the pipe, the radius is 0.150 m. What is the speed of the water at this point if the volume flow rate in the pipe is 1.20 m³/s? (b) At a second point in the pipe, the water speed is 3.80 m/s. What is the radius of the pipe at this point?

45. • **Home repair.** You need to extend a 2.50-inch-diameter pipe, but you have only a 1.00-inch-diameter pipe on hand. You make a fitting to connect these pipes end to end. If the water is flowing at 6.00 cm/s in the wide pipe, how fast will it be flowing through the narrow one?

46. •• A fluid is flowing through a rubber hose. (a) If you squeeze the hose in one place to half its original diameter, what happens to the speed of the fluid at that place? (b) What would you have to do to the hose's cross-sectional area to make the fluid's speed five times slower than at the rest of the hose? (c) What would you have to do to the diameter of the hose to make the fluid's speed five times faster than at the rest of the hose?

13.6 Bernoulli's Equation
13.7 Applications of Bernoulli's Equation

47. • A small circular hole 6.00 mm in diameter is cut in the side of a large water tank, 14.0 m below the water level in the tank. The top of the tank is open to the air. Find the speed at which the water shoots out of the tank.

48. • A sealed tank containing seawater to a height of 11.0 m also contains air above the water at a gauge pressure of 3.00 atm. Water flows out from the bottom through a small hole. Calculate the speed with which the water comes out of the tank.

49. • What gauge pressure is required in the city water mains for a stream from a fire hose connected to the mains to reach a vertical height of 15.0 m? (Assume that the mains have a much larger diameter than that of the fire hose.)

50. • At one point in a pipeline, the water's speed is 3.00 m/s and the gauge pressure is 4.00×10^4 Pa. Find the gauge pressure at a second point in the line 11.0 m lower than the first if the pipe diameter at the second point is twice that at the first.

51. •• **Lift on an airplane.** Air streams horizontally past a small airplane's wings such that the speed is 70.0 m/s over the top surface and 60.0 m/s past the bottom surface. If the plane has a mass of 1340 kg and a wing area of 16.2 m², what is the net vertical force (including the effects of gravity) on the airplane? The density of the air is 1.20 kg/m³.

52. •• **Old pipes!** You have bought an old house to restore, and you find that a portion of one of the horizontal water pipes is corroded inside, blocking 40% of the area. The water coming into this region is moving at 8.5 cm/s just before the blocked segment of pipe. (a) What is the speed of the water as it goes through the partially blocked segment? (b) By how many pascals does the pressure in the blocked segment decrease compared with the pressure in the normal pipe?

53. •• Water discharges from a horizontal cylindrical pipe at the rate of 465 cm³/s. At a point in the pipe where the radius is 2.05 cm, the absolute pressure is 1.60×10^5 Pa. What is the pipe's radius at a constriction if the pressure there is reduced to 1.20×10^5 Pa?

54. •• **Artery blockage.** A medical technician is trying to determine what percentage of a patient's artery is blocked by plaque. To do this, she measures the blood pressure just before the region of blockage and finds that it is 1.20×10^4 Pa, while in the region of blockage it is 1.15×10^4 Pa. Furthermore, she knows that blood flowing through the normal artery just before the point of blockage is traveling at 30.0 cm/s, and the specific gravity of this

patient's blood is 1.06. What percentage of the cross-sectional area of the patient's artery is blocked by the plaque?

55. •• At a certain point in a horizontal pipeline, the water's speed is 2.50 m/s and the gauge pressure is 1.80×10^4 Pa. Find the gauge pressure at a second point in the line if the cross-sectional area at the second point is twice that at the first.

*13.8 Real Fluids: Viscosity and Turbulence

56. • With what terminal speed would a steel ball bearing 2.00 mm in diameter fall in a liquid of viscosity $0.150 \ N \cdot s/m^2$ if we could neglect buoyancy?

57. •• What speed must a gold sphere of radius 3.00 mm have in castor oil for the viscous drag force to be one-fourth of the weight of the sphere? The density of gold is 19,300 kg/m^3 and the viscosity of the oil is $0.986 \ N \cdot s/m^2$.

58. •• A copper sphere with a mass of 0.20 g and a density of 8900 kg/m^3 is observed to fall with a terminal speed of 6.0 cm/s in an unknown liquid. Find the viscosity of the unknown liquid if its buoyancy can be neglected.

59. •• **Clogged artery.** Viscous blood is flowing through an BIO artery partially clogged by cholesterol. A surgeon wants to remove enough of the cholesterol to double the flow rate of blood through this artery. If the original diameter of the artery is D, what should be the new diameter (in terms of D) to accomplish this for the same pressure gradient?

General Problems

60. •• The deepest point known in any of the earth's oceans is in the Marianas Trench; it is 10.92 km deep. (a) Assuming water to be incompressible, what is the pressure at this depth? Use the density of seawater. (b) The actual pressure is 1.16×10^8 Pa; your calculated value will be less because the density actually varies with depth. Using the bulk modulus of water and the actual pressure, find the density of the water at the bottom of the Marianas Trench.

61. •• A U-shaped tube open to the air at both ends contains some mercury. A quantity of water is carefully poured into the left arm of the U-shaped tube until the vertical height of the water column is 15.0 cm (Figure 13.44). (a) What is the gauge pressure at the water–mercury interface? (b) Calculate the vertical distance h from the top of the mercury in the right-hand arm of the tube to the top of the water in the left-hand arm.

▲ **FIGURE 13.44** Problem 61.

62. •• An open barge has the dimensions shown in Figure 13.45. If the barge is made out of 4.0-cm-thick steel plate on each of its four sides and its bottom, what mass of coal can the barge carry in fresh water without sinking? Is there enough room in the barge to hold this amount of coal? (The density of coal is about 1500 kg/m^3.)

▲ **FIGURE 13.45** Problem 62.

63. •• A piece of wood is 0.600 m long, 0.250 m wide, and 0.080 m thick. Its density is 600 kg/m^3. What volume of lead must be fastened underneath it to sink the wood in calm water so that its top is just even with the water level? What is the mass of this volume of lead?

64. •• The densities of air, helium, and hydrogen (at $p = 1.0$ atm and $T = 20°$ C) are 1.20 kg/m^3, 0.166 kg/m^3, and 0.0838 kg/m^3, respectively. (a) What is the volume, in cubic meters, displaced by a hydrogen-filled airship that has a total lift of 120 kN? (The *lift* is the amount by which the buoyant force exceeds the weight of the gas that fills the airship.) b) What would be the lift if helium were used instead of hydrogen? In view of your answer, why is helium used in modern airships such as advertising blimps?

65. •• In seawater, a life preserver with a volume of 0.0400 m^3 will support a 75.0 kg person (average density 980 kg/m^3), with 20% of the person's volume above water when the life preserver is fully submerged. What is the density of the material composing the life preserver?

66. •• Block A in Figure 13.46 hangs by a cord from spring balance D and is submerged in a liquid C contained in beaker B. The mass of the beaker is 1.00 kg; the mass of the liquid is 1.80 kg. Balance D reads 3.50 kg and balance E reads 7.50 kg. The volume of block A is 3.80×10^{-3} m^3. (a) What is the density of the liquid? (b) What will each balance read if block A is pulled up out of the liquid?

▲ **FIGURE 13.46** Problem 66.

67. •• A hunk of aluminum is completely covered with a gold shell to form an ingot of weight 45.0 N. When you suspend the ingot from a spring balance and submerge the ingot in water, the balance reads 39.0 N. What is the weight of the gold in the shell?

68. •• A liquid is used to make a mercury-type barometer, as described in Section 13.2. The barometer is intended for spacefaring astronauts. At the surface of the earth, the column of liquid rises to a height of 2185 mm, but on the surface of Planet X, where the acceleration due to gravity is one-fourth of its value on earth, the column rises to only 725 mm. Find (a) the density of the liquid and (b) the atmospheric pressure at the surface of Planet X.

69. •• An open cylindrical tank of acid rests at the edge of a table 1.4 m above the floor of the chemistry lab. If this tank springs a small hole in the side at its base, how far from the foot of the table will the acid hit the floor if the acid in the tank is 75 cm deep?

70. •• **Airplane design.** Modern airplane design calls for a lift, due to the net force of the moving air on the wing, of about 2000 N per square meter of wing area. Assume that air flows past the wing of an aircraft with streamline flow. If the speed of flow past the lower wing surface is 120 m/s, what is the required speed over the upper surface to give a lift of 2000 N/m^2? The density of the air is 1.20 kg/m^3.

71. •• **Exploring Europa's oceans.** Europa, a satellite of Jupiter, appears to have an ocean beneath its icy surface. Proposals have been made to send a robotic submarine to Europa to see if there might be life there. There is no atmosphere on Europa,

and we shall assume that the surface ice is thin enough that we can neglect its weight and that the oceans are fresh water having the same density as on the earth. The mass and diameter of Europa have been measured to be 4.78×10^{22} kg and 3130 km, respectively. (a) If the submarine intends to submerge to a depth of 100 m, what pressure must it be designed to withstand? (b) If you wanted to test this submarine before sending it to Europa, how deep would it have to go in our oceans to experience the same pressure as the pressure at a depth of 100 m on Europa?

72. •• The horizontal pipe shown in Figure 13.47 has a cross-sectional area of 40.0 cm^2 at the wider portions and 10.0 cm^2 at the constriction. Water is flowing in the pipe, and the discharge from the pipe is 6.00×10^{-3} m^3/s (6.00 L/s). Find (a) the flow speeds at the wide and the narrow portions; (b) the pressure difference between these portions; (c) the difference in height between the mercury columns in the U-shaped tube.

40.0 cm^2 10.0 cm^2

▲ **FIGURE 13.47** Problem 72.

73. •• **Venturi meter.** The Venturi meter is a device used to measure the speed of a fluid traveling through a pipe. Two cylinders are inserted in small holes in the pipes, as shown in

▲ **FIGURE 13.48** Problem 73.

Figure 13.48. Since the cross-sectional area is different at the two places, the speed and pressure will be different there also. The difference (h) in the heights of the two columns can easily be measured, as can the cross-sectional areas A_1 and A_2. Notice that points 1 and 2 in the figure are both at the same vertical height. (a) Show that $\Delta p = \rho g h$, where ρ is the density of the fluid and Δp is the pressure difference between points 1 and 2. (b) Apply Bernoulli's equation and the continuity condition to show that the speed at point 1 is given by the equation $v_1 = \sqrt{\dfrac{2gh}{(A_1/A_2)^2 - 1}}$. (c) How would you find the speed at point 2?

74. •• **Compressible fluids.** Throughout this chapter, we have dealt only with incompressible fluids. But under very high pressure, fluids do, in fact, compress. (a) Show that the continuity condition for compressible fluids is $\rho_1 A_1 v_1 = \rho_2 A_2 v_2$, where ρ is the density of the fluid. (b) Show that your result reduces to the familiar result for incompressible fluids.

14 TEMPERATURE AND HEAT

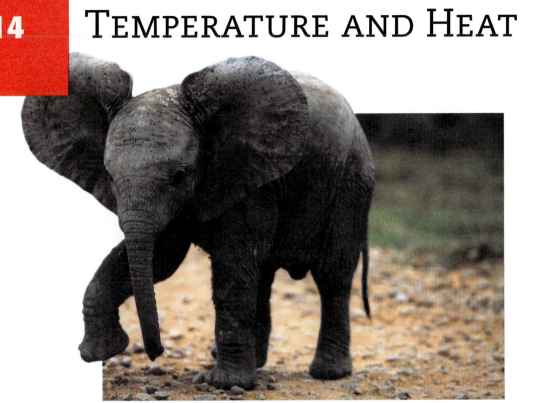

Which season do you like better, summer or winter? Whatever your choice, you use a lot of physics to keep comfortable in changing weather conditions. Your body's core needs to be kept at constant temperature. The body has effective temperature-control mechanisms, but sometimes it needs help. On a hot day, you wear less clothing, to improve heat transfer from your body to the air and to allow better cooling by evaporation of perspiration. You probably drink cold beverages, possibly with ice in them, and sit near a fan or in an air-conditioned room. On a cold day, you wear more clothes or stay indoors where it's warm. When you're outside, you keep active and drink hot liquids to stay warm. The concepts in this chapter will help you understand the basic physics of keeping warm or cool.

First we need to define temperature, including temperature scales and ways to measure temperature. Next we discuss changes in dimensions and in the volumes of materials caused by temperature changes. We'll encounter the concept of *heat,* which describes energy transfer caused by temperature differences, and we'll learn to calculate the *rates* of such energy transfers. This chapter lays the groundwork for our later study of *thermodynamics,* the study of energy transformations and their relationships to the properties of matter. Thermodynamics forms an indispensable part of the foundation of physics, chemistry, and the life sciences, and its applications turn up in such diverse places as car engines, refrigerators, biochemical processes, and the structure of stars.

Large animals have a relatively small ratio of heat-dissipating surface area to heat-producing internal volume, so they often have special systems to help them get rid of unwanted heat. People sweat, dogs pant, and African elephants send blood into their large, thin-skinned, highly vascularized ears.

14.1 Temperature and Thermal Equilibrium

The concept of **temperature** is rooted in qualitative ideas of "hot" and "cold" based on our sense of touch. An object that feels hot usually has a higher temperature than when it feels cold. That's pretty vague, of course, but many properties of matter that we can measure quantitatively depend on temperature. The length

441

of a metal rod increases as the rod becomes hotter. The pressure of gas in a container increases with temperature; a steam boiler may explode if it gets too hot. When a material is extremely hot, it glows "red hot" or "white hot," the color depending on its temperature.

Temperature is also related to the kinetic energies of the molecules of a material. In the next chapter, we'll look at that relationship in detail. It's important to understand, however, that temperature and heat can and must be defined independently of any detailed molecular picture.

Thermometers

Temperature is a measure of "hotness" or "coldness" on some scale. But *what* scale? We can use any measurable property of a system that varies with its hotness or coldness to assign numbers to various states of hotness and coldness. Figure 14.1a shows a familiar type of **thermometer** (a device used to measure temperature). When the system becomes hotter, the liquid (usually mercury or ethanol) expands and rises in the tube, and the value of *L* increases. Another simple system is a quantity of gas in a constant-volume container (Figure 14.1b). The pressure *p*, measured by the gauge, increases or decreases as the gas becomes hotter or colder. A third example is the electrical resistance *R* of a conducting wire, which also varies when the wire becomes hotter or colder. Each of these properties gives us a number (*L*, *p*, or *R*) that varies with hotness and coldness, so each property can be used to make a thermometer.

Thermal Equilibrium

To measure the temperature of an object, you place the thermometer in contact with the object. If you want to know the temperature of a cup of hot coffee, you stick the thermometer in the coffee. As the two interact, the thermometer becomes hotter and the coffee cools off a little. After the thermometer settles down to a steady value, you read the temperature. The system has reached an *equilibrium* condition, in which the interaction between the thermometer and the coffee causes no further change in the temperature of any part of the system. We call this a state of **thermal equilibrium.**

In a state of thermal equilibrium, the thermometer and the coffee have the same temperature. How do we know this? Consider the interaction of any two systems *A* and *B*. System *A* might be a hot potato and *B* a pan of cold water. We may use any kind of thermometer to monitor their temperatures; for example, we could use the tube-and-liquid system (Figure 14.1a) for system *A* and the container of gas and pressure gauge (Figure 14.1b) for system *B*. In general, when the two systems come into contact, the values of *L* and *p* change as the systems move toward thermal equilibrium. Initially, one system is hotter than the other; during the interaction, each system changes the temperature of the other.

If the systems are separated by an insulating material, or **insulator,** such as wood, plastic foam, or fiberglass, they influence each other more slowly. An *ideal* insulator is a material that permits *no* interactions at all between the two systems. It *prevents* the systems from attaining thermal equilibrium if they aren't in thermal equilibrium at the start. This is why camping coolers are made with insulating materials. We don't want the ice and cold food inside to warm up and attain thermal equilibrium with the hot summer air outside; the insulation delays this process, although not forever.

Zeroth Law of Thermodynamics

Now consider three systems *A*, *B*, and *C* that are initially *not* in thermal equilibrium (Figure 14.2). We surround them with an ideal insulating box so that they cannot interact with anything except each other. We separate *A* and *B* with an ideal insulating wall (the green slab in Figure 14.2a), but we let system *C* interact

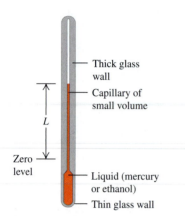

Thick glass wall

Capillary of small volume

L

Zero level

Liquid (mercury or ethanol)

Thin glass wall

(a) Changes in temperature cause the liquid's volume to change.

p

Container of gas at constant volume

(b) Changes in temperature cause the pressure of the gas to change.

▲ **FIGURE 14.1** Two types of thermometer.

with both *A* and *B*. This interaction is shown in the figure by a gold slab representing a thermal **conductor**—a material that *permits* thermal interactions through it. We wait until thermal equilibrium is attained; then *A* and *B* are each in thermal equilibrium with *C*. But are they in thermal equilibrium *with each other?*

To find out, we separate *C* from *A* and *B* with an ideal insulating wall (see Figure 14.2b), and then we replace the insulating wall between *A* and *B* with a *conducting* wall that lets *A* and *B* interact. What happens? Experiment shows that *nothing* happens: The states of *A* and *B* do not change. We thus conclude that if *C* is initially in thermal equilibrium with both *A* and *B*, then *A* and *B* are also in thermal equilibrium with each other. This principle is called the **zeroth law of thermodynamics.** It may seem trivial and obvious, but even so, it needs to be verified by experiment.

(a) If systems *A* and *B* are each in thermal equilibrium with system *C* …

(b) … then systems *A* and *B* are in thermal equilibrium with each other.

▲ **FIGURE 14.2** The zeroth law of thermodynamics.

Zeroth law of thermodynamics
Two systems that are each in thermal equilibrium with a third system are in thermal equilibrium with each other.

The importance of this law was recognized only after the first, second, and third laws of thermodynamics had been named. Since it is fundamental to all of them, the label "zeroth" is appropriate.

The temperature of a system determines whether the system is in thermal equilibrium with another system. **Two systems are in thermal equilibrium if and only if they have the same temperature.** When the temperatures of two systems are different, the systems *cannot* be in thermal equilibrium. A thermometer actually measures *its own* temperature, but when a thermometer is in thermal equilibrium with another object, the temperatures of the two must be equal. A temperature scale, such as the Celsius or Fahrenheit scale, is just a particular scheme for assigning numbers to temperatures.

14.2 Temperature Scales

To make the thermometer in Figure 14.1a useful, we need to give it a scale with numbers on it. These numbers are arbitrary; historically, many different schemes have been used. Suppose we label the thermometer's liquid level when it is at the freezing temperature of pure water "zero" and the level at the boiling temperature "100"; then we divide the distance between these two points into 100 equal intervals called *degrees*. The result is the **Celsius temperature scale** (formerly called the *centigrade scale* in English-speaking countries). We interpolate between these reference temperatures 0°C and 100°C, or extrapolate beyond them, by using the liquid-in-tube thermometer or one of the other thermometers mentioned in Section 14.1. The temperature for a state colder than freezing water is a negative number. The Celsius scale, shown on the left side of Figure 14.3, is used, both in everyday life and in science and industry, everywhere in the world except the United States and a few other English-speaking countries.

The right side of Figure 14.3 shows the **Fahrenheit temperature scale,** still used in everyday life in the United States. The freezing temperature of water is assigned the value 32°F (32 degrees Fahrenheit), and the boiling temperature of water is 212°F, both at normal atmospheric pressure. Thus, there are 180 degrees between freezing and boiling, compared with 100 on the Celsius scale. One Fahrenheit degree represents only $\frac{100}{180}$, or $\frac{5}{9}$ as large a temperature change as one Celsius degree.

To convert temperatures from Celsius to Fahrenheit, we note that a Celsius temperature T_C is the number of Celsius degrees above freezing; to obtain the number of Fahrenheit degrees above freezing, we must multiply T_C by $\frac{9}{5}$. But freezing on the Fahrenheit scale is 32°F, so to obtain the actual Fahrenheit

▲ **FIGURE 14.3** The Celsius and Fahrenheit temperature scales compared.

▲ **Some like it hot.** We usually think of the boiling point of water as being 100°C, but remember that this is true only at normal atmospheric pressure. At higher pressures, water remains liquid at temperatures above 100°C. The photo shows a hydrothermal vent on the ocean floor. The water emerging from such a vent may be as hot as 400°C, but it remains liquid because of the great pressure due to the overlying water. Amazingly, the mineral "chimneys" built by these "smokers" host a rich population of microorganisms that can survive at temperatures higher than 110°C. Indeed, some *grow best* at temperatures above 100°C and find temperatures below 80°C (176°F) too cold for growth.

temperature T_F, we must first multiply the Celsius value by $\frac{9}{5}$ and then add 32°. Symbolically,

$$T_F = \frac{9}{5}T_C + 32°. \tag{14.1}$$

To convert Fahrenheit to Celsius, we first subtract 32° to obtain the number of Fahrenheit degrees above freezing and then multiply by $\frac{5}{9}$ to obtain the number of Celsius degrees above freezing—that is, the Celsius temperature. In symbols,

$$T_C = \frac{5}{9}(T_F - 32°). \tag{14.2}$$

We don't recommend memorizing Equations 14.1 and 14.2. Instead, try to understand the reasoning that led to them well enough that you can derive them on the spot when you need them. Check your reasoning with the relation 100°C = 212°F.

It's useful to distinguish between an actual temperature on a certain scale and a temperature *interval*, representing a *difference*, or change, in temperature. To make this distinction, we state an actual temperature of 20° as 20°C (20 degrees Celsius) and a temperature *interval* of 10° as 10 C° (10 Celsius degrees). Thus, a beaker of water heated from 20°C to 30°C undergoes a temperature change of 10 C°. We'll use this notation consistently throughout this book.

When we calibrate two thermometers, such as a liquid-in-tube system and a gas thermometer, so that they agree at 0°C and 100°C, they may not agree exactly at intermediate temperatures. The expansion properties of a gas may not match exactly the properties of a liquid. Ideally, we'd like to define a temperature scale that doesn't depend on the properties of a particular material. The gas thermometer, which we'll discuss next, comes close. In Chapter 16 we'll learn how to establish a scale that is truly independent of the material used.

The Kelvin Scale

In Section 14.1, we mentioned a thermometer that makes use of the variation in pressure of a gas with changing temperature. The gas, often helium, is placed in a constant-volume container (Figure 14.4a), and its pressure is measured by one of the devices described in Section 13.2. To calibrate a constant-volume gas ther-

(a) A constant-volume gas thermometer

(b) Graphs of pressure versus temperature at constant volume for three gases

▲ **FIGURE 14.4** Use of a constant-volume gas thermometer to find the temperature at which a gas would have zero pressure (if it were still gaseous). This is the zero temperature on the Kelvin scale.

mometer, we measure the pressure at two temperatures, say, 0°C and 100°C, plot these points on a graph, and draw a straight line between them (Figure 14.4b). Then, from the graph, we can read the temperature corresponding to any other pressure.

By extrapolating this graph to lower and lower pressures, we see that there is a hypothetical temperature at which the gas pressure would become zero. We might expect that this temperature would be different for different gases, but it actually turns out to be the same for many different gases (at least in the limit of very low gas concentrations), namely, $-273.15°C$. We'll call this temperature *absolute zero*. We can't actually observe this zero-pressure condition, because gases liquefy and even solidify at very low temperatures; then the proportional relationship between pressure and temperature no longer holds. However, we can use this extrapolated zero-pressure temperature as the basis for a new temperature scale with its zero at that temperature.

This is the **Kelvin temperature scale,** named for Lord Kelvin (1824–1907). The units are the same size as those of the Celsius scale, but the zero is shifted so that the zero point is at absolute zero: $0\text{ K} = -273.15°C$ and $273.15\text{ K} = 0°C$; thus,

$$T_K = T_C + 273.15° \tag{14.3}$$

A common room temperature, $20°C\ (= 68°F)$, is $20 + 273.15$, or about 293 K. In SI nomenclature, "degree" is not used with the Kelvin scale; the room temperature 20°C is read "293 kelvins," not "293 degrees Kelvin." We capitalize Kelvin when it refers to the temperature scale, but the *unit* of temperature is the *kelvin*, not capitalized, but abbreviated K.

Figure 14.5 summarizes the relations among the Celsius, Fahrenheit, and Kelvin scales. The Kelvin scale is called an **absolute temperature scale,** and its zero point is called **absolute zero.** To define more completely what we mean by absolute zero, we need to use thermodynamic principles that we'll develop in Chapter 16.

▲ FIGURE 14.5 Relationships among Kelvin, Celsius, and Fahrenheit temperature scales. Temperatures have been rounded off to the nearest degree.

EXAMPLE 14.1 **Body temperature**

Normal internal body temperature for an average healthy human is 98.6°F. **(a)** Find this temperature in degrees Celsius and in kelvins. **(b)** When a human is relaxing on a couch, the skin temperature is about 2 C° lower than the internal temperature. How much lower is the skin temperature, in Fahrenheit degrees and in kelvins?

SOLUTION

SET UP AND SOLVE Part (a): To convert from Fahrenheit to Celsius temperatures, we first subtract 32° to obtain the number of Fahrenheit degrees above freezing and then multiply by $\frac{5}{9}$ to find the

number of Celsius degrees above freezing (i.e., the Celsius temperature). Thus, in degrees Celsius, normal body temperature is

$$T_C = \tfrac{5}{9}(T_F - 32°) = \tfrac{5}{9}(98.6° - 32°) = 37.0°C.$$

Continued

To find this temperature in kelvins, we add 273.15 K:

$$T_K = T_C + 273.15° = 37.0° + 273.15°$$
$$= 310.1 \text{ K } (= 310.1 \text{ kelvins}).$$

Part (b): To convert the number of Celsius degrees to the number of Fahrenheit degrees in a temperature interval, we multiply by 1 in the form (9 F°/5 C°). But one Celsius degree equals one kelvin, so to find the same interval on the Kelvin scale, we just multiply by 1:

$$2 \text{ Celsius degrees} = 2 \text{ C°} = (9 \text{ F°}/5 \text{ C°})2 \text{ C°} = 3.6 \text{ F°}$$

and

$$2 \text{ C°} = 2 \text{ K}.$$

REFLECT Note again that the degree symbol and the word *degree* are not used for the Kelvin scale. Also, for any calculations of temperature *changes*, the numbers of degrees on the Celsius and Kelvin scales are equal, but the number of degrees on the Fahrenheit scale is $\frac{9}{5}$ as great as either of these.

Practice Problem: On a stormy day in Orlando, Florida, the temperature dropped by 31.5 F°. What is this temperature change in Celsius degrees and in kelvins? *Answer:* $\Delta T = -17.5 \text{ C°} = -17.5 \text{ K}.$

14.3 Thermal Expansion

Most materials expand when their temperatures increase. Bridge decks need special joints and supports to allow for expansion. A completely filled and tightly capped bottle of water cracks when it is heated, but you can loosen a metal jar lid by running hot water on it. These are all examples of *thermal expansion.*

Linear Expansion

Suppose a rod of material has a length L_0 at some initial temperature T_0. When the temperature changes by a small amount ΔT, the length changes by ΔL (Figure 14.6). Experiment shows that if ΔT is not too large (say, less than 100 C° or so), ΔL is *directly proportional* to ΔT. If two rods made of the same material have the same temperature change, but one is twice as long as the other, then the *change* in its length is also twice as great. Therefore, ΔL must also be proportional to L_0. Introducing a proportionality constant α (which is different for different materials), we may express this relation in an equation:

For moderate temperature changes, ΔL is directly proportional to ΔT:

ΔL is also directly proportional to L_0:

▲ **FIGURE 14.6** The dependence of linear thermal expansion on the change in temperature and the initial length.

Thermal expansion
When the temperature of a solid object changes, the change in length, ΔL, is proportional to the change in temperature, ΔT:

$$\Delta L = \alpha L_0 \, \Delta T. \tag{14.4}$$

The proportionality constant α is called the **coefficient of linear expansion.** If an object has length L_0 at temperature T_0, then its length L at a temperature $T = T_0 + \Delta T$ is

$$L = L_0 + \Delta L = L_0(1 + \alpha \, \Delta T). \tag{14.5}$$

Units: The units of α are K^{-1} or $(\text{C°})^{-1}$. (Remember that a temperature *interval* is the same in Celsius and Kelvin.) In the discussion that follows, we'll usually use K^{-1}.

We can think of α as the fractional change in length of an object during a temperature change of 1 C°. For many materials, every linear dimension changes according to Equation 14.4 or 14.5. Thus, L could be the thickness of a rod, the length of the side of a square sheet, or (as we'll see in a minute) the diameter of a hole. Some materials, such as wood or single crystals, expand differently in different directions. We won't consider this complication.

We can understand thermal expansion qualitatively on a molecular basis. Picture the interatomic forces in a solid as springs (Figure 14.7). Each atom vibrates

Average distance between atoms

▲ **FIGURE 14.7** We can envision the forces between neighboring atoms in a solid by imagining the atoms to be connected by springs.

▶ **The heat is on.** While the coefficient of linear expansion of a material may seem like a text-book concept, we depend on it daily. Circuit breakers and mechanical thermostats are based on a *bimetallic strip*—a flat strip made by welding together two thin strips of metal so that one metal forms the top face of the composite strip and the other forms the bottom face. If the two metals have different coefficients of linear expansion α, the bimetallic strip bends when heated because the metal with the higher value of α expands more than the other metal. (If the strip is chilled, it bends in the opposite direction.) In a thermostat or circuit breaker, the bimetallic strip is used as part of an electrical contact. If the temperature gets too high (or too low), the bending of the strip breaks the contact. A thermostat responds to the temperature of the local air; a circuit breaker responds to the heating produced by the electrical current flowing through it. A dangerous current overload trips the breaker.

about its equilibrium position. When the temperature increases, the average distance between molecules also increases. As the atoms get farther apart, every dimension increases.

When you heat an object that has a hole in it, the hole gets bigger. Figure 14.8 shows what happens. If you heat a flat plate of material, its area increases. If you now cut a section from the center of the plate, both the cutout and the remaining plate (with a hole in it) behave as they did previously: The cut-out piece and the hole it came from both get bigger. When you heat an object with a hole in it, the *hole gets bigger*.

The direct proportionality between ΔL and ΔT expressed by Equation 14.4 isn't exact; it's *approximately* correct for sufficiently small temperature changes. For a given material, α varies somewhat with the initial temperature T_0 and the size of the temperature interval. We'll ignore this complication. Average values of α for several materials are listed in Table 14.1. Within the precision of these values, we don't need to worry about whether the initial temperature T_0 is 0°C, 20°C, or some other temperature. We also note that α is usually a very small number; even for a temperature change of 100 C°, the fractional change in length $\Delta L/L_0$ is on the order of $\frac{1}{1000}$. But don't be misled by this small number: The expansion of a 100 m bridge by 0.1 m has to be taken seriously!

COLD

HOT

A plate expands when heated. (Expansion exaggerated!)

A cutout expands as it would have done if still part of the plate—so the *hole must expand, too.*

▲ **FIGURE 14.8** One way to understand why a hole in a solid object expands (rather than shrinks) when the object is heated.

PROBLEM-SOLVING STRATEGY 14.1 **Thermal expansion** (MP)

This strategy also applies to problems involving an expansion in *volume*, which we'll consider later in this section.

SET UP

1. Identify which of the quantities in Equation 14.4 or 14.5 are known and which are unknown. Often, you will be given two temperatures and will have to compute ΔT. Or you may be given an initial temperature T_0 and may have to find a final temperature corresponding to a given change in length or volume. In this case, find ΔT first; then the final temperature is $T_0 + \Delta T$.

SOLVE

2. Consistency of units is crucial, as always. L_0 and ΔL (or V_0 and ΔV) must have the same units, and if you use a value of α in K^{-1}, then ΔT must be in kelvins.

REFLECT

3. Remember that dimensions of holes in a material expand with temperature just the same way as any other linear dimensions do.

TABLE 14.1   Coefficients of linear expansion for selected materials

Material	α (K^{-1} or $C^{\circ-1}$)
Quartz (fused)	0.04×10^{-5}
Invar (nickel–iron alloy)	0.09×10^{-5}
Glass	$0.4{-}0.9 \times 10^{-5}$
Steel	1.2×10^{-5}
Copper	1.7×10^{-5}
Brass	2.0×10^{-5}
Aluminum	2.4×10^{-5}

EXAMPLE 14.2 **Change in length of a measuring tape**

A surveyor uses a steel measuring tape that is exactly 50.000 m long at a temperature of 20°C. What is its length on a hot summer day when the temperature is 35°C?

SOLUTION

SET UP AND SOLVE We have $L_0 = 50.000$ m, $T_0 = 20°C$, and $T = 35°C$. We use Equation 14.4 to find ΔL (Note that because ΔL is usually much smaller than L_0, we need to keep more significant figures in the lengths than in the temperatures.) From Table 14.1, the coefficient of linear expansion for steel is 1.2×10^{-5} K^{-1}. From Equation 14.4,

$$\Delta L = \alpha L_0 \Delta T$$
$$= (1.2 \times 10^{-5} \text{ K}^{-1})(50 \text{ m})(35°C - 20°C)$$
$$= 9.0 \times 10^{-3} \text{ m} = 9.0 \text{ mm.}$$

The new length is

$$L = L_0 + \Delta L = 50.000 \text{ m} + 0.0090 \text{ m} = 50.009 \text{ m.}$$

REFLECT The measuring tape lengthens by 9 mm, or 0.018%. In surveying a baseball field, this amount is negligible, but not when measuring the length of a steel bridge. Note that, although L_0 is given to five significant figures, we need only two of them to compute ΔL.

Practice Problem: A concrete slab forming part of a driveway is 20.000 m long when the temperature is 20°C. How much does the driveway increase in length when the temperature increases to 30°C? The coefficient of linear expansion for concrete is 1.2×10^{-5} K^{-1}. *Answer:* $\Delta L = 2.4$ mm.

EXAMPLE 14.3 **Measuring a true distance**

The surveyor in Example 14.2 measures a distance when the temperature is 35°C and obtains the result 35.794 m. What is the actual distance?

SOLUTION

SET UP AND SOLVE From Equation 14.5, the ratio L/L_0 for any specific material depends only on the temperature change. At 35°C, the distance between two successive meter marks on the tape is a little more than a meter, by the ratio

$$\frac{L}{L_0} = \frac{L_0(1 + \alpha T)}{L_0} = \frac{50.009 \text{ m}}{50.000 \text{ m}}.$$

Thus, the true distance is

$$\frac{50.009 \text{ m}}{50.000 \text{ m}}(35.794 \text{ m}) = 35.800 \text{ m.}$$

REFLECT The term $(1 + \alpha \Delta T)$ for a particular material depends only on the temperature change, within the limits of precision of Equation 14.5.

Volume Expansion

Increases in temperature usually cause increases in *volume* for both solid and liquid materials. Experiments show that if the temperature change ΔT is not too great (less than 100 C° or so), the increase in volume, ΔV, is approximately proportional to the temperature change. The change in volume is also proportional to the initial volume V_0, just as with linear expansion, so we obtain the following relationship:

TABLE 14.2 **Coefficients of volume expansion**

Material	β (K^{-1})
Solids	
Quartz (fused)	0.12×10^{-5}
Invar	0.27×10^{-5}
Glass	1.2–2.7×10^{-5}
Steel	3.6×10^{-5}
Copper	5.1×10^{-5}
Brass	6.0×10^{-5}
Aluminum	7.2×10^{-5}
Liquids	
Mercury	18×10^{-5}
Glycerin	49×10^{-5}
Ethanol	75×10^{-5}
Carbon disulfide	115×10^{-5}

Volume expansion

When the temperature of an object changes, the change ΔV in its volume is proportional to the temperature change ΔT. That is,

$$\Delta V = \beta V_0 \Delta T \qquad (14.6)$$

and

$$V = V_0(1 + \beta \Delta T). \qquad (14.7)$$

The constant β characterizes the volume expansion properties of a particular material; it is called the **coefficient of volume expansion.** The units of β are

K^{-1}. As with linear expansion, β varies somewhat with temperature, and Equation 14.6 is an approximate relation that works well for small temperature changes. For many substances, β decreases at low temperatures. Table 14.2 lists values of β in the neighborhood of room temperature for several substances. Note that the values for liquids are much larger than those for solids.

For solid materials that expand equally in all directions, there is a simple relation between the volume expansion coefficient β and the linear expansion coefficient α. Expansion in each of the three directions contributes to changes in volume. Detailed analysis shows that the two coefficients are related simply by $\beta = 3\alpha$. We invite you to check this relationship for a few materials listed in Tables 14.1 and 14.2.

EXAMPLE 14.4 **Expansion of mercury**

A glass flask filled with a volume of 200 cm³ is filled to the brim with mercury at 20°C. When the temperature of the system is raised to 100°C, does the mercury overflow? If so, by how much? The coefficient of volume expansion of the glass is 1.2×10^{-5} K^{-1}.

SOLUTION

SET UP Both the flask and the mercury expand. The mercury overflows because its coefficient of volume expansion (from Table 14.2) is much greater than that of the glass: 18×10^{-5} K^{-1} versus 1.2×10^{-5} K^{-1}.

SOLVE The increase in volume of the flask is $\Delta V_{\text{flask}} = \beta_{\text{flask}} V_0 \Delta T$, and the increase in the volume of mercury is $\Delta V_{\text{mercury}} = \beta_{\text{mercury}} V_0 \Delta T$:

$$\Delta V_{\text{mercury}} = (18 \times 10^{-5} \text{ K}^{-1})(200 \text{ cm}^3)(100°C - 20°C)$$
$$= 2.9 \text{ cm}^3;$$
$$\Delta V_{\text{flask}} = (1.2 \times 10^{-5} \text{ K}^{-1})(200 \text{ cm}^3)(100°C - 20°C)$$
$$= 0.19 \text{ cm}^3.$$

The volume of mercury that overflows is the difference between these values:

$$\Delta V_{\text{mercury}} - \Delta V_{\text{flask}} = 2.9 \text{ cm}^3 - 0.19 \text{ cm}^3 = 2.7 \text{ cm}^3.$$

REFLECT This is basically the way a mercury-in-glass thermometer works, except that instead of letting the mercury overflow and run all over the place, the thermometer has it rise inside a sealed tube as T increases.

Practice Problem: Suppose we replace the mercury with ethanol (less poisonous than mercury and more suitable for very cold weather). How much ethanol runs over? *Answer:* 11.8 cm³

Thermal Expansion of Water

Above 4°C, liquid water expands with increasing temperature. However, between 0°C (the freezing point) and 4°C, water *decreases* in volume with increasing temperature; in this range, its coefficient of volume expansion is *negative*. Thus, water has its greatest density at 4°C. Water also expands when it freezes; that's why ice humps up in the middle of the compartments in an ice cube tray and why pipes full of water burst if allowed to freeze. Most other materials contract when they freeze.

This anomalous behavior of water has an important effect on plant and animal life in lakes. When a lake cools, the cooled water at the surface flows to the bottom because of its greater density. But when the temperature goes below 4°C, this flow ceases, and the water near the surface remains colder (and less dense) than that at the bottom. As the surface freezes, the ice floats because it is less dense than water. The water at the bottom remains at 4°C until nearly the entire lake is frozen. If water behaved like most substances, contracting continuously on cooling and freezing, lakes would freeze from the bottom up. Circulation due to density differences would continuously carry warmer (less dense) water to the surface for efficient cooling, and lakes would freeze solid much more easily. This would destroy all plant and animal life that can withstand cold water, but not freezing. All life forms known on earth depend on chemical systems based on aqueous solutions; if water did not have this special property, the evolution of various life-forms would have taken a very different course.

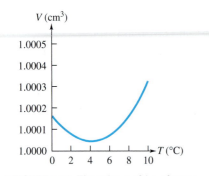

▲ FIGURE 14.9 The volume of 1 g of water in the temperature range from 0°C to 10°C. The fact that water is denser at about 4°C than at the freezing point is vitally important for the ecology of lakes and streams.

▲ FIGURE 14.10 The interlocking teeth of an expansion joint on a bridge. These joints are needed to accommodate changes in length that result from thermal expansion.

The anomalous expansion of water in the temperature range from 0°C to 10°C is shown in Figure 14.9.

Thermal Stress

If we clamp the ends of a rod rigidly to prevent expansion or contraction and then raise or lower the temperature, a compressive or tensile stress called **thermal stress** develops. The rod would like to expand or contract, but the clamps won't let it. The resulting stress may become large enough to strain the rod irreversibly or even break it. Concrete highways and bridge decks usually have gaps between sections, filled with a flexible material or bridged by interlocking teeth (Figure 14.10), to permit expansion and contraction of the concrete. If one end of a steel bridge is rigidly fastened to its abutment, the other end usually rests on rollers.

To calculate the thermal stress in a clamped rod, we compute the amount the rod *would* expand (or contract) if it were not held and then find the stress needed to compress (or stretch) it back to its original length. Suppose a rod with length L_0 and cross-sectional area A is held at constant length while the temperature is reduced (negative ΔT), causing a tensile stress. Then the fractional change in length if the rod were free to contract would be

$$\frac{\Delta L}{L_0} = \alpha \, \Delta T.$$

Both ΔL and ΔT are negative. The tension F must increase enough to produce an equal and opposite fractional change in length. From the definition of Young's modulus Y (Equation 11.4),

$$Y = \frac{F/A}{\Delta L/L_0} \qquad \text{and} \qquad \frac{\Delta L}{L_0} = \frac{F}{AY}.$$

If the *total* fractional change in length is zero, then

$$\alpha \, \Delta T + \frac{F}{AY} = 0, \qquad \text{or} \qquad F = -AY\alpha \, \Delta T. \qquad (14.8)$$

For a decrease in temperature, ΔT is negative, so F is positive. The tensile *stress* F/A in the rod is

$$\frac{F}{A} = -Y\alpha \, \Delta T. \qquad (14.9)$$

If ΔT is positive, F and F/A are negative, corresponding to *compressive* force and stress.

EXAMPLE 14.5 **Stress on a spacer**

An aluminum cylinder 10 cm long, with a cross-sectional area of 20 cm², is to be used as a spacer between two steel walls. At 17.2°C, it just slips in between the walls. Then it warms to 22.3°C. Calculate the stress in the cylinder and the total force it exerts on each wall, assuming that the walls are perfectly rigid and a constant distance apart.

SOLUTION

SET UP Figure 14.11 shows our sketch. We use Equation 14.9, which relates the stress F/A (compressive in this case) to the temperature change. From Table 11.1, $Y = 0.70 \times 10^{11}$ Pa, and from Table 14.1, $\alpha = 2.4 \times 10^{-5}$ K^{-1}. The temperature change is $\Delta T = 5.1$ K, and the cross-sectional area of the cylinder is 20 cm² $= 20 \times 10^{-4}$ m².

▲ FIGURE 14.11 Our sketch for this problem.

Continued

SOLVE From Equation 14.9, the stress F/A is

$$\frac{F}{A} = -Y\alpha\,\Delta T$$

$$= -(0.70 \times 10^{11}\,\text{Pa})(2.4 \times 10^{-5}\,\text{K}^{-1})(5.1\,\text{K})$$

$$= -8.6 \times 10^6\,\text{Pa (about } -1240\,\text{lb/in.}^2).$$

The total force F exerted by the cylinder on a wall is

$$F = -AY\alpha\,\Delta T = (20 \times 10^{-4}\,\text{m}^2)(-8.6 \times 10^6\,\text{Pa})$$

$$= -1.7 \times 10^4\,\text{N (about 3800 lb)}.$$

REFLECT The negative sign indicates compressive rather than tensile stress. The stress is independent of the length and cross-sectional area of the cylinder. The total force is nearly 2 tons.

Thermal stresses can be induced by non-uniform expansion due to temperature differences. Have you ever broken a glass jar by pouring boiling water into it? Thermal stress caused by temperature differences exceeded the breaking stress of the material, and it cracked. The same phenomenon makes ice cubes crack when they're dropped into a hot liquid. Heat-resistant glasses such as Pyrex™ have exceptionally low expansion coefficients and high strength.

14.4 Quantity of Heat

When you put a cold spoon into a cup of hot coffee, the spoon warms up and the coffee cools off as they approach thermal equilibrium. What kind of interaction is taking place to cause these temperature changes? During this interaction, *something* is transferred from the coffee to the spoon. We'll call this interaction a **heat transfer** or a *heat flow* from the coffee to the spoon. But what *is* this "something" that flows from the coffee to the spoon?

The answer to this question emerged gradually during the 18th and 19th centuries. Sir James Joule (1818–1889) discovered that water can be warmed by vigorous stirring with a paddle wheel (Figure 14.12a) and that *the rise in temperature is directly proportional to the work done* (and energy added) in turning the wheel. Since the same temperature change could have been caused by putting the water in contact with some hotter object (Figure 14.12b), that interaction must also involve an energy exchange. This experiment and many similar ones, have established the fact that heat flow is *energy transfer* and that there is an equivalence between heat and work: The same change of state of a system (such as a change in temperature or volume) can be produced by heat flow, work, or a combination of the two.

Energy transfer that takes place solely because of a temperature difference is called *heat flow,* or *heat transfer,* and energy transferred in this way is called **heat.** For example, cold water in a steam boiler is converted to steam by contact with a metal pipe kept at a high temperature by a hot flame from burning coal or gas. Having received energy from the flame, the water (as steam) has a greater ability to do *work* (by pushing against a turbine blade or the piston in a steam engine) than does an equal mass of cold liquid water.

> **NOTE** ▶ The term *heat* always refers to the *transfer* of energy from one object or system to another due to a temperature difference, never to the amount of energy *contained within* a particular system. There is no such thing as "the heat *in* an object"; **the concept of heat has meaning only as energy in transit.** A detailed study of the relationship between heat and work leads to the *first law of thermodynamics,* which we'll study in detail in the next chapter. ◀

Because heat is energy transferred from one system to another, the SI unit of quantity of heat is the joule. The International Committee on Weights and Measures recommends use of the joule as the basic unit of energy in all forms, including heat. We'll follow that recommendation in this book. However, several older,

The water warms as the paddle does work on it; the temperature rise is proportional to the amount of work done.

(a) Raising the temperature of water by doing work on it

Direct heating can produce the same temperature change as doing work on the water.

(b) Raising the temperature of water by direct heating

▲ **FIGURE 14.12** The temperature of a system may be changed by either (a) doing work on the system or (b) adding heat to it.

non-SI units are also in common use for heat. The most familiar of these is the calorie.

The familiar "Calorie" found on food labels is actually a kilocalorie (kcal), equal to 1000 cal. The kilocalorie, also called the food calorie, is sometimes written with a capital C (Calorie) to distinguish it from the calorie just defined. But as Figure 14.13 shows, much of the world worries about the joule content of their food, not the calorie (or Calorie) content.

A corresponding unit of quantity of heat that uses Fahrenheit degrees and British units is the **British thermal unit,** or Btu. One Btu is defined as the quantity of heat required to raise the temperature of 1 standard pound (weight) of water 1 F° from 63°F to 64°F.

Because heat is energy in transit, there must be a definite relation between the preceding units and the familiar energy unit, the joule. Experiments similar in concept to Joule's have shown that

▲ **FIGURE 14.13** Packaged foods sold in many countries outside the United States, such as these sugar cubes from Germany, list their energy content in joules as well as calories.

$$1 \text{ cal} = 4.186 \text{ J},$$

$$1 \text{ kcal} = 1000 \text{ cal} = 4186 \text{ J},$$

$$1 \text{ Btu} = 778 \text{ ft} \cdot \text{lb} = 252 \text{ cal} = 1055 \text{ J}.$$

Specific Heat Capacity

We use the symbol Q for quantity of heat (amount of energy transferred). The quantity of heat Q required to increase the temperature T of a mass m of a certain material by a small amount from T_1 to T_2 is found to be approximately proportional to the temperature change $\Delta T = T_2 - T_1$. To raise the temperature of a certain mass of substance from 20°C to 40°C ($\Delta T = 20$ K) requires approximately twice as much heat as the amount needed to raise it from 20°C to 30°C ($\Delta T = 10$ K). The heat required for a given temperature change is also proportional to the mass m of substance. Thus, when you heat water to make tea, you need twice as much heat for two cups as for one if the temperature interval is the same. Finally, the quantity of heat needed also depends on the nature of the material; to raise the temperature of 1 kilogram of water by 1 C° requires almost five times as much heat as for 1 kilogram of aluminum and the same temperature change.

Putting all these relationships together, we have the definition of specific heat capacity:

In Equation 14.10, Q and ΔT can be either positive or negative. When they are positive, heat enters the object and its temperature increases; when they are negative, heat leaves the object and its temperature decreases.

NOTE ▶ Remember that Q does not represent a change in the amount of heat *contained* in an object; that is a meaningless concept. Heat is always energy *in transit* as a result of a temperature difference. There is no such thing as "the amount of heat in an object." The term *heat capacity* is unfortunate because it tends to suggest the erroneous idea that an object *contains* a certain amount of heat. ◀

The specific heat capacity of water is approximately

$$c_{\text{water}} = 4190 \text{ J}/(\text{kg} \cdot \text{K}), 1 \text{ cal}/(\text{g} \cdot \text{K}), \text{ or } 1 \text{ Btu}/(\text{lb} \cdot \text{F}°).$$

Specific heat capacities vary somewhat with the initial temperature and the temperature interval. For example, the specific heat capacity of water varies by almost 1% in the temperature range from 0°C to 100°C. In the problems and examples in this chapter, we'll usually ignore this small variation. Table 14.3 lists specific heat capacities for several common materials.

TABLE 14.3 **Mean specific heat capacities (constant pressure, temperature range 0°C to 100°C)**

| Material | Specific heat capacity (c) | |
	J/(kg·K)	cal/(g·K)
Solids		
Lead	0.13×10^3	0.031
Mercury	0.14×10^3	0.033
Silver	0.23×10^3	0.056
Copper	0.39×10^3	0.093
Iron	0.47×10^3	0.112
Marble ($CaCO_3$)	0.88×10^3	0.21
Salt	0.88×10^3	0.21
Aluminum	0.91×10^3	0.217
Beryllium	1.97×10^3	0.471
Ice ($-25°C$ to $0°C$)	2.01×10^3	0.48
Liquids		
Ethylene glycol	2.39×10^3	0.57
Ethanol	2.43×10^3	0.58
Water	4.19×10^3	1.00

Quantitative Analysis 14.1

The meaning of c

In the equation $Q = mc \, \Delta T$, m represents the mass in grams of the sample and c represents

A. the amount of heat required to raise the temperature of m grams of sample by 1 C°.
B. the amount of heat required to raise the temperature of 1 gram of the sample by 1 C°.
C. the amount of heat required to raise the temperature of m grams of the sample by ΔT.

SOLUTION The specific heat capacity c is a property of a particular material; it doesn't depend on *how much* of the material is present. It's also independent of the temperature interval: if we double ΔT, the total amount of heat doubles, but c doesn't change. Thus, neither A nor C can be right. The correct answer is B: c is the amount of heat needed *per unit mass* and *per unit temperature change*.

EXAMPLE 14.6 **Running a fever**

During a bout with the flu, an 80 kg man ran a fever of 2.0 C°; that is, his body temperature was 39.0°C (or 102.2°F) instead of the normal 37.0°C (or 98.6°F). Assuming that the human body is mostly water, how much heat was required to raise his temperature by that amount?

SOLUTION

SET UP AND SOLVE The temperature change is $\Delta T = 39.0°C - 37.0°C = 2.0 \text{ C}° = 2.0 \text{ K}$. From Table 14.3, the specific heat capacity of water is $4190 \text{ J}/(\text{kg} \cdot \text{K})$. From Equation 14.10,

$$Q = mc \, \Delta T = (80 \text{ kg})[4190 \text{ J}/(\text{kg} \cdot \text{K})](2.0 \text{ K}) =$$
$$= 6.7 \times 10^5 \text{ J}.$$

REFLECT This amount of heat is equal to 1.6×10^5 cal, or 160 kcal (160 food calories). This is roughly half the calorie intake from eating 1 ounce of milk chocolate.

Practice Problem: If a 35 kg child has a temperature of 104°F = 40°C, how much heat was needed to raise her temperature to that value from an initial value of 37°C? *Answer:* 4.4×10^5 J.

EXAMPLE 14.7 **Circuit meltdown**

You are designing an electronic circuit element made of 23 mg of silicon. The electric current through it adds energy at the rate of 7.4 mW = 7.4×10^{-3} J/s. If your design doesn't allow any heat transfer out of the element, at what rate does its temperature increase? The specific heat capacity of silicon is $705 \text{ J}/(\text{kg} \cdot \text{K})$.

Continued

SOLUTION

SET UP AND SOLVE In 1 second, $Q = (7.4 \times 10^{-3} \text{ J/s})(1 \text{ s}) = 7.4 \times 10^{-3}$ J. From Equation 14.10, the temperature change in 1 second is

$$\Delta T = \frac{Q}{mc} = \frac{7.4 \times 10^{-3} \text{ J}}{(23 \times 10^{-6} \text{ kg})[705 \text{ J}/(\text{kg} \cdot \text{K})]} = 0.46 \text{ K}.$$

Alternatively, we can divide both sides of this equation by Δt and rearrange factors:

$$\frac{\Delta T}{\Delta t} = \frac{Q/\Delta t}{mc}$$

$$= \frac{7.4 \times 10^{-3} \text{ J/s}}{(23 \times 10^{-6} \text{ kg})[705 \text{ J}/(\text{kg} \cdot \text{K})]} = 0.46 \text{ K/s}.$$

REFLECT At this rate of temperature rise (27 K every minute), the circuit element would quickly self-destruct. Heat transfer is an important design consideration in electronic circuit elements.

NOTE ▶ We conclude this section with a short sermon. It is absolutely essential for you to keep clearly in mind the distinction between *temperature* and *heat*. Temperature depends on the physical state of a material and is a quantitative description of its hotness or coldness. Heat is energy transferred from one object to another because of a temperature difference. We can change the temperature of an object by adding heat to it or taking heat away from it or by adding or subtracting energy in other ways, such as doing mechanical work. If we cut an object in half, each half has the same temperature as the whole; but to raise the temperature of each half by a given interval, we add *half* as much heat as for the whole. ◀

Conceptual Analysis 14.2

Heat versus temperature

As Table 14.3 shows, the specific heat capacity of water is about 10 times that of iron. If you take equal masses of water and iron, initially in thermal equilibrium, and add 50 J of heat to each, which of the following statements is true?

A. They remain in thermal equilibrium.
B. They are no longer in thermal equilibrium; the iron is warmer.
C. They are no longer in thermal equilibrium; the water is warmer.

SOLUTION Because water has a larger specific heat capacity than iron, a greater amount of heat is needed to cause a given temperature change for a given mass of water than for an equal mass of iron. If the heat added is the same for both, it follows that the temperature change of the water is less than that of the iron. If they were initially at the same temperature, then, after the additions of heat, the iron is warmer than the water. The correct answer is B.

14.5 Phase Changes

We've discussed the energy transfer (heat) involved in changing an object's temperature. Heat is also involved in *phase changes,* such as the melting of ice or boiling of water. Once we understand these additional heat relationships, we can analyze a variety of problems involving quantity of heat Q.

We use the term **phase** to describe a specific state of matter, such as solid, liquid, or gas. The compound H_2O exists in the *solid phase* as ice, in the *liquid phase* as water, and in the *gaseous phase* as steam. A transition from one phase to another is called a **phase change** or phase transition. For any given pressure, a phase change usually takes place at a definite temperature and is usually accompanied by the absorption or emission of heat and a change in volume and density.

A familiar example of a phase change is the melting of ice. When we add heat to ice at 0°C and normal atmospheric pressure, the temperature of the ice *does not* increase. Instead, some of the ice melts to form liquid water. If we add the heat slowly, to maintain the system very close to thermal equilibrium, the temperature remains at 0°C until all the ice is melted. The effect of adding heat to this system is not to raise its temperature, but to change its *phase* from solid to liquid.

▶ **Flaking out?** Snow and ice are two familiar forms of the solid phase of water. Why do they look so different? Air always contains water vapor. When air above the freezing temperature of water cools to the point that it can't retain all its water vapor (i.e., the relative humidity exceeds 100%), some vapor condenses to liquid in the form of rain, fog, or dew. If the air cools further, the liquid water freezes to form hail or sleet. But if the temperature is below the freezing point of water, the water vapor goes directly from the gaseous to the solid phase. (This is the reverse of *sublimation*, where a solid material goes directly into the vapor phase.) Suspended in air, the ice crystals grow slowly, preserving their natural six-fold symmetry and forming snowflakes. A similar process causes frost to form on the cooling coils of a refrigerator.

To change 1 kg of ice at 0°C to 1 kg of liquid water at 0°C and normal atmospheric pressure requires 3.34×10^5 J of heat. The heat required, per unit mass is called the **heat of fusion** (or sometimes *latent* heat of fusion), denoted by L_f. Thus, the heat of fusion L_f of water, at normal atmospheric pressure, is

$$L_f = 3.34 \times 10^5 \text{ J/kg} = 79.6 \text{ cal/g} = 143 \text{ Btu/lb}.$$

More generally, to melt a mass m of material that has a heat of fusion L_f requires a quantity of heat Q given by

$$Q = mL_f.$$

This process is *reversible:* To freeze liquid water to ice at 0°C, we have to *remove* heat. The magnitude is the same, but in this case Q is negative because heat is removed rather than added. To cover both possibilities and to include other kinds of phase changes, we write

$$Q = \pm mL. \tag{14.11}$$

The plus sign (heat entering) is used when the material melts, the minus sign (heat leaving) when it freezes. The heat of fusion is different for different materials, and it also varies somewhat with pressure.

At any given pressure, there is a unique temperature at which liquid water and ice can coexist in a condition called **phase equilibrium.** The freezing temperature is always the same as the melting temperature.

We can tell this whole story again, changing the names of the characters, for *boiling*, or *evaporation*, a phase transition between the liquid and gaseous phases. The corresponding heat (per unit mass) is called the **heat of vaporization,** L_v. At normal atmospheric pressure, the heat of vaporization L_v for water is

$$L_v = 2.26 \times 10^6 \text{ J/kg} = 539 \text{ cal/g} = 970 \text{ Btu/lb}.$$

Note that over five times as much heat is required to vaporize a quantity of water at 100°C as is required to raise its temperature from 0°C to 100°C.

Both L_v and the boiling temperature of a material depend on pressure. Water boils at a lower temperature (about 95°C) in Denver than in Pittsburgh because Denver is at a higher elevation and the average atmospheric pressure is less. The heat of vaporization is somewhat greater at this lower pressure, about 2.27×10^6 J/kg.

Like melting, boiling is a reversible transition. When heat is removed from a gas at the boiling temperature, the gas returns to the liquid phase, or *condenses*, giving up to its surroundings the same quantity of heat (heat of vaporization) as was needed to vaporize it. At a given pressure, the boiling and condensation temperatures are the same.

Table 14.4 lists heats of fusion and vaporization for several materials, with the corresponding melting and boiling temperatures at normal atmospheric pressure. Very few *elements* have melting temperatures in the vicinity of ordinary room temperatures; one of the few is the metal gallium, shown in Figure 14.14.

▲ **FIGURE 14.14** The metal gallium melts in your hand. This element is one of the few having a melting temperature near room temperature.

TABLE 14.4 **Heats of fusion and vaporization**

Substance	Normal melting point*		Heat of fusion, L_f, J/kg	Normal boiling point*		Heat of vaporization, L_v, J/kg
	K	°C		K	°C	
Helium	†	†	†	4.216	−268.93	20.9×10^3
Hydrogen	13.84	−259.31	58.6×10^3	20.26	−252.89	452×10^3
Nitrogen	63.18	−209.97	25.5×10^3	77.34	−195.81	201×10^3
Oxygen	54.36	−218.79	13.8×10^3	90.18	−182.97	213×10^3
Ethyl alcohol	159	−114	104.2×10^3	351	78	854×10^3
Mercury	234	−39	11.8×10^3	630	357	272×10^3
Water	273.15	0.00	334×10^3	373.15	100.00	2256×10^3
Sulfur	392	119	38.1×10^3	717.75	444.60	326×10^3
Lead	600.5	327.3	24.5×10^3	2023	1750	871×10^3
Antimony	903.65	630.50	165×10^3	1713	1440	561×10^3
Silver	1233.95	960.80	88.3×10^3	2466	2193	2336×10^3
Gold	1336.15	1063.00	64.5×10^3	2933	2660	1578×10^3
Copper	1356	1083	134×10^3	1460	1187	5069×10^3

* At normal atmospheric pressure.

†A pressure in excess of 25 atmospheres is required to make helium solidify. At 1 atmosphere pressure, helium
remains a liquid down to absolute zero.

Conceptual Analysis 14.3

Getting burned

As a theoretical possibility, which (if any) of the following choices would transfer more heat to your skin and thus
cause a worse burn?

A. Allowing 1 g of boiling water (at 100°C) to cool to body temperature in your hand.
B. Allowing 1 g of steam at 100°C to condense to liquid water at
100°C in your hand.
C. The heat transfer is the same in both cases.

SOLUTION When 1 g of liquid water cools from 100°C to 20°C,
it gives off 4.186 J for each C° drop in temperature, for a total of
335 J. When 1 g of steam at 100°C condenses to liquid water at
the same temperature, it gives off an amount of heat equal to the
heat of vaporization, about 2260 J. The total amount of heat
given off by the condensing steam is over six times as great as the
amount given off by the cooling water. Answer B is correct.

Figure 14.15 shows how temperature varies with time when heat is added
continuously to a specimen of ice with an initial temperature below 0°C. The
temperature rises (from a to b) until the melting point is reached. Then, as more

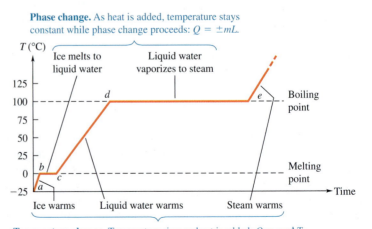

Phase change. As heat is added, temperature stays
constant while phase change proceeds: $Q = \pm mL$.

Temperature change. Temperature rises as heat is added: $Q = mc\Delta T$.

▲ **FIGURE 14.15** A plot of temperature versus time for a sample of ice to
which heat is added continuously.

heat is added (from *b* to *c*), the temperature remains constant until all the ice has melted. Next, the temperature starts to rise again (from *c* to *d*) until the boiling temperature is reached. At that point, the temperature is again constant (from *d* to *e*) until all the water is transformed into the vapor phase. If the rate of heat input is constant, the slope of the line for the liquid phase is smaller than that of the solid phase because, as Table 14.3 indicates, the specific heat capacity of ice is only about half that of liquid water.

Conceptual Analysis 14.4

Water and ice

What happens when a lump of ice at 0°C is placed in a beaker of water at 0°C in a room at 0°C?

A. Nothing.
B. All the ice melts.
C. Only some of the ice melts.
D. Only some of the water freezes.

SOLUTION The system is in thermal equilibrium; all parts are at the same temperature, and there is no heat transfer when the ice is placed in the beaker of water. If there were freezing or melting, there would have to be heat transfer. Therefore, nothing happens; the correct answer is A.

A substance can sometimes evaporate directly from the solid to the gaseous phase; this process is called **sublimation,** and the solid is said to *sublime*. The corresponding heat is called the **heat of sublimation,** L_s. Liquid carbon dioxide cannot exist at a pressure lower than about 5×10^5 Pa (about 5 atm), so "dry ice" (solid carbon dioxide) sublimes at atmospheric pressure. Sublimation of water from frozen food causes freezer burn, and it is the reason clothes can dry on a clothesline even at subfreezing temperatures. The reverse process, a phase change from gas to solid, occurs when frost forms on cold objects such as the cooling coils in a refrigerator.

The temperature-control mechanisms of many warm-blooded animals make use of the heat of vaporization, removing heat from the body by sweating or panting, both of which depend on evaporating water from the body. Evaporative cooling enables humans to maintain normal body temperature in hot, dry desert climates, where the air temperature may reach 55°C (about 130°F). The skin temperature may be as much as 30 C° cooler than the surrounding air. Under these conditions, a normal person may perspire several liters per day. Unless this lost water is replaced, dehydration, heat stroke, and death result. Old-time desert rats (such as the author) state that in the desert, any canteen that holds less than a gallon should be viewed as a toy!

Evaporative cooling is also used to cool buildings in hot, dry climates and to condense and recirculate "used" steam in coal-fired or nuclear-powered electric-generating plants. That's what is going on in the large cone-shaped concrete towers that you see at such plants.

Chemical reactions such as combustion involve definite quantities of heat. Complete combustion of 1 gram of gasoline produces about 46,000 J, or 11,000 cal, so the **heat of combustion** L_c of gasoline is

$$L_c = 46,000 \text{ J/g} = 46 \times 10^6 \text{ J/kg}.$$

Earlier, we mentioned that the energy value of food is measured in kilocalories (or Calories with a capital C), where 1 kcal = 1000 cal = 4186 J. When we say that a gram of peanut butter "contains 6 Calories," we mean that if we burned it completely—allowed it to undergo complete combustion with oxygen—it would release 6 kcal (25,000 J) of heat. In the body, essentially the same combustion takes place, although slowly and by means of enzyme-mediated reactions in cells. Not all of the energy liberated in the body's "burning" of food is available for mechanical work. We'll study the *efficiency* of energy conversion in Chapter 16.

14.6 Calorimetry

"Calorimetry" means "measuring heat." We've discussed the energy transfer (heat) involved in temperature changes and in phases changes. Now we're ready to look at some examples of calorimetry calculations (calculations with heat). The basic principle is simple: When heat flow occurs between two objects that are isolated from their surroundings, the amount of heat lost by one object must equal the amount of heat gained by the other. Heat is energy in transit, so this principle is really just another form of conservation of energy. We take each quantity of heat *added to* an object as *positive* and each quantity *leaving* an object as *negative*. When several objects interact, the *algebraic sum* of the quantities of heat transferred to *all* of them must be zero. The basic principle can be stated very simply as

$$\Sigma Q = 0.$$

Calorimetry, dealing entirely with one conserved scalar quantity, is in many ways the simplest of all physical theories!

▲ **Meat, not heat.** A calorimeter is a device used to measure heat production or consumption by an isolated system. Typically, the calorimeter is a benchtop piece of equipment used in an analytical laboratory to study, for example, the amount of heat generated by chemical reactions. However, the calorimeter can also be used to measure heat production in a much larger isolated system, such as the farm animal shown here. The cow is fed a strictly controlled diet in this room-sized calorimeter for several days, and the amount of heat produced by the animal's metabolism is carefully measured. In this way, agricultural scientists have been able to determine which types of animal feed are most efficient at promoting weight gain without excessive loss of energy as heat.

PROBLEM-SOLVING STRATEGY 14.2 Calorimetry problems

SET UP

1. To avoid confusion about algebraic signs when calculating quantities of heat, use Equations 14.10 and 14.11 consistently for each object. Each Q is positive when heat enters an object and negative when it leaves. The algebraic sum of all the Q's must be zero.

SOLVE

2. Often you will need to find an unknown temperature. Represent it by an algebraic symbol such as T. Then, if an object has an initial temperature of 20°C and an unknown final temperature T, the temperature change for the object is $\Delta T = T_{final} - T_{initial} = T - 20°C$ (*not* 20°C − T) . . . and so on.

3. Compute the heat added to each interacting object, and then equate the algebraic sum of all the quantities of heat to zero (representing conservation of energy). When heat leaves an object, consider it as negative heat added to the object.

REFLECT

4. In problems in which a phase change takes place, as when ice melts, you may not know in advance whether *all* of the material undergoes a phase change or only part of it does. You can always assume one or the other, and if the resulting calculation gives an absurd result (such as a final temperature that is higher or lower than *all* of the initial temperatures), you know that the initial assumption was wrong. Back up and try again!

EXAMPLE 14.8 Coffee in a metal cup

A Turkish restaurant serves coffee in copper mugs (with the inside tin plated to avoid copper poisoning). A waiter fills a cup having a mass of 0.100 kg and initially at 20.0°C with 0.300 kg of coffee that is initially at 70.0°C. What is the final temperature after the coffee and the cup attain thermal equilibrium? (Assume that coffee has the same specific heat capacity as water and that there is no heat exchange with the surroundings.)

Continued

SOLUTION

SET UP AND SOLVE Call the final temperature T. The (negative) change in temperature of the coffee is $\Delta T_{coffee} = T - 70°C$, and the (positive) change in temperature of the cup is $\Delta T_{copper} = T - 20°C$. We need to find the heat lost by the coffee and gained by the copper cup and then set the algebraic sum equal to zero. Because the coffee loses heat, it has a negative value of Q:

$$Q_{coffee} = mc_{water}\Delta T_{coffee}$$
$$= (0.300\ kg)[4190\ J/(kg \cdot K)](T - 70.0°C).$$

(Note that ΔT_{coffee} is negative in this expression.) The heat gained by the copper cup is

$$Q_{copper} = mc_{copper}\Delta T_{copper}$$
$$= (0.100\ kg)[390\ J/(kg \cdot K)](T - 20.0°C).$$

(Note that ΔT_{copper} is positive in this expression.) We equate the sum of these two quantities of heat to zero, obtaining an algebraic equation for T:

$$Q_{coffee} + Q_{copper} = 0,$$
or
$$(0.300\ kg)[4190\ J/(kg \cdot K)](T - 70.0°C)$$
$$+ (0.100\ kg)[390\ J/(kg \cdot K)](T - 20.0°C) = 0.$$

Solving this equation for T, we find $T = 68.5°C$.

REFLECT The final temperature is much closer to the initial temperature of the coffee than to that of the cup; water has a much larger specific heat capacity than copper, and we have three times as much mass of water. We can also find the quantities of heat by substituting this value for T back into the original equations. When we do this, we find that $Q_{coffee} = -1890\ J$ and $Q_{copper} = +1890\ J$; Q_{coffee} is negative, as expected.

Practice Problem: Find the final temperature if the cup is a heavy ceramic cup with a mass of 0.200 kg and specific heat capacity $c = 800\ J/kg \cdot K$. *Answer: 64.3°C.*

EXAMPLE 14.9 **Chilling your soda**

A physics student wants to cool 0.25 kg of Diet Omni-Cola (mostly water) initially at 20°C by adding ice initially at $-20°C$. How much ice should she add so that the final temperature will be 0°C with all the ice melted? Assume that the heat capacity of the paper container may be neglected.

SOLUTION

SET UP AND SOLVE The ice *gains* the heat (positive Q) required to warm it from $-20°C$ to 0°C and to melt all of it. The cola *loses* (negative Q) the same amount of heat. Let the unknown mass of ice be m. The (negative) heat transfer to the Omni-Cola is

$$Q_{Omni} = m_{Omni}c_{water}\Delta T_{Omni}$$
$$= (0.25\ kg)[4190\ J/(kg \cdot K)](0°C - 20°C)$$
$$= -21,000\ J.$$

The specific heat capacity of ice (not the same as that for liquid water) is about $2.0 \times 10^3\ J/kg \cdot K$. The heat needed to warm a mass m of ice from $-20°C$ to 0°C is

$$Q_{ice} = mc_{ice}\Delta T_{ice}$$
$$= m[2.0 \times 10^3\ J/(kg \cdot K)][0°C - (-20°C)]$$
$$= m(4.0 \times 10^4\ J/kg).$$

The additional heat needed to melt the ice is the mass of the ice times the heat of fusion:

$$Q_{melt} = mL_f$$
$$= m(3.34 \times 10^5\ J/kg.)$$

The sum of these three quantities must equal zero:

$$Q_{Omni} + Q_{ice} + Q_{melt} = -21,000\ J + m(40,000\ J/kg)$$
$$+ m(334,000\ J/kg) = 0.$$

Solving this equation for m, we get $m = 0.056\ kg = 56\ g$ (two or three medium-size ice cubes).

REFLECT A final state with all the ice melted isn't a very satisfying outcome. We probably want to add a couple of extra ice cubes so that the drink will stay cold for a while even though the temperature of the surrounding air may be considerably higher than 0°C.

14.7 Heat Transfer

In Section 14.1, we spoke qualitatively about *conductors* and *insulators*—materials that permit or prevent heat transfer between objects. We weren't concerned with how quickly or slowly the transfer takes place. But if you're boiling water to make tea or trying to build an energy-efficient house, you need to know how quickly or slowly heat is transferred. In this section, we'll study the three mechanisms of heat transfer—conduction, convection, and radiation—and the relation of the rate of heat transfer to the properties of the system. *Conduction* occurs within an object or between two objects that are in actual contact with each other.

▲ **FIGURE 14.16** Steady-state heat flow due to conduction in a uniform rod.

Heat current $H = kA \dfrac{T_H - T_C}{L}$

Doubling the cross-sectional area of the conductor doubles the heat current ($H \propto A$):

Doubling the length of the conductor halves the heat current ($H \propto 1/L$):

▲ **FIGURE 14.17** The relationship of heat current to the area and length of a conductor.

TABLE 14.5 Thermal conductivities

Material	k (W/(m·K))
Metals	
Lead	34.7
Steel	50.2
Brass	109
Aluminum	205
Copper	385
Silver	406
Other solids (representative values)	
Styrofoam™	0.01
Fiberglass	0.04
Wood	0.12–0.04
Insulating brick	0.15
Red brick	0.6
Concrete	0.8
Glass	0.8
Ice	1.6
Gases	
Air	0.024
Helium	0.14

Convection depends on the motion of mass (such as air or water) from one region of space to another, and *radiation* is heat transfer by electromagnetic radiation, such as sunshine, with no need for matter to be present in the space between objects. We'll consider these three kinds of processes in turn.

Conduction

If you hold one end of a copper rod and place the other end in a flame, the end you are holding gets hotter and hotter, even though it isn't in direct contact with the flame. Heat reaches the cooler end by **conduction** through the material. On the atomic level, the atoms in the hotter regions have more kinetic energy, on the average, than their cooler neighbors. They jostle their neighbors, giving them some of their energy. The neighbors then jostle *their* neighbors, and so it goes through the material. The atoms themselves do not move from one region of the material to another, but their energy does.

In metals, electron motion provides another mechanism for heat transfer. Most metals are good conductors of electricity because some electrons can leave their parent atoms and wander through the crystal lattice. These free electrons can carry energy from the hotter to the cooler regions of the metal. Good thermal conductors such as silver, copper, aluminum, and gold are also good electrical conductors.

Heat transfer occurs only between regions at different temperatures, and the direction of heat flow is always from higher to lower temperature. Figure 14.16 shows a rod of conducting material with cross-sectional area A and length L. The left end of the rod is kept at a temperature T_H and the right end at a lower temperature T_C, and heat flows from left to right. We assume that the rod is insulated, so that heat flows only from one end to the other, not in or out at the sides.

In discussing the rate of heat transfer with time, we'll change our notation slightly: We'll use ΔQ (rather than just Q) for the quantity of heat transferred in a time Δt. Then the rate of heat flow with time (heat transferred per unit time) is $\Delta Q/\Delta t$. We call this rate the **heat current** and denote it by H. That is, $H = \Delta Q/\Delta t$. Experiments show that the heat current is proportional to the cross-sectional area A. If we place two identical rods side by side, the total heat flow is twice as great as for each individual rod (Figure 14.17). It is also proportional to the temperature difference $(T_H - T_C)$. Finally, it is *inversely* proportional to the length L: Roughly speaking, if the heat has twice as far to go, it takes twice as long to get there.

Introducing a proportionality constant k called the **thermal conductivity** of the material, we have

$$H = \frac{\Delta Q}{\Delta t} = kA \frac{T_H - T_C}{L}. \tag{14.12}$$

The quantity $(T_H - T_C)/L$ is the temperature difference *per unit length*; it is called the **temperature gradient.** The numerical value of k depends on the material of the rod. Materials with large k are good conductors of heat; materials with small k are poor conductors (and thus good insulators). Equation 14.12 also gives the heat current through a slab, or *any* homogeneous object with uniform cross-sectional area A perpendicular to the direction of flow; L is the length of the heat-flow path.

The units of heat current H are units of energy per unit time, or power; the SI unit of heat current is the joule per second, or watt (W). We can find the units of k by solving Equation 14.12 for k. We invite you to verify that the SI units of k are W/(m · K). Some numerical values of k are given in Table 14.5. This table makes it clear why copper and aluminum are often used in the bottoms of cooking pans.

The thermal conductivity of "dead" (nonmoving) air is very small. A wool sweater is warm because it traps air between the fibers. In fact, many insulating

▶ **Hot-and-cold fish.** Most fish are the same temperature as the surrounding water because the heat their bodies generate is lost by conduction to the water as their blood circulates through the gills. However, some large predatory fishes, such as these bluefin tuna, use a special technique to warm key body parts—their central swimming muscles, their brains, and the retinas of their eyes, for example. Warming these organs allows the fishes to hunt effectively in cold water. To keep a body part warm, the arteries entering it run in intimate contact with the veins leaving it, allowing rapid transfer of heat by conduction between the vessels. The heat in the venous blood leaving the body part passes to the cold arterial blood approaching it; by the time the arterial blood reaches the part in question, it is warm. Thus, the "countercurrent" flow of blood in the adjoining vessels traps heat in a particular region.

materials, such as Styrofoam™ and fiberglass, are mostly dead air. Figure 14.18 shows a "space-age" ceramic material with highly unusual thermal properties, including very small conductivity.

 Quantitative Analysis 14.5 **Big house, little house**

Two neighboring houses are built of the same materials, but one is twice as long, high, and wide as the other and also has walls twice as thick. To keep the two houses equally warm on a cold day, at what rate must the heater in the big house supply heat, compared with the heater in the small house?

A. at twice the rate.
B. at four times the rate.
C. at 16 times the rate.

SOLUTION We assume that the walls, roofs, and basement floors (if any) participate equally in the heat loss from the houses. The larger house is twice as large in each dimension, so it has four times the surface area as the smaller one. If the walls of the two houses were the same thickness, the larger one would lose heat at four times the rate of the small one. But its walls are twice as thick; therefore, the rate of heat flow for a given area is only half as great. We conclude that the larger house loses heat at a rate two times as great as the smaller one. The correct answer is A.

PROBLEM-SOLVING STRATEGY 14.3 **Heat conduction**

SET UP

1. Identify the direction of heat flow in the problem (from hot to cold). In Equation 14.12, L is always measured along that direction and A is always an area perpendicular to that direction. Often, when a box or other container has an irregular shape, but uniform wall thickness, you can approximate it as a flat slab with the same thickness and total wall area.

SOLVE

2. In some problems, the heat flows through two different materials in succession. The temperature at the interface between the two materials is then intermediate between T_H and T_C; represent it by a symbol such as T. The temperature differences for the two materials are then $(T_H - T)$ and $(T - T_C)$. In steady-state heat flow, the same heat has to pass through both materials in succession, so the heat current H must be *the same* in both materials.
3. If there are two *parallel* heat flow paths, so that some heat flows through each, then the total H is the sum of the quantities H_1 and H_2 for the separate paths. An example is heat flow from inside to outside a house, both through the glass in a window and through the surrounding frame. In this case, the temperature difference is the same for the two paths, but L, A, and k may be different.
4. As always, it is essential to use a consistent set of units. If you use a value of k expressed in $W/(m \cdot K)$, don't use distances in cm, heat in calories, or T in °F!

REFLECT

5. Ask whether your results make sense. If you find that Styrofoam™ conducts heat better than copper, you've made a mistake!

▲ **FIGURE 14.18** This protective tile, developed for use in the space shuttle, has extraordinary thermal properties. The extremely small thermal conductivity and small heat capacity of the material make it possible to hold the tile by its edges, even though it is hot enough to emit the light needed for this photograph.

EXAMPLE 14.10 Conduction through a Styrofoam™ cooler

The Styrofoam™ box in Figure 14.19 is used to keep drinks cold at a picnic. The total wall area (including the lid) is 0.80 m², and the wall thickness is 2.0 cm. The box is filled with ice and cans of Omni-Cola, keeping the inner surface at 0°C. What is the rate of heat flow into the box if the temperature of the outside surface is 30°C? How much ice melts in one day (24 h)?

► **FIGURE 14.19**

SOLUTION

SET UP Figure 14.20 shows our sketch. We assume that the total heat flow is approximately the same as it would be through a flat slab of area 0.80 m² and thickness 2.0 cm = 0.020 m. We find k from Table 14.5. The heat of fusion of ice is 3.34×10^5 J/kg. There are 86,400 s in one day.

SOLVE From Equation 14.12, the heat current H (rate of heat flow) is

$$H = kA\frac{T_2 - T_1}{L}$$

$$= [0.010 \text{ W}/(\text{m} \cdot \text{K})](0.80 \text{ m}^2)\frac{30°C - 0°C}{0.020 \text{ m}}$$

$$= 12 \text{ W}.$$

The total heat flow Q in one day is

$$Q = Ht = (12 \text{ J/s})(86,400 \text{ s}) = 1.04 \times 10^6 \text{ J}.$$

The mass of ice melted by this quantity of heat is

$$m = \frac{Q}{L_f} = \frac{1.04 \times 10^6 \text{ J}}{3.34 \times 10^5 \text{ J/kg}} = 3.1 \text{ kg}.$$

▲ **FIGURE 14.20** Our sketch for this problem.

REFLECT A typical bag of ice you buy at the market is 8 lb = 3.6 kg. So this amount is roughly equal to one 8 lb bag of ice.

Practice Problem: This same Styrofoam™ cooler is sitting in the sun, and the outside temperature reaches 40°C. How much time passes before the 8 lb of ice is completely melted? *Answer: t = 21 h.*

EXAMPLE 14.11 Conduction in two bars in series

A steel bar 10.0 cm long is welded end to end to a copper bar 20.0 cm long. Each bar has a square cross section 2.00 cm on a side. The free end of the steel bar is in contact with steam at 100°C, and the free end of the copper bar is in contact with ice at 0°C. Find the temperature at the junction of the two bars and the total rate of heat flow.

SOLUTION

SET UP Figure 14.21 shows our sketch; we use the subscripts s and c for steel and copper, respectively. The key to the solution is the fact that the heat currents in the two bars must be equal; otherwise, some sections would have more heat flowing in than out, or the reverse, and steady-state conditions could not exist.

SOLVE Let T be the unknown junction temperature; we use Equation 14.12 for each bar and equate the two expressions:

$$\frac{k_s A(100°C - T)}{L_s} = \frac{k_c A(T - 0°C)}{L_c}.$$

▲ **FIGURE 14.21** Our sketch for this problem.

Continued

The areas A are equal and may be divided out. Substituting numerical values, we find that

$$\frac{[50.2 \ \text{W}/(\text{m} \cdot \text{K})](100°\text{C} - T)}{0.100 \ \text{m}}$$
$$= \frac{[385 \ \text{W}/(\text{m} \cdot \text{K})](T - 0°\text{C})}{0.200 \ \text{m}}.$$

Rearranging and solving for T, we obtain

$$T = 20.7°\text{C}.$$

To find the total heat current H, we substitute this value for T back into either of the previous expressions:

$$H = \frac{[50.2 \ \text{W}/(\text{m} \cdot \text{K})](0.0200 \ \text{m})^2(100°\text{C} - 20.7°\text{C})}{0.100 \ \text{m}}$$
$$= 15.9 \ \text{W}$$

or

$$H = \frac{[385 \ \text{W}/(\text{m} \cdot \text{K})](0.0200 \ \text{m})^2(20.7°\text{C} - 0°\text{C})}{0.200 \ \text{m}}$$
$$= 15.9 \ \text{W}.$$

REFLECT Even though the steel bar is shorter, the temperature drop across it is much greater than that across the copper bar because steel is a much poorer conductor of heat.

Practice Problem: If we change the length of the steel bar, what length is needed in order to make the temperature at the junction 50.0°C? *Answer:* 2.60 cm.

EXAMPLE 14.12 **Conduction in two bars in parallel**

Suppose the two bars in Example 14.11 are separated. One end of each bar is placed in contact with steam at 100°C, and the other end of each bar contacts ice at 0°C. What is the *total* rate of heat flow in the two bars?

SOLUTION

SET UP Figure 14.22 shows our sketch. In this case the bars are in parallel rather than in series. As before, we use the subscripts s and c for steel and copper, respectively.

SOLVE The total heat current H is now the *sum* of the currents in the two bars. The temperature difference between ends is the same for both bars: $T_H - T_C = 100°\text{C} - 0°\text{C} = 100 \ \text{K}$. We find that

$$H = \frac{\Delta Q}{\Delta t} = k_c A_c \frac{T_{H,c} - T_{C,c}}{L_c} + k_s A_s \frac{T_{H,s} - T_{C,s}}{L_s}$$
$$= \frac{[385 \ W/(\text{m} \cdot \text{K})](0.0200 \ \text{m})^2(100 \ \text{K})}{0.200 \ \text{m}}$$
$$+ \frac{[50.2 \ \text{W}/(\text{m} \cdot \text{K})](0.0200 \text{m})^2(100 \ \text{K})}{0.100 \ \text{m}}$$
$$= 77.0 \ \text{W} + 20.1 \ \text{W} = 97.1 \ \text{W}.$$

REFLECT The heat flow in the copper bar is much greater than that in the steel bar, even though the steel bar is longer, because its thermal conductivity is much larger. The total heat flow is

▲ **FIGURE 14.22** Our sketch for this problem.

much greater than that in Example 14.11, partly because the total cross section for heat flow is greater and partly because the full 100 C° temperature difference acts across each bar.

Practice Problem: Suppose we increase the cross-sectional area of the steel bar. What cross-sectional area would be needed to make the heat currents in the two bars equal? *Answer:* 15.3 cm².

Convection

Convection is the transfer of heat by the motion of a mass of fluid from one region of space to another. Familiar examples include hot-air and hot-water home heating systems, the cooling system of an automobile engine, and the heating and cooling of the body by the flow of blood. If the fluid is circulated by a blower or pump, the process is called *forced convection;* if the flow is caused by differences in density due to thermal expansion, such as hot air rising, the process is called *natural convection* or *free convection.*

EXAMPLE 14.14 Radiation from the human body

If the total surface area of a woman's body is 1.2 m² and her skin temperature is 30°C, find the total rate of radiation of energy from her body. She also *absorbs* radiation from her surroundings. If the surroundings are at a temperature of 20°C, what is her *net* rate of heat loss by radiation? The emissivity of the body is very close to unity, irrespective of skin pigmentation.

SOLUTION

SET UP We need to convert the temperatures to absolute (Kelvin) temperatures: 30°C = 303 K and 20°C = 293 K. The rate of radiation of energy per unit area is given by Equation 14.13.

SOLVE Taking $e = 1$, we find that

$$H = Ae\sigma T^4$$
$$= (1.2 \text{ m}^2)(1)[5.67 \times 10^{-8} \text{ W}/(\text{m}^2 \cdot \text{K}^4)](303 \text{ K})^4$$
$$= 574 \text{ W}.$$

This loss is partly offset by the *absorption* of radiation, which depends on the temperature of the surroundings. The *net* rate of radiative energy transfer is given by Equation 14.14:

$$H = Ae\sigma(T^4 - T_s^4)$$
$$= (1.2 \text{ m}^2)(1)[(5.67 \times 10^{-8} \text{ W}/(\text{m}^2 \cdot \text{K}^4)]$$
$$\cdot [(303 \text{ K})^4 - (293 \text{ K})^4]$$
$$= 72 \text{ W}.$$

REFLECT The heat produced by the human body at rest is about 75 W. Thus, this net rate of radiation is sufficient to prevent overheating. But when additional heat is produced by even mild exertion, heat must be removed by other means, such as evaporative cooling.

▲ **See my heat.** Just as an ordinary photograph captures visible light from an object, an infrared image captures heat released in the form of long-wavelength infrared radiation (infrared light). We cannot see infrared light without the help of special cameras or goggles. However, the venomous snakes known as pit vipers, which include the rattlesnakes and water moccasins, have special "pit organs" on their snout that are sensitive to infrared radiation. These snakes hunt mostly at night; their pit organs help them to "see" their warm-blooded prey in the cool darkness.

An object that is a good absorber must also be a good emitter. An ideal radiator, with an emissivity of unity, is also an ideal absorber, absorbing *all* of the radiation that strikes it. Such an ideal surface is called an ideal blackbody, or simply a **blackbody.** Conversely, an ideal *reflector,* which absorbs *no* radiation at all, is a highly ineffective radiator. This is the reason for the silver coatings on vacuum, or thermos, bottles, which were invented by Sir James Dewar (1842–1923). A vacuum bottle has double glass walls, and the air is pumped out of the spaces between the walls, eliminating nearly all heat transfer by conduction and convection. The silver coating on the walls reflects most of the radiation from the contents back into the container, and the wall itself is a very poor emitter. Thus, a vacuum bottle can keep coffee or soup hot for several hours. The Dewar flask, used to store very cold liquefied gases, is exactly the same in principle.

Heat transfer by radiation is important in some surprising places. A premature baby in an incubator can be cooled dangerously by radiation if the walls of the incubator happen to be cold, even when the *air* in the incubator is warm. Some incubators regulate the air temperature by measuring the baby's skin temperature.

We can study the infrared radiation emitted by an object by using a camera with infrared-sensitive film or by means of a device, similar to a television camera, that is sensitive to infrared radiation. The resulting picture is called a *thermograph.* The rate of emission of energy depends strongly on temperature, so thermography permits the detailed study of temperature distributions, with a precision as great as 0.1 C°. Thermography is used to study energy losses in heated buildings, and it has several important medical applications. Various tumors, such as breast cancer, cause local temperature variations, and growths as small as 1 cm can be detected. Circulatory disorders that cause local temperature anomalies can be studied, and thermography has many other applications.

*14.8 Solar Energy and Resource Conservation

The principles of heat transfer that we've studied in this chapter have many practical applications in a civilization such as ours, with growing energy consumption and dwindling energy resources. A substantial fraction of all the energy consumption in the United States is used to heat and cool homes and other buildings,

▶ **Baked in a convection oven?** The volcanic Hawaiian Islands are a by-product of the earth's convective cooling system. Earth's deep interior generates heat, mainly by the decay of radioactive elements and the slow solidification of the liquid core. The temperature difference between the hot interior and the cold crust sets up density differences that cause the solid rock of the earth's crust and mantle to flow in (very) slow convective motions, carrying heat from the interior to the surface. The Hawaiian islands are built by a dramatic type of convective flow called a *mantle plume*—a vertical jet of hot rock that may rise from near the core itself. As this plume approaches the surface, the reduction in pressure causes some of the plume's rock to melt, creating the lava that builds the islands. In the foreground we see a cinder cone on the peak of Mauna Kea; in the background is the silhouette of Mauna Loa.

We invite you to check for consistency of units in Equation 14.13. Emissivity *e* is often larger for dark surfaces than for light ones. The emissivity of a smooth copper surface is about 0.3, but *e* for a dull black surface is nearly unity.

 Quantitative Analysis 14.6 **Raising the temperature**

If the Kelvin temperature of a spherical object were increased by 20%, by approximately what factor would the rate of radiated energy emitted from its surface be changed?

A. 1.2.
B. 1.4.
C. 1.7.
D. 2.0.

SOLUTION The rate of radiation of energy is proportional to the fourth power of the absolute temperature. If the temperature increases by a factor of 1.2, the rate of radiation increases by a factor of $(1.2)^4$, or 2.07 (to three significant figures). The closest answer to this is D, the correct answer.

EXAMPLE 14.13 **Radiation from a hot plate**

A thin, square steel plate 10 cm on a side is heated in a blacksmith's forge to a temperature of 800°C. If the emissivity is 0.60, what is the plate's rate of radiation of energy?

SOLUTION

SET UP The total surface area of the plate, including both sides, is $2(0.10 \text{ m})^2 = 0.020 \text{ m}^2$. We must convert the temperature to the Kelvin scale: 800°C = 1073 K.

SOLVE Equation 14.13 gives

$$H = Ae\sigma T^4$$
$$= (0.020 \text{ m}^2)(0.60)[5.67 \times 10^{-8} \text{ W}/(\text{m}^2 \cdot \text{K}^4)](1073 \text{ K})^4$$
$$= 900 \text{ W}.$$

REFLECT This rate of emission of energy is comparable to the output of a small electric space heater.

Practice Problem: What temperature would be required for this plate to radiate at the rate of 1500 W? *Answer:* 950°C.

While an object at absolute (Kelvin) temperature *T* is radiating, its surroundings, at temperature T_s, are also radiating, and the object *absorbs* some of this radiation. If it is in thermal equilibrium with its surroundings, the rates of radiation and absorption must be equal. For this to be true, the rate of absorption must be given in general by $H = Ae\sigma T_s^4$. Then the *net* rate of radiation from an object at temperature *T* with surroundings at temperature T_s is

$$H_{net} = Ae\sigma T^4 - Ae\sigma T_s^4 = Ae\sigma(T^4 - T_s^4). \tag{14.14}$$

In this equation, a positive value of *H* means a net heat flow *out of* the object. Equation 14.14 shows that, for radiation, as for conduction and convection, the heat current depends on the temperature *difference* between two objects.

EXAMPLE 14.14 **Radiation from the human body**

If the total surface area of a woman's body is 1.2 m^2 and her skin temperature is 30°C, find the total rate of radiation of energy from her body. She also *absorbs* radiation from her surroundings. If the surroundings are at a temperature of 20°C, what is her *net* rate of heat loss by radiation? The emissivity of the body is very close to unity, irrespective of skin pigmentation.

SOLUTION

SET UP We need to convert the temperatures to absolute (Kelvin) temperatures: 30°C = 303 K and 20°C = 293 K. The rate of radiation of energy per unit area is given by Equation 14.13.

SOLVE Taking $e = 1$, we find that

$$H = Ae\sigma T^4$$
$$= (1.2 \text{ m}^2)(1)[5.67 \times 10^{-8} \text{ W}/(\text{m}^2 \cdot \text{K}^4)](303 \text{ K})^4$$
$$= 574 \text{ W}.$$

This loss is partly offset by the *absorption* of radiation, which depends on the temperature of the surroundings. The *net* rate of radiative energy transfer is given by Equation 14.14:

$$H = Ae\sigma(T^4 - T_s^4)$$
$$= (1.2 \text{ m}^2)(1)[(5.67 \times 10^{-8} \text{ W}/(\text{m}^2 \cdot \text{K}^4)]$$
$$\cdot [(303 \text{ K})^4 - (293 \text{ K})^4]$$
$$= 72 \text{ W}.$$

REFLECT The heat produced by the human body at rest is about 75 W. Thus, this net rate of radiation is sufficient to prevent over-heating. But when additional heat is produced by even mild exertion, heat must be removed by other means, such as evaporative cooling.

▲ **See my heat.** Just as an ordinary photograph captures visible light from an object, an infrared image captures heat released in the form of long-wavelength infrared radiation (infrared light). We cannot see infrared light without the help of special cameras or goggles. However, the venomous snakes known as pit vipers, which include the rattlesnakes and water moccasins, have special "pit organs" on their snout that are sensitive to infrared radiation. These snakes hunt mostly at night; their pit organs help them to "see" their warm-blooded prey in the cool darkness.

An object that is a good absorber must also be a good emitter. An ideal radiator, with an emissivity of unity, is also an ideal absorber, absorbing *all* of the radiation that strikes it. Such an ideal surface is called an ideal blackbody, or simply a **blackbody.** Conversely, an ideal *reflector*, which absorbs *no* radiation at all, is a highly ineffective radiator. This is the reason for the silver coatings on vacuum, or thermos, bottles, which were invented by Sir James Dewar (1842–1923). A vacuum bottle has double glass walls, and the air is pumped out of the spaces between the walls, eliminating nearly all heat transfer by conduction and convection. The silver coating on the walls reflects most of the radiation from the contents back into the container, and the wall itself is a very poor emitter. Thus, a vacuum bottle can keep coffee or soup hot for several hours. The Dewar flask, used to store very cold liquefied gases, is exactly the same in principle.

Heat transfer by radiation is important in some surprising places. A premature baby in an incubator can be cooled dangerously by radiation if the walls of the incubator happen to be cold, even when the *air* in the incubator is warm. Some incubators regulate the air temperature by measuring the baby's skin temperature.

We can study the infrared radiation emitted by an object by using a camera with infrared-sensitive film or by means of a device, similar to a television camera, that is sensitive to infrared radiation. The resulting picture is called a *thermograph*. The rate of emission of energy depends strongly on temperature, so thermography permits the detailed study of temperature distributions, with a precision as great as 0.1 C°. Thermography is used to study energy losses in heated buildings, and it has several important medical applications. Various tumors, such as breast cancer, cause local temperature variations, and growths as small as 1 cm can be detected. Circulatory disorders that cause local temperature anomalies can be studied, and thermography has many other applications.

*14.8 Solar Energy and Resource Conservation

The principles of heat transfer that we've studied in this chapter have many practical applications in a civilization such as ours, with growing energy consumption and dwindling energy resources. A substantial fraction of all the energy consumption in the United States is used to heat and cool homes and other buildings,

The areas A are equal and may be divided out. Substituting numerical values, we find that

$$\frac{[50.2 \text{ W}/(\text{m} \cdot \text{K})](100°\text{C} - T)}{0.100 \text{ m}}$$
$$= \frac{[385 \text{ W}/(\text{m} \cdot \text{K})](T - 0°\text{C})}{0.200 \text{ m}}.$$

Rearranging and solving for T, we obtain

$$T = 20.7°\text{C}.$$

To find the total heat current H, we substitute this value for T back into either of the previous expressions:

$$H = \frac{[50.2 \text{ W}/(\text{m} \cdot \text{K})](0.0200 \text{ m})^2(100°\text{C} - 20.7°\text{C})}{0.100 \text{ m}}$$
$$= 15.9 \text{ W}$$

or

$$H = \frac{[385 \text{ W}/(\text{m} \cdot \text{K})](0.0200 \text{ m})^2(20.7°\text{C} - 0°\text{C})}{0.200 \text{ m}}$$
$$= 15.9 \text{ W}.$$

REFLECT Even though the steel bar is shorter, the temperature drop across it is much greater than that across the copper bar because steel is a much poorer conductor of heat.

Practice Problem: If we change the length of the steel bar, what length is needed in order to make the temperature at the junction 50.0°C? *Answer:* 2.60 cm.

EXAMPLE 14.12 Conduction in two bars in parallel

Suppose the two bars in Example 14.11 are separated. One end of each bar is placed in contact with steam at 100°C, and the other end of each bar contacts ice at 0°C. What is the *total* rate of heat flow in the two bars?

SOLUTION

SET UP Figure 14.22 shows our sketch. In this case the bars are in parallel rather than in series. As before, we use the subscripts s and c for steel and copper, respectively.

SOLVE The total heat current H is now the *sum* of the currents in the two bars. The temperature difference between ends is the same for both bars: $T_H - T_C = 100°\text{C} - 0°\text{C} = 100 \text{ K}$. We find that

$$H = \frac{\Delta Q}{\Delta t} = k_c A_c \frac{T_{H,c} - T_{C,c}}{L_c} + k_s A_s \frac{T_{H,s} - T_{C,s}}{L_s}$$
$$= \frac{[385 \text{ W}/(\text{m} \cdot \text{K})](0.0200 \text{ m})^2(100 \text{ K})}{0.200 \text{ m}}$$
$$+ \frac{[50.2 \text{ W}/(\text{m} \cdot \text{K})](0.0200\text{m})^2(100 \text{ K})}{0.100 \text{ m}}$$
$$= 77.0 \text{ W} + 20.1 \text{ W} = 97.1 \text{ W}.$$

REFLECT The heat flow in the copper bar is much greater than that in the steel bar, even though the copper bar is longer, because its thermal conductivity is much larger. The total heat flow is

▲ **FIGURE 14.22** Our sketch for this problem.

much greater than that in Example 14.11, partly because the total cross section for heat flow is greater and partly because the full 100 C° temperature difference acts across each bar.

Practice Problem: Suppose we increase the cross-sectional area of the steel bar. What cross-sectional area would be needed to make the heat currents in the two bars equal? *Answer:* 15.3 cm².

Convection

Convection is the transfer of heat by the motion of a mass of fluid from one region of space to another. Familiar examples include hot-air and hot-water home heating systems, the cooling system of an automobile engine, and the heating and cooling of the body by the flow of blood. If the fluid is circulated by a blower or pump, the process is called *forced convection;* if the flow is caused by differences in density due to thermal expansion, such as hot air rising, the process is called *natural convection* or *free convection*.

Day: The land is warmer than the water; convection draws a sea breeze onshore.

Night: The land is colder than the water; convection sends a land breeze offshore.

▲ **FIGURE 14.23** Convective currents in the air determine daytime sea breezes and nighttime land breezes near shore.

▲ **FIGURE 14.24** Heat transfer by radiation from the sun. The heat is not dangerous to human skin, but the ultraviolet radiation is.

Convection in the atmosphere plays a dominant role in determining weather patterns (Figure 14.23), and convection in the oceans is an important global heat-transfer mechanism. On a smaller scale, glider pilots make use of thermal updrafts from the warm earth. But sometimes the air cools enough as it rises to form thunderheads, which contain convection currents that can tear a glider to pieces.

The most important mechanism for heat transfer within the human body is forced convection of blood, with the heart serving as the pump. The total rate of heat loss from the body is on the order of 100 to 200 W (2000 to 4000 kcal per day). A dry, unclothed body in still air loses about 75 W by radiation, but during vigorous exercise and plentiful perspiration, evaporative cooling with convection is the dominant mechanism.

Convective heat transfer is a complex process, and there is no simple equation to describe it. Here are a few experimental facts: The heat current due to convection is directly proportional to the surface area involved. This is the reason for the large surface areas of radiators and cooling fins. In some cases, it is approximately proportional to the $\frac{5}{4}$ power of the temperature difference between the surface and the main body of fluid. The viscosity of fluids slows natural convection near a stationary surface. In air, this effect produces a surface film; forced convection decreases the thickness of this film, increasing the rate of heat transfer. This is the reason for the "wind-chill factor": You get cold faster in a cold wind than in still air with the same temperature.

Radiation

Heat transfer by **radiation** depends on electromagnetic waves such as visible light, infrared, and ultraviolet radiation. Everyone has felt the warmth of the sun's radiation (Figure 14.24) and the intense heat from a charcoal grill or the glowing coals in a fireplace. Heat from these very hot objects reaches you not by conduction or convection in the intervening air, but by *radiation*. This kind of heat transfer would occur even if there were nothing but vacuum between you and the source of heat.

Every object, even at ordinary temperatures, emits energy in the form of electromagnetic radiation. At ordinary temperatures, say, 20°C, nearly all the energy is carried by infrared waves with wavelengths much longer than those of visible light. As the temperature rises, the wavelengths shift to shorter values. At 800°C, an object emits enough visible radiation to be self-luminous and appears "red hot," although even at this temperature most of the energy is carried by infrared waves. At 3000°C, the temperature of an incandescent lamp filament, the radiation contains enough visible light that the object appears "white hot."

The rate of energy radiation from a surface is proportional to the surface area A. The rate increases very rapidly with temperature, in proportion to the fourth power of the absolute (Kelvin) temperature. The rate also depends on the nature of the surface; this dependence is described by a quantity e called the **emissivity,** a dimensionless number between 0 and 1. The heat current $H = \Delta Q / \Delta t$ due to radiation from a surface area A with emissivity e at absolute (Kelvin) temperature T can be expressed as

$$H = Ae\sigma T^4, \tag{14.13}$$

where σ is a fundamental physical constant called the **Stefan–Boltzmann constant.** This relation is called the **Stefan–Boltzmann law,** in honor of its late-19th-century discoverers. The numerical value of σ is found experimentally to be

$$\sigma = 5.6705 \times 10^{-8} \text{ W}/(\text{m}^2 \cdot \text{K}^4).$$

to maintain a comfortable temperature and humidity inside when the outside temperature is much hotter or much colder.

For space heating, the objective is to prevent as much heat flow as possible from inside to outside; heating units replace the inevitable loss of heat. Walls insulated with material of low thermal conductivity, storm windows, and multiple-layer glass windows all help to reduce heat loss. It has been estimated that if all buildings used such materials, the total energy needed for space heating would be reduced by at least one-third.

Air-conditioning in summer poses the reverse problem: Heat flows from outside to inside, and energy must be expended in refrigeration units to remove it. Again, appropriate insulation can decrease this energy cost considerably.

Direct conversion of solar energy is a promising development in energy technology. Near the earth, the rate of energy transfer due to solar radiation is about 1400 W for each square meter of surface area. Not all of this energy reaches the earth's surface; even on a clear day, about one-fourth of the energy is absorbed by the earth's atmosphere. In a typical household solar heating system, large black plates facing the sun are backed with pipes through which water circulates. The black surface absorbs most of the sun's radiation; the heat is transferred by conduction to the water and then by forced convection to radiators inside the house. Heat loss by convection of air near the solar collecting panels is reduced by covering them with glass, with a thin air space between the glass and the panel. An insulated heat reservoir stores the energy collected for use at night and on cloudy days. Many larger-scale solar-energy conversion systems, including windmills, are also currently under study; a few examples are discussed in Section 16.9.

From an environmental standpoint, solar energy has multiple advantages over the use of fossil fuels (burning of coal or oil) or nuclear power. Fossil fuels are being used up; solar power continues indefinitely. Obtaining fossil fuels may involve strip mining, with its associated destruction of landscape and elimination of other useful land functions, such as farming or timber. Offshore oil drilling is a source of ocean water pollution. Air pollution from combustion products is a familiar problem, as is acid rain, which is directly attributable to coal smoke in many cases. Excess atmospheric carbon dioxide produced by the combustion of hydrocarbons is a major contributor to the so-called greenhouse effect. Many responsible scientists believe that the long-range effects on our climate will be serious or even catastrophic unless greenhouse gas emission is substantially reduced.

Nuclear power poses radiation hazards and the problem of disposing of radioactive waste material. Solar power avoids all these problems. Some practical problems still need to be worked out, however, including high installation costs and the need for energy storage facilities for nighttime and cloudy days.

Intelligent consideration of the effects of solar radiation in the design of buildings can also reduce energy consumption in heating and cooling. In recent years, there has been considerable growth in awareness of the need to design buildings with energy conservation in mind. The need to conserve is pressing and will undoubtedly become more so in years to come.

▲ **Driving off using the sunset.** Solar energy represents an almost limitless source of energy if we can figure out how to convert it efficiently into usable forms such as mechanical, chemical, or electrical energy. Thanks to ultralight materials and efficient solar panels and energy converters, the Nuna 2, pictured here, can reach speeds of over 100 mph (160 km/hr)! This car, designed and built in the Netherlands by physics and engineering students, shows how limitless human imagination, creativity, and innovation can be with enough study and hard work.

SUMMARY

Temperature and Temperature Scales

(Sections 14.1 and 14.2) Two objects in **thermal equilibrium** must have the same temperature. A conducting material between two objects permits interaction leading to thermal equilibrium; an insulating material prevents or impedes this interaction. The **Celsius** and **Fahrenheit** temperature scales are based on the freezing ($0°C = 32°F$) and boiling ($100°C = 212°F$) temperatures of water, related by the formulas $T_F = \frac{9}{5}T_C + 32°$ and $T_C = \frac{5}{9}(T_F - 32°)$ (Equations 14.1 and 14.2).

The **Kelvin** scale has its zero at the extrapolated zero-pressure temperature for a gas thermometer, which is $-273.15°C$. Thus, $0\ \text{K} = -273.15°C$, and $T_K = T_C + 273.15$ (Equation 14.3).

 If A and B are each in thermal equilibrium with C ...

 ... then A and B are in thermal equilibrium with each other.

Thermal Expansion

(Section 14.3) The change ΔL in any linear dimension L_0 of a solid object with a temperature change ΔT is approximately $\Delta L = \alpha L_0 \Delta T$ (Equation 14.4), where α is the **coefficient of linear expansion.** The change ΔV in the volume V_0 of any solid or liquid material with a temperature change ΔT is approximately $\Delta V = \beta V_0 \Delta T$ (Equation 14.6), where β is the **coefficient of volume expansion.** For many solids, $\beta = 3\alpha$.

$$L = L_0 + \Delta L$$
$$= L_0(1 + \alpha \Delta T)$$

Heat, Phase Changes, and Calorimetry

(Sections 14.4–14.6) Heat is energy transferred from one object to another as a result of a temperature difference. The quantity of heat Q required to raise the temperature of a mass m of material by a small amount ΔT is $Q = mc\Delta T$ (Equation 14.10), where c is the **specific heat capacity** of the material.

To change a mass m of a material to a different phase (such as liquid to solid or liquid to vapor) at the same temperature requires the addition or subtraction of a quantity of heat Q given by $Q = \pm mL$ (Equation 14.11), where L is the **heat of fusion, heat of vaporization,** or **heat of sublimation.**

Calculations with heat are called **calorimetry calculations:** In an isolated system whose parts interact by heat exchange, the algebraic sum of the Q's for all parts of the system must be zero.

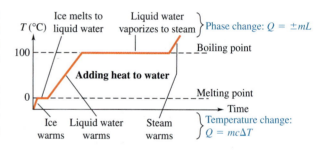

Heat Transfer

(Section 14.7) The three mechanisms of heat transfer are conduction, convection, and radiation. **Conduction** is transfer of energy of molecular motion within materials without bulk motion of the materials. **Convection** involves the motion of a mass from one region to another. **Radiation** is energy transfer through electromagnetic radiation.

The **heat current** H for conduction depends on the area A through which the heat flows, the length L of the heat path, the temperature difference $(T_H - T_C)$, and the thermal conductivity k of the material, according to the equation

$$H = kA\frac{T_H - T_C}{L}. \qquad (14.12)$$

The heat current H due to radiation is given by $H = Ae\sigma T^4$ (Equation 14.13), where A is the surface area, e is the **emissivity** of the surface (a pure number between 0 and 1), T is the absolute (Kelvin) temperature, and σ is the Stefan–Boltzmann constant.

$$H = kA\frac{T_H - T_C}{L}$$

Continued

Solar Energy and Resource Conservation

(Section 14.8) A substantial fraction of all energy consumption in the United States is used to heat and cool homes and other buildings. Insulation in walls and multiple-layer glass windows can reduce heat flow by at least a third.

In a typical household solar heating system, large black plates facing the sun are backed with pipes through which water circulates. The black surface absorbs most of the sun's radiation; the heat is transferred by conduction to the water and then by forced convection to radiators inside the house.

(MP) For instructor-assigned homework, go to www.masteringphysics.com

Conceptual Questions

1. When a block with a hole in it is heated, why doesn't the material around the hole expand into the hole and make it smaller? Explain this behavior by looking at the forces operating at the molecular level.

2. You have a drink that you want to cool off. You could put in 100 g of ice or 100 g of water, both at 0°C. Which one would be more effective in cooling your drink? Why?

3. A thermostat for controlling household heating systems often contains a bimetallic element consisting of two parallel strips of different metals welded together along their length. When the temperature changes, this composite strip bends one way or the other. Why?

4. Why is it sometimes possible to loosen caps on screw-top bottles by dipping the capped bottle briefly into hot water?

5. Galileo supposedly designed a thermometer consisting of hollow metal spheres suspended in a liquid inside a vertical glass cylinder. At a low temperature, all the spheres were at the top of the liquid. As the temperature of the room (and hence of the liquid and the spheres) rose, the spheres, one by one, would descend from the top. Each sphere was marked with the temperature at which it descended. (Replicas of this thermometer are available today, one of which sits on the author's fireplace mantel.) Explain the physical principles behind the operation of this device. What do you suppose is different about the properties of the spheres?

6. Builders usually put steel bars (called *rebar*) inside of concrete slabs for reinforcement. Since the concrete and rebar are made of different materials, it might seem that they should expand at different rates when heated and that the rebar should actually *weaken* the concrete. So why does adding rebar strengthen concrete? What might happen if a metal other than steel were used?

7. Suppose you have a thermos bottle half full of cold coffee. Could you warm it up to drinking temperature by shaking it? Is this possible *in principle?* Is it feasible *in practice?* Why or why not?

8. You've probably seen what happens to lettuce or other vegetables if they freeze accidentally in the refrigerator. Freezing cells, as opposed to just making them cold, can kill them by causing them to burst. Why does a cell burst when frozen?

9. True or false? When two objects at different temperatures are placed in contact, the rise in temperature of the cooler object must equal the drop in temperature of the warmer one.

10. If you have wet hands and pick up a piece of metal that is below the freezing point of water, you may stick to it. This doesn't happen with wood. Why this difference in behavior?

11. If you add heat slowly to ice at 0°C, why doesn't the temperature of the ice increase? What becomes of this heat energy? Likewise, if you add heat to boiling water, the temperature remains at 100°C. What is happening to the heat you add?

12. Some people claim that ice cubes freeze faster if the trays are filled with hot water because hot water cools off faster than cold water. Is this plausible? Why or why not?

13. A person pours a cup of hot coffee, intending to drink it 5 minutes later. To have it as hot as possible for drinking, should she put the cold milk into it now or wait until just before she drinks it? Explain your reasoning.

14. If you put your hand into boiling water at 212°F, you will immediately get a serious burn. Yet you readily reach into a much hotter 400°F oven without danger. Why the difference? (*Hint:* What are the significant differences between the properties of the air in the oven and the boiling water?)

15. You are going away for the weekend and plan to turn down your home thermostat to conserve energy. Your neighbor suggests that you not turn it down, because the walls and floors of your home will get cold and have to be reheated when you get back, which will take more energy than you save. Should you follow your neighbor's advice? Consider all three forms of heat transfer (conduction, convection, and radiation).

16. Why is snow, which is made up of ice crystals, a much better insulator than ice?

17. You are putting insulation in your walls. The insulation you have purchased is 6 in. thick, but the space in your walls is just 4 in. deep. If you squeeze the insulation into the 4 in. space, will it provide the same insulating value as if you put it in a 6 in. space? Why or why not?

18. Give some good reasons why the equation $H = e\sigma A T^4$ is valid only if the temperature is expressed in kelvins (rather than degrees Fahrenheit or Celsius).

Multiple-Choice Problems

1. If heat Q is required to increase the temperature of a metal object from 4°C to 6°C, the amount of heat necessary to increase its temperature from 6°C to 12°C is most likely
   A. Q.   B. $2Q$.   C. $3Q$.   D. $4Q$.

2. A metal bar expands by 1.0 mm when its temperature is increased by 1.0 C°. Which of the following statements about this bar must be true? (There may be more than one correct choice.)
   A. It will expand by more than 1.0 mm if its temperature is increased by 1.0 K.
   B. It will expand by less than 1.0 mm if its temperature is increased by 1.0 F°.
   C. It will expand by 2.00 mm if its temperature is increased by 2.0 K.
   D. It will expand by more than 2.0 mm if its temperature is increased by 2.0 F°.

3. If an amount of heat Q is needed to increase the temperature of a solid metal sphere of diameter D from 4°C to 7°C, the amount of heat needed to increase the temperature of a solid sphere of diameter $2D$ of the same metal from 4°C to 7°C is
   A. Q.   B. $2Q$.   C. $4Q$.   D. $8Q$.

4. If you mix 100 g of ice at 0°C with 100 g of boiling water at 100°C in a perfectly insulated container, the final stabilized temperature will be
   A. 0°C.
   B. between 0°C and 50°C.
   C. 50°C.
   D. between 50°C and 100°C.

5. A sphere radiates energy at a rate of 1.00 J/s when its temperature is 100°C. At what rate will it radiate energy if its temperature is increased to 200°C? (Neglect any heat transferred back into the sphere.)
   A. 1.27 J/s.   B. 2.00 J/s.   C. 2.59 J/s.   D. 16.0 J/s.

6. A solid cylindrical metal rod of diameter D with insulation wrapped around it conducts 50.0 J/s of heat from a hot to a cold reservoir. If the diameter of this rod were reduced to $D/2$ the heat it would conduct would be
   A. 200 J/s.   B. 100 J/s.   C. 25 J/s.   D. 12.5 J/s.

7. The wall of a furnace conducts 1000 cal/min of heat out of the furnace and into the factory. If the wall's thickness is doubled, but nothing else changes (including the inner and outer surface temperatures), the amount of heat it conducts into the factory will be
   A. 4000 cal/min.
   B. 2000 cal/min.
   C. 500 cal/min.
   D. 250 cal/min.

8. A thin metal rod expands 1.5 mm when its temperature is increased by 2.0 C°. If an identical rod of the same material, except *twice as long,* also has its temperature increased by 2.0 C°, it will expand
   A. 0.75 mm.   B. 1.0 mm.   C. 3.0 mm.   D. 6.0 mm.

9. If a sphere originally radiates 100 J/s, how much energy will it radiate per second if its absolute temperature is doubled and its diameter is halved? (Neglect any heat transferred into the sphere.)
   A. 100 J/s.   B. 200 J/s.   C. 400 J/s.   D. 800 J/s.

10. A cylindrical metal bar conducts heat at a rate R from a hot reservoir to a cold reservoir. If both its *length* and *diameter* are doubled, it will conduct heat at a rate
    A. R.   B. $2R$.   C. $4R$.   D. $8R$.

11. Two rods P and Q of identical shape and size, but made of different metals, are joined end to end. The left end of rod P is kept at 100°C while the right end of rod Q is at 0°C, causing heat to flow down the rods. The graph in Figure 14.25 shows the temperature distribution along the rods from the hot end to the cold end. Which rod has the higher thermal conductivity?
    A. rod P.
    B. rod Q.
    C. We cannot tell from the available data.

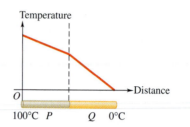

▲ **FIGURE 14.25** Multiple-choice problem 11.

12. The thermal conductivity of concrete is 0.80 W/(m · K), and the thermal conductivity of a certain wood is 0.10 W/(m · K). How thick would a solid concrete wall have to be to have the same rate of heat flow as an 8.0-cm-thick solid wall of this wood? Both walls have the same surface area and the same interior and exterior temperatures.
    A. 1.0 cm.   B. 16 cm.   C. 32 cm.   D. 64 cm.

13. The graph in Figure 14.26 shows the temperature as a function of time for a sample of material being heated at a constant rate. What segment or segments of this graph show the sample existing in two phases (or states)?
    A. OA.
    B. AB.
    C. OA and BC.

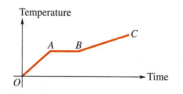

▲ **FIGURE 14.26** Multiple-choice problem 13.

14. For the sample in the previous question, what segment of the graph shows the specific heat capacity of the sample to be *greatest?*
    A. OA.   B. AB.   C. BC.

15. You enter a cold room containing a wooden table and a steel table; both have been there for a long time. Why does the steel table feel much colder than the wooden one?
    A. Steel is a much better conductor of heat than wood is.
    B. The steel stores much more cold than the wood does.
    C. Steel has a higher specific heat capacity than wood has.
    D. The temperature of the steel table is lower than that of the wooden table.

Problems

14.2 Temperature Scales

1. • (a) While vacationing in Europe, you feel sick and are told that you have a temperature of 40.2°C. Should you be concerned? What is your temperature in °F? (b) The morning weather report in Sydney predicts a high temperature of 12°C. Will you need to bring a jacket? What is this temperature in °F? (c) A friend has suggested that you go swimming in a pool having water of temperature 350 K. Is this safe to do? What would this temperature be on the Fahrenheit and Celsius scales?

2. • **Temperatures in biomedicine.** (a) **Normal body temperature.** The average normal body temperature measured in the mouth is 310 K. What would Celsius and Fahrenheit thermometers read for this temperature? (b) **Elevated body temperature.** During very vigorous exercise, the body's temperature can go as high as 40°C. What would Kelvin and Fahrenheit thermometers read for this temperature? (c) **Temperature difference in the body.** The surface temperature of the body is normally about 7 C° lower than the internal temperature. Express this temperature difference in kelvins and in Fahrenheit degrees. (d) **Blood storage.** Blood stored at 4.0°C lasts safely for about 3 weeks, whereas blood stored at −160°C lasts for 5 years. Express both temperatures on the Fahrenheit and Kelvin scales. (e) **Heat stroke.** If the body's temperature is above 105°F for a prolonged period, heat stroke can result. Express this temperature on the Celsius and Kelvin scales.

3. • (a) On January 22, 1943, the temperature in Spearfish, South Dakota, rose from −4.0°F to 45.0°F in just 2 minutes. What was the temperature change in Celsius degrees and in kelvins? (b) The temperature in Browning, Montana, was 44.0°F on January 23, 1916, and the next day it plummeted to −56.0°F. What was the temperature change in Celsius degrees and in kelvins?

4. • **Inside the earth and the sun.** (a) Geophysicists have estimated that the temperature at the center of the earth's core is 5000°C (or more), while the temperature of the sun's core is about 15 million K. Express both of these temperatures in Fahrenheit degrees.

5. •• (a) At what temperature do the Fahrenheit and Celsius scales coincide? (b) Is there any temperature at which the Kelvin and Celsius scales coincide?

6. •• (W) Deduce a formula for converting (a) Fahrenheit degrees directly to Kelvin degrees, (b) Kelvin degrees directly to Fahrenheit degrees. (c) Use your formulas to find the temperature at which the Fahrenheit and Kelvin scales coincide.

14.3 Thermal Expansion

7. • The Eiffel Tower in Paris is 984 ft tall and is made mostly of steel. If this is its height in winter when its temperature is −8.00°C, how much additional vertical distance must you cover if you decide to climb it during a summer heat wave when its temperature is 40.0°C? (b) Express the coefficient of linear expansion of steel in terms of Fahrenheit degrees.

8. • A steel bridge is built in the summer when its temperature is 35.0°C. At the time of construction, its length is 80.00 m. What is the length of the bridge on a cold winter day when its temperature is −12.0°C?

9. • A metal rod is 40.125 cm long at 20.0°C and 40.148 cm long at 45.0°C. Calculate the average coefficient of linear expansion of the rod's material for this temperature range.

10. • (a) Steel train rails are laid in 12.0-m-long segments placed end to end. The rails are laid on a winter day when their temperature is −2.00°C. How much space must be left between adjacent rails if they are just to touch on a summer day when their temperature is 33.0°C? (b) If the rails are mistakenly laid in contact with each other, what is the stress in them on a summer day when their temperature is 33.0°C?

11. • An underground tank with a capacity of 1700 L (1.70 m³) is completely filled with ethanol that has an initial temperature of 19.0°C. After the ethanol has cooled off to the temperature of the tank and ground, which is 10.0°C, how much air space will there be above the ethanol in the tank? (See Table 14.2, and assume that the volume of the tank doesn't change appreciably.)

12. • A copper cylinder is initially at 20.0°C. At what temperature will its volume be 0.150% larger than it is at 20.0°C?

13. • A glass volumetric flask has a capacity of 500.00 mL at room temperature (20.0°C). What is its capacity at a temperature of 5.0°C if the coefficient of *linear* expansion for this glass is $1.20 \times 10^{-5} (\text{C}°)^{-1}$?

14. •• A surveyor's 30.0 m steel tape is correct at a temperature of 20.0°C. The distance between two points, as measured by this tape on a day when its temperature is 5.00°C, is 25.970 m. What is the true distance between the points?

15. •• A glass flask whose volume is 1000.00 cm³ at 0.0°C is completely filled with mercury at this temperature. When flask and mercury are warmed to 55.0°C, 8.95 cm³ of mercury overflow. Compute the coefficient of volume expansion of the glass. (Consult Table 14.2.)

16. •• The volume of 1 g of water is 1.0002 cm³, 1.0000 cm³, 1.0258 cm³, and 1.0434 cm³ at 0°C, 4°C, 75°C, and 100°C, respectively. Find the average coefficient of volume expansion of water in the temperature range (a) from 0°C to 4°C, (b) from 75°C to 100°C.

17. •• The markings on an aluminum ruler and a brass ruler begin at the left end; when the rulers are at 0.00°C, they are perfectly aligned. How far apart will the 20.0 cm marks be on the two rulers at 100.0°C if the left-hand ends are kept precisely aligned?

14.4 Quantity of Heat

18. • (a) How much heat is required to raise the temperature of 0.250 kg of water from 20.0°C to 30.0°C? (b) If this amount of heat is added to an equal mass of mercury that is initially at 20.0°C, what is its final temperature?

19. • One of the moving parts of an engine contains 1.60 kg of aluminum and 0.300 kg of iron and is designed to operate at 210°C. How much heat is required to raise its temperature from 20.0° to 210°C?

20. • In an effort to stay awake for an all-night study session, a student makes a cup of coffee by first placing a 200.0 W electric immersion heater in 0.320 kg of water. (a) How much heat must be added to the water to raise its temperature from 20.0°C to 80.0°C? (b) How much time is required if all of the heater's power goes into heating the water?

21. • **Heat loss during breathing.** In very cold weather, a significant mechanism for heat loss by the human body is energy expended in warming the air taken into the lungs with each

breath. (a) On a cold winter day when the temperature is $-20°C$, what is the amount of heat needed to warm to internal body temperature $(37°C)$ the 0.50 L of air exchanged with each breath? Assume that the specific heat capacity of air is $1020 \text{ J}/(\text{kg} \cdot \text{K})$ and that 1.0 L of air has a mass of 1.3 g. (b) How much heat is lost per hour if the respiration rate is 20 breaths per minute?

22. • A nail driven into a board increases in temperature. If 60% of the kinetic energy delivered by a 1.80 kg hammer with a speed of 7.80 m/s is transformed into heat that flows into the nail and does not flow out, what is the increase in temperature of an 8.00 g aluminum nail after it is struck 10 times?

23. • (a) What is the maximum amount of heat generated when the driver of a 1525 kg car traveling at 25.0 m/s hits the brakes and brings the car to a stop in 17 s? (b) If the car is all iron and all the heat goes into the car, by how much will its temperature increase? (See Table 14.3.)

24. • The nominal food-energy value of 1.0 g of butter is about 7.2 food calories. If all this energy could be converted completely to mechanical energy, how much butter would be required to power a 65 kg mountaineer on her journey from Lupine Meadows (elevation 2070 m) to the summit of Grand Teton (4196 m)?

25. • How fast would a 4.50 g bullet have to be traveling so that it increased the temperature of 1.0 L of water by 1.0 C° if it gave all of its kinetic energy to the water?

26. • From a height of 35.0 m, a 1.25 kg bird dives (from rest) into a small fish tank containing 50.0 kg of water. What is the maximum rise in temperature of the water if the bird gives it all of its mechanical energy?

27. •• A 15.0 g bullet traveling horizontally at 865 m/s passes through a tank containing 13.5 kg of water and emerges with a speed of 534 m/s. What is the maximum temperature increase that the water could have as a result of this event?

28. •• **Maintaining body temperature.** While running, a 70 kg **BIO** student generates thermal energy at a rate of 1200 W. To maintain a constant body temperature of 37°C, this energy must be removed by perspiration or other mechanisms. If these mechanisms failed and the heat could not flow out of the student's body, for what amount of time could a student run before irreversible body damage occurred? (Protein structures in the body are damaged irreversibly if the body temperature rises to 44°C or above. The specific heat capacity of a typical human body is $3480 \text{ J}/(\text{kg} \cdot \text{K})$, slightly less than that of water. The difference is due to the presence of protein, fat, and minerals, which have lower specific heat capacities.)

29. •• A technician measures the specific heat capacity of an unidentified liquid by immersing an electrical resistor in it. Electrical energy is converted to heat, which is then transferred to the liquid for 120 s at a constant rate of 65.0 W. The mass of the liquid is 0.780 kg, and its temperature increases from 18.55°C to 22.54°C. (a) Find the average specific heat capacity of the liquid in this temperature range. Assume that negligible heat is transferred to the container that holds the liquid and that no heat is lost to the surroundings. (b) Suppose that in this experiment heat transfer from the liquid to the container or its surroundings cannot be ignored. Is the result calculated in part (a) an overestimate or an underestimate of the average specific heat capacity? Explain.

30. •• Much of the energy of falling water in a waterfall is converted into heat. If all the mechanical energy is converted into heat that stays in the water, how much of a rise in temperature occurs in a 100 m waterfall?

14.5 Phase Changes

31. • Consult Table 14.4. (a) How much heat is required to melt 0.150 kg of lead at 327.3°C? (b) How much heat would be needed to evaporate this lead at 1750°C? (c) If the total heat added from parts (a) and (b) were put into ice at 0.00°C, how many grams of the ice would it melt?

32. • **A two-ton air conditioner.** The capacity of commercial air conditioners is sometimes expressed in "tons," the number of tons of ice that can be frozen from water at 0°C in 24 h by the unit. (a) How much energy does a 2.0 ton air conditioner remove from a room in 24 hours? (b) Express the capacity of a 2.0 ton air conditioner in watts.

33. • **Treatment for a stroke.** One suggested treatment for a **BIO** person who has suffered a stroke is to immerse the patient in an ice-water bath at 0°C to lower the body temperature, which prevents damage to the brain. In one set of tests, patients were cooled until their internal temperature reached 32.0°C. To treat a 70.0 kg patient, what is the minimum amount of ice (at 0°C) that you need in the bath so that its temperature remains at 0°C? The specific heat capacity of the human body is $3480 \text{ J}/(\text{kg} \cdot \text{C}°)$, and recall that normal body temperature is 37.0°C.

34. • A container holds 0.550 kg of ice at $-15.0°C$. The mass of the container can be ignored. Heat is supplied to the container at the constant rate of 800.0 J/min for 500.0 min. (a) After how many minutes does the ice *start* to melt? (b) After how many minutes, from the time when the heating is first started, does the temperature begin to rise above 0.00°C? (c) Plot a curve showing the temperature as a function of the time elapsed.

35. • What must the initial speed of a lead bullet be at a temperature of 25°C so that the heat developed when it is brought to rest will be just sufficient to melt it? Assume that all the initial mechanical energy of the bullet is converted to heat and that no heat flows from the bullet to its surroundings. (Typical rifles have muzzle speeds around 350 m/s.)

36. • **Evaporative cooling.** The evaporation of sweat is an **BIO** important mechanism for temperature control in some warm-blooded animals. (a) What mass of water must evaporate from the skin of a 70.0 kg man to cool his body 1.00 C°? The heat of vaporization of water at body temperature (37°C) is 2.42×10^6 J/kg. The specific heat capacity of a typical human body is $3480 \text{ J}/(\text{kg} \cdot \text{K})$. (b) What volume of water must the man drink to replenish the evaporated water? Compare this result with the volume of a soft-drink can, which is 355 cm^3.

37. •• An ice-cube tray contains 0.350 kg of water at 18.0°C. How much heat must be removed from the water to cool it to 0.00°C and freeze it? Express your answer in joules and in calories.

38. •• How much heat is required to convert 12.0 g of ice at $-10.0°C$ to steam at 100.0°C? Express your answer in joules and in calories.

39. •• **Steam burns vs. water burns.** What is the amount of **BIO** heat entering your skin when it receives the heat released (a) by 25.0 g of steam initially at 100.0°C that cools to 34.0°C? (b) by 25.0 g of water initially at 100.0°C that cools

to 34.0°C? (c) What do these results tell you about the relative severity of steam and hot-water burns?

40. •• **Bicycling on a Warm Day.** If the air temperature is the
BIO same as the temperature of your skin (about 30°C), your body cannot get rid of heat by transferring it to the air. In that case, it gets rid of the heat by evaporating water (sweat). During bicycling, a typical 70 kg person's body produces energy at a rate of about 500 W due to metabolism, 80% of which is converted to heat. (a) How many kilograms of water must the person's body evaporate in an hour to get rid of this heat? The heat of vaporization of water at body temperature is 2.42×10^6 J/kg. (b) The evaporated water must, of course, be replenished, or the person will dehydrate. How many 750 mL bottles of water must the bicyclist drink per hour to replenish the lost water? (Recall that the mass of a liter of water is 1.0 kg.)

41. •• **Overheating.** (a) By how much would the body tempera-
BIO ture of the bicyclist in the previous problem increase in an hour if he were unable to get rid of the excess heat? (b) Is this temperature increase large enough to be serious? To find out, how high a fever would it be equivalent to, in °F? [Recall that the normal internal body temperature is 98.6°F and the specific heat capacity of the body is 3480 J/(kg·C°).]

14.6 Calorimetry

42. • You have 750 g of water at 10.0°C in a large insulated beaker. How much boiling water at 100.0°C must you add to this beaker so that the final temperature of the mixture will be 75°C?

43. •• A 0.500 kg chunk of an unknown metal that has been in boiling water for several minutes is quickly dropped into an insulating Styrofoam™ beaker containing 1.00 kg of water at room temperature (20.0°C). After waiting and gently stirring for 5.00 minutes, you observe that the water's temperature has reached a constant value of 22.0°C. (a) Assuming that the Styrofoam™ absorbs a negligibly small amount of heat and that no heat was lost to the surroundings, what is the specific heat capacity of the metal? (b) Which is more useful for storing energy from heat, this metal or an equal weight of water? Explain. (c) What if the heat absorbed by the Styrofoam™ actually is not negligible. How would the specific heat capacity you calculated in part (a) be in error? Would it be too large, too small, or still correct? Explain your reasoning.

44. •• A copper pot with a mass of 0.500 kg contains 0.170 kg of water, and both are at a temperature of 20.0°C. A 0.250 kg block of iron at 85.0°C is dropped into the pot. Find the final temperature of the system, assuming no heat loss to the surroundings.

45. •• In a physics lab experiment, a student immersed 200 one-cent coins (each having a mass of 3.00 g) in boiling water. After they reached thermal equilibrium, she quickly fished them out and dropped them into 0.240 kg of water at 20.0°C in an insulated container of negligible mass. What was the final temperature of the coins? [One-cent coins are made of a metal alloy—mostly zinc—with a specific heat capacity of 390 J/(kg·K).]

46. •• A laboratory technician drops an 85.0 g solid sample of unknown material at a temperature of 100.0°C into a calorimeter. The calorimeter can is made of 0.150 kg of copper and contains 0.200 kg of water, and both the can and water are initially at 19.0°C. The final temperature of the system is measured to be

26.1°C. Compute the specific heat capacity of the sample. (Assume no heat loss to the surroundings.)

47. •• A 4.00 kg silver ingot is taken from a furnace, where its temperature is 750°C, and placed on a very large block of ice at 0.00°C. Assuming that all the heat given up by the silver is used to melt the ice and that not all the ice melts, how much ice is melted?

48. •• An insulated beaker with negligible mass contains 0.250 kg of water at a temperature of 75.0°C. How many kilograms of ice at a temperature of −20.0°C must be dropped in the water so that the final temperature of the system will be 30.0°C?

49. •• A glass vial containing a 16.0 g sample of an enzyme is cooled in an ice-and-water bath initially at 0.00°C. The bath contains water and 0.120 kg of ice. The sample has a specific heat capacity of 2250 J/(kg·K); the glass vial has a mass of 6.0 g and a specific heat capacity of 2800 J/(kg·K). How much ice melts to cool the enzyme sample from room temperature (19.5°C) to the temperature of the ice bath?

14.7 Heat Transfer

50. • A slab of a thermal insulator with a cross-sectional area of 100 cm² is 3.00 cm thick. Its thermal conductivity is 0.075 W/(m·K). If the temperature difference between opposite faces is 80 C°, how much heat flows through the slab in 1 day?

51. • **Heat flow through the earth.** The thermal gradient near the earth's surface is around 20 to 30 K/km. (We'll use an average of 25 K/km.) The thermal conductivity of rocks varies, so we'll use an average of 3.0 W/(m·K). (a) How many joules of heat reach each square meter of the earth's land surface during a typical day? (The majority of this heat comes from the decay of radioactive atoms in the earth's interior.) (b) What happens to the heat? Why is the earth not getting hotter and hotter?

52. • An electric kitchen range has a total wall area of 1.40 m² and is insulated with a layer of fiberglass 4.0 cm thick. The inside surface of the fiberglass has a temperature of 175°C, and its outside surface is at 35°C. The fiberglass has a thermal conductivity of 0.040 W/(m·K). (a) How much heat per second flows through the insulation, assuming that it may be treated as a flat slab with an area of 1.40 m²? (b) What electrical power input to the heating element is required to maintain the inside temperature of the fiberglass?

53. • **Conduction through the skin.** The blood plays an impor-
BIO tant role in removing heat from the body by bringing this heat directly to the surface where it can radiate away. Nevertheless, this heat must still travel through the skin before it can radiate away. We shall assume that the blood is brought to the bottom layer of skin at a temperature of 37°C and that the outer surface of the skin is at 30.0°C. Skin varies in thickness from 0.50 mm to a few millimeters on the palms and soles, so we shall assume an average thickness of 0.75 mm. A 165 lb, 6 ft person has a surface area of about 2.0 m² and loses heat at a net rate of 75 W while resting. On the basis of our assumptions, what is the thermal conductivity of this person's skin?

54. •• A pot with a steel bottom 8.50 mm thick rests on a hot stove. The area of the bottom of the pot is 0.150 m². The water inside the pot is at 100.0°C, and 0.390 kg are evaporated every 3.00 min. Find the temperature of the lower surface of the pot, which is in contact with the stove.

55. •• A carpenter builds an exterior house wall with a layer of wood 3.0 cm thick on the outside and a layer of Styrofoam™

insulation 2.2 cm thick on the inside wall surface. The wood has a thermal conductivity of $0.080 \, \text{W}/(\text{m} \cdot \text{K})$, and the Styrofoam™ has a thermal conductivity of $0.010 \, \text{W}/(\text{m} \cdot \text{K})$. The interior surface temperature is 19.0°C, and the exterior surface temperature is −10.0°C. (a) What is the temperature at the plane where the wood meets the Styrofoam™? (b) What is the rate of heat flow per square meter through this wall?

56. •• Suppose that the rod in Figure 14.27 is made of copper, is 45.0 cm long, and has a cross-sectional area of $1.25 \, \text{cm}^2$. Let $T_H = 100.0°C$ and $T_C = 0.0°C$. (a) What is the final steady-state temperature gradient along the rod? (b) At what rate does heat flow through this rod? (c) What is the final steady-state temperature at a point in the rod 12.0 cm from its left end?

▲ **FIGURE 14.27** Problem 56.

57. •• One end of an insulated metal rod is maintained at 100°C, while the other end is maintained at 0°C by an ice–water mixture. The rod is 60.0 cm long and has a cross-sectional area of $1.25 \, \text{cm}^2$. The heat conducted by the rod melts 8.50 g of ice in 10.0 min. Find the thermal conductivity k of the metal.

58. •• A long rod that is insulated to prevent heat loss along its sides is in perfect thermal contact with boiling water (at atmospheric pressure) at one end and with an ice–water mixture at the other (Figure 14.28). The rod consists of a 1.00 m section of copper (one end in steam) joined end-to-end to a length L_2 of steel (one end in ice). Both sections of the rod have cross-sectional areas of $4.00 \, \text{cm}^2$. The temperature of the copper–steel junction is 65.0°C after a steady state has been set up. (a) How much heat per second flows from the steam bath to the ice–water mixture? (b) What is the length L_2 of the steel section?

▲ **FIGURE 14.28** Problem 58.

59. •• **Mammal insulation.** Animals in cold climates often
BIO depend on *two* layers of insulation: a layer of body fat [of thermal conductivity $0.20 \, \text{W}/(\text{m} \cdot \text{K})$] surrounded by a layer of air trapped inside fur or down. We can model a black bear (*Ursus americanus*) as a sphere 1.5 m in diameter having a layer of fat 4.0 cm thick. (Actually, the thickness varies with the season, but we are interested in hibernation, when the fat layer is thickest.) In studies of bear hibernation, it was found that the outer surface layer of the fur is at 2.7°C during hibernation, while the inner surface of the fat layer is at 31.0°C. (a) What is the temperature at the fat–inner fur boundary, and (b) how thick should the air layer (contained within the fur) be so that the bear loses heat at a rate of 50.0 W?

60. • What is the rate of energy radiation per unit area of a blackbody at a temperature of (a) 273 K? (b) 2730 K?

61. • **Radiation by the body.** The amount of heat radiated by the
BIO body depends on its surface temperature and area. Typically, this temperature is about 30°C (although it can vary). The surface area depends on the person's height and weight. An empirical formula for the surface area of a person's body is

$$A(\text{in m}^2) = (0.202)M^{0.425} h^{0.725},$$

where M is the person's mass (in kilograms) and h is his or her height (in meters). (a) What would be the surface area of a 165 lb (75 kg), 6 ft (1.83 m) person? (This is a good chance to use the y^x key of your calculator.) (b) How much heat would the person radiate away per second at a skin temperature of 30°C? (At the low temperatures of room-temperature objects, nearly all the heat radiated is infrared radiation, for which the emissivity is essentially 1, regardless of the amount of skin pigment.) (c) How much *net* heat would radiation remove from the person's body if the air temperature is 20°C? (d) Take measurements on your own body to test the validity of the area formula. Treat yourself as a sphere and several cylinders.

62. • **How large is the sun?** By measuring the spectrum of wavelengths of light from our sun, we know that its surface temperature is 5800 K. By measuring the rate at which we receive its energy on earth, we know that it is radiating a total of $3.92 \times 10^{26} \, \text{J/s}$ and behaves nearly like an ideal blackbody. Use this information to calculate the diameter of our sun.

63. •• **Basal metabolic rate.** The basal metabolic rate is the rate
BIO at which energy is produced in the body when a person is at rest. A 75 kg (165 lb) person of height 1.83 m (6 ft) would have a body surface area of approximately 2.0 m². (a) What is the net amount of heat this person could radiate per second into a room at 18°C (about 65°F) if his skin's surface temperature is 30°C? (At such temperatures, nearly all the heat is infrared radiation, for which the body's emissivity is 1.0, regardless of the amount of pigment.) (b) Normally, 80% of the energy produced by metabolism goes into heat, while the rest goes into things like pumping blood and repairing cells. Also normally, a person at rest can get rid of this excess heat just through radiation. Use your answer to part (a) to find this person's basal metabolic rate.

64. • The emissivity of tungsten is 0.35. A tungsten sphere with a radius of 1.50 cm is suspended within a large evacuated enclosure whose walls are at 290 K. What power input is required to maintain the sphere at a temperature of 3000 K if heat conduction along the supports is negligible?

65. • **Size of a lightbulb filament.** The operating temperature of a tungsten filament in an incandescent lightbulb is 2450 K, and its emissivity is 0.35. Find the surface area of the filament of a 150 W bulb if all the electrical energy consumed by the bulb is radiated by the filament as light. (In reality, only a small fraction of the radiation appears as visible light.)

66. •• A sphere of radius R and absolute surface temperature T radiates at a rate H. At what rate (in terms of H) will it radiate if (a) its temperature is doubled, (b) its diameter is doubled, (c) both its temperature and its diameter are doubled? (d) What should be its temperature (in terms of T) so that its radiation rate is doubled? (e) What should be its radius (in terms of R) so that its radiation rate is to be cut in half?

General Problems

67. •• An 8.50 kg block of ice at 0°C is sliding on a rough horizontal icehouse floor (also at 0°C) at 15.0 m/s. Assume that half of any heat generated goes into the floor and the rest goes into the ice. (a) How much ice melts after the speed of the ice has been reduced to 10.0 m/s? (b) What is the maximum amount of ice that will melt?

68. • An aluminum cube 0.100 m on a side is heated from 10.0°C to 50.0°C. What is the change in its density?

69. •• **Global warming.** As the earth warms, sea level will rise due to melting of the polar ice and thermal expansion of the oceans. Estimates of the expected temperature increase vary, but 3.5 C° by the end of the century has been plausibly suggested. If we assume that the temperature of the oceans also increases by this amount, how much will sea level rise by the year 2100 due only to the thermal expansion of the water? Assume, reasonably, that the ocean basins do not expand appreciably. The average depth of the ocean is 4000 m, and the coefficient of volume expansion of water at 20°C is $0.207 \times 10^{-3} (C°)^{-1}$.

70. •• **Giant stars.** In 2003, astronomers discovered some of the brightest stars in the universe. Their surface temperature is about 80,000°C, and they are estimated to be about 10 to 20 times more massive than our sun. For the sake of simplicity, assume that their average density is the same as that of our sun. (a) Find the radius of the largest of these stars in terms of the radius R of our sun. (b) Find the amount of energy the largest such star emits per second in terms of the energy H that our sun emits per second, given that our sun's surface temperature is 5800 K.

71. •• **On-demand water heaters.** Conventional hot-water heaters consist of a tank of water maintained at a fixed temperature. The hot water is to be used when needed. The drawback is that energy is wasted because the tank loses heat when it is not in use, and you can run out of hot water if you use too much. Some utility companies are encouraging the use of *on-demand* water heaters (also known as *flash heaters*), which consist of heating units to heat the water as you use it. No water tank is involved, so no heat is wasted. A typical household shower flow rate is 2.5 gal/min (9.46 L/min) with the tap water being heated from 50°F (10°C) to 120°F (49°C) by the on-demand heater. What rate of heat input (either electrical or from gas) is required to operate such a unit, assuming that all the heat goes into the water?

72. •• **Burning fat by exercise.** Each pound of fat contains
BIO 3500 *food* calories. When the body metabolizes food, 80% of this energy goes to heat. Suppose you decide to run without stopping, an activity that produces 1290 W of metabolic power for a typical person. (a) For how many hours must you run to burn up 1 lb of fat? Is this a realistic exercise plan? (b) If you followed your planned exercise program, how much heat would your body produce when you burn up a pound of fat? (c) If you needed to get rid of all of this excess heat by evaporating water (i.e., sweating), how many liters would you need to evaporate? The heat of vaporization of water at body temperature is 2.42×10^{6} J/kg.

73. •• **Shivering.** You have no doubt noticed that you usually
BIO shiver when you get out of the shower. Shivering is the body's way of generating heat to restore its internal temperature to the normal 37°C, and it produces approximately 290 W of heat power per square meter of body area. A 68 kg (150 lb), 1.78 m (5 foot, 10 inch) person has approximately 1.8 m² of surface area. How long would this person have to shiver to raise his or her body temperature by 1.0 C°, assuming that none of this heat is lost by the body? The specific heat capacity of the body is about 3500 J/(kg · K).

74. •• A steel tank is completely filled with 2.80 m³ of ethanol when both the tank and the ethanol are at a temperature of 32.0°C. When the tank and its contents have cooled to 18.0°C, what additional volume of 18.0°C ethanol can be put into the tank?

75. •• **Pasta time!** You are making pesto for your pasta and have a cylindrical measuring cup 10.0 cm high made of ordinary glass ($\beta = 2.7 \times 10^{-5} (C°)^{-1}$) and that is filled with olive oil ($\beta = 6.8 \times 10^{-4} (C°)^{-1}$) to a height of 1.00 mm below the top of the cup. Initially, the cup and oil are at a kitchen temperature of 22.0°C. You get a phone call and forget about the olive oil, which you inadvertently leave on the hot stove. The cup and oil heat up slowly and have a common temperature. At what temperature will the olive oil start to spill out of the cup?

76. •• A copper calorimeter can with mass 0.100 kg contains 0.160 kg of water and 0.018 kg of ice in thermal equilibrium at atmospheric pressure. If 0.750 kg of lead at a temperature of 255°C is dropped into the can, what is the final temperature of the system if no heat is lost to the surroundings?

77. •• A piece of ice at 0°C falls from rest into a lake whose temperature is 0°C, and 1.00% of the ice melts. Compute the minimum height from which the ice has fallen.

78. •• **Spacecraft reentry.** A spacecraft made of aluminum circles the earth at a speed of 7700 m/s. (a) Find the ratio of its kinetic energy to the energy required to raise its temperature from 0°C to 600°C. (The melting point of aluminum is 660°C; assume that its specific heat capacity of 910 J/(kg · K) remains constant.) (b) Discuss the bearing of your answer on the problem of the reentry of a manned space vehicle into the earth's atmosphere.

79. •• **Hot air in a physics lecture.** (a) A typical student listening attentively to a physics lecture has a heat output of 100 W. How much heat energy does a class of 90 physics students release into a lecture hall over the course of a 50 min lecture? (b) Assume that all the heat energy in part (a) is transferred to the 3200 m³ of air in the room. The air has a specific heat capacity of 1020 J/(kg · K) and a density of 1.20 kg/m³. If none of the heat escapes and the air-conditioning system is off, how much will the temperature of the air in the room rise during the 50 min lecture? (c) If the class is taking an exam, the heat output per student rises to 280 W. What is the temperature rise during 50 min in this case?

80. •• As an attentive scientist, you put heat into a 0.500 kg sample of solid material at the rate of 10.0 kJ/min while recording its temperature as a function of time. You plot your data and obtain the graph shown in Figure 14.29. (a) What is the latent heat of fusion for this substance? (b) What are the specific heat capacities of the liquid and solid states of the material?

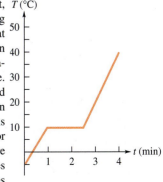

▲ **FIGURE 14.29** Problem 80.

81. •• A vessel whose walls are thermally insulated contains 2.10 kg of water and 0.20 kg of ice, all at a temperature of 0.0°C. The outlet of a tube leading from a boiler in which water is boiling at atmospheric pressure is inserted into the water. How many grams of steam must condense to raise the temperature of the system to 30.0°C? Neglect the heat transferred to the container.

82. •• **Time for a lake to freeze over.** When the air temperature is below 0°C, the water at the surface of a lake freezes to form a sheet of ice. If the upper surface of an ice sheet 25.0 cm thick is at −10.0°C and the bottom surface is at 0.00°C, calculate the time it will take to add 2.0 mm to the thickness of this sheet.

83. •• **Jogging in the heat of the day.** You have probably seen **BIO** people jogging in extremely hot weather and wondered "Why?" As we shall see, there are good reasons not to do this! When jogging strenuously, an average runner of mass 68 kg and surface area 1.85 m² produces energy at a rate of up to 1300 W, 80% of which is converted to heat. The jogger radiates heat, but actually absorbs more from the hot air than he radiates away. At such high levels of activity, the skin's temperature can be elevated to around 33°C instead of the usual 30°C. (We shall neglect conduction, which would bring even more heat into his body.) The only way for the body to get rid of this extra heat is by evaporating water (sweating). (a) How much heat per second is produced just by the act of jogging? (b) How much *net* heat per second does the runner gain just from radiation if the air temperature is 40.0°C (104°F)? (Remember that he radiates out, but the environment radiates back in.) (c) What is the *total* amount of excess heat this runner's body must get rid of per second? (d) How much water must the jogger's body evaporate every minute due to his activity? The heat of vaporization of water at body temperature is 2.42×10^6 J/kg. (e) How many 750 mL bottles of water must he drink after (or preferably before!) jogging for a half hour? Recall that a liter of water has a mass of 1.0 kg.

84. •• **Overheating while jogging.** (a) If the jogger in the previ- **BIO** ous problem were not able to get rid of the excess heat, by how much would his body temperature increase above the normal 37°C in a half hour of jogging? The specific heat capacity for a human is about 3500 J/(kg · K). (b) How high a fever (in °F) would this temperature increase be equivalent to? Is the increase large enough to be of concern? (Recall that normal body temperature is 98.6°F.)

85. •• A thirsty nurse cools a 2.00 L bottle of a soft drink (mostly water) by pouring it into a large aluminum mug of mass 0.257 kg and adding 0.120 kg of ice initially at −15.0°C. If the soft drink and mug are initially at 20.0°C, what is the final temperature of the system, assuming no heat losses?

86. •• **Incandescent lighting.** Ninety-five percent of the electrical energy consumed by a 60 W incandescent lightbulb is converted to heat. The spherical glass envelope of the bulb has a radius of 2.5 cm and is 0.50 mm thick. The thermal conductivity of the glass is 0.80 W/(m · K). What is the temperature difference between the inside and outside surfaces of the glass after steady-state heat flow has been established?

87. •• A camping icebox has a wall area of 2.00 m² and a thickness of 3.00 cm and is made of an insulating material having a thermal conductivity of 0.050 W/(m · K). The temperature of the outside surface of the icebox is 20.0°C, and the inside wall of the box is maintained at 5.00°C by ice. The melted ice drains from the box at a temperature of 2.50°C. How many kilograms of ice should you buy for a 10-hour picnic?

88. •• **The effect of urbanization on plant growth.** A study **BIO** published in July 2004 indicated that temperature increases in urban areas in the eastern United States are causing plants to bud up to 7 days early compared with plants in rural areas just a few miles away, thereby disrupting biological cycles. Average temperatures in the urban areas were up to 3.5 C° higher than in the rural areas. By what percent will the radiated heat per square meter increase due to such a temperature difference if the rural temperature was 0°C on the average?

89. •• **Basal metabolic rate.** The energy output of an animal **BIO** engaged in an activity is called the basal metabolic rate (BMR) and is a measure of the conversion of food energy into other forms of energy. A simple calorimeter to measure the BMR consists of an insulated box with a thermometer to measure the temperature of the air. The air has a density of 1.29 kg/m³ and a specific heat capacity of 1020 J/(kg · K). A 50.0 g hamster is placed in a calorimeter that contains 0.0500 m³ of air at room temperature. (a) When the hamster is running in a wheel, the temperature of the air in the calorimeter rises 1.8 C° per hour. How much heat does the running hamster generate in an hour? (Assume that all this heat goes into the air in the calorimeter. Neglect the heat that goes into the walls of the box and into the thermometer, and assume that no heat is lost to the surroundings.) (b) Assuming that the hamster converts seed into heat with an efficiency of 10% and that hamster seed has a food energy value of 24 J/g, how many grams of seed must the hamster eat per hour to supply the energy found in part (a)?

90. •• (W) Two solid spheres having the same emissivity and density radiate at the same temperature. One sphere has twice the mass of the other. Find the ratio of the radiation rate of the large sphere to that of the small sphere.

91. •• (W) **Why do the seasons lag?** In the northern hemisphere, June 21 (the summer solstice) is both the longest day of the year and the day on which the sun's rays strike the earth most vertically, hence delivering the greatest amount of heat to the surface. Yet the hottest summer weather usually occurs about a month or so later. Let us see why this is the case. Because of the large specific heat capacity of water, the oceans are slower to warm up than the land (and also slower to cool off in winter). In addition to perusing pertinent information in the tables included in this book, it is useful to know that approximately two-thirds of the earth's surface is ocean composed of salt water having a specific heat capacity of 3890 J/(kg · K) and that the oceans, on the average, are 4000 m deep. Typically, an average of 1050 W/m² of solar energy falls on the earth's surface, and the oceans absorb essentially all of the light that strikes them. However most of that light is absorbed in the upper 100 m of the surface. Depths below that do not change temperature seasonally. Assume that the sunlight falls on the surface for only 12 hours per day and that the ocean retains all the heat it absorbs. What will be the rise in temperature of the upper 100 m of the oceans during the month following the summer solstice? Does this seem to be large enough to be perceptible?

15 THERMAL PROPERTIES OF MATTER

You can't see air molecules, but they're moving all around you. Did you know that in one day you are hit 10^{32} times by air molecules? And did you know that the average speed of an air molecule is about 1000 mi/h? Or that the impacts of these molecules on a surface are responsible for the pressure that air exerts on that surface?

To understand and relate such facts, we need to be able to use both *macroscopic* (bulk) and *microscopic* viewpoints. The **macroscopic** perspective deals with large-scale variables such as pressure, volume, temperature, and mass of substance. In contrast, the **microscopic** point of view investigates small-scale quantities such as the speeds, kinetic energies, momenta, and masses of the individual molecules that make up a substance. Where these two perspectives overlap, they must be consistent. For example, the (microscopic) collision forces that occur when air molecules strike a surface (such as your skin) cause (macroscopic) atmospheric pressure.

In this chapter, we'll use both macroscopic and microscopic approaches to gain an understanding of the thermal properties and behavior of matter. One of the simplest kinds of matter to understand is the *ideal gas*. For this class of materials, we'll relate pressure, volume, temperature, and amount of substance to one another and to the speeds and masses of individual molecules. We will explore the molecular basis of the heat capacities of both gases and solids, and we will take a look at the various *phases* of matter—gas, liquid, and solid—and the conditions under which each occurs.

As we'll learn in this chapter, unconfined gases expand when heated. When hot ground heats the overlying air, the air expands and rises, forming a *thermal*. Thermals can lift soaring birds to great heights.

15.1 The Mole and Avogadro's Number

In our study of mechanics, we've usually described a quantity of a material or substance in terms of the *mass* of material. In this chapter, where we explore the relation between mechanics and thermal phenomena, we'll often find it useful to

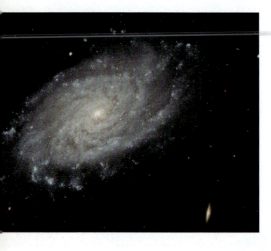

◄ **One trillionth of a mole of stars.** A typical fair-sized spiral galaxy like our own Milky Way contains roughly 100 billion (10^{11}) stars. That's a lot of stars . . . But remember that a mole of any substance contains 6.022×10^{23} (Avogadro's number) of molecules. A mole of water, which you can hold in your hand, thus contains *one trillion* (10^{12}) times more molecules than there are stars in our galaxy.

describe a quantity of material in terms of the number of *moles* of the material rather than the mass. So we'll begin by discussing what we mean by a mole.

One **mole** of any pure chemical element or compound contains **a definite number of molecules**—the same number for all elements and compounds. The official SI definition of the mole is as follows:

> **Definition of the mole**
> One mole (1 mol) is the amount of substance that contains as many elementary entities as there are atoms in 0.012 kilogram of carbon 12.

In our discussion, the "elementary entities" are molecules. (In a monatomic substance such as carbon or helium, each molecule is a single atom, but in this discussion we'll still call it a molecule.)

The number of molecules in a mole is called **Avogadro's number,** denoted by N_A. The numerical value is

$$N_A = 6.022 \times 10^{23} \text{ molecules/mol}.$$

Figure 15.1 shows 1 mole of each of several familiar substances.

The **molar mass** M of a substance is the mass of 1 mole; this is equal to the mass m of a single molecule, multiplied by Avogadro's number N_A:

$$M = N_A m. \tag{15.1}$$

Molar mass is sometimes called "molecular mass" or "molecular weight." Both these terms are unfortunate, the first because M is *not* the mass of a molecule, the second because we are talking about mass, not weight. In this chapter, we'll use "molar mass" consistently.

We'll denote the number of moles of substance by n. In this chapter, we'll usually denote the total mass of substance by m_{total} (because later we'll want to use m as the mass of a single molecule). The total mass is equal to the number of moles multiplied by the mass per mole:

$$m_{total} = nM. \tag{15.2}$$

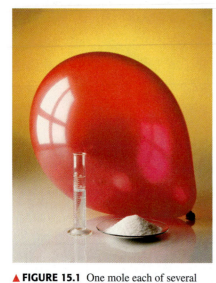

▲ **FIGURE 15.1** One mole each of several familiar substances.

EXAMPLE 15.1 **Mass of a hydrogen atom**

Find the mass of a single hydrogen atom and the mass of an oxygen molecule (consisting of two oxygen atoms and written O_2).

SOLUTION

SET UP From the periodic table of the elements (Appendix D), we find that the molar mass of hydrogen (i.e., the mass per mole of hydrogen atoms) is 1.008 g/mol. The molar mass of oxygen is 16.0 g/mol, so the molar mass of O_2 is 32.0 g/mol.

SOLVE We use Equation 15.1. The mass m_H of a single hydrogen atom is

$$m_H = \frac{M_H}{N_A} = \frac{1.008 \text{ g/mol}}{6.022 \times 10^{23} \text{ molecules/mol}}$$
$$= 1.674 \times 10^{-24} \text{ g/atom}.$$

The mass of a single molecule of O_2 is

$$m_{O_2} = \frac{32.0 \text{ g/mol}}{6.022 \times 10^{23} \text{ molecules/mol}}$$
$$= 53.1 \times 10^{-24} \text{ g/molecule}.$$

REFLECT A water molecule (H_2O) consists of one oxygen atom and two hydrogen atoms, but we can now see that the oxygen atom accounts for nearly 90% of its mass.

Practice Problem: Find the total mass of a molecule of nitrogen dioxide (NO_2), a component of smog. What fraction of this total mass is the mass of the nitrogen atom? *Answers:* 7.64×10^{-23} g/molecule, 0.30.

15.2 Equations of State

The conditions in which a particular material exists are described by physical quantities such as pressure, volume, and temperature. Usually we also need to specify the amount of substance in a system. For example, a tank of oxygen in a welding outfit has a pressure gauge and a label stating its volume. We could add a thermometer and place the tank on a scale. These variables (pressure, volume, and temperature) describe the **state** of the material, and they are called **state variables** or **state coordinates.** The amount of substance can be described by its total mass or the number of moles.

The volume V of a substance usually depends on its pressure p, temperature T, and amount of substance, measured either as mass m_{total} or number of moles n. Ordinarily, we can't change one of these variables without causing a change in another. When the tank of oxygen gets hotter, the pressure increases. When the tank gets too hot, the pressure causes it to explode; this happens occasionally with overheated steam boilers (Figure 15.2).

In a few cases, the relationship among p, V, T, and m_{total} (or n) is simple enough that we can express it as an equation called the **equation of state.** When it's too complicated for that, we can use graphs or numerical tables. Even then, the relation among the variables still exists; we call it an equation of state even when we don't know the actual equation.

In this discussion, we'll consider only **equilibrium states**—that is, states in which the temperature and pressure are uniform throughout the system. In principle, when a system changes from one state to another, *non-equilibrium* states must occur during the transition. For example, when a material expands, there must be mass in motion; this requires acceleration and non-uniform pressure. Similarly, when heat conduction occurs, different regions must have different temperatures. We'll assume that such changes occur so slowly that the system is always very nearly in an equilibrium state.

The Ideal-Gas Equation

Gases at low pressures have particularly simple equations of state. Figure 15.3 shows an experimental setup to study the behavior of a gas. The cylinder has a movable piston and is equipped with a pressure gauge and a thermometer. We can vary the pressure, volume, and temperature, and we can pump any desired mass of any gas into the cylinder. Measurements of the behavior of various gases at low pressures lead to several conclusions:

- First, **the volume V is proportional to the number of moles n and thus to the number of molecules.** Thus, if we double the number of moles, keeping the pressure and temperature constant, the volume doubles.
- Second, **the volume varies *inversely* with the pressure p.** Hence, if we double the pressure, holding the temperature T and amount of substance n constant, we compress the gas to one-half of its initial volume. This relation is called **Boyle's law,** after Robert Boyle (1627–1691), a contemporary of Newton. It states that $pV = $ constant when n and T are constant.
- Third, **the pressure is directly proportional to the absolute (Kelvin) temperature.** Thus, if we double the absolute temperature, keeping the volume and quantity of material constant, the pressure doubles. This is called **Charles's law,** after Jacques Charles (1746–1823). It states that $p = ($constant$)T$ when n and V are constant.

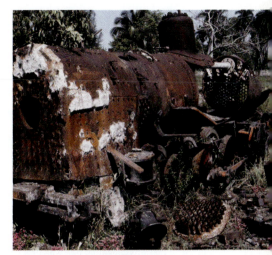

▲ **FIGURE 15.2** An overheated steam boiler can explode with great violence. This photo shows the rusted wreckage of a steam locomotive destroyed by a boiler explosion.

▲ **FIGURE 15.3** A hypothetical setup for studying the behavior of gases.

These three relationships can be combined neatly into a single equation:

Ideal-gas equation

For an ideal gas (defined in the following paragraphs), and as an approximation of real gas behavior, the product of pressure p and volume V is proportional to the product of the number n of moles of gas and the absolute temperature T:

$$pV = nRT. \tag{15.3}$$

The proportionality constant R is called the **ideal-gas constant.** Its numerical value depends on the units used for p, V, and T. In SI units, in which the unit of p is the Pa ($=N/m^2$) and the unit of V is the cubic meter (m^3), $R = 8.3145 \ J/mol \cdot K$.

▲ **Martian dust devil.** This photo shows a dust devil that was caught on film while passing the *Mars Spirit Rover.* Although Mars is bitterly cold and has an atmosphere much thinner than earth's, the physics of dust devils is the same on both planets. First, a patch of sun-warmed ground transfers heat to the overlying air. By the ideal-gas equation ($pV = nRT$), this increase in the temperature of the air must increase the product pV. The air is not confined, so its volume V increases, lowering its density and causing it to rise buoyantly. As it rises, surrounding air flows in to take its place. If this surrounding air has a net rotation (as it often does), conservation of angular momentum causes the air to spin faster as it moves inward, creating the dust devil. On earth, where heating can be strong and the atmosphere is dense and energetic, this basic process results not just in dust devils, but in tornadoes and in great storms such as hurricanes and typhoons.

We call Equation (15.3) the **ideal-gas equation.** We might expect that the constant R in this equation would have different values for different gases, but it turns out to have the same value for *all* gases, at least at sufficiently high temperatures and low pressures. Note that the units of pressure times volume are the same as the units of work or energy (e.g., N/m^2 times m^3); that's why R has units of energy per mole per unit of absolute temperature.

In chemical calculations, volumes are sometimes expressed in liters (L) and pressures in atmospheres (atm). In this system,

$$R = 0.08206 \ L \cdot atm/(mol \cdot K).$$

We can express Equation 15.3 in terms of the mass m_{total} of material, using Equation 15.2:

$$pV = \frac{m_{total}}{M} RT.$$

From this relationship, we can get an expression for the density (mass per unit volume, $\rho = m_{total}/V$) of the gas:

$$\rho = \frac{pM}{RT}. \tag{15.4}$$

We can now define an ideal gas as **a gas for which Equation 15.3 holds precisely for *all* pressures and temperatures.** This is an idealized model; no real gas behaves exactly like an ideal gas. However, most real gases show nearly ideal behavior at very low pressures and high temperatures, when the gas molecules are far apart and in rapid motion. The match is reasonably good (within a few percent) at moderate pressures (such as a few atmospheres) and at temperatures well above those at which the gas liquefies.

For a *constant mass* (or constant number of moles) of an ideal gas, the product nR is constant, so the quantity pV/T is also constant. Thus, using the subscripts 1 and 2 to refer to any two states of the same mass of a gas, we have

$$\frac{p_1 V_1}{T_1} = \frac{p_2 V_2}{T_2} = \text{constant.} \tag{15.5}$$

Quantitative Analysis 15.1

A compressed gas

If a gas in a 1.0 L box at 800 K is compressed to a volume of 0.50 L while its pressure changes from 1.0 atm to 0.5 atm, what is the resulting temperature in kelvins? (Assume no phase change.)

A. 800 K.   B. 600 K.   C. 400 K.   D. 200 K.

The amount of gas doesn't change, so nR is constant, and we can use Equation 15.5, $p_1 V_1/T_1 = p_2 V_2/T_2$. Now we notice that the

change of state involves *halving* both the volume and the pressure. If we rearrange the equation to solve for T_2/T_1, we see that $T_2/T_1 = p_2 V_2/p_1 V_1 = \frac{1}{4}$. Thus, the final absolute temperature is one-quarter of the original temperature, or 200 K. (Because our equation did not use the ideal-gas constant, the units used for pressure and volume did not matter, as long as they were the same for both states. However, for any ideal-gas calculation, temperature *must* be in kelvins.)

PROBLEM-SOLVING STRATEGY 15.1   **Using the ideal-gas law**

SET UP

1. List your known and unknown quantities. If the problem involves two different states of the same quantity of gas, designate one as state 1 and the other as state 2.

2. As always, be sure to use a consistent set of units. First decide which value of the gas constant R you are going to use, and then convert the units of the other quantities accordingly. You may have to convert atmospheres to pascals or liters to cubic meters. Sometimes the statement of the problem will make one system of units clearly more convenient than others. Decide on your system, and stick to it!

3. Don't forget that T must always be an *absolute* temperature. If you are given temperatures in degrees Celsius, be sure to add 273 to convert to kelvins.

4. You may sometimes have to convert between total mass m_{total} and number of moles n. The relationship is $m_{total} = Mn$, where M is the molar mass. Here's a tricky point: If you replace n in Equation 15.3 by (m_{total}/M), you *must* use the same mass units for m_{total} and M. So if M is in grams per mole (the usual units for molar mass), then m must also be in grams. If you want to use m_{total} in kilograms, then you must convert M to kilograms per mole. For example, the molar mass of oxygen is 32 g/mol or 32×10^{-3} kg/mol. Be careful!

SOLVE

5. If you are dealing with only one state of the system, you will use Equation 15.3, the ideal-gas equation. If you are dealing with two states of the same quantity of gas, *and* you know all but one of the p, V, and T values, you can use Equation 15.5; otherwise you have to use Equation 15.3.

REFLECT

6. The mathematical relations are simple, but it's easy to make mistakes with units and conversions of units. Be sure to carry units through your calculations; be especially careful to distinguish between grams, kilograms, and moles.

EXAMPLE 15.2   **Volume of a gas at STP**

The condition called **standard temperature and pressure** (STP) for a gas is defined to be a temperature of 0°C = 273 K and a pressure of 1 atm = 1.013×10^5 Pa. If you want to keep a mole of an ideal gas in your room at STP, how big a container do you need?

SOLUTION

SET UP If we use the ideal-gas equation with SI units, we need to express R in units of $J/(mol \cdot K)$. The temperature in the ideal-gas equation must be an absolute temperature, expressed in kelvins.

SOLVE We rearrange the ideal-gas equation, solving for volume:

$$pV = nRT,$$
$$V = \frac{nRT}{p} = \frac{(1 \text{ mol})[8.314 \text{ J}/(\text{mol} \cdot \text{K})](273 \text{ K})}{1.013 \times 10^5 \text{ Pa}}$$
$$= 0.0224 \text{ m}^3 = 22.4 \text{ L}.$$

REFLECT This is about the size of a 5-gallon gasoline can.

Practice Problem: How many moles would your entire room hold at STP if the room had dimensions of 3 m × 3 m × 2 m? *Answer:* $n = 800$ mol.

EXAMPLE 15.3 Mass of air in a scuba tank

A typical tank used for scuba diving (Figure 15.4) has a volume of 11.0 L (about 0.4 ft^3) and a maximum gauge pressure of 2.10×10^7 Pa (about 3000 lb/in^2 gauge). The "empty" tank contains 11.0 L of air at 21°C and 1 atm (1.013×10^5 Pa). The air is hot when it comes out of the compressor; when the tank is filled, the temperature is 42°C and the gauge pressure is 2.10×10^7 Pa. What mass of air was added? (Air is a mixture of gases: about 78% nitrogen, 21% oxygen, and 1% miscellaneous gases; its average molar mass is 28.8 g/mol = 28.8×10^{-3} kg/mol.)

▶ **FIGURE 15.4**

SOLUTION

SET UP First we find the number of moles in the tank, at the beginning and at the end. We must remember to convert the temperatures from Celsius to kelvin and to convert the pressures from gauge to absolute by adding 1.013×10^5 Pa.

SOLVE From Equation 15.3, the number of moles n_1 in the "empty" tank is

$$n_1 = \frac{pV}{RT} = \frac{(1.013 \times 10^5 \text{ Pa})(11.0 \times 10^{-3} \text{ m}^3)}{[8.314 \text{ J}/(\text{mol} \cdot \text{K})](294 \text{ K})} = 0.456 \text{ mol}.$$

The number of moles n_2 in the "full" tank is

$$n_2 = \frac{(2.11 \times 10^7 \text{ Pa})(11.0 \times 10^{-3} \text{ m}^3)}{[8.314 \text{ J}/(\text{mol} \cdot \text{K})](315 \text{ K})} = 88.6 \text{ mol}.$$

We added 88.6 mol − 0.456 mol = 88.1 mol to the tank. The average molar mass of air is 28.8×10^{-3} kg/mol, so the added mass is $(88.1 \text{ mol})(28.8 \times 10^{-3} \text{ kg/mol}) = 2.54$ kg.

REFLECT Because the amount of gas was not the same for the two states of the system, Equation 15.5 isn't applicable; we have to use the ideal-gas equation, Equation 15.3.

EXAMPLE 15.4 Density of air

Find the density of air at 20°C and normal atmospheric pressure.

SOLUTION

SET UP AND SOLVE We use Equation 15.4, taking care to convert T to kelvins. As in the previous example, the average molar mass of air is 28.8 g/mol = 28.8×10^{-3} kg/mol. From Equation 15.4,

$$\rho = \frac{pM}{RT} = \frac{(1.013 \times 10^5 \text{ Pa})(28.8 \times 10^{-3} \text{ kg/mol})}{[8.314 \text{ J}/(\text{mol} \cdot \text{K})](293 \text{ K})}$$
$$= 1.20 \text{ kg/m}^3.$$

REFLECT Remember that the density of water is an easy-to-remember 1.00×10^3 kg/m^3. Thus, the density of air at normal atmospheric pressure and ordinary temperatures is roughly a thousandth that of water.

When we deal with *mixtures* of ideal gases, the concept of **partial pressure** is useful. In a mixture, the partial pressure of each gas is the pressure that gas would exert if it occupied the entire volume by itself. The actual total pressure of the mixture is the sum of the partial pressures of the components. In air at normal atmospheric pressure, the partial pressure of nitrogen is about 0.8 atm, or 0.8×10^5 Pa, and the partial pressure of oxygen is about 0.2 atm, or 0.2×10^5 Pa.

The ability of the human body to absorb oxygen from the atmosphere depends critically on the partial pressure of oxygen. Absorption drops sharply when the partial pressure of oxygen is less than about 0.13×10^5 Pa, corresponding to an elevation above sea level of approximately 4700 m (15,000 ft). At partial pressures less than 0.11×10^5 Pa, oxygen absorption is not sufficient to maintain life. There is no permanently maintained human habitation on earth above 16,000 ft, although survival for short periods of time is possible at higher elevations. At the summit of Mount Everest (elevation 8882 m, or 29,141 ft) the partial pressure of

▶ **Scuba hazards.** Scuba divers must breathe gas that is at the same pressure as the surrounding water; otherwise they couldn't inflate their lungs once they dove more than a short distance below the surface. However, that means that the partial pressures of some of the gases in the mix rise as the diver descends. Certain gases become toxic at elevated partial pressures. Nitrogen, which is harmless at its normal atmospheric partial pressure of 0.80 atm, becomes a narcotic at elevated pressures. A diver breathing ordinary compressed air begins to act drunk below about 30 m because of nitrogen narcosis. Oxygen also has toxic effects at elevated partial pressures, depending on the partial pressure and the length of exposure. To counteract these problems, technical divers sometimes use special gas mixtures (typically nitrogen–oxygen or helium–oxygen mixtures) chosen to fit the depth and duration of the intended dive.

oxygen is only about 0.07×10^5 Pa, and climbers nearly always carry oxygen tanks. For similar reasons, jet airplanes, which typically fly at altitudes of 8000 to 12,000 m, *must* have pressurized cabins for passenger comfort and health.

pV Diagrams

For a given quantity of a material, the equation of state is a relation among the three state coordinates: pressure p, volume V, and temperature T. A useful graphical representation of this relation is a set of graphs of pressure as a function of volume, each for a particular constant temperature. Such a diagram is called a ***pV diagram.*** Each curve, representing behavior at a specific temperature, is called an **isotherm,** or a *pV isotherm.* ("Isotherm" means "same temperature.")

Figure 15.5 shows pV isotherms for a constant amount of an ideal gas. The highest temperature is T_4; the lowest is T_1. The figure is a graphical representation of the ideal-gas equation of state. We can read off the volume V corresponding to any given pressure p and temperature T in the range shown.

Figure 15.6 shows a pV diagram for a material that *does not* obey the ideal-gas equation. At high temperatures such as T_4, the curves resemble the ideal-gas curves of Figure 15.5. However, at temperatures below T_c, the isotherms develop flat parts—regions where the material can be compressed without an increase in pressure. Observation of the gas shows that it is *condensing* from the vapor (gas) to the liquid phase. The flat parts of the isotherms in the shaded area of Figure 15.6 represent conditions of liquid–vapor *phase equilibrium.* As the volume decreases, more and more material goes from vapor to liquid, but the pressure does not change. To keep the temperature constant, we have to remove heat—the heat of vaporization we discussed in Section 14.5.

When we compress a gas such as that in Figure 15.6 at a constant temperature T_2, it is vapor until point a is reached. There it begins to liquefy; as the volume decreases further and heat of vaporization is removed, more material liquefies, with *both* pressure and temperature remaining constant. At point b, *all* the material is in the liquid state. After this, any further compression results in a very rapid rise in pressure because, in general, liquids are much less compressible than gases. At a lower constant temperature T_1, the gas behaves similarly, but the onset of condensation occurs at lower pressure and greater volume than at the constant temperature T_2.

We'll use pV diagrams often in this chapter and the next. We'll show that the area under a pV curve (regardless of whether it is or is not an isotherm) represents the *work* done by the system during a change in volume. This work, in turn, is directly related to heat transfer and changes in the *internal energy* of the system, which we'll study later in this chapter.

Another diagram that's useful, especially for describing phases of matter and phase transitions, is a graph with axes p and T, called a **phase diagram.** We learned in Section 14.5 that each phase is stable only in certain ranges of temperature and pressure. Ordinarily, a transition from one phase to another takes place under conditions of **phase equilibrium** between the two phases. For a given

Each curve represents pressure as a function of volume for an ideal gas at a single temperature.

▲ **FIGURE 15.5** Isotherms, or constant-temperature curves, for a constant amount of an ideal gas.

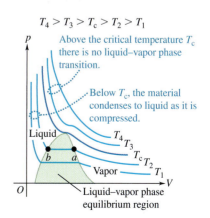

▲ **FIGURE 15.6** A pV diagram for a non-ideal gas, showing pV isotherms for temperatures above and below the critical temperature T_c.

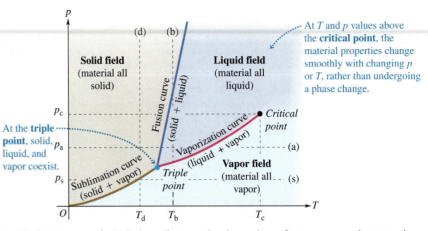

▲ **FIGURE 15.7** A typical pT phase diagram, showing regions of temperature and pressure in which the various phases exist and where phase changes occur.

pressure, this occurs at only one specific temperature. A phase diagram shows what phase occurs for each possible combination of temperature and pressure.

A typical example is shown in Figure 15.7. Each point on the diagram represents a pair of values of p and T. The three colored areas labeled "solid field," "liquid field," and "vapor field" represent points at which the material consists of a single phase: solid, liquid, and vapor, respectively. At any point along the three colored lines separating these fields, the material consists of two coexisting phases. On the sublimation curve, solid and vapor coexist; on the fusion curve, solid and liquid coexist; and on the vaporization curve, liquid and vapor coexist. When a material is at a point on one of these lines, a phase change can proceed.

If we increase the temperature of a substance, keeping the pressure constant, it passes through a sequence of states represented by points on a horizontal line such as the dashed gray line (a) in the figure. The melting and boiling temperatures at this pressure are the temperatures at which this line intersects the fusion and vaporization curves, respectively. If we *compress* a material by increasing the pressure while we hold the temperature constant, as represented by a vertical dashed line such as line (b), the material passes from vapor to liquid and then to solid at the points where the line crosses the vaporization curve and fusion curve, respectively.

When the pressure is low enough, constant-pressure heating can transform a substance from solid directly to vapor, as shown by line (s). As we learned in Chapter 14, this process is called *sublimation;* it occurs at a pressure and temperature corresponding to the intersection of the line and the sublimation curve. At atmospheric pressure, solid carbon dioxide (dry ice) undergoes sublimation; no liquid phase can exist at this pressure. When a substance with an initial temperature lower than the temperature at the point labeled "triple point" is compressed by increasing its pressure, it goes directly from the vapor to the solid phase, as shown by line (d). The melting of ice under pressure is what makes ice skating possible.

TABLE 15.1   Triple-point data

Substance	Temperature, K	Pressure, Pa
Hydrogen	13.8	0.0704×10^5
Neon	24.57	0.432×10^5
Nitrogen	63.18	0.125×10^5
Oxygen	54.36	0.00152×10^5
Ammonia	195.40	0.0607×10^5
Carbon dioxide	216.55	5.17×10^5
Water	273.16	0.00610×10^5

Triple Point

The intersection point of the equilibrium curves in Figure 15.7 is called the **triple point.** For any substance, this point represents the unique pressure–temperature combination at which *all three* phases can coexist. We call these the triple-point pressure and temperature. Triple-point data for a few substances are given in Table 15.1.

Critical Point

Figure 15.6 shows that a liquid–vapor phase transition occurs only when the temperature and pressure are less than those at the point lying at the top of the tongue-shaped area labeled "liquid–vapor equilibrium region." This point corresponds to the endpoint at the top of the vaporization curve in Figure 15.7. It is called the **critical point,** and the corresponding values of p and T are called the critical pressure p_c and critical temperature T_c. A gas at a temperature *above* the critical temperature doesn't separate into two phases when it is compressed isothermally (along a vertical line to the right of the critical point in Figure 15.7). Instead, its properties change gradually and continuously from those we ordinarily associate with a gas (low density and high compressibility) to those of a liquid (high density and low compressibility) *without a phase transition.* Similarly, when a material is heated at a constant pressure greater than the critical-point pressure (a horizontal line above the critical point in Figure 15.7), its properties change gradually from liquid-like to gas-like.

If the preceding discussion stretches your credulity, here's another point of view: Look at liquid–vapor phase transitions at successively higher points on the vaporization curve. As we approach the critical point, the *differences* in physical properties, such as density, bulk modulus, optical properties, and viscosity, between the liquid and vapor phases become smaller and smaller. Exactly *at the* critical point they all become zero, and at this point the distinction between liquid and vapor disappears. The heat of vaporization also grows smaller and smaller as we approach the critical point, and it too becomes zero at the critical point.

Table 15.2 lists critical constants for a few substances. The very low critical temperatures of hydrogen and helium show why these gases defied attempts to liquefy them for many years. For carbon dioxide, the triple-point temperature is $-56.6°C$ and the triple-point pressure is 5.11 atm. At atmospheric pressure, CO_2 can exist only as a solid or vapor—hence the name "dry ice." Liquid CO_2 can exist only at a pressure greater than 5.11 atm.

Many substances can exist in more than one solid phase. A familiar example is carbon, which exists as noncrystalline lampblack (roughly, soot) and crystalline graphite and diamond. (Graphite is the main constituent of pencil leads; it is also used in dry lubricants.) Water is another example: At least eight types of ice, differing in crystal structure and physical properties, have been observed at very high pressures.

▲ **How hot is hot?** For industrial applications, we often need to measure very hot and very cold temperatures, and the measurements involved require special thermometers such as the platinum resistance thermometer. Of course, these thermometers must be calibrated with the use of reproducible temperatures other than the freezing and boiling points of pure water used by the Fahrenheit and Celsius scales. The photo shows the calibration of a platinum resistance thermometer for high temperatures, using the freezing point of molten silver ($961°C = 1234$ K). Calibration of thermometers for low-temperature use can be done at the triple point of argon, where solid, liquid, and gaseous phases coexist ($-189.3°C = 83.8$ K). Some of these platinum resistance thermometers are sensitive enough to measure temperatures with an accuracy of ± 0.05 C° over a range of temperatures from $-190°C$ to over 1000°C.

TABLE 15.2 Critical-point data

Substance	Critical temperature, K	Critical pressure, Pa
Helium ($^4_2$He)	5.3	2.29×10^5
Hydrogen	33.3	13.0×10^5
Nitrogen	126.2	33.9×10^5
Oxygen	154.8	50.8×10^5
Ammonia	405.5	112.8×10^5
Carbon dioxide	304.2	73.9×10^5
Water	647.4	221.2×10^5

15.3 Kinetic Theory of an Ideal Gas

8.1–8.3

We've studied several properties of matter in bulk, including elasticity, density, surface tension, equations of state, and heat capacities, with only passing references to molecular structure. Now we want to look in more detail at the relation of bulk (macroscopic) behavior to microscopic structure. We begin with a general discussion of the molecular structure of matter. Then, in the next two sections, we'll develop the *kinetic-molecular model* of an ideal gas and derive the equation of state and an expression for molar heat capacity from this molecular model.

Molecular Properties of Matter

All familiar matter is made up of atoms or groups of connected atoms. For convenience, we'll use the term **molecule** to refer to the smallest unit of a substance, even in cases where this unit is a single atom. Individual atoms are on the order of 10^{-10} m in size; the largest molecules contain many atoms and are 10,000 or more times that large. In gases, the molecules move nearly independently; in liquids and solids, they are held together by intermolecular forces that are electrical in nature, arising from interactions of the electrically charged particles that make up the molecules. Gravitational forces between molecules are negligible in comparison with electrical forces.

When molecules of a gas are far apart, the electrical forces between them are very small and usually attractive. As a gas is compressed and its molecules are brought closer together, the attractive forces increase. At sufficiently small separations, the intermolecular attractions are large enough to make the material condense into a liquid or solid.

Molecules are always in motion; their kinetic energies usually increase with temperature. In *solids,* molecules vibrate about more or less fixed centers. In a crystalline solid, these centers are arranged in a recurring *crystal lattice.* Figure 15.8 shows the cubic crystal structure of sodium chloride (ordinary table salt). A scanning tunneling microscope photograph of the surface of a silicon crystal is shown in Figure 15.9. Each "bead" is a silicon atom.

In a *liquid,* the intermolecular distances are usually only slightly greater than in the solid phase of the same substance, but the molecules have much greater freedom of movement. Liquids show regularity of structure only in the immediate neighborhood of a few molecules.

The molecules of a *gas* are usually widely separated and exert only very small attractive forces on one another. A gas molecule moves in a straight line until it collides with another molecule or with a wall of the container. In molecular terms, an *ideal gas* is a gas whose molecules exert *no* attractive forces on one another and therefore have no *potential* energy.

At low temperatures, most common substances are in the solid phase. As the temperature rises, a substance melts and then vaporizes. From a *molecular* point of view, these transitions are in the direction of increasing molecular kinetic energy. Thus, temperature and molecular kinetic energy are closely related.

Kinetic Molecular Theory of an Ideal Gas

The goal of any molecular theory of matter is to understand the *macroscopic* properties of matter in terms of its atomic or molecular structure and behavior. Such theories are of tremendous practical importance; once we have this understanding, we can *design* materials to have specific desired properties. Such analysis has led to the development of high-strength steels, glasses with special optical properties, semiconductor materials for electronic devices, and countless other materials that are essential to contemporary technology.

One of the simplest examples of a molecular theory is the kinetic-molecular model of an ideal gas. With the help of this model, we can understand the relation

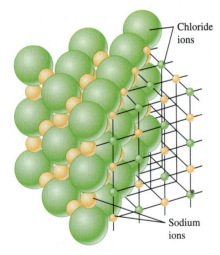

Chloride ions

Sodium ions

▲ **FIGURE 15.8** Schematic representation of the cubic crystal structure of sodium chloride (table salt).

▲ **FIGURE 15.9** A scanning tunneling microscope image of silicon atoms on the surface of a silicon crystal. The regularity of the crystal structure is easy to see.

of ideal-gas behavior, including the ideal-gas equation of state (Equation 15.3) and the molar heat capacities of gases, to Newton's laws. The development that follows has several steps, and you may need to go over it several times to grasp how it all goes together. Don't get discouraged!

Here are the assumptions of the kinetic-molecular model:

1. A container with volume V contains a very large number N of identical molecules, each with mass m. The container has perfectly rigid walls that do not move.
2. The molecules behave as point particles; their size is small in comparison to the average distance between particles and to the dimensions of the container.
3. The molecules are in constant random motion; they obey Newton's laws. Each molecule occasionally makes a perfectly elastic (energy-conserving) collision with a wall of the container.
4. During collisions, the molecules exert *forces* on the walls of the container; these forces create the *pressure* that the gas exerts. In a typical collision (Figure 15.10), the velocity component v_y parallel to the wall is unchanged, and the component v_x perpendicular to the wall changes direction, but not magnitude.

Here's our program, one step at a time:

Step 1: We find the total change in momentum associated with each collision.
Step 2: We find the *number* of collisions per unit time for a certain wall area A.
Step 3: We find the total change in momentum per unit time due to these collisions and, from that, the force on area A needed to cause that change in momentum.
Step 4: Finally, we can obtain an expression for the pressure, which is force per unit area, and compare it with the ideal-gas equation.

We'll take these steps in order. Here we go:

Step 1. Let $|v_x|$ be the magnitude of the x component of velocity of a molecule of the gas. For now, we assume that all molecules have the same $|v_x|$. That isn't right, but making this temporary assumption helps to clarify the basic ideas. We will show later that the assumption isn't really necessary. For each collision, the x component of momentum changes from $-m|v_x|$ to $+m|v_x|$, so the *change* in the x component of momentum is $m|v_x| - (-m|v_x|) = 2m|v_x|$.

Step 2. If a molecule is going to collide with a given wall area A during a small time interval Δt, then, at the beginning of Δt, it must be within a distance $|v_x| \Delta t$ from the wall (Figure 15.11) and it must be headed toward the wall. So the number of molecules that collide with A during Δt is equal to the number of molecules that are within a cylinder with base area A and length $|v_x| \Delta t$ and that have their v_x aimed toward the wall. The volume of such a cylinder is $A|v_x| \Delta t$.

Assuming that the number of molecules per unit volume (N/V) is uniform, the *number* of molecules in this cylinder is $(N/V)(A|v_x| \Delta t)$. On the average, half of these molecules are moving toward the wall and half away from it. So the number of collisions with wall area A during Δt is

$$\tfrac{1}{2}\left(\frac{N}{V}\right)(A|v_x| \Delta t).$$

Step 3. The total change in momentum, ΔP_x, due to all these collisions during time Δt is the *number* of collisions multiplied by the change in momentum in one collision, $2m|v_x|$:

$$\Delta P_x = \tfrac{1}{2}\left(\frac{N}{V}\right)(A|v_x| \Delta t)(2m|v_x|) = \frac{NAmv_x^2 \, \Delta t}{V}.$$

(We're using capital P for momentum and small p for pressure. Also, capital V denotes volume, and small v represents a velocity component. Be careful!) The

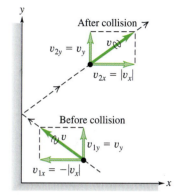

▲ **FIGURE 15.10** Elastic collision of a molecule with an idealized container wall. The component v_y parallel to the wall does not change; the component v_x perpendicular to the wall reverses direction. The speed v does not change.

▲ **FIGURE 15.11** Molecules moving toward the wall with speed $|v_x|$ collide with area A during the time interval Δt only if they are within a distance $|v_x| \Delta t$ of the wall at the beginning of the interval. All such molecules are contained within a volume $A|v_x| \Delta t$.

rate of change of the momentum component P_x with time is the preceding expression divided by Δt:

$$\frac{\Delta P_x}{\Delta t} = \frac{NAmv_x^2}{V}.$$

According to Newton's second law, this rate of change of momentum equals the force exerted by the wall area A on the molecules. From Newton's *third* law, this force is equal and opposite to the force exerted *on* the wall *by* the molecules.

Step 4. The pressure p of the gas is the magnitude of the force per unit area, and we obtain

$$p = \frac{F}{A} = \frac{Nmv_x^2}{V}, \qquad pV = Nmv_x^2. \tag{15.6}$$

Now we need one additional step: We need to express v_x^2 in this equation in terms of the average value of v^2 for all the molecules. First, the square of the speed of an individual molecule (v^2) is related to the sum of the squares of the components $(v_x, v_y$ and $v_z)$: $v^2 = v_x^2 + v_y^2 + v_z^2$. Second, we can take the *average* of this expression for all the molecules in the gas: When we do, we get $(v^2)_{av} = (v_x^2)_{av} + (v_y^2)_{av} + (v_z^2)_{av}$. Third, there is no distinction among the x, y, and z axis directions, so it must be true that $(v_x^2)_{av} = (v_y^2)_{av} = (v_z^2)_{av}$, and it follows that $(v^2)_{av} = 3(v_x^2)_{av}$, or $(v_x^2)_{av} = (\frac{1}{3})(v^2)_{av}$.

We see that we didn't really need the initial assumption that all molecules had the same value of $|v_x|$, because in this step we work with *average values* of the velocity components. When we replace v_x^2 with $(v_x^2)_{av}$ in Equation 15.6, we get

$$pV = \tfrac{1}{3}Nm(v^2)_{av} = \tfrac{2}{3}N[\tfrac{1}{2}m(v^2)_{av}].$$

We notice that $\frac{1}{2}m(v^2)_{av}$ is the average *translational kinetic energy* of a single molecule. The product of this quantity and the total number N of molecules equals the *total* random kinetic energy K_{tr} of translational motion of *all* the molecules. (The notation K_{tr} reminds us that this energy is associated with *translational* motion and anticipates the possibility of additional energies associated with rotational and vibrational motion of molecules.) Hence, the product pV equals two-thirds of the total translational kinetic energy:

$$pV = \tfrac{2}{3}K_{tr}.$$

Now here comes the *coup de grace:* We compare this result with the ideal-gas equation, $pV = nRT$, which is based on experimental studies of gas behavior. For the two equations to agree, we must have the following relationship:

Kinetic energy of gas molecules

For an ideal gas, the total translational kinetic energy K_{tr} of all the molecules is proportional to the absolute (Kelvin) temperature T and to the quantity of gas (as measured by the number of moles, n):

$$K_{tr} = \tfrac{3}{2}nRT. \tag{15.7}$$

We'll use this important result several times in the discussion that follows.

The average translational kinetic energy of a *single* molecule is the total translational kinetic energy K_{tr} of *all* the molecules, divided by the number N of molecules:

$$K_{av} = \frac{K_{tr}}{N} = \tfrac{1}{2}m(v^2)_{av} = \frac{3nRT}{2N}.$$

▶ **Hold your hydrogen.** The cloud of gas and dust from which our solar system formed consisted mostly of diatomic hydrogen gas (H_2). However, earth and its sister rocky planets have practically no hydrogen gas in their atmospheres, whereas the gas giants, such as Jupiter, have a lot. Why? The main reason concerns mass—of hydrogen and of planets. Hydrogen is the least massive element; H_2 has a molar mass of 2.01 g/mol. Therefore, H_2 molecules have a higher average speed at a given temperature than more massive molecules. On a small planet like earth, a significant fraction of any H_2 molecules in the atmosphere are moving faster than the planet's escape speed and can simply fly off into outer space. Thus, small planets leak hydrogen until essentially none remains in their atmospheres. The gas giants, being far more massive, have enough gravity to keep their hydrogen.

Earth and
Jupiter to scale

Also, the total number of molecules, N, is the number of moles, n, multiplied by Avogadro's number N_A (i.e., $N = nN_A$), so the average translational kinetic energy per molecule is

$$K_{av} = \frac{3nRT}{2(nN_A)} = \tfrac{3}{2}\frac{R}{N_A}T.$$

The ratio R/N_A occurs frequently in molecular theory. It is called the **Boltzmann constant,** denoted by k and defined as

$$k = \frac{R}{N_A} = \frac{8.314 \text{ J/mol} \cdot \text{K}}{6.022 \times 10^{23} \text{ molecules/mol}}$$
$$= 1.381 \times 10^{-23} \text{ J/molecule} \cdot \text{K}.$$

We can rewrite the expression for K_{av} (the average translational kinetic energy of a single molecule) in terms of k as

$$K_{av} = \tfrac{1}{2}m(v^2)_{av} = \tfrac{3}{2}kT. \qquad (15.8)$$

This result shows that, for an ideal gas, the average translational kinetic energy *per molecule* depends only on the temperature, not on the pressure, volume, or kind of molecule involved. We can obtain an equivalent statement by using the relation $M = N_A m$. The average translational kinetic energy *per mole* (which also depends only on T) is

$$N_A \tfrac{1}{2}m(v^2)_{av} = N_A(\tfrac{3}{2}kT) = \tfrac{3}{2}RT.$$

Finally, it's often useful to rewrite the ideal-gas equation on a molecular basis. We use $N = N_A n$ and $R = N_A k$ to obtain the following alternative form:

$$pV = NkT. \qquad (15.9)$$

This equation shows that we can think of k as a gas constant on a "per molecule" basis instead of the usual "per-mole" basis with the gas constant R.

Quantitative Analysis 15.2

A cooled gas

An ideal gas is cooled at constant volume until the pressure is half the original pressure. When this happens, the average translational kinetic energy of the gas molecules is

A. twice the original.

B. unchanged.

C. half the original.

SOLUTION According to the ideal-gas equation, $pV = nRT$, if V is constant and p is reduced by a factor of one-half, the absolute temperature must also decrease by a factor of one-half. According to Equation 15.8, the average translational kinetic energy is proportional to the absolute temperature, so it too decreases by a factor of one-half. The correct answer is C.

◀ **It could have been so nice there!** Science fiction authors once envisioned Venus as a cloud-shrouded tropical swamp planet—and indeed, when it formed, Venus probably had at least as much water as our own world. But Venus is now utterly dry, with a dense carbon dioxide atmosphere that keeps it hotter than a pizza oven. Where did the water go? Being closer to the sun, Venus was always warmer than earth. If it ever had oceans, they soon vaporized. With no oceans, carbon dioxide could not form limestone (as it does on earth), but instead stayed in the atmosphere. The thick, hot atmosphere let water vapor rise to altitudes at which UV light could split water molecules, releasing hydrogen atoms. Because of their low mass, these atoms easily reached escape speed and disappeared into outer space. Eventually, the water was gone. That is how our sister planet became an arid furnace. We're so lucky . . . .

Molecular Speeds in an Ideal Gas

From Equations 15.8 and 15.9, we can obtain an expression for the square root of $(v^2)_{av}$, called the **root-mean-square speed** v_{rms} of molecules in an ideal gas:

$$v_{rms} = \sqrt{(v^2)_{av}} = \sqrt{\frac{3kT}{m}} = \sqrt{\frac{3RT}{M}}. \tag{15.10}$$

This quantity increases with temperature, as we should expect; it also varies inversely with the square root of the molecular or molar mass.

To compute the rms speed, we square each molecular speed, add, divide by the number of molecules, and take the square root. That is, v_{rms} is the *root* of the *mean* of the *squares*. Example 15.6 illustrates this procedure.

We've mentioned that the molecules in a gas don't all have the same speed. Figure 15.12 is a graph of the relative numbers of molecules with various speeds for three different temperatures. As the temperature increases, the curve flattens and the peak moves to higher speed. This speed distribution curve is called the *Maxwell–Boltzmann* distribution.

Number of molecules

▲ **FIGURE 15.12** The distribution of speeds for the molecules of a gas at three different temperatures.

PROBLEM-SOLVING STRATEGY 15.2 **Kinetic-molecular theory** (MP)

As usual, using a consistent set of units is essential. Following are several places where caution is needed:

1. The usual units for molar mass M are grams per mole; the molar mass of O_2 is 32 g/mol, for example. These units are often omitted in tables. When you use SI units in equations, such as Equation 15.10, you *must* express M in kilograms per mole by multiplying the value shown in the table by $(1 \text{ kg}/10^3 \text{ g})$. Thus, in SI units, M for O_2 is 32×10^{-3} kg/mol.

2. Are you working on a "per molecule" basis or a "per mole" basis? Remember that m is the mass of a molecule and M is the mass of a mole. N is the number of molecules, and n is the number of moles; k is the gas constant per molecule, and R is the gas constant per mole. Although N, the number of molecules, is in one sense a dimensionless number, you can do a complete unit check if you think of N as having the unit "molecules;" then m has the unit "mass per molecule" and k has the unit "joules per molecule per kelvin."

3. Remember that T is always *absolute* (Kelvin) temperature.

EXAMPLE 15.5 Kinetic energy of a molecule

(a) What is the average translational kinetic energy of a molecule of oxygen (O_2) at a temperature of 27°C, assuming that oxygen can be treated as an ideal gas? **(b)** What is the *total* translational kinetic energy of the molecules in 1 mole of oxygen at this temperature? **(c)** Compare the root-mean-square speeds of oxygen and nitrogen (N_2) molecules at this temperature (assuming that they can be treated as ideal gases). The mass of an oxygen molecule is $m_{O_2} = 5.31 \times 10^{-26}$ kg, and the mass of a molecule of nitrogen is $m_{N_2} = 4.65 \times 10^{-26}$ kg.

Continued

SOLUTION

SET UP AND SOLVE **Part (a):** First we convert the temperature to kelvins: 27°C = 300 K. Then we use Equation 15.8: For one molecule,

$$K_{av} = \tfrac{1}{2}m(v^2)_{av} = \tfrac{3}{2}kT$$
$$= \tfrac{3}{2}(1.38 \times 10^{-23} \text{ J/K})(300 \text{ K}) = 6.21 \times 10^{-21} \text{ J}.$$

Part (b): Using Equation 15.7 (for 1 mole), we obtain

$$K_{tr} = \tfrac{3}{2}nRT = \tfrac{3}{2}(1 \text{ mol})[8.315 \text{ J/(mol} \cdot \text{K)}](300 \text{ K}) = 3740 \text{ J}.$$

Part (c): From Equation 15.10, we find that

$$v_{rms,O_2} = \sqrt{\frac{3kT}{m_{O_2}}} = \sqrt{\frac{3(1.38 \times 10^{-23} \text{ J/K})(300 \text{ K})}{5.31 \times 10^{-26} \text{ kg}}}$$
$$= 484 \text{ m/s},$$

$$v_{rms,N_2} = \sqrt{\frac{3kT}{m_{N_2}}} = \sqrt{\frac{3(1.38 \times 10^{-23} \text{ J/K})(300 \text{ K})}{4.65 \times 10^{-26} \text{ kg}}}$$
$$= 517 \text{ m/s}.$$

Thus, the ratio of the rms speed of N_2 molecules to that of O_2 molecules is 1.07.

ALTERNATIVE SOLUTION

$$v_{rms,O_2} = \sqrt{\frac{3RT}{M_{O_2}}} = \sqrt{\frac{3(8.314 \text{ J/mol} \cdot \text{K})(300 \text{ K})}{32 \times 10^{-3} \text{ kg/mol}}} = 484 \text{ m/s},$$

$$v_{rms,N_2} = \sqrt{\frac{3RT}{M_{N_2}}} = \sqrt{\frac{3(8.314 \text{ J/mol} \cdot \text{K})(300 \text{ K})}{28 \times 10^{-3} \text{ kg/mol}}} = 517 \text{ m/s}.$$

REFLECT These speeds are roughly 1000 mi/h. At any temperature, rms molecular speeds are inversely proportional to the square root of molar mass. Note that we have to be careful throughout to distinguish between "per molecule" and "per mole" quantities.

Practice Problem: What is the root-mean-square speed of a diatomic hydrogen molecule (H_2) at 300 K, assuming that it can be treated as an ideal gas? The mass of a hydrogen molecule is 3.348×10^{-27} kg. *Answer:* $v_{rms} = 1930$ m/s.

EXAMPLE 15.6 **Gang of five**

Five ideal-gas molecules chosen at random are found to have speeds of 500, 600, 700, 800, and 900 m/s, respectively. Find the rms speed for this collection. Is it the same as the *average* speed of these molecules?

SOLUTION

SET UP AND SOLVE The average value of v^2 for the molecules is

$$(v^2)_{av} = [(500 \text{ m/s})^2 + (600 \text{ m/s})^2 + (700 \text{ m/s})^2$$
$$+ (800 \text{ m/s})^2 + (900 \text{ m/s})^2]/5$$
$$= 5.10 \times 10^5 \text{ m}^2/\text{s}^2.$$

The square root of this is v_{rms}:

$$v_{rms} = 714 \text{ m/s}.$$

The *average* speed v_{av} is given by

$$v_{av} = \frac{500 \text{ m/s} + 600 \text{ m/s} + 700 \text{ m/s} + 800 \text{ m/s} + 900 \text{ m/s}}{5}$$
$$= 700 \text{ m/s}.$$

REFLECT In general, v_{rms} and v_{av} are not the same. Roughly speaking, v_{rms} gives greater weight to the larger speeds than does v_{av}.

Practice Problem: Suppose we double all the speeds in this example. How do v_{av} and v_{rms} change? *Answers:* $v_{av} = 1400$ m/s, $v_{rms} = 1428$ m/s.

EXAMPLE 15.7 **Volume of a gas at STP, revisited**

Find the number of molecules and the number of moles in 1 cubic meter of air at atmospheric pressure and 0°C.

SOLUTION

SET UP AND SOLVE We use the alternative form of the ideal-gas equation, $pV = NkT$ (Equation 15.9):

$$N = \frac{pV}{kT} = \frac{(1.013 \times 10^5 \text{ Pa})(1 \text{ m}^3)}{(1.38 \times 10^{-23} \text{ J/K})(273 \text{ K})}$$
$$= 2.69 \times 10^{25}.$$

The number of moles n is

$$n = \frac{N}{N_A} = \frac{2.69 \times 10^{25} \text{ molecules}}{6.022 \times 10^{23} \text{ molecules/mol}} = 44.7 \text{ mol}.$$

Continued

The total volume is 1.00 m³, so the volume of 1 mole is

$$\frac{1.00 \text{ m}^3}{44.7 \text{ mol}} = 0.0224 \text{ m}^3/\text{mol} = 22.4 \text{ L}/\text{mol}.$$

REFLECT This is the same result that we obtained in Example 15.2 (Section 15.2), using only macroscopic quantities.

15.4 Heat Capacities

In Section 14.4, we defined specific heat capacities in terms of the measured amount of heat needed to change the temperature of a specified quantity of material by a particular amount (in SI units, 1 K and 1 kg). We didn't attempt to *predict* heat capacities on the basis of more fundamental considerations. In some simple cases, these numbers *can* be predicted on theoretical grounds, using the relation between heat and molecular energy.

Especially when we deal with heat capacities of gases, it's often more convenient to describe the quantity of substance in terms of the number of *moles* rather than the mass m_{total} of material. We define the **molar heat capacity** (also called molar specific heat) of a substance as follows:

> **Molar heat capacity**
>
> The amount of heat Q needed for a certain temperature change ΔT is proportional to the temperature change and to the number of moles of substance; that is,
>
> $$Q = nC \, \Delta T, \tag{15.11}$$
>
> where C is a quantity, different for different materials, called the *molar heat capacity* for the material. The SI units of C are $\text{J}/(\text{mol} \cdot \text{K})$.

Comparing Equations 14.10 ($Q = m_{total}c \, \Delta T$) and 15.11 ($Q = nC \, \Delta T$), and recalling that $m_{total} = Mn$, we see that the molar heat capacity C of a material is related to its specific heat capacity c by the equation

$$C = Mc, \quad \text{(Relation of specific and molar heat capacities)} \tag{15.12}$$

where M is the molar mass of the material. That is, heat per mole equals heat per unit mass times amount of mass per mole. For example, the molar heat capacity of liquid water is about $(4186 \text{ J}/(\text{kg} \cdot \text{K}))(18 \times 10^{-3} \text{ kg}/\text{mol}) = 75 \text{ J}/(\text{mol} \cdot \text{K})$.

In our discussion of heat capacities in this chapter, we'll keep the volume of material constant so that there is no energy transfer through mechanical work. If we were to let a gas expand, it would do work (force times distance) on the moving walls of its container. We'll return to this more general case in Section 15.7. For now, with the volume held constant, we'll denote the molar heat capacity at constant volume as C_V.

Molar Heat Capacities of Gases

In this section, we present a brief introduction to the analysis of heat capacities of gases on the basis of the simple kinetic-molecular model we discussed in the last section. In that model, the molecular energy consists only of the kinetic energy K_{tr} associated with the translational motion of pointlike molecules. This energy is directly proportional to the absolute temperature T, as shown by Equation 15.7: $K_{tr} = \frac{3}{2}nRT$. When the temperature changes by a small amount ΔT, the corresponding change in kinetic energy is

$$\Delta K_{tr} = \tfrac{3}{2}nR \, \Delta T.$$

From the definition of molar heat capacity at constant volume, C_V, we also have

$$Q = nC_V \,\Delta T,$$

where Q is the heat input needed for a temperature change ΔT. Now if K_{tr} represents the total molecular energy, as we have assumed, then Q and ΔK_{tr} must be *equal*. Equating the last two equations, we get

$$nC_V \,\Delta T = \tfrac{3}{2}nR \,\Delta T, \qquad (15.13)$$

$$C_V = \tfrac{3}{2}R \qquad \text{(monatomic gas)}$$

This surprisingly simple result says that the molar heat capacity (at constant volume) of *every* gas whose molecules can be represented as points is equal to $3R/2$. In SI units,

$$C_V = \tfrac{3}{2}[8.314 \text{ J}/(\text{mol} \cdot \text{K})] = 12.47 \text{ J}/(\text{mol} \cdot \text{K}).$$

For comparison, Table 15.3 gives *measured* values of C_V for several gases. We see that, for monatomic gases, our prediction is right on the money, but that it is way off for diatomic and polyatomic gases.

Thus, our point-molecule model works for monatomic gases, but for diatomic and polyatomic molecules we need something more sophisticated. For example, we can picture a diatomic molecule as *two* point masses, like a little elastic dumbbell. Such a molecule can have additional kinetic energy associated with *rotation* about axes through its center of mass, and the atoms may also have a back-and-forth *vibrating* motion along the line joining them, with additional kinetic and potential energies. Hence, the molar heat capacities for diatomic gases should be greater than those for monatomic gases. These possibilities are shown in Figure 15.13.

Equation 15.7 $\left(K_{tr} = \tfrac{3}{2}nRT\right)$ shows that the average random *translational* kinetic energy of the molecules of an ideal gas is proportional to the absolute temperature T of the gas. It turns out that the additional energy of rotational and vibrational motion is also proportional to T. A diatomic molecule has an additional average *rotational* kinetic energy of kT per molecule or RT per mole. Thus, we expect a diatomic molecule to have an average kinetic energy of $K = \tfrac{3}{2}kT + kT = \tfrac{5}{2}kT$ per molecule or $\tfrac{5}{2}RT$ per mole, and the molar heat capacity should be $\tfrac{5}{2}R$. In SI units,

$$C_V = \tfrac{5}{2}R = \tfrac{5}{2}[8.314 \text{ J}/(\text{mol}\cdot\text{K})] = 20.8 \text{ J}/(\text{mol}\cdot\text{K}) \qquad \text{(diatomic gas).} \quad (15.14)$$

We note that this value agrees, within a few percent, with the measured molar heat capacities of the diatomic gases listed in Table 15.3.

Vibrational motion can also contribute to the heat capacities of gases. Molecular bonds are not rigid; they can stretch and bend, and the resulting vibrations lead to additional degrees of freedom and additional energies. Because of quantum effects, including these energies in our formulation would be more complex than for the rotational energies of diatomic molecules, and we won't attempt a quantitative discussion. In Table 15.3, the large values of C_V for some polyatomic molecules show the contributions of vibrational energy. In addition, a molecule with three or more atoms that are not in a straight line has an average rotational kinetic energy of $\tfrac{3}{2}kT$ rather than just kT.

15.5 The First Law of Thermodynamics

Energy relationships are of central importance in the study of energy-conversion devices such as engines, batteries, and refrigerators and also in the functioning of living organisms. We've studied energy transfer through mechanical work

TABLE 15.3 Molar heat capacities of gases

Type of gas	Gas	$C_V(\text{J}/(\text{mol}\cdot\text{K}))$
Monatomic	He	12.47
	Ar	12.47
Diatomic	H_2	20.42
	N_2	20.76
	O_2	21.10
	CO	20.85
Polyatomic	CO_2	28.46
	SO_2	31.39
	H_2S	25.95

(a) Translational motion

(b) Rotational motion

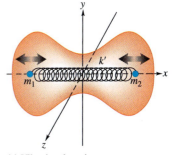

(c) Vibrational motion

▲ **FIGURE 15.13** A diatomic molecule can move in three ways: (a) by translational motion of the whole molecule through space, (b) by rotation of the molecule about an axis, and (c) by vibration of the two atoms on their springlike mutual bond.

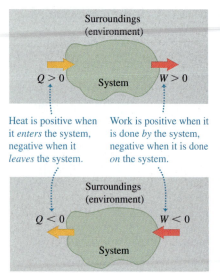

Heat is positive when it *enters* the system, negative when it *leaves* the system.

Work is positive when it is done *by* the system, negative when it is done *on* the system.

▲ **FIGURE 15.14** A thermodynamic system may exchange energy with its surroundings by means of heat (which may enter or leave the system) and work (which may be done by or on the system).

▲ **FIGURE 15.15** The catastrophic eruption of Mt. St. Helens on May 18, 1980, a dramatic illustration of the enormous pressure developed in a confined hot gas. The eruption column is driven in part by this pressure and in part by the buoyancy of the hot gas, which is much less dense than the surrounding air.

(Chapter 7) and through heat transfer (Chapters 14 and 15). Now we're ready to combine and generalize those principles. *Thermodynamics* is the study of energy relationships that involve heat, mechanical work, and other aspects of energy and energy transfer. The first law of thermodynamics extends the principle of conservation of energy to include heat as well as mechanical energy.

Energy, Heat, and Work

To state energy relationships precisely, we'll always use the concept of a *thermodynamic system,* and we'll discuss *heat* and *work* as two means of transferring energy into or out of such a system. The system might be a quantity of expanding steam in a turbine, the refrigerant in an air conditioner, some other specific quantity of material, or, sometimes, a particular device or an organism. A **thermodynamic system** (Figure 15.14) is a system that can interact (and exchange energy) with its surroundings, or environment, in at least two ways, one of which is heat transfer. A familiar example of a thermodynamic system is a quantity of gas confined in a cylinder with a piston, similar to the cylinders in internal-combustion engines. Energy can be added to the system by conduction of heat, and the system can also do *work* as the gas exerts a force on the piston and moves it through a displacement. With thermodynamic systems, as with all others, it's essential to define clearly at the start exactly what is and is not included in the system. Only then can we describe unambiguously the energy transfers into and out of that system.

Thermodynamics has its roots in practical problems. The engine in an automobile and the jet engines in an airplane use the heat of combustion of their fuel to perform mechanical work in propelling the vehicle. Muscle tissue in living organisms metabolizes chemical energy in food and performs mechanical work on the organism's surroundings. A steam engine or steam turbine uses the heat of combustion of coal or some other fuel to perform mechanical work such as driving an electric generator or pulling a train.

In all these situations, we describe the energy relations in terms of the quantity of heat Q added *to* the system and the work W done *by* the system. Both Q and W may be positive or negative. Figure 15.14 shows the sign conventions we'll use. As in the preceding chapter, a positive value of Q represents heat flow *into* the system, with a corresponding input of energy to it. Negative Q represents heat flow *out of* the system. A positive value of W represents work done *by* the system as it pushes outward against its surroundings, such as work done by an expanding gas. Thus, positive work corresponds to energy *leaving* the system. Negative W, such as work done *on a gas* by its surroundings while the gas is being compressed, represents energy *entering* the system. We'll use these rules consistently in the examples in this chapter and the next.

NOTE ▶ There is no uniformity in the literature concerning the signs of Q and W. In particular, W is sometimes defined with the opposite sign, as work done *on* the system rather than *by* it. The moral is, when you read other references, be careful! ◀

In this discussion, we'll be concerned mostly with *equilibrium* processes. In such processes, heat transfer takes place so slowly that the system is always very nearly in thermal equilibrium. (That is, the temperature is uniform throughout the system.). Also, changes in volume take place slowly enough so that the system is always very nearly in *mechanical equilibrium.* (That is, the pressure is uniform throughout the system.) Including both conditions, we speak of states of **thermodynamic equilibrium.** In non-equilibrium processes, there is no such thing as a single temperature or pressure for the system as a whole.

▶ **Your typical steamship.** It's a truism that the industrial revolution was powered by steam. In a steam engine, water is boiled to create steam, which later cools and condenses. The resulting changes in pressure and volume do work, such as moving a piston. We've all seen historical images of steam locomotives and steamships. What you may not realize is that today's nuclear submarines are . . . steamships. A reactor core is simply a source of heat. To do work with that heat—and, not incidentally, to prevent the core from overheating and melting down—the reactor uses steam. And what better method? Steam power is, after all, a mature technology.

Work Done during Volume Changes

A gas in a cylinder with a movable piston is a simple example of a thermodynamic system. Internal-combustion engines, steam engines, and compressors in refrigerators and air conditioners all use some version of such a system. In the next several sections, we'll use the gas-in-cylinder system to explore several kinds of processes that involve energy transformations. We'll look first at the *work* done by the system during a change in volume. When a gas expands, it pushes on its boundary surfaces as they move outward; an expanding gas always does positive work. The same thing is true of any solid or fluid material confined under pressure. Figure 15.15 shows an impressive example of the work done by expanding gases.

Figure 15.16 shows a solid or fluid in a cylinder with a movable piston. Suppose that the cylinder has cross-sectional area A and that the pressure exerted by the system at the piston face is p. Then the magnitude F of the total force exerted on the piston by the system is $F = pA$. When the piston moves out a small distance Δx, the work W done by the force is

$$W = F \Delta x = pA \Delta x. \qquad (15.15)$$

The change in volume is $\Delta V = A \Delta x$, so we can express the work done by the system as

$$W = p \Delta V.$$

(We assume that the process proceeds so slowly that mechanical equilibrium is maintained; then, at any instant, the pressure is the same throughout the system.) If the pressure remains constant while the volume changes by a finite amount—say, from V_1 to V_2—the total work done by the system is

$$W = p(V_2 - V_1) \qquad \text{(constant pressure only).} \qquad (15.16)$$

But what if the pressure is *not* constant during the expansion? Suppose, for example, that we let an ideal gas expand, keeping its temperature constant. Then the product pV is constant, so as the volume V increases, the pressure p must decrease. This situation is similar to one in which work is done by a varying force, a phenomenon we studied in Chapter 7, and we can handle it in the same way. We divide the total change in volume into many small changes ΔV_1, $\Delta V_2, \ldots$, each so small that we can consider the pressure to be constant within each one. Calling the various pressures $p_1, p_2, \ldots$, we represent the total work as

$$W = p_1 \Delta V_1 + p_2 \Delta V_2 + \cdots.$$

As we take the ΔV's smaller and smaller, this approximation becomes more and more precise.

We can also draw a graph showing the variation of p with V, as in Figure 15.17a, with pressure p on the vertical axis and volume V on the horizontal axis. Then each product $p_1 \Delta V_1$, $p_2 \Delta V_2$, and so on, corresponds to the area of one of the rectangles in Figure 15.17b, and the sum of these areas is approximately equal to the total area under the curve between V_1 and V_2. As the ΔV's become smaller and smaller, the approximation gets better and better. So we have the following general result:

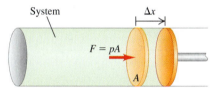

▲ **FIGURE 15.16** The work done by the system during the small expansion Δx is $\Delta W = F \Delta x = pA \Delta x$.

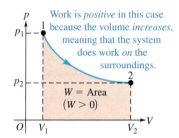

(a) pV diagram for a system undergoing a change in volume with varying pressure

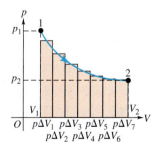

(b) The curve in **(a)** treated as a series of small constant-pressure intervals

▲ **FIGURE 15.17** The work done by a system equals the area under the curve on a pV diagram.

The volume *decreases* ($V_2 < V_1$), meaning that the surroundings do work on the system. Thus, work is *negative*.

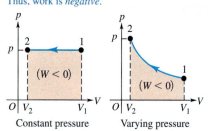

▲ FIGURE 15.18 Two cases in which the work is negative (meaning that work is done *on* the system, reducing its volume).

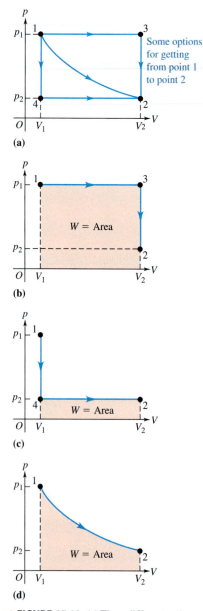

▲ FIGURE 15.19 (a) Three different paths between state 1 and state 2. (b)–(d) The work done by the system during a transition between two states depends on the path chosen.

Graphical representation of work during a volume change

The work W done by a system is equal to the area under the curve on a pV diagram.

According to the sign rule that we stated earlier in this section, W is always the work done *by* the system, and it is always *positive* when a system *expands*. When a system expands from state 1 to state 2 as shown in Figure 15.17, the area is positive. In a *compression* from state 1 to state 2 (Figure 15.18), the change in volume is negative, and the total work done by the system on the piston by the system is negative. This corresponds to a *negative* area; thus, when a system is compressed, its volume decreases, and it does *negative* work on its surroundings.

A particular case that occurs often in problems is the *isothermal* (constant-temperature) expansion of an ideal gas. As the gas expands, the pressure decreases, so we can't use Equation 15.16. Methods of calculus can be used to show that when n moles of an ideal gas expand from volume V_1 to volume V_2 at constant temperature T, the total work W done by the gas is

$$W = nRT \ln \frac{V_2}{V_1}, \qquad (15.17)$$

where "ln" stands for the natural logarithm (i.e., the logarithm to the base e).

When a system changes from an initial state to a final state, it passes through a series of intermediate states; we call this series of states a **path.** There are always infinitely many different possibilities for these intermediate states. When they are all equilibrium states, the path can be plotted on a pV diagram (Figure 15.19). Point 1 represents an initial state (1) with pressure p_1 and volume V_1, and point 2 represents a final state (2) with pressure p_2 and volume V_2. For example (Figure 15.19b), we could keep the pressure constant at p_1 while the system expands to volume V_2 (point 3 on the diagram) and then reduce the pressure to p_2 (probably by decreasing the temperature) while keeping the volume constant at V_2 (to point 2 on the diagram). The work done by the system during this process is the area under the line $1 \to 3$; the system does no work during the constant-volume process $3 \to 2$. Or the system might traverse the path $1 \to 4 \to 2$ (Figure 15.19c); in that case, the work is the area under the line $4 \to 2$. The smooth curve from 1 to 2 is another possibility (Figure 15.19d), and the work done in that case is different from that done in each of the other paths. If the system passes through non-equilibrium states during a change of state, we may not be able to speak of a pressure or temperature for the system as a whole. There is still a path for such a change of state, but it can't be represented in terms of points and curves on a pV diagram.

We conclude that **the work done by the system depends not only on the initial and final states, but also on the intermediate states—that is, on the path.** Furthermore, we can take the system through a series of states forming a closed loop, such as $1 \to 3 \to 2 \to 4 \to 1$. In this case, the final state is the same as the initial state, but the total work done by the system is *not* zero. (In fact, it is represented on the graph by the *area* enclosed by the loop; can you prove that?) It follows that it doesn't make sense to talk about the amount of work contained in a system. In a particular state, a system may have definite values of the state coordinates p, V, and T, but it wouldn't make sense to say that it has a definite value of W.

Heat Transfer during Volume Changes

Heat transfer and work are two means by which the energy of a thermodynamic system may increase or decrease. We've just seen that when a thermodynamic system undergoes a change of state, the *work* done by the system depends not

(a) System does work on piston; hot plate adds heat to system ($W > 0$ and $Q > 0$).

(b) System does no work; no heat enters or leaves system ($W = 0$ and $Q = 0$).

▲ **FIGURE 15.20** (a) Slow, controlled isothermal expansion of a gas from an initial state 1 to a final state 2 with the same temperature, but lower pressure. (b) Rapid, uncontrolled expansion of the same gas starting at the same state 1 and ending at the same state 2.

only on the initial and final states, but also on the series of intermediate states through which it passes—that is, on the *path* from the initial state to the final state. Next we'll show that this is also true for the *heat* added to a system.

Here's an example: We want to change the volume of a certain quantity of an ideal gas from 2.0 L to 5.0 L while keeping the temperature constant at $T = 300$ K. Figure 15.20 shows two different ways we can do this. In Figure 15.20a, the gas is contained in a cylinder with a piston and has an initial volume of 2.0 L. We let the gas expand slowly, supplying heat from the electric heater to keep the temperature at 300 K. After expanding in this slow, controlled, isothermal manner, the gas reaches its final volume of 5.0 L; it absorbs a definite amount of heat in the process.

Figure 15.20b shows a different process leading to the same final state. The container is surrounded by insulating walls and is divided by a thin, breakable partition into two compartments. The lower part has a volume of 2.0 L, and the upper part has a volume of 3.0 L. In the lower compartment, we place the same amount of the same gas as in Figure 15.20a, again at $T = 300$ K. The initial state is the same as before. Now we break the partition; the gas undergoes a rapid, uncontrolled expansion, with no heat passing through the insulating walls. The final volume is 5.0 L, the same as in Figure 15.20a. This uncontrolled expansion of a gas into vacuum is called a **free expansion.** During the process, the gas is *not* in thermodynamic equilibrium.

Experiments have shown that when an ideal gas undergoes a free expansion, there is no temperature change. Therefore, the final equilibrium state of the gas is the same as that in Figure 15.20a. The intermediate states (pressures and volumes) during the transition from state 1 to state 2 are entirely different in the two cases; Figures 15.20a and 15.20b represent *two different paths* connecting the *same states* 1 and 2. For path (b), *no* heat is transferred into the system, and it does no work. **Like work, heat depends not only on the initial and final states, but also on the path.** The free expansion involves non-equilibrium states that can't be described by a single temperature or pressure for the system as a whole.

Because of this dependence on the path, it doesn't make sense to say that a system "contains" a certain quantity of heat. Suppose we were to assign an arbitrary value to "the heat in an object" in some standard reference state. Then, presumably, the heat in the object in some other state would equal the heat in the object in the reference state plus the heat added when the object goes into the second state. But that notion is ambiguous: The heat added depends on the *path* we take from the reference state to the second state. Thus, there is no consistent way to define "heat in an object;" it isn't a useful concept. It *does* make sense, however, to speak of the amount of *internal energy* in a body; this important concept is our next topic.

Activ
Physics
ONLINE
8.5

Internal Energy and the First Law

The concept of internal energy is one of the most important concepts in thermodynamics. We can look at it in various ways, some simple, some subtle. Let's start with the simple. Matter consists of atoms and molecules, and these are made up of particles having kinetic and potential energies. We tentatively define the **internal energy** of a system as the sum of all the kinetic and potential energies of its constituent particles. We use the symbol U for internal energy. During a change of state of the system, the internal energy may change from an initial value U_1 to a final value U_2; we denote the change in internal energy as $\Delta U = U_2 - U_1$.

We also know that heat transfer is energy transfer. When we add a quantity of heat Q to a system and it does no work during the process, the internal energy should increase by an amount equal to Q; that is, $\Delta U = Q$. When a system does work W by expanding against its surroundings and no heat is added during the process, energy leaves the system and the internal energy decreases. That is, when W is positive, ΔU is negative, and conversely, so $\Delta U = -W$. When *both* heat transfer *and* work occur, the *total* change in internal energy is $U_2 - U_1 = \Delta U = Q - W$. We can rearrange this set of equations into the following form:

> **First law of thermodynamics**
>
> When heat Q is added to a system, some of this added energy remains within the system, changing its internal energy by an amount ΔU. The remainder leaves the system as the system does work W against its surroundings. Because W and Q may be positive, negative, or zero, we also expect ΔU to be positive, negative, or zero, depending on the process. We thus have
>
> $$Q = \Delta U + W, \qquad \text{or} \qquad U_2 - U_1 = \Delta U = Q - W. \qquad (15.18)$$

The first law of thermodynamics represents a generalization of the principle of conservation of energy to include energy transfer through heat as well as mechanical work. Actually *calculating* this energy for any real system, however, would be hopelessly complicated. By contrast, if we use Equation 15.18 to define changes in internal energy for thermodynamic processes, then we have to ask whether these changes may depend on the path taken as the system moves from one state to another. We've already seen that both work and heat exchange depend on the path taken; might this also be true for internal energy? If so, it wouldn't make sense to speak of the internal energy of an object, and it couldn't be the basis for an enlarged conservation law.

The only way to resolve such questions is through *experiment.* We study the properties of various materials; in particular, we measure Q and W for various changes of state and various paths in order to learn whether ΔU is or is not the same for different paths. The results of many such investigations are clear and unambiguous: ΔU *is independent of the path.* The change in internal energy of a system during any thermodynamic process depends only on the initial and final states, *not* on the path leading from one to the other. An equivalent statement is that the internal energy U of a system is a function of the state coordinates p, V, and T alone (actually, of any two of these, since the three variables are related by the equation of state).

Now let's return to the first law of thermodynamics. To say that the first law, given by Equation 15.18, represents conservation of energy for thermodynamic processes is correct—as far as it goes. But an important *additional* part of the content of the first law is the fact that internal energy depends only on the state of a system. In changes of state, the change in internal energy is path-independent.

If we take a system through a process that eventually returns it to its initial state (a *cyclic* process), the *total* internal energy change must be zero. Then

$$U_2 = U_1 \quad \text{and} \quad Q = W.$$

If a net quantity of work W is done by the system during this process, an equal amount of energy must have flowed into the system as heat Q. But there is no reason why either Q or W individually has to be zero.

An *isolated* system is a system that does no work on its surroundings and has no heat flow. For any process taking place in an isolated system,

$$W = Q = 0 \quad \text{and} \quad U_2 - U_1 = \Delta U = 0.$$

In other words, *the internal energy of an isolated system is constant.*

Conceptual Analysis 15.3

An expanding gas

When an ideal gas in a well-insulated container expands slowly by pushing a piston, the temperature of the gas drops because

A. the gas must do work, so its internal energy must decrease, and temperature is related to internal energy.

B. the molecules have more room to move around, which means that they can travel at a lower speed, and temperature is related to molecular speed.

C. pushing the piston robs the gas of heat, and loss of heat means that the temperature of the gas will drop.

SOLUTION The first law of thermodynamics says that $\Delta U = Q - W$. In this case the container is insulated, so $Q = 0$. The gas expands, so W is positive; therefore, ΔU must be negative. A is a correct answer. B is not correct: It's true that the molecules have room to move, but their slower speed is a consequence of doing work against the moving piston. C is not correct: The problem states that the container is well insulated, so there is no heat transfer.

PROBLEM-SOLVING STRATEGY 15.3   **First law of thermodynamics**

SET UP

1. As usual, consistent units are essential. If p is in pascals and V is in cubic meters, then W is in joules. If p and V are not in pascals and cubic meters, respectively, you may want to convert them into those units. If a heat capacity is given in terms of calories, the simplest procedure is usually to convert it to joules. Be especially careful with moles. When you use $n = m_{total}/M$ to convert between mass and number of moles, remember that if m_{total} is in kilograms, M must be in *kilograms* per mole. The usual units for M are *grams* per mole; be careful!

SOLVE

2. The internal energy change ΔU in any thermodynamic process or series of processes is independent of the path, no matter whether the substance is an ideal gas or not. This is of the utmost importance in the problems in this chapter and the next. Sometimes you will be given enough information about one path between given initial and final states to calculate ΔU for that path. Then you can use the fact that ΔU is the same for every other path between the same two states to relate the various energy quantities for other paths.

3. When a process consists of several distinct steps, it often helps to make a chart showing Q, W, and ΔU for each step. Put these quantities for each step on a different line, and arrange them so that the Q's, W's, and ΔU's form columns. Then you can apply the first law to each line; in addition, you can add each column and apply the first law to the sums. Do you see why?

REFLECT

4. Ask yourself whether the entries in the table in point 3 are consistent. For example, if you find that Q for a certain process is positive, but W and ΔU are both negative, you know that there's something wrong.

EXAMPLE 15.8 **Thermodynamics of boiling water**

One gram of water $(1\ cm^3)$ becomes $1671\ cm^3$ of steam when boiled at a constant pressure of 1 atm $(1.013 \times 10^5\ Pa)$. The heat of vaporization at this pressure is $L_v = 2.256 \times 10^6\ J/kg = 2256\ J/g$. Compute **(a)** the work done by the water when it vaporizes; **(b)** its increase in internal energy.

SOLUTION

SET UP AND SOLVE Part (a): For a constant-pressure process, we may use Equation 15.16, $W = p(V_2 - V_1)$, to compute the work done by the vaporizing water.

The work done by the vaporizing water is

$$W = p(V_2 - V_1)$$
$$= (1.013 \times 10^5\ Pa)(1671 \times 10^{-6}\ m^3 - 1 \times 10^{-6}\ m^3)$$
$$= 169\ J.$$

Part (b): We find the heat added to the water and then use the first law of thermodynamics. The heat added to the water is the heat of vaporization, $Q = mL_v$:

$$Q = mL_v$$
$$= (1\ g)(2256\ J/g)$$
$$= 2256\ J.$$

From the first law of thermodynamics, Equation 15.18, the change in internal energy is

$$\Delta U = Q - W$$
$$= 2256\ J - 169\ J$$
$$= 2087\ J.$$

REFLECT To vaporize 1 gram of water, we have to add 2256 J of heat. Most (2087 J) of this added energy remains in the system as an increase in its internal energy. The remaining 169 J leaves the system as the system does work against its surroundings while expanding from liquid to vapor. The increase in internal energy is associated mostly with the intermolecular forces that hold the molecules together in the liquid state. Because these forces are attractive, the associated potential energies are greater after work has been done on the molecules to pull them apart in forming the vapor state. It's like increasing the potential energy by pulling an elevator farther from the center of the earth.

Practice Problem: Suppose water is boiled in a pressure chamber in which the pressure is 2.00 atm, the heat of vaporization is 2200 J/g, and 1.00 kg of steam has a volume of $0.824\ m^3$. Determine the work done and the increase in internal energy. *Answers:* 167 J, 2033 J.

EXAMPLE 15.9 **An isothermal expansion**

Figure 15.21 shows a slow, controlled isothermal expansion of 3.0 moles of an ideal gas. The initial volume of the gas is 4.0 L and the final volume is 5.0 L. While the gas expands, heat is supplied from a flame to maintain the temperature at 300 K. How much work does the gas do during the expansion? What is the change in the internal energy of the gas?

State 1   State 2

$n = 3.0\ mol$
$T = 300\ K$
$V_1 = 4.0\ L$ $V_2 = 5.0\ L$

▶ **FIGURE 15.21**

SOLUTION

SET UP AND SOLVE From Equation 15.17,

$$W = nRT \ln\!\left(\frac{V_2}{V_1}\right)$$

$$= (3.0\ mol)[8.314\ J/(mol \cdot K)](300\ K) \ln\!\left(\frac{5.0\ L}{4.0\ L}\right)$$

$$= 1700\ J.$$

Because the temperature is constant and the substance is an ideal gas, the change in internal energy is zero.

REFLECT Because the internal energy does not change, all of the heat entering the system goes into work.

Practice Problem: If 2000 J of heat is added isothermally to 3.5 moles of an ideal gas with an initial volume of 3.0 L and a constant temperature of 300 K, what is the final volume of the gas? *Answer:* $V_2 = 3.8\ L$.

EXAMPLE 15.10 A series of thermodynamic processes

A series of thermodynamic processes is shown in the pV diagram of Figure 15.22. In process ab, 150 J of heat are added to the system, and in process bd, 600 J of heat are added. Find **(a)** the internal energy change in process ab; **(b)** the internal energy change in process abd; **(c)** the total heat added in process acd.

▶ **FIGURE 15.22** pV diagram showing various thermodynamic processes.

SOLUTION

SET UP AND SOLVE **Part (a):** No change in volume occurs during process ab, so $W_{ab} = 0$ and $\Delta U_{ab} = Q_{ab} = 150$ J.

Part (b): Process bd occurs at constant pressure, so the work done by the system during this expansion is

$$W_{bd} = p(V_2 - V_1)$$
$$= (8.0 \times 10^4 \text{ Pa})(5.0 \times 10^{-3} \text{ m}^3 - 2.0 \times 10^{-3} \text{ m}^3)$$
$$= 240 \text{ J}.$$

The total work for process abd is

$$W_{abd} = W_{ab} + W_{bd} = 0 + 240 \text{ J} = 240 \text{ J},$$

and the total heat added is

$$Q_{abd} = Q_{ab} + Q_{bd} = 150 \text{ J} + 600 \text{ J} = 750 \text{ J}.$$

Applying Equation 15.18 to process abd, we find that

$$\Delta U_{abd} = Q_{abd} - W_{abd} = 750 \text{ J} - 240 \text{ J} = 510 \text{ J}.$$

Part (c): Because ΔU is independent of the path, the internal energy change is the same for path acd as for abd; that is,

$$\Delta U_{acd} = \Delta U_{abd} = 510 \text{ J}.$$

The total work for the path acd is

$$W_{acd} = W_{ac} + W_{cd} = p(V_2 - V_1) + 0$$
$$= (3.0 \times 10^4 \text{ Pa})(5.0 \times 10^{-3} \text{ m}^3 - 2.0 \times 10^{-3} \text{ m}^3)$$
$$= 90 \text{ J}.$$

Now we apply Equation 15.18 to process acd:

$$Q_{acd} = \Delta U_{acd} + W_{acd} = 510 \text{ J} + 90 \text{ J} = 600 \text{ J}.$$

We see that although ΔU is the same (510 J) for abd and acd, W (240 J versus 90 J) and Q (750 J versus 600 J) are quite different for the two processes.

Here is a tabulation of the various quantities:

Step	Q	W	$\Delta U = Q - W$
ab	150 J	0	150 J
bd	600 J	240 J	360 J
abd	750 J	240 J	510 J

Step	Q	W	$\Delta U = Q - W$
ac	?	90 J	?
cd	?	0	?
acd	600 J	90 J	510 J

REFLECT The fact that ΔU is the same for all paths between given initial and final states plays a crucial role in this solution

15.6 Thermodynamic Processes

Here are four thermodynamic processes that occur often enough in practical problems to be worth some discussion. Their characteristics can be summarized briefly as "no heat transfer," "constant volume," "constant pressure," and "constant temperature," respectively. These four processes for an ideal gas are shown on the pV diagram in Figure 15.23.

Activ Physics ONLINE   8.4, 8.6, 8.8–8.11

Adiabatic Process

An **adiabatic process** is a process in which there is no heat transfer into or out of a system; in other words, $Q = 0$. We can prevent heat flow either by surrounding the system with thermally insulating material or by carrying out the process so quickly that there is not enough time for any appreciable heat flow. From the first law, we find that, for every adiabatic process,

$$U_2 - U_1 = \Delta U = -W \qquad \text{(adiabatic process)}. \qquad (15.19)$$

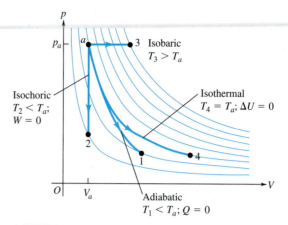

▲ **FIGURE 15.23** Four different processes for a constant amount of an ideal gas, all starting at state a. The temperature increases only during the isobaric expansion.

When a system expands under adiabatic conditions, W is positive, ΔU is negative, and the internal energy decreases. When a system is *compressed* adiabatically, W is negative and U increases. An increase in internal energy is often, though not always, accompanied by a rise in temperature.

The compression stroke in an internal-combustion engine is an example of a process that is approximately adiabatic. The temperature rises as the air–fuel mixture in the cylinder is compressed. Similarly, the expansion of the burned fuel during the power stroke is an approximately adiabatic expansion with a drop in temperature.

Isochoric Process

An **isochoric process** is a *constant-volume* process. When the volume of a thermodynamic system is constant, the system does no work on its surroundings. Then $W = 0$, and

$$U_2 - U_1 = \Delta U = Q \qquad \text{(isochoric process).} \qquad (15.20)$$

In an isochoric process, all the energy added as heat remains in the system as an increase in its internal energy. Heating a gas in a closed constant-volume container is an example of an isochoric process.

Isobaric Process

An **isobaric process** is a *constant-pressure* process. In general, for an isobaric process, *none* of the three quantities ΔU, Q, and W in the first law is zero, but calculating W is easy, as we saw in Section 15.5. Figure 15.24 shows how an isobaric process looks on a pV diagram. For an isobaric process,

$$W = p(V_2 - V_1) \qquad \text{(isobaric process).} \qquad (15.16)$$

Example 15.8 is an example of an isobaric process.

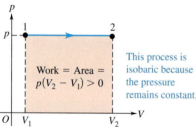

This process is isobaric because the pressure remains constant.

▲ **FIGURE 15.24** A pV diagram for an isobaric process.

Isothermal Process

An **isothermal process** is a *constant-temperature* process. For a process to be isothermal, the system must remain in thermal equilibrium. This means that any heat flow into or out of the system must occur slowly enough to maintain thermal equilibrium. In general, *none* of the quantities ΔU, Q, and W is zero. Example 15.9 is an example of an isothermal process.

In some special cases (including ideal gases), the internal energy of a system depends *only* on its temperature, not on its pressure or volume. For such systems, if the temperature is constant, the internal energy is also constant; then $\Delta U = 0$

and $Q = W$. That is, any energy entering the system as heat Q must leave it again as work W done by the system. Example 15.9, involving an ideal gas, is an example of an isothermal process in which U is also constant. For most systems other than ideal gases, the internal energy depends on pressure as well as temperature, so U may vary even when T is constant.

15.7 Properties of an Ideal Gas

We stated in Section 15.5 that, for an ideal gas, the internal energy U depends only on temperature, not on pressure or volume. How do we know this? Let's think again about the free-expansion experiment described in Section 15.5. A thermally insulated container with rigid walls is divided into two compartments by a partition (Figure 15.25). One compartment contains a quantity of an ideal gas, and the other is evacuated.

When the partition is removed or broken, the gas expands to fill both parts of the container. This process is called a *free expansion.* The gas does no work because the walls of the container don't move. Both Q and W are zero, so the internal energy U is constant. This is true of any substance, whether it is an ideal gas or not.

Does the temperature of a gas change during a free expansion? Suppose it *does* change, while the internal energy stays the same. In that case, the internal energy must depend on both temperature and volume, or both temperature and pressure, but certainly not on temperature alone. But if T is the *same* after the free expansion as before, a process for which we know that U is constant even though both p and V change, then we have to conclude that U depends *only* on T, not on p or V.

Many experiments have shown that when an ideal gas undergoes a free expansion, its temperature *does not* change. The conclusion is that **the internal energy of an ideal gas depends only on its temperature, not on its pressure or volume.** This property, in addition to the ideal-gas equation of state, is part of the ideal-gas model. In the next chapter, we'll use the preceding property several times, so make sure that you understand it.

For non-ideal gases, some temperature change occurs during free expansions, even though the internal energy is constant. This shows that the internal energy cannot depend *only* on temperature; it must depend on pressure as well. From a microscopic viewpoint, this dependence on pressure is not surprising. Non-ideal gases usually have attractive intermolecular forces. When molecules move farther apart, the associated potential energies increase. If the total internal energy is constant, the kinetic energies must decrease. Temperature is directly related to molecular *kinetic* energy, so, for a non-ideal gas, a free expansion is usually accompanied by a *drop* in temperature.

ActivPhysics ONLINE 8.7

▲ **FIGURE 15.25** When the partition is broken, the gas expands freely into the vacuum region.

Heat Capacities of an Ideal Gas

We defined molar heat capacity in Section 15.4. The molar heat capacity of a substance depends on the conditions under which the heat is added. It is usually easiest to measure the heat capacity of a gas in a closed container under constant-volume conditions. The corresponding heat capacity is the **molar heat capacity at constant volume,** denoted by C_V. Heat capacity measurements for solids and liquids are usually carried out in the atmosphere under constant atmospheric pressure, and we call the resulting heat capacity the **molar heat capacity at constant pressure,** denoted by C_p. If neither p nor V is constant, we have an infinite number of possible heat capacities.

To measure C_V for a gas, we add heat to raise the temperature of the gas in a rigid container with constant volume. To measure C_p, we add heat while letting the gas expand just enough to keep the pressure constant as the temperature rises.

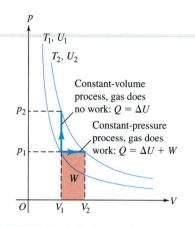

▲ FIGURE 15.26 Constant-volume and constant-pressure processes for a sample of an ideal gas. For an ideal gas, U depends only on T.

Why should these two molar heat capacities be different? The answer lies in the first law of thermodynamics. In a constant-volume temperature change, the system does no work, and the change in internal energy, ΔU, equals the heat added, Q. In a constant-pressure temperature change, by contrast, the volume *must* increase; otherwise, the pressure could not remain constant. As the material expands, it does an amount of work W. According to the first law,

$$Q = \Delta U + W.$$

For a given temperature change, the heat input for a constant-pressure process must be *greater* than that for a constant-volume process because additional energy is needed to account for the work W done during the expansion, so C_p is greater than C_V. The pV diagram in Figure 15.26 shows this relationship. For air, C_p is 40% greater than C_V.

In fact, there's a simple relation between C_V and C_p for an ideal gas. We'll omit the details of the derivation; the result is

$$C_p = C_V + R. \tag{15.21}$$

For an ideal gas, C_p is always greater than C_V; the difference is the gas constant R. (Of course, R must be expressed in the same units as C_V and C_p, such as $J/(\text{mol} \cdot K)$.)

C_p versus C_V

The main reason more heat is needed to raise the temperature of an ideal gas by a given amount at constant pressure than at constant volume is that

A. at constant volume the molecules remain the same mean distance apart.

B. at constant pressure some energy must be provided to increase the volume occupied by the gas.

C. at constant pressure some energy must be provided to separate the molecules, which are subject to cohesive forces of attraction.

SOLUTION For an ideal gas, the molecules have no appreciable interaction, so answers A and C are eliminated. As the gas expands during the constant-pressure process, it has to do work against the walls of its container as the volume increases. This work represents an additional energy requirement; B is correct.

Measured values of C_p and C_V are given in Table 15.4 for several real gases at low pressures; the difference in most cases is approximately $8.31 \, J/(\text{mol} \cdot K)$, as Equation 15.21 predicts. The table also shows that the molar heat capacity of a gas is related to its molecular structure, as we discussed in Section 15.4. In fact, the first two columns of Table 15.4 are the same as those in Table 15.3.

NOTE ▶ Here's a final reminder: For an ideal gas, the change in internal energy for *any* infinitesimal process is given by $\Delta U = nC_V \Delta T$, *whether the volume is constant or not.* This relation, which comes in handy in the next conceptual analysis example, holds for other substances *only* when the volume is constant. ◀

TABLE 15.4 Molar heat capacities of gases at low pressure

Type of gas	Gas	$C_V(J/(\text{mol} \cdot K))$	$C_p(J/(\text{mol} \cdot K))$	$C_p - C_V(J/(\text{mol} \cdot K))$	γ
Monatomic	He	12.47	20.78	8.31	1.67
	Ar	12.47	20.78	8.31	1.67
Diatomic	H_2	20.42	28.74	8.32	1.41
	N_2	20.76	29.07	8.31	1.40
	O_2	20.85	29.17	8.31	1.40
	CO	20.85	29.16	8.31	1.40
Polyatomic	CO_2	28.46	36.94	8.48	1.30
	SO_2	31.39	40.37	8.98	1.29
	H_2S	25.95	34.60	8.65	1.33

A compressed gas

An ideal gas in a container is compressed to half its original volume with no change in temperature. The internal energy of the gas is then

A. half its original value, because of the heat released.
B. unchanged, because the temperature is unchanged.
C. twice its original value, because the energy comes from work on the gas.
D. unchanged, because no heat is absorbed or released.

SOLUTION The internal energy of an ideal gas depends only on its temperature. In this case the temperature doesn't change, so the internal energy is also unchanged (answer B). Heat is released, and work is done on the gas, but these two quantities exactly balance each other. Thus, answers A, C, and D can't be correct.

Adiabatic Process for an Ideal Gas

An adiabatic process, defined in Section 15.5, is a process in which no heat transfer takes place between a system and its surroundings. In an adiabatic process, $Q = 0$ and (from the first law) $\Delta U = -W$. Zero heat transfer is an idealization, but a process is approximately adiabatic if the system is well insulated or if the process takes place so quickly that there is not enough time for any appreciable heat flow to occur.

An adiabatic process for an ideal gas is shown on the pV diagram of Figure 15.27. As the gas expands from volume V_a to V_b, its temperature drops because it does positive work, decreasing its internal energy. If point a, representing the initial state, lies on an isotherm at temperature $T + \Delta T$, then point b for the final state is on a different isotherm at a lower temperature T. An adiabatic curve at any point is always *steeper* than the isotherm passing through the same point. For an adiabatic *compression* from V_b to V_a, the situation is reversed and the temperature rises.

The air in the output pipes of air compressors used in gasoline stations and paint-spraying equipment and to fill scuba tanks is always warmer than the air entering the compressor because of the approximately adiabatic compression. When air is compressed in the cylinders of a diesel engine during the compression stroke, it gets so hot that fuel injected into the cylinders ignites spontaneously.

The first law of thermodynamics, together with the ideal-gas equation of state, can be used to derive a relation between pressure and volume for an adiabatic process for an ideal gas. This relation depends on the ratio of the two molar heat capacities at constant pressure and at constant volume. We'll denote this ratio by γ; that is, $\gamma = C_p/C_V$. For diatomic gases, γ is approximately 1.40, as Table 15.4 shows.

We recall that for an *isothermal* (constant-temperature) process, the product pV is constant, so p is inversely proportional to V. It turns out that for an *adiabatic* process, the product pV^γ is constant, and p is proportional to $1/V^\gamma$. So when V increases, the pressure p decreases more rapidly for an adiabatic process than an isothermal process. This is to be expected, because the temperature of an ideal gas always decreases when it expands isothermally.

When an ideal gas expands from state (p_1, V_1) to state (p_2, V_2), the state coordinates are related by

$$p_1 V_1^\gamma = p_2 V_2^\gamma = \text{constant}. \qquad (15.22)$$

We can combine this result with the ideal-gas equation of state to obtain the following relation between volume and temperature:

$$T_1 V_1^{\gamma-1} = T_2 V_2^{\gamma-1}. \qquad (15.23)$$

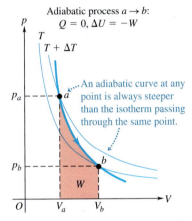

Adiabatic process $a \to b$:
$Q = 0$, $\Delta U = -W$

An adiabatic curve at any point is always steeper than the isotherm passing through the same point.

▲ **FIGURE 15.27** A pV diagram of an adiabatic process for an ideal gas. As the gas expands from V_a to V_b, its temperature drops from $T + \Delta T$ to T, corresponding to the decrease in internal energy due to the work W done by the gas (represented by the shaded area).

EXAMPLE 15.11 **Adiabatic compression in a diesel engine**

The compression ratio of a certain diesel engine is 15 to 1; this means that air in the cylinders is compressed to one-fifteenth of its initial volume (Figure 15.28). If the initial pressure is 1.01×10^5 Pa and the initial temperature is 27°C (300 K), find the final pressure and the temperature after compression. Air is mostly a mixture of diatomic oxygen and nitrogen; treat it as an ideal gas with $\gamma = 1.40$.

▶ **FIGURE 15.28**

SOLUTION

SET UP We solve Equation 15.22 for p_2. We don't need to know V_1 or V_2, but only their ratio. Similarly, we solve Equation 15.23 for T_2 and use the ratio of the initial and final volumes.

SOLVE We have $p_1 = 1.01 \times 10^5$ Pa, $T_1 = 300$ K, and $V_1/V_2 = 15$. From Equation 15.22,

$$p_2 = p_1\left(\frac{V_1}{V_2}\right)^{\gamma} = (1.01 \times 10^5 \text{ Pa})(15)^{1.40}$$
$$= 44.8 \times 10^5 \text{ Pa} = 44 \text{ atm}.$$

From Equation 15.23,

$$T_2 = T_1\left(\frac{V_1}{V_2}\right)^{\gamma-1} = (300 \text{ K})(15)^{0.40} = 886 \text{ K} = 613° \text{ C}.$$

REFLECT If the compression had been isothermal, the final pressure would have been 15 atm, but because the temperature also increases during an adiabatic compression, the final pressure is much greater, about 650 psi. The high temperature attained during compression causes the fuel to ignite spontaneously, without the need for spark plugs, when it is injected into the cylinders near the end of the compression stroke.

SUMMARY

The Mole and Avogadro's Number

(Section 15.1) **Avogadro's number** $(N_A = 6.022 \times 10^{23}$ molecules/mol$)$ is the number of molecules in a mole. The **molar mass** of a substance is the mass of the substance in 1 mole.

Equations of State

(Section 15.2) The pressure, volume, and temperature of a given quantity of a substance are called state variables; they are related by an equation of state. The equation of state for an ideal gas is the **ideal-gas equation:** $pV = nRT$ (Equation 15.3); R is the **ideal-gas constant.**

Kinetic Theory of an Ideal Gas

(Section 15.3) The average translational kinetic energy of n moles of an ideal gas is directly proportional to the absolute temperature of the gas: $K_{tr} = \frac{3}{2}nRT$ (Equation 15.7). This relation can be expressed for a single particle in the gas by using Boltzmann's constant $k = R/N_A$: $K_{av} = \frac{1}{2}m(v^2)_{av} = \frac{3}{2}kT$ (Equation 15.8).

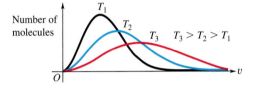

Heat Capacities

(Section 15.4) The **molar heat capacity** is the amount of heat required to change the temperature of 1 mole of material by 1 kelvin. The molar heat capacity at constant volume is the same for *every* ideal monatomic gas: $C_V = \frac{3}{2}R$ (Equation 15.13) For an ideal diatomic gas, including rotational, but not vibrational, kinetic energy, $C_V = \frac{5}{2}R$ (Equation 15.14).

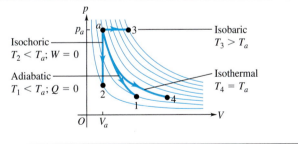

Translational motion   Rotational motion   Vibrational motion

The First Law of Thermodynamics

(Section 15.5) The **first law of thermodynamics** states that when heat Q is added to a system while work W is done by the system, the internal energy U changes by an amount $\Delta U = Q - W$ (Equation 15.18). The internal energy of any thermodynamic system depends only on its state. The change in internal energy in any process depends only on the initial and final states, not on the path taken.

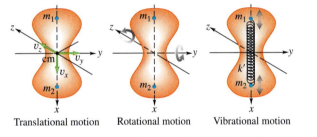

Surroundings (environment)

Thermodynamic Processes

(Section 15.6) Four common kinds of thermodynamic processes are as follows:

- **Adiabatic process:** No heat transfer in or out of a system; $Q = 0$.
- **Isochoric process:** Constant volume; $W = 0$.
- **Isobaric process:** Constant pressure; $W = p(V_2 - V_1)$.
- **Isothermal process:** Constant temperature.

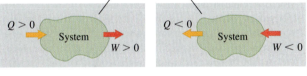

Properties of an Ideal Gas

(Section 15.7) The internal energy of an ideal gas depends only on its temperature, not its pressure or volume. For non-ideal gases, and for solids and liquids, the internal energy generally depends on both pressure and temperature. The molar heat capacities C_V and C_p of an ideal gas are related by $C_p = C_V + R$ (Equation 15.25). The ratio of C_p to C_V is denoted by γ: $\gamma = C_p/C_V$ (Equation 15.26). For an adiabatic process taking place in an ideal gas, the quantities $TV^{\gamma-1}$ and pV^γ are constant.

Adiabatic process $a \rightarrow b$:
$Q = 0, \Delta U = -W$

An adiabatic curve at any point is always steeper than the isotherm passing through the same point.

Conceptual Questions

1. In the ideal-gas equation, could you give the temperature in degrees Celsius rather than in kelvins if you used an appropriate numerical value of the gas constant R?

2. True or false? Equal masses of two different gases placed in containers of equal volume at equal temperature must exert equal pressures.

3. Suppose you turn on a fan in an insulated room. Will the fan make the room cooler? If not, will it still make *you* feel cooler? Explain your reasoning.

4. The ideal-gas law is sometimes written in the form $p_1 V_1/T_1 = p_2 V_2/T_2$. Are there any extra limitations on this form of the law, or is it just as general as the form $pV = nRT$?

5. By thinking about matter on the microscopic level, explain why heat flows from a hot to a cold object, but not the other way around. (*Hint:* Look at the transfer of energy during molecular collisions.)

6. (a) If you double the absolute temperature of an ideal gas, what happens to the average kinetic energy of its molecules? To the root-mean-square speed of its molecules? (b) If you double the speeds of the molecules of an ideal gas, what happens to the absolute temperature of this gas?

7. Chemical reaction rates slow down as the temperature is decreased. (This is why we put food in the refrigerator to preserve it.) By thinking about matter on the microscopic (molecular) level, explain why this happens.

8. The *mean free path* of a gas molecule is the average distance the molecule travels before colliding with another molecule. Does this mean free path increase, decrease, or stay the same if the gas is compressed?

9. True or false? When two ideal gases are mixed, they must have the same average molecular speed when they have reached thermal equilibrium.

10. A process called *gaseous diffusion* is sometimes used to separate isotopes of uranium, such as ^{235}U and ^{238}U. (Isotopes of an element are atoms of the element that have different masses.) Speculate on how this process might work.

11. In a constant-volume process, $\Delta U = nC_V \Delta T$; in a constant-pressure process, it is *not* true that $\Delta U = nC_p \Delta T$. Why not?

12. Give good physical reasons that C_p should be greater than C_V.

13. Since C_V is defined with specific reference to a constant-volume process, how can it be correct that, for an ideal gas, $\Delta U = nC_V \Delta T$ even when the volume is not constant?

14. The ratio γ found in Equations 15.22 and 15.23 must always be greater than 1. Why?

15. Do Equations 15.22 and 15.23 hold for adiabatic processes for liquids and solids? Why or why not?

Multiple-Choice Problems

1. To double both the pressure and the volume of a fixed amount of an ideal gas, you would multiply its absolute temperature by
   A. 1 (i.e., keep the temperature the same).
   B. 2.
   C. 4.
   D. 16.

2. Oxygen molecules are 16 times more massive than hydrogen molecules. If samples of these two gases are at the *same temperature*, what must be true about the motion of the molecules? (There may be more than one correct choice.)
   A. The rms molecular speed is the same for both gases.
   B. The average kinetic energy is the same for both gases.
   C. The rms speed of the hydrogen molecules is 4 times greater than that of the oxygen molecules.
   D. The rms speed of the hydrogen molecules is 16 times greater than that of the oxygen molecules.

3. An ideal gas in a cubical box having sides of length L exerts a pressure p on the walls of the box. If all of this gas is put into a box having sides of length $2L$ without changing its temperature, the pressure it exerts on the walls of the larger box will be
   A. $4p$.   B. $p/2$.   C. $p/4$.   D. $p/8$.

4. If you mix different amounts of two ideal gases that are originally at different temperatures, what must be true of the final state after the temperature stabilizes? (There may be more than one correct choice.)
   A. Both gases will reach the same final temperature.
   B. The final rms molecular speed will be the same for both gases.
   C. The final average kinetic energy will be the same for both gases.

5. If you double the rms speed of the molecules of an ideal gas, which of the following statements is or are true about the gas?
   A. Its absolute temperature is doubled.
   B. Its Celsius temperature is doubled.
   C. Its absolute temperature is quadrupled.
   D. Its Celsius temperature is quadrupled.

6. In an ideal gas, which of the following quantities can be determined by measuring *just* the temperature of the gas?
   A. The average kinetic energy of the molecules.
   B. The total kinetic energy of the molecules.
   C. The pressure of the gas.

7. The mass of 1 mole of helium gas is 4.0 g, and the mass of 1 mole of neon gas is 20.0 g. (Both gases are monatomic.) If an amount of heat Q must be added to 4.0 g of He to increase its temperature by 1.0 F° at constant volume, how much heat is needed to raise 20.0 g of Ne by 1.0 F° at constant volume?
   A. Q.   B. $5Q$.   C. $25Q$.

8. If the rms molecular speed of an ideal gas at an absolute temperature T is v, its rms molecular speed at an absolute temperature $2T$ is
   A. $\sqrt{2}v$.   B. $2v$.   C. $2\sqrt{2}v$.   D. $4v$.

9. The formula $\Delta U = nC_V \Delta T$ for the change in the internal energy of a fixed amount of an ideal gas is valid
   A. only for constant-volume processes.
   B. only for adiabatic processes.
   C. only for isobaric processes.
   D. for *any* process involving that fixed amount of the gas.

10. For the process shown in the pV diagram in Figure 15.29, the total work in going from a to d along the path shown is
    A. 15×10^5 J.   B. 9×10^5 J.
    C. 6×10^5 J.   D. 1×10^5 J.

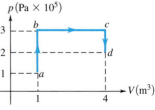

▶ **FIGURE 15.29** Multiple-choice problem 10.

11. You have two boxes, one containing some hot gas and the other containing some cold gas. *This is all you know about these boxes.* What can you validly conclude about the characteristics of the gas in the boxes? (There may be more than one correct choice.)
    A. The molecules in the hot gas are moving faster, on average, than those in the cold gas.
    B. The molecules of the hot gas have greater average kinetic energy than those of the cold gas.
    C. The molecules of the hot gas have more *total* kinetic energy than those of the cold gas.
    D. The pressure of the hot gas is greater than that of the cold gas.

12. The gas shown in Figure 15.30 is in a completely insulated rigid container. Weight is added to the frictionless piston, compressing the gas. As this is done,
    A. the temperature of the gas stays the same because the container is insulated.
    B. the temperature of the gas increases because heat is added to the gas.
    C. the temperature of the gas increases because work is done on the gas.
    D. the pressure of the gas stays the same because the temperature of the gas is constant.

▲ FIGURE 15.30 Multiple-choice problem 12.

13. Which of the following must be true about an ideal gas that undergoes an isothermal *expansion?* (There may be more than one correct choice.)
    A. No heat enters the gas.
    B. The pressure of the gas decreases.
    C. The internal energy of the gas does not change.
    D. The gas does positive work.

14. Ideal gas is intitially confined to one side of a perfectly insulated rigid chamber by a movable frictionless piston, as shown in Figure 15.31. (The other side of the chamber is evacuated.) What is true of this gas after the piston is suddenly pulled to the right end of the chamber? (There may be more than one correct choice.)
    A. The expansion causes the temperature of the gas to decrease.
    B. The pressure of the gas decreases.
    C. The temperature of the gas does not change.
    D. The expansion causes the internal energy of the gas to decrease.

▲ FIGURE 15.31 Multiple-choice problem 14.

15. Suppose that, in the previous problem, the piston is not pulled but instead is allowed to move slowly to the right as it is hit by the gas molecules. What is true about this gas just as the piston reaches the right end of the chamber? (There may be more than one correct choice.)
    A. The expansion causes the temperature of the gas to decrease.
    B. The pressure of the gas decreases.

C. The temperature of the gas does not change.
D. The expansion causes the internal energy of the gas to decrease.

Problems

15.1 Equations of State

1. • A cylindrical tank has a tight-fitting piston that allows the volume of the tank to be changed. The tank originally contains 0.110 m^3 of air at a pressure of 3.40 atm. The piston is slowly pulled out until the volume of the gas is increased to 0.390 m^3. If the temperature remains constant, what is the final value of the pressure?

2. • Helium gas with a volume of 2.60 L under a pressure of 1.30 atm and at a temperature of 41.0°C is warmed until both the pressure and volume of the gas are doubled. (a) What is the final temperature? (b) How many grams of helium are there? The molar mass of helium is 4.00 g/mol.

3. • A 3.00 L tank contains air at 3.00 atm and 20.0°C. The tank is sealed and cooled until the pressure is 1.00 atm. (a) What is the temperature then in degrees Celsius, assuming that the volume of the tank is constant? (b) If the temperature is kept at the value found in part (a) and the gas is compressed, what is the volume when the pressure again becomes 3.00 atm?

4. • A 20.0 L tank contains 0.225 kg of helium at 18.0°C. The molar mass of helium is 4.00 g/mol. (a) How many moles of helium are in the tank? (b) What is the pressure in the tank, in pascals and in atmospheres?

5. • A room with dimensions 7.00 m by 8.00 m by 2.50 m is filled with pure oxygen at 22.0°C and 1.00 atm. The molar mass of oxygen is 32.0 g/mol. (a) How many moles of oxygen are required? (b) What is the mass of this oxygen, in kilograms?

6. • A tank contains 0.460 kg of nitrogen gas at a pressure of 50.0 atm. What mass of oxygen would an identical tank contain, also at 50.0 atm and at the same temperature? The molar mass of nitrogen (N_2) is 28.0 g/mol, and that of oxygen (O_2) is 32.0 g/mol.

7. • A large cylindrical tank contains 0.750 m^3 of nitrogen gas at 27°C and 1.50×10^5 Pa (absolute pressure). The tank has a tight-fitting piston that allows the volume to be changed. What will be the pressure if the volume is decreased to 0.480 m^3 and the temperature is increased to 157°C.

8. • **Planetary atmospheres.** (a) Calculate the density of the atmosphere at the surface of Mars (where the pressure is 650 Pa and the temperature is typically 253 K, with a CO_2 atmosphere), Venus (with an average temperature of 730 K and pressure of 92 atm, with a CO_2 atmosphere), and Saturn's moon Titan (where the pressure is 1.5 atm and the temperature is −178°C, with a N_2 atmosphere). (b) Compare each of these densities with that of the earth's atmosphere, as determined in Example 15.4. Consult the periodic chart in Appendix D to determine molar masses.

9. • A metal tank with a volume of 3.10 L will burst if the absolute pressure of the gas it contains exceeds 100 atm. (a) If 11.0 mol of an ideal gas is put into the tank at a temperature of 23.0°C, to what temperature can the gas be warmed before the tank ruptures? Neglect the thermal expansion of the tank. (b) On the basis of your answer to part (a), is it reasonable to neglect the thermal expansion of the tank? Explain.

10. • **Lung volume.** The total lung volume for a typical person is
BIO 6.00 L. A person fills her lungs with air at an absolute pressure
of 1.00 atm. Then, holding her breath, she compresses her
chest cavity, decreasing her lung volume to 5.70 L. What is the
pressure of the air in her compressed lungs, assuming that the
temperature of the air remains constant?

11. • A Jaguar XK8 convertible has an eight-cylinder engine. At
the beginning of its compression stroke, one of the cylinders
contains 499 cm^3 of air at atmospheric pressure $(1.01 \times 10^5$ Pa$)$ and a temperature of 27.0°C. At the end of the stroke,
the air has been compressed to a volume of 46.2 cm^3 and the
gauge pressure has increased to 2.72×10^6 Pa. Compute the
final temperature.

12. •• A diver observes a bubble of air rising from the bottom of
a lake (where the absolute pressure is 3.50 atm) to the surface
(where the pressure is 1.00 atm). The temperature at the bottom is 4.0°C and the temperature at the surface is 23.0°C.
(a) What is the ratio of the volume of the bubble as it reaches
the surface to its volume at the bottom? (b) Would it be safe
for the diver to hold his breath while ascending from the bottom of the lake to the surface? Why or why not?

13. •• (a) Use the ideal-gas law to estimate the number of air
molecules in your beloved physics lab, assuming that all the
air is N$_2$. (b) Calculate the particle density in the lab (i.e., the
number of molecules per cubic centimeter).

14. •• If a certain amount of ideal gas occupies a volume V at STP
on earth, what would be its volume (in terms of V) on Venus,
where the temperature is 1003°C and the pressure is 92 atm?

15.2 Phases of Matter

15. • Calculate the volume of 1.00 mol of liquid water at a temperature of 20°C (at which its density is 998 kg/m^3), and compare this volume with the volume occupied by 1.00 mol of
water at the critical point. (See Table 15.2.) Water has a molar
mass of 18.0 g/mol.

16. •• Solid water (ice) is slowly warmed from a very low temperature. (a) What minimum external pressure p_1 must be
applied to the solid if a melting phase transition is to be
observed? Describe the sequence of phase transitions that
occur if the applied pressure p is such that $p < p_1$. (b) Above
a certain maximum pressure p_2, no boiling transition is
observed. What is this pressure? Describe the sequence of
phase transitions that occur if $p_1 < p < p_2$.

17. •• A physicist places a piece of ice at 0.00°C and a beaker of
water at 0.00°C inside a glass box and closes the lid of the box.
All the air is then removed from the box. If the ice, water, and
beaker are all maintained at a temperature of 0.00°C, describe
the final equilibrium state inside the box.

15.3 Kinetic Theory of an Ideal Gas

18. • Find the mass of a single sulfur (S) atom and an ammonia
(NH$_3$) molecule. Use the periodic table in Appendix D to find
the molar masses.

10. • How many water molecules are there in a 1.00 L bottle of
water? The molar mass of water is 18.0 g/mol.

20. • In the air we breathe at 72°F and 1.0 atm pressure, how
many molecules does a typical cubic centimeter contain,
assuming that the air is all N$_2$?

21. • **Fusion reactor.** A deuteron, $^2_1$H, is the nucleus of a hydrogen isotope and consists of one proton and one neutron. The
plasma of deuterons in a nuclear fusion reactor must be heated
to about 300 million K. (a) What is the root-mean-square
speed of the deuterons? Is this a significant fraction of the
speed of light, c? (b) What would be the temperature of the
plasma if the deuterons had an rms speed equal to $0.10c$?

22. • **Smoke gets in your eyes.** Smoke particles in the air typically have masses on the order of 10^{-16} kg. The Brownian
motion (rapid, irregular movement) of these particles, resulting
from collisions with air molecules, can be observed with a
microscope. Find the root-mean-square speed of Brownian
motion for a particle with a mass of 3.00×10^{-16} kg in air at
300 K.

23. • Oxygen (O$_2$) has a molar mass of 32.0 g/mol. (a) What is
the root-mean-square speed of an oxygen molecule at a temperature of 300 K? (b) What is its average translational kinetic
energy at that speed?

24. • Suppose some insects have speeds of 10.00 m/s, 8.00 m/s,
7.00 m/s, and 2.00 m/s. Find (a) the rms speed of these critters
and (b) their average speed.

25. •• In a gas at standard temperature and pressure, what is the
length of the side of a cube that contains a number of molecules equal to the population of the earth (about 6 billion people at present)?

26. •• At what temperature is the root-mean-square speed of
nitrogen molecules equal to the root-mean-square speed of
hydrogen molecules at 20.0°C? (*Hint:* The periodic table in
Appendix D shows the molar mass (in g/mol) of each element
under the chemical symbol for that element. The molar mass
of H$_2$ is twice the molar mass of hydrogen atoms, and similarly
for N$_2$.)

27. •• **Where is the hydrogen?** The average temperature of
the atmosphere near the surface of the earth is about 20°C.
(a) What is the root-mean-square speed of hydrogen molecules, H$_2$, at this temperature? (b) The escape speed from
the earth is about 11 km/s. Is the average H$_2$ molecule moving
fast enough to escape? (c) Compare the rms speeds of oxygen
(O$_2$) and nitrogen (N$_2$) with that of H$_2$. (d) So why has the
hydrogen been able to escape the earth's gravity, but the heavier gases (such as O$_2$ and N$_2$) have not, even though none of
these gases has an rms speed equal to the escape speed of the
earth? (*Hint:* Do *all* the molecules have the rms speed, or are
some moving faster? Since the rms speed for H$_2$ is greater than
that of O$_2$ and N$_2$, which gas would have a higher percentage
of its molecules moving fast enough to escape?)

28. •• A flask contains a mixture of neon (Ne), krypton (Kr), and
radon (Rn) gases. Compare (a) the average kinetic energies of
the three types of atoms; (b) their root-mean-square speeds.
(*Hint:* The periodic table in Appendix D shows the molar mass
(in g/mol) of each element.)

29. •• **Gaseous diffusion of uranium.** (a) A process called
gaseous diffusion is often used to separate isotopes of uranium,
such as ^{235}U and ^{238}U. (Isotopes of an element are atoms of the
element that have different masses.) The only gaseous compound of uranium at ordinary temperatures is uranium hexafluoride, UF$_6$. Speculate on how ^{235}UF$_6$ and ^{238}UF$_6$ molecules
might be separated by diffusion. (b) The molar masses of ^{235}UF$_6$
and ^{238}UF$_6$ molecules are 0.349 kg/mol and 0.352 kg/mol,
respectively. If uranium hexafluoride acts as an ideal gas, what
is the ratio of the root-mean-square speed of ^{235}UF$_6$ molecules
to that of ^{238}UF$_6$ molecules at any given temperature?

30. •• **Breathing at high altitudes.** If you have ever hiked or
BIO climbed to high altitudes in the mountains, you surely have
noticed how short of breath you get. This occurs because the
air is thinner, so each breath contains fewer O_2 molecules than
at sea level. At the top of Mt. Everest, the pressure is only
$\frac{1}{3}$ atm. Air contains 21% O_2 and 78% N_2, and an average human
breath is 0.50 L of air. At the top of Mt. Everest, (a) how many
O_2 molecules does each breath contain when the temperature is
$-15°F$, and (b) what percent is this of the number of O_2 molecules you would get from a breath at sea level at $-15°F$?

31. •• **How often do we need to breathe?** A resting person
BIO requires 14.5 L of O_2 per hour to maintain metabolic activities.
Such a person breathes in 0.50 L of air at approximately 20°C
with each breath. The inhaled air is 20.9% O_2, while the
exhaled air is 16.3% O_2. (a) How many breaths per minute
does a resting person need to take to provide the necessary
oxygen? (b) How many O_2 molecules does a resting person
inhale per breath?

15.4 Heat Capacities

32. • (a) How much heat does it take to increase the temperature
of 2.50 moles of an ideal monatomic gas from 25.0°C to
55.0°C if the gas is held at constant volume? (b) How much
heat is needed if the gas is diatomic rather than monatomic?
(c) Sketch a pV diagram for these processes.

33. • (a) If you supply 1850 J of heat to 2.25 moles of an ideal
diatomic gas initially at 10.0°C in a perfectly rigid container,
what will be the final temperature of the gas? (b) Suppose the
gas in the container were an ideal monatomic gas instead. How
much heat would you need to add to produce the same temperature change? (c) Sketch a pV diagram of these processes.

34. • Compute the specific heat capacity (in J/(kg · K)) at constant volume of nitrogen (N_2) gas, and compare it with the
specific heat capacity of liquid water. Use Appendix D to
determine the molar mass of N_2.

35. • (a) According to the rule of Dulong and Petit, the molar heat
capacity of elemental solids is $3R$. Thus, what should be the
specific heat capacity of copper in J/(kg · K)? (The molar mass
of copper is 63.55 g/mol.) (b) Compare your calculated value
from part (a) with the one given in Table 14.3. Does copper
obey this rule exactly?

36. •• Assume that the gases in this problem can be treated as ideal
over the temperature ranges involved, and consult Appendix D
to determine the necessary molar masses. (a) How much heat is
needed to raise the temperature of 75.0 g of N_2 from 12.1°C to
49.5°C at constant volume? (b) If instead you want to produce
the same temperature change in 75.0 g of O_2 at constant volume,
how much heat do you need?

15.5 The First Law of Thermodynamics

37. • A metal cylinder with rigid walls contains 2.50 mol of oxygen gas. The gas is cooled until the pressure decreases to
30.0% of its original value. You can ignore the thermal contraction of the cylinder. (a) Draw a pV diagram of this process.
(b) Calculate the work done by the gas.

38. • A gas under a constant pressure of 1.50×10^5 Pa and with
an initial volume of 0.0900 m^3 is cooled until its volume
becomes 0.0600 m^3. (a) Draw a pV diagram of this process.
(b) Calculate the work done by the gas.

39. • Two moles of an ideal gas are heated at constant pressure
from $T = 27°C$ to $T = 107°C$. (a) Draw a pV diagram for this
process. (b) Calculate the work done by the gas.

40. • (a) If 1.75 moles of an ideal gas are slowly compressed at a
constant temperature of 22.0°C from a volume of 6.32 L to
one of 1.24 L, how much work is done *by* the gas and *on* the
gas? (b) Draw a pV diagram of this process.

41. •• **Work done in a**
cyclic process. In Figure 15.32, consider the
closed loop $1 \rightarrow 2 \rightarrow$
$3 \rightarrow 4 \rightarrow 1$. This is a
cyclic process in which
the initial and final states
are the same. (a) Find
the total work done by
the system in this pro-
cess, and show that it is
equal to the area enclosed by the loop. (b) How is the work
done during the process in part (a) related to the work
done if the loop is traversed in the opposite direction,
$1 \rightarrow 4 \rightarrow 3 \rightarrow 2 \rightarrow 1$. Explain. (c) How much work is done in
the cycle $3 \rightarrow 4 \rightarrow 2 \rightarrow 3$?

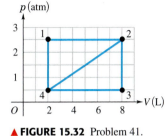

▲ **FIGURE 15.32** Problem 41.

42. •• **Work done by the lungs.** The graph in Figure 15.33 shows
BIO a pV diagram of the air in a human lung when a person is
inhaling and then exhaling a deep breath. Such graphs,
obtained in clinical practice, are normally somewhat curved,
but we have modeled one as a set of straight lines of the same
general shape. (*Important:* The pressure shown is the *gauge*
pressure, *not* the absolute pressure.) (a) How many joules of
net work does this person's lung do during one complete
breath? (b) The process illustrated here is somewhat different
from those we have been studying, because the pressure
change is due to changes in the amount of gas in the lung, not
to temperature changes. (Think of your own breathing. Your
lungs do not expand because they've gotten hot.) If the temperature of the air in the lungs remains a reasonable 20°C,
what is the maximum number of moles in this person's lungs
during a breath?

▲ **FIGURE 15.33** Problem 42.

43. • In a certain chemical process, a lab technician supplies
254 J of heat to a system. At the same time, 73 J of work
are done on the system by its surroundings. What is the
increase in the internal energy of the system?

44. • A gas in a cylinder expands from a volume of 0.110 m³ to 0.320 m³. Heat flows into the gas just rapidly enough to keep the pressure constant at 1.80×10^5 Pa during the expansion. The total heat added is 1.15×10^5 J. (a) Find the work done by the gas. (b) Find the change in internal energy of the gas.

45. • A gas in a cylinder is held at a constant pressure of 2.30×10^5 Pa and is cooled and compressed from 1.70 m³ to 1.20 m³. The internal energy of the gas decreases by 1.40×10^5 J. (a) Find the work done by the gas. (b) Find the amount of the heat that flowed into or out of the gas, and state the direction (inward or outward) of the flow.

46. • **Boiling water at high pressure.** When water is boiled under a pressure of 2.00 atm, the heat of vaporization is 2.20×10^6 J/kg and the boiling point is 120°C. At this pressure and temperature, 1.00 kg of water has a volume of 1.00×10^3 m³, and 1.00 kg of steam has a volume of 0.824 m³. (a) Compute the work done when 1.00 kg of steam is formed at this temperature. (b) Compute the increase in internal energy of the water.

47. •• When a system is taken from state a to state b in Figure 15.34 along the path acb, 90.0 J of heat flows into the system and 60.0 J of work is done by the system. (a) How much heat flows into the system along path adb if the work done by the system is 15.0 J? (b) When the system is returned from b to a along the curved path, the absolute value of the work done by the system is 35.0 J. Does the system absorb or liberate heat? How much heat? (c) If $U_a = 0$ and $U_d = 8.0$ J, find the heat absorbed in the processes ad and db.

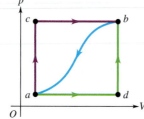

▲ **FIGURE 15.34** Problem 47.

15.6 Thermodynamic Processes

15.7 Properties of an Ideal Gas

48. • During an isothermal compression of an ideal gas, 335 J of heat must be removed from the gas to maintain a constant temperature. How much work is done by the gas during the process?

49. • You are keeping 1.75 moles of an ideal gas in a container surrounded by a large ice-water bath that maintains the temperature of the gas at 0.00°C. (a) How many joules of work would have to be done on this gas to compress its volume from 4.20 L to 1.35 L? (b) How much heat came into (or out of) the gas during this process? Was it into or out of?

50. • Suppose you do 457 J of work on 1.18 moles of ideal He gas in a perfectly insulated container. By how much does the internal energy of this gas change? Does it increase or decrease?

51. • We want to raise the temperature of 5.00 moles of an ideal gas from $-10.0°$ C to $+70.0°$ C. Calculate the amount of heat (in joules) needed if the gas is (a) ideal argon (Ar) at a fixed volume of 8.20 m³, (b) ideal helium (He) at a constant pressure of 1.11 atm, (c) ideal nitrogen (N_2) at a constant pressure of 1.3 atm, and (d) ideal chlorine (Cl_2) at a constant volume of 22.9 L.

52. •• Figure 15.35 shows a pV diagram for an ideal gas in which its pressure tripled from a to b when 534 J of heat was put into the gas. (a) How much work was done on or by the gas between a and b? (b) Without doing any calculations, decide whether the temperature of this gas increased, decreased, or remained the same between a and b. Explain your reasoning. (c) By how much did the internal energy of the gas change between a and b? Did it increase or decrease? (d) What is the temperature of the gas at point b in terms of its temperature at a, T_a?

▲ **FIGURE 15.35** Problem 52.

53. •• Figure 15.36 shows a pV diagram for an ideal gas in which its absolute temperature at b is one-fourth of its absolute temperature at a. (a) What volume does this gas occupy at point b? (b) How many joules of work was done by or on the gas in this process? Was it done by or on the gas? (c) Did the internal energy of the gas increase or decrease from a to b? How do you know? (d) Did heat enter or leave the gas from a to b? How do you know?

▲ **FIGURE 15.36** Problem 53.

54. •• The pV diagram in Figure 15.37 shows a process abc involving 0.450 mole of an ideal gas. (a) What was the temperature of this gas at points a, b, and c? (b) How much work was done by or on the gas in this process? (c) How much heat had to be put in during the process to increase the internal energy of the gas by 15,000 J?

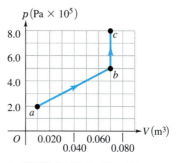

▲ **FIGURE 15.37** Problem 54.

55. •• The process abc shown in the pV diagram in Figure 15.38 involves 0.0175 mole of an ideal gas. (a) What was the lowest temperature the gas reached in this process? Where did it occur? (b) How much work was done by or on

▲ **FIGURE 15.38** Problem 55.

the gas from a to b; from b to c? (c) If 215 J of heat was put into the gas during abc, how many of those joules went into internal energy?

56. •• In the process illustrated by the pV diagram in Figure 15.39, the temperature of the ideal gas remains constant at 85°C. (a) How many moles of gas are involved? (b) What volume does this gas occupy at a? (c) How much work was done by or on the gas from a to b? (d) By how much did the internal energy of the gas change during this process?

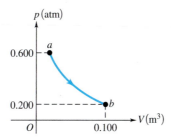

▲ FIGURE 15.39 Problem 56.

57. • A cylinder contains 0.250 mol of carbon dioxide (CO_2) gas at a temperature of 27.0°C. The cylinder is provided with a frictionless piston, which maintains a constant pressure of 1.00 atm on the gas. The gas is heated until its temperature increases to 127.0°C. Assume that the CO_2 may be treated as an ideal gas. (a) Draw a pV diagram of this process. (b) How much work is done by the gas in the process? (c) On what is this work done? (d) What is the change in internal energy of the gas? (e) How much heat was supplied to the gas? (f) How much work would have been done if the pressure had been 0.50 atm?

58. •• **Heating air in the lungs.** Human lung capacity varies from about 4 L to 6 L, so we shall use an average of 5.0 L. The air enters at the ambient temperature of the atmosphere and must be heated to internal body temperature at an approximately constant pressure of 1.0 atm in our model. Suppose you are outside on a winter day when the temperature is −10°F. (a) How many moles of air does your lung hold if the 5.0 L is at the internal body temperature of 37°C? (b) How much heat must your body have supplied to get the 5.0 L of air up to internal body temperature, assuming that the atmosphere is all N_2? (See Table 15.4.) (c) Suppose instead that you manage to inhale the full 5.0 L of air in one breath and hold it in your lungs without expanding (or contracting) them. How much heat would your body have had to supply in that case to raise the air up to internal body temperature?

59. •• The graph in Figure 15.40 shows a pV diagram for 1.10 moles of *ideal* oxygen, O_2. (a) Find the temperature at points a, b, c, and d. (b) How many joules of heat enters (or leaves) the oxygen in segment (i) ab, (ii) bc, (iii) cd, (iv) da? (c) In each of the preceding segments, does the heat enter or leave the gas? How do you know?

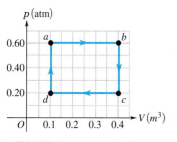

▲ FIGURE 15.40 Problem 59.

60. • An ideal gas at 4.00 atm and 350 K is permitted to expand adiabatically to 1.50 times its initial volume. Find the final pressure and temperature if the gas is (a) monatomic with $C_p/C_V = \frac{5}{3}$, (b) diatomic with $C_p/C_V = \frac{7}{5}$.

61. • The engine of a Ferrari F355 F1 sports car takes in air at 20.0°C and 1.00 atm and compresses it adiabatically to 0.0900 times the original volume. The air may be treated as an ideal gas with $\gamma = 1.40$. (a) Draw a pV diagram of this process. (b) Find the final temperature and pressure of the air in the engine.

62. • Propane gas (C_3H_8) behaves like an ideal gas with $\gamma = 1.127$. (a) Determine the molar heat capacity of propane gas at constant volume and the molar heat capacity at constant pressure. (b) How much heat would it take to raise the temperature of 2.25 moles of propane from −15°C to 45°C if this gas were heated (i) in a rigid tank or (ii) in a flexible tank that always maintained the same pressure on the gas?

63. •• During an adiabatic expansion, the temperature of 0.450 mol of argon (Ar) drops from 50.0°C to 10.0°C. Argon is monatomic and may be treated as an ideal gas. (a) Draw a pV diagram of this process. (b) How much work does the gas do? (c) What is the change in internal energy of the gas?

64. •• In the pV diagram shown in Figure 15.41, 85.0 J of work was done by 0.0650 mole of ideal gas during an adiabatic process. (a) How much heat entered or left this gas from a to b? (b) By how many joules did the internal energy of the gas change? (c) What is the temperature of the gas at b?

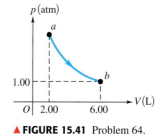

▲ FIGURE 15.41 Problem 64.

General Problems

65. • Modern vacuum pumps make it easy to attain pressures on the order of 10^{-13} atm in the laboratory. At a pressure of 9.00×10^{-14} atm and an ordinary temperature of 300 K, how many molecules are present in 1.00 cm³ of gas?

66. •• **How many atoms are you?** Estimate the number of atoms in the body of a 65 kg physics student. Note that the human body is mostly water, which has molar mass 18.0 g/mol, and that each water molecule contains three atoms.

67. •• **The effect of altitude on the lungs.** (a) Calculate the *change* in air pressure you will experience if you climb a 1000 m mountain, assuming that the temperature and air density do not change over this distance and that they were 22°C and 1.2 kg/m³, respectively, at the bottom of the mountain. (b) If you took a 0.50 L breath at the foot of the mountain and managed to hold it until you reached the top, what would be the volume of this breath when you exhaled it there?

68. •• (a) Calculate the mass of nitrogen present in a volume of 3000 cm³ if the temperature of the gas is 22.0°C and the absolute pressure is 2.00×10^{-13} atm, a partial vacuum easily obtained in laboratories. The molar mass of nitrogen (N_2) is 28.0 g/mol. (b) What is the density (in kg/m³) of the N_2?

69. • An automobile tire has a volume of 0.0150 m³ on a cold day when the temperature of the air in the tire is 5.0°C and atmospheric pressure is 1.02 atm. Under these conditions, the gauge pressure is measured to be 1.70 atm (about 25 lb/in²). After the

car is driven on the highway for 30 min, the temperature of the air in the tires has risen to 45.0°C and the volume to 0.0159 m³. What is the gauge pressure at that time?

70. •• Nitrogen gas in an expandable container is cooled from 50.0°C to 10.0°C with the pressure held constant at 3.00×10^5 Pa. The total heat liberated by the gas is 2.50×10^4 J. Assume that the gas may be treated as ideal. (a) Find the number of moles of gas. (b) Find the change in internal energy of the gas. (c) Find the work done by the gas. (d) How much heat would be liberated by the gas for the same temperature change if the volume were constant?

71. •• **The surface of the sun.** The surface of the sun has a temperature of about 5800 K and consists largely of hydrogen atoms. (a) Find the rms speed of a hydrogen atom at this temperature. (The mass of a single hydrogen atom is 1.67×10^{-27} kg.) (b) What would be the mass of an atom that had half the rms speed of hydrogen?

72. • The speed of propagation of a sound wave in air at 27°C is about 350 m/s. Calculate, for comparison, v_{rms} for nitrogen (N_2) molecules at this temperature. The molar mass of nitrogen is 28.0 g/mol.

73. •• Helium gas expands slowly to twice its original volume, doing 300 J of work in the process. Find the heat added to the gas and the change in internal energy of the gas if the process is (a) isothermal, (b) adiabatic, (c) isobaric.

74. •• A cylinder with a piston contains 0.250 mol of ideal oxygen at a pressure of 2.40×10^5 Pa and a temperature of 355 K. The gas first expands isobarically to twice its original volume. It is then compressed isothermally back to its original volume, and finally it is cooled isochorically to its original pressure. (a) Show the series of processes on a pV diagram. (b) Compute the temperature during the isothermal compression. (c) Compute the maximum pressure. (d) Compute the total work done by the piston on the gas during the series of processes.

75. •• Use the conditions and processes of the previous problem to compute (a) the work done by the oxygen, the heat added to it, and the change in its internal energy during the initial expansion, (b) the work done, the heat added, and the change in internal energy during the final cooling, and (c) the change in internal energy during the isothermal compression.

76. •• (a) One-third of a mole of He gas is taken along the path abc shown as the solid line in Figure 15.42. Assume that the gas may be treated as ideal. How much heat is transferred into or out of the gas? (b) If the gas instead went from state a to state c along the horizontal dashed line in Fig. 15.42, how

much heat would be transferred into or out of the gas? (c) How does Q in part (b) compare against Q in part (a)? Explain.

77. •• A bicyclist uses a tire pump whose cylinder is initially full of air at an absolute pressure of 1.01×10^5 Pa. The length of stroke of the pump (the length of the cylinder) is 36.0 cm. At what part of the stroke (i.e., what length of the air column) does air begin to enter a tire in which the gauge pressure is 2.76×10^5 Pa? Assume that the temperature remains constant during the compression.

78. •• **The bends.** If deep-sea divers rise to the surface too quickly, BIO nitrogen bubbles in their blood can expand and prove fatal. This phenomenon is known as the *bends*. If a scuba diver rises quickly from a depth of 25 m in Lake Michigan (which is fresh water), what will be the volume at the surface of an N_2 bubble that occupied 1.0 mm³ in his blood at the lower depth? Does it seem that this difference is large enough to be a problem? (Assume that the pressure difference is due only to the changing water pressure, not to any temperature difference, an assumption that is reasonable, since we are warm-blooded creatures.)

79. •• Figure 15.43 shows a pV diagram for 0.0040 mole of *ideal* H_2 gas. The temperature of the gas does not change during segment bc. (a) What volume does this gas occupy at point c? (b) Find the temperature of the gas at points a, b, and c. (c) How much heat went into or out of the gas during segments ab, ca, and bc? Indicate whether the heat has gone into or out of the gas. (d) Find the change in the internal energy of this hydrogen during segments ab, bc, and ca. Indicate whether the internal energy increased or decreased during each of these segments.

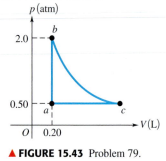

▲ FIGURE 15.43 Problem 79.

80. •• The graph in Figure 15.44 shows a pV diagram for 3.25 moles of *ideal* helium (He) gas. Part ca of this process is isothermal. (a) Find the pressure of the He at point a. (b) Find the temperature of the He at points a, b, and c. (c) How much heat entered or left the He during segments ab, bc, and ca? In each segment, did the heat enter or leave? (d) By how much did the internal energy of the He change from a to b, from b to c, and from c to a? Indicate whether this energy increased or decreased.

▲ FIGURE 15.44 Problem 80.

81. •• A welder using a tank of volume 0.0750 m³ fills it with oxygen (molar mass = 32.0 g/mol) at a gauge pressure of 3.00×10^5 Pa and temperature of 37.0°C. The tank has a small leak, and in time some of the oxygen leaks out. On a day when the temperature is 22.0°C, the gauge pressure of the oxygen in the tank is 1.80×10^5 Pa. Find (a) the initial mass of oxygen, (b) the mass of oxygen that has leaked out.

82. •• **Diesel ignition.** Conventional engines ignite their fuel by using the spark from a spark plug. But in a diesel engine, the

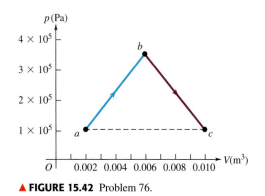

▲ FIGURE 15.42 Problem 76.

air enters the chamber at the temperature of the atmosphere and is compressed by the piston until it reaches 550°C, at which time the fuel is injected into the chamber and ignited by the hot air. There is no spark plug and no heat is put into the air. (One of the drawbacks of diesel engines is that they are hard to start in cold weather, as we shall shortly see.) Suppose that a certain chamber has a maximum volume of 0.50 L and uses 0.050 mole of air. We can model the air as all ideal N_2 and use the appropriate values from Table 15.4. (a) If the air temperature is 20°C, what is the volume of the air (which started at 0.50 L) when it has been compressed enough so that its temperature has risen to 550°C? (b) What is the change in the internal energy of the air during this compression? (c) How much work did the piston do on this gas while compressing it? (d) Suppose it is a cold winter morning, with the air temperature 10° F. If the piston compressed the air by the same amount as before, what will be the highest temperature the gas will reach in this case? (e) Do you now see why a diesel engine is hard to start in cold weather? Can you suggest any reasonable technological solutions to help start a diesel engine on a cold day?

83. •• Initially at a temperature of 80.0°C, 0.28 m³ of air expands at a constant gauge pressure of 1.38×10^5 Pa to a volume of 1.42 m³ and then expands further adiabatically to a final volume of 2.27 m³ and a final gauge pressure of 2.29×10^4 Pa. Draw a pV diagram for this sequence of processes, and compute the total work done by the air. C_V for air is 20.8 J/(mol · K).

84. •• In a cylinder, 4.00 mol of helium initially at 1.00×10^6 Pa and 300 K expands until its volume doubles. Compute the work done by the gas if the expansion is (a) isobaric, (b) adiabatic. (c) Show each process on a pV diagram. In which case is the magnitude of the work done by the gas the greatest? (d) In which case is the magnitude of the heat transfer greatest? (e) In which case is the magnitude of the change in internal energy greatest?

85. •• Two moles of helium are initially at a temperature of 27.0°C and occupy a volume of 0.0300 m³. The helium first expands at constant pressure until its volume has doubled. Then it expands adiabatically until the temperature returns to its initial value. Assume that the helium can be treated as an ideal gas. (a) Draw a diagram of the process in the pV-plane. (b) What is the total heat supplied to the helium in the process? (c) What is the total change in internal energy of the helium? (d) What is the total work done by the helium? (e) What is the final volume of the helium?

86. •• • A hot-air balloon stays aloft because hot air at atmospheric pressure is less dense than cooler air at the same pressure. (The calculation of the buoyant force is discussed in Chapter 13.) If the volume of the balloon is 500.0 m³ and the surrounding air is at 15.0°C, what must the temperature of the air in the balloon be for it to lift a total load of 290 kg (in addition to the mass of the hot air)? The density of air at 15.0°C and atmospheric pressure is 1.23 kg/m³.

THE SECOND LAW OF THERMODYNAMICS

In this chapter we'll encounter the concept of *entropy,* which represents the fact that order tends to disintegrate spontaneously into disorder. To fend off entropy, our bodies require a constant input of energy— which we take in the form of food.

When you put 0.1 kg of boiling water and 0.1 kg of ice in an insulated cup, you end up with 0.2 kg of water at about 10°C. That's not surprising. But you'd be very surprised if you came back later and found that the water had turned back to 0.1 kg of ice and 0.1 kg of boiling water. That wouldn't violate the first law of thermodynamics; energy would be conserved. But it doesn't happen in nature. Why not? Why does a power plant convert less than half of the heat from burning coal into electrical energy, discarding the remainder of the heat? Why does heat always flow spontaneously from hotter places to cooler places, never the reverse? When you drop ink into water, it mixes spontaneously, coloring the water, but it never spontaneously unmixes. Why not? What do all these things have in common?

A study of inherently one-way processes, such as the flow of heat from hotter to colder regions and the conversion of work into heat by friction, leads to the *second law of thermodynamics.* This law places fundamental limitations on the efficiency of an engine or a power plant and on the minimum energy input needed to operate a refrigerator. So the second law is directly relevant to many important practical problems. We can also state the second law in terms of the concept of *entropy,* a quantitative measure of the degree of disorder, or randomness, of a system.

16.1 Directions of Thermodynamic Processes

Heat flows spontaneously from a hotter object to a cooler object, never the reverse. Spontaneous heat flow from a cool object to a hot object would not violate the first law, but it doesn't happen in nature. Or suppose all the air in a box could rush to one side, leaving vacuum in the other side, the reverse of the free

516

expansion we described in Section 15.5. This phenomenon doesn't occur in nature either, although the first law doesn't forbid it. It's easy to convert mechanical energy completely into heat; we do this every time we use a car's brakes to stop it. It is not so easy to convert heat into mechanical energy. Many would-be inventors have proposed cooling some air to extract heat from it and then converting that heat to mechanical energy to propel a car or an airplane. None has ever succeeded; no one has ever built a machine that converts heat *completely* into mechanical energy.

What all these examples have in common is a preferred *direction.* In each case, a process proceeds spontaneously in one direction, but not in the other. Still, despite the fact that there is a preferred direction for every natural process, we can think of a class of idealized processes that are *reversible.* We say that a system undergoes a **reversible process** if the system is always very close to being in thermodynamic equilibrium, within itself and with its surroundings. When this is the case, any change of state that takes place can be reversed (i.e., made to go the other way) by making only an infinitesimal change in the conditions of the system. For example, heat flow between two objects whose temperatures differ only infinitesimally can be reversed by making only a very small change in one temperature or the other. Thus, a gas expanding slowly and adiabatically can be compressed slowly and adiabatically by an infinitesimal increase in pressure.

Reversible processes are thus **equilibrium processes.** In contrast, heat flow with a finite (as opposed to an infinitesimal) temperature difference, the free expansion of a gas, and the conversion of work to heat by friction are all **irreversible processes:** No small change in conditions could make any of them go to the other way. They are also all *non-equilibrium* processes.

> ### Reversible process
> A reversible process is a transition from one state of a thermodynamic system to another, during which the system is always very close to a state of mechanical and thermal equilibrium (including uniform temperature and pressure).

A reversible process is an idealization that can never be precisely attained in the real world. But by making the temperature gradients and the pressure differences in the substance very small, we can keep the system very close to equilibrium states.

Finally, we'll find that there is a relation between the direction of a process and the *disorder,* or *randomness,* of the resulting state. For example, imagine a tedious sorting job, such as alphabetizing a thousand book titles written on file cards. Throw the alphabetized stack of cards into the air. Do they come down in alphabetical order? No, their tendency is to come down in a random, or disordered, state. In the free expansion of a gas that we saw in Figure 15.25, the air is more disordered after it has expanded into the entire container than when it was confined in one side, because the molecules are scattered over more space.

Similarly, macroscopic kinetic energy is energy associated with organized, coordinated motions of many molecules in a moving macroscopic object, but heat transfer involves changes in energy of random, disordered molecular motion. Therefore the conversion of mechanical energy into heat involves an increase in randomness, or disorder.

In the sections that follow, we'll introduce the second law of thermodynamics by considering two broad classes of devices: *heat engines,* which are partly successful in converting heat into work, and *refrigerators,* which are partly successful in transporting heat from cooler to hotter objects.

▲ **Near-reversible control.** The energy released by the sun comes from nuclear fusion reactions in its core. The rate of these reactions depends sensitively on temperature: A slight increase in temperature would cause a large increase in energy output. For life on earth, it is essential that the sun's brightness be steady. Luckily, the rate of fusion is controlled by a "thermostat." Energy escapes from the core rather slowly. Suppose the rate of fusion increased slightly. Then the extra heat output would cause the core to swell and thus to cool down, reducing the fusion rate. (The core consists of a plasma rather than a gas per se, but thermodynamically, it behaves like a gas.) Similarly, a drop in the rate of fusion would cause the core to shrink and heat up, increasing the rate again. Inferno though it is, the core is always close to equilibrium, so that a slight change in conditions can reverse the direction of a thermodynamic process.

Conceptual Analysis 16.1

Reversible versus irreversible processes

Which of the following mechanical processes are not reversible, in the sense that energy converted from one form to another cannot be completely converted from the second form back to the first form?

A. A ball is tossed upward, gaining height.
B. A moving cart is caught by a spring, stretching the spring.
C. A moving block slides to a stop because of friction.

SOLUTION Processes A and B involve only mechanical energy. In each, the system is given some kinetic energy, which is then transformed into potential energy. In A, the kinetic energy is recovered as the ball falls back to its original elevation; in B, the kinetic energy is recovered when the spring is permitted to relax back to its original length. If friction can be neglected, processes A and B are reversible. Process C is not reversible, because mechanical energy is converted to internal energy and there is no way to convert it back to mechanical energy without supplying some work from outside the system.

16.2 Heat Engines

8.12, 8.13 **Activ Physics** ONLINE

The essence of a technological society is its ability to use sources of mechanical energy other than muscle power. Sometimes mechanical energy is directly available; water power is an example. But most of our energy comes from the burning of fossil fuels (coal, oil, and gas) and from nuclear reactions. These processes supply energy that is transferred as *heat*. This transformation of energy is directly useful for heating buildings, for cooking, and for chemical and metallurgical processing. But to run an electrical generator or to operate a machine or propel a vehicle, we need *mechanical* energy.

Thus, it's important to know how to take heat from a source and convert as much of it as possible into mechanical energy or work. This is what happens in gasoline and Diesel engines in automobiles and trucks, jet engines in airplanes, steam turbines in electric power plants, and many other systems. A device that transforms heat partly into work or mechanical energy is called a **heat engine.** In a heat engine, a quantity of matter inside the engine undergoes addition and subtraction of heat, expansion and compression, and, sometimes, a phase change. We call this matter the **working substance** of the engine. In internal combustion engines (such as automobile engines), the working substance is a mixture of air and fuel; in a steam engine or steam turbine, it is water.

The simplest kind of engine to analyze is one in which the working substance undergoes a **cyclic process—a sequence of processes that eventually leaves the substance in the same state as that in which it started.** In a steam turbine, the water is recycled and used over and over. Internal combustion engines do not use the same air over and over, but we can still analyze them in terms of cyclic processes that approximate their actual operation.

All the heat engines just mentioned absorb heat from a source at a relatively high temperature, perform some mechanical work, and discard some heat at a lower temperature. As far as the engine is concerned, the discarded heat is wasted. In internal combustion engines, the waste heat is discarded in the hot exhaust gases and the cooling system; in a steam engine or steam turbine, the waste heat is the heat that must be taken out of the used steam in order to condense and recycle the water.

When a system is carried through a cyclic process, its initial and final internal energies are equal, so the change ΔU in internal energy of the system is zero. Thus, for any cyclic process, the first law of thermodynamics requires that

$$\Delta U = Q - W = 0 \quad \text{and} \quad Q = W.$$

That is, **in a cyclic process, the net heat Q flowing into the engine equals the net work W done by the engine.**

When we analyze heat engines, it helps to think of two objects with which the working substance of the engine can interact. One of these, called the *hot reservoir*, can give the working substance large amounts of heat at a constant temperature T_H without appreciably changing its own temperature. The other object,

▲ **Earth power.** One type of heat engine uses the earth itself as a source of heat. At the Svartsengi geothermal power plant in Iceland, the hot reservoir is a subsurface body of hot volcanic rock. (Iceland is one of the most active volcanic regions in the world.) The rock heats the local briny groundwater to temperatures of 240°C. Drill holes bring this water to the surface as high-pressure steam. The steam is used both to power turbines for electrical generation and to heat fresh water, which is distributed by the surrounding towns for home heating and hot water. The condensed steam is then released into the Blue Lagoon next to the power plant, where bathers can relax in 40°C waters even in the middle of an Icelandic winter. The power plant pumps about 150 MJ/s (150 MW) of heat from below ground and produces about 50 MW of electricity.

called the *cold reservoir,* can absorb large amounts of discarded heat from the engine at a constant lower temperature T_C. In a steam-turbine system, the flames and hot gases in the boiler are the hot reservoir, and the cold water and air used to condense and cool the used steam are the cold reservoir.

We denote the quantities of heat transferred from the hot and cold reservoirs as Q_H and Q_C, respectively. A quantity of heat Q is positive when heat is transferred *from* a reservoir *into* the working substance. When heat leaves the working substance, Q is negative. Thus, in a heat engine, Q_H is positive, but Q_C is negative, representing heat *leaving* the working substance. When the working substance does positive work on its surroundings, W is positive. These sign conventions are consistent with the rules that we stated in Chapter 15; we'll continue to use those rules here. Sometimes it clarifies the relationships to state them in terms of the absolute values of the Q's and W's, because absolute values are always positive. When we do this, our notation will show it explicitly.

We can represent the energy transformations in a heat engine by the *energy-flow diagram* of Figure 16.1. The engine itself is represented by the circle. The amount of heat Q_H supplied to the engine by the hot reservoir is proportional to the width of the incoming "pipeline" at the top of the diagram. The width of the outgoing pipeline at the bottom is proportional to the magnitude $|Q_C|$ of the heat discarded. The branch line to the right represents that portion of the heat supplied that the engine converts to mechanical work W.

When an engine repeats the same cycle over and over, Q_H and Q_C represent the quantities of heat absorbed and rejected, respectively, by the engine *during one cycle; Q_H is positive, Q_C negative.* The *net* heat Q absorbed per cycle is

$$Q = Q_H + Q_C = |Q_H| - |Q_C|. \tag{16.1}$$

The useful output of the engine is the net work W done by the working substance; from the first law,

$$W = Q = Q_H + Q_C = |Q_H| - |Q_C|. \tag{16.2}$$

Ideally, we would like to convert *all* the heat Q_H into work; in that case, we would have $Q_H = W$ and $Q_C = 0$. Experience shows that this is impossible; there is always some heat wasted, and Q_C can never be zero. We define the **thermal efficiency** of an engine, denoted by e, as the quotient of W and Q_H:

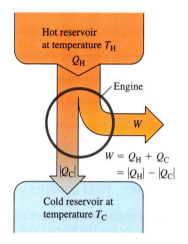

▲ FIGURE 16.1 Schematic energy-flow diagram for a heat engine.

Thermal efficiency of a heat engine
The thermal efficiency of a heat engine is the useful work W done by the engine, divided by the heat input Q_H:

$$e = \frac{W}{Q_H}. \tag{16.3}$$

The thermal efficiency e represents the fraction of Q_H that *is* converted to work. To put it another way, e is what you get, divided by what you pay for. This is always less than 1, an all-too-familiar experience! In terms of the flow diagram of Figure 16.1, the most efficient engine is the one for which the branch pipeline representing the work output is as wide as possible and the exhaust pipeline representing the heat thrown away is as narrow as possible.

When we substitute the two expressions for W given by Equation 16.2 into Equation 16.3, we get the following equivalent expressions for e:

$$e = \frac{W}{Q_H} = 1 + \frac{Q_C}{Q_H} = 1 - \frac{|Q_C|}{|Q_H|}. \tag{16.4}$$

Note that e is a quotient of two energy quantities and thus is a pure number, without units. Of course, we must always express W, Q_H, and Q_C in the same units.

▲ **Zero power.** Using knowledge of the principles of physics and energy conservation, architects are designing homes of the future that will consume no net power. These homes, called "zero-power homes," are designed to generate as much power as they consume, allowing their owners to have an annual energy bill of $0. They can do this by using a combination of rooftop photovoltaic cells, solar water heaters, state-of-the-art insulation, energy-efficient appliances, and computer-controlled power distribution systems. Some can even generate excess power, which can be sold back to "the grid" to generate income. Of course, this net negative energy use does not violate the laws of thermodynamics: The house is not a closed system. The negative energy use by these homes results from the efficient collection and use of the vast amounts of solar energy reaching the homes each year.

To complete the definition of the Kelvin scale, we assign the arbitrary value of 273.16 K to the temperature of the triple point of water. As we discussed in Section 15.2, this is the unique temperature at which gas, liquid, and solid phases of water can coexist in phase equilibrium. When a substance is taken around a Carnot cycle, the ratio of the heat absorbed to the heat rejected, $|Q_H|/|Q_C|$, is equal to the ratio of the temperatures of the reservoirs, *as expressed on the gas scale,* defined in Section 14.2. Since, on both scales, the triple point of water is chosen to be 273.16 K, it follows that *the Kelvin and the ideal-gas scales are identical.*

The zero point on the Kelvin scale is called **absolute zero.** There are theoretical reasons for believing that absolute zero cannot be attained experimentally, although temperatures below 10^{-7} K have been achieved. The more closely we approach absolute zero, the more difficult it is to get yet closer. Absolute zero can also be interpreted on a molecular level, although this must be done with some care. Because of quantum effects, it would *not* be correct to say that at $T = 0$, all molecular motion ceases. At absolute zero, the system has its *minimum* possible total energy (kinetic plus potential). One statement of the *third law of thermodynamics* is that it is impossible to reach absolute zero in a finite number of thermodynamic steps.

*16.9 Energy Resources: A Case Study in Thermodynamics

The laws of thermodynamics place very general limitations on the conversion of energy from one form to another. In these times of increasing energy demand and diminishing resources, such matters are of the utmost practical importance. We conclude this chapter with a brief discussion of a few energy-conversion systems, present and proposed.

About half of the electric power generated in the United States is obtained from coal-fired steam-turbine generating plants. Modern boilers can transfer about 80% to 90% of the heat of combustion of coal into steam. The theoretical maximum thermal efficiency of the turbine, given by Equation 16.9, is usually limited to about 0.55, and the actual efficiency is typically 90% of this value, or approximately 0.50. The efficiency of large generators in converting mechanical power to electrical power is very high, typically 99%. Thus, the overall thermal efficiency of such a plant is roughly (0.85) (0.50) (0.99), or at most about 40%.

The Tennessee Valley Authority's Kingston power plant has a generating capacity of about 1 gigawatt $(1000\text{ MW, or }10^9\text{ W})$ of electrical power. The steam is heated to about 540°C $(1000°F)$ at a pressure of more than 120 atm $(1.24 \times 10^7\text{ Pa, or }1800\text{ psi})$. The plant burns 14,000 tons of coal per day (13 million kg, the equivalent of 140 railroad cars), and the overall thermal efficiency is about 35%.

In a nuclear power plant, the heat that generates steam is supplied by a nuclear reaction rather than the chemical reaction of burning coal. The steam turbines in nuclear power plants have the same theoretical efficiency limit as those in coal-fired plants. At present, it is not practical to run nuclear reactors at temperatures and pressures as high as those in coal boilers, so the thermal efficiency of a nuclear plant is somewhat lower, typically 30%.

In the year 2005, about 20% of the world's electric power supply came from nuclear power plants. High construction costs, questions of public safety, and the problem of disposal of radioactive waste have slowed the development of additional nuclear power. However, there is also increasing concern about the environmental impact of coal-burning power plants. The health hazards of coal smoke are serious and well documented, and the burning of coal contributes to global warming through the greenhouse effect. It is important to manage our

The mass burned per hour is

$$(5.0 \text{ g/s})\left(\frac{3600 \text{ s}}{1 \text{ h}}\right) = 18{,}000 \text{ g/h} = 18 \text{ kg/h}.$$

REFLECT The efficiency from part (a) is a fairly typical figure for cars and trucks if W includes only the work actually delivered to the wheels. The density of gasoline is about 0.70 g/cm^3; the volume of fuel burned per hour is about $25{,}700 \text{ cm}^3$, 25.7 L, or 6.8 gallons of gasoline per hour. If the truck is traveling at 55 mi/h (88 km/h), that volume represents fuel consumption of about 8.1 miles per gallon (mpg) (3.4 km/L).

Each cylinder in the engine goes through one cycle for every two revolutions of the crankshaft. For a four-cylinder engine, 100 cycles per second corresponds to 50 crankshaft revolutions per second, or 3000 rev/min (typical for highway speeds).

Practice Problem: A gasoline engine with a thermal efficiency of 28% has a power output of 50 hp. How much heat must be supplied per second to the engine? *Answer:* $Q_H = 133 \text{ kJ}$.

16.3 Internal Combustion Engines

The gasoline engine, used in automobiles and many other types of machinery, is a familiar example of a heat engine. Figure 16.3 shows the sequence of processes. First, a mixture of air and gasoline vapor flows into a cylinder through an open intake valve while the piston descends, increasing the volume of the cylinder from a minimum of V (when the piston is all the way up) to a maximum of rV (when it is all the way down). The quantity r is called the **compression ratio;** for present-day automobile engines, it is typically about 8.

At the end of this *intake stroke,* the intake valve closes and the air–gasoline mixture is compressed, quickly and approximately adiabatically, to volume V during the *compression stroke.* The mixture is then ignited by the spark plug, and the heated gas expands, again approximately adiabatically, back to volume rV. As it does so, it pushes on the piston and does work on it; this is the *power stroke.* Finally, the exhaust valve opens and the combustion products are pushed out (during the *exhaust stroke*), leaving the cylinder ready for the next intake stroke.

The Otto Cycle

Figure 16.4 is a pV diagram showing an idealized model of the thermodynamic processes in a gasoline engine. This model is called the **Otto cycle.** We'll assume that the gasoline–air mixture behaves as an ideal gas. At point a, the mixture has entered the cylinder. The mixture is compressed adiabatically (line ab) and is then ignited. Heat Q_H (heat of combustion) is added to the system by the burning

Intake stroke: Piston moves down, causing a partial vacuum in cylinder; gasoline–air mixture enters through intake valve.

Compression stroke: Intake valve closes; mixture is compressed as piston moves up.

Ignition: Spark plug ignites mixture.

Power stroke: Hot burned mixture expands, pushing piston down.

Exhaust stroke: Exhaust valve opens; piston moves up, expelling exhaust and leaving cylinder ready for next intake stroke.

▲ **FIGURE 16.3** Cycle of a four-stroke internal combustion engine.

Otto cycle

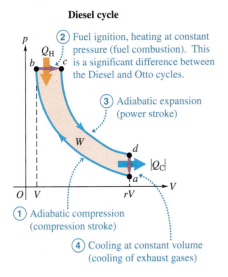

▲ **FIGURE 16.4** The pV diagram for the Otto cycle, an idealized model of the thermodynamic processes that take place in a gasoline engine.

Diesel cycle

▲ **FIGURE 16.5** The pV diagram for the Diesel cycle.

gasoline (line bc), and the power stroke is the adiabatic expansion cd. The gas is cooled to the temperature of the outside air (da); during process (da), heat Q_C is released. In practice, this same air does not enter the engine again, but since an equivalent amount does enter, we may consider the process to be cyclic.

It's possible, although a bit complicated, to calculate the efficiency e of this idealized cycle; we'll omit the details. The result is surprisingly simple; it depends only on the compression ratio r and the ratio $\gamma = C_p/C_V$ of the molar heat capacities at constant volume and at constant pressure, which we introduced in Section 15.7. It turns out that the efficiency for the idealized Otto cycle is given by

$$e = 1 - \frac{1}{r^{\gamma-1}}. \tag{16.5}$$

The quantities r and γ are pure numbers, and they are always greater than 1. As we would expect, the thermal efficiency given by Equation 16.5 is always less than 1, even for this idealized model. With $r = 8$ and $\gamma = 1.4$ (the value for air), the theoretical efficiency is $e = 0.56$, or 56%. The efficiency can be increased by increasing r. However, doing this also increases the temperature reached by the air–fuel mixture at the end of the adiabatic compression. If the temperature is too high, the mixture explodes spontaneously during compression instead of burning evenly after the spark plug ignites it. This is called *pre-ignition,* or *detonation;* it causes a knocking sound and can damage the engine. The octane rating of a gasoline is a measure of its antiknock qualities. The maximum practical compression ratio for high-octane, or "premium," gasoline is about 10. Higher ratios can be used with more exotic fuels.

The Otto cycle is a highly idealized model. It assumes that the air–fuel mixture behaves as an ideal gas; it neglects friction, turbulence, loss of heat to cylinder walls, incomplete combustion, and many other effects that combine to reduce the efficiency of a real engine. Thermal efficiencies of real gasoline engines are typically around 20%.

The Diesel Cycle

The Diesel engine is similar in operation to the gasoline engine. The most important difference is that, at the beginning of the compression stroke, the cylinder contains air, but no fuel. A little before the beginning of the power stroke, the injectors start to inject fuel directly into the cylinder, just fast enough to keep the pressure approximately constant during the first part of the power stroke. Because of the high temperature developed during the adiabatic compression, the fuel ignites spontaneously as it is injected; no spark plugs are needed.

The idealized **Diesel cycle** is shown in the pV diagram of Figure 16.5. Starting at point a, air is compressed adiabatically to point b, heated (by the heat of combustion) at constant pressure to point c, expanded adiabatically to point d, and cooled at constant volume to point a. Because there is no fuel in the cylinder

◀ **Peanut power.** As we've learned, the key feature of the Diesel engine is that the fuel is ignited, not by a spark, but by the heat from adiabatic compression during the compression stroke. Thus, there's no real connection between Diesel engines and "diesel fuel." In fact, the original Diesel engine, invented in 1892 by Rudolph Diesel, ran on peanut oil! Diesel saw this property as a key feature of his engine: In addition to being far more efficient than steam engines, it could run on fuel produced by local agriculture, which was independent of the fossil fuel monopolies of the day. In the 1920s, the engine was modified to run on "diesel" fossil fuel, which was inexpensive. Now, however, there is renewed interest in "bio-diesel"—basically, vegetable oil. This fuel can be produced anywhere plants grow, and it does not contribute to global warming: The carbon dioxide released when it burns equals the carbon dioxide taken up by the plants that produced it.

during most of the compression stroke, pre-ignition cannot occur, and the compression ratio r can be much higher than for a gasoline engine. This feature improves the efficiency of the engine and ensures reliable ignition when the fuel is injected (because of the high temperature reached during the adiabatic compression). Values of r of 15 to 20 are typical; with these values and $\gamma = 1.4$, the theoretical efficiency of the idealized Diesel cycle is about 0.65 to 0.70. As with the Otto cycle, the efficiency of any actual engine is substantially less than this. Diesel engines are usually more efficient than gasoline engines. They are also heavier (per unit power output) and often harder to start.

16.4 Refrigerators

We can think of a **refrigerator** as a heat engine operating in reverse. A heat engine takes heat from a hot place and gives off heat to a colder place. A refrigerator does the opposite; it takes heat from a cold place (the inside of the refrigerator) and gives it off to a warmer place (usually the air in the room where the refrigerator is located). A heat engine has a net *output* of mechanical work; the refrigerator requires a net *input* of mechanical work, as shown in Figure 16.6, an energy-flow diagram for a refrigerator. With the symbols we used in Section 16.2, Q_C is positive for a refrigerator, but both W and Q_H are negative, so $|W| = -W$ and $|Q_H| = -Q_H$.

For a cyclic process, the first law gives $\Delta U = 0$ and

$$Q_H + Q_C - W = 0, \quad \text{or} \quad -Q_H = Q_C - W.$$

Or, because both Q_H and W are negative,

$$|Q_H| = |Q_C| + |W|. \quad (16.6)$$

Thus, as the diagram shows, the heat $|Q_H|$ leaving the working substance and given to the hot reservoir is always *greater* than the heat Q_C taken from the cold reservoir. Note that the absolute-value relation given by Equation 16.6 is valid for both heat engines and refrigerators.

From an economic point of view, the best refrigeration cycle is one that removes the greatest amount of heat Q_C from the refrigerator for the least expenditure of mechanical work W. The relevant ratio is therefore $Q_C/|W|$. We call this the **performance coefficient,** denoted by K. Also, from Equation 16.6, we have $|W| = |Q_H| - |Q_C|$, so K can be expressed as follows:

Performance coefficient of a refrigerator

$$K = \frac{Q_C}{|W|} = \frac{|Q_C|}{|Q_H| - |Q_C|}. \quad (16.7)$$

As always, we measure Q_H, Q_C and W all in the same energy units; K is then a dimensionless number.

The principles of the common refrigeration cycle are shown schematically in Figure 16.7. The fluid "circuit" contains a refrigerant (the working substance). The left side of the circuit (including the cooling coils inside the refrigerator) is at low temperature and low pressure; the right side (including the condenser coils outside the refrigerator) is at high temperature and high pressure. Ordinarily, both sides contain liquid and vapor in phase equilibrium.

The compressor takes in fluid, compresses it adiabatically, and delivers it to the condenser coil at high pressure. The temperature of the fluid is then higher than that of the air surrounding the condenser, so the refrigerant gives off heat $|Q_H|$ and partially condenses to liquid. The fluid then expands adiabatically, at a rate controlled by the expansion valve, into the evaporator. As it does so, it cools

▲ **Cooling power.** The modern refrigerator is based on the physical principle that, as a gas expands or a liquid evaporates, it absorbs heat from its surroundings. The ancient Egyptians used this principle to make ice by setting water out in clay pots on cold, windy nights and keeping the pots wet on the outside. Mechanical refrigerators from the early 20th century, like the one shown here, used alternate compression and expansion of a volatile gas, such as ether or ammonia, to cool a closed container. As the gas is compressed on the outside of the container, it heats up, and this heat is released into the room. The compressed gas is allowed to expand in cooling coils inside the container, where it absorbs heat from the container, lowering the container's temperature. The net effect is that heat is transferred from a cold area to a warm area, but not without an energy cost: the energy required to compress the gas in each cycle.

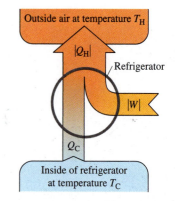

▲ **FIGURE 16.6** Schematic energy-flow diagram for a refrigerator.

(a)

(b)

▲ **FIGURE 16.7** Principle of the mechanical refrigeration cycle.

considerably, enough so that the fluid in the evaporator coil is colder than its surroundings. The fluid absorbs heat Q_C from its surroundings, cooling them while partially vaporizing. It then enters the compressor to begin another cycle. The compressor, usually driven by an electric motor, requires energy input and does work $|W|$ *on* the working substance during each cycle.

An air conditioner operates on exactly the same principle. In this case, the refrigerator box becomes a room or an entire building. The evaporator coils are inside, the condenser is outside, and fans circulate air through these components (Figure 16.8). In large installations, the condenser coils are often cooled by water. For air conditioners, the quantities of greatest practical importance are the *rate* of heat removal (the heat current H from the region being cooled) and the *power* input $P = W/t$ to the compressor. If heat Q_C is removed in time t, then $H = Q_C/t$. We can then express the performance coefficient as

$$K = \frac{Q_C}{|W|} = \frac{Ht}{Pt} = \frac{H}{P}.$$

▲ **FIGURE 16.8** An air conditioner works on the same principle as a refrigerator.

Typical room air conditioners have heat removal rates H of 5000 to 10,000 Btu/h, or about 1500 to 3000 W, and require a power input of about 500 to 1000 W. Performance coefficients are typically about 3, with somewhat larger values for larger-capacity units. Unfortunately, K is usually expressed commercially in mixed units, with H in Btu per hour and P in watts. In these units, H/P is called the **energy efficiency rating (EER).** Because 1 W = 3.413 Btu/h, the EER is numerically 3.413 times as large as the dimensionless K. Room air conditioners typically have an EER of about 10. The units, customarily omitted, are $(Btu/h)/W$.

A variation on this theme is the **heat pump,** used to heat buildings by cooling the outside. It functions like a refrigerator turned inside out. The evaporator coils are outside, where they take heat from cold air or water, and the condenser coils are inside, where they give off heat to the inside region. With proper design, the heat $|Q_H|$ delivered to the inside during each cycle can be considerably greater than the work $|W|$ required to get it there. Heat pumps are typically designed so that they can be run as air conditioners in the summer (by reversing the pumps so that the condenser becomes the evaporator and vice versa). In this mode, a heat pump has no extra efficiency over a standard air conditioner.

For example, suppose you have an air conditioner with $K = 3$. In normal use, the unit removes 300 J of heat from the inside of the house while expending 100 J of electrical energy and discarding 400 J to the outside. But if you mount the air conditioner backwards, so that 400 J goes *into* the house and 300 J is taken from the outside environment, you are getting a total of 400 J of heat into the house while paying the electric company for only 100 J of electrical energy.

Nevertheless, some work is *always* needed to transfer heat from a colder to a hotter object. Heat flows spontaneously from hotter to colder, and to reverse this flow requires the addition of work from the outside. Experience shows that it is impossible to make a refrigerator that transports heat from a cold object to a hotter object without the addition of work. If no work were needed, the performance coefficient would be infinite. We call such a device a *workless refrigerator;* it is a mythical beast, like the unicorn, the frictionless plane, and the free lunch.

Conceptual Analysis 16.2

Heating up or cooling down?

One method sometimes used in an attempt to cool a kitchen on a hot day is to leave the refrigerator door open. Does this actually cool the kitchen?

A. Yes, because refrigerators function on the same principle as air conditioners.
B. No, it actually warms the kitchen.
C. There is no net effect. The heat that is absorbed in the front of the refrigerator is offset by heat dissipated from the back of the refrigerator.

SOLUTION It is true that refrigerators and air conditioners function in the same way, but air conditioners move heat from the inside to the outside of the building, whereas refrigerators move heat from the refrigerator box to the rest of the kitchen. We've learned that, to move heat from the refrigerator box to the warmer kitchen, the refrigerator must convert work to heat. This additional heat is also released to the kitchen. Thus, the refrigerator *always* adds net heat to the kitchen, whether its door is open or shut. Opening the door makes the refrigerator work harder and thus heats the kitchen *more* than if you kept the door shut. Answer B is correct.

Conceptual Analysis 16.3

Efficient heating

Which of the following key advantages does a heat pump have over an ordinary electric (hot-wire) heater for heating a house?

A. The heat pump can be used as an air conditioner in the summer.
B. The heat pump pulls in warm air from the outside to add to the heat it produces.
C. The heat pump uses work to bring additional heat from the outside to the inside of the house.

SOLUTION As we've discussed, a heat pump is basically an air conditioner installed backward; indeed, most heat pumps are designed to switch direction and work as air conditioners when needed. Thus, A is correct. C is also correct; a standard hot-wire heater converts electrical energy to heat on a joule-for-joule basis, but a heat pump uses work (obtained from electric energy) to move heat from the outside to the inside *and also* converts this work to additional heat released inside the house. B is not correct: A heat pump moves heat, not hot air, from the outside to the inside.

16.5 The Second Law of Thermodynamics

Experimental evidence strongly suggests that it is impossible to build a heat engine that converts heat completely to work—that is, an engine with 100% thermal efficiency. This impossibility is the basis of one form of the **second law of thermodynamics:**

> **Second law of thermodynamics (engine statement)**
> It is impossible for any system to undergo a process in which it absorbs heat from a reservoir at a single temperature and converts the heat completely into mechanical work with the system ending in the same state in which it began.

We'll call this the "engine" statement of the second law.

The basis of the second law of thermodynamics lies in the difference between the nature of internal energy and that of macroscopic mechanical energy. In a moving object, the molecules have random motion, but superimposed on this is a coordinated motion of every molecule in the direction of the object's velocity. The kinetic energy associated with this *coordinated* macroscopic motion is what we call the kinetic energy of the moving object. The kinetic and potential energies associated with the *random* motion of the object's molecules constitute the internal energy. When a moving object comes to rest as result of friction or an inelastic collision, the organized part of the motion is converted to random motion. **Since we cannot control the motions of individual molecules, we cannot convert this random motion completely back to organized motion.** We can convert *part* of it, and that is what a heat engine does.

If the second law were *not* true, we could power an automobile or run a power plant simply by cooling the surrounding air and thus taking energy from it. Neither of these impossible scenarios violates the *first* law of thermodynamics. The second law is not a deduction from the first, but stands by itself as a separate law of nature. The first law denies the possibility of creating or destroying energy; the second law limits the *availability* of energy and the ways in which it can be used and converted.

Our analysis of refrigerators in Section 16.4 forms the basis for an alternative statement of the second law of thermodynamics. Heat flows spontaneously from hotter to colder objects, never the reverse. A refrigerator does take heat from a colder to a hotter object, but its operation depends on an input of mechanical energy or work. Generalizing this observation, we state the following principle:

> **Second law of thermodynamics (refrigerator statement)**
> It is impossible for any process to have as its sole result the transfer of heat from a cooler to a hotter object.

We'll call this the "refrigerator" statement of the second law. It may not seem to be very closely related to the "engine" statement. In fact, though, the two statements are completely equivalent. For example, if we could build a workless refrigerator, violating the "refrigerator" statement of the second law, we could use it in conjunction with a heat engine to pump the heat rejected by the engine back into the hot reservoir, to be reused. This composite machine (Figure 16.9a) would violate the "engine" statement of the second law because its net effect would be to take a net quantity of heat $Q_H - |Q_C|$ from the hot reservoir and convert it completely to work W.

Alternatively, if we could make an engine with 100% thermal efficiency, in violation of the first statement, we could run it by taking heat from the hot reservoir. Then we could use the work output to drive a refrigerator that pumps heat

If a workless refrigerator were possible, it could be used in conjunction with an ordinary heat engine to form a 100%-efficient engine, converting heat $Q_H - |Q_C|$ completely to work.

(a) The "engine" statement of the second law

If a 100%-efficient engine were possible, it could be used in conjunction with an ordinary refrigerator to form a workless refrigerator, transferring heat Q_C from the cold to the hot reservoir with no net input of work.

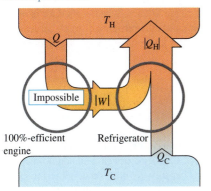

(b) The "refrigerator" statement of the second law

▲ **FIGURE 16.9** Energy-flow diagrams for equivalent forms of the second law. Since either of these machines is impossible, the other must be also.

from the cold reservoir to the hot (Figure 16.9b). This composite device would violate the "refrigerator" statement because its net effect would be to take heat Q_C from the cold reservoir and deliver it to the hot reservoir without requiring any input of work. Thus, any device that violates one form of the second law can also be used to make a device that violates the other form. In other words, if violations of the first form are impossible, so are violations of the second!

The conversion of work to heat, as in friction or viscous fluid flow, and heat flow from hot to cold across a finite temperature gradient are *irreversible* processes. The "engine" and "refrigerator" statements of the second law state that these processes can be only partially reversed. Here are two other examples: Gases always seep through an opening spontaneously from a region of high pressure to a region of low pressure; and gases left by themselves always tend to mix, never to unmix. Figure 16.10 shows two liquids mixing spontaneously.

The second law of thermodynamics is an expression of the inherent one-way aspect of these and many other irreversible processes. Energy conversion is an essential aspect of all plant and animal life and of many mechanical devices, so the second law of thermodynamics is of the utmost fundamental importance in the world we live in.

▲ **FIGURE 16.10** These liquids mix spontaneously—and they never spontaneously unmix.

16.6 The Carnot Engine: The Most Efficient Heat Engine

According to the second law, no heat engine can have 100% efficiency. But how great an efficiency *can* an engine have, given two heat reservoirs at temperatures T_H and T_C? This question was answered in 1824 by the French engineer Sadi Carnot (1796–1832), who developed a hypothetical, idealized heat engine that has the *maximum possible* efficiency consistent with the second law. In his honor, the cycle of this engine is called the **Carnot cycle.**

To understand the rationale of the Carnot cycle, we return to a recurrent theme in this chapter: *reversibility* and its relation to directions of thermodynamic processes. The conversion of work to heat is an irreversible process; the purpose of a heat engine is a *partial* reversal of this process: the conversion of heat to work with as great efficiency as possible. For maximum heat-engine efficiency, therefore, *we must avoid all irreversible processes.* This requirement turns out to be enough to determine the basic sequence of steps in the Carnot cycle, as we'll show next.

Heat flow through a finite temperature drop is an irreversible process. Therefore, during heat transfer in the Carnot cycle, there must be *no* finite temperature differences. When the engine takes heat from the hot reservoir at temperature T_H, the working substance of the engine must also be at T_H; otherwise, irreversible heat flow would occur. Similarly, when the engine discards heat to the cold reservoir at T_C, the engine itself must be at T_C. That is, every process that involves heat transfer must be *isothermal* at either T_H or T_C.

Conversely, in any process in which the temperature of the working substance of the engine is intermediate between T_H and T_C, there must be *no* heat transfer between the engine and either reservoir, because such heat transfer cannot be reversible. Therefore, any process in which the temperature T of the working substance changes must be adiabatic. The bottom line is that *every process* in our idealized cycle must be either *isothermal* or *adiabatic*. In addition, thermal and mechanical equilibrium must be maintained at all times, so that each process is completely reversible.

Activ
ONLINE
Physics   8.14

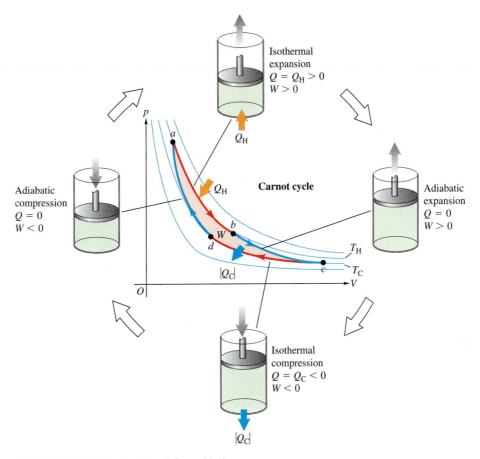

Isothermal
expansion
$Q = Q_H > 0$
$W > 0$

Adiabatic
compression
$Q = 0$
$W < 0$

Carnot cycle

Adiabatic
expansion
$Q = 0$
$W > 0$

Isothermal
compression
$Q = Q_C < 0$
$W < 0$

▲ **FIGURE 16.11** The Carnot cycle for an ideal gas.

The Carnot Cycle

The Carnot cycle consists of two isothermal and two adiabatic processes. Figure 16.11 shows a Carnot cycle using an ideal gas in a cylinder with a piston as its working substance. It consists of the following steps:

1. The gas expands isothermally at temperature T_H, absorbing heat Q_H (ab).
2. It expands adiabatically until its temperature drops to T_C (bc).
3. It is compressed isothermally at T_C, rejecting heat $|Q_C|$ (cd).
4. It is compressed adiabatically back to its initial state at temperature T_H (da).

When the working substance in a Carnot engine is an ideal gas, it's a straightforward calculation to find the heat and work for each step. Then from these quantities we can obtain the thermal efficiency, using the definition of e (Equation 16.4). The details of the calculations are a little involved, so we'll simply state the results here, without any derivation.

The ratio Q_C/Q_H of the two quantities of heat turns out to be equal (apart from a negative sign) to the ratio of the absolute temperatures of the reservoirs:

$$\frac{Q_C}{Q_H} = -\frac{T_C}{T_H}. \qquad (16.8)$$

Combining this equation with the general expression for the thermal efficiency of *any* heat engine, $e = 1 + Q_C/Q_H$ (Equation 16.4), we find that the thermal efficiency of the Carnot engine depends only on the temperatures T_H and T_C:

Thermal efficiency of Carnot engine

$$e_{\text{Carnot}} = 1 - \frac{T_C}{T_H} = \frac{T_H - T_C}{T_H}. \qquad (16.9)$$

This surprisingly simple result says that the thermal efficiency of the Carnot engine depends only on the ratio T_C/T_H of the absolute temperatures of the two heat reservoirs. Note that the temperatures must be *absolute* (Kelvin). The efficiency is large when the temperature *difference* is large, and it is very small when the temperatures are nearly equal. The efficiency can never be exactly 1 unless $T_C = 0$. As we shall see later, this, too, is impossible.

EXAMPLE 16.2 **A Carnot engine**

A Carnot engine takes 2000 J of heat from a reservoir at 500 K, does some work, and discards some heat to a reservoir at 350 K. How much work does it do, how much heat is discarded, and what is its efficiency?

SOLUTION

SET UP AND SOLVE From Equation 16.8, the heat Q_C discarded by the engine is

$$Q_C = -Q_H \frac{T_C}{T_H} = -(2000 \text{ J}) \frac{350 \text{ K}}{500 \text{ K}}$$
$$= -1400 \text{ J}.$$

Then, from the first law, the work W done by the engine is

$$W = Q_H + Q_C = 2000 \text{ J} + (-1400 \text{ J})$$
$$= 600 \text{ J}.$$

From Equation 16.9, the thermal efficiency is

$$e_{\text{Carnot}} = 1 - \frac{T_C}{T_H} = 1 - \frac{350 \text{ K}}{500 \text{ K}} = 0.30 = 30\%.$$

Alternatively, from the basic definition of thermal efficiency,

$$e = \frac{W}{Q_H} = \frac{600 \text{ J}}{2000 \text{ J}} = 0.30 = 30\%.$$

REFLECT The efficiency of any engine is always less than 1. For the Carnot engine, the greater the ratio of T_H to T_C, the greater is the efficiency.

Practice Problem: What temperature T_H would the high-temperature reservoir need to have in order to increase the efficiency to $e = 0.50$? *Answer: 700 K.*

Carnot Refrigerator

Because each step in the Carnot cycle is reversible, the *entire cycle* may be reversed, converting the engine into a refrigerator. The performance coefficient of the Carnot refrigerator is obtained by combining the general definition of K, Equation 16.7, with Equation 16.8 for the Carnot cycle. We first rewrite Equation 16.7 as

$$K = \frac{|Q_C|}{|Q_H| - |Q_C|} = \frac{|Q_C|/|Q_H|}{1 - |Q_C|/|Q_H|}.$$

From Equation 16.8, $|Q_C|/|Q_H| = T_C/T_H$. Substituting this into the previous equation, we find that

$$K_{\text{Carnot}} = \frac{T_C}{T_H - T_C}. \qquad (16.10)$$

When the temperature difference $T_H - T_C$ is small, K is much larger than 1; in this case, a lot of heat can be "pumped" from the lower to the higher temperature with only a little expenditure of work. But the greater the temperature difference, the smaller K is and the more work is required to transfer a given quantity of heat.

EXAMPLE 16.3 **A Carnot refrigerator**

If the Carnot engine described in Example 16.2 is run backwards as a refrigerator, what is its performance coefficient?

Continued

SOLUTION

SET UP AND SOLVE We use the values from Example 16.2, with all the signs reversed because the cycle is run backwards:

$$Q_C = +1400 \text{ J}, \quad Q_H = -2000 \text{ J}, \quad W = -600 \text{ J}.$$

From Equation 16.7, the performance coefficient K is

$$K = \frac{Q_C}{|W|} = \frac{1400 \text{ J}}{600 \text{ J}} = 2.33.$$

Because the cycle is a Carnot cycle, we may also use Equation 16.10:

$$K = \frac{T_C}{T_H - T_C} = \frac{350 \text{ K}}{500 \text{ K} - 350 \text{ K}} = 2.33.$$

REFLECT For a Carnot cycle, e and K depend only on the temperatures, as shown by Equations 16.9 and 16.10, and we don't need to calculate Q and W. For cycles containing irreversible processes, however, these equations are not valid, and more detailed calculations are necessary.

Practice Problem: Suppose you want to increase the performance coefficient K in Example 16.3. Would it be better to decrease T_H by 50 K or increase T_C by 50 K? *Answer:* Increase T_C.

The Carnot Cycle and the Second Law

We can prove that **no engine can be more efficient than a Carnot engine operating between the same two temperatures.** The key to the proof is the preceding observation that, since each step in the Carnot cycle is reversible, the *entire cycle* may be reversed. Run backward, the engine becomes a refrigerator. Suppose we have a super-efficient engine that is more efficient than a Carnot engine (Figure 16.12). The Carnot engine, run backward as a refrigerator with negative work $-W$, takes in heat Q_C from the cold reservoir and expels heat $|Q_H|$ to the hot reservoir. The super-efficient engine expels heat $|Q_C|$, but to do this, it takes in a greater amount of heat $Q_H + Q$. Its work output is then $W + Q$, and the net effect of the two machines together is to take a quantity of heat Q and convert it completely into work. Doing this, however, violates the "engine" statement of the second law. We could construct a similar argument that a super-efficient engine could be used to violate the "refrigerator" statement of the second law. (Note that we don't have to assume that the super-efficient engine is reversible.)

Thus, the statement that no engine can be more efficient than a Carnot engine is yet another equivalent statement of the second law of thermodynamics. It also follows directly that **all Carnot engines operating between the same two temperatures have the same efficiency, irrespective of the nature of the working substance.** Although we discussed Equation 16.9 in the context of a Carnot engine using an ideal gas as its working substance, that equation is in fact valid for *any* Carnot engine, no matter what its working substance.

Equation 16.9 also shows how to maximize the efficiency of a real engine, such as a steam turbine in an electric generating plant. The intake temperature T_H must be made as high as possible and the exhaust temperature T_C as low as possi-

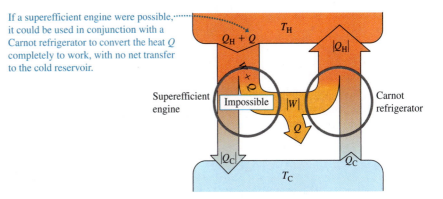

▲ **FIGURE 16.12** If there were a more efficient engine than a Carnot engine, it could be used in conjunction with a Carnot refrigerator to construct the impossible device shown here.

ble. The exhaust temperature can't be lower than the lowest temperature available for cooling the exhaust—usually the temperature of the air, or perhaps of river or lake water if this is available at the plant. The vapor pressures of all liquids increase rapidly with increasing temperature, so T_H is limited by the mechanical strength of the boiler. At 540°C $(1000°F)$, the vapor pressure of water is about 125×10^5 Pa (120 atm, or 1800 psi), and this is about the maximum practical pressure in large present-day steam boilers.

The unavoidable exhaust heat loss in electric power plants creates a serious environmental problem. When a lake or river is used for cooling, the temperature of the body of water may be raised several degrees. Such a temperature change has a severely disruptive effect on the overall ecological balance, since relatively small temperature changes can have significant effects on metabolic rates in plants and animals. Because **thermal pollution,** as this effect is called, is an inevitable consequence of the second law of thermodynamics, careful planning is essential to minimize the ecological impact of new power plants.

16.7 Entropy

The second law of thermodynamics, as we have stated it, is a rather strange beast, compared with many familiar physical laws. It is not an equation or a quantitative relationship, but rather a statement of *impossibility*. However, the second law *can* be stated as a quantitative relation by use of the concept of *entropy,* the subject of this section.

We've talked about several processes that proceed naturally in the direction of increasing disorder. Irreversible heat flow increases disorder because the molecules are initially sorted into hotter and cooler regions, and this sorting is lost when the system comes to thermal equilibrium. Adding heat to an object increases its disorder because it increases average molecular speeds and therefore the randomness of molecular motion. Free expansion of a gas increases its disorder because the molecules have greater randomness of *position* after the expansion than before. **Entropy** provides a *quantitative* measure of disorder.

Entropy and Disorder

To introduce the concept of entropy, let's consider an infinitesimal isothermal expansion of an ideal gas. We add heat Q and let the gas expand just enough so that the temperature remains constant. Because the internal energy of an ideal gas depends only on its temperature, the internal energy is also constant. Thus, from the first law, the work W done by the gas is equal to the heat Q added. That is,

$$Q = W = p \, \Delta V = \frac{nRT}{V} \Delta V \quad \text{and} \quad \frac{Q}{T} = nR \frac{\Delta V}{V}.$$

The gas is in a more disordered state after the expansion than before because the molecules are moving in a larger volume and have more randomness of position. The fractional change in volume $\Delta V/V$ is a measure of the increase in disorder, and it is proportional to the quantity Q/T. We introduce the symbol S for the entropy of the system in a particular state, and we *define* the entropy change $\Delta S = S_2 - S_1$ during a reversible isothermal process at absolute temperature T as follows:

Definition of entropy change in a reversible isothermal process
In a reversible isothermal process from state 1 to state 2, the change in entropy $\Delta S = S_2 - S_1$ of a system equals the heat Q added to or removed from the system, divided by the absolute temperature T:

$$\Delta S = S_2 - S_1 = \frac{Q}{T}. \tag{16.11}$$

Unit: Energy divided by temperature: J/K.

Conceptual Analysis 16.4   Increasing entropy

An amount of heat Q is added to each of two quantities of an ideal gas. Gas A is at absolute temperature T, and gas B is at absolute temperature $2T$. Each gas is allowed to expand isothermally. Which gas undergoes the greater entropy change?

A. gas A.
B. gas B.
C. Both have the same entropy change.

SOLUTION For each gas, the change in entropy for the isothermal process is the amount of heat added, divided by the absolute temperature. The absolute temperature for gas B is twice as great as that for gas A, and the two amounts of heat are the same. So the entropy change of B is half that of A. The correct answer is A.

EXAMPLE 16.4   Entropy change in melting ice

Compute the change in entropy of 1.00 kilogram of ice at 0°C when it is melted and converted to water at 0°C.

SOLUTION

SET UP The temperature T is constant at 273 K, and the heat of fusion Q needed to melt the ice is $Q = mL_f = (1.00 \text{ kg})(334 \times 10^3 \text{ J/kg}) = 334 \times 10^3 \text{ J}$.

SOLVE From Equation 16.11, the increase in entropy of the system is

$$\Delta S = \frac{Q}{T} = \frac{3.34 \times 10^5 \text{ J}}{273 \text{ K}} = 1220 \text{ J/K}.$$

REFLECT The entropy of the system increases as heat is added to it. The disorder increases because the water molecules in the liq-

uid state have more freedom to move than when they were locked in a crystal structure. In any *isothermal* reversible process, the change of entropy equals the heat transferred divided by the absolute temperature. When we refreeze the water, its entropy change is $\Delta S = -1220 \text{ J/K}$.

Practice Problem: When 50 g of liquid water at 0°C freezes into a 50 g ice cube at 0°C, what is the change in entropy of the material? *Answer:* $\Delta S = -61 \text{ J/K}$.

We can generalize the definition of entropy change to include *any* reversible process leading from one state to another, whether it is isothermal or not. We represent the process as a series of infinitesimal reversible steps. During a typical step, an infinitesimal quantity of heat ΔQ is added to the system at absolute temperature T. Then we sum the quotients $\Delta Q/T$ for the entire process. If T varies during the process, then carrying out this sum requires calculus.

Because entropy is a measure of the disorder of a system in any specific state, it must depend only on the current state of the system, not on its past history. We'll show later, by using the second law of thermodynamics, that this is indeed the case. When a system proceeds from an initial state with entropy S_1 to a final state with entropy S_2, the change in entropy $\Delta S = S_2 - S_1$, defined by Equation 16.11, does not depend on the path leading from the initial to the final state, but is the same for *all possible* processes leading from state 1 to state 2. Thus, if the entropy of one state of a system is assigned a certain value, the entropies of all other states of that system also have definite values, and those values depend only on the state of the system. We recall that *internal energy,* which was introduced in Chapter 15, also has this property, although entropy and internal energy are very different quantities.

As with internal energy, the preceding discussion does not define entropy itself, but only the *change* in entropy in any given process. To complete the definition, we may arbitrarily assign a value to the entropy of a system in one specified reference state and then calculate the entropy of any other state with reference to this assigned value.

EXAMPLE 16.5 An adiabatic expansion

A gas expands adiabatically and reversibly. What is its change in entropy?

SOLUTION

SET UP AND SOLVE In an adiabatic process, no heat enters or leaves the system; $Q = 0$, and there is *no* change in entropy: $\Delta S = 0$. Every *reversible* adiabatic process is a constant-entropy process.

REFLECT The increase in disorder resulting from the gas occupying a greater volume after the expansion is exactly balanced by the decrease in disorder associated with the lowered temperature of the gas and its decreased molecular speeds.

EXAMPLE 16.6 Entropy and the Carnot cycle

The Carnot engine in Example 16.2 (Section 16.6) takes 2000 J of heat from a reservoir at 500 K, does some work, and discards some heat to a reservoir at 350 K. Find the total entropy change in the engine during one cycle.

SOLUTION

SET UP AND SOLVE During the isothermal expansion at 500 K, the engine takes in 2000 J and its entropy change is

$$\Delta S = \frac{Q}{T} = \frac{2000 \text{ J}}{500 \text{ K}} = 4.0 \text{ J/K}.$$

During the isothermal compression at 350 K, the engine gives off 1400 J of heat and its entropy change is

$$\Delta S = \frac{-1400 \text{ J}}{350 \text{ K}} = -4.0 \text{ J/K}.$$

The entropy change of the engine during each of the two adiabatic processes is zero. Thus, the total entropy change in the engine during one cycle is $4.0 \text{ J/K} + 0 - 4.0 \text{ J/K} + 0 = 0$.

REFLECT The total entropy change of the two heat reservoirs is also zero, although each individual reservoir has a nonzero entropy change. This cycle contains no irreversible processes, and the total entropy change of the system and its surroundings is zero.

Entropy in Irreversible Processes

In an idealized reversible process involving only equilibrium states, the total entropy change of the system and its surroundings is zero. But all *irreversible* processes involve an increase in entropy. Unlike energy, entropy is *not* a conserved quantity. The entropy of an isolated system can change, but, as we shall see, it can never decrease. **An entropy increase occurs in every natural (irreversible) process if all systems taking part in the process are included.** Example 16.7 (below) illustrates an increase in entropy during an irreversible process in an isolated system.

The fact that entropy is a function only of the *state* of a system shows us how to compute entropy changes in *irreversible* (non-equilibrium) processes, to which Equation 16.11 is not applicable. We simply invent a path connecting the given initial and final states that *does* consist entirely of reversible equilibrium processes, and we compute the total entropy change for that alternative path. It is not the actual path, but the entropy change must be the same as that for the actual path.

EXAMPLE 16.7 A free expansion

A thermally insulated box is divided by a partition into two compartments, each having volume V. (Figure 16.13). Initially, one compartment contains n moles of an ideal gas at temperature T, and the other compartment is evacuated. We then break the partition, and the gas expands to fill both compartments. What is the entropy change in this free-expansion process?

Continued

SOLUTION

SET UP For the given process, $Q = 0$, $W = 0$, $\Delta U = 0$, and therefore (because the system is an ideal gas), $\Delta T = 0$. We might think that the entropy change is zero, because there is no heat exchange. But Equation 16.11 is valid only for *reversible* processes; the free expansion described here is *not* reversible, and there is an entropy change. To calculate ΔS, we use the fact that the entropy change depends only on the initial and final states. We can devise a *reversible* process having the same end points, use Equation 16.11 to calculate its entropy change, and thus determine the entropy change in the original process.

SOLVE The appropriate reversible process in this case is an isothermal expansion from V to $2V$ at temperature T, shown on the pV diagram of Figure 16.13c. The gas does work during this substitute expansion, so heat must be supplied to keep the internal energy constant. The total heat equals the total work, which is given by Equation 15.17:

$$W = Q = nRT \ln \frac{V_2}{V_1}.$$

Thus, the entropy change is

$$\Delta S = \frac{Q}{T} = \frac{nRT \ln \frac{2V}{V}}{T} = nR \ln 2,$$

and this is also the entropy change for the free expansion. For 1 mole,

$$\Delta S = (1 \text{ mol})[8.314 \text{ J}/(\text{mol} \cdot \text{K})](0.693)$$
$$= 5.76 \text{ J/K}.$$

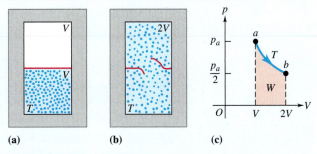

▲ **FIGURE 16.13** (a, b) Free expansion of an insulated ideal gas, an irreversible process. (c) An example of a reversible process that has the same initial and final states as the free expansion and thus has the same change in entropy.

REFLECT The entropy change ΔS is proportional to the amount of substance (n moles) and is independent of the temperature T (provided that it is constant). The increase in disorder is due to the increased randomness of position resulting from the increase in volume.

Practice Problem: In a free expansion, 2.00 mol of an ideal gas expands from an initial volume of 1.50 L to a final volume of 6.00 L. What is the increase in entropy? *Answer:* 23.1 J/K.

EXAMPLE 16.8 **Mixing hot and cold water**

Suppose 1.00 kg of water at 100°C is placed in thermal contact with 1.00 kg of water at 0°C. Find the approximate total change in entropy when the hot water cools to 99°C and the cold water warms to 1°C. Assume that the specific heat capacity of water is constant at 4190 J/(kg · K) over the given temperature range.

SOLUTION

SET UP AND SOLVE This process involves irreversible heat flow because of the temperature differences. The first 4190 J of heat transferred cools the hot water to 99°C (372 K) and warms the cold water from 0°C to 1°C (274 K). The net change of entropy of the hot water is approximately

$$\Delta S_{\text{hot}} = \frac{-4190 \text{ J}}{372 \text{ K}} = -11.3 \text{ J/K}.$$

(During this process, the temperature actually varies from 373 K to 372 K, but the resulting error in the calculation is very small.) The change of entropy of the cold water is approximately

$$\Delta S_{\text{cold}} = \frac{+4190 \text{ J}}{274 \text{ K}} = +15.3 \text{ J/K}.$$

The total change of entropy of the system during this process is

$$\Delta S_{\text{hot}} + \Delta S_{\text{cold}} = -11.3 \text{ J/K} + 15.3 \text{ J/K} = +4.0 \text{ J/K}.$$

Further increases in entropy occur as the system approaches thermal equilibrium at 50°C (323 K). Because the two temperatures vary continuously during this heat exchange, we would need methods of calculus to calculate the entropy changes precisely. It turns out that the total entropy change of the hot water is $\Delta S_{\text{hot}} = -603 \text{ J/K}$, the total entropy change of the cold water is $\Delta S_{\text{cold}} = 705 \text{ J/K}$, and the total entropy change of the system is $705 \text{ J/K} - 603 \text{ J/K} = 102 \text{ J/K}$.

REFLECT The total entropy of the final state is greater than that of the initial state, corresponding to increasing disorder as the distinction between the hotter and colder molecules gradually disappears. We could have reached the same end state by simply mixing the two quantities of water, also an irreversible process. The entropy depends only on the state of the system, and the total entropy change would be the same, 102 J/K.

Practice Problem: Repeat the approximate calculation for the total entropy change when the hot water cools from 76°C to 75°C and the cool water warms from 24°C to 25°C. *Answer:* 2.0 J/K.

▲ **Zero power.** Using knowledge of the principles of physics and energy conservation, architects are designing homes of the future that will consume no net power. These homes, called "zero-power homes," are designed to generate as much power as they consume, allowing their owners to have an annual energy bill of $0. They can do this by using a combination of rooftop photovoltaic cells, solar water heaters, state-of-the-art insulation, energy-efficient appliances, and computer-controlled power distribution systems. Some can even generate excess power, which can be sold back to "the grid" to generate income. Of course, this net negative energy use does not violate the laws of thermodynamics: The house is not a closed system. The negative energy use by these homes results from the efficient collection and use of the vast amounts of solar energy reaching the homes each year.

To complete the definition of the Kelvin scale, we assign the arbitrary value of 273.16 K to the temperature of the triple point of water. As we discussed in Section 15.2, this is the unique temperature at which gas, liquid, and solid phases of water can coexist in phase equilibrium. When a substance is taken around a Carnot cycle, the ratio of the heat absorbed to the heat rejected, $|Q_H|/|Q_C|$, is equal to the ratio of the temperatures of the reservoirs, *as expressed on the gas scale,* defined in Section 14.2. Since, on both scales, the triple point of water is chosen to be 273.16 K, it follows that *the Kelvin and the ideal-gas scales are identical.*

The zero point on the Kelvin scale is called **absolute zero.** There are theoretical reasons for believing that absolute zero cannot be attained experimentally, although temperatures below 10^{-7} K have been achieved. The more closely we approach absolute zero, the more difficult it is to get yet closer. Absolute zero can also be interpreted on a molecular level, although this must be done with some care. Because of quantum effects, it would *not* be correct to say that at $T = 0$, all molecular motion ceases. At absolute zero, the system has its *minimum* possible total energy (kinetic plus potential). One statement of the *third law of thermodynamics* is that it is impossible to reach absolute zero in a finite number of thermodynamic steps.

*16.9 Energy Resources: A Case Study in Thermodynamics

The laws of thermodynamics place very general limitations on the conversion of energy from one form to another. In these times of increasing energy demand and diminishing resources, such matters are of the utmost practical importance. We conclude this chapter with a brief discussion of a few energy-conversion systems, present and proposed.

About half of the electric power generated in the United States is obtained from coal-fired steam-turbine generating plants. Modern boilers can transfer about 80% to 90% of the heat of combustion of coal into steam. The theoretical maximum thermal efficiency of the turbine, given by Equation 16.9, is usually limited to about 0.55, and the actual efficiency is typically 90% of this value, or approximately 0.50. The efficiency of large generators in converting mechanical power to electrical power is very high, typically 99%. Thus, the overall thermal efficiency of such a plant is roughly (0.85)(0.50)(0.99), or at most about 40%.

The Tennessee Valley Authority's Kingston power plant has a generating capacity of about 1 gigawatt $(1000 \text{ MW, or } 10^9 \text{ W})$ of electrical power. The steam is heated to about 540°C $(1000°F)$ at a pressure of more than 120 atm $(1.24 \times 10^7 \text{ Pa, or } 1800 \text{ psi})$. The plant burns 14,000 tons of coal per day (13 million kg, the equivalent of 140 railroad cars), and the overall thermal efficiency is about 35%.

In a nuclear power plant, the heat that generates steam is supplied by a nuclear reaction rather than the chemical reaction of burning coal. The steam turbines in nuclear power plants have the same theoretical efficiency limit as those in coal-fired plants. At present, it is not practical to run nuclear reactors at temperatures and pressures as high as those in coal boilers, so the thermal efficiency of a nuclear plant is somewhat lower, typically 30%.

In the year 2005, about 20% of the world's electric power supply came from nuclear power plants. High construction costs, questions of public safety, and the problem of disposal of radioactive waste have slowed the development of additional nuclear power. However, there is also increasing concern about the environmental impact of coal-burning power plants. The health hazards of coal smoke are serious and well documented, and the burning of coal contributes to global warming through the greenhouse effect. It is important to manage our

Entropy and the Second Law

The mixing of substances at different temperatures and the flow of heat from a higher to a lower temperature are characteristic of *all* natural (that is, irreversible) processes. When all the entropy changes in the process are included, the increases in entropy are always found to be greater than the decreases. In the special case of a *reversible* process, the increases and decreases are equal. Thus, we can state the following general principle: **When all systems taking part in a process are included, the total entropy either remains constant or increases.** Put another way, **no process is possible in which the total entropy decreases when all systems taking part in the process are included.** This alternative statement of the second law of thermodynamics, in terms of entropy, is equivalent to the "engine" and "refrigerator" statements discussed earlier.

The increase of entropy in every natural (irreversible) process measures the increase in disorder, or randomness, in the universe associated with that process. Consider again the example of mixing hot and cold water. We *might* have used the hot and cold water as the high- and low-temperature reservoirs of a heat engine. While removing heat from the hot water and giving heat to the cold water, we could have obtained some mechanical work. But once the hot and cold water have been mixed and have come to a uniform temperature, this opportunity to convert heat to mechanical work is lost irretrievably. The lukewarm water will never *unmix* itself and separate into hotter and colder portions. No decrease in *energy* occurs when the hot and cold water are mixed. What has been lost is not *energy,* but *opportunity*—the opportunity to convert part of the heat from the hot water into mechanical work. When entropy increases, energy becomes less *available,* and the universe has become more random, or "run down."

▲ **Flower power.** Sometimes the second law of thermodynamics is invoked to make the process of evolution seem impossible. If the universe tends toward disorder (increasing entropy), how could complex life forms have evolved from simpler, primitive forms? Similarly, it would seem impossible that a complex plant or animal could develop from a single cell. The flaw in this reasoning is that neither the earth nor an organism is a closed system. The earth constantly receives energy from the sun (and radiates "waste" heat to space). Organisms also constantly consume energy and transform it to power their activities. You eat food; plants use sunlight; the embryo in a bird's egg uses chemical energy stored in the yolk and white. If you were sealed off from a suitable source of energy, you would quickly die—and then, indeed, entropy would take its course.

*16.8 The Kelvin Temperature Scale

When we studied temperature scales in Chapter 14, we expressed the need for a temperature scale that doesn't depend on the properties or behavior of any particular material. We can now use the Carnot cycle to define such a scale. We've learned that the efficiency of a Carnot engine operating between two heat reservoirs at absolute temperatures T_H and T_C is independent of the nature of the working substance and that it depends only on the temperatures. If several Carnot engines with different working substances operate between the same two heat reservoirs, their thermal efficiencies are all the same:

$$e = \frac{Q_H + Q_C}{Q_H} = 1 + \frac{Q_C}{Q_H}.$$

Therefore, the ratio Q_C/Q_H is the same for *all* Carnot engines operating between two given temperatures T_H and T_C.

Kelvin proposed that we *define* the ratio of the temperatures, T_C/T_H, to be equal to the magnitude of the ratio Q_C/Q_H of the quantities of heat absorbed and rejected:

$$\frac{T_C}{T_H} = \frac{|Q_C|}{|Q_H|} = -\frac{Q_C}{Q_H}. \tag{16.12}$$

Equation 16.12 looks identical to Equation 16.8, but there is a subtle and crucial difference. The temperatures in Equation 16.8 are based on an ideal-gas thermometer, as defined in Section 14.2. But Equation 16.12 *defines* a temperature scale that is based on the Carnot cycle and the second law of thermodynamics and is independent of the behavior of any particular substance. Thus, the **Kelvin temperature scale** is truly *absolute.*

called the *cold reservoir,* can absorb large amounts of discarded heat from the engine at a constant lower temperature T_C. In a steam-turbine system, the flames and hot gases in the boiler are the hot reservoir, and the cold water and air used to condense and cool the used steam are the cold reservoir.

We denote the quantities of heat transferred from the hot and cold reservoirs as Q_H and Q_C, respectively. A quantity of heat Q is positive when heat is transferred *from* a reservoir *into* the working substance. When heat leaves the working substance, Q is negative. Thus, in a heat engine, Q_H is positive, but Q_C is negative, representing heat *leaving* the working substance. When the working substance does positive work on its surroundings, W is positive. These sign conventions are consistent with the rules that we stated in Chapter 15; we'll continue to use those rules here. Sometimes it clarifies the relationships to state them in terms of the absolute values of the Q's and W's, because absolute values are always positive. When we do this, our notation will show it explicitly.

We can represent the energy transformations in a heat engine by the *energy-flow diagram* of Figure 16.1. The engine itself is represented by the circle. The amount of heat Q_H supplied to the engine by the hot reservoir is proportional to the width of the incoming "pipeline" at the top of the diagram. The width of the outgoing pipeline at the bottom is proportional to the magnitude $|Q_C|$ of the heat discarded. The branch line to the right represents that portion of the heat supplied that the engine converts to mechanical work W.

When an engine repeats the same cycle over and over, Q_H and Q_C represent the quantities of heat absorbed and rejected, respectively, by the engine *during one cycle;* Q_H is positive, Q_C negative. The *net* heat Q absorbed per cycle is

$$Q = Q_H + Q_C = |Q_H| - |Q_C|. \tag{16.1}$$

The useful output of the engine is the net work W done by the working substance; from the first law,

$$W = Q = Q_H + Q_C = |Q_H| - |Q_C|. \tag{16.2}$$

Ideally, we would like to convert *all* the heat Q_H into work; in that case, we would have $Q_H = W$ and $Q_C = 0$. Experience shows that this is impossible; there is always some heat wasted, and Q_C can never be zero. We define the **thermal efficiency** of an engine, denoted by e, as the quotient of W and Q_H:

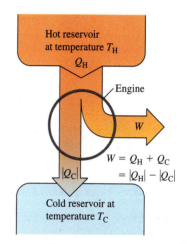

▲ **FIGURE 16.1** Schematic energy-flow diagram for a heat engine.

> **Thermal efficiency of a heat engine**
> The thermal efficiency of a heat engine is the useful work W done by the engine, divided by the heat input Q_H:
>
> $$e = \frac{W}{Q_H}. \tag{16.3}$$

The thermal efficiency e represents the fraction of Q_H that *is* converted to work. To put it another way, e is what you get, divided by what you pay for. This is always less than 1, an all-too-familiar experience! In terms of the flow diagram of Figure 16.1, the most efficient engine is the one for which the branch pipeline representing the work output is as wide as possible and the exhaust pipeline representing the heat thrown away is as narrow as possible.

When we substitute the two expressions for W given by Equation 16.2 into Equation 16.3, we get the following equivalent expressions for e:

$$e = \frac{W}{Q_H} = 1 + \frac{Q_C}{Q_H} = 1 - \frac{|Q_C|}{|Q_H|}. \tag{16.4}$$

Note that e is a quotient of two energy quantities and thus is a pure number, without units. Of course, we must always express W, Q_H, and Q_C in the same units.

PROBLEM-SOLVING STRATEGY 16.1 **Heat engines**

We suggest that you reread the strategy in Section 15.5; those suggestions are equally useful throughout the present chapter. The following points may need additional emphasis:

1. Be very careful with the sign conventions for W and the various Q's. W is positive when the system expands and does work, negative when it is compressed. Each Q is positive if it represents heat entering the working substance of the engine or other system, negative when heat leaves the system. When in doubt, use the first law, if possible, to check consistency. When you know that a quantity is negative, such as Q_C in the preceding discussion, it sometimes helps to write it as $Q_C = -|Q_C|$.
2. As always, unit consistency is essential. Be careful not to mix thermal units such as calories or Btu with mechanical quantities such as joules. We suggest you convert everything to joules whenever possible. Efficiency ratings of air conditioners are usually expressed in a peculiar mix of British and SI units; be careful!
3. Some problems deal with power rather than energy quantities. Power is work done per unit time $(P = W/t)$, and the rate of heat transfer (heat current) H is heat transferred per unit time $(H = Q/t)$. Sometimes it helps to ask, "What is W or Q in 1 second (or 1 hour)?"

EXAMPLE 16.1 **Fuel consumption in a truck**

A gasoline engine in a large truck takes in 2500 J of heat and delivers 500 J of mechanical work per cycle. The heat is obtained by burning gasoline with heat of combustion $L_c = 5.0 \times 10^4$ J/g. **(a)** What is the thermal efficiency of this engine? **(b)** How much heat is discarded in each cycle? **(c)** How much gasoline is burned during each cycle? **(d)** If the engine goes through 100 cycles per second, what is its power output in watts? In horsepower? **(e)** How much gasoline is burned per second? Per hour?

SOLUTION

SET UP It's often useful to make an energy-flow sketch for heat-engine problems; Figure 16.2 shows what we draw. We are given that $Q_H = 2500$ J and $W = 500$ J.

SOLVE Part (a): The thermal efficiency is found from Equation 16.3:

$$e = \frac{W}{Q_H} = \frac{500 \text{ J}}{2500 \text{ J}} = 0.20 = 20\%.$$

Part (b): From Equation 16.2, the heat Q_C discarded per cycle is the difference between the heat absorbed (Q_H) and the work W done by the engine:

$$W = Q_H + Q_C,$$
$$500 \text{ J} = 2500 \text{ J} + Q_C,$$
$$Q_C = -2000 \text{ J}.$$

Thus, 2000 J of heat leaves the engine during each cycle.

Part (c): Let m be the mass of gasoline burned during each cycle; then Q_H is m times the heat of combustion: $Q_H = mL_c$. Thus,

$$m = Q_H/L_c = (2500 \text{ J})/(5.0 \times 10^4 \text{ J/g}) = 0.050 \text{ g}.$$

▲ **FIGURE 16.2** Our sketch for this problem.

Part (d): The power P (rate of doing work) is the work per cycle multiplied by the number of cycles per second.

$$P = (500 \text{ J/cycle})(100 \text{ cycles/s}) = 50,000 \text{ W} = 50 \text{ kW}, \quad \text{or}$$
$$P = (50,000 \text{ W})(1 \text{ hp}/746 \text{ W}) = 67 \text{ hp}.$$

Part (e): The mass of gasoline burned per second is the mass burned per cycle multiplied by the number of cycles per second:

$$(0.050 \text{ g/cycle})(100 \text{ cycles/s}) = 5.0 \text{ g/s}.$$

Continued

development of energy resources so as to minimize the risks to human life and health, and nuclear power continues to receive attention as a future energy resource. We noted at the end of Section 16.6 that thermal pollution from both coal-fired and nuclear plants poses serious environmental problems.

Solar energy is an inviting possibility. The power per unit surface area in the sun's radiation (before it passes through the earth's atmosphere) is approximately $1.4 \, \text{kW/m}^2$. A maximum of about $1.0 \, \text{kW/m}^2$ reaches the surface of the earth on a clear day, and the average over a 24-hour period is about $0.2 \, \text{kW/m}^2$. This radiation can be collected and used to heat water for home use (Figure 16.14a).

A different solar-energy scheme is to use banks of photovoltaic (PV) cells (Figure 16.14b) for the direct conversion of solar energy to electricity. Such a system is not a heat engine in the usual sense and is not limited by the Carnot efficiency. There are other fundamental limitations on photocell efficiency, but 50% seems attainable in multilayer semiconductor photocells. Because of high capital costs, the price of PV-produced energy is about 25 cents per kilowatt-hour (compared with about 12 cents for conventional coal-fired steam-turbine plants). But such a system offers many advantages, such as lack of noise, lack of moving parts, minimal maintenance requirements, and freedom from pollution. Capital costs are likely to drop with improved technology, and PV systems continue to be studied and developed.

The energy of wind, fundamentally solar in origin, can be gathered and converted by "wind farms" of windmills (Figure 16.14c). The largest wind farms are located in California, where the state government encourages their use. However, the Great Plains states alone have enough wind energy to theoretically meet the electrical power needs of the entire United States. As with PV systems, the capital costs of such systems are higher than for coal-fired generating plants of equal capacity.

Biomass is yet another mechanism for using solar energy. Plants absorb solar energy and store it; the energy can be utilized by burning the plant matter or by using fermentation and distillation to make alcohols. Ethanol made from fermented corn is used in the United States as a gasoline additive, although its cost is not quite competitive at present crude-oil price levels. An important feature of biomass materials is that they take as much carbon dioxide out of the atmosphere when they grow as is released when they burn; thus, they don't contribute to the greenhouse effect.

An indirect scheme for the collection and conversion of solar energy would use the temperature gradient in the oceans. In the Caribbean, for example, the water temperature near the surface is about 25°C, and at a depth of a few hundred meters it is about 10°C. The second law of thermodynamics forbids cooling the ocean and converting the extracted heat completely into work, but there is nothing to forbid running a heat engine between those two temperatures. The thermodynamic efficiency would be very low (about 5%), but a vast supply of energy would be available.

The present level of activity in energy-conversion research in the United States is rather low in comparison to the period of the 1970s, when we experienced a serious energy shortage. The disadvantages of excessive reliance on nonrenewable resources such as oil—especially imported oil—are not hard to see. Critics have accused the U.S government of not having a coherent and effective energy policy compared with other countries. As we humans use up our available fossil-fuel resources, and as developing countries require more of the world's supply, we will certainly have to become more active in developing alternative energy sources. The principles of thermodynamics will play a central role in this development.

Absorber plate covered by glass

Tubes carry heated fluid

Insulation

(a) Passive solar collecting panel for home water heating

(b) A telephone powered by photovoltaic cells

(c) Windmills generating electricity

▲ **FIGURE 16.14** Three sources of energy other than the burning of fossil fuels.

SUMMARY

Directions of Thermodynamic Processes

(Section 16.1) Heat flows spontaneously from a hotter object to a cooler object, never the reverse. A **reversible process (equilibrium process)** is a process whose direction can be reversed by an infinitesimal change in the conditions of the process.

Heat Engines

(Section 16.2) A **heat engine** takes heat Q_H from a source, converts part of it to work W, and discards the remainder, $|Q_C|$, at a lower temperature. The **thermal efficiency** e of a heat engine is

$$e = \frac{W}{Q_H} = 1 + \frac{Q_C}{Q_H} = 1 - \frac{|Q_C|}{|Q_H|}. \qquad (16.4)$$

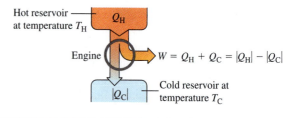

Internal Combustion Engines and Refrigerators

(Sections 16.3–16.4) An idealized model of the thermodynamic processes that take place in a gasoline engine is called the **Otto cycle.** The theoretical efficiency of the Otto cycle is about 50%; those of real gasoline engines are typically around 20%.

A **refrigerator** takes heat Q_C from a cold place, has an input W of work, and discards heat $|Q_H|$ at a warmer place. The **performance coefficient** K of a refrigerator is defined as

$$K = \frac{Q_C}{|W|} = \frac{|Q_C|}{|Q_H| - |Q_C|}. \qquad (16.7)$$

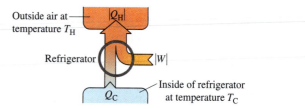

The Second Law of Thermodynamics

(Section 16.5) The **second law of thermodynamics** describes the directionality of natural thermodynamic processes. It can be stated in several equivalent forms. The "engine" statement is "No cyclic process can convert heat completely into work." The "refrigerator" statement is "No cyclic process can transfer heat from a cold place to a hotter place with no input of mechanical work."

The Carnot Engine: The Most Efficient Heat Engine

(Section 16.6) The **Carnot cycle** operates between two heat reservoirs at temperatures T_H and T_C and uses only reversible processes. Its thermal efficiency is

$$e_{\text{Carnot}} = 1 - \frac{T_C}{T_H} = \frac{T_H - T_C}{T_H}. \qquad (16.9)$$

No engine operating between the same two temperatures can be more efficient than a Carnot engine. All Carnot engines operating between the same two temperatures have the same efficiency.

Entropy

(Section 16.7) **Entropy** is a quantitative measure of the disorder of a system. The entropy change in a reversible isothermal process is $\Delta S = Q/T$ (Equation 16.11), where T is absolute temperature. The second law can be stated in terms of entropy: The entropy of an isolated system may increase, but can never decrease. When a system interacts with its surroundings, the total entropy of system and surroundings can never decrease.

Continued

*The Kelvin Temperature Scale

(**Section 16.8**) The Kelvin temperature scale is based on the efficiency of the Carnot cycle and is independent of the properties of any specific material. The zero point on the Kelvin scale is absolute zero.

*Energy Resources: A Case Study in Thermodynamics

(**Section 16.9**) About half of the electric power generated in the United States is obtained from coal-fired steam-turbine generating plants. The theoretical maximum thermal efficiency of the turbine, given by Equation 16.9, is usually limited to about 0.55, and the actual overall efficiency is about 40%. In a nuclear power plant, the heat that generates steam is supplied by a nuclear reaction rather than the chemical reaction of burning coal; the thermal efficiency of a nuclear plant is typically 30%. Other sources of energy include the sun, wind, ethanol from fermented corn, and thermal gradients in the ocean.

(**MP**) For instructor-assigned homework, go to www.masteringphysics.com

Conceptual Questions

1. Household refrigerators have arrays or coils of tubing on the outside, usually at the back or bottom. When the refrigerator is running, the tubing becomes quite hot. Where does the heat come from?
2. A chef tries to cool his kitchen on a hot day by leaving the door of the walk-in refrigerator open. Will this strategy work? Would the result be different if the chef used an old-fashioned icebox (which is simply an insulated box with a compartment holding ice)?
3. The overall efficiency of a car is a measure of how effectively it converts the energy of the gasoline it uses into miles driven, and we normally express it as miles per gallon of gas. This efficiency is limited by much more than the thermodynamic efficiency of the engine. What other things use up the energy of the gasoline to limit the overall efficiency of a car? Without altering a car's engine, in what ways could you improve its overall efficiency?
4. A growing plant creates a highly complex and organized structure out of simple materials, such as air, water, and minerals. Does this violate the second law of thermodynamics? What is the plant's ultimate source of energy?
5. Why must a room air conditioner be placed in a window rather than just set on the floor and plugged in? Why can a refrigerator be set on the floor and plugged in?
6. If you pour a cup of hot water into a cup of cold water, you wind up with two cups of lukewarm water. (a) Is this process reversible or irreversible? Why? (b) Does the entropy increase or decrease? How can this be, since no heat was added to (or removed from) the system?
7. How can the thermal conduction of heat from a hot object to a cold object increase entropy when the same amount of heat that flows out of the hot object flows into the cold one?
8. How can the free expansion of a gas into a vacuum increase entropy when no heat is added to (or subtracted from) this gas?
9. Does the second law of thermodynamics say that heat can *never* go from a cold object to a hot object? Explain.
10. The first law of thermodynamics is basically just a statement of the conservation of energy. Is the same true for the second law of thermodynamics?
11. In what ways is a heat pump different from (or similar to) a refrigerator?
12. Does the second law of thermodynamics say that entropy (disorder) can never decrease? Explain and give a few examples to illustrate your answer.
13. *Why* does heat *not* flow from a cold to a hot object? How does heat "know" it should obey the second law of thermodynamics? Explain by thinking about collisions at the molecular level.
14. Some people have suggested that the idea that life originated from nonliving materials violates the second law of thermodynamics because the molecules would have to go from a less ordered to a more ordered state, decreasing entropy. What is wrong with this argument?
15. What are the numerical limits on the value of the thermal efficiency e of a heat engine? On the coefficient of performance K of a refrigerator?
16. The first law of thermodynamics is sometimes paraphrased as "You can't get something for nothing." The second law has been paraphrased as "You can't even break even." Explain why these statements are good summaries of those two laws.
17. Would it be more economical to run a refrigerator with a high or a low coefficient of performance? Why?

Multiple-Choice Problems

1. An insulated box has a barrier that confines a gas to only one side of the box. The barrier springs a leak, allowing the gas to

flow and occupy both sides of the box. Which statement best describes the entropy of this system?

A. The entropy is greater in the first state, with all the gas on one side of the box.

B. The entropy is greater in the second state, with the gas on both sides of the box.

C. The entropy is the same in both states, since no heat was added to the gas and its temperature did not change.

2. Suppose you put a hot object in contact with a cold object and observe (with some wonder) that heat flows from the cold object to the hot object, making the cold one colder and the hot one hotter. This process would violate

A. only the first law of thermodynamics.

B. only the second law of thermodynamics.

C. both the first and the second laws of thermodynamics.

3. If you increase the temperature of *both* the hot and cold reservoirs of a Carnot heat engine by the *same* number of degrees, the efficiency of this engine

A. increases.

B. decreases.

C. does not change.

4. The thermal efficiency formula $e = W/Q_H$ is valid for which of the following heat engines? (There may be more than one correct choice.)

A. Carnot engine.

B. Otto engine.

C. Diesel engine.

D. Any other type of heat engine.

5. The thermal efficiency formula $e = 1 - T_C/T_H$ is valid for which of the following heat engines? (There may be more than one correct choice.)

A. Carnot engine.

B. Otto engine.

C. Diesel engine.

D. Any other type of heat engine.

6. A refrigerator consumes a certain amount of electrical energy in order to operate. In terms of the thermodynamic cycle of this refrigerator, this electrical energy is equal to

A. the work done on the gas.

B. the heat extracted from the food in the refrigerator.

C. the heat expelled into the room.

D. the sum of all three quantities in choices A, B, and C.

7. Which of the following statements is a consequence of the *second* law of thermodynamics? (There may be more than one correct choice.)

A. The efficiency of a heat engine can never be greater than unity.

B. Heat can never flow from a cold object to a hot object unless work is done.

C. Energy is conserved in all thermodynamics processes.

D. Even a perfect heat engine cannot convert all of the heat put into it to work.

8. You want to increase the efficiency of a Carnot heat engine by changing the temperature of either its hot or its cold reservoir by the same number of degrees ΔT. Which of the following choices will produce the *greater* increase in its thermodynamic efficiency?

A. Increase the temperature of the hot reservoir by ΔT.

B. Decrease the temperature of the cold reservoir by ΔT.

C. It would not matter. Both choices would produce the same increase in efficiency, since ΔT is the same for both.

9. Two Carnot heat engines operate between the same hot and cold reservoirs, but one has a greater compression ratio than the other. Which statement is true about their thermal efficiencies?

A. The one with the greater compression ratio will have the greater efficiency.

B. The one with the greater compression ratio will have the lesser efficiency.

C. Both will have the same efficiency.

10. You put 250 g of water into the freezer and make ice cubes. Which of the following statements is true about this process? (There may be more than one correct choice.)

A. The entropy of the water increases.

B. The entropy of the room increases.

C. The amount of heat removed from the water is equal to the amount of heat ejected into the room.

D. More heat is ejected into the room than was removed from the water.

E. The work done by the refrigerator is equal to the heat removed from the water.

11. If you mix cold milk with hot coffee in an insulated Styrofoam™ cup, which of the following things happen? (There may be more than one correct choice.)

A. The entropy of the milk increases.

B. The entropy of the coffee decreases by the same amount that the entropy of the milk increased.

C. The net entropy of the coffee–milk mixture does not change, because no heat was added to this system.

D. The entropy of the coffee–milk mixture increases.

12. Which of the following changes will *increase* the thermodynamic efficiency of an Otto cycle heat engine? (There may be more than one correct choice.)

A. Increase its compression ratio.

B. Use a gas with a larger γ.

C. Use a gas with a smaller γ.

D. Increase the temperature of its hot reservoir.

13. Which of the following statements about entropy is correct? (There may be more than one correct choice.)

A. As a car slows down due to road friction on its tires, the entropy of the world increases.

B. When water is evaporated to make steam, the water's entropy decreases.

C. When water freezes to make ice, the water's entropy decreases.

D. When simple molecules are combined to make complex DNA, the entropy of those molecules increases.

14. If we run an ideal Carnot heat engine in *reverse,* which of the following statements about it must be true? (There may be more than one correct choice.)

A. Heat enters the gas at the cold reservoir and goes out of the gas at the hot reservoir.

B. The amount of heat transferred at the hot reservoir is equal to the amount of heat transferred at the cold reservoir.

C. It is able to perform a net amount of useful work, such as pumping water from a well, during each cycle.

D. It can transfer heat from a cold object to a hot object.

15. Which of the following processes would be a *violation* of the second law of thermodynamics? (There may be more than one correct choice.)

A. All the kinetic energy of an object is transformed into heat.

B. All the heat put into the operating gas of a heat engine during one cycle is transformed into work.

C. A refrigerator removes 100 cal of heat from milk while using only 75 cal of electrical energy to operate.

D. A heat engine does 25 J of work while expelling only 10 J of heat to the cold reservoir.

Problems

16.2 Heat Engines

1. • If a heat engine is 33% efficient, how much work can you get by putting in 150 J of heat, and how much heat do you waste, during each cycle?

2. • Each cycle, a certain heat engine expels 250 J of heat when you put in 325 J of heat. Find the efficiency of this engine and the amount of work you get out of the 325 J heat input.

3. • A diesel engine performs 2200 J of mechanical work and discards 4300 J of heat each cycle. (a) How much heat must be supplied to the engine in each cycle? (b) What is the thermal efficiency of the engine?

4. • An aircraft engine takes in 9000 J of heat and discards 6400 J each cycle. (a) What is the mechanical work output of the engine during one cycle? (b) What is the thermal efficiency of the engine?

5. • **A gasoline engine.** A gasoline engine takes in 1.61×10^4 J of heat and delivers 3700 J of work per cycle. The heat is obtained by burning gasoline with a heat of combustion of 4.60×10^4 J/g. (a) What is the thermal efficiency of the engine? (b) How much heat is discarded in each cycle? (c) What mass of fuel is burned in each cycle? (d) If the engine goes through 60.0 cycles per second, what is its power output in kilowatts? In horsepower?

6. • A gasoline engine has a power output of 180 kW (about 241 hp). Its thermal efficiency is 28.0%. (a) How much heat must be supplied to the engine per second? (b) How much heat is discarded by the engine per second?

7. • A certain nuclear power plant has a mechanical power output (used to drive an electric generator) of 330 MW. Its rate of heat input from the nuclear reactor is 1300 MW. (a) What is the thermal efficiency of the system? (b) At what rate is heat discarded by the system?

8. •• Figure 16.15 shows a pV diagram for a heat engine that uses 1.40 moles of an ideal diatomic gas. (a) How much heat goes into this gas per cycle, and where in the cycle does it occur? (b) How much heat is ejected by the gas per cycle, and where does it occur? (c) How much work does this engine do each cycle? (d) What is the thermal efficiency of the engine?

9. •• The pV diagram in Figure 16.16 shows a cycle of a heat engine that uses 0.250 mole of an ideal gas having $\gamma = 1.40$. The curved part ab of the cycle is adiabatic. (a) Find the pressure of the gas at point a. (b) How much heat enters this gas per cycle, and where does it happen? (c) How much heat leaves this gas in a cycle, and where does it occur? (d) How much work does this engine do in a cycle? (e) What is the thermal efficiency of the engine?

16.3 Internal Combustion Engines

10. • An Otto engine uses a gas having $\gamma = 1.40$ and has a compression ratio of 8.50. (a) Out of every gallon of fuel this engine burns, what fraction is wasted (i.e., produces energy that is wasted)? (b) If you could change the compression ratio to 10.0 instead, what percentage of the fuel would be wasted?

11. • What compression ratio r must an Otto cycle have to achieve an ideal efficiency of 65.0% if the gas used in the chamber has $\gamma = 1.40$?

12. • For an Otto engine with a compression ratio of 7.50, you have your choice of using an ideal monatomic or ideal diatomic gas. Which one would give you greater efficiency? Calculate the efficiency in both cases to find out.

13. •• For an Otto cycle with a compression ratio of 9.50 and a gas having $\gamma = 1.40$, the temperature of the gasoline–air mixture when it enters the cylinder is 22.0°C (point a of Figure 16.4). (a) What is the temperature at the end of the compression stroke (point b)? (b) The initial pressure of the gasoline–air mixture (point a) is 8.50×10^4 Pa, slightly below atmospheric pressure. What is the pressure at the end of the compression stroke?

16.4 Refrigerators

14. • In one cycle, a freezer uses 785 J of electrical energy in order to remove 1750 J of heat from its freezer compartment at 10°F. (a) What is the coefficient of performance of this freezer? (b) How much heat does it expel into the room during this cycle?

15. • A refrigerator has a coefficient of performance of 2.10. Each cycle, it absorbs 3.40×10^4 J of heat from the cold reservoir. (a) How much mechanical energy is required each cycle to operate the refrigerator? (b) During each cycle, how much heat is discarded to the high-temperature reservoir?

16. • A window air-conditioner unit absorbs 9.80×10^4 J of heat per minute from the room being cooled and in the same period deposits 1.44×10^5 J of heat into the outside air. What is the power consumption of the unit in watts?

17. •• A freezer has a coefficient of performance of 2.40. The freezer is to convert 1.80 kg of water at 25.0°C to 1.80 kg of ice at −5.0°C in 1 hour. (a) What amount of heat must be removed from the water at 25.0°C to convert it to ice at −5.0°C? (b) How much electrical energy is consumed by the freezer during this hour? c) How much wasted heat is rejected to the room in which the freezer sits?

18. •• A refrigerator has a coefficient of performance of 2.25, runs on an input of 95 W of electrical power, and keeps its inside compartment at 5°C. If you put a dozen 1.0 L plastic bottles of water at 31°C into this refrigerator, how long will it take for them to be cooled down to 5°C? (Ignore any heat that leaves the plastic.)

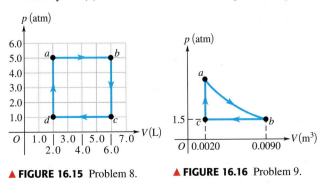

▲ **FIGURE 16.15** Problem 8. ▲ **FIGURE 16.16** Problem 9.

16.6 The Carnot Engine: The Most Efficient Heat Engine

19. • A Carnot engine whose high-temperature reservoir is at 620 K takes in 550 J of heat at this temperature in each cycle and gives up 335 J to the low-temperature reservoir. (a) How much mechanical work does the engine perform during each cycle? (b) What is the temperature of the low-temperature reservoir? (c) What is the thermal efficiency of the cycle?

20. • A heat engine is to be built to extract energy from the temperature gradient in the ocean. If the surface and deepwater temperatures are 25°C and 8°C, respectively, what is the maximum efficiency such an engine can have?

21. • You are designing a heat engine to waste as little heat as possible. Your project plans require a thermal efficiency of 67%, and the lowest temperature available to you is 65°F. (a) What should be the temperature of the hot reservoir (in °F) to achieve the required efficiency? (b) For every 100 J of heat absorbed at the hot reservoir, how much work will it do and how much will be wasted per cycle?

22. • A Carnot engine is operated between two heat reservoirs at temperatures of 520 K and 300 K. (a) If the engine receives 6.45 kJ of heat energy from the reservoir at 520 K in each cycle, how many joules per cycle does it reject to the reservoir at 300 K? (b) How much mechanical work is performed by the engine during each cycle? (c) What is the thermal efficiency of the engine?

23. • A Carnot refrigerator is operated between two heat reservoirs at temperatures of 320 K and 270 K. (a) If the refrigerator receives 415 J of heat energy from the reservoir at 270 K during each cycle, how many joules of heat energy does it deliver to the reservoir at 320 K? (b) If the refrigerator goes through 165 cycles each minute, what power input is required to operate the refrigerator? (c) What is the coefficient of performance of the refrigerator?

24. •• An ice-making machine operates in a Carnot cycle. It takes heat from water at 0.0°C and rejects heat to a room at 24.0°C. Suppose that 85.0 kg of water at 0.0°C are converted to ice at 0.0°C. (a) How much heat is rejected to the room? (b) How much energy must be supplied to the device?

25. •• A Carnot freezer that runs on electricity removes heat from the freezer compartment, which is at −10°C, and expels it into the room at 20°C. You put an ice-cube tray containing 375 g of water at 18°C into the freezer. (a) What is the coefficient of performance of this freezer? (b) How much energy is needed to freeze this water? (c) How much electrical energy must be supplied to the freezer to freeze the water? (d) How much heat does the freezer expel into the room while freezing the ice?

26. •• Fill in the details of the derivation of Equation 16.8.

27. •• The *pV* diagram in Figure 16.17 shows a general Carnot cycle for an engine, with the hot and cold thermal reservoir segments identified. Segments *ab* and *cd* are isothermal, while the other two are adiabatic. (a) If this engine is used as a heat engine, what is the direction of the cycle, clockwise or coun-

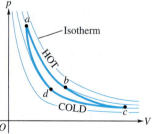

▲ **FIGURE 16.17** Problem 27.

terclockwise? In which segments does heat enter the gas, and in which ones does it leave the gas? (b) If the engine is used as a refrigerator, what is the direction of the cycle? In which segments does heat enter the gas, and in which ones does it leave the gas? Also, which segments take place at the inside of the refrigerator, and which ones occur in the air of the room in which the refrigerator is operating? (c) If the engine is used as a heat pump–air conditioner, what is the direction of the cycle, and in which segments does heat enter the gas and in which ones does it leave the gas? Which segments take place inside of the house and which ones occur outside? (d) If the engine is used as a heat pump–house heater, what is the direction of the cycle? In which segments does heat enter the gas and in which ones does it leave the gas? Which segments take place inside of the house and which ones occur outside?

28. •• (a) Show that the efficiency e of a Carnot engine and the coefficient of performance K of a Carnot refrigerator are related by $K = (1 - e)/e$. The engine and refrigerator operate between the same hot and cold reservoirs. (b) What is K for the limiting values $e \rightarrow 1$ and $e \rightarrow 0$? Explain.

16.7 Entropy

29. • A sophomore with nothing better to do adds heat to 0.350 kg of ice at 0.00°C until it is all melted. (a) What is the change in entropy of the water? (b) The source of the heat is a very massive body at a temperature of 25.0°C. What is the change in entropy of this body? (c) What is the total change in entropy of the water and the heat source?

30. • A 4.50 kg block of ice at 0.00°C falls into the ocean and melts. The average temperature of the ocean is 3.50°C, including all the deep water. By how much does the melting of this ice change the entropy of the world? Does it make it larger or smaller? (*Hint:* Do you think that the ocean will change temperature appreciably as the ice melts?)

31. •• A heat engine in a large factory operates between a cold reservoir at 20.0°C and a hot reservoir at 250°C and does 375 J of work per cycle. But this engine is only 75% as efficient as a Carnot engine operating between these same temperatures. (a) How much heat per cycle is exchanged at the hot and cold reservoirs? (b) By how much does this engine change the entropy of the factory during each cycle?

32. •• A large factory furnace maintained at 175°C at its outer surface is wrapped in an insulating blanket of thermal conductivity 0.055 W/(m · K) which is thick enough that the outer surface of the insulation is at 42°C while heat escapes from the furnace at a steady rate of 125 W for each square meter of surface area. By how much does each square meter of the furnace change the entropy of the factory every second?

33. •• A 10.0 L gas tank containing 3.20 moles of ideal He gas at 20.0°C is placed inside a completely evacuated insulated bell jar of volume 35.0 L. A small hole in the tank allows the He to leak out into the jar until the gas reaches a final equilibrium state with no more leakage. (a) What is the change in entropy of this system due to the leaking of the gas? (b) Is the process reversible or irreversible? How do you know?

34. • You mix 100.0 g of water at 85.0°C with the same amount of water at 20.0°C in an insulated beaker. (a) Calculate the approximate change in entropy of the water when the hot water has cooled by 1.00°C and the cool water has warmed up

by the same amount. (b) Is this process reversible or irreversible? How do you know?

35. •• You pour 0.500 kg of water at 98.0°C into the same amount of water at 92.0°C in an insulated flask. Calculate the approximate change in entropy of the water by the time the temperature of this mixture has stabilized. (*Hint:* Use Example 16.8 as a guide and proceed in 1.00°C increments until you reach the final temperature.)

36. •• Three moles of an ideal gas undergo a reversible isothermal compression at 20.0°C. During this compression, 1850 J of work is done on the gas. What is the change in entropy of the gas?

37. •• **Entropy change due to driving.** Premium gasoline produces 1.23×10^8 J of heat per gallon when it is burned at a temperature of approximately 400°C (although the amount can vary with the fuel mixture). If the car's engine is 25% efficient, three-fourths of that heat is expelled into the air, typically at 20°C. If your car gets 35 miles per gallon of gas, by how much does the car's engine change the entropy of the world when you drive 1.0 mile? Does it decrease or increase it?

38. •• **Entropy of metabolism.** An average sleeping person
BIO metabolizes at a rate of about 80 W by digesting food or burning fat. Typically, 20% of this energy goes into bodily functions, such as cell repair, pumping blood, and other uses of mechanical energy, while the rest goes to heat. Most people get rid of all of this excess heat by transferring it (by conduction and the flow of blood) to the surface of the body, where it is radiated away. The normal internal temperature of the body (where the metabolism takes place) is 37°C, and the skin is typically 7 C° cooler. By how much does the person's entropy change per second due to this heat transfer?

39. •• **Entropy change from digesting fat.** Digesting fat pro-
BIO duces 9.3 food calories per gram of fat, and typically 80% of this energy goes to heat when metabolized. The body then moves all this heat to the surface by a combination of thermal conductivity and motion of the blood. The internal temperature of the body (where digestion occurs) is normally 37°C, and the surface is usually about 30°C. By how much does the digestion and metabolism of a 2.50 g pat of butter change your body's entropy? Does it increase or decrease?

*16.9 Energy Resources: A Case Study in Thermodynamics

40. • **Solar collectors.** A well-insulated house of moderate size in a temperate climate requires an average heat input rate of 20.0 kW. If this heat is to be supplied by a solar collector with an average (night and day) energy input of 300 W/m² and a collection efficiency of 60.0%, what area of solar collector is required?

41. • **Solar power.** A solar power plant is to be built with an average power output capacity of 2500 MW in a location where the average power from the sun's radiation is 200 W/m² at the earth's surface. What land area (in km² and mi²) must the solar collectors occupy if they are (a) photocells with 42% efficiency, (b) mirrors that generate steam for a turbine-generator unit with an overall efficiency of 21%?

42. •• **Fossil-fuel versus solar heating.** (a) A homeowner in a cold climate has a coal-burning furnace that burns 9000 kg (about 10 tons) of coal during a winter. The heat of combustion of coal is 2.50×10^7 J/kg. If stack losses (the amount of

heat energy lost up the chimney) are 20%, how many joules were actually used to heat the house? (b) The homeowner proposes to install a solar heating system, heating large tanks of water by solar radiation during the summer and using the stored energy for heating during the winter. Find the dimensions required of the storage tank, assuming it to be a cube, for it to store a quantity of energy equal to that computed in part (a). Assume that the water is raised to 49.0°C (120°F) in the summer and cooled to 27.0°C (80°F) in the winter.

43. •• **Solar water heater.** A solar water heater for domestic hot-water supply uses solar collecting panels with a collection efficiency of 50% in a location where the average solar-energy input is 200 W/m². If the water comes into the house at 15.0°C and is to be heated to 60.0°C, what volume of water can be heated per hour if the area of the collector is 30.0 m²?

General Problems

44. •• A certain heat engine operating on a Carnot cycle absorbs 150 J of heat per cycle at its hot reservoir at 135°C and has a thermal efficiency of 22.0%. (a) How much work does this engine do per cycle? (b) How much heat does the engine waste each cycle? (c) What is the temperature of the cold reservoir? (d) By how much does the engine change the entropy of the world each cycle? (e) What mass of water could this engine pump per cycle from a well 35.0 m deep?

45. •• A heat engine takes 0.350 mol of an ideal diatomic gas around the cycle shown in the *pV* diagram of Figure 16.18. Process $1 \to 2$ is at constant volume, process $2 \to 3$ is adiabatic, and process $3 \to 1$ is at a constant pressure of 1.00 atm. The value of γ for this gas is 1.40. (a) Find the pressure and volume at points 1, 2, and 3. (b) Calculate Q, W, and ΔU for each of the three processes. (c) Find the net work done by the gas in the cycle. (d) Find the net heat flow into the engine in one cycle. (e) What is the thermal efficiency of the engine? How does this efficiency compare with that of a Carnot-cycle engine operating between the same minimum and maximum temperatures T_1 and T_2?

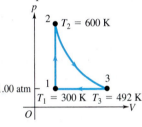

▲ **FIGURE 16.18** Problem 45.

46. •• As a budding mechanical engineer, you are called upon to design a Carnot engine that has 2.00 moles of He gas (see Table 15.4) as its working substance and that operates from a high-temperature reservoir at 500°C. The engine is to lift a 15.0 kg weight 2.00 m per cycle, using 500 J of heat input. The gas in the engine chamber can have a minimum volume of 5.00 L during the cycle. (a) Draw a *pV* diagram for this cycle. In your diagram, show where heat enters and leaves the gas. (b) What must be the temperature of the cold reservoir? (c) What is the thermal efficiency of the engine? (d) How much heat energy does this engine waste per cycle? (e) What is the maximum pressure that the gas chamber will have to withstand?

47. •• The Kwik-Freez Appliance Co. wants you to design a food freezer that will keep the freezing compartment at −5.0°C and will operate in a room at 20.0°C. The freezer is to make 5.00

kg of ice at 0.0°C, starting with water at 20.0°C. Find the least possible amount of electrical energy needed to make this ice and the smallest possible amount of heat expelled into the room.

48. •• An ideal Carnot engine operates between 500°C and 100°C with a heat input of 250 J per cycle. What minimum number of cycles are necessary for the engine to lift a 500 kg rock through a height of 100 m?

49. •• A cylinder contains oxygen gas (O_2) at a pressure of 2.00 atm. The volume is 4.00 L, and the temperature is 300 K. Assume that the oxygen may be treated as an ideal gas. The oxygen is carried through the following processes:
   (i)   Heated at constant pressure from the initial state (state 1) to state 2, which has $T = 450$ K.
   (ii) Cooled at constant volume to 250 K (state 3).
   (iii) Compressed at constant temperature to a volume of 4.00 L (state 4).
   (iv) Heated at constant volume to 300 K, which takes the system back to state 1.
   (a) Show these four processes in a pV diagram, giving the numerical values of p and V in each of the four states. (b) Calculate Q and W for each of the four processes. (c) Calculate the net work done by the oxygen. (d) What is the efficiency of this device as a heat engine? How does this efficiency compare with that of a Carnot-cycle engine operating between the same minimum and maximum temperatures of 250 K and 450 K?

50. •• **Human entropy.** A person having skin of surface area
   BIO 1.85 m^2 and temperature 30.0°C is resting in an insulated room where the ambient air temperature is 20.0°C. In this state, a person gets rid of excess heat by radiation. By how much does the person change the entropy of the air in this room each second? (Recall that the room radiates back into the person and that the emissivity of the skin is 1.00.)

51. •• **Heat pump.** A certain heat pump operates on a Carnot cycle. (a) If the outside temperature in winter is −5.0°C and the inside temperature is 17.0°C, how many joules of heat will the heat pump deliver to the inside for each joule of electrical energy used to run the unit, assuming an ideal Carnot cycle? (b) Suppose you have the option of burning natural gas to heat your home, rather than using a heat pump. How much energy would the natural gas have to provide in order to deliver the same amount of heat to the inside of the house as in part (a)?

52. •• **Heat pump.** Consider a Carnot heat pump delivering heat to the inside of a house to maintain it at 68°F. Show that the heat pump delivers *less* heat for each joule of electrical energy used to operate the unit as the outside temperature *decreases*. Notice that this behavior is opposite to that of a Carnot *heat engine*, which becomes *more* efficient as the difference in reservoir temperatures increases.

53. •• **A human engine.** You decide to use your body as a Carnot
   BIO heat engine. The operating gas is in a tube with one end in your mouth (where the temperature is 37.0°C) and the other end at the surface of your skin, at 30.0°C. (a) What is the maximum efficiency of such a heat engine? Would it be a very use-

ful engine? (b) Suppose you want to use this human engine to lift a 2.50 kg box from the floor to a tabletop 1.20 m above the floor. How much must you increase the gravitational potential energy and how much heat input is needed to accomplish this? (c) How many 350 calorie (those are *food* calories, remember) candy bars must you eat to lift the box in this way? Recall that 80% of the food energy goes into heat.

54. •• A Carnot engine whose low-temperature reservoir is at −90.0° C has an efficiency of 40.0%. An engineer is assigned the problem of increasing the engine's efficiency to 45.0%. (a) By how many Celsius degrees must the temperature of the high-temperature reservoir be increased if the temperature of the low-temperature reservoir remains constant? (b) By how many Celsius degrees must the temperature of the low-temperature reservoir be decreased if that of the high-temperature reservoir remains constant?

55. •• **Entropy change due to the sun.** Our sun radiates from a surface at 5800 K (with an emissivity of 1.0) into the near vacuum of space, which is at a temperature of 3 K. (a) By how much does our sun change the entropy of the universe every second? (Consult Appendix F.) (b) Is the process reversible or irreversible? Is your answer to part (a) consistent with this conclusion? Explain.

56. •• One end of a copper rod is immersed in boiling water at 100°C and the other end in an ice–water mixture at 0°C. The sides of the rod are insulated. After steady-state conditions have been achieved in the rod, 0.160 kg of ice melts in a certain time interval. For this time interval, find (a) the entropy change of the boiling water, (b) the entropy change of the ice–water mixture, (c) the entropy change of the copper rod, (d) the total entropy change of the entire system.

57. •• The pV diagram in Figure 16.19 shows a heat engine operating on 0.850 mol of H_2. (See Table 15.4.) Segment ca is isothermal. (a) Without doing any calculations, identify the segments during which heat enters the gas and those during which it leaves the gas. Explain your reasoning. (b) Find the thermal efficiency of this heat engine, treating the gas as ideal.

▲ **FIGURE 16.19** Problem 57.

58. •• Calculate the coefficient of performance of the engine in the previous problem if it is run in reverse, as a refrigerator.

59. •• A certain heat engine absorbs 125.0 J of heat each cycle at its hot reservoir of 145°C and ejects 107.5 J at its cold reservoir of 10.0°C. (a) How much work does this engine perform per cycle? (b) What is the thermal efficiency of the engine? (c) What entropy change does the engine produce each cycle? (d) What is the greatest efficiency possible between the two heat reservoirs?

MATHEMATICS REVIEW

A study of physics at the level of this textbook requires some basic math skills. The relevant math topics are summarized in this appendix. We strongly recommend that you review this material and become comfortable with it as quickly as possible so that, during your physics course, you can focus on the physics concepts and procedures that are being introduced, without being distracted by unfamiliarity with the math that is being used.

A.1 Exponents

Exponents are used frequently in physics. When we write 3^4, the superscript 4 is called an **exponent** and the **base number** 3 is said to be raised to the fourth power. The quantity 3^4 is equal to $3 \times 3 \times 3 \times 3 = 81$. Algebraic symbols can also be raised to a power—for example, x^4. There are special names for the operation when the exponent is 2 or 3. When the exponent is 2, we say that the quantity is **squared;** thus, x^2 is x squared. When the exponent is 3, the quantity is **cubed;** hence, x^3 is x cubed.

Note that $x^1 = x$, and the exponent is typically not written. Any quantity raised to the zero power is defined to be unity (that is, 1). Negative exponents are used for reciprocals: $x^{-4} = 1/x^4$. The exponent can also be a fraction, as in $x^{1/4}$. The exponent $\frac{1}{2}$ is called a **square root,** and the exponent $\frac{1}{3}$ is called a **cube root.**

For example, $\sqrt{6}$ can also be written as $6^{1/2}$. Most calculators have special keys for calculating numbers raised to a power—for example, a key labeled y^x or one labeled x^2.

Exponents obey several simple rules, which follow directly from the meaning of raising a quantity to a power:

1. When the product of two powers of the same quantity are multiplied, the exponents are added:

$$(x^n)(x^m) = x^{n+m}.$$

   For example, $(3^2)(3^3) = 3^5 = 243$. To verify this result, note that $3^2 = 9$, $3^3 = 27$, and $(9)(27) = 243$.

   A special case of this rule is $(x^n)(x^{-n}) = x^{n+(-n)} = x^0 = 1$.

2. The product of two different base numbers raised to the same power is the product of the base numbers, raised to that power:

$$(x^n)(y^n) = (xy)^n.$$

   For example, $(2^4)(3^4) = 6^4 = 1296$. To verify this result, note that $2^4 = 16$, $3^4 = 81$, and $(16)(81) = 1296$.

3. When a power is raised to another power, the exponents are multiplied:

$$(x^n)^m = x^{nm}.$$

   For example, $(2^2)^3 = 2^6 = 64$. To verify this result, note that $2^2 = 4$, so $(2^2)^3 = (4)^3 = 64$.

If the base number is negative, it is helpful to know that $(-x)^n = (-1)^n x^n$, and $(-1)^n$ is $+1$ if n is even and -1 if n is odd.

EXAMPLE A.1 **Simplifying an exponential expression**

Simplify the expression $\dfrac{x^3 y^{-3} x y^{4/3}}{x^{-4} y^{1/3} (x^2)^3}$, and calculate its numerical value when $x = 6$ and $y = 3$.

SOLUTION

SET UP AND SOLVE We simplify the expression as follows:

$$\frac{x^3 x}{x^{-4}(x^2)^3} = x^3 x^1 x^4 x^{-6} = x^{3+1+4-6} = x^2; \quad \frac{y^{-3} y^{4/3}}{y^{1/3}} = y^{-3+\frac{4}{3}-\frac{1}{3}} = y^{-2}.$$

Therefore,

$$\frac{x^3 y^{-3} x y^{4/3}}{x^{-4} y^{1/3} (x^2)^3} = x^2 y^{-2} = x^2 \left(\frac{1}{y}\right)^2 = \left(\frac{x}{y}\right)^2.$$

For $x = 6$ and $y = 3$, $\left(\dfrac{x}{y}\right)^2 = \left(\dfrac{6}{3}\right)^2 = 4$.

If we evaluate the original expression directly, we obtain

$$\frac{x^3 y^{-3} x y^{4/3}}{x^{-4} y^{1/3} (x^2)^3} = \frac{(6^3)(3^{-3})(6)(3^{4/3})}{(6^{-4})(3^{1/3})([6^2]^3)} = \frac{(216)(1/27)(6)(4.33)}{(1/1296)(1.44)(46{,}656)} = 4.00,$$

which checks.

REFLECT This example demonstrates the usefulness of the rules for manipulating exponents.

EXAMPLE A.2 **Solving an exponential expression for the base number**

If $x^4 = 81$, what is x?

SOLUTION

SET UP AND SOLVE We raise each side of the equation to the $\frac{1}{4}$ power: $(x^4)^{1/4} = (81)^{1/4}$. $(x^4)^{1/4} = x^1 = x$, so $x = (81)^{1/4}$ and $x = +3$ or $x = -3$. Either of these values of x gives $x^4 = 81$.

REFLECT Notice that we raised *both sides* of the equation to the $\frac{1}{4}$ power. As explained in Section A.3, an operation performed on both sides of an equation does not affect the equation's validity.

A.2 Scientific Notation and Powers of 10

In physics, we frequently encounter very large and very small numbers, and it is important to use the proper number of significant figures when expressing a quantity. We can deal with both these issues by using **scientific notation,** in which a quantity is expressed as a decimal number with one digit to the left of the decimal point, multiplied by the appropriate power of 10. If the power of 10 is positive, it is the number of places the decimal point is moved to the right to obtain the fully written-out number. For example, $6.3 \times 10^4 = 63{,}000$. If the power of 10 is negative, it is the number of places the decimal point is moved to the left to obtain the fully written-out number. For example, $6.56 \times 10^{-3} = 0.00656$. In going from 6.56 to 0.00656, the decimal point is moved three places to the left, so 10^{-3} is the correct power of 10 to use when the number is written in scientific notation. Most calculators have keys for expressing a number in either decimal (floating-point) or scientific notation.

When two numbers written in scientific notation are multiplied (or divided), multiply (or divide) the decimal parts to get the decimal part of the result, and multiply (or divide) the powers of 10 to get the power-of-10 portion of the result. You may have to adjust the location of the decimal point in the answer to express it in scientific notation. For example,

$$(8.43 \times 10^8)(2.21 \times 10^{-5}) = (8.43 \times 2.21)(10^8 \times 10^{-5})$$
$$= (18.6) \times (10^{8-5}) = 18.6 \times 10^3$$
$$= 1.86 \times 10^4.$$

Similarly,

$$\frac{5.6 \times 10^{-3}}{2.8 \times 10^{-6}} = \left(\frac{5.6}{2.8}\right) \times \left(\frac{10^{-3}}{10^{-6}}\right) = 2.0 \times 10^{-3-(-6)} = 2.0 \times 10^3.$$

Your calculator can handle these operations for you automatically, but it is important for you to develop good "number sense" for scientific notation manipulations.

A.3 Algebra

Solving Equations

Equations written in terms of symbols that represent quantities are frequently used in physics. An **equation** consists of an equals sign and quantities to its left and to its right. Every equation tells us that the combination of quantities on the left of the equals sign has the same value as (is equal to) the combination on the right of the equals sign. For example, the equation $y + 4 = x^2 + 8$ tells us that $y + 4$ has the same value as $x^2 + 8$. If $x = 3$, then the equation $y + 4 = x^2 + 8$ says that $y = 13$.

Often, one of the symbols in an equation is considered to be the *unknown,* and we wish to solve for the unknown in terms of the other symbols or quantities. For example, we might wish to solve the equation $2x^2 + 4 = 22$ for the value of x. Or we might wish to solve the equation $x = v_0 t + \frac{1}{2}at^2$ for the unknown a in terms of x, t, and v_0.

An equation can be solved by using the following rule:

An equation remains true if any operation performed on one side of the equation is also performed on the other side. The operations could be (a) adding or subtracting a number or symbol, (b) multiplying or dividing by a number or symbol, or (c) raising each side of the equation to the same power.

EXAMPLE A.3 **Solving a numerical equation**

Solve the equation $2x^2 + 4 = 22$ for x.

SOLUTION

SET UP AND SOLVE First we subtract 4 from both sides. This gives $2x^2 = 18$. Then we divide both sides by 2 to get $x^2 = 9$. Finally, we raise both sides of the equation to the $\frac{1}{2}$ power. (In other words, we take the square root of both sides of the equation.) This gives $x = \pm\sqrt{9} = \pm 3$. That is, $x = +3$ or $x = -3$. We can verify our answers by substituting our result back into the original equation: $2x^2 + 4 = 2(\pm 3)^2 + 4 = 2(9) + 4 = 18 + 4 = 22$, so $x = \pm 3$ does satisfy the equation.

REFLECT Notice that a square root always has *two* possible values, one positive and one negative. For instance, $\sqrt{4} = \pm 2$, because $(2)(2) = 4$ and $(-2)(-2) = 4$. Your calculator will give you only a positive root; it's up to you to remember that there are actually two. Both roots are correct mathematically, but in a physics problem only one may represent the answer. For instance, if you can get dressed in $\sqrt{4}$ minutes, the only physically meaningful root is 2 minutes!

EXAMPLE A.4 **Solving a symbolic equation**

Solve the equation $x = v_0t + \frac{1}{2}at^2$ for a.

SOLUTION

SET UP AND SOLVE We subtract v_0t from both sides. This gives $x - v_0t = \frac{1}{2}at^2$.

Now we multiply both sides by 2 and divide both sides by t^2, giving $a = \dfrac{2(x - v_0t)}{t^2}$.

REFLECT As we've indicated, it makes no difference whether the quantities in an equation are represented by variables (such as x, v, and t) or by numerical values.

The Quadratic Formula

Using the methods of the previous subsection, we can easily solve the equation $ax^2 + c = 0$ for x:

$$x = \pm\sqrt{\frac{-c}{a}}.$$

For example, if $a = 2$ and $c = -8$, the equation is $2x^2 - 8 = 0$ and the solution is

$$x = \pm\sqrt{\frac{-(-8)}{2}} = \pm\sqrt{4} = \pm 2.$$

The equation $ax^2 + bx = 0$ is also easily solved by factoring out an x on the left side of the equation, giving $x(ax + b) = 0$. (To *factor out* a quantity means to isolate it so that the rest of the expression is either multiplied or divided by that quantity.) The equation $x(ax + b) = 0$ is true (that is, the left side equals zero) if either $x = 0$ or $x = -\frac{b}{a}$. Those are the equation's two solutions. For example, if $a = 2$ and $b = 8$, the equation is $2x^2 + 8x = 0$ and the solutions are $x = 0$ and $x = -\frac{8}{2} = -4$.

But if the equation is in the form $ax^2 + bx + c = 0$, with a, b, and c all nonzero, we cannot use our standard methods to solve for x. Such an equation is called a **quadratic equation,** and its solutions are expressed by the **quadratic formula:**

Quadratic formula

For a quadratic equation in the form $ax^2 + bx + c = 0$, where a, b, and c are real numbers and $a \neq 0$, the solutions are given by the quadratic formula:

$$x = \frac{-b \pm \sqrt{b^2 - 4ac}}{2a}$$

In general, a quadratic equation has two roots (solutions). But if $b^2 - 4ac = 0$, then the two roots are equal. By contrast, if $b^2 < 4ac$, then $b^2 - 4ac$ is negative, and both roots are complex numbers and cannot represent physical quantities. In such a case, the original quadratic equation has mathematical solutions, but no physical solutions.

EXAMPLE A.5 **Solving a quadratic equation**

Find the values of x that satisfy the equation $2x^2 - 2x = 24$.

SOLUTION

SET UP AND SOLVE First we write the equation in the standard form $ax^2 + bx + c = 0$: $2x^2 - 2x - 24 = 0$. Then $a = 2$, $b = -2$, and $c = -24$. Next, the quadratic formula gives the two roots as

$$x = \frac{-(-2) \pm \sqrt{(-2)^2 - 4(2)(-24)}}{(2)(2)} = \frac{+2 \pm \sqrt{4 + 192}}{4} = \frac{2 \pm 14}{4},$$

so $x = 4$ or $x = -3$. If x represents a physical quantity that takes only nonnegative values, then the negative root $x = -3$ is nonphysical and is discarded.

REFLECT As we've mentioned, when an equation has more than one mathematical solution or root, it's up to *you* to decide whether one or the other or both represent the true physical answer. (If neither solution seems physically plausible, you should review your work.)

Simultaneous Equations

If a problem has two unknowns—for example, x and y—then it takes two independent equations in x and y (that is, two equations for x and y, where one equation is not simply a multiple of the other) to determine their values uniquely. Such equations are called **simultaneous equations** (because you solve them together). A typical procedure is to solve one equation for x in terms of y and then substitute the result into the second equation to obtain an equation in which y is the only unknown. You then solve this equation for y and use the value of y in either of the original equations in order to solve for x. In general, to solve for n unknowns, we must have n independent equations.

EXAMPLE A.6 **Solving two equations in two unknowns**

Solve the following pair of equations for x and y:

$$x + 4y = 14$$
$$3x - 5y = -9$$

SOLUTION

SET UP AND SOLVE The first equation gives $x = 14 - 4y$. Substituting this for x in the second equation yields, successively, $3(14 - 4y) - 5y = -9$, $42 - 12y - 5y = -9$, and $-17y = -51$. Thus, $y = \frac{-51}{-17} = 3$. Then $x = 14 - 4y = 14 - 12 = 2$. We can verify that $x = 2$, $y = 3$ satisfies both equations.

An alternative approach is to multiply the first equation by -3, yielding $-3x - 12y = -42$. Adding this to the second equation gives, successively, $3x - 5y + (-3x) + (-12y) = -9 + (-42)$, $-17y = -51$, and $y = 3$, which agrees with our previous result.

REFLECT As shown by the alternative approach, simultaneous equations can be solved in more than one way. The basic method we describe is easy to keep straight; other methods may be quicker, but may require more insight or forethought. Use the method you're comfortable with.

A pair of equations in which all quantities are symbols can be combined to eliminate one of the common unknowns.

EXAMPLE A.7 **Solving two symbolic equations in two unknowns**

Use the equations $v = v_0 + at$ and $x = v_0 t + \frac{1}{2}at^2$ to obtain an equation for x that does not contain a.

SOLUTION

SET UP AND SOLVE We solve the first equation for a:

$$a = \frac{v - v_0}{t}.$$

We substitute this expression into the second equation:

$$x = v_0 t + \frac{1}{2}\left(\frac{v - v_0}{t}\right)t^2 = v_0 t + \frac{1}{2}vt - \frac{1}{2}v_0 t = \frac{1}{2}v_0 t + \frac{1}{2}vt = \left(\frac{v_0 + v}{2}\right)t.$$

REFLECT When you solve a physics problem, it's often best to work with symbols for all but the final step of the problem. Once you've arrived at the final equation, you can plug in numerical values and solve for an answer.

A.4 Logarithmic and Exponential Functions

The base-10 logarithm, or **common logarithm** (log), of a number y is the power to which 10 must be raised to obtain y: $y = 10^{\log y}$. For example, $1000 = 10^3$, so $\log(1000) = 3$; you must raise 10 to the power 3 to obtain 1000. Most calculators have a key for calculating the log of a number.

Sometimes we are given the log of a number and are asked to find the number. That is, if $\log y = x$ and x is given, what is y? To solve for y, write an equation in which 10 is raised to the power equal to either side of the original equation: $10^{\log y} = 10^x$. But $10^{\log y} = y$, so $y = 10^x$. In this case, y is called the **antilog** of x. For example, if $\log y = -2.0$, then $y = 10^{-2.0} = 1.0 \times 10^{-2.0} = 0.010$.

The log of a number is positive if the number is greater than 1. The log of a number is negative if the number is less than 1, but greater than zero. The log of zero or of a negative number is not defined, and $\log 1 = 0$.

Another base that occurs frequently in physics is the quantity $e = 2.718. \ldots$ The **natural logarithm** (ln) of a number y is the power to which e must be raised to obtain y: $y = e^{\ln y}$. If $x = \ln y$, then $y = e^x$. Most calculators have keys for $\ln x$ and for e^x. For example, $\ln 10.0 = 2.30$, and if $\ln x = 3.00$, then $x = 10^{3.00} = 20.1$. Note that $\ln 1 = 0$.

Logarithms with any choice of base, including base 10 or base e, obey several simple and useful rules:

1. $\log(ab) = \log a + \log b$.

2. $\log\left(\dfrac{a}{b}\right) = \log a - \log b$.

3. $\log(a^n) = n \log a$.

A particular example of the second rule is

$$\log\left(\frac{1}{a}\right) = \log 1 - \log a = -\log a,$$

since $\log 1 = 0$.

EXAMPLE A.8   **Solving a logarithmic equation**

If $\frac{1}{2} = e^{-\alpha T}$, solve for T in terms of α.

SOLUTION

SET UP AND SOLVE We take the natural logarithm of both sides of the equation: $\ln\left(\frac{1}{2}\right) = -\ln 2$ and $\ln\left(e^{-\alpha T}\right) = -\alpha T$. The equation thus becomes $-\alpha T = -\ln 2$, and it follows that $T = \frac{\ln 2}{\alpha}$.

REFLECT The equation $y = e^{\alpha x}$ expresses y in terms of the exponential function $e^{\alpha x}$. The general rules for exponents in Appendix A.1 apply when the base is e, so $e^x e^y = e^{x+y}$, $e^x e^{-x} = e^{x+(-x)} = e^0 = 1$, and $(e^x)^2 = e^{2x}$.

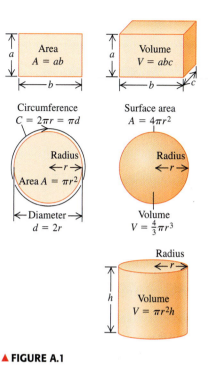

▲ **FIGURE A.1**

A.5 Areas and Volumes

Figure A.1 illustrates the formulas for the areas and volumes of common geometric shapes:

- A rectangle with length a and width b has area $A = ab$.
- A rectangular solid (a box) with length a, width b, and height c has volume $V = abc$.
- A circle with radius r has diameter $d = 2r$, circumference $C = 2\pi r = \pi d$, and area $A = \pi r^2 = \pi d^2/4$.
- A sphere with radius r has surface area $A = 4\pi r^2$ and volume $V = \frac{4}{3}\pi r^3$.
- A cylinder with radius r and height h has volume $V = \pi r^2 h$.

A.6 Plane Geometry and Trigonometry

Following are some useful results about angles:

1. Interior angles formed when two straight lines intersect are equal. For example, in Figure A.2, the two angles θ and ϕ are equal.
2. When two parallel lines are intersected by a diagonal straight line, the alternate interior angles are equal. For example, in Figure A.3, the two angles θ and ϕ are equal.
3. When the sides of one angle are each perpendicular to the corresponding sides of a second angle, then the two angles are equal. For example, in Figure A.4, the two angles θ and ϕ are equal.
4. The sum of the angles on one side of a straight line is 180°. In Figure A.5, $\theta + \phi = 180°$.
5. The sum of the angles in any triangle is 180°.

Similar Triangles

Triangles are **similar** if they have the same shape, but different sizes or orientations. Similar triangles have equal angles and equal ratios of corresponding sides. If the two triangles in Figure A.6 are similar, then $\theta_1 = \theta_2$, $\phi_1 = \phi_2$, $\gamma_1 = \gamma_2$, and $\dfrac{a_1}{a_2} = \dfrac{b_1}{b_2} = \dfrac{c_1}{c_2}$.

If two similar triangles have the same size, they are said to be **congruent.** If triangles are congruent, one can be rotated to where it can be placed precisely on top of the other.

Right Triangles and Trig Functions

In a **right triangle,** one angle is 90°. Therefore, the other two acute angles (*acute* means less than 90°) have a sum of 90°. In Figure A.7, $\theta + \phi = 90°$. The side

Interior angles formed when two straight lines intersect are equal:
$$\theta = \phi$$

▲ **FIGURE A.2**

When two parallel lines are intersected by a diagonal straight line, the alternate interior angles are equal:
$$\theta = \phi$$

▲ **FIGURE A.3**

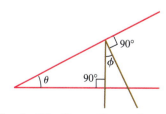

When the sides of one angle are each perpendicular to the corresponding sides of a second angle, then the two angles are equal:
$$\theta = \phi$$

▲ **FIGURE A.4**

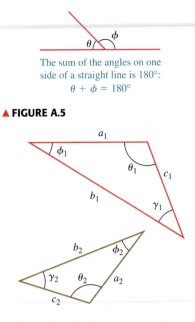

The sum of the angles on one side of a straight line is 180°:
$$\theta + \phi = 180°$$

▲ FIGURE A.5

Two similar triangles: Same shape but not necessarily the same size

▲ FIGURE A.6

Hypotenuse c, ϕ, a, 90°, θ, b

For a right triangle:
$$\theta + \phi = 90°$$
$$c^2 = a^2 + b^2 \text{ (Pythagorean theorem)}$$

▲ FIGURE A.7

opposite the right angle is called the **hypotenuse** (side c in the figure). In a right triangle, the square of the length of the hypotenuse equals the sum of the squares of the lengths of the other two sides. For the triangle in Figure A.7, $c^2 = a^2 + b^2$. This formula is called the **Pythagorean theorem.**

If two right triangles have the same value for one acute angle, then the two triangles are similar and have the same ratio of corresponding sides. This true statement allows us to define the functions **sine, cosine,** and **tangent** that are ratios of a pair of sides. These functions, called **trigonometric** functions or **trig functions,** depend only on one of the angles in the right triangle. For an angle θ, these functions are written $\sin\theta$, $\cos\theta$, and $\tan\theta$.

In terms of the triangle in Figure A.7, the sine, cosine, and tangent of the angle θ are as follows:

$$\sin\theta = \frac{\text{opposite side}}{\text{hypotenuse}} = \frac{a}{c}.$$

$$\cos\theta = \frac{\text{adjacent side}}{\text{hypotenuse}} = \frac{b}{c}.$$

$$\tan\theta = \frac{\text{opposite side}}{\text{adjacent side}} = \frac{a}{b}.$$

Note that $\tan\theta = \frac{\sin\theta}{\cos\theta}$. For angle ϕ, $\sin\phi = \frac{b}{c}$, $\cos\phi = \frac{a}{c}$, and $\tan\phi = \frac{b}{a}$.

In physics, angles are expressed in either degrees or radians, where π radians $= 180°$. (For more on radians, see Section 9.1.) Most calculators have a key for switching between degrees and radians. Always be sure that your calculator is set to the appropriate angular measure.

Inverse trig functions, denoted, for example, by $\sin^{-1}x$ (or $\arcsin x$), have a value equal to the angle that has the value x for the trig function. For example, $\sin 30° = 0.500$, so $\sin^{-1}(0.500) = \arcsin(0.500) = 30°$. Note that $\sin^{-1}x$ does *not* mean $\frac{1}{\sin x}$.

EXAMPLE A.9 **Using trigonometry I**

A right triangle has one angle of 30° and one side with length 8.0 cm, as shown in Figure A.8. What is the angle ϕ, and what are the lengths x and y of the other two sides of the triangle?

▲ FIGURE A.8

SOLUTION

SET UP AND SOLVE $\phi + 30° = 90°$, so $\phi = 60°$.

$$\tan 30° = \frac{8.0\text{ cm}}{x}, \text{ so } x = \frac{8.0\text{ cm}}{\tan 30°} = 13.9\text{ cm.}$$

To find y, we use the Pythagorean theorem: $y^2 = (8.0\text{ cm})^2 + (13.9\text{ cm})^2$, so $y = 16.0$ cm.

Or we can say $\sin 30° = 8.0\text{ cm}/y$, so $y = 8.0\text{ cm}/\sin 30° = 16.0$ cm, which agrees with the previous result.

REFLECT Notice how we used the Pythagorean theorem in combination with a trig function. You will use these tools constantly in physics, so make sure that you can employ them with confidence.

EXAMPLE A.10 **Using trigonometry II**

A right triangle has two sides with lengths as specified in Figure A.9. What is the length x of the third side of the triangle, and what is the angle θ, in degrees?

▲ **FIGURE A.9**

SOLUTION

SET UP AND SOLVE The Pythagorean theorem applied to this right triangle gives $(3.0\ \text{m})^2 + x^2 = (5.0\ \text{m})^2$, so $x = \sqrt{(5.0\ \text{m})^2 - (3.0\ \text{m})^2} = 4.0\ \text{m}$. (Since x is a length, we take the positive root of the equation.) We also have

$$\cos\theta = \frac{3.0\ \text{m}}{5.0\ \text{m}} = 0.600, \text{ so } \theta = \cos^{-1}(0.600) = 53.1°.$$

REFLECT In this case, we knew the lengths of two sides, but none of the acute angles, so we used the Pythagorean theorem first and then an appropriate trig function.

In a right triangle, all angles are in the range from 0° to 90°, and the sine, cosine, and tangent of the angles are all positive. This must be the case, since the trig functions are ratios of lengths. But for other applications, such as finding the components of vectors, calculating the oscillatory motion of a mass on a spring, or describing wave motion, it is useful to define the sine, cosine, and tangent for angles outside that range. Graphs of $\sin\theta$ and $\cos\theta$ are given in Figure A.10. The values of $\sin\theta$ and $\cos\theta$ vary between $+1$ and -1. Each function is periodic, with a period of 360°. Note the range of angles between 0° and 360° for which each function is positive and negative. The two functions $\sin\theta$ and $\cos\theta$ are 90° out of phase (that is, out of step). When one is zero, the other has its maximum magnitude.

For any triangle (see Figure A.11)—in other words, not necessarily a right triangle—the following two relations apply:

1. $\dfrac{\sin\alpha}{a} = \dfrac{\sin\beta}{b} = \dfrac{\sin\gamma}{c}$ (law of sines).

2. $c^2 = a^2 + b^2 - 2ab\cos\gamma$ (law of cosines).

Some of the relations among trig functions are called trig identities. The following table lists only a few, those most useful in introductory physics:

▲ **FIGURE A.10**

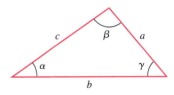

▲ **FIGURE A.11**

Useful trigonometric identities

$\sin(-\theta) = -\sin(\theta)$ ($\sin\theta$ is an odd function)
$\cos(-\theta) = \cos(\theta)$ ($\cos\theta$ is an even function)
$\sin 2\theta = 2\sin\theta\cos\theta$
$\cos 2\theta = \cos^2\theta - \sin^2\theta = 2\cos^2\theta - 1 = 1 - 2\sin^2\theta$
$\sin(\theta \pm \phi) = \sin\theta\cos\phi \pm \cos\theta\sin\phi$
$\cos(\theta \pm \phi) = \cos\theta\cos\phi \mp \sin\theta\sin\phi$
$\sin(180° - \theta) = \sin\theta$
$\cos(180° - \theta) = -\cos\theta$
$\sin(90° - \theta) = \cos\theta$
$\cos(90° - \theta) = \sin\theta$

THE INTERNATIONAL SYSTEM OF UNITS

The Système International d'Unités, abbreviated SI, is the system developed by the General Conference on Weights and Measures and adopted by nearly all the industrial nations of the world. The following material is adapted from B. N. Taylor, ed., National Institute of Standards andTechnology Spec. Pub. 811 (U.S. Govt. Printing Office, Washington, DC, 1995). See also **http://physics.nist.gov/cuu**

Quantity	Name of unit	Symbol	Equivalent units
SI base units			
length	meter	m	
mass	kilogram	kg	
time	second	s	
electric current	ampere	A	
thermodynamic temperature	kelvin	K	
amount of substance	mole	mol	
luminous intensity	candela	cd	
SI derived units			
area	square meter	m^2	
volume	cubic meter	m^3	
frequency	hertz	Hz	s^{-1}
mass density (density)	kilogram per cubic meter	kg/m^3	
speed, velocity	meter per second	m/s	
angular velocity	radian per second	rad/s	
acceleration	meter per second squared	m/s^2	
angular acceleration	radian per second squared	rad/s^2	
force	newton	N	$kg \cdot m/s^2$
pressure (mechanical stress)	pascal	Pa	N/m^2
kinematic viscosity	square meter per second	m^2/s	
dynamic viscosity	newton-second per square meter	$N \cdot s/m^2$	
work, energy, quantity of heat	joule	J	$N \cdot m$
power	watt	W	J/s
quantity of electricity	coulomb	C	$A \cdot s$
potential difference, electromotive force	volt	V	$J/C, W/A$
electric field strength	volt per meter	V/m	N/C
electric resistance	ohm	Ω	V/A
capacitance	farad	F	$A \cdot s/V$
magnetic flux	weber	Wb	$V \cdot s$
inductance	henry	H	$V \cdot s/A$
magnetic flux density	tesla	T	Wb/m^2
magnetic field strength	ampere per meter	A/m	
magnetomotive force	ampere	A	
luminous flux	lumen	lm	$cd \cdot sr$
luminance	candela per square meter	cd/m^2	
illuminance	lux	lx	lm/m^2
wave number	1 per meter	m^{-1}	
entropy	joule per kelvin	J/K	
specific heat capacity	joule per kilogram-kelvin	$J/(kg \cdot K)$	
thermal conductivity	watt per meter-kelvin	$W/(m \cdot K)$	

Quantity	Name of unit	Symbol	Equivalent units
radiant intensity	watt per steradian	W/sr	
activity (of a radioactive source)	becquerel	Bq	s^{-1}
radiation dose	gray	Gy	J/kg
radiation dose equivalent	sievert	Sv	J/kg
SI supplementary units			
plane angle	radian	rad	
solid angle	steradian	sr	

Definitions of SI Units

meter (m) The *meter* is the length equal to the distance traveled by light, in vacuum, in a time of 1/299,792,458 second.

kilogram (kg) The *kilogram* is the unit of mass; it is equal to the mass of the international prototype of the kilogram. (The international prototype of the kilogram is a particular cylinder of platinum-iridium alloy that is preserved in a vault at Sèvres, France, by the International Bureau of Weights and Measures.)

second (s) The *second* is the duration of 9,192,631,770 periods of the radiation corresponding to the transition between the two hyperfine levels of the ground state of the cesium-133 atom.

ampere (A) The *ampere* is that constant current that, if maintained in two straight parallel conductors of infinite length, of negligible circular cross section, and placed 1 meter apart in vacuum, would produce between these conductors a force equal to 2×10^{-7} newton per meter of length.

kelvin (K) The *kelvin,* unit of thermodynamic temperature, is the fraction 1/273.16 of the thermodynamic temperature of the triple point of water.

ohm (V) The *ohm* is the electric resistance between two points of a conductor when a constant difference of potential of 1 volt, applied between these two points, produces in this conductor a current of 1 ampere, this conductor not being the source of any electromotive force.

coulomb (C) The *coulomb* is the quantity of electricity transported in 1 second by a current of 1 ampere.

candela (cd) The *candela* is the luminous intensity, in a given direction, of a source that emits monochromatic radiation of frequency 540×10^{12} hertz and that has a radiant intensity in that direction of 1/683 watt per steradian.

mole (mol) The *mole* is the amount of substance of a system that contains as many elementary entities as there are carbon atoms in 0.012 kg of carbon 12. The elementary entities must be specified and may be atoms, molecules, ions, electrons, other particles, or specified groups of such particles.

newton (N) The *newton* is that force that gives to a mass of 1 kilogram an acceleration of 1 meter per second per second.

joule (J) The *joule* is the work done when the point of application of a constant force of 1 newton is displaced a distance of 1 meter in the direction of the force.

watt (W) The *watt* is the power that gives rise to the production of energy at the rate of 1 joule per second.

volt (V) The *volt* is the difference of electric potential between two points of a conducting wire carrying a constant current of 1 ampere, when the power dissipated between these points is equal to 1 watt.

weber (Wb) The *weber* is the magnetic flux that, linking a circuit of one turn, produces in it an electromotive force of 1 volt as it is reduced to zero at a uniform rate in 1 second.

lumen (lm) The *lumen* is the luminous flux emitted in a solid angle of 1 steradian by a uniform point source having an intensity of 1 candela.

farad (F) The *farad* is the capacitance of a capacitor between the plates of which there appears a difference of potential of 1 volt when it is charged by a quantity of electricity equal to 1 coulomb.

henry (H) The *henry* is the inductance of a closed circuit in which an electromotive force of 1 volt is produced when the electric current in the circuit varies uniformly at a rate of 1 ampere per second.

radian (rad) The *radian* is the plane angle between two radii of a circle that cut off on the circumference an arc equal in length to the radius.

steradian (sr) The *steradian* is the solid angle that, having its vertex in the center of a sphere, cuts off an area of the surface of the sphere equal to that of a square with sides of length equal to the radius of the sphere.

SI Prefixes The names of multiples and submultiples of SI units may be formed by application of the prefixes listed in Appendix F.

The Greek Alphabet

Name	Capital	Lowercase	Name	Capital	Lowercase
Alpha	A	α	Nu	N	ν
Beta	B	β	Xi	Ξ	ξ
Gamma	Γ	γ	Omicron	O	o
Delta	Δ	δ	Pi	Π	π
Epsilon	E	ϵ	Rho	P	ρ
Zeta	Z	ζ	Sigma	Σ	σ
Eta	H	η	Tau	T	τ
Theta	Θ	θ	Upsilon	Υ	υ
Iota	I	ι	Phi	Φ	ϕ
Kappa	K	κ	Chi	X	χ
Lambda	Λ	λ	Psi	Ψ	ψ
Mu	M	μ	Omega	Ω	ω

PERIODIC TABLE OF THE ELEMENTS

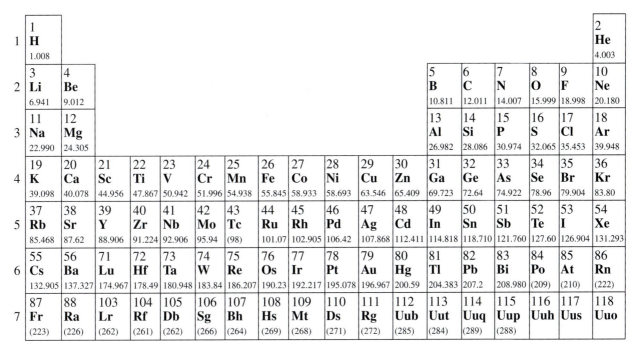

Group 1 2 3 4 5 6 7 8 9 10 11 12 13 14 15 16 17 18
Period

Period	1	2	3	4	5	6	7	8	9	10	11	12	13	14	15	16	17	18
1	1 **H** 1.008																	2 **He** 4.003
2	3 **Li** 6.941	4 **Be** 9.012											5 **B** 10.811	6 **C** 12.011	7 **N** 14.007	8 **O** 15.999	9 **F** 18.998	10 **Ne** 20.180
3	11 **Na** 22.990	12 **Mg** 24.305											13 **Al** 26.982	14 **Si** 28.086	15 **P** 30.974	16 **S** 32.065	17 **Cl** 35.453	18 **Ar** 39.948
4	19 **K** 39.098	20 **Ca** 40.078	21 **Sc** 44.956	22 **Ti** 47.867	23 **V** 50.942	24 **Cr** 51.996	25 **Mn** 54.938	26 **Fe** 55.845	27 **Co** 58.933	28 **Ni** 58.693	29 **Cu** 63.546	30 **Zn** 65.409	31 **Ga** 69.723	32 **Ge** 72.64	33 **As** 74.922	34 **Se** 78.96	35 **Br** 79.904	36 **Kr** 83.80
5	37 **Rb** 85.468	38 **Sr** 87.62	39 **Y** 88.906	40 **Zr** 91.224	41 **Nb** 92.906	42 **Mo** 95.94	43 **Tc** (98)	44 **Ru** 101.07	45 **Rh** 102.905	46 **Pd** 106.42	47 **Ag** 107.868	48 **Cd** 112.411	49 **In** 114.818	50 **Sn** 118.710	51 **Sb** 121.760	52 **Te** 127.60	53 **I** 126.904	54 **Xe** 131.293
6	55 **Cs** 132.905	56 **Ba** 137.327	71 **Lu** 174.967	72 **Hf** 178.49	73 **Ta** 180.948	74 **W** 183.84	75 **Re** 186.207	76 **Os** 190.23	77 **Ir** 192.217	78 **Pt** 195.078	79 **Au** 196.967	80 **Hg** 200.59	81 **Tl** 204.383	82 **Pb** 207.2	83 **Bi** 208.980	84 **Po** (209)	85 **At** (210)	86 **Rn** (222)
7	87 **Fr** (223)	88 **Ra** (226)	103 **Lr** (262)	104 **Rf** (261)	105 **Db** (262)	106 **Sg** (266)	107 **Bh** (264)	108 **Hs** (269)	109 **Mt** (268)	110 **Ds** (271)	111 **Rg** (272)	112 **Uub** (285)	113 **Uut** (284)	114 **Uuq** (289)	115 **Uup** (288)	116 **Uuh**	117 **Uus**	118 **Uuo**

Lanthanoids	57 **La** 138.905	58 **Ce** 140.116	59 **Pr** 140.908	60 **Nd** 144.24	61 **Pm** (145)	62 **Sm** 150.36	63 **Eu** 151.964	64 **Gd** 157.25	65 **Tb** 158.925	66 **Dy** 162.500	67 **Ho** 164.930	68 **Er** 167.259	69 **Tm** 168.934	70 **Yb** 173.04
Actinoids	89 **Ac** (227)	90 **Th** (232)	91 **Pa** (231)	92 **U** (238)	93 **Np** (237)	94 **Pu** (244)	95 **Am** (243)	96 **Cm** (247)	97 **Bk** (247)	98 **Cf** (251)	99 **Es** (252)	100 **Fm** (257)	101 **Md** (258)	102 **No** (259)

For each element the average molar mass of the mixture of isotopes occurring in nature is shown. For elements having no stable molar isotope, the approximate molar mass of the longest-lived isotope is shown in parentheses. For elements that have been predicted but not yet detected, no molar mass is given. All molar masses are expressed in atomic mass units ($1\,\text{u} = 1.66053873(13) \times 10^{-27}\,\text{kg}$), equivalent to grams per mole (g/mol).

UNIT CONVERSION FACTORS

LENGTH

$1\ m = 100\ cm = 1000\ mm = 10^6\ \mu m = 10^9\ nm$
$1\ km = 1000\ m = 0.6214\ mi$
$1\ m = 3.281\ ft = 39.37\ in.$
$1\ cm = 0.3937\ in.$
$1\ in. = 2.540\ cm$
$1\ ft = 30.48\ cm$
$1\ yd = 91.44\ cm$
$1\ mi = 5280\ ft = 1.609\ km$
$1\ \text{Å} = 10^{-10}\ m = 10^{-8}\ cm = 10^{-1}\ nm$
$1\ \text{nautical mile} = 6080\ ft$
$1\ \text{light year} = 9.461 \times 10^{15}\ m$

AREA

$1\ cm^2 = 0.155\ in.^2$
$1\ m^2 = 10^4\ cm^2 = 10.76\ ft^2$
$1\ in.^2 = 6.452\ cm^2$
$1\ ft^2 = 144\ in.^2 = 0.0929\ m^2$

VOLUME

$1\ \text{liter} = 1000\ cm^3 = 10^{-3}\ m^3$
$\qquad\quad = 0.03531\ ft^3 = 61.02\ in.^3$
$1\ ft^3 = 0.02832\ m^3 = 28.32\ \text{liters} = 7.477\ \text{gallons}$
$1\ \text{gallon} = 3.788\ \text{liters}$

TIME

$1\ min = 60\ s$
$1\ h = 3600\ s$
$1\ d = 86,400\ s$
$1\ y = 365.24\ d = 3.156 \times 10^7\ s$

ANGLE

$1\ rad = 57.30° = 180°/\pi$
$1° = 0.01745\ rad = \pi/180\ rad$
$1\ \text{revolution} = 360° = 2\pi\ rad$
$1\ \text{rev}/\text{min (rpm)} = 0.1047\ rad/s$

SPEED

$1\ m/s = 3.281\ ft/s$
$1\ ft/s = 0.3048\ m/s$
$1\ mi/min = 60\ mi/h = 88\ ft/s$
$1\ km/h = 0.2778\ m/s = 0.6214\ mi/h$
$1\ mi/h = 1.466\ ft/s = 0.4470\ m/s = 1.609\ km/h$
$1\ \text{furlong}/\text{fortnight} = 1.662 \times 10^{-4}\ m/s$

ACCELERATION

$1\ m/s^2 = 100\ cm/s^2 = 3.281\ ft/s^2$
$1\ cm/s^2 = 0.01\ m/s^2 = 0.03281\ ft/s^2$
$1\ ft/s^2 = 0.3048\ m/s^2 = 30.48\ cm/s^2$
$1\ mi/h \cdot s = 1.467\ ft/s^2$

MASS

$1\ kg = 10^3\ g = 0.0685\ \text{slug}$
$1\ g = 6.85 \times 10^{-5}\ \text{slug}$
$1\ \text{slug} = 14.59\ kg$
$1\ u = 1.661 \times 10^{-27}\ kg$
$1\ kg\ \text{has a weight of } 2.205\ lb \text{ when } g = 9.80\ m/s^2$

FORCE

$1\ N = 10^5\ dyn = 0.2248\ lb$
$1\ lb = 4.448\ N = 4.448 \times 10^5\ dyn$

PRESSURE

$1\ Pa = 1\ N/m^2 = 1.450 \times 10^{-4}\ lb/in.^2 = 0.209\ lb/ft^2$
$1\ bar = 10^5\ Pa$
$1\ lb/in.^2 = 6895\ Pa$
$1\ lb/ft^2 = 47.88\ Pa$
$1\ atm = 1.013 \times 10^5\ Pa = 1.013\ bar$
$\qquad\quad = 14.7\ lb/in.^2 = 2117\ lb/ft^2$
$1\ mm\ Hg = 1\ torr = 133.3\ Pa$

ENERGY

$1\ J = 10^7\ \text{ergs} = 0.239\ cal$
$1\ cal = 4.186\ J\ \text{(based on 15° calorie)}$
$1\ ft \cdot lb = 1.356\ J$
$1\ Btu = 1055\ J = 252\ cal = 778\ ft \cdot lb$
$1\ eV = 1.602 \times 10^{-19}\ J$
$1\ kWh = 3.60 \times 10^6\ J$

MASS–ENERGY EQUIVALENCE

$1\ kg \leftrightarrow 8.988 \times 10^{16}\ J$
$1\ u \leftrightarrow 931.5\ MeV$
$1\ eV \leftrightarrow 1.074 - 10^{-9}\ u$

POWER

$1\ W = 1\ J/s$
$1\ hp = 746\ W = 550\ ft \cdot lb/s$
$1\ Btu/h = 0.293\ W$

Appendix F

NUMERICAL CONSTANTS

Fundamental Physical Constants*

Name	Symbol	Value
Speed of light in vacuum	c	2.99792458×10^8 m/s
Magnitude of charge of electron	e	$1.60217653(14) \times 10^{-19}$ C
Gravitational constant	G	$6.6742(10) \times 10^{-11}$ N $\cdot$ m^2/kg^2
Planck's constant	h	$6.6260693(11) \times 10^{-34}$ J $\cdot$ s
Boltzmann constant	k	$1.3806505(24) \times 10^{-23}$ J/K
Avogadro's number	N_A	$6.0221415(10) \times 10^{23}$ molecules/mol
Gas constant	R	$8.314472(15)$ J/(mol $\cdot$ K)
Mass of electron	m_e	$9.1093826(16) \times 10^{-31}$ kg
Mass of proton	m_p	$1.67262171(29) \times 10^{-27}$ kg
Mass of neutron	m_n	$1.67492728(29) \times 10^{-27}$ kg
Permeability of vacuum	μ_0	$4\pi \times 10^{-7}$ Wb/T $\cdot$ m/A
Permittivity of vacuum	$\epsilon_0 = 1/\mu_0 c^2$	$8.854187817 \cdots \times 10^{-12}$ C^2/(N $\cdot$ m^2)
	$1/4\pi\epsilon_0$	$8.987551787 \cdots \times 10^9$ N $\cdot$ m^2/C^2

Other Useful Constants*

Mechanical equivalent of heat		4.186 J/cal (15° calorie)
Standard atmospheric pressure	1 atm	1.01325×10^5 Pa
Absolute zero	0 K	-273.15°C
Electron volt	1 eV	$1.60217653(14) \times 10^{-19}$ J
Unified atomic mass unit	1 u	$1.66053886(28) \times 10^{-27}$ kg
Electron rest energy	$m_e c^2$	$0.510998918(44)$ MeV
Volume of ideal gas (0°C and 1 atm)		$22.413996(39)$ liter/mol
Acceleration due to gravity (standard)	g	9.80 m/s^2

*Source: National Institute of Standards and Technology (**http://physics.nist.gov/cuu**). Numbers in parentheses show the uncertainty in the final digits of the main number; for example, the number 1.6454(21) means 1.6454 ± 0.0021. Values shown without uncertainties are exact.

Astronomical Data[†]

Body	Mass (kg)	Radius (m)	Orbit radius (m)	Orbit period
Sun	1.99×10^{30}	6.96×10^{8}	—	—
Moon	7.35×10^{22}	1.74×10^{6}	3.84×10^{8}	27.3 d
Mercury	3.30×10^{23}	2.44×10^{6}	5.79×10^{10}	88.0 d
Venus	4.87×10^{24}	6.05×10^{6}	1.08×10^{11}	224.7 d
Earth	5.97×10^{24}	6.38×10^{6}	1.50×10^{11}	365.3 d
Mars	6.42×10^{23}	3.40×10^{6}	2.28×10^{11}	687.0 d
Jupiter	1.90×10^{27}	6.91×10^{7}	7.78×10^{11}	11.86 y
Saturn	5.68×10^{26}	6.03×10^{7}	1.43×10^{12}	29.45 y
Uranus	8.68×10^{25}	2.56×10^{7}	2.87×10^{12}	84.02 y
Neptune	1.02×10^{26}	2.48×10^{7}	4.50×10^{12}	164.8 y
Pluto	1.31×10^{22}	1.15×10^{6}	5.91×10^{12}	247.9 y

[†]Source: NASA Jet Propulsion LaboratorySolar System Dynamics Group (**http://ssd.jpl.nasa.gov**), and P. Kenneth Seidelmann, ed., ***Explanatory Supplement to the Astronomical Almanac*** (University Science Books, Mill Valley, CA, 1992), pp. 704–706. For each body, "radius" is its radius at its equator and "orbit radius" is its average distance from the sun (for the planets) or from the earth (for the moon).

Prefixes for Powers of 10

Power of ten	Prefix	Abbreviation	Pronunciation
10^{-24}	yocto-	y	*yoc*-toe
10^{-21}	zepto-	z	*zep*-toe
10^{-18}	atto-	a	*at*-toe
10^{-15}	femto-	f	*fem*-toe
10^{-12}	pico-	p	*pee*-koe
10^{-9}	nano-	n	*nan*-oe
10^{-6}	micro-	μ	*my*-crow
10^{-3}	milli-	m	*mil*-i
10^{-2}	centi-	c	*cen*-ti
10^{3}	kilo-	k	*kil*-oe
10^{6}	mega-	M	*meg*-a
10^{9}	giga-	G	*jig*-a or *gig*-a
10^{12}	tera-	T	*ter*-a
10^{15}	peta-	P	*pet*-a
10^{18}	exa-	E	*ex*-a
10^{21}	zetta-	Z	*zet*-a
10^{24}	yotta-	Y	*yot*-a

Examples:

1 femtometer = 1 fm = 10^{-15} m
1 picosecond = 1 ps = 10^{-12} s
1 nanocoulomb = 1 nC = 10^{-9} C
1 microkelvin = 1 μK = 10^{-6} K

1 millivolt = 1 mV = 10^{-3} V
1 kilopascal = 1 kPa = 10^{3} Pa
1 megawatt = 1 MW = 10^{6} W
1 gigahertz = 1 GHz = 10^{9} Hz

ANSWERS TO ODD-NUMBERED PROBLEMS

Chapter 1

Conceptual Questions

1. The number π is the ratio of two lengths: the circumference of a circle divided by its diameter. Consequently, π is dimensionless; it has no units and is thus a constant.

3. In this context, "yard" refers to a volume equal to a cubic yard, yd^3.

5. Numerous possibilities exist, such as the time of swing of a pendulum of a certain length; the time required for an object to fall from a specific height; the pulse rate of a healthy adult; the flow rate of a specific volume of sand (e.g., an hourglass); and the constant-frequency electric signal generated by the vibrations of a quartz crystal. Each of these potential standards, however, has deficiencies and is thus less accurate than the atomic standard.

7. No, the formula cannot be correct. V has units of length cubed (e.g., m^3), r and h each have the units of length and π is dimensionless; therefore, $\pi r^3 h$ has units of length raised to the fourth power (e.g., m^4), which is dimensionally incorrect.

9. Measure the height of a stack of 100 pages, and divide that distance by 100 to obtain the thickness of a single page.

11. Consider the SI System of units: A has units of m^2; V has units of m^3; C has units of m; R has units of m. If we compare the equivalency of only the units for each formula, we obtain (a) $\{m^2\} \neq \{m\}$; (b) $\{m^3\} \neq \{m^2\}$; (c) $\{m^2\} = \{m^2\}$; (d) $\{m^3\} = \{m^3\}$; (e) $\{m\} \neq \{m^2\}$; (f) $\{m^3\} = \{m^3\}$. Therefore, formulas (a), (b), and (e) cannot be correct.

13. (a) Yes, since scalar addition only involves adding numbers. (b) No, because vector addition is not done simply by adding magnitudes. The magnitude of the vector sum depends on the direction, as well as the magnitude, of each vector being added. For example, if two vectors have equal magnitude, but lie in opposite directions, their vector sum is zero.

15. No, the magnitude of such a vector can never be zero. By definition, the magnitude of a vector $\vec{A}$ is related to its com-

ponents by $A = \sqrt{A_x^2 + A_y^2}$. Thus, A is zero if, and only if, A_x and A_y are both zero.

Multiple-Choice Problems

1. B
3. C
5. B
7. B
9. C
11. B
13. D

Problems

1. (a) 2.40 grams/day
   (b) 1.20×10^{-4} grams/day
   (c) 0.500 grams/day (d) 1.50 kilohms
   (e) 20 milliamps
3. (a) 4.10×10^5 μg/day (b) 0.900 g/day
   (c) 2 tablets/day (d) 0.070 mg/day
5. (a) 1.00×10^3 kg/m^3
   (b) 1.05 g/cm^3 (c) 1.00 kg, 2.20 lb
7. (a) 2330 km/h (b) 648 m/s
9. 15.9 km/L
11. $6.39 per gallon
13. (a) 3600 s
    (b) 8.64×10^4 s (c) 3.15×10^7 s
15. (a) 3.14; 3.1416; 3.1415927
    (b) 2.72; 2.7183; 2.7182818
    (c) 3.61; 3.6056; 3.6055513
17. (a) 0.9969 to 0.9981 (b) 0.061 to 0.078
    (c) 0.061 to 0.079
19. (a) 5.50 g/cm^3
    (b) 1.1×10^6 g/cm^3
    (c) 4.7×10^{14} g/cm^3
21. 9.0 cm
23. 18.9 g
25. 19,000
27. 11,000
29. 10^{12}; no
31. 3×10^9 beats; 4×10^7 gallons
33. 9×10^{14}; 3×10^6 per person
35. (b) one-fourth lap: 106 ft; 45° with respect to radius drawn to initial position. one-half lap: 150 ft; 180° with respect to radius drawn to initial position. one lap: 0
39. (a) 4.7 m, 8.1 m (b) −15.6 km, 15.6 km
    (c) 3.82 cm, −5.07 cm
41. (a) 6.4 m; 51° (b) 6.7 km; 243°
    (c) 19 m/s; 298° (d) 14 N; 124°
43. (a) 10.0 lb; 37° (b) 39 m/s; 232°
    (c) 2500 km; 127° (d) 89.9 N; 323°

45. (a) 5.40 cm, −1.50 cm (b) 5.60 cm, 344° counterclockwise from $+x$ axis (c) 2.80 cm, −6.00 cm (d) 6.62 cm, 295° counterclockwise from $+x$ axis
47. (b) 53 N; 45°
49. (a) 5.06 km; 20.2° north of west
51. 142 g to 149 g
53. (a) 2200 g (b) 2.1 m
55. 6.7×10^{-2} L $= 67$ cm^3
57. (a) 5.7×10^6 steps (b) 120 days
59. 19 μg $= 1.9 \times 10^{-5}$ g
61. 143 m; 41° south of west
63. 3.30 N
65. 160 N, 13° below the horizontal

Chapter 2

Conceptual Questions

1. (a) The magnitude of the displacement equals the distance traveled only when the motion is always in the same direction and lies along a straight line in space. An example is a car traveling due east on a straight, level road. (b) A car travels due east for 0.4 mi and then due west for 0.1 mi. The displacement has magnitude 0.3 mi, while the distance traveled is 0.5 mi. (c) No.

3. The average velocity equals the instantaneous velocity if the velocity is constant.

5. (a) True. The average speed can be zero only if the object is not moving. (b) False. If the object returns to its starting point, then its displacement is zero and its average velocity is zero; however, the distance it traveled is not zero, and thus its average speed is nonzero. An example is a car that travels 50 m north for 5 s and then 50 m south for 5 s. For the 10-second interval, the average velocity is zero, but the average speed is $(100 \text{ m})/(10 \text{ s}) = 10$ m/s.

7. No, velocity and acceleration are different physical quantities with different units and cannot be compared.

9. In each of these cases, the slope of velocity versus time is the acceleration. The sign of the slope gives the sign of the acceleration, in terms of the direction taken to be positive for plotting the velocity. Consequently, a positive slope indicates that the object is either speeding up in the positive x direction or slowing

down in the negative x direction. Similarly, a negative slope indicates an increasing speed in the negative x direction or a decreasing speed in the positive x direction. A zero slope implies constant speed and thus no acceleration.

11. (a) The velocity must be positive, since x is increasing in the positive x direction. The intervals between time values, Δt, and between displacements, Δx, are both constants for all five intervals; thus, the velocity is constant and the acceleration is zero. (b) For each time interval, the average velocity is $v_{av,x} = \Delta x/\Delta t = (0.25\text{ m})/(2.00\text{ s}) = 0.125\text{ m/s}$. Since the velocity does not change, $a_{av,x} = \Delta v_x/\Delta t = (0.0\text{ m/s})/(2.00\text{ s}) = 0.0\text{ m/s}^2$ for each time interval. (c) The displacement is $7.75\text{ m} - 6.50\text{ m} = 1.25\text{ m}$.

13. False. "Negative acceleration" has meaning only in reference to a choice of positive coordinate direction, and we are free to choose any direction we wish to be positive x and positive y. The correct statement is "If the acceleration and velocity have opposite directions, then the object must be slowing down." One example is an object dropped from the roof of a building. If we take upward to be $+y$, then the acceleration is negative, but the object is speeding up; its velocity is growing increasingly negative and is in the same direction as the acceleration.

15. (a) Since all three objects have the same v at A and at B, Δv is the same for all three. And given that $a_{av} = \Delta v/\Delta t$, a_{av} is the same for all three objects. (b) At A, they all have the same velocity. By comparing the slope of a tangent line drawn to the $v–t$ graph for each object at point A, we can conclude that the acceleration is different for all three objects.

17. (a) Since the object's velocity is always positive, the object does not reverse its direction of motion. (b) No, the object is always moving away from its starting point; the velocity is always in the same direction. (c) Yes, $v = 0$ at the beginning and at the end of the motion. (d) Yes, initially the object has a positive acceleration; however, the acceleration subsequently decreases in magnitude, passes through zero, and then becomes increasingly negative (increasing in magnitude).

Multiple-Choice Problems

1. C, D
3. C, D
5. D
7. A, D
9. B
11. A
13. B, D
15. C

Problems

1. (a) $x_A = -5\text{ cm}$, $x_B = +45\text{ cm}$, $x_C = +15\text{ cm}$, $x_D = -5\text{ cm}$ (b) (i) $+50\text{ cm}$; 50 cm (ii) -30 cm; 30 cm (iii) -20 cm; 20 cm (iv) 0; 100 cm
3. 1.3 m/s; 2.0 m/s
5. (a) 3.0 m/s; 1.5 m/s; 1.8 m/s (b) same
7. (a) 7.0 m (b) (i) 1.0 m/s (ii) 3.0 m/s (iii) 5.0 m/s (iv) 7.0 m/s (v) 4.0 m/s
9. (a) 15.0 mi/h (b) 22.0 ft/s (c) 6.70 m/s
11. (a) 5.0 m (b) $1.1 \times 10^7\text{ yr}$
13. 30 nm
15. (a) $9.47 \times 10^{15}\text{ m}$ (b) 0.300 m; $3.44 \times 10^{-7}\text{ m}$ (c) 8.33 min (d) 2.56 s (e) 1.67 h
17. 40 min
19. (a) IV (b) I (c) V (d) II (e) III
23. (a) (in m/s^2) 0, 1.0, 1.5, 2.5, 2.5, 2.5, 1.0, 0; no; yes (b) 3.0 m/s^2; 1.0 m/s^2; 0
27. (a) 6.3 ft/s^2 (b) 347 ft
29. (a) $4.61 \times 10^3\text{ m/s}^2 = 470g$; upward (b) 18.7 ms
31. (a) $30\text{ m/s}^2 = 3g$ (b) no; different distances in the same time
33. 38 cm
35. (a) $4.42 \times 10^5\text{ m/s}^2 = 4.51 \times 10^4g$ (b) 0.758 ms
37. (a) $5.4\text{ m/s}^2 = 18\text{ ft/s}^2$ (b) 220 ft
39. (a) braking: -26.5 ft/s^2; speeding up: 6.67 ft/s^2 (b) 90.4 mph; a_x not constant (c) 3.32 s
41. $4A$; $2C$
43. (a) $R/2^{1/3}$ (b) $1/2^{2/3}$
45. (a) 62.5 km (b) 175 m/s
47. (a) 2000 m (b) $2T$
49. (a) 30.6 m (b) 24.5 m/s
51. (a) 33.5 m (b) 15.8 m/s
53. (a) 0.250 s: 40.9 m aboveground; 2.55 m/s upward. 1.00 s: 40.1 m aboveground; 4.80 m/s downward (b) 3.41 s (c) 28.4 m/s (d) 41.2 m
55. (a) 70.6 m (b) 15.3 s
57. (a) 4.93 s (b) 36.3 m/s
59. (a) 3.3 s (b) $9H$
61. (a) 107 mph (b) 107 mph
63. (a) 9.9 m/s, downward (b) 9.9 m/s, upward
65. 98.1 km/h
67. 1300 yr
69. (a) 48 mph (b) travel times at each speed are not the same
71. (a) $H/6$ (b) 24.0 s
73. (a) $3.1 \times 10^6\text{ m/s}^2 = 3.2 \times 10^5g$ (b) 1.6 ms (c) no
75. 3.60 m from point directly below the drop
77. (a) 1670 m/s (b) 310 s (c) $21\text{ m/s}^2 = 2.2g$; 65 s
79. $-2.2 \times 10^{-6}\text{ mm/day}^2$; $-2.9 \times 10^{-19}\text{ mm/s}^2$
81. (a) 628 m (b) 0; 9.8 m/s^2 downward (c) 36.4 s; 111 m/s
83. (a) 20.0 cm/s, to the right (b) 40.0 cm/s, to the right

(c) $0 < t < 6.0\text{ s}$ and $9.0\text{ s} < t < 10.0\text{ s}$; $6.0\text{ s} < t < 9.0\text{ s}$; 6.0 s and 9.0 s (d) 40.0 cm/s^2, to the left (e) 6.0 s, 9.0 s (f) $0 < t < 3.0\text{ s}$, $6.0\text{ s} < t < 7.0\text{ s}$, $9.0\text{ s} < t < 10.0\text{ s}$; $5.0\text{ s} < t < 6.0\text{ s}$, $7.0\text{ s} < t < 9.0\text{ s}$; 6.0 s, 9.0 s (g) no; acceleration not constant
85. (a) $20.5\text{ m/s}^2 = 2.09g_E = 5.53g_M$, upward (b) 8.67 m/s^2, upward; 40.9 s (c) 24 m; 3.6 s
87. (a) 383 m (b) overestimated

Chapter 3

Conceptual Questions

1. The acceleration is downward at all points in the motion. The football's velocity has a constant nonzero horizontal component, so the velocity is never vertical and therefore never parallel to the acceleration. At the highest point in the trajectory, the vertical component of the velocity is zero; thus, the velocity is horizontal, and the acceleration and velocity are perpendicular at this point.

3. The constant speed of the elevator does not affect the rate at which the object falls relative to the elevator. She obtains $a = 9.8\text{ m/s}^2$ downward for either direction of the elevator's motion.

5. As it falls, the package retains the same horizontal component of velocity that it had in the airplane. The package and airplane travel horizontally at the same speed; thus, relative to the pilot, the package falls straight downward. A person at rest on the ground sees the package move with constant horizontal velocity and with a vertical velocity of increasing magnitude. Relative to this person, the path of the package is a parabola.

7. The time in the air is governed solely by the vertical component of the motion: $t = 2v_{0y}/g = 2v_0\sin\theta_0/g$. To achieve the maximum time in the air, maximize $\sin\theta_0$ by launching the projectile straight upward at a launch angle of $90°$ with respect to the horizontal. Since the horizontal component of velocity would be zero, the range would be zero ($x = (v_0\cos 90°)t$).

9. (a) Yes, at the maximum height of the projectile's motion, the vertical component of its velocity is zero and thus its velocity is purely horizontal. (b) No, since the projectile's velocity has a constant nonzero horizontal component, the velocity is never vertical.

11. Two aspects of this path violate the physical principles of projectile motion: (1) The horizontal component of the velocity must be constant; this path provides for a varying horizontal velocity component that equals zero at the path's

endpoints. (2) The shape of the path must be parabolic; this path is a semicircle.

13. The arrow and the target fall with the same downward acceleration, regardless of the magnitude of the initial velocity of the arrow.

15. The trajectory does not allow for a constant horizontal velocity component; the horizontal component varies from zero, to a maximum nonzero value at the peak of travel, and back to zero. Also, this path does not have the requisite parabolic shape that results from motion having a constant downward acceleration and a constant horizontal velocity component.

Multiple-Choice Problems

1. B
3. C
5. A
7. B
9. C
11. A
13. D
15. D
17. B

Problems

1. (a) 1.09 km/s; -0.24 km/s
   (b) 1.12 km/s; $12.4°$ below $+x$ axis
3. (a) 2.0 m, 1.0 m (b) 2.2 m, $26.6°$ counterclockwise from $+x$ axis (c) 5.3 m/s; 3.3 m/s (d) 6.2 m/s; $32°$ counterclockwise from $+x$ axis
5. (a) $(v_x)_{av} = 3.8$ m/s; $(v_y)_{av} = 3.8$ m/s; $(a_x)_{av} = 0.46$ m/s²; $(a_y)_{av} = -0.46$ m/s²
   (b) $(v_x)_{av} = 3.8$ m/s; $(v_y)_{av} = 0$; $(a_x)_{av} = 0$; $(a_y)_{av} = -0.46$ m/s²
   (c) $(v_x)_{av} = -3.8$ m/s; $(v_y)_{av} = -3.8$ m/s; $(a_x)_{av} = -0.46$ m/s²; $(a_y)_{av} = 0.46$ m/s²
   (d) $(v_x)_{av} = (v_y)_{av} = 0$; $(a_x)_{av} = (a_y)_{av} = 0$ (e) 5.4 m/s; no; distance traveled is larger than displacement
7. (a) 0.64 ft (b) 5.76 ft
9. (a) 0.391 s (b) 3.58 m/s (c) 5.24 m/s at $46.9°$ below horizontal
11. 3.32 m
13. (a) 30.6 m/s (b) 36.3 m/s
15. (a) 13 m/s, 20 m/s (b) 20 m (c) 2.0 s (d) 13 m/s, horizontal; 9.80 m/s², downward (e) 4.0 s (f) 52 m
17. (a) 0.682 s, 2.99 s (b) 24.0 m/s, 11.3 m/s; 24.0 m/s, -11.3 m/s (c) 30.0 m/s at $36.9°$ below the horizontal
19. (a) 118 ft/s (b) 54.4 ft
21. (a) 4.00 m/s (b) 1.47 m
23. (a) $53.1°$ (b) 15.0 m/s; 9.80 m/s², downward (c) 15.9 m; 17.7 m/s
25. (a) $45°$ (b) 23.0 m (c) 5.75 m
27. 111 m/s; $45°$
29. 370 m; $45°$

31. 2.7 m/s
33. (a) 2.97×10^4 m/s
    (b) 5.91×10^{-3} m/s²
    (c) 4.78×10^4 m/s; 3.97×10^{-2} m/s²
35. 1.64×10^{-3} m/s²
37. 25 m/s² $= 2.5g$
39. (a) $14°$ north of west (b) 310 km/h
41. (a) $28°$ north of east (b) 3.7 m/s, east (c) 217 s
43. (a) $24°$ west of south (b) 5.5 hr
45. 9.87 m/s
47. 55.5 m, south
49. 630 m
51. 29.5 m
53. (a) 9.16 m/s² (b) 2.72 s (c) 8.45 m
55. (a) 16.6 m/s (b) 10.8 m/s; $40.1°$ below the horizontal
57. (a) 4.25 m/s (b) 10.6 m
61. 8.58 m/s $= 19.2$ mph
63. 14.4 m/s $= 32.2$ mph
65. (a) 17.8 m/s (b) in river, 28.4 m from the near bank
67. (a) 49 m/s (b) 50 m
69. (a) 863 m (b) 4360 m

Chapter 4

Conceptual Questions

1. The force is applied at the wheels by the surface of the road.
3. Use Newton's second law. Apply a known force that imparts rectilinear motion, and measure the acceleration that is produced. If the person is initially at rest and the force is applied for time t, the acceleration is $a = v/t$, where v is the final speed of the person. The mass is then calculated as $m = F/a$.
5. The bus must be slowing down (braking). The friction force on the ball is small; consequently, the ball continues to move with its initial velocity: the velocity of the bus prior to braking.
7. By Newton's third law, the magnitude of the force the compact exerts on the SUV equals the magnitude of the force the SUV exerts on the compact. The effect of the force on the motion—the acceleration that is produced—is greater for the compact, and thus for its passengers, since the compact has less mass.
9. The elevator is in a free fall, with a downward acceleration of 9.8 m/s². Consequently, the elevator and the briefcase have the same downward acceleration and fall together.
11. The impact force gives the car a large forward acceleration. Consequently, the car seat imparts a forward force, proportional to the forward acceleration, on the passenger's torso. However, if the car does not have a headrest, or if the headrest is improperly adjusted, the motion of the passenger's unsupported head follows Newton's first law. The head, which was not acted upon by an outside

force, initially maintains the speed of the car and thus moves backward *relative* to the passenger's torso. Next, the head is rapidly thrust forward. This back-and-forth or "whipping" motion can cause injury to the neck.

13. While the ball is in the air, there is no horizontal force on it, and it travels in a straight line in accordance with Newton's first law. If the plane turns, the ball no longer travels in a straight line relative to the passenger to whom the ball was thrown. There is now a net horizontal force on the passenger, causing him to accelerate in the new direction of the plane; but there is no corresponding force on the ball. The passenger thus cannot catch the ball.

15. With no air resistance, all objects fall with the same acceleration and thus have identical speeds when they reach the ground. The pillow is softer, so it travels through a greater distance as it comes to rest. The pillow therefore has a smaller magnitude of acceleration than the rock, and the stopping force on the pillow is less. By Newton's third law, since your head exerts less force on the pillow than on the rock, the pillow exerts less force on your head.

17. (a) You feel this because the seat exerts a forward force on you, while your body exerts a backward reaction force on the seat. You feel as though you are being pushed back, but you are actually being pushed forward. (b) The free-body diagram is sketched in the figure below. $\vec{F}_1$ and $\vec{F}_2$ are the horizontal and vertical components, respectively, of the force the car seat exerts on you. F_2 equals the weight mg of the person, while F_1 produces the horizontal acceleration.

Multiple-Choice Problems

1. C
3. B
5. D
7. B
9. A
11. A, D
13. B
15. B

Problems

1. 7.1 N to the right; 7.1 N downward
3. 241 N; 287 N

5. (a) $F_{1x} = 844$ N, $F_{1y} = 507$ N;
   $F_{2x} = -418$ N, $F_{2y} = 668$ N;
   $F_{3x} = -248$ N, $F_{3y} = -328$ N
   (b) 866 N; 78.1°
7. (a) 4.31 m/s² (b) 215 m
9. (a) 680 N (b) the ground
11. 90.9 kg
13. (a) 2.72 kg; 0.186 slug (b) 29.0 lb;
   129 N
15. (a) 2.06×10^{-6} N (b) 1.21×10^{-4} N
   (c) 10.1 lb; 4.6 kg
17. (a) 1 kg stone (b) 1 slug stone (c) 1 slug
   stone (d) 1 slug stone (e) 1 kg stone
19. (a) 138 N (b) 138 N (c) 1350 N for
   both (a) and (b) (d) the same, 138 N
21. (a) 3.71 m/s² (b) 8.69 kg
23. (a) 2.45 m/s² (b) 191 m
25. (a) earth (b) 4 N; the book (c) no
   (d) 4 N; the earth; the book; upward
   (e) 4 N; the hand; the book; downward
   (f) second (g) third
27. (a) (i) P (the push), w (gravity), n (normal) (ii) same as (i), but P absent
   (iii) w (gravity) (b) P, force of bottle on
   hand; n, downward force of bottle on
   tabletop; w, bottle pulling up on earth
37. (a) 490 N (b) 735 N (c) 612 N
39. (a) 502 N (b) 345 N (c) 424 N
41. (b) 7.43×10^{-4} s (c) 848 N
43. (a) 784 N (b) 47.4 N
45. (a) 21.2 m/s² (b) 1700 N (c) 1700 N;
   173 kg
47. (b) friction force exerted by the pavement (c) 1.04×10^4 N
49. (b) 0.049 N (c) 410w
51. (a) 4.8 m/s (b) 16 m/s² (d) 2360 N
53. (a) 140 N
55. (a) 64.4 kg (b) (i) 631 N (ii) 108 N
57. (a) 539 N (b) 81 N, upward
   (c) 1.47 m/s², upward

Chapter 5

Conceptual Questions

1. No, the object is in equilibrium only if
   the vector sum of all of the forces on it is
   zero. With only one applied force, the
   net force cannot be zero.
3. The chain and sprocket convert the
   downward force on the pedal to a rotation of the rear wheel.
5. The coefficient of static friction is much
   less for icy pavement.
7. The vertical component of the vector $\vec{T}$
   must equal the weight of the object.
   Since the magnitude of any vector is
   greater than either of its components, T
   must be greater than the weight of the
   object.
9. With no friction, the weight W will
   accelerate downward when the system is
   released. This downward acceleration is
   possible only if a net downward force
   exists. The downward force W on the
   weight must therefore be greater than

the upward tensile force in the wire. The
tension will be less than W.
11. (a) No, without friction, there would be
   no horizontal force on you. (b) Yes, you
   could push down on the rung of a ladder,
   and the ladder would exert an upward
   normal force on you. (c) No, the pole
   could not exert a vertical force, parallel
   to the pole, without friction. (d) Yes,
   you could push down on the ground, and
   the ground would push up on you.
   (e) No, without friction, the ground
   could not exert the horizontal force on
   the wheels necessary for traction.
   (f) No, without friction, there would be
   no horizontal force on the car; therefore,
   the car could travel only in a straight
   line.
13. The correct statement is "Friction
   always opposes the *relative* motion
   between two surfaces." A counterexam-
   ple is friction causing the acceleration of
   an object. A simple example involves a
   stationary object on a sheet of paper that
   rests on a tabletop. When you pull the
   paper, the friction exerted by the paper
   on the object accelerates the object in
   the direction of your tug.
15. Tendons, skin, and cartilage are all
   elastic.

Multiple-Choice Problems

1. A
3. B
5. A
7. A
9. A
11. C
13. D

Problems

1. (a) 3.6 kg (b) 410 kg (c) 6×10^3 kg
3. (a) 25.0 N (b) 50.0 N
5. (a) 2.54×10^3 N (b) 1.01°
7. (a) N/m²; kg/(m · s²) (b) 25 cm²
9. (a) 47.0 N (b) 85.2 N
11. (b) 649 N; 314 N; 813 N (c) no
13. (b) 2.65 N (c) 0.193 N
15. (a) $w\sin\alpha$ (b) $2w\sin\alpha$ (c) $w\cos\alpha$ for
   each block
17. (a) 4.41×10^4 N (b) 60 times the weight
19. 250W
21. (a) 3.4 m/s (c) 2.2W
23. (a) 48.0 N (b) $a = 2.65$ m/s², downward (c) 0
25. (b) 2.08 m/s²; 3.07 N
27. (a) 4.0 m/s², down the slope
   (b) 4.0 m/s², down the slope
   (c) 4.0 m/s², down the slope
29. (b) up the ramp (c) 50.0 kg box:
   0.612 m/s² up the ramp; 30.0 kg box:
   0.612 m/s² downward
31. (a) 0 (b) 6.0 N (c) 16.0 N (d) 8.0 N
33. (a) 266 lb (b) 0
35. 0.16

37. 8D
39. (a) 22.0 N (b) 1.96 m/s², opposite to the
   motion
41. $\mu_s = \tan\theta_1$; $\mu_k = \tan\theta_2$
43. 50°
45. (a) 283 N (b) 7.39 m/s²
47. (a) $T = \dfrac{M(a + \mu g)}{\cos\phi + \mu\sin\phi}$
   (b) (i) $T = Ma/\cos\phi$
   (ii) $T = M(a + \mu g)$
49. (b) 2.4×10^{-5} kg/m
51. (a) W (b) $W/4$ (c) $W/9$
55. (a) 357 N/m (b) 2.08 kg
57. (a) 0.93 N/cm (b) 10 mm
59. (a) yes; graph of m versus x is a straight
   line (b) 24.5 N/m (c) 94 cm
61. (a) 15.2 cm (b) 17.6 cm
63. (a) 4.4 m/s (b) 440 m/s², upward;
   2.5×10^4 N (c) 7.0 ms
65. (d) 70 N/cm
67. (a) 621 N (b) 161 N
69. (a) 1.10×10^8 N (b) 5W (c) 8.4 s
71. (a) 12.0 N (b) 15.0 N
73. (a) yes; the graph of W versus L is a
   straight line (b) 50.0 N/m (c) 4.0 N
75. (a) 2.0×10^4 N (b) 6.19×10^3 N
   (c) 3.26×10^4 N
77. (a) 250 N/m (b) 5.23 m/s²; in the backward direction
79. 4.71 s
81. (a) without: 0.20 kg/m; with: 20 kg/m
   (b) without: 55 m/s; with: 5.5 m/s
83. (b) 20 N (c) 100 N
85. 2.0 kg box: 7.5 m/s²; 3.0 kg box:
   5.0 m/s²
87. g/μ_s

Chapter 6

Conceptual Questions

1. False. They are not in equilibrium. They
   have an acceleration (toward the earth),
   because the direction of their velocity is
   continually changing due to the gravitational pull of the earth, which is a net
   force on them. In their circular orbit,
   their velocity vector is continually
   pulled toward the earth, and they do not
   travel in a straight line, but they also do
   not get any closer to the earth.
3. This is incorrect. The magnitude of the
   force of the earth on the apple equals the
   magnitude of the force of the apple on
   the earth. Equal forces have different
   effects on the two objects because the
   mass of the earth is much greater than
   the mass of the apple. The same magnitude of force produces a much larger
   acceleration for the apple.
5. No, there is no way to tell the difference
   without making observations outside the
   laboratory.
7. (a) No. The gravitational pull on the
   1.0 kg object is $F_g = G\dfrac{(1.0 \text{ kg})m_p}{R_p^2}$,

where m_p is the mass of the planet and R_p is its radius. If the planets have different radii, then the gravitational pulls will be different; the planet of smaller radius exerts a greater pull. (b) Yes. The gravitational pull is $F_g = G\dfrac{(1.0\text{ kg})m_p}{r^2}$,

where r is the distance of the object from the center of the planet. At the same r and for planets of the same m_p, the force F_g will be the same.

9. False. F_g is proportional to $1/r^2$, where r is the distance of the object from the center of the earth. Doubling the height above the surface does not double the distance from the center of the earth.

11. (a) It is a good idea. For an unbanked highway $f_s = m\dfrac{v^2}{R}$. f_s can become as small as required by this equation as the speed is reduced. But f_s cannot be greater than $\mu_s n$, and too great a speed can cause skidding. (b) It is not a good idea. At the posted speed, the horizontal component of the normal force gives the inward force needed to keep the car in a circular path. As v is reduced, there can be too much inward force, and the car slides to the bottom of the roadway.

13. (a) The car turns while the person tends to continue traveling in a straight line. There is no outward force on the person. (b) The free-body diagram is given in the figure below. The acceleration $\vec{a}_{rad}$ is inward toward the center of the curve. $\vec{F}$ is the force exerted by the car on the person.

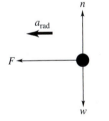

15. First, there is no outward force on the satellite. Second, the forces on the satellite do not balance. There is, however, a net inward force (gravity) that produces the inward acceleration associated with the circular motion. The free-body diagram is given in the figure below.

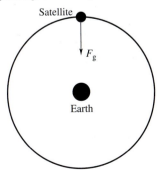

Multiple-Choice Problems

1. D
3. C
5. C
7. C
9. D
11. B
13. A
15. C

Problems

3. (b) 77 N (c) 12 times weight of hand
5. (b) 6.19 s (c) no
7. (a) 35.0 km/s (b) 5.47×10^{22} N
9. 20.0 m/s = 44.7 mph
11. (a) 5.24 m/s (b) highest: 833 N; lowest: 931 N (c) 14.2 s (d) 1760 N
13. (a) 1.73 m/s² (c) 0.0115 N, upward (d) 9.8×10^{-3} N
15. (a) 1.3 m/s (b) 3.1 m/s on earth
17. 1.87×10^{-34} N
19. 2.18
21. (b) 169
23. 36.6 cm from M
25. (a) $3F$ (b) $9F$ (c) $F/4$ (d) $16F$ (e) $\sqrt{2}d$
27. (a) 2.25×10^{25} kg (b) $3.76 m_E$
29. 433 N
31. 9×10^{13} N
33. (a) 175 min (b) 3.71 m/s²
35. 7.46×10^3 m/s
37. (a) 86,164 s = 24 h (c) 3.58×10^7 m
39. 2.01×10^{30} kg
41. (a) 8.87×10^{-3} m (b) 3.88×10^{20} N
43. (b) 370 km
45. (a) 1.62 m/s² (b) 0.69 N (c) 4.2 N
47. (a) to the right (b) 42 m
49. (b) 0.28 (c) no
51. (a) 2.9×10^{15} kg; 7.7×10^{-3} m/s² (b) 6.2 m/s; yes
53. (a) 4.56×10^{25} kg (b) 15.4 hours
55. 34.4 N
57. (a) 31.0 N (b) 3.53 m/s
59. (a) 1.54×10^7 m (b) 23.5 m/s²; 2.4g
61. 473.4 N

Chapter 7

Conceptual Questions

1. The force one surface exerts on the other displaces the atoms of the surface from their equilibrium positions and imparts oscillatory motion to them. The energy associated with this motion is thermal energy.

3. Kinetic energy is a scalar and has no direction and no components. It is incorrect to speak of its components.

5. The force of the rope on the object does work on the object. The force of the object on the rope does work on the rope. Thus, each force performs work on a different object; the work done on the rope is not part of the net work done on the object. The nonzero net work done

on the object by the rope provides kinetic energy to the object.

7. In the absence of friction in the jack mechanism, the same work is done in both cases. When the jack is used, a smaller force is exerted over a larger distance to do the same amount of work as lifting the car directly.

9. The elastic potential energy of the compressed spring is converted into thermal energy, which is dispersed within the solution.

11. The kinetic energy comes from potential energy stored in your tensed muscles. When you jump, you push downward on the floor with a force greater than your weight. By Newton's third law, the floor pushes up on you with an upward force of the same magnitude. The work this force does on you increases your kinetic energy and lifts you into the air. You could not jump if you were floating in outer space, since there is nothing to exert a force on you.

13. The change in kinetic energy is proportional to the change in v^2. For 15 mph to 20 mph, the change in v^2 is 175 mph². For 10 mph to 15 mph, the change in v^2 is 125 mph². Thus, the change is greater for 15 mph to 20 mph.

15. Energy is transported from the sun to the earth by electromagnetic waves, such as visible light, that are radiated by the sun. Part of this energy is converted to chemical energy by plants, using photosynthesis. This chemical energy is ingested when we eat the plants or eat an animal that has eaten the plants. Our bodies convert the chemical energy (food energy) into mechanical energy through the operation of our muscles.

Multiple-Choice Problems

1. B
3. A
5. C
7. A, D
9. A, D, E
11. B, D
13. B, D
15. C

Problems

1. 300 J
3. 5.22×10^4 J
5. (a) 3.60 J (b) -0.900 J (c) 0 (d) 0 (e) 2.70 J
7. (a) 74 N (b) 330 J (c) -330 J (d) 0; 0 (e) 0
9. (a) 37,500 J, 9.0 food calories (b) converted to other forms of energy
11. (a) 324 J (b) -324 J (c) 0
13. 4.21 g
15. (a) 7.07 m/s (b) 3/4
17. 74.2 J

19. (a) 38.6 m (b) 154 m (c) converted to thermal energy
21. (a) 30.3 m/s (b) 46.9 m
23. (a) 0.0399 (b) 0.160
25. (a) 2.6×10^4 N/m (b) 650 N
27. 0.290 m, 0.375 J
29. (a) 6.2 J (b) 11.2 J
31. 420 J; from potential energy stored in his tensed muscles
33. 8.2 kg
35. (a) 199 N/m (b) 69.3 cm, 47.8 J
37. (a) 2.08×10^5 N/m (b) no
39. (a) 920 (b) 180 m
41. 1.1×10^3 jumps; 37 min.; no
43. (a) 7.24×10^3 J (b) 7.24×10^3 J, 120 m/s; 14 m/s, 32 mph (c) 4850 ft; 9700 ft
45. (a)–(d) $\sqrt{v_0^2 + 2gh}$ (e) unchanged
47. (a) 2.0 m/s (b) 9.8×10^{-7} J, 2.0 J/kg (c) 200 m, 63 m/s (d) 5.9 J/kg (e) in its tensed legs
49. $2.42v$
51. $4K$
53. 7.38 cm
55. 127 J, converted to thermal energy
57. 0.233 J
59. 5.2 m/s
61. (a) 300 N (b) (i) 56% (ii) 33%
63. (a) 3.6×10^5 J (b) 100 m/s; no (c) 520 m; no
65. (a) $4.39 (b) $0.13
67. 29.6 kW
69. (a) 1.3×10^3 km² (b) 36 km, 22 mi; yes
71. (a) 0.134 hp (b) 56 kW (c) 2.68×10^{-3} hp (d) 5.25×10^{23} hp (e) 28 kWh
73. running: 1.3×10^6 J; walking: 1.7×10^6 J; walking, because it lasts longer
75. (a) 1.3×10^5 J (b) 1.5 W (c) kinetic energy, thermal energy
77. (a) 1.0×10^5 N/m, 250 J (b) 0.46 m/s
79. (a) (i) 0 (ii) 0 (b) (i) 0 (ii) −25.1 J
81. 3.00 m/s
83. (a) same for both (b) same for both (c) 50 g object (d) same for both (e) 50 g object
85. 2.1 m/s, 1.9 N
87. 2.24×10^5 J
89. (c) 1.3×10^5 N (d) 4.2×10^5 N/m, 24 m/s = 54 mph (e) larger x_{max}; no
91. (a) 68 cm (b) flex when land; joints and muscles absorb energy (c) less flexible and bones more fragile
93. 10 m/s
95. (a) no (b) yes, $150
97. 50.0 m
99. (a) 8.8 m (b) will slide back down
101. 3.89 m; 9.44 m/s
103. (a) earth: 2.66×10^{33} J; moon: 3.85×10^{28} J (b) earth: 6.36×10^{17} megatons of TNT; moon: 9.20×10^{12} megatons of TNT
105. (a) 0.053 gallon (b) 19
107. 3.6×10^{13} J; 8.6×10^{-3} megaton bombs
109. (a) yes (b) 250 N/m (c) 28.3 cm (d) 70.8 N
111. 125.6 m

Chapter 8

Conceptual Questions

1. The free-body diagrams are given in the figure below. n_{BA} is the normal force that B exerts on A, n_{AB} is the normal force that A exerts on B, and n is the normal force that the table exerts on B. f_{BA} is the friction force that B exerts on A, f_{AB} is the friction force that A exerts on B, and f is the friction force that the table exerts on B. (a) For block A, n_{BA}, f_{BA}, and w_A are all external forces. (b) For block B, n, n_{AB}, f_{AB}, f, P, and w_B are all external forces. (c) P, f, n, w_A, and w_B are external forces; n_{BA}, n_{AB}, f_{BA}, and f_{AB} are internal forces.

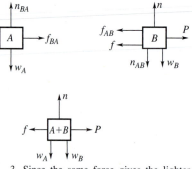

3. Since the same force gives the lighter fragment a greater acceleration, the lighter fragment gains more velocity in the same time.
5. The follow-through increases the time the force acts and therefore increases the impulse applied to the ball. This in turn increases the final momentum and speed of the struck object.
7. The ball has a larger range when the cannon is fastened to the ground. The final momentum of the cannonball is equal to the impulse applied to it, which is the product of the force and the time the force acts. When the cannon recoils, the ball reaches the end of the barrel more quickly and the impulse is reduced.
9. (a) Yes. $K = p^2/2m$, so if $p = 0$, then $K = 0$. (b) No. The system can have zero total momentum because the objects have equal nonzero momenta in opposite directions. But the kinetic energy of each object does not depend on the direction of the object's velocity and thus is never negative. Therefore, the kinetic energies do not add to zero. (c) Yes. The only way the total kinetic energy can be zero is for each object to be at rest.
11. If a drop is considered to be the system, the system is not isolated. The drop gains momentum as it falls, because of the external force of gravity. When the

drop strikes the ground, the momentum of the drop is removed by the net upward impulse due to the force exerted by the ground. If the drop and earth are considered to be an isolated system, the total momentum is zero before the drop starts to fall; remains zero as the drop falls, because the earth moves toward the drop; and is zero after the drop lands and both drop and earth come to rest.
13. Since the change in momentum is greater when the bullets bounce off, the impulse applied by the plate is greater in that case. By Newton's third law, the impulse applied to the plate is also greater.
15. No. The horizontal component of momentum must be conserved. It is nonzero just before the explosion, so it cannot be zero immediately after the explosion.

Multiple-Choice Problems

1. A, D
3. A, B, C
5. C
7. C
9. B
11. B, D
13. A, C, D
15. D

Problems

1. (a) 44 kg · m/s (b) 0 (c) −12 kg · m/s (d) −2 kg · m/s
3. (a) −30 kg · m/s; −55 kg · m/s (b) 0; 52 kg · m/s (c) 0; −3 kg · m/s
5. (a) 6.5 kg · m/s; 150 J (b) (i) 73 m/s (ii) 110 m/s
7. (a) $3p$ (b) $\sqrt{3}p$
9. 2.5×10^{-23} m/s
11. 9.9 cm/s
13. (a) 0.790 m/s (b) −0.0023 J
15. (a) 5.00 m/s, east (b) 5.71 m/s, east (c) 3.78 m/s, east (d) 5.00 m/s, east
17. 0.960 m/s
19. 1.8 m
21. (a) 15.0 m/s (b) 25.0%; converted to other forms
23. 0.0300 J; converted to other forms
25. 229 m/s
27. 0.763 m/s at 27.6° south of east
29. (a) 7.1 m/s (b) 5.2 m/s
31. (a) 0.300 kg: 0.27 m/s to the right; 0.150 kg: 1.07 m/s to the right (b) 0.300 kg: 0.011 J; 0.150 kg: 0.086 J
33. (a) proton: 154 km/s to the left; alpha particle: 104 km/s to the right (b) 3.58×10^{-17} J (c) total kinetic energy of the system is conserved
35. V for bowling ball; $2V$ for Ping Pong™ ball
37. (a) 5.22 kg · m/s (b) 261 N
39. (a) 4.2 kg · m/s; 140 N (b) −7.3 kg · m/s; −240 N
41. (a) 120.0 N/s, to the left (b) (i) 80 m/s, to the left (ii) 50 m/s, to the left

43. 2.1 m/s
45. along the line connecting the atoms, 0.048 nm from the oxygen atom
47. (a) 3.70×10^9 m (b) 4.48×10^5 m (c) star moves in orbit of larger radius
49. (a) 0.40 m above and 0.70 m to the right of the 20 N weight (b) moves closer to the center of the sphere
51. (a) 16.0 m behind leading car (b) 5.04×10^4 kg · m/s (c) 16.8 m/s (d) 5.04×10^4 kg · m/s; same
53. (a) 80.0 N (b) Yes. Eject gas in the appropriate direction.
55. 2.4 km/s
57. (a) 7.4 m/s^2 (b) 3.8×10^3 kg/s (c) 9.2 km/s
59. 11.9 m/s; 24.5 m/s
61. (a) 14.6 m/s, at 31.0° from the original direction of the bullet (b) no; $\Delta K = -189$ J
63. (a) 0.0914 (b) 0.332
65. (a) $v_A = v/3$, $v_B = 4v/3$ (b) $v_A = -v/3$, $v_B = 2v/3$
67. 1.53 m/s
69. 391 m/s
71. 0.105 m/s
73. (a) 6.79 m/s (b) 55.2 J
75. (a) 4.3 km/s (b) 4.8×10^{32} J (c) 1.1×10^{17} megaton bombs
77. 960 m/s
79. 15
81. 4.98×10^5 m/s
83. (a) A: v_0 to the left; B: v_0 to the right; elastic (b) both carts are at rest; inelastic
85. 250 J
87. (a) 67.5 cm/s; 185 cm/s (b) 197 cm/s; 20.0°

Chapter 9

Conceptual Questions

1. The tangential acceleration is parallel to the instantaneous velocity at each point and is equal to the rate of change of the speed of the point. The radial acceleration is associated with the rate of change of the direction of the point's velocity.
3. Yes, the point has both tangential and radial acceleration. The tangential acceleration has a constant magnitude $r\alpha$. It is tangential to the circular path and changes direction as the flywheel rotates. The radial acceleration is $r\omega^2$ and is not constant in magnitude, since α changes ω. The radial acceleration is directly radially inward and changes direction as the flywheel rotates.
5. (a) Yes, the ring is a collection of point masses, all the same distance R from the axis. (b) No, the point mass has $I = MR^2$, and the solid uniform disk has $I = \frac{1}{2}MR^2$. The mass of the disk is spread between the axis and a distance R from the axis, so I for the disk is less than MR^2.
7. Some of the energy supplied to the bike goes into rotational kinetic energy of the

wheels, rather than translational kinetic energy of the bike. The amount of translational kinetic energy lost to rotation of the wheels increases as the mass of the wheels increases.

9. When the raw egg rolls, only the liquid near the shell rotates, whereas all the contents of the hard-boiled egg rotate. The raw egg therefore has a smaller moment of inertia and will reach the bottom of the slope first.
11. The moment of inertia is proportional to the mass. It is a measure of the resistance of the object to changes in its rotation, just as the mass is a measure of the resistance of an object to changes in its translational motion. The moment of inertia differs from mass in two ways: It has units of kg · m^2, whereas mass has units of kg, and the moment of inertia depends not only on the amount of mass, but also on how the mass is distributed relative to the axis of rotation.
13. His legs and arms move in circular arcs relative to his hips and shoulders, respectively.
15. The acceleration depends on the slope of the hill. If the slope changes along the path, then the translational acceleration of the ball changes and constant-acceleration equations cannot be used.

Multiple-Choice Problems

1. B
3. C
5. A
7. B
9. C
11. C
13. B
15. A

Problems

1. 17.2°
3. (a) 0.105 rad/s; 1.75×10^{-3} rad/s; 1.45×10^{-4} rad/s (b) 1 min; 1 hr; 12 hr
5. (a) 2.25 s (b) 2.79 rad/s
7. 45.3°
9. (a) 200 rad/s (b) 3.1×10^{-3} s (c) 170 rpm (d) 0.032 s
11. (a) 2.33 rad/s^2 (b) 818°
13. 0.0135 rad/s^2
15. (a) 12.5 s (b) 7.96 rev
17. (a) 300 rpm (b) 75.0 s; 312 rev
19. 10.5 rad/s
21. 0.85 m/s
23. (a) 18.0 m/s^2 (b) 3.00 m/s, 18.0 m/s^2
25. 28 rpm
27. (a) 47.6 rad/s (b) (i) 1.88 rad/s (ii) 4.29 rad/s (c) 129 m
29. (a) 1.57×10^5 rad/s^2 (b) 864 m/s^2
31. $\frac{11}{16}mL^2$
33. (a) 0.0640 kg · m^2 (b) 0.0320 kg · m^2 (c) 0.0320 kg · m^2
35. (a) $m/2$ (b) 8/3
37. 4.44 N

39. 0.600 kg · m^2
41. (a) 225 m (b) 56.3 m
43. (a) 0.664 m (b) 7.69 rad/s
45. (a) 140 J (b) 33%
47. (a) 106 J (b) 0.904% (c) 28.6% (d) 1.50%
49. (a) 67.9 rad/s (b) 8.35 J
51. (a) cylinder: 3.23 m; sphere: 3.02 m (c) no
53. (a) 3.76 m (b) 8.58 m/s
55. 18.4 rad/s^2
57. (a) 84.0 rev (b) 5.95 mi (c) 583 mi
59. (a) -0.784 J (b) 5.42 rad/s (c) 5.42 m/s (d) 4.43 m/s
61. (a) 2.63×10^{33} J (b) 2.57×10^{29} J (c) 9.77×10^{-3}%
63. 96 days
65. (a) 3.3 kg · m^2 (b) 93 J
67. 12:33 A.M., 1:38 A.M., 2:44 A.M., 3:45 A.M., 4:54 A.M., 6:00 A.M., 7:05 A.M., 8:11 A.M., 9:16 A.M., 10:21 A.M., 11:27 A.M., and same times in P.M.
69. (a) H (b) $5H/7$ (c) in (b), stone ends up with rotational kinetic energy
71. (a) 1.05 rad/s (b) 5.0 J (c) 78.5 J (d) 6.4%
73. (a) 23.0 m

Chapter 10

Conceptual Questions

1. The extra length increases the torque applied to the bolt; the force exerted on the wrench by the mechanic acts with a longer moment arm. The increased torque can shear the bolt.
3. To prevent the bricks from falling, two criteria must be met. First, the center of gravity of the top brick cannot extend past the right-hand edge of the brick beneath it, so the minimum overlap is 6 inches. Second, the center of gravity of the two-brick combination cannot lie beyond the edge of the table. To determine the maximum x, assume the first criteria is just met—the top brick extends 6 in. beyond the bottom brick. As Figure 1 shows, the center of gravity of the two-brick combination is then 9 in. to the left of the right-hand edge of the top brick. Therefore, the greatest x can be is 9.0 in.
5. (a) Yes, you can change the location of your center of mass by changing the shape of your body. This changes the way that your mass is distributed. (b) Yes, you can change your moment of inertia with respect to some axis by moving your arms or legs to change how your mass is distributed with respect to the axis.
7. The refrigerator starts to slide when the horizontal applied force exceeds the maximum possible static friction force. The size of the static friction force is

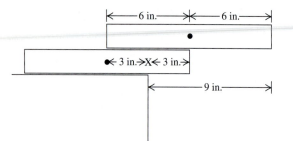

▲ **FIGURE 1.**

proportional to the weight of the refrigerator and to the coefficient of static friction between the refrigerator and the floor. Consider an axis at the forward, lower corner of the refrigerator. The refrigerator starts to tip when the torque due to the applied force exceeds the torque due to the weight of the refrigerator. The torque due to the applied force depends on the applied force and on where the force is applied. The gravity torque depends on the weight of the refrigerator and the width of the refrigerator. Therefore, whether the refrigerator starts to slide or starts to tip first depends on: μ_s, the width of the refrigerator and the height at which the force is applied. The higher up you push, the more likely the refrigerator is to tip.

9. A glass tips when its center of gravity is pushed beyond the edge of its base. The answer to both questions depends on the location of the center of gravity. For a given base, the glass is easier to tip the higher its center of gravity. For a center of gravity at a given height, the more narrow the base the easier it is for the glass to tip. If the water lowers the center of gravity, it makes the glass harder to tip. If the water raises the center of gravity, it makes the glass easier to tip. The water also increases the weight of the object so more force is required to tilt it.

11. Torques tending to close the door are opposed by torques applied by the object. The moment arm for the force exerted by the object is very small, so the force is very large and pulls horizontally against the hinges.

13. A free-body diagram for the hammer is sketched in Figure 2. The person using the hammer to pull the nail exerts a force $\vec{P}$ at the end of the handle. The nail exerts a downward force with magnitude F on the claw of the hammer and by Newton's third law the hammer exerts an upward force with magnitude $F' = F$ on the nail. The magnitude of the torque due to $\vec{P}$ equals the magnitude of the torque due to $\vec{F}$. But the force $\vec{P}$ has a much larger moment arm than $\vec{F}$, so $F \gg P$ and F' is large.

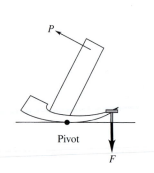

▲ **FIGURE 2.**

15. Since angular momentum is given by $L = I\omega$ and rotational kinetic energy is given by $K_{rot} = \frac{1}{2}I\omega^2$, $K_{rot} = \dfrac{L^2}{2I}$. If they have the same L they will have the same K_{rot} only if they have the same I. And since $L = \sqrt{2I(K_{rot})}$, if they have the same rotational kinetic energy they will have the same angular momentum only if they have the same I. And rotational kinetic energy is a scalar whereas angular momentum is a vector. Even if they have the same magnitude of angular momentum, the angular momenta of the two objects could be different if they are in different directions.

Multiple-Choice Problems

1. C
3. E
5. B
7. A
9. C
11. C
13. C
15. D

Problems

1. (a) 40.0 N · m, counterclockwise
   (b) 34.6 N · m, counterclockwise
   (c) 20.0 N · m, counterclockwise
   (d) 17.3 N · m, clockwise (e) 0 (f) 0
3. 0.726 N · m, clockwise
5. 2.50 N · m, counterclockwise
7. 3.22 rad/s²
9. 0.482
11. (a) 2.23 m/s² (b) 15.2 N (c) 4.46 rad/s²
13. (a) 3.16 × 10⁴ N (b) 2.60 × 10⁴ N;
   2.67 × 10⁴ N
15. (a) 5.88 m/s² (b) 49.0 N (c) 33.4 rad/s²

17. (a) 4.86 m/s² (b) 1.40 × 10³ N; static
19. (a) 8.98 rad/s (b) 9.88 × 10³ J
   (c) 494 W
21. (a) 358 N · m (b) 1.79 × 10³ N
   (c) 83.8 m/s
23. 4.71 × 10⁻⁶ kg · m²/s
25. (a) 0 (b) 44.8 kg · m²/s, counterclockwise
27. (a) 45,000 N · m (b) 45,000 kg · m²/s²
29. 1.14 rev/s
31. (a) 1.71 rad/s (b) external force but no external torque
33. 0.924 rad/s
35. (a) only rotational equilibrium (b) neither (c) only translational equilibrium (d) only translational equilibrium (e) both
37. 49.9 cm
39. hand: 272 N; foot: 130 N
41. (a) 1200 N (b) from the ground
43. (a) 625 N (b) 500 N; 75 N
45. (b) 87.5 N; 250 N (c) 87.5 N
47. (b) 530 N (c) 600 N; 270 N
49. (a) 370 N (b) when he just starts to raise it off the ground (c) no
51. 140 N by each hinge
53. (b) 781 N
55. 1.10 × 10⁵ N · m
57. 2.4 × 10⁻¹² N · m
59. (a) 2.9 cm (b) shift upper body backward (c) unnatural posture and curved back strains the back muscles
61. (a) 390 N (b) 173 N
63. (a) 9.58 × 10³ N; 1.36 × 10⁴ N
   (b) 3.23 × 10⁴ N
65. (a) 1.28 rad/s (b) 0.631 rad/s
   (c) 1.26 m
67. 0.730 m/s²; 6.09 rad/s²; 36.3 N; 21.1 N
69. (a) 0.92 rad/s² (b) no; α not constant (c) 1.78 rad/s
71. (a) 19.2 cm to the right; 8.2 cm above the shoulder joint (b) 32.5 N (c) 0; 11.4 N, upward
73. (a) 750 N, upward (b) 2310 N
   (c) 1160 N; 2750 N; 2980 N
75. (a) 4.25 m/s (b) 4.52 m/s² (c) 15.8 N; 11.3 N
77. person above: 590 N; person below: 1370 N; above
79. (a) 0.374 km/s (b) maximum speed at minimum distance and minimum speed at maximum distance (c) 154
81. 3200 J
83. (a) foot: 200 N; hand: 175 N (b) foot: –92 N; hand: 92 N

Chapter 11

Conceptual Questions

1. Swinging of a playground swing; this motion is simple harmonic only for small amplitudes and the motion also loses mechanical energy due to dissipative forces. Pistons in a car engine; force doesn't precisely obey Hooke's law.

3. The negative work done by friction removes kinetic energy from the object. The object slows down and takes more time to complete one cycle, for example more time to move from the initial maximum displacement to equilibrium, than when friction is absent. The period is increased by friction.

5. The period decreases. The effect is the same as increasing g by taking pendulum to another planet; the restoring force is increased.

7. Molecules in a gas have space in between them and can be pushed closer together. In a liquid or solid the molecules are more closely packed together. An attempt to push them together is opposed by a large repulsive force.

9. In a satellite the pendulum is in free-fall. There is no restoring force and the pendulum does not swing back and forth when released with an initial displacement. For a mass on a spring the restoring force is applied by the spring, and this force is not affected by being in orbit. The period of a mass on a spring could be used as a time-keeping device but a pendulum could not.

11. The circular frequency $\omega = \dfrac{2\pi}{T} = 2\pi f$

is proportional to the number of complete swings the pendulum makes each second. It is inversely proportional to the time for one complete swing. The angular velocity is the rate at which the angular position of the pendulum is changing and is proportional to the linear speed of the pendulum bob along its path. The circular frequency describes a full cycle of the motion and is constant during the motion. The angular velocity changes during the motion. It is zero at the maximum displacement and is a maximum as the pendulum bob passes through its lowest point.

13. Concrete is brittle and fairly easily broken up into pieces. But concrete columns are capable of supporting very large weights, such as in bridges and buildings. Concrete can withstand much larger compressive stress than tensile stress.

15. It is easy to compress Styrofoam into a smaller volume but it is difficult to do so for most woods (balsa wood is an exception). Therefore, wood must have a much larger bulk modulus than Styrofoam.

Multiple-Choice Problems

1. A
3. B
5. C
7. A, C, D
9. C
11. B
13. B
15. C

Problems

1. (a) 1.03×10^9 Pa (b) 1.47×10^{-3} (c) 7.01×10^{11} Pa
3. (a) 1.6×10^6 Pa (b) -8.0×10^{-6} (c) -2.0×10^{-5} m
5. relaxed: 3.3×10^4 Pa; maximum tension: 6.7×10^5 Pa
7. 1.4 mm
9. (a) 2.2 mm (b) smaller
11. (a) 24% (b) 12%
13. (a) -0.0531 m^3 (b) 1.09×10^3 kg/m^3
15. decrease 9.1 mL
17. 3.4×10^6 N
19. $8.6°$
21. 10.2 m/s^2
23. (a) 2.15×10^{-3} s; 2.93×10^3 rad/s (b) 2.00×10^4 Hz; 1.26×10^5 rad/s (c) 1.3×10^{-15} s to 2.3×10^{-15} s; 4.3×10^{14} Hz to 7.5×10^{14} Hz (d) 2.0×10^{-7} s; 3.1×10^7 rad/s
25. (a) 0.120 m (b) 1.60 s (c) 0.625 Hz
27. (a) 4.0 ms (b) 250 Hz (c) 1600 rad/s
29. (a) 0.0284 J (b) 0.0138 m (c) 0.615 m/s
31. (a) 0.376 m (b) 59.2 m/s^2 (c) 118 N
33. $A/\sqrt{2}$
35. (a) 0.80 s (b) 1.25 Hz (c) 7.85 rad/s (d) 3.0 cm (e) 148 N/m
37. (a) 23.6 cm/s (b) 185 cm/s^2 (c) maximum speed at $x = 0$; maximum acceleration at $x = \pm A$
39. 1.05×10^3 N/m
41. (a) 1.60 s (b) 0.625 Hz (c) 3.93 rad/s (d) 5.1 cm; 0.4 s, 1.2 s, 1.8 s (e) 79 cm/s^2; 0.4 s, 1.2 s, 1.8 s (f) 4.9 kg
43. (b) 9.99×10^{-15} g = 9.99 fg
45. 1.88 s
47. 2.60 s
49. (a) $\sqrt{2}\,T$ (b) $L/9$ (c) $L_{new} = 10L$ (d) $T/\sqrt{10}$ (e) $T_{new} = T$
51. (a) 0.543 J (b) converted to other forms by dissipative forces
53. (a) 0, 0.80 s, 1.60 s, 2.40 s, 3.20 s (b) 0.0533 J (c) 0.0218 J; converted to other forms by nonconservative forces
55. (a) 6.72×10^3 m/s^2 (b) 3.02×10^3 N (c) 18.3 m/s; 75.6 J
57. 29.4 m/s^2
59. 9.08×10^{24} kg
61. $\mu_s(m + M)g/k$
63. 3.3 mm
65. (a) 4.2×10^4 N (b) 64 m
67. (a) 1.56 m (b) steel: 1.0×10^8 Pa; brass: 5.00×10^7 Pa (c) steel: 5.0×10^{-4}; brass: 5.6×10^{-4}
69. (a) 0.18 mm (b) 0.19 mm
71. (a) 1004 kg/m^3; 100.4% (b) no
73. 0.0541 L

Chapter 12

Conceptual Questions

1. There is kinetic energy of the moving string and the elastic potential energy of the string when it is displaced from equilibrium. The kinetic energy could be transferred to an object attached to the end of the string.

3. Sound waves require a medium and cannot propagate through empty space.

5. The harmonic content (the extent to which frequencies higher than the fundamental are present) is different for the same note produced by different instruments.

7. This would be an example of resonance. When the sung note has the same frequency as one of the normal-mode frequencies of the glass, large amplitude standing waves can be set up in the glass.

9. The observed frequency of the rotating fork is shifted by the Doppler effect. Its pitch is increased when it is moving toward the listener and is decreased when it is moving away from the listener. The listener therefore hears two different frequencies from the two forks and beats occur.

11. Changing the tension in the string changes the speed of transverse waves on the string and this alters the standing wave frequencies for the string. The notes of a piano are produced by mallets striking stretched wires and the piano is tuned by adjusting the tension in these wires.

13. The sound you hear results from standing waves in the air column inside the bottle. As the bottle fills, this air column gets shorter and the frequencies of the standing waves increase.

15. Sound is a compression wave traveling through a medium. When a tree falls in the forest, it produces such a longitudinal wave in the air around it. The sound wave is produced and travels through the air, whether anyone is there to hear it or not.

Multiple-Choice Problems

1. A
3. A
5. B
7. B, C
9. A
11. D
13. C
15. C

Problems

1. (a) 1.7 cm to 17 m (b) 4.3×10^{14} Hz to 7.5×10^{14} Hz (c) 1.5 cm (d) 6.4 cm
3. 2.2 km/s
5. 258 m/s
7. (a) 16.3 m/s (b) 0.136 m (c) 23.1 m/s; 0.192 m (both increase by a factor of $\sqrt{2}$)
9. (a) $\sqrt{2}\,V$ (b) V (c) $V/\sqrt{3}$ (d) $\sqrt{2}\,V$ (e) $2\sqrt{5}\,V$
11. (a) 25.0 Hz, 0.0400 s, 19.6 rad/m (b) $y(x, t) = -(0.0700 \text{ m}) \sin 2\pi \cdot \left(\dfrac{t}{0.0400 \text{ s}} - \dfrac{x}{0.320 \text{ m}}\right)$ (c) 0.0495 m

13. 0.469 g/cm
17. (a) 408 Hz (b) 24th
19. (a) 45.0 cm (b) no; 440 Hz is lowest frequency possible
23. (a) fundamental: 0.60 m; 1st overtone: 0.30 m, 0.90 m; 2nd overtone: 0.20 m, 0.60 m, 1.00 m (b) fundamental: 0; 1st overtone: 0, 0.80 m; 2nd overtone: 0, 0.48 m, 0.96 m
25. (a) 35.2 Hz (b) 17.6 Hz
27. (a) 16.0 cm, 8.0 cm, 5.3 cm, 4.0 cm; 2210 Hz, 4420 Hz, 6630 Hz, 8840 Hz (b) 32.0 cm, 10.7 cm, 6.4 cm, 4.6 cm; 1110 Hz, 3330 Hz, 5550 Hz, 7770 Hz
29. 39.1 cm; yes
31. (a) 70 Hz (b) 93 Hz
33. (a) 0.237 m (b) 0.711 m (c) 0.474 m
35. (a) $n(820\ Hz)$, $n = 1, 2, 3, \ldots$ (b) $(2n + 1)(410\ Hz)$, $n = 0, 1, 2, \ldots$
37. (a) 90 m (b) 102 kHz (c) 1.4 cm (d) 4.4 mm to 8.8 mm (e) 6.2 MHz
39. (b) 10.9 m
41. (a) $3.16 \times 10^{-7}\ W/m^2$ (b) $1.58 \times 10^{-3}\ W/m^2$ (c) $6.31 \times 10^{-13}\ W/m^2$
43. 3.2×10^{-3}
45. 15.0 cm
47. (a) 5.5 μJ (b) 2.3 m/s; 31,000 times faster
49. (a) 3.16 (b) 20 dB (c) 3.0 dB
51. 17 Hz
53. (a) 11.6 Hz, 7.6 Hz (b) 11.6 Hz
55. (a) 0.798 m (b) 0.922 m (c) 431 Hz (d) 373 Hz
57. 780 m/s
59. (a) 548 Hz (b) 652 Hz
61. (a) 7.02 m/s; toward (b) 1404 Hz
63. (a) $3f_S$ (b) f_S (c) pitches are unaltered but music is heard in reverse
65. 5.362×10^{14} Hz; 559.5 nm
67. 3.19 cm/s
69. (a) 0.0133 s, 75 Hz, 0.50 m (b) 2nd (c) 37.5 m/s (d) 0.356 g
71. (a) 148 N (b) 26%
73. 0.858 m/s
75. (a) 6.74 cm (b) 147 Hz
77. (a) 0.25 m/s (b) 0.91 m
79. 320 Hz
81. (a) 38 Hz (b) no
83. 5 kg

Chapter 13

Conceptual Questions

1. The pressure in a fluid depends only on height, not the shape of the container. The height of both columns is the same because the pressure at the bottom of each column of water must be the same, if the water is not flowing in either direction. The water in the funnel is supported partly by the rest of the water and partly by the sides of the funnel.

3. Hot air has a smaller density than the surrounding air so the buoyancy force is larger than the weight when the balloon is filled with hot air. The density of the air in the balloon depends on the temperature of this air; the ascent or descent of the balloon is controlled by varying the temperature of the air in the balloon.

5. The pressure difference would be $(0.01)(1.0 \times 10^5\ Pa) = 1.0 \times 10^3$ Pa. For a door with area 2 m^2 the net force keeping the door closed would be 2×10^3 N. This is about 450 pounds. It would take a very strong person to pull the door open. But all that would be required would be to open it slightly, so air can move from the high pressure to the low pressure side. Once the pressure is equalized the door will easily open the rest of the way.

7. The volume flow rate is vA. When A is smaller, v must be larger. The escaping air makes more noise because it is moving faster as it enters the surrounding air.

9. When the marble is sitting in the floating box it must cause an amount of water to be displaced that is equal to the weight of the marble. When the marble is sitting at the bottom of the beaker the buoyant force on it is less than its weight, since it sinks, so it is displacing less than its weight of water. The marble causes less water to be displaced when it has been dropped into the water, so the water level in the beaker falls.

11. The pressure inside the rocket ship pushes the air through the hole. The vacuum doesn't pull the air out; the vacuum exerts no force.

13. (a) The average density of the submarine must equal that of the surrounding water when the submarine floats at equilibrium at some depth. The density of water increases with depth below the surface, so the average density of the submarine is different when it is floating at different depths. (b) The submarine could rise by decreasing its average density and descend by increasing its average density. It could do this either by pushing some water out of tanks within the submarine and replacing that water by air, or by letting more water into these tanks.

15. The balloons move forward toward the front of the car. The air in the car has the same acceleration as the car. The force that produces this acceleration for a volume of the air is exerted by the surrounding air. When this volume is replaced by a helium-filled balloon, the force on the balloon exerted by the surrounding air is the same as when just air was in the volume. But the helium-filled balloon has less mass than the same volume of air

(the balloon rises if released), so the same force produces a greater acceleration when applied to the balloon and the balloon has a greater forward acceleration than does the air inside the car.

Multiple-Choice Problems

1. B
3. A, D
5. A
7. C
9. D
11. C
13. E
15. A

Problems

1. 7.02×10^3 kg/m^3; yes
3. 41.8 N; no
5. (a) 19.3 cm (b) 2.29 million dollars
7. (a) 8ρ (b) $L/3^{1/3}$
9. (a) no; $2\rho_1\rho_2/(\rho_1 + \rho_2)$ (b) yes
11. (a) 5.25 kg (b) 1.3 N (c) 1.1×10^{-9} g
13. (a) 2.52×10^6 Pa (b) 1.78×10^5 N
15. 1.5×10^7 Pa to 3.2×10^7 Pa
17. 93.5 mm of Hg
19. (a) 1.36 cm (b) 10.3 m
21. (a) 864 kg/m^3 (b) 0.0475 atm
23. (a) 706 Pa (b) 3160 Pa
25. 117/77
27. (a) 4.64 m (b) 1.45 mm
29. (a) 3.4 L (b) 56 N
31. (a) 5.75 m^3 (b) 1150 kg
33. 0.562 m^3
35. (a) 6370 N (b) 558 kg (c) 85.9%
37. (a) 1.02×10^3 kg/m^3 (b) 8.0%
39. 2.86 Pa
41. 20.0
43. (a) 2.33 m/s (b) 5.21 m/s
45. 37.5 cm/s
47. 16.6 m/s
49. 1.47×10^5 Pa
51. 500 N, downward
53. 0.41 cm
55. 2.03×10^4 Pa
57. 9.59 cm/s
59. $(2^{1/4})D$
61. (a) 1.47×10^3 Pa (b) 13.9 cm
63. 4.66×10^{-4} m^3; 5.27 kg
65. 732 kg/m^3
67. 33.5 N
69. 2.05 m
71. (a) 1.30×10^5 Pa (b) 13.3 m
73. (c) Use $v_1A_1 = v_2A_2$.

Chapter 14

Conceptual Questions

1. When the material is heated the average distance between the atoms or molecules in the material increases uniformly in all directions. The piece of material with the hole expands just like the piece without the hole, and the hole expands just like a solid piece of the material.

3. The two metals have different coefficients of linear expansion. The strips are in good thermal contact, so when the temperature changes both strips have the same ΔT. The strip with the larger α has a greater change of length. If ΔT is positive the composite strip bends such that the material with the larger α is on the outside of the curve. If ΔT is negative the composite strip bends such that the material with the larger α is on the inside of the curve.

5. The spheres have an average density that is slightly less than the density of the liquid at low temperatures. And the spheres differ a little from one another in their average densities. As the temperature of the liquid increases, it expands and its density decreases. When the average density of a particular sphere exceeds that of the liquid, that sphere sinks to the bottom of the cylinder. This occurs at different temperatures for different spheres, with the ones with the greater average density descending first. The volume of each sphere also increases as the temperature increases, so its average density decreases, but the coefficient of volume expansion for the liquid is much larger than for the solid spheres and the expansion of the liquid dominates.

7. This is possible in principle. Shaking the thermos gives the coffee kinetic energy that is converted to thermal energy when the coffee comes to rest. This is not practical. To raise the temperature of 0.1 kg of coffee (mostly water) 10 C° requires about 4000 J of energy. The 0.1 kg of coffee would have to fall through a distance of 4000 m to acquire this much kinetic energy.

9. False. Conservation of energy requires that the amount of heat that flows into the cooler object equals the amount of heat energy that flows out of the warmer object. But the temperature changes associated with these heat flows depend on the mass and specific heat capacities of the objects. Equal heat flows need not mean equal temperature changes.

11. Phase transitions happen at fixed temperatures. As long as two phases are present the temperature of the system remains at the phase transition temperature. The heat added during the phase change is required for the phase change and doesn't produce a temperature change.

13. There will be small effects due to different emissivity of the coffee when its color changes. But the predominant effect on the rate of heat transfer is the temperature difference between the coffee and its surroundings; the greater the temperature difference the greater the rate of heat loss to the environment. The heat loss during the five minutes is less if the cream is added at the beginning of the period, so the coffee is cooler as it sits during the five-minute period.

15. No. The heat your furnace must provide equals the heat that passes out of the house into the environment. The rate of heat transfer decreases when the temperature difference between the house and its surroundings is less. Less heat is lost while you are away if the house is at a lower temperature during that time.

17. No. The insulating property of the material depends primarily on the air pockets within the material. Compressing the insulation increases its thermal conductivity and therefore reduces its insulating value. Also, the rate of heat conduction is indirectly proportional to the thickness of the insulation. Therefore, even for the same thermal conductivity heat will be conducted at a greater rate for a 4 in. space than for a 6 in. space.

Multiple-Choice Problems

1. C
3. D
5. C
7. C
9. C
11. A
13. B
15. A

Problems

1. (a) Yes. 104.4°F (b) Yes. 54°F (c) No. 77°C, 171°F
3. (a) 27.2 C° 27.2 K (b) −55.6 C°, −55.6 K
5. (a) −40.0° (b) No
7. (a) 6.8 in. (b) 6.7×10^{-6} $(F°)^{-1}$
9. 2.3×10^{-5} $(C°)^{-1}$
11. 11 L
13. 499.73 mL
15. 1.7×10^{-5} $(C°)^{-1}$
17. 0.008 cm
19. 3.03×10^{5} J
21. (a) 38 J (b) 4.5×10^{4} J
23. (a) 4.77×10^{5} J (b) 0.666 C°
25. 1.36×10^{3} m/s
27. 0.0613 C°
29. (a) 2.51×10^{3} J/(kg · K) (b) overestimate
31. (a) 3680 J (b) 1.31×10^{5} J (c) 0.404 kg
33. 3.7 kg
35. 357 m/s
37. 1.43×10^{5} J, 34.2 kcal
39. (a) 6.33×10^{4} J (b) 6.91×10^{3} J (c) steam burns are more severe
41. (a) 5.9 C° (b) 109°F; yes
43. (a) 215 J/(kg · K) (b) water (c) too small

45. 35.1°C
47. 2.10 kg
49. 3.08 g
51. (a) 6480 J (b) radiated into space at same rate
53. 4.0×10^{-3} W/(m · C°)
55. (a) −5.8°C (b) 11 W/m²
57. 227 W/(m · K)
59. (a) 29.6°C (b) 9.1 cm
61. (a) 1.96 m² (b) 937 W (c) 118 W
63. (a) 140 W (b) 180 W
65. 2.1 cm²
67. (a) 0.793 g (b) 1.43 g
69. 2.9 m
71. 26 kW
73. 456 s
75. 37.5°C
77. 340 m
79. (a) 2.7×10^{7} J (b) 6.89 C° (c) 19.3 C°
81. 140 g
83. (a) 1.04×10^{3} J/s (b) 87.1 J/s (c) 1130 J/s (d) 28 g (e) 1.1 bottles
85. 14.1°C
87. 5.2 kg
89. (a) 118 J (b) 49.3 g
91. 3.4 C°; yes

Chapter 15

Conceptual Questions

1. No. The conversion from kelvins to Celsius degrees involves an additive rather than a multiplicative factor, so the conversion factor cannot be absorbed into the gas constant. For example, there are negative temperatures on the Celsius scale and negative values for T don't make sense in the ideal gas equation, no matter what the value is for the gas constant.

3. No, the fan does not make the room cooler. Electrical energy is provided to the room at the fan and the fan does not remove energy from the room, so operation of the fan in the room increases the temperature of the room. The fan moves the air and the air flowing past you moves thermal energy away from your body and makes you feel cooler.

5. In a hot object the random motions of the atoms (or molecules) are more energetic than in a cold object. When the two objects are in contact their atoms collide and in the collision kinetic energy is transferred from the atoms in the hot object to the atoms in the cold object.

7. As the temperature is decreased the average kinetic energy of the molecules in the material decreases. Collisions between molecules in the material become less frequent and are less energetic.

9. False. At thermal equilibrium the two kinds of atoms have the same temperature and the same average kinetic energy. To have the same average kinetic energy, the lighter atoms have a greater speed.

11. For any process of an ideal gas, $\Delta U = nC_V \Delta T$. The constants C_V and C_p are defined by the equations for the heat flow for constant volume ($Q = nC_V \Delta T$) and constant pressure ($Q = nC_p \Delta T$) processes. For a constant volume process, $W = 0$ and $Q = nC_V \Delta T$ so by $\Delta U = Q - W$, $\Delta U = nC_V \Delta T$. For a constant pressure process, $Q = nC_p \Delta T$, but $W \neq 0$ and ΔU is not equal to Q.

13. For an ideal gas U depends only on T. Since $\Delta U = nC_V \Delta T$ for constant volume, ΔU is also given by this expression for any process.

15. No. To derive these equations we used the ideal gas law. The equation of state for liquids and solids differs greatly from the ideal gas law, so equations 15.22 and 15.23 don't apply.

Multiple-Choice Problems

1. C
3. D
5. C
7. A
9. D
11. B
13. B, C, D
15. A, B, D

Problems

1. 0.959 atm
3. (a) $-175°C$ (b) 1.00 L
5. (a) 5.78×10^3 mol (b) 185 kg
7. 3.36×10^5 Pa
9. (a) $70.2°C$ (b) yes
11. $503°C$
13. (a) 3×10^{27} molecules (b) 3×10^{19} molecules/cm^3
15. 18 cm^3; 56 cm^3
17. solid and vapor, with no liquid
19. 3.35×10^{35} molecules
21. (a) 1.9×10^6 m/s; no (b) 7.3×10^{10} K
23. (a) 4.84×10^2 m/s (b) 6.21×10^{-21} J
25. 6.1×10^{-6} m
27. (a) 1.90 km/s (b) no (c) O_2: 0.477 km/s; N_2: 0.510 km/s (d) some molecules move faster than v_{rms}
29. (a) the different isotopes have different v_{rms} (b) 1.004
31. (a) 10.5 breaths/min (b) 2.62×10^{21} molecules
33. (a) $49.6°C$ (b) 1110 J
35. (a) 392 J/(kg·K) (b) 390 J/(kg·K) in Table 14.3
37. (b) 0
39. (b) 1.33×10^3 J
41. (a) 1.2×10^3 J (b) negative of work done in (a) (c) 600 J
43. 327 J
45. (a) -1.15×10^5 J (b) 2.55×10^5 J; heat flows out of the gas
47. (a) 45.0 J (b) liberates 65.0 J (c) ad: 23.0 J db: 22.0 J
49. (a) -4510 J (b) 4510 J out of gas

51. (a) 4490 J (b) 8310 J (c) 11,600 J (d) 8310 J
53. (a) 0.125 L (b) 57.0 J done on gas (c) decreased (d) left the gas
55. (a) 278 K (b) 162 J done by gas (c) 53 J
57. (b) 208 J (c) on the piston (d) 712 J (e) 930 J (f) 208 J
59. (a) $T_a = 665$ K; $T_b = 2660$ K; $T_c = 887$ K; $T_d = 222$ K (b) (i) 6.39×10^4 J (ii) 4.05×10^4 J (iii) 2.13×10^4 J (iv) 1.01×10^4 J (c) (i) enters (ii) leaves (iii) leaves (iv) enters
61. (b) $495°C$; 29.1 atm
63. (b) 224 J (c) -224 J
65. 2.20×10^6 molecules
67. (a) 1.18×10^4 Pa (b) 0.5667
69. 1.92 atm
71. (a) 1.2×10^4 m/s (b) 6.68×10^{-27} kg
73. (a) $Q = 300$ J; $\Delta U = 0$ (b) $Q = 0$; $\Delta U = -300$ J (c) $Q = 750$ J; $\Delta U = 450$ J
75. (a) $W = 738$ J; $Q = 2588$ J; $\Delta U = 1850$ J (b) $W = 0$; $Q = -1850$ J; $\Delta U = -1850$ J (c) 0
77. 9.6 cm
79. (a) 0.80 L (b) $T_a = 305$ K; $T_b = T_c = 1220$ K (c) ab: 76 J into gas; ca: 107 J out of gas; bc: 56 J into gas (d) ab: $\Delta U = 76$ J; bc: $\Delta U = 0$; ca: $\Delta U = -76$ J
81. (a) 0.373 kg (b) 0.098 kg
83. 4.18×10^5 J
85. (b) 1.25×10^4 J (c) 0 (d) 1.25×10^4 J (e) 0.169 m^3

Chapter 16

Conceptual Questions

1. For a refrigerator device, $|Q_H| = |Q_C| + |W|$. This says that the heat energy $|Q_H|$ deposited into the room is the same as the heat energy $|Q_C|$ removed from the food compartment plus the amount of mechanical energy required to operate the refrigerator (inputed to the device as electrical energy). The tubing is where heat flows from the device into the room.

3. Energy is lost due to friction within the car's drive train, due to work done against wind resistance, and due to work done by friction between the tires and the road and by friction during braking. You can improve the car's efficiency by giving it an aerodynamic shape that reduces wind resistance and by using materials and lubrication that reduce friction work.

5. For an air conditioner or refrigerator the amount of heat $|Q_H|$ that flows out of the device is greater than the heat $|Q_C|$ that flows into the device. In fact, $|Q_H| = |Q_C| + |W|$, where $|W|$ is the energy supplied to operate the device. If an air

conditioner is set on the floor and plugged in, $|Q_C|$ is removed from the room but $|Q_H|$ is ejected into the room. Since $|Q_H|$ is larger than $|Q_C|$, the room is heated rather than cooled. A refrigerator also adds heat to the room in which it is placed. That heat must be removed, for example by a window air conditioner, or else the room will be heated.

7. The change in entropy depends not only on the heat flow but is also inversely proportional to the Kelvin temperature at which that heat flow occurs. The negative heat flow out of the hot object occurs at a higher temperature than the positive heat flow into the cold object, so the positive entropy change is greater than the negative entropy change and the net entropy change is positive.

9. No. The second law says this can never be the sole result of a process for an isolated system. But a device can cause this to happen if mechanical energy is inputed to the device. A refrigerator is an example of a device that moves heat from a cold object (the food) to a warm object (the room).

11. Both devices move heat energy from a cooler object to a warmer object. For a refrigerator the purpose of the device is to remove heat from the cooler object (the food compartment). The heat deposited into the warmer object (the room) is waste heat. For a heat pump operating in the winter, the purpose of the device is to deposit heat into the warmer object (the interior of the building).

13. In a hot object the random motions of the atoms (or molecules) are more energetic than in a cold object. When the two objects are in contact their atoms collide and in the collision kinetic energy is transferred from the atoms in the hot object to the atoms in the cold object. In the collisions energy is transferred in this direction and not in the reverse direction.

15. The efficiency of a heat engine is the ratio of the magnitude of the work output to the magnitude of the energy input. The work output ranges from zero to the amount of the energy input so the efficiency lies between 0 and 1 (or 100%). The coefficient of performance K of a refrigerator is the ratio of the magnitude of heat $|Q_C|$ removed at the low temperature reservoir to the magnitude of the work $|W|$ required to operate the device. This ratio can be very small (small $|Q_C|$, large $|W|$) or very large (large $|Q_C|$, small $|W|$), so K ranges from zero to infinity.

17. The coefficient of performance of a refrigerator is the ratio of the magnitude

of the heat $|Q_C|$ removed at the low temperature reservoir to the magnitude of the work $|W|$ required to operate the device. Removal of $|Q_C|$ is the useful action of the device and $|W|$ is what you have to pay for, so it is most economical to operate a refrigerator with a large coefficient of performance.

Multiple-Choice Problems

1. B
3. B
5. A
7. B, D
9. C
11. A, D
13. A, C
15. B

Problems

1. 50 J; 100 J
3. (a) 6500 J (b) 34%
5. (a) 23% (b) 12,400 J (c) 0.350 g
   (d) 222 kW, 298 hp
7. (a) 25% (b) 970 MW
9. (a) 12.3 atm (b) 5470 J; process ca
   (c) 3723 J; process bc (d) 1747 J
   (e) 31.9%
11. 13.8

13. (a) 453.2°C (b) 1.99×10^6 Pa
15. (a) 1.62×10^4 J (b) 5.02×10^4 J
17. (a) 8.09×10^5 J (b) 3.37×10^5 J
    (c) 1.14×10^6 J
19. (a) 215 J (b) 378 K (c) 39.1%
21. (a) 1128°F (b) 67 J; 33 J
23. (a) 492 J (b) 212 W (c) 5.4
25. (a) 8.77 (b) 1.54×10^5 J
    (c) 1.76×10^4 J (d) 1.72×10^5 J
27. (a) clockwise; heat enters in ab and leaves in cd (b) counterclockwise; heat enters in dc and leaves in ba; dc inside refrigerator and ba in room (c) counterclockwise; heat enters in dc and leaves in ba; dc inside house and ba outside (d) counterclockwise; heat enters in dc and leaves in ba; dc outside house and ba inside
29. (a) 428 J/K (b) −392 J/K (c) 36 J/K
31. (a) hot: 1.14×10^3 J; cold: 765 J
    (b) 0.43 J/K
33. (a) 33.3 J/K (b) irreversible since $\Delta S > 0$
35. 0.186 J/K
37. 3780 J/K; increase
39. −5.8 J/K; decrease
41. (a) 29.8 km²; 11.5 mi² (b) 59.5 km²; 23.0 mi²

43. 57.3 L
45. (a) $p_1 = 1.00$ atm, $V_1 = 8.62$ L;
    $p_2 = 2.00$ atm, $V_2 = 8.62$ L;
    $p_3 = 1.00$ atm, $V_3 = 14.1$ L (b) $1 \rightarrow 2$:
    $Q = 2183$ J, $W = 0$, $\Delta U = 2183$ J;
    $2 \rightarrow 3$: $Q = 0$, $W = 786$ J,
    $\Delta U = -786$ J; $3 \rightarrow 1$: $Q = -1960$ J,
    $W = -559$ J, $\Delta U = -1400$ J (c) 227 J
    (d) 227 J (e) $e = 10.4\%$;
    $e_{Carnot} = 50.0\%$
47. 1.95×10^5 J; 2.28×10^6 J
49. (a) $p_1 = 2.00$ atm, $V_1 = 4.00$ L;
    $p_2 = 2.00$ atm, $V_2 = 6.00$ L;
    $p_3 = 1.11$ atm, $V_3 = 6.00$ L;
    $p_4 = 1.67$ atm, $V_4 = 4.00$ L
    (b) $1 \rightarrow 2$: $Q = 1422$ J, $W = 405$ J;
    $2 \rightarrow 3$: $Q = -1355$ J, $W = 0$; $3 \rightarrow 4$:
    $Q = W = -274$ J; $4 \rightarrow 1$: $Q = 339$ J,
    $W = 0$ (c) 131 J (d) $e = 7.5\%$;
    $e_{Carnot} = 44\%$
51. (a) 13.2 J (b) 13.2 J
53. (a) 2.26%; no (b) 29.4 J; 1.30×10^3 J
    (c) 1.11×10^{-3} candy bars
55. (a) 1.30×10^{26} J/K (b) irreversible;
    $\Delta S > 0$
57. (a) enters: ab; leaves: bc, ca (b) 14.0%
59. (a) 17.5 J (b) 14.0% (c) 0.0808 J/K
    (d) 32.3%